Source Readings
IN ECONOMIC THOUGHT

Norton Readings in Economics

READINGS IN MONEY AND BANKING
Edited by C. R. Whittlesey

READINGS IN BUSINESS CYCLES AND NATIONAL INCOME
Edited by Alvin H. Hansen *and* Richard V. Clemence

SOURCE READINGS IN ECONOMIC THOUGHT
Edited by Philip C. Newman, Arthur D. Gayer, *and* Milton H. Spencer

Source Readings IN ECONOMIC THOUGHT

Edited by

PHILIP C. NEWMAN · ARTHUR D. GAYER

MILTON H. SPENCER

W · W · NORTON & COMPANY · INC · *New York*

PRINTED IN THE UNITED STATES OF AMERICA
FOR THE PUBLISHERS BY THE VAIL-BALLOU PRESS
789

CONTENTS

Preface xi

PART ONE

GREEK ECONOMIC THOUGHT

Plato (427?–347? B.C.) 2

On the State, *from The Republic* 2

Aristotle (384–322 B.C.) 6

On the State, Property, and Money, *from Politics* 6

On Money, *from The Nicomachean Ethics* 12

PART TWO

MEDIEVAL ECONOMIC THOUGHT

St. Thomas Aquinas (1225?–1274) 16

Of Cheating 17

Of Usury 19

PART THREE

MERCANTILISM

Thomas Mun (1571–1641) 24

England's Treasure by Forraign Trade 24

Philipp Wilhelm von Hornick (1638–1712) 38

Austria over All if She Only Will 38

Edward Misselden (1608–1654) 43

Of Exchanges in Generall 43

Sir James Steuart (1712–1780) 49

On Government Regulation 49

On Population 50

PART FOUR

THE FORERUNNERS OF ECONOMIC LIBERALISM

Sir Dudley North (1641–1691) 54

The Preface *to Discourses upon Trade* 54

Concerning the Abatement of Interest 57

Sir William Petty (1623–1687) 60
A Treatise of Taxes and Contributions 60
The Table, *from The Political Anatomy of Ireland* 66

Richard Cantillon (1680?–1734) 68
On the Nature of Commerce in General 69

David Hume (1711–1776) 86
Of Money, *from Political Discourses* 86

PART FIVE

THE PHYSIOCRATS

François Quesnay (1694–1774) 93
Explanation of the Economic Table 93

Pierre-Paul Mercier de la Rivière (1720–1793) 99
The Natural and Essential Order of Political Societies 99

Anne Robert Jacques Turgot (1727–1781) 106
On Capital and Interest 106

PART SIX

CLASSICAL ECONOMICS

Adam Smith (1723–1790) 120
An Inquiry into the Nature and Causes of the Wealth of Nations—
Introduction and Plan of the Work 122
Of the Improvement in the Productive Powers of Labour 123
Of the Nature, Accumulation, and Employment of Stock 148
Of Systems of Political Œconomy 151
Of the Revenue of the Sovereign or Commonwealth 155

Jean Baptiste Say (1767–1832) 157
Of the Vent or Demand for Products 158

Jeremy Bentham (1748–1832) 165
The Principle of Utility 166

Thomas Robert Malthus (1766–1834) 170
An Essay on the Principle of Population 171
On the Progress of Wealth, *from Principles of Political Economy* 177

David Ricardo (1772–1823) 191
Principles of Political Economy and Taxation 192
The High Price of Bullion 215

John Stuart Mill (1806–1873) 226
Of International Values 227
Of Property 231

PART SEVEN

REACTIONS AGAINST CLASSICISM: SOCIALISM

Jean Charles Léonard Simonde de Sismondi (1773–1842) 236
New Principles of Political Economy 236

Karl Heinrich Marx (1818–1883) 240
A Contribution to the Critique of Political Economy 242
Money, and the Buying and Selling of Labour-Power, *from Capital* 243
The So-called Primitive Accumulation, *from Capital* 252
Production, Consumption, Value, and Price, *from Capital* 264
Crises, *from Theories of Surplus Value* 274

Henry George (1839–1897) 287
Progress and Poverty 288

Rudolf Hilferding (1877–1941) 292
The Ideology of Imperialism 292

PART EIGHT

REACTIONS AGAINST CLASSICISM: ECONOMIC NATIONALISM

Friedrich List (1789–1846) 297
The National System of Political Economy 298

PART NINE

LOCATION THEORY

Johann Heinrich von Thuenen (1783–1850) 320
The Isolated State 320

Alfred Weber (1868–) 331
The Theory of Location in its Relation to General Economics (by Andreas Predöhl) 331

August Loesch (1906–1945) 337
The Nature of Economic Regions 337

PART TEN

MARGINALISM

Carl Menger (1840–1921) 347
Economy and Economic Goods 348
The Theory of Value 354

Friedrich von Wieser (1851–1926) 378
The Austrian School and the Theory of Value 378
The Economic Principle in State Economy, *from Social Economics* 387

William Stanley Jevons (1835–1882) 390
Theory of Political Economy 391

John Bates Clark (1847–1938) 411
The Distribution of Wealth 412

Alfred Marshall (1842–1924) 423
Principles of Economics 424
Elements of Economics of Industry 434
The Social Possibilities of Economic Chivalry 441
Employment in British and German Steel Industries 446

PART ELEVEN

MATHEMATICAL ECONOMICS

Antoine Augustin Cournot (1801–1877) 451
Of the Competition of Producers 452

Marie Esprit Léon Walras (1834–1910) 460
Geometrical Theory of the Determination of Prices 461

Vilfredo Pareto (1848–1923) 476
Manual of Political Economy 477

PART TWELVE

REACTIONS AGAINST ORTHODOXY: THE GERMAN HISTORICAL SCHOOL

Werner Sombart (1863–1941) 491
Capitalism 492
The Modern Business Man, *from The Quintessence of Capitalism* 499
The Growth of a Capitalistic Point of View in Economic Life, *from The Jews and Modern Capitalism* 504

Max Weber (1864–1920) 508
The Protestant Ethic and the Spirit of Capitalism 509

PART THIRTEEN

REACTIONS AGAINST ORTHODOXY: INSTITUTIONALISM

Thorstein Bunde Veblen (1857–1929) 523
The Limitations of Marginal Utility 524
The Theory of Business Enterprise 530

Wesley Clair Mitchell (1874–1948) 543
The Role of Money in Economic Theory 544
Quantitative Analysis in Economic Theory 548

John Rogers Commons (1862–1945) 556
Institutional Economics 557

John Atkinson Hobson (1858–1940) 575
Work and Wealth 576
The Physiology of Industry 588

PART FOURTEEN

NEO-CLASSICAL ECONOMICS: IMPERFECT-COMPETITION AND OLIGOPOLY THEORIES

Piero Sraffa (1898–) 592
The Laws of Returns under Competitive Conditions 592

Edward Hastings Chamberlin (1899–) 605
The Theory of Monopolistic Competition 605

Heinrich von Stackelberg (1905–1946) 623
Market Structure and Equilibrium 624

Oskar Morgenstern (1902–) 633
The Theory of Economic Behavior (by Leonid Hurwicz) 634
Oligopoly, Monopolistic Competition, and the Theory of Games 648

PART FIFTEEN

WELFARE ECONOMICS

Arthur Cecil Pigou (1877–) 659
The Economics of Welfare 659
Some Aspects of Welfare Economics 675

PART SIXTEEN

ECONOMIC STABILITY AND EMPLOYMENT

Knut Wicksell (1851–1926) 687
The Influence of the Rate of Interest on Prices 687

Bertil Ohlin (1899–) 693
Some Notes on the Stockholm Theory of Savings and Investment 694

John Maynard Keynes (1883–1946) 712
The General Theory, *from The General Theory of Employment, Interest and Money* 713
The General Theory of Employment 714
The Theory of the Rate of Interest 722
The Theory of Prices, *from The General Theory of Employment, Interest and Money* 726
Concluding Notes on Social Philosophy, *from The General Theory of Employment, Interest and Money* 738

Joseph Alois Schumpeter (1883–1950) 746
The Explanation of the Business Cycle 747
The Instability of Capitalism 755
Crumbling Walls, *from Capitalism, Socialism, and Democracy* 758

PREFACE

The purpose of this book is to serve either as the basic text or as supplementary reading for courses in the history of economic thought, modern economic thought, or economic theory. The range of the selections stretching from Plato to Schumpeter, the emphasis on the period since Jevons and Marshall, and the primary concern with selections central to economic analysis are intended to make the book suitable for all three courses.

It is obviously impossible to include all the important figures of economic thought between the covers of one book, especially when the selections from the really indispensable writers, like Smith and Keynes, must be long enough to be fairly representative of their thinking. If anyone is disturbed at the omission of his favorite sage or selection, may we say that our "first approximation" of desirable selections was as large again as this volume. Something had to give or the book would have been priced out of the market.

The average student, advanced undergraduate or graduate, should have no difficulty with most of the selections. Even in the section on the mathematical economists we were careful to leave out otherwise excellent material where the mathematics might be too much for the average reader.

Considerations of space have made it necessary to dispense with some representatives of certain "schools" of economic thought, especially where they contribute chiefly by restating and elaborating prior doctrines. It is for this reason that figures like Böhm-Bawerk are not included. At the same time, a special effort has been made to include selections from writers who are exceptionally inaccessible and not found in any anthology; examples of this category are Misselden, North, and Steuart.

In all cases an effort has been made to keep the selections long enough to present the views of each writer and encourage further reading on the part of the student, and especially full treatment has been given to the "giants" of economic thought.

The book owes much to the generous assistance of many people. A book of readings cannot come into being without the permission of authors, publishers, and journals to reproduce portions of books and articles; with few exceptions, the editors of the present volume have been well treated on this score, and they wish to make general acknowledgment at this point. Specific acknowledgments are made in the body of the text.

Fortunately, several translations of works not previously available in English—Menger and Marx, for example—were completed during the period that this work was in preparation, greatly facilitating our efforts. In addition, several selections were especially translated for the present volume. Dr. Louis Siegelman of Cornell University is responsible for the translation of parts of Pareto's *Manuale di Economia Politica,* while Herbert and Marilyn Ranschberg of Queens College translated parts of Stackelberg's *Marktform und Gleichgewicht.* Mark Blaug helped check translations and also was of great aid in improving many introductions and selections. Professor Ruth E. Newman made significant contributions in improving the style and content of the entire work. We also appreciate the dogged perseverance of Arno von Borkenhorst.

Professor Josef Soudek of Queens College made many valuable suggestions about selections and helped choose the portions of foreign works to be translated. Dr. Paul Sweezy made suggestions about the inclusion of Rudolf Hilferding; Professors Morgenstern, Pigou, and Hicks were kind enough to engage in correspondence about the compressibility of their principal works. Where they could not be compressed to the satisfaction of their authors, the works were omitted. Dr. William Jaffe of Northwestern University was kind enough to suggest the selection from Walras.

A word about the division of labor among the editors: The tragic death of Professor Gayer in September, 1951, removed at once an able coworker and beloved friend when the book was barely beyond the preliminary planning stage. The finished work is as we then conceived it; but the final selections were made and edited jointly by the two remaining editors, while Dr. Newman has assumed primary responsibility for the introductions and general organization.

P.C.N.
M.H.S.

PART ONE

Greek Economic Thought

Greek economic thought, like that of other pre-capitalistic civilizations, is to be found in legal codes and in religious and philosophic writings. The Socratic philosophers, our chief sources for the economic thought of the Greeks, intertwined economics with philosophy, ethics, and politics. Because to the Socratics all economic problems were basically moral problems, there is a strong moral and ascetic strain in Greek economics.

Greek economic life was so limited in development that it was impossible for Greek thinkers to develop a cohesive, extensive, or integrated system of economic thought. Yet there was sufficient development for Aristotle to discuss division of labor and value in exchange with great acumen, and for the chief Socratic philosophers—Plato, Xenophon, and Aristotle—to protest against the incipient merchant capitalism and money greed of their age. However, neither these writers nor the other Greek writers who did any thinking in economic terms developed any sustained analysis of economic factors in their writings.

Since the Greeks believed that the citizen existed for the state, it is not surprising that they regarded the goal of economics as the furthering of human welfare and emphasized economic policy as opposed to "pure" theory. Because control by the state was a part of every man's life, many Greek thinkers, especially Plato, had leanings toward socialism.

As a result of the great influence of Aristotle on certain medieval thinkers, medieval economic thought, especially as expressed by the Scholastics, presents in certain respects an unbroken continuity with the Greeks. There is, however, very little Greek influence discernible in later phases of the history of economic thought.

The following sections present typical selections from the writings of Plato and Aristotle, two of the outstanding contributors to Greek economic thought. Certain aspects of Greek economics will become more apparent in the discussions of these individual writers.

PLATO

(427?–347? B.C.)

The Greek philosopher, Plato, was born of noble parents, who gave him every educational advantage of that time. While still a youth he became both pupil and friend of Socrates. Plato founded a school in the Grove of Academus, the Academy, where he taught mathematics and philosophy until his death. He established his reputation as a philosopher by the publication of the *Republic,* in which he showed what he considered to be the ideal republic. This was the first of the utopias, aristocratic and communistic at the same time, where philosophers would rule, private property and family would be abolished, and education based on ability would fit each person for his role in the community.

The selection that follows is from the *Republic,* Book II. Here Plato shows that the division of labor, that is, the development of specialization and exchange, is responsible for the creation of the city-state. The division of labor, he points out, is a result of the inability of individuals to satisfy their manifold wants. At the same time, he demonstrates the disadvantages of self-sufficiency. Interestingly, this passage is one of the important sources of concepts later refined by Hutcheson and Adam Smith in their discussions of productivity. Plato's analysis, however, is not with any specific idea of "productivity." Rather, he is concerned in general with the greater utility and the plenitude and the superior quality of the goods produced. The division of labor produces exchange, and both become the pillars on which the state and the subsequent social order exist. Under this organization, the class hierarchy guarantees that the just state will be maintained in equilibrium.

Although Plato's ideas are certainly primitive and fairly restricted in scope, they show a clear advance in economic thinking over what was merely ethical generalization by Old Testament and certain Oriental thinkers. Plato's pupil Aristotle carried these ideas further, and as will be shown, developed a theory of money and value.

Plato's expository form is a dialogue of Socrates with Adeimantus. Those words of Adeimantus that are merely affirmation or acknowledgment of what Socrates says are excised without indication from the text here presented, which is otherwise the Jowett translation.

ON THE STATE *

A State arises, as I conceive, out of the needs of mankind; no one is self-sufficing, but all of us have many wants. . . .

Then, as we have many wants, and many persons are needed to supply them, one takes a helper for one purpose and another for another; and when these partners and helpers are gathered together in one habitation the body of inhabitants is termed a State.

And they exchange with one another, and one gives, and another receives, under the idea that the exchange will be for their good.

Then let us begin and create in idea a State; and yet the true creator is necessity, who is the mother of our invention.

Now the first and greatest of necessities is food, which is the condition of life and existence.

* From *The Republic,* translated by Benjamin Jowett.

The second is a dwelling, and the third clothing and the like.

And now let us see how our city will be able to supply this great demand: We may suppose that one man is a husbandman, another a builder, some one else a weaver—shall we add to them a shoemaker, or perhaps some other purveyor to our bodily wants?

The barest notion of a State must include four or five men.

And how will they proceed? Will each bring the result of his labours into a common stock?—the individual husbandman, for example, producing for four, and labouring four times as long and as much as he need in the provision of food with which he supplies others as well as himself; or will he have nothing to do with others and not be at the trouble of producing for them, but provide for himself alone a fourth of the food in a fourth of the time, and in the remaining three-fourths of his time be employed in making a house or a coat or a pair of shoes, having no partnership with others, but supplying himself all his own wants? . . .

And will you have a work better done when the workman has many occupations, or when he has only one?

When he has only one.

Further, there can be no doubt that a work is spoilt when not done at the right time.

For business is not disposed to wait until the doer of the business is at leisure; but the doer must follow up what he is doing, and make the business his first object.

And if so, we must infer that all things are produced more plentifully and easily and of a better quality when one man does one thing which is natural to him and does it at the right time, and leaves other things.

Then more than four citizens will be required; for the husbandman will not make his own plough or mattock, or other implements of agriculture, if they are to be good for anything. Neither will the builder make his tools—and he too needs many; and in like manner the weaver and shoemaker.

Then carpenters, and smiths, and many other artisans, will be sharers in our little State, which is already beginning to grow.

Yet even if we add neatherds, shepherds, and other herdsmen, in order that our husbandmen may have oxen to plough with, and builders as well as husbandmen may have draught cattle, and curriers and weavers fleeces and hides,—still our State will not be very large.

Then, again, there is the situation of the city—to find a place where nothing need be imported is well-nigh impossible.

Then there must be another class of citizens who will bring the required supply from another city.

But if the trader goes empty-handed, having nothing which they require who would supply his need, he will come back empty-handed.

And therefore what they produce at home must be not only enough for themselves, but such both in quantity and quality as to accommodate those from whom their wants are supplied.

Then more husbandmen and more artisans will be required.

Not to mention the importers and exporters, who are called merchants.

And if merchandise is to be carried over the sea, skilful sailors will also be needed, and in considerable numbers.

Then, again, within the city, how will they exchange their productions? To secure such an exchange was, as you will remember, one of our principal objects when we formed them into a society and constituted a State.

Clearly they will buy and sell.

Then they will need a market-place, and a money-token for purposes of exchange.

Suppose now that a husbandman, or an artisan, brings some production to market, and he comes at a time when there is no one to exchange with him,—is he to leave his calling and sit idle in the market-place?

Not at all; he will find people there who, seeing the want, undertake the office of salesmen. In well-ordered states they are commonly those who are the weakest in bodily strength, and therefore of little use for any other purpose; their duty is to be in the market, and to give money in exchange for goods to those who desire to sell and to take money from those who desire to buy.

This want, then, creates a class of retail-traders in our State. Is not 'retailer' the term which is applied to those who sit in the market-place engaged in buying and selling, while those who wander from one city to another are called merchants?

And there is another class of servants, who are intellectually hardly on the level of companionship; still they have plenty of bodily strength for labour, which accordingly they sell, and are called, if I do not mistake, hirelings, hire being the name which is given to the price of their labour. . . .

And now, Adeimantus, is our State matured and perfected?

I think so.

Where, then, is justice, and where is injustice, and in what part of the State did they spring up?

Probably in the dealings of these citizens with one another. I cannot imagine that they are more likely to be found anywhere else. . . .

Let us then consider, first of all, what will be their way of life, now that we have thus established them. Will they not produce corn, and wine, and clothes, and shoes, and build houses for themselves? And when they are housed, they will work, in summer, commonly, stripped and barefoot, but in winter substantially clothed and shod. They will feed on barley-meal and flour of wheat, baking and kneading them, making noble cakes and loaves; these they will serve up on a mat of reeds or on clean leaves, themselves reclining the while upon beds strewn with yew or myrtle. And they and their children will feast, drinking of the wine which they have made, wearing garlands on their heads, and hymning the praises of the gods, in happy converse with one another. And they will take care that their families do not exceed their means; having an eye to poverty or war. . . .

Of course they must have a relish—salt, and olives, and cheese, and they will boil roots and herbs such as country people prepare; for a dessert we shall give them figs, and peas, and beans; and they will roast myrtleberries and acorns at the fire, drinking in moderation. . . .

The question which you would have me consider is, not only how a State, but how a luxurious State is created; and possibly there is no harm in this, for in such a State we shall be more likely to see how justice and injustice originate. In my opinion the true and healthy constitution of the State is the one which I have described. But if you wish also to see a State at fever heat, I have no objection. For I suspect that many will not be satisfied with the simpler way of life. They will be for adding sofas, and tables, and other furniture; also dainties, and perfumes, and incense, and courtesans, and cakes, all these not of one sort only, but in every variety; we must go beyond the necessaries of which I was at first speaking, such as houses, and clothes, and shoes: the arts of the painter and the embroiderer will have to be set in motion, and gold and ivory and all sorts of materials must be procured.

Then we must enlarge our borders; for the original healthy State is no longer sufficient. Now will the city have to fill and swell with a multitude of callings which are not required by any natural want; such as the whole tribe of hunters and actors, of whom one large class have to do with forms and colours; another will be the votaries of music—poets and their attendant train of rhapsodists, players, dancers, contractors; also makers of divers kinds of articles, including women's dresses. And we shall want more servants. Will not tutors be also in request, and nurses wet and dry, tirewomen and barbers, as well as confectioners and cooks; and swineherds, too, who were not needed and therefore had no place in the former edition of our State, but are needed now? They must not be forgotten: and there will be animals of many other kinds, if people eat them. . . .

And the country which was enough to support the original inhabitants will be too small now, and not enough.

Then a slice of our neighbours' land will be wanted by us for pasture and tillage, and they will want a slice of ours, if, like ourselves, they exceed the limit of necessity, and give themselves up to the unlimited accumulation of wealth.

And so we shall go to war. Shall we not?

Most certainly.

Then, without determining as yet whether war does good or harm, thus much we may affirm, that now we have discovered war to be derived from causes which are also the causes of almost all the evils in States, private as well as public.

ARISTOTLE

(384–322 B.C.)

The most important contribution to Greek economic thought was made by the philosopher Aristotle, one of the greatest thinkers of all time. Born at Stagira, the son of a physician, he was long a student of Plato at Athens and later became tutor to Alexander the Great of Macedon. Subsequently he returned to Athens and founded a school, the Lyceum. During the anti-Macedonian reaction in 323 B.C. he fled to Chalcia, where he died the following year.

While his writings on politics, ethics, and logic were secondary to those of Plato in his own day, his philosophy was later taken over by both Islamic and Catholic thinkers. In fact, during the Middle Ages it was heretical to question what was, in large part, Aristotelian doctrine. In the realm of political philosophy, his *Politics* has been an influential text almost from its initial publication.

In the first book of the *Politics* he treats many economic questions, such as exchange, division of labor, money, interest, and usury. To be sure, there is no continual, sustained analysis, but even his scattered ideas, notably on private property, usury, and the just price, had a great influence on subsequent economic thought, especially in the Middle Ages. It should be borne in mind, however, that he was the product of a relatively undeveloped economy, the small Greek city-state, and the simplicity of the economic organization that he saw around him may have led him to oversimplification and generalization.

Economics, from the Greek *oikonomia,* is etymologically "management of the household," and Aristotle's predecessors had analyzed all economics as "matters of the household." At one point (*Politics* I, 1252 A 7–13) he criticized Plato and Xenophon for not seeing the differences between the economics of a state and of a household, but in his discussion of money, he himself fell into the same error.

The following selections are from Aristotle's *Politics* and the *Nicomachean Ethics.*

ON THE STATE, PROPERTY, AND MONEY *

When several villages are united in a single community, perfect and large enough to be nearly or quite self-sufficing, the state comes into existence, originating in the bare needs of life, and continuing in existence for the sake of a good life. And therefore, if the earlier forms of society are natural, so is the state, for it is the end of them, and the [completed] nature is the end. For what each thing is when fully developed, we call its nature, whether we are speaking of a man, a horse, or a family. Besides, the final cause and end of a thing is the best, and to be self-sufficing is the end and the best.

Hence it is evident that the state is a creation of nature, and that man is by nature a political animal. And he who by nature and not by mere accident is without a state, is either above humanity, or below it; he is the 'Tribeless, lawless, hearthless one,' whom Homer denounces—the outcast who is a lover of war; he may be compared to an unprotected piece in the game of draughts.

* From *Politics,* translated by Benjamin Jowett.

Now the reason why man is more of a political animal than bees or any other gregarious animals is evident. Nature, as we often say, makes nothing in vain, and man is the only animal whom she has endowed with the gift of speech. And whereas mere sound is but an indication of pleasure or pain, and is therefore found in other animals (for their nature attains to the perception of pleasure and pain and the intimation of them to one another, and no further), the power of speech is intended to set forth the expedient and inexpedient, and likewise the just and the unjust. And it is a characteristic of man that he alone has any sense of good and evil, of just and unjust, and the association of living beings who have this sense makes a family and a state.

Thus the state is by nature clearly prior to the family and to the individual, since the whole is of necessity prior to the part; for example, if the whole body be destroyed, there will be no foot or hand, except in an equivocal sense, as we might speak of a stone hand; for when destroyed the hand will be no better. But things are defined by their working and power; and we ought not to say that they are the same when they are no longer the same, but only that they have the same name. The proof that the state is a creation of nature and prior to the individual is that the individual, when isolated, is not self-sufficing; and therefore he is like a part in relation to the whole. But he who is unable to live in society, or who has no need because he is sufficient for himself, must be either a beast or a god: he is no part of a state. A social instinct is implanted in all men by nature, and yet he who first founded the state was the greatest of benefactors. For man, when perfected, is the best of animals, but, when separated from law and justice, he is the worst of all; since armed injustice is the more dangerous, and he is equipped at birth with the arms of intelligence and with moral qualities which he may use for the worst ends. Wherefore, if he have not virtue, he is the most unholy and the most savage of animals, and the most full of lust and gluttony. But justice is the bond of men in states, and the administration of justice, which is the determination of what is just, is the principle of order in political society.

Seeing then that the state is made up of households, before speaking of the state we must speak of the management of the household. The parts of the household are the persons who compose it, and a complete household consists of slaves and freemen. Now we should begin by examining everything in its least elements; and the first and least parts of a family are master and slave, husband and wife, father and children. We have therefore to consider what each of these three relations is and ought to be:—I mean the relation of master and servant, of husband and wife, and thirdly of parent and child. And there is another element of a household, the so-called art of money-making, which, according to some, is identical with household management, according to others, a principal part of it; the nature of this art will also have to be considered by us. . . .

Let us now enquire into property generally, and into the art of money-making . . . The first question is whether the art of money-making is the same with the art of managing a household or a part of it, or instrumental to it; and if the last, whether in the way that the art of making shuttles is instrumental to the art of weaving, or in the way that the casting of bronze is instrumental to the art of the statuary, for they are not instrumental in the same way, but the one provides tools and the other material; and by material I mean the substratum out of which any work is made; thus wool is the material of the weaver, bronze of the statuary. Now it is easy to see that the art of household management is not identical with the art of money-making, for the one uses the material which the other provides. And the art which uses household stores can be no other than the art of household management. There is, however, a doubt whether the art of money-making is a part of household management or a distinct art. [They appear to be connected]; for the money-maker has to consider whence money and property can be procured; but there are many sorts of property and wealth:—there is husbandry and the care and provision of food in general; are these parts of the money-making art or distinct arts? . . .

Of the art of acquisition then there is one kind which is natural and is a part of the management of a household. Either we must suppose the necessaries of life to exist previously, or the art of household management must provide a store of them for the common use of the family or state. They are the elements of true wealth; for the amount of property which is needed for a good life is not unlimited, although Solon in one of his poems says that,

'No bound to riches has been fixed for man.'

. . . Let us begin our discussion of the question with the following considerations:—

Of everything which we possess there are two uses: both belong to the thing as such, but not in the same manner, for one is the proper, and the other the improper or secondary use of it. For example, a shoe is used for wear, and is used for exchange; both are uses of the shoe. He who gives a shoe in exchange for money or food to him who wants one, does indeed use the shoe as a shoe, but this is not its proper or primary purpose, for a shoe is not made to be an object of barter. The same may be said of all possessions, for the art of exchange extends to all of them, and it arises at first in a natural manner from the circumstance that some have too little, others too much. Hence we may infer that retail trade is not a natural part of the art of money-making; had it been so, men would have ceased to exchange when they had enough. And in the first community, which is the family, this art is obviously of no use, but only begins to be useful when the society increases. For the members of the family originally had all things in common; in a more divided state of society they still shared in many things, but they were different things which they had to give in exchange for what they wanted, a kind of barter which is still practised among barbarous nations who exchange with one another the necessaries of life and nothing more; giving and receiving wine, for example, in exchange for corn and the like. This sort of barter is not part of the money-making art and is not contrary to nature, but is needed for the satisfaction of men's natural wants. The other or more complex form of exchange grew out of the simpler. When the inhabitants of one country became more dependent on those of another, and they imported what they needed, and exported the surplus, money necessarily came into use. For the various necessaries of life are not easily carried about, and hence men agreed to employ in their dealings with each other something which was intrinsically useful and easily applicable to the purposes of life, for example, iron, silver, and the like. Of this the value was at first measured by size and weight, but in process of time they put a stamp upon it, to save the trouble of weighing and to mark the value.

When the use of coin had once been discovered, out of the barter of necessary articles arose the other art of money-making, namely, retail trade; which was at first probably a simple matter, but became more complicated as soon as men learned by experience whence and by what exchanges the greatest profit might be made. Originating in the use of coin, the art of money-making is generally thought to be chiefly concerned with it, and to be the art which produces wealth and money; having to consider how they may be accumulated. Indeed, wealth is assumed by many to be only a quantity of coin, because the art of money-making and retail trade are concerned with coin. Others maintain that coined money is a mere sham, a thing not natural, but conventional only, which would have no value or use for any of the purposes of daily life if another commodity were substituted by the users. And, indeed, he who is rich in coin may often be in want of necessary food. But how can that be wealth of which a man may have a great abundance and yet perish with hunger, like Midas in the fable, whose insatiable prayer turned everything that was set before him into gold?

Men seek after a better notion of wealth and of the art of making money than the mere acquisition of coin, and they are right. For natural wealth and the natural art of money-making are a different thing; in their true form they are part of the management of a household; whereas retail trade is the art of producing wealth, not in every way, but by exchange. And it seems to be concerned with coin; for coin is the starting-point and the goal of exchange. And there is no bound to the wealth which springs from this art of money-making. As in the art of medicine there is no limit to the pursuit of health, and as in the other arts there is no limit to the pursuit of their several ends, for they aim at accomplishing their ends to the uttermost; (but of the means there is a limit, for the end is always the limit), so, too, in this art of money-making there is no limit of the end, which is wealth of the spurious kind, and the acquisition of money. But the art of household management has a limit; the unlimited acquisition of money is not its business. And, therefore, in one point of view, all wealth must have a limit; nevertheless, as a matter of fact, we find the opposite to be the case; for all money-makers increase their hoard of coin without limit. The source of the confusion is the near connexion between the two kinds of money-making; in either, the instrument [i.e. wealth] is the same, although the use is different, and so they pass into one another; for each is a use of the same property, but with a difference: accumulation is the end in the one case, but there is a further end in the other. Hence some persons are led to believe that making money is the object of household management, and the whole idea of their lives is that they ought either to increase their money without limit, or at any rate not to lose it. The origin of this disposition in men is that they are intent upon living only, and not upon living well; and, as their desires are unlimited, they also desire that the means of gratifying them should be without limit. Even those who aim at a good life seek the means of obtaining bodily pleasures; and, since the enjoyment of these appears to depend on property, they are absorbed in making money: and so there arises the second species of money-making. For, as their enjoyment is in excess, they seek an art which produces the excess of enjoyment; and, if they are not able to supply their pleasures by the art of money-making, they try other arts, using in turn every faculty in a manner contrary to nature. The quality of courage, for example, is not intended to make money, but to inspire confidence; neither is this the aim of the general's or of the physician's art; but the one aims at victory and the other at health. Nevertheless, some men turn every quality or art into a means of making money; this they conceive to be the end, and to the promotion of the end all things must contribute.

Thus, then, we have considered the art of money-making, which is unnecessary, and why men want it; and also the necessary art of money-making, which we have seen to be different from the other, and to be a natural part of the art of managing a household, concerned with the provision of food, not, however, like the former kind, unlimited, but having a limit.

And we have found the answer to our original question. Whether the art of money-making is the business of the manager of a household and of the statesman or not their business?—viz. that it is an art which is presupposed by them. For political science does not make men, but takes them from nature and uses them; and nature provides them with food from the element of earth, air, or sea. At this stage begins the duty of the manager of a household, who has to order the things which nature supplies;—he may be compared to the weaver who has not to make but to use wool, and to know what sort of wool is good and serviceable or bad and unserviceable. Were this otherwise, it would be difficult to see why the art of money-making is a part of the management of a household and the art of medicine not; for surely the members of a household must have health just as they must have life or any other necessary. And as from one point of view the master of the house and the ruler of the state have to consider about health, from another point of view not they but the physician; so in one way the art of household management, in another way the subordinate art, has to consider about money. But, strictly speaking, as I have already said, the means of life must be provided beforehand by nature; for the business of nature is to furnish food to that which is born, and the food of the offspring always remains over in the parent. Wherefore the art of making money out of fruits and animals is always natural.

Of the two sorts of money-making one, as I have just said, is a part of household management, the other is retail trade: the former necessary and honourable, the latter a kind of exchange which is justly censured; for it is unnatural, and a mode by which men gain from one another. The most hated sort, and with the greatest reason, is usury, which makes a gain out of money itself, and not from the natural use of it. For money was intended to be used in exchange, but not to increase at interest. And this term usury, which means the birth of money from money, is applied to the breeding of money because the offspring resembles the parent. Wherefore of all modes of making money this is the most unnatural.

. . . It would be well also to collect the scattered stories of the ways in which individuals have succeeded in amassing a fortune; for all this is useful to persons who value the art of making money. There is the anecdote of Thales the Milesian and his financial device, which involves a principal of universal application, but is attributed to him on account of his reputation for wisdom. He was reproached for his poverty, which was supposed to show that philosophy was of no use. According to the story, he knew by his skill in the stars while it was yet winter that there would be a great harvest of olives in the coming year; so, having a little capital, he gave earnest-money for the use of all the olive-presses in Chios and Miletus, which he hired at a low price because no one bid against him. When the harvest-time came, and many wanted them all at once and of a sudden, he let them out at any rate which he pleased, and made a quantity of money. Thus he showed the world that philosophers can easily be rich if they like, but that their ambition is of another sort. He is supposed to have given a striking proof of his wisdom, but, as I was saying, his device for getting money is of universal application, and is nothing but the creation of a monopoly. It is an art often practised by cities when they are in want of money; they make a monopoly of provisions.

There was a man of Sicily, who, having money deposited with him, bought up all the iron from the iron mines; afterwards, when the merchants from their various markets came to buy, he was the only seller, and without much increasing the price he gained 200 per cent. Which when Dionysius heard, he told him that he might take away his money, but that he must not remain at Syracuse, for he thought that the man had discovered a way of making money which was injurious to his own interests. He had the same idea as Thales; they both contrived to create a monopoly for themselves. And statesmen ought to knew these things; for a state is often as much in want of money and of such devices for obtaining it as a household, or even more so; hence some public men devote themselves entirely to finance.

ON MONEY *

There are some who hold that retaliation [this word must not be understood as meaning only requital of *evil*] is absolutely just. This was the doctrine of the Pythagoreans, who defined justice absolutely as retaliation on one's neighbour.

But retaliation does not accord with the conception of either distributive or corrective justice, although corrective justice is certainly what is intended by the Rhadamanthine rule: "As a man's action, such his fate; / Then justice shall be true and straight." The law of retaliation and the law of corrective justice in many cases do not agree. For instance, if a person who strikes another is a magistrate, he ought not to be struck in return, and if a person strikes a magistrate, he ought not only to be struck but to be punished. Again, it makes a great difference whether what is done to a person is done with his consent or against it, *and the law of retaliation takes no account of this difference.* Still in such associations as depend upon exchange it is this kind of justice, viz. retaliation, which is the bond of union; but it is proportionate, and not equal retaliation; for it is proportionate requital which holds a state together.

People seek to requite either evil or good. It looks like slavery not to requite evil; and if they do not requite good, no interchange *of services* takes place, and it is this interchange which holds society together. It is thus that men build a temple of the Graces in their streets to ensure reciprocity, as being the peculiar characteristic of grace; for it is our duty to return the service of one who has been gracious to us, and to take the initiative in showing grace ourselves.

Now, proportionate requital is produced by cross-conjunction. Thus let *A* represent a builder, *B* a cobbler, *C* a house, and *D* a shoe. Then the builder ought to receive from the cobbler some part of his work, and to give him his own work in return. If then there is proportionate equality in the first instance, and retaliation *or reciprocity* follows, the result of which we are speaking will be attained. Otherwise the exchange will not be equal or permanent. For there is no reason why the work of the one should not be superior to that of the other, and therefore they ought to be equalized. (This is equally the case with all the arts; they would be destroyed, if the effect upon the patient were not, in kind, quantity and quality, the same as the effort of the agent.) For association is formed, not by two doctors, but by a doctor and a husbandman, and generally by people who are different, and not equal, and who need to be equalized. It follows that such things as are the subjects of exchange must in some sense be comparable. This is the reason for the invention of money. Money is a sort of medium or mean; for it measures everything and consequently measures among other things excess or defect, e.g. the number of shoes which are equivalent to a house or a meal. As a builder then is to a cobbler, so must

* From *The Nicomachean Ethics,* translated by J. E. C. Welldon (London, Macmillan and Co., Ltd., New York, The Macmillan Co., 1892).

so many shoes be to a house or a meal; for otherwise there would be no exchange or association. But this will be impossible, unless the shoes and the house or meal are in some sense equalized. Hence arises the necessity of a single universal standard of measurement, as was said before. This standard is in truth the demand for mutual services, which holds society together; for if people had no wants, or their wants were dissimilar, there would be either no exchange, or it would not be the same as it is now.

Money is a sort of recognized representative of this demand. That is the reason why it is called money, because it has not a natural but a conventional existence, and because it is in our power to change it, and make it useless.

Retaliation or reciprocity will take place, when the terms have been so equated that, as a husbandman is to a cobbler, so is the cobbler's ware to the husbandman's. But we must bring the terms to a figure of proportion not after the exchange has taken place—or one of the two extremes will have both advantages *i.e. will have its superiority counted twice over*—but when both parties still retain their own wares; they will then be equal and capable of association, because it is possible to establish the proper equality between them. Thus let *A* be a husbandman, *C* food, *B* a cobbler, and *D* his wares, which are equated *to the food.* But if this kind of reciprocity were impossible, there would be no association.

The fact that it is demand which is like a principle of unity binding society together is evident because, if there is no mutual demand on the part of two persons, if neither of them or one only needs the services of the other, they do not effect an exchange, whereas, if somebody wants what somebody else has, e.g. wine, they effect an exchange, giving the wine e.g. in return for the right of importing corn. Here then the wine and the corn must be equated.

Money is serviceable with a view to future exchange; it is a sort of security which we possess that, if we do not want a thing now, we shall be able to get it when we do want it; for if a person brings money, it must be in his power to get what he wants.

It is true that money is subject to the same laws as other things; its value is not always the same; still it tends to have a more constant value than any thing else. All things, then, must have a pecuniary value, as this will always facilitate exchange, and so will facilitate association.

Money therefore is like a measure that equates things, by making them commensurable; for association would be impossible without exchange, exchange without equality, and equality without commensurability.

Although it is in reality impossible that things which are so widely different should become commensurable, they may become sufficiently so for practical purposes. There must be some single standard then, and that a standard upon which the world agrees; hence it is called money, for it is this which makes all things commensurable, as money is the universal standard of measurement. Let *A* be a house, *B* ten minae, *C* a couch. Now *A* is half *B,* if the house is worth, or is equal to, five minae. Again, the couch *C* is the tenth part of *B*. It is clear then that the number of couches which are equal to a house is five. It is clear too that this was the method of exchange before the invention of money; for it makes no difference whether it is five couches or the value of five couches that we give in exchange for a house.

PART TWO

Medieval Economic Thought

Most writers regard the Middle Ages as the period extending from the fall of the Roman Empire in the fifth century A.D. to the middle of the fifteenth century. It covered over a thousand years of history, and it is inconceivable that there was no "economic thought" over so many years—even in the so-called Dark Ages.

The structure of medieval society was feudal; hereditary land was owned by nobles, or rather, "held" for the Crown, and worked by serfs. The basic economy, like that of Greece and Rome before it, was mainly agricultural. Handicrafts, trade, and finance were to be found only in the free cities. The Catholic Church, itself a great landholding institution, was dominant all over Europe, the more so because it was unified at a time when the temporal lords were not. Its canon law influenced almost all socio-economic activities, including business and trade.

The theological jurists, called canonists, tried to work out a way of regulating evils which they felt could not be entirely prevented. In this category were interest on money, moneylending in general, monopoly, and trade for selfish advantage. In these matters they were greatly influenced by Aristotle; their pronouncements of policy on many economic and business matters were the same as his.

With the rise of trade after the twelfth century, the Church lawyers were forced more and more to discuss questions like the "just price," the "just wage," and the legitimacy of interest and profit. From such considerations they were led incidentally to problems of value and distribution, the relationship of cost of production to price, and taxation; only incidentally, however, because the central theme of medieval thought was the ethical and moral significance of the business or economic action of the individual, be he peasant or prince.

The most influential of the medieval thinkers was the scholastic philosopher, St. Thomas Aquinas, whose writings cover almost every facet of human relations and summarize the best of medieval doctrine on economic questions. The following section is drawn from his works.

ST. THOMAS AQUINAS

(1225?–1274)

St. Thomas Aquinas, perhaps the greatest Catholic philosopher of all time, dominated the surge of Catholic intellectualism in the thirteenth century. He was born in Italy, near Naples, and entered the Dominican order, teaching at various times in Naples, Cologne, and Paris.

His great contribution, the *Summa Theologica,* was an attempt to harmonize Christianity with Aristotelian philosophy. The resultant doctrine has been called the *Thomistic synthesis.*

It was difficult to reconcile the traditional aversion of the Church to business, acquisition, and interest with the needs of the growing bourgeoisie of the towns. The growth and trade and, to some extent, small-scale industry during the later Middle Ages wrought changes in a society that had previously been dominated materially by feudal landholders and spiritually by the Church. The aversion of the Church to business and moneylending became more and more incongruous as the property of the Church grew and as it became an important borrower and lender of money.

Consequently, although St. Thomas' teachings possess a core of medievalism, they are rather advanced in some aspects. He held, for example, that private property is best, not because of any natural law, but because it has been proved best through experience. But while the ownership of goods should be private, the right to use these goods should be held in common, so that the needy may have their share. Commerce and trade are morally lawful only if pursued for a lawful end, such as the seeking of modest gain for a livelihood or the acquisition of gain which is regarded, not as an extorted profit, but as a reward for the merchant's labor. Charging interest on loans is morally wrong because payment is exacted for use which is inseparable from the thing used—money. Also, a person is entitled to income only because he labors or because he risks something; since a borrower gains as a fruit of his own labor, not as fruit of the loan, and since lending money is not considered a risk, interest cannot be justified. All goods and commodities must be sold at the just price, defined as one which will enable a seller to maintain the customary standard of living of his class.

In keeping with his principle that the usufruct of all goods should be shared in common, St. Thomas drew the further conclusion that the needy have a "natural" right to superfluous income. The Church and the State must be against poverty because it causes so many sins and crimes.

It is impossible in this context to examine fully the illuminating commentaries in many fields by St. Thomas. The English translation of his *Summa Theologica* alone runs to some twenty volumes, while the French edition of his complete works by Fretté and Maré runs to thirty-four volumes. In many ways he was politically democratic; for example, he believed that citizens should participate in their government and that the state exists for the individual, not the individual for the state. And yet he held that slavery was in accordance with natural law and compatible with the welfare of the community. Also, he felt it best for women to be dominated by men.

St. Thomas enjoys a higher authority among Catholics than any other writer on social subjects, especially since his views were endorsed by Pope Leo XIII in his encyclical *Aeterni Patris* in 1879. In the twentieth century there has been a neo-Thomist revival of modest proportions. Notable figures in this revival include Cardinal Mercier and Jacques Maritain in France and a group, including Mortimer Adler and Robert Maynard Hutchins, at the University of Chicago in the United States.

OF CHEATING, WHICH IS COMMITTED IN BUYING AND SELLING *

Whether It Is Lawful to Sell a Thing for More Than Its Worth?

It is altogether sinful to have recourse to deceit in order to sell a thing for more than its just price, because this is to deceive one's neighbour so as to injure him. . . .

But, apart from fraud, we may speak of buying and selling in two ways. First, as considered in themselves, and from this point of view, buying and selling seem to be established for the common advantage of both parties, one of whom requires that which belongs to the other, and vice versa . . . Now whatever is established for the common advantage, should not be more of a burden to one party than to another, and consequently all contracts between them should observe equality of thing and thing. Again, the quality of a thing that comes into human use is measured by the price given for it, for which purpose money was invented . . . Therefore if either the price exceed the quantity of the thing's worth, or, conversely, the thing exceed the price, there is no longer the equality of justice: and consequently, to sell a thing for more than its worth, or to buy it for less than its worth, is in itself unjust and unlawful.

Secondly we may speak of buying and selling, considered as accidentally tending to the advantage of one party, and to the disadvantage of the other: for instance, when a man has great need of a certain thing, while another man will suffer if he be without it. In such a case the just price will depend not only on the thing sold, but on the loss which the sale brings on the seller. And thus it will be lawful to sell a thing for more than it is worth in itself, though the price paid be not more than it is worth to the owner. Yet if the one man derive a great advantage by becoming possessed of the other man's property, and the seller be not at a loss through being without that thing, the latter ought not to raise the price, because the advantage accruing to the buyer, is not due to the seller, but to a circumstance affecting the buyer. Now no man should sell what is not his, though he may charge for the loss he suffers.

On the other hand if a man find that he derives great advantage from something he has bought, he may, of his own accord, pay the seller something over and above: and this pertains to his honesty.

. . . According to the Divine law, it is reckoned unlawful if the equality of justice be not observed in buying and selling: and he who has received more than he ought must make compensation to him that has suffered loss, if the loss be considerable. I add this condition, because the just price of things is not fixed with mathematical precision, but depends on a kind of estimate, so that a slight addition or subtraction would not seem to destroy the equality of justice. . . .

* Reprinted from the *Summa Theologica* with the permission of Benziger Brothers, Inc., publishers and copyright owners.

Whether a Sale Is Rendered Unlawful through a Fault in the Thing Sold?

. . . A threefold fault may be found pertaining to the thing which is sold. One, in respect of the thing's substance: and if the seller be aware of a fault in the thing he is selling, he is guilty of a fraudulent sale, so that the sale is rendered unlawful. Hence we find it written against certain people (Isa. i. 22): *Thy silver is turned into dross, thy wine is mingled with water:* because that which is mixed is defective in its substance.

Another defect is in respect of quantity which is known by being measured: wherefore if anyone knowingly make use of a faulty measure in selling, he is guilty of fraud, and the sale is illicit. . . .

A third defect is on the part of the quality, for instance, if a man sell an unhealthy animal as being a healthy one: and if anyone do this knowingly he is guilty of a fraudulent sale, and the sale, in consequence, is illicit.

In all these cases not only is the man guilty of a fraudulent sale, but he is also bound to restitution. But if any of the foregoing defects be in the thing sold, and he knows nothing about this, the seller does not sin, because he does that which is unjust materially, nor is his deed unjust . . . Nevertheless he is bound to compensate the buyer, when the defect comes to his knowledge. Moreover what has been said of the seller applies equally to the buyer. For sometimes it happens that the seller thinks his goods to be specifically of lower value, as when a man sells gold instead of copper, and then if the buyer be aware of this, he buys it unjustly and is bound to restitution: and the same applies to a defect in quantity as to a defect in quality. . . .

Whether the Seller Is Bound to State the Defects of the Thing Sold?

. . . It is always unlawful to give anyone an occasion of danger or loss, although a man need not always give another the help or counsel which would be for his advantage in any way; but only in certain fixed cases, for instance when someone is subject to him, or when he is the only one who can assist him. Now the seller who offers goods for sale, gives the buyer an occasion of loss or danger, by the very fact that he offers him defective goods, if such defect may occasion loss or danger to the buyer: —loss, if, by reason of this defect, the goods are of less value, and he takes nothing off the price on that account:—danger, if this defect either hinder the use of the goods or render it hurtful, for instance, if a man sells a lame for a fleet horse, a tottering house for a safe one, rotten or poisonous food for wholesome. Wherefore if suchlike defects be hidden, and the seller does not make them known, the sale will be illicit and fraudulent, and the seller will be bound to compensation for the loss incurred.

On the other hand, if the defect be manifest, for instance if a horse have but one eye, or if the goods though useless to the buyer, be useful to someone else, provided the seller take as much as he ought from the price, he is not bound to state the defect of the goods, since perhaps, on account of that defect the buyer might want him to allow a greater rebate than he need. Wherefore the seller may look to his own indemnity, by withholding the defect of the goods. . . .

Whether, in Trading, It Is Lawful to Sell a Thing at a Higher Price Than What Was Paid for It?

. . . A tradesman is one whose business consists in the exchange of things. According to the Philosopher . . . exchange of things is twofold; one, natural as it were, and necessary, whereby one commodity is exchanged for another, or money taken in exchange for a commodity, in order to satisfy the needs of life. Suchlike trading, properly speaking, does not belong to tradesmen, but rather to housekeepers or civil servants who have to provide the household or the state with the necessaries of life. The other kind of exchange is either that of money for money, or of any commodity for money, not on account of the necessities of life, but for profit, and this kind of exchange, properly speaking, regards tradesmen, according to the Philosopher . . . The former kind of exchange is commendable because it supplies a natural need: but the latter is justly deserving of blame, because, considered in itself, it satisfies the greed for gain, which knows no limit and tends to infinity. Hence trading, considered in itself, has a certain debasement attaching thereto, in so far as, by its very nature, it does not imply a virtuous or necessary end. Nevertheless gain which is the end of trading, though not implying, by its nature, anything virtuous or necessary, does not, in itself, connote anything sinful or contrary to virtue: wherefore nothing prevents gain from being directed to some necessary or even virtuous end, and thus trading becomes lawful. Thus, for instance, a man may intend the moderate gain which he seeks to acquire by trading for the upkeep of his household, or for the assistance of the needy: or again, a man may take to trade for some public advantage, for instance, lest his country lack the necessaries of life, and seek gain, not as an end, but as payment for his labour. . . .

OF THE SIN OF USURY, WHICH IS COMMITTED IN LOANS *

We must now consider the sin of usury, which is committed in loans: and under this head there are four points of inquiry: (1) Whether it is a sin to take money as a price for money lent, which is to receive usury? (2) Whether it is lawful to lend money for any other kind of consideration,

* Reprinted from the *Summa Theologica* with the permission of Benziger Brothers, Inc., publishers and copyright owners.

by way of payment for the loan? (3) Whether a man is bound to restore just gains derived from money taken in usury? (4) Whether it is lawful to borrow money under a condition of usury?

Whether It Is a Sin to Take Usury for Money Lent?

. . . To take usury for money lent is unjust in itself, because this is to sell what does not exist, and this evidently leads to inequality which is contrary to justice.

In order to make this evident, we must observe that there are certain things the use of which consists in their consumption: thus we consume wine when we use it for drink, and we consume wheat when we use it for food. Wherefore in suchlike things the use of the thing must not be reckoned apart from the thing itself, and whoever is granted the use of the thing, is granted the thing itself; and for this reason, to lend things of this kind is to transfer the ownership. Accordingly if a man wanted to sell wine separately from the use of the wine, he would be selling the same thing twice, or he would be selling what does not exist, wherefore he would evidently commit a sin of injustice. In like manner he commits an injustice who lends wine or wheat, and asks for double payment, viz. one, the return of the thing in equal measure, the other, the price of the use, which is called usury.

On the other hand there are things the use of which does not consist in their consumption: thus to use a house is to dwell in it, not to destroy it. Wherefore in such things both may be granted: for instance, one man may hand over to another the ownership of his house while reserving to himself the use of it for a time, or vice versa, he may grant the use of the house, while retaining the ownership. For this reason a man may lawfully make a charge for the use of his house, and, besides this, revendicate the house from the person to whom he has granted its use, as happens in renting and letting a house.

Now money, according to the Philosopher, . . . was invented chiefly for the purpose of exchange: and consequently the proper and principal use of money is its consumption or alienation whereby it is sunk in exchange. Hence it is by its very nature unlawful to take payment for the use of money lent, which payment is known as usury: and just as a man is bound to restore other ill-gotten goods, so is he bound to restore the money which he has taken in usury. . . .

Whether It Is Lawful to Ask for Any Other Kind of Consideration for Money Lent?

. . . According to the Philosopher . . . *a thing is reckoned as money if its price can be measured by money.* Consequently, just as it is a sin against justice, to take money, by tacit or express agreement, in return for lending money or anything else that is consumed by being used, so also is it a like sin, by tacit or express agreement to receive anything whose price can be measured by money. Yet there would be no sin in receiving something of the kind, not as exacting it, nor yet as though it were due on account of some agreement tacit or expressed, but as a gratuity: since, even before lending the money, one could accept a gratuity, nor is one in a worse condition through lending.

On the other hand it is lawful to exact compensation for a loan, in respect of such things as are not appreciated by a measure of money, for instance, benevolence, and love for the lender, and so forth. . . .

Whether a Man Is Bound to Restore Whatever Profits He Has Made Out of Money Gotten by Usury?

. . . There are certain things whose use is their consumption, and which do not admit of usufruct, according to law . . . Wherefore if suchlike things be extorted by means of usury, for instance money, wheat, wine and so forth, the lender is not bound to restore more than he received (since what is acquired by such things is the fruit not of the thing but of human industry), unless indeed the other party by losing some of his own goods be injured through the lender retaining them: for then he is bound to make good the loss.

On the other hand there are certain things whose use is not their consumption: such things admit of usufruct, for instance house or land property and so forth. Wherefore if a man has by usury extorted from another his house or land, he is bound to restore not only the house or land but also the fruits accruing to him therefrom, since they are the fruits of things owned by another man and consequently are due to him. . . .

Whether It Is Lawful to Borrow Money under a Condition of Usury?

. . . It is by no means lawful to induce a man to sin, yet it is lawful to make use of another's sin for a good end, since even God uses all sin for some good, since He draws some good from every evil as stated in the *Enchiridion* . . . Hence when Publicola asked whether it were lawful to make use of an oath taken by a man swearing by false gods (which is a manifest sin, for he gives Divine honour to them) Augustine . . . answered that he who uses, not for a bad but for a good purpose, the oath of a man that swears by false gods, is a party, not to his sin of swearing by demons, but to his good compact whereby he kept his word. If, however, he were to induce him to swear by false gods, he would sin.

Accordingly we must also answer to the question in point that it is by no means lawful to induce a man to lend under a condition of usury; yet it is lawful to borrow for usury from a man who is ready to do so and is a usurer by profession; provided the borrower have a good end in view, such as the relief of his own or another's need. Thus too it is lawful for a man who has fallen among thieves to point out his property to them (which they sin in taking) in order to save his life, after the example of the ten men who said to Ismahel . . . *Kill us not: for we have stores in the field.*

PART THREE
Mercantilism

Mercantilism is the term used to describe the economic thought and economic policy which dominated Europe from the sixteenth to the eighteenth century. It necessarily varied from period to period and from land to land, and no one writer has definitely restated mercantilistic doctrine in the same way that St. Thomas restated Scholastic thought.

The age of mercantilism was extremely dynamic. New nation-states were forming and expanding, and the first great European wave of overseas expansion was taking place. Commerce and manufactures were encroaching on what used to be the exclusive domain of agriculture. Whereas the goal of human effort during the Middle Ages had been the attainment of personal salvation, mercantilist policy saw in the individual an instrumentality for aggrandizement of the power of the state.

The extreme mercantilists wished to increase national power by the closest sort of economic regulation, especially of foreign trade. The goal was to have a favorable balance of trade with every country with which the nation traded. An industry manufacturing for export was to be preferred over one manufacturing for the domestic market.

Since most mercantilist writers had a primitive labor theory of production, they considered it good policy to regulate wages downward in order to improve the competitive position of the nation in the export market. For the same reason, and also because of the demand for soldiers, most mercantilists were in favor of a large population.

One school of mercantilist thought, bullionism, emphasized that a nation's wealth was to be measured by the amount of bullion it possessed. Many countries severely restricted the export of bullion because they mistakenly identified money with wealth. For the same reason mercantilists abhorred unsold stocks of commodities, in contrast to the medieval thinkers who desired an increasing abundance of goods and services. This change in attitude resulted from the growing importance and value of money in trade. In the Middle Ages goods had been exchanged for goods, so it was manifestly unwise to diminish one's stock of commodities. But in the mercantilist period even the more enlightened writers like Mun, Petty, and Davenant believed in increasing the stock of money within a country regardless of whether they knew how this money was to be used. The extreme bullionists went further still and wanted to restrict bullion exports entirely. Most mercantilists believed that plentiful and cheap money was beneficial to a nation and made trade flourish, but did not seem to see the inflationary consequences of such a policy.

Most nations tightly controlled trade and industry during this period. Elizabethan England and Colbertian France are extreme examples of attempts to regulate a country to prosperity.

This was an age of colonization, and colonies were regarded as existing for the benefit of the mother country. The onerous and vexatious regulations and taxes which led to the American Revolution were a logical part of British mercantilist policy. In many cases colonial areas were exploited by great chartered companies, like the Hudson Bay Company and the East India Company, which had special grants of monopoly from the Crown.

To summarize, mercantilism was never a definite unified body of doctrine (Adam Smith to the contrary notwithstanding), never completely dominated all minds even at the height of its influence, and has never completely disappeared. Except perhaps for England during the period of laissez-faire (approximately 1815–1914), no Western nation since the seventeenth century has been free of mercantilist ideas.

No one writer can give the student a fair and complete picture of mercantilism. The selection from Thomas Mun is of interest because he was the writer against whom Adam Smith trained his guns and because his expositions are fuller than those of his contemporaries. Von Hornick's piece is considered an outstanding example of mercantilism on the Continent. Steuart has been called "the last of the mercantilists," and the brief quotations indicating his great faith in government control are classic.

THOMAS MUN

(1571–1641)

Mun was perhaps the most important writer of the mercantilist era, and his *England's Treasure by Forraign Trade* was the outstanding exposition of advanced mercantilist doctrine. He was one of the first to show that as long as the total exports of a nation exceeded its imports, a favorable balance of trade with each individual nation was unnecessary.

Thomas Mun was born in London, the son of a prosperous mercer of that city. For some time he was active and successful in foreign trade. He became a member of the board of the East India Company in 1615 and subsequently was placed on its commission on trade. In 1621 he published a pamphlet, *A Discourse of Trade from England unto the East Indies,* in which he defended the East India Company against charges of enriching itself at the expense of the public. The company had been severely attacked by extreme bullionists because it exported bullion from England to India. Mun and other defenders pointed out that this bullion brought back into the English treasury many times the amount exported.

Mun's great work, *England's Treasure by Forraign Trade,* was published twenty-three years after his death by his son John, who stated that the manuscript had been bequeathed to him. In it, Mun took exception to the arguments of certain of his contemporaries, notably Malynes and Misselden. He was opposed especially to Misselden's argument that undervaluation of silver caused an injurious contraction of the currency. Naturally, he also defended the exportation of bullion. He contended that this export was like the seed cast by the farmer and was, in the long run, more than repaid in kind. This bullion purchased raw material to be brought to England, processed, and then again exported in a vastly more valuable form. He also pointed out that the longer the voyage, the greater the profit for England, because of charges for "Shipping, Wages, Victuals, Insurance, Interest, Customes, Imposts, and the like." For several centuries afterward, England continued to gain much treasure through these invisible items. He warned the rulers against hoarding bullion and urged them to spend the money on public works and armament. In a very significant statement Mun held that "a Prince (in this case) is like the stomach in the body, which if it cease to digest and distribute to the other members, it doth no sooner corrupt them, but it destroyes it self." Although this statement may not present a full analysis of the circulation of wealth throughout the community, Mun certainly understood the sterility of hoarded treasure and the fact that it is employment, goods, and services which make for prosperity.

The last part of his study is devoted to an analysis of what constitutes a balance of trade. Note that Mun's contemporary Misselden also considers the balance of trade.

ENGLAND'S TREASURE BY FORRAIGN TRADE *

The means to enrich this Kingdom, and to encrease our Treasure

Although a Kingdom may be enriched by gifts received, or by purchase taken from some other Nations, yet these are things uncertain and of small consideration when they happen. The ordinary means therefore to

* From *England's Treasure by Forraign Trade,* reprinted from the first edition of 1664 and published for the Economic History Society (Oxford, Basil Blackwell, 1928).

encrease our wealth and treasure is by *Forraign Trade,* wherein wee must ever observe this rule; to sell more to strangers yearly than wee consume of theirs in value. For suppose that when this Kingdom is plentifully served with the Cloth, Lead, Tinn, Iron, Fish and other native commodities, we doe yearly export the overplus to forraign Countries to the value of twenty two hundred thousand pounds; by which means we are enabled beyond the Seas to buy and bring in forraign wares for our use and Consumptions, to the value of twenty hundred thousand pounds; By this order duly kept in our trading, we may rest assured that the Kingdom shall be enriched yearly two hundred thousand pounds, which must be brought to us in so much Treasure; because that part of our stock which is not returned to us in wares must necessarily be brought home in treasure. . . .

The particular ways and means to encrease the exportation of our commodities, and to decrease our Consumption of forraign wares

The revenue or stock of a Kingdom by which it is provided of forraign wares is either *Natural* or *Artificial.* The Natural wealth is so much only as can be spared from our own use and necessities to be exported unto strangers. The Artificial consists in our manufactures and industrious trading with forraign commodities, concerning which I will set down such particulars as may serve for the cause we have in hand.

1. First, although this Realm be already exceeding rich by nature, yet might it be much encreased by laying the waste grounds (which are infinite) into such employments as should no way hinder the present revenues of other manured lands, but hereby to supply our selves and prevent the importations of Hemp, Flax, Cordage, Tobacco, and divers other things which now we fetch from strangers to our great impoverishing.

2. We may likewise diminish our importations, if we would soberly refrain from excessive consumption of forraign wares in our diet and rayment, with such often change of fashions as is used, so much the more to encrease the waste and charge; which vices at this present are more notorious amongst us than in former ages. Yet might they easily be amended by enforcing the observation of such good laws as are strictly practised in other Countries against the said excesses; where likewise by commanding their own manufactures to be used, they prevent the coming in of others, without prohibition, or offence to strangers in their mutual commerce.

3. In our exportations we must not only regard our own superfluities, but also we must consider our neighbours necessities, that so upon the wares which they cannot want, nor yet be furnished thereof elsewhere, we may (besides the vent of the Materials) gain so much of the manufacture as we can, and also endeavour to sell them dear, so far forth as the high price cause not a less vent in the quantity. But the superfluity of our commodities which strangers use, and may also have the same from other

Nations, or may abate their vent by the use of some such like wares from other places, and with little inconvenience; we must in this case strive to sell as cheap as possible we can, rather than to lose the utterance of such wares. . . . So that by these alterations we learn, that it is in vain to expect a greater revenue of our wares than their condition will afford, but rather it concerns us to apply our endeavours to the times with care and diligence to help our selves the best we may, by making our cloth and other manufactures without deceit, which will encrease their estimation and use.

4. The value of our exportations likewise may be much advanced when we perform it our selves in our own Ships, for then we get only not the price of our wares as they are worth here, but also the Merchants gains, the charges of ensurance, and fraight to carry them beyond the seas. . . .

5. The frugal expending likewise of our own natural wealth might advance much yearly to be exported unto strangers; and if in our rayment we will be prodigal, yet let this be done with our own materials and manufactures, as Cloth, Lace, Imbroderies, Cutworks and the like, where the excess of the rich may be the employment of the poor, whose labours notwithstanding of this kind, would be more profitable for the Commonwealth, if they were done to the use of strangers.

6. The Fishing in his Majesties seas of *England, Scotland* and *Ireland* is our natural wealth, and would cost nothing but labour, which the *Dutch* bestow willingly, and thereby draw yearly a very great profit to themselves by serving many places of Christendom with our Fish, for which they return and supply their wants both of forraign Wares and Mony, besides the multitude of Mariners and Shipping, which hereby are maintain'd, whereof a long discourse might be made to shew the particular manage of this important business. Our Fishing plantation likewise in *New-England, Virginia, Groenland,* the *Summer Islands* and the *New-found-land,* are of the like nature, affording much wealth and employments to maintain a great number of poor, and to encrease our decaying trade.

7. A Staple or Magazin for forraign Corn, Indico, Spices, Raw-silks, Cotton wool or any other commodity whatsoever, to be imported will encrease Shipping, Trade, Treasure, and the Kings customes, by exporting them again where need shall require, which course of Trading, hath been the chief means to raise *Venice, Genoa,* the *low-Countreys,* with some others; and for such a purpose *England* stands most commodiously, wanting nothing to this performance but our own diligence and endeavour.

8. Also wee ought to esteem and cherish those trades which we have in remote or far Countreys, for besides the encrease of Shipping and Mariners thereby, the wares also sent thither and receiv'd from thence are far more profitable unto the kingdom than by our trades neer at hand; As for example; suppose Pepper to be worth here two Shillings the pound constantly, if then it be brought from the *Dutch* at *Amsterdam,* the Merchant may give there twenty pence the pound, and gain well by the bargain; but if he fetch this Pepper from the *East-indies,* he must not give above three pence the pound at the most, which is a mighty advantage,

not only in that part which serveth for our own use, but also for that great quantity which (from hence) we transport yearly unto divers other Nations to be sold at a higher price: whereby it is plain, that we make a far greater stock by gain upon these *Indian* Commodities, than those Nations doe where they grow, and to whom they properly appertain, being the natural wealth of their Countries. . . .

9. It would be very beneficial to export money as well as wares, being done in trade only, it would encrease our Treasure; but of this I write more largely in the next Chapter to prove it plainly.

10. It were policie and profit for the State to suffer manufactures made of forraign Materials to be exported custome-free, as Velvets and all other wrought Silks, Fustians, thrown Silks and the like, it would employ very many poor people, and much encrease the value of our stock yearly issued into other Countreys, and it would (for this purpose) cause the more forraign Materials to be brought in, to the improvement of His Majesties Customes. I will here remember a notable increase in our manufacture of winding and twisting only of forraign raw Silk, which within 35. years to my knowledge did not employ more than 300. people in the City and suburbs of London, where at this present time it doth set on work above fourteen thousand souls, as upon diligent enquiry hath been credibly reported unto His Majesties Commissioners for Trade. And it is certain, that if the said forraign Commodities might be exported from hence, free of custome, this manufacture would yet encrease very much, and decrease as fast in *Italy* and in the *Netherlands*. . . .

11. It is needful also not to charge the native commodities with too great customes, lest by indearing them to the strangers use, it hinder their vent. And especially forraign wares brought in to be transported again should be favoured, for otherwise that manner of trading (so much importing the good of the Commonwealth) cannot prosper nor subsist. But the Consumption of such forraign wares in the Realm may be the more charged, which will turn to the profit of the kingdom in the *Ballance of the Trade,* and thereby also enable the King to lay up the more Treasure out of his yearly incomes, as of this particular I intend to write more fully in his proper place, where I shall shew how much money a Prince may conveniently lay up without the hurt of his subjects.

12. Lastly, in all things we must endeavour to make the most we can of our own, whether it be *Natural* or *Artificial;* And forasmuch as the people which live by the Arts are far more in number than they who are masters of the fruits, we ought the more carefully to maintain those endeavours of the multitude, in whom doth consist the greatest strength and riches both of King and Kingdom: for where the people are many, and the arts good, there the traffique must be great, and the Countrey rich. The *Italians* employ a greater number of people, and get more money by their industry and manufactures of the raw Silks of the Kingdom of *Cicilia,* than the King of *Spain* and his Subjects have by the revenue of this rich commodity. But what need we fetch the example so far, when

we know that our own natural wares doe not yield us so much profit as our industry? For Iron oar in the Mines is of no great worth, when it is compared with the employment and advantage it yields being digged, tried, transported, bought, sold, cast into Ordnance, Muskets, and many other instruments of war for offence and defence, wrought into Anchors, bolts, spikes, nayles and the like, for the use of Ships, Houses, Carts, Coaches, Ploughs, and other instruments for Tillage. Compare our Fleece-wools with our Cloth, which requires shearing, washing, carding, spinning, Weaving, fulling, dying, dressing and other trimmings, and we shall find these Arts more profitable than the natural wealth, whereof I might instance other examples, but I will not be more tedious, for if I would amplify upon this and the other particulars before written, I might find matter sufficient to make a large volume, but my desire in all is only to prove what I propound with brevity and plainness.

The Exportation of our Moneys in Trade of Merchandize is a means to encrease our Treasure

This Position is so contrary to the common opinion, that it will require many and strong arguments to prove it before it can be accepted of the Multitude, who bitterly exclaim when they see any monies carried out of the Realm; affirming thereupon that wee have absolutely lost so much Treasure, and that this is an act directly against the long continued laws made and confirmed by the wisdom of this Kingdom in the High Court of Parliament, and that many places, nay *Spain* it self which is the Fountain of Mony, forbids the exportation thereof, some cases only excepted. To all which I might answer, that *Venice, Florence, Genoa,* the *Low Countreys* and divers other places permit it, their people applaud it, and find great benefit by it; but all this makes a noise and proves nothing, we must therefore come to those reasons which concern the business in question.

First, I will take that for granted which no man of judgment will deny, that we have no other means to get Treasure but by forraign trade, for Mines wee have none which do afford it, and how this money is gotten in the managing of our said Trade I have already shewed, that it is done by making our commodities which are exported yearly to over ballance in value the forraign wares which we consume; so that it resteth only to shew how our monyes may be added to our commodities, and being jointly exported may so much the more encrease our Treasure.

Wee have already supposed our yearly consumptions of forraign wares to be for the value of twenty hundred thousand pounds, and our exportations to exceed that two hundred thousand pounds, which sum wee have thereupon affirmed is brought to us in treasure to ballance the accompt. But now if we add three hundred thousand pounds more in ready money unto our former exportations in wares, what profit can we have (will some men say) although by this means we should bring in so much ready mony more than wee did before, seeing that wee have carried out the like value.

To this the answer is, that when wee have prepared our exportations of wares, and sent out as much of every thing as wee can spare or vent abroad: It is not therefore said that then we should add our money thereunto to fetch in the more mony immediately, but rather first to enlarge our trade by enabling us to bring in more forraign wares, which being sent out again will in due time much encrease our Treasure.

For although in this manner wee do yearly multiply our importations to the maintenance of more Shipping and Mariners, improvment of His Majesties Customs and other benefits: yet our consumption of those forraign wares is no more than it was before; so that all the said encrease of commodities brought in by the means of our ready mony sent out as is afore written, doth in the end become an exportation unto us of a far greater value than our said moneys were, which is proved by three several examples following.

1. For I suppose that 100000. *l.* being sent in our Shipping to the East Countreys, will buy there one hundred thousand quarters of wheat cleer aboard the Ships, which being after brought into *England* and housed, to export the same at the best time for vent thereof in *Spain* or *Italy,* it cannot yield less in those parts than two hundred thousand pounds to make the Merchant but a saver, yet by this reckning wee see the Kingdom hath doubled that Treasure.

2. Again this profit will be far greater when wee trade thus in remote Countreys, as for example, if wee send one hundred thousand pounds into the *East-Indies* to buy Pepper there, and bring it hither, and from hence send it for *Italy* or *Turkey,* it must yield seven hundred thousand pounds at least in those places, in regard of the excessive charge which the Merchant disburseth in those long voyages in Shipping, Wages, Victuals, Insurance, Interest, Customes, Imposts, and the like, all which notwithstanding the King and the Kingdom gets.

3. But where the voyages are short & the wares rich, which therefore will not employ much Shipping, the profit will be far less. As when another hundred thousand pounds shall be employed in *Turkey* in raw Silks, and brought hither to be after transported from hence into *France,* the *Low Countreys,* or *Germany,* the Merchant shall have good gain, although he sell it there but for one hundred and fifty thousand pounds: and thus take the voyages altogether in their *Medium,* the moneys exported will be returned unto us more than Trebled. But if any man will yet object, that these returns come to us in wares, and not really in mony as they were issued out,

The answer is (keeping our first ground) that if our consumption of forraign wares be no more yearly than is already supposed, and that our exportations be so mightily encreased by this manner of Trading with ready money as is before declared: It is not then possible but that all the over-ballance or difference should return either in mony or in such wares as we must export again, which, as is already plainly shewed will be still a greater means to encrease our Treasure.

For it is in the stock of the Kingdom as in the estates of private men, who having store of wares, doe not therefore say that they will not venture out or trade with their mony (for this were ridiculous) but do also turn that into wares, whereby they multiply their Mony, and so by a continual and orderly change of one into the other grow rich, and when they please turn all their estates into Treasure; for they that have Wares cannot want mony.

Neither is it said that Mony is the Life of Trade, as if it could not subsist without the same; for we know that there was great trading by way of commutation or barter when there was little mony stirring in the world. The *Italians* and some other Nations have such remedies against this want, that it can neither decay nor hinder their trade, for they transfer bills of debt, and have Banks both publick and private, wherein they do assign their credits from one to another daily for very great sums with ease and satisfaction by writings only, whilst in the mean time the Mass of Treasure which gave foundation to these credits is employed in Forraign Trade as a Merchandize, and by the said means they have little other use of money in those countreys more than for their ordinary expences. It is not therefore the keeping of our mony in the Kingdom, but the necessity and use of our wares in forraign Countries, and our want of their commodities that causeth the vent and consumption on all sides, which makes a quick and ample Trade. If wee were once poor, and now having gained some store of mony by trade with resolution to keep it still in the Realm; shall this cause other Nations to spend more of our commodities than formerly they have done, whereby we might say that our trade is Quickned and Enlarged? no verily, it will produce no such good effect: but rather according to the alteration of times by their true causes wee may expect the contrary; for all men do consent that plenty of mony in a Kingdom doth make the native commodities dearer, which as it is to the profit of some private men in their revenues, so is it directly against the benefit of the Publique in the quantity of the trade; for as plenty of mony makes wares dearer, so dear wares decline their use and consumption . . . . And although this is a very hard lesson for some great landed men to learn, yet I am sure it is a true lesson for all the land to observe, lest when wee have gained some store of mony by trade, wee lose it again by not trading with our mony. I knew a Prince in *Italy* (of famous memory) *Ferdinando the first,* great Duke of *Tuscanie,* who being very rich in Treasure, endevoured therewith to enlarge his trade by issuing out to his Merchants great sums of money for very small profit; I my self had forty thousand crowns of him *gratis* for a whole year, although he knew that I would presently send it away in *Specie* for the parts of *Turkey* to be employed in wares for his Countries, he being well assured that in this course of trade it would return again (according to the old saying) with a Duck in the mouth. This noble and industrious Prince by his care and diligence to countenance and favour Merchants in their affairs, did so encrease the practice thereof, that there is scarce a Nobleman or Gentleman in all his dominions that doth not Merchandize either by himself or in partnership with others, whereby within these thirty years the trade to his port of *Leghorn* is so much encreased, that of a poor little town (as I my self knew it) it is now become a fair and strong City, being one of the most famous places for trade in all Christendom. . . .

There is yet an objection or two as weak as all the rest: that is, if wee trade with our Mony wee shall issue out the less wares; as if a man should say, those Countreys which heretofore had occasion to consume our Cloth, Lead, Tin, Iron, Fish, and the like, shall now make use of our monies in the place of those necessaries, which were most absurd to affirm, or that the Merchant had not rather carry out wares by which there is ever some gains expected, than to export mony which is still but the same without any encrease.

But on the contrary there are many Countreys which may yield us very profitable trade for our mony, which otherwise afford us no trade at all, because they have no use of our wares, as namely the *East-Indies* for one in the first beginning thereof, although since by industry in our commerce with those Nations we have brought them into the use of much of our Lead, Cloth, Tin, and other things, which is a good addition to the former vent of our commodities.

Again, some men have alleged that those Countries which permit mony to be carried out, do it because they have few or no wares to trade withall: but wee have great store of commodities, and therefore their action ought not to be our example.

To this the answer is briefly, that if we have such a quantity of wares as doth fully provide us of all things needful from beyond the seas: why should we then doubt that our monys sent out in trade, must not necessarily come back again in treasure; together with the great gains which it may procure in such manner as is before set down? And on the other side, if those Nations which send out their monies do it because they have but few wares of their own, how come they then to have so much Treasure as we ever see in those places which suffer it freely to be exported at all times and by whomsoever? I answer, *Even by trading with their Moneys;* for by what other means can they get it, having no Mines of Gold or Silver?

Thus may we plainly see, that when this weighty business is duly considered in his end, as all our humane actions ought well to be weighed, it is found much contrary to that which most men esteem thereof, because they search no further than the beginning of the work, which mis-informs theïr judgments, and leads them into error: For if we only behold the actions of the husbandman in the seed-time when he casteth away much good corn into the ground, we will rather accompt him a mad man than a husbandman: but when we consider his labours in the harvest which is the end of his endeavours, we find the worth and plentiful encrease of his actions. . . .

It will not increase our treasure to enjoyn the Merchant that exporteth Fish, Corn or Munition, to return all or part of the value in Money

Victuals and Munition for war are so pretious in a Commonwealth, that either it seemeth necessary to restrain the exportation altogether, or (if the plenty permits it) to require the return thereof in so much treasure; which appeareth to be reasonable and without difficulty, because *Spain* and other Countries do willingly part with their money for such wares, although in other occasions of trade they straightly prohibit the exportation thereof: all which I grant to be true, yet notwithstanding we must consider that all the ways and means which (in course of trade) force treasure into the Kingdom, do not therefore make it ours: for this can be done onely by a lawful gain, and this gain is no way to be accomplished but by the overballance of our trade, and this overballance is made less by restrictions: therefore such restrictions do hinder the increase of our treasure. The Argument is plain, and needs no other reasons to strengthen it, except any man be so vain to think that restrictions would not cause the less wares to be exported. But if this likewise should be granted, yet to enjoyn the Merchant to bring in money for Victuals and Munition carried out, will not cause us to have one peny the more in the Kingdom at the years end; for whatsoever is forced in one way must out again another way: because onely so much will remain and abide with us as is gained and incorporated into the estate of the Kingdom by the overballance of the trade.

This may be made plain by an example taken from an Englishman, who had occasion to buy and consume the wares of divers strangers for the value of six hundred pounds, and having wares of his own for the value of one thousand pounds, he sold them to the said strangers, and presently forced all the money from them into his own power; yet upon cleering of the reckoning between them there remained onely four hundred pounds to the said Englishman for overballance of the wares bought and sold; so the rest which he had received was returned back from whence he forced it. And this shall suffice to shew that whatsoever courses we take to force money into the Kingdom, yet so much onely will remain with us as we shall gain by the ballance of our trade. . . .

Whether it be necessary for great Princes to lay up store of Treasure

Before we set down the quantity of Treasure which Princes may conveniently lay up yearly without hurting the Common-wealth, it will be fit to examine whether the act it self of Treasuring be necessary: for in common conference we ever find some men who do so much dote or hope upon the Liberality of Princes, that they term it baseness, and conceive it needless for them to lay up store of Treasure, accounting the honour and safety of great Princes to consist more in their Bounty, than in their Money, which they labour to confirm by the examples of *Caesar, Alexander,* and others, who hating covetousness, atchieved many acts and victories by lavish gifts and liberal expences. Unto which they add also the *little fruit* which came by that *great summ of money* which King *David* laid up and left to his son *Solomon,* who notwithstanding this, and all his other rich Presents and wealthy Traffique in a quiet reign, consumed all with pomp and vain delights, excepting only that which was spent in building of the Temple. . . . A Prince who hath store of mony hates peace, despiseth the friendship of his Neighbours and Allies, enters not only into unnecessary, but also into dangerous Wars, to the ruin and over-throw (sometimes) of his own estate: All which, with divers other weak arguments of this kind, (which for brevity I omit) make nothing against the lawful gathering and massing up of Treasure by wise and provident Princes, if they be rightly understood.

For first, concerning those worthies who have obtained to the highest top of *honour* and *dignity,* by their great gifts and expences, who knows not that this hath been done rather upon the spoils of their Enemies than out of their own Cofers, which is indeed a Bounty that causeth neither loss nor peril? Whereas on the countrary, those Princes which do not providently lay up Treasure, or do imoderately consume the same when they have it, will sodainly come to want and misery; for there is nothing doth so soon decay as Excessive Bounty, in using whereof they want the means to use it. And this was King *Solomons* case, notwithstanding, his infinite Treasure, which made him overburthen his Subjects in such a manner, that (for this cause) many of them rebelled against his Son *Rehoboam,* who thereby lost a great part of his dominions, being so grosly mis-led by his young Counsellors. Therefore a Prince that will not oppress his people, and yet be able to maintain his Estate, and defend his Right, that will not run himself into Poverty, Contempt, Hate, and Danger, must lay up treasure, and be thrifty, for further proof whereof I might yet produce some other examples, which here I do omit as needless.

Only I will add this as a necessary rule to be observed, that when more treasure must be raised than can be received by the ordinary taxes, it ought ever to be done with equality to avoid the hate of the people, who are never pleased except their contributions be granted by general consent: For which purpose the invention of Parliaments is an excellent policie of Government, to keep a sweet concord between a King and his Subjects, by restraining the Insolency of the Nobility, and redressing the Injuries of the Commons, without engaging a Prince to adhere to either party, but indifferently to favour both. There could nothing be devised with more judgment for the common quiet of a Kingdom, or with greater care for the safety of a King, who hereby hath also good means to dispatch those things by others, which will move envy, and to execute that himself which will merit thanks.

How much Treasure a Prince may conveniently lay up yearly

Thus far we have shewed the ordinary and extraordinary incomes of Princes, the conveniency thereof, and to whom only it doth necessarily and justly belong, to take the extraordinary contributions of their Subjects. It resteth now to examine what proportion of treasure each particular Prince may conveniently lay up yearly. This business doth seem at the first to be very plain and easy, for if a Prince have two millions yearly revenue, and spend but one, why should he not lay up the other? Indeed I must confess that this course is ordinary in the means and gettings of private men, but in the affairs of Princes it is far different, there are other circumstances to be considered; for although the revenue of a King should be very great, yet if the gain of the Kingdom be but small, this latter must ever give rule and proportion to that Treasure, which may conveniently be laid up yearly, for if he should mass up more money than is gained by the over-ballance of his forraign trade, he shall not *Fleece,* but *Flea* his Subjects, and so with their ruin overthrow himself for want of future sheerings. To make this plain, suppose a Kingdom to be so rich by nature and art, that it may supply it self of forraign wares by trade, and yet advance yearly 200000 *l.* in ready mony: Next suppose all the Kings revenues to be 900000 *l.* and his expences but 400000 *l.* whereby he may lay up 300000 *l.* more in his Coffers yearly than the whole Kingdom gains from strangers by forraign trade; who sees not then that all the mony in such a State, would suddenly be drawn into the Princes treasure, whereby the life of lands and arts must fail and fall to the ruin both of the publick and private wealth? So that a King who desires to lay up much mony must endeavour by all good means to maintain and encrease his forraign trade, because it is the sole way not only to lead him to his own ends, but also to enrich his Subjects to his farther benefit: for a Prince is esteemed no less powerful by having many rich and well affected Subjects, than by possessing much treasure in his Coffers.

But here we must meet with an Objection, which peradventure may be made concerning such States (whereof I have formerly spoken) which are of no great extent, and yet bordering upon mighty Princes, are therefore constrained to lay extraordinary taxes upon their subjects, whereby they procure to themselves very great incomes yearly, and are richly provided against any Forraign Invasions; yet have they no such great trade with Strangers, as that the overbalance or gain of the same may suffice to lay up the one half of that which they advance yearly, besides their own expences.

To this the answer is, that stil the gain of their Forraign Trade must be the rule of laying up their treasure, the which although it should not be much yearly, yet in the time of a long continued peace, and being well managed to advantage, it will become a great summe of money, able to make a long defence, which may end or divert the war. Neither are all the advances of Princes strictly tied to be massed up in treasure, for they have other no less necessary and profitable wayes to make them rich and powerfull, by issuing out continually a great part of the mony of their yearly Incomes to their subjects from whom it was first taken; as namely, by employing them to make Ships of War, with all the provisions thereunto belonging, to build and repair Forts, to buy and store up Corn in the Granaries of each Province for a years use (at least) aforehand, to serve in occasion of Dearth, which cannot be neglected by a State but with great danger, to erect Banks with their money for the encrease of their subjects trade, to maintain in their pay, Collonels, Captains, Souldiers, Commanders, Mariners, and others, both by Sea and Land, with good discipline, to fill their Store-houses (in sundry strong places) and to abound in Gunpowder, Brimstone, Saltpeter, Shot, Ordnance, Musquets, Swords, Pikes, Armours, Horses, and in many other such like Provisions fitting War; all which will make them to be feared abroad, and loved at home, especially if care be taken that all (as neer as possible) be made out of the Matter and Manufacture of their own subjects, which bear the burden of the yearly Contributions; for a Prince (in this case) is like the stomach in the body, which if it cease to digest and distribute to the other members, it doth no sooner corrupt them, but it destroyes it self.

Thus we have seen that a small State may lay up a great wealth in necessary provisions, which are Princes Jewels, no less precious than their Treasure, for in time of need they are ready, and cannot otherwise be had (in some places) on the suddain, whereby a State may be lost, whilest Munition is in providing: so that we may account that Prince as poor who can have no wares to buy at his need, as he that hath no money to buy wares; for although *Treasure is said to be the sinews of the War,* yet this is so because it doth provide, unite & move the power of men, victuals, and munition where and when the cause doth require; but if these things be wanting in due time, what shall we then do with our mony? the consideration of this, doth cause divers well-governed States to be exceeding provident and well furnished of such provisions, especially those Granaries and Storehouses with that famous *Arsenal* of the *Venetians,* are to be admired for the magnificence of the buildings, the quantity of the Munitions and Stores both for Sea and Land, the multitude of the workmen, the diversity and excellency of the Arts, with the order of the government. They are rare and worthy things for Princes to behold and imitate; for Majesty without providence of competent force, and ability of necessary provisions is unassured. . . .

The order and means whereby we may draw up the ballance of our Forraign Trade

Now, that we have sufficiently proved the Ballance of our Forraign Trade to be the true rule of our Treasure; It resteth that we shew by whom and in what manner the said ballance may bedrawn up at all times, when it shall please the State to discover how we prosper or decline in this great and weighty business, wherein the Officers of his Majesties Customes are the onely Agents to be employed, because they have the accounts of all the wares which are issued out or brought into the Kingdome; and although (it is true) they cannot exactly set down the cost and charges of other mens goods bought here or beyond the seas; yet nevertheless, if they ground themselves upon the book of Rates, they shall be able to make such an estimate as may well satisfie this enquiry: for it is not expected that such an account can possibly be drawn up to a just ballance, it will suffice onely that the difference be not over great.

First therefore, concerning our Exportations, when we have valued their first cost, we must add twenty-five *per cent.* thereunto for the charges here, for fraight of Ships, ensurance of the *Adventure,* and the *Merchants* Gains; and for our Fishing Trades, which pay no Custome to his Majesty, the value of such Exportations may be easily esteem'd by good observations which have been made, and may continually be made, according to the increase or decrease of those affairs, the present estate of this commodity being valued at one hundred and forty thousand pounds issued yearly. Also we must add to our Exportations all the moneys which are carried out in Trade by license from his Majesty.

Secondly, for our Importations of Forraign Wares, the Custome-books serve onely to direct us concerning the quantity, for we must not value they as they are rated here, but as they cost us with all charges laden into our Ships beyond the Seas, in the respective places where they are bought: for the Merchants gain, the charges of Insurance, Fraight of Ships, Customes, Imposts, and other Duties here, which doe greatly indear them unto our use and consumption, are notwithstanding but Commutations amongst our selves, for the Stranger hath no part thereof: wherefore our said Importations ought to be valued at twenty five *per cent.* less than they are rated to be worth here. And although this may seem to be too great allowance upon many rich Commodities, which come but from the *Low Countreys* and other places neer hand, yet will it be found reasonable, when we consider it in gross Commodities, and upon Wares laden in remote Countreys, as our Pepper, which cost us, with charges, but four pence the pound in the *East Indies,* and it is here rated at twenty pence the pound: so that when all is brought into a *medium,* the valuation ought to be made as afore-written. And therefore, the order which hath been used to multiply the full rates upon wares inwards by twenty, would produce a very great errour in the Ballance, for in this manner the ten thousand bags of Pepper, which this year we have brought hither from the *East Indies,* should be valued at very near two hundred and fifty thousand pounds, whereas all this Pepper in the Kingdomes accompt, cost not above fifty thousand pounds, because the Indians have had no more of us, although we paid them extraordinary dear prices for the same. All the other charges (as I have said before) is but a change of effects amongst our selves, and from the Subject to the King, which cannot impoverish the Common-wealth. But it is true; that whereas nine thousand bags of the said Pepper are already shipped out for divers forraign parts; These and all other Wares, forraign or domestick, which are thus transported Outwards, ought to be cast up by the rates of his Majesties Custome-money, multiplyed by twenty, or rather by twenty five (as I conceive) which will come neerer the reckoning, when we consider all our Trades to bring them into a *medium*.

Thirdly, we must remember, that all Wares exported or imported by Strangers (in their shipping) be esteemed by themselves, for what they carry out, the Kingdom hath only the first cost and the custom: And what they bring in, we must rate it as it is worth here, the Custom, Impost, and pety charges only deducted.

Lastly, there must be good notice taken of all the great losses which we receive at Sea in our Shipping either outward or homeward bound: for the value of the one is to be deducted from our Exportations, and the value of the other is to be added to our Importations: for to lose and to consume doth produce one and the same reckoning. Likewise if it happen that His Majesty doth make over any great sums of mony by Exchange to maintain a forraign war, where we do not feed and clothe the Souldiers, and Provide the armies, we must deduct all this charge out of our Exportations or add it to our Importations; for this expence doth either carry out or hinder the coming in of so much Treasure. And here we must remember the great collections of mony which are supposed to be made throughout the Realm yearly from our Recusants by Priests and Jesuits, who secretly convey the same unto their Colleges, Cloysters and Nunneries beyond the Seas, from whence it never returns to us again in any kind; therefore if this mischief cannot be prevented, yet it must be esteemed and set down as a cleer loss to the Kingdome, except (to ballance this) we will imagine that as great a value may perhaps come in from forraign Princes to their Pensioners here for Favours or Intelligence, which some States account good Policy, to purchase with great Liberality; the receipt whereof notwithstanding is plain Treachery.

There are yet some other petty things which seem to have reference to this Ballance, of which the said Officers of His Majesties Customs can take no notice, to bring them into the accompt. As namely, the expences of travailers, the gifts to Ambassadors and Strangers, the fraud of some rich goods not entred into the Custom-house, the gain which is made here by Strangers by change and re-change, Interest of mony, ensurance upon English mens goods and their lives: which can be little when the charges of their living here is deducted; besides that the very like advantages are as amply ministred unto the English in forraign Countreys, which doth counterpoize all these things, and therefore they are not considerable in the drawing up of the said Ballance.

PHILIPP WILHELM VON HORNICK

(1638–1712)

The son of a high administrative official, von Hornick studied and received his doctorate in law at the University of Inglestadt in Austria. Then he returned to Vienna, where he practiced law and wrote several anti-French polemics in which he claimed Charlemagne's ancient empire for Austria. More important, however, especially for economists, is his *Oesterreich über Alles, wann Es Nur Will* (*Austria over All, if She Only Will*), published anonymously in 1684. This extremely popular pamphlet went through twelve editions and won for von Hornick a post as privy councilor with the Cardinal of Passau.

The work is thoroughly mercantilist and autarchic. Von Hornick tried to show how Austria could become wealthy and self-sufficient if she consumed only what she produced and produced what she consumed. He urged a census of resources and a progressive population policy. Foreign goods were to be totally excluded even if they were better and cheaper than Austrian goods. Gold and silver were not to leave the country under any pretext; all necessary and unavoidable imports were to be paid for by the export of commodities.

In truly mercantilist fashion he argued that political considerations always outweighed economic considerations; the cornerstone of his policy was the aggrandizement of Austrian power. Some of his arguments have not been surpassed by modern protectionists, and the policies he laid down have been aped consciously or unconsciously by many underdeveloped countries wishing to industrialize.

It is apparent from an examination of the document that von Hornick has great faith in his arguments and expects his readers to take them on faith as well. For example, he does not seem to take seriously the possibility of sharp retaliation by the countries whose exports Austria is urged to cut off. And his confidence in state regulation as a cure-all is naïve and trusting—but very typical of the age.

AUSTRIA OVER ALL IF SHE ONLY WILL *

Nine Principal Rules of National Economy

If the might and eminence of a country consist in its surplus of gold, silver, and all other things necessary or convenient for its *subsistence*, derived, so far as possible, from its own resources, without *dependence* upon other countries, and in the proper fostering, use, and application of these, then it follows that a general national *economy* (*Landes-Oeconomie*) should consider how such a surplus, fostering, and enjoyment can be brought about, without *dependence* upon others, or where this is not feasible in every respect, with as little *dependence* as possible upon foreign countries, and sparing use of the country's own cash. For this purpose the following nine rules are especially serviceable.

First, to inspect the country's soil with the greatest care, and not to leave the agricultural possibilities or a single corner or clod of earth

* From *Austria over All if She Only Will.* Reprinted by permission of the publishers from Arthur Eli Monroe, *Early Economic Thought*. Cambridge, Mass.: Harvard University Press, Copyright, 1924, by The President and Fellows of Harvard College.

unconsidered. Every useful form of *plant* under the sun should be experimented with, to see whether it is adapted to the country, for the distance or nearness of the sun is not all that counts. Above all, no trouble or expense should be spared to discover gold and silver.

Second, all commodities found in a country, which cannot be used in their natural state, should be worked up within the country; since the payment for *manufacturing* generally exceeds the value of the raw material by two, three, ten, twenty, and even a hundred fold, and the neglect of this is an abomination to prudent managers.

Third, for carrying out the above two rules, there will be need of people, both for producing and cultivating the raw materials and for working them up. Therefore, attention should be given to the population, that it may be as large as the country can support, this being a well-ordered state's most important concern, but, unfortunately, one that is often neglected. And the people should be turned by all possible means from idleness to remunerative *professions;* instructed and encouraged in all kinds of *inventions,* arts, and trades; and, if necessary, instructors should be brought in from foreign countries for this.

Fourth, gold and silver once in the country, whether from its own mines or obtained by *industry* from foreign countries, are under no circumstances to be taken out for any purpose, so far as possible, or allowed to be buried in chests or coffers, but must always remain in *circulation;* nor should much be permitted in uses where they are at once *destroyed* and cannot be utilized again. For under these conditions, it will be impossible for a country that has once acquired a considerable supply of cash, especially one that possesses gold and silver mines, ever to sink into poverty; indeed, it is impossible that it should not continually increase in wealth and property. Therefore,

Fifth, the inhabitants of the country should make every effort to get along with their domestic products, to confine their luxury to these alone, and to do without foreign products as far as possible (except where great need leaves no alternative, or if not need, wide-spread, unavoidable abuse, of which Indian spices are an example). And so on.

Sixth, in case the said purchases were indispensable because of necessity or *irremediable* abuse, they should be obtained from these foreigners at first hand, so far as possible, and not for gold or silver, but in exchange for other domestic wares.

Seventh, such foreign commodities should in this case be imported in unfinished form, and worked up within the country, thus earning the wages of *manufacture* there.

Eighth, opportunities should be sought night and day for selling the country's superfluous goods to these foreigners in manufactured form, so far as this is necessary, and for gold and silver; and to this end, *consumption,* so to speak, must be sought in the farthest ends of the earth, and developed in every possible way.

Ninth, except for important considerations, no importation should be allowed under any circumstances of commodities of which there is a sufficient supply of suitable quality at home; and in this matter neither sympathy nor compassion should be shown foreigners, be they friends, kinsfolk, *allies,* or enemies. For all friendship ceases, when it involves my own weakness and ruin. And this holds good, even if the domestic commodities are of poorer quality, or even higher priced. For it would be better to pay for an article two dollars which remain in the country than only one which goes out, however strange this may seem to the ill-informed.

There is no need of further elucidating these fundamental rules of a general national *economy.* Their reasonableness is obvious to every man of intelligence. . . .

How to Institute Reforms in the National Economy Properly

. . . I should like to begin with the above-mentioned fifth rule, and advise the Austrians to be content for a while with their own goods, with their own manufactures, however bad they may be at first, and to refrain from foreign ones, keeping their good gold and silver in their pockets. This would fit in with all the other rules, and everything else would follow from this alone. For the ninth rule is practically included in this fifth one; and if people would use nothing but domestic *manufactures,* the children and inhabitants of the country would be compelled (most of them gladly) to turn their hands to their own *manufactures,* and to work up the domestic raw materials. In this way the second rule would be greatly furthered. And since artisans go where they can get a living, and many foreigners would necessarily be out of work as a result of the prohibition of their *products,* and sometimes even lack our raw materials, they would be compelled to come to Austria, in order to seek work, necessary raw materials, and their living, and to settle there . . .

What is to be done about those merchants who are engaged solely in the importing business? They will be ruined.—An advantage! For they are the very fellows who are impoverishing the country. It is therefore better that they should collapse than the commonwealth. They will be able to hold out, however, until they obtain *commissions* from domestic wholesalers or financiers, or *credit* from them, or book-keeping with the *manufacturers,* or some other position or service (of which there will then be a hundred times as many as there are ruined merchants), or invest any *capital* they may have in domestic *manufactures.* If they do not wish to be employed by the domestic *factories,* however, and they have no *capital* to invest, then such worthless rascals, who act only to the advantage of foreigners and to the harm of Austria, and who have not been able to do any more than earn their daily bread, are no more worthy of sympathy than downright fools.

Our Austrian manufactures will not be as good as the foreign ones.—Such a claim is in many cases a delusion of the Devil, who is hostile to the prosperity of Austria. Granted, however, that this would be an unavoidable evil, still it would not be unendurable. I will cite the prohibition of

Hungarian wine in Austria, Styria, and elsewhere. If you ask why wines are prohibited which are better than the domestic ones, and even cheaper, the answer will be: That the domestic gifts of Providence may be utilized and prudently *consumed,* not despised, thrown away, or ruined; that the highlands may be *benefited,* and the limited cultivation of vineyards, an important source of regalian revenue, may not be abandoned; that thereby so much more money may stay in our pockets. It is the same with Hungarian salt, to which the Austrian is inferior. And yet the former is kept out and the latter retains control of the field. It is quite the proper thing, however, and can be applied *ad literam* to domestic *manufactures.* For if we have such *principles* in a few things, why do we not *extend* them to the great and many? . . .

It is to be feared that we shall have to live at the mercy of domestic artisans and business-men, since they will raise their prices excessively when they are not restrained by foreigners.—If the government supervises things as it should, and checks wantonness, this will not have to be feared. And if manufactures eventually become extensive, the people themselves will strive for money and bread, and make goods cheap through their plentifulness. Where foodstuffs, house-rent, and wages of servants, as well as raw materials or goods, are inexpensive, as with us, and where wares are not brought from a distance and consequently are subject to no heavy charges for freight, tolls, or risks, it is hardly possible that they should be higher-priced than foreign ones (especially if the market is certain, and the goods do not have to lie long at *interest*). It might even be said that strangers do not make us gifts of these things, either; and it would be better, after all, if something must be sacrificed, to be a victim to one's own countryman rather than to a stranger, and to console one's self with the fact, already alluded to above, that it is better, although not every peasant can understand it, to pay two dollars for a domestic article, which remains in the country, than only one for a foreign one, which is exported. For what once goes out stays out. But what remains in domestic *circulation* involves no loss to the *public,* but is an advantage in several ways. The merchant himself, who invested it, can profit by it again. The state is to be thought of as a rich man, who has his money in many purses. If he takes something out of one and puts it into the other, he becomes no poorer thereby. For, although one purse becomes lighter, the other becomes that much heavier. He is master, however, of one as well as of the other. And this must be a leading *principle* of national *economy,* or things will not go well.

But those nations whose manufactures we propose to prohibit will be angry, and cut us off from such things as we may still need from them; our domestic goods hitherto taken by them will be left on our hands; our alliances and we ourselves will be deserted in time of need.—Let them be angry who will. If they are enemies, we do not need to spare their feelings; if they are friends, they will excuse us if we, by eventually developing a good *economy,* get into a *position* not only to help ourselves, but also in case of need to be of more *real* service to them. We see how France is angry at the way England consigns to the flames all French wares that are discovered. And after all, let him who stands behind Job take a friendship which really aims only at plundering our purse. We have learned how much friends give us for nothing in an emergency.

EDWARD MISSELDEN

(1608–1654)

In Misselden's time controversy raged over the chartered East India Company's export of bullion to India. The extreme bullionists were opposed to any export of specie, while the Company defended itself by showing that bullion export was capital investment, resulting ultimately in the augmentation of bullion in England.

On this question Misselden was on both sides of the fence. When he was in the employ of the Merchants Adventurers he wrote a pamphlet attacking the East India Company. A year later, after joining the East India Company, he reversed his position and wrote his justly famous *Circle of Commerce* (1623), in which he defended the free sale of foreign exchange and attacked Gerard de Malynes, a confirmed bullionist. In this pamphlet Misselden introduced the term *balance of trade,* which had not been used previously (unless by Mun) and actually drew one up for the England of his time. He also emphasized the modern view that one must examine a nation's entire balance of trade in order to see whether bullion export is dangerous.

While Misselden wanted government regulation in many fields, and favored the chartered companies, he nevertheless advocated freedom in trade and commerce.

OF EXCHANGES IN GENERALL *

The *Politique Exchange,* is when mony is exchanged value for value, according to the *extrinsique* or outward valuation. Such as is the *intrinsique* finenes to the *natural Exchange,* such is the *extrinsique* value to the *Politique Exchange.* Wherein Merchants are wont to reckon the certaine value of mony in finenes, at an uncertaine valuation, in denomination and accompt: sometimes at a higher, sometimes at a lower rate. Which is therefore in Merchants termes, called the *price,* or *course,* or *rate* of the *Exchange.* And this valuation is thus uncertaine, because it is greater or lesse, according to the circumstances of *time,* and *place,* and *persons.* Of *time,* when money is taken by *Exchange* for longer or shorter time. Of *place,* where mony is more plentifull or scarse. Of *persons,* when the party taking mony, is of greater or lesse credit, or hath more or lesse need thereof. In all these respects, the rates of monies delivered and taken by *Exchange,* are alwayes more or lesse. For as it is a common thing amongst men, to sell one & the same commodity, to divers men at divers prises: so is it also in *Exchange,* when one and the same finenes of mony, is answered by a different value in denomination or accompt. Neither is there any certainty of gaine to the deliverer of mony in the first *Exchange,* although he seem to have some advantage in the price thereof above the value of fine silver; nor of losse to the taker, though hee seeme to have some disadvantage in the price thereof under the value of fine silver: because the deliverer may perhaps be subject to remit his mony backe, in

* From *The Circle of Commerce* (London, 1623).

the second or forrain *Exchange,* as much under the value of fine silver, as he had before above the value in the first *Exchange:* And it may fall out also, that the taker may gaine by the rising of the *Exchange* abroad; that, which hee seemed to lose by the falling thereof at home. And if it happen that the mony delivered in the first *Exchange,* bee not remitted in the second *Exchange,* but otherwise employed in trade; that alter's not the case, by *Malynes* owne rule; which is, *That commodities are bought and sold according to the publike measure of the Exchange.* So that in these *Exchanges,* there is no certainty of gaine or losse to the parties taking or delivering of mony, untill the time be run out, and the returne come backe, from those parts and places, whether the mony was first delivered by *Exchange:* during which time, the manifold occurrents which are contingent to trade, may vary the gaine or losse to either party. . . .

The Provinciall Exchange, is that generall permutation before noted, *which one Country maketh with another, in mony, in Merchandize, in all kind of Commerce.* And therefore it may well bee sad to bee the *Periphery or Circumference of the Circle of Commerce;* and *The Ballance of trade,* the very *Center* of this *Circle.* For as in the *Personall Exchange* betweene man and man, the gaine or losse of such Exchanging cannot bee knowne, but by the returne of the mony exchanged: that is, till that mony bee come backe in *Exchange,* which was at first delivered, as is before declared: So also in the *Provinciall Exchange* betweene Country and Country, the gaine or losse which one Kingdome maketh upon another, cannot bee knowne untill the Returnes thereof bee made: that is, till the forraine Commodities bee brought in, for the Native Commodities issued and carried out; and both cast into the *Ballance of Trade,* to bee waighed and tried one against the other.

For as a paire of Scales or Ballance, is an Invention to shew us the waight of things, whereby we may discerne the heavy from the light, and how one thing differeth from another in the Scale of waight: So is also this *Ballance of Trade,* an excellent and politique Invention, to shew us the difference of waight in the *Commerce* of one Kingdome with another: that is, whether the Native Commodities exported, and all the forraine Commodities Imported, doe ballance or overballance one another in the *Scale of Commerce.*

If the Native Commodities exported doe waigh downe and exceed in value the forraine Commodities imported; it is a rule that never faile's, that then the Kingdome growe's rich, and prosper's in estate and stocke: because the overplus thereof must needs come in, in treasure. But if the Forraine Commodities imported, doe exceed in value the Native Commodities exported; it is a manifest signe that then trade decayeth, and the stocke of the Kingdome wasteth apace: because the overplus must needs goe out in treasure. As for example: If this Kingdome send out Clothes and other the Native Commodities thereof into forrain parts, which are there sold for one thousand pounds of our money in value; and receive backe againe in returne, the forraine Commodities of other Kingdomes to the value of eight hundred pounds, for the thousand pounds sent out, it is manifest that the other two hundred pounds, being also due to this Kingdome, must needs come in, in treasure, to ballance and make even the thousand pounds at first sent out. Which of necessity, must either come in, in mony or merchandize: if not in mony, then in merchandize: if not in merchandize, then in mony: and consequently the more come's in, in mony, the lesse in merchandize: and the lesse in merchandize the more in mony. But if this Kingdome shall receive in, twelve hundred pounds in value of the forraine Commodities of other Kingdomes, for the thousand pounds sent out, then it is manifest, that this Kingdome spendeth more of the forraine, then other Kingdomes doe spend of our Native Commodities, by two hundred pounds in the value of one thousand pounds: whereby this Kingdome is become so much in debt to those forraine Kingdomes: which of necessity must goe out from hence in treasure, to satisfie that which was brought in, more then that which was carried out. And this experiment is therefore called *The Ballance of Trade*. . . .

And now we will come to the *Positive Constitution* of our owne *Forme*, to bring to the *Ballance*, the state of the present time and trade: wherein I will give you a taste of one yeeres collections of the Kingdomes trade, in this forme following. viz.

THE BALLANCE OF TRADE OF THE KINGDOME IS DEBITOR, FOR ALL THE EXPORTATIONS OF THE MERCHANDIZE THEREOF, FOR ONE WHOLE YEARE, FROM CHRISTMAS AN. 1621. TO CHRISTMAS AN. 1622. AS FOLLOWETH.

	li.	*sh.*	*d.*
Custome of the Port of London	50406	06.	04
Custome of the Out-ports	26756	18.	00
The Custome of Wrappers of Clothes, Bayes, and Cottons, free of Custome, being the tenth part of 50000. pounds, which is the Custome of them all	05000	00.	00
The Custome of the Fish of our owne fishing, and which is freed from Custome by Statute, by computation	07000	00.	00
The Custome of Goods shipt out by Certificate: viz. of forraine goods brought in, and for want of vent in the Kingdome, shipt out again: which are freed of Custome by his Majesties gracious graunt of Privy Seale	08050	00.	00
The Totall of all the Custome is	97213	04.	04
	li.	*sh.*	*d.*
Which Totall being multiplied by twenty, because the Custome is valued by twelve pence in the pound, produceth the value of all the Goods Exported to amount unto	1944264	07.	01
The Net Custome of which value, at twelve pence in the pound, the Wrappers, Fish, and Goods shipt out by certificate deducted, is the 2. summes first before mentioned, and is	0077163	04.	04

The Impost of Bayes, Tinne, Lead, and Pewter, which onely are imposed outwards, amounteth to	0007370	01.	05
The Merchants gaine, fraight, and petty charges upon 1944264. li. being the whole value of the Exportations as above appeareth, at 15. per Cento, is	0291639	00.	00
The Totall Exportations with charges, Amount to	2320436	12.	10

THE BALLANCE OF THE TRADE OF THE KINGDOME IS CREDITOR, FOR ALL THE IMPORTATIONS OF THE MERCHANDIZE THEREOF, FOR ONE WHOLE YEARE, FROM CHRISTMAS AN. 1621. TO CHRISTMAS AN. 1622. AS FOLLOWETH.

	li.	*sh.*	*d.*
The Custome of the Port of London	68280	09.	01
The Custome of the Out-Ports	19579	02.	06
The Custome of Wines of all sortes, all other Merchandize being included in the former, is	03200	00.	00
The Custome amounts to	91059	11.	07
One third part thereof to be added, for the underrating of Goods in Custome, to that they are worth, or cost, is	30353	03.	10
Also the allowance of 5. per Cento upon 91059. 11. 7. is	04552	19.	07
The Totall Summe amounts to	125965	15.	00
Which totall, being multiplied by 20 produceth the value of all the Goods Imported, to amount unto	2519315	00.	00
Fine Goods secretly conveied inwards, more then outwards.	0100000	00.	00
The Totall Importations amount to	2619315	00.	00
The Totall Exportations	2320436	12.	10
The Remainder sheweth, that there is more imported this yeare then was Exported, by the summe of	0298878	07.	02

So then wee see it to our griefe, that wee are fallen into a great *Underballance of Trade* with other Nations. Wee felt it before in sense; but now we know it by science: wee found it before in operation; but now wee see it in speculation: Trade alas, faile's and faint's, and we in it.

And now we are come to the *End* of this *Ballance of Trade,* which in *Place* is last, but in *Purpose* first & chiefs't, according to that in Philosophy, *Finis est Principium in Intentione: The End is the beginning, in purpose and intent.*

A *Merchant* when hee will informe himselfe how his Estate standeth, is said to take a *Ballance* of his Estate: wherin he collecteth and considereth all his *Wares,* and *Monyes,* and *Debts,* as if hee would cast every-thing into the *Scale* to bee tried by waight: Which is therefore in *Merchants* and *Accomptants* termes, so called a *Ballance* of Accompt, or a *Ballance of Trade.* And to what *End* doth he this: Surely to try in what Estate he is: whether he goeth forward or backward, whether he hath got or lost. And if it appeare to him by his *Ballance,* that his *Gaine* doth not answere his *Expence;* the first and last is, he must either *Gaine more,* or *Spend lesse,* or els looke to come behind hand.

A *Father* or *Master of a Family,* doth thus also consider his Estate, by comparing his *Expence* with his *Revenue:* and if he finde, that his *Expence* exceedeth his *Revenue;* either he must *Lessen his charge,* or els *Consume his Estate.*

The *Royall Merchant, the Regall Father of that great family of a Kingdome,* if *Hee* will know the Estate of his *Kingdome, Hee* will compare the *Gaine* thereof with the *Expence;* that is, the *Native Commodities issued and sent out,* with *the Forraine Commodities received in:* and if it appeare that the *Forraine Commodities* doe exceed the *Native:* either he must *increase the Native,* or *Lessen the Forraine,* or else looke for nothing else, but *The decay of Trade:* and therein *The losse of his Revenue,* and *Impoverishing of his People.*

So then, the *End* of the *Ballance of Trade,* may be said either to be *Propior,* or *Remotior.* There's *One End neerer hand;* There's *Another End farther off. One End* of it is, to finde out *The cause of the Malady: The other,* to present a *Medicable Remedy,* for the decay of trade.

Hic labor hoc opus erat: in both these I bestowed my former time and paines, in that *Little tract of Trade,* wherein I marshalled those *Causes* and *Remedies,* into their rancks, in the best order I could: and to which I referre those, that desire more distinctly to understand the same, lest I should seem to *Tautologize,* after *Malynes* manner, in unnecessary repetitions. For as all those *Causes* doe forcibly conduce unto the *Underballancing of Trade:* so also the removing of them, must needs concurre unto the *Remedy* thereof: and you may safely conclude, that untill the Kingdome come to an *Over-ballance of Trade,* the *causes* of the decay of Trade cannot be taken away: for the *Decay of Trade,* and the *Over-ballance of Trade,* cannot stand together.

. . . And this is the first *End* of our *Ballance of Trade.* It shewe's us our Case in what Estate we stand: It shewe's the Causes of our Decay of trade: It represents those causes in Capitall Characters, that he that run's may reade *Excesse* and *Idlenes.*

What's the other *End* of it? Surely to direct us to the *Remedy:* which in a word, is nothing els, but to make our *Importations lesse,* and our *Exportations more.* Our *Importations* may be lessened, by a restraint of such superfluous and unnecessary things, as either we have of our own, or can make our owne, as may best concurre with the *Policy of Trade,* and the *Wisdome of the State,* to which as it become's me, I humbly commend the same.

Our *Exportations* may be Improved, either by *Precept,* or *Practice. Longum Iter per præcepta, breue per Exemplum. Example is the best precept.* Wee are sent *to* the *Belgicke Pismire* to learne a *Precept,* and why not to the *Belgicke Grashopper?* For *The Grashopper hath no King, yet they march out, all in Troupes.* Wee need goe no further then the *Low Countries,* to learne this *Lesson.* Although, the *Kingdome of Naples,* the *Signory of Venice,* the *Common-wealthes of Genoa, Florence, Milan, Marcelles,* and many others, might teach us the same thing; yet the *Low Countries* doe seeme to be an *Epitome* of all the Rest. Which certainly for *Policy* and *Industry,* may read a Lecture to all the other people of the world. There you shall see, their Gates stand wide open: you may carry out as much money as you will: It is there held no *Paradoxe,* to let mony goe out, and yet not to want it within: because they have an Eie to the *Ballance of Trade;* whereby they are assured, that although it may goe out at one dore, yet it will come in at another. But there you shall see no *Excesse* in superfluous consumptions of forraine Commodities. No *Projects,* nor *Projectors,* but for the Common-good. All kind of *Manufactures* invented, that will fit the times, and please the mindes of forrain Nations. Their own Commodities eased of charge, the forraine Imposed. Frugality, industry, policy, all working together for the publike. All kinde of *Staples,* of *Corne,* of *Wine,* of *Cloth,* of *Fish,* of *Silk,* of *Spices,* of *Flaxe,* of *Hempe,* of what not? And all these, not to breed or feed home-bred *Consumption,* but to maintain *Trade* and *Forraine Negotiation.* For indeed their whole Country is nothing els, but a *Magazin,* a Staple, a Receptacle, of the Comodities of all other Countries. And this is a living *Precept,* a Patterne, a Forme, a plat-forme for our Imitation, for the encrease of our *Exportation:* and this will restore our ancient *Ballance of Trade.*

SIR JAMES STEUART

(1712–1780)

The most mature English mercantilist writing is exemplified in the works of Sir James Steuart. Steuart was a contemporary of Adam Smith, who directed his *Wealth of Nations* at him as much as at Thomas Mun, although Smith never mentioned his fellow Scot by name.

Sir James was born in Scotland and educated at the University of Edinburgh, and became a barrister. He then toured Europe for five years, observing economic conditions at first hand. At this time, too, he may have visited the Jacobite lodge in Rome, since he was later involved in the abortive plot to set Bonnie Prince Charlie on the throne of England. After the Jacobite defeat at Culloden, Steuart had to go into exile, and he was not permitted to return to Scotland for two decades.

This exile was not wholly unprofitable, for Steuart maintained his interest in economics by observing European conditions; he particularly devoted himself to the study of monetary problems. In 1758 he published *A Dissertation upon the Doctrine and Principles of Money Applied to the German Coins* at Tuebingen. During this period he also compiled the notes on which he later based his major work, *An Inquiry into the Principles of Political Economy,* which finally saw publication in 1767. Although the book is unevenly written and not well integrated, it has many merits and sold well until *The Wealth of Nations* swept it and other competitive commentaries into obscurity.

In his labor theory of value Steuart anticipated Smith by a decade, and he discussed the influence of supply and demand on price. His treatment of population problems was the best in the English language before Malthus.

Like Smith, Steuart believed that self-interest was the most powerful force to motivate economic behavior, but he felt that because individual self-interest didn't always coincide with the public welfare, government regulation was essential, to protect the public weal.

The following selections, all taken from the *Principles of Political Economy,* underline Steuart's essential economic philosophy. At the time he was writing, such doctrines were an integral part of general thinking, woven into scores of laws and regulations. These passages must be read within that framework in order to be appreciated. They show why Steuart has been called "the last of the mercantilists."

ON GOVERNMENT REGULATION *

The principle of self-interest will serve as a general key to this inquiry; and it may, in one sense, be considered as the ruling principle of my subject, and may therefore be traced throughout the whole. This is the main spring, and only motive which a statesman should make use of, to engage a free people to concur in the plans which he lays down for their government. . . .

From this principle, men are engaged to act in a thousand different ways, and every action draws after it certain necessary consequences. The question therefore constantly under consideration comes to be, what will

* From *An Inquiry into the Principles of Political Œconomy,* in *The Works, Political, Metaphisical, and Chronological, of the Late Sir James Steuart,* collected by his son (London, 1805).

mankind find it their interest to do, under such and such circumstances? . . .

The best way to govern a society, and to engage every one to conduct himself according to a plan, is for the statesman to form a system of administration, the most consistent possible with the interest of every individual, and never to flatter himself that his people will be brought to act in general, and in matters which purely regard the public, from any other principle than private interest. . . .

Public spirit, in my way of treating this subject, is as superfluous in the governed, as it ought to be all-powerful in the statesman; at least, if it is not altogether superfluous, it is fully as much so, as miracles are in a religion once fully established. Both are admirable at setting out, but would shake everything loose, were they to continue to be common and familiar. Were miracles wrought every day, the laws of nature would no longer be laws: and were every one to act for the public, and neglect himself, the statesman would be bewildered, and the supposition is ridiculous.

I expect, therefore, that every man is to act for his own interest in what regards the public; and, politically speaking, every one ought to do so. It is the combination of every private interest which forms the public good, and of this the public, that is, the statesman only, can judge. . . .

Were the principle of public spirit carried farther; were a people to become quite disinterested; there would be no possibility of governing them. Every one might consider the interest of his country in a different light, and many might join in the ruin of it, by endeavouring to promote its advantages. . . .

Now as I suppose my statesman to do his duty in the most minute particulars, so I allow every one of his subjects to follow the dictates of his private interest. All I require is an exact obedience to the laws. This also is the interest of every one; for he who transgresses ought most undoubtedly to be punished: and this is all the public spirit which any perfect government has occasion for. . . .

The statesman who resolves to improve this infant trade into foreign commerce, must examine the wants of other nations, and consider the productions of his own country. He must then determine, what kinds of manufactures are best adapted for supplying the first, and for consuming the latter. He must introduce the use of such manufactures among his subjects; and endeavour to extend his population and his agriculture, by encouragements given to these new branches of consumption. He must provide his people with the best masters; he must supply them with every useful machine; and above all, he must relieve them of their work.

ON POPULATION *

Thus the generative faculty resembles a spring loaded with a weight, which always exerts itself in proportion to the diminution of resistance:

* From *An Inquiry into the Principles of Political Œconomy*, etc.

when food has remained some time without augmentation or diminution, generation will carry numbers as high as possible; if then food come to be diminished, the spring is overpowered; the force of it becomes less than nothing, Inhabitants will diminish, at least, in proportion to the overcharge. If, upon the other hand, food be increased, the spring which stood at o, will begin to exert itself in proportion as the resistance diminishes; people will begin to be better fed; they will multiply, and, in proportion as they increase in numbers, the food will become scarce again.

. . . The generative faculty in man (which we have compared to a spring), and the care and love we have for our children, first prompt us to multiply, and then engage us to divide what we have with our little ones. Thus from dividing and subdividing it happens, that in every country where food is limited to a certain quantity, the inhabitants must be subsisted in a regular progression, descending down from plenty and ample subsistence, to the last periods of want, and even sometimes starving for hunger.

Although the examples of this last extremity are not common in some countries, yet I believe they are more so than is generally imagined; and the other stages of want are productive of many diseases, and of a decay which extinguishes the faculty of generation, or which weakens it, so as to produce children less vigorous and less healthy. I appeal to experience, if this reasoning be not just. . . .

Children produced from parents who are able to maintain them, and bring them up to a way of getting bread for themselves, do really multiply and serve the state. Those born of parents whose subsistence is precarious, or which is proportioned to their own physical necessary only, have a precarious existence, and will undoubtedly begin their life by being beggars. Many such will perish for want of food, but many more for want of ease; their mendicity will be accompanied with that of their parents, and the whole will go to ruin . . . and as by far the greater part of inhabitants are in the lower classes, it becomes the duty of a statesman to provide against such evils, if he intends, usefully to increase the number of his people.

. . . I believe, it will be found, that a sufficient abundance of children are born already; and that we have neither occasion for concubinage, or polygamy, to increase their numbers. But we want a right method of taking care of those we have, in order to produce a multiplication proportioned to the possibility of our providing nourishment and employment. I have therefore proposed, that a statesman, well informed of the situation of his people, the state of every class, the number of marriages found in each, should say, let a particular encouragement be given to so many marriages among the lower classes and let these be distributed in a certain proportion for every parish, city, borough, &c. in the country; let rules be laid down to direct a preference in case of a competition, between different couples; and let the consequence of this approbation be, to relieve the parents of all children above what they can maintain, as has been said. I propose no new limitations upon marriage, because I am a friend to liberty, and because such limitations would shock the spirit of the times. I therefore would strongly recommend hospitals for foundlings over all the country; and still more strongly the frugal maintenance of children in such hospitals, and their being bred up early to fill and recruit the lowest classes of the people.

PART FOUR

The Forerunners of Economic Liberalism

Since the seventeenth and eighteenth centuries were periods of transition, it is not surprising to find writers who combined elements of mercantilism and of the physiocratic and classical schools that were to follow. Sir Josiah Child, for instance, retained the mercantilist belief in the desirability of a favorable balance of trade and the importance of a numerous population, but recognized that the export of precious metals was sometimes beneficial. Nicholas Barbon and Sir Dudley North were other important writers of the late seventeenth century who argued, like Child, that the stock of goods and services in a country was its true wealth. North especially pleaded for free trade and regarded the trading world as one "nation."

Sir William Petty, whose chief works were published between 1662 and 1691, was a rare genius who anticipated both Smith and Marx on many counts and who founded the science of statistics. Certain features of his economics are mercantilist; others, such as his theory of public works, are far in advance of his time.

Between 1750 and 1770 there appeared works by Richard Cantillon and David Hume which helped bridge the gap between mercantilism and economic liberalism. The intellectual climate in France and England had changed by this time; mercantilism was on the defensive, the physiocrats were already publishing their great works, and Adam Smith's *Wealth of Nations* was only a few years off.

The writers who follow in this section, then, although they cannot be conveniently fitted into a neat pigeonhole, made contributions of stature and originality.

SIR DUDLEY NORTH

(1641–1691)

One of the more important figures in the transition from mercantilism to free trade in England was Sir Dudley North. He has been called the first free-trader and one-worlder and in this respect is one of the outstanding predecessors of Adam Smith. His views on capital formation and interest are also remarkably modern.

North went to Turkey as a young man and spent eighteen years there in the employ of the Turkey Company. He returned to England a rich man, entered politics, and in 1684 was named commissioner of customs.

The *Discourses upon Trade* (London, 1691) has an unusual history. Shortly after Sir Dudley's death his own brother claimed he couldn't find a copy, and the book remained lost for over a century. There was suspicion that it was suppressed by the authorities because of its advanced views. Finally, in 1822, a copy was found at an auction of a gentleman's library.

In the following selection his opposition to arbitary regulation of commerce is clearly revealed.

DISCOURSES UPON TRADE *

The Preface

Methinks when I meet with a great deal of Firsting, and Seconding, I smell one who conceits himself an Author, a Creature as fulsome as any other sort of Impertinents. If there be Reason, and that understood, what could the formal Methodist add? Let me have the Cockle, and who will take the gay shell.

Now after all this it will be unjust, not to say somewhat of the Subject-matter of these Discourses, which is Commerce and Trade; and the Author's [1] manner of Treating it.

He seems to be of a Temper different from most, who have medled with this Subject in Publick; for it is manifest, his Knowledge and Experience of Trade is considerable, which could not be attained, unless he were a Trader himself; and yet it is not to be collected from any thing he says, of what Nature his dealing hath been; for he speaks impartially of Trade in general, without warping to the Favour of any particular Interest. It hath been observed formerly, when Merchants have been consulted, and the Questions concerned only Trade in general, they agreed in Opinion; but when opposite Interests were concerned, they differed *toto cœlo.* As for his Opinion touching Interest of Money, wherein he is clear, that it should be left freely to the Market, and not be restrained by Law, he is lyable to the same suspicion, which attends those of a different Judgment; that is, partiality to his own Interest; the difference is only in the supposed Cause, which in the one, is Wealth, and in the other Want. He

*From *Discourses upon Trade* (London, 1691).

1 [The author of the Preface is actually Sir Dudley North himself.—*Editor.*]

hath given his Judgment with his Reasons, which every one is free to canvas; and there is no other means whereby a wise and honest Person can justifie his Opinions in Publick Concerns.

In the next place, I find Trade here Treated at another rate, than usually hath been; I mean Philosophically: for the ordinary and vulgar conceits, being meer Husk and Rubbish, are waived; and he begins at the quick, from Principles indisputably true; and so proceeding with like care, comes to a Judgment of the nicest Disputes and Questions concerning Trade. And this with clearness enough, for he reduceth things to their Extreams, wherein all discriminations are most gross and sensible, and then shews them; and not in the state of ordinary concerns, whereof the terms are scarce distinguishable.

This Method of Reasoning hath been introduc'd with the new Philosophy, the old dealt in Abstracts more than Truths; and was employed about forming Hypotheses, to fit abundance of precarious and insensible Principles; such as the direct or oblique course of the Atomes in *vacuo,* Matter and Form, Privation, solid Orbs, *fuga vacui,* and many others of like nature; whereby they made sure of nothing; but upon the appearance of *Des Cartes'* excellent dissertation *de Methodo,* so much approved and accepted in our Ages, all those Chymera's soon dissolved and vanisht.

And hence it is, that Knowledge in great measure is become Mechanical; which word I need not interpret farther, than by noting, it here means, built upon clear and evident Truths. But yet this great Improvement of Reason which the World hath lately obtained, is not diffus'd enough, and resides chiefly with the studious and learned, the common People having but a small share; for they cannot abstract, so as to have a true and just thought of the most ordinary things, but are possest and full of the vulgar Errors of sense: Except in some few things that fall within the compass of their day-labour, and so gives them an Experience; As when a Common-Seaman, with all his Ignorance, proves a better Mechanick, for actual Service, than the Professor himself, with all his Learning.

The case of Trade is the same; for although to buy and sell, be the Employment of every man, more or less; and the Common People, for the most part, depend upon it for their daily subsistence; yet there are very few who consider Trade in general upon true Principles, but are satisfied to understand their own particular Trades, and which way to let themselves into immediate gain. And out of this active Sphere nothing is so fallacious, and full of Error, as mens Notions of Trade. And there is another Reason, why this matter seems less understood, than in truth it is. For whenever Men consult for the Publick Good, as for the advancement of Trade, wherein all are concerned, they usually esteem the immediate Interest of their own to be the common Measure of Good and Evil. And there are many, who to gain a little in their own Trades, care not how much others suffer; and each Man strives, that all others may be forc'd in their dealings, to act subserviently for his Profit, but under the covert of the Publick.

So Clothiers would have men be forc'd to buy their Manufacture; and I may mention such as sell Wool, they would have men forc'd to buy of them at an high Price, though the Clothier loseth. The Tinners would have their Tin dear, though the Merchant profits little: And in general all those who are lazy, and do not, or are not active enough and cannot, look out, to vent the Product of their Estates, or to Trade with it themselves, would have all Traders forc'd by Laws, to bring home to them sufficient Prizes, whether they gain or lose by it. And all the while, not one of them will endure to be under a force, to Sell, or Let their own Estates at lower rates, than the free Market of things will produce.

Now it is no wonder, that out of these Ingredients a strange Medley of Error should result, whereby seldom any Publick Order, which hath been establisht, and intended, or at least pretended for the good of Trade in general, hath had a suitable Effect; but on the contrary, hath for the most part proved prejudicial, and thereupon, by common consent, been discontinued. But this is too copious Matter for a Preface, and tho' many Instances occur, I leave all, and return to the matter of Vulgar Errors in Trade.

It is not long since there was a great noise with Inquiries into the Balance of Exportation and Importation; and so into the Balance of Trade, as they called it. For it was fancyed that if we brought more Commodities in, than we carried out, we were in the High-way to Ruin. In like manner have we heard much said against the *East-India* Trade, against the *French* Trade, with many other like politick conceits in Trade; most of which, Time and better Judgment hath disbanded; but others succeed in their room, according as new Persons find Encouragement to invent, and inspire, for promoting their private Interest, by imposing on those, who desire to be cunning. And now we complain for want of Money in specie, that Bullion is Exported or mis-employed to other uses, than making Money; and ascribe the deadness of Trade, especially of Corn, and Cattel in the Country, to this; and hope by a Regulation of the Bullion-Trade, and stinting the Price, except it be in Money, to make a through Reformation, and give new Life to all things, with much more, *ejusdem farina,* which I do not particularize, this being enough for a taste.

Now it may appear strange to hear it said,

That the whole World as to Trade, is but as one Nation or People, and therein Nations are as Persons.

That the loss of a Trade with one Nation, is not that only, separately considered, but so much of the Trade of the World rescinded and lost, for all is combined together.

That there can be no Trade unprofitable to the Publick; for if any prove so, men leave it off; and wherever the Traders thrive, the Publick, of which they are a part, thrives also.

That to force Men to deal in any prescrib'd manner, may profit such as happen to serve them; but the Publick gains not, because it is taking from one Subject, to give to another.

That no Laws can set Prices in Trade, the Rates of which, must and will make themselves: But when such Laws do happen to lay any hold, it is so much Impediment to Trade, and therefore prejudicial.

That Money is a Merchandize, whereof there may be a glut, as well as a scarcity, and that even to an Inconvenience.

That a People cannot want Money to serve the ordinary dealing, and more than enough they will not have.

That no Man shall be the richer for the making much Money, nor have any part of it, but as he buys it for an equivalent price.

That the free Coynage is a perpetual Motion found out, whereby to Melt and Coyn without ceasing, and so to feed Goldsmiths and Coyners at the Publick Charge.

That debasing the Coyn is defrauding one another, and to the Publick there is no sort of Advantage from it; for that admits no Character, or Value, but Intrinsick.

That the sinking Money by Allay or Weight is all one.

That Exchange and ready Money, are the same, nothing but Carriage and re-carriage being saved.

That Money Exported in Trade is an increase to the Wealth of the Nation; but spent in War, and Payments abroad, is so much Impoverishment. . . .

Concerning the Abatement of Interest

. . . The Question to be considered is, Whether the Government have reason by a Law, to prohibit the taking more than 4*l.* *per Cent.* Interest for Money lent, or to leave the Borrower and Lender to make their own Bargains.

In the Disquisition of this, many things are to be considered, and particularly such as relate to Trade, of which a true Notion will set right a World of Mistakes, wherefore that now shall be chiefly treated of.

Trade is nothing else but a Commutation of Superfluities; for instance: I give of mine, what I can spare, for somewhat of yours, which I want, and you can spare.

Thus Trade, whilst it is restrained within the limits of a Town, Country, or Nation, signifieth only the Peoples supplying each other with Conveniences, out of what that Town, Country, or Nation affords.

And in this, he who is most diligent, and raiseth most Fruits, or maketh most of Manufactory, will abound most in what others make, or raise; and consequently be free from Want, and enjoy most Conveniences, which is truly to be Rich, altho' there were no such thing as Gold, Silver, or the like amongst them.

Mettals are very necessary for many Uses, and are to be reckon'd among the Fruits and Manufactories of the World. And of these, Gold and Silver being by nature very fine, and more scarce than others, are higher prized; and a little of them is very reasonably esteem'd equal in value with a great quantity of other Mettals, &c. For which reason, and moreover that they are imperishable, as well as convenient for easie stowage and removal, and not from any Laws, they are made a Standard, or common Measure to deal with; and all Mankind concur in it, as every one knows, therefore I need not inlarge further in this matter.

Now it is to be consider'd, that Mankind being fallen into a way of commuting in this manner, to serve their occasions, some are more provident, others more profuse; some by their Industry and Judgment raise more Fruits from the Earth, than they consume in supplying their own occasions; and then the surplus remains with them, and is Property or Riches.

And Wealth thus contracted, is either commuted for other Mens Land (supposing all men to have had some) or massed up in heaps of Goods; be the same of Mettals, or any thing valuable. And those are the Rich, who transmit what they have to their Posterity; whereby particular Families become rich; and of such are compounded Cities, Countries, Nations, &c.

And it will be found, that as some particular men in a Town grow richer, and thrive better than others; so also do Nations, who by Trade serving the occasions of their Neighbours, supply themselves with what they have occasion for from abroad; which done, the rest is laid up, and is Silver, Gold, &c. for as I said, these being commutable for every thing, and of small bulk, are still preferr'd to be laid up, till occasion shall call them out to supply other Necessaries wanted.

Now Industry and Ingenuity having thus distinguisht Men into Rich and Poor; What is the consequence? One rich Man hath Lands, not only more than he can manage, but so much, that letting them out to others, he is supplied with a large over-plus, so needs no farther care.

Another rich Man hath Goods; that is, Mettals, Manufactures, &c. in great quantity, with these he serves his own occasions, and then commutes the rest in Trade; that is, supplies others with what they want, and takes in exchange what they had of, beyond their own occasions, whereby managing cunningly, he must always advance.

Now as there are more Men to Till the Ground than have Land to Till, so also there will be many who want Stock to manage; and also (when a Nation is grown rich) there will be Stock for Trade in many hands, who either have not the skill, or care not for the trouble of managing it in Trade.

But as the Landed Man letts his Land, so these still lett their Stock; this latter is call'd Interest, but is only Rent for Stock, as the other is for Land. And in several Languages, hiring of Money, and Lands, are Terms of common use; and it is so also in some Counties in *England*.

Thus to be a Landlord, or a Stock-lord is the same thing; the Landlord hath the advantage only in this: That his Tenant cannot carry away the Land, as the Tenant of the other may the Stock; and therefore Land ought to yield less profit than Stock, which is let out at the greater hazard.

These things consider'd, it will be found, that as plenty makes cheapness in other things, as Corn, Wool, &c. when they come to Market in greater Quantities than there are Buyers to deal for, the Price will fall; so if there be more Lenders than Borrowers, Interest will also fall; wherefore it is not low Interest makes Trade, but Trade increasing, the Stock of the Nation makes Interest low.

It is said, that in *Holland* Interest is lower than in *England.* I answer; It is, because their Stock is greater than ours. I cannot hear that they ever made a Law to restrain Interest, but am certainly informed, that at this day, the Currant Interest between Merchant and Merchant, when they disburse Money for each others Account, is 6 *per Cent.* and the Law justifies it.

SIR WILLIAM PETTY

(1623–1687)

Like the French economist Quesnay, Sir William Petty started life as a physician, studying medicine at Oxford and on the Continent. For a time he was professor of anatomy and medicine at Oxford. Later he was in charge of a survey of lands forfeited in Ireland during the rebellion against Cromwell. This survey was to be the basis for redistribution of the lands to those who had helped suppress the rebellion.

After experimenting with shipbuilding in England for several years, he returned to Ireland in 1666 to manage his landed estates and devoted himself to advocating political and economic reforms and to writing on economic subjects. He was much in advance of his time, especially in the fields of statistics and monetary economics.

Although his writings are numerous, even taken together they do not present an integrated view of economic society, like Smith's *Wealth of Nations* or Ricardo's *Principles*. Nevertheless, they do contain sections of great interest and importance. He was one of the first English economists to enunciate a labor theory of value. Also, he may be regarded as the founder of the science of statistics. In his *Discourses on Political Arithmetic* (1691), he stated that his aim was to deal with economic subjects "in terms of Number, Weight, or Measure," thus anticipating modern statistical method.

His other important works are *Quantulumcunque, or a Tract Concerning Money* (1682), the *Treatise of Taxes and Contributions* (1662, 1667, 1685), and *The Political Anatomy of Ireland* (1672). The following selections are from the two last-named works. They showed Petty's realism, his penchant for measurement, and his formulation of a labor theory of value, according to which, for instance, the value of an Irish cabin is determined by the number of days' subsistence required by the laborers involved in its construction.

A TREATISE OF TAXES AND CONTRIBUTIONS *

Of the Several Wayes of Taxe

Of the several wayes of Taxe, and first, of setting a part, a proportion of the whole Territory for Publick uses, in the nature of Crown Lands; and secondly, by way of Assessment, or Land-taxe

Supposing, that the several causes of Publick Charge are lessened as much as may be, and that the people be well satisfied, and contented to pay their just shares of what is needfull for their Government and Protection, as also for the Honour of their Prince and Countrey: It follows now to propose the several wayes, and expedients, how the same may be most easily, speedily, and insensibly collected. The which I shall do, by exposing the conveniencies and inconveniences of some of the principal wayes of Levyings, used of later years within the several States of *Europe:* unto which others of smaller and more rare use may be referred.

Imagine then, a number of people, planted in a Territory, who had upon Computation concluded, that two Millions of pounds *per annum,* is

* From *The Economic Writings of Sir William Petty,* Volume I, edited by Charles Henry Hull (Cambridge, the University Press, 1899).

necessary to the publick charges. Or rather, who going more wisely to work, had computed a twenty fifth part of the proceed of all their Lands and Labours, were to be the *Excisum,* or the part to be cut out, and laid aside for publick uses. Which proportions perhaps are fit enough to the affairs of *England,* but of that hereafter.

Now the question is, how the one or the other shall be raised. The first way we propose, is, to Excize the very Land it self in kinde; that is, to cut out of the whole twenty five Millions, which are said to be in *England* and *Wales,* as much Land *in specie,* as whereof the Rack-rent would be two Millions, *viz.* about four Millions of Acres, which is about a sixth part of the whole; making the said four Millions to be Crown Lands, and as the four Counties intended to be reserved in *Ireland* upon the forfeitures were. Or else to excize a sixth part of the rent of the whole, which is about the proportion, that the Adventurers and Souldiers in *Ireland* retribute to the King, as Quit Rents. Of which two wayes, the latter is manifestly the better, the King having more security, and more obligees; provided the trouble and charge of this universal Collection, exceed not that of the other advantage considerably.

This way in a new State would be good, being agreed upon, as it was in *Ireland,* before men had even the possession of any Land at all; wherefore whosoever buyes Land in *Ireland* hereafter, is no more concerned with the Quit Rents wherewith they are charged, then if the Acres were so much the fewer; or then men are, who buy Land, out of which they know Tythes are to be paid. And truly that Countrey is happy, in which by Original Accord, such a Rent is reserved, as whereby the Publick charge may be born, without contingent, sudden, superadditions, in which lies the very *Ratio* of the burthen of all Contributions and Exactions. For in such cases, as was said before, it is not onely the Landlord payes, but every man who eats but an Egg, or an Onion of the growth of his Lands; or who useth the help of any Artisan, which feedeth on the same.

But if the same were propounded in *England, viz.* if an aliquot part of every Landlords Rent were excinded or retrenched, then those whose Rents were settled, and determined for long times to come, would chiefly bear the burthen of such an Imposition, and others have a benefit thereby. For suppose *A.* and *B.* have each of them a parcel of Land, of equal goodness and value; suppose also that *A.* hath let his parcel for twenty one years at twenty pound *per annum,* but that *B.* is free; now there comes out a Taxe of a fifth part; hereupon *B.* will not let under 25 *l.* that his remainder may be twenty, whereas *A.* must be contented with sixteen neat; nevertheless the Tenants of *A.* will sell the proceed of their bargain at the same rate, that the Tenants of *B.* shall do. The effect of all this is; First, that the Kings fifth part of *B.* his Farm shall be greater then before. Secondly, that the Farmer to *B.* shall gain more then before the Taxe. Thirdly, that the Tenant or Farmer of *A.* shall gain as much as the King and Tenant to *B.* both. Fourthly, the Tax doth ultimately light upon the Landlord *A.* and the Consumptioners. From whence it follows, that a Land-taxe resolves into an irregular Excize upon consumptions, that those bear it most, who least complain. And lastly, that some Landlords may gain, and onely such whose Rents are predetermined shall loose; and that doubly, *viz.* one way by the [not?] raising of their revenues, and the other by enhansing the prices of provisions upon them.

Another way is an Excisum out of the Rent of Houseing, which is much more uncertain then that of Land. For an House is of a double nature, *viz.* one, wherein it is a way and means of expence; the other, as 'tis an Instrument and Tool of gain: for a Shop in *London* of less capacity and less charge in building then a fair Dining-Room in the same House unto which both do belong, shall nevertheless be of the greater value; so also shall a Dungeon, Sellar, then a pleasant Chamber; because the one is expence, the other profit. Now the way [of a] Land-taxe rates housing, as of the latter nature, but the Excize, as of the former. . . .

But before we talk too much of Rents [in order to Taxes], we should endeavour to explain the mysterious nature of them, with reference as well to Money, the rent of which we call usury; as to that of Lands and Houses, afore-mentioned.

Suppose a man could with his own hands plant a certain scope of Land with Corn, that is, could Digg, or Plough, Harrow, Weed, Reap, Carry home, Thresh, and Winnow so much as the Husbandry of this Land requires; and had withal Seed wherewith to sowe the same. I say, that when this man hath subducted his seed out of the proceed of his Harvest, and also, what himself hath both eaten and given to others in exchange for Clothes, and other Natural necessaries; that the remainder of Corn is the natural and true Rent of the Land for that year; and the *medium* of seven years, or rather of so many years as makes up the Cycle, within which Dearths and Plenties make their revolution, doth give the ordinary Rent of the Land in Corn.

But a further, though collaterall question may be, how much English money this Corn or Rent is worth? I answer, so much as the money, which another single man can save, within the same time, over and above his expence, if he imployed himself wholly to produce and make it; *viz.* Let another man go travel into a Countrey where is Silver, there Dig it, Refine it, bring it to the same place where the other man planted his Corn; Coyne it, &c. the same person, all the while of his working for Silver, gathering also food for his necessary livelihood, and procuring himself covering, &c. I say, the Silver of the one, must be esteemed of equal value with the Corn of the other: the one being perhaps twenty Ounces and the other twenty Bushels. From whence it follows, that the price of a Bushel of this Corn to be an Ounce of Silver.

And forasmuch as possibly there may be more Art and Hazzard in working about the Silver, then about the Corn, yet all comes to the same pass; for let a hundred men work ten years upon Corn, and the same number of men, the same time, upon Silver; I say, that the neat proceed of the Silver is the price of the whole neat proceed of the Corn, and like parts of the one, the price of like parts of the other. Although not so many of those who wrought in Silver, learned the Art of refining and coining, or out-lived the dangers and diseases of working in the Mines. And this also is the way of pitching the true proportion, between the values of Gold and Silver, which many times is set but by popular errour, sometimes more, sometimes less, diffused in the world; which errour (by the way) is the cause of our having been pestred with too much Gold heretofore, and wanting it now.

This, I say, to be the foundation of equallizing and ballancing of values; yet in the superstructures and practices hereupon, I confess there is much variety, and intricacy; of which hereafter.

The world measures things by Gold and Silver, but principally the latter; for there may not be two measures, and consequently the better of many must be the onely of all; that is, by fine silver of a certain weight: but now if it be hard to measure the weight and fineness of silver, as by the different reports of the ablest Saymasters I have known it to be; and if silver granted to be of the same fineness and weight, rise and fall in its price, and be more worth at one place then another, not onely for being farther from the Mines, but for other accidents, and may be more worth at present, then a moneth or other small time hence; and if it differ in its proportion unto the several things valued by it, in several ages upon the increase and diminution thereof, we shall endeavour to examine some other natural Standards and Measures, without derogating from the excellent use of these.

Our Silver and Gold we call by severall names, as in *England* by pounds, shillings, and pence, all which may be called and understood by either of the three. But that which I would say upon this matter is, that all things ought to be valued by two natural Denominations, which is Land and Labour; that is, we ought to say, a Ship or garment is worth such a measure of Land, with such another measure of Labour; forasmuch as both Ships and Garments were the creatures of Lands and mens Labours thereupon: This being true, we should be glad to finde out a natural Par between Land and Labour, so as we might express the value by either of them alone as well or better then by both, and reduce one into the other as easily and certainly as we reduce pence into pounds. Wherefore we would be glad to finde the natural values of the Fee simple of Land, though but no better then we have done that of the *usus fructus* above-mentioned, which we attempt as followeth.

Having found the Rent or value of the *usus fructus per annum,* the question is, how many years purchase (as we usually say) is the Fee simple naturally worth? If we say an infinite number, then an Acre of Land would be equal in value to a thousand Acres of the same Land; which is absurd, an infinity of unites being equal to an infinity of thousands. Wherefore we must pitch upon some limited number, and that I apprehend to be the number of years, which I conceive one man of fifty years old, another of twenty eight, and another of seven years old, all being alive together may be thought to live; that is to say, of a Grandfather, Father, and Childe; few men having reason to take care of more remote Posterity: for if a man be a great Grandfather, he himself is so much the nearer his end, so as there are but three in a continual line of descent usually co-existing together; and as some are Grandfathers at forty years, yet as many are not till above sixty, and *sic de cæteris.*

Wherefore I pitch the number of years purchase, that any Land is naturally worth, to be the ordinary extent of three such persons their lives. Now in *England* we esteem three lives equal to one and twenty years, and consequently the value of Land, to be about the same number of years purchase. Possibly if they thought themselves mistaken in the one, (as the observator on the Bills of Mortality thinks they are) they would alter in the other, unless the consideration of the force of popular errour and dependance of things already concatenated, did hinder them.

This I esteem to be the number of years purchase where Titles are good, and where there is a moral certainty of enjoying the purchase. But in other Countreys Lands are worth nearer thirty years purchase, by reason of the better Titles, more people, and perhaps truer opinion of the value and duration of three lives.

And in some places, Lands are worth yet more years purchase by reason of some special honour, pleasures, priviledge or jurisdiction annexed unto them.

On the other hand, Lands are worth fewer years purchase (as in *Ireland*) for the following reasons, which I have here set down, as unto the like whereof the cause of the like cheapness in any other place may be imputed.

First, In *Ireland,* by reason of the frequent Rebellions, (in which if you are conquered, all is lost; or if you conquer, yet you are subject to swarms of thieves and robbers) and the envy which precedent missions of English have against the subsequent, perpetuity it self is but forty years long, as within which time some ugly disturbance hath hitherto happened almost ever since the first coming of the English thither.

2. The Claims upon Claims which each hath to the others Estates, and the facility of making good any pretence whatsoever by the favour of some one or other of the many Governours and Ministers which within forty years shall be in power there; as also by the frequency of false testimonies, and abuse of solemn Oaths.

3. The paucity of Inhabitants, there being not above the $\frac{1}{5}$th part so many as the Territory would maintain, and of those but a small part do work at all, and yet a smaller work so much as in other Countreys.

4. That a great part of the Estates, both real and personal in *Ireland,* are owned by Absentees, and such as draw over the profits raised out of *Ireland* refunding nothing; so as *Ireland* exporting more then it imports doth yet grow poorer to a paradox.

Of Usury

What reason there is for taking or giving Interest or Usury for any thing which we may certainly have again whensoever we call for it, I see not; nor why Usury should be scrupled, where money or other necessaries valued by it, is lent to be paid at such a time and place as the Borrower chuseth, so as the Lender cannot have his money paid him back where and when himself pleaseth, I also see not. Wherefore when a man giveth out his money upon condition that he may not demand it back until a certain time to come, whatsoever his own necessities shall be in the mean time, he certainly may take a compensation for this inconvenience which he admits against himself: And this allowance is that we commonly call Usury.

And when one man furnisheth another with money at some distant place, and engages under great Penalties to pay him there, and at a certain day besides; the consideration for this, is that we call Exchange or local Usury.

As for example, if a man wanting money at *Carlisle* in the heat of the late Civil Wars, when the way was full of Souldiers and Robbers, and the passage by Sea very long, troublesome, and dangerous, and seldom passed; why might not another take much more than an 100 l. at *London* for warranting the like Summe to be paid at *Carlisle* on a certain day?

Now the Questions arising hence are; what are the natural Standards of Usury and Exchange? As for Usury, the least that can be, is the Rent of so much Land as the money lent will buy, where the security is undoubted; but where the security is casual, then a kinde of ensurance must be enterwoven with the simple natural Interest, which may advance the Usury very conscionably unto any height below the Principal it self. Now if things are so in *England,* that really there is no such security as abovementioned, but that all are more or less hazardous, troublesome, or chargeable to make, I see no reason for endeavoring to limit Usury upon time, any more then that upon place, which the practice of the world doth not, unless it be that those who make such Laws were rather Borrowers then Lenders: But of the vanity and fruitlessness of making Civil Positive Laws against the Laws of Nature, I have spoken elsewhere, and instanced in several particulars.

As for the natural measures of Exchange, I say, that in times of Peace, the greatest Exchange can be but the labour of carrying the money *in specie,* but where are hazards [and] emergent uses for money more in one place then another, &c. or opinions of these true or false, the Exchange will begoverned by them.

Parallel unto this, is something which we omitted concerning the price of Land; for as great need of money heightens Exchange, so doth great need of Corn raise the price of that likewise, and consequently of the Rent of the Land that bears Corn, and lastly of the Land it self; as for example, if the Corn which feedeth *London,* or an Army, be brought forty miles thither, then the Corn growing within a mile of *London,* or the quarters of such Army, shall have added unto its natural price, so much as the charge of bringing it thirty nine miles doth amount unto: And unto perishable Commodities, as fresh fish, fruits, &c. the ensurance upon the hazard of corrupting, &c. shall be added also; and finally, unto him that eats these things there (suppose in Taverns) shall be added the charge of all the circumstancial appurtenances of House-rent, Furniture, Attendance, and the Cooks skill as well as his labour to accompany the same.

Hence it comes to pass, that Lands intrinsically alike near populous places, such as where the perimeter of the Area that feeds them is great, will not onely yield more Rent for these Reasons, but also more years purchase then in remote places, by reason of the pleasure and honour extraordinary of having Lands there.

THE TABLE *

But to make nearer approaches to the perfection of this Work, 'twould be expedient to know the Content of Acres of every Parish, and withal, what quantity of Butter, Cheese, Corn, and Wooll, was raised out of it for three years consequent; for thence the natural Value of the Land may be known, and by the number of People living within a Market-days Journey, and the Value of their housing, which shews the Quality and Expence of the said People; I would hope to come to the knowledg of the Value of the said Commodities, and consequently the Value of the Land, by deducting the hire of Working-People in it. And this brings me to the most important Consideration in Political Oeconomies, *viz.* how to make a *Par* and *Equation* between Lands and Labour, so as to express the Value of any thing by either alone. To which purpose, suppose two Acres of Pasture-land inclosed, and put thereinto a wean'd Calf, which I suppose in twelve Months will become 1 *C.* heavier in eatable Flesh; then 1 *C.* weight of such Flesh, which I suppose fifty days Food, and the Interest of the Value of the Calf, is the value or years Rent of the Land. But if a mans labour —— for a year can make the said Land to yield more than sixty days Food of the same, or of any other kind, then that overplus of days food is the Wages of the Man; both being expressed by the number of days food. That some Men will eat more than others, is not material, since by a days food we understand $1/100$ part of what 100 of all Sorts and Sizes will eat, so as to Live, Labour, and Generate. And that a days food of one sort, may require more labour to produce, than another sort, is also not material, since we understand the easiest-gotten food of the respective Countries of the World.

As for example, I suppose a pint of Oatmeal equal to half a pint of Rice, or a quart of Milk, or a pound of Bread, or a pound and quarter of Flesh, *&c.* each, in the respective place where each is the easiest gotten food. But if Rice be brought out of *India* into *Ireland,* or Oatmeal car-

* From *The Political Anatomy of Ireland,* in *The Economic Writings of Sir William Petty,* Volume I, edited by Charles Henry Hull (Cambridge, the University Press, 1899).

ried from *Ireland* thither; then in *India* the pint of Oatmeal must be dearer than half a pint of Rice, by the freight and hazard of Carriage, *& vice-versa, & sic de cæteris.* For, as for pleasant tast, I question whether there be any certainty, or regularity of the same in Nature, the same depending upon Novelty, opinion of Virtue, the recommendation of others, *&c.* Wherefore the days food of an adult Man, at a Medium, and not the days labour, is the common measure of Value, and seems to be as regular and constant as the value of fine Silver. For an ounce, suppose, of Silver in *Peru* is equivalent to a days food, but the same in *Russia* is equivalent to four days food, by reason of the Freight, and hazard in carrying the same from *Peru* to *Russia;* and in *Russia* the price of Silver shall grow to be worth more days labour, if a Workman can by the esteem and request of Silver Utensils earn more than he can on other materials. Wherefore I valued an *Irish* Cabbin at the number of days food, which the Maker spent in building of it.

By the same way we must make a Par and Equation between Art and Simple Labour; for if by such Simple Labour I could dig and prepare for Seed a hundred Acres in a thousand days; suppose then, I spend a hundred days in studying a more compendious way, and in contriving Tools for the same purpose; but in all that hundred days dig nothing, but in the remaining nine hundred days I dig two hundred Acres of Ground; then I say, that the said Art which cost but one hundred days Invention is worth one Mans labour for ever; because the new Art, and one Man, perform'd as much as two Men could have done without it.

By the same way we make an Equation between Art and Opinion. For it a Picture-maker, suppose, makes Pictures at 5 *l.* each; but then, find that more Persons would employ him at that rate than his time would extend to serve them in, it will certainly come to pass that this Artist will consider whether as many of those who apply to him at 5 *l.* each Picture, will give 6 *l.* as will take up his whole time to accommodate; and upon this Computation he pitcheth the Rate of his Work.

By the same way also an Equation may be made between drudging Labour, and Favour, Acquaintance, Interest, Friends, Eloquence, Reputation, Power, Authority, *&c.* All which I thought not amiss to intimate as of the same kind with finding an Equation between Land and Labour, all these not very pertinent to the Proportionation of the several Counties of *Ireland.*

Wherefore to return to the matter in hand, I say, that the Quantity of Commodity produced, and the Quantity of the —— shews the effects of the Land; and the number of People living thereupon, with the Quality of their housing, shews the Value of the Commodity; for one days delicate and exquisit Food may be worth ten of ordinary. Now the Nature of Peoples feeding may be estimated by the visible part of their Expence, which is their housing. But such helps of knowing the Value of Lands, I am not yet able to furnish.

RICHARD CANTILLON

(1680?–1734)

An outstanding example of work of great merit which had little or no influence on its own time is Richard Cantillon's *Essai sur la Nature du Commerce en General* (*On the Nature of Commerce in General*). Although it is not really comparable to Smith's *Wealth of Nations,* it is certainly the most unified exposition of economics published prior to 1776.

Little is known of Cantillon's life except that he was born in Ireland and lived in France for many years. By profession he was a financier and banker; this experience doubtless accounts for his profound grasp of monetary economics. He was probably acquainted with the physiocrats; in any case, they were familiar with Cantillon's work, since he is discussed in *L'Ami des Hommes,* one of their chief publications. Many of Cantillon's ideas are similar to physiocratic concepts. Unlike the physiocrats, however, Cantillon did not regard land as the sole source of wealth.

Exactly when Cantillon wrote the *Essai* is unknown. It was not published until twenty years after his death, and even then failed to arouse any great interest and soon was forgotten. Interest in it was not revived until 1881, when Stanley Jevons discovered a copy and tried to point out to his contemporaries the great merit of this neglected work. Finally, in 1931, the Royal Economic Society published the *Essai,* edited by Henry Higgs and accompanied by Jevons' article from the 1881 *Contemporary Review*.

Cantillon's analysis of money and foreign trade is of unusually high caliber. He anticipated the classicists cost-of-production theory of value and also showed that market value (which he distinguishes from long-run "intrinsic" value) is affected by supply and demand. Furthermore, he gave a remarkably clear analysis of the self-regulating nature of the price mechanism—of the interdependence of cost, supply, demand, and price.

His analysis of the role of inflation in foreign trade is likewise remarkable. He demonstrated how an influx of bullion will raise the price level of commodities within the country itself and thus cut down on export possibilities, since other countries will prefer to use cheaper sources of supply. Thus he showed that much of the bullion flowing in would have to be shipped out again to make up for the adverse foreign trade balance. For example, the Spaniards had to go to the ends of the earth to find gold and silver, which they then had to send to the French and other European nations which manufactured the goods Spain needed.

As for interest, Cantillon states that the rate must be sufficient to compensate the lender for his risk while it still enables the borrower to make a profit on the borrowed money after paying the interest.

Cantillon's *Essai,* from which extensive selections follow, was the first systematic exposition of economics in the history of the science. Here is stated the dogma, later taken over by the physiocrats, that land is the ultimate source of all wealth, and here the interaction of value and market price on each other is spelled out. The student will note too the strikingly modern quality of Cantillon's discussion of international trade.

ON THE NATURE OF COMMERCE IN GENERAL *

I. The number of Laborers, Artisans, & other people working in a state adjusts itself naturally to the need of them

If all the Laborers in a Village bring up several Sons in the same work, there will be too many Laborers to cultivate the land belonging to this Village, & the Superfluous adults will have to seek their living somewhere else, ordinarily in the Cities: if some stay with their Fathers, since they will not find enough work, they will live in great poverty, & will not marry, not having the means to raise children, or if they marry, the children born soon die of misery along with the Father & the Mother, as we see every day in France.

Thus if working conditions remain the same in the Village, & it gets its living by working the same amount of land, it will not increase in population in a thousand years. . . .

It is easy to see from the same line of reasoning that the Laborers, Artisans & others, who earn their living by work, must adjust their numbers to the employment & to the need of them in the Towns & Cities. . . .

It often happens that the Laborers & Artisans have not enough employment, when there are too many of them to share the work. It also happens that they are deprived of the employment they had, by accidents & by a variation in consumption; it will also happen that they have too much work, according to circumstances: in any case, when they lack employment, they leave the Villages, Towns, or Cities where they live, in such numbers that the number left is always adjusted to the employment which suffices to give them a living; & when a permanent increase of work develops, it is profitable, & enough others come to share the work.

From this reasoning it is easy to understand that the charity Schools in England & the projects in France for increasing the number of Artisans are quite useless. If the King of France sent a hundred thousand of his Subjects to Holland at his expense, to learn the Shipping trade, they would be useless when they returned, if no more Ships were sent to Sea than formerly. It is true that it would be a great advantage for a State to teach its Subjects to make the Manufactures which it is customary to import from Abroad, & all the products bought there; but I am now considering only a State by itself.

Since the Artisans earn more than the Laborers, they are in a better position than the latter to have their children learn a trade; & there can never be a lack of Artisans in a State, when there is enough work to give them regular employment.

* From *On the Nature of Commerce in General.* Reprinted by permission of the publishers from Arthur Eli Monroe, *Early Economic Thought.* Cambridge, Mass.: Harvard University Press, Copyright, 1924, by The President and Fellows of Harvard College.

II. The price & intrinsic value of a thing in general is the measure of the land & the labor which enters into its production

One Acre of land produces more wheat, or supports more Sheep, than another Acre: the labor of one man is dearer than that of another man, according to skill & circumstances, as has already been explained. If two Acres of land are of the same quality, one will support as many Sheep & will produce the same quantity of wool as the other Acre, assuming the same labor; & the wool produced by the one will sell for the same price as that which is produced by the other.

If the Wool in one case is worked up into a suit of coarse cloth, & the Wool in the other into a suit of fine cloth; since this last suit will require more labor & more expensive labor than is put into the coarse cloth, it will sometimes be ten times dearer, although both suits contain the same amount of Wool & of the same quality. The quantity of the produce of land, & the quantity as well as the quality of the labor, will necessarily enter into the price.

A pound of Flax worked up into fine Brussels Lace, requires the labor of fourteen persons for a year, or the work of one person for fourteen years . . . The price paid for this lace suffices to pay for the support of one person for fourteen years, & to pay in addition the profits of all the Entrepreneurs & Merchants involved.

The Spring of fine steel, which regulates an English Watch, ordinarily sells at a price which makes the ratio between the material & the work or between the steel & the Spring as one to one, with the result that the labor here makes almost the entire value of this Spring . . .

On the other hand, the price of the Hay from a Meadow, brought to market, or of a Wood which you desire to cut down, depends upon the material, or upon the produce of the land, according to its quality.

The price of a jar of water from the river Seine is nothing, because it is an immense supply which never dries up; but people give a penny for it in the streets of Paris, which is the price or measure of the labor of the water Carrier.

From these arguments & examples, I think it will be understood that the price or the intrinsic value of a thing is the measure of the amount of land & of labor which enters into its production, taking into account the quality or produce of the land & the quality of the labor.

But it often happens that several things which now have this intrinsic value do not sell in the Market according to this value: that will depend upon the whims & fancies of men, & upon the amount they consume.

If a Lord cuts canals & builds terraces in his Garden, their intrinsic value will be in proportion to the land & labor; but the price in fact will not always follow this proportion: if he offers to sell this Garden, it may happen that nobody will give him half as much as he has spent on it; & it may also happen, if several persons desire it, that he will be paid twice its intrinsic value, that is, the value of the land & of the amount he has spent on it.

If the Farmers in a State sow more wheat than ordinarily, that is to say, much more wheat than is needed for the year's consumption, the intrinsic & real value of the wheat will correspond to the land & labor which enter into its production: but since there is too great an abundance of it, & more Sellers than Buyers, the price of wheat in the Market will necessarily fall below the intrinsic price or value. If, on the contrary, the Farmers sow less wheat than is needed for the consumption, there will be more Buyers than Sellers, & the price of wheat in the Market will rise above its intrinsic value.

There is never any variation in the intrinsic value of things; but the impossibility of adjusting the production of merchandise & commodities to the consumption of them in a State causes a daily variation, & a perpetual flux & reflux in the prices of the Market. However, in well regulated Societies, the Market prices of commodities & merchandise of which the consumption is fairly constant & uniform do not vary greatly from the intrinsic value; & when there do not happen to be too sterile or too abundant years, the Magistrates of the Cities are always in a position to fix the Market price of many things, such as bread & meat, without giving anyone cause for complaint.

Land is the material, & labor is the form, of all commodities & merchandise; & since those who work must necessarily live on the produce of the Land, it seems as if we could find a relation between the value of labor & that of the produce of Land: that will be the subject of the following Chapter.

III. Of the par or ratio between the value of land and the value of labor

. . . If the Proprietor of a great Estate undertakes to exploit it himself, he will employ Slaves, or free People, to work on it: if he employs several Slaves, he will need Inspectors to make them work; he will also have to have Slave Artisans, to provide all the conveniences & comforts of life for himself, & for those whom he employs; he will have to have trades taught to others to continue the work.

In this economy, he will have to furnish a simple subsistence to his slave Laborers & the wherewithal to bring up their Children. He will have to give their Inspectors advantages in proportion to the trust & authority they have; he will have to maintain the Slaves, to whom he is having Trades taught, during the time of their Apprenticeship without return, & to grant the Slave artisans who work, & to their Inspectors, who have to be experienced in the Trades, a more nourishing subsistence compared with that of the Slave laborers, &c., because the loss of an Artisan would be greater than that of a Laborer, & because they ought to be given better care, seeing that it is always an expense to have a trade taught to replace them.

On this assumption, the work of the humblest adult slave, is worth at least & corresponds to the amount of land which the Proprietor is obliged to employ for his food & other necessaries, & also to twice as much land as it takes to bring up a Child till old enough to work, inasmuch as half of the Children born die before the age of seventeen years, according to the calculations & observations of the famous Doctor Halley: thus it is necessary to bring up two Children in order that one may reach working age, & it would seem that this reckoning would not suffice to keep up the supply of labor, since adult Men die at all ages.

It is true that the half of the Children born who die before the age of seventeen years, die for the most part during the first years of their life rather than later, since a full third of those born die during the first year. This circumstance appears to diminish the expense required to bring up a Child till old enough to work: but as the Mothers lose a good deal of time in taking care of their Children in sickness & childhood, & since even the adult Daughters do not equal the work of the Males, & earn barely enough to keep them; it seems that to bring up one of two Children to manhood or working age, it is necessary to employ as much produce of Land as for the subsistence of an adult Slave, whether the Proprietor raises these Children in his own house or has them brought up, *or the slave Father brings them up in a separate House or Hamlet. Thus I conclude that the daily work of the humblest Slave, corresponds in value to twice the produce of Land on which he subsists, whether the Proprietor gives it to him for his own subsistence & that of his Family;* or has him supported with his Family in his own House. It is a matter which does not admit of exact calculation, & in which precision is not even very necessary; it suffices if we do not get too far from reality.

If the Proprietor employs Vassals or free Peasants on his work, he will probably support them somewhat better than Slaves, & this according to the custom of the place; but again, on this supposition, the work of the free Laborer should correspond in value to twice the produce of land required for his support; but it would always be more advantageous for the Proprietor to support Slaves, rather than free Peasants, since, when he has raised too many of them for his work, he will be able to sell the superfluous ones like cattle, & will be able to get a price for them in proportion to the amount he has expended to bring them up to manhood or working age; except in cases of old age & infirmity.

We can likewise estimate the work of Artisan slaves at twice the produce of land which they consume; that of the Inspectors of work likewise, according to the favors & advantages which are given them over & above those who work under their direction.

The Laborers or Artisans, when they have their double portion in their proper degree, if they are married employ one portion for their own support, & the other for that of their Children.

If they are Bachelors, they will put aside a small part of their double portion, to get into a position where they can marry, & to collect a little fund for house-keeping; but the greater number will consume the double portion for their own support.

For example, the married Peasant will be satisfied to live on bread, cheese, vegetables, &c., will rarely eat meat, will drink little wine or beer, will have only old & rough clothes, which he will wear as long as he can: he will employ the surplus of his double portion in bringing up & supporting his Children; while the bachelor Peasant will eat meat as often as he can, & will buy himself new clothes, &c., & consequently will employ his double portion for his own support; thus he will consume twice as much produce of land on his person as the married Peasant does.

I do not consider here the expenses of the Wife, I assume that her work is barely enough for her own support, & when a great number of little Children are seen in one of those poor households, I assume that some charitable persons are contributing something to their subsistence, without which the Husband & the Mother have to deprive themselves of a part of their necessaries to support their Children.

In order to understand this better, it is necessary to know that a poor Peasant can support himself, at the lowest calculation, on the produce of an Acre & a half of land, living on bread & vegetables, wearing clothes of Hemp, & wooden shoes, &c., whereas, if he can buy himself wine & meat, clothes of broadcloth, &c., he will be able to spend, without drunkenness or gluttony, & without any excess, the produce of from four to ten Acres of land of average quality, taking the greater part of the lands of Europe, one with another. . . .

This is why I did not specify how much Land corresponds in value to the work of the humblest Peasant or Laborer, when I said that it is worth twice the produce of the Land which serves to support him; for that varies according to the standard of living in the different Countries. . . .

The Silver or Coin, which finds in exchange the proportions between values, is the most certain measure for judging the par between Land & Labor, & the relation of one to the other in the different Countries where this Par varies according to the greater or less produce of Land which is attributed to those who labor.

For example, if one Man earns an ounce of silver every day by his labor, & if another earns only half an ounce in the same place; it may be concluded that the first has once again as much produce of Land to spend as the second.

Sir William Petty, in a little Manuscript of the year 1685, considers this par, as an Equation between Land & Labor, the most important consideration in political Arithmetic; but the analysis which he made of it in passing is bizarre & not in accord with the rules of nature, simply because he did not keep to causes & principles, but only to effects; as Messrs. Locke & d'Avenant, & all the other English Authors who have written upon this subject, have done since.

IV. The circulation & exchange of commodities & merchandise, as well as their production, are carried on in Europe by Entrepreneurs, & subject to risk

The Farmer is an Entrepreneur who promises to pay the Proprietor, for his Farm or Land, a definite sum of money (which is ordinarily assumed to be equal in value to a third of the produce of the Land), without having any assurance as to the profit he will make from this enterprise. He employs a part of this Land to pasture Herds, to produce grain, wine, hay, &c. according to his ideas, without being able to foresee which of these kinds of commodities will bring the best price. This price of the commodities will depend in part upon the Seasons, & in part upon consumption; if there is an abundance of wheat in relation to consumption, it will be cheap; if there is a scarcity, it will be dear. Who can foresee the number of births & deaths among the Inhabitants of the State in the course of the year? Who can foresee the increase or diminution of expenditure which may arise among the Families? Yet the price of the Farmer's commodities naturally depends upon these events which he cannot foresee, & consequently he carries on the enterprise of his Farm with uncertainty.

The City consumes more than half of the Farmer's commodities. He takes them to Market there, or he sells them in the Market of the nearest Town, or some even set up as Entrepreneurs to do this transporting. The latter undertake to pay the Farmer a definite price for his commodities, which is that of the Market that day, to get an uncertain price in the City, which must nevertheless repay them the expenses of carriage, & leave them a profit for their enterprise; yet the daily variation in the prices of commodities in the City, though not considerable, renders their profit uncertain.

The Entrepreneur or Merchant who transports commodities from the Country to the City, cannot remain there to sell them at retail when they come to be consumed: not one Family in the City will undertake to buy all at once the commodities it might consume; since each Family may increase or decrease in number as well as in consumption, or at least vary in the kinds of commodities which it will consume: Families lay in stocks of wine alone. In any case, the greater number of the Inhabitants of the City, who live only from hand to mouth, & who nevertheless are the largest consumers, will not be able to lay in stocks of commodities from the Country.

As a result, several persons in the City set up as Merchants or Entrepreneurs, to buy the commodities of the Country from those who bring them in, or to have them brought in on their own account: they pay a fixed price for them according to that of the place where they buy, to resell them in large or small quantities at an uncertain price.

These Entrepreneurs are the wholesale Merchants of wool and grain, the Bakers, Butchers, Manufacturers, & all Merchants of all kinds who buy the commodities & materials of the Country, to work them up & resell them as the Inhabitants need to consume them.

These Entrepreneurs can never know the volume of consumption in their City, nor even how long their Customers will buy of them, seeing that their Rivals will try in every way to get away their Business: all this causes so much uncertainty among all these Entrepreneurs that we see failures among them every day.

The Manufacturer who has purchased the wool of the Merchant, or of the Farmer directly, cannot know what profit he will make from his enterprise, in the sale of his cloths & stuffs to the Merchant draper. If the latter has not a fairly good market, he will not load up with the cloths & stuffs of the Manufacturer, still less if these stuffs go out of style.

The Draper is an Entrepreneur who buys cloths & stuffs from the Manufacturer at a fixed price, to resell them at an uncertain price, because he can not foresee the volume of consumption; it is true that he can fix a price & refuse to sell unless he gets it, but if his Customers leave him to buy cheaper of somebody else, he will run up expenses while waiting to sell at the price he proposes, & that will ruin him as much or more than if he sold without profit.

Merchants in shops & Retailers of all kinds are Entrepreneurs who buy at a definite price & resell in their Shops or in the public Squares at an uncertain price. What encourages & maintains Entrepreneurs of these kinds in a State is the fact that the Consumers, who are their Customers, prefer to pay a little more in order to find at hand what they need in small quantities, rather than to lay in a stock of it, & that the greater part of them have not the means to lay in such a stock, buying at first hand.

All these Entrepreneurs become consumers & Customers of each other; the Draper, of the wine Merchant; the latter, of the Draper: they adjust their numbers in the State to their Customers or to their market. If there are too many Hatters in a City or in a street for the number of persons who buy hats there, those having the fewest customers will have to become bankrupt; if there are too few, it will be a profitable enterprise, which will encourage some new Hatters to open shop there, & it is thus that Entrepreneurs of all kinds, at their own risk, adjust their numbers in a State. . . .

It might perhaps be argued that all the Entrepreneurs seek to secure all they can in their state, & to cheat their Customers, but that is outside my subject.

From all these arguments & an infinity of others which might be advanced upon a question which concerns all the Inhabitants of a State, we may conclude that, with the exception of the Prince & the Proprietors of Lands, all the Inhabitants of a State are dependent; that they may be divided into two classes, namely, Entrepreneurs & Wage-earners; & that the Entrepreneurs work for uncertain wages, so to speak, & all others for certain wages while they have them, although their functions & their rank are very disproportionate. The General who has a salary, the Courtier who has a pension, & the Domestic who has wages, are in the latter class. All the others are Entrepreneurs, whether they establish themselves with a capital to carry on their enterprise, or are Entrepreneurs of their own work without any capital, & they may be considered as living subject to uncertainty; even Beggars & Robbers are Entrepreneurs of this class. Finally, all the Inhabitants of a State draw their subsistence & their benefits from the fund of the Proprietors of Lands, & are dependent.

It is true, however, that if some Inhabitant receiving high wages, or some Entrepreneur of importance, has saved up some property or wealth, that is, if he has stores of wheat, of wool, of copper, of gold or silver, or of some commodity of merchandise having a stable use or sale in a State & having a real or intrinsic value, he may properly be regarded as independent to the extent of this fund. He can dispose of it to buy a mortgage, & a rent upon Lands, & upon the funds of the State when it makes loans secured by lands: he may even live much better than the Proprietors of small estates, & even buy some of these.

But commodities & merchandise, even gold & silver, are much more subject to accidents & losses than landed property; & however they have been earned or saved, they have always been drawn from the fund of the existing Proprietors, either by profit, or by savings of wages destined for one's subsistence.

The number of Proprietors of money, in a great State, is often pretty considerable; & although the value of all the money which circulates in the State does not exceed the ninth or tenth part of the value of the commodities derived from the land at the present time, nevertheless since the Proprietors of money lend considerable sums from which they draw interest, either by mortgages on land, or by the commodities & merchandise itself of the State, the sums owed them generally exceed all the actual money of the State, & they often become such a powerful group that they would in certain cases rival the Proprietors of lands, if the latter were not often likewise Proprietors of money, & if the Proprietors of large sums of money were not always seeking also to become Proprietors of lands.

It is always true, however, that all the sums which they have earned or saved have been drawn from the fund of the existing Proprietors; but since several of the latter ruin themselves every day in a State, & since the others who acquire ownership of their lands take their place, the independence which is given by the ownership of lands pertains only to those who retain possession of them; & since all lands always have an existing Master or Proprietor, I always assume that it is from the fund of the latter that all the Inhabitants of the State draw their subsistence & all their riches. If these Proprietors all limited themselves to living on their rents, this would not be doubtful, and in that case it would be much more difficult for the other Inhabitants to enrich themselves at their expense.

I shall establish as a principle, therefore, that the Proprietors of lands are alone naturally independent in a State; that all the other orders are dependent, either as Entrepreneurs, or as wage-earners, & that all the exchange & circulation in the State is carried on by the intervention of these Entrepreneurs.

V. Of Market Prices

Suppose the Butchers on the one hand & the Buyers on the other. The price of meat will be determined after some altercations; & a pound of Beef will bear about the same ratio to a piece of money, that all the Beef offered for sale in the Market bears to all the money brought thither to buy Beef.

This proportion is settled by altercation. The Butcher holds out for a price according to the number of buyers he sees; the Buyers, on their part, offer less according as they believe that the Butcher will have less market: the price settled upon by some is ordinarily followed by the others. Some are more skillful in getting good prices for their merchandise, others more adroit in discrediting it. Though this method of fixing the prices of things in the Market has no just or geometrical basis, since it often depends upon the eagerness or the facility of a small number of Buyers or of Sellers; yet it does not seem possible to arrive at it in any other more suitable way. It remains true that the quantity of commodities or of merchandise offered for sale, compared with the demand or with the number of Buyers, is the basis upon which people fix, or always think they fix, the prevailing Market prices; & that in general these prices do not differ much from the intrinsic value. . . .

It often happens that the Sellers, desiring to keep their prices too high in the Market, lose the opportunity to sell their commodities or merchandise on good terms, & suffer a loss. It also happens that by keeping up these prices they will often be able to sell to better advantage another day.

Distant Markets may always have an influence on the prices of the Market where one happens to be: if wheat is extremely dear in France, its price will rise in England & in the other neighboring Countries.

VI. Of the increase & the decrease in the quantity of Money in a State

If mines of gold or silver are discovered in a State, & if considerable quantities of material are taken from them, the Proprietor of these Mines, the Entrepreneurs, & all those who work in them will not fail to increase their expenditures in proportion to the riches & the profits which they will make: they will also lend at interest the sums of money which they have over and above what they need for their expenses. All this money, lent as well as spent, will enter into circulation, & will not fail to raise the price of commodities & merchandise in all the channels of circulation which it enters. The increase of money will bring about an increase of expenditure, & this increase of expenditure will bring about an increase of Market prices in the years of most active trade, & by degrees in the least active.

Everybody agrees that the abundance of money, or its increase in trade, raises the price of all things. The quantity of money brought from America to Europe during the last two centuries demonstrates this truth by experience.

Mr. Locke lays it down as a fundamental Maxim that the quantity of commodities & merchandise, as compared with the quantity of money, determines Market price. I have tried to explain his idea in the preceding Chapters: he realized well that the abundance of money makes everything dear, but he did not analyze how that takes place. The great difficulty of this analysis consists in discovering by what path & in what proportion the increase of money raises the price of things.

I have already remarked that an acceleration, or a greater speed, in the circulation of money in trade amounts to the same thing as an increase in standard money, up to a certain degree. I have also remarked that an increase or decrease in the prices of a distant Market, whether in the State or Abroad, has an influence upon the current prices of the Market. On the other hand, money circulates in detail through such a great number of channels, that it seems impossible not to lose sight of it; for after having been collected to make large sums, it is distributed in the tiny streams of trade, & subsequently is gradually accumulated again to make large payments. For those operations it is necessary to exchange coins of gold, silver, & copper constantly, according to the briskness of this trade. It therefore happens ordinarily that people do not notice the increase or decrease in the money supply in a State, because it slips away to foreign countries, or is introduced into the State, by paths & in proportions which are so imperceptible that it is impossible to determine exactly the quantity which comes into the State, or which goes out of it.

However, all these operations take place before our eyes, & everyone has a direct part in them. Hence I think I may venture some reflections upon this subject, though I cannot treat it in an exact & precise manner.

I hold that in general an increase in the monetary stock causes in a State a proportional increase in consumption, which by degrees produces the rise of prices.

If the increase in the money supply comes from Mines of gold or silver in a State, the Proprietor of these Mines, the Entrepreneurs, the Smelters, the Refiners, & in general all those working in them will not fail to increase their expenditures in proportion to their gains. They will consume in their households more meat & more wine or beer than they used to, they will acquire the habit of wearing better clothes, finer linen, of having better furnished Houses, & other refinements. Consequently they will give employment to several Artisans who did not have so much work formerly, & who for the same reason will increase their expenditures also; all this increase of expenditures on meat, wine, wool, &c., necessarily diminishes the share of the other Inhabitants of the State who do not participate at first in the riches from the Mines in question. The altercations of the Market, or the demand for meat, wine, wool, &c., being stronger than usual, will not fail to raise their price. These high prices will induce the Farmers to employ more land to produce these things another year: these same Farmers will profit from this increase of price, & will increase the expenditures of their families like the others. Those, therefore, who will suffer from this dearness, & from the increased consumption, will be at first the Proprietors of lands, during the term of their Leases, then their servants, & all the workmen or people working for fixed wages who support their families thereby. All these will have to diminish their expenditures in proportion to the new consumption; which will oblige a great many of them to leave the State to seek their fortunes elsewhere. The Proprietors will dismiss many of them, & the others will eventually demand an increase in wages in order to be able to live according to their customary standard. This, roughly, is how a considerable increase of money from Mines increases consumption; & while diminishing the number of inhabitants, brings about a greater expenditure among those who remain.

If more money is taken from the Mines, the prices of all things will be increased by this abundance of money to such an extent, that not only will the Proprietors of lands increase their Rents considerably at the expiration of their Leases, & resume their former standard of living, increasing proportionately the wages of those who serve them; but the Artisans & Workmen will ask such high prices for their products that it will be quite profitable to bring them from Abroad, where they are made much cheaper. This will naturally induce several people to import quantities of Manufactured goods made in foreign Countries, where they may be had cheaply: which will imperceptibly ruin the Artisans & Manufacturers of the State who could not live on such low wages, in view of the high prices.

When the too great abundance of money from the Mines has diminished the population of a State, accustomed those who remain to excessive expenditure, carried the produce of land & the work of Artisans to excessive prices, ruined the Manufacturers of the State, through the use made by the Proprietors of land & those who work in the Mines of goods from foreign countries, the money produced by the Mines will necessarily be transferred to Foreigners to pay for what we import from them: which will imperceptibly impoverish this State, & render it in some ways dependent upon foreign countries to which money has to be sent every year. as it is drawn from the Mines. The great circulation of money, which at first was general, ceases; poverty & misery follow, & the working of the Mines appears to be only for the advantage of those employed in them, & for the Foreigners who profit from it. . . .

Now if the increase of money in the State is derived from a balance of trade with Foreigners (that is, by sending them products & Manufactures of greater value & quantity than we import from them & consequently receiving the surplus in money), this annual increase of money will enrich a great number of Merchants & Entrepreneurs in the State, & will give employment to many Artisans & Workmen who furnish the products which are sent Abroad whence this money is obtained. This will gradually increase the consumption of these industrious inhabitants, & will raise the prices of land & labor. But the industrial Classes, who are eager to accumulate property, will not increase their expenditures at first; they will wait until they have accumulated a good fortune, from which they can obtain a sure interest independently of their trade. When a great number of inhabitants have acquired considerable fortunes from this money which enters constantly & annually into the State, they will not fail to increase their consumption & to make all things dear. Although this dearness involves them in even greater expenditures than they had at first intended to make, they will not for the most part give them up, as long as they have any capital left; since nothing is easier or more agreeable than to increase the expenditures of families, but nothing is more difficult or more disagreeable than to reduce them.

If an annual & constant balance has caused a considerable increase of money in a State, it will not fail to increase consumption, to raise the price of everything, & even to diminish the number of inhabitants, unless an additional amount of commodities is obtained from Abroad in proportion to the increase of consumption. Moreover, States which have acquired a considerable abundance of money ordinarily import many things from neighboring countries where money is scarce, & where everything is consequently cheap: but since money has to be sent for that, the balance of trade will become smaller. The cheapness of land & labor in foreign countries where money is scarce will naturally cause Manufactures & other industries to be set up there like those of the State, but which will not at first be as perfect or as well liked.

In this situation, the State can subsist amid an abundance of money, consume all its produce & even much of the produce of foreign countries, & still over & above all that keep a small balance of trade over Foreign Countries, or at least keep this balance many years at par; that is, to import in exchange for its products & its Manufactures, as much money from these foreign countries as it has to send them in exchange for commodities or the produce of land which it imports from them. If this State is a maritime State, the facility & cheapness of its shipping for the transport of its products & its Manufactures into foreign countries may compensate in some measure for the dearness of labor which the excessive supply of money causes there; with the result that the products & the Manufactures of the State, dear as they are, will not cease to be sold in distant foreign countries, at lower prices sometimes than the Manufactures of another State where labor is cheaper.

The expenses of carriage increase considerably the prices of things transported into distant countries; but these expenses are rather moderate in maritime States, where there is regular transportation to all Ports abroad, so that Ships ready to sail are almost always to be found there, which load with all the merchandise entrusted to them, for a very reasonable freight charge.

It is not so in States where navigation is not flourishing; there it is necessary to build ships expressly for the transport of merchandise, which sometimes wipes out all the profit; & the expenses of operation are always high, which discourages commerce altogether. . . .

The increase in the quantity of money in a State may also be caused, without any balance of commerce, by subsidies paid to this State by foreign Powers; by the expenses of numerous Ambassadors, or Travellers, who may be led to go there for political reasons, or by curiosity, or for pleasure; by the transfer of the property & fortunes of Families, who from motives of religious liberty, or for other reasons, leave their native land to take up their residence in this State. In all these cases, the sums which come into the State always cause an increase of expenditures & consumption there, & consequently raise the prices of everything in the channels of trade which the money enters. . . .

VII. Continuation of the same subject of the increase & diminution of the amount of money in a State

Since gold, silver, & copper have an intrinsic value in proportion to the land & labor which enter into their production, in the localities where they are mined, & also to the expenses of importing or introducing them into States which have no Mines, the quantity of money, like that of all other commodities, determines its value in the altercations of Markets as compared with all other things.

If England begins to use gold, silver & copper for the first time in barter, money will be esteemed, according to the amount of it in circulation, in proportion to its value compared with all other commodities & merchandise, & this valuation will be arrived at roughly by the altercations of the Markets. Upon the basis of these valuations, Proprietors of lands & Entrepreneurs will fix the wages of the Servants & Workmen they employ, at so much per day or per year, in such a way that they & their families may be able to live on the wages given them.

Let us suppose, now, that as a result of the residence of Ambassadors & foreign Travellers in England, as much money has been introduced into that country's circulation as there was originally; this money will pass at first into the hands of numerous Artisans, Domestics, Entrepreneurs, & others who will have taken part in the work on the equipages, entertainments, &c. of these Foreigners: the Manufacturers, Farmers & other Entrepreneurs will be aware of this increase of money which will accustom many persons to making greater expenditures than in the past, which will consequently raise the prices in the Markets. . . . Many exchanges which formerly took place by barter will now be made with the help of ready money, & consequently there will be more rapidity in the circulation of money than there was at the beginning in England.

I conclude from all this that as a result of the introduction of a double quantity of money into a State, the prices of commodities & merchandise are not always doubled. A River which follows a winding course will not flow twice as fast, if the volume of its waters is doubled.

The proportion of dearness, which the increase & the quantity of money introduce into the State, will depend on the effect produced by this money on consumption & on circulation. Through whatever hands the money introduced passes, it will naturally increase consumption; but this increase will be greater or less according to circumstances; it will affect certain kinds of commodities or merchandise more or less, according to the tastes of those who acquire the money. The prices in the Markets will rise more for some kinds than for others, however plentiful money may be. In England, the price of meat might triple, without the price of wheat rising more than a quarter.

It is always permitted in England to import grain from foreign countries, but the importation of cattle is not allowed. As a result, however considerable the increase of money may be in England, the price of wheat can never rise higher there than in other countries where money is scarce, except by the amount of the expenses & risks involved in importing wheat from these same foreign countries.

It is not the same with the price of cattle, which will necessarily be in proportion to the quantity of money offered for meat, as compared with the amount of this meat & the number of cattle raised there.

An ox weighing eight hundred pounds sells nowadays in Poland & in Hungary for two or three ounces of silver, while in the London Market it is generally sold for more than forty ounces of silver. However, a quarter of grain does not sell in London for twice as much as in Poland & in Hungary.

The increase of money increases the price of commodities & merchandise only by the cost of transportation, when this transportation is permitted. But in many cases this transportation would cost more than the value of the article; which makes forests useless in many places. The same transportation is the reason why milk, fresh butter, fresh vegetables, game, &c. are worth almost nothing in the Provinces at a distance from the Capital.

I conclude that an increase of money in a State always leads to an increase of consumption there & the habit of making greater expenditures. But the dearness caused by this money does not affect all kinds of commodities & merchandise equally, in proportion to the quantity of this money; unless what is introduced is continued in the same channels of circulation as the original money; that is, unless those who offered one ounce of silver in the Markets are the same & the only ones who now offer two ounces there, since the doubling of the weight of the money in circulation, which never happens. I take it that when a substantial addition is made to the money of a State, the new money gives a new turn to consumption, & even a rapidity to circulation; but it is not possible to determine the exact degree.

VIII. Of the interest of money & its causes

As the prices of things are determined in the altercations of the markets by the quantity of things offered for sale in proportion to the amount of money offered for them, or, what is the same thing, by the numerical proportion between the Sellers & the Buyers; similarly the interest of money in a State is determined by the numerical proportion between the Lenders & the Borrowers.

Although money passes as a pledge in exchange, yet it does not multiply, & does not produce any interest by merely circulating. The necessities of Men seem to have introduced the practice of interest. A Man who lends his money upon good security, or upon land mortgages, runs at least the risk of the enmity of the Borrower, or that of the expenses of law suits & losses; but when he lends without security, he runs the risk of losing all. Because of these reasons, Men in need must have at first tempted the Lenders by the attraction of a profit; & this profit must have been in proportion to the needs of the Borrowers & to the fear & the avarice of the Lenders. This, it seems to me, was the original source of interest. But its constant practice in States appears to be founded upon the profits which Entrepreneurs can make out of it.

Land produces naturally, aided by the labor of Man, four, ten, twenty, fifty, a hundred, a hundred & fifty times the quantity of wheat sown, according to the quality of the land & the industry of the Inhabitants. It multiplies fruits & Cattle. The Farmer who cultivates it ordinarily has two thirds of the produce, of which one third pays his expenses & his support, the other remains to him as the profit on his enterprise.

If the Farmer has enough funds to carry on his enterprise, if he has all the tools & the equipment necessary, the horses for cultivating, the cattle needed to develop the land, &c., he will take for himself, all expenses paid, a third of the produce of the Farm. But if an experienced Laborer, living by his labor at wages from hand to mouth, & having no land, can find someone willing to lend him land, or money to buy some, he will be in a position to give this Lender all of the third rent, or a third of the produce of a Farm of which he will become the Farmer or Entrepreneur. However, he will consider his position better than formerly, seeing that he will find his subsistence in the second rent, & will become a Master, whereas before he was a Servant: so that if, through his great economy, & by depriving himself of certain necessaries, he can gradually accumulate a small capital, he will have to borrow less & less every year, & will succeed in time in appropriating all the third rent for himself.

If this new Entrepreneur finds an opportunity to buy wheat or cattle on credit, to pay for them after a considerable time & when he will be in a position to make money by the sale of the produce of his Farm, he will readily pay a higher price for them than that of the market for cash: & this method will be the same as if he borrowed money to buy the wheat for cash, paying as interest the difference between the price for cash & for credit: but in whatever way he borrows, whether cash or merchandise, he has to have something left to live on from his enterprise, or else he will be bankrupt. This risk will cause people to demand of him twenty to thirty per cent profit or interest upon the amount of money or upon the value of the commodities or merchandise lent to him.

In another case, a master Hatter, who has some capital to carry on his hat Manufacture, either to hire a house, buy beavers, wool, dye, &c., or to pay every week the subsistence of his Workmen, must not only obtain his living out of this enterprise, but also a profit similar to that of the Farmer, who has the third part for himself. This living, like this profit, must be derived from the sale of the hats, of which the price must pay not only for the materials but also for the support of the Hatter & of his Workmen, & also the profit in question.

But a Journeyman Hatter, experienced, but without capital, can undertake the same Manufacture, borrowing money & materials, & giving up the profit to anyone willing to lend him money, or to anyone willing to entrust him with beaver, wool, &c., for which he will pay only after considerable time & when he has sold his hats. If, at the maturity of his notes, the Lender of the money calls for his capital again, or if the wool Merchant & the other Lenders do not wish to trust him any longer, he will have to give up his enterprise; in which case he will perhaps prefer to become bankrupt. But if he is steady & industrious, he will be able to make his creditors see that he has, in money or in hats, approximately the value of the capital he borrowed, & they will probably prefer to continue to trust him & to be satisfied, for the present, with their interest or profit. Which will enable him to continue, & perhaps he will gradually accumulate some capital by depriving himself of a few necessaries. With this help he will have to borrow less & less every year, & when he has accumulated sufficient capital to carry on his Manufacture, which will always be in proportion to the market he has, the profit will all remain to him, & he will grow rich, if he does not increase his expenditures.

It is well to note that the living expenses of such a Manufacturer are of relatively small value, compared to that of the sums he borrows in his business, or of the materials entrusted to him; & consequently the Lenders do not run a great risk of losing their capital, if he is an honest & industrious man: but as it is very possible that he may not be, the Lenders will always demand of him a profit or interest of twenty to thirty per cent of the value of the loan: besides it will be only those who have a good opinion of him who will trust him. We can reason in the same way with respect to all Masters, Artisans, Manufacturers, & other Entrepreneurs in the State, who conduct enterprises of which the capital exceeds considerably the value of their annual subsistence.

But if a water Carrier in Paris sets up as an Entrepreneur of his own work, all the capital he will need will be the price of two buckets, which he will be able to buy for an ounce of silver, after which all that he earns becomes profit. If he earns by his labor fifty ounces of silver per year, the sum of his capital or loan will be to that of his profit as one to fifty. That is, he will make five thousand per cent, while the Hatter will not make fifty per cent, & will even be obliged to pay twenty to thirty per cent of it to the Lender.

However, a Lender of money will prefer to lend a thousand ounces of silver to a Hatter at twenty per cent interest, rather than to lend a thousand ounces to a thousand water Carriers at five hundred per cent interest. The water Carriers will soon spend on their subsistence not only the money they earn by their daily work, but all that is lent to them. These capitals that are lent to them are small in proportion to the sum they need for their subsistence: whether they have much or little employment, they can easily spend all they earn. Thus the earnings of these humble Entrepreneurs cannot be determined. One might well say that a water Carrier makes five thousand per cent of the value of the buckets which constitute the capital of his enterprise, & even ten thousand per cent, if by strenuous work he earned a hundred ounces a year. But since he can spend the hundred ounces on his living expenses, as well as the fifty, it is only by knowing how much he does spend for his living that one can tell how much clear profit he has.

It is always necessary to deduct the subsistence & living expenses of the Entrepreneurs before deciding about their profit. That is what we did in the example of the Farmer, & in that of the Hatter: & this is what cannot be determined for the humble Entrepreneurs: & so they generally become bankrupt, if they have any debts.

It is customary for the Brewers of London to lend some barrels of beer to the Entrepreneurs of Taverns, & when the latter pay for the first barrels, more are lent to them. If the consumption in these Taverns becomes large, these Brewers sometimes make a profit of five hundred per cent per year; & I have heard it said that the big Brewers do not fail to make money, as long as only half of the Taverns go bankrupt on them in the course of the year.

All the Merchants in the State make a regular practice of entrusting merchandise or commodities to Retailers on credit, & adjust their rate of profit, or their interest, to the risk they run. . . .

. . . high interest rates are not only tolerated, but are even in a way useful & necessary in a State. Those who buy fish in the streets pay this heavy interest in the increased price which they give; this is a convenience to them, & they do not feel the loss of it. Similarly an Artisan who drinks a mug of beer, & pays a price for it which allows the Brewer a profit of five hundred per cent, enjoys this convenience, & does not feel the loss at all on such small transactions.

DAVID HUME

(1711–1776)

Hume, one of the great English utilitarian philosophers, is important here because of his writings in economics. From 1734 to 1762 he devoted himself to writing, producing among other works his most important book, *A Treatise of Human Nature* (three volumes, 1739–1740). Between 1763 and 1769 he amassed a small fortune in the British diplomatic service, which he entered as secretary to Lord Hertford; he then retired to Edinburgh, where he remained for the rest of his life the intellectual leader of a group which included men like Adam Smith.

In ethics, philosophy, and politics, as well as in economics, Hume's point of view is dominated by the principle of utility—the promotion of human happiness. In this respect he was the spiritual godfather of Jeremy Bentham and the Philosophic Radicals.

As far as technical economics is concerned, his chief contributions were in the fields of foreign trade and money. His emphasis on foreign trade, his belief that the merchant occupies a high place in society, and his advocacy of state controls reveal his mercantilist leanings. In some respects, however, such as his specie-flow analysis, he deviated sharply from mercantilist doctrines. This analysis is first found in his essay *Of Money* (1752), where he argues that in the long run an influx of specie into a country might benefit the national treasury but not private individuals; that although some financial gain might accrue to private individuals in the beginning, eventually the rise in price resulting from the specie inflow would cancel out the advantages. This price adjustment illustrates his view that money has no intrinsic value, but is merely a symbol or measure of value. He also held that the rate of interest is dependent not upon the quantity of money, as was then generally believed, but on the combination of the supply and demand of loan funds and the rate of profit.

According to Hume the seeds of a favorable balance of trade lie in an unfavorable balance of trade. If a country were to lose bullion through excessive imports, that very result would lower domestic prices and inhibit further imports to a point where an export surplus would be achieved and the lost treasure brought back. Hume's theory of the automatic equilibrium of international trade is one of his important contributions to economics.

The following passage gives the crux of Hume's quantity theory of money. Briefly put, it holds that the proportion between money in circulation and commodities for sale in the market determines the level of prices.

OF MONEY *

Money is not, properly speaking, one of the subjects of commerce; but only the instrument, which men have agreed upon to facilitate the exchange of one commodity for another. 'Tis none of the wheels of trade: 'Tis the oil, which renders the motion of the wheels more smooth and easy. If we consider any one kingdom by itself, 'tis evident, that the greater or less plenty of money is of no consequence; since the prices of commodities are always proportion'd to the plenty of money . . . 'Tis

* From "Of Money," in *Political Discourses* (Edinburgh, 1752).

only the *public,* that draws any advantage from the greater plenty of money; and that only in its wars and negociations with foreign states. And this is the reason, why all rich and trading countries, from *Carthage* to *Britain* and *Holland,* have employ'd mercenary troops, which they hir'd from their poorer neighbours. Were they to make use of their native subjects, they would find less advantage from their superior riches, and from their great plenty of gold and silver; since the pay of all their servants must rise in proportion to the public opulence. Our small army in *Britain* of 20,000 men are maintain'd at as great expence as a *French* army thrice as numerous. The *English* fleet, during the late war, requir'd as much money to support it as all the *Roman* legions, which kept the whole world in subjection, during the time of the emperors.

The greater number of people and their greater industry are serviceable in all cases; at home and abroad, in private and in public. But the greater plenty of money is very limited in its use, and may even sometimes be a loss to a nation in its commerce with foreigners.

There seems to be a happy concurrence of causes in human affairs, which check the growth of trade and riches, and hinder them from being confin'd entirely to one people; as might naturally at first be dreaded from the advantages of an establish'd commerce. Where one nation has got the start of another in trade, 'tis very difficult for the latter to regain the ground it has lost; because of the superior industry and skill of the former, and the greater stocks, which its merchants are possest of, and which enable them to trade for so much smaller profits. But these advantages are compensated, in some measure, by the low prices of labour in every nation, that has not an extensive commerce, and does not very much abound in gold and silver. Manufactures, therefore, gradually shift their places, leaving those countries and provinces, which they have already enrich'd, and flying to others, whither they are allur'd by the cheapness of provisions and labour; till they have enrich'd these also, and are again banish'd by the same causes. And in general, we may observe, that the dearness of every thing, from plenty of money, is a disadvantage, that attends an establish'd commerce, and sets bounds to it in every country, by enabling the poorer states to undersell the richer in all foreign markets.

. . . Since the discovery of the mines in *America,* industry has encreas'd in all the nations of *Europe,* except in the possessors of those mines; and this may justly be ascrib'd, amongst other reasons, to the encrease of gold and silver. Accordingly we find, that in every kingdom, into which money begins to flow in greater abundance than formerly, every thing takes a new face; labour and industry gain life; the merchant becomes more enterprizing; the manufacturer more diligent and skillful; and even the farmer follows his plough with greater alacrity and attention. This is not easily to be accounted for, if we consider only the influence, which a greater abundance of coin has in the kingdom itself, by heightening the price of commodities, and obliging every one to pay a greater number of these little yellow or white pieces for every thing he purchases. And as to foreign trade, it appears, that great plenty of money is rather disadvantageous, by raising the price of every kind of labour.

To account, then, for this phænomenon, we must consider, that tho' the high price of commodities be a necessary consequence of the encrease of gold and silver, yet it follows not immediately upon that encrease; but some time is requir'd before the money circulate thro' the whole state, and make its effects be felt on all ranks of people. At first, no alteration is perceiv'd; by degrees, it raises the price first of one commodity, then of another; till the whole at last rises to a just proportion, with the new quantity of specie, which is in the kingdom. In my opinion, 'tis only in this interval or intermediate situation, betwixt the acquisition of money and rise of prices, that the encreasing quantity of gold and silver is favourable to industry. When any quantity of money is imported into a nation, it is not at first disperst into many hands; but is confin'd to the coffers of a few persons, who immediately seek to employ it to the best advantage. . . .

From the whole of this reasoning we may conclude, that 'tis of no manner of consequence, with regard to the domestic happiness of a state, whether money be in a greater or less quantity. The good policy of the magistrate consists only in keeping it, if possible, still encreasing; because, by that means, he keeps a spirit of industry alive in the nation, and encreases the stock of labour, wherein consists all real power and riches. A nation, whose money decreases, is actually, at that time, much weaker and more miserable, than another nation, who possesses no more money, but is on the encreasing hand. This will be easily accounted for, if we consider, that the alterations in the quantity of money, either on the one side or the other, are not immediately attended with proportionable alterations in the prices of commodities. There is always an interval before matters be adjusted to their new situation; and this interval is as pernicious to industry, when gold and silver are diminishing, as it is advantageous, when these metals are encreasing. The workman has not the same employment from the manufacturer and merchant; tho' he pays the same price for everything in the market. The farmer cannot dispose of his corn and cattle; tho' he must pay the same rent to his landlord. The poverty and beggary and sloth, which must ensue, are easily foreseen.

. . . There are some kingdoms, . . . where money is so scarce, that the landlord can get none at all from his tenants; but is oblig'd to take his rent in kind, and either to consume it himself, or transport it to places, where he may find a market. In those countries, the prince can levy few or no taxes, but in the same manner: And as he will receive very small benefit from impositions so pay'd, 'tis evident, that such a kingdom has very little force even at home; and cannot maintain fleets and armies to the same extent, as if every part of it abounded in gold and silver. . . .

To these difficulties I answer, that the effect, here suppos'd to flow from scarcity of money, really arises from the manners and customs of the inhabitants, and that we mistake, as is usual, a collateral effect for a cause. . . .

It seems a maxim almost self-evident, that the prices of every thing depend on the proportion betwixt commodities and money, and that any considerable alteration on either of these has the same effect either of heightening or diminishing the prices. Encrease the commodities, they become cheaper: Encrease the money, they rise in their value. As on the other hand, a diminution of the former, and that of the latter have contrary tendencies.

'Tis also evident, that the prices do not so much depend on the absolute quantity of commodities and of money, which are in a nation; as on that of the commodities, which come or may come to market, and of the money, which circulates. If the coin be lockt up in chests, 'tis the same thing with regard to prices, as if it were annihilated: If the commodities be hoarded in granaries, a like effect follows. As the money and commodities, in these cases, never meet, they cannot affect each other. Were we, at any time, to form conjectures concerning the prices of provisions, the corn, which the farmer must reserve for the maintenance of himself and family, ought never to enter into the estimation. 'Tis only the overplus, compar'd to the demand, that determines the value.

To apply these principles, we must consider, that in the first and more uncultivated ages of any state, e're fancy has confounded her wants with those of nature, men, contented with the productions of their own fields, or with those rude preparations, which they themselves can work upon them, have little occasion for exchange, or at least for money, which, by agreement, is the common measure of exchange. The wool of the farmer's own flock, spun in his own family, and wrought by a neighbouring weaver, who receives his payment in corn or wool, suffices for furniture and cloathing. The carpenter, the smith, the mason, the taylor are retain'd by wages of a like nature; and the landlord himself, dwelling in the neighbourhood, is contented to receive his rent in the commodities rais'd by the farmer. The greatest part of these he consumes at home, in rustic hospitality: The rest, perhaps, he disposes of for money to the neighbouring town, whence he draws the materials of his expence and luxury.

But after men begin to refine on all these enjoyments, and live not always at home, nor are contented with what can be rais'd in their neighbourhood, there is more exchange and commerce of all kinds, and more money enters into that exchange. The tradesmen will not be paid in corn; because they want something more than barely to eat. The farmer goes beyond his own parish for the commodities he purchases, and cannot always carry his commodities to the merchant, who supplies him. The landlord lives in the capital or in a foreign country; and demands his rent in gold and silver, which can easily be transported to him. Great undertakers and manufacturers and merchants arise in every commodity; and these can conveniently deal in nothing but in specie. And consequently, in this situation of society, the coin enters into many more contracts, and by that means is much more employ'd than in the former.

The necessary effect is, that provided the money does not encrease in the nation, every thing must become much cheaper in times of industry and refinement, than in rude, uncultivated ages. 'Tis the proportion betwixt the money, that circulates, and the commodities in the market, that determines the prices. Goods, that are consum'd at home, or exchang'd with other goods in the neighbourhood, never come to market; they affect not, in the least, the current specie; with regard to it they are as if totally annihilated; and consequently this method of using them sinks the proportion on the side of the commodities, and encreases the prices. But after money enters into all contracts and sales, and is every where the measure of exchange, the same national cash has a much greater task to perform; all commodities are then in the market; the sphere of circulation is enlarg'd; 'tis the same case as if that individual sum were to serve a larger kingdom; and therefore, the proportion being here diminish'd on the side of the money, every thing must become cheaper, and the prices gradually fall.

By the most exact computations, that have been form'd all over *Europe,* after making allowance for the change in the numerary value or the denomination, 'tis found, that the prices of all things have only risen three, or at most four times since the discovery of the *West Indies*. But will any one assert, that there is no more than four times the coin in *Europe,* that was in the fifteenth century and the centuries preceding it? . . .

Were the question propos'd, which of these methods of living in the people, the simple or the refin'd, is the most advantageous to the state or public, I shou'd, without much scruple, prefer the latter, in a view to politics at least; and should produce this as an additional reason for the encouragement of trade and manufactures. . . .

Here then we may learn the fallacy of the remark, often to be met with in historians, and even in common conversation, that any particular state is weak, tho' fertile, populous, and well cultivated, merely because it wants money. It appears, that the want of money can never injure any state within itself: For men and commodities are the real strength of any community. 'Tis the simple manner of living which here hurts the public, by confining the gold and silver to few hands, and preventing its universal diffusion and circulation. On the contrary, industry and refinements of all kinds incorporate it with the whole state, however small its quantity may be: They digest it into every vein, so to speak; and make it enter into every transaction and contract. No hand is entirely empty of it; and as the prices of every thing fall by that means, the sovereign has a double advantage: He may draw money by his taxes from every part of the state, and what he receives goes farther in every purchase and payment.

PART FIVE

The Physiocrats

The science of political economy as an integrated body of concepts begins to emerge for the first time in the writings of the physiocrats. The writings of this school mark the first clear separation of economics from the body of moral philosophy.

The fundamental idea of physiocratic doctrine is the notion of the exclusive productivity of agriculture and the barrenness of trade and industry. Agriculture alone produces a *produit net*—a surplus over and above what is required for the maintenance of agricultural labor. From this surplus all other classes in society are supported.

This conception was embodied in Quesnay's *Tableau Économique* as a closed circular flow representing the distribution of this *net product* among the classes of society. It has been said that the *Tableau Économique* was suggested to Quesnay by Harvey's discovery of the circulation of blood in the human body. This view supplanted the conception of the body as an aggregate of independent parts and showed it to be a unified organ wherein all parts are interrelated. In the *Tableau,* goods are the "blood" and money the "blood vessels." Monetary terms are used to describe the distribution and exchange of goods, the uses of the *produit net.* This view of society enabled the physiocrats to picture the economic process as self-regulating and self-perpetuating, expressive of the law of nature in the economic realm.

Physiocratic reasoning, it has been said, rests on a philosophic confusion between economic value and physical matter. This interpretation overlooks the historical environment of physiocracy. The *Tableau* is a precise reflection of French society about the middle of the eighteenth century. Under the feudal system the peasants and artisans gained little more than their subsistence, while the riches accumulated in the hands of the nobility. These riches were derived from the labor of the cultivators, and for this reason the latter were "productive." The urban traders and artisans did not pay rents and did not add to the wealth of the privileged class, and for this reason they were "unproductive." French industry at this time was luxury industry, catering to the feudal aristocracy whose consumption absorbed nearly the whole industrial output. This fact explains the dependent position of industry and trade in the physiocratic system. For the physiocrats, the entrepreneur appeared as an employee of the nobility, belonging rather to the sphere of consumption than to the sphere of production.

The physiocrats wished to tax only the nobility because the other classes were already held down to the subsistence level. To burden the "sterile" classes would only make luxury goods more expensive. To burden the productive class of agricultural workers would only lower the revenue. Hence the nobility alone was taxable and the *impôt unique*—the single tax—was to fall on land not merely because agriculture was productive but because the total income of society flowed into the hands of the nobility.

The physiocratic emphasis on natural law and a divinely ordained social order was a reaction against the straitjacket mercantilism of Colbert and the *ancien régime.* Since industry did not create wealth, only transformed it, regulation was useless and possibly harmful. The "natural order" must not be tampered with. The prescription for government action was *laissez faire, laissez passer,* and practical recommendations centered about the promotion of agriculture: free trade, reduction of court luxuries, improvement of transportation, and nonintervention by the state.

By demonstrating the stability of the economic order as an automatic mechanism the physiocrats established political economy as a separate discipline of study. As long as economic processes are the result of administrative action, there is nothing to investigate except the political decisions themselves. The moment the economic order is viewed as a mechanism with independent laws of development, a science which makes these laws explicit is called for. The physiocrats were in the truest sense the founders of economic science.

FRANÇOIS QUESNAY
(1694–1774)

François Quesnay was the leader of the first "school" of economics, the physiocrats. He was the court physician of Louis XV and Mme. de Pompadour and did not turn to economics until late in life. His famous *Tableau Économique* (*Economic Table*), written for the king of France in 1758, purports to depict the flow of goods and money in a nation. Thus it was the first attempt to analyze the flow of wealth on a macro-economic basis. Macro-economics describes economic activities in terms of large aggregates, in contrast to micro-economics, which describes economic activities in terms of individuals. Because he originated this approach, many great economists, of as diverse backgrounds as Smith, Marx, and Keynes, have paid tribute to the prescient work of Quesnay.

Quesnay did not write voluminously, but his ideas gained wide acceptance even in his own day because of his great influence on his colleagues and disciples.

In reading the following piece, one should remember that Quesnay is describing the agriculture of northern France, with which he was personally acquainted. In this section of France large-scale farming was general, with wealthy peasants paying rent to a landowner. Quesnay's attitude toward agriculture is revealed again in his articles on "Farmers" and "Grain," written for the *Encyclopédie* (1756, 1757), in which he advocates more intensive methods of farming and the abolition of taxes and restrictions of a mercantilist nature.

Like other physiocrats, Quesnay was no revolutionary, and he upheld the sanctity and desirability of private property to a point where he held the landowner (not the actual farmer) to be "productive," while claiming that manufacturers, merchants, and artisans were not! Agricultural laborers were not even mentioned.

In the following selection Quesnay describes the flow of goods and services in economic life.

EXPLANATION OF THE ECONOMIC TABLE *

The *productive Expenditures* are employed in agriculture, meadows, pastures, forests, mines, fishing, &c. to perpetuate riches in the form of grain, beverages, wood, cattle, raw materials for the handicrafts, &c.

The *sterile Expenses* are made upon handicraft products, housing, clothing, interest on money, servants, commercial expenses, foreign commodities, &c.

The sale of the net product which the Cultivator has produced during the preceding year, by means of the *annual Advances* of 600 livres employed in agriculture by the Farmer, furnishes the proprietor a *revenue* of 600 livres.

The *annual advances* of 300 livres in sterile expenses are employed for the capital & the expenses of commerce, for the purchase of raw materials for the handicrafts, & for the subsistence & other needs of the artisan until he has finished & sold his product.

* From *Explanation of the Economic Table.* Reprinted by permission of the publishers from Arthur Eli Monroe, *Early Economic Thought.* Cambridge, Mass.: Harvard University Press, Copyright, 1924, by The President and Fellows of Harvard College.

Of the 600 livres of *revenue,* one half is spent by the Proprietor on purchases from the productive class, such as bread, wine, meat, &c., & the other half on purchases from the sterile class, such as clothing, furnishings, implements, &c.

These expenditures may incline more or less to one side or the other, as the spender goes in more or less for luxury in the way of subsistence or luxury in the form of ornamentation. Here the average situation is taken, where the reproductive expenditures renew the same revenue from year to year. But it is easy to see what changes would be caused in the annual reproduction of revenue, as the sterile expenditures or the productive expenditures became more or less important than the other: it is easy, I say, to tell this from the very changes which would take place in the table. For, suppose that luxury in the form of ornamentation should increase by a sixth in the case of the Proprietor, by a sixth in the case of the Artisan, & by a sixth in the case of the Cultivator, the reproduction of revenue would fall from 600 livres to 500 livres. If, on the contrary, an increase of expenditure of the same extent occurred in the consumption or the exportation of raw materials, the reproduction of revenue would rise from 600 livres to 700 livres, & so on. Thus we see that an excess of luxury in the way of decoration may quickly ruin with magnificence an opulent Nation.

The 300 livres of revenue which were devoted to productive expenditures in the table bring back to this class, in money, *advances* which reproduce 300 livres net, which make up a part of the reproduction of the Proprietor's revenue; And by the distribution of the remaining sums which return to this same class, the total revenue is reproduced yearly. These 300 livres I say, which return to the productive class at first through the sale of the products which the Proprietor buys of them, are spent by the Farmer, half upon the consumption of products furnished by this same class, & the other half upon clothing, implements, tools, &c. which he buys of the sterile class. And they arise again with the net product.

The 300 livres of the Proprietor's revenue which were devoted to sterile expenditures are spent by the artisan, half on productive expenditures in the purchase of subsistence, raw materials, & for foreign commerce; the other half is distributed among the sterile class itself for living expenses, & to restore the *advances*. This circulation & this reciprocal distribution continues by subdivisions in the same order, down to the last penny of the sums which pass reciprocally from one class of expenditures to the other class of expenditures.

Circulation brings 600 livres to the sterile class, from which it is necessary to deduct 300 livres for the *annual advances,* leaving 300 livres for wages. These wages are equal to the 300 livres which this class receives from the productive class, & the advances are equal to the 300 livres of revenue which go to this same sterile class.

The productions of the other class amount to 1200 livres, after deducting taxes, tithes, & interest on the advances of the Husbandman, which will be considered separately, in order to avoid undue complications in

ECONOMIC TABLE

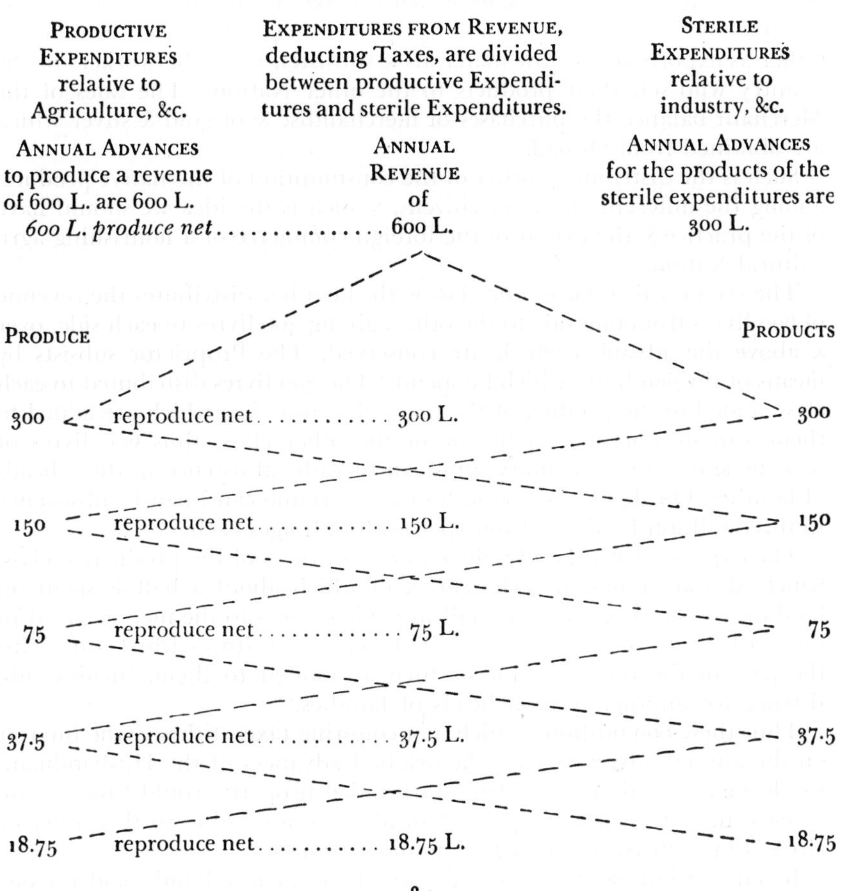

&c

TOTAL REPRODUCTION.............. 600 L. of revenue; besides the annual expenditures of 600 L. and the interest on the original advances of the Husbandman, amounting to 300 L., which the land restores: Thus the reproduction is 1500 L., including the revenue of 600 L. which is the basis of the calculation, apart from taxes deducted, and the advances required for its annual reproduction, &c.

analyzing the expenditures. In the expenditure of the 1200 livres of production, the Proprietor of the revenue buys 300 livres of them. Another 300 livres goes to the sterile class, of which a half, or 150 livres, is consumed for subsistence by this class; the other half, or 150 livres, being taken for foreign commerce, which comes under this same class. Finally, 300 livres are consumed in the productive class, by the men who produce them, & 300 livres for feeding & care of the cattle. Thus of the 1200 livres of product this class expends 600 livres, & its *advances* of 600 livres are returned to it in money through the sales which it makes to the Proprietor & to the sterile class. An eighth of the total product enters into foreign commerce, either as exports or for raw materials & subsistence for the workers of the country who sell their products to the other Nations. The sales of the Merchant balance the purchases of merchandise & of gold & silver which are obtained from abroad.

Such is the distributive order of the consumption of the native products among the different classes of citizens, & such is the idea we should have of the practice & the extent of the foreign commerce of a flourishing agricultural Nation.

The reciprocal traffic of one class with the other distributes the revenue of 600 livres from one side to the other; giving 300 livres to each side, over & above the advances which are conserved. The Proprietor subsists by means of the 600 livres which he spends. The 300 livres distributed to each class, added to the product of the taxes, the tithe, &c., which are added to them, can support a man in one or the other class: thus 600 livres of revenue & the supplementary sums can furnish subsistence to three heads of families. On this basis, 600 millions of revenue can furnish subsistence to three million families of four persons of all ages each.

The expenses furnished by the *annual advances* of the productive class, which also are renewed each year, & of which about a half is spent on food for the cattle & the other half in paying wages to the men engaged in the work of this class, add 300 millions of expenditures which can, with the part of the other products which are added to them, furnish subsistence for another million heads of families.

Thus these 900 millions, which, not counting taxes, tithes, & the interest on the annual advances & on the original advances of the Husbandman, would be renewed annually from the landed property, could furnish subsistence to sixteen million persons of all ages, according to this order of circulation & distribution of the annual revenues.

By circulation we mean here the purchases at first hand, paid for out of the revenue which is distributed among all the classes of men, excepting commerce, which multiplies purchases & sales without multiplying things, & which is only an increase of sterile expenditures.

The *riches of the productive class* of a Nation where the Proprietors of the land have constantly 600 millions of revenue may be evaluated as follows.

A revenue of 600 millions for the Proprietors assumes in addition 300 millions in taxes, & 150 millions for the tithe of the annual product, including all the charges, levied on those subject to the tithe: This makes a total of 1 billion 50 millions, including the revenue: In addition there are the reproduction of 1 billion 50 millions of annual advances, & 110 millions of interest on these advances at 10 per 100: making a grand total of 2,210,000,000 livres.

In a kingdom having many vineyards, forests, meadows, &c. there would be only about two-thirds of these 2 billions 210 millions which would be obtained by the labor of the plow. This part would require, in a good State of large-scale cultivation carried on by horses, the employment of three hundred thirty-three thousand three hundred thirty-four plows at 120 acres of land per plow, three hundred thirty-three thousand three hundred thirty-four men to direct them, & 40 million acres of land.

This culture may, with 5 or 6 billions of advances, be extended in France to more than 60 million acres.

We are not speaking here of small-scale cultivation carried on with oxen, in which more than a million plows would be needed, & about 2,000,000 men to exploit 40 million acres of land, which would yield only two-fifths as much as large-scale cultivation does. This small-scale cultivation to which the Cultivators are reduced, from lack of riches to make the original advances, is carried on at the expense of the landed property itself, employed to a great extent for the expenses, & by excessive annual expenditures for the subsistence of the multitude of men occupied in this form of cultivation, which absorb almost all the product. This ungrateful cultivation, which reveals the poverty & the ruin of the Nations where it prevails, has nothing to do with the order of the Table, which is arranged on the basis of half of the employment of a plow, where the annual advances can, in conjunction with the fund of original advances, produce one hundred per cent.

The total original advances required for the establishment of a plow in large-scale cultivation, for the first fund for the purchase of cattle, tools, seed, food, up-keep, wages, &c. in the course of two years' work before the first harvest, are estimated at 10,000 livres; thus the total for three hundred thirty-three thousand three hundred thirty-four plows is 3,333,340,000 livres. (See the articles *Farms, Farmers, Grains,* in the *Encyclopédie.*)

The interest on these advances should amount to at least 10 per 100, for the products of agriculture are exposed to ruinous accidents, which in ten years destroy the value of at least one year's crop. These advances demand, moreover, much up-keep & renewals; hence the total of interest on the original advances for establishing the Husbandmen is 333,322,000 livres.

The meadows, vineyards, ponds, forests, &c. require slight original advances on the part of the Farmers. The value of these advances may be reduced, including the original expenses for plantings & other work done at the expense of the Proprietors, to 1,000,000,000 livres.

But vineyards & gardens require large annual advances, which, taken in connection with those of the other parts, may on the average be included in the total of annual advances set forth above.

The total annual reproduction in net product, in annual advances with the interest thereon, & in interest on the original advances, reckoned in conformity with the order of the table, is 2,543,322,000 livres.

The territory of France could produce as much & even much more.

Of this sum of 2,543,322,000 livres, 525 millions constitute half of the reproduction of the annual advances employed in feeding the cattle: leaving (if all taxes go back into circulation, & if they do not encroach upon the advances of the Husbandmen) 2,018,322,000 livres.

This makes, FOR THE EXPENDITURE OF MEN, *on the average 504,580,500 livres for each million heads of families, or for each head of a family 562 livres, which accidents reduce to about 530 livres.* On this footing a State is rich, & men live comfortably there. . . .

We are speaking of an opulent Nation which possesses a territory & advances which yield annually, & without wasting away, 1 billion 50 millions of net product; but all these riches kept up successively by this annual product may be destroyed or lose their value, in the decadence of an agricultural Nation, by the mere wasting away of the productive advances, which may make great headway in a short time as a result of eight principal causes.

1. A bad system of taxation, encroaching upon the advances of the Cultivators. *Noli me tangere* is the motto of these advances.
2. Increase of taxes through expenses of collection.
3. Excess of luxurious expenditure on decoration.
4. Excess of expenses for litigation.
5. Lack of foreign trade in the produce of the land.
6. Lack of freedom in domestic trade in native commodities & in agriculture.
7. Personal vexations of the inhabitants of the rural districts.
8. Failure of the annual net product to return to the productive class.

PIERRE-PAUL MERCIER DE LA RIVIÈRE

(1720–1793)

The major contribution of Mercier de la Rivière, a French public official, writer, and thinker, formed an essential part of physiocratic doctrine. From 1747 to 1759 Mercier de la Rivière was a member of the Parlement of Paris. Shortly afterward he was made intendant of the colony of Martinique, where he soon antagonized his mercantilist superiors by applying the principles of free trade. After a long and losing battle with the French court, he was finally recalled in 1764. Soon after his retirement he wrote *L'Ordre Naturel et Essentiel des Sociétés Politiques* (*The Natural and Essential Order of Political Societies,* 1767). The book was an immediate sensation and gained fame for its author, who was invited to visit the court of Catherine the Great. Soon he was sent back by the irate Catherine, who complained of his lack of tact, saying that "he thought we were walking along on all fours, and tried to set us up on our hind legs."

Although his book contains many fine passages, it is also marked by a number of errors and exaggerations. These are in keeping with the teachings of other physiocratic writers, however. Not only is agriculture regarded as the source of all wealth and the single tax on the net product of agriculture as the only justifiable tax, but the autocratic emperor of China is set up as a model sovereign. Mercier de la Rivière recognizes the possibility of abuse of power by an unwise sovereign but suggests that the sovereign would either see the error of his ways or be deposed by force. In 1767 one of his disciples, Dupont de Nemours, published an abridgement of *L'Ordre Naturel,* entitled *De l'Origine et des Progrès d'une Science Nouvelle* (*On the Origin and Progress of a New Science*).

Mercier de la Rivière made his major contribution by combining two important eighteenth-century notions. He applied to economic questions one of the essential ideas of the Enlightenment—the concept of a natural order of society in which resources and needs are self-adjusting, without requiring state intervention—and made it an integral part of physiocratic doctrine. In the following selection his concept of the natural order is used tellingly as an argument for laissez-faire and free trade.

THE NATURAL AND ESSENTIAL ORDER OF POLITICAL SOCIETIES *

Preface

By uniting to live in society men have no other aim than to establish among themselves rights of both common and individual property with the aid of which they are able to procure for themselves all the happiness and enjoyment of which mankind is capable. I am writing, therefore, for the benefit of every member of society, for I am dealing with the means through which society must, of necessity and always, give the greatest permanency and the greatest value to the rights of common and individual property and thus arrive at the greatest possible perfection.

Wherever knowledge permits us to penetrate beneath the surface of

* From *The Natural and Essential Order of Political Societies,* reprinted from *Introduction to Contemporary Civilization in the West* (New York, Columbia University Press, 1946).

things, we discover an end as well as the means appropriate to its realization; we do not discern anything which is not governed by laws peculiar to its existence and which does not obey these laws so that it may attain with their aid everything which is compatible both with the nature of its being and the manner of its existence. It has occurred to me that man has not been less well treated. His particular abilities which make him the master of the earth permit me to believe that, in the general plan of the creation, there is a share of happiness for man and an order designed to assure its enjoyment.

Certain of this idea and convinced that the divine light in us is not given to us without purpose, I have arrived at the conclusion that this purpose consists in understanding the order in accordance with which our life must be organized if we are to achieve our happiness. Turning to the search for, and the study of, this order I began to realize that our natural state of existence is that of living in society; that our greatest happiness can be realized only in society; that the organization of men in society and their happiness as a result of this organization is the intention of the creator; that, consequently, we have to consider society as the work of God, and the fundamental laws of the social order as part of the general and immutable laws of the creation. The first difficulties encountered in this manner of looking upon man are due to the evils which result from our life in society. However, after realizing that even among the most useful things there is not one which may not become pernicious by our abusing it, I have felt it necessary to inquire whether the natural laws of society are the real causes of these evils or whether the latter are not rather the necessary consequences of our ignorance of the meaning of these laws. My investigations into this subject have led me from doubt to final certainty; they have convinced me that there is a natural order for the government of men united in society—an order which assures us necessarily of all the temporal happiness which is ours during our stay on earth and of all the enjoyments which we can reasonably hope for and to which we can add nothing without injuring ourselves; an order for the understanding of which nature has given us adequate intellectual powers and which needs only to be understood in order to be followed; an order in which everything is necessarily for the best, where all interests are so perfectly adjusted to each other and so inseparably united with each other that, from the sovereign to the last of his subjects, the happiness of one group cannot be increased without, at the same time, increasing the happiness of all other groups; an order, finally, the sanctity and usefulness of which demonstrates the existence of a benevolent deity and thus prepares and induces man, out of gratitude, to love and to worship God, and to seek, out of self-interest, the state of perfection which comes closest to God's will. The more I endeavoured to struggle against this certainty, the more I prepared the way for its final victory over me. May God give me the ability to demonstrate this truth, as I see it and as I feel it, to others. May it please God that this truth is spread everywhere; so that it may transform our vices into virtues and that happiness be given to all mankind.

Chapter II

Realization of the physical necessity of society leads directly to an understanding of what is absolutely just and what is absolutely unjust. . . .

The just may be defined as an order of duties and rights which are of the nature of physical necessity and thus absolute in character. Similarly, the unjust is everything which is in opposition to this order. . . .

It is not because men live in society that they have mutual duties and rights; it is because they have, by nature and of necessity, mutual duties and rights that they live, by nature and of necessity, in society. These duties and rights, which are of an absolute necessity in the physical order, represent the absolutely just.

I do not think that anyone will deny the existence of the natural right to secure one's own survival. This basic right is, indeed, only the result of a basic duty which is imposed upon man under penalty of pain or even death. Without this right his condition would be worse than that of animals. For all animals enjoy a similar right. Now, it must be clear that man's right to secure his own survival includes the right to acquire, by his own work, those things that are useful to his existence as well as the right to keep them after their acquisition. It is evident that this second right is only part of the first, for one cannot be said to have acquired what one has not the right to keep; thus the right to acquire and the right to keep form together only one and the same right although considered at different times.

It is thus from nature herself that man has received the exclusive property of his person and of those things which he acquires by his own work. I use the term exclusive property because if it were not exclusive it would not be a property right. . . .

In order to be able to fulfill the basic duty which nature has imposed upon him, and also in order to exist, man by absolute necessity has the right to secure his survival; in order to exercise this right it is absolutely necessary that others should not have the right to prevent him from doing so. The exclusive property of his person, which I am going to call personal property (*proprieté personelle*) is thus for each man a right by absolute necessity; and since this exclusive personal property would be nil without the exclusive ownership right to those things which man acquires by his labor, this second exclusive right of property, to which I shall give the name of negotiable property (*proprieté mobilère*) is an absolute necessity, like the first from which it is derived.

Thus we are already far advanced in our understanding of what is absolutely just and absolutely unjust. Once it is realized that it is absolutely necessary that personal and movable property are exclusive rights we are able to realize that each man has also duties which are of absolute necessity. These duties consist in the obligation not to invade the property rights of others, for it is evident that without these duties rights would cease to exist. . . .

In this manner the absolutely just reveals itself in all its simplicity: as soon as we understand the physical necessity of living in society, we also recognize the necessity, and consequently the absolute justice, of each man being the exclusive owner of his person and of those things which he acquires by his labor; we realize also the necessity and the absolute justice of each man making it his duty to respect the property rights of other men, and that thus among men rights do not exist without duties. . . .

I shall close this chapter with an observation about the inequality of conditions among men. Those who complain about this inequality do not realize that it reflects merely the very essence of justice: when I acquire the exclusive property of a given object no other man can be at the same time owner of that object. The law of property is the same for all men. The rights to property are equal for all but they are not all of equal worth, because their worth is absolutely independent of the natural law of property. Each man acquires in proportion to his abilities . . . and these abilities differ in different persons.

Apart from the various degrees of ability there are always, in the multitude of possible chances, constellations of circumstances which are either more or less fortunate. It is thus for two reasons that there must develop great differences in the state of affairs of human beings united in society. Therefore one ought not to consider an inequality of conditions an abuse which has its origin only in society. Even if it were possible to dissolve society, it would still be impossible to do away with inequalities which have their roots in the inequality of physical abilities as well as a multitude of purely accidental events, the course of which is independent of our wills. Thus, no matter what situation we may assume to exist, we would never be able to make the conditions of man equal, unless, by changing the laws of nature, we equalized for each man both physical abilities and accidental events. . . .

I admit, however, that the inequalities in the status of man in any given society may have been caused by great disorders which often tend to increase inequalities beyond their natural and necessary proportions. But does this mean that one ought to establish complete equality of conditions? Obviously not, for in order to do so, it would be necessary to destroy all property and consequently society. What is needed is rather to correct the disorders which cause what is no evil at all to become one, by their creating conditions which make only rights belong to some and only duties belong to others.

Chapter VI

Property and, consequently, security and liberty of enjoyment are the essence of the natural and fundamental order of society. This order is part of the physical order, and therefore its principal characteristics are in no way arbitrary. On the contrary, they are simple, clear, immutable, and in the highest degree advantageous for society as a whole, as well as for each of its members.

It is important not to confuse the supra-natural order with the natural order: the former reflects the will of God which is known only by revelation; and only those to whom God has revealed the existence of this supra-natural order are capable of perceiving it. In contrast, the natural order can be understood by all men with the aid of their reasoning power alone. . . .

The natural order is a perfect adjustment of physical means, which nature has chosen in order to produce necessarily the physical effects which she expects from them. I call these means physical means because in nature everything is physical; thus the natural order of which the social order is a part, is and can only be a physical order. . . . As soon as this fundamental truth is recognized it becomes obvious that the social order is not at all arbitrary in character, that it is not the work of man but is, on the contrary, the work of the creator of nature in the same way as all other branches of the physical order whose parts are absolutely and forever independent of our will. Consequently we have to regard the permanent laws of this physical order as the essential basis of all positive legislation and of all social institutions. . . .

It can thus truly be said that there is nothing more simple and more self-evident than the basic and invariable principles of the natural and fundamental order of society. In order to understand these principles, not only with respect to their natural origin and their essence but also as far as their practical consequences are concerned, it is necessary to understand the physical order. Once this order is understood the fundamental principle of the natural order of society and its practical consequences are likewise seen. No human power would ever think of making positive laws to the effect that sowing is to take place during the harvesting season and that harvesting is to be undertaken during the season of sowing. . . .

. . . The greatest possible happiness of the community as a whole consists in the greatest possible abundance of useful goods and in the greatest possible liberty to make use of these goods. I have made it clear that this maximum of enjoyment is the necessary consequence of the establishment of the right of property and that it is only by establishing this right that we are able to attain happiness. Now it is evident that, what secures the best possible state of affairs for the community procures also the same advantage for each individual member of society in view of the fact that each individual is called upon, by the natural order of things, to share in the happiness which all possess in common.

In order to prove this last proposition it will suffice to point out that a great output of commodities can acquire great utility only with the aid of industry, and that it is necessary for society to have an industrial class which, by aiding the agricultural class, acquires the right to share in the abundance of the crops. It is thus clear that the number of goods available to the agricultural class can be increased only by also increasing their quantity for all other persons who by their work tend to provide a greater variety and a greater number of goods to the farmer. Finally it is obvious that the volume of the annual crop is the determinant of population and of everything which determines the political power of society. In other words, the greatest possible increase of farm output is what makes for the best possible political order and gives it a maximum of power and security. . . .

Chapter XXXVI

. . . I have pointed out that the natural and fundamental order of society calls for the greatest possible freedom of foreign trade in the common interest of both the sovereign and the nation. It is now necessary to demonstrate the truth of this thesis in greater detail. In order to do this it will be sufficient to present simply and clearly the elementary concepts of commerce, and thus to indicate the real significance of the terms which are in daily use without being fully understood. . . .

If I speak here of domestic trade it is because I am convinced that today there exists general agreement about the necessity of leaving domestic trade as free as possible. Consumption is the measure of production, for goods which are not consumed degenerate into glut without utility and value, and there would be no further investment in their production. To recognize this truth is equivalent to realizing at the same time that freedom of domestic trade promotes production by making consumption possible.

However, . . . the development of greater free trade is constantly delayed by prejudices. People are convinced that profits made by foreign merchants within a given country as a result of exports and imports represent an increase of wealth for this nation. This error would be of no consequence if it did not induce governments to put all kinds of restrictions and taxes on consumption and consumers in the belief that these restrictions affect only the middlemen; governments also tend frequently to sacrifice the freedom of domestic trade to the private interests of sellers by granting them special privileges. The effect of these privileges, which reduce competition, is to put into the hands of a sterile class a part of the wealth which otherwise could be invested for productive purposes. . . .

No matter what form trade may take it always represents an exchange of commodities with commodities. The act of selling or buying is only an act of exchanging even if the transaction involves the use of money, for money is only a commodity. The aim of this exchange is enjoyment or consumption: that is to say, trade may be defined briefly as the exchange of useful commodities in order to distribute them to the final consumers for whose enjoyment they are destined. . . .

The exchange of a commodity for money is called selling, and men attach such interest to this form of trade that they like to be able always to sell for money and not to buy with money. This interest is an incomprehensible mania no matter how one looks at it. Without concerning myself with all aspects of this mania I shall attack its principle by pointing out that the sales which one wants to make for money can take place only if and as long as one buys with money. It is absolutely necessary that the sellers and buyers provide each other through their purchases with money which they in turn have received as a result of their sales. A wage earner sells his services and his talent and pays with his wages for what he consumes. The farmer sells his crop after transferring part of what he receives to the sovereign and the owner of the land, and uses the surplus in order to pay for what he consumes. The sovereign and the landowner also must be regarded as sellers of commodities through the intermediary of the farmer. With the price of these sales they pay for what they consume. The rentier receives an income which is the fruit of the wealth which he has sold either for a limited period or for ever, and with this income he pays for what he consumes. The owner of a house sells the annual yield of the investment involved in the acquisition and the maintenance of the house. The sale of this annual yield provides him annually with the means of payment for what he consumes. Thus, if we consider trade as a multitude of sales and purchases made with money, everybody is a buyer only to the extent to which he is a seller, and since buying is paying, the buyer can do so only to the extent that he sells, because it is only by selling that he is able to obtain the money to pay for what he buys. From the fact that every buyer must be a seller and can buy only insofar as he sells, a further conclusion follows: namely, that every seller must be also a buyer and can sell only insofar as he buys, and that each seller must through his purchases provide others with the money to buy the commodities which he intends to sell them.

Is it not evident then that, if the sales which we make to each other balance in terms of money, I can buy from you only if you buy from me, and that between you and me the sum total of our sales and that of our respective purchases must be equal? How could I possibly pay you if you, after having sold to me commodities worth 100 francs wanted to buy from me only commodities worth 50 francs? And if I were able to pay you once how could I possibly continue to give you more money than I receive? A third person, perhaps, buys from me, but who is going to buy from him? And how can he buy if he does not sell? You may extend the chain of sellers and buyers as long as you wish, it will always be necessary that each purchase is paid by the product of a sale, and that everybody is both buyer and seller in money for equal sums. As soon as money becomes the only means of exchange, everything would be lost if money ceased to circulate. It is absolutely necessary that money be spent.

ANNE ROBERT JACQUES TURGOT

(1727–1781)

Turgot was one of the most famous men to be associated with the physiocratic school. The son of a prominent government official, he began his career by taking holy orders but after a few years found that he was better fitted for government service. He was successively a judge, intendant of Limoges, and finally, comptroller-general of France. His effort to institute reforms in the French economy, especially in the direction of free trade, antagonized powerful elements whose special privileges he was threatening, and they finally induced King Louis XVI to dismiss him. Nevertheless, his reforms in Limoges, which first brought him to public attention, were incalculable: He improved the system of tax collection, constructed new roads, increased the facilities for grain trading, established freedom for working in several professions, created bureaus of charity, and increased educational facilities. And in spite of his dismissal, his theories were later adjudged so sound that today he has an honored place among the great ministers of France.

Though the physiocrats claimed him as one of their own. Turgot was too independent a thinker really to belong to any "school." He was a friend and disciple of Quesnay, but he sometimes referred to other physiocrats contemptuously. Although he accepted much of their doctrine as expressed by Quesnay, he minimized the contrast between sterile industry and productive agriculture, devoted much space to a subjective theory of value, and developed analyses of capital and interest which were more modern than those of his contemporaries.

Among Turgot's important works is *Valeurs et Monnaies*. The following selection is from the *Reflexions sur la Formation et la Distribution des Richesses* (*On the Formation and Distribution of Riches*). It was written in 1766 but not published until 1769–1770.

ON CAPITAL AND INTEREST *

I have already remarked that all kinds of work, whether in agriculture or in industry, require advances, and I have shown how land, through the fruits and plants which it produces spontaneously for the support of men and animals, and through the trees from which men made their first tools, had furnished the first advances for agriculture, and even for the first objects wrought by individuals for their own use. For example, it is land which furnished the stone, the clay, and wood from which the first houses were built, and before the division of labor, when the man who tilled the soil provided for his other needs by his own labor, no other advances were needed: but when a large part of society depended on the labor of their hands for a livelihood, those who lived on wages in this way had to begin by having something in advance, either to procure the materials upon

* From *On the Formation and Distribution of Riches.* Reprinted by permission of the publishers from Arthur Eli Monroe, *Early Economic Thought.* Cambridge, Mass.: Harvard University Press, Copyright, 1924, by The President and Fellows of Harvard College.

which they worked, or to live on while awaiting the payment of their wages.

In early times an employer used to furnish materials himself, and pay the workman his wages from day to day. The Farmer or Proprietor himself gave the spinner the hemp he had gathered, and supported her while she was working; he then turned the thread over to the weaver, to whom he gave every day the wages agreed upon; but these small daily advances can suffice only for coarse handicraft operations. A great many trades, even among those followed by the poorest members of Society, require that the same material should pass through a great many different hands, and undergo very long, difficult, and varied preparation.—I have already referred to the preparation of leather for shoes: anyone who has seen a tanner's shop realizes how utterly impossible it is for one man, or even several poor men, to lay in a stock of hides, lime, tanbark, tools, etc., erect the buildings required for establishing a tannery, and live for several months until the leather is sold. In this industry and in many others, do not the workmen have to learn the trade before venturing to touch the materials, which they would spoil in their first attempts? This makes another advance necessary. Who, then, will bring together the materials for the work, the ingredients and tools required for their preparation? Who will have canals, markets, and buildings of all kinds erected? Who will support, until the leather has been sold, this large number of workmen, no one of whom could prepare a single hide by himself, and no one of whom could live on the profit from the sale of a single finished piece? Who will pay the expenses of learners and apprentices? Who will provide them with subsistence until they are trained by having worked up by degrees from simple tasks suited to their age to work requiring the greatest strength and skill? It will be one of these owners of *capitals* or accumulated moveable values (*valeurs mobiliaires*) who will employ them, partly in advances for construction and the purchase of material, partly for the daily wages of the workmen engaged in preparing them. It is he who will wait until the sale of the leather returns him not only all his advances, but also a profit sufficient to recompense him for what he could have earned on his money, if he had used it to buy land; and, in addition, for the wages due him for his labor, his oversight, his risk, and even his skill; for, at the same profit, he would doubtless have preferred to live without any trouble on the revenue from the land he might have acquired with the same capital. As this capital returns to him through the sale of the products, he employs it in new purchases to supply and maintain his manufacture by this continual circulation: he lives on his profits, and lays aside what he can spare to increase his capital and put it into his business by increasing the amount of his advances, in order to increase his profits still more.

The whole class engaged in supplying the immense variety of industrial products required to satisfy the different needs of Society, is therefore subdivided, so to speak, into two categories: that of the manufacturing Entrepreneurs, Master craftsmen, all owners of large capitals, which they turn to account by employing people by means of their advances; and the second, which is composed of simple Artisans, who have no property but their hands, who advance nothing but their daily work and receive no profit except their wages.

In speaking first of the employment of capitals in manufacturing enterprises, my object was to present a more obvious example of the necessity and the effect of large advances and of their regular circulation; but I reversed the natural order somewhat, which would have required me to begin by speaking of agricultural enterprises, which likewise are carried on, extended, and made profitable only by means of large advances. It is the owners of large capitals who, in order to employ them to advantage in agricultural enterprises, lease estates and pay the Proprietors big rentals for them, undertaking to make all the advances for cultivation.—Their position must be the same as that of the manufacturing Entrepreneurs: like them they have to make the first advances for the enterprise, to provide themselves with cattle, horses, agricultural implements, and to buy the first seed; like them they have to support and provide subsistence for the ploughmen, reapers, threshers, servants, and workmen of all kinds, who have only their hands, advance only their labor, and earn only their wages; like them they have to take in, besides the recovery of their capitals, that is, of all their original and annual advances, (1) a profit equal to the revenue they might have made on their capital without any work; (2) the wages and price of their labor, their risk, and their industry; (3) the means of replacing annually the wasting away of the equipment used in their enterprise, the cattle that die, the tools that wear out, etc.

All this must be deducted from the price of the produce of the land; the surplus enables the Cultivator to pay the Proprietor for the permission given him by the latter to use his land for the establishing of his enterprise. It is the price of the lease, the revenue of the Proprietor, the *net product,* for what the land produces up to the amount required to cover the advances of all kinds, and the profits of the one who makes them, cannot be considered a *revenue,* but only as *recovery of the expenses of cultivation,* inasmuch as, if the Cultivator did not obtain them, he would be careful not to employ his riches and his trouble in cultivating somebody else's land.

The competition of rich entrepreneurs engaged in agriculture establishes the current price of leases in proportion to the fertility of the land and the price at which its produce sells, always according to the estimates which the farmers make of all their expenses and the profit they should make on their advances: they can pay the Proprietor only the surplus.

But when the competition between them is very keen, they pay him all this surplus, the Proprietor leasing his land only to the one who offers the highest rent.

When, on the contrary, there are no rich men with large capitals to invest in agricultural enterprises, when, as a result of the low price of agricultural products, or any other cause, the harvests do not suffice to assure the Entrepreneurs, in addition to the recovery of their investment, profits at least equal to what they would earn on their money by employing it in any other way, there are no Farmers desirous of leasing land.

The Proprietors are compelled to have them cultivated by Tenants or Metayers who are unable to make any advances and to cultivate efficiently.

The Proprietor in this case makes small advances himself, which yield him a very small revenue: if the land belongs to a Proprietor who is poor, or in debt, or careless, or to a Widow or a Minor, it remains uncultivated. . . .

It follows from the foregoing that the class of Cultivators is divided, like the manufacturing class, into two categories of men—the Entrepreneurs or Capitalists, who make all the advances, and the simple Wage-earners. It is also evident that it is the capitals alone which develop and sustain great agricultural enterprises; which give lands a constant rental value, if I may so express myself; which assure the Proprietors a steady revenue as large as possible.

The Entrepreneurs, whether in agriculture or in manufacturing, obtain their advances and their profits only by the sale of the produce of the land or the manufactured articles.

It is always the needs and the means of the consumer that determine selling prices; but the consumer does not always need the goods manufactured or produced, at the time of the harvest or when the products are finished.

The Entrepreneurs, however, need to get their funds back immediately and regularly, in order to put them into their business again. Plowing and sowing must follow the harvest without interruption, the workmen in a manufactory must be kept busy, new production must be started as the earlier is finished, materials must be replaced as they are used up. The operations of a going enterprise are not to be interrupted with impunity, and they are not to be resumed whenever one wishes.

The Entrepreneur, therefore, has the greatest interest in getting his funds back promptly, through the sale of his crops and his products. On the other hand, the consumer is interested in finding the things he needs, when he wishes them, and where he wishes them; it would be very inconvenient for him to have to buy his supply for the whole year at the time of the harvest.

Among the articles of common consumption there are many which require long and expensive labor, labor which cannot be undertaken with profit except upon a very large quantity of material, so large that the consumption of a small number of people, or of a small district, could not provide a market for the products of a single plant.

Enterprises of this sort are therefore necessarily limited in number, at a considerable distance from each other, and consequently very far from the homes of most of the consumers; there is no one, above the level of extreme misery, who is not in a position to consume several things not produced or made except at a great distance from his home, and equally distant from each other. A man who could procure what he consumes only by purchasing directly from producer or maker would do without many things or would spend his life in travelling.

This double interest on the part of the producer and the consumer, the first in finding a sale, and the second in finding what he wishes to buy, without losing valuable time waiting for a buyer or looking for a seller, must have given some third parties the idea of intervening between them.—This is the purpose of the profession of Merchants, who buy commodities from the producer to get together a stock or store, where the consumer comes to supply his needs.

In this way, the entrepreneur, assured of a sale and of the return of his funds, devotes himself to new production without anxiety and without interruption, and the consumer finds what he needs available at all times.

From the Huckster who displays her herbs in the market, to the Merchant of Nantes or Cadiz, who extends his purchases and sales as far as India and America, the profession of Merchant, or commerce properly so called, is divided into an infinite number of branches, and, so to speak, of grades. . . . But all have this in common that they *buy to sell again,* and that their first purchases are an advance which comes back to them only after a time. It must come back to them, like that of the Entrepreneurs in agriculture and manufacturing, not only entire within a certain period, in order to be put back into new purchases, but also (1) with a profit equal to the revenue they might make on their capital without any work; and (2) with the wages and price of their labor, their risks, and their skill. Without the assurance of this return and these indispensable profits, no Merchant would go in to commerce; none could keep on with it; it is on this basis that he regulates his purchases, estimating the amount and the price of the things he can expect to sell in a certain time. The Retailer learns by experience, by the success of limited experiments made cautiously, about how great are the needs of the consumers he is in a position to supply. The Merchant obtains information through Correspondents concerning the abundance or scarcity and the price of merchandise in the different countries to which he extends his trading; he directs his speculations accordingly; he sends commodities from places where they are cheap to places where they are dearer; with the understanding, of course, that the expenses of transportation enter into the calculation of the advances which have to come back to him.

Since commerce is necessary, and it is impossible to undertake any kind of commerce without advances in proportion to its extent, this makes another employment for moveable riches, a further use which the owner of a mass of saved and accumulated values, of a sum of money, in a word, of a capital, can make of it to earn a profit, to procure his subsistence, and to increase his riches if possible.

It is evident from what has just been said how agriculture, manufacturing of all kinds, and all the branches of commerce are carried on by means of a mass of *capitals* or accumulated moveable riches, which, having been at first advanced by the Entrepreneurs in each of these different classes of work, must return to them every year with a regular profit: the capital, in order to be put back and advanced anew in continuing the same enterprises; the profit, for the more or less comfortable support of the Entrepreneurs. It is this continual advance and return of capitals which constitutes *what ought to be called the circulation of money,* that useful and fruitful circulation which enlivens all the works of Society, which sustains movement and life in the body politic, and which may well be compared to the circulation of the blood in animal bodies. For if, through any derangement in the scale of expenses of the different classes of Society, the Entrepreneurs cease recovering their advances with the profit they have a right to expect, it is evident that they will be obliged to cut down their operations; that the sum of labor, of consumption of agricultural products, of production, and of revenue will be proportionately diminished; that poverty will take the place of riches, and that Wage-earners, failing to find work, will sink into deepest misery.

It is hardly necessary to remark that enterprises of all kinds, but especially in manufacturing, and still more in commerce, could only have been very limited before the introduction of gold and silver in commerce, since it was almost impossible to accumulate considerable capitals, and even more difficult to multiply and divide payments as much as is necessary to facilitate and multiply exchanges to the extent required by a vigorous commerce and circulation. Only agriculture could maintain itself to some extent, since cattle are the principal object of the advances it requires; it is even probable that there were then no entrepreneurs in agriculture except the Proprietors. . . .

Since capitals are the indispensable basis of all enterprises, since money is a principal means for saving small gains, accumulating profits, and becoming rich, those who along with skill and diligence have no capitals, or not enough for the enterprises they wish to establish, do not find it hard to resolve to give the owners of capitals or money, who are willing to trust them with it, a share of the profits they expect to obtain in addition to recovering their advances.

The owners of money weigh the risk which their capital may run, if the enterprise does not succeed, against the advantage of enjoying a steady profit without working, and determine on this basis whether to demand more or less profit or interest on their money, or to consent to lend it for the interest offered them by the borrower. This makes another outlet for the owner of money, lending at interest or trading in money. For we should make no mistake about it; lending at interest is simply a kind of trading, in which the Lender is a man who sells the *use* of his money, and the Borrower a man who buys it, just as the Proprietor of an estate and his Farmer sell and buy respectively the *use* of leased property.

This was expressed perfectly by the name the Romans gave to interest on money loans, *usura pecuniæ,* a word whose French translation has become odious as a result of the false ideas which people have had about interest on money. . . .

The value of silver in the market depends only on the quantity of this metal employed in current trade; but the rate of interest depends on the amount of values accumulated and laid aside to form capitals. It makes no difference whether these values are in metal or in some other kind of property, provided they may easily be converted into money.

The mass of metal in a State is far from being as large as the sum of values lent at interest in the course of a year; but all these capitals, in furnishings, merchandise, tools, cattle, take the place of this money and represent it. A note signed by a man known to own property worth *a hundred thousand francs,* and who promises to pay *a hundred thousand francs* at the end of a certain period, passes during this period for *a hundred thousand francs.* All the capitals of the man who signed this note are security for its payment, whatever the nature of the property he possesses, provided they have a value of *a hundred thousand francs.*

It is therefore not the quantity of money in the form of metal which causes interest on money to rise or fall, or which causes more money to be offered for lending; it is solely the sum of capitals in commerce, that is to say, the actual sum of moveable values of all kinds, accumulated, saved by degrees from revenues and profits, to be employed in obtaining further revenues and further profits for the owner. It is these accumulated savings that are offered to borrowers, and the more there are of them, the lower the interest on money is, unless the number of borrowers be increased in proportion.

The spirit of economy in a Nation tends to increase continually the sum of its capitals, to increase the number of lenders, to diminish the number of borrowers. Luxurious habits have precisely the opposite effect; and from what has already been said about the use of capitals in all agricultural, industrial, or commercial enterprises, one can judge whether luxury enriches a Nation or impoverishes it.

Since interest on money has been falling steadily in Europe for several centuries, we must conclude that the spirit of economy has been more general than the spirit of luxury. It is only rich people who indulge in luxuries, and among the rich all those who are reasonable limit themselves to spending their revenue, and are careful not to trench upon their capitals. Those who wish to become rich are much more numerous in a Nation than the rich; now in the present state of things, when all land is occupied, there is only one means of becoming rich: To have or to obtain, in some way, an annual revenue or profit in excess of what is absolutely necessary for subsistence, to lay aside this surplus every year to form a capital, by means of which an increase of annual revenue or profit may be obtained, which may in turn be saved and converted into capital. . . .

It is evident that the annual products which can be derived from capitals invested in these different ways are mutually limited, and are all dependent upon the current rate of interest on money. . . .

A man who lends his money at interest enjoys his income with even less trouble and restraint than the owner of land; but the insolvency of his debtor may cause him to lose his capital.

He will therefore not be satisfied with an interest equal to the revenue from the land he could buy with the same capital.

The interest on money loans should therefore be higher than the revenue of land purchased for the same capital; for if the lender had an opportunity to buy an estate yielding an equal revenue, he would prefer this investment.

For similar reasons, money invested in agriculture, industry, or commerce should yield a profit greater than the revenue from the same capital invested in land, or the interest on the same money loaned; for these investments require, in addition to the capital advanced, much care and labor, and if they were not lucrative, it would be much better to procure an equal revenue, which could be enjoyed without doing anything. Besides the interest on his capital, therefore, the entrepreneur must obtain every year a profit to recompense him for his trouble, his labor, his skill, and his risks, and to provide him, moreover, with the wherewithal to replace the annual wasting away of the advances, which he has to convert from the beginning into things subject to change and exposed to all kinds of accidents.

The different employments of capitals, then, yield very unequal returns; but this inequality does not prevent them from exercising a mutual influence upon each other, and from establishing a kind of equilibrium among themselves, as between two liquids of different densities, communicating with each other through the arm of an inverted siphon of which they occupy the two branches; they would not come to the same level, but the height of one could not increase without the other also rising in the opposite branch.

Suppose a great many owners of estates suddenly desire to sell them: It is evident that the price of land will fall, and that a smaller sum will buy a greater revenue. That cannot come about without the interest on money becoming higher; for the owners of money will prefer to buy estates rather than to lend at an interest no higher than the revenue from the estates they might buy. If, therefore, the borrowers wish to obtain money, they will be obliged to pay a higher rental for it. If the interest on money becomes higher, people will prefer to lend it, rather than utilize it, at greater trouble and risk, in agricultural, industrial, or commercial enterprises; and only those enterprises will be carried on which yield, in addition to the wages of labor, a profit much greater than the rate of interest on money loans. In short, when the profits yielded by any employment of money increase or diminish, capitals flow into them from other employments, or are withdrawn to be put into the other employments; which necessarily changes the relation between the capital and the annual return in each of these employments. In general, money invested in land yields less than money loans, and money loans yield less than money employed in industrial enterprises; but the return on money employed in any way whatever cannot increase or diminish, without causing all the other employments to experience a proportionate increase or diminution.

The current interest on money loans may therefore be regarded as a kind of thermometer of the abundance or scarcity of capitals in a Nation, and of the extent of the enterprises of all kinds to which it can devote itself: it is evident that the lower the rate of interest is, the greater the value of land is. A man with rents amounting to fifty thousand livres has property worth only a million, if land sells for only the twentieth penny; he has two millions, if land sells for the fortieth penny.

If interest is five per cent, all uncleared land which will not yield five per cent, over and above replacing the advances and recompensing the Farmer for his trouble, will be left idle; all forms of manufacturing or commerce which will not yield five per cent, over and above wages for the trouble and risk of the Entrepreneur, will not exist.

If there is a neighboring Nation where interest on money is only two per cent, it will not only carry on all the commerce from which the Nation where interest is five per cent is excluded, but its Manufacturers and its Merchants, being able to get along with less profit, will offer their commodities at lower prices in all markets, and will get control of almost all the trade in everything not preserved to the Nation where money is worth five per cent by special circumstances or excessive costs of transportation.

The rate of interest may be regarded as a kind of level below which all labor, all cultivation, all industry, all commerce cease. It is like a sea spread over a vast territory: the summits of the mountains rise above the waters, forming fertile and cultivated islands. If this sea happens to be drained away, the hillsides, then the plains and the valleys, appear as the water subsides, and become covered with vegetation of all kinds. The water only has to rise or fall a foot to flood immense stretches of shore or return them to cultivation.—It is the abundance of capitals which enlivens all enterprises, and low interest on money is at once the effect and the index of the abundance of capitals. . . .

We have seen that every rich man is necessarily the owner of a capital in moveable riches, or of an estate equivalent to a capital. Every landed estate is equivalent to a capital; and so every Proprietor is a capitalist, but not every Capitalist is proprietor of a landed estate; and the owner of a moveable capital has a choice of employing it to acquire land or of investing it in enterprises of the agricultural class or of the industrial class. The capitalist who has become an entrepreneur in agriculture or industry is no more disposable, either himself or his profits, than the mere laborer in these two classes; both are bound up with the continuation of their enterprises. The Capitalist who becomes a mere moneylender makes loans to a Proprietor or to an Entrepreneur. If he lends to a Proprietor, he seems to belong to the class of Proprietors; he becomes a joint owner of the property; the revenue from the land is pledged to pay the interest on his loan; the value of the property is pledged to secure his capital as far as required. If the lender of money has lent to an entrepreneur, it is certain that his person belongs to the disposable class; but his capital remains involved in the advances for the enterprise, and cannot be withdrawn without injuring the enterprise, unless replaced by a capital of equal value.

It is true that the interest which he receives on this capital appears to be disposable, since the entrepreneur and the enterprise can do without it; and it also seems as if we might conclude that in the profits of the two classes engaged in labor, whether agricultural or industrial, there is a disposable portion, namely, what corresponds to the interest on the advances, calculated at the current rate on money loans; and it also seems that this conclusion conflicts with our statement that only the class of Proprietors had a revenue properly so called, a disposable revenue, and that all the members of the two other classes had only wages or profits.—This deserves some explanation.

If we consider the thousand crowns received every year by a man who has lent sixty thousand francs to a Merchant, from the point of view of what he can do with them, there is no doubt that they are perfectly disposable, since the enterprise can get along without them.

But it does not follow that they are disposable in the sense that the State can with impunity appropriate a part of them for public needs. These thousand crowns are not a return made gratuitously by agriculture or commerce to the man who made the advances; it is the price and the condition of this advance, without which the enterprise could not continue. —If this return is diminished, the capitalist will withdraw his money, and the enterprise will come to an end. This return should therefore be inviolate and enjoy complete immunity, since it is the price of an advance made to the enterprise without which the enterprise could not continue. To touch it would mean raising the price of the advances for all enterprises, and consequently diminishing the enterprises themselves, that is to say, agriculture, industry and commerce.

This answer should lead us to conclude that if we said that the capitalist who had lent to a Proprietor *seemed* to belong to the proprietary class, this *appearance* had something equivocal about it which needed to be cleared up.

As a matter of fact, it is perfectly true that the interest on his money is no more disposable, that is to say, no more fit to be trenched upon, than the interest on money lent to Entrepreneurs in agriculture and commerce. This interest is equally a price freely agreed upon, and it can no more be trenched upon without changing the rate of interest: it makes little difference to whom the loan was made; if the rate of interest changes and increases for the Proprietor, it will change and increase for the Cultivator, the Manufacturer, and the Merchant. In short, the Capitalist lender of money should be regarded as a dealer in a commodity absolutely necessary for the production of riches, and which cannot bear too low a price. It is as foolish to burden his trade with a tax as to levy a tax on the manure used to fertilize land. Let us conclude from this that the lender of money belongs indeed to the disposable class, with respect to his person, because he does not have to work; but not with respect to the character of his riches, whether the interest on his money be paid by the Proprietor of land from a part of his revenue, or by an Entrepreneur from a part of his profits pledged to pay the interest on advances.

PART SIX
Classical Economics

The term *classical* is generally used to describe the doctrines formulated by the men who founded English political economy and by their immediate followers. The foremost writers commonly associated with classical economics are Adam Smith, Thomas Malthus, and David Ricardo. Other important figures are Jeremy Bentham, whose utilitarian theories were incorporated into post-Ricardian economics, and John Stuart Mill, who wrote an elegant restatement of classical doctrine in 1848. According to some authorities, the classical era ended with the publication in 1857 of Cairnes' *The Character and Logical Method of Political Economy.*

Thus classical doctrine dominated English economic thought for about seventy-five years, and it was influential to a lesser extent through most of the nineteenth century and even later. When Alfred Marshall wrote his restatement of economics in 1890, he specifically made the point that the marginal-utility economists had misrepresented Ricardo, and he reformulated the classical cost-of-production theory as a co-determinant of value. As a result, many of the more important classical doctrines became part of modern British economics.

When the classical doctrine was introduced at the end of the eighteenth century, France, with its famous physiocratic school, dominated economics. Therefore it was natural for Adam Smith, publishing in 1776, to adopt many physiocratic ideas, such as belief in an omnipotent and benevolent natural order, in laissez-faire, and in the right to own private property. Like the physiocrats, the classical economists were very keen dissectors of the time and country in which they lived, and they too regarded the distribution of the social product among the various social classes as the foremost problem in economics. To be sure, the physiocrats were by no means the only influence on Adam Smith, as will be shown in the section on his thinking. The direction of influence was reversed when the teachings of Adam Smith were introduced into France by J. B. Say, who incorporated them into a systematic treatise. Thereafter they dominated orthodox French economics until the last quarter of the nineteenth century. Classical doctrine was also influential in the United States, and for a brief interlude, even in Germany.

The founders of the classical school lived during the British Industrial Revolution, when a new class of merchants and factory owners was rising to make England the workshop of the world. The economists attempted to depict faithfully the actions and the underlying motivation of the businessmen of their day. The methodology of classical economics, especially as exemplified by Ricardo, was one of isolating abstraction.[1] In what the theorists considered a "normal" or "natural" capitalistic economy, men were guided solely by self-interest and an overwhelming desire for maximum profit. Being practical men, the classicists realized that forces other than self-interest existed, but the application of these forces to business affairs was considered a deviation from the norm. What they were seeking were the broad basic principles which would explain the society—at least the business society—of their own time.

The Benthamite philosophy, which dominated classical economics after Ricardo, held that since there was no conflict between self-interest and the public good, government could achieve the greatest good of the greatest number by encouraging the selfishness and self-interest of individuals. The concept of the economic man guided solely by self-interest ran through all classical doctrine, but because the classical writers were seldom, if ever, explicit about the underlying Benthamite social philosophy, they were accused of apologizing for unregulated capitalism, exalting selfishness, and neglecting all ethical considerations.

In addition to the abstract deductive method, there were other elements common to almost all the classical writers. First and foremost was the labor theory of value. Almost all the members of the school regarded labor as the ultimate source of the only accurate measure of value. Therefore, paradoxically enough, the school which has often been denounced for justifying capitalism was also the progenitor of Marxian economics. From Ricardo on, the school has been associated with the notorious "iron law of wages," according to which wages tend to fluctuate around the subsistence level. Together with Malthus' pessimistic population doctrine—that population normally tends to outstrip the means of subsistence—this wage theory helped earn for the classicists a reputation for pessimism. Critics like Carlyle called their economics the "dismal science."

Members of the classical school, notably Ricardo, Malthus, and West, also evolved a theory of rent. In general, this theory held that differentials in production costs between more fertile and less fertile land, as population increases, account for the phenomenon of rent.

Much opprobrium has fallen on the classical school because of the use of their doctrines by individualists like Bastiat in France and by propagandist societies such as the Manchester school. These groups were opposed to almost all government regulation in the economic sphere, including labor legislation and social security of any kind. This position earned them the hatred of labor as well as of other underprivileged groups,

[1] The abstract deductive method which one tends to associate with classicism is really Ricardian, since both Adam Smith and Malthus used the historical inductive method. In his long correspondence with Ricardo, Malthus often objected to the highly rarefied abstraction in Ricardo's method. But Malthus' *Principles of Political Economy* became a neglected work, while Ricardo became the chief spokesman for the classical school.

and because these interest groups used many of the arguments of the classical economists and cited them as authorities, much of the hatred and distrust was transferred to the school.

So far, our remarks have concerned the school as a whole. The following section includes discussions of the individual writers in the school and excerpts illustrating the position of each.

ADAM SMITH

(1723–1790)

Born in Scotland, Adam Smith is considered to be the founder of English classical economics, and along with Ricardo he is regarded as one of the most influential writers in that tradition. He taught logic and moral philosophy at Scottish universities, and his *Theory of Moral Sentiments* (1759), a treatise on moral philosophy which also included topics of economic interest, appeared some time before he left his professorship at Glasgow University.

From 1764 to 1766 he traveled in Europe as tutor to the Duke of Buccleuch, and in Paris he met such eminent thinkers as Voltaire, Turgot, and Quesnay, all protagonists of the physiocratic doctrine. Much of his work may be traced to this influence. His major work, *The Wealth of Nations* (1776), was written on his mother's farm in Kirkcaldy, Scotland, where he lived, jobless, until a short time after his book appeared. He was appointed commissioner of customs at Edinburgh in 1778 and held this post until his death.

Adam Smith's course in moral philosophy at Glasgow University consisted of four parts.[1] The first was devoted to natural theology, adducing the principles of being and the attributes of God, and describing the principles of the human mind upon which religion is based. The second part was devoted to ethics, and here he developed the principles which formed the basis of his *Theory of Moral Sentiments.* This was a two-volume essay which argued that moral approbation and disapprobation are ultimately expressions of sympathy with the feeling of an assumed impartial spectator; conscience itself is no more than a reflection of the views of this spectator, and sympathy with his views is the basis of all moral feeling.

The third part of the course dealt with justice; here Smith traced the progress of jurisprudence and the effect of measures contributing to the accumulation of property. The fourth part was a discussion of political regulations which were based on expedience, not justice, and which were calculated to increase the riches, power, and prosperity of the state. Questions were raised about commercial and financial policy, ecclesiastical and military establishments, and the like. Eventually he developed this section in *The Wealth of Nations.*

The Wealth of Nations was an immediate success. Although Smith was a college professor who had lived a reflective life on the whole and who had not engaged in active business up to the time of publication of his work, he had associated closely with several different circles of people with diversified interests and had learned from all of them.

The plan of *The Wealth of Nations* is as follows: Book I argues that labor is the source of the annual wealth of nations. Increases in the amount of productive labor and in the productivity of the individual laborer are the source of increases in national wealth. Division of labor is the principal cause of the increased productivity of labor. The division of labor depends on the "propensity to truck, barter, and exchange." He is therefore led to consider money as a medium of exchange and subsequently, to examine the problem of value and price determination. Price is broken down into components: wages, profits, and rent; and the theory of distribution follows. Book II takes up the nature of capital accumulation and the distinction between productive and unproductive labor. Book III is a historical digression, and Book IV contains a critique of mercantilism and physiocracy. Finally, the last book deals with public finance.

The entire work is a masterful synthesis

[1] A complete set of notes was taken by a member of this class in moral philosophy and over a century later was edited and published by Professor Edward Cannan as *Lectures on Justice, Police, Revenue and Arms Delivered in the University of Glasgow by Adam Smith.*

of centuries of accumulated but separate economic ideas. The influence of the physiocrats is manifested in his concern with the problem of economic surplus and his stress on harmony and the natural order. His value theory owes much to Petty, Locke, and Cantillon. His theory of money stems from the writing of Locke and Hume. The principles of self-interest and social harmony exemplify the influence of Mandeville and Hutcheson. But everywhere Smith's analysis is more than a synthesis. By and large, Smith's discussion, though never entirely original, is always a substantial improvement over the statements of his predecessors.

Impressive as is *The Wealth of Nations,* consistency is not always one of its outstanding features. The labor theory of value is limited in its original form to precapitalist times (witness the beaver and deer example, p. 131); in early societies labor costs constitute the sum total of value, but with the development of capitalism a margin for profit must be introduced. Elsewhere Smith drops this theory altogether and advances a mechanical cost-of-production theory. Price is resolved into wages, profit, and rent.

It is not always clear whether labor is the cause of the value of a good ("the toil and trouble of acquiring it") or the measure of value ("the quantity of labour which it enables him [the owner] to purchase or command"). It was left to Ricardo to iron out the inconsistencies of this view.

In fact, Smith's value theory has meant many things to many men. Ricardo and Marx drew a pure labor-value theory from it. Others perceived a supply-and-demand analysis, and even the utility theorists claimed Smith as their authority. This confusion as to interpretation occurs also in connection with Smith's doctrines of "laissez-faire," and "free trade" and his "quantity theory of money." Smith was the great eclectic, and there are few important economic ideas which cannot be traced to his book.

Reading *The Wealth of Nations* today is much like reading the Bible, in that on almost every page we meet some familiar concept or well-worn truth. The distinction between natural price and market price, the concept of fixed and circulating capital, the inverse relation of wages and profits, the tendency for a declining rate of profit, the Malthusian theory of population, the subsistence theory of wages, the theory of rent, the competitive equalization of net advantages, the invisible hand, the four canons of taxation—these are the stock in trade of hundreds of economics texts.

We must remember, however, that Smith's approach to economic problems is essentially different from the modern one. He conceived the "economic problem" to be man's struggle to conquer nature in the production of material wealth. In the modern view, on the other hand, the basic problem is how to allocate given resources among different uses so as to maximize the consumer's satisfaction. Smith's concern was rather with ways of increasing the productivity of labor and widening the scope of the market. Hence his stress on capital accumulation, productive labor, and free trade.

The influence of Smith's writings reached out beyond the borders of economic science. He became the apostle of economic liberalism. No other writer in the history of economic thought was to have such influence upon succeeding generations. His approach to economic questions and his organization of the science was to cast a mold for the whole body of nineteenth-century economic thought. His substantive theory provided scores of economists with points of departure for elaboration and refinement. His views on public policy became the semi-official doctrine of the British government, leaving their imprint on parliamentary debates and governmental reports.

In the following selections from *The Wealth of Nations* the most significant aspects of Smith's thinking are represented.

AN INQUIRY INTO THE NATURE AND CAUSES OF THE WEALTH OF NATIONS—INTRODUCTION AND PLAN OF THE WORK *

The annual labour of every nation is the fund which originally supplies it with all the necessaries and conveniencies of life which it annually consumes, and which consist always either in the immediate produce of that labour, or in what is purchased with that produce from other nations.

According, therefore, as this produce, or what is purchased with it, bears a greater or smaller proportion to the number of those who are to consume it, the nation will be better or worse supplied with all the necessaries and conveniencies for which it has occasion.

But this proportion must, in every nation, be regulated by two different circumstances; first, by the skill, dexterity, and judgment with which its labour is generally applied; and, secondly, by the proportion between the number of those who are employed in useful labour, and that of those who are not so employed. Whatever be the soil, climate, or extent of territory of any particular nation, the abundance or scantiness of its annual supply must, in that particular situation, depend upon those two circumstances.

The abundance or scantiness of this supply, too, seems to depend more upon the former of those two circumstances than upon the latter. Among the savage nations of hunters and fishers, every individual who is able to work, is more or less employed in useful labour, and endeavours to provide, as well as he can, the necessaries and conveniences of life, for himself, or such of his family or tribe as are either too old, or too young, or too infirm to go a hunting and fishing. Such nations, however, are so miserably poor, that from mere want, they are frequently reduced, or, at least, think themselves reduced, to the necessity sometimes of directly destroying, and sometimes of abandoning their infants, their old people, and those afflicted with lingering diseases, to perish with hunger, or to be devoured by wild beasts. Among civilized and thriving nations, on the contrary, though a great number of people do not labour at all, many of whom consume the produce of ten times, frequently of a hundred times more labour than the greater part of those who work; yet the produce of the whole labour of the society is so great, that all are often abundantly supplied, and a workman, even of the lowest and poorest order, if he is frugal and industrious, may enjoy a greater share of the necessaries and conveniencies of life than it is possible for any savage to acquire. . . .

Whatever be the actual state of the skill, dexterity, and judgment with which labour is applied in any nation, the abundance or scantiness of its annual supply must depend, during the continuance of that state, upon the proportion between the number of those who are annually employed

* From *An Inquiry into the Nature and Causes of the Wealth of Nations,* in *Select Chapters and Passages from* The Wealth of Nations *of Adam Smith,* edited by W. J. Ashley (New York and London, Macmillan and Co., 1894).

in useful labour, and that of those who are not so employed. The number of useful and productive labourers, it will hereafter appear, is everywhere in proportion to the quantity of capital stock which is employed in setting them to work, and to the particular way in which it is so employed. . . .

Nations, tolerably well advanced as to skill, dexterity, and judgment, in the application of labour, have followed very different plans in the general conduct or direction of it; and those plans have not all been equally favourable to the greatness of its produce. The policy of some nations has given extraordinary encouragement to the industry of the country; that of others to the industry of towns. Scarce any nation has dealt equally and impartially with every sort of industry. Since the downfall of the Roman empire, the policy of Europe has been more favourable to arts, manufactures, and commerce, the industry of towns, than to agriculture, the industry of the country. . . .

Though these different plans were, perhaps, first introduced by the private interests and prejudices of particular orders of men, without any regard to, or foresight of, their consequences upon the general welfare of the society; yet they have given occasion to very different theories of political œconomy; of which some magnify the importance of that industry which is carried on in towns, others of that which is carried on in the country. Those theories have had a considerable influence, not only upon the opinions of men of learning, but upon the public conduct of princes and sovereign states. . . .

OF THE CAUSES OF IMPROVEMENT IN THE PRODUCTIVE POWERS OF LABOUR, AND OF THE ORDER ACCORDING TO WHICH ITS PRODUCE IS NATURALLY DISTRIBUTED AMONG THE DIFFERENT RANKS OF THE PEOPLE *

Of the Division of Labour

The greatest improvement in the productive powers of Labour, and the greater skill, dexterity, and judgment with which it is anywhere directed, or applied, seem to have been the effects of the division of labour. . . .

To take an example, therefore, from a very trifling manufacture; but one in which the division of labour has been very often taken notice of, the trade of the pin-maker; a workman not educated to this business (which the division of labour has rendered a distinct trade), nor acquainted with the use of the machinery employed in it (to the invention of which the same division of labour has probably given occasion), could scarce, perhaps, with his utmost industry, make one pin in a day, and certainly could not make twenty. But in the way in which this business is now carried on, not only the whole work is a peculiar trade, but it is divided into a num-

* From *The Wealth of Nations;* see credit note, page 122.

ber of branches, of which the greater part are likewise peculiar trades. One man draws out the wire, another straightens it, a third cuts it, a fourth points it, a fifth grinds it at the top for receiving the head: to make the head requires two or three distinct operations; to put it on is a peculiar business; to whiten the pins is another; it is even a trade by itself to put them into the paper; and the important business of making a pin is, in this manner, divided into about eighteen distinct operations, which, in some manufactories, are all performed by distinct hands, though in others the same man will sometimes perform two or three of them. I have seen a small manufactory of this kind where ten men only were employed, and where some of them consequently performed two or three distinct operations. But though they were very poor, and therefore but indifferently accommodated with the necessary machinery, they could, when they exerted themselves, make among them about twelve pounds of pins in a day. There are in a pound upwards of four thousand pins of a middling size. Those ten persons, therefore, could make among them upwards of forty-eight thousand pins in a day. Each person, therefore, making a tenth part of forty-eight thousand pins, might be considered as making four thousand eight hundred pins in a day. But if they had all wrought separately and independently, and without any of them having been educated to this peculiar business, they certainly could not each of them have made twenty, perhaps not one pin in a day; that is, certainly, not the two hundred and fortieth, perhaps not the four thousand eight hundredth part of what they are at present capable of performing, in consequence of a proper division and combination of their different operations.

In every other art and manufacture, the effects of the division of labour are similar to what they are in this very trifling one; though, in many of them, the labour can neither be so much subdivided, nor reduced to so great a simplicity of operation. The division of labour, however, so far as it can be introduced, occasions, in every art, a proportionable increase of the productive powers of labour. The separation of different trades and employments from one another, seems to have taken place, in consequence of this advantage. This separation, too, is generally carried furthest in those countries which enjoy the highest degree of industry and improvement; what is the work of one man in a rude state of society, being generally that of several in an improved one. . . .

This great increase of the quantity of work, which, in consequence of the division of labour, the same number of people are capable of performing, is owing to three different circumstances; first, to the increase of dexterity in every particular workman; secondly, to the saving of the time which is commonly lost in passing from one species of work to another; and lastly, to the invention of a great number of machines which facilitate and abridge labour, and enable one man to do the work of many.

First, the improvement of the dexterity of the workman necessarily increases the quantity of the work he can perform; and the division of labour, by reducing every man's business to some one simple operation, and by making this operation the sole employment of his life, necessarily increases very much the dexterity of the workman. A common smith, who, though accustomed to handle the hammer, has never been used to make nails, if upon some particular occasion he is obliged to attempt it, will scarce, I am assured, be able to make above two or three hundred in a day, and those, too, very bad ones. A smith who has been accustomed to make nails, but whose sole or principal business has not been that of a nailer, can seldom with his utmost diligence make more than eight hundred or a thousand nails in a day. . . .

Secondly, the advantage which is gained by saving the time commonly lost in passing from one sort of work to another, is much greater than we should at first view be apt to imagine it. It is impossible to pass very quickly from one kind of work to another, that is carried on in a different place, and with quite different tools. A country weaver, who cultivates a small farm, must lose a good deal of time in passing from his loom to the field, and from the field to his loom. When the two trades can be carried on in the same workhouse, the loss of time is no doubt much less. . . .

Thirdly, and lastly, everybody must be sensible how much labour is facilitated and abridged by the application of proper machinery. It is unnecessary to give any example. I shall only observe, therefore, that the invention of all those machines by which labour is so much facilitated and abridged, seems to have been originally owing to the division of labour. Men are much more likely to discover easier and readier methods of attaining any object, when the whole attention of their minds is directed towards that single object, than when it is dissipated among a great variety of things. But in consequence of the division of labour, the whole of every man's attention comes naturally to be directed towards some one very simple object. It is naturally to be expected, therefore, that some one or other of those who are employed in each particular branch of labour should soon find out easier and readier methods of performing their own particular work, wherever the nature of it admits of such improvement. . . .

It is the great multiplication of the productions of all the different arts, in consequence of the division of labour, which occasions, in a well-governed society, that universal opulence which extends itself to the lowest ranks of the people. Every workman has a great quantity of his own work to dispose of beyond what he himself has occasion for; and every other workman being exactly in the same situation, he is enabled to exchange a great quantity of his own goods for a great quantity, or, what comes to the same thing, for the price of a great quantity of theirs. He supplies them abundantly with what they have occasion for, and they accommodate him as amply with what he has occasion for, and a general plenty diffuses itself through all the different ranks of society. . . .

Of the Principle Which Gives Occasion to the Division of Labour

This division of labour, from which so many advantages are derived, is not originally the effect of any human wisdom, which foresees and intends that general opulence to which it gives occasion. It is the necessary, though very slow and gradual, consequence of a certain propensity in human nature which has in view no such extensive utility; the propensity to truck, barter, and exchange one thing for another.

Whether this propensity be one of those original principles in human nature, of which no further account can be given; or whether, as seems more probable, it be the necessary consequence of the faculties of reason and speech, it belongs not to our present subject to inquire. It is common to all men, and to be found in no other race of animals, which seem to know neither this nor any other species of contracts. . . .

As it is by treaty, by barter, and by purchase, that we obtain from one another the greater part of those mutual good offices which we stand in need of, so it is this same trucking disposition which originally gives occasion to the division of labour. In a tribe of hunters or shepherds a particular person makes bows and arrows, for example, with more readiness and dexterity than any other. He frequently exchanges them for cattle or for venison with his companions; and he finds at last that he can in this manner get more cattle and venison, than if he himself went to the field to catch them. From a regard to his own interest, therefore, the making of bows and arrows grows to be his chief business, and he becomes a sort of armourer. Another excels in making the frames and covers of their little huts or movable houses. He is accustomed to be of use in this way to his neighbours, who reward him in the same manner with cattle and with venison, till at last he finds it his interest to dedicate himself entirely to this employment, and to become a sort of house-carpenter. In the same manner a third becomes a smith, or a brazier; a fourth a tanner or dresser of hides or skins, the principal part of the cloathing of savages. And thus the certainty of being able to exchange all that surplus part of the produce of his own labour, which is over and above his own consumption, for such parts of the produce of other men's labour as he may have occasion for, encourages every man to apply himself to a particular occupation, and to cultivate and bring to perfection whatever talent or genius he may possess for that particular species of business. . . .

Among men, . . . the most dissimilar geniuses are of use to one another; the different produces of their respective talents, by the general disposition to truck, barter, and exchange, being brought, as it were, into a common stock, where every man may purchase whatever part of the produce of other men's talents he has occasion for.

That the Division of Labour Is Limited by the Extent of the Market

As it is the power of exchanging that gives occasion to the division of labour, so the extent of this division must always be limited by the extent of that power, or, in other words, by the extent of the market. When the market is very small, no person can have any encouragement to dedicate himself entirely to one employment, for want of the power to exchange all that surplus part of the produce of his own labour, which is over and above his own consumption, for such part of the produce of other men's labour as he has occasion for.

There are some sorts of industry, even of the lowest kind, which can be carried on nowhere but in a great town. A porter, for example, can find employment and subsistence in no other place. . . .

As, by means of water-carriage, a more extensive market is open to every sort of industry than what land-carriage alone can afford it, so it is upon the sea-coast, and along the banks of navigable rivers, that industry of every kind naturally begins to subdivide and improve itself; and it is frequently not till a long time after that those improvements extend themselves to the inland parts of the country. . . .

Since such therefore are the advantages of water-carriage, it is natural that the first improvements of art and industry should be made where this conveniency opens the whole world for a market to the produce of every sort of labour, and that they should always be much later in extending themselves into the inland parts of the country. The inland parts of the country can for a long time have no other market for the greater part of their goods, but the country which lies round about them, and separates them from the sea-coast, and the great navigable rivers. The extent of their market, therefore, must for a long time be in proportion to the riches and populousness of that country, and consequently their improvement must always be posterior to the improvement of that country. . . .

The nations that, according to the best authenticated history, appear to have been first civilized, were those that dwelt round the coast of the Mediterranean Sea. That sea, by far the greatest inlet that is known in the world, having no tides, nor consequently any waves except such as are caused by the wind only, was, by the smoothness of its surface, as well as by the multitude of its islands, and the proximity of its neighbouring shores, extremely favourable to the infant navigation of the world; when, from their ignorance of the compass, men were afraid to quit the view of the coast, and from the imperfection of the art of ship-building, to abandon themselves to the boisterous waves of the ocean. . . .

Of the Origin and Use of Money

When the division of labour has been once thoroughly established, it is but a very small part of a man's wants which the produce of his own labour can supply. He supplies the far greater part of them by exchanging that surplus part of the produce of his own labour, which is over and above his own consumption, for such parts of the produce of other men's labour as he has occasion for. Every man thus lives by exchanging, or becomes in some measure a merchant, and the society itself grows to be what is properly a commercial society.

But, when the division of labour first began to take place, this power of exchanging must frequently have been very much clogged and embarrassed in its operations. One man, we shall suppose, has more of a certain commodity than he himself has occasion for, while another has less. The former consequently would be glad to dispose of, and the latter to purchase, a part of this superfluity. But, if this latter should chance to have nothing that the former stands in need of, no exchange can be made between them. The butcher has more meat in his shop than he himself can consume, and the brewer and the baker would each of them be willing to purchase a part of it. But they have nothing to offer in exchange, except the different productions of their respective trades, and the butcher is already provided with all the bread and beer which he has immediate occasion for. No exchange can, in this case, be made between them. . . .

In the rude ages of society, cattle are said to have been the common instrument of commerce; and, though they must have been a most inconvenient one, yet in old times we find things were frequently valued according to the number of cattle which had been given in exchange for them. . . .

In all countries, however, men seem at last to have been determined by irresistible reasons to give the preference, for this employment, to metals above every other commodity. Metals cannot only be kept with as little loss as any other commodity, scarce anything being less perishable than they are, but they can likewise, without any loss, be divided into any number of parts, as by fusion those parts can easily be re-united again; a quality which no other equally durable commodities possess, and which more than any other quality renders them fit to be the instruments of commerce and circulation. . . .

Those metals seem originally to have been made use of for this purpose in rude bars, without any stamp or coinage. . . .

The use of metals in this rude state was attended with two very considerable inconveniencies; first, with the trouble of weighing; and, secondly, with that of assaying them. . . . We should find it excessively troublesome, if every time a poor man had occasion either to buy or sell a farthing's worth of goods, he was obliged to weigh the farthing. The operation of assaying is still more difficult, still more tedious, and, unless a part of the metal is fairly melted in the crucible, with proper dissolvents, any conclusion that can be drawn from it, is extremely uncertain. Before the institution of coined money, however, unless they went through this tedious and difficult operation, people must always have been liable to the grossest frauds and impositions. . . . To prevent such abuses, to facilitate exchanges, and thereby to encourage all sorts of industry and commerce, it has been found necessary, in all countries that have made any considerable advances towards improvement, to affix a public stamp upon certain quantities of such particular metals as were in those countries commonly made use of to purchase goods. Hence the origin of coined money, and of those public offices called mints; institutions exactly of the same nature with those of the aulnagers and stampmasters of woollen and linen cloth. All of them are equally meant to ascertain, by means of a public stamp, the quantity and uniform goodness of those different commodities when brought to market.

The first public stamps of this kind that were affixed to the current metals, seem in many cases to have been intended to ascertain, what it was both most difficult and most important to ascertain, the goodness or fineness of the metal . . .

The inconveniency and difficulty of weighing those metals with exactness gave occasion to the institution of coins, of which the stamp, covering entirely both sides of the piece and sometimes the edges too, was supposed to ascertain not only the fineness, but the weight of the metal. Such coins therefore were received by tale as at present, without the trouble of weighing. . . .

It is in this manner that money has become, in all civilized nations, the universal instrument of commerce, by the intervention of which goods of all kinds are bought and sold, or exchanged for one another.

What are the rules which men naturally observe in exchanging them either for money or for one another, I shall now proceed to examine. These rules determine what may be called the relative or exchangeable value of goods.

The word VALUE, it is to be observed, has two different meanings, and sometimes expresses the utility of some particular object, and sometimes the power of purchasing other goods which the possession of that object conveys. The one may be called "value in use"; the other, "value in exchange." The things which have the greatest value in use have frequently little or no value in exchange; and, on the contrary, those which have the greatest value in exchange have frequently little or no value in use. Nothing is more useful than water: but it will purchase scarce anything; scarce anything can be had in exchange for it. A diamond, on the contrary, has scarce any value in use, but a very great quantity of other goods may frequently be had in exchange for it.

In order to investigate the principles which regulate the exchangeable commodities, I shall endeavour to show,

I. What is the real measure of this exchangeable value; or, wherein consists the real price of all commodities.

II. What are the different parts of which this real price is composed or made up.

III. And what are the different circumstances which sometimes raise some or all of these different parts of price above, and sometimes sink them below, their natural or ordinary rate; or, what are the causes which sometimes hinder the market price, that is, the actual price, of commodities, from coinciding exactly with what may be called their natural price. . . .

Of the Real and Nominal Price of Commodities, or of Their Price in Labour, and Their Price in Money

Every man is rich or poor according to the degree in which he can afford to enjoy the necessaries, conveniencies, and amusements of human life. But after the division of labour has once thoroughly taken place, it is but a very small part of these with which a man's own labour can supply him. The far greater part of them he must derive from the labour of other people, and he must be rich or poor according to the quantity of that labour which he can command, or which he can afford to purchase. The value of any commodity, therefore, to the person who possesses it, and who means not to use or consume it himself, but to exchange it for other commodities, is equal to the quantity of labour which it enables him to purchase or command. Labour, therefore, is the real measure of the exchangeable value of all commodities. . . .

But though labour be the real measure of the exchangeable value of all commodities, it is not that by which their value is commonly estimated. It is often difficult to ascertain the proportion between two different quantities of labour. The time spent in two different sorts of work will not always alone determine this proportion. The different degrees of hardship endured, and of ingenuity exercised, must likewise be taken into account. . . . In exchanging indeed the different productions of different sorts of labour for one another, some allowance is commonly made for both. It is adjusted, however, not by any accurate measure, but by the higgling and the bargaining of the market, according to that sort of rough equality which, though not exact, is yet sufficient for carrying on the business of common life.

Every commodity, besides, is more frequently exchanged for, and thereby compared with, other commodities than with labour. It is more natural therefore to estimate its exchangeable value by the quantity of some other commodity, than by that of the labour which it can purchase. The greater part of people too understand better what is meant by a quantity of a particular commodity than by a quantity of labour. The one is a plain and palpable object; the other an abstract notion, which, though it can be made sufficiently intelligible, is not altogether so natural and obvious.

But, when barter ceases, and money has become the common instrument of commerce, every particular commodity is more frequently exchanged for money than for any other commodity. . . . Hence it comes to pass, that the exchangeable value of every commodity is more frequently estimated by the quantity of money, than by the quantity either of labour or of any other commodity which can be had in exchange for it.

Gold and silver, however, like every other commodity, vary in their value, are sometimes cheaper and sometimes dearer, sometimes of easier and sometimes of more difficult purchase. The quantity of labour which any particular quantity of them can purchase or command, or the quantity of other goods which it will exchange for, depends always upon the fertility or barrenness of the mines which happen to be known about the time when such exchanges are made. The discovery of the abundant mines of America reduced, in the sixteenth century, the value of gold and silver in Europe to about a third of what it had been before. As it costs less labour to bring those metals from the mine to the market, so when they were brought thither they could purchase or command less labour; and this revolution in their value, though perhaps the greatest, is by no means the only one of which history gives some account. But as a measure of quantity, such as the natural foot, fathom, or handful, which is continually varying in its own quantity, can never be an accurate measure of the quantity of other things; so a commodity, which is itself continually varying in its own value, can never be an accurate measure of the value of other commodities. Equal quantities of labour must, at all times and places, be of equal value to the labourer. . . . Labour alone, . . . never varying in its own value, is alone the ultimate and real standard by which the value of all commodities can at all times and places be estimated and compared. It is their real price; money is their nominal price only.

But though equal quantities of labour are always of equal value to the labourer, yet to the person who employs him they appear sometimes to be of greater and sometimes of smaller value. He purchases them sometimes with a greater and sometimes with a smaller quantity of goods, and to him the price of labour seems to vary like that of all other things. It appears to him dear in the one case, and cheap in the other. In reality, however, it is the goods which are cheap in the one case, and dear in the other.

In this popular sense, therefore, Labour, like commodities, may be said to have a real and a nominal price. Its real price may be said to consist in the quantity of the necessaries and conveniencies of life which are given for it; its nominal price, in the quantity of money. The labourer is rich or poor, is well or ill rewarded, in proportion to the real, not to the nominal price of his labour. . . .

Of the Component Parts of the Price of Commodities

In that early and rude state of society which precedes both the accumulation of stock and the appropriation of land, the proportion between the quantities of labour necessary for acquiring different objects seems to be the only circumstance which can afford any rule for exchanging them for one another. If among a nation of hunters, for example, it usually costs twice the labour to kill a beaver which it does to kill a deer, one beaver should naturally exchange for, or be worth two deer. It is natural that what is usually the produce of two days' or two hours' labour, should be worth double of what is usually the produce of one day's or one hour's labour.

If the one species of labour should be more severe than the other, some allowance will naturally be made for this superior hardship; and the produce of one hour's labour in the one way may frequently exchange for that of two hours' labour in the other.

Or if the one species of labour requires an uncommon degree of dexterity and ingenuity, the esteem which men have for such talents, will naturally give a value to their produce, superior to what would be due to the time employed about it. Such talents can seldom be acquired but in consequence of long application, and the superior value of the produce may frequently be no more than a reasonable compensation for the time and labour which must be spent in acquiring them. In the advanced state of society, allowances of this kind, for superior hardship and superior skill, are commonly made in the wages of labour; and something of the same kind must probably have taken place in its earliest and rudest period.

In this state of things, the quantity of labour commonly employed in acquiring or producing any commodity, is the only circumstance which can regulate the quantity of labour which it ought commonly to purchase, command, or exchange for.

As soon as stock has accumulated in the hands of particular persons, some of them will naturally employ it in setting to work industrious people, whom they will supply with materials and subsistence, in order to make a profit by the sale of their work, or by what their labour adds to the value of the materials. In exchanging the complete manufacture either for money, for labour, or for other goods, over and above what may be sufficient to pay the price of the materials, and the wages of the workmen, something must be given for the profits of the undertaker of the work who hazards his stock in this adventure. The value which the workmen add to the materials, therefore, resolves itself in this case into two parts, of which the one pays their wages, the other the profits of their employer upon the whole stock of materials and wages which he advanced. He could have no interest to employ them, unless he expected from the sale of their work something more than what was sufficient to replace his stock to him; and he could have no interest to employ a great stock rather than a small one, unless his profits were to bear some proportion to the extent of his stock.

The profits of stock, it may perhaps be thought, are only a different name for the wages of a particular sort of labour, the labour of inspection and direction. They are, however, altogether different, are regulated by quite different principles, and bear no proportion to the quantity, the hardship, or the ingenuity of this supposed labour of inspection and direction. They are regulated altogether by the value of the stock employed, and are greater or smaller in proportion to the extent of this stock. . . . In the price of commodities, therefore, the profits of stock constitute a component part altogether different from the wages of labour, and regulated by quite different principles.

In this state of things, the whole produce of labour does not always belong to the labourer. He must in most cases share it with the owner of the stock which employs him. Neither is the quantity of labour commonly employed in acquiring or producing any commodity the only circumstance which can regulate the quantity which it ought commonly to purchase, command, or exchange for. An additional quantity, it is evident, must be due for the profits of the stock which advanced the wages and furnished the materials of that labour.

As soon as the land of any country has all become private property, the landlords, like all other men, love to reap where they never sowed, and demand a rent even for its natural produce. The wood of the forest, the grass of the field, and all the natural fruits of the earth, which, when land was in common, cost the labourer only the trouble of gathering them, come, even to him, to have an additional price fixed upon them. Men must then pay for the licence to gather them; and in exchanging them either for money, for labour, or for other goods, over and above what is due, both for the labour of gathering them, and for the profits of the stock which employs that labour, some allowance must be made for the price of the licence, which constitutes the first rent of land. In the price, therefore, of the greater part of commodities the rent of land comes in this manner to constitute the third source of value. . . .

The real value of all the different component parts of price, it must be observed, is measured by the quantity of labour which they can, each of them, purchase or command. Labour measures the value not only of that part of price which resolves itself into labour, but of that which resolves itself into rent, and of that which resolves itself into profit.

In every society the price of every commodity finally resolves itself into some one or other, or all of those three parts; and in every improved society, all the three enter more or less, as component parts, into the price of the far greater part of commodities. . . .

Of the Natural and Market Price of Commodities

. . . When the price of any commodity is neither more nor less than what is sufficient to pay the rent of the land, the wages of the labour, and the profits of the stock employed in raising, preparing, and bringing it to market, according to their natural rates, the commodity is then sold for what may be called its natural price. . . .

The actual price at which any commodity is commonly sold is called its market price. It may either be above, or below, or exactly the same with its natural price.

The market price of every particular commodity is regulated by the proportion between the quantity which is actually brought to market, and the demand of those who are willing to pay the natural price of the commodity, or the whole value of the rent, labour, and profit, which must be paid in order to bring it thither. Such people may be called the effectual demanders, and their demand the effectual demand; since it may be sufficient to effectuate the bringing of the commodity to market. It is different from the absolute demand. A very poor man may be said in some sense to have a demand for a coach and six; he might like to have it; but his demand is not an effectual demand, as the commodity can never be brought to the market in order to satisfy it. . . .

When the quantity brought to market is just sufficient to supply the effectual demand and no more, the market price naturally comes to be either exactly, or as nearly as can be judged of, the same with the natural price. The whole quantity upon hand can be disposed of for this price, and cannot be disposed of for more. The competition of the different dealers obliges them all to accept of this price, but does not oblige them to accept of less.

The quantity of every commodity brought to market naturally suits itself to the effectual demand. It is the interest of all those who employ their land, labour, or stock, in bringing any commodity to market, that the quantity never should exceed the effectual demand; and it is the interest of all other people that it never should fall short of that demand.

If at any time it exceeds the effectual demand, some of the component parts of its price must be paid below their natural rate. If it is rent, the interest of the landlords will immediately prompt them to withdraw a part of their land; and if it is wages or profit, the interest of the labourers in the one case, and of their employers in the other, will prompt them to withdraw a part of their labour or stock from this employment. The quantity brought to market will soon be no more than sufficient to supply the effectual demand. All the different parts of its price will rise to their natural rate, and the whole price to its natural price.

If, on the contrary, the quantity brought to market should at any time fall short of the effectual demand, some of the component parts of its price must rise above their natural rate. If it is rent, the interest of all other landlords will naturally prompt them to prepare more land for the raising of this commodity; if it is wages or profit, the interest of all other labourers and dealers will soon prompt them to employ more labour and stock in preparing and bringing it to market. The quantity brought thither will soon be sufficient to supply the effectual demand. All the different parts of its price will soon sink to their natural rate, and the whole price to its natural price.

The natural price, therefore, is, as it were, the central price, to which the prices of all commodities are continually gravitating. Different accidents may sometimes keep them suspended a good deal above it, and sometimes force them down even somewhat below it. But whatever may be the obstacles which hinder them from settling in this centre of repose and continuance, they are constantly tending towards it. . . .

The occasional and temporary fluctuations in the market price of any commodity fall chiefly upon those parts of its price which resolve themselves into wages and profit. That part which resolves itself into rent is less affected by them. A rent certain in money is not in the least affected by them either in its rate or in its value. A rent which consists either in a certain proportion or in a certain quantity of the rude produce, is no doubt affected in its yearly value by all the occasional and temporary fluctuations in the market price of that rude produce; but it is seldom affected by them in its yearly rate. In settling the terms of the lease, the landlord and farmer endeavour, according to their best judgment, to adjust that rate, not to the temporary and occasional, but to the average and ordinary price of the produce.

Such fluctuations affect both the value and the rate either of wages or of profit, according as the market happens to be either over-stocked or under-stocked with commodities or with labour; with work done, or with work to be done. A public mourning raises the price of black cloth (with which the market is almost always under-stocked upon such occasions), and augments the profits of the merchant who possess any considerable quantity of it. It has no effect upon the wages of the weavers. The market is under-stocked with commodities, not with labour; with work done, not with work to be done. It raises the wages of journeymen tailors. The market is here under-stocked with labour. There is an effectual demand for more labour, for more work to be done than can be had. It sinks the price of coloured silks and cloths, and thereby reduces the profits of the merchants who have any considerable quantity of them upon hand. It sinks too the wages of the workmen employed in preparing such commodities, for which all demand is stopped for six months, perhaps for a twelvemonth. The market is here over-stocked both with commodities and with labour.

But, though the market price of every particular commodity is in this manner continually gravitating, if one may say so, towards the natural price, yet sometimes particular accidents, sometimes natural causes, and sometimes particular regulations of police, may, in many commodities, keep up the market price, for a long time together, a good deal above the natural price.

When by an increase in the effectual demand, the market price of some particular commodity happens to rise a good deal above the natural price, those who employ their stocks in supplying that market are generally careful to conceal this change. If it was commonly known, their great profit would tempt so many new rivals to employ their stocks in the same way, that, the effectual demand being fully supplied, the market price would soon be reduced to the natural price, and perhaps for sometime even below it. If the market is at a great distance from the residence of those who supply it, they may sometimes be able to keep the secret for several years together, and may so long enjoy their extraordinary profits without any new rivals. Secrets of this kind, however, it must be acknowledged, can seldom be long kept; and the extraordinary profit can last very little longer than they are kept.

Secrets in manufactures are capable of being longer kept than secrets in trade. A dyer who has found the means of producing a particular colour with materials which cost only half the price of those commonly made use of, may, with good management, enjoy the advantage of his discovery as long as he lives, and even leave it as a legacy to his posterity. His extraordinary gains arise from the high price which is paid for his private labour. They properly consist in the high wages of that labour. But as they are repeated upon every part of his stock, and as their whole amount bears, upon that account, a regular proportion to it, they are commonly considered as extraordinary profits of stock.

Such enhancements of the market price are evidently the effects of particular accidents, of which, however, the operation may sometimes last for many years together.

Some natural productions require such a singularity of soil and situation, that all the land in a great country, which is fit for producing them, may not be sufficient to supply the effectual demand.The whole quantity brought to market, therefore, may be disposed of to those who are willing to give more than what is sufficient to pay the rent of the land which produced them, together with the wages of the labour, and the profits of the stock which were employed in preparing and bringing them to market, according to their natural rates. Such commodities may continue for whole centuries together to be sold at this high price; and that part of it which resolves itself into the rent of land is in this case the part which is generally paid above its natural rate. The rent of the land which affords such singular and esteemed productions, like the rent of some vineyards in France of a peculiarly happy soil and situation, bears no regular proportion to the rent of other equally fertile and equally well-cultivated land in its neighbourhood. The wages of the labour, and the profits of the stock employed in bringing such commodities to market, on the contrary, are seldom out of their natural proportion to those of the other employments of labour and stock in their neighbourhood.

Such enhancements of the market price are evidently the effect of natural causes which may hinder the effectual demand from ever being fully supplied, and which may continue, therefore, to operate forever.

A monopoly granted either to an individual or to a trading company has the same effect as a secret in trade or manufactures. The monopolists, by keeping the market constantly under-stocked, by never fully supplying the effectual demand, sell their commodities much above the natural price, and raise their emoluments, whether they consist in wages or profit, greatly above their natural rate.

The price of monopoly is, upon every occasion, the highest which can be got. The natural price, or the price of free competition, on the contrary, is the lowest which can be taken, not upon every occasion, indeed, but for any considerable time together. The one is upon every occasion the highest which can be squeezed out of the buyers, or which, it is supposed, they will consent to give: the other is the lowest which the sellers can commonly afford to take, and at the same time continue their business.

The exclusive privileges of corporations, statutes of apprenticeship and all those laws which restrain, in particular employments, the competition to a smaller number than might otherwise go into them, have the same tendency, though in a less degree. They are a sort of enlarged monopolies, and may frequently, for ages together, and in whole classes of employments, keep up the market price of particular commodities above the natural price, and maintain both the wages of the labour and the profits of the stock employed about them somewhat above their natural rate.

Such enhancements of the market price may last as long as the regulations of police which give occasion to them. . . .

Of the Wages of Labour

. . . What are the common wages of labour depends everywhere upon the contract usually made between those two parties, whose interests are by no means the same. The workmen desire to get as much, the masters to give as little, as possible. The former are disposed to combine in order to raise, the latter in order to lower, the wages of labour. . . .

But though in disputes with their workmen, masters must generally have the advantage, there is, however, a certain rate below which it seems impossible to reduce, for any considerable time, the ordinary wages even of the lowest species of labour.

A man must always live by his work, and his wages must at least be sufficient to maintain him. They must even upon most occasions be somewhat more; otherwise it would be impossible for him to bring up a family, and the race of such workmen could not last beyond the first generation. . . .

There are certain circumstances, however, which sometimes give the labourers an advantage, and enable them to raise their wages considerably above this rate; evidently the lowest which is consistent with common humanity.

When in any country the demand for those who live by wages; labourers, journeymen, servants of every kind, is continually increasing; when every year furnishes employment for a greater number than had been employed the year before, the workmen have no occasion to combine in order to raise their wages. The scarcity of hands occasions a competition among masters, who bid against one another in order to get workmen, and thus voluntarily break through the natural combination of masters not to raise wages.

The demand for those who live by wages, it is evident, cannot increase but in proportion to the increase of the funds which are destined for the payment of wages. These funds are of two kinds: first, the revenue which is over and above what is necessary for the maintenance; and secondly, the stock which is over and above what is necessary for the employment of their masters. . . .

The demand for those who live by wages, therefore, necessarily increases with the increase of the revenue and stock of every country, and cannot possibly increase without it. The increase of revenue and stock is the increase of national wealth. The demand for those who live by wages, therefore, naturally increases with the increase of national wealth, and cannot possibly increase without it.

It is not the actual greatness of national wealth, but its continual increase, which occasions a rise in the wages of labour. It is not, accordingly, in the richest countries, but in the most thriving, or in those which are growing rich the fastest, that the wages of labour are highest. England is certainly in the present times, a much richer country than any part of North America. The wages of labour, however, are much higher in North America than in any part of England. . . . The demand for labourers, the funds destined for maintaining them, increase, it seems, still faster than they can find labourers to employ. . . .

In Great Britain the wages of labour seem, in the present times, to be evidently more than what is precisely necessary to enable the labourer to bring up a family. . . .

First, in almost every part of Great Britain there is a distinction, even in the lowest species of labour, between summer and winter wages. Summer wages are always highest. But on account of the extraordinary expense of fuel, the maintenance of a family is most expensive in winter. Wages therefore being highest when this expense is lowest, it seems evident that they are not regulated by what is necessary for this expense; but by the quantity and supposed value of the work. A labourer, it may be said indeed, ought to save part of his summer wages in order to defray his winter expense; and that through the whole year they do not exceed what is necessary to maintain his family through the whole year. . . .

Secondly, the wages of labour do not in Great Britain fluctuate with the price of provisions. These vary everywhere from year to year, frequently from month to month. But in many places the money price of labour remains uniformly the same sometimes for half a century together. If in these places therefore the labouring poor can maintain their families in dear years, they must be at their ease in times of moderate plenty, and in affluence in those of extraordinary cheapness. . . .

Thirdly, as the price of provisions varies more from year to year than the wages of labour, so on the other hand, the wages of labour vary more from place to place than the price of provisions. The prices of bread and butcher's meat are generally the same, or very nearly the same, through the greater part of the United Kingdom. These and most other things which are sold by retail, the way in which the labouring poor buy all things, are generally fully as cheap or cheaper in great towns than in the remoter parts of the country, for reasons which I shall have occasion to explain hereafter. But the wages of labour in a great town and its neighbourhood are frequently a fourth or a fifth part, twenty or five-and-twenty per cent. higher than at a few miles distance. . . . If the labouring poor, therefore, can maintain their families in those parts of the kingdom where the price of labour is lowest, they must be in affluence where it is highest.

Fourthly, the variations in the price of labour not only do not correspond either in place or time with those in the price of provisions, but they are frequently quite opposite.

. . . Oatmeal supplies the common people in Scotland with the greatest and the best part of their food, which is in general much inferior to that of their neighbours of the same rank in England. This difference, however, in the mode of their subsistence is not the cause, but the effect of the difference in their wages; though, by a strange misapprehension, I have frequently heard it represented as the cause. It is not because one man keeps a coach while his neighbour walks a-foot, that the one is rich and the other poor; but because the one is rich he keeps a coach, and because the other is poor he walks a-foot. . . .

The liberal reward of labour, by enabling them to provide better for their children, and consequently to bring up a greater number, naturally tends to widen and extend those [subsistence] limits. It deserves to be remarked too, that it necessarily does this as nearly as possible in the proportion which the demand for labour requires. If this demand is continually increasing, the reward of labour must necessarily encourage in such a manner the marriage and multiplication of labourers, as may enable them to supply that continually increasing demand by a continually increasing population. If the reward should at any time be less than what was requisite for this purpose, the deficiency of hands would soon raise it; and if it should at any time be more, their excessive multiplication would soon lower it to this necessary rate. The market would be so much understocked with labour in the one case, and so much over-stocked in the other, as would soon force back its price to that proper rate which the circumstances of the society required. It is in this manner that the demand for men, like that for any other commodity, necessarily regulates the production of men; quickens it when it goes on too slowly, and stops it when it advances too fast. It is this demand which regulates and determines the state of propagation in all the different countries of the world, in North America, in Europe, and in China; which renders it rapidly progressive in the first, slow and gradual in the second, and altogether stationary in the last. . . .

The liberal reward of labour, as it encourages the propagation, so it increases the industry of the common people. The wages of labour are the encouragement of industry, which, like every other human quality, improves in proportion to the encouragement it receives. A plentiful subsistence increases the bodily strength of the labourer, and the comfortable hope of bettering his condition, and of ending his days perhaps in ease and plenty, animates him to exert that strength to the utmost. Where wages are high, accordingly, we shall always find the workmen more active, diligent, and expeditious, than where they are low; in England, for example, than in Scotland; in the neighbourhood of great towns, than in remote country places. . . .

The increase in the wages of labour necessarily increases the price of many commodities, by increasing that part of it which resolves itself into wages, and so far tends to diminish their consumption both at home and abroad. The same cause, however, which raises the wages of labour, the increase of stock, tends to increase its productive powers, and to make a smaller quantity of labour produce a greater quantity of work. The owner of the stock which employs a great number of labourers, necessarily endeavours, for his own advantage, to make such a proper division and distribution of employment, that they may be enabled to produce the greatest quantity of work possible. For the same reason he endeavours to supply them with the best machinery which either he or they can think of. What takes place among the labourers in a particular workhouse, takes place, for the same reason, among those of a great society. The greater their number, the more they naturally divide themselves into different classes and subdivisions of employment. More heads are occupied in inventing the most proper machinery for executing the work of each, and it is, therefore, more likely to be invented. There are many commodities, therefore, which, in consequence of these improvements, come to be produced by so much less labour than before, that the increase of its price is more than compensated by the diminution of its quantity.

Of the Profits of Stock

The rise and fall in the profits of stock depend upon the same causes with the rise and fall in the wages of labour, the increasing or declining state of the wealth of the society; but those causes affect the one and the other very differently.

The increase of stock, which raises wages, tends to lower profit. When the stocks of many rich merchants are turned into the same trade, their mutual competition naturally tends to lower its profit; and when there is a like increase of stock in all the different trades carried on in the same society, the same competition must produce the same effect in them all.

It is not easy, it has already been observed, to ascertain what are the average wages of labour even in a particular place and at a particular time. We can, even in this case, seldom determine more than what are the most usual wages. But even this can seldom be done with regard to the profits of stock. Profit is so very fluctuating, that the person who carries on a particular trade cannot always tell you himself what is the average of his annual profit. It is affected, not only by every variation of price in the commodities which he deals in, but by the good or bad fortune both of his rivals and of his customers, and by a thousand other accidents to which goods when carried either by sea or by land, or even when stored in a warehouse, are liable. It varies, therefore, not only from year to year, but from day to day, and almost from hour to hour. To ascertain what is the average profit of all the different trades carried on in a great kingdom must be much more difficult; and to judge of what it may have been formerly, or in remote periods of time, with any degree of precision, must be altogether impossible.

But though it may be impossible to determine with any degree of precision, what are or were the average profits of stock, either in the present, or in ancient times, some notion may be formed of them from the interest of money. It may be laid down as a maxim, that wherever a great deal can be made by the use of money, a great deal will commonly be given for the use of it; and that wherever little can be made by it, less will commonly be given for it. Accordingly, therefore, as the usual market rate of interest varies in any country, we may be assured that the ordinary profits of stock must vary with it, must sink as it sinks and rise as it rises. The progress of interest, therefore, may lead us to form some notion of the progress of profit. . . .

It generally requires a greater stock to carry on any sort of trade in a town than in a country village. The great stocks employed in every branch of trade, and the number of rich competitors, generally reduce the rate of profit in the former below what it is in the latter. But the wages of labour are generally higher in a great town than in a country village. In a thriving town the people who have great stocks to employ frequently cannot get the number of workmen they want, and therefore bid against one another in order to get as many as they can, which raises the wages of labour, and lowers the profits of stock. In the remote parts of the country there is frequently not stock sufficient to employ all the people, who therefore bid against one another in order to get employment, which lowers the wages of labour, and raises the profits of stock. . . .

In our North American and West Indian colonies, not only the wages of labour, but the interest of money, and consequently the profits of stock, are higher than in England. . . . High wages of labour and high profits of stock, however, are things, perhaps, which scarce ever go together, except in the peculiar circumstances of new colonies. A new colony must always for some time be more under-stocked in proportion to the extent of its territory, and more under-peopled in proportion to the extent of its stock, than the greater part of other countries. They have more land than they have stock to cultivate. What they have, therefore, is applied to the cultivation only of what is most fertile and most favourably situated, the land near the sea shore, and along the banks of navigable rivers. Such land, too, is frequently purchased at a price below the value even of its natural produce. Stock employed in the purchase and improvement of such lands must yield a very large profit, and consequently afford to pay a very large interest. Its rapid accumulation in so profitable an employment enables the planter to increase the number of his hands faster than he can find them in a new settlement. Those whom he can find, therefore, are very liberally rewarded. As the colony increases, the profits of stock gradually diminish. When the most fertile and best situated lands have been all occupied, less profit can be made by the cultivation of what is inferior both in soil and situation, and less interest can be afforded for the stock which is so employed. In the greater part of our colonies, accordingly, both the legal and the market rate of interest have been considerably reduced during the course of the present century. As riches, improvement, and population have increased, interest has declined. The wages of labour do not sink with the profits of stock. The demand for labour increases with the increase of stock, whatever be its profits. . . .

The acquisition of new territory, or of new branches of trade, may sometimes raise the profits of stock, and with them the interest of money, even in a country which is fast advancing in the acquisition of riches. The stock of the country not being sufficient for the whole accession of business, which such acquisitions present to the different people among whom it is divided, is applied to those particular branches only which afford the greatest profit. Part of what had before been employed in other trades, is necessarily withdrawn from them, and turned into some of the new and more profitable ones. In all those old trades, therefore, the competition comes to be less than before. The market comes to be less fully supplied with many different sorts of goods. Their price necessarily rises more or less, and yields a greater profit to those who deal in them, who can, therefore, afford to borrow at a higher interest. For some time after the conclusion of the late war, not only private people of the best credit, but some of the greatest companies in London, commonly borrowed at five per cent., who before that had not been used to pay more than four, and four and a half per cent. The great accession both of territory and trade, by our acquisitions in North America and the West Indies, will sufficiently account for this, without supposing any diminution in the capital stock of the society. . . .

The diminution of the capital stock of the society, or of the funds destined for the maintenance of industry, however, as it lowers the wages of labour, so it raises the profits of stock, and consequently the interest of money. By the wages of labour being lowered, the owners of what stock remains in the society can bring their goods at less expense to market than before, and less stock being employed in supplying the market than before, they can sell them dearer. Their goods cost them less, and they get more for them. Their profits, therefore, being augmented at both ends, can well afford a large interest. . . .

In a country which had acquired that full complement of riches which the nature of its soil and climate, and its situation with respect to other countries, allowed it to acquire; which could, therefore, advance no further, and which was not going backwards, both the wages of labour and the profits of stock would probably be very low. In a country fully peopled in proportion to what either its territory could maintain or its stock employ, the competition for employment would necessarily be so great as to reduce the wages of labour to what was barely sufficient to keep up the number of labourers, and, the country being already fully peopled, that number could never be augmented. In a country fully stocked in proportion to all the business it had to transact, as great a quantity of stock would be employed in every particular branch as the nature and extent of the trade would admit. The competition, therefore, would everywhere be as great, and consequently the ordinary profit as low as possible. . . .

The lowest ordinary rate of profit must always be something more than what is sufficient to compensate the occasional losses to which every employment of stock is exposed. It is this surplus only which is neat or clear profit. What is called gross profit comprehends frequently, not only this surplus, but what is retained for compensating such extraordinary losses. The interest which the borrower can afford to pay is in proportion to the clear profit only.

The lowest ordinary rate of interest must, in the same manner, be something more than sufficient to compensate the occasional losses to which lending, even with tolerable prudence, is exposed. Were it not more, charity or friendship could be the only motives for lending.

In a country which had acquired its full complement of riches, where in every particular branch of business there was the greatest quantity of stock that could be employed in it, as the ordinary rate of clear profit would be very small, so the usual market rate of interest which could be afforded out of it would be so low as to render it impossible for any but the very wealthiest people to live upon the interest of their money. All people of small or middling fortunes would be obliged to superintend themselves the employment of their own stocks. It would be necessary that almost every man should be a man of business, or engage in some sort of trade. The province of Holland seems to be approaching near to this state. It is there unfashionable not to be a man of business. . . .

The highest ordinary rate of profit may be such as, in the price of the greater part of commodities, eats up the whole of what should go to the rent of the land, and leaves only what is sufficient to pay the labour of preparing and bringing them to market, according to the lowest rate at which labour can anywhere be paid, the bare subsistence of the labourer. The workman must always have been fed in some way or other while he was about the work; but the landlord may not always have been paid. The profits of the trade which the servants of the East India Company carry on in Bengal may not perhaps be very far from this rate.

The proportion which the usual market rate of interest ought to bear to the ordinary rate of clear profit, necessarily varies as profit rises or falls. Double interest is in Great Britain reckoned what the merchants call a good, moderate, reasonable profit; terms which I apprehend mean no more than a common and usual profit. In a country where the ordinary rate of clear profit is eight or ten per cent., it may be reasonable that one half of it should go to interest, wherever business is carried on with borrowed money. The stock is at the risk of the borrower, who, as it were, insures it to the lender; and four or five per cent. may, in the greater part of trades, be both a sufficient profit upon the risk of this insurance, and a sufficient recompense for the trouble of employing the stock. But the proportion between interest and clear profit might not be the same in countries where the ordinary rate of profit was either a good deal lower, or a good deal higher. If it were a good deal lower, one half of it perhaps could not be afforded for interest; and more might be afforded if it were a good deal higher.

In countries which are fast advancing to riches, the low rate of profit may, in the price of many commodities, compensate the high wages of labour, and enable those countries to sell as cheap as their less thriving neighbours, among whom the wages paid for labour may be lower. . . .

Of the Rent of Land

Rent, considered as the price paid for the use of land, is naturally the highest which the tenant can afford to pay in the actual circumstances of the land. In adjusting the terms of the lease, the landlord endeavours to leave him no greater share of the produce than what is sufficient to keep up the stock from which he furnishes the feed, pays the labour, and purchases and maintains the cattle and other instruments of husbandry, together with the ordinary profits of farming stock in the neighbourhood. This is evidently the smallest share with which the tenant can content himself without being a loser, and the landlord seldom means to leave him any more. Whatever part of the produce, or, what is the same thing, whatever part of its price, is over and above this share, he naturally endeavours to reserve to himself as the rent of his land, which is evidently the highest the tenant can afford to pay in the actual circumstances of the land. . . .

The rent of land, it may be thought, is frequently no more than a reasonable profit or interest for the stock laid out by the landlord upon its improvement. This, no doubt, may be partly the case upon some occasions; for it can scarce ever be more than partly the case. The landlord demands a rent even for unimproved land, and the supposed interest or profit upon the expense of improvement is generally an addition to this original rent. Those improvements, besides, are not always made by the stock of the landlord, but sometimes by that of the tenant. When the lease comes to be renewed, however, the landlord commonly demands the same augmentation of rent, as if they had been all made by his own. . . .

The rent of land, therefore, considered as the price paid for the use of the land, is naturally a monopoly price. It is not at all proportioned to what the landlord may have laid out upon the improvement of the land, or to what he can afford to take; but to what the farmer can afford to give.

Such parts only of the produce of land can commonly be brought to market of which the ordinary price is sufficient to replace the stock which must be employed in bringing them thither, together with its ordinary profits. If the ordinary price is more than this, the surplus part of it will naturally go to the rent of the land. If it is not more, though the commodity may be brought to market, it can afford no rent to the landlord. Whether the price is, or is not more, will depend upon the demand.

There are some parts of the produce of land for which the demand must always be such as to afford a greater price than what is sufficient to bring them to market; and there are others for which it either may or may not be such as to afford this greater price. The former must always afford a rent to the landlord. The latter sometimes may, and sometimes may not, according to different circumstances.

Rent, it is to be observed, therefore, enters into the composition of the price of commodities in a different way from wages and profit. High or low wages and profit are the causes of high or low price; high or low rent is the effect of it. It is because high or low wages and profit must be paid, in order to bring a particular commodity to market, that its price is high or low; but it is because its price is high or low, a great deal more, or very little more, or no more, than what is sufficient to pay those wages and profit, that it affords a high rent, a low rent, or no rent at all. . . .

OF THE PRODUCE OF LAND WHICH ALWAYS AFFORDS RENT

. . . The rent of land not only varies with its fertility, whatever be its produce, but with its situation, whatever be its fertility. Land in the neighbourhood of a town gives a greater rent than land equally fertile in a distant part of the country. Though it may cost no more labour to cultivate the one than the other, it must always cost more to bring the produce of the distant land to market. A greater quantity of labour, therefore, must be maintained out of it; and the surplus, from which are drawn both the profit of the farmer and the rent of the landlord, must be diminished. But in remote parts of the country the rate of profits, as has already been shown, is generally higher than in the neighbourhood of a large town. A smaller proportion of this diminished surplus, therefore, must belong to the landlord. . . .

CONCLUSION OF THE CHAPTER

I shall conclude this very long chapter with observing, that every improvement in the circumstances of the society tends either directly or indirectly to raise the real rent of land, to increase the real wealth of the landlord, his power of purchasing the labour, or the produce of the labour of other people.

The extension of improvement and cultivation tends to raise it directly. The landlord's share of the produce necessarily increases with the increase of the produce.

That rise in the real price of those parts of the rude produce of land, which is first the effect of extended improvement and cultivation, and afterwards the cause of their being still further extended, the rise in the price of cattle, for example, tends too to raise the rent of land directly, and in a still greater proportion. The real value of the landlord's share, his real command of the labour of other people, not only rises with the real value of the produce, but the proportion of his share to the whole produce rises with it. That produce, after the rise in its real price, requires no more labour to collect it than before. A smaller proportion of it will, therefore, be sufficient to replace, with the ordinary profit, the stock which employs that labour. A greater proportion of it must, consequently, belong to the landlord.

All those improvements in the productive powers of labour, which tend directly to reduce the real price of manufactures, tend indirectly to raise the real rent of land. The landlord exchanges that part of his rude produce, which is over and above his own consumption, or what comes to the same thing, the price of that part of it, for manufactured produce. Whatever reduces the real price of the latter, raises that of the former. An equal quantity of the former becomes thereby equivalent to a greater quantity of the latter; and the landlord is enabled to purchase a greater quantity of the conveniencies, ornaments, or luxuries, which he has occasion for.

Every increase in the real wealth of the society, every increase in the quantity of useful labour employed within it tends indirectly to raise the real rent of land. A certain proportion of this labour naturally goes to the land. A greater number of men and cattle are employed in its cultivation, the produce increases with the increase of the stock which is thus employed in raising it, and the rent increases with the produce.

The contrary circumstances, the neglect of cultivation and improvement, the fall in the real price of any part of the rude produce of land, the rise in the real price of manufactures from the decay of manufacturing art and industry, the declension of the real wealth of the society, all tend, on the other hand, to lower the real rent of land, to reduce the real wealth of the landlord, to diminish his power of purchasing either the labour, or the produce of the labour of other people.

The whole annual produce of the land and labour of every country, or what comes to the same thing, the whole price of that annual produce, naturally divides itself, it has already been observed, into three parts,—the rent of land, the wages of labour, and the profits of stock; and constitutes a revenue to three different orders of people,—to those who live by rent, to those who live by wages, and to those who live by profit. These are the three great original and constituent orders of every civilized society, from whose revenue that of every other order is ultimately derived.

The interest of the first of those three great orders, it appears from what has been just now said, is strictly and inseparably connected with the general interest of the society. Whatever either promotes or obstructs the one, necessarily promotes or obstructs the other. When the public deliberates concerning any regulation of commerce or police, the proprietors of land never can mislead it, with a view to promote the interest of their own particular order; at least, if they have any tolerable knowledge of that interest. They are, indeed, too often defective in this tolerable knowledge. They are the only one of the three orders whose revenue costs them neither labour nor care, but comes to them, as it were, of its own accord, and independent of any plan or project of their own. That indolence, which is the natural effect of the ease and security of their situation, renders them too often, not only ignorant, but incapable of that application of mind which is necessary in order to foresee and understand the consequences of any public regulation.

The interest of the second order, that of those who live by wages, is as strictly connected with the interest of the society as that of the first. The wages of the labourer, it has already been shown, are never so high as when the demand for labour is continually rising, or when the quantity employed is every year increasing considerably. When this real wealth of the society becomes stationary, his wages are soon reduced to what is barely enough to enable him to bring up a family, or to continue the race of labourers. When the society declines, they fall even below this. The order of proprietors may, perhaps, gain more by the prosperity of the society than that of labourers; but there is no order that suffers so cruelly from decline. But though the interest of the labourer is strictly connected with that of the society, he is incapable either of comprehending that interest, or of understanding its connexion with his own. His condition leaves him no time to receive the necessary information, and his education and habits are commonly such as to render him unfit to judge even though he was fully informed. In the public deliberations, therefore, his voice is little heard and less regarded, except upon some particular occasions, when his clamour is animated, set on, and supported by his employers, not for his, but their own particular purposes.

His employers constitute the third order, that of those who live by profit. It is the stock that is employed for the sake of profit, which puts into motion the greater part of the useful labour of every society. The plans and projects of the employers of stock regulate and direct all the most important operations of labour, and profit is the end proposed by all those plans and projects. But the rate of profit does not, like rent and wages, rise with the prosperity and fall with the declension of the society. On the contrary, it is naturally low in rich and high in poor countries, and it is always highest in the countries which are going fastest to ruin. The interest of this third order, therefore, has not the same connexion with the general interest of the society as that of the other two. Merchants and master manufacturers are, in this order, the two classes of people who commonly employ the largest capitals, and who by their wealth draw to themselves the greater share of the public consideration. As during their whole lives they are engaged in plans and projects, they have frequently more acuteness of understanding than the greater part of country gentlemen. As their thoughts, however, are commonly exercised rather about the interest of their own particular branch of business, than about that of the society, their judgment, even when given with the greatest candour,—which it has not been upon every occasion,—is much more to be depended upon with regard to the former of those two objects than with regard to the latter. Their superiority over the country gentleman is, not so much in their knowledge of the public interest, as in their having a better knowledge of their own interest than he has of his. It is by this superior knowledge of their own interest that they have frequently imposed upon his generosity, and persuaded him to give up both his own interest and that of the public, from a very simple but honest conviction, that their interest, and not his, was the interest of the public. The interest of the dealers, however, in any particular branch of trade or manufactures, is always in some respects different from, and even opposite to, that of the public. To widen the market and to narrow the competition is always the interest of the dealers. To widen the market may frequently be agreeable enough to the interest of the public; but to narrow the competition must always be against it, and can serve only to enable the dealers, by raising their profits above what they naturally would be, to levy, for their own benefit, an absurd tax upon the rest of their fellow-citizens. The proposal of any new law or regulation of commerce which comes from this order, always ought to be listened to with great precaution, and ought never to be adopted till after having been long and carefully examined, not only with the most scrupulous, but with the most suspicious attention. It comes from an order of men, whose interest is never exactly the same with that of the public, who have generally an interest to deceive and even to oppress the public, and who accordingly have, upon many occasions, both deceived and oppressed it. . . .

OF THE NATURE, ACCUMULATION, AND EMPLOYMENT OF STOCK *

Of the Accumulation of Capital, or of Productive and Unproductive Labour

There is one sort of labour which adds to the value of the subject upon which it is bestowed: there is another which has no such effect. The former, as it produces a value, may be called productive; the latter, unproductive labour. Thus the labour of a manufacturer adds, generally, to the value of the materials which he works upon, that of his own maintenance, and of his master's profit. The labour of a menial servant, on the contrary, adds to the value of nothing. Though the manufacturer has his wages advanced to him by his master, he, in reality, costs him no expense, the value of those wages being generally restored, together with a profit, in the improved value of the subject upon which his labour is bestowed. But the maintenance of a menial servant never is restored. A man grows rich by employing a multitude of manufacturers: he grows poor by maintaining a multitude of menial servants. The labour of the latter, however, has its value, and deserves its reward as well as that of the former. But the labour of the manufacturer fixes and realizes itself in some particular subject or vendible commodity, which lasts for some time at least after that labour is past. It is, as it were, a certain quantity of labour stocked and stored up to be employed, if necessary, upon some other occasion. That subject, or what is the same thing, the price of that subject, can afterwards, if necessary, put into motion a quantity of labour equal to that which had originally produced it. The labour of the menial servant, on the contrary, does not fix or realize itself in any particular subject or vendible commodity. The services of the menial generally perish in the very instant of their

* From *The Wealth of Nations;* see credit note, page 122.

performance, and seldom leave any trace or value behind them, for which an equal quantity of service could afterwards be procured.

The labour of some of the most respectable orders in the society is, like that of menial servants, unproductive of any value, and does not fix or realize itself in any permanent subject, or vendible commodity, which endures after that labour is past, and for which an equal quantity of labour could afterwards be procured. The sovereign, for example, with all the officers both of justice and war who serve under him, the whole army and navy, are unproductive labourers. They are the servants of the public, and are maintained by a part of the annual produce of the industry of other people. Their service, how honourable, how useful, or how necessary soever, produces nothing for which an equal quantity of service can afterwards be procured. The protection, security, and defence of the commonwealth, the effect of their labour this year, will not purchase its protection, security, and defence for the year to come. In the same class must be ranked, some both of the gravest and most important, and some of the most frivolous professions: churchmen, lawyers, physicians, men of letters of all kinds; players, buffoons, musicians, opera-singers, opera-dancers, etc. The labour of the meanest of these has a certain value, regulated by the very same principles which regulate that of every other sort of labour; and that of the noblest and most useful produces nothing which could afterwards purchase or procure an equal quantity of labour. Like the declamation of the actor, the harangue of the orator, or the tune of the musician, the work of all of them perishes in the very instant of its production.

Both productive and unproductive labourers, and those who do not labour at all, are all equally maintained by the annual produce of the land and labour of the country. This produce, how great soever, can never be infinite, but must have certain limits. According, therefore, as a smaller or greater proportion of it is in any one year employed in maintaining unproductive hands, the more in the one case and the less in the other will remain for the productive, and the next year's produce will be greater or smaller accordingly; the whole annual produce, if we except the spontaneous productions of the earth, being the effect of productive labour.

Though the whole annual produce of the land and labour of every country is, no doubt, ultimately destined for supplying the consumption of its inhabitants, and for procuring a revenue to them, yet when it first comes either from the ground, or from the hands of the productive labourers, it naturally divides itself into two parts. One of them, and frequently the largest, is, in the first place, destined for replacing a capital, or for renewing the provisions, materials, and finished work, which had been withdrawn from a capital; the other for constituting a revenue either to the owner of this capital, as the profit of his stock; or to some other person, as the rent of his land. Thus, of the produce of land, one part replaces the capital of the farmer; the other pays his profit and the rent of the landlord; and thus constitutes a revenue both to the owner of this capital as the profits of his stock, and to some other person as the rent of his land. Of the produce of a great manufacture, in the same manner, one part, and that always the largest, replaces the capital of the undertaker of the work; the other pays his profit, and thus constitutes a revenue to the owner of this capital.

That part of the annual produce of the land and labour of any country which replaces a capital, never is immediately employed to maintain any but productive hands. It pays the wages of productive labour only. That which is immediately destined for constituting a revenue either as profit or as rent, may maintain indifferently either productive or unproductive hands.

Whatever part of his stock a man employs as a capital, he always expects it to be replaced to him with a profit. He employs it, therefore, in maintaining productive hands only; and after having served in the function of a capital to him, it constitutes a revenue to them. Whenever he employs any part of it in maintaining unproductive hands of any kind, that part is, from that moment, withdrawn from his capital, and placed in his stock reserved for immediate consumption.

Unproductive labourers, and those who do not labour at all, are all maintained by revenue; either, first, by that part of the annual produce which is originally destined for constituting a revenue to some particular persons, either as the rent of land or as the profits of stock; or, secondly, by that part which, though originally destined for replacing a capital and for maintaining productive labourers only, yet when it comes into their hands, whatever part of it is over and above their necessary subsistence, may be employed in maintaining indifferently either productive or unproductive hands. Thus, not only the great landlord or the rich merchant, but even the common workman, if his wages are considerable, may maintain a menial servant; or he may sometimes go to a play or a puppet-show, and so contribute his share towards maintaining one sett of unproductive labourers; or he may pay some taxes, and thus help to maintain another sett, more honourable and useful, indeed, but equally unproductive. No part of the annual produce, however, which had been originally destined to replace a capital, is ever directed towards maintaining unproductive hands, till after it has put into motion its full complement of productive labour, or all that it could put into motion in the way in which it was employed. The workman must have earned his wages by work done, before he can employ any part of them in this manner. That part, too, is generally but a small one. It is his spare revenue only, of which productive labourers have seldom a great deal. They generally have some, however, and in payment of taxes the greatness of their number may compensate, in some measure, the smallness of their contribution. The rent of land and the profits of stock are everywhere, therefore, the principal sources from which unproductive hands derive their subsistence. These are the two sorts of revenue of which the owners have generally most to spare. They might both maintain indifferently either productive or unproductive hands. They seem, however, to have some predilection for the latter. The expense of a great lord feeds generally more idle than industrious people. The rich merchant, though with his capital he maintains industrious people only, yet by his expense, that is, by the employment of his revenue, he feeds commonly the very same sort as the great lord.

The proportion, therefore, between the productive and unproductive hands, depends very much in every country upon the proportion between that part of the annual produce, which, as soon as it comes either from the ground or from the hands of the productive labourers, is destined for replacing a capital, and that which is destined for constituting a revenue, either as rent, or as profit. This proportion is very different in rich from what it is in poor countries. . . .

Parsimony, and not industry, is the immediate cause of the increase of capital. Industry, indeed, provides the subject which parsimony accumulates. But whatever industry might acquire, if parsimony did not save and store up, the capital would never be the greater.

Parsimony, by increasing the fund which is destined for the maintenance of productive hands, tends to increase the number of those hands whose labour adds to the value of the subject upon which it is bestowed. It tends therefore to increase the exchangeable value of the annual produce of the land and labour of the country. It puts into motion an additional quantity of industry, which gives an additional value to the annual produce.

What is annually saved is as regularly consumed as what is annually spent, and nearly in the same time too; but it is consumed by a different sett of people. That portion of his revenue which a rich man annually spends, is in most cases consumed by idle guests and menial servants, who leave nothing behind them in return for their consumption. That portion which he annually saves, as for the sake of the profit it is immediately employed as a capital, is consumed in the same manner, and nearly in the same time too, but by a different sett of people, by labourers, manufacturers and artificers, who reproduce with a profit the value of their annual consumption. His revenue, we shall suppose, is paid him in money. Had he spent the whole, the food, clothing, lodging, which the whole could have purchased, would have been distributed among the former sett of people. By saving a part of it, as that part is for the sake of the profit immediately employed as a capital either by himself or by some other person, the food, cloathing, and lodging, which may be purchased with it, are necessarily reserved for the latter. The consumption is the same, but the consumers are different. . . .

OF SYSTEMS OF POLITICAL ŒCONOMY *

Of Restraints upon the Importation from Foreign Countries of Such Goods as Can Be Produced at Home

By restraining, either by high duties, or by absolute prohibitions, the importation of such goods from foreign countries as can be produced at

* From *The Wealth of Nations;* see credit note, page 122.

home, the monopoly of the home market is more or less secured to the domestic industry employed in producing them. . . .

To give the monopoly of the home market to the produce of domestic industry, in any particular art or manufacture, is in some measure to direct private people in what manner they ought to employ their capitals, and must, in almost all cases, be either a useless or a hurtful regulation. If the produce of domestic can be brought there as cheap as that of foreign industry, the regulation is evidently useless. If it cannot, it must generally be hurtful. It is the maxim of every prudent master of a family, never to attempt to make at home what it will cost him more to make than to buy. The taylor does not attempt to make his own shoes, but buys them of the shoemaker. The shoemaker does not attempt to make his own cloaths, but employs a taylor. The farmer attempts to make neither the one nor the other, but employs those different artificers. All of them find it for their interest to employ their whole industry in a way in which they have some advantage over their neighbours, and to purchase with a part of its produce, or, what is the same thing, with the price of a part of it, whatever else they have occasion for.

What is prudence in the conduct of every private family, can scarce be folly in that of a great kingdom. If a foreign country can supply us with a commodity cheaper than we ourselves can make it, better buy it of them with some part of the produce of our own industry, employed in a way in which we have some advantage. The general industry of the country, being always in proportion to the capital which employs it, will not thereby be diminished, no more than that of the above-mentioned artificers; but only left to find out the way in which it can be employed with the greatest advantage. It is certainly not employed to the greatest advantage when it is thus directed towards an object which it can buy cheaper than it can make. The value of its annual produce is certainly more or less diminished, when it is thus turned away from producing commodities evidently of more value than the commodity which it is directed to produce. According to the supposition, that commodity could be purchased from foreign countries cheaper than it can be made at home. It could, therefore, have been purchased with a part only of the commodities, or, what is the same thing, with a part only of the price of the commodities, which the industry employed by an equal capital would have produced at home had it been left to follow its natural course. The industry of the country, therefore, is thus turned away from a more to a less advantageous employment, and the exchangeable value of its annual produce, instead of being increased, according to the intention of the lawgiver, must necessarily be diminished by every such regulation.

By means of such regulations, indeed, a particular manufacture may sometimes be acquired sooner than it could have been otherwise, and after a certain time may be made at home as cheap or cheaper than in the foreign country. But though the industry of the society may be thus carried with advantage into a particular channel sooner than it could have been otherwise, it will by no means follow that the sum total, either of its industry, or of its revenue, can ever be augmented by any such regulation. The industry of the society can augment only in proportion as its capital augments, and its capital can augment only in proportion to what can be gradually saved out of its revenue. But the immediate effect of every such regulation is to diminish its revenue, and what diminishes its revenue is certainly not very likely to augment its capital faster than it would have augmented of its own accord, had both their capital and their industry been left to find out their natural employments. . . .

The natural advantages which one country has over another in producing particular commodities are sometimes so great, that it is acknowledged by all the world to be in vain to struggle with them. By means of glasses, hotbeds, and hot-walls, very good grapes can be raised in Scotland, and very good wine too can be made of them at about thirty times the expense for which at least equally good can be brought from foreign countries. Would it be a reasonable law to prohibit the importation of all foreign wines merely to encourage the making of claret and burgundy in Scotland? But if there would be a manifest absurdity in turning towards any employment thirty times more of the capital and industry of the country than would be necessary to purchase from foreign countries an equal quantity of the commodities wanted, there must be an absurdity, though not altogether so glaring, yet exactly of the same kind, in turning towards any such employment a thirtieth, or even a three hundredth part more of either. Whether the advantages which one country has over another be natural or acquired, is in this respect of no consequence. As long as the one country has those advantages, and the other wants them, it will always be more advantageous for the latter rather to buy of the former than to make. It is an acquired advantage only which one artificer has over his neighbour who exercises another trade; and yet they both find it more advantageous to buy of another than to make what does not belong to their particular trades. . . .

There seem, however, to be two cases in which it will generally be advantageous to lay some burden upon foreign, for the encouragement of domestic industry.

The first is, when some particular sort of industry is necessary for the defence of the country. The defence of Great Britain, for example, depends very much upon the number of its sailors and shipping. The act of navigation, therefore, very properly endeavours to give the sailors and shipping of Great Britain the monopoly of the trade of their own country, in some cases, by absolute prohibitions, and in others by heavy burdens upon the shipping of foreign countries. . . .

The second case in which it will generally be advantageous to lay some burden upon foreign for the encouragement of domestic industry, is when some tax is imposed at home upon the produce of the latter. In this case, it seems reasonable that an equal tax should be imposed upon the like produce of the former. This would not give the monopoly of the home market to domestic industry, nor turn towards a particular employment a greater share of the stock and labour of the country than what would naturally go to it. It would only hinder any part of what would naturally go to it from being turned away by the tax into a less natural direction, and would leave the competition between foreign and domestic industry, after the tax, as nearly as possible upon the same footing as before it. . . .

Conclusion of the Mercantile System

. . . Consumption is the sole end and purpose of all production; and the interest of the producer ought to be attended to, only so far as it may be necessary for promoting that of the consumer. The maxim is so perfectly self-evident, that it would be absurd to attempt to prove it. But in the mercantile system, the interest of the consumer is almost constantly sacrificed to that of the producer; and it seems to consider production, and not consumption, as the ultimate end and object of all industry and commerce. . . .

It cannot be very difficult to determine who have been the contrivers of this whole mercantile system; not the consumers, we may believe, whose interest has been entirely neglected, but the producers, whose interest has been so carefully attended to; and among this latter class our merchants and manufacturers have been by far the principal architects. . . .

Of the Agricultural Systems, or of Those Systems of Political Œconomy Which Represent the Produce of Land as Either the Sole or the Principal Source of the Revenue and Wealth of Every Country

. . . Every system which endeavours, either, by extraordinary encouragements, to draw towards a particular species of industry a greater share of the capital of the society than what would naturally go to it; or, by extraordinary restraints, to force from a particular species of industry some share of the capital which would otherwise be employed in it, is in reality subversive of the great purpose which it means to promote. It retards, instead of accelerating, the progress of the society towards real wealth and greatness; and diminishes, instead of increasing, the real value of the annual produce of its land and labour.

All systems either of preference or of restraint, therefore, being thus completely taken away, the obvious and simple system of natural liberty establishes itself of its own accord. Every man, as long as he does not violate the laws of justice, is left perfectly free to pursue his own interest his own way, and to bring both his industry and capital into competition with those of any other man, or order of men. The sovereign is completely discharged from a duty, in the attempting to perform which he must always be exposed to innumerable delusions, and for the proper performance of which no human wisdom or knowledge could ever be sufficient: the duty of superintending the industry of private people, and of directing it towards the employments most suitable to the interest of the society. According to the system of natural liberty, the sovereign has only three duties to attend to; three duties of great importance, indeed, but plain and intelligible to common understandings: first, the duty of protecting the society from the violence and invasion of other independent societies; secondly, the duty of protecting, as far as possible, every member of the society from the injustice or oppression of every other member of it, or the duty of establishing an exact administration of justice; and thirdly, the duty of erecting and maintaining certain public works and certain public institutions, which it can never be for the interest of any individual, or small number of individuals, to erect and maintain, because the profit could never repay the expense to any individual or small number of individuals, though it may frequently do much more than repay it to a great society. . . .

OF THE REVENUE OF THE SOVEREIGN OR COMMONWEALTH *

Of the Expenses of the Sovereign or Commonwealth—Institutions for the Education of Youth

. . . In the progress of the division of labour, the employment of the far greater part of those who live by labour, that is, of the great body of the people, comes to be confined to a few very simple operations; frequently to one or two. But the understandings of the greater part of men are necessarily formed by their ordinary employments. The man whose whole life is spent in performing a few simple operations, of which the effects too are, perhaps, always the same, or very nearly the same, has no occasion to exert his understanding, or to exercise his invention in finding out expedients for removing difficulties which never occur. He naturally loses, therefore, the habit of such exertion, and generally becomes as stupid and ignorant as it is possible for a human creature to become. The torpor of his mind renders him, not only incapable of relishing or bearing a part in any rational conversation, but of conceiving any generous, noble, or tender sentiment, and consequently of forming any just judgment concerning many even of the ordinary duties of private life. Of the great and extensive interests of his country he is altogether incapable of judging; and, unless very particular pains have been taken to render him otherwise, he is equally incapable of defending his country in war. The uniformity of his stationary life naturally corrupts the courage of his mind, and makes him regard with abhorrence the irregular, uncertain, and adventurous life of a soldier. It corrupts even the activity of his body, and renders him incapable of exerting his strength and vigour and perseverance in any other employment than that to which he has been bred. His dexterity at his own particular trade seems, in this manner, to be acquired at the expense of his intellectual, social, and martial virtues. But in every improved and civilized society this is the state into which the labouring poor, that

* From *The Wealth of Nations;* see credit note, page 122.

is, the great body of the people, must necessarily fall, unless government takes some pains to prevent it. . . .

Of the Sources of the General or Public Revenue of the Society—Of Taxes

. . . It is necessary to premise the four following maxims with regard to taxes in general.

I. The subjects of every state ought to contribute towards the support of the government, as nearly as possible, in proportion to their respective abilities; that is, in proportion to the revenue which they respectively enjoy under the protection of the state. . . . In the observation or neglect of this maxim consists, what is called, the equality or inequality of taxation. . . .

II. The tax which each individual is bound to pay, ought to be certain, and not arbitrary. The time of payment, the manner of payment, the quantity to be paid, ought all to be clear and plain to the contributor, and to every other person. . . . The certainty of what each individual ought to pay is, in taxation, a matter of so great importance, that a very considerable degree of inequality, it appears, I believe, from the experience of all nations, is not near so great an evil as a very small degree of uncertainty.

III. Every tax ought to be levied at the time, or in the manner, in which it is most likely to be convenient for the contributor to pay it. A tax upon the rent of land or of houses, payable at the same term at which such rents are usually paid, is levied at the time when it is most likely to be convenient for the contributor to pay; or, when he is most likely to have wherewithal to pay. Taxes upon such consumable goods as are articles of luxury are all finally paid by the consumer, and generally in a manner that is very convenient for him. He pays them by little and little, as he has occasion to buy the goods. As he is at liberty too, either to buy, or not to buy, as he pleases, it must be his own fault if he ever suffers any considerable inconveniency from such taxes.

IV. Every tax ought to be so contrived as both to take out and to keep out of the pockets of the people as little as possible over and above what it brings into the public treasury of the state.

JEAN BAPTISTE SAY

(1767–1832)

Say was a member of a Protestant family which fled from France at the time of the revocation of the Edict of Nantes and returned to France in the middle of the eighteenth century. During the French Revolution he remained unobtrusive, and after a brief period of favor during Napoleon's ascendancy, his career was blocked because of his extremely liberal position on economic questions. The publication of his *Traité d'Économie Politique* (*A Treatise on Political Economy*) in 1803 hastened his disgrace. After Waterloo he inaugurated a free course of lectures in economics in Paris, and later he became a professor at the Conservatoire des Arts et Métiers.

His major work is the *Treatise on Political Economy,* which was the first popular book on economics published on the European continent. Both the terminology which he developed and his division of economic activity into the production, distribution, and consumption of wealth have become classic. Although Say has been best known as the man who systematized Adam Smith's concepts and introduced them to French readers, he was more than a mere popularizer. In fact, he became the founder of a school of his own, the liberal-optimistic school which dominated economic thinking in France for three-quarters of a century thereafter.

Say regarded economics as a natural science and assumed that wealth is created, distributed, and consumed in accordance with the laws of nature and without the necessity for any government interference. His famous Law of Markets (*loi des débouchés*), the argument of which is given in the following selection, was the extreme of naïve optimism. He claimed that overproduction and market gluts were impossible, since every supply creates its own demand.

Say's analysis of value marks a clear break with the classical school. As a result of his writings the labor theory of value ceased to exert any influence among French economists. Following Galiani and Condillac, he made value dependent upon scarcity and utility. According to Say, the cost of production influenced price by causing changes in supply, while consumer estimates of utility determined the level of demand. The value of the productive factors, land, labor, and capital, derived from the value of their products. Profit was the reward for the productive services of the entrepreneur in combining the factors of production.

In much of his work, Say was apparently groping toward an equilibrium analysis of the economic process along the lines of the mathematical school that was to follow him. He regarded economics as a positive science yielding no ethical evaluations or imperative directions to legislators. He went far beyond Adam Smith in his aversion to government control, claiming that it was objectionable even when it was indispensable.

The various propositions concerning the impossibility of general overproduction that came to be called Say's Law of Markets dominated nineteenth-century economic thought, appearing emphatically in the writings of men like James Mill and Ricardo. As a model of a barter economy, given the assumptions of freely competitive conditions (that is, perfect knowledge and perfect mobility in the use of resources), the theory was a useful simplifying abstraction which focused attention on the function of prices in the allocation of resources. The limiting assumptions of the model were ignored, however, and Say's Law was interpreted literally as a description of the actual operation of the economy. Consequently, business cycles came to be regarded as short-run phenomena, deviations, so to speak, from the long-run tendencies toward general stability.

Say's Law of Markets did not go unchallenged by dissenters like Malthus and Sismondi. But such heterodoxy had little influence on the body of received doctrine.

It was not until 1936, more than one hundred years later, that the Law of Markets was given its final quietus by John Maynard Keynes in his *General Theory of Employment, Interest and Money.*

OF THE VENT OR DEMAND FOR PRODUCTS *

It is common to hear adventures in the different channels of industry assert, that their difficulty lies not in the production, but in the disposal of commodities; that produce would always be abundant, if there were but a ready demand, or vent. When the vent for their commodities is slow, difficult, and productive of little advantage, they pronounce money to be scarce; the grand object of their desire is, a consumption brisk enough to quicken sales and keep up prices. But ask them what peculiar causes and circumstances facilitate the demand for their products, and you will soon perceive that most of them have extremely vague notions of these matters; that their observation of facts is imperfect, that their explanation still more so; that they treat doubtful points as matter of certainty, often pray for what is directly opposite to their interests and importunately solicit from authority a protection of the most mischievous tendency.

To enable us to form clear and correct practical notions in regard to the vents for the products of industry, we must carefully analyse the best established and most certain facts, and apply to them the inferences we have already deduced from a similar way of proceeding; and thus perhaps we may arrive at new and important truths, that may serve to enlighten the views of the agents of industry, and to give confidence to the measures of governments anxious to afford them encouragement.

A man, who applies his labour to the investing of objects with value by the creation of utility of some sort, cannot expect such a value to be appreciated and paid for, unless where other men have the means of purchasing it. Now, of what do those means consist? Of other values, of other products, likewise the fruits of industry, capital, and land. Which leads us to a conclusion, that may at first sight appear paradoxical; viz. that it is production which opens a demand for products.

Should a tradesman say, "I do not want other products for my woollens, I want money," there could be little difficulty in convincing him, that his customers cannot pay him in money, without having first procured it by the sale of some other commodities of their own. "Yonder farmer," he may be told, "will buy your woollens, if his crops be good, and will buy more or less according to their abundance or scantiness; he can buy none at all, if his crops fail altogether. Neither can you buy his wool or his corn yourself, unless you contrive to get woollens or some other article to buy withal. You say, you only want money; I say, you want other commodities, and not money. For what, in point of fact, do you want the money? Is it not for the purchase of raw materials or stock for your trade, or victuals

* From *A Treatise on Political Economy,* translated by C. R. Prinsep (Boston, 1824).

for your support? [1] Wherefore, it is products that you want, and not money. The silver coin you will have received on the sale of your own products, and given in the purchase of those of other people, will the next moment execute the same office between other contracting parties, and so from one to another to infinity; just as a public vehicle successively transports objects one after another. If you cannot find a ready sale for your commodity, will you say, it is merely for want of a vehicle to transport it? For after all, money is but the agent of the transfer of values. Its whole utility has consisted in conveying to your hands the value of the commodities, which your customer has sold, for the purpose of buying again from you; and the very next purchase you make, it will again convey to a third person the value of the products you may have sold to others. So that you will have bought, and every body must buy, the objects of want or desire, each with the value of his respective products transformed into money for the moment only. Otherwise, how could it be possible that there should now be bought and sold in France five or six times as many commodities, as in the miserable reign of Charles VI.? Is it not obvious, that five or six times as many commodities must have been produced, and that they must have served to purchase one or the other?"

Thus, to say that sales are dull, owing to the scarcity of money, is to mistake the means for the cause; an error that proceeds from the circumstance, that almost all produce is in the first instance exchanged for money, before it is ultimately converted into other produce; and the commodity, which recurs so repeatedly in use, appears to vulgar apprehension the most important of commodities, and the end and object of all transactions, whereas it is only the medium. Sales cannot be said to be dull because money is scarce, but because other products are so. There is always money enough to conduct the circulation and mutual interchange of other values, when those values really exist. Should the increase of traffic require more money to facilitate it, the want is easily supplied, and is a strong indication of prosperity—a proof that a great abundance of values has been created, which it is wished to exchange for other values. In such cases, merchants know well enough how to find substitutes for the product serving as the medium of exchange or money; [2] and money itself soon pours in, for this reason, that all produce naturally gravitates to that place where it is most in demand. It is a good sign when the business is too great for the money; just in the same way as it is a good sign when the goods are too plentiful for the warehouses.

When a superabundant article can find no vent, the scarcity of money has so little to do with the obstruction of its sale, that the sellers would gladly

1 Even when money is obtained with a view to hoard or bury it, the ultimate object is always to employ it in a purchase of some kind. The heir of the lucky finder uses it in that way, if the miser do not; for money, as money, has no other use than to buy with.

2 By bills at sight or after date, bank-notes, running-credits, write-offs, &c. as at London and Amsterdam.

receive its value in goods for their own consumption at the current price of the day: they would not ask for money, or have any occasion for that product, since the only use they could make of it would be to convert it forthwith into articles of their own consumption.[3]

This observation is applicable to all cases, where there is a supply of commodities or of services in the market. They will universally find the most extensive demand in those places, where the most values are produced; because in no other places are the sole means of purchase created, *i.e.* values. Money performs but a momentary function in this double exchange; and when the transaction is finally closed, it will always be found, that one kind of produce has been exchanged for another.

It is worth while to remark, that a product is no sooner created, than it, from that instant, affords a market for other products to the full extent of its own value. When the producer has put the finishing hand to his product, he is most anxious to sell it immediately, lest its value should vanish in his hands. Nor is he less anxious to dispose of the money he may get for it; for the value of money is also perishable. But the only way of getting rid of money is in the purchase of some product or other. Thus, the mere circumstance of the creation of one product immediately opens a vent for other products.

For this reason, a good harvest is favourable, not only to the agriculturist, but likewise to the dealers in all commodities generally. The greater the crop, the larger are the purchases of the growers. A bad harvest, on the contrary, hurts the sale of commodities at large. And so it is also with the products of manufacture and commerce. The success of one branch of commerce supplies more ample means of purchase, and consequently opens a vent for the products of all the other branches; on the other hand, the stagnation of one channel of manufacture, or of commerce, is felt in all the rest.

But it may be asked, if this be so, how does it happen, that there is at times so great a glut of commodities in the market, and so much difficulty in finding a vent for them? Why cannot one of these super-abundant commodities be exchanged for another? I answer, that the glut of a particular commodity arises from its having outrun the total demand for it in one of two ways; either because it has been produced in excessive abundance, or because the produce of other commodities has fallen short.

It is because the production of some commodities has declined, that other commodities are superabundant. To use a more hackneyed phrase, people have bought less, because they have made less profit; and they have

[3] I speak here of their aggregate consumption, whether unproductive and designed to satisfy the personal wants of themselves and their families, or expended in the sustenance of reproductive industry. The woollen or cotton manufacturer operates a two-fold consumption of wool and cotton, 1. For his personal wear. 2. For the supply of his manufacture; but, be the purpose of his consumption what it may, whether personal gratification or reproduction, he must needs buy what he consumes with what he produces.

made less profit for one of two causes; either they have found difficulties in the employment of their productive means, or these means have themselves been deficient.

It is observable, moreover, that precisely at the same time that one commodity makes a loss, another commodity is making excessive profit. And, since such profits must operate as a powerful stimulus to the cultivation of that particular kind of produce, there must needs be some violent means, or some extraordinary cause, a political or natural convulsion, or the avarice or ignorance of authority, to perpetuate this scarcity on the one hand, and consequent glut on the other. No sooner is the cause of this political disease removed, than the means of production feel a natural impulse towards the vacant channels, the replenishment of which restores activity to all the others. One kind of production would seldom outstrip the rest, and its products be disproportionately cheapened, were production left entirely to itself.

Should a producer imagine, that many other classes, yielding no material products, are his customers and consumers equally with the classes that raise themselves a product of their own; as, for example, public functionaries, physicians, lawyers, churchmen, &c., and thence infer, that there is a class of demand other than that of the actual producers, he would but expose the shallowness and superficiality of his ideas. A priest goes to a shop to buy a gown or a surplice; he takes the value, that is to make the purchase, in the form of money. Whence had he that money? From some tax-gatherer, who has taken it from a tax-payer. But whence did this latter derive it? From the value he has himself produced. This value, first produced by the tax-payer, and afterwards turned into money, and given to the priest for his salary, has enabled him to make the purchase. The priest stands in the place of the producer, who might himself have laid the value of his product on his own account, in the purchase, perhaps not of a gown or surplice, but of some other more serviceable product. The consumption of the particular product, the gown or surplice, has but supplanted that of some other product. It is quite impossible that the purchase of one product can be effected, otherwise than by the value of another.

From this important truth may be deduced the following important conclusions:—

1. That, in every community, the more numerous are the producers, and the more various their productions, the more prompt, numerous, and extensive are the vents for those productions; and, by a natural consequence, the more profitable are they to the producers; for price rises with the demand. But this advantage is to be derived from real production alone, and not from a forced circulation of products; for a value once created is not augmented in its passage from one hand to another, nor by being seized and expended by the government, instead of by an individual. The man, that lives upon the productions of other people, origi-

nates no demand for those productions; he merely puts himself in the place of the producer, to the great injury of production, as we shall presently see.

2. That each individual is interested in the general prosperity of all, and that the success of one branch of industry promotes that of all the others. In fact, whatever profession or line of business a man may devote himself to, he is the better paid and the more readily finds employment, in proportion as he sees others thriving equally around him. A man of talent, that scarcely vegetates in a retrograde state of society, would find a thousand ways of turning his faculties to account in a thriving community that could afford to employ and reward his ability. A merchant established in a rich and populous town, sells to a much larger amount than one who sets up in a poor district, with a population sunk in indolence and apathy. What could an active manufacturer, or an intelligent merchant, do in a small deserted and semi-barbarous town in a remote corner of Poland or Westphalia? Though in no fear of a competitor, he could sell but little, because little was produced; whilst at Paris, Amsterdam, or London, in spite of the competition of a hundred dealers in his own line, he might do business on the largest scale. The reason is obvious: he is surrounded with people who produce largely in an infinity of ways, and who make purchases, each with his respective products, that is to say, with the money arising from the sale of what he may have produced.

This is the true source of the gains made by the towns' people out of the country people, and again by the latter out of the former; both of them have wherewith to buy more largely, the more amply they themselves produce. A city, standing in the centre of a rich surrounding country, feels no want of rich and numerous customers; and, on the other side, the vicinity of an opulent city gives additional value to the produce of the country. The division of nations into agricultural, manufacturing, and commercial, is idle enough. For the success of a people in agriculture is a stimulus to its manufacturing and commercial prosperity: and the flourishing condition of its manufacture and commerce reflects a benefit upon its agriculture also.

The position of a nation, in respect of its neighbours, is analogous to the relation of one of its provinces to the others, or of the country to the town: it has an interest in their prosperity, being sure to profit by their opulence. The government of the United States, therefore, acted most wisely, in their attempt, about the year 1802, to civilize their savage neighbours, the Creek Indians. The design was, to introduce habits of industry amongst them, and make them producers, capable of carrying on a barter trade with the States of the Union; for there is nothing to be got by dealing with a people that have nothing to pay. It is useful and honourable to mankind, that one nation among so many should conduct itself uniformly upon liberal principles. The brilliant results of this enlightened policy will demonstrate, that the systems and theories really destructive and fallacious are the exclusive and jealous maxims acted upon by the old

European governments, and by them most impudently styled *practical truths,* for no other reason, as it would seem, than because they have the misfortune to put them in practice. The United States will have the honour of proving experimentally, that true policy goes hand in hand with moderation and humanity.

3. From this fruitful principle, we may draw this further conclusion, that it is no injury to the internal or national industry and production to buy and import commodities from abroad; for nothing can be bought from strangers, except with native products, which find a vent in this external traffic. Should it be objected, that this foreign produce may have been bought with specie, I answer, specie is not always a native product, but must have been bought itself with the products of native industry; so that, whether the foreign articles be paid for in specie or in home produce, the vent for national industry is the same in both cases.

4. The same principle leads to the conclusion, that the encouragement of mere consumption is no benefit to commerce; for the difficulty lies in supplying the means, not in stimulating the desire of consumption; and we have seen, that production alone, furnishes those means. Thus, it is the aim of good government to stimulate production, of bad government to encourage consumption.

For the same reason that the creation of a new product is the opening of a new market for other products, the consumption or destruction of a product is the stoppage of a vent for them. This is no evil, where the end of the product has been answered by its destruction, which end is the satisfying of some human want, or the creation of some new product designed for such a satisfaction. Indeed, if the nation be in a thriving condition, the gross national reproduction exceeds the gross consumption. The consumed products have fulfilled their office, as it is natural and fitting they should; the consumption, however, has opened no new market, but just the reverse.

Having once arrived at the clear conviction, that the general demand for produce is brisk in proportion to the activity of production, we need not trouble ourselves much to enquire towards what channel of industry production may be most advantageously directed. The products created give rise to various degrees of demand, according to the wants, the manners, the comparative capital, industry, and natural resources of each country; the articles most in request, owing to the competition of buyers, yield the best interest of money to the capitalist, the largest profits to the adventurer, and the best wages to the labourer; and the agency of their respective services is naturally attracted by these advantages towards those particular channels.

In a community, city, province, or nation, that produces abundantly, and adds every moment to the sum of its products, almost all the branches of commerce, manufacture, and generally of industry, yield handsome profits, because the demand is great, and because there is always a large quantity of produce in the market, ready to bid for new productive services. And, *vice versa,* wherever, by reason of the blunders of the nation or its government, production is stationary, or does not keep pace with consumption, the demand gradually declines, the value of the products is less than the charges of their production; no productive exertion is properly rewarded; profits and wages decrease; the employment of capital becomes less advantageous and more hazardous; it is consumed piecemeal, not through extravagance, but through necessity, and because the sources of profit are dried up. The labouring classes experience a want of work; families before in tolerable circumstances are more cramped and confined; and those before in difficulties, are left altogether destitute. Depopulation, misery, and returning barbarism, occupy the place of abundance and happiness.

Such are the concomitants of declining production, which are only to be remedied by frugality, intelligence, activity, and freedom.

JEREMY BENTHAM

(1748–1832)

Although Bentham's direct contribution to economic doctrine is limited mainly to his *Defence of Usury* (1787), which is a minor classic in economics, he exercised also a great deal of influence on the development of economic theory through his formulation of a concept of human nature to which many nineteenth-century economists subscribed.

Bentham was born in London in 1748. His father, a lawyer, sent the boy to Oxford, and later to Lincoln's Inn to study law. However, Bentham was by nature a scholar, with little taste for law practice. His father wisely decided to finance a scholarly, cloistered environment for him, and Bentham devoted his life to study and writing. His life spanned the entire era of classical political economy. His first book, the *Fragment on Government* (1776), appeared in the same year as *The Wealth of Nations,* and one of his last books was edited by John Stuart Mill.

Most of Bentham's writings are concerned one way or another with the formulation and application of a calculus of behavior based on the principle of utility. Bentham's "felicific calculus"—an apparatus which could measure the precise pain-pleasure relationship resulting from any human act—was intended to provide for social science what Newton's law of gravitation provided for the physical sciences. Bentham argued that pain and pleasure, the two forces which control human behavior, could be measured by taking into account the four dimensions that affect them: (1) intensity, (2) duration, (3) certainty, (4) propinquity, or nearness. Bentham believed that upon these were based the actual calculations made by individuals in the process of acting. The felicific calculus, however, is more than a picture of the decisions that enter into human conduct. It is also a criterion of right and wrong. Those acts which contribute to the "greatest happiness of the greatest number" are right, for they ensure maximum happiness for the entire community. Acts which diminish this maximized happiness are wrong.

Bentham's analysis is made in terms of small increments of pain and pleasure and lacks only the concept of a margin to constitute the theory of utility as it is found in Jevons. Bentham faced all the difficulties that have continued to plague utility theory since his time, such as the measurability of intensities of feeling and the comparability of feelings among individuals. He never arrived at any definite answers to these questions, and contradictory views can be found in his writings.

Bentham did not receive recognition until he was fairly advanced in age. James Mill was primarily responsible for acquainting economists and social thinkers of the period with Bentham's views. Eventually Bentham and Mill joined forces and formed a group of writers and thinkers dedicated to the principle of utilitarianism and actively devoted to social reform. The principle of utility was applied by Bentham and his disciples to the discussion of all sorts of problems in constitutional and criminal law, education, marriage, the relationship between church and state, and other aspects of political science.

The philosophy of hedonism, with its view of the rational and passive character of human nature and its stress on the principle of self-interest, had undeniable influence on economic thinking. John Stuart Mill, Jevons, and Edgeworth were self-declared Benthamites, and utilitarian views appear in most of the disciples of Ricardo. Strangely enough, however, Ricardo himself, though he was a friend of James Mill, was not a Benthamite and made no use of the utility calculus. In terms of the development of classical political economy there was a lag in the influence of Bentham's views.

In the following selection from Bentham's classic *An Introduction to the Principles of Morals and Legislation* (1789), the author states his hedonistic philosophy in some detail.

OF THE PRINCIPLE OF UTILITY *

Nature has placed mankind under the governance of two sovereign masters, *pain* and *pleasure*. It is for them alone to point out what we ought to do, as well as to determine what we shall do. On the one hand the standard of right and wrong, on the other the chain of causes and effects, are fastened to their throne. They govern us in all we do, in all we say, in all we think: every effort we can make to throw off our subjection, will serve but to demonstrate and confirm it. In words a man may pretend to abjure their empire: but in reality he will remain subject to it all the while. The *principle of utility* recognises this subjection, and assumes it for the foundation of that system, the object of which is to rear the fabric of felicity by the hands of reason and of law. Systems which attempt to question it, deal in sounds instead of sense, in caprice instead of reason, in darkness instead of light.

But enough of metaphor and declamation: it is not by such means that moral science is to be improved.

The principle of utility is the foundation of the present work: it will be proper therefore at the outset to give an explicit and determinate account of what is meant by it. By the principle of utility is meant that principle which approves or disapproves of every action whatsoever, according to the tendency which it appears to have to augment or diminish the happiness of the party whose interest is in question: or, what is the same thing in other words, to promote or to oppose that happiness. I say of every action whatsoever; and therefore not only of every action of a private individual, but of every measure of government.

By utility is meant that property in any object, whereby it tends to produce benefit, advantage, pleasure, good, or happiness (all this in the present case comes to the same thing), or (what comes again to the same thing) to prevent the happening of mischief, pain, evil, or unhappiness to the party whose interest is considered: if that party be the community in general, then the happiness of the community: if a particular individual, then the happiness of that individual.

The interest of the community is one of the most general expressions that can occur in the phraseology of morals: no wonder that the meaning of it is often lost. When it has a meaning, it is this. The community is a fictitious *body*, composed of the individual persons who are considered as constituting as it were its *members*. The interest of the community then is, what?—the sum of the interests of the several members who compose it.

It is in vain to talk of the interest of the community, without understanding what is the interest of the individual. A thing is said to promote the interest, or to be *for* the interest, of an individual, when it tends to add to the sum total of his pleasures: or, what comes to the same thing, to diminish the sum total of his pains.

* From *An Introduction to the Principles of Morals and Legislation,* in *The Works of Jeremy Bentham,* edited bv Sir John Bowring (Edinburgh, 1843).

An action then may be said to be conformable to the principle of utility, or, for shortness sake, to utility (meaning with respect to the community at large), when the tendency it has to augment the happiness of the community is greater than any it has to diminish it.

A measure of government (which is but a particular kind of action, performed by a particular person or persons) may be said to be conformable to or dictated by the principle of utility, when in like manner the tendency which it has to augment the happiness of the community is greater than any which it has to diminish it.

When an action, or in particular a measure of government, is supposed by a man to be conformable to the principle of utility, it may be convenient, for the purposes of discourse, to imagine a kind of law or dictate, called a law or dictate of utility: and to speak of the action in question, as being conformable to such law or dictate.

A man may be said to be a partizan of the principle of utility, when the approbation or disapprobation he annexes to any action, or to any measure, is determined, by and proportioned to the tendency which he conceives it to have to augment or to diminish the happiness of the community: or in other words, to its conformity or unconformity to the laws or dictates of utility.

Of an action that is conformable to the principle of utility, one may always say either that it is one that ought to be done, or at least that it is not one that ought not to be done. One may say also, that it is right it should be done; at least that it is not wrong it should be done: that it is a right action; at least that it is not a wrong action. When thus interpreted, the words *ought,* and *right* and *wrong,* and others of that stamp, have a meaning: when otherwise, they have none.

Has the rectitude of this principle been ever formally contested? It should seem that it had, by those who have not known what they have been meaning. Is it susceptible of any direct proof? It should seem not: for that which is used to prove every thing else, cannot itself be proved: a chain of proofs must have their commencement somewhere. To give such proof is as impossible as it is needless.

Not that there is or ever has been that human creature breathing, however stupid or perverse, who has not on many, perhaps on most occasions of his life, deferred to it. By the natural constitution of the human frame, on most occasions of their lives men in general embrace this principle, without thinking of it: if not for the ordering of their own actions, yet for the trying of their own actions, as well as of those of other men. There have been, at the same time, not many, perhaps, even of the most intelligent, who have been disposed to embrace it purely and without reserve. There are even few who have not taken some occasion or other to quarrel with it, either on account of their not understanding always how to apply it, or on account of some prejudice or other which they were afraid to examine into, or could not bear to part with. For such is the stuff that man is made of: in principle and in practice, in a right track and in a wrong one, the rarest of all human qualities is consistency.

When a man attempts to combat the principle of utility, it is with reasons drawn, without his being aware of it, from that very principle itself. His arguments, if they prove any thing, prove not that the principle is *wrong*, but that, according to the applications he supposes to be made of it, it is *misapplied*. . . .

Among principles adverse to that of utility, that which at this day seems to have most influence in matters of government, is what may be called the principle of sympathy and antipathy. By the principle of sympathy and antipathy, I mean that principle which approves or disapproves of certain actions, not on account of their tending to augment the happiness, nor yet on account of their tending to diminish the happiness of the party whose interest is in question, but merely because a man finds himself disposed to approve or disapprove of them: holding up that approbation or disapprobation as a sufficient reason for itself, and disclaiming the necessity of looking out for any extrinsic ground. Thus far in the general department of morals: and in the particular department of politics, measuring out the quantum (as well as determining the ground) of punishment, by the degree of the disapprobation.

It is manifest, that this is rather a principle in name than in reality: it is not a positive principle of itself, so much as a term employed to signify the negation of all principle. What one expects to find in a principle is something that points out some external consideration, as a means of warranting and guiding the internal sentiments of approbation and disapprobation: this expectation is but ill fulfilled by a proposition, which does neither more nor less than hold up each of those sentiments as a ground and standard for itself. . . .

The various systems that have been formed concerning the standard of right and wrong, may all be reduced to the principle of sympathy and antipathy. One account may serve for all of them. They consist all of them in so many contrivances for avoiding the obligation of appealing to any external standard, and for prevailing upon the reader to accept of the author's sentiment or opinion as a reason, and that a sufficient one, for itself. The phrases different, but the principle the same.[1] . . .

1 . . . These principles, if such they can be called, it is more frequent to see applied to morals than to politics: but their influence extends itself to both. In politics, as well as morals, a man will be at least equally glad of a pretence for deciding any question in the manner that best pleases him, without the trouble of inquiry. If a man is an infallible judge of what is right and wrong in the actions of private individuals, why not in the measures to be observed by public men in the direction of those actions? Accordingly (not to mention other chimeras) I have more than once known the pretended law of nature set up in legislative debates, in opposition to arguments derived from the principle of utility.

"But is it never, then, from any other considerations than those of utility, that we derive our notions of right and wrong?" I do not know: I do not care. Whether a moral sentiment can be originally conceived from any other source than a view of utility, is one question: whether upon examination and reflection it can, in point of fact, be actually persisted in and justified on any other ground, by a person reflecting within himself, is another: whether in point of right it can properly be justified on any other ground, by

OBJECTIONS TO THE PRINCIPLE OF UTILITY ANSWERED [2]

Trifling scruples and trifling verbal difficulties may be raised in opposition to the principle of utility, but no real and distinct objection can be opposed to it. Indeed, how can it be combated, if not by reasons drawn from the principle itself? . . .

Evil may be done, whilst it is believed that the *principle of utility* is followed. A feeble and limited mind may deceive itself, by considering only a part of the good and evil. A man under the influence of passion may deceive himself, by setting an extreme value upon one advantage which hides from him the inconveniences attending upon it. What constitutes a wicked man, is the habit of seeking pleasures hurtful to others; and even this supposes the absence of many kinds of pleasures. But we ought not to charge upon this principle the faults which are opposed to it, and which it alone can serve to remove. If a man calculate badly, it is not arithmetic which is in fault, it is himself. . . .

Every one will constitute himself judge of his own utility; this is and this ought to be, otherwise man would not be a reasonable being. He who is not a judge of what is suitable for himself, is less than an infant, is a fool. The obligation which binds men to their engagements, is nothing but a feeling of an interest of a superior class, which outweighs an inferior interest. Men are not always held by the particular utility of a certain engagement; but in the case in which the engagement becomes burthensome to one of the parties, they are still held by the general utility of engagements—by the confidence that each enlightened man wishes to have placed in his word, that he may be considered as trustworthy, and enjoy the advantages attached to probity and esteem. It is not the engagement which constitutes the obligation by itself; for there are some void engagements; there are some unlawful. Why? Because they are considered as hurtful. It is the utility of the contract which gives it force. . . .

The most exalted acts of virtue may be easily reduced to a calculation of good and evil. This is neither to degrade nor to weaken them, but to represent them as the effects of reason, and to explain them in a simple and intelligible manner. . . .

---

a person addressing himself to the community, is a third. The two first are questions of speculation: it matters not, comparatively speaking, how they are decided. The last is a question of practice: the decision of it is of as much importance as that of any can be. . . .

[2] The following paragraphs are from Dumont's *Traités de Legislation.*

THOMAS ROBERT MALTHUS

(1766–1834)

Thomas Malthus, another important figure of the classical period of political economy, was an economist, sociologist, and utilitarian moralist. His theory of population was incorporated into Ricardian economics as the principal explanation for fluctuations in the supply of labor and hence for the rate of wages in the long run. He was one of the first writers to enunciate the classical differential theory of rent, later taken over and modified by Ricardo.

Malthus was born in England in 1776, the son of a country gentleman of studious and philosophic outlook. After some years of private tutoring, he entered Cambridge in 1784 as a student candidate for the Anglican ministry. After taking holy orders, he continued as a graduate student for many years; it was not until 1797 that he accepted his first parish post. In the next year he published anonymously his famous *Essay on the Principle of Population as it Affects the Future Improvement of Society*. He opposed the prevailing expectation of continuing social improvement by emphasizing the fact that the procreative powers of the human race were enough to inundate the earth if they were not held in check by "misery and vice." According to Malthus, since population increases geometrically while food resources increase only arithmetically, there is continuous pressure on the means of subsistence. The *Essay* excited a good deal of controversy and brought the author into public notice, and Malthus decided to visit the Continent in order to test his theories empirically. He then wrote an enlarged but less provocative revision, in which he modified many of his more extreme views and suggested moral restraint from marriage as one means of balancing subsistence and population. About this time Malthus was appointed professor of history and economics at the new college founded by the East India Company at Haileybury, and he remained there for the rest of his days.

In 1820 he published the unduly neglected *Principles of Political Economy*, in which he took specific issue with Ricardian doctrine. Adopting Smith's rather than Ricardo's labor theory of value, Malthus developed the concept of "effective demand"—demand effective in the sense that it could insure a continuous supply of goods. To him, the effective demand for a commodity was measured by the amount of labor which it could command: the outlay on wages and materials plus an average rate of profit. The maintenance of continuous production depended on the existence of effective demand at the price which covered the producer's expenditures plus profit. Since the wage bill of productive labor was, by definition, less than the sum of the values of its product, the effective demand would not be adequate to maintain production and gluts would result. Thus supply did not create its own demand and overproduction was inevitable. The solution for the deadlock, said Malthus, lay with the body of unproductive consumers (like landlords) who made it possible for demand to remain effective because they consumed without producing. In addition to unproductive consumption, public works would help to stave off gluts and overproduction.

Malthus carried on a long correspondence with Ricardo and Say in an effort to convince them of his views, but met with little success. Ricardo was quite incapable of grasping the pragmatic and empirical approach of Malthus, even as the latter was incapable of appreciating the abstract subtleties of Ricardian value theory and the rigor of its deductive reasoning. As a result of the growing dominance of Ricardian economics, Malthus' book passed into oblivion. A century went by before the problem of effective demand rose again to public notice: in his *General Theory*, John Maynard Keynes paid tribute to the pioneering work of Malthus on this subject.

Our first selection comprises the essentials of Malthus' contribution to population theory; the second presents his theory of market gluts.

AN ESSAY ON THE PRINCIPLE OF POPULATION *

The Increase of Population and Food

In the northern states of America, where the means of subsistence have been more ample, the manners of the people more pure, and the checks to early marriages fewer, than in any of the modern states of Europe, the population has been found to double itself, for above a century and a half successively, in less than twenty-five years. Yet, even during these periods, in some of the towns, the deaths exceeded the births, a circumstance which clearly proves that, in those parts of the country which supplied this deficiency, the increase must have been much more rapid than the general average.

In the back settlements, where the sole employment is agriculture, and vicious customs and unwholesome occupations are little known, the population has been found to double itself in fifteen years. Even this extraordinary rate of increase is probably short of the utmost power of population. Very severe labour is requisite to clear a fresh country; such situations are not in general considered as particularly healthy; and the inhabitants, probably, are occasionally subject to the incursions of the Indians, which may destroy some lives, or at any rate diminish the fruits of industry.

According to a table of Euler, calculated on a mortality of 1 in 36, if the births be to the deaths in the proportion of 3 to 1, the period of doubling will be only 12 years and 4–5ths. And this proportion is not only a possible supposition, but has actually occurred for short periods in more countries than one.

Sir William Petty supposes a doubling possible in so short a time as ten years.

But, to be perfectly sure that we are far within the truth, we will take the slowest of these rates of increase, a rate in which all concurring testimonies agree, and which has been repeatedly ascertained to be from procreation only.

It may safely be pronounced, therefore, that population, when unchecked, goes on doubling itself every twenty-five years, or increases in a geometrical ratio.

The rate according to which the productions of the earth may be supposed to increase, it will not be so easy to determine. Of this, however, we may be perfectly certain, that the ratio of their increase in a limited territory must be of a totally different nature from the ratio of the increase of population. A thousand millions are just as easily doubled every twenty-five years by the power of population as a thousand. But the food to support the increase from the greater number will by no means be obtained

* From *An Essay on the Principle of Population,* sixth edition (London, 1826).

with the same facility. Man is necessarily confined in room. When acre has been added to acre till all the fertile land is occupied, the yearly increase of food must depend upon the melioration of the land already in possession. This is a fund, which, from the nature of all soils, instead of increasing, must be gradually diminishing. But population, could it be supplied with food, would go on with unexhausted vigour; and the increase of one period would furnish the power of a greater increase the next, and this without any limit. . . .

Europe is by no means so fully peopled as it might be. In Europe there is the fairest chance that human industry may receive its best direction. The science of agriculture has been much studied in England and Scotland; and there is still a great portion of uncultivated land in these countries. Let us consider at what rate the produce of this island might be supposed to increase under circumstances the most favourable to improvement.

If it be allowed that by the best possible policy, and great encouragements to agriculture, the average produce of the island could be doubled in the first twenty-five years, it will be allowing, probably, a greater increase than could with reason be expected.

In the next twenty-five years, it is impossible to suppose that the produce could be quadrupled. It would be contrary to all our knowledge of the properties of land. The improvement of the barren parts would be a work of time and labour; and it must be evident to those who have the slightest acquaintance with agricultural subjects, that in proportion as cultivation extended, the additions that could yearly be made to the former average produce must be gradually and regularly diminishing. That we may be the better able to compare the increase of population and food, let us make a supposition, which, without pretending to accuracy, is clearly more favourable to the power of production in the earth, than any experience we have had of its qualities will warrant.

Let us suppose that the yearly additions which might be made to the former average produce, instead of decreasing, which they certainly would do, were to remain the same; and that the produce of this island might be increased every twenty-five years, by a quantity equal to what it at present produces. The most enthusiastic speculator cannot suppose a greater increase than this. In a few centuries it would make every acre of land in the island like a garden.

If this supposition be applied to the whole earth, and if it be allowed that the subsistence for man which the earth affords might be increased every twenty-five years by a quantity equal to what it at present produces, this will be supposing a rate of increase much greater than we can imagine that any possible exertions of mankind could make it.

It may be fairly pronounced, therefore, that, considering the present average state of the earth, the means of subsistence, under circumstances the most favourable to human industry, could not possibly be made to increase faster than in an arithmetical ratio.

The necessary effects of these two different rates of increase, when brought together, will be very striking. Let us call the population of this island eleven millions; and suppose the present produce equal to the easy support of such a number. In the first twenty-five years the population would be twenty-two millions, and the food being also doubled, the means of subsistence would be equal to this increase. In the next twenty-five years, the population would be forty-four millions, and the means of subsistence only equal to the support of thirty-three millions. In the next period the population would be eighty-eight millions, and the means of subsistence just equal to the support of half that number. And, at the conclusion of the first century, the population would be a hundred and seventy-six millions, and the means of subsistence only equal to the support of fifty-five millions, leaving a population of a hundred and twenty-one millions totally unprovided for.

Taking the whole earth, instead of this island, emigration would of course be excluded; and, supposing the present population equal to a thousand millions, the human species would increase as the numbers, 1, 2, 4, 8, 16, 32, 64, 128, 256, and subsistence as 1, 2, 3, 4, 5, 6, 7, 8, 9. In two centuries the population would be to the means of subsistence as 256 to 9; in three centuries as 4096 to 13, and in two thousand years the difference would be almost incalculable.

In this supposition no limits whatever are placed to the produce of the earth. It may increase for ever and be greater than any assignable quantity; yet still the power of population being in every period so much superior, the increase of the human species can only be kept down to the level of the means of subsistence by the constant operation of the strong law of necessity, acting as a check upon the greater power.

Of the general Checks to Population, and the Mode of their Operation

The ultimate check to population appears then to be a want of food, arising necessarily from the different ratios according to which population and food increase. But this ultimate check is never the immediate check, except in cases of actual famine.

The immediate check may be stated to consist in all those customs, and all those diseases, which seem to be generated by a scarcity of the means of subsistence; and all those causes, independent of this scarcity, whether of a moral or physical nature, which tend prematurely to weaken and destroy the human frame.

These checks to population, which are constantly operating with more or less force in every society, and keep down the number to the level of the means of subsistence, may be classed under two general heads—the preventive, and the positive checks.

The preventive check, as far as it is voluntary, is peculiar to man, and arises from that distinctive superiority in his reasoning faculties, which enables him to calculate distant consequences. The checks to the indefinite increase of plants and irrational animals are all either positive, or, if preventive, involuntary. But man cannot look around him, and see the distress which frequently presses upon those who have large families; he cannot contemplate his present possessions or earnings, which he now nearly consumes himself, and calculate the amount of each share, when with very little addition they must be divided, perhaps, among seven or eight, without feeling a doubt whether, if he follow the bent of his inclinations, he may be able to support the offspring which he will probably bring into the world. In a state of equality, if such can exist, this would be the simple question. In the present state of society other considerations occur. Will he not lower his rank in life, and be obliged to give up in great measure his former habits? Does any mode of employment present itself by which he may reasonably hope to maintain a family? Will he not at any rate subject himself to greater difficulties, and more severe labour, than in his single state? Will he not be unable to transmit to his children the same advantages of education and improvement that he had himself possessed? Does he even feel secure that, should he have a large family, his utmost exertions can save them from rags and squalid poverty, and their consequent degradation in the community? And may he not be reduced to the grating necessity of forfeiting his independence, and of being obliged to the sparing hand of Charity for support?

These considerations are calculated to prevent, and certainly do prevent, a great number of persons in all civilized nations from pursuing the dictate of nature in an early attachment to one woman.

If this restraint do not produce vice, it is undoubtedly the least evil that can arise from the principle of population. Considered as a restraint on a strong natural inclination, it must be allowed to produce a certain degree of temporary unhappiness; but evidently slight, compared with the evils which result from any of the other checks to population; and merely of the same nature as many other sacrifices of temporary to permanent gratification, which it is the business of a moral agent continually to make.

When this restraint produces vice, the evils which follow are but too conspicuous. A promiscuous intercourse to such a degree as to prevent the birth of children, seems to lower, in the most marked manner, the dignity of human nature. It cannot be without its effect on men, and nothing can be more obvious than its tendency to degrade the female character, and to destroy all its most amiable and distinguishing characteristics. Add to which, that among those unfortunate females, with which all great towns abound, more real distress and aggravated misery are, perhaps, to be found, than in any other department of human life.

When a general corruption of morals, with regard to the sex, pervades all the classes of society, its effects must necessarily be, to poison the springs of domestic happiness, to weaken conjugal and parental affection, and to lessen the united exertions and ardour of parents in the care and education of their children;—effects which cannot take place without a decided diminution of the general happiness and virtue of the society; particularly as the necessity of art in the accomplishment and conduct of intrigues, and in the concealment of their consequences necessarily leads to many other vices.

The positive checks to population are extremely various, and include every cause, whether arising from vice or misery, which in any degree contributes to shorten the natural duration of human life. Under this head, therefore, may be enumerated all unwholesome occupations, severe labour and exposure to the seasons, extreme poverty, bad nursing of children, great towns, excesses of all kinds, the whole train of common diseases and epidemics, wars, plague, and famine.

On examining these obstacles to the increase of population which I have classed under the heads of preventive and positive checks, it will appear that they are all resolvable into moral restraint, vice, and misery.

Of the preventive checks, the restraint from marriage which is not followed by irregular gratifications may properly be termed moral restraint.

Promiscuous intercourse, unnatural passions, violations of the marriage bed, and improper arts to conceal the consequences of irregular connexions, are preventive checks that clearly come under the head of vice.

Of the positive checks, those which appear to arise unavoidably from the laws of nature, may be called exclusively misery; and those which we obviously bring upon ourselves, such as wars, excesses, and many others which it would be in our power to avoid, are of a mixed nature. They are brought upon us by vice, and their consequences are misery.

The sum of all these preventive and positive checks, taken together, forms the immediate check to population; and it is evident that, in every country where the whole of the procreative power cannot be called into action, the preventive and the positive checks must vary inversely as each other; that is, in countries either naturally unhealthy, or subject to a great mortality, from whatever cause it may arise, the preventive check will prevail very little. In those countries, on the contrary, which are naturally healthy, and where the preventive check is found to prevail with considerable force, the positive check will prevail very little, or the mortality be very small.

In every country some of these checks are, with more or less force, in constant operation; yet, notwithstanding their general prevalence, there are few states in which there is not a constant effort in the population to increase beyond the means of subsistence. This constant effort as constantly tends to subject the lower classes of society to distress, and to prevent any great permanent melioration of their condition.

These effects, in the present state of society, seem to be produced in the following manner. We will suppose the means of subsistence in any country just equal to the easy support of its inhabitants. The constant effort towards population, which is found to act even in the most vicious societies, increases the number of people before the means of subsistence are increased. The food, therefore, which before supported eleven millions, must now be divided among eleven millions and a half. The poor consequently must live much worse, and many of them be reduced to severe distress. The number of labourers also being above the proportion of work in the market, the price of labour must tend to fall, while the price of provisions would at the same time tend to rise. The labourer therefore must do more work, to earn the same as he did before. During this season of distress, the discouragements to marriage and the difficulty of rearing a family are so great, that the progress of population is retarded. In the mean time, the cheapness of labour, the plenty of labourers, and the necessity of an increased industry among them, encourage cultivators to employ more labour upon their land, to turn up fresh soil, and to manure and improve more completely what is already in tillage, till ultimately the means of subsistence may become in the same proportion to the population, as at the period from which we set out. The situation of the labourer being then again tolerably comfortable, the restraints to population are in some degree loosened; and, after a short period, the same retrograde and progressive movements, with respect to happiness, are repeated.

This sort of oscillation will not probably be obvious to common view; and it may be difficult even for the most attentive observer to calculate its periods. Yet that, in the generality of old states, some alternation of this kind does exist though in a much less marked, and in a much more irregular manner, than I have described it, no reflecting man, who considers the subject deeply, can well doubt. . . .

A circumstance which has, perhaps, more than any other, contributed to conceal this oscillation from common view, is the difference between the nominal and real price of labour. It very rarely happens that the nominal price of labour universally falls; but we well know that it frequently remains the same, while the nominal price of provisions has been gradually rising. This, indeed, will generally be the case, if the increase of manufactures and commerce be sufficient to employ the new labourers that are thrown into the market, and to prevent the increased supply from lowering the money-price. But an increased number of labourers receiving the same money-wages will necessarily, by their competition, increase the money-price of corn. This is, in fact, a real fall in the price of labour; and, during this period, the condition of the lower classes of the community must be gradually growing worse. But the farmers and capitalists are growing rich from the real cheapness of labour. Their increasing capitals enable them to employ a greater number of men; and, as the population had probably suffered some check from the greater difficulty of supporting a family, the demand for labour, after a certain period, would be great in proportion to the supply, and its price would of course rise, if left to find its natural level; and thus the wages of labour, and consequently the condition of the lower classes of society, might have progressive and retrograde movements, though the price of labour might never nominally fall.

In savage life, where there is no regular price of labour, it is little to be doubted that similar oscillations took place. When population has increased nearly to the utmost limits of the food, all the preventive and the positive checks will naturally operate with increased force. Vicious habits with respect to the sex will be more general, the exposing of children more frequent, and both the probability and fatality of wars and epidemics will be considerably greater; and these causes will probably continue their operation till the population is sunk below the level of the food; and then the return to comparative plenty will again produce an increase, and, after a certain period, its further progress will again be checked by the same causes.

But without attempting to establish these progressive and retrograde movements in different countries, which would evidently require more minute histories than we possess, and which the progress of civilization naturally tends to counteract, the following propositions are intended to be proved:—

1. Population is necessarily limited by the means of subsistence.

2. Population invariably increases where the means of subsistence increase, unless prevented by some very powerful and obvious checks.

3. These checks, and the checks which repress the superior power of population, and keep its effects on a level with the means of subsistence, are all resolvable into moral restraint, vice and misery.

ON THE PROGRESS OF WEALTH *

It has been thought by some very able writers, that, although there may easily be a glut of particular commodities, there cannot possibly be a glut of commodities in general; because, according to their own view of the subject, commodities being always exchanged for commodities, one half will always furnish a market for the other half, and production being thus the sole source of demand, an excess in the supply of one article merely proves a deficiency in the supply of some other, and a general excess is impossible. M. Say . . . has indeed gone so far as to state that the consumption of a commodity by taking it out of the market diminishes demand, and the production of a commodity proportionately increases it.

This doctrine, however, as generally applied, appears to me to be utterly unfounded, and completely to contradict the great principles which regulate supply and demand.

It is by no means true, as a matter of fact, that commodities are always exchanged for commodities. An immense mass of commodities is exchanged directly, either for productive labour, or personal services: and it is quite obvious, that this mass of commodities, compared with the labour with which it is to be exchanged, may fall in value from a glut just as any one commodity falls in value from an excess of supply, compared either with labour or money.

In the case supposed there would evidently be an unusual quantity of

* From *Principles of Political Economy,* second edition (London, 1836).

commodities of all kinds in the market, owing to those who had been before engaged in personal services having been converted, by the accumulation of capital, into productive labourers; while the number of labourers altogether being the same, and the power and will to purchase for consumption among landlords and capitalists being by supposition diminished, commodities would necessarily fall in value compared with labour, so as very greatly to lower profits, and to check for a time further production. But this is precisely what is meant by the term glut, which, in this case, is evidently general not partial.

M. Say, Mr. Mill, and Mr. Ricardo, the principal authors of these new doctrines, appear to me to have fallen into some fundamental errors in the view which they have taken of this subject.

In the first place, they have considered commodities as if they were so many mathematical figures, or arithmetical characters, the relations of which were to be compared, instead of articles of consumption, which must of course be referred to the numbers and wants of the consumers.

If commodities were only to be compared and exchanged with each other, then indeed it would be true that, if they were all increased in their proper proportions to any extent, they would continue to bear among themselves the same relative value; but, if we compare them, as we certainly ought to do, with the means of producing them, and with the numbers and wants of the consumers, then a great increase of produce with comparatively stationary numbers or with wants diminished by parsimony, must necessarily occasion a great fall of value estimated in labour, so that the same produce, though it might have *cost* the same quantity of labour as before, would no longer *command* the same quantity; and both the power of accumulation and the motive to accumulate would be strongly checked.

It is asserted that effectual demand is nothing more than the offering of one commodity in exchange for another which has cost the same quantity of labour. But is this all that is necessary to effectual demand? Though each commodity may have cost the same quantity of labour in its production, and they may be exactly equivalent to each other in exchange, yet why may not both be so plentiful as not to command more labour, than they have cost, that is, to yield no profit, and in this case, would the demand for them be effectual? Would it be such as to encourage their continued production? Unquestionably not. Their relation to each other may not have changed; but their relation to the wants of the society, and their relation to labour, may have experienced a most important change.

It will be readily allowed that a new commodity thrown into the market, which, in proportion to the labour employed upon it, is of higher exchangeable value than usual, is precisely calculated to increase demand; because it implies, not a mere increase of quantity, but an increase of value owing to a better adaptation of the produce to the tastes, wants and consumption of the society. But to fabricate or procure commodities of this kind is the grand difficulty; and they certainly do not naturally and necessarily follow an accumulation of capital and increase of commodities, most particularly when such accumulation and increase have been occasioned by economy of consumption, or a discouragement to the indulgence of those tastes and wants, which are the very elements of demand and of value.

Mr. Ricardo, though he maintains as a general position that capital cannot be redundant, is obliged to make the following concession. He says, "There is only one case, and that will be temporary, in which the accumulation of capital with a low price of food may be attended with a fall of profits; and that is, when the funds for the maintenance of labour increase much more rapidly than population;—wages will then be high and profits low. If every man were to forego the use of luxuries and be intent only on accumulation, a quantity of necessaries might be produced for which there could not be any immediate consumption. Of commodities so limited in number, there might undoubtedly be an universal glut; and consequently there might neither be demand for an additional quantity of such commodities, nor profits on the employment of more capital. If men ceased to consume, they would cease to produce." Mr. Ricardo then adds, "This admission does not impugn the general principle." In this last remark I can by no means agree with him. It appears to me most completely to impugn the general principle. Even if we suppose with Mr. Ricardo, what is not true, that an increase of population would certainly remedy the evil; yet as from the nature of a population, an increase of labourers cannot be brought into the market, in consequence of a particular demand, till after the lapse of sixteen or eighteen years, and the conversion of revenue [1] into capital by saving, may take place much more rapidly; a country is always liable to an increase in the quantity of the funds for the maintenance of labour faster than the increase of population. But if, whenever this occurs, there may be an universal glut of commodities, how can it be maintained, as a general position, that capital is never redundant; and that because commodities may retain the same relative values, a glut can only be partial, not general?

Another fundamental error into which the writers above-mentioned and their followers appear to have fallen is, the not taking into consideration the influence of so general and important a principle in human nature, as indolence or love of ease.

It has been supposed that, if a certain number of farmers and a certain number of manufacturers had been exchanging their surplus food and clothing with each other, and their powers of production were suddenly so increased that both parties could, with the same labour, produce luxuries in addition to what they had before obtained, there could be no sort of difficulty with regard to demand, as part of the luxuries which the farmer produced would be exchanged against part of the luxuries produced by the manufacturer; and the only result would be, the happy

1 [By "revenue" Malthus means "income."—*Editor.*]

one of both parties being better supplied and having more enjoyments.

But in this intercourse of mutual gratifications, two things are taken for granted, which are the very points in dispute. It is taken for granted that luxuries are always preferred to indolence, and that an adequate proportion of the profits of each party is consumed as revenue. What would be the effect of a desire to save under such circumstances, shall be considered presently. The effect of a preference of indolence to luxuries would evidently be to occasion a want of demand for the returns of the increased powers of production supposed, and to throw labourers out of employment. The cultivator, being now enabled to obtain the necessaries and conveniences to which he had been accustomed, with less toil and trouble, and his tastes for ribands, lace and velvet not being fully formed, might be very likely to indulge himself in indolence, and employ less labour on the land; while the manufacturer, finding his velvets rather heavy of sale, would be led to discontinue their manufacture, and to fall almost necessarily into the same indolent system as the farmer. That an efficient taste for luxuries and conveniences, that is, such a taste as will properly stimulate industry, instead of being ready to appear at the moment it is required, is a plant of slow growth, the history of human society sufficiently shows; and that it is a most important error to take for granted, that mankind will produce and consume all that they have the power to produce and consume, and will never prefer indolence to the rewards of industry, will sufficiently appear from a slight review of some of the nations with which we are acquainted. . . .

It has been said, that it is specifically the deficiency of production on the part of the indolent, which occasions the want of demand for the products of the industrious; and that, if the idle were made to produce, the surplus would disappear. But this remark is evidently beside the question. The real question is, whether under the actual habits and tastes of the society, any number of persons who might be inclined to save and produce, if they suited their produce to these habits and tastes, would be secure of finding such a demand for all they could bring into the market as to prevent the possibility of what is called a glut, or a great fall of profits in a large mass of commodities. What might happen under different tastes and habits is entirely a different question.

It has also been said, that there is never an indisposition to consume, that the indisposition is to produce. Yet, what is the disposition of those master manufacturers, and merchants who produce very largely and consume sparingly? Is their will to purchase commodities for their consumption proportioned to their power? Does not the use which they make of their capital clearly show that their will is to produce, not to consume? and in fact, if there were not in every country some who were indisposed to consume to the value of what they produced, how could the national capital ever be increased?

A third very serious error of the writers above referred to, and practically the most important of the three, consists in supposing that accumulation ensures demand; or that the consumption of the labourers employed by those whose object is to save, will create such an effectual demand for commodities as to encourage a continued increase of produce. . . .

It is not, of course, meant to be stated that parsimony, or even a temporary diminution of consumption,[2] is not often in the highest degree useful, and sometimes absolutely necessary to the progress of wealth. A state may certainly be ruined by extravagance; and a diminution of the actual expenditure may not only be necessary on this account, but when the capital of a country is deficient, compared with the demand for its products, a temporary economy of consumption is required, in order to provide that supply of capital which can alone furnish the means of an increased consumption in future. All that is contended for is, that no nation can *possibly* grow rich by an accumulation of capital, arising from a permanent diminution of consumption; because such accumulation being beyond what is wanted in order to supply the effectual demand for produce, a part of it would very soon lose both its use and its value, and cease to possess the character of wealth.

The laws which regulate the rate of profits and the progress of capital, bear a very striking and singular resemblance to the laws which regulate the rate of wages and the progress of population.

Mr. Ricardo has very clearly shewn that the rate of profits must diminish, and the progress of accumulation be finally stopped, under the most favourable circumstances, by the increasing difficulty of procuring the food of the labourer. I, in like manner, endeavoured to shew in my Essay on the Principle of Population that, under circumstances the most favourable to cultivation which could possibly be supposed to operate in the actual state of the earth, the real wages of the labourer would gradually become more scanty, and the progress of population be finally stopped by the increasing difficulty of procuring the means of subsistence.

But Mr. Ricardo has not been satisfied with proving the position just stated. He has not been satisfied with shewing that the difficulty of procuring the food of the labourer is the only *absolutely necessary* cause of the fall of profits, in which I am ready fully and entirely to agree with him: but he has gone on to say, that, there is *no other cause* of the fall of profits in the actual state of things that has any degree of permanence.[3] In this latter statement he appears to me to have fallen into precisely the same kind of error as I should have fallen into, if, after having shewn that the unrestricted power of population was beyond comparison greater than the power of the earth to produce food under the most favourable circumstances possible, I had allowed that population could not be redundant unless the powers of the earth to keep up with the progress of

[2] Parsimony, or the conversion of revenue into capital, may take place without any diminution of consumption, if the revenue increases first.

[3] By this expression I mean such a degree of permanence as to be called the ordinary rate of profits.

population had been tried to the uttermost. But I all along said, that population might be redundant, and greatly redundant, compared with the demand for it and the actual means of supporting it, although it might most properly be considered as deficient, and greatly deficient, compared with the extent of territory, and the powers of such territory to produce additional means of subsistence; that, in such cases, notwithstanding the acknowledged deficiency of population, and the obvious desirableness of having it greatly increased, it was useless and foolish directly to encourage the birth of more children, as the effect of such encouragement, without a demand for labour and the means of paying it properly, could only be increased misery and mortality with little or no final increase of population.

Now the same kind of reasoning ought, I think, to be applied to the rate of profits and the progress of capital. Fully acknowledging that there is hardly a country in the four quarters of the globe where capital is not deficient, and in most of them very greatly deficient, compared with the territory and even the number of people; and fully allowing at the same time the extreme desirableness of an increase of capital, I should say that, where the state of the demand for commodities was such as to afford much less than ordinary profits to the producer, and the capitalists were at a loss where and how to employ their capitals to advantage, the saving from revenue to add still more to these capitals would only tend prematurely to diminish the motive to accumulation, and still further to distress the capitalists, with little increase of a wholesome and effective capital.

What is wanted in both these cases, prior to the increase of capital and population, is an effectual demand for commodities, that is, a demand by those who are able and willing to pay an adequate price for them; and though high profits are not followed by an increase of capital, so certainly as high wages are by an increase of population, yet it will be found that they are so followed more generally than they appear to be, because, in many countries, profits are often thought to be high, owing to the high interest of money, when they are really low; and because, universally, risk in employing capital has precisely the same effect in diminishing the motive to accumulate and the reward of accumulation, as low profits. At the same time it will be allowed that determined extravagance, and a determined indisposition to save, may keep profits permanently high. The most powerful stimulants may, under peculiar circumstances, be resisted; yet still it will not cease to be true that the natural and legitimate encouragement to the increase of capital is that increase of the power and will to save which is held out by certain and steady profits; and under circumstances in any degree similar, such increase of power and will to save must almost always be accompanied by a proportionate increase of capital.

One of the most striking instances of the truth of this remark, and a further proof of a singular resemblance in the laws that regulate the increase of capital and of population, is to be found in the rapidity with which the loss of capital is recovered during a war which does not interrupt commerce. The loans to government convert capital into revenue, and increase demand at the same time that they at first diminish the means of supply. The necessary consequence must be an increase of profits. This naturally increases both the power and the reward of accumulation; and if only the same habits of saving prevail among the capitalists as before, the recovery of the lost stock must be rapid, just for the same kind of reason that the recovery of population is so rapid after some great mortality.

Application of some of the preceding Principles to the Distresses of the Labouring Classes since 1815, with General Observations

It has been said that the distresses of the labouring classes since 1815 are owing to a deficient capital, which is evidently unable to employ all that are in want of work.

That the capital of the country does not bear an adequate proportion to the population; that the capital and revenue together do not bear so great a proportion as they did before 1815; and that such a disproportion will at once account for very great distress among the labouring classes, I am most ready to allow. But it is a very different thing to allow that the capital is deficient compared with the population; and to allow that it is deficient compared with the demand for it, and the demand for the commodities procured by it.* The two cases are very frequently confounded, because they both produce distress among the labouring classes; but they are essentially distinct. They are attended with some very different symptoms, and require to be treated in a very different manner.

If one fourth of the capital of a country were suddenly destroyed, or entirely transferred to a different part of the world, without any other cause occurring of a diminished demand for commodities, this scantiness of capital would certainly occasion great inconvenience to consumers, and great distress among the working classes; but it would be attended with great advantages to the remaining capitalists. Commodities, in general, would be scarce, and bear a high price on account of the deficiency in the means of producing them. Nothing would be so easy as to find a profitable employment for capital; but it would by no means be easy to find capital for the number of employments in which it was deficient; and consequently the rate of profits would be very high. In this state of things there would be an immediate and pressing demand for capital, on account of there being an immediate and pressing demand for commodities;

* It is a contradiction in terms, to say that labour is redundant compared with capital, and that capital is at the same time redundant compared with labour:—but it is no contradiction in terms to say that both labourers and capital may be redundant, compared with the means of employing them profitably. I have never maintained the former position, though I have been charged with so doing; but the latter has been so fully established by experience, that I am surprized at the pertinacity with which theoretical writers continue to refuse their assent to it.

and the obvious remedy would be, the supply of the demand in the only way in which it could take place, namely, by saving from revenue to add to capital. This supply of capital would, as I have before stated, take place just upon the same principle as a supply of population would follow a great destruction of people on the supposition of there being an immediate and pressing want of labour evinced by the high real wages given to the labourer.

On the other hand, if the capital of the country were diminished by the failure of demand in some large branches of trade, which had before been very prosperous, and absorbed a great quantity of stock; or even if, while capital were suddenly destroyed, the revenue of the landlords was diminished in a greater proportion owing to peculiar circumstances, the state of things, with the exception of the distresses of the poor, would be almost exactly reversed. The remaining capitalists would be in no respect benefited by events which had diminished demand in a still greater proportion than they had diminished the supply. Commodities would be every where cheap. Capital would be seeking employment, but would not easily find it; and the profits of stock would be low. There would be no pressing and immediate demand for capital, because there would be no pressing and immediate demand for commodities; and, under these circumstances, the saving from revenue to add to capital, instead of affording the remedy required, would only aggravate the distresses of the capitalists, and fill the stream of capital which was flowing out of the country. The distresses of the capitalists would be aggravated, just upon the same principle as the distresses of the labouring classes would be aggravated if they were encouraged to marry and increase, after a considerable destruction of people, although accompanied by a still greater destruction of capital which had kept the wages of labour very low. There might certainly be a great deficiency of population, compared with the territory and powers of the country, and it might be very desirable that it should be greater; but if the wages of labour were still low, notwithstanding the diminution of people, to encourage the birth of more children would be to encourage misery and mortality rather than population.

Now I would ask, to which of these two suppositions does the present state of this country [1] bear the nearest resemblance? Surely to the latter. That a great loss of capital has lately been sustained, is unquestionable. During nearly the whole of the war, owing to the union of great powers of production with a great effectual consumption and demand, the prodigious destruction of capital by the government was much more than recovered. To doubt this would be to shut our eyes to the comparative state of the country in 1792 and 1813. The two last years of the war were, however, years of extraordinary expense, and being followed immediately by a period marked by a very unusual stagnation of effectual demand, the destruction of capital which took place in those years was not probably recovered. But this stagnation itself was much more disastrous in its effects

1 Written in 1820.

upon the national capital, and still more upon the national revenue, than any previous destruction of stock. It commenced certainly with the extraordinary fall in the value of the raw produce of the land, to the amount, it has been supposed, of nearly one third. When this fall had diminished the capitals of the farmers, and still more the revenues both of landlords and farmers, and of all those who were otherwise connected with the land, their power of purchasing manufactures and foreign products was of necessity greatly diminished. The failure of home demand filled the warehouses of the manufacturers with unsold goods, which urged them to export more largely at all risks. But this excessive exportation glutted all the foreign markets, and prevented the merchants from receiving adequate returns; while, from the diminution of the home revenues, aggravated by a sudden and extraordinary contraction of the currency, even the comparatively scanty returns obtained from abroad found a very insufficient domestic demand, and the profits and consequent expenditure of merchants and manufacturers were proportionably lowered. While these unfavourable changes were taking place in rents and profits, the powerful stimulus which had been given to population by the continued demand for labour during the war, occasioned the pouring in of fresh supplies of labour, which, aided by the disbanded soldiers and sailors, and the failure of demand arising from the losses of the farmers and merchants, reduced generally both wages and profits, and left the country with a greatly diminished capital and revenue;—not merely in proportion to the alteration of the value of the currency, but in reference to the bullion value of its produce, and the command of this bullion value over labour, at the price at which it was actually employed. For the four or five years since the war, on account of the change in the distribution of the national produce, and the want of effectual consumption and demand occasioned by it, a check has been given to the rate of production, and the population, under its former impulse, has increased, not only faster than the demand for labour, but faster than the actual produce; yet this produce, though deficient, compared with the population, is redundant, compared with the effectual demand for it and the revenue which is to purchase it. Though labour is cheap, there is neither the power nor the will to employ it all; because not only has the capital of the country diminished, compared with the number of labourers, but, owing to the diminished revenues of the country, the commodities which those labourers would produce are not in such request as to ensure tolerable profits to the reduced capital.

But when profits are low and uncertain, when capitalists are quite at a loss where they can safely employ their capitals, and when on these accounts capital is flowing out of the country; in short, when all the evidence which the nature of the subject admits, distinctly proves that there is no effective demand for capital at home, is it not contrary to the general principles of political economy, is it not a vain and fruitless opposition to that first, greatest, and most universal of all its principles, the principle of supply and demand, to recommend saving, and the conversion of more revenue into capital? Is it not just the same sort of thing as to recommend marriage when people are starving and emigrating? . . .

If a large country, of considerable fertility, and sufficient inland communications, were surrounded by an impassable wall, we all agree that it might be tolerably rich, though not so rich as if it enjoyed the benefit of foreign commerce. Now, supposing such a country gradually to indulge in a considerable consumption, to call forth and employ a great quantity of ingenuity in production, and to save only yearly that portion of its revenue which it could most advantageously add to its capital, expending the rest in consumable commodities and personal services, it might evidently, under such a balance of produce and consumption, be increasing in wealth and population with considerable rapidity. But if, upon the principle laid down by M. Say, that the consumption of a commodity is a diminution of demand, the society were greatly and generally to slacken their consumption, and add to their capitals, there cannot be the least doubt, on the principle of demand and supply, that the profits of capitalists would soon be greatly reduced, though there were no poor land in cultivation; and the population would be thrown out of work and would be starving, although without a single tax, or any restrictions on trade.

. . . When Hume and Adam Smith prophesied that a little increase of national debt beyond the then amount of it, would probably occasion bankruptcy; the main cause of their error was the very natural one, of not being able to see the vast increase of productive power to which the nation would subsequently attain. An expenditure, which would have absolutely crushed the country in 1770, might be little more than what was necessary to call forth its prodigious powers of production in 1816. But just in proportion to this power of production, and to the facility with which a vast consumption could be supplied, consistently with a rapid accumulation of capital, would be the distress felt by capitalists and labourers upon any great and sudden diminution of expenditure.

On this account there is reason to doubt the policy of raising the supplies of a long and expensive war within the year, a policy which has been recommended by very able writers. If the country were poor, such a system of taxation might completely keep down its efforts. It might every year positively diminish its capital, and render it every year more ruinous to furnish the same supplies; till the country would be obliged to submit to its enemies from the absolute inability of continuing to oppose them with effect. On the other hand, if the country were rich, and had great powers of production, which were likely to be still further called forth by the stimulus of a great effective consumption, it might be able to pay the heavy taxes imposed upon it, out of its revenue, and yet find the means of adequate accumulation; but if this process were to last for any time, and the habits of the people were accommodated to this scale of public and private expenditure, it is scarcely possible to doubt that, at the end of the war, when so large a mass of taxes would at once be restored to the payers of them, the just balance of produce and consumption would be completely destroyed, and a period would ensue, longer or shorter, according to circumstances, in which a very great stagnation would be felt in every branch of productive industry, attended by its usual concomitant general distress. The evil occasioned by imposing a tax is very rarely compensated by the taking it off. We should constantly keep in mind that the tendency to expenditure in individuals has most formidable antagonists in the love of indolence, and in the desire of saving, in order to better their condition and provide for a family; and that all theories founded upon the assumption that mankind always produce and consume as much as they have the power to produce and consume, are founded upon a want of knowledge of the human character and of the motives by which it is usually influenced.

It will be said, perhaps, that as the capital of the country compared with its population has been diminished since the war, partly by the unrecovered destruction which it sustained during the last two years of the contest, and still more by the sudden want of demand which occurred on its termination; how is the lost capital ever to be recovered, except by accumulation? Now it is perfectly true that the recovery and increase of our capital can take place in no other way than by accumulation. But in looking to this most desirable object, it is absolutely necessary that we should listen to the dictates of those great general laws which seldom fail to direct us in the right course. If population were ever so deficient in a state compared with its territory, yet, if the wages of labour still continued very scanty, and the people were emigrating, the great general laws of demand and supply would instruct us that some previous change in the state of things was necessary, before we ought to wish for an increased proportion of marriages, which in fact, under the actual circumstances, would not accomplish the object aimed at. In the same manner, if a portion of our capital be destroyed, and yet the profits of the remainder are low, and accompanied with frequent losses, and a tendency to emigrate, surely the great general laws of demand and supply cannot more clearly shew us that something else is wanted before we can accumulate with effect.

What is now wanted in this country is an increased national revenue,—an increase in the exchangeable value of the whole produce estimated in bullion,—and in the command of this bullion over labour. When we have attained this, which can only be attained by increased and steady profits, we may then begin again to accumulate, and our accumulation will then be effectual. But if, instead of saving from increased profits, we save from diminished expenditure; if, at the very time that the supply of commodities compared with the demand for them, clearly admonishes us that the proportion of capital to revenue is already too great, we go on saving from our revenue to add still further to our capital, all general principles concur in shewing that we must of necessity be aggravating instead of alleviating our distresses.

But how, it will be asked, are we to obtain this increase of revenue?

What steps are we to take in order to raise the exchangeable value of the whole produce, and prepare the way for the future saving which is acknowledged to be necessary? These questions I have endeavoured to answer in . . . this very long Chapter *On the immediate Causes of the Progress of Wealth,* where it has appeared that a union of the means of distribution with the powers of production is absolutely necessary to create an adequate stimulus to the continued increase of wealth; and that the three causes, which, by favouring distribution, tend most to keep up and increase the exchangeable value of the whole produce, are, the division of landed property, the extension of domestic and foreign trade, and the maintenance of such a proportion of unproductive consumers as is best adapted to the powers of production.

. . . With regard to the first main cause which I have mentioned, as tending to increase the exchangeable value of the national produce, namely the division of landed property, I have given my reasons for thinking that, in the actual and peculiar state of this country, the abolition of the law of primogeniture would produce more evil than good; and there is no other way in which a different division of land could be effected, consistently with an adequate respect for the great fundamental law of property, on which all progress in civilization, improvement, and wealth, must ever depend. But if the *distribution* of wealth to a certain extent be one of the main causes of its increase, while it is unadvisable directly to interfere with the present division of land in this country, it may justly become a question, whether the evils attendant on the national debt are not more than counterbalanced by the distribution of property and increase of the middle classes of society, which it must necessarily create; and whether by saving, in order to pay it off, we are not submitting to a painful sacrifice, which, if it attains its object, whatever other good it may effect, will leave us with a much less favourable distribution of wealth? By greatly reducing the national debt, if we are able to accomplish it, we may place ourselves perhaps in a more safe position, and this no doubt is a most important consideration; but grievously will those be disappointed who think that, either by greatly reducing or at once destroying it, we can enrich ourselves, and employ all our labouring classes.

With regard to the second main cause of an increase in the exchangeable value of the whole produce—namely, the extension of domestic and foreign trade, it is well known that we can by no means command either of these at pleasure, but we may do much to impede both. We cannot indeed reasonably attribute any sudden deficiency of trade to causes which have been of long duration; yet there can be little doubt that our commerce has been much impaired by unnecessary restraints, and that much benefit might be derived from the removal of them. While it is necessary to raise a large sum by taxation for the expenses of the government and the payment of the interest of the national debt, it would by no means be advisable to neglect so fair and fruitful a resource as the customs. In regulating these taxes, it is also natural that those foreign commodities should be taxed the highest, which are either of the same kind as the native commodities which have been taxed, or such as, for special reasons of health, happiness, or safety, it is desirable to grow largely at home. But there seems to be no reason for the absolute prohibition of any commodities whatever; and there is little doubt that, upon this principle, a much greater freedom might be given to foreign commerce, at the same time that a greater revenue might be derived from the customs. . . .

In all cases where, under peculiar circumstances, the distress of the country would be aggravated by the opening of certain trades, which had before been subject to restrictions, the exchangeable value of the whole produce estimated in labour, would for a time be diminished. But, in general, as I have endeavoured to shew, . . . the natural and permanent tendency of all extension of trade both domestic and foreign, is to increase the exchangeable value of the whole produce. This is more especially the case when, instead of changing the channels of commerce, we are able to make large and distinct additions to them. The good is then unalloyed by partial and temporary evil. This better distribution of the produce of the country, this better adaptation of it to the wants and tastes of the consumers, will at once give it a greater market value, and at once increase the national revenue, the rate of steady profits, and the wages of labour.

With regard to the third cause of an increase in the exchangeable value of the whole produce, the maintenance of unproductive consumers—though many have no power to be of use in this respect, others may do something; and it must certainly be advantageous that the truth, whatever it may be, relating to the effects of unproductive consumers, should be fully known, that we may not aim at what will obstruct the progress of wealth, and clamour at what is calculated to advance it. Whatever it may be thought advisable to do respecting the diminution of unproductive consumers, with a view to the placing ourselves in a safer position, we shall be led to proceed with more deliberation, if we are not hurried on by the impression that, by this diminution, we are affording immediate relief to the labouring classes.

It is also of importance to know that, in our endeavours to assist the working classes in a period like the present, it is desirable to employ them in those kinds of labour, the results of which do not come for sale into the market, such as roads and public works. The objection to employing a large sum in this way, raised by taxes, would not be its tendency to diminish the capital employed in productive labour; because this, to a certain extent, is exactly what is wanted; but it might, perhaps, have the effect of concealing too much the failure of the national demand for labour, and prevent the population from gradually accommodating itself to a reduced demand. This however might be, in a considerable degree, corrected by the wages given. And altogether I should say, that the employment of the poor in roads and public works, and a tendency among landlords and persons of property to build, to improve and beautify their grounds, and to employ workmen and menial servants, are the means most within our power and most directly calculated to remedy the evils arising from that disturbance in the balance of produce and consumption, which has been occasioned by the sudden conversion of soldiers, sailors, and various other classes which the war employed, into productive labourers.

If by the operation of these three causes, either separately or conjointly, we can make the supply and demand bear a more advantageous proportion to each other, so as to increase the exchangeable value of the whole produce, the rate of profits may then permanently rise as high as the quality of the soil in cultivation combined with the actual skill of the cultivators will allow, which is far from being the case at present. And as soon as the capitalists can begin to save from steady and improving profits, instead of from diminished expenditure, that is, as soon as the national revenue, estimated in bullion, and in the command of this bullion over labour, begins yearly and steadily to increase, we may then begin safely and effectively to recover our lost capital by the usual process of saving a portion of our increased revenue to add to it.

DAVID RICARDO

(1772–1823)

David Ricardo was born in London of Jewish parents. His father was a broker on the Exchange, and Ricardo received training in finance at an early age. After his marriage caused a rift with his father, he entered business independently as a loan broker. He prospered rapidly and used his leisure to study. In 1799 he discovered the book that was to stimulate his interest in economics, *The Wealth of Nations.* In the years that followed he handled large government loans in the Napoleonic Wars and became a pamphleteer on topics of economic interest. His friends included James Mill and Jeremy Bentham, and to Mill's coaching in particular he owed his greatest debt as a writer.

In 1814 he retired from active business and began to write his famous *Principles of Political Economy and Taxation,* which appeared in 1817. During this period he carried on a vigorous correspondence with Malthus and other writers, in which he elaborated his theory in some detail. The *Principles* was an immediate success, and a school of disciples formed within a few years. Ricardo's influence was pervasive and lasting: Ricardian economics became a synonym for classical political economy. Fifty years were to pass before that influence waned.

Ricardo's concern was primarily with secular trends in the production of wealth and with the distribution of the national income among the various classes of society. Ricardo reformulated Smith's theory of value, emphasizing that the amount of embodied labor determines the relative value of commodities. "Labor" includes both the present and the past labor which is stored up in implements and machinery. To escape the difficulties arising from the fact that different technical conditions in different industries would cause wage changes to affect values and prices unequally, Ricardo assumed that capital and labor are everywhere combined in the same proportions. Consequently in his theory differences in capital structure exert no influence on the price structure—prices conform to labor values.

Ricardo's rent theory denies the existence of absolute rent and attempts to explain rent as a pure surplus, resulting from differences of soil fertility. Production on marginal land yields no rent, but on the more productive soil an unearned increment arises which accrues to the owner of the land. Rent does not enter into the creation of value or the determination of prices, since the price depends upon the labor required to cultivate the rentless margin.

Wages tend to remain at the level of subsistence as a result of the operation of the Malthusian law of population. Ricardo treated profit as a residuum—total product minus the sum of rent and wages. Profit was not distinguished from interest because the historical bifurcation of the rentier and the entrepreneur had not yet come about. Profits tend to fall in the long run because diminishing returns in agriculture will yield proportionately higher costs and lower returns. The secular constancy of real wages and the upward drift of money wages, as a result of the rising prices of necessities, result in falling profits as returns are reduced. A growing population leads to more extensive and intensive cultivation, to the accumulation of capital, and consequently to falling profits and rising rents. Landlords reap a double gain through rising rents and through rising prices for agricultural products as a result of the limited supply of lands. Thus economic progress affects rents, profits, and wages in a conflicting manner, indicating the presence of opposing interests between landlords on the one hand and capitalists and laborers on the other. In the later editions of his *Principles* Ricardo suggested as a further source of conflict among the classes of society the introduction of technical innovations which he believed could cause a permanent displacement of labor. (See "On Machinery," p. 211.)

Ricardo's analysis included policy recommendations with regard to the dominant social and economic problems of his day. The period following the Napoleonic Wars witnessed a growing conflict of interest between the manufacturing classes who wished to compete on the international market by reducing the price of foodstuff, thus lowering wages and the cost of production, and the landlords who desired to maintain the high price of grain by preventing the importation of cheaper corn. Ricardo's theory showed that economic progress would best be served by importing the food supply and paying for imports with manufactured goods, that is, by repealing the Corn Laws and establishing free trade. His theory therefore provided the supporters of free trade with an admirable rationale. The abolition of the Corn Laws in order to lower the price of corn was justified on economic grounds, and the interest of the landed classes was shown to be in conflict with the interest of society as a whole.

The following selections are from Ricardo's *Principles* and his essay on *The High Price of Bullion* (1809). The essay, which was incorporated in the famous report of the Bullion Committee, sets forth his explanation of the great rise in prices which followed the suspension of specie payments in 1797. The exposition of the "currency principle" of banking has become a classic in the field.

PRINCIPLES OF POLITICAL ECONOMY AND TAXATION *

On Value

THE VALUE OF A COMMODITY, OR THE QUANTITY OF ANY OTHER COMMODITY FOR WHICH IT WILL EXCHANGE, DEPENDS ON THE RELATIVE QUANTITY OF LABOUR WHICH IS NECESSARY FOR ITS PRODUCTION, AND NOT ON THE GREATER OR LESS COMPENSATION WHICH IS PAID FOR THAT LABOUR

It has been observed by Adam Smith that "the word Value has two different meanings, and sometimes expresses the utility of some particular object, and sometimes the power of purchasing other goods which the possession of that object conveys. The one may be called *value in use;* the other *value in exchange.* The things," he continues, "which have the greatest value in use, have frequently little or no value in exchange; and, on the contrary, those which have the greatest value in exchange, have little or no value in use." Water and air are abundantly useful; they are indeed indispensable to existence, yet, under ordinary circumstances, nothing can be obtained in exchange for them. Gold, on the contrary, though of little use compared with air or water, will exchange for a great quantity of other goods.

Utility then is not the measure of exchangeable value, although it is absolutely essential to it. If a commodity were in no way useful—in other words, if it could in no way contribute to our gratification—it would be destitute of exchangeable value, however scarce it might be, or whatever quantity of labour might be necessary to procure it.

Possessing utility, commodities derive their exchangeable value from two sources: from their scarcity, and from the quantity of labour required to obtain them.

There are some commodities, the value of which is determined by their

* From *The Principles of Political Economy and Taxation* (London, 1817).

scarcity alone. No labour can increase the quantity of such goods, and therefore their value cannot be lowered by an increased supply. Some rare statues and pictures, scarce books and coins, wines of a peculiar quality, which can be made only from grapes grown on a particular soil, of which there is a very limited quantity, are all of this description. Their value is wholly independent of the quantity of labour originally necessary to produce them, and varies with the varying wealth and inclinations of those who are desirous to possess them.

These commodities, however, form a very small part of the mass of commodities daily exchanged in the market. By far the greatest part of those goods which are the objects of desire are procured by labour; and they may be multiplied, not in one country alone, but in many, almost without any assignable limit, if we are disposed to bestow the labour necessary to obtain them.

In speaking, then, of commodities, of their exchangeable value, and of the laws which regulate their relative prices, we mean always such commodities only as can be increased in quantity by the exertion of human industry, and on the production of which competition operates without restraint.

In the early stages of society, the exchangeable value of these commodities, or the rule which determines how much of one shall be given in exchange for another, depends almost exclusively on the comparative quantity of labour expended on each. . . .

That this is really the foundation of the exchangeable value of all things, excepting those which cannot be increased by human industry, is a doctrine of the utmost importance in political economy . . .

If the quantity of labour realised in commodities regulate their exchangeable value, every increase of the quantity of labour must augment the value of that commodity on which it is exercised, as every diminution must lower it.

Adam Smith, who so accurately defined the original source of exchangeable value, and who was bound in consistency to maintain that all things became more or less valuable in proportion as more or less labour was bestowed on their production, has himself erected another standard measure of value, and speaks of things being more or less valuable in proportion as they will exchange for more or less of this standard measure. Sometimes he speaks of corn, at other times of labour, as a standard measure; not the quantity of labour bestowed on the production of any object, but the quantity which it can command in the market: as if these were two equivalent expressions, and as if, because a man's labour had become doubly efficient, and he could therefore produce twice the quantity of a commodity, he would necessarily receive twice the former quantity in exchange for it.

If this indeed were true, if the reward of the labourer were always in proportion to what he produced, the quantity of labour bestowed on a commodity, and the quantity of labour which that commodity would purchase, would be equal, and either might accurately measure the variations of other things; but they are not equal; the first is under many circumstances an invariable standard, indicating correctly the variations of other things; the latter is subject to as many fluctuations as the commodities compared with it. Adam Smith, after most ably showing the insufficiency of a variable medium, such as gold and silver, for the purpose of determining the varying value of other things, has himself, by fixing on corn or labour, chosen a medium no less variable.

Gold and silver are no doubt subject to fluctuations from the discovery of new and more abundant mines; but such discoveries are rare, and their effects, though powerful, are limited to periods of comparatively short duration. They are subject also to fluctuation from improvements in the skill and machinery with which the mines may be worked; as in consequence of such improvements a greater quantity may be obtained with the same labour. They are further subject to fluctuation from the decreasing produce of the mines, after they have yielded a supply to the world for a succession of ages. But from which of these sources of fluctuation is corn exempted? Does not that also vary, on one hand, from improvements in agriculture, from improved machinery and implements used in husbandry, as well as from the discovery of new tracts of fertile land, which in other countries may be taken into cultivation, and which will affect the value of corn in every market where importation is free? Is it not on the other hand subject to be enhanced in value from prohibitions of importation, from increasing population and wealth, and the greater difficulty of obtaining the increased supplies, on account of the additional quantity of labour which the cultivation of inferior land requires? Is not the value of labour equally variable; being not only affected, as all other things are, by the proportion between the supply and demand, which uniformly varies with every change in the condition of the community, but also by the varying price of food and other necessaries, on which the wages of labour are expended?

In the same country double the quantity of labour may be required to produce a given quantity of food and necessaries at one time that may be necessary at another and a distant time; yet the labourer's reward may possibly be very little diminished. If the labourer's wages at the former period were a certain quantity of food and necessaries, he probably could not have subsisted if that quantity had been reduced. Food and necessaries in this case will have risen 100 per cent. if estimated by the *quantity* of labour necessary to their production, while they will scarcely have increased in value if measured by the quantity of labour for which they will *exchange*. . . .

It cannot then be correct to say with Adam Smith, "that as labour may sometimes *purchase* a greater and sometimes a smaller quantity of goods, it is their value which varies, not that of the labour which purchases them;" and therefore, "that labour, *alone never varying in its own value,* is alone the ultimate and real standard by which the value of all commodities can at all times and places be estimated and compared;"—but it is correct to say, as Adam Smith had previously said, "that the proportion between the quantities of labour necessary for acquiring different objects seems to be the only circumstance which can afford any rule for exchanging them for one another;" or in other words that it is the comparative quantity of commodities which labour will produce that determines their present or past relative value, and not the comparative quantities of commodities which are given to the labourer in exchange for his labour. . . .

LABOUR OF DIFFERENT QUALITIES DIFFERENTLY REWARDED. THIS NO CAUSE OF VARIATION IN THE RELATIVE VALUE OF COMMODITIES

In speaking, however, of labour, as being the foundation of all value, and the relative quantity of labour as almost exclusively determining the relative value of commodities, I must not be supposed to be inattentive to the different qualities of labour, and the difficulty of comparing an hour's or a day's labour in one employment with the same duration of labour in another. The estimation in which different qualities of labour are held comes soon to be adjusted in the market with sufficient precision for all practical purposes, and depends much on the comparative skill of the labourer and intensity of the labour performed. The scale, when once formed, is liable to little variation. If a day's labour of a working jeweller be more valuable than a day's labour of a common labourer, it has long ago been adjusted and placed in its proper position in the scale of value.

In comparing, therefore, the value of the same commodity at different periods of time, the consideration of the comparative skill and intensity of labour required for that particular commodity needs scarcely to be attended to, as it operates equally at both periods. One description of labour at one time is compared with the same description of labour at another; if a tenth, a fifth, or a fourth has been added or taken away, an effect proportioned to the cause will be produced on the relative value of the commodity.

If a piece of cloth be now of the value of two pieces of linen, and if, in ten years hence, the ordinary value of a piece of cloth should be four pieces of linen, we may safely conclude that either more labour is required to make the cloth, or less to make the linen, or that both causes have operated.

As the inquiry to which I wish to draw the reader's attention relates to the effect of the variations in the relative value of commodities, and not in their absolute value, it will be of little importance to examine into the comparative degree of estimation in which the different kinds of human labour are held. We may fairly conclude that whatever inequality there might originally have been in them, whatever the ingenuity, skill, or time necessary for the acquirement of one species of manual dexterity more than another, it continues nearly the same from one generation to another; or at least that the variation is very inconsiderable from year to year, and therefore can have little effect, for short periods, on the relative value of commodities. . . .

NOT ONLY THE LABOUR APPLIED IMMEDIATELY TO COMMODITIES AFFECT THEIR VALUE, BUT THE LABOUR ALSO WHICH IS BESTOWED ON THE IMPLEMENTS, TOOLS, AND BUILDINGS, WITH WHICH SUCH LABOUR IS ASSISTED

Even in that early state to which Adam Smith refers, some capital, though possibly made and accumulated by the hunter himself, would be necessary to enable him to kill his game. Without some weapon, neither the beaver nor the deer could be destroyed, and therefore the value of these animals would be regulated, not solely by the time and labour necessary to their destruction, but also by the time and labour necessary for providing the hunter's capital, the weapon, by the aid of which their destruction was effected.

Suppose the weapons necessary to kill the beaver was constructed with much more labour than that necessary to kill the deer, on account of the greater difficulty of approaching near to the former animal, and the consequent necessity of its being more true to its mark; one beaver would naturally be of more value than two deer, and precisely for this reason, that more labour would, on the whole, be necessary to its destruction. Or suppose that the same quantity of labour was necessary to make both weapons, but that they were of very unequal durability; of the durable implement only a small portion of its value would be transferred to the commodity, a much greater portion of the value of the less durable implement would be realised in the commodity which it contributed to produce.

All the implements necessary to kill the beaver and deer might belong to one class of men, and the labour employed in their destruction might be furnished by another class; still, their comparative prices would be in proportion to the actual labour bestowed, both on the formation of the capital and on the destruction of the animals. Under different circumstances of plenty or scarcity of capital, as compared with labour, under different circumstances of plenty or scarcity of the food and necessaries essential to the support of men, those who furnished an equal value of capital for either one employment or for the other might have a half, a fourth, or an eighth of the produce obtained, the remainder being paid as wages to those who furnished the labour; yet this division could not affect the relative value of these commodities, since whether the profits of capital were greater or less, whether they were 50, 20, or 10 per cent., or whether the wages of labour were high or low, they would operate equally on both employments.

If we suppose the occupations of the society extended, that some provide canoes and tackle necessary for fishing, others the seed and rude machinery first used in agriculture, still the same principle would hold true, that the exchangeable value of the commodities produced would be in proportion to the labour bestowed on their production; not on their immediate production only, but on all those implements or machines required to give effect to the particular labour to which they were applied.

If we look to a state of society in which greater improvements have been made, and in which arts and commerce flourish, we shall still find that commodities vary in value conformably with this principle: in estimating the exchangeable value of stockings, for example, we shall find that their value, comparatively with other things, depends on the total quantity of labour necessary to manufacture them and bring them to market. First, there is the labour necessary to cultivate the land on which the raw cotton is grown; secondly, the labour of conveying the cotton to the country where the stockings are to be manufactured, which includes a portion of the labour bestowed in building the ship in which it is conveyed, and which is charged in the freight of the goods; thirdly, the labour of the spinner and weaver; fourthly, a portion of the labour of the engineer, smith, and carpenter, who erected the buildings and machinery, by the help of which they are made; fifthly, the labour of the retail dealer, and of many others, whom it is unnecessary further to particularise. The aggregate sum of these various kinds of labour determines the quantity of other things for which these stockings will exchange, while the same consideration of the various quantities of labour which have been bestowed on those other things will equally govern the portion of them which will be given for the stockings. . . .

On Rent

It remains however to be considered whether the appropriation of land, and the consequent creation of rent, will occasion any variation in the relative value of commodities independently of the quantity of labour necessary to production. In order to understand this part of the subject we must inquire into the nature of rent, and the laws by which its rise or fall is regulated.

Rent is that portion of the produce of the earth which is paid to the landlord for the use of the original and indestructible powers of the soil. It is often, however, confounded with the interest and profit of capital, and, in popular language, the term is applied to whatever is annually paid by a farmer to his landlord. If, of two adjoining farms of the same extent, and of the same natural fertility, one had all the conveniences of farming buildings, and, besides, were properly drained and manured, and advantageously divided by hedges, fences, and walls, while the other had none of these advantages, more remuneration would naturally be paid for the use of one than for the use of the other; yet in both cases this remuneration would be called rent. But it is evident that a portion only of the money annually to be paid for the improved farm would be given for the original and indestructible powers of the soil; the other portion would be paid for the use of the capital which had been employed in ameliorating the quality of the land, and in erecting such buildings as were necessary to secure and preserve the produce. Adam Smith sometimes speaks of rent in the strict sense to which I am desirous of confining it, but more often in the popular sense in which the term is usually employed. He tells us that the demand for timber, and its consequent high price, in the more southern countries of Europe caused a rent to be paid for forests in Norway, which could before afford no rent. Is it not, however, evident that the person who paid what he thus calls rent, paid it in consideration of the valuable commodity which was then standing on the land, and that he actually repaid himself with a profit by the sale of the timber? If, indeed, after the timber was removed, any compensation were paid to the landlord for the use of the land, for the purpose of growing timber or any other produce, with a view to future demand, such compensation might justly be called rent, because it would be paid for the productive powers of the land; but in the case stated by Adam Smith, the compensation was paid for the liberty of removing and selling the timber, and not for the liberty of growing it. He speaks also of the rent of coal mines, and of stone quarries, to which the same observation applies—that the compensation given for the mine or quarry is paid for the value of the coal or stone which can be removed from them, and has no connection with the original and indestructible powers of the land. This is a distinction of great importance in an inquiry concerning rent and profits; for it is found that the laws which regulate the progress of rent are widely different from those which regulate the progress of profits, and seldom operate in the same direction. In all improved countries, that which is annually paid to the landlord, partaking of both characters, rent and profit, is sometimes kept stationary by the effects of opposing causes; at other times advances or recedes as one or the other of these causes preponderates. In the future pages of this work, then, whenever I speak of the rent of land, I wish to be understood as speaking of that compensation which is paid to the owner of land for the use of its original and indestructible powers.

On the first settling of a country in which there is an abundance of rich and fertile land, a very small proportion of which is required to be cultivated for the support of the actual population, or indeed can be cultivated with the capital which the population can command, there will be no rent; for no one would pay for the use of land when there was an abundant quantity not yet appropriated, and, therefore, at the disposal of whosoever might choose to cultivate it.

On the common principles of supply and demand, no rent could be paid for such land, for the reason stated why nothing is given for the use of air and water, or for any other of the gifts of nature which exist in boundless quantity. With a given quantity of materials, and with the assistance of the pressure of the atmosphere, and the elasticity of steam, engines may perform work, and abridge human labour to a very great extent; but no charge is made for the use of these natural aids, because they are inexhaustible and at every man's disposal. In the same manner, the brewer, the distiller, the dyer, make incessant use of the air and water for the production of their commodities; but as the supply is boundless, they bear no price. If all land had the same properties, if it were unlimited in quantity, and uniform in quality, no charge could be made for its use, unless where it possessed peculiar advantages of situation. It is only, then, because land is not unlimited in quantity and uniform in quality, and because, in the progress of population, land of an inferior quality, or less advantageously situated, is called into cultivation, that rent is ever paid for the use of it. When, in the progress of society, land of the second degree of fertility is taken into cultivation, rent immediately commences on that of the first quality, and the amount of that rent will depend on the difference in the quality of these two portions of land.

When land of the third quality is taken into cultivation, rent immediately commences on the second, and it is regulated as before by the difference in their productive powers. At the same time, the rent of the first quality will rise, for that must always be above the rent of the second by the difference between the produce which they yield with a given quantity of capital and labour. With every step in the progress of population, which shall oblige a country to have recourse to land of a worse quality, to enable it to raise its supply of food, rent, on all the more fertile land, will rise.

Thus suppose land—No. 1, 2, 3—to yield, with an equal employment of capital and labour, a net produce of 100, 90, and 80 quarters of corn. In a new country, where there is an abundance of fertile land compared with the population, and where therefore it is only necessary to cultivate No. 1, the whole net produce will belong to the cultivator, and will be the profits of the stock which he advances. As soon as population had so far increased as to make it necessary to cultivate No. 2, from which ninety quarters only can be obtained after supporting the labourers, rent would commence on No. 1; for either there must be two rates of profit on agricultural capital, or ten quarters, or the value of ten quarters must be withdrawn from the produce of No. 1 for some other purpose. Whether the proprietor of the land, or any other person, cultivated No. 1, these ten quarters would equally constitute rent; for the cultivator of No. 2 would get the same result with his capital whether he cultivated No. 1, paying ten quarters for rent, or continued to cultivate No. 2, paying no rent. In the same manner it might be shown that when No. 3 is brought into cultivation, the rent of No. 2 must be ten quarters, or the value of ten quarters, whilst the rent of No. 1 would rise to twenty quarters; for the cultivator of No. 3 would have the same profits whether he paid twenty quarters for the rent of No. 1, ten quarters for the rent of No. 2, or cultivated No. 3 free of all rent.

It often, and, indeed, commonly happens, that before No. 2, 3, 4, or 5, or the inferior lands are cultivated, capital can be employed more productively on those lands which are already in cultivation. It may perhaps be found that by doubling the original capital employed on No. 1, though the produce will not be doubled, will not be increased by 100 quarters, it may be increased by eighty-five quarters, and that this quantity exceeds what could be obtained by employing the same capital on land No. 3.

In such case, capital will be preferably employed on the old land, and will equally create a rent; for rent is always the difference between the produce obtained by the employment of two equal quantities of capital and labour. If, with a capital of £1000 a tenant obtain 100 quarters of wheat from his land, and by the employment of a second capital of £1000 he obtain a further return of eighty-five, his landlord would have the power, at the expiration of his lease, of obliging him to pay fifteen quarters or an equivalent value for additional rent; for there cannot be two rates of profit. If he is satisfied with a diminution of fifteen quarters in the return for his second £1000, it is because no employment more profitable can be found for it. The common rate of profit would be in that proportion, and if the original tenant refused, some other person would be found willing to give all which exceeded that rate of profit to the owner of the land from which he derived it.

In this case, as well as in the other, the capital last employed pays no rent. For the greater productive powers of the first £1000, fifteen quarters, is paid for rent, for the employment of the second £1000 no rent whatever is paid. If a third £1000 be employed on the same land, with a return of seventy-five quarters, rent will then be paid for the second £1000, and will be equal to the difference between the produce of these two, or ten quarters; and at the same time the rent for the first £1000 will rise from fifteen to twenty-five quarters; while the last £1000 will pay no rent whatever.

If, then, good land existed in a quantity much more abundant than the production of food for an increasing population required, or if capital could be indefinitely employed without a diminished return on the old land, there could be no rise of rent; for rent invariably proceeds from the employment of an additional quantity of labour with a proportionally less return.

The most fertile and most favourably situated land will be first cultivated, and the exchangeable value of its produce will be adjusted in the same manner as the exchangeable value of all other commodities, by the total quantity of labour necessary in various forms, from first to last, to produce it and bring it to market. When land of an inferior quality is taken into cultivation, the exchangeable value of raw produce will rise, because more labour is required to produce it.

The exchangeable value of all commodities, whether they be manufactured, or the produce of the mines, or the produce of land, is always regulated, not by the less quantity of labour that will suffice for their production under circumstances highly favourable, and exclusively enjoyed by those who have peculiar facilities of production; but by the greater quantity of labour necessarily bestowed on their production by those who have no such facilities; by those who continue to produce them under the most unfavourable circumstances; meaning—by the most unfavourable circumstances, the most unfavourable under which the quantity of produce required renders it necessary to carry on the production.

Thus, in a charitable institution, where the poor are set to work with the funds of benefactors, the general prices of the commodities, which are the produce of such work, will not be governed by the peculiar facilities afforded to these workmen, but by the common, usual, and natural difficulties which every other manufacturer will have to encounter. The manufacturer enjoying none of these facilities might indeed be driven altogether from the market if the supply afforded by these favoured workmen were equal to all the wants of the community; but if he continued the trade, it would be only on condition that he should derive from it the usual and general rate of profits on stock; and that could only happen when his commodity sold for a price proportioned to the quantity of labour bestowed on its production.

It is true, that on the best land, the same produce would still be obtained with the same labour as before, but its value would be enhanced in consequence of the diminished returns obtained by those who employed fresh labour and stock on the less fertile land. Notwithstanding, then, that the advantages of fertile over inferior lands are in no case lost, but only transferred from the cultivator, or consumer, to the landlord, yet, since more labour is required on the inferior lands, and since it is from such land only that we are enabled to furnish ourselves with the additional supply of raw produce, the comparative value of that produce will continue permanently above its former level, and make it exchange for more hats, cloth, shoes, etc., etc., in the production of which no such additional quantity of labour is required.

The reason, then, why raw produce rises in comparative value is because more labour is employed in the production of the last portion obtained, and not because a rent is paid to the landlord. The value of corn is regulated by the quantity of labour bestowed on its production on that quality of land, or with that portion of capital, which pays no rent. Corn is not high because a rent is paid, but a rent is paid because corn is high; and it has been justly observed that no reduction would take place in the price of corn although landlords should forego the whole of their rent. Such a measure would only enable some farmers to live like gentlemen, but would not diminish the quantity of labour necessary to raise raw produce on the least productive land in cultivation.

Nothing is more common than to hear of the advantages which the land possesses over every other source of useful produce, on account of the surplus which it yields in the form of rent. Yet when land is most abundant, when most productive, and most fertile, it yields no rent; and it is only when its powers decay, and less is yielded in return for labour, that a share of the original produce of the more fertile portions is set apart for rent. It is singular that this quality in the land, which should have been noticed as an imperfection compared with the natural agents by which manufacturers are assisted, should have been pointed out as constituting its peculiar pre-eminence. If air, water, the elasticity of steam, and the pressure of the atmosphere were of various qualities; if they could be appropriated, and each quality existed only in moderate abundance, they, as well as the land, would afford a rent, as the successive qualities were brought into use. With every worse quality employed, the value of the commodities in the manufacture of which they were used would rise, because equal quantities of labour would be less productive. Man would do more by the sweat of his brow and nature perform less; and the land would be no longer pre-eminent for its limited powers.

If the surplus produce which land affords in the form of rent be an advantage, it is desirable that, every year, the machinery newly constructed should be less efficient than the old, as that would undoubtedly give a greater exchangeable value to the goods manufactured, not only by that machinery but by all the other machinery in the kingdom; and a rent would be paid to all those who possessed the most productive machinery.

The rise of rent is always the effect of the increasing wealth of the country, and of the difficulty of providing food for its augmented population. It is a symptom, but it is never a cause of wealth; for wealth often increases most rapidly while rent is either stationary, or even falling. Rent increases most rapidly as the disposable land decreases in its productive powers. Wealth increases most rapidly in those countries where the disposable land is most fertile, where importation is least restricted, and where, through agricultural improvements, productions can be multiplied without any increase in the proportional quantity of labour, and where consequently the progress of rent is slow. . . .

[1]. . . The interest of the landlord is always opposed to that of the consumer and manufacturer. Corn can be permanently at an advanced price only because additional labour is necessary to produce it; because its cost of production is increased. The same cause invariably raises rent, it is therefore for the interest of the landlord that the cost attending the production of corn should be increased. This, however, is not the interest of the consumer; to him it is desirable that corn should be low relatively to money and commodities, for it is always with commodities or money that corn is purchased. Neither is it the interest of the manufacturer that corn should be at a high price, for the high price of corn will occasion high wages, but will not raise the price of his commodity. Not only, then, must more of his commodity, or, which comes to the same thing, the value of more of his commodity, be given in exchange for the corn which he himself consumes, but more must be given, or the value of more, for wages to his workmen, for which he will receive no remuneration. All classes, therefore, except the landlords, will be injured by the increase in the price of corn. . . .[1]

[1] From a later chapter on the "Doctrine of Adam Smith Concerning the Rent of Land."

On Natural and Market Price

In making labour the foundation of the value of commodities, and the comparative quantity of labour which is necessary to their production, the rule which determines the respective quantities of goods which shall be given in exchange for each other, we must not be supposed to deny the accidental and temporary deviations of the actual or market price of commodities from this, their primary and natural price.

In the ordinary course of events, there is no commodity which continues for any length of time to be supplied precisely in that degree of abundance which the wants and wishes of mankind require, and therefore there is none which is not subject to accidental and temporary variations of price.

It is only in consequence of such variations that capital is apportioned precisely, in the requisite abundance and no more, to the production of the different commodities which happen to be in demand. With the rise or fall of price, profits are elevated above, or depressed below, their general level; and capital is either encouraged to enter into, or is warned to depart from, the particular employment in which the variation has taken place.

Whilst every man is free to employ his capital where he pleases, he will naturally seek for it that employment which is most advantageous; he will naturally be dissatisfied with a profit of 10 per cent., if by removing his capital he can obtain a profit of 15 per cent. This restless desire on the part of all the employers of stock to quit a less profitable for a more advantageous business has a strong tendency to equalise the rate of profits of all, or to fix them in such proportions as may, in the estimation of the parties, compensate for any advantage which one may have, or may appear to have, over the other. It is perhaps very difficult to trace the steps by which this change is effected: it is probably effected by a manufacturer not absolutely changing his employment, but only lessening the quantity of capital he has in that employment. . . .

A capitalist, in seeking profitable employment for his funds, will naturally take into consideration all the advantages which one occupation possesses over another. He may therefore be willing to forego a part of his money profit in consideration of the security, cleanliness, ease, or any other real or fancied advantage which one employment may possess over another.

If from a consideration of these circumstances, the profits of stock should be so adjusted that in one trade they were 20, in another 25, and in another 30 per cent., they would probably continue permanently with that relative difference, and with that difference only; for if any cause should elevate the profits of one of these trades 10 per cent., either these profits would be temporary, and would soon again fall back to their usual station, or the profits of the others would be elevated in the same proportion.

The present time appears to be one of the exceptions to the justness of this remark. The termination of the war has so deranged the division which before existed of employments in Europe, that every capitalist has not yet found his place in the new division which has now become necessary.

Let us suppose that all commodities are at their natural price, and consequently that the profits of capital in all employments are exactly at the same rate, or differ only so much as, in the estimation of the parties, is equivalent to any real or fancied advantage which they possess or forego. Suppose now that a change of fashion should increase the demand for silks and lessen that for woollens; their natural price, the quantity of labour necessary to their production, would continue unaltered, but the market price of silks would rise and that of woollens would fall; and consequently the profits of the silk manufacturer would be above, whilst those of the woollen manufacturer would be below, the general and adjusted rate of profits. Not only the profits, but the wages of the workmen, would be affected in these employments. This increased demand for silks would, however, soon be supplied by the transference of capital and labour from the woollen to the silk manufacture; when the market prices of silks and woollens would again approach their natural prices, and then the usual profits would be obtained by the respective manufacturers of those commodities.

It is then the desire, which every capitalist has, of diverting his funds from a less to a more profitable employment that prevents the market price of commodities from continuing for any length of time either much above or much below their natural price. It is this competition which so adjusts the changeable value of commodities that, after paying the wages for the labour necessary to their production, and all other expenses required to put the capital employed in its original state of efficiency, the remaining value or overplus will in each trade be in proportion to the value of the capital employed.

In the seventh chapter of the *Wealth of Nations,* all that concerns this question is most ably treated. Having fully acknowledged the temporary effects which, in particular employments of capital, may be produced on the prices of commodities, as well as on the wages of labour, and the profits of stock, by accidental causes, without influencing the general price of commodities, wages, or profits, since these effects are equally operative in all stages of society, we will leave them entirely out of our consideration whilst we are treating of the laws which regulate natural prices, natural wages, and natural profits, effects totally independent of these accidental causes. In speaking, then, of the exchangeable value of commodities, or the power of purchasing possessed by any one commodity, I mean always that power which it would possess if not disturbed by any temporary or accidental cause, and which is its natural price.

On Wages

Labour, like all other things which are purchased and sold, and which may be increased or diminished in quantity, has its natural and its market price. The natural price of labour is that price which is necessary to enable the labourers, one with another, to subsist and to perpetuate their race, without either increase or diminution.

The power of the labourer to support himself, and the family which may be necessary to keep up the number of labourers, does not depend on the quantity of money which he may receive for wages, but on the quantity of food, necessaries, and conveniences become essential to him from habit which that money will purchase. The natural price of labour, therefore, depends on the price of the food, necessaries, and conveniences required for the support of the labourer and his family. With a rise in the price of food and necessaries, the natural price of labour will rise; with the fall in their price, the natural price of labour will fall.

With the progress of society the natural price of labour has always a tendency to rise, because one of the principal commodities by which its natural price is regulated has a tendency to become dearer from the greater difficulty of producing it. As, however, the improvements in agriculture, the discovery of new markets, whence provisions may be imported, may for a time counteract the tendency to a rise in the price of necessaries, and may even occasion their natural price to fall, so will the same causes produce the correspondent effects on the natural price of labour.

The natural price of all commodities, excepting raw produce and labour, has a tendency to fall in the progress of wealth and population; for though, on one hand, they are enhanced in real value, from the rise in the natural price of the raw material of which they are made, this is more than counterbalanced by the improvements in machinery, by the better division and distribution of labour, and by the increasing skill, both in science and art, of the producers.

The market price of labour is the price which is really paid for it, from the natural operation of the proportion of the supply to the demand; labour is dear when it is scarce and cheap when it is plentiful. However much the market price of labour may deviate from its natural price, it has, like commodities, a tendency to conform to it.

It is when the market price of labour exceeds its natural price that the condition of the labourer is flourishing and happy, that he has it in his power to command a greater proportion of the necessaries and enjoyments of life, and therefore to rear a healthy and numerous family. When, however, by the encouragement which high wages give to the increase of population, the number of labourers is increased, wages again fall to their natural price, and indeed from a reaction sometimes fall below it.

When the market price of labour is below its natural price, the condition of the labourers is most wretched: then poverty deprives them of those comforts which custom renders absolute necessaries. It is only after their privations have reduced their number, or the demand for labour has increased, that the market price of labour will rise to its natural price, and that the labourer will have the moderate comforts which the natural rate of wages will afford.

Notwithstanding the tendency of wages to conform to their natural rate, their market rate may, in an improving society, for an indefinite period, be constantly above it; for no sooner may the impulse which an increased capital gives to a new demand for labour be obeyed, than another increase of capital may produce the same effect; and thus, if the increase of capital be gradual and constant, the demand for labour may give a continued stimulus to an increase of people.

Capital is that part of the wealth of a country which is employed in production, and consists of food, clothing, tools, raw materials, machinery, etc., necessary to give effect to labour.

Capital may increase in quantity at the same time that its value rises. An addition may be made to the food and clothing of a country at the same time that more labour may be required to produce the additional quantity than before; in that case not only the quantity but the value of capital will rise.

Or capital may increase without its value increasing, and even while its value is actually diminishing; not only may an addition be made to the food and clothing of a country, but the addition may be made by the aid of machinery, without any increase, and even with an absolute diminution in the proportional quantity of labour required to produce them. The quantity of capital may increase, while neither the whole together, nor any part of it singly, will have a greater value than before, but may actually have a less.

In the first case, the natural price of labour, which always depends on the price of food, clothing, and other necessaries, will rise; in the second, it will remain stationary or fall; but in both cases the market rate of wages will rise, for in proportion to the increase of capital will be the increase in the demand for labour; in proportion to the work to be done will be the demand for those who are to do it.

In both cases, too, the market price of labour will rise above its natural price; and in both cases it will have a tendency to conform to its natural price, but in the first case this agreement will be most speedily effected. The situation of the labourer will be improved, but not much improved; for the increased price of food and necessaries will absorb a large portion of his increased wages; consequently a small supply of labour, or a trifling increase in the population, will soon reduce the market price to the then increased natural price of labour.

In the second case, the condition of the labourer will be very greatly improved; he will receive increased money wages without having to pay any increased price, and perhaps even a diminished price for the commodities which he and his family consume; and it will not be till after a great addition has been made to the population that the market price of labour will again sink to its then low and reduced natural price.

Thus, then, with every improvement of society, with every increase in its capital, the market wages of labour will rise; but the permanence of their rise will depend on the question whether the natural price of labour has also risen; and this again will depend on the rise in the natural price of those necessaries on which the wages of labour are expended.

It is not to be understood that the natural price of labour, estimated even in food and necessaries, is absolutely fixed and constant. It varies at different times in the same country, and very materially differs in different countries. It essentially depends on the habits and customs of the people. . . .

From manufactured commodities always falling and raw produce always rising, with the progress of society, such a disproportion in their relative value is at length created, that in rich countries a labourer, by the sacrifice of a very small quantity only of his food, is able to provide liberally for all his other wants.

Independently of the variations in the value of money, which necessarily affect money wages, but which we have here supposed to have no operation, as we have considered money to be uniformly of the same value, it appears then that wages are subject to a rise or fall from two causes:—

First, the supply and demand of labourers.

Secondly, the price of the commodities on which the wages of labour are expended.

In different stages of society, the accumulation of capital, or of the means of employing labour, is more or less rapid, and must in all cases depend on the productive powers of labour. The productive powers of labour are generally greatest when there is an abundance of fertile land: at such periods accumulation is often so rapid that labourers cannot be supplied with the same rapidity as capital.

It has been calculated that under favourable circumstances population may be doubled in twenty-five years; but under the same favourable circumstances the whole capital of a country might possibly be doubled in a shorter period. In that case, wages during the whole period would have a tendency to rise, because the demand for labour would increase still faster than the supply.

In new settlements, where the arts and knowledge of countries far advanced in refinement are introduced, it is probable that capital has a tendency to increase faster than mankind; and if the deficiency of labourers were not supplied by more populous countries, this tendency would very much raise the price of labour. In proportion as these countries become populous, and land of a worse quality is taken into cultivation, the tendency to an increase of capital diminishes; for the surplus produce remaining, after satisfying the wants of the existing population, must necessarily be in proportion to the facility of production, viz. to the smaller number of persons employed in production. Although, then, it is probable that, under the most favourable circumstances, the power of production is still greater than that of population, it will not long continue so; for the land being limited in quantity, and differing in quality, with every increased portion of capital employed on it there will be a decreased rate of production, whilst the power of population continues always the same.

In those countries where there is abundance of fertile land, but where, from the ignorance, indolence, and barbarism of the inhabitants, they are exposed to all the evils of want and famine, and where it has been said that population presses against the means of subsistence, a very different remedy should be applied from that which is necessary in long settled countries, where, from the diminishing rate of the supply of raw produce, all the evils of a crowded population are experienced. In the one case, the evil proceeds from bad government, from the insecurity of property, and from a want of education in all ranks of the people. To be made happier they require only to be better governed and instructed, as the augmentation of capital, beyond the augmentation of people, would be the inevitable result. No increase in the population can be too great, as the powers of production are still greater. In the other case, the population increases faster than the funds required for its support. Every exertion of industry, unless accompanied by a diminished rate of increase in the population, will add to the evil, for production cannot keep pace with it. . . .

On Profits

The profits of stock, in different employments, having been shown to bear a proportion to each other, and to have a tendency to vary all in the same degree and in the same direction, it remains for us to consider what is the cause of the permanent variations in the rate of profit, and the consequent permanent alterations in the rate of interest.

We have seen that the price [1] of corn is regulated by the quantity of labour necessary to produce it, with that portion of capital which pays no rent. We have seen, too, that all manufactured commodities rise and fall in price in proportion as more or less labour becomes necessary to their production. Neither the farmer who cultivates that quantity of land which regulates price, nor the manufacturer who manufactures goods, sacrifice any portion of the produce for rent. The whole value of their commodities is divided into two portions only: one constitutes the profits of stock, the other the wages of labour.

Supposing corn and manufactured goods always to sell at the same price, profits would be high or low in proportion as wages were low or high. But suppose corn to rise in price because more labour is necessary to produce it; that cause will not raise the price of manufactured goods in the production of which no additional quantity of labour is required. If, then, wages continued the same, the profits of manufacturers would remain the

[1] The reader is desired to bear in mind that, for the purpose of making the subject more clear, I consider money to be invariable in value, and therefore every variation of price to be referable to an alteration in the value of the commodity.

same; but if, as is absolutely certain, wages should rise with the rise of corn, then their profits would necessarily fall. . . .

On the Influence of Demand and Supply on Prices

It is the cost of production which must ultimately regulate the price of commodities, and not, as has been often said, the proportion between the supply and demand: the proportion between supply and demand may, indeed, for a time, affect the market value of a commodity, until it is supplied in greater or less abundance, according as the demand may have increased or diminished; but this effect will be only of temporary duration.

Diminish the cost of production of hats, and their price will ultimately fall to their new natural price, although the demand should be doubled, trebled, or quadrupled. Diminish the cost of subsistence of men, by diminishing the natural price of the food and clothing by which life is sustained, and wages will ultimately fall, notwithstanding that the demand for labourers may very greatly increase.

The opinion that the price of commodities depends solely on the proportion of supply to demand, or demand to supply, has become almost an axiom in political economy, and has been the source of much error in that science. It is this opinion which has made Mr. Buchanan maintain that wages are not influenced by a rise or fall in the price of provisions, but solely by the demand and supply of labour; and that a tax on the wages of labour would not raise wages, because it would not alter the proportion of the demand of labourers to the supply.

The demand for a commodity cannot be said to increase if no additional quantity of it be purchased or consumed; and yet under such circumstances its money value may rise. Thus, if the value of money were to fall, the price of every commodity would rise, for each of the competitors would be willing to spend more money than before on its purchase; but though its price rose 10 or 20 per cent., if no more were bought than before, it would not, I apprehend, be admissible to say that the variation in the price of the commodity was caused by the increased demand for it. Its natural price, its money cost of production, would be really altered by the altered value of money; and without any increase of demand, the price of the commodity would be naturally adjusted to that new value.

"We have seen," says M. Say, "that the cost of production determines the lowest price to which things can fall: the price below which they cannot remain for any length of time, because production would then be either entirely stopped or diminished." Vol. ii. p. 26.

He afterwards says that the demand for gold having increased in a still greater proportion than the supply, since the discovery of the mines, "its price in goods, instead of falling in the proportion of ten to one, fell only in the proportion of four to one;" that is to say, instead of falling in proportion as its natural price had fallen, fell in proportion as the supply exceeded the demand.—*"The value of every commodity rises always in a direct ratio to the demand, and in an inverse ratio to the supply."*

The same opinion is expressed by the Earl of Lauderdale.

"With respect to the variations in value, of which everything valuable is susceptible, if we could for a moment suppose that any substance possessed intrinsic and fixed value, so as to render an assumed quantity of it constantly, under all circumstances, of an equal value, then the degree of value of all things, ascertained by such a fixed standard, would vary according to the proportion *betwixt the quantity of them* and the demand for them, and every commodity would, of course, be subject to a variation in its value, from four different circumstances:

1. "It would be subject to an increase of its value, from a diminution of its quantity.

2. "To a diminution of its value, from an augmentation of its quantity.

3. "It might suffer an augmentation in its value, from the circumstance of an increased demand.

4. "Its value might be diminished by a failure of demand.

"As it will, however, clearly appear that no commodity can possess fixed and intrinsic value, so as to qualify it for a measure of the value of other commodities, mankind are induced to select, as a practical measure of value, that which appears the least liable to any of these four sources of variations, *which are the sole causes of alteration of value.*

"When, in common language, therefore, we express the *value* of any commodity, it may vary at one period from what it is at another, in consequence of eight different contingencies:—

1. "From the four circumstances above stated, in relation to the commodity of which we mean to express the value.

2. "From the same four circumstances, in relation to the commodity we have adopted as a measure of value."

This is true of monopolised commodities, and, indeed, of the market price of all other commodities for a limited period. If the demand for hats should be doubled, the price would immediately rise, but that rise would be only temporary, unless the cost of production of hats or their natural price were raised. If the natural price of bread should fall 50 per cent. from some great discovery in the science of agriculture, the demand would not greatly increase, for no man would desire more than would satisfy his wants, and as the demand would not increase, neither would the supply; for a commodity is not supplied merely because it can be produced, but because there is a demand for it. Here, then, we have a case where the supply and demand have scarcely varied, or, if they have increased, they have increased in the same proportion; and yet the price of bread will have fallen 50 per cent., at a time, too, when the value of money had continued invariable.

Commodities which are monopolised, either by an individual or by a company, vary according to the law which Lord Lauderdale has laid down: they fall in proportion as the sellers augment their quantity, and rise in proportion to the eagerness of the buyers to purchase them; their price has no necessary connection with their natural value: but the prices of commodities which are subject to competition, and whose quantity may be increased in any moderate degree, will ultimately depend, not on the state of demand and supply, but on the increased or diminished cost of their production.

On Machinery

In the present chapter I shall enter into some inquiry respecting the influence of machinery on the interests of the different classes of society, a subject of great importance, and one which appears never to have been investigated in a manner to lead to any certain or satisfactory results. It is more incumbent on me to declare my opinion on this question, because they have, on further reflection, undergone a considerable change; and although I am not aware that I have ever published anything respecting machinery which it is necessary for me to retract, yet I have in other ways given my support to doctrines which I now think erroneous; it therefore becomes a duty in me to submit my present views to examination, with my reasons for entertaining them.

Ever since I first turned my attention to questions of political economy, I have been of opinion that such an application of machinery to any branch of production as should have the effect of saving labour was a general good, accompanied only with that portion of inconvenience which in most cases attends the removal of capital and labour from one employment to another. It appeared to me that, provided the landlords had the same money rents, they would be benefited by the reduction in the prices of some of the commodities on which those rents were expended, and which reduction of price could not fail to be the consequence of the employment of machinery. The capitalist, I thought, was eventually benefited precisely in the same manner. He, indeed, who made the discovery of the machine, or who first usefully applied it, would enjoy an additional advantage by making great profits for a time; but, in proportion as the machine came into general use, the price of the commodity produced would, from the effects of competition, sink to its cost of production, when the capitalist would get the same money profits as before, and he would only participate in the general advantage as a consumer, by being enabled, with the same money revenue, to command an additional quantity of comforts and enjoyments. The class of labourers also, I thought, was equally benefited by the use of machinery, as they would have the means of buying more commodities with the same money wages, and I thought that no reduction of wages would take place because the capitalist would have the power of demanding and employing the same quantity of labour as before, although he might be under the necessity of employing it in the production of a new or, at any rate, of a different commodity. If, by improved machinery, with the employment of the same quantity of labour, the quantity of stockings could be quadrupled, and the demand for stockings were only doubled, some labourers would necessarily be discharged from the stocking trade; but as the capital which employed them was still in being, and as it was the interest of those who had it to employ it productively, it appeared to me that it would be employed on the production of some other commodity useful to the society, for which there could not fail to be a demand; for I was, and am, deeply impressed with the truth of the observation of Adam Smith, that "the desire for food is limited in every man by the narrow capacity of the human stomach, but the desire of the conveniences and ornaments of building, dress, equipage, and household furniture, seems to have no limit or certain boundary." As, then, it appeared to me that there would be the same demand for labour as before, and that wages would be no lower, I thought that the labouring class would, equally with the other classes, participate in the advantage, from the general cheapness of commodities arising from the use of machinery.

These were my opinions, and they continue unaltered, as far as regards the landlord and the capitalist; but I am convinced that the substitution of machinery for human labour is often very injurious to the interests of the class of labourers.

My mistake arose from the supposition that whenever the net income of a society increased, its gross income would also increase; I now, however, see reason to be satisfied that the one fund, from which landlords and capitalists derive their revenue, may increase, while the other, that upon which the labouring class mainly depend, may diminish, and therefore it follows, if I am right, that the same cause which may increase the net revenue of the country may at the same time render the population redundant, and deteriorate the condition of the labourer.

A capitalist, we will suppose, employs a capital of the value of £20,000, and that he carries on the joint business of a farmer and a manufacturer of necessaries. We will further suppose that £7000 of this capital is invested in fixed capital, viz. in buildings, implements, etc., etc., and that the remaining £13,000 is employed as circulating capital in the support of labour. Let us suppose, too, that profits are 10 per cent., and consequently that the capitalist's capital is every year put into its original state of efficiency and yields a profit of £2000.

Each year the capitalist begins his operations by having food and necessaries in his possession of the value of £13,000, all of which he sells in the course of the year to his own workmen for that sum of money, and, during the same period, he pays them the like amount of money for wages: at the end of the year they replace in his possession food and necessaries of the value of £15,000, £2000 of which he consumes himself, or disposes of as may best suit his pleasure and gratification. As far as these products are concerned, the gross produce for that year is £15,000, and the net produce £2000. Suppose, now, that the following year the capitalist employs half his men in constructing a machine, and the other half in producing food and necessaries as usual. During that year he would pay the sum of £13,000 in wages as usual, and would sell food and necessaries to the same amount to his workmen; but what would be the case the following year?

While the machine was being made, only one-half of the usual quantity of food and necessaries would be obtained, and they would be only one-half the value of the quantity which was produced before. The machine would be worth £7500, and the food and necessaries £7500, and, therefore, the capital of the capitalist would be as great as before; for he would have, besides these two values, his fixed capital worth £7000, making in the whole £20,000 capital, and £2000 profit. After deducting this latter sum for his own expenses, he would have a no greater circulating capital than £5500 with which to carry on his subsequent operations; and, therefore, his means of employing labour would be reduced in the proportion of £13,000 to £5500, and, consequently, all the labour which was before employed by £7500 would become redundant.

The reduced quantity of labour which the capitalist can employ, must, indeed, with the assistance of the machine, and after deductions for its repairs, produce a value equal to £7500, it must replace the circulating capital with a profit of £2000 on the whole capital; but if this be done, if the net income be not diminished, of what importance is it to the capitalist whether the gross income be of the value of £3000, of £10,000, or of £15,000?

In this case, then, although the net produce will not be diminished in value, although its power of purchasing commodities may be greatly increased, the gross produce will have fallen from a value of £15,000 to a value of £7500; and as the power of supporting a population, and employing labour, depends always on the gross produce of a nation, and not on its net produce, there will necessarily be a diminution in the demand for labour, population will become redundant, and the situation of the labouring classes will be that of distress and poverty.

As, however, the power of saving from revenue to add to capital must depend on the efficiency of the net revenue, to satisfy the wants of the capitalist, it could not fail to follow from the reduction in the price of commodities consequent on the introduction of machinery that with the same wants he would have increased means of saving—increased facility of transferring revenue into capital. But with every increase of capital he would employ more labourers; and, therefore, a portion of the people thrown out of work in the first instance would be subsequently employed; and if the increased production, in consequence of the employment of the machine, was so great as to afford, in the shape of net produce, as great a quantity of food and necessaries as existed before in the form of gross produce, there would be the same ability to employ the whole population, and, therefore, there would not necessarily be any redundancy of people.

All I wish to prove is that the discovery and use of machinery may be attended with a diminution of gross produce; and whenever that is the case, it will be injurious to the labouring class, as some of their number will be thrown out of employment, and population will become redundant compared with the funds which are to employ it.

The case which I have supposed is the most simple that I could select; but it would make no difference in the result if we supposed that the machinery was applied to the trade of any manufacturer—that of a clothier, for example, or of a cotton manufacturer. If, in the trade of a clothier, less cloth would be produced after the introduction of machinery, for a part of that quantity which is disposed of for the purpose of paying a large body of workmen would not be required by their employer. In consequence of using the machine, it would be necessary for him to reproduce a value only equal to the value consumed, together with the profits on the whole capital. £7500 might do this as effectually as £15,000 did before, the case differing in no respect from the former instance. It may be said, however, that the demand for cloth would be as great as before, and it may be asked from whence would this supply come? But by whom would the cloth be demanded? By the farmers and the other producers of necessaries, who employed their capitals in producing these necessaries as a means of obtaining cloth: they gave corn and necessaries to the clothier for cloth, and he bestowed them on his workmen for the cloth which their work afforded him.

This trade would now cease; the clothier would not want the food and clothing, having fewer men to employ and having less cloth to dispose of. The farmers and others, who only produced necessaries as means to an end, could no longer obtain cloth by such an application of their capitals, and, therefore, they would either themselves employ their capitals in producing cloth, or would lend them to others, in order that the commodity really wanted might be furnished; and that for which no one had the means of paying, or for which there was no demand, might cease to be produced. This, then, leads us to the same result; the demand for labour would diminish, and the commodities necessary to the support of labour would not be produced in the same abundance.

If these views be correct, it follows, first, that the discovery and useful application of machinery always leads to the increase of the net produce of the country, although it may not, and will not, after an inconsiderable interval, increase the value of that net produce.

Secondly, that an increase of the net produce of a country is compatible with a diminution of the gross produce, and that the motives for employing machinery are always sufficient to ensure its employment if it will increase the net produce, although it may, and frequently must, diminish both the quantity of the gross produce and its value.

Thirdly, that the opinion entertained by the labouring class, that the employment of machinery is frequently detrimental to their interests, is not founded on prejudice and error, but is conformable to the correct principles of political economy.

Fourthly, that if the improved means of production, in consequence of the use of machinery, should increase the net produce of a country in a degree so great as not to diminish the gross produce (I mean always quantity of commodities, and not value), then the situation of all classes will be improved. The landlord and capitalist will benefit, not by an increase of rent and profit, but by the advantages resulting from the expenditure of the same rent and profit on commodities very considerably reduced in value, while the situation of the labouring classes will also be considerably improved; First, from the increased demand for menial servants; secondly, from the stimulus to savings from revenue which such an abundant net produce will afford; and, thirdly, from the low price of all articles of consumption on which their wages will be expended.

THE HIGH PRICE OF BULLION *

§ 1. The precious metals employed for circulating the commodities of the world, previously to the establishment of banks, have been supposed by the most approved writers on political economy to have been divided into certain proportions among the different civilized nations of the earth, according to the state of their commerce and wealth, and therefore according to the number and frequency of the payments which they had to perform. While so divided they preserved every where the same value, and as each country had an equal necessity for the quantity actually in use, there could be no temptation offered to either for their importation or exportation.

Gold and silver, like other commodities, have an intrinsic value, which is not arbitrary, but is dependent on their scarcity, the quantity of labour bestowed in procuring them, and the value of the capital employed in the mines which produce them.

"The quality of utility, beauty, and scarcity," says Dr Smith, "are the original foundation of the high price of those metals, or of the great quantity of other goods, for which they can every where be exchanged. This value was antecedent to, and independent of, their being employed as coin, and was the quality which fitted them for that employment."

If the quantity of gold and silver in the world employed as money were exceedingly small, or abundantly great, it would not in the least affect the proportions in which they would be divided among the different nations—the variation in their quantity would have produced no other effect than to make the commodities for which they were exchanged comparatively dear or cheap. The smaller quantity of money would perform the functions of a circulating medium, as well as the larger. Ten millions would be as effectual for that purpose as 100 millions. Dr Smith observes, "that the most abundant mines of the precious metals would add little to the wealth of the world. A produce of which the value is principally derived from its scarcity is necessarily degraded by its abundance."

If in the progress towards wealth, one nation advanced more rapidly than the others, that nation would require and obtain a greater proportion of the money of the world. Its commerce, its commodities, and its payments, would increase, and the general currency of the world would be divided according to the new proportions. All countries, therefore, would contribute their share to this effectual demand.

In the same manner, if any nation wasted part of its wealth, or lost part

* From *The High Price of Bullion* (London, 1809).

of its trade, it could not retain the same quantity of circulating medium which it before possessed. A part would be exported, and divided among the other nations till the usual proportions were re-established.

While the relative situation of countries continued unaltered, they might have abundant commerce with each other, but their exports and imports would on the whole be equal. England might possibly import more goods from, than she would export to, France, but she would in consequence export more to some other country, and France would import more from that country; so that the exports and imports of all countries would balance each other; bills of exchange would make the necessary payments, but no money would pass because it would have the same value in all countries.

§ 2. If a mine of gold were discovered in either of these countries, the currency of that country would be lowered in value in consequence of the increased quantity of the precious metals brought into circulation, and would therefore no longer be of the same value as that of other countries. Gold and silver, whether in coin or in bullion, obeying the law which regulates all other commodities, would immediately become articles of exportation; they would leave the country where they were cheap, for those countries where they were dear, and would continue to do so, as long as the mine should prove productive, and till the proportion existing between capital and money in each country before the discovery of the mine, were again established, and gold and silver restored every where to one value. In return for the gold exported, commodities would be imported; and though what is usually termed the balance of trade would be against the country exporting money or bullion, it would be evident that she was carrying on a most advantageous trade, exporting that which was no way useful to her, for commodities which might be employed in the extension of her manufactures, and the increase of her wealth.

If instead of a mine being discovered in any country, a bank were established, such as the Bank of England, with the power of issuing its notes for a circulating medium; after a large amount had been issued, either by way of loan to merchants, or by advances to Government, thereby adding considerably to the sum of the currency, the same effect would follow as in the case of the mine. The circulating medium would be lowered in value, and goods would experience a proportionate rise. The equilibrium between that and other nations would only be restored by the exportation of part of the coin.

The establishment of the bank, and the consequent issue of its notes, therefore, as well as the discovery of the mine, operate as an inducement to the exportation either of bullion, or of coin, and are beneficial only in as far as that object may be accomplished. The bank substitutes a currency of no value for one most costly, and enables us to turn the precious metals (which, though a very necessary part of our capital, yield no revenue), into a capital which will yield one. Dr A. Smith compares the advantages attending the establishment of a bank to those which would be obtained by converting our highways into pastures and corn fields, and procuring a road through the air. The highways, like the coin, are highly useful, but neither yield any revenue. Some people might be alarmed at the specie leaving the country, and might consider that as a disadvantageous trade which required us to part with it; indeed the law so considers it by its enactments against the exportation of specie; but a very little reflection will convince us that it is our choice, and not our necessity, that sends it abroad; and that it is highly beneficial to us to exchange that commodity which is superfluous, for others which may be made productive.

§ 3. The exportation of the specie may at all times be safely left to the discretion of individuals; it will not be exported more than any other commodity, unless its exportation should be advantageous to the country. If it be advantageous to export it, no laws can effectually prevent its exportation. Happily, in this case, as well as in most others in commerce, where there is free competition, the interests of the individual and that of the community are never at variance.

Were it possible to carry the law against melting, or exporting of coin, into strict execution, at the same time that the exportation of gold bullion was freely allowed, no advantage could accrue from it, but great injury must arise to those who might have to pay, possibly, two ounces or more of coined gold for one of uncoined gold. This would be a real depreciation of our currency, raising the prices of all other commodities in the same proportion as it increased that of gold bullion. The owner of money would in this case suffer an injury equal to what a proprietor of corn would suffer, were a law to be passed prohibiting him from selling his corn for more than half its market value. The law against the exportation of the coin has this tendency, but is so easily evaded, that gold in bullion has always been nearly of the same value as gold in coin.

§ 4. Thus, then, it appears that the currency of one country can never for any length of time be much more valuable, as far as equal quantities of the precious metals are concerned, than that of another; that excess of currency is but a relative term; that if the circulation of England were 10 millions, that of France 5 millions, that of Holland 4 millions, &c., &c., whilst they kept their proportions, though the currency of each country were doubled or trebled, neither country would be conscious of an excess of currency. The prices of commodities would every where rise, on account of the increase of currency, but there would be no exportation of money from either. But if these proportions be destroyed by England alone doubling her currency, while that of France, Holland, &c., &c., continued as before, we should then be conscious of an excess in our currency, and for the same reason the other countries would feel a deficiency in theirs, and part of our excess would be exported till the proportions of ten, five, four, &c., were again established.

If in France an ounce of gold were more valuable than in England, and would therefore in France purchase more of any commodity common to both countries, gold would immediately quit England for such purpose, and we should send gold in preference to any thing else, because it would be the cheapest exchangeable commodity in the English market; for if gold be dearer in France than in England, goods must be cheaper; we should not therefore send them from the dear to the cheap market, but, on the contrary, they would come from the cheap to the dear market, and would be exchanged for our gold.

§ 5. The Bank might continue to issue their notes, and the specie be exported with advantage to the country, while their notes were payable in specie on demand, because they could never issue more notes than the value of the coin which would have circulated had there been no bank.

If they attempted to exceed this amount, the excess would be immediately returned to them for specie; because our currency, being thereby diminished in value, could be advantageously exported, and could not be retained in our circulation. These are the means, as I have already explained, by which our currency endeavours to equalize itself with the currencies of other countries. As soon as this equality was attained, all advantage arising from exportation would cease; but if the Bank, assuming that because a given quantity of circulating medium had been necessary last year, therefore the same quantity must be necessary this, or for any other reason, continued to re-issue the returned notes, the stimulus which a redundant currency first gave to the exportation of the coin would be again renewed with similar effects; gold would be again demanded, the exchange would become unfavourable, and gold bullion would rise, in a small degree, above its Mint price, because it is legal to export bullion, but illegal to export the coin, and the difference would be about equal to the fair compensation for the risk.

In this manner, if the Bank persisted in returning their notes into circulation, every guinea might be drawn out of their coffers.

If, to supply the deficiency of their stock of gold, they were to purchase gold bullion at the advanced price, and have it coined into guineas, this would not remedy the evil; guineas would be still demanded, but, instead of being exported, would be melted, and sold to the Bank as bullion at the advanced price. "The operations of the Bank," observed Dr Smith, alluding to an analogous case, "were, upon this account, somewhat like the web of Penelope,—the work that was done in the day was undone in the night." The same sentiment is expressed by Mr Thornton:—"Finding the guineas in their coffers to lessen every day, they must naturally be supposed to be desirous of replacing them by all effectual and not extravagantly expensive means. They will be disposed, to a certain degree, to buy gold, though at a losing price, and to coin it into new guineas; but they will have to do this at the very moment when many are privately melting what is coined. The one party will be melting and selling while the other is buying and coining. And each of these two contending businesses will now be carried on, not on account of an actual exportation of each melted guinea to Hamburgh, but the operation, or at least a great part of it.

will be confined to London, the coiners and the melters living on the same spot, and giving constant employment to each other.

"The Bank," continues Mr Thornton, "if we suppose it, as we now do, to carry on this sort of contest with the melters, is obviously waging a very unequal war; and even though it should not be tired early, it will be likely to be tired sooner than its adversaries."

The Bank would be obliged, therefore, ultimately to adopt the only remedy in their power to put a stop to the demand for guineas. They would withdraw part of their notes from circulation, till they should have increased the value of the remainder to that of gold bullion, and, consequently, to the value of the currencies of other countries. All advantage from the exportation of gold bullion would then cease, and there would be no temptation to exchange bank notes for guineas.

§ 6. In this view of the subject, then, it appears that the temptation to export money in exchange for goods, or what is termed an unfavourable balance of trade, never arises but from a redundant currency. But Mr Thornton, who has considered this subject very much at large, supposes that a very unfavourable balance of trade may be occasioned to this country by a bad harvest, and the consequent importation of corn; and that there may be at the same time an unwillingness in the country to which we are indebted to receive our goods in payment; the balance due to the foreign country must therefore be paid out of that part of our currency consisting of coin, and that hence arises the demand for gold bullion, and its increased price. He considers the Bank as affording considerable accommodation to the merchants, by supplying with their notes the void occasioned by the exportation of the specie.

As it is acknowledged by Mr Thornton, in many parts of his work, that the price of gold bullion is rated in gold coin, and as it is also acknowledged by him that the law against melting gold coin into bullion, and exporting it, is easily evaded, it follows, that no demand for gold bullion, arising from this or any other cause, can raise the money price of that commodity. The error of this reasoning proceeds from not distinguishing between an increase in the value of gold, and an increase in its money price.

If there were a great demand for corn, its money price would advance, because, in comparing corn with money, we in fact compare it with another commodity; and, for the same reason, when there is a great demand for gold, its corn price will increase; but in neither case will a bushel of corn be worth more than a bushel of corn, or an ounce of gold more than an ounce of gold. An ounce of gold bullion could not, whatever the demand might be, whilst its price was rated in gold coin, be of more value than an ounce of coined gold, or 3*l.* 17s. 10½d.

If this argument should not be considered as conclusive, I should urge that a *void* in the currency, as here supposed, can only be occasioned by the annihilation or limitation of paper currency, and then it would speedily be filled by importations of bullion, which its increased value, in consequence of the diminution of circulating medium, would infallibly attract to the advantageous market. However great the scarcity of corn might be, the exportation of money would be limited by its increasing scarcity. Money is in such general demand, and, in the present state of civilization, is so essential to commercial transactions, that it can never be exported to excess; even in a war, such as the present, when our enemy endeavours to interdict all commerce with us, the value which the currency would bear from its increasing scarcity would prevent the exportation of it from being carried so far as to occasion a void in the circulation.

Mr Thornton has not explained to us why any unwillingness should exist in the foreign country to receive our goods in exchange for their corn; and it would be necessary for him to show, that if such an unwillingness were to exist, we should agree to indulge it so far as to consent to part with our coin.

If we consent to give coin in exchange for goods, it must be from choice, not necessity. We should not import more goods than we export, unless we had a redundancy of currency, which it therefore suits us to make a part of our exports. The exportation of the coin is caused by its cheapness, and is not the effect, but the cause of an unfavourable balance: we should not export it, if we did not send it to a better market, or if we had any commodity which we could export more profitably. It is a salutary remedy for a redundant currency; and as I have already endeavoured to prove that redundancy or excess is only a relative term, it follows that the demand for it abroad arises only from the comparative deficiency of the currency of the importing country, which there causes its superior value.

It resolves itself entirely into a question of interest. If the sellers of the corn to England, to the amount, I will suppose, of a million, could import goods which cost a million in England, but would produce, when sold abroad, more than if the million had been sent in money, goods would be preferred; if otherwise, money would be demanded.

It is only after a comparison of the value in their markets and in our own of gold and other commodities, and because gold is cheaper in the London market than in theirs, that foreigners prefer gold in exchange for their corn. If we diminish the quantity of currency, we give an additional value to it: this will induce them to alter their election, and prefer the commodities. If I owed a debt in Hamburgh of 100*l.*, I should endeavour to find out the cheapest mode of paying it. If I send money, the expense attending its transportation being, I will suppose, 5*l.*, to discharge my debt will cost me 105*l.* If I purchase cloth here, which, with the expenses attending its exportation, will cost me 106*l.*, and which will in Hamburgh sell for 100*l.*, it is evidently more to my advantage to send the money. If the purchase and expenses of sending hardware to pay my debt will take 107*l.*, I should prefer sending cloth to hardware, but I would send neither in preference to money, because money would be the cheapest exportable commodity in the London market. The same reasons would operate with the exporter of the corn, if the transaction were on his own account.

But if the Bank, "fearful for the safety of their establishment," and knowing that the requisite number of guineas would be withdrawn from their coffers at the Mint price, should think it necessary to diminish the amount of their notes in circulation, the proportion between the value of the money, of the cloth, and of the hardware, would no longer be as 105, 106, and 107; but the money would become the most valuable of the three, and therefore would be less advantageously employed in discharging the foreign debts.

If, which is a much stronger case, we agreed to pay a subsidy to a foreign power, money would not be exported whilst there were any goods which could more cheaply discharge the payment. The interest of individuals would render the exportation of the money unnecessary.

§ 7. Thus, then, specie will be sent abroad to discharge a debt only when it is superabundant; only when it is the cheapest exportable commodity. If the Bank were at such a time paying their notes in specie, gold would be demanded for that purpose. It would be obtained there at its Mint price, whereas its price as bullion would be something above its value as coin, because bullion could, and coin could not, be legally exported.

It is evident, then, that a depreciation of the circulating medium is the necessary consequence of its redundance; and that in the common state of the national currency this depreciation is counteracted by the exportation of the precious metals.

Such, then, appear to me to be the laws that regulate the distribution of the precious metals throughout the world, and which cause and limit their circulation from one country to another, by regulating their value in each. But before I proceed to examine on these principles the main object of my inquiry, it is necessary that I should show what is the standard measure of value in this country, and of which, therefore, our paper currency ought to be the representative, because it can only be by a comparison to this standard that its regularity, or its depreciation, may be estimated.

§ 8. No permanent measure of value can be said to exist in any nation while the circulating medium consists of two metals, because they are constantly subject to vary in value with respect to each other. However exact the conductors of the Mint may be, in proportioning the relative value of gold to silver in the coins, at the time when they fix the ratio, they cannot prevent one of these metals from rising, while the other remains stationary, or falls in value. Whenever this happens, one of the coins will be melted to be sold for the other. Mr Locke, Lord Liverpool, and many other writers, have ably considered this subject, and have all agreed, that the only remedy for the evils in the currency proceeding from this source, is the making one of the metals only the standard measure of value. Mr Locke considered silver as the most proper metal for this purpose, and proposed that gold coins should be left to find their own value, and pass for a greater or lesser number of shillings, as the market price of gold might vary with respect to silver.

Lord Liverpool, on the contrary, maintained that gold was not only the most proper metal for a general measure of value in this country, but that, by the common consent of the people, it had become so, was so considered by foreigners, and that it was best suited to the increased commerce and wealth of England.

He, therefore, proposed, that gold coin only should be a legal tender for sums exceeding one guinea, and silver coins for sums not exceeding that amount. As the law now stands, gold coin is a legal tender for all sums; but it was enacted in the year 1774, "That no tender in payment of money made in the silver coin of this realm, of any sum exceeding the sum of twenty-five pounds at any one time, shall be reputed in law, or allowed to be legal tender within Great Britain or Ireland, for more than according to its value by weight, after the rate of 5s. 2d. for each ounce of silver." The same regulation was revived in 1798, and is now in force.

For many reasons given by Lord Liverpool, it appears, proved beyond dispute, that gold coin has been for near a century the principal measure of value; but this is, I think, to be attributed to the inaccurate determination of the Mint proportions. Gold has been valued too high; no silver, therefore, can remain in circulation which is of its standard weight.

If a new regulation were to take place, and silver to be valued too high, or (which is the same thing) if the market proportions between the prices of gold and silver were to become greater than those of the Mint, gold would then disappear, and silver become the standard currency.

This may require further explanation. The relative value of gold and silver in the coins is as 15 9/124 to 1. An ounce of gold which is coined into 3*l.* 17s. 10½d. of gold coin, is worth, according to the Mint regulation, 15 9/142 ounces of silver, because that weight of silver is also coined into 3*l.* 17s. 10½d. of silver coin. Whilst the relative value of gold to silver is in the market under 15 to 1, which it has been for a great number of years till lately, gold coin would necessarily be the standard measure of value, because neither the Bank nor any individual would send 15 9/142 ounces of silver to the Mint to be coined into 3*l.* 17s. 10½d., when they could sell that quantity of silver in the market for more than 3*l.* 17s. 10½d. in gold coin; and this they could do by the supposition, that less than 15 ounces of silver would purchase an ounce of gold.

But if the relative value of gold to silver be more than the Mint proportion of 15 9/124 to 1, no gold would then be sent to the Mint to be coined, because as either of the metals are a legal tender to any amount, the possessor of an ounce of gold would not send it to the Mint to be coined into 3*l.* 17s. 10½d. of gold coin, whilst he could sell it, which he could do in such a case, for more than 3*l.* 17s. 10½d. of silver coin. Not only would not gold be carried to the Mint to be coined, but the illicit trader would melt the gold coin, and sell it as bullion for more than its nominal value in the silver coin. Thus, then, gold would disappear from circulation, and silver coin become the standard measure of value. As gold has lately experienced a considerable rise compared with silver (an ounce of standard gold, which, on an average of many years, was of equal value to 14¾ ounces of standard silver, being now in the market of the same value as 15½ ounces), this would be the case now were the Bank restriction bill repealed, and the coinage of silver freely allowed at the Mint, in the same manner as that of gold; but in an act of Parliament of 39 Geo. III. is the following clause:—

"Whereas inconvenience may arise from any coinage of silver until such regulations may be formed as shall appear necessary; and whereas from the present low price of silver bullion, owing to temporary circumstances, a small quantity of silver bullion has been brought to the Mint to be coined, and there is reason to suppose that a still further quantity may be brought; and it is, therefore, necessary to suspend the coining of silver for the present; be it therefore enacted, That from and after the passing of this act, no silver bullion shall be coined at the Mint, nor shall any silver coin that may have been coined there be delivered, any law to the contrary notwithstanding." This law is now in force.

It would appear, therefore, to have been the intention of the legislature to establish gold as the standard of currency in this country. Whilst this law is in force, silver coin must be confined to small payments only, the quantity in circulation being barely sufficient for that purpose. It might be for the interest of a debtor to pay his large debts in silver coin if he could get silver bullion coined into money; but being prevented by the above law from doing so, he is necessarily obliged to discharge his debt with gold coin, which he could obtain at the Mint with gold bullion to any amount. Whilst this law is in force, gold must always continue to be the standard of currency.

Were the market value of an ounce of gold to become equal to thirty ounces of silver, gold would nevertheless be the measure of value, whilst this prohibition continued in force. It would be of no avail, that the possessor of 30 ounces of silver should know that he once could have discharged a debt of 3*l.* 17s. 10½d. by procuring 15⁹⁄₁₂₄ ounces of silver to be coined at the Mint, as he would in this case have no other means of discharging his debt but by selling his 30 oz. of silver at the market value, that is to say, for one ounce of gold, or 3*l.* 17s. 10½d. of gold coin.

The public has sustained, at different times, very serious loss from the depreciation of the circulating medium, arising from the unlawful practice of clipping the coins.

In proportion as they become debased, so the prices of every commodity for which they are exchangeable rise in nominal value, not excepting gold and silver bullion: accordingly we find, that before the recoinage in the reign of King William the Third, the silver currency had become so degraded, that an ounce of silver, which ought to be contained in 62 pence, sold for 77 pence; and a guinea, which was valued at the Mint at 20 shillings, passed in all contracts for 30 shillings. This evil was then remedied by the recoinage. Similar effects followed from the debasement of the gold currency, which were again corrected in 1774 by the same means.

§ 9. Our gold coins have, since 1774, continued nearly at their standard purity; but our silver currency has again become debased. By an assay at the Mint in 1798, it appears that our shillings were found to be 24 per cent., and our sixpences 38 per cent., under their Mint value; and I am informed, that by a late experiment they were found considerably more deficient. They do not, therefore, contain as much pure silver as they did in the reign of King William. This debasement, however, did not operate previously to 1798, as on the former occasion. At that time both gold and silver bullion rose in proportion to the debasement of the silver coin. All foreign exchanges were against us full 20 per cent., and many of them still more. But although the debasement of the silver coin had continued for many years, it had neither, previously to 1798, raised the price of gold nor silver, nor had it produced any effect on the exchanges. This is a convincing proof, that gold coin was, during that period, considered as the standard measure of value. Any debasement of the gold coin would then have produced the same effects on the prices of gold and silver bullion, and on the foreign exchanges, which were formerly caused by the debasement of the silver coins.

While the currency of different countries consists of the precious metals, or of a paper money which is at all times exchangeable for them; and while the metallic currency is not debased by wearing or clipping, a comparison of the weight and degree of fineness of their coins will enable us to ascertain their par of exchange. Thus the par of exchange between Holland and England is stated to be about eleven florins, because the pure silver contained in eleven florins is equal to the pure silver contained in twenty standard shillings.

This par is not, nor can it be, absolutely fixed; because gold coin being the standard of commerce in England, and silver coin in Holland, a pound sterling, or 20/21 of a guinea, may at different times be more or less valuable than twenty standard shillings, and therefore more or less valuable than its equivalent of eleven florins. Estimating the par either by silver or by gold will be sufficiently exact for our purpose.

If I owe a debt in Holland, by knowing the par of exchange, I also know the quantity of our money which will be necessary to discharge it.

If my debt amount to 1,100 florins, and gold have not varied in value, 100*l.* in our pure gold coin will purchase as much Dutch currency as is necessary to pay my debt. By exporting the 100*l.* therefore in coin, or (which is the same thing) paying a bullion merchant the 100*l.* in coin, and allowing him the expenses attending its transportation, such as freight, insurance, and his profit, he will sell me a bill which will discharge my debt; at the same time he will export the bullion to enable his correspondent to pay the bill when it shall become due.

§ 10. These expenses, then, are the utmost limits of an unfavourable exchange. However great my debt may be, though it equalled the largest subsidy ever given by this country to an ally; while I could pay the bullion merchant in coin of standard value, he would be glad to export it, and to sell me bills. But if I pay him for his bill in a debased coin, or in a depreciated paper-money, he will not be willing to sell me his bill at this rate; because if the coin be debased it does not contain the quantity of pure gold or silver which ought to be contained in 100*l.*, and he must therefore export an additional number of such debased pieces of money to enable him to pay my debt of 100*l.*, or its equivalent, 1,100 florins. If I pay him in paper-money, as he cannot send it abroad, he will consider whether it will purchase as much gold or silver bullion as is contained in the coin for which it is a substitute; if it will do this, paper will be as acceptable to him as coin; but if it will not, he will expect a further premium for his bill, equal to the depreciation of the paper.

While the circulating medium consists, therefore, of coin undebased, or of paper-money immediately exchangeable for undebased coin, the exchange can never be more above, or more below par, than the expenses attending the transportation of the precious metals. But when it consists of a depreciated paper-money, it necessarily will fall according to the degree of the depreciation.

The exchange will, therefore, be a tolerably accurate criterion by which we may judge of the debasement of the currency, proceeding either from a clipped coinage or a depreciated paper-money.

JOHN STUART MILL

(1806–1873)

John Stuart Mill was the son of James Mill, the confidant and assistant of Jeremy Bentham and David Ricardo. We have seen in our section on Bentham how the elder Mill helped form that able group of social reformers known as the "Philosophic Radicals." Theirs was a utilitarian philosophy based on the ethical criterion of the "greatest good for the greatest number" and the psychological theory of the association of ideas. James Mill's *Analysis of the Phenomena of the Human Mind* (1829) has been said to mark the beginning of modern associationist psychology.

Educated at home by his father, John Stuart Mill received a remarkable upbringing based on the utilitarian faith in education and training as vehicles of social progress. At an unbelievably early age he was introduced to Latin, Greek, mathematics, and philosophy. In his youth personal contact with his father's circle helped make him a thorough utilitarian, trained to carry on his father's ideas and ambitions. He believed that a better social order could be attained through the combination of reason and human liberty.

In 1819 the elder Mill obtained a post in the London office of the East India Company, and soon after he was able to obtain employment there for his son. John Stuart rose rapidly in the company, and when it was dissolved in 1858, he was given an ample pension for life. After office hours he wrote for periodicals and promoted utilitarian societies. Later he devoted himself to studies dealing with man's relationship to his environment—philosophy, sociology, and economics.

After a time he began to question some aspects of utilitarian philosophy, especially its neglect of forces other than self-interest, such as feelings and conscience, as motivators of human action. When he was in his late twenties his attitude toward utilitarianism underwent a change which he likened, in his *Autobiography,* to a religious conversion. It was not until after the death of his father in 1836, however, that he finally broke with utilitarianism, and even then some facets of that doctrine never left him.

Mill's chief contribution to economics consisted in the collection and systematization of the writings of the post-Ricardian school. His major work, the *Principles of Political Economy* (1848), was considered to be the standard restatement of economic theory until the publication of Jevons' *Theory* in 1871. Today it is regarded as a well-written but essentially shallow book. It contains nothing original except the concept of the "stationary state" and the addition of the concept of "reciprocal demand" to the Ricardian theory of international trade. (See "Of International Values," p. 227.)

Mill's socialist sympathies emerge clearly in his treatment of the critique of capitalism made by the early English and French utopian socialists. Mill envisioned socialist society as an equalitarian one which would preserve the best features of capitalism. His view of the role of the state is never clearly defined, however. In the *Principles* (Book V, Chapter 11) he lays down a laissez-faire position for the state but lists so many exceptions that the rule is almost vitiated. Again, in his famous essay "On Liberty" (1859) he stresses the necessary relationship between individual liberty and free competition but is not altogether successful in reconciling his sympathies for reform with the implications of his theoretical reasoning.

OF INTERNATIONAL VALUES *

The values of commodities produced at the same place, or in places sufficiently adjacent for capital to move freely between them—let us say, for simplicity, of commodities produced in the same country—depend (temporary fluctuations apart) upon their cost of production. But the value of a commodity brought from a distant place, especially from a foreign country, does not depend on its cost of production in the place from whence it comes. On what, then, does it depend? The value of a thing in any place depends on the cost of its acquisition in that place; which, in the case of an imported article, means the cost of production of the thing which is exported to pay for it.

Since all trade is in reality barter, money being a mere instrument for exchanging things against one another, we will, for simplicity, begin by supposing the international trade to be in form, what it always is in reality, an actual trucking of one commodity against another. As far as we have hitherto proceeded, we have found all the laws of interchange to be essentially the same, whether money is used or not; money never governing, but always obeying, those general laws.

If, then, England imports wine from Spain, giving for every pipe of wine a bale of cloth, the exchange value of a pipe of wine in England will not depend upon what the production of the wine may have cost in Spain, but upon what the production of the cloth has cost in England. Though the wine may have cost in Spain the equivalent of only ten days' labour, yet, if the cloth costs in England twenty days' labour, the wine, when brought to England, will exchange for the produce of twenty days' English labour, *plus* the cost of carriage; including the usual profit on the importer's capital, during the time it is locked up, and withheld from other employment.

The value, then, in any country, of a foreign commodity, depends on the quantity of home produce which must be given to the foreign country in exchange for it. In other words, the values of foreign commodities depend on the terms of international exchange. What, then, do these depend upon? What is it which, in the case supposed, causes a pipe of wine from Spain to be exchanged with England for exactly that quantity of cloth? We have seen that it is not their cost of production. If the cloth and the wine were both made in Spain, they would exchange at their cost of production in Spain; if they were both made in England, they would exchange at their cost of production in England: but all the cloth being made in England, and all the wine in Spain, they are in circumstances to which we have already determined that the law of cost of production is not applicable. We must accordingly, as we have done before in a similar embarrassment, fall back upon an antecedent law, that of supply and demand: and in this we shall again find the solution of our difficulty. . . .

* From *Principles of Political Economy,* edited by W. J. Ashley (London and New York, Longmans, Green and Co., 1909). Reprinted by permission of the publishers.

It may be considered . . . as established, that when two countries trade together in two commodities, the exchange value of these commodities relatively to each other will adjust itself to the inclinations and circumstances of the consumers on both sides, in such manner that the quantities required by each country, of the articles which it imports from its neighbour, shall be exactly sufficient to pay for one another. As the inclinations and circumstances of consumers cannot be reduced to any rule, so neither can the proportions in which the two commodities will be interchanged. We know that the limits, within which the variation is confined, are the ratio between their costs of production in the one country, and the ratio between their costs of production in the other. Ten yards of cloth cannot exchange for more than 20 yards of linen, nor for less than 15. But they may exchange for any intermediate number. The ratios, therefore, in which the advantage of the trade may be divided between the two nations are various. The circumstances on which the proportionate share of each country more remotely depends, admit only of a very general indication.

It is even possible to conceive an extreme case, in which the whole of the advantage resulting from the interchange would be reaped by one party, the other country gaining nothing at all. There is no absurdity in the hypothesis that, of some given commodity, a certain quantity is all that is wanted at any price; and that, when that quantity is obtained, no fall in the exchange value would induce other consumers to come forward, or those who are already supplied to take more. Let us suppose that this is the case in Germany with cloth. Before her trade with England commenced, when 10 yards of cloth cost her as much labour as 20 yards of linen, she nevertheless consumed as much cloth as she wanted under any circumstances, and, if she could obtain it at the rate of 10 yards of cloth for 15 of linen, she would not consume more. Let this fixed quantity be 1000 times 10 yards. At the rate, however, of 10 for 20, England would want more linen than would be equivalent to this quantity of cloth. She would, consequently, offer a higher value for linen; or, what is the same thing, she would offer her cloth at a cheaper rate. But, as by no lowering of the value could she prevail on Germany to take a greater quantity of cloth, there would be no limit to the rise of linen or fall of cloth, until the demand of England for linen was reduced by the rise of its value, to the quantity which 1000 times 10 yards of cloth would purchase. It might be, that to produce this diminution of the demand a less fall would not suffice than that which would make 10 yards of cloth exchange for 15 of linen. Germany would then gain the whole of the advantage, and England would be exactly as she was before the trade commenced. It would be for the interest, however, of Germany herself to keep her linen a little below the value at which it could be produced in England, in order to keep herself from being supplanted by the home producer. England, therefore, would always benefit in some degree by the existence of the trade, though it might be a very trifling one.

In this statement, I conceive, is contained the first elementary principle of International Values. I have, as is indispensable in such abstract and hypothetical cases, supposed the circumstances to be much less complex than they really are: in the first place, by suppressing the cost of carriage; next, by supposing that there are only two countries trading together; and lastly, that they trade only in two commodities. To render the exposition of the principle complete it is necessary to restore the various circumstances thus temporarily left out to simplify the argument. Those who are accustomed to any kind of scientific investigation will probably see, without formal proof, that the introduction of these circumstances cannot alter the theory of the subject. Trade among any number of countries, and in any number of commodities, must take place on the same essential principles as trade between two countries and in two commodities. . . .

Let us now introduce a greater number of commodities than the two we have hitherto supposed. Let cloth and linen, however, be still the articles of which the comparative cost of production in England and in Germany differs the most; so that, if they were confined to two commodities, these would be the two which it would be most their interest to exchange. . . . Let us suppose, then, that the demand of England for linen is either so much greater than that of Germany for cloth, or so much more extensible by cheapness, that if England had no commodity but cloth which Germany would take, the demand of England would force up the terms of interchange to 10 yards of cloth for only 16 of linen, so that England would gain only the difference between 15 and 16, Germany the difference between 16 and 20. But let us now suppose that England has also another commodity, say iron, which is in demand in Germany, and that the quantity of iron which is of equal value in England with 10 yards of cloth, (let us call this quantity a hundredweight) will, if produced in Germany, cost as much labour as 18 yards of linen, so that if offered by England for 17 it will undersell the German producer. In these circumstances, linen will not be forced up to the rate of 16 yards for 10 of cloth, but will stop, suppose at 17; for although, at that rate of interchange, Germany will not take enough cloth to pay for all the linen required by England, she will take iron for the remainder, and it is the same thing to England whether she gives a hundredweight of iron or 10 yards of cloth, both being made at the same cost. If we now superadd coals or cottons on the side of England, and wine, or corn, or timber, on the side of Germany, it will make no difference in the principle. The exports of each country must exactly pay for the imports; meaning now the aggregate exports and imports, not those of particular commodities taken singly. The produce of fifty days' English labour, whether in cloth, coals, iron, or any other exports, will exchange for the produce of forty, or fifty, or sixty days' German labour, in linen, wine, corn, or timber, according to the international demand. There is some proportion at which the demand of the two countries for each other's products will exactly correspond: so that the things supplied by England to Germany will be completely paid for, and no more, by those supplied by Germany to England. This accordingly will be the ratio in which the produce of English and the produce of German labour will exchange for one another.

If, therefore, it be asked what country draws to itself the greatest share of the advantage of any trade it carries on, the answer is, the country for whose productions there is in other countries the greatest demand, and a demand the most susceptible of increase from additional cheapness. In so far as the productions of any country possess this property, the country obtains all foreign commodities at less cost. It gets its imports cheaper, the greater the intensity of the demand in foreign countries for its exports. It also gets its imports cheaper, the less the extent and intensity of its own demand for them. The market is cheapest to those whose demand is small. A country which desires few foreign productions, and only a limited quantity of them, while its own commodities are in great request in foreign countries, will obtain its limited imports at extremely small cost, that is, in exchange for the produce of a very small quantity of its labour and capital.

Lastly, having introduced more than the original two commodities into the hypothesis, let us also introduce more than the original two countries. After the demand of England for the linen of Germany has raised the rate of interchange to 10 yards of cloth for 16 of linen, suppose a trade opened between England and some other country which also exports linen. And let us suppose that, if England had no trade but with the third country, the play of international demand would enable her to obtain from it, for 10 yards of cloth or its equivalent, 17 yards of linen. She evidently would not go on buying linen from Germany at the former rate: Germany would be undersold, and must consent to give 17 yards, like the other country. In this case, the circumstances of production and of demand in the third country are supposed to be in themselves more advantageous to England than the circumstances of Germany; but this supposition is not necessary: we might suppose that if the trade with Germany did not exist, England would be obliged to give to the other country the same advantageous terms which she gives to Germany; 10 yards of cloth for 16, or even less than 16, of linen. Even so, the opening of the third country makes a great difference in favour of England. There is now a double market for English export, while the demand of England for linen is only what it was before. This necessarily obtains for England more advantageous terms of interchange. The two countries, requiring much more of her produce than was required by either alone, must, in order to obtain it, force an increased demand for their exports, by offering them at a lower value.

It deserves notice, that this effect in favour of England from the opening of another market for her exports, will equally be produced even though the country from which the demand comes should have nothing to sell which England is willing to take. Suppose that the third country, though requiring cloth or iron from England, produces no linen, nor any other article which is in demand there. She however produces exportable articles, or she would have no means of paying for imports: her exports, though not suitable to the English consumer, can find a market somewhere. As we are only supposing three countries, we must assume her to find this market in Germany, and to pay for what she imports from England by orders on her German customers. Germany, therefore, besides having to pay for her own imports, now owes a debt to England on account of the third country, and the means for both purposes must be derived from her exportable produce. She must therefore tender that produce to England on terms sufficiently favourable to force a demand equivalent to this double debt. Everything will take place precisely as if the third country had bought German produce with her own goods, and offered that produce to England in exchange for hers. There is an increased demand for English goods, for which German goods have to furnish the payment; and this can only be done by forcing an increased demand for them in England, that is, by lowering their value. Thus an increase of demand for a country's exports in any foreign country enables her to obtain more cheaply even those imports which she procures from other quarters. And conversely, an increase of her own demand for any foreign commodity compels her, *cæteris paribus,* to pay dearer for all foreign commodities.

The law which we have now illustrated, may be appropriately named, the Equation of International Demand. It may be concisely stated as follows. The produce of a country exchanges for the produce of other countries, at such values as are required in order that the whole of her exports may exactly pay for the whole of her imports. This law of International Values is but an extension of the more general law of Value, which we called the Equation of Supply and Demand. We have seen that the value of a commodity always so adjusts itself as to bring the demand to the exact level of the supply. But all trade, either between nations or individuals, is an interchange of commodities, in which the things that they respectively have to sell constitute also their means of purchase: the supply brought by the one constitutes his demand for what is brought by the other. So that supply and demand are but another expression for reciprocal demand: and to say that value will adjust itself so as to equalize demand with supply, is in fact to say that it will adjust itself so as to equalize the demand on one side with the demand on the other. . . .

OF PROPERTY *

The laws and conditions of the Production of wealth partake of the character of physical truths. There is nothing optional or arbitrary in them. Whatever mankind produce, must be produced in the modes, and under the conditions, imposed by the constitution of external things, and by the inherent properties of their own bodily and mental structure. Whether they like it or not, their productions will be limited by the amount of their previous accumulation, and, that being given, it will be proportional to their energy, their skill, the perfection of their machinery, and

* From *Principles of Political Economy,* edited by W. J. Ashley (London and New York, Longmans, Green and Co., 1909). Reprinted by permission of the publishers.

their judicious use of the advantages of combined labour. Whether they like it or not, a double quantity of labour will not raise, on the same land, a double quantity of food, unless some improvement takes place in the processes of cultivation. Whether they like it or not, the unproductive expenditure of individuals will *pro tanto* tend to impoverish the community, and only their productive expenditure will enrich it. . . .

It is not so with the Distribution of wealth. That is a matter of human institution solely. The things once there, mankind, individually or collectively, can do with them as they like. They can place them at the disposal of whomsoever they please, and on whatever terms. Further, in the social state, in every state except total solitude, any disposal whatever of them can only take place by the consent of society, or rather of those who dispose of its active force. Even what a person has produced by his individual toil, unaided by any one, he cannot keep, unless by the permission of society. Not only can society take it from him, but individuals could and would take it from him, if society only remained passive; if it did not either interfere *en masse,* or employ and pay people for the purpose of preventing him from being disturbed in the possession. The distribution of wealth, therefore, depends on the laws and customs of society. . . .

We proceed, then, to the consideration of the different modes of distributing the produce of land and labour, which have been adopted in practice, or may be conceived in theory. . . .

The assailants of the principle of individual property may be divided into two classes: those whose scheme implies absolute equality in the distribution of the physical means of life and enjoyment, and those who admit inequality, but grounded on some principle, or supposed principle, of justice or general expediency, and not, like so many of the existing social inequalities, dependent on accident alone. . . . The characteristic name for [the first] economical system is Communism, a word of continental origin, only of late introduced into this country. The word Socialism, which originated among the English Communists, and was assumed by them as a name to designate their own doctrine, is now [1849], on the Continent, employed in a larger sense; not necessarily implying Communism, or the entire abolition of private property, but applied to any system which requires that the land and the instruments of production should be the property, not of individuals, but of communities or associations, or of the government. Among such systems, the two of highest intellectual pretension are those which, from the names of their real or reputed authors, have been called St. Simonism and Fourierism; the former defunct as a system, but which during the few years of its public promulgation sowed the seeds of nearly all the Socialist tendencies which have since spread so widely in France: the second, still [1865] flourishing in the number, talent, and zeal of its adherents.

Whatever may be the merits or defects of these various schemes, they cannot be truly said to be impracticable. No reasonable person can doubt that a village community, composed of a few thousand inhabitants, cultivating in joint ownership . . . could raise an amount of production sufficient to maintain them in comfort; and would find the means of obtaining, and if need be, exacting, the quantity of labour necessary for this purpose, from every member of the association who was capable of work. . . .

If . . . the choice were to be made between Communism with all its chances, and the present [1852] state of society with all its sufferings and injustices; if the institution of private property necessarily carried with it as a consequence, that the produce of labour should be apportioned as we now see it, almost in an inverse ratio to the labour—the largest portions to those who have never worked at all, the next largest to those whose work is almost nominal, and so in a descending scale, the remuneration dwindling as the work grows harder and more disagreeable, until the most fatiguing and exhausting bodily labour cannot count with certainty on being able to earn even the necessaries of life; if this or Communism were the alternative, all the difficulties, great or small, of Communism would be but as dust in the balance. But to make the comparison applicable, we must compare Communism at its best, with the régime of individual property, not as it is, but as it might be made. The principle of private property has never yet had a fair trial in any country; and less so, perhaps, in this country than in some others. The social arrangements of modern Europe commenced from a distribution of property which was the result, not of just partition, or acquisition by industry, but of conquest and violence: and notwithstanding what industry has been doing for many centuries to modify the work of force, the system still retains many and large traces of its origin. The laws of property have never yet conformed to the principles on which the justification of private property rests. They have made property of things which never ought to be property, and absolute property where only a qualified property ought to exist. They have not held the balance fairly between human beings, but have heaped impediments upon some, to give advantage to others; they have purposely fostered inequalities, and prevented all from starting fair in the race. That all should indeed start on perfectly equal terms is inconsistent with any law of private property: but if as much pains as has been taken to aggravate the inequality of chances arising from the natural working of the principle, had been taken to temper that inequality by every means not subversive of the principle itself; if the tendency of legislation had been to favour the diffusion, instead of the concentration of wealth—to encourage the subdivision of the large masses, instead of striving to keep them together; the principle of individual property would have been found to have no necessary connexion with the physical and social evils which almost all Socialist writers assume to be inseparable from it.

PART SEVEN
Reactions against Classicism: Socialism

Almost from its inception the classical school of economics met with criticism from various sides. We have seen, for example, how Malthus differed with Ricardo on a number of important issues but went unheeded in his own time. Lord Lauderdale and later John Stuart Mill took issue with the individualism, automatism, and pessimism that characterized latter-day classical economics. However, the main tenets of classicism showed a remarkable persistence in English economic thought throughout the nineteenth century and proved most difficult to crack; Jevons, for one, complained bitterly again and again of the entrenchment of the supporters of classicism and of their success in fighting his own new doctrines.

On the Continent, however, conditions were different: classical doctrine met with considerable opposition in France and especially in Germany. In France, Smith's doctrines had been introduced by Say and at first had been well received. However, after the Napoleonic Wars a whole galaxy of French socialist writers arose, including such thinkers on economic topics as Sismondi, Saint-Simon, Fourier, Cabet, Blanc, and Proudhon. For France had developed its industry greatly under Napoleon, and many of the abuses incident to the rise of industrialism, such as business crises, child labor, unemployment, and long hours, aroused vehement protest.

The early nineteenth-century socialists, both in England and on the Continent, were products of the Enlightenment, distrustful of authority and confident that the power of reason could enable mankind to solve human problems. These were all men of vision who sought to propagandize for a new social order. Sometimes they even set up small-scale models of the orders they conceived, to show how attractive the new life could be. But although all of them bitterly criticized the ills of capitalism and a competitive society, none of them envisioned overthrowing the existing order and none of them participated actively in politics. Almost all of these so-called utopians were of middle-class background, and they could see no reason why the soundness of their arguments should not persuade the owners of property to end abuses voluntarily and instead support plans for reform. Such support was most usually not forthcoming, of course, and the movements consequently lost their momentum. But one cannot say that the utopian socialists always labored in vain. They made socialism a flaming issue in their day and disseminated its ideas to America as well as to other countries on the Continent. Furthermore, both the great British consumer coöperative movement and Fabian socialism owe a great deal to the socialist enthusiasts of this period.

Both Pierre Joseph Proudhon and Henry George are examples of reformist socialists, although some of their followers may resent the label. Neither wanted to eliminate capitalism; indeed, Proudhon's hatred of communism gained him the undying enmity of Karl Marx. At the same time, his proposal to replace the Bank of France by a "people's bank" dealing in labor exchange notes was bitterly denounced by the propertied class. He was a defender of private property although he wished to eliminate the rentier, the man who lives off his property. Proudhon was thus the spiritual progenitor of a long line of thinkers who wished to retain capitalism as a whole, but only after reforming one or another of its aspects. Henry George was another who believed that capitalism need not be destroyed, if only the right to receive rent, which he considered to be unearned increment, were abolished.

There is room in this section for only a few of the many writers who represent various aspects of socialism. The utopian socialists have been almost entirely omitted because their contribution to economic theory was slight. Sismondi and Henry George typify the reformist thinkers who criticized unrestrained capitalism but advocated neither the violent overthrow of the system nor the communal ownership of the instruments of production. By far the most important of the socialist writers is Karl Marx. Another German, Rudolf Hilferding, made a significant attempt to extend Marxian analysis to fields which Marx failed to cover fully, notably imperialism and finance capitalism.

For further reading, Eduard Bernstein's *Evolutionary Socialism* and the *Fabian Essays* of the British Fabian Society are especially recommended.

JEAN CHARLES LÉONARD SIMONDE DE SISMONDI

(1773–1842)

Jean Simonde de Sismondi was born in Geneva, a scion of the aristocratic family of Simonde, victims of the conquest of their native city of Pisa by Florence in the sixteenth century.

His father, who had jeopardized the family fortunes by unwise investments, placed the young Sismondi in business to try to recoup the losses. Sismondi upheld his father's faith in him by showing great acumen in business affairs; he rose rapidly, accumulating along the way much of the firsthand knowledge which stood him in good stead in his later economic studies.

The repercussions of the French Revolution finally became felt in Geneva, and in 1792 Sismondi was imprisoned with his father. In 1793 the family escaped to England, where the young Sismondi became an enthusiastic observer of English political institutions: "the noble English liberty, the habeas corpus, the trial by jury, and fixed laws."

After a brief return to Geneva resulted in another brush with the authorities, the Sismondi family settled on a farm in Tuscany to await the time when they would be welcome in their own country. On the farm Sismondi wrote a treatise on the agriculture of Tuscany, the *Tableau de l'Agriculture Toscane* (*Table of Tuscan Agriculture,* 1801), and laid the foundation for his work on politics and Italian history, the *Histoire des Républiques Italiennes du Moyen Âge* (*History of the Italian Republics,* sixteen volumes, 1807–1818), which was published only after Sismondi's later return to Geneva. This time he remained there, becoming secretary of the chamber of commerce of the province of Leman.

Among his early economic works is the *Traité de la Richesse Commerciale* (*Treatise on Commercial Wealth,* 1803), in which he followed the doctrines of Adam Smith rather uncritically. Later, however, his historical studies led him to doubt the infallibility of Smith, and these doubts appeared in an article, "Political Economy," written for the *Edinburgh Encyclopedia* in 1818. In the following year his ideas were published in expanded form as *Nouveaux Principes d'Économie Politique* (*New Principles of Political Economy*). In this book he criticized classical political economy, attacked the concentration of wealth, and traced the depression phase of the business cycle to underconsumption, which has become a major concept in modern theory. It is from the *New Principles* that the following selection has been taken. In it Sismondi tries to show that crises and unemployment are unavoidable corollaries of capitalism.

NEW PRINCIPLES OF POLITICAL ECONOMY *

It is of some consequence to the happiness of citizens whether every one's share of comfort and enjoyment approaches equality or whether a few have all the superfluity, while the masses are reduced to the bare necessaries of life. Whether the national income is distributed in one manner or in the other is also of some consequence to the progress of national wealth. . . .

* From *New Principles of Political Economy*. The selection from Donald O. Wagner, *Social Reformers.*

The concentration of fortunes in the hands of a few men narrows the domestic market, and industry is more and more reduced to seek an outlet in foreign markets, where it is threatened with the greatest convulsions.

All states whose production exceeds their consumption turn their eyes toward this foreign market, and as its bounds are unknown its extent seems unlimited. But with the perfection of navigation, the opening of routes and better assurance of protection it becomes apparent that the market of the universe is quite as limited as that of each nation was formerly, and that the reliance of all producers upon the foreign market has everywhere raised production above demand. It becomes plain also that, as the great reduction in price offered by the producers of one country to the consumers of another is a decree of death to the producers of the latter country, the resistance to this commercial aggression, though violent and disorderly, is almost always popular, however contrary it may appear to be to the interest of the consumers. The latter comprise, however, all the inhabitants of the country. . . .

When one scans the reports of trade, the newspapers, and accounts of travellers, one sees everywhere proofs of this superabundant production which outstrips consumption and is regulated not by demand but by the amount of capital seeking employment. One sees proof also of this activity of the merchants which leads them to rush *en masse* into every new market and exposes them by turns to ruinous losses in every trade from which they anticipated profit. . . .

The opening of the immense market which Spanish America offered to industrious producers seemed to me the event which might do most to relieve English manufactures. The British government was of the same opinion, and in the seven years which passed after the commercial crisis of 1819 an unheard-of effort was put forth to introduce English commerce into . . . distant parts . . . But however large the market presented by free America, it would not have sufficed to absorb all the merchandise that England had produced in excess of consumption if the borrowing of the new republics had not suddenly augmented immeasurably their means of buying English merchandise. Each American state borrowed from England a sum sufficient to put its government in operation, and although this was capital funds, it was spent immediately within the year . . . to buy English merchandise. . . . As long as this strange commerce lasted, as long as Englishmen asked only that Americans be good enough to buy English merchandise with English capital and consume it for love of them, the prosperity of English manufacturing seemed glittering. . . . But when the capital was spent and the time for payment arrived, the veil suddenly dropped, the illusion vanished, and distress, even more severe than it had been in 1818, began once more.

The crisis therefore has returned more sharply than ever: no orders in the factories; no sales; insufficient wages for the workers, a large number of whom can find no work; the capital of the manufacturers tied up in finished goods which tax all their warehouses: such are the signs of the existing distress and of the growing disproportion between production and consumption. . . .

However, I am far from saying that the evil is irremediable: the nation has great resources and the ministry is very skillful. But an experience so dearly bought should at last spread enlightenment; it should cause the fact to be recognized that consumption is not the necessary consequence of production; that the glutting of the market is, on the contrary, the inevitable result of the system into which we have precipitated ourselves. . . .

The division of labor requires that business be conducted on a very large scale, since each workman who is restricted to a single operation must find a means of keeping himself constantly occupied. More circulating capital is therefore required. Moreover the multiplication of machines which displace or reduce human labor requires an expensive establishment to begin with, a first cost which is only returned piecemeal: it therefore presupposes the possession of unemployed capital which can be spared from present use in order to establish a kind of perpetual rent.

The increasing division of labor is, as we have seen, the principal cause of the increase of the powers of production. Each person does better the thing he is confined to; and when finally his work is reduced to the simplest operation, he comes to do it with so much ease and rapidity that the eye cannot follow him and one scarcely comprehends how the hand of man can attain such a degree of dexterity and speed.

Frequently this division of labor makes it apparent that the worker is no longer even the equal of a machine—a machine can in fact replace him. Several great inventions in mechanics as applied to the arts have been the result of such observation on the part of the worker or his employer. But by this division man loses in intelligence, health, and good humor everything he gains in the ability to produce wealth. . . .

When a technical invention augments the productive powers of man, doubtless it should not be employed to the disadvantage of those whom it ought to serve. If it is not called forth by any new demand for labor, if it does not put the goods produced within the reach of new consumers, it should not at the very least displace or render useless a certain number of producers whether native or foreign. But there is no way of directly checking the revolution which the invention produces. It would be both useless and dangerous to suppress the invention itself. If we were to prevent the adoption of a new machine in our own workshops our neighbors would not be so scrupulous: they would make war on our workmen with their steam engines, their spinning machines, and all their new inventions. It is a war to the death in which one is forced to defend oneself but which one is imprudent to commence.

No spectacle is more amazing, more terrifying perhaps, than that presented by England in the midst of an opulence which at first is so dazzling to the eye. If one is not content to consider merely the colossal wealth of the peers of the realm to whom £20,000 is only a moderate income, if one estimates their luxury at its true value and according to the enjoyment it procures—an insulting luxury which displays itself in sumptuous carriages, numerous lackeys running through the streets with raised staffs, and fox-hunting turn-outs of a score of horses and two-score dogs that cost two thousand pounds a year—one feels some indignation in comparing such prodigality with the suffering of the poor. The highways are traversed alternately by troops of beggars discharged from the factories and by bands of ragged Irishmen who apply at farm after farm for any kind of agricultural work at a greatly reduced wage. The former like the latter ask alms only when work is denied them; but all the places are filled. The farm laborer, the cottager, sees with bitterness these strangers competing with him for work which before was hardly sufficient to support himself. In the cities, in the capital, at Hyde Park Corner, where the most splendid carriages follow each other with the speed of light, groups of ten or twenty factory workers, sitting motionless with despair in their eyes and their limbs exhausted with fear, fail to excite even a moment's notice. A third of the factories are closed, still another third will have to close soon, and all the stores are over-stocked. Merchandise is everywhere offered for sale at a price so low as not to pay half the cost of making it; and all the letters from South America announce that the immense cargoes sent there in the course of trade can be sold for scarcely enough to cover the freight. Amidst this universal distress, when the workman is everywhere turned away and the English nation has yielded its place to steam engines that do everything men used to do, rewards are still offered to the inventor of new machines which would render useless the workers who still find a livelihood. . . .

I desire urban as well as rural industry to be divided amongst a great number of independent workshops and not combined under a single head who commands hundreds or thousands of workers. I desire manufacturing capital to be divided amongst a great number of middling capitalists and not united in the possession of one man who is master of several millions; I want the industrious workman to have the prospect, almost the certainty, of becoming the partner of his master, so that he will marry only when he has a share in the business instead of growing old without hope of advancement as he does to-day. But to bring about these reforms I ask only the slow and indirect means of legislation, only the execution of complete justice between master and workman. This would require the former to assume all the responsibility for the evil he does the latter. Let the law constantly favor the division and not the accumulation of inheritances; let it compel the master to find a pecuniary and political advantage in binding his workmen more closely to himself, in hiring them for longer periods, in sharing his profits with them, and perhaps private interest, being better directed, will itself repair the evil it has done society.

KARL HEINRICH MARX

(1818–1883)

Karl Marx, one of the leading figures of the nineteenth century, was especially important in the development of economic thought. Because he formulated the basic views held by the Communist Party and because his doctrine is revolutionary, there has been a tendency among academic economists to mention him only as an object of attack. Although his arguments have many weaknesses, nevertheless, his study of the operations of the capitalistic system has suggested numerous areas of investigation to other schools of economists, notably the German historical and the American institutional schools. His analysis of trade cycles, for instance, has proved very stimulating to subsequent writers.

For an understanding of Marx's economic views an examination of the *Communist Manifesto* and other incendiary Marxist publications is unnecessary; discussion may be confined to pertinent sections of his analytical works, *Capital* for example, with special reference to his theory of value and his theory of economic development.

Karl Heinrich Marx was born in Treves, Germany, the son of a successful lawyer and philosopher who, although born a Jew, embraced Christianity when Karl was a boy. The young Marx studied at the Gymnasium of his native city and later at the universities of Bonn and Berlin. At Berlin he joined the Young Hegelians, and this radical connection prevented Marx from obtaining a college teaching post. In 1841, however, the University of Jena awarded him the degree of doctor of philosophy. A brief excursion into journalism with the *Rheinische Zeitung* ended early in 1843 when the paper was suppressed. Shortly afterward he married Jenny von Westphalen, daughter of the privy councilor of Treves.

In 1844 Marx went to Paris, but the next year trouble with the authorities caused him to move again, this time to Belgium. Here he wrote *La Misère de la Philosophie* (*The Poverty of Philosophy,* 1847), in which he attacked Proudhon's proposal to turn workers into property owners through corporate organizations.

By this time he had begun collaboration with Friedrich Engels, a fellow Rhinelander of socialist and Hegelian leanings, whose father was a wealthy industrialist with factories in Germany and England. In Brussels they were the center of a group of working-class radicals called the Communist League, but the revolution of 1848 alarmed the Belgian government, which expelled the whole group from the country.

Marx returned to Germany, but after the reaction of 1849 he found himself unwelcome there as well, and following a brief stay in Paris he went to London, where he remained comparatively inactive until 1862. Here he lived in the slums in extreme poverty, depending for bare survival on free-lance writing and the benevolence of Engels, who had re-entered his father's business in Manchester. He spent innumerable days in the British Museum, studying the great economists and reading the many "blue books" on industrial and labor conditions put out by government investigating committees. His conclusions may be found in the first volume of *Das Kapital* (*Capital,* 1867), a massive work showing tremendous research and great erudition.

Meanwhile, the International Workingmen's Association, a group of radicals from many lands, was formed in 1864, and Marx and Engels became active in its affairs. However, internal dissension, especially between Marx and the anarchist Bakunin, helped destroy the organization. In 1879 Marx withdrew from active participation in working-class politics and tried to finish his major work. In 1878 his failing health forced him to give up work on *Capital,* and he died five years later.

Engels' labor on Marx's notes for three years afterward made possible publication of the second and third volumes of

Capital (1885–1894). And in 1910 Karl Kautsky, a German socialist, brought out a four-volume work, *Theorien über den Mehrwert* (*Theories of Surplus Value*, 1905–1910), from still other notes.

Marx's analysis of the capitalistic system is, of course, controversial, but there is no question that he turned economics away from arid speculation on abstract premises in a search for the "eternal verities." Because he concentrated on the historical features of specific situations, his theory shows a genuine note of reality. His was the first large-scale attempt to examine the actual workings of the capitalist process, and many later writers—Sombart, Veblen, Keynes, Mitchell, and Schumpeter, to name a few—owe a great deal to Marx's pioneering studies, although they may reject some or many of his conclusions.

Among Marx's major contributions to economic thought are the economic interpretation of history, the labor theory of surplus value, and a theory of capitalistic concentration. And while he developed no explicit theory of imperfect competition, the roots of such a theory are present in both his theory of capitalistic concentration and his theory of exploitation. Also, although he never presented a thoroughly integrated theory of the business cycle, he was one of the first writers to note the normality of trade fluctuations under capitalism. His analysis of effective demand in Volume II of *Capital* is in the modern tradition and is far superior to the crude underconsumption theories of his socialist predecessors.

Of course, even the most creative genius borrows from his predecessors. Marx was a keen student of the history of economic thought, knew the works of preceding economists in great detail, and borrowed from them. Among those he found most useful were Saint-Simon and, above all, Ricardo, whose labor theory of value (see pp. 192–197) was to become one of the cornerstones of socialist theory in Marx's hands. Moreover, Marx's theory of distribution showed the landlord fattening on the growth of society without contributing to its welfare. But while both regarded the value of a commodity as determined and measured by the labor-time expended on it, Ricardo seemed to regard this "law" as holding true for all periods of civilization, while Marx viewed it as a law of production under one stage of human development, namely capitalism.

The first selection, which anticipates the later analysis in *Capital*, is taken from *Zur Kritik der Politischen Oekonomie* (*A Contribution to the Critique of Political Economy*, 1859), a work which represents the first two chapters of a huge manuscript designed to cover the entire field of economics.[1]

The second and third selections are from Volume I of *Capital*. The first of these gives Marx's explanation of how surplus value is created in the capitalistic process and how this process is dependent upon the separation of the worker from his instruments of production. The next, in which he eloquently discusses the evolution of the proletariat, is an excellent example of his fusing of analytical and historical materials.

The fourth selection, from Volume II of *Capital*, gives the gist of Marx's theory of capital reproduction. The last, from *Theories of Surplus Value*, analyzes the role of capital accumulation and effective demand in business cycles. This section has not been available hitherto in English.

[1] This work, comprising some 1472 manuscript pages arranged in twenty-three volumes, was completed in 1863 but has never been published in full. Instead, Marx undertook the more modest task of completing a four-volume work on capitalism (*Capital*), of which only one volume was published during his lifetime.

A CONTRIBUTION TO THE CRITIQUE OF POLITICAL ECONOMY *

I was led by my studies to the conclusion that legal relations as well as forms of state could neither be understood by themselves, nor explained by the so-called general progress of the human mind, but that they are rooted in the material conditions of life, which are summed up by Hegel after the fashion of the English and French of the eighteenth century under the name "civic society;" the anatomy of that civic society is to be sought in political economy. . . . The general conclusion at which I arrived and which, once reached, continued to serve as the leading thread in my studies, may be briefly summed up as follows: In the social production which men carry on they enter into definite relations that are indispensable and independent of their will; these relations of production correspond to a definite stage of development of their material powers of production. The sum total of these relations of production constitutes the economic structure of society—the real foundation, on which rise legal and political superstructures and to which correspond definite forms of social consciousness. The mode of production in material life determines the general character of the social, political and spiritual processes of life. It is not the consciousness of men that determines their existence, but, on the contrary, their social existence determines their consciousness. At a certain stage of their development, the material forces of production in society come in conflict with the existing relations of production, or—what is but a legal expression for the same thing—with the property relations within which they had been at work before. From forms of development of the forces of production these relations turn into their fetters. Then comes the period of social revolution. With the change of the economic foundation the entire immense superstructure is more or less rapidly transformed. In considering such transformations the distinctions should always be made between the material transformation of the economic conditions of production which can be determined with the precision of natural science, and the legal, political, religious, aesthetic or philosophic—in short ideological forms in which men become conscious of this conflict and fight it out. Just as our opinion of an individual is not based on what he thinks of himself, so can we not judge of such a period of transformation by its own consciousness; on the contrary, this consciousness must rather be explained from the contradictions of material life, from the existing conflict between the social forces of production and the relations of production. No social order ever disappears before all the productive forces, for which there is room in it, have been developed; and new higher relations of production never appear before the material conditions of their existence have matured in the womb of the old society. Therefore, mankind always takes up only such problems as it can solve; since, looking at

* From *A Contribution to the Critique of Political Economy,* translated by N. I. Stone (Chicago, Charles H. Kerr & Co., 1904).

the matter more closely, we will always find that the problem itself arises only when the material conditions necessary for its solution already exist or are at least in the process of formation. In broad outlines we can designate the Asiatic, the ancient, the feudal, and the modern bourgeois methods of production as so many epochs in the progress of the economic formation of society. The bourgeois relations of production are the last antagonistic form of the social process of production—antagonistic not in the sense of individual antagonism, but of one arising from conditions surrounding the life of individuals in society; at the same time the productive forces developing in the womb of bourgeois society create the material conditions for the solution of that antagonism. This social formation constitutes, therefore, the closing chapter of the prehistoric stage of human society.

MONEY, AND THE BUYING AND SELLING OF LABOUR-POWER *

Contradictions in the General Formula of Capital

The creation of surplus-value, and therefore the conversion of money into capital, can . . . be explained neither on the assumption that commodities are sold above their value, nor that they are bought below their value.

The problem is in no way simplified by introducing irrelevant matters after the manner of Col. Torrens: "Effectual demand consists in the power and inclination (!), on the part of consumers, to give for commodities, either by immediate or circuitous barter, some greater portion of . . . capital than their production costs." In relation to circulation, producers and consumers meet only as buyers and sellers. To assert that the surplus-value acquired by the producer has its origin in the fact that consumers pay for commodities more than their value, is only to say in other words: The owner of commodities possesses, as a seller, the privilege of selling too dear. The seller has himself produced the commodities or represents their producer, but the buyer has to no less extent produced the commodities represented by his money, or represents their producer. The distinction between them is, that one buys and the other sells. The fact that the owner of the commodities, under the designation of producer, sells them over their value, and under the designation of consumer, pays too much for them, does not carry us a single step further.

To be consistent therefore, the upholders of the delusion that surplus-value has its origin in a nominal rise of prices or in the privilege which the seller has of selling too dear, must assume the existence of a class that only buys and does not sell, *i.e.,* only consumes and does not produce. The existence of such a class is inexplicable from the standpoint we have so far reached, viz., that of simple circulation. But let us anticipate. The money with which such a class is constantly making purchases, must constantly

* From *Capital,* translated by Samuel Moore and Edward Aveling (London, William Glaisher, Ltd., 1886). The wording of this heading was devised for this compilation.

flow into their pockets, without any exchange, gratis, by might or right, from the pockets of the commodity-owners themselves. To sell commodities above their value to such a class, is only to crib back again a part of the money previously given to it. . . .

Turn and twist then as we may, the fact remains unaltered. If equivalents are exchanged, no surplus-value results, and if non-equivalents are exchanged, still no surplus-value. Circulation, or the exchange of commodities, begets no value.

The reason is now therefore plain why, in analysing the standard form of capital, the form under which it determines the economical organisation of modern society, we entirely left out of consideration its most popular, and, so to say, antediluvian forms, merchants' capital and money-lenders' capital.

The circuit M—C—M′, buying in order to sell dearer, is seen most clearly in genuine merchants' capital. But the movement takes place entirely within the sphere of circulation. Since, however, it is impossible, by circulation alone, to account for the conversion of money into capital, for the formation of surplus-value, it would appear, that merchants' capital is an impossibility, so long as equivalents are exchanged; that, therefore, it can only have its origin in the twofold advantage gained, over both the selling and the buying producers, by the merchant who parasitically shoves himself in between them. It is in this sense that Franklin says, "war is robbery, commerce is generally cheating." If the transformation of merchants' money into capital is to be explained otherwise than by the producers being simply cheated, a long series of intermediate steps would be necessary, which, at present, when the simple circulation of commodities forms our only assumption, are entirely wanting.

What we have said with reference to merchants' capital, applies still more to money-lenders' capital. In merchants' capital, the two extremes, the money that is thrown upon the market, and the augmented money that is withdrawn from the market, are at least connected by a purchase and a sale, in other words by the movement of the circulation. In money-lenders' capital the form M—C—M′ is reduced to the two extremes without a mean, M—M′, money exchanged for more money, a form that is incompatible with the nature of money, and therefore remains inexplicable from the standpoint of the circulation of commodities. Hence Aristotle: "since chrematistic is a double science, one part belonging to commerce, the other to economic, the latter being necessary and praiseworthy, the former based on circulation and with justice disapproved (for it is not based on Nature, but on mutual cheating), therefore the usurer is most rightly hated, because money itself is the source of his gain, and is not used for the purposes for which it was invented. For it originated for the exchange of commodities, but interest makes out of money, more money. . . . Interest is money of money, so that of all modes of making a living, this is the most contrary to nature."

In the course of our investigation, we shall find that both merchants' capital and interest-bearing capital are derivative forms, and at the same time it will become clear, why these two forms appear in the course of history before the modern standard form of capital.

We have shown that surplus-value cannot be created by circulation, and, therefore, that in its formation, something must take place in the background, which is not apparent in the circulation itself. But can surplus-value possibly originate anywhere else than in circulation, which is the sum total of all the mutual relations of commodity-owners, as far as they are determined by their commodities? Apart from circulation, the commodity-owner is in relation only with his own commodity. So far as regards value, that relation is limited to this, that the commodity contains a quantity of his own labour, that quantity being measured by a definite social standard. This quantity is expressed by the value of the commodity, and since the value is reckoned in money of account, this quantity is also expressed by the price, which we will suppose to be £10. But his labour is not represented both by the value of the commodity, and by a surplus over that value, not by a price of 10 that is also a price of 11, not by a value that is greater than itself. The commodity owner can, by his labour, create value, but not self-expanding value. He can increase the value of his commodity, by adding fresh labour, and therefore more value to the value in hand, by making, for instance, leather into boots. The same material has now more value, because it contains a greater quantity of labour. The boots have therefore more value than the leather, but the value of the leather remains what it was; it has not expanded itself, has not, during the making of the boots, annexed surplus value. It is therefore impossible that outside the sphere of circulation, a producer of commodities can, without coming into contact with other commodity owners, expand value, and consequently convert money or commodities into capital.

It is therefore impossible for capital to be produced by circulation, and it is equally impossible for it to originate apart from circulation. It must have its origin both in circulation and yet not in circulation.

We have, therefore, got a double result.

The conversion of money into capital has to be explained on the basis of the laws that regulate the exchange of commodities, in such a way that the starting point is the exchange of equivalents. Our friend, Moneybags, who as yet is only an embryo capitalist, must buy his commodities at their value, must sell them at their value, and yet at the end of the process must withdraw more value from circulation than he threw into it at starting. His development into a full-grown capitalist must take place, both within the sphere of circulation and without it. These are the conditions of the problem Hic Rhodus, hic salta!

The Buying and Selling of Labour-Power

The change of value that occurs in the case of money intended to be converted into capital, cannot take place in the money itself, since in its function of means of purchase and of payment, it does no more than realise the price of the commodity it buys or pays for; and, as hard cash, it is value petrified, never varying. Just as little can it originate in the second act of circulation, the re-sale of the commodity, which does no more than transform the article from its bodily form back again into its money-form. The change must, therefore, take place in the commodity bought by the first act, M—C, but not in its value, for equivalents are exchanged, and the commodity is paid for at its full value. We are, therefore, forced to the conclusion that the change originates in the use-value, as such, of the commodity, *i.e.,* in its consumption. In order to be able to extract value from the consumption of a commodity, our friend, Moneybags, must be so lucky as to find, within the sphere of circulation, in the market, a commodity, whose use-value possesses the peculiar property of being a source of value, whose actual consumption, therefore, is itself an embodiment of labour, and, consequently, a creation of value. The possessor of money does find on the market such a special commodity in capacity for labour or labour-power.

By labour-power or capacity for labour is to be understood the aggregate of those mental and physical capabilities existing in a human being, which he exercises whenever he produces a use-value of any description.

But in order that our owner of money may be able to find labour-power offered for sale as a commodity, various conditions must first be fulfilled. The exchange of commodities of itself implies no other relations of dependence than those which result from its own nature. On this assumption, labour-power can appear upon the market as a commodity, only if, and so far as, its possessor, the individual whose labour-power it is, offers it for sale, or sells it, as a commodity. In order that he may be able to do this, he must have it at his disposal, must be the untrammelled owner of his capacity for labour, *i.e.,* of his person. He and the owner of money meet in the market, and deal with each other as on the basis of equal rights, with this difference alone, that one is buyer, the other seller; both, therefore, equal in the eyes of the law. The continuance of this relation demands that the owner of the labour-power should sell it only for a definite period, for if he were to sell it rump and stump, once for all, he would be selling himself, converting himself from a free man into a slave, from an owner of a commodity into a commodity. He must constantly look upon his labour-power as his own property, his own commodity, and this he can only do by placing it at the disposal of the buyer temporarily, for a definite period of time. By this means alone can he avoid renouncing his rights of ownership over it.

The second essential condition to the owner of money finding labour-power in the market as a commodity is this—that the labourer instead of being in the position to sell commodities in which his labour is incorporated, must be obliged to offer for sale as a commodity that very labour-power, which exists only in his living self.

In order that a man may be able to sell commodities other than labour-power, he must of course have the means of production, as raw material, implements, &c. No boots can be made without leather. He requires also the means of subsistence. Nobody—not even "a musician of the future"—can live upon future products, or upon use-values in an unfinished state; and ever since the first moment of his appearance on the world's stage, man always has been, and must still be a consumer, both before and while he is producing. In a society where all products assume the form of commodities, these commodities must be sold after they have been produced; it is only after their sale that they can serve in satisfying the requirements of their producer. The time necessary for their sale is superadded to that necessary for their production.

For the conversion of his money into capital, therefore, the owner of money must meet in the market with the free labourer, free in the double sense, that as a free man he can dispose of his labour-power as his own commodity, and that on the other hand he has no other commodity for sale, is short of everything necessary for the realisation of his labour-power.

The question why this free labourer confronts him in the market, has no interest for the owner of money, who regards the labour market as a branch of the general market for commodities. And for the present it interests us just as little. We cling to the fact theoretically, as he does practically. One thing, however, is clear—nature does not produce on the one side owners of money or commodities, and on the other men possessing nothing but their own labour-power. This relation has no natural basis, neither is its social basis one that is common to all historical periods. It is clearly the result of a past historical development, the product of many economical revolutions, of the extinction of a whole series of older forms of social production.

So, too, the economical categories, already discussed by us, bear the stamp of history. Definite historical conditions are necessary that a product may become a commodity. It must not be produced as the immediate means of subsistence of the producer himself. Had we gone further, and inquired under what circumstances all, or even the majority of, products take the form of commodities, we should have found that this can only happen with production of a very specific kind, capitalist production. Such an inquiry, however, would have been foreign to the analysis of commodities. Production and circulation of commodities can take place, although the great mass of the objects produced are intended for the immediate requirements of their producers, are not turned into commodities, and consequently social production is not yet by a long way dominated in its length and breadth by exchange-value. The appearance of products as commodities presupposes such a development of the social division of labour, that the separation of use-value from exchange-value, a separation which first begins with barter, must already have been completed. But such a degree of development is common to many forms of society, which in other respects present the most varying historical features. On the other hand, if we consider money, its existence implies a definite stage in the exchange of commodities. The particular functions of money which it performs, either as the mere equivalent of commodities, or as means of circulation, or means of payment, as hoard or as universal money, point, according to the extent and relative preponderance of the one function or the other, to very different stages in the process of social production. Yet we know by experience that a circulation of commodities relatively primitive, suffices for the production of all these forms. Otherwise with capital. The historical conditions of its existence are by no means given with the mere circulation of money and commodities. It can spring into life, only when the owner of the means of production and subsistence meets in the market with the free labourer selling his labour-power. And this one historical condition comprises a world's history. Capital, therefore, announces from its first appearance a new epoch in the process of social production.

We must now examine more closely this peculiar commodity, labour-power. Like all others it has a value. How is that value determined?

The value of labour-power is determined, as in the case of every other commodity, by the labour-time necessary for the production, and consequently also the reproduction, of this special article. So far as it has value, it represents no more than a definite quantity of the average labour of society incorporated in it. Labour-power exists only as a capacity, or power of the living individual. Its production consequently presupposes his existence. Given the individual, the production of labour-power consists in his reproduction of himself or his maintenance. For his maintenance he requires a given quantity of the means of subsistence. Therefore the labour-time requisite for the production of labour-power reduces itself to that necessary for the production of those means of subsistence; in other words, the value of labour-power is the value of the means of subsistence necessary for the maintenance of the labourer. Labour-power, however, becomes a reality only by its exercise; it sets itself in action only by working. But thereby a definite quantity of human muscle, nerve, brain, &c., is wasted, and these require to be restored. This increased expenditure demands a larger income. If the owner of labour-power works to-day, to-morrow he must again be able to repeat the same process in the same conditions as regards health and strength. His means of subsistence must therefore be sufficient to maintain him in his normal state as a labouring individual. His natural wants, such as food, clothing, fuel, and housing, vary according to the climatic and other physical conditions of his country. On the other hand, the number and extent of his so-called necessary wants, as also the modes of satisfying them, are themselves the product of historical development, and depend therefore to a great extent on the degree of civilisation of a country, more particularly on the conditions under which, and consequently on the habits and degree of comfort in which, the class of free labourers has been formed. In contradistinction therefore to the case of other commodities, there enters into the determination of the value of labour-power a historical and moral element. Nevertheless, in a given country, at a given period, the average quantity of the means of subsistence necessary for the labourer is practically known.

The owner of labour-power is mortal. If then his appearance in the market is to be continuous, and the continuous conversion of money into capital assumes this, the seller of labour-power must perpetuate himself, "in the way that every living individual perpetuates himself, by procreation." The labour-power withdrawn from the market by wear and tear and death, must be continually replaced by, at the very least, an equal amount of fresh labour-power. Hence the sum of the means of subsistence necessary for the production of labour-power must include the means necessary for the labourer's substitutes, *i.e.*, his children, in order that this race of peculiar commodity-owners may perpetuate its appearance in the market.

In order to modify the human organism, so that it may acquire skill and handiness in a given branch of industry, and become labour-power of a special kind, a special education or training is requisite, and this, on its part, costs an equivalent in commodities of a greater or less amount. This amount varies according to the more or less complicated character of the labour-power. The expenses of this education (excessively small in the case of ordinary labour-power), enter pro tanto into the total value spent in its production.

The value of labour-power resolves inself into the value of a definite quantity of the means of subsistence. It therefore varies with the value of these means or with the quantity of labour requisite for their production.

Some of the means of subsistence, such as food and fuel, are consumed daily, and a fresh supply must be provided daily. Others such as clothes and furniture last for longer periods and require to be replaced only at longer intervals. One article must be bought or paid for daily, another weekly, another quarterly, and so on. But in whatever way the sum total of these outlays may be spread over the year, they must be covered by the average income, taking one day with another. If the total of the commodities required daily for the production of labour-power be equal to A, and those required weekly be equal to B, and those required quarterly be equal to C, and so on, the daily average of these commodities is equal to

$$\frac{365A + 52B + 4C + \&c.}{365}$$

Suppose that in this mass of commodities requisite for the average day there are embodied 6 hours of social labour, then there is incorporated daily in labour-power half a day's average social labour, in other words, half a day's labour is requisite for the daily production of labour-power. This quantity of labour forms the value of a day's labour-power or the value of the labour-power daily reproduced. If half a day's average social labour is incorporated in three shillings, then three shillings is the price corresponding to the value of a day's labour-power. If its owner therefore offers it for sale at three shillings a day, its selling price is equal to its value, and according to our supposition, our friend Moneybags, who is intent upon converting his three shillings into capital, pays this value.

The minimum limit of the value of labour-power is determined by the value of the commodities, without the daily supply of which the labourer cannot renew his vital energy, consequently by the value of those means of subsistence that are physically indispensable. If the price of labour-power fall to this minimum, it falls below its value, since under such circumstances it can be maintained and developed only in a crippled state. But the value of every commodity is determined by the labour-time requisite to turn it out so as to be of normal quality.

It is a very cheap sort of sentimentality which declares this method of determining the value of labour-power, a method prescribed by the very nature of the case, to be a brutal method, and which wails with Rossi that, "To comprehend capacity for labour (puissance de travail) at the same time that we make abstraction from the means of subsistence to the labourers during the process of production, is to comprehend a phantom (être de raison). When we speak of labour, or capacity for labour, we speak at the same time of the labourer and his means of subsistence, of labourer and wages." When we speak of capacity for labour, we do not speak of labour, any more than when we speak of capacity for digestion, we speak of digestion. The latter process requires something more than a good stomach. When we speak of capacity for labour, we do not abstract from the necessary means of subsistence. On the contrary, their value is expressed in its value. If his capacity for labour remains unsold, the labourer derives no benefit from it, but rather he will feel it to be a cruel nature-imposed necessity that this capacity has cost for its production a definite amount of the means of subsistence and that it will continue to do so for its reproduction. He will then agree with Sismondi: "that capacity for labour. . . . is nothing unless it is sold."

One consequence of the peculiar nature of labour-power as a commodity is, that its use-value does not, on the conclusion of the contract between the buyer and seller, immediately pass into the hands of the former. Its value, like that of every other commodity, is already fixed before it goes into circulation, since a definite quantity of social labour has been spent upon it; but its use-value consists in the subsequent exercise of its force. The alienation of labour-power and its actual appropriation by the buyer, its employment as a use-value, are separated by an interval of time. But in those cases in which the formal alienation by sale of the use-value of a commodity, is not simultaneous with its actual delivery to the buyer, the money of the latter usually functions as means of payment. In every country in which the capitalist mode of production reigns, it is the custom not to pay for labour-power before it has been exercised for the period fixed by the contract, as for example, the end of each week. In all cases, therefore, the use-value of the labour-power is advanced to the capitalist: the labourer allows the buyer to consume it before he receives payment of the price; he everywhere gives credit to the capitalist. That this credit is no mere fiction, is shown not only by the occasional loss of wages on the bankruptcy of the capitalist, but also by a series of more enduring consequences. Nevertheless, whether money serves as a means of purchase or as a means of payment, this makes no alteration in the nature of the exchange of commodities. The price of the labour-power is fixed by the contract, although it is not realised till later, like the rent of a house. The labour-power is sold, although it is only paid for at a later period. It will, therefore, be useful, for a clear comprehension of the relation of the parties, to assume provisionally, that the possessor of labour-power, on the occasion of each sale, immediately receives the price stipulated to be paid for it.

We now know how the value paid by the purchaser to the possessor of this peculiar commodity, labour-power, is determined. The use-value which the former gets in exchange, manifests itself only in the actual usufruct, in the consumption of the labour-power. The money owner buys everything necessary for this purpose, such as raw material, in the market, and pays for it at its full value. The consumption of labour-power is at one and the same time the production of commodities and of surplus value. The consumption of labour-power is completed, as in the case of every other commodity, outside the limits of the market or of the sphere of circulation. Accompanied by Mr. Moneybags and by the possessor of labour-power, we therefore take leave for a time of this noisy sphere, where everything takes place on the surface and in view of all men, and follow them both into the hidden abode of production, on whose threshold there stares us in the face "No admittance except on business." Here we shall see, not only how capital produces, but how capital is produced. We shall at last force the secret of profit making.

This sphere that we are deserting, within whose boundaries the sale and purchase of labour-power goes on, is in fact a very Eden of the innate rights of man. There alone rule Freedom, Equality, Property and Bentham. Freedom, because both buyer and seller of a commodity, say of labour-power, are constrained only by their own free will. They contract as free agents, and the agreement they come to, is but the form in which they give legal expression to their common will. Equality, because each enters into relation with the other, as with a simple owner of commodities, and they exchange equivalent for equivalent. Property, because each disposes only of what is his own. And Bentham, because each looks only to himself. The only force that brings them together and puts them in relation with each other, is the selfishness, the gain and the private interests of each. Each looks to himself only, and no one troubles himself about the rest, and just because they do so, do they all, in accordance with the pre-established harmony of things, or under the auspices of an all-shrewd providence, work together to their mutual advantage, for the common weal and in the interest of all.

On leaving this sphere of simple circulation or of exchange of commodities, which furnishes the "Free-trader Vulgaris" with his views and ideas, and with the standard by which he judges a society based on capital and wages, we think we can perceive a change in the physiognomy of our dramatis personæ. He, who before was the money owner, now strides in front as capitalist; the possessor of labour-power follows as his labourer. The one with an air of importance, smirking, intent on business; the other, timid and holding back, like one who is bringing his own hide to market and has nothing to expect but—a hiding.

THE SO-CALLED PRIMITIVE ACCUMULATION *

The Secret of Primitive Accumulation

We have seen how money is changed into capital; how through capital surplus-value is made, and from surplus-value more capital. But the accumulation of capital presupposes surplus-value; surplus-value presupposes capitalistic production; capitalistic production presupposes the pre-existence of considerable masses of capital and of labour-power in the hands of producers of commodities. The whole movement, therefore, seems to turn in a vicious circle, out of which we can only get by supposing a primitive accumulation (previous accumulation of Adam Smith) preceding capitalistic accumulation; an accumulation not the result of the capitalist mode of production, but its starting point.

This primitive accumulation plays in Political Economy about the same part as original sin in theology. Adam bit the apple, and thereupon sin fell on the human race. Its origin is supposed to be explained when it is told as an anecdote of the past. In times long gone by there were two sorts of people; one, the diligent, intelligent, and, above all, frugal élite; the other, lazy rascals, spending their substance, and more, in riotous living. The legend of theological original sin tells us certainly how man came to be condemned to eat his bread in the sweat of his brow; but the history of economic original sin reveals to us that there are people to whom this is by no means essential. Never mind! Thus it came to pass that the former sort accumulated wealth, and the latter sort had at last nothing to sell except their own skins. And from this original sin dates the poverty of the great majority that, despite all its labour, has up to now nothing to sell but itself, and the wealth of the few that increases constantly although they have long ceased to work. Such insipid childishness is every day preached to us in the defence of property. M. Thiers, *e.g.,* had the assurance to repeat it with all the solemnity of a statesman, to the French people, once so *spirituel.* But as soon as the question of property crops up, it becomes a sacred duty to proclaim the intellectual food of the infant as the one thing fit for all ages and for all stages of development. In actual history it is notorious that conquest, enslavement, robbery, murder, briefly force, play the great part. In the tender annals of Political Economy, the idyllic reigns from time immemorial. Right and "labour" were from all time the sole means of enrichment, the present year of course always excepted. As a matter of fact, the methods of primitive accumulation are anything but idyllic.

* From *Capital,* translated by Samuel Moore and Edward Aveling (London, William Glaisher, Ltd., 1886). The heading is the title of Part VIII in the source.

In themselves, money and commodities are no more capital than are the means of production and of subsistence. They want transforming into capital. But this transformation itself can only take place under certain circumstances that centre in this, *viz.*, that two very different kinds of commodity-possessors must come face to face and into contact; on the one hand, the owners of money, means of production, means of subsistence, who are eager to increase the sum of values they possess, by buying other people's labour-power; on the other hand, free labourers, the sellers of their own labour-power, and therefore the sellers of labour. Free labourers, in the double sense that neither they themselves form part and parcel of the means of production, as in the case of slaves, bondsmen, &c., nor do the means of production belong to them, as in the case of peasant-proprietors; they are, therefore, free from, unencumbered by, any means of production of their own. With this polarisation of the market for commodities, the fundamental conditions of capitalist production are given. The capitalist system presupposes the complete separation of the labourers from all property in the means by which they can realise their labour. As soon as capitalist production is once on its own legs, it not only maintains this separation, but reproduces it on a continually extending scale. The process, therefore, that clears the way for the capitalist system, can be none other than the process which takes away from the labourer the possession of his means of production; a process that transforms, on the one hand, the social means of subsistence and of production into capital, on the other, the immediate producers into wage-labourers. The so-called primitive accumulation, therefore, is nothing else than the historical process of divorcing the producer from the means of production. It appears as primitive, because it forms the pre-historic stage of capital and of the mode of production corresponding with it.

The economic structure of capitalistic society has grown out of the economic structure of feudal society. The dissolution of the latter set free the elements of the former.

The immediate producer, the labourer, could only dispose of his own person after he had ceased to be attached to the soil and ceased to be the slave, serf, or bondman of another. To become a free seller of labour-power, who carries his commodity wherever he finds a market, he must further have escaped from the regime of the guilds, their rules for apprentices and journeymen, and the impediments of their labour regulations. Hence, the historical movement which changes the producers into wage-workers, appears, on the one hand, as their emancipation from serfdom and from the fetters of the guilds, and this side alone exists for our bourgeois historians. But, on the other hand, these new freedmen became sellers of themselves only after they had been robbed of all their own means of production, and of all the guarantees of existence afforded by the old feudal arrangements. And the history of this, their expropriation, is written in the annals of mankind in letters of blood and fire.

The industrial capitalists, these new potentates, had on their part not only to displace the guild masters of handicrafts, but also the feudal lords, the possessors of the sources of wealth. In this respect their conquest of social power appears as the fruit of a victorious struggle both against feudal lordship and its revolting prerogatives, and against the guilds and the fetters they laid on the free development of production and the free exploitation of man by man. The chevaliers d'industrie, however, only succeeded in supplanting the chevaliers of the sword by making use of events of which they themselves were wholly innocent. They have risen by means as vile as those by which the Roman freed-man once on a time made himself the master of his *patronus.*

The starting-point of the development that gave rise to the wage-labourer as well as to the capitalist, was the servitude of the labourer. The advance consisted in a change of form of this servitude, in the transformation of feudal exploitation into capitalist exploitation. To understand its march, we need not go back very far. Although we come across the first beginnings of capitalist production as early as the 14th or 15th century, sporadically, in certain towns of the Mediterranean, the capitalistic era dates from the 16th century. Wherever it appears, the abolition of serfdom has been long effected, and the highest development of the middle ages, the existence of sovereign towns, has been long on the wane.

In the history of primitive accumulation, all revolutions are epoch-making that act as levers for the capitalist class in course of formation; but, above all, those moments when great masses of men are suddenly and forcibly torn from their means of subsistence, and hurled as free and "unattached" proletarians on the labour market. The expropriation of the agricultural producer, of the peasant, from the soil, is the basis of the whole process. The history of this expropriation, in different countries, assumes different aspects, and runs through its various phases in different orders of succession, and at different periods. In England alone, which we take as our example, has it the classic form.

Expropriation of the Agricultural Population from the Land

In England, serfdom had practically disappeared in the last part of the 14th century. The immense majority of the population consisted then, and to a still larger extent, in the 15th century, of free peasant proprietors, whatever was the feudal title under which their right of property was hidden. In the larger seignorial domains, the old bailiff, himself a serf, was displaced by the free farmer. The wage-labourers of agriculture consisted partly of peasants, who utilised their leisure time by working on the large estates, partly of an independent special class of wage-labourers, relatively and absolutely few in numbers. The latter also were practically at the same time peasant farmers, since, besides their wages, they had alloted to them arable land to the extent of 4 or more acres, together with their cottages. Besides they, with the rest of the peasants, enjoyed the usufruct of the common land, which gave pasture to their cattle, furnished them with timber, fire-wood, turf, &c. In all countries of Europe, feudal production is characterised by division of the soil amongst the greatest possible number of sub-feudatories. The might of the feudal lord, like that of the sovereign, depended not on the length of his rent roll, but on the number of his subjects, and the latter depended on the number of peasant proprietors. Although, therefore, the English land, after the Norman conquest, was distributed in gigantic baronies, one of which often included some 900 of the old Anglo-Saxon lordships, it was bestrewn with small peasant properties, only here and there interspersed with great seignorial domains. Such conditions, together with the prosperity of the towns so characteristic of the 15th century, allowed of that wealth of the people which Chancellor Fortescue so eloquently paints in his "Laudes legum Angliæ;" but it excluded the possibility of capitalistic wealth.

The prelude of the revolution that laid the foundation of the capitalist mode of production, was played in the last third of the 15th, and the first decade of the 16th century. A mass of free proletarians was hurled on the labour-market by the breaking-up of the bands of feudal retainers, who, as Sir James Steuart well says, "everywhere uselessly filled house and castle." Although the royal power, itself a product of bourgeois development, in its strife after absolute sovereignty forcibly hastened on the dissolution of these bands of retainers, it was by no means the sole cause of it. In insolent conflict with king and parliament, the great feudal lords created an incomparably larger proletariat by the forcible driving of the peasantry from the land, to which the latter had the same feudal right as the lord himself, and by the usurpation of the common lands. The rapid rise of the Flemish wool manufactures, and the corresponding rise in the price of wool in England, gave the direct impulse to these evictions. The old nobility had been devoured by the great feudal wars. The new nobility was the child of its time, for which money was the power of all powers. Transformation of arable land into sheep-walks was, therefore, its cry. . . .

Legislation was terrified at this revolution. . . . An Act of 1533 recites that some owners possess 24,000 sheep, and limits the number to be owned to 2000. The cry of the people and the legislation directed, for 150 years after Henry VII., against the expropriation of the small farmers and peasants, were alike fruitless. . . .

The process of forcible expropriation of the people received in the 16th century a new and frightful impulse from the Reformation, and from the consequent colossal spoliation of the church property. The Catholic church was, at the time of the Reformation, feudal proprietor of a great part of the English land. The suppression of the monasteries, &c., hurled their inmates into the proletariat. The estates of the church were to a large extent given away to rapacious royal favourites, or sold at a nominal price to speculating farmers and citizens, who drove out, *en masse,* the hereditary sub-tenants and threw their holdings into one. The legally guaranteed property of the poorer folk in a part of the church's tithes was tacitly confiscated. . . .

After the restoration of the Stuarts, the landed proprietors carried, by legal means, an act of usurpation, effected everywhere on the Continent without any legal formality. They abolished the feudal tenure of land, *i.e.,* they got rid of all its obligations to the State, "indemnified" the State by taxes on the peasantry and the rest of the mass of the people, vindicated for themselves the rights of modern private property in estates to which they had only a feudal title, and, finally, passed those laws of settlement, which *mutatis mutandis,* had the same effect on the English agricultural labourer, as the edict of the Tartar Boris Godunof on the Russian peasantry.

. . . The bourgeois capitalists favoured the operation with the view, among others, to promoting free trade in land, to extending the domain of modern agriculture on the large farm-system, and to increasing their supply of the free agricultural proletarians ready to hand. Besides, the new landed aristocracy was the natural ally of the new bankocracy, of the newly-hatched *haute finance,* and of the large manufacturers, then depending on protective duties. . . .

The advance made by the 18th century shows itself in this, that the law itself becomes now the instrument of the theft of the people's land, although the large farmers make use of their little independent methods as well. The parliamentary form of the robbery is that of Acts for enclosures of Commons, in other words, decrees by which the landlords grant themselves the people's land as private property, decrees of expropriation of the people. Sir F. M. Eden refutes his own crafty special pleading, in which he tries to represent communal property as the private property of the great landlords who have taken the place of the feudal lords, when he, himself, demands a "general Act of Parliament for the enclosure of Commons," (admitting thereby that a parliamentary *coup d'état* is necessary for its transformation into private property), and moreover calls on the legislature for the indemnification for the expropriated poor.

Whilst the place of the independent yeoman was taken by tenants at will, small farmers on yearly leases, a servile rabble dependent on the pleasure of the landlords, the systematic robbery of the Communal lands helped especially, next to the theft of the State domains, to swell those large farms, that were called in the 18th century capital farms or merchant farms, and to "set free" the agricultural population as proletarians for manufacturing industry. . . .

The spoliation of the church's property, the fraudulent alienation of the State domains, the robbery of the common lands, the usurpation of feudal and clan property, and its transformation into modern private property under circumstances of reckless terrorism, were just so many idyllic methods of primitive accumulation. They conquered the field for capitalistic agriculture, made the soil part and parcel of capital, and created for the town industries the necessary supply of a "free" and outlawed proletariat.

Bloody Legislation against the Expropriated, from the End of the 15th Century. Forcing Down of Wages by Acts of Parliament.

The proletariat created by the breaking up of the bands of feudal retainers and by the forcible expropriation of the people from the soil, this "free" proletariat could not possibly be absorbed by the nascent manufactures as fast as it was thrown upon the world. On the other hand, these men, suddenly dragged from their wonted mode of life, could not as suddenly adapt themselves to the discipline of their new condition. They were turned *en masse* into beggars, robbers, vagabonds, partly from inclination, in most cases from stress of circumstances. Hence at the end of the 15th and during the whole of the 16th century, throughout Western Europe a bloody legislation against vagabondage. The fathers of the present working-class were chastised for their enforced transformation into vagabonds and paupers. Legislation treated them as "voluntary" criminals, and assumed that it depended on their own goodwill to go on working under the old conditions that no longer existed. . . .

Thus were the agricultural people, first forcibly expropriated from the soil, driven from their homes, turned into vagabonds, and then whipped, branded, tortured by laws grotesquely terrible, into the discipline necessary for the wage system.

. . . The advance of capitalist production developes a working-class, which by education, tradition, habit, looks upon the conditions of that mode of production as self-evident laws of nature. The organization of the capitalist process of production, once fully developed, breaks down all resistance. The constant generation of a relative surplus-population keeps the law of supply and demand of labour, and therefore keeps wages, in a rut that corresponds with the wants of capital. The dull compulsion of economic relations completes the subjection of the labourer to the capitalist. Direct force, outside economic conditions, is of course still used, but only exceptionally. In the ordinary run of things, the labourer can be left to the "natural laws of production," *i.e.,* to his dependence on capital, a dependence springing from, and guaranteed in perpetuity by, the conditions of production themselves. It is otherwise during the historic genesis of capitalist production. The bourgeoisie, at its rise, wants and uses the power of the state to "regulate" wages, *i.e.,* to force them within the limits suitable for surplus-value making, to lengthen the working-day and to keep the labourer himself in the normal degree of dependence. This is an essential element of the so-called primitive accumulation. . . .

Genesis of the Capitalist Farmer

Now that we have considered the forcible creation of a class of outlawed proletarians, the bloody discipline that turned them into wage-labourers, the disgraceful action of the state which employed the police to accelerate the accumulation of capital by increasing the degree of exploitation of labour, the question remains: whence came the capitalists originally? For the expropriation of the agricultural population creates, directly, none but great landed proprietors. As far, however, as concerns the genesis of the farmer, we can, so to say, put our hand on it, because it is a slow process evolving through many centuries. The serfs, as well as the free small proprietors, held land under very different tenures, and were therefore emancipated under very different economic conditions. In England the first form of the farmer is the bailiff, himself a serf. His position is similar to that of the old Roman *villicus,* only in a more limited sphere of action. During the second half of the 14th century he is replaced by a farmer, whom the landlord provides with seed, cattle and implements. His condition is not very different from that of the peasant. Only he exploits more wage-labour. Soon he becomes a métayer, a half-farmer. He advances one part of the agricultural stock, the landlord the other. The two divide the total product in proportions determined by contract. This form quickly disappears in England, to give place to the farmer proper, who makes his own capital breed by employing wage-labourers, and pays a part of the surplus product, in money or in kind, to the landlord as rent. So long, during the 15th century, as the independent peasant and the farm-labourer working for himself as well as for wages, enriched themselves by their own labour, the circumstances of the farmer, and his field of production, were equally mediocre. The agricultural revolution which commenced in the last third of the 15th century, and continued during almost the whole of the 16th (excepting, however, its last decade), enriched him just as speedily as it impoverished the mass of the agricultural people.

The usurpation of the common lands allowed him to augment greatly his stock of cattle, almost without cost, whilst they yielded him a richer supply of manure for the tillage of the soil. To this, was added in the 16th century, a very important element. At that time the contracts for farms ran for a long time, often for 99 years. The progressive fall in the value of the precious metals, and therefore of money, brought the farmers golden fruit. Apart from all the other circumstances discussed above, it lowered wages. A portion of the latter was now added to the profits of the farm. The continuous rise in the price of corn, wool, meat, in a word of all agricultural produce, swelled the money capital of the farmer without any action on his part, whilst the rent he paid, (being calculated on the old value of money) diminished in reality. Thus they grew rich at the expense both of their labourers and their landlords. No wonder therefore, that England, at the end of the 16th century, had a class of capitalist farmers, rich, considering the circumstances of the time.

Reaction of the Agricultural Revolution on Industry. Creation of the Home Market for Industrial Capital.

The expropriation and expulsion of the agricultural population, intermittent but renewed again and again, supplied, as we saw, the town industries with a mass of proletarians entirely unconnected with the corporate guilds and unfettered by them . . . In spite of the smaller number of its cultivators, the soil brought forth as much or more produce, after as before, because the revolution in the conditions of landed property was accompanied by improved methods of culture, greater co-operation, concentration of the means of production, &c., and because not only were the agricultural wage-labourers put on the strain more intensely, but the field of production on which they worked for themselves, became more and more contracted. With the setting free of a part of the agricultural population, therefore, their former means of nourishment were also set free. They were now transformed into material elements of variable capital. The peasant, expropriated and cast adrift, must buy their value in the form of wages, from his new master, the industrial capitalist. That which holds good of the means of subsistence holds with the raw materials of industry dependent upon home agriculture. They were transformed into an element of constant capital. Suppose, *e.g.*, a part of the Westphalian peasants, who, at the time of Frederic II., all span flax, forcibly expropriated and hunted from the soil; and the other part that remained, turned into day-labourers of large farmers. At the same time arise large establishments for flax-spinning and weaving, in which the men "set free" now work for wages. . . . The expropriation and eviction of a part of the agricultural population not only set free for industrial capital, the labourers, their means of subsistence, and material for labour; it also created the home market.

. . . Formerly, the peasant family produced the means of subsistence and the raw materials, which they themselves, for the most part, consumed. These raw materials and means of subsistence have now become commodities; the large farmer sells them, he finds his market in manufactures. Yarn, linen, coarse woollen stuffs—things whose raw materials had been within the reach of every peasant family, had been spun and woven by it for its own use—were now transformed into articles of manufacture, to which the country districts at once served for markets. The many scattered customers, whom stray artizans until now had found in the numerous small producers working on their own account, concentrate themselves now into one great market provided for by industrial capital. Thus, hand in hand with the expropriation of the self-supporting peasants, with their separation from their means of production, goes the destruction of rural domestic industry, the process of separation between manufacture and agriculture. . . . It will be remembered that manufacture, properly so-called, conquers but partially the domain of national production, and always rests on the handicrafts of the town and the domestic industry of the rural districts as its ultimate basis. If it destroys these in one form, in particular branches, at certain points, it calls them up again elsewhere, because it needs them for the preparation of raw material up to a certain point. It produces, therefore, a new class of small villagers who, while following the cultivation of the soil as an accessary calling, find their chief occupation in industrial labour, the products of which they sell to the manufacturers directly, or through the medium of merchants. . . .

Genesis of the Industrial Capitalist

The genesis of the industrial capitalist did not proceed in such a gradual way as that of the farmer. Doubtless many small guild-masters, and yet more independent small artisans, or even wage-labourers, transformed themselves into small capitalists, and (by gradually extending exploitation of wage-labour and corresponding accumulation) into full-blown capitalists. In the infancy of capitalist production, things often happened as in the infancy of mediæval towns, where the question, which of the escaped serfs should be master and which servant, was in great part decided by the earlier or later date of their flight. The snail's-pace of this method corresponded in no wise with the commercial requirements of the new world-market that the great discoveries of the end of the 15th century created. But the middle ages had handed down two distinct forms of capital, which mature in the most different economic social formations, and which, before the era of the capitalist mode of production, are considered as capital quand même—usurer's capital and merchant's capital.

"At present, all the wealth of society goes first into the possession of the capitalist . . . . he pays the landowner his rent, the labourer his wages, the tax and tithe gatherer their claims, and keeps a large, indeed the largest, and a continually augmenting share, of the annual produce of labour for himself. The capitalist may now be said to be the first owner of all the wealth of the community, though no law has conferred on him the right to this property . . . . this change has been effected by the taking of interest on capital . . . . and it is not a little curious that all the lawgivers of Europe endeavoured to prevent this by statutes, viz., statutes against usury. . . . . The power of the capitalist over all the wealth of the country is a complete change in the right of property, and by what law, or series of laws, was it effected?" [1] The author should have remembered that revolutions are not made by laws.

The money capital formed by means of usury and commerce was prevented from turning into industrial capital, in the country by the feudal constitution, in the towns by the guild organisation. These fetters vanished with the dissolution of feudal society, with the expropriation and partial eviction of the country population. The new manufactures were established at sea-ports, or at inland points beyond the control of the old municipalities and their guilds. Hence in England an embittered struggle of the corporate towns against these new industrial nurseries.

The discovery of gold and silver in America, the extirpation, enslavement and entombment in mines of the aboriginal population, the beginning of the conquest and looting of the East Indies, the turning of Africa into a warren for the commercial hunting of black-skins, signalised the rosy

[1] "The Natural and Artificial Rights of Property Contrasted." Lond., 1832, pp. 98–99. Author of the anonymous work: 'Th. Hodgskin.'

dawn of the era of capitalist production. These idyllic proceedings are the chief momenta of primitive accumulation. On their heels treads the commercial war of the European nations, with the globe for a theatre. It begins with the revolt of the Netherlands from Spain, assumes giant dimensions in England's anti-jacobin war, and is still going on in the opium wars against China, &c.

The different momenta of primitive accumulation distribute themselves now, more or less in chronological order, particularly over Spain, Portugal, Holland, France, and England. In England at the end of the 17th century, they arrive at a systematical combination, embracing the colonies, the national debt, the modern mode of taxation, and the protectionist system. These methods depend in part on brute force, *e.g.*, the colonial system. But they all employ the power of the State, the concentrated and organised force of society, to hasten, hothouse fashion, the process of transformation of the feudal mode of production into the capitalist mode, and to shorten the transition. Force is the midwife of every old society pregnant with a new one. It is itself an economic power.

Of the Christian colonial system, W. Howitt, a man who makes a speciality of Christianity, says: "The barbarities and desperate outrages of the so-called Christian race, throughout every region of the world, and upon every people they have been able to subdue, are not to be paralleled by those of any other race, however fierce, however untaught, and however reckless of mercy and of shame, in any age of the earth." The history of the colonial administration of Holland—and Holland was the head capitalistic nation of the 17th century—"is one of the most extraordinary relations of treachery, bribery, massacre, and meanness." Nothing is more characteristic than their system of stealing men, to get slaves for Java. The men stealers were trained for this purpose. The thief, the interpreter, and the seller, were the chief agents in this trade, native princes the chief sellers. . . .

The English East India Company, as is well known, obtained, besides the political rule in India, the exclusive monopoly of the tea-trade, as well as of the Chinese trade in general, and of the transport of goods to and from Europe. But the coasting trade of India and between the islands, as well as the internal trade of India, were the monopoly of the higher employés of the company. The monopolies of salt, opium, betel and other commodities, were inexhaustible mines of wealth. The employés themselves fixed the price and plundered at will the unhappy Hindus. The Governor-General took part in this private traffic. . . .

The colonial system ripened, like a hot-house, trade and navigation. The "societies Monopolia" of Luther were powerful levers for concentration of capital. The colonies secured a market for the budding manufactures, and, through the monopoly of the market, an increased accumulation. The treasures captured outside Europe by undisguised looting, enslavement, and murder, floated back to the mother-country and were there turned into capital. Holland, which first fully developed the colonial system, in 1648 stood already in the acme of its commercial greatness. It was "in almost exclusive possession of the East Indian trade and the commerce between the south-east and north-west of Europe. Its fisheries, marine, manufactures, surpassed those of any other country. The total capital of the Republic was probably more important than that of all the rest of Europe put together." Gülich forgets to add that by 1648, the people of Holland were more overworked, poorer and more brutally oppressed than those of all the rest of Europe put together. . . .

The system of public credit, *i.e.* of national debts, whose origin we discover in Genoa and Venice as early as the middle ages, took possession of Europe generally during the manufacturing period. The colonial system with its maritime trade and commercial wars served as a forcing-house for it. Thus it first took root in Holland. National debts, *i.e.,* the alienation of the state—whether despotic, constitutional or republican—marked with its stamp the capitalistic era. The only part of the so-called national wealth that actually enters into the collective possessions of modern peoples is—their national debt. Hence, as a necessary consequence, the modern doctrine that a nation becomes the richer the more deeply it is in debt. Public credit becomes the *credo* of capital. And with the rise of national debt-making, want of faith in the national debt takes the place of the blasphemy against the Holy Ghost, which may not be forgiven.

The public debt becomes one of the most powerful levers of primitive accumulation. As with the stroke of an enchanter's wand, it endows barren money with the power of breeding and thus turns it into capital, without the necessity of its exposing itself to the troubles and risks inseparable from its employment in industry or even in usury. The state-creditors actually give nothing away, for the sum lent is transformed into public bonds, easily negotiable, which go on functioning in their hands just as so much hard cash would. But further, apart from the class of lazy annuitants thus created, and from the improvised wealth of the financiers, middlemen between the government and the nation—as also apart from the tax-farmers, merchants, private manufacturers, to whom a good part of every national loan renders the service of a capital fallen from heaven—the national debt has given rise to joint-stock companies, to dealings in negotiable effects of all kinds, and to agiotage, in a word to stock-exchange gambling and the modern bankocracy.

At their birth the great banks, decorated with national titles, were only associations of private speculators, who placed themselves by the side of governments, and, thanks to the privileges they received, were in a position to advance money to the state. Hence the accumulation of the national debt has no more infallible measure than the successive rise in the stock of these banks, whose full development dates from the founding of the Bank of England in 1694. The Bank of England began with lending its money to the Government at 8%; at the same time it was empowered by Parliament to coin money out of the same capital, by lending it again to the public in the form of bank-notes. It was allowed to use these notes for discounting bills, making advances on commodities, and for buying the precious metals. It was not long ere this credit-money, made by the bank itself, became the coin in which the Bank of England made its loans to the state, and paid, on account of the state, the interest on the public debt. It was not enough that the bank gave with one hand and took back more with the other; it remained, even whilst receiving, the eternal creditor of the nation down to the last shilling advanced. Gradually it became inevitably the receptacle of the metallic hoard of the country, and the centre of gravity of all commercial credit. . . .

With the national debt arose an international credit system, which often conceals one of the sources of primitive accumulation in this or that people. Thus the villanies of the Venetian thieving system formed one of the secret bases of the capital-wealth of Holland to whom Venice in her decadence lent large sums of money. So also was it with Holland and England. By the beginning of the 18th century the Dutch manufactures were far outstripped. Holland had ceased to be the nation preponderant in commerce and industry. One of its main lines of business, therefore, from 1701–1776, is the lending out of enormous amounts of capital, especially to its great rival England. The same thing is going on to-day between England and the United States. A great deal of capital, which appears to-day in the United States without any certificate of birth, was yesterday, in England, the capitalised blood of children.

As the national debt finds its support in the public revenue, which must cover the yearly payments for interest, &c., the modern system of taxation was the necessary complement of the system of national loans. The loans enable the government to meet extraordinary expenses, without the taxpayers feeling it immediately, but they necessitate, as a consequence, increased taxes. On the other hand, the raising of taxation caused by the accumulation of debts contracted one after another, compels the government always to have recourse to new loans for new extraordinary expenses. Modern fiscality, whose pivot is formed by taxes on the most necessary means of subsistence (thereby increasing their price), thus contains within itself the germ of automatic progression. Over-taxation is not an incident, but rather a principle. In Holland, therefore, where this system was first inaugurated, the great patriot, De Witt, has in his "Maxims" extolled it as the best system for making the wage-labourer submissive, frugal, industrious, and overburdened with labour. The destructive influence that it exercises on the condition of the wage-labourer concerns us less however, here, than the forcible expropriation, resulting from it, of peasants, artisans, and in a word, all elements of the lower middle-class. On this there are not two opinions, even among the bourgeois economists. Its expropriating efficacy is still further heightened by the system of protection, which forms one of its integral parts.

The great part that the public debt, and the fiscal system corresponding with it, has played in the capitalisation of wealth and the expropriation of the masses, has led many writers, like Cobbett, Doubleday and others, to seek in this, incorrectly, the fundamental cause of the misery of the modern peoples.

The system of protection was an artificial means of manufacturing manufacturers, of expropriating independent labourers, of capitalising the national means of production and subsistence, of forcibly abbreviating the transition from the mediæval to the modern mode of production. . . .

Colonial system, public debts, heavy taxes, protection, commercial wars, &c., these children of the true manufacturing period, increase gigantically during the infancy of Modern Industry. The birth of the latter is heralded by a great slaughter of the innocents. . . .

With the development of capitalist production during the manufacturing period, the public opinion of Europe had lost the last remnant of shame and conscience. The nations bragged cynically of every infamy that served them as a means to capitalistic accumulation. Read, *e.g.*, the naïve Annals of Commerce of the worthy A. Anderson. Here it is trumpetted forth as a triumph of English statecraft that at the Peace of Utrecht, England extorted from the Spaniards by the Asiento Treaty the privilege of being allowed to ply the negro-trade, until then only carried on between Africa and the English West Indies, between Africa and Spanish America as well. England thereby acquired the right of supplying Spanish America until 1743 with 4800 negroes yearly. This threw, at the same time, an official cloak over British smuggling. Liverpool waxed fat on the slave-trade. This was its method of primitive accumulation. . . .

Whilst the cotton industry introduced child-slavery in England, it gave in the United States a stimulus to the transformation of the earlier, more or less patriarchal slavery, into a system of commercial exploitation. In fact, the veiled slavery of the wage-workers in Europe needed, for its pedestal, slavery pure and simple in the new world.

Tantæ molis erat, to establish the "eternal laws of Nature" of the capitalist mode of production, to complete the process of separation between labourers and conditions of labour, to transform, at one pole, the social means of production and subsistence into capital, at the opposite pole, the mass of the population into wage-labourers, into "free labouring poor," that artificial product of modern society. If money, according to Augier, "comes into the world with a congenital blood-stain on one cheek," capital comes dripping from head to foot, from every pore, with blood and dirt.

PRODUCTION, CONSUMPTION, VALUE, AND PRICE *

Simple Reproduction

THE FORMULATION OF THE QUESTION

. . . So long as we looked upon the production of value and the value of products from the point of view of individual capital, it was immaterial

* From *Capital*, in *A Handbook of Marxism*, edited by Emile Burns (New York, International Publishers, 1935). The wording of this heading was devised for this compilation. The material selected by Burns is from Volumes II and III.

for the analysis which was the natural form of the product in commodities, whether it was, for instance, that of a machine, of corn, or of looking-glasses. It was always but a matter of illustration, and any line of production could serve that purpose. What we had to consider was the immediate process of production itself, which presented itself at every point as the process of some individual capital. So far as reproduction was concerned, it was sufficient to assume that that portion of the product in commodities, which represented capital in the sphere of circulation, found an opportunity to reconvert itself into its elements of production and thus into its form of productive capital. It likewise sufficed to assume that both the labourer and the capitalist found in the market those commodities for which they spend their wages and surplus-value. This merely formal manner of presentation does not suffice in the study of the total social capital and of the value of its products. The reconversion of one portion of the value of the product into capital, the passing of another portion into the individual consumption of the capitalist and working classes, form a movement within the value of the product itself which is created by the total capital; and this movement is not only a reproduction of value, but also of material, and is, therefore, as much conditioned on the relative proportions of the elements of value of the total social product as on its use-value, its material substance.

Simple reproduction on the same scale appears as an abstraction, inasmuch as the absence of all accumulation or reproduction on an enlarged scale is an irrelevant assumption in capitalist society, and, on the other hand, conditions of production do not remain exactly the same in different years (as was assumed). The assumption is that a social capital of a given magnitude produces the same quantity of value in commodities this year as last, and supplies the same quantity of wants, although the forms of the commodities may be changed in the process of reproduction. However, while accumulation does take place, simple reproduction is always a part of it and may, therefore, be studied in itself, being an actual factor in accumulation. . . .

THE TWO DEPARTMENTS OF SOCIAL PRODUCTION

The total product, and therefore the total production, of society, is divided into two great sections:

I. *Means of Production,* commodities having a form in which they must, or at least may, pass over into productive consumption.

II. *Means of Consumption,* commodities having a form in which they pass into the individual consumption of the capitalist and working classes.

In each of these two departments, all the various lines of production belonging to them form one single great line of production, the one that of the means of production, the other that of articles of consumption. The aggregate capital invested in each of these two departments of production constitutes a separate section of the entire social capital.

In each department, the capital consists of two parts:

(1) *Variable Capital.* This capital, so far as its value is concerned, is equal to the value of the social labour-power employed in this line of production, in other words equal to the sum of the wages paid for this labour-power. So far as its substance is concerned, it consists of the active labour-power itself, that is to say, of the living labour set in motion by this value of capital.

(2) *Constant Capital.* This is the value of all the means of production employed in this line. These, again, are divided into *fixed* capital, such as machines, instruments of labour, buildings, labouring animals, etc., and *circulating* capital, such as materials of production, raw and auxiliary materials, half-wrought articles, etc.

The value of the total annual product created with the capital of each of the two great departments of production consists of one portion representing the constant capital *c* consumed in the process of production and transferred to the product, and of another portion added by the entire labour of the year. This latter portion, again, consists of one part reproducing the advanced variable capital *v,* and of another representing an excess over the variable capital, the surplus-value *s.* And just as the value of every individual commodity, so that of the entire annual product of each department consists of $c + v + s$.

The portion *c* of the value, representing the constant capital *consumed* in production, is not identical with the value of the constant capital *invested* in production. It is true that the materials of production are entirely consumed and their values completely transferred to the product. But of the invested *fixed* capital, only a portion is consumed and its value transferred to the product. Another portion of the fixed capital, such as machines, buildings, etc., continues to exist and serve the same as before, merely depreciating to the extent of the annual wear and tear. This persistent portion of the fixed capital does not exist for us, when we consider the value of the product. It is a portion of the value of capital existing independently beside the new value in commodities produced by this capital. This was shown previously in the analysis of the value of the product of some individual capital (Volume I, Chapter VI). However, for the present we must leave aside the method of analysis employed there. We saw in the study of the value of the product of individual capital that the value withdrawn from the fixed capital by wear and tear was transferred to the product in commodities created during the time of wear, no matter whether any portion of this fixed capital is reproduced in its natural form out of the value thus transferred or not. At this point, however, in the study of the social product as a whole and of its value, we must for the present leave out of consideration that portion of value which is transferred from the fixed capital to the annual product by wear and tear, unless this fixed capital is reproduced *in natura* during the year. In one of the following sections of this chapter we shall return to this point.

We shall base our analysis of simple reproduction on the following diagram, in which *c* stands for constant capital, *v* for variable capital, and *s* for surplus value, the rate of surplus value between *v* and *s* being assumed at 100 per cent. The figures may indicate millions of francs, marks, pounds sterling, or dollars.

I. Production of Means of Production.
Capital .... 4000*c* + 1000*v* = 5000.
Product in Commodities .. 4000*c* + 1000*v* + 1000*s* = 6000.
These exist in the form of means of production.

II. Production of Means of Consumption.
Capital .... 2000*c* + 500*v* = 2500.
Product in Commodities .. 2000*c* + 500*v* + 500*s* = 3000.
These exist in articles of consumption.

Recapitulation: Total annual product in commodities:

I. 4000*c* + 1000*v* + 1000*s* = 6000 means of production.
II. 2000*c* + 500*v* + 500*s* = 3000 articles of consumption.

Total value 9000, exclusive of the fixed capital persisting in its natural form, according to our assumption.

Now, if we examine the transactions required on the basis of simple reproduction, where the entire surplus value is unproductively consumed, leaving aside for the present the mediation of the money circulation, we obtain at the outset three great points of vantage.

(1) The 500*v*, representing wages of the labourers, and 500*s*, representing surplus value of the capitalists, in department II, must be spent for articles of consumption. But their value exists in the articles of consumption to the amount of 1000, held by the capitalists of department II, which reproduce the 500*v* and represent the 500*s*. The wages and surplus value of department II, then, are exchanged within this department for products of this same department. By this means, a quantity of articles of consumption equal to 1000 (500*v* + 500*s*) disappear out of the total product of department II.

(2) The 1000*v* and 1000*s* of department I must likewise be spent for articles of consumption, in other words, for some of the products of department II. Hence they must be exchanged for the remaining 2000*c* of constant value, which is equal in amount to them. Department II receives in return an equal quantity of means of production, the product of I, in which the value of 1000*v* and 1000*s* of I is incorporated. By this means, 2000*c* of II and (1000*v* + 1000*s*) of I disappear out of the calculation.

(3) Nothing remains now but 4000*c* of I. These consist of means of production which can be used up only in department I. They serve for the reproduction of its consumed constant capital, and are disposed of by the mutual exchange between the individual capitalists of I, just as are

the ($500v + 500s$) in II by an exchange between the capitalists and labourers, or between the individual capitalists, of II. . . .

Accumulation and Reproduction on an Enlarged Scale

It has been shown in Volume I, how accumulation works in the case of the individual capitalist. By the conversion of the commodity-capital into money, the surplus-product, in which the surplus value is incorporated, is also monetised. The capitalist reconverts the surplus value thus monetised into additional natural elements of his productive capital. In the next cycle of production the increased capital furnishes an increased product. But what happens in the case of the individual capital, must also show in the annual reproduction of society as a whole, just as we have seen it done in the case of reproduction on a simple scale, where the successive precipitation of the depreciated elements of fixed capitals in the form of money, accumulated as a hoard, also makes itself felt in the annual reproduction of society.

If a certain individual capital amounts to $400c + 100v$, with an annual surplus value of $100s$, then the product in commodities amounts to $400c + 100v + 100s$. This amount of 600 is converted into money. Of this money, again, $400c$ are converted into the natural form of constant capital, $100v$ into labour power, and—provided that the entire surplus value is accumulated—$100s$ are converted into additional constant capital by their transformation into natural elements of productive capital. The following assumptions go with this case: (1) That this amount is sufficient under the given technical conditions either to expand the existing constant capital, or to establish a new industrial business. But it may also happen that surplus value must be converted into money and this money hoarded for a much longer time, before these steps may be taken, before actual accumulation, or expansion of production, can take place. (2) It is furthermore assumed that production on an enlarged scale has actually been in process previously. For in order that the money (the surplus value hoarded as money) may be converted into elements of productive capital, these elements must be available on the market as commodities. It makes no difference whether they are bought as finished products, or made to order. They are not paid for until they are finished, and at any rate, until actual reproduction of an enlarged scale, an expansion of hitherto normal production, has taken place so far as they are concerned. They had to be present potentially, that is to say, in their elements, for it required only an impulse in the form of an order, that is to say, a purchase preceding their actual existence and anticipating their sale, in order to stimulate their production. The money on one side in that case calls forth expanded reproduction on the other, because the possibility for it exists without the money. For money in itself is not an element of actual reproduction. . . .

A. Diagram of Simple Reproduction.

$$\left.\begin{array}{l} \text{I. } 4000c + 1000v + 1000s = 6000 \\ \text{II. } 2000c + 500v + 500s = 3000 \end{array}\right\} \text{Total, 9000.}$$

B. Initial Diagram for Accumulation on an Expanded Scale.

I. $4000c + 1000v + 1000s = 6000$ }
II. $1500c + 750v + 750s = 3000$ } Total, 9000.

Assuming that in diagram B one half of the surplus value of I, amounting to 500, is accumulated, we have first to accomplish the change of place between $(1000v + 500s)$ I, or 1500 I $(v + s)$, and 1500 II c. Department I then keeps $4000c$ and $500s$, the last sum being accumulated. The exchange between $(1000v + 500s)$ I and 1500 II c is a process of simple reproduction, which has been examined previously.

Let us now assume that 400 of the 500 I s are to be converted into constant capital, and 100 into variable capital. The transactions within the $400s$ of I, which are to be capitalized, have already been discussed. They can be immediately annexed to I c, and in that case we get in department I $4400c + 1000v + 100s$ (these last to be converted into $100v$).

Department II buys from I for the purpose of accumulation the 100 I s (existing in means of production), which thus become additional constant capital in department II, while the 100 in money, which this department pays for them, are converted into the money-form of the additional variable capital of I. We then have for I a capital of $4400c + 1100v$ (these last in money), a total of 5500.

Department II has now $1600c$ for its constant capital. In order to be able to operate this, it must advance $50v$ in money for the purchase of new labour power, so that its variable capital grows from 750 to 800. This expansion of the constant and variable capital of II by a total of 150 is supplied out of its surplus value. Hence only 600 of the 750 II s remain for the consumption of the capitalists of II, whose annual product is now distributed as follows:

II. $1600c + 800v + 600s$ (fund for consumption), a total of 3000. The $150s$, produced in articles of consumption, which have been converted into $(100c + 50v)$ II, pass entirely into the consumption of the labourers in this form, 100 being consumed by the labourers of I (100 I v), and 50 by the labourers of II (50 II v), as explained above. Department II, where the total product is prepared in a form suitable for accumulation, must indeed reproduce surplus value in the form of necessary articles of consumption exceeding the other portions by 100. If reproduction really starts on an expanded scale, then the 100 of variable money capital of I flow back to II through the hands of the labourers of I, while II transfers $100s$ in commodities to I and at the same time 50 in commodities to its own labourers.

The change made in the arrangement for the purpose of accumulation now presents the following aspect:

I. $4400c + 1100v + 500$ fund for consumption $= 6000$
II. $1600c + 800v + 600$ fund for consumption $= 3000$

Total, as before, 9000

Of these amounts, the following are capital:

$$\left.\begin{array}{l} \text{I. } 4400c + 1100v \text{ (money)} = 5500 \\ \text{II. } 1600c + 800v \text{ (money)} = 2400 \end{array}\right\} \text{Total, } 7900$$

while production started out with

$$\left.\begin{array}{l} \text{I. } 4000c + 1000v = 5000 \\ \text{II. } 1500c + 750v = 2250 \end{array}\right\} \text{Total, } 7250$$

Now, if actual accumulation takes place on this basis, that is to say, if reproduction is actually undertaken with this increased capital, we obtained at the end of next year:

$$\left.\begin{array}{l} \text{I. } 4400c + 1100v + 1100s = 6600 \\ \text{II. } 1600c + 800v + 800s = 3200 \end{array}\right\} \text{Total, } 9800.$$

Market Prices and Market Values

. . . Whatever may be the way in which the prices of the various commodities are first fixed or mutually regulated, the law of value always dominates their movements. If the labour time required for the production of these commodities is reduced, prices fall; if it is increased, prices rise, other circumstances remaining the same.

Aside from the fact that prices and their movements are dominated by the law of value, it is quite appropriate, under these circumstances, to regard the value of commodities not only theoretically, but also historically, as existing prior to the prices of production. This applies to conditions, in which the labourer owns his means of production, and this is the condition of the land-owning farmer and of the craftsman in the old world as well as the new. This agrees also with the view formerly expressed by me that the development of products into commodities arises through the exchange between different communes, not through that between the members of the some commune. It applies not only to this primitive condition, but also to subsequent conditions based on slavery or serfdom, and to the guild organisation of handicrafts, so long as the means of production installed in one line of production cannot be transferred to another line except under difficulties, so that the various lines of production maintain, to a certain degree, the same mutual relations as foreign countries or communistic groups.

In order that the prices at which commodities are exchanged with one another may correspond approximately to their values, no other conditions are required but the following: (1) The exchange of the various commodities must no longer be accidental or occasional; (2) So far as the direct exchange of commodities is concerned, these commodities must be produced on both sides in sufficient quantities to meet mutual requirements, a thing easily learned by experience in trading, and therefore a natural outgrowth of continued trading; (3) So far as selling is concerned, there must be no accidental or artificial monopoly which may enable either of the contracting sides to sell commodities above their value or compel others to sell below value. An accidental monopoly is one which a buyer or seller acquires by an accidental proportion of supply to demand.

The assumption that the commodities of the various spheres of production are sold at their value implies, of course, only that their value is the centre of gravity around which prices fluctuate, and around which their rise and fall tends to an equilibrium. We shall also have to note a *market value,* which must be distinguished from the individual value of the commodities produced by the various producers. Of this more anon. The individual value of some of these commodities will be below the market value, that is to say, they require less labour-time for their production than is expressed in the market value, while that of others will be above the market value. We shall have to regard the market-value on one side as the average value of the commodities produced in a certain sphere, and on the other side as the individual value of commodities produced under the average conditions of their respective sphere of production and constituting the bulk of the products of that sphere. It is only extraordinary combinations of circumstances under which commodities produced under the least or most favourable conditions regulate the market value, which forms the centre of fluctuation for the market prices, which are the same, however, for the same kind of commodities. If the ordinary demand is satisfied by the supply of commodities of average value, that is to say, of a value midway between the two extremes, then those commodities, whose individual value stands below the market value, realise an extra surplus-value, or surplus-profit, while those, whose individual value stands above the market value, cannot realise a portion of the surplus value contained in them. . . .

No matter what may be the way in which prices are regulated, the result always is the following:

(1) The law of value dominates the movements of prices, since a reduction or increase of the labour time required for production causes the prices of production to fall or to rise. It is in this sense that Ricardo (who doubtless realised that his prices of production differed from the value of commodities) says that "the inquiry to which he wishes to draw the reader's attention relates to the effect of the variations in the relative value of commodities, and not in their absolute value."

(2) The average profit which determines the prices of production must always be approximately equal to that quantity of surplus value which falls to the share of a certain individual capital in its capacity as an aliquot part of the total social capital. Take it that the average rate of profit, and therefore the average profit, are expressed by an amount of money of a higher value than the money value of the actual average surplus value. So far as the capitalists are concerned in that case, it is immaterial whether they charge one another a profit of 10 or of 15 per cent. The one of these percentages does not cover any more actual commodity value than the other, since the overcharge in money is mutual.

But so far as the labourer is concerned (the assumption being that he receives the normal wages, so that the raising of the average profit does not imply an actual deduction from his wages, in other words, does not express something entirely different from the normal surplus value of the capitalist), the rise in the price of commodities due to a raising of the average profit must be accompanied by a corresponding rise of the money expression for the variable capital. As a matter of fact, such a general nominal raising of the rate of profit and the average profit above the limit provided by the proportion of the actual surplus value to the total invested capital is not possible without carrying in its wake an increase of wages, and also an increase in the prices of the commodities which constitute the constant capital. The same is true of the opposite case, that of a reduction of the rate of profit in this way. Now, since the total value of the commodities regulates the total surplus value, and this the level of the average profit and the average rate of profit—always understanding this as a general law, as a principle regulating the fluctuations—it follows that the law of value regulates the prices of production.

Competition first brings about, in a certain individual sphere, the establishment of an equal market value and market price by averaging the various individual values of the commodities. The competition of the capitals in the different spheres then results in the price of production which equalises the rates of profit between the different spheres. This last process requires a higher development of capitalist production than the previous process.

In order that commodities of the same sphere of production, the same kind, and approximately the same quality may be sold at their value, the following two requirements must be fulfilled:

(1) The different individual values must have been averaged into *one* social value, the above-named market value, and this implies a competition between the producers of the same kind of commodities, and also the existence of a common market, on which they offer their articles for sale. In order that the market price of identical commodities, which however are produced under different individual circumstances, may correspond to the market value, may not differ from it by exceeding it or falling below it, it is necessary that the different sellers should exert sufficient pressure upon one another to bring that quantity of commodities on the market which social requirements demand, in other words, that quantity of commodities whose market value society can pay. If the quantity of products exceeds this demand, then the commodities must be sold below their market value; vice versa, if the quantity of products is not large enough to meet this demand, or, what amounts to the same, if the pressure of competition among the sellers is not strong enough to bring this quantity of products to market, then the commodities are sold above their market value. If the market value is changed, then there will also be a change in the conditions under which the total quantity of commodities can be sold. If the market value falls, then the average social demand increases (always

referring to the solvent demand) and can absorb a larger quantity of commodities within certain limits. If the market value rises, then the solvent social demand for commodities is reduced and smaller quantities of them are absorbed. Hence if supply and demand regulate the market price, or rather the deviations of market prices from market values, it is true, on the other hand, that the market value regulates the proportions of supply and demand, or the centre around which supply and demand cause the market prices to fluctuate.

If we look closer at the matter, we find that the conditions determining the value of some individual commodity become effective, in this instance, as conditions determining the value of the total quantities of a certain kind. For, generally speaking, capitalist production is from the outset a mass production. And even other, less developed, modes of production carry small quantities of products, the result of the work of many small producers, to market as co-operative products, at least in the main lines of production, concentrating and accumulating them for sale in the hands of relatively few merchants. Such commodities are regarded as co-operative products of an entire line of production, or of a greater or smaller part of this line.

We remark by the way that the "social demand," in other words, that which regulates the principle of demand, is essentially conditioned on the mutual relations of the different economic classes and their relative economic positions, that is to say, first, on the proportion of the total surplus value to the wages, and secondly, on the proportion of the various parts into which surplus value is divided (profit, interest, ground-rent, taxes, etc.). And this shows once more that absolutely nothing can be explained by the relation of supply and demand, unless the basis has first been ascertained, on which this relation rests. . . .

(2) To say that a commodity has a use-value is merely to say that it satisfies some social want. So long as we were dealing simply with individual commodities, we could assume that the demand for any one commodity—its price implying its quantity—existed without inquiring into the extent to which this demand required satisfaction. But this question of the extent of a certain demand becomes essential, whenever the product of some entire line of production is placed on one side, and the social demand for it on the other. In that case it becomes necessary to consider the amount, the quantity, of this social demand.

In the foregoing statements referring to market value, the assumption was that the mass of the produced commodities remains the same given quantity, and that a change takes place only in the proportions of the elements constituting this mass and produced under different conditions, so that the market value of the same mass of commodities is differently regulated. Let us suppose that this mass is of a quantity equal to the ordinary supply, leaving aside the possibility that a portion of the produced commodities may be temporarily withdrawn from the market. Now, if the demand for this mass also remains the same, then this commodity will be sold at its market value; no matter which one of the three aforementioned cases may regulate this market value. This mass of commodities does not only satisfy a demand, but satisfies it to its full social extent. On the other hand, if the quantity is smaller than the demand for it, then the market prices differ from the market values. And the first differentiation is that the market value is always regulated by the commodity produced under the least favourable circumstances, if the supply is too small, and by the commodity produced under the most favourable conditions, if the supply is too large. In other words, one of the extremes determines the market value, in spite of the fact that the proportion of the masses produced under different conditions ought to bring about a different result. If the difference between demand and supply of the product is very considerable, then the market price will likewise differ considerably from the market value in either direction. Now, the difference between the quantity of the produced commodities and the quantity of commodities which fixes their sale at their market value may be due to two reasons. Either the quantity itself varies, by decreasing or increasing, so that there would be a reproduction on a different scale than the one which regulated a certain market value. If so, then the supply changes while the demand remains unchanged, and we have a relative over-production or under-production. Or, the reproduction, and the supply, remain the same, while the demand is reduced or increased, which may take place for several reasons. If so, then the absolute magnitude of the supply is unchanged, while its relative magnitude, compared to the demand, has changed. The effect is the same as in the first case, only it acts in the opposite direction. Finally, if changes take place on both sides, either in opposite directions, or, if in the same direction, not to the same extent, in other words, if changes take place on both sides which alter the former proportion between these sides, then the final result must always lead to one of the two above-mentioned cases.

CRISES *

In world market crises the contradictions and antagonisms of bourgeois production break through to the surface. But instead of investigating the nature of the conflicting elements which force their way through in the catastrophe, the apologists content themselves with denying the catastrophe itself; and, faced with its regular recurrence, with insisting that production would never lead to crises if it were carried on according to the textbooks. The apologetics consist, then, in falsifying the simplest economic relations, and especially in stubbornly maintaining the unity in face of the contradiction. . . .

In order to prove that capitalist production cannot lead to general crises, all its conditions and definite forms, all its principles and *differentiae specificae* (specific differences) are denied; in short, capitalist pro-

* From *Theories of Surplus Value,* translated by G. A. Bonner and Emile Burns (New York, International Publishers, 1952).

duction itself is denied. And in fact what is demonstrated is that if the capitalist mode of production—instead of being a specifically developed, unique form of social production—were a mode of production dating back to the crudest beginnings of social production, the antagonisms and contradictions peculiar to it, and therefore also their explosion in crises, would not exist.

"Productions," Ricardo, following Say, observes, "are always bought by productions, or by services; money is only the medium by which the exchange is effected."

Here therefore, in the first place, the *commodity,* in which the antagonism between exchange value and use value exists, is transformed into a simple product (use value), and consequently the exchange of commodities is transformed into a mere bartering of products, of simple use values. This is to go back not only to before capitalist production, but to before simple commodity production; and the most developed phenomenon of capitalist production—world market crisis—is flatly denied by the flat denial of the first condition of capitalist production, namely, that the product is a commodity and must therefore take the form of money and pass through the process of metamorphosis. Instead of speaking of wage labour, the term used is "services," a word in which the specific characteristic of wage labour and of its use—namely, that it increases the value of the commodities for which it is exchanged, that it produces surplus value—is again disregarded, and with it also the specific relation whereby money and commodities are transformed into capital. "Service" is labour considered only as *use value* (a secondary matter in capitalist production), just in the same way as in the word *"productions"* the essence of the *commodity* and of the contradiction contained in it is suppressed. Then, quite consistently, *money* is conceived as merely the intermediary in the exchange of products, not as an essential and necessary form of existence of the commodity, which must present itself as exchange value—general social labour. Inasmuch as, through the transformation of the commodity into mere use value (product), the essence of exchange value is expunged, it is then easy to deny—or rather it is then necessary to deny—*money* as an essential and independent form of the commodity in the process of the metamorphosis from its original form. In this way, therefore, crises are reasoned out of existence through losing sight of or denying the first preconditions of capitalist production: the nature of the product as a commodity, the duplication of the commodity in commodity and money, the consequent separate phases in the exchange of commodities, and finally the relation of money or commodities to wage labour. . . .

Ricardo says: "No man produces but with a view to consume or sell, and he never sells but with an intention to purchase some other commodity, which may be immediately useful to him, or which may contribute to future production. By producing, then, he necessarily becomes either the consumer of his own goods, or the purchaser and consumer of the goods of some other person. It is not to be supposed that he should, for any length of time, be ill-informed of the commodities which he can most advantageously produce, to attain the object which he has in view, namely, the possession of other goods; and, therefore, it is not probable that he will continually produce a commodity for which there is no demand."

This is the childish babble of a Say, but it is not worthy of Ricardo. In the first place no capitalist produces in order to consume his product. And when we are speaking of capitalist production, then it is correct to say "No man produces with a view to consume his own product," even if he uses portions of his product for industrial consumption. But here it is private consumption that is in question. In the earlier passage, it was forgotten that the product is a commodity. Now even the social division of labour is forgotten. In conditions in which men produce for themselves, there are in fact no crises, but also no capitalist production. Nor have we ever heard that the ancients, with their slave production, at any time experienced crises, although among the ancients too individual producers went bankrupt. The first part of the alternative is nonsense. So is the second. A man who has produced has not the choice whether he will sell or not. He *must* sell. And in crises appears precisely the circumstance that he cannot sell, or only below the price of production, or even that he must sell at a positive loss. What does it avail him or us, therefore, that he has produced in order to sell? What concerns us is precisely to discover what has cut across this good intention of his.

Further: "No man sells but with a view to purchase some other commodity, which may be immediately useful to him, or which may contribute to future production." What a pleasant portrayal of bourgeois relations! Ricardo even forgets that a man may sell in order to pay, and that these compulsory sales play a very significant role in crises. The immediate purpose of the capitalist when he sells is to transform his commodities or rather his commodity capital back again into money capital, and thereby to realise his profit. Consumption—revenue—is consequently not the determining motive of this process, which it is, however, for the man who only sells commodities in order to transform them into means of subsistence. But this is not capitalist production, in which revenue appears as a result but not as the determining purpose. Everyone sells with the immediate aim of selling; that is, in order to transform commodities into money.

During the crisis the man may be very pleased when he has made a sale, without any immediate thought of a purchase. However, if the value that has been realised is now again to function as capital it must pass through the process of reproduction, that is, be exchanged once more for labour and commodities. But crisis is precisely the moment of disturbance and interruption in the process of reproduction. And this disturbance cannot be explained by the fact that it does not take place in periods when there is no crisis. . . .

What has to be done, however, is to follow through the further development of the potential crisis—the real crisis can only be presented on the basis of the real movement of capitalist production, competition and credit

—in so far as crisis arises from the forms characteristic of capital, its *properties* as capital, and not from its mere existence as commodity and as money. The mere direct *process of production* of capital cannot by itself add anything new in this connection. In order to exist at all, the conditions for it are assumed. For that reason, in the first section dealing with capital—the immediate process of production—no new element of crisis has to be added. *By its nature* crisis is present in it. For the process of production is appropriation and therefore production of surplus value. But this cannot appear in the process of production itself, because the latter is not concerned with the realisation of both the reproduced value, and the surplus value. Crisis can only appear in the process of circulation, which in essence is at the same time the process of reproduction.

Here it must further be noted that we must examine the process of circulation or process of reproduction *before* examining already existing capital—capital and profit—as we have to show not only how capital produces, but how capital is produced. The actual movement, however, starts from the capital in hand—that is, the actual movement that is based on developed capitalist production, beginning out of itself and presupposing itself. . . .

The circulation process as a whole or the whole process of reproduction of capital is the unity of its production phase with its circulation phase, a process which runs through both those processes as its phases. Therein lies a further developed possibility or abstract form of crisis. The economists who deny crises therefore insist only on the unity of these two phases. If they were only separate without being a unity, then no forcible restoration of their unity would be possible, no crisis. If they were only a unity without being separate, then no forcible separation would be possible, which again is crisis. It is the forcible restoration of unity between independent phases, and the forcible separation from each other of processes which in essence are one.

Therefore:

1. The general *possibility* of crises is given in the process of *metamorphosis of capital* itself, and in fact in a twofold way: in so far as money functions as *means of circulation,* through the separation of purchase and sale; and in so far as it functions as *means of payment,* where it has two separate aspects, as *measure of value* and as *realisation of value.* These two aspects become separated. If in the interval between them the value has altered, the commodity at the moment of its sale is not worth what it was worth at the moment when money functioned as measure of value and therefore of the reciprocal obligations; then the obligation cannot be met from the proceeds of sale of the commodities, and therefore the whole series of transactions, which depend in a backward chain on this one transaction, cannot be settled. If even for a certain time the commodities cannot be sold, although their value has not changed—in such a case money cannot function as means of payment, since it has to function as such within a definite term laid down in advance. But as the same sum of money func-

tions here for a series of mutual transactions and obligations, the inability to pay appears not at one point only but at many, and hence crisis.

These are the formal possibilities of crises. The first-mentioned forms are possible without the latter; that is to say, crises are possible without credit, without money functioning as means of payment. But the latter forms are not possible without the former, that is, without the separation between purchase and sale. But in the latter case crisis appears not only because commodities are unsaleable, but also when they cannot be sold within a certain period; and in this case crisis arises and derives its character not only from the fact that commodities cannot be sold, but from the non-fulfilment of a whole series of payments which depend on the sale of these particular commodities within this particular period of time. This is the characteristic form of money crises.

Therefore if a crisis appears because purchase and sale become separated, it develops *as a money crisis* when money has developed as *means of payment,* and this *second form* of crises follows as a matter of course when the first makes its appearance. In investigating why the general possibility of crises becomes *an actual crisis,* in investigating the conditions of crisis, it is therefore quite superfluous to concern ourselves with those crises which arise from the development of money as means of payment. Precisely for this reason the economists like to advance this self-explanatory form as the cause of crises. In so far as the development of money as means of payment is linked with the development of credit and of surplus credit, it is true that the causes of the latter have to be investigated; but this is not yet the place to do it.

2. In so far as crises result from changes and revolutions in prices which do not coincide with changes in the values of commodities, they naturally cannot be investigated when we are considering capital in general, when it is assumed that prices are identical with the values of commodities.

3. The general possibility of crises is the formal metamorphosis of capital itself, the separation in time and space of purchase and sale. But this is never the cause of crisis. For it is nothing but the most general form of crisis, that is, crisis itself in its most generalised expression. It cannot however be said that the abstract form of crisis is the cause of crisis. If we seek its cause, what we want to know is why its abstract form, the form of its possibility, develops from possibility into actuality.

4. The general conditions of crises, in so far as they are independent of price fluctuations (and whether these are linked with the credit system or not; price fluctuations as distinct from fluctuations of value), must be explicable from the general conditions of capitalist production.

[We find, then, as factors in a crisis:]

The reconversion of money into capital. A definite level of production or reproduction is assumed. The fixed capital can here be considered as given, remaining the same and not entering into the process of realisation. As the reproduction of the raw material is dependent not only on the labour expended on it, but on the productivity of this labour in association with natural conditions, it is possible [even with the method of production remaining the same] for the mass of the product of the same quantity of labour to fall (with bad harvests). The value of the raw material therefore rises, while its mass falls. The proportions in which money has to flow back into the various component parts of the capital, in order to continue production on the former level, are disturbed. More must be paid out for raw material, less remains for labour, and the same quantity of labour as before cannot be absorbed. In the first place, this is not physically possible, because there is a deficiency of raw material; secondly, because a greater part of the value of the product has to be transformed into raw material, and consequently a smaller part can be transformed into variable capital. Reproduction can not be repeated at the same level. A part of the fixed capital stays idle, a part of the workers is thrown out on the streets. The rate of profit falls, because the value of the constant capital compared with the variable has risen and less variable capital is employed. The fixed charges—interest, rent—which are based on the anticipation of stable rates of profit and of exploitation of labour, remain the same, and in part cannot be paid. Hence crisis. Crisis of labour and crisis of capital. This is therefore an interruption of the reproduction process resulting from an increased value of the part of the constant capital that has to be replaced out of the value of the product. In this case, although the rate of profit falls, there is a rise in the price of the product. If this product enters into other spheres of production as a means of production, the rise in its price results in the same disturbance of reproduction in these spheres. If it enters into general consumption as a means of subsistence, it either enters also into the consumption of the workers or it does not. In the first case, the effects are the same as that of a disturbance in the variable capital, which is dealt with later. But in so far as it enters generally into consumption, the result may be (unless the consumption of it falls) a fall in the demand for other products. Hence their reconversion into money at their value will be hindered to a corresponding degree, and thus the other side of their reproduction—not the reconversion of money into productive capital, but the reconversion of commodities into money—will be disturbed. In any case the mass of profit and the mass of wages in this branch of industry falls, and this means a fall in part of the necessary returns from the sale of commodities of other branches of production.

This shortage of raw material may however also make its appearance apart from the influence of harvests or of the natural productivity of the labour which supplies the raw material. If for example an undue portion of the [accumulated] surplus value, of the surplus capital, is [expended] on machinery, etc., in a particular branch of production, the raw material, although it would have been adequate for the old level of production, will be inadequate for the new. This therefore results from the disproportionate conversion of the surplus capital into its different elements. It is a case of *overproduction of fixed capital* and produces exactly the same phenomena as in the first case.

General and Partial Overproduction

In Chapter XXI Ricardo says: "Too much of a *particular* commodity may be produced, of which there may be such a glut in the market as not to repay the capital expended on it; but this cannot be the case with respect to *all* commodities."

That only *particular* but not *all* kinds of commodities can constitute a glut in the market, and that consequently overproduction can always only be partial, is a paltry evasion. In the first place, if the mere nature of a commodity is considered, there is nothing in it which would prevent *all* commodities being in over supply on the market and therefore all falling below their price. What is involved here is precisely the moment of crisis. In fact, all commodities [may be in over supply] except *money*. The necessity for *the* commodity to transform itself into money means only that the necessity exists for *all* commodities. And inasmuch as there is a difficulty in a single commodity making this metamorphosis, the difficulty can exist for all commodities. The general nature of the metamorphosis of commodities—which includes the separation of purchase and sale as well as their unity—instead of excluding the *possibility* of a general glut, is rather *the* possibility of a general glut.

Moreover, in the background of Ricardo's arguments and similar arguments put forward by others there is in fact not only the relation of purchase and sale, but also that of demand and supply, which we have to consider only when we investigate the competition of capitals. Just as Mill says that purchase is sale, etc., so is demand supply and supply demand; but they are equally separate, and can assume independence of each other. At a given moment the supply of all commodities may be greater than the demand for all commodities, because the demand for the general commodity, money, exchange value, is greater than the demand for all particular commodities; in other words, because the compulsion for the commodity to take the form of money, to realise its exchange value, is greater than the compulsion for the commodity to be reconverted into use value. If the relation between demand and supply is conceived in a wider and more concrete way, there enters into it the relation between production and consumption. Here again there must be borne in mind the *unity* of these two phases, which exists in their nature and forcibly asserts itself precisely in crisis, against the equally existent, and for bourgeois production even characteristic, separation and opposition of the two.

As for the antithesis between partial and universal overproduction—that is, in so far as the former is emphasised only as a means of getting rid of the latter—the following further points may be noted:

First: A general rise of prices in all articles of capitalist production usually precedes a crisis. Consequently they all have a share in the following crash, and all constitute an overloading of the market at the prices which they had before the crash. The market can absorb a mass of commodities at falling prices, prices that have fallen below their prices of production, which it could not absorb at their former market prices. The excess of commodities is always relative, that is, it is an excess at certain prices. The prices at which the commodities are then absorbed are ruinous for the producer or merchant.

Secondly:

For a crisis (and therefore also overproduction) to be general, it is sufficient for it to grip the principal articles of trade. . . .

Expansion of Production and Expansion of the Market

. . . The word *overproduction* in itself leads to error. So long as the most urgent needs of a great part of society are not satisfied, or *only* its most immediate needs, there can naturally be absolutely no talk of an *overproduction of products*—in the sense that the mass of products would be excessive in relation to the need for them. What must be said is the opposite: that in this sense, on the basis of capitalistic production, there is constant *underproduction*. The limit of production is the *capitalist's profit,* and not at all the *need of the producers.* But overproduction of *products* and overproduction of *commodities* are two completely different things. If Ricardo thinks that the form *commodity* makes no difference to the product, and further, that the *circulation of commodities* is only formally different from barter, that in this circulation exchange value is only a form, without significance, of the exchange of things, and that therefore money is a merely formal means of circulation, this is in fact the outcome of his presupposition that the bourgeois mode of production is the absolute mode of production, and consequently is a mode of production without any precise specific character, that what is specific in it is only formal. It is therefore not possible for him to admit that the bourgeois mode of production contains within itself a barrier to the free development of the productive forces, a barrier which comes to the surface in crises, and incidentally in *overproduction*—the basic phenomenon in crises.

Ricardo saw . . . that the limitless "desire" for all kinds of use values is constantly satisfied, on the basis of a state of things in which the mass of producers remains more or less restricted to necessities, in which this very considerable mass of producers therefore remains more or less excluded from the consumption of wealth—in so far as wealth oversteps the circle of the necessary means of subsistence.

Incidentally, this is also the case, and to a still higher degree, in the ancient form of production based on slavery. But the ancients never even thought of transforming the surplus product into capital. At least, only to a small extent. The widespread occurrence among them of the amassing of treasure in the narrow sense shows how much surplus product lay completely idle. They converted a great part of the surplus product into unproductive expenditure on works of art, religious monuments and public works. Still less was their production directed to the unfettering and development of the material forces of production—division of labour, machinery, use of natural forces and science in private production. Broadly speaking they never got beyond handicraft labour. The wealth which they produced for private consumption was consequently relatively small, and only seems large because it was amassed in the hands of a few people, who, incidentally, did not know what to do with it. If consequently there was no *overproduction* among the ancients, there was nevertheless *overconsumption* on the part of the rich, which in the final periods of Rome and Greece broke out into insane extravagance. The few trading peoples among them lived partly at the expense of all these essentially poor nations. It is the absolute development of the productive forces, and hence mass production, with the mass of producers confined within the circle of the necessary means of subsistence on the one hand, and on the other hand the barrier set by the capitalists' profit, which forms the basis of modern overproduction.

All the difficulties which Ricardo and others raise against overproduction, etc., rest on the fact that they either look on bourgeois production as a mode of production in which no distinction exists between purchase and sale—direct barter—or they regard it as *social* production, of such a kind that society distributes its means of production and productive forces as if according to a plan, in the degree and measure in which they are necessary for the satisfaction of its various needs; so that to each sphere of production falls the quota of social capital required for the satisfaction of the need to which it corresponds. This fiction arises entirely from the inability to grasp the specific form of bourgeois production; and this inability in turn from the obsession that bourgeois production is production pure and simple. Just like a man who believes in a particular religion and sees in it religion pure and simple, with only *false* religions outside it.

On the contrary, it would be much more pertinent to ask: on the basis of capitalist production, in which everyone works for himself, and particular labour must at the same time appear as its opposite, abstract general labour, and in this form as social labour—how can the necessary balance and interdependence of the various spheres of production, their dimensions and the proportions between them, be possible except through the constant neutralisation of a constant disharmony? This moreover is admitted when adjustments through competition are spoken of; for these adjustments always presuppose that there is something to be adjusted, and harmony therefore is always only a result of the movement which neutralises the existing disharmony. For this reason, too, Ricardo admits the glut of the market for particular commodities; and then a general simultaneous glut in the market is said to be *impossible*. Consequently the impossibility of overproduction for any particular sphere of production is not denied. What is said to be [impossible] is the *simultaneity* of this phenomenon for all spheres of production, and hence general overproduction. This last phrase is always to be taken *cum grano salis,* for in times of general overproduction the overproduction in some spheres is always only the *result,* the *consequence,* of overproduction in the leading articles of commerce; [in these it is] always only *relative,* overproduction because overproduction exists in other spheres. Apologetics twists this precisely into its opposite. Overproduction in the leading articles of commerce, in which alone active overproduction manifests itself—these are in general articles which can only be produced in the mass and on a factory scale, also in agriculture—[is supposed only to exist] because overproduction exists in the articles in which relative or passive overproduction appears. According to this idea overproduction only exists because overproduction is not universal. The relativity of overproduction—that actual overproduction in some spheres leads to it in others—is expressed in this way: There is no universal overproduction, because if overproduction were universal, all spheres of production would retain the same relation to one another; therefore universal overproduction is equivalent to proportional production, which excludes overproduction. And this is supposed to be an argument against overproduction. That is to say, on the ground that universal overproduction in the absolute sense would not be overproduction, but only a greater than usual development of productive power in all spheres of production, it is said that actual overproduction, which is precisely not this non-existent, self-abrogating overproduction, does not exist—although it only exists because it is not this. If this miserable sophistry is more closely examined, we get the following result. Overproduction takes place, say, in iron, cotton goods, linen, silk, cloth, etc. It cannot then be said, for example, that too little coal has been produced and that therefore this overproduction has occurred; for the overproduction of iron, etc., involves an exactly similar overproduction of coal, just as an overproduction of woven cloth involves that of yarn. (Overproduction of yarn as compared with cloth, iron as against machinery, etc., would be possible. This would always be a relative overproduction of constant capital.) There can therefore be no question of the overproduction of articles whose overproduction is implied because they enter as elements, raw materials, auxiliary materials or means of labour into the articles the positive overproduction of which is precisely the fact to be explained (the "particular commodity of which too much has been produced, of which there may be such a glut in the market as not to repay the capital expended on it"). The discussion concerns other articles which directly belong to other spheres of production, and can neither be subsumed under the leading articles of commerce which, according to the assumption, have been overproduced; nor do they belong to spheres in which, because they form the intermediate product for the leading articles of commerce, production must have advanced at least as much as in the final phases of the product—although there is no reason why they themselves should not have gone still further ahead, and thus have brought about an overproduction within the other overproduction. For example, although sufficient coal must have been produced in order to keep going all the industries into which coal enters as a necessary condition of production, and therefore the overproduction of coal is implied in the overproduction of iron, yarn, etc. (the coal having been produced only in proportion to the production of iron and yarn), it is *also* possible that more coal was produced than even the overproduction in iron, yarn, etc., required. This is not only possible, but very probable. For the production of coal and yarn and of those other spheres of production which produce only the conditions and earlier phases of the product to be completed in another sphere, is not governed by the immediate demand, by the immediate production or reproduction, but by the *degree, measure, proportion* in which these are expanding. And it is self-evident that in this calculation the goal may be overshot. Nevertheless [overproduction is said to originate from the fact that] there has not been enough produced, there has been underproduction, of other articles, such as for example pianofortes, precious stones, and so forth. The absurdity of this statement emerges all the more clearly when it is given an international setting, as Say and others after him have done. Thus, for example, England has not overproduced, but Italy has underproduced. If Italy, firstly, had had capital enough to replace the English capital that had been exported to Italy in the form of commodities; and secondly had so invested this capital that it produced the specific articles which English capital needed (partly to replace itself and partly to replace the revenue flowing from it) there would have been no overproduction. That is, there would not have existed the fact of actual—in relation to the *actual* production in Italy—existing overproduction in England, but only the fact of *imaginary underproduction in Italy*—imaginary, because it presupposes a capital in Italy and a development of the productive forces which did not exist there; and secondly because it makes the same utopian presupposition that this *non*-existing capital in Italy had been applied exactly as required in order that the English supplies and Italian demand, English and Italian production, should be complementary to each other. This means in other words nothing [but]: No overproduction would occur if demand and supply corresponded to each other; if capital were distributed in such proportions in all spheres of production that the production of one article involved the consumption of the other and thus its own consumption. There would be no overproduction, if there were no overproduction. But as capitalistic production is only able to let itself go without restraint in certain spheres, in definite conditions, no capitalistic production at all would be possible if it had to develop in all spheres *simultaneously* and *in equal degree*. Because in these spheres absolute overproduction takes place, relative overproduction takes place also in the spheres where there has not been overproduction. This explanation of overproduction in one direction by underproduction in another means nothing [but]: If production were proportionate, there would be no overproduction. Ditto, if demand and supply corresponded to each other. Ditto, if all spheres comprised equal opportunities of capitalistic production and its expansion—division of labour, machinery, export to distant markets, production on a mass scale, etc. Or in still more abstract form: if all countries which trade with one another possessed an equal capacity for production, and indeed for different and complementary production. That is to say: overproduction takes place, because all these pious wishes are not fulfilled. Or in even more abstract form: there would be no overproduction at one point if overproduction took place at all points in equal degree. But capital is not large enough to overproduce in this universal way, and consequently universal overproduction occurs.

Let us examine this fantasy still more closely:

It is admitted that there can be overproduction in each *particular branch of production*. The one circumstance that might prevent overproduction in *all* at the same time is, so it is alleged, that commodity exchanges against commodity, that is to say, they take refuge in the conditions of barter which they assume. But this way of escape is cut off by the very fact that trade in commodities is not barter, and therefore the seller of a commodity is not necessarily at the same time the purchaser of another. This whole subterfuge therefore rests on abstracting from *money*, and abstracting from the fact that what is in question is not the exchange of products but the circulation of commodities, for which the separation of purchase and sale is essential.

The circulation of capital in itself comprises *possibilities* of interruptions. For example, in the reconversion of money into its conditions of production the point is not only to transform money back again into the same use values (in kind), but it is essential for the repetition of the process of reproduction that these use values are to be had at their old value (lower is naturally still better). The very significant part of these elements of reproduction which consists of raw materials can however rise in price for two reasons: *first* if the instruments of production increase in quicker proportion than the raw materials can be provided within a definite period of time. *Secondly,* as a result of the variable character of harvests. That is why weather conditions, as Tooke rightly observes, play such an important role in modern industry. That is also true of the means of subsistence in relation to wages. The reconversion from money into commodity can therefore come up against difficulties and bring about possibilities of crisis, just as well as the conversion of commodity into money. In so far as simple circulation is considered—not the circulation of capital—this difficulty does not arise.

There are besides a number of other factors, conditions and possibilities of crisis which can only be considered when examining the concrete relations, in particular of the competition of capitals and of credit.

The overproduction of commodities is denied, though the overproduction of capital is admitted. But capital itself consists of commodities, or in so far as it consists of money it must be reconverted into commodities of one kind or another in order to be able to function as capital. What then does overproduction of capital mean? Overproduction of quantities of value destined to produce surplus value, or, if considered in their material content, overproduction of commodities destined for reproduction—that is, reproduction on too large a scale, which is the same thing as overproduction pure and simple. Defined more exactly, this in turn means nothing but that too much has been produced for the purpose of enrichment, or that too large a part of the product has been destined, not for consumption as revenue, but for making more money, for accumulation; not to satisfy the personal requirements of its possessor, but to secure for him abstract social riches, money and more power over the labour of others—capital—or to increase the power in his hands. That is what some say. Ricardo denies it. How then do the others explain the overproduction of commodities? That production is not sufficiently widely diversified, that certain articles of consumption have not been produced in sufficiently great quantities. It is clear that this cannot refer to industrial consumption; for the manufacturer who overproduces in linen thereby of necessity increases his demand for yarn, machinery, labour, etc. Therefore the reference must be to personal consumption. Too much linen has been produced, but perhaps too few oranges. Previously money was denied, for the purpose of [denying] the separation between purchase and sale. Here, capital is denied, in order to transform the capitalists into people who carry out the simple operation C–M–C, and for individual consumption, not as capitalists with the aim of getting richer, with the aim of reconverting a part of the surplus value into capital. But the statement that there is *too much capital* in fact means nothing but that too little is consumed, and in the given conditions can be consumed, as *revenue* (Sismondi). Why then does the producer of linen demand of the producer of corn that he consume more linen, or the latter demand of the former that he consume more corn? Why does the man who deals in linen not himself realise a larger part of his revenue, his surplus value, in linen, and the farmer in corn? Each of them individually will admit that, apart from the limit to his requirements, what prevents him from doing this is his need to capitalise it. But collectively they will not admit it.

In this treatment we have completely abstracted from that element of crises which arises from the fact that commodities are reproduced more cheaply than they have been produced. Hence depreciation of the commodities on the market.

In the general crises on the world market, all the contradictions of bourgeois production break through collectively; in particular crises (particular as to content and in extent) they appear only in a scattered, isolated and one-sided form.

Overproduction is specifically conditioned by the general law of the production of capital: production is in accordance with the productive forces, that is, with the possibility that the given quantity of capital has of exploiting the maximum quantity of labour, without regard to the actual limits of the market, the needs backed by the ability to pay; and this takes place through the constant expansion of reproduction and accumulation, and therefore the constant reconversion of revenue into capital; while on the other hand the mass of producers remain restricted to the average level of needs, and on the basis of capitalist production must remain so restricted.

HENRY GEORGE

(1839–1897)

Henry George was born in Philadelphia of middle-class, strongly religious parents, whose zeal for the faith is reflected in their son's unmistakable tendency to be missionary in all his writings. Of formal learning he had little, quitting school at thirteen to become an errand boy and clerk. He went to sea while still in his teens but after voyaging to Australia and India, returned home and became an itinerant printer. Eventually he settled in San Francisco, where he turned his hand to newspaper work and in short order fell in love, married, and lost his job. For years he lived in the starkest poverty, augmenting his occasional work as a printer with door-to-door selling. Finally his fortunes improved; he rose from printer to managing editor of the San Francisco *Times*.

He next turned his attention to politics and ran for the state legislature. He was defeated by the opposition of the Central Pacific Railroad on the issue of the land subsidy the railroad was receiving from the state. George vehemently opposed this subsidy and the land speculation occasioned by the completion of the railroad between Sacramento and Oakland. The origin of his opposition to land monopoly and exploitation is to be found in this period. In 1871 he sketched the bare outlines of his later theory in a pamphlet entitled *Our Land and Land Policy*, but not until 1879 did his famous *Progress and Poverty*, in which his theme was fully elaborated, finally appear. To Henry George it seemed certain that poverty is caused by the monopolization of land by the few. Since land should belong to all, he felt, ownership by a few deprives the rest of their birthright. According to this supposition, all rent is unearned increment. The injustice to the landless grows when, as a result of natural progress, the value of land is augmented and rent increases correspondingly.

The rest of George's life was spent in propagating his new ideas. Shortly after the publication of *Progress and Poverty* in 1879 he moved to New York, where he lived by writing and lecturing, and in 1881–1882 he traveled through England and Ireland as a correspondent for the New York *Irish World* and analyzed the Irish land question from his particular point of view.

Politics claimed him again during his later years. He ran twice for mayor of New York. The first time, in 1886, he narrowly missed election and claimed that he was counted out at the polls. In 1897 the strain of campaigning proved too much for him, and he died of a stroke on the eve of the election.

Estimates of Henry George's influence vary. The appeal of his program was wide, and many wealthy men became his enthusiastic supporters—probably because his program offered no threat to capitalism. However, except for a few mavericks like John R. Commons, he influenced academic economists very little. His influence on organized labor was also slight, since the exploited workingman could hardly be drawn to a program which emphasized a single tax on land as the panacea for all economic ills and disregarded all other forms of exploitation.

In the following selections from *Progress and Poverty* George proposes and justifies his remedy: the confiscation of rent through the single tax. Wealth results from the combination of land and labor, said George. The only rewards to which these factors of production are entitled are those which can be produced on no-rent land. As the result of progress, land of various grades of fertility is worked by equivalent labor. Since rent is the surplus from the more fertile grades of land, wages tend to equal the yield of labor at the margin. Hence rent represents the monopoly power of the owner, who is able to exact payment for the right to work the more fertile land.

The right to work the land belongs to everyone, and it therefore follows, according to George, that private ownership and monopoly of land deprives mankind of its just due. His remedy was to tax away land values. The details of how this single tax would end poverty are spelled out in the selections following.

PROGRESS AND POVERTY *

The Statics of the Problem

If production had not passed the simple stage in which all labor is directly applied to the land and all wages are paid in its produce, the fact that when the land owner takes a larger portion the laborer must put up with a smaller portion could not be lost sight of.

But the complexities of production in the civilized state, in which so great a part is borne by exchange, and so much labor is bestowed upon materials after they have been separated from the land, though they may to the unthinking disguise, do not alter the fact that all production is still the union of the two factors, land and labor, and that rent (the share of the land holder) cannot be increased except at the expense of wages (the share of the laborer) and interest (the share of capital). Just as the portion of the crop, which in the simpler forms of industrial organization the owner of agricultural land receives at the end of the harvest as his rent, lessens the amount left to the cultivator as wages and interest, so does the rental of land on which a manufacturing or commercial city is built lessen the amount which can be divided as wages and interest between the laborer and capital there engaged in the production and exchange of wealth.

In short, the value of land depending wholly upon the power which its ownership gives of appropriating wealth created by labor, the increase of land values is always at the expense of the value of labor. . . .

The True Remedy

. . . There is but one way to remove an evil—and that is, to remove its cause. Poverty deepens as wealth increases, and wages are forced down while productive power grows, because land, which is the source of all wealth and the field of all labor, is monopolized. To extirpate poverty, to make wages what justice commands they should be, the full earnings of the laborer, we must therefore substitute for the individual ownership of land a common ownership. Nothing else will go to the cause of the evil —in nothing else is there the slightest hope.

This, then, is the remedy for the unjust and unequal distribution of wealth apparent in modern civilization, and for all the evils which flow from it:

We must make land common property. . . .

* From *Progress and Poverty,* fiftieth anniversary edition (New York, Robert Schalkenbach Foundation, 1951).

How Equal Rights to the Land May Be Asserted and Secured

. . . I do not propose either to purchase or to confiscate private property in land. The first would be unjust; the second, needless. Let the individuals who now hold it still retain, if they want to, possession of what they are pleased to call *their* land. Let them continue to call it *their* land. Let them buy and sell, and bequeath and devise it. We may safely leave them the shell, if we take the kernel. *It is not necessary to confiscate land; it is only necessary to confiscate rent*. . . .

We already take some rent in taxation. We have only to make some changes in our modes of taxation to take it all.

What I, therefore, propose, as the simple yet sovereign remedy, which will raise wages, increase the earnings of capital, extirpate pauperism, abolish poverty, give remunerative employment to whoever wishes it, afford free scope to human powers, lessen crime, elevate morals, and taste, and intelligence, purify government and carry civilization to yet nobler heights, is—*to appropriate rent by taxation.*

In this way the State may become the universal landlord without calling herself so, and without assuming a single new function. In form, the ownership of land would remain just as now. No owner of land need be dispossessed, and no restriction need be placed upon the amount of land any one could hold. For, rent being taken by the State in taxes, land, no matter in whose name it stood, or in what parcels it was held, would be really common property, and every member of the community would participate in the advantages of its ownership.

Now, insomuch as the taxation of rent, or land values, must necessarily be increased just as we abolish other taxes, we may put the proposition into practical form by proposing—

To abolish all taxation save that upon land values.

As we have seen, the value of land is at the beginning of society nothing, but as society develops by the increase of population and the advance of the arts, it becomes greater and greater. In every civilized country, even the newest, the value of the land taken as a whole is sufficient to bear the entire expenses of government. In the better developed countries it is much more than sufficient. Hence it will not be enough merely to place all taxes upon the value of land. It will be necessary, where rent exceeds the present governmental revenues, commensurately to increase the amount demanded in taxation, and to continue this increase as society progresses and rent advances. But this is so natural and easy a matter, that it may be considered as involved, or at least understood, in the proposition to put all taxes on the value of land. That is the first step, upon which the practical struggle must be made. When the hare is once caught and killed, cooking him will follow as a matter of course. When the common right to land is so far appreciated that all taxes are abolished save those which fall upon rent, there is no danger of much more than is necessary to induce them to collect the public revenues being left to individual land holders. . . .

Of the Effect upon the Production of Wealth

. . . To abolish the taxation which, acting and reacting, now hampers every wheel of exchange and presses upon every form of industry, would be like removing an immense weight from a powerful spring. Imbued with fresh energy, production would start into new life, and trade would receive a stimulus which would be felt to the remotest arteries. The present method of taxation operates upon exchange like artificial deserts and mountains; it costs more to get goods through a custom house than it does to carry them around the world. It operates upon energy, and industry, and skill, and thrift, like a fine upon those qualities. If I have worked harder and built myself a good house while you have been contented to live in a hovel, the tax-gatherer now comes annually to make me pay a penalty for my energy and industry, by taxing me more than you. If I have saved while you wasted, I am mulct, while you are exempt. If a man build a ship we make him pay for his temerity, as though he had done an injury to the state; if a railroad be opened, down comes the tax-collector upon it, as though it were a public nuisance; if a manufactory be erected we levy upon it an annual sum which would go far toward making a handsome profit. We say we want capital, but if any one accumulate it, or bring it among us, we charge him for it as though we were giving him a privilege. We punish with a tax the man who covers barren fields with ripening grain, we fine him who puts up machinery, and him who drains a swamp. How heavily these taxes burden production only those realize who have attempted to follow our system of taxation through its ramifications, for, as I have before said, the heaviest part of taxation is that which falls in increased prices. But manifestly these taxes are in their nature akin to the Egyptian Pasha's tax upon date-trees. If they do not cause the trees to be cut down, they at least discourage the planting.

To abolish these taxes would be to lift the whole enormous weight of taxation from productive industry. The needle of the seamstress and the great manufactory; the cart-horse and the locomotive; the fishing boat and the steamship; the farmer's plow and the merchant's stock, would be alike untaxed. All would be free to make or to save, to buy or to sell, unfined by taxes, unannoyed by the tax-gatherer. . . .

And to shift the burden of taxation from production and exchange to the value or rent of land would not merely be to give new stimulus to the production of wealth; it would be to open new opportunities. For under this system no one would care to hold land unless to use it, and land now withheld from use would everywhere be thrown open to improvement.

The selling price of land would fall; land speculation would receive its death blow; land monopolization would no longer pay. Millions and millions of acres from which settlers are now shut out by high prices would be abandoned by their present owners or sold to settlers upon nominal terms. And this not merely on the frontiers, but within what are now considered well settled districts. Within a hundred miles of San Francisco would be thus thrown open land enough to support, even with present modes of cultivation, an agricultural population equal to that now scattered from the Oregon boundary to the Mexican line—a distance of 800 miles. In the same degree would this be true of most of the Western States, and in a great degree of the older Eastern States, for even in New York and Pennsylvania is population yet sparse as compared with the capacity of the land. And even in densely populated England would such a policy throw open to cultivation many hundreds of thousands of acres now held as private parks, deer preserves, and shooting grounds.

For this simple device of placing all taxes on the value of land would be in effect putting up the land at auction to whomsoever would pay the highest rent to the state. The demand for land fixes its value, and hence, if taxes were placed so as very nearly to consume that value, the man who wished to hold land without using it would have to pay very nearly what it would be worth to any one who wanted to use it.

And it must be remembered that this would apply, not merely to agricultural land, but to all land. Mineral land would be thrown open to use, just as agricultural land; and in the heart of a city no one could afford to keep land from its most profitable use, or on the outskirts to demand more for it than the use to which it could at the time be put would warrant. Everywhere that land had attained a value, taxation, instead of operating, as now, as a fine upon improvement, would operate to force improvement.

RUDOLF HILFERDING

(1877–1941)

Hilferding was an orthodox Marxist who dared to be a critic on at least some points of Marxist doctrine. Austrian-born, he was educated at the University of Vienna. He then moved to Germany, where he became a leading social democrat and later served as minister of finance under the Weimar Republic. He fled to France when Hitler came to power and committed suicide in 1941, some months after his arrest by German military police during the invasion.

His most famous book, *Das Finanz Kapital* (*Finance Capitalism,* 1910) is chiefly concerned with problems of monopoly, the business cycle, and tariffs. It is Hilferding's thesis that the monopoly and concentration of capital are controlled by the banks, which are dominant in the mature phases of capitalistic development. He greatly elaborates Marx's contributions on the subject of the development of corporation finance. His is the classic Marxian exposition of the formation of the monopoly price, which can hardly be explained by the labor theory of value. Corporate organization results in the separation of ownership from control and in unproductive mergers and consolidations for the purpose of making possible promoter's profits. When national monopolies compete in the international sphere, profits drop; therefore, international cartels are formed, which in turn seek to penetrate the economies of primitive countries unable to protect themselves through tariffs. This is an elaboration of the Marxian account of imperialism, familiar to readers of Rosa Luxemburg and Nikolai Lenin.

In the following selection Hilferding describes in burning language the ideology of capitalistic imperialism.

THE IDEOLOGY OF IMPERIALISM *

[The ideology of finance capital] is entirely opposed to that of liberalism; finance capital wants not freedom but dominance; it has no taste for the independence of the individual capitalist but rather demands his regimentation; it abhors the anarchy of competition and desires organization, to be sure only to be able to resume competition on a higher level. In order to achieve this and at the same time to maintain and augment its power, it needs the state to guarantee the home market through protection and thereby to facilitate the conquest of foreign markets. It requires a politically powerful state which need take no account of the opposed interests of other states in formulating its commercial policy. It needs a strong state which recognizes finance capital's interests abroad and uses political power to extort favorable treaties from smaller states, a state which can exert its influence all over the world in order to be able to turn the entire world into a sphere for investment. Finance capital, finally, needs a state which is strong enough to carry out a policy of expansion and to gather in new colonies. Where liberalism was an opponent of state power politics and wished to insure its own dominance against the older

* From *Das Finanzkapital,* translated by Paul Sweezy in *Theory of Capitalist Development* (New York, Oxford University Press, Inc., 1942). This heading is Sweezy's.

power of aristocracy and bureaucracy, to which end it confined the state's instruments of power within the smallest possible compass, there finance capital demands power politics without limit; and it would do so even if the outlays for army and navy did not directly assure to the most powerful capitalist groups an important market with enormous monopolistic profits.

The demand for a policy of expansion revolutionizes the entire *Weltanschauung* of the bourgeoisie. The bourgeoisie ceases to be peaceful and humanitarian. The old freetraders believed in free trade not only as the best economic policy, but also as the beginning of an era of peace. Finance capital has long since abandoned any such notions. It does not believe in the harmony of capitalist interests, but knows that the competitive struggle approaches ever closer to a political battle for power. The ideal of peace dies out; in place of the ideal of humanity steps that of the might and power of the state. The modern state, however, had its origin in the strivings of nations toward unity. The national aspiration, which found its natural limit in the formation of the nation as the foundation of the state —because it recognized the right of every nation to its own state form and therefore saw the borders of the state in the natural borders of the nation —is now transformed into the aspiration of one nation for dominance over others. As an ideal there now appears the conquest of world mastery for one's own nation, a striving as unlimited as capital's striving for profit from which it springs. Capital becomes the conqueror of the world, and with every new land conquered sets a new border which must be overstepped. This striving becomes an economic necessity, since any holding back lowers the profit of finance capital, reduces its ability to compete and finally can make of a smaller economic region a mere tributary of a larger one. Economically grounded, it is ideologically justified by that remarkable twisting of the national idea, which no longer recognizes the right of every nation to political self-determination and independence, and which is no longer an expression of the democratic belief in the equality of all nationalities. Rather the economic advantage of monopoly is mirrored in the favored place which must be ascribed to one's own nation. The latter appears as chosen above all others. Since the subordination of foreign nations proceeds by force, that is to say in a very natural way, it appears to the dominant nation that it owes its mastery to its special natural qualities, in other words to its racial characteristics. Thus in racial ideology there emerges a scientifically-cloaked foundation for the power lust of finance capital, which in this way demonstrates the cause and necessity of its operations. In place of the democratic ideal of equality steps an oligarchical ideal of mastery.

If in the field of foreign policy this ideal seems to include the whole nation, in internal affairs it stresses the standpoint of mastery as against the working class. At the same time, the growing power of the workers increases the effort of capital to enhance the state power as security against the demands of the proletariat.

In this way the ideology of imperialism arises on the grave of the old liberal ideals. It scoffs at the naïveté of liberalism. What an illusion, in a world of capitalistic struggle where the superiority of arms alone decides, to believe in a harmony of interests! What an illusion to look forward to the reign of eternal peace and to preach international law where only force decides the fate of peoples! What idiocy to want to extend the legal relations existing within a state beyond its borders! What irresponsible business disturbances are created by this humanitarian nonsense which makes a problem out of the workers; discovers social reform at home; and, in the colonies, wants to abolish contract slavery, the only possibility of rational exploitation! Eternal justice is a lovely dream, but one never even built a railroad out of moralizing. How can we conquer the world if we want to wait for competition to get religion [*auf die Bekehrung der Konkurrenz warten wollen*]?

In place of the faded ideals of the bourgeoisie, however, imperialism injects this dissolution of all illusions only to awaken a new and greater illusion. Imperialism is sober in weighing the real conflict of capitalist interest groups which both quarrel and unite among themselves. But it becomes transported and intoxicated when it reveals its own ideal. The imperialist wants nothing for himself; he is also, however, no illusionist and dreamer who dissolves the hopeless confusion of races in all stages of civilization and with all sorts of possibilities for development into the bloodless concept of mankind. With hard, clear eyes he looks at the crowd of peoples and perceives above them all his own nation. It is real; it lives in the mighty state, always becoming greater and more powerful; and its glorification justifies all his strivings. The renunciation of individual interest in favor of the higher general interest, which constitutes the condition of every vital social ideology, is thereby achieved; the state, which is extraneous to the people, and the nation are thereby bound together; and the national idea is made the driving force of policy. Class antagonisms are abolished in the service of the totality. Common action of the nation united for the goal of national greatness takes the place of class struggle which for the possessing class is both fruitless and dangerous.

This ideal which seems to unite shattered bourgeois society with a new bond, must receive an even more ecstatic acceptance since all the time the disintegration of bourgeois society proceeds apace.

PART EIGHT

Reactions against Classicism: Economic Nationalism

Since England was the country that benefited first from the Industrial Revolution, she had a natural competitive advantage over her less industrialized rivals. Advocates of free trade and laissez-faire, like Smith and Ricardo, had urged that England concentrate on manufactures and use the proceeds from the sale of manufactured goods to purchase food and raw materials. With the finest industries, navy, merchant marine, and colonial empire in the world, Britain was certainly in excellent position to gain from free trade. Free trade, of course, meant freedom for British merchants to conquer world markets. In spite of the propagandizing of the Anti-Corn-Law League and other free-trade organizations, however, it was not until 1849 that duties on food imports disappeared. Since this was seventy-three years after the publication of *The Wealth of Nations,* it becomes obvious that Smith's free-trade theories did not immediately sweep everything from their path, even in England, the country which was in the best position to benefit from them. By 1860, however, free trade not only was firmly established in England but had spread to France, primarily as a result of the propagandizing of Say and Bastiat. In that year France and England agreed to a mutual lowering of tariff duties.

It is apparent, however, that the free-trade argument which was accepted by industrialized England would not hold so well in agricultural countries wishing to foster new industries. In the United States, for example, the northern states, which wanted to encourage manufacturing, supported protection and all it implied. Alexander Hamilton's 1791 *Report on Manufactures* was one of the neo-mercantilist documents published in this country that advocated just such a system of national protection, with strong tariff walls behind which the infant industries might grow and prosper. During the Napoleonic Wars small industries sprang up in the northeastern states, sheltered by the absence of British competition. The owners of these industries naturally were loath to relinquish their newly found advantage and pressed strongly for a tariff system.

These developments were most illuminating to the German economist Friedrich List, who found during a sojourn in America that his nationalist philosophy was strengthened by the prosperity he witnessed. He felt that in the experience of America was an example for the German states to follow and an answer to the theories of the classical school.

It must be remembered that at this time Germany was feeling a strong surge of nationalism after the great victory over Napoleon by the German states under the leadership of Prussia. Furthermore, the mercantilist goal of state power had never really died in Germany, and philosophers such as Fichte and Hegel, presenting concepts that exalted the good of the state above the needs or desires of individuals, were highly revered. This was also the era of economic coöperation, the prelude to the political unity of the various German states through the instrumentality of the *Zollverein* (customs union).

List has been selected to represent the protectionist school because his was the first resounding attack on the ideal of unrestricted free trade which had had such great influence all over Europe and because of the literary and expository merits of his *National System of Political Economy*. List was also one of the founders of the famous German historical school, which is discussed later in this volume.

FRIEDRICH LIST

(1789–1846)

Friedrich List was born in Reutlingen, Germany, the son of a prosperous tanner. He was educated in the spirit of the Enlightenment and studied the writings of the classical economists. In 1817 he was appointed professor of administration and politics at the University of Tuebingen, and he was also political adviser to the government of Württemburg.

At this time there was no Germany proper; instead there were hundreds of petty duchies and principalities, all levying tolls, tariffs, and duties on one another. List formed an association of German businessmen, the purpose of which was to do away with internal tariff barriers, to unify Germany economically as an antecedent to political union, and to secure tariff protection from the cheap goods of more advanced industrial countries. In 1820 he was elected to the legislature of Württemburg, but soon after he was in trouble with the authorities because of his advocacy of liberal reforms. When he was sentenced to ten months' imprisonment for inciting insurrection, List fled the country and lived as a fugitive for several years. On his visit to Württemburg in 1824 he was actually arrested but was later released on the promise to emigrate to America. There he lived in the German colonies around Reading, Pennsylvania, and Baltimore, Maryland, and prospered financially as a promoter of railroad and mining enterprises. His American experiences confirmed his prior view that the teachings of Adam Smith and David Ricardo were not applicable to an undeveloped country which was striving for industrialization.

In 1827 appeared his first book advocating economic nationalism, *Outlines of American Political Economy,* and in 1832 he visited his native Germany at a time when agitation for a customs union of the various German principalities and states was at its height. When the *Zollverein* (customs union) came into existence, it adopted the reasonable Prussian tariff of ten percent ad valorem, which many German manufacturers—and List—felt was insufficient. In the heat of this debate he published *Das Nationale System der Politischen Ökonomie* (*The National System of Political Economy,* 1841), which became not only the bible of protectionism but also one of the finest examples of the method of the historical school.

In general, his thesis was that the dominant theory of the classical school, which advocated unrestricted competition, failed to recognize that every nation was not an England. When a country was undeveloped and just starting to industrialize, a protective tariff might be very necessary during the infant-industry stage. He further noted that there were as yet only *national* economies rather than the cosmopolitan economy the classical writers seemed to take for granted. The goal of political economy was therefore to be the economic development of the nation. The higher price that consumers might have to pay for some product because of tariffs could be regarded as a capital investment in infant industries by the payer of the higher price.

It should again be noted that List was one of the first economists to use the historical method, depending on concrete example rather than abstract theory to buttress his arguments.

THE NATIONAL SYSTEM OF POLITICAL ECONOMY

Introduction *

In no branch of political economy is there such a divergence of opinions between theorists and practical men as in regard to international commerce and commercial policy. . . . Poor, weak, and barbarous countries have become, mainly as a result of wise commercial policy, empires abounding in wealth and power, while other countries, for opposite reasons, have sunk from a high level of national importance into insignificance. . . . The more rapid the growth of a spirit of industrial invention and improvement, of social and political reform, the wider becomes the gap between stationary and progressive nations, and the more dangerous it is to remain on the further side. If in the past centuries were required for Great Britain to succeed in monopolizing the most important manufacture of those days, the wool industry, later decades were sufficient in the case of the far more important cotton industry, and in our own time a few years' start enabled her to annex the whole linen industry of the Continent.

And at no former date has the world seen a manufacturing and commercial supremacy like that which in our own day, endowed with such immense power, has followed so systematic a policy, and has striven so hard to monopolize all manufactures, all commerce, all shipping, all the chief colonies, all the ocean, and to make the rest of the world, like the Hindus, its serfs in all industrial and commercial relations.

Alarmed at the effects of this policy, nay, rather forced by the convulsions which it produced, we have lately seen a country whose civilization seemed little adapted for manufacturing, we have seen Russia seek her salvation in the system of prohibition so much abhorred by orthodox theory. What has been the result? National prosperity.

On the other hand, North America, which was attaining a high position under protection, was attracted by the promises of the theory, and induced to open her ports again to English goods. What was the fruit of free competition? Convulsion and ruin.

Such experiences are well fitted to awake doubts whether the theory is so infallible as it pretends to be; whether the common practice is so insane as it is depicted by the theory; to arouse fears lest our nationality might be in danger of perishing at last from an error in the theory, like the patient who followed a printed prescription and died of a misprint; and to produce a suspicion that this much-praised theory may be built like the old Greek horse, with vast womb and lofty sides, only to conceal men and weapons and to induce us to pull down our walls of defence with our own hands.

This much at least is certain, that although the great questions of com-

* From "Introduction to the *National System of Political Economy,*" in *Life of Friedrich List and Selections from His Writings,* by Margaret E. Hirst (New York, Charles Scribner's Sons, London, Smith, Elder & Co., 1909).

mercial policy have been discussed by the keenest brains of all nations in books and legislative assemblies, yet the gulf between theory and practice which has existed since the time of Quesnay and Smith is not only not filled up, but gapes wider and wider each year. And of what use is a science to us, if it throws no light on the path which practice ought to follow. . . .

In fact, we believe that we can prove the responsibility for the divergence between the theory and practice of commercial policy to rest as much with the theorists as with the practical men. In questions of international trade, political economy must derive its teaching from experience, must adapt its measures to the needs of the present and to the particular circumstances of each nation, without neglecting the claims of the future and of mankind as a whole. Accordingly it founds itself upon philosophy, politics, and history.

Philosophy demands, in the interests of the future and of mankind, an even closer friendship among nations, avoidance of war as far as possible, the establishment and development of international law, the change of what we call the law of nations into the law of federated states, freedom of international intercourse, both in intellectual and material things; and, finally, the alliance of all nations under the rule of law—that is, a universal union.

But politics demands, in the interests of each separate nation, guarantees for its independence and continued existence, special regulations to help its progress in culture, prosperity, and power, to build its society into a perfectly complete and harmoniously developed body politic, self-contained and independent. . . .

But the practice and theory of political economy in their present forms each takes sides with a faction, the one supporting the special claims of nationality, the other the one-sided demands of cosmopolitanism.

Practice, or, in other words, the so-called mercantile system, commits the great error of maintaining the absolute and universal advantage and necessity of restriction, because it has been advantageous and beneficial to certain nations at certain periods of their development. It does not see that restriction is only the means, and freedom is the end. Looking only at the nation, never at the individual, only at the present, never at the future, it is exclusively political and national in thought, and is devoid of philosophical outlook or cosmopolitan feeling. The ruling theory, on the contrary, founded by Adam Smith on the dreams of Quesnay, has in view only the cosmopolitan claims of the future, indeed of the most distant future. Universal union and absolute freedom of international trade, which at the present time are a cosmopolitan dream only to be realized perhaps after the lapse of centuries, can (according to the theory) be realized at the present time. It does not understand the needs of the present and the meaning of nationality—in fact, it ignores national existence, and with it the principle of national independence. In its exclusive cosmopolitanism, it considers mankind only as a whole, and the welfare of the whole race, not caring for the nation or national welfare, it shudders at the teachings of politics, and condemns theory and practice as mere worthless routine. . . .

We thus see of what great practical importance the question of international free trade is at present, and how necessary it is that a thorough and unbiassed inquiry should at last be undertaken to see whether and how far theory and practice are guilty of error in this matter. Thus the problem of harmonizing the two might be solved, or, at least, a serious attempt made to solve it. In very truth the author must explain (not from mock modesty, but from a real and deep-rooted mistrust of his powers) that it is only after a mental struggle of many years' standing, after he has a hundred times questioned the correctness of his views and a hundred times found them true, only after he has a hundred times tested the views and principles opposed to his own and a hundred times realized their error, that he has determined to venture the solution of this problem. This is no vain attempt to contradict ancient authorities and to found new theories. If he had been an Englishman he would scarcely have doubted the main principles of Adam Smith's system.

It was the state of his own country which more than twenty years ago roused in him the first doubts in its infallibility. It has been the state of his own country which has induced him since then, in many unsigned articles, and, finally, in longer essays under his own name, to develop views opposed to the prevailing theory. And to-day it is still mainly the interests of Germany which have emboldened him to come forward with this book. . . .

Maintenance, development, and perfecting of national spirit at present is, and must be, a chief object of national endeavour. It is no wrong and selfish aim, but a rational one, in perfect harmony with the true interests of mankind in general. It leads naturally to a final alliance of nations under the rule of law, the universal union, which can only contribute to the well-being of the human race if it is realized in the form of a confederation. A union proceeding from the overwhelming political strength and wealth of a single nation, and thus basing itself upon the subjection and dependence of all other nations, would, on the contrary, result in the destruction of all national characteristics and all international emulation; it is opposed both to the interest and sentiment of nations, since they all feel themselves destined to independence and the attainment of a high level of wealth and political importance. Such a union would only be a repetition of the former attempt by Rome, carried out indeed by means of manufactures and commerce instead of by cold steel as in former times, but none the less leading back to barbarism. The civilization, political development, and strength of nations are mainly dependent on their economic circumstances; and the converse is also true. The more its economy is developed and perfected, the more civilized and powerful is the nation; the higher the level of its civilization and power, the higher the level of its economic development. . . .

Every nation, which attaches any value to its independence and continued existence, must strive to pass with all speed from a lower stage of culture to a higher, and to combine within its own territory agriculture, manufactures, shipping, and commerce. The transition from savagery to the pastoral state, and from the latter to the agricultural state, are best effected by free trade with civilized, that is, manufacturing and commercial nations. The transition from an agricultural community into the class of agricultural, commercial, and manufacturing nations could only take place under free trade if the same process of development occurred simultaneously in all nations destined to manufactures, if nations put no hindrance in the way of one another's economic development, if they did not check one another's progress through war and tariffs. But since individual nations, through specially favourable circumstances, gained an advantage over others in manufactures, trade, and shipping, and since they early understood the best means of getting and maintaining through these advantages political ascendency, they have accordingly invented a policy which aimed, and still aims, at obtaining a monopoly in manufactures and trade, and at checking the progress of less advanced nations. The combination of the details of this policy (prohibition of imports, import duties, restrictions on shipping, bounties on exports) is known as the tariff system. . . .

Hence there is a cosmopolitan and a political economy, a theory of exchange values and a theory of productive powers, two doctrines which are essentially distinct and which must be developed independently. The productive powers of a nation are not only limited by the industry, thrift, morality, and intelligence of its individual members, and by its natural resources or material capital, but also by its social, political, and municipal laws and institutions, and especially by the securities for the continued existence, independence, and power of the nationality. However industrious, thrifty, enterprising, moral, and intelligent the individuals may be, without national unity, national division of labour, and national co-operation of productive powers the nation will never reach a high level of prosperity and power, or ensure to itself the lasting possession of its intellectual, social, and material goods. The principle of division of labour has not been fully grasped up to the present. Productivity depends not only on the division of various manufacturing operations among many individuals, but still more on the moral and physical co-operation of these individuals for a common end.

Thus the principle is applicable not merely to single factories or estates, but to the whole agricultural, manufacturing, and commercial forces of a nation. Division of labour and co-operation of productive powers exist where the intellectual activity of a nation bears a proper ratio to its material production, where agriculture, industry, and trade are equally and harmoniously developed.

In a purely agricultural nation, even when it enjoys free trade with manufacturing and commercial nations, a great part of its productive powers and natural resources lies idle and unused. Its intellectual and political development and its powers of defence are hampered. It can have no shipping of importance, no extensive trade. All its prosperity, so far as it results from international trade, can be interrupted, injured, or ruined by foreign regulations or by war.

Manufacturing power, on the contrary, promotes science, art, and political development, increases the well-being of the people, the population, national revenue, and national power, provides the country with the means of extending its commerce to all quarters of the world and of founding colonies, and nourishes the fishing industry, shipping and the navy. Through it alone can home agriculture be raised to a high pitch of development. Agriculture and manufactures in one and the same nation, united, that is, under one political authority, live in perpetual peace. Their mutual relations cannot be disturbed by war or foreign measures, consequently they ensure to the nation continued advance in well-being, civilization, and power. Nature lays down certain conditions for the existence of agriculture and manufactures, but these conditions are not always the same. . . .

Four distinct periods can be recognized in the economic development of nations by means of international trade. In the first, home agriculture is fostered by the importation of foreign manufactured goods and the export of agricultural products and raw materials. In the second, home manufactures arise by the side of foreign imports. In the third, home manufactures supply the greater part of the home-market. In the fourth, large quantities of home-manufactured goods are exported and raw materials and agricultural products imported from abroad.

The tariff system, as a means of advancing the economic development of the nation by regulation of its foreign trade, must constantly follow the principle of national industrial *education*.

It is madness to attempt to help home agriculture by protection, since home agriculture can only be advanced on economic principles by the development of home manufactures, and the exclusion of foreign raw materials and agricultural products can only depress home manufactures.

The economic betterment of a nation which is at a low level of intelligence and culture, or in which the population is small in relation to the extent and productivity of its territory, is best accomplished through free trade with highly cultivated, rich, and industrious nations. In the case of such a country every restriction of trade, intended to plant manufacturing industry within its borders, is premature and injurious, not only to the welfare of mankind in general, but to the progress of the nation itself. Only when the intellectual, political, and economic education of the nation has so far advanced as a result of free trade that its further progress would be checked and hindered by the import of foreign manufactures and the lack of a sufficient market for its own goods, can protective measures be justified.

The territory of some nations is not of great extent nor supplied with many natural resources, the mouths of its rivers are not within its boundaries, and it does not form a homogeneous whole. Such a nation cannot apply the protective system at all, or only with imperfect success until it has first supplied its deficiencies by conquest or treaty.

Manufacturing power embraces so many branches of science and knowledge, and presupposes so much experience, skill, and practice, that national industrial development can only be gradual. Any exaggeration or hastening of protection punishes itself by diminished national prosperity. The most injurious and objectionable course is the sudden and complete isolation of the country by prohibition. Yet even this can be justified if, separated from other countries by a long war, it has suffered from an involuntary prohibition of foreign manufactures, and has been forced to supply itself. In this case a gradual transition from prohibition to protection should be effected by deciding beforehand upon a system of gradually diminishing duties. But a nation which desires to pass from a non-protective policy to protection must, on the contrary, begin with low taxes, which increase gradually upon a pre-determined scale. Taxes predetermined in this way must be maintained intact by statesmen. They must not lower the taxes before the time, though they may raise them if they seem insufficient.

Excessively high import duties, which entirely cut off foreign competition, injure the country which imposes them, since its manufacturers are not forced to compete with foreigners, and indolence is fostered. If home manufactures do not prosper under moderate and gradually increasing duties, this is a proof that the country has not the necessary qualifications for the development of its own manufacturing system. Duties in a branch of industry that is already protected should not fall so low, that the existence of the industry is endangered by foreign competition. Support of existing manufactures, and protection for the essentials of national industry must be unalterable principles. Foreign competition, accordingly, can be allowed only a share in the yearly increase of consumption. The duties must be raised as soon as the foreigner gains the greater part or the whole of the yearly increase.

A nation like England, whose manufacturing power has a long start of all other countries, best maintains and extends its industrial and commercial supremacy by the freest possible trade. In its case cosmopolitan and political principles are identical. This explains the preference of distinguished English statesmen for absolute free trade and the unwillingness of wise financiers in other countries to apply this principle under the existing conditions of the world. For the last quarter of a century the system of prohibition and protection has worked to the disadvantage of England and the advantage of her rivals. Most disadvantageous of all are its restrictions on the importation of foreign raw materials and food stuffs.

Commercial unions and commercial treaties are the most effective means of facilitating intercourse between different nations. But commercial treaties are only legitimate and valuable when they involve mutual benefits. They are injurious and illegitimate when the development of a manufacturing power in one country is sacrificed in order to gain concessions for the exports of its agricultural products to another country. . . . Even if protection temporarily enhances prices, yet it ensures cheapness in the future as a result of home competition. For a perfectly developed industry can fix a much lower price for its products than the cost of transport and of trader's profits allow when raw materials and food must be exported and manufactures imported.

The loss which a nation incurs by protection is only one of *values,* but it gains *powers* by which it is enabled to go on producing permanently inestimable amounts of value. This loss in value should be regarded merely as the price paid for the industrial education of the nation.

Protection to manufactures does not injure the agriculturists of the protected nation. Through the growth of a home manufacturing power, wealth, population, and with them the demand for agricultural products will vastly increase. Consequently there will be a considerable rise in the rents and selling prices of landed property, while as time goes by the manufactured products required by agriculturists will fall in price. These gains will outweigh the losses sustained by the agriculturists through the temporary rise in the prices of manufactured goods.

Similarly, both home and foreign trade gain from protection, since both are of importance only in the case of countries which can supply their own markets with manufactures, consume their own agricultural products, and exchange their own manufacturing surplus for foreign raw materials and food stuffs. Merely agricultural nations of the temperate zone have an insignificant home and foreign trade; foreign trade in such cases is generally in the hands of the manufacturing and commercial nations who hold intercourse with them.

Moderate protection does not grant a monopoly to home manufactures, only a guarantee against loss for those individuals who have devoted their capital, talent, and labour to new and untried industries. There can be no monopoly since home competition takes the place of foreign, and it is open to each member of the state to share in the benefits it offers to individuals. There is merely a monopoly for the inhabitants of one country against those of foreign countries, who themselves possess at home a similar monopoly. But this monopoly is useful, not only because it wakes productive forces lying idle and dormant in the nation, but because it attracts to the country foreign productive forces (material and intellectual capital, *entrepreneurs,* skilled and unskilled workmen).

In the case of many nations of long standing culture the export of raw materials and agricultural products, and the import of foreign manufactures, can no longer benefit their powers of production. Such nations suffer many serious evils if they do not foster their own manufactures. Their agriculture must necessarily be crippled, since, if important home manufactures arose, the increased population would find employment there, and the consequent great demand for agricultural products would make agriculture on a large scale very profitable and favour its development. But in the case supposed the surplus population could only be employed in agriculture. The result would be a subdivision of land and increase of small cultivators which would be most injurious to the power, civilization, and wealth of the nation.

An agricultural population consisting for the most part of peasant proprietors can neither contribute large quantities of products to the home trade nor exercise an important demand for manufactures. In such a case the consumption of each individual is limited for the most part to what he himself produces. Under these conditions the nation can never develop any satisfactory system of transport, and can never possess the incalculable advantages arising from such a system. The inevitable result is national weakness, moral and material, individual and political. These consequences are the more dangerous when neighbouring nations pursue the opposite course, when they advance as we fall back, when yonder the hope of better things to come increases the courage, power, and enterprise of the citizens, while here courage and spirit are more and more depressed by the outlook into a hopeless future. History affords striking examples of whole nations falling into ruin because they did not know how to undertake at the right moment the great task of planting their own manufactures, and a powerful industry and commerce, by which they could insure to themselves intellectual, economic, and political independence.

Private Economy and National Economy *

. . . 'What is prudence in the conduct of every private family,' says Adam Smith, 'can scarce be folly in that of a great kingdom.' Every individual in pursuing his own interests necessarily promotes thereby also the interests of the community. It is evident that every individual, inasmuch as he knows his own local circumstances best and pays most attention to his occupation, is far better able to judge than the statesman or legislator how his capital can most profitably be invested. . . . Adam Smith concludes from this: 'Restrictions on trade imposed on the behalf of the internal industry of a country, are mere folly; every nation, like every individual, ought to buy articles where they can be procured the cheapest; in order to attain to the highest degree of national prosperity, we have simply to follow the maxim of letting things alone (laisser faire et laisser aller).' Smith and Say compare a nation which seeks to promote its industry by protective duties, to a tailor who wants to make his own boots, and to a bootmaker who would impose a toll on those who enter his door, in order to promote his prosperity. As in all errors of the popular school, so also in this one does Thomas Cooper go to extremes in his book which is directed against the American system of protection. 'Politi-

* From *The National System of Political Economy,* translated by Sampson S. Lloyd (London and New York, Longmans, Green and Co., 1904).

cal economy,' he alleges, 'is almost synonymous with the private economy of all individuals; *politics* are no essential ingredient of *political economy;* it is folly to suppose that the community is something quite different from the individuals of whom it is composed. Every individual knows best how to invest his labour and his capital. The wealth of the community is nothing else than the aggregate of the wealth of all its individual members; and if every individual can provide best for himself, that nation must be the richest in which every individual is most left to himself.' . . .

How? Is the wisdom of private economy, also wisdom in national economy? Is it in the nature of individuals to take into consideration the wants of future centuries, as those concern the nature of the nation and the State? Let us consider only the first beginning of an American town; every individual left to himself would care merely for his own wants, or at the most for those of his nearest successors, whereas all individuals united in one community provide for the convenience and the wants of the most distant generations; they subject the present generation for this object to privations and sacrifices which no reasonable person could expect from individuals. Can the individual further take into consideration in promoting his private economy, the defence of the country, public security, and the thousand other objects which can only be attained by the aid of the whole community? Does not the State require individuals to limit their private liberty according to what these objects require? Does it not even require that they should sacrifice for these some part of their earnings, of their mental and bodily labour, nay, even their own life? We must first root out, as Cooper does, the very ideas of 'State' and 'nation' before this opinion can be entertained.

No; that may be wisdom in national economy which would be folly in private economy, and *vice versâ;* and owing to the very simple reason, that a tailor is no nation and a nation no tailor, that one family is something very different from a community of millions of families, that one house is something very different from a large national territory. Nor does the individual merely by understanding his own interests best, and by striving to further them, if left to his own devices, always further the interests of the community. We ask those who occupy the benches of justice, whether they do not frequently have to send individuals to the treadmill on account of their excess of inventive power, and of their all too great industry. Robbers, thieves, smugglers, and cheats know their own local and personal circumstances and conditions extremely well, and pay the most active attention to their business; but it by no means follows therefrom, that society is in the best condition where such individuals are least restrained in the exercise of their private industry.

In a thousand cases the power of the State is compelled to impose restrictions on private industry. It prevents the shipowner from taking on board slaves on the west coast of Africa, and taking them over to America. It imposes regulations as to the building of steamers and the rules of navigation at sea, in order that passengers and sailors may not be sacrificed to the avarice and caprice of the captains. In England certain rules have recently been enacted with regard to shipbuilding, because an infernal union between assurance companies and shipowners has been brought to light, whereby yearly thousands of human lives and millions in value were sacrificed to the avarice of a few persons. In North America millers are bound under a penalty to pack into each cask not less than 198 lbs. of good flour, and for all market goods market inspectors are appointed, although in no other country is individual liberty more highly prized. Everywhere does the State consider is to be its duty to guard the public against danger and loss, as in the sale of necessaries of life, so also in the sale of medicines, &c.

But the cases which we have mentioned (the school will reply) concern unlawful damages to property and to the person, not the honourable exchange of useful objects, not the harmless and useful industry of private individuals; to impose restrictions on these latter the State has no right whatever. Of course not, so long as they remain harmless and useful; that which, however, is harmless and useful in itself, in general commerce with the world, can become dangerous and injurious in national internal commerce, and *vice versâ*. In time of peace, and considered from a cosmopolitan point of view, privateering is an injurious profession; in time of war, Governments favour it. The deliberate killing of a human being is a crime in time of peace, in war it becomes a duty. Trading in gunpowder, lead, and arms in time of peace is allowed; but whoever provides the enemy with them in time of war, is punished as a traitor.

For similar reasons the State is not merely justified in imposing, but bound to impose, certain regulations and restrictions on commerce (which is in itself harmless) for the best interests of the nation. By prohibitions and protective duties it does not give directions to individuals how to employ their productive powers and capital (as the popular school sophistically alleges); it does not tell the one, 'You must invest your money in the building of a ship, or in the erection of a manufactory'; or the other, 'You must be a naval captain or a civil engineer'; it leaves it to the judgment of every individual how and where to invest his capital, or to what vocation he will devote himself. It merely says, 'It is to the advantage of our nation that we manufacture these or the other goods ourselves; but as by free competition with foreign countries we can never obtain possession of this advantage, we have imposed restrictions on that competition, so far as in our opinion is necessary, to give those among us who invest their capital in these new branches of industry, and those who devote their bodily and mental powers to them, the requisite guarantees that they shall not lose their capital and shall not miss their vocation in life; and further to stimulate foreigners to come over to our side with their productive powers. In this manner, it does not in the least degree restrain private industry; on the contrary, it secures to the personal, natural, and moneyed powers of the nation a greater and wider field of activity. It does not thereby do something which its individual citizens could understand better and do better than it; on the contrary, it does something which the individuals, even if they understood it, would not be able to do for themselves.

The allegation of the school, that the system of protection occasions unjust and anti-economical encroachments by the power of the State against the employment of the capital and industry of private individuals, appears in the least favourable light if we consider that it is the *foreign* commercial regulations which allow such encroachments on *our* private industry to take place, and that only by the aid of the system of protection are we enabled to counteract those injurious operations of the foreign commercial policy. If the English shut out our corn from their markets, what else are they doing than compelling our agriculturists to grow so much less corn than they would have sent out to England under systems of free importation? If they put such heavy duties on our wool, our wines, or our timber, that our export trade to England wholly or in great measure ceases, what else is thereby effected than that the power of the English nation restricts proportionately our branches of production? In these cases a direction is evidently given by *foreign legislation* to *our* capital and *our* personal productive powers, which but for the regulations made by it they would scarcely have followed. It follows from this, that were we to disown giving, by means of *our* own legislation, a direction to our own national industry in accordance with our own national interests, we could not prevent foreign nations from regulating our national industry after a fashion which corresponds with their own real or presumed advantage, and which in any case operates disadvantageously to the development of our own productive powers. But can it possibly be wiser on our part, and more to the advantage of those who nationally belong to us, for us to allow our private industry to be regulated by a foreign national Legislature, in accordance with foreign national interests, rather than regulate it by means of our own Legislature and in accordance with our own interests? Does the German or American agriculturist feel himself less restricted if he has to study every year the English Acts of Parliament, in order to ascertain whether that body deems it advantageous to encourage or to impose restrictions on his production of corn or wool, than if his own Legislature imposes certain restrictions on him in respect of foreign manufactured goods, but at the same time insures him a market for all his products, of which he can never again be deprived by foreign legislation?

If the school maintains that protective duties secure to the home manufacturers a monopoly to the disadvantage of the home consumers, in so doing it makes use of a weak argument. For as every individual in the nation is free to share in the profits of the home market which is thus secured to native industry, this is in no respect a private monopoly, but a privilege, secured to all those who belong to our nation, as against those who nationally belong to foreign nations, and which is the more righteous and just inasmuch as those who nationally belong to foreign nations possess themselves the very same monopoly, and those who belong to us are merely thereby put on the same footing with them. It is neither a privilege to the exclusive advantage of the producers, nor to the exclusive disadvantage of the consumers; for if the producers at first obtain higher prices, they run great risks, and have to contend against those considerable losses and sacrifices which are always connected with all beginnings in manufacturing industry. But the consumers have ample security that these extraordinary profits shall not reach unreasonable limits, or become perpetual, by means of the competition at home which follows later on, and which, as a rule, always lowers prices further than the level at which they had steadily ranged under the free competition of the foreigner. If the agriculturists, who are the most important consumers to the manufacturers, must also pay higher prices, this disadvantage will be amply repaid to them by increased demands for agricultural products, and by increased prices obtained for the latter.

It is a further sophism, arrived at by confounding the theory of mere values with that of the powers of production, when the popular school infers from the doctrine, '*that the wealth of the nation is merely the aggregate of the wealth of all individuals in it, and that the private interest of every individual is better able than all State regulations to incite to production and accumulation of wealth,*' the conclusion that the national industry would prosper best if only every individual were left undisturbed in the occupation of accumulating wealth. That doctrine can be conceded without the conclusion resulting from it at which the school desires thus to arrive; for the point in question is not (as we have shown in a previous chapter) that of immediately increasing by commercial restrictions the amount of *the values of exchange* in the nation, but of increasing *the amount of its productive powers.* But that the aggregate of the productive powers of the nation is not synonymous with the aggregate of the productive powers of all individuals, each considered separately—that the total amount of these powers depends chiefly on social and political conditions, but especially on the degree in which the nation has rendered effectual the division of labour and the confederation of the powers of production within itself—we believe we have sufficiently demonstrated in the preceding chapters. . . .

Nationality and the Economy of the Nation

. . . The system of the school suffers, as we have already shown, . . . from three main defects: firstly, from boundless *cosmopolitanism,* which neither recognises the principle of nationality, nor takes into consideration the satisfaction of its interests; secondly, from a dead *materialism,* which everywhere regards chiefly the mere exchangeable value of things without taking into consideration the mental and political, the present and the future interests, and the productive powers of the nation; thirdly, from *a disorganising particularism* and *individualism,* which, ignoring the nature and character of social labour and the operation of the union of powers in their higher consequences, considers private industry only as it would develop itself under a state of free interchange with society (i.e. with the whole human race) were that race not divided into separate national societies.

Between each individual and entire humanity, however, stands THE NATION, with its special language and literature, with its peculiar origin and history, with its special manners and customs, laws and institutions, with the claims of all these for existence, independence, perfection, and continuance for the future, and with its separate territory; a society which, united by a thousand ties of mind and of interests, combines itself into one independent whole, which recognises the law of right for and within itself, and in its united character is still opposed to other societies of a similar kind in their national liberty, and consequently can only under the existing conditions of the world maintain self-existence and independence by its own power and resources. As the individual chiefly obtains by means of the nation and in the nation mental culture, power of production, security, and prosperity, so is the civilisation of the human race only conceivable and possible by means of the civilisation and development of the individual nations.

Meanwhile, however, an infinite difference exists in the condition and circumstances of the various nations; we observe among them giants and dwarfs, well-formed bodies and cripples, civilised, half-civilised, and barbarous nations; but in all of them, as in the individual human being, exists the impulse of self-preservation, the striving for improvement which is implanted by nature. It is the task of politics to civilise the barbarous nationalities, to make the small and weak ones great and strong, but, above all, to secure to them existence and continuance. It is the task of national economy to accomplish *the economical development of the nation,* and to prepare it for admission into the universal society of the future. . . .

A large population, and an extensive territory endowed with manifold national resources, are essential requirements of the normal nationality; they are the fundamental conditions of mental cultivation as well as of material development and political power. A nation restricted in the number of its population and in territory, especially if it has a separate language, can only possess a crippled literature, crippled institutions for promoting art and science. A small State can never bring to complete perfection within its territory the various branches of production. In it all protection becomes mere private monopoly. Only through alliances with more powerful nations, by partly sacrificing the advantages of nationality, and by excessive energy, can it maintain with difficulty its independence.

A nation which possesses no coasts, mercantile marine, or naval power, or has not under its dominion and control the mouths of its rivers, is in its foreign commerce dependent on other countries; it can neither establish colonies of its own nor form new nations; all surplus population, mental and material means, which flows from such a nation to uncultivated countries, is lost to its own literature, civilisation and industry, and goes to the benefit of other nationalities.

A nation not bounded by seas and chains of mountains lies open to the attacks of foreign nations, and can only by great sacrifices, and in any case only very imperfectly, establish and maintain a separate tariff system of its own.

Territorial deficiencies of the nation can be remedied either by means of hereditary succession, as in the case of England and Scotland; or by purchase, as in the case of Florida and Louisiana; or by conquests, as in the case of Great Britain and Ireland.

In modern times a fourth means has been adopted, which leads to this object in a manner much more in accordance with justice and with the prosperity of nations than conquest, and which is not so dependent on accidents as hereditary succession, namely, the union of the interests of various States by means of free conventions. . . .

As respects their economy, nations have to pass through the following stages of development: original barbarism, pastoral condition, agricultural condition, agricultural-manufacturing condition, and agricultural-manufacturing-commercial condition.

The industrial history of nations, and of none more clearly than that of England, proves that the transition from the savage state to the pastoral one, from the pastoral to the agricultural, and from agriculture to the first beginnings in manufacture and navigation, is effected most speedily and advantageously by means of free commerce with further advanced towns and countries, but that a perfectly developed manufacturing industry, an important mercantile marine, and foreign trade on a really large scale, can only be attained by means of the interposition of the power of the State.

The less any nation's agriculture has been perfected, and the more its foreign trade is in want of opportunities of exchanging the excess of native agricultural products and raw materials for foreign manufactured goods, the deeper that the nation is still sunk in barbarism and fitted only for an absolute monarchical form of government and legislation, the more will free trade (i.e. the exportation of agricultural products and the importation of manufactured goods) promote its prosperity and civilisation.

On the other hand, the more that the agriculture of a nation, its industries, and its social, political, and municipal conditions, are thoroughly developed, the less advantage will it be able to derive for the improvement of its social conditions, from the exchange of native agricultural products and raw materials for foreign manufactured goods, and the greater disadvantages will it experience from the successful competition of a foreign manufacturing power superior to its own.

Solely in nations of the latter kind, namely, those which possess all the necessary mental and material conditions and means for establishing a manufacturing power of their own, and of thereby attaining the highest degree of civilisation, and development of material prosperity and political power, but which are retarded in their progress by the competition of a foreign manufacturing Power which is already farther advanced than their own—only in such nations are commercial restrictions justifiable for the purpose of establishing and protecting their own manufacturing power; and even in them it is justifiable only until that manufacturing power is strong enough no longer to have any reason to fear foreign competition, and thenceforth only so far as may be necessary for protecting the inland manufacturing power in its very roots.

The system of protection would not merely be contrary to the principles of cosmopolitical economy, but also to the rightly understood advantage of the nation itself, were it to exclude foreign competition at once and altogether, and thus isolate from other nations the nation which is thus protected. If the manufacturing Power to be protected be still in the first period of its development, the protective duties must be very moderate, they must only rise gradually with the increase of the mental and material capital, of the technical abilities and spirit of enterprise of the nation. Neither is it at all necessary that all branches of industry should be protected in the same degree. Only the most important branches require special protection, for the working of which much outlay of capital in building and management, much machinery, and therefore much technical knowledge, skill, and experience, and many workmen are required, and whose products belong to the category of the first necessaries of life, and consequently are of the greatest importance as regards their total value as well as regards national independence (as, for example, cotton, woollen and linen manufactories, &c.). If these main branches are suitably protected and developed, all other less important branches of manufacture will rise up around them under a less degree of protection. It will be to the advantage of nations in which wages are high, and whose population is not yet great in proportion to the extent of their territory, e.g. in the United States of North America, to give less protection to manufactures in which machinery does not play an important part, than to those in which machinery does the greater part of the work, providing that those nations which supply them with similar goods allow in return free importation to their agricultural products.

The popular school betrays an utter misconception of the nature of national economical conditions if it believes that such nations can promote and further their civilisation, their prosperity, and especially their social progress, equally well by the exchange of agricultural products for manufactured goods, as by establishing a manufacturing power of their own. A mere agricultural nation can never develop to any considerable extent its home and foreign commerce, its inland means of transport, and its foreign navigation, increase its population in due proportion to their well-being, or make notable progress in its moral, intellectual, social, and political development: it will never acquire important political power, or be placed in a position to influence the cultivation and progress of less advanced nations and to form colonies of its own. A mere agricultural State is an infinitely less perfect institution than an agricultural-manufacturing State. The former is always more or less economically and politically dependent on those foreign nations which take from it agricultural products in exchange for manufactured goods. It cannot determine for itself how much it will produce; it must wait and see how much others will buy from it. These latter, on the contrary (the agricultural-manufacturing States), produce for themselves large quantities of raw materials and provisions, and supply merely the deficiency by importation from the purely agricultural nations. The purely agricultural nations are thus in the first place dependent for their power of effecting sales on the chances of a more or less plentiful harvest in the agricultural-manufacturing nations; in the next place they have to compete in these sales with other purely agricultural nations, whereby their power of sale, in itself very uncertain, thus becomes still more uncertain. Lastly, they are exposed to the danger of being totally ruined in their trading with foreign manufacturing nations by wars, or new foreign tariff regulations whereby they suffer the double disadvantage of finding no buyers for their surplus agricultural products, and of failing to obtain supplies of the manufactured goods which they require. An agricultural nation is, as we have already stated, an individual with *one* arm, who makes use of a foreign arm, but who cannot make sure of the use of it in all cases; an agricultural-manufacturing nation is an individual who has *two* arms *of his own* always at his disposal.

It is a fundamental error of the school when it represents the system of protection as a mere device of speculative politicians which is contrary to nature. History is there to prove that protective regulations originated either in the natural efforts of nations to attain to prosperity, independence, and power, or in consequence of wars and of the hostile commercial legislation of predominating manufacturing nations.

The idea of independence and power originates in the very idea of 'the nation.' The school never takes this into consideration, because it does not make the economy of the separate nation, but the economy of society generally, i.e. of the whole human race, the object of its investigations. If we imagine, for instance, that all nations were united by means of a universal confederation, their individual independence and power would cease to be an object of regard. The security for the independence of every nation would in such a case rest on the legal provisions of the universal society, just as e.g. the security of the independence of the states of Rhode Island and Delaware lies in the union of all the free states constituting the American Union. Since the first foundation of that Union it has never yet occurred to any of these smaller states to care for the enlargement of its own political power, or to consider its independence less secured than is that of the largest states of the Union.

In proportion, however, as the principle of a universal confederation of nations is reasonable, in just the same degree would a given nation act contrary to reason if, in anticipation of the great advantages to be expected from such a union, and from a state of universal and perpetual peace, it were to regulate the principles of its national policy as though this universal confederation of nations existed already. We ask, would not every sane person consider a government to be insane which, in consideration of the benefits and the reasonableness of a state of universal and perpetual peace, proposed to disband its armies, destroy its fleet, and demolish its fortresses? But such a government would be doing nothing different in principle from what the popular school requires from governments when, because of the advantages which would be derivable from general free trade, it urges that they should abandon the advantages derivable from protection.

War has a ruinous effect on the reciprocal commercial relations between nation and nation. The agriculturist living in one country is by it forcibly separated from the manufacturer living in another country. While, however, the manufacturer (especially if he belongs to a nation powerful at sea, and carrying on extensive commerce) readily finds compensation from the agriculturists of his own country, or from those of other accessible agricultural countries, the inhabitant of the purely agricultural country suffers doubly through this interruption of intercourse.

The market for his agricultural products will fail him entirely, and he will consequently lose the means of paying for those manufactured goods which have become necessaries to him owing to previously existing trade; his power both of production and consumption will be diminished.

If, however, one agricultural nation whose production and consumption are thus diminished by war has already made considerable advances in population, civilisation, and agriculture, manufactures and factories will spring up in it in consequence of the interruption of international commerce by war. War acts on it like a prohibitive tariff system. It thereby becomes acquainted with the great advantages of a manufacturing power of its own, it becomes convinced by practical experience that it has gained more than it has lost by the commercial interruptions which war has occasioned. The conviction gains ground in it, that it is called to pass from the condition of a mere agricultural State to the condition of an agricultural-manufacturing State, and in consequence of this transition, to attain to the highest degree of prosperity, civilisation, and power. But if after such a nation has already made considerable progress in the manufacturing career which was opened to it by war, peace is again established, and should both nations then contemplate the resumption of their previously existing commercial intercourse, they will both find that during the war new interests have been formed, which would be destroyed by re-establishing the former commercial interchange. The former agricultural nation will feel, that in order to resume the sale of its agricultural products to the foreigner, it would have to sacrifice its own manufacturing industry which has in the meanwhile been created; the manufacturing nation will feel that a portion of its home agricultural production, which has been formed during the war, would again be destroyed by free importation. Both, therefore, try to protect these interests by means of imposing duties on imports. This is the history of commercial politics during the last fifty years.

It is war that has called into existence the more recent systems of protection; and we do not hesitate to assert, that it would have been to the interest of the manufacturing nations of the second and third rank to retain a protective policy and further develop it, even if England after the conclusion of peace had not committed the monstrous mistake of imposing restrictions on the importation of necessaries of life and of raw materials, and consequently of allowing the motives which had led to the system of protection in the time of the war, to continue during peace. As an uncivilised nation, having a barbarous system of agriculture, can make progress only by commerce with civilised manufacturing nations, so after it has attained to a certain degree of culture, in no other way can it reach the highest grade of prosperity, civilisation, and power, than by possessing a manufacturing industry of its own. A war which leads to the change of the purely agricultural State into an agricultural-manufacturing State is therefore a blessing to a nation, just as the War of Independence of the United States of North America, in spite of the enormous sacrifices which it required, has become a blessing to all future generations. But a peace which throws back into a purely agricultural condition a nation which is fitted to develop a manufacturing power of its own, becomes a curse to it, and is incomparably more injurious to it than a war.

It is fortunate for the manufacturing Powers of the second and third rank, that England after the restoration of the general peace has herself imposed a limit to her main tendency (of monopolising the manufacturing market of the whole earth), by imposing restrictions on the importation of foreign means of subsistence and raw materials. Certainly the English agriculturists, who had enjoyed a monopoly of supplying the English market with products during the war, would of course have painfully felt the foreign competition, but that only at first; at a later period (as we will show more particularly elsewhere), these losses would have been made up to them tenfold by the fact that England had obtained a monopoly of manufacturing for the whole world. But it would have been still more injudicious if the manufacturing nations of the second and third rank, after their own manufacturing power had just been called into existence, in consequence of wars lasting for twenty-five years, and after (in consequence of twenty-five years' exclusion of their agricultural products from the English market) that power has been strengthened so far that possibly it only required another ten or fifteen years of strict protection in order to sustain successfully free competition with English manufactures—if (we say) these nations, after having endured the sacrifices of half a century, were to give up the immense advantages of possessing a manufacturing power of their own, and were to descend once more from the high state of culture, prosperity, and independence, which is peculiar to agricultural-manufacturing countries, to the low position of dependent agricultural nations, merely because it now pleases the English nation to perceive its error and the closely impending advances of the Continental nations which enter into competition with it.

Supposing also that the manufacturing interest of England should obtain sufficient influence to force the House of Lords, which chiefly consists of large landed proprietors, and the House of Commons, composed mostly of country squires. to make concessions in respect of the importation of agricultural products, who would guarantee that after a lapse of a few years a new Tory ministry would not under different circumstances again pass a new Corn Law? Who can guarantee that a new naval war or a new Continental system may not separate the agriculturists of the Continent from the manufacturers of the island kingdom, and compel the Continental nations to recommence their manufacturing career, and to spend their best energies in overcoming its primary difficulties, merely in order at a later period to sacrifice everything again at the conclusion of peace?

In this manner the school would condemn the Continental nations for ever to be rolling the stone of Sisyphus, for ever to erect manufactories in time of war in order to allow them to fall to ruin in time of peace.

To results so absurd as these the school could never have arrived had it not (in spite of the name which it gives to the science which it professes) completely excluded politics from that science, had it not completely ignored the very existence of nationality, and left entirely out of consideration the effects of war on the commercial intercourse between separate nations.

How utterly different is the relation of the agriculturist to the manufacturer if both live in one and the same country, and are consequently really connected with one another by perpetual peace. Under those circumstances, every extension or improvement of an already existing manufactory increases the demand for agricultural products. This demand is no uncertain one; it is not dependent on foreign commercial regulations or foreign commercial fluctuations, on foreign political commotions or wars, on foreign inventions and improvements, or on foreign harvests; the native agriculturist has not to share it with other nations, it is certain to him every year. However the crops of other nations may turn out, whatever misunderstandings may spring up in the political world, he can depend on the sale of his own produce, and on obtaining the manufactured goods which he needs at suitable and regular prices. On the other hand, every improvement of the native agriculture, every new method of culture, acts as a stimulant on the native manufacture, because every augmentation of native agricultural production must result in a proportionate augmentation of native manufacturing production. Thus, by means of this reciprocal action, progress is insured for all time to both these main sources of the nation's strength and support.

Political power not merely secures to the nation the increase of its prosperity by foreign commerce and by colonies abroad, it also secures to it the possession of internal prosperity, and secures to it its own existence, which is far more important to it than mere material wealth. England has obtained political power by means of her navigation laws; and by means of political power she has been placed in a position to extend her manufacturing power over other nations. Poland, however, was struck out of the list of nations because she did not possess a vigorous middle class, which could only have been called into existence by the establishment of an internal manufacturing power.

The school cannot deny that the internal market of a nation is ten times more important to it than its external one, even where the latter is in the most flourishing condition; but it has omitted to draw from this the conclusion, which is very obvious, that it is ten times more important to cultivate and secure the home market, than to seek for wealth abroad, and that only in those nations which have developed their internal industry to a high degree can foreign commerce attain importance. . . .

Science must not deny the nature of special national circumstances, nor ignore and misrepresent it, in order to promote cosmopolitical objects. Those objects can only be attained by paying regard to nature, and by trying to lead the separate nations in accordance with it to a higher aim. We may see what small success has hitherto attended the doctrines of the school in practice. This is not so much the fault of practical statesmen, by whom the character of the national circumstances has been comprehended tolerably correctly, as the fault of the theories themselves, the practice of which (inasmuch as they are opposed to all experience) must necessarily err. Have those theories prevented nations (like those of South America) from introducing the protectionist system, which is contrary to the requirements of their national circumstances? Or have they prevented the extension of protectionism to the production of provisions and raw materials, which, however, needs no protection, and in which the restriction of commercial intercourse must be disadvantageous under all circumstances to both nations—to that which imposes, as well as to that which suffers from such restrictions? Has this theory prevented the finer manufactured goods, which are essentially articles of luxury, from being comprehended among objects requiring protection, while it is nevertheless clear that these can be exposed to competition without the least danger to the prosperity of the nation? No; the theory has till now not effected any thorough reform, and further will never effect any, so long as it stands opposed to the very nature of things. But it can and must effect great reforms as soon as it consents to base itself on that nature.

It will first of all establish a benefit extending to all nations, to the prosperity and progress of the whole human race, if it shows that the prevention of free trade in natural products and raw materials causes to the nation itself which prevents it the greatest disadvantage, and that the system of protection can be justified solely and only for the purpose of the *industrial development* of the nation. It may then, by thus basing the system of protection as regards manufactures on correct principles, induce nations which at present adopt a rigidly prohibitive system, as e.g. the French, to give up the prohibitive system by degrees. The manufacturers will not oppose such a change as soon as they become convinced that the theorists, very far from planning the ruin of existing manufactures, consider their preservation and their further development as the basis of every sensible commercial policy.

PART NINE
Location Theory

The same conditions of political decentralization and delayed economic development which made the Germany of the early nineteenth century receptive to protectionist views like those of List also encouraged the growth of other theories different from British classical economics.

The classical economists almost uniformly ignore problems of location; implicit in their economic theory is the assumption that all factors of production, commodities, and consumers are concentrated at a single spot, and problems of transportation can therefore be ignored. The first economist to develop a complete theory of location, paying systematic attention to these problems, was Johann Heinrich von Thuenen. In his *Isolated State* (1826) he considers the location of different forms of agricultural products in relation to the market and shows how the perishability and relative value of various items determines the distance from the market at which their production is most profitable.

Von Thuenen was largely ignored in English-speaking countries, where Ricardo's differential-rent theory was generally accepted during the nineteenth century. In Germany, however, his work was well known, and from Germany in 1909 came the first general location theory (one not confined to agriculture), that of Alfred Weber. In the tradition of von Thuenen, Weber analyzes the economic forces set in motion when people settle a primitive area and erect an isolated economic system. Unlike von Thuenen, however, he concentrates on industry. Using locational diagrams, he attempts to show how the eventual location of an industry will be determined by the relative effect upon costs of nearness to the market, nearness to raw materials, and nearness to an adequate supply of labor.

Among others who in recent years have contributed to location theory are the Swedish economist Palander, who developed and refined Weber's techniques, and August Loesch, who abandoned the assumption of perfect competition and tried to create a model applicable to monopolistic and imperfect-competition situations.

JOHANN HEINRICH VON THUENEN

(1783–1850)

One of the most original thinkers in the field of economics, Johann Heinrich von Thuenen, was born in 1783. His father was a landholder in Oldenberg, and he himself spent most of his life on his country estate. Except for a short period during which he attended the University of Goettingen he had no formal education. While still in his twenties he bought an estate in Mecklenburg, near Rostock, where he remained for the rest of his life, developing a model farm and collecting data useful in the formulation of his economic theory.

His chief work, *Der Isolierte Staat* (*The Isolated State*), first appeared in 1826. His "state" consists of a city surrounded by a uniformly fertile plain ending in an impassable wilderness which cuts off all contact with the outside world. The question then arises, How will the use of the land vary as the distance from the market (the city) increases? In developing his answer to this question, von Thuenen originated the first complete theory of location and anticipated the conclusions of the marginal-utility economists.

In general, his answer is that as one moves away from the city, production becomes less intensive and is devoted increasingly to items which are relatively nonperishable and which are valuable enough to bear the cost of transportation. Consequently, a series of concentric rings will develop around the city, each devoted primarily to a particular type of land-use. For instance, the first ring will be devoted to the production of items like green vegetables and dairy products, which (in the nineteenth century) are difficult to transport and store. Moving outward, in the subsequent rings one encounters forestry (for building materials and fuel), extensive farming of various types, in which grain becomes an increasingly important crop, and, in the fourth main ring, stock-raising.

The areas further away from the city cannot be cultivated as intensively as those close by because total costs would be excessive. Wherever his lands are located, the cultivator must decide just how many units of labor will bring him the maximum rent. That is to say, the expenditure of labor should stop at the point at which the cost of adding one more unit of labor exactly equals the value of the added yield. Without using the term, von Thuenen applied this concept of margin both to rent and interest and to a theory of wages. Unlike some of the earlier economists, however, he was interested in the welfare of the laborer and sought a way to include in his earnings some of the surplus over the margin which would otherwise be retained by the landlord. Eventually he evolved the formula $W = \sqrt{ap}$, where W is a just wage, a is the cost of labor, and p represents the product. He used this formula on his own estate and was so enamored of it that he wished it to be the only inscription on his tombstone.

Von Thuenen's contributions were largely ignored by English economists. In Germany, however, location theory was highly developed.

THE ISOLATED STATE *

Part I

Finally I should like to ask the readers who intend to devote their time and attention to this work not to be deterred by the initial assumptions which deviate from reality and not to consider them as arbitrary and

* From *Der Isolierte Staat,* Volumes I and II, reprinted from *Readings in Economics,* edited by K. William Kapp and Lore L. Kapp (New York, Barnes & Noble, Inc., 1949).

without purpose. On the contrary, these assumptions are necessary in order to clearly understand the effect which a given variable has. In actual life we have only a vague idea of the effect and operation of any single variable because it appears always in conflict with other variables operating at the same time. This procedure has thrown light on so many problems in my life and seems to me to be so generally applicable that I consider it the most important feature of my work.

ASSUMPTIONS

Let us suppose a very large town located in the center of a fertile plain void of navigable rivers or canals. The plain is of equal fertility and can be cultivated everywhere. At a considerable distance from the town lies an impenetrable wilderness which separates this state completely from the rest of the world. The town, which is the only one in the plain, has to provide the state with all manufactured products and the surrounding rural areas are the only suppliers of foodstuffs for the town. Salt and other mines which satisfy the need for salt and metals for the entire state are assumed to be located in proximity to the town.

THE PROBLEM

The question is, how will agricultural production develop under these circumstances and how will the shorter or longer distance from the city affect the cultivation of the soil if it is to be carried on in the most rational manner? Generally speaking, it is clear that close to the town there will be produced such crops as, in relation to their value, have a considerable weight or take much space and such crops as require transportation costs so heavy that they cannot be brought to the town from the more distant areas. Likewise, perishable goods will be produced in the neighborhood of the town because these have to be consumed while they are fresh. The greater the distance from the town, the more it will be found that land will be used for the production of goods which, in relation to their value, require lower costs of transportation. For this reason, there will develop pretty definite and distinct concentric circles around the town in which either this or that crop will be the main crop. Insofar as we consider the production of a particular crop the main goal of economic activities, we shall find in each of the different circles radically different economic arrangements since the whole character of economic life changes with the cultivation of a different crop.

FIRST CIRCLE: FREE ECONOMY

The more delicate garden products—which either cannot be transported on wagons over longer distances (like cauliflower, strawberries, lettuce, and others) and therefore have to be carried to the city, or which can be sold only in small quantities and while they are still fresh—can be cultivated only in closest proximity of the town. For this reason, truck gardening will take place in its immediate neighborhood.

In addition to the more delicate garden products, fresh milk is one of the needs of the town; its production also will have to take place in this first circle. For the transport of milk is not only difficult and expensive, but milk becomes, particularly in times of great heat, unpalatable after a few hours; therefore it cannot be brought to the city from great distances.

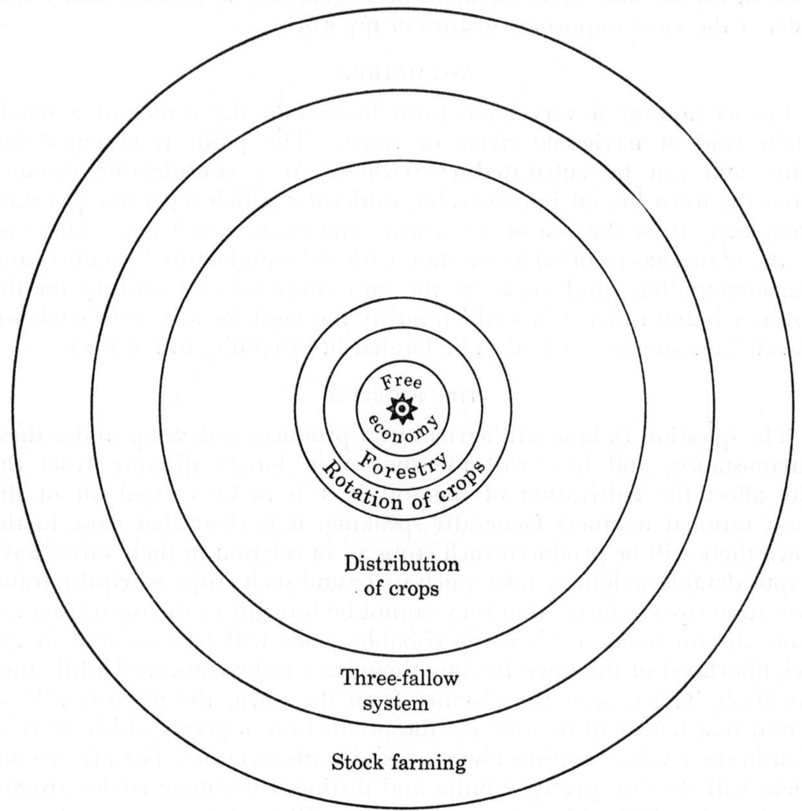

The price of milk must be at a level high enough so that the land used for its production would not yield greater returns if it were used for another product. Since rent is relatively high in this first circle, any crop which requires a great amount of labor is out of the question. The task, then, is to obtain a maximum amount of cattle feed with a minimum amount of labor. In other words, cattle will be fed in the barn, and an effort will be made to grow as much clover as possible; for, in a given area under these conditions, it is an established fact that a much greater number of cattle can be maintained if the clover is cut at the right time than if the same area is used for pasture, where the plants will be continuously disturbed in their growth through being crushed and eaten by the animals. But if the use of land for pastures should be preferred because of the greater cleanliness, the area devoted to pastures can be only small—and cattle, nevertheless, will have to be fed with green cut clover and the leftovers of potatoes, cabbage, turnips, etc.

The distinguishing characteristic of this circle is that manure is bought primarily from the town and is not produced on the estates themselves as in the more distant areas. This gives the first circle an advantage over the more distant ones and makes it possible to sell products which the other circles must retain in order to maintain the fertility of the soil.

In this circle the sale of hay and straw is, in addition to the production of milk, the main objective. Because the more distant areas cannot compete in these products, their price will have to be high enough to make the land yield the highest possible returns. Grains will play only a subordinate role because they can be produced more cheaply in the distant circles owing to lower rent and lower wages. Indeed, the cultivation of grain could be abandoned altogether if it were not for the fact that grain is required for the production of straw; by sowing it closely, part of the grain yield will be sacrificed in order to have more straw. In addition to milk, hay, and straw, the first circle must supply the city with all those products which would become too expensive if transported over larger distances. These are potatoes, cabbage, turnips, green clover, and others.

No part of the land in this first circle will be left fallow for two reasons: first, because rent is too high to keep part of the land unutilized; second, because the availability of unlimited amounts of manure makes it possible to raise the fertility of the soil in such a way that a maximum of output will be reached even without resting the soil by keeping it fallow.

Crops will be rotated in such a manner that each crop finds the soil in a favorable condition for it; however, crops which are disadvantageous for the area, in the light of the cost-price situation, will not be grown merely for the sake of rotation. In other words, we see here in operation the so-called free economy, which does not admit of any generalization and prediction as far as the rotation of crops is concerned.

The purchase of manure from the city is most advantageous for that part of the circle which is closest to the city. With greater distance from the city this advantage declines rapidly owing to the fact that not only the shipment of the manure but also the mode of cultivation of crops is rendered more expensive. With greater distance from the city, an area is soon reached where it becomes doubtful that it is still advantageous to obtain manure from the town. Finally, we reach that area where it is definitely more advantageous to produce the manure than to purchase it; here then is the limit of the first and the beginning of the second circle. . . .

THE MEANING OF RENT

We have to make a precise distinction between the revenues of the estate and the rent of the land as such. An estate is always equipped with buildings, enclosures, trees, and other objects of value which can be separated from the land. Revenues of an estate are, therefore, not wholly the result of the land, but are in part interest on the capital represented by these objects of value. Land rent is that part of the revenue of the estate which is derived from land as such and which remains after deduction of interest on the value of buildings, timber, enclosures, and of all other valuable objects separable from the land.

It is true, in buying an estate on which all buildings, trees, and enclosures have burned down, one calculates, in order to arrive at an estimate of its value, first the approximate net revenue of the estate after it has been equipped with buildings, etc.; but then one deducts the interest on the capital required for the construction of buildings, etc., and determines the purchase price in accordance with the remaining rent. . . .

These exists no definite relationship between the amount of capital invested in an estate and the rent from the land itself; in fact, any relationship may be observed depending upon differences in the prices of the product, in the quality of soil, etc. Adam Smith's concept of rent [revenue of the estate] in no way provides a standard of measurement of land-rent proper. By dividing the price of commodities into three parts—wages, interest, and rent, while rent in the sense in which Adam Smith uses the term includes again an indeterminate amount of interest on capital—one loses all conceptual clarity and precision. . . .

ACCORDING TO WHICH LAW IS THE PRICE OF GRAIN DETERMINED?

. . . The town can obtain the required amount of grain only if it pays a price high enough to cover at least the costs of production and transportation of the most distant producer whose grain it still requires. . . . Not only for our isolated state but also in reality is the price of grain determined in accordance with the following law: the price of corn must be high enough so that the land-rent on that estate which has the highest production and shipping costs and the output of which is still required to satisfy the demand does not fall below zero. In other words, the price of grain is neither arbitrary nor accidental but is determined in accordance with definite rules.

A permanent change of demand produces a permanent change in the price of grain. . . . If consumption increased, the hitherto cultivated area could no longer satisfy the demand of the town and the inadequate supply would cause prices to rise. As a result of the higher price, the more distant estates which so far had not yielded any land-rent would be enabled to obtain a surplus which is the basis of land-rent. The area beyond these estates could be cultivated with profit and the area under cultivation would expand up to the point where production of grain still yielded a land-rent. As soon as this happened, production and consumption would again be in equilibrium; but the price of grain would have been permanently raised. . . .

ORIGIN OF LAND-RENT

If rye from the most distant estates and rye from the area nearest the town were brought to the market, at the same time, it is impossible that the rye from the greater distance could be sold below a certain amount which measures its cost. [Thünen has assumed a price of one and one-half (1.5) "Taler" per "Scheffel" = 1.5 bushels of grain.] By contrast, the producer living nearer the town could sell his rye for approximately one-third the amount (½ Taler) and he would still cover his total costs of production and transportation. Now, the latter can neither be compelled nor be expected to sell a commodity of equal quality at a lower price than that which the former obtains. As far as the buyer is concerned, the rye produced near the town has the same value as the rye from the more distant estate, and it is of no concern to him which of the two has cost more to produce. What the producer from the neighborhood of the town obtains for his rye over and above his costs of production is for him a pure gain. Because this gain is permanent and is made year in and year out, the land of his estate yields an annual rent. In other words, the land-rent of an estate originates in the advantage which it has due to its location or to the quality of its soil over and above the poorest (most inferior) estate which is still needed to produce for the satisfaction of the demand. The value of this advantage, expressed in money or grain, measures the size of the rent. . . .

Part II

THE FORMATION OF CAPITAL THROUGH LABOR

Suppose that the worker, if diligent and thrifty, can produce by his hands 10 per cent more than he requires for his necessary subsistence—says 1.1*s* or 110*c* in the year. Then, after deducting what he must spend for his own support there remains 110*c* — 100*c* = 10*c*.

In the course of ten years, then, he may accumulate a store on which he can live for a year without working; or he may for the one whole year devote his labor to the making of useful tools—that is, to the creation of capital. Let us follow him now in the labor that creates the capital. With a hewn flint he manages to make wood into a bow and arrow. A fishbone serves for the arrow's point. From the stalk of the plantain and the fibrous covering of the cocoanut, he makes ropes or strings; the one he uses to string the bow, with the other he makes fishing nets. In the following year he applies himself again to the production of means of subsistence; but he is now provided with bow, arrows, and nets and with the help of those tools his work is much more remunerative, the product of his work much greater.

Suppose that in this way the product of his work, after deducting what he must spend to keep the tools in a state of good repair, rises from 110*c* to 150*c*; then he can put aside in one year 50*c*, and he needs to devote only two years now to the production of the means of subsistence, after which he can again spend a whole year in the making of bows and nets.

Now he himself can make no use of these, since the tools made in the previous year are sufficient for his needs; but he can lend them to a worker who up till now has worked without capital. This second worker has been producing 110*c;* if then he is lent the capital, on which the laborer who made it has expended a year's labor, his production, if he keeps up the value of the tools lent him and returns them, is 150*c.*[1] The extra production got by means of capital amounts therefore to 40*c*. This worker can consequently pay a rent of 40*c* for the borrowed capital, and this sum the worker who produced the capital draws in perpetuity for his one year's labor. Here we have the origin and ground of interest, and its relation to capital. As the wages of labor are to the amount of rent which the same labor, if applied to the production of capital, creates, so is capital to interest. In the present case the wage of a year's work is 110*c;* the rent brought in by the capital—that is, the result of a year's labor—is 40*c*. The ratio therefore is 110*c:* 40*c* = 100: 36.4, and the rate of interest is 36.4 per cent. . . .

The next question which arises is whether the accumulation of capital will continue or cease once the point has been reached where every laborer is provided with a capital equipment which required one year's labor for its production? If we contrast the laborer who owns bow, arrows, and nets with another who, although likewise only sparsely equipped with capital tools, is nevertheless provided with spades, hatchets, and nails . . . we shall discover—if we assume equal skill, equal diligence, equal effort and physical strength—a different productivity of labor. The second laborer who is equipped with spade and hatchet will have produced a greater product at the end of the year than the first. Spades and hatchets are themselves the products of human labor, and the incentive for their production and thus for the accumulation of capital lies precisely in the great usefulness which these tools possess. In producing bow and arrows, etc., the individual laborer did not need the aid of other laborers. In contrast, the production and processing of iron requires a division of labor; in this case, the workers engaged in the creation of capital must be regarded as an association formed for a common purpose and based upon an agreement as to the division of the common product.

Let us assume that finally every laborer is equipped with the aforementioned iron tool and that the tool used represents the annual output of

[1] But how can the object lent be kept and returned in equally good condition and equal in value? This, I admit, does not hold in the case of individual objects, but it certainly does in the totality of objects lent within a nation. If, e.g., any one hires out one hundred buildings for one hundred years, under the condition that the hirer annually erect a new building, the hundred buildings do retain equal value in spite of the annual wear and tear. In this inquiry we must necessarily direct our attention to the whole, and if here only two persons are represented as dealing with one another, it is simply a picture by which we may make clear the movement that goes on simultaneously over the whole nation.

one worker employed in the creation of capital; under these circumstances each laborer works with a capital, the production of which has required two years. This would still be a very incomplete provision of capital. Production of capital continues therefore so that each laborer is step by step provided with capital of 3, 4, 5, and more years of effort; with the greater amount of capital, output per man will increase more and more.

The question now is: Will the increase of output be proportional to the increase of capital? For example, will the application of a quantity of capital produced with a labor of three years yield a rent three times as great as the capital produced with one year's effort—that is to say $3 \times 40c = 120c$?

We know that not every amount of capital in the form of tools, machines, and buildings will make labor proportionately more effective. . . . No matter how useful an instrument or a machine may be, there is always a limit beyond which a further addition of the implement ceases to be useful and to yield a rent. Once this limit has been reached, labor devoted to the creation of capital has to be diverted to the production of other valuable commodities even though the latter may be less useful and may yield a smaller rent than the former.

In other words, the laborer engaged in the production of capital will, in his own interest, devote his labor first to the production of the tools and machines which contribute most to his physical power and render his work most effective; after these tools are available in sufficient quantities, he will turn to the production of implements and machines which, although still very useful, are nevertheless less effective than the ones produced first —with the result that he will have to be satisfied with a lower rent in the event that he loans the implement to others.

Here we come upon the reason for the phenomenon which will be of extreme importance in the following analysis—namely, *that each additional [unit of] capital yields lower rents than the preceding one.* This phenomenon can be observed also in those cases where, instead of the product of a year's labor, money is the standard of measurement of capital. . . .

WAGES AND INTEREST RATES

. . . As pointed out above, the newly added capital tends to increase output per laborer to a lesser degree than the preceding unit of invested capital. The question is now what series of figures will illustrate the decreasing efficiency of capital. Later, when the basic characteristics of such a series will have revealed themselves more completely, we shall make the examination of the relationship between capital and output per laborer the subject of a special study. For the time being, we have merely to find a series of figures which decline progressively, and this requirement is fulfilled by a geometrical series whose base number is a fraction like $9/10$, $(9/10)^2$, $(9/10)^3$, $(9/10)^4$. . . . In order to base our investigation upon definite figures and thereby be able to proceed further, I assume for the moment that the output of one laborer is increased as follows:

through the application of the first unit of capital representing one year's labor by 40c
through the application of the second unit of capital representing one year's labor by .... 9/10 × 40c = 36c
through the application of the third unit of capital representing one year's labor by .... 9/10 × 36c = 32.4c

Completion of this calculation yields the following table:

		Total Product
The labor of one man without capital produces,		110c
the first unit of capital (of one year's labor) adds	40c	150c
" 2nd " " " " " " " "	9/10 × 40 = 36c	186c
" 3rd " " " " " " " "	9/10 × 36 = 32.4c	218.4c
" 4th " " " " " " " "	9/10 × 32.4 = 29.2c	247.6c
" 5th " " " " " " " "	9/10 × 29.2 = 26.3c	273.9c
" 6th " " " " " " " "	9/10 × 26.3 = 23.7c	297.6c
" 7th " " " " " " " "	9/10 × 23.7 = 21.3c	318.9c
" 8th " " " " " " " "	9/10 × 21.3 = 19.2c	338.1c
" 9th " " " " " " " "	9/10 × 19.2 = 17.3c	355.4c
" 10th " " " " " " " "	9/10 × 17.3 = 15.6c	371c
" 11th " " " " " " " "	9/10 × 15.6 = 14.0c	385c
" 12th " " " " " " " "	9/10 × 14.0 = 12.6c	397.6c
" 13th " " " " " " " "	9/10 × 12.6 = 11.3c	408.9c
" 14th " " " " " " " "	9/10 × 11.3 = 10.2c	419.1c

In the nation here under discussion there is as yet no capitalist for whom others work, but everyone works for himself. There are, however, two classes of laborers—namely, those occupied with the creation of capital and those who work with loaned capital for their own account. I shall call laborers of the second group simply "laborers" without any distinguishing adjective. What these laborers retain of their output after deduction of the interest on capital loaned is the wage of their labor. If society finds itself in a state of economic development and wealth where everyone is provided with a capital of one year's labor, the lenders of that amount of capital obtain a rent of 40*c*. If the accumulation of capital continues to the point where each laborer has available an amount of capital of two years' labor, the lenders cannot obtain 40*c* for the second unit of capital but only 36*c* because the laborer cannot produce more than 36*c*; he would forgo its use if a higher rent were asked for it.

Now, will the laborers continue to pay 40*c* for the first unit of capital of one year's labor, or will they pay only 36*c* as they do for the second unit? If any one of the laborers engaged in the production of capital has completed the creation of the second unit and offers it to a laborer at a rent of 36*c*, the latter who has been paying his creditor 40*c* for the capital of one year's labor will serve notice to this creditor, discontinue his contract, and take the less expensive capital instead. The worker engaged in the creation of capital who has been served notice that his capital will no longer be used has, however, produced also a second unit of capital and now has two units of capital to lend. These two units can find no application if he is not willing to be satisfied with a rent of 36*c* per unit of capital of one year's effort. Since these units are completely useless to him, he will have to agree to lend both the first and the second unit of capital for 36*c*.

It may be objected that the capital which resulted from the first year's labor consists of implements of another kind than that produced by the second year's labor, and that consequently one cannot take the place of the other and can be no measure for it. This, however, is not the case; because of the increase of capital, the return from labor directed toward the creation of capital has declined in a proportion of 40:36 and labor devoted to the creation of capital is now remunerated at a rate of 36*c* no matter whether it is concerned with the production of bows and nets or of hatchets and spades. For if one kind of labor received a higher remuneration than the other, so many more laborers would devote themselves to this field of production that the equilibrium would be reestablished. Just as the price of a commodity cannot be different for different buyers and cannot be determined in accordance with the subjective value which it possesses for the individual buyer, but has to be the same for all commodities, so the price of capital—i.e., the rent one has to pay for it—cannot be fixed in accordance with the usefulness which the total capital yields to the person who obtains the loan. In other words, commodities of equal value—units of capital the production of which requires the same labor—cannot have two different prices at any given time.

The rent which the total capital yields if it is lent is determined by the use of the last unit of capital still applied. This is one of the most important conclusions in the theory of interest.

According to the preceding table, the laborer who works with a capital of two years' labor earns:

through his own labor	110*c*
through the application of the first unit of capital	40*c*
through the application of the second unit of capital	36*c*
Thus, the product of his labor amounts to	186*c*
of which amount he has to pay to the capitalist for two units of capital at 36*c*	72*c*
In other words, he keeps for himself	114*c*
as against 110*c* which he would keep if he had applied one unit of capital of one year's labor.	

If the laborer applies three units of capital of three years' labor, his return would be:

from his own labor	110c
from the first unit of capital	40c
from the second unit of capital	36c
from the third unit of capital	32.4c
Total	218.4c
of which amount he pays to the capitalist the rent of three units of capital at 32.4c =	97.2c
He retains	121.2c

Thus the diminution of rent in the course of the increase of capital accrues to the worker and has the effect of raising the wages of his labor.

ALFRED WEBER

(1868–)

Von Thuenen's theory of agricultural location later served as a model for further investigations in the location-theory field in Germany. At the turn of the century Alfred Weber used von Thuenen's method in the field of industrial location. For many years, economics was static, in respect to both time and space, so Weber's model involved comparative statics. Nevertheless, his was the first general location theory, as opposed to one restricted to agriculture. In 1909 appeared his *Reine Theorie des Standorts,* Part I of the great *Über den Standort der Industrien (On the Location of Industries*) which Weber edited and which proved to be a landmark in this field of investigation. Soon a multitude of Weber's students were writing able monographs expanding the master's findings or attempting to prove them empirically. Since there is no complete translation of Weber's work available in English, and since his theory is too comprehensive to permit of easy juxtaposition of excerpts, the editor preferred to present a concise summary of Weber's theory by Professor Andreas Predöhl of the University of Kiel.

THE THEORY OF LOCATION IN ITS RELATION TO GENERAL ECONOMICS *

I. THE PRESENT STATUS OF THE THEORY OF LOCATION

The problem of location of economic activities, though it is one of the most vital economic questions, has been dealt with as yet rather inadequately in economics. It is barely touched upon in the general systematic treatises. It is mentioned frequently, but treated poorly, in many monographs dealing with particular industries. In addition to these monographic studies there are a few discussions of "theories" of location (some of them historical, some of them theoretical, in nature) consisting merely of a catalogue of factors that determine location. These more or less descriptive classifications considerably fall short of the achievements of economic theory in general.

There are also some geographical studies. The question why a certain industry occupies a certain place on the surface of the earth at the first glance seems to be a purely geographical question. Accordingly, geographers everywhere have dealt with problems of location. But, without prejudice to the value of these investigations as geographical studies, it is to be emphasized that they cannot, from the nature of the case, serve the requirements of an economic theory of location. Economic geography, as long as it is true geography and not merely a name for a certain aspect of applied economics, is entirely different from, and by no means a substitute for, economics of location. The economist must approach this subject in terms of economic principles; he must reckon with geographical

* By Andreas Predöhl. From "The Theory of Location in Its Relation to General Economics," *Journal of Political Economy,* June, 1928, pp. 371–379.

facts, but he subordinates them to economic considerations, i.e., he interprets them as costs and prices, and he groups them into the general framework of economic relations.

Besides geographical investigations there are some noteworthy historical approaches to the problems of location. These are of great value as treatments of the historical or sociological background of an economic theory of location, but they are not theory of location proper.

There are only two outstanding economic theories of location. Both are German, but as a matter of chance rather than as a matter of a natural outgrowth of the trend of German economics. They are Heinrich von Thünen's theory of location of agriculture dealt with in his famous book *Der isolierte Staat,* and Alfred Weber's theory of location of manufacturing industries. Both have had little influence outside their country of origin. Although Thünen's work is quoted frequently, that particular part dealing with location is hardly mentioned in the non-German literature; and even in Germany, well known and frequently utilized though it is, it has not been improved significantly during the century of its existence, but has lived a rather unproductive life in German textbooks. Guided by Thünen's theory of location of agriculture, Weber noticed the lack of a satisfactory theory of location of manufacturing industries and built up in juxtaposition to Thünen's work his exhaustive theory on this subject, first published in 1909. In its field this theory had a great influence in Germany, not only stimulating monographic investigations of location, but also decidedly influencing all other succeeding investigations. But outside of Germany it seems to have become buried in the stacks of the larger libraries.

The contributions of Thünen and Weber are far superior to other achievements in this field. Although Thünen's theory in its empirical-realistic parts is no longer fully applicable because of the great changes in the factual situation, his scheme of circles of agricultural activities around a central town, supposed to be the consuming center, is as useful as ever, and is a stimulating starting-point for research in this field. Weber's theory has those weaknesses almost inevitably connected with a first approach to a new problem, but the theory of location of manufacturing industries has been improved but little since his work was published. Only two later attempts have been made to construct a general theory of location. Furlan's short mathematical sketch, however, covers but a small part of the field, while Engländer is too much biased in favor of his own general economic theory, which is a kind of economic psychology, to be able to give more than a system of cases. Any progress in this field of the theory of location may still be expected to start from the results attained by Alfred Weber.

II. ALFRED WEBER'S THEORY OF LOCATION

As Weber's theory is little known in non-German-speaking countries, it seems expedient to give, in the shortest compass possible, a survey of its main contents. This survey cannot, of course, include the elaborate arguments and the careful modifications made in the process of moving from abstraction to reality; it must be confined to the principles, with some emphasis upon those matters which serve as starting-points for further discussion.

The theory, in the main, is confined to the integrated processes of the manufacturing and marketing of distinct products. Modifications dealing with the cases of disintegrated processes, and processes through which different products are produced jointly, are made in the latter parts of the work. The factors determining location of such processes are conceived of as being specific advantages of cost in certain places. Since the attempt is made to construct a theory that can be applied everywhere and at any time (a so-called "pure theory"), Weber considers only those advantages of cost that affect all industries and do not depend on the peculiarities of our present economic system. In order to find those costs Weber imagines a manufacturing process changing its location, and watches the changes of cost.

Three groups of cost are found which generally change when locality is changed: cost of transportation, cost of raw material and fuel, and cost of labor. Weber simplifies this grouping by including cost of raw material and fuel in transportation cost. In other words, whenever the raw material or fuel at one source has a higher price than at another, he treats the situation in terms of the more expensive source being farther from the possible industrial location; with the result that only two kinds of cost need to be considered: cost of transportation and cost of labor. In dealing with these, transportation cost is first considered, and then labor cost is introduced. Fixed places of consumption and fixed centers of suitable labor are assumed.

Confining the attention solely to transportation cost as affecting the local distribution of manufacturing industries, these industries will be located at points of lowest transportation cost. Weber's method involves, first, selecting (from the standpoint of a given consuming center) those sources of raw materials and fuel that involve lowest transportation cost, thus forming what Weber calls the "locational figure" of the industry (a triangle, a quadrangle, or a more complicated figure, consisting of the consuming point and the sources of raw materials and fuel to be used). It involves, second, the determination of the point at which the lowest transportation cost occurs with respect to this locational figure, either at the consuming point or at one of the sources of raw materials or fuel, or at an intermediate point. This will be the point at which the manufacturing process is to be located.

The transportation cost is worked out by Weber in terms of the weights to be carried and the distances to be covered. All other factors determining transportation cost are translated into weight and distance by means of imaginary additions to, or subtractions from, the actual weights and distances. Therefore the locational figure as well as the localization of the manufacturing process with respect to its locational figure are determined by the lowest ton-miles. Each corner of the figure (namely, the consuming point and all sources of raw materials and fuel used) attract the manufacturing process with a distinct force. The consuming point pulls with the weight of the finished product; each source of raw material and fuel pulls with the weight of its material.

Whether the consuming point or some source of raw material or fuel will pull with the greater force depends decidedly on the characteristics of the material used. Some materials are converted into finished products without any loss of weight, whereas others undergo varying reductions of weight. Only weight-losing materials can attract the manufacturing process, because only in the case of such materials is the weight of the finished product lower than the weight of the material; in all other cases the weight of the finished product is at least equal to the weight of the material. However, not only the localized raw materials are to be considered, but also those raw materials that are to be found everywhere. These so-called "ubiquitous materials" do not have a part in forming the locational figure, but they do have a part in deciding the struggle between the point of consumption and the sources of localized raw materials; for the weight of the finished product is composed not only of that part of the weight of the *localized* materials that enters the weight of the finished product, but also of that part of the weight of the *ubiquitous* materials that enters the weight of the finished product, wherever location may be. Thus, location depends on the amount of weight-losing materials compared with the amount of ubiquitous materials entering the weight of the finished product.

Weber presents the results of his analysis of transportation costs in the form of principles, explains the application of the principles to possible cases, and devotes extended discussions to ramifications of the simple assumptions of the theory. He introduces, then, as a second factor of location, the differences of cost of labor in different places. The favorable centers of labor are conceived of as attracting the industries from the points of lowest transportation cost to points where labor cost is lower but transportation cost is higher. A less costly center of labor diverts the industrial process from its cheapest transportation point whenever the savings in labor cost at the favorable labor place are larger than the additional transportation cost. Weber incloses the point of lowest transportation cost in figures whose perimeters are lines connecting the points of equal additional transportation cost, so-called "iso-dapanes." Among them is one iso-dapane connecting the points where the additional transportation cost just counterbalances the savings of labor cost, the so-called "critical iso-dapane." If the favorable labor place is situated *within* the critical iso-dapane it diverts the manufacturing process; if it is *outside,* the manufacturing process remains at the point of lowest transportation cost.

As Weber explains the point of lowest transportation cost definitely and in quantitative terms by means of weight and distance, so also he introduces weight and distance to explain definitely and in quantitative terms the attraction exerted by the favorable labor place upon the manufacturing process. He finds, on the one side, that the attraction exerted by the favorable center of labor depends on the ratio of the labor cost of the manufacturing industry to the weight of the product: this he calls its "labor cost index." He finds, on the other side, that the divertibility of the manufacturing industry depends on the weight to be transported during the whole process of production: this he calls its "locational weight." And he finds that whether the industry actually will be diverted depends upon the two in combination—upon the ratio of the labor cost to the locational weight; this he calls its "labor coefficient."

Having discussed these two main factors of location, transportation cost and labor cost, Weber introduces another group of factors that he considers to be of a decidedly different nature—the "agglomerating" and the "deglomerating" factors. The transportation and labor factors distribute the industries over the surface, fixing them at places of what Weber calls lowest regional cost. The agglomerating factors tend to draw together the industries of such a region into more or less big agglomerations; the deglomerating factors have a dispersing effect. Agglomerating factors are such matters as savings of overhead cost, savings due to closer proximity of auxiliary industries, savings due to better connections with marketing organizations, etc.; the main deglomerating factor is rent, which increases with increasing local concentration of industries. Weber expresses both sets of factors, agglomerating and deglomerating, by a single resultant "agglomerating force" which he introduces as altering the distribution of manufacturing industries as that would be determined by the regional factors. This agglomerating force is treated as a factor quite independent of these other factors, although the attraction of industries to sources of raw materials by favorable transportation cost, or to favorable labor places by low labor cost, is itself a cause of agglomeration. The "agglomerating force" in reality merely reinforces an agglomeration caused by the transportation and labor factors.

The discussion of the agglomerating force resembles very much that of the labor factor. Here, also, "iso-dapanes" are constructed around the points of lowest regional cost; and a critical iso-dapane is conceived of as being the line where the attracting forces of the original points are counterbalanced by the agglomerating force. The main differences are that the places of agglomeration are not fixed places, as are the favorable labor places, and that their force of attraction is not fixed, as is that of the labor place. The agglomerating force will be effective only if critical iso-dapanes of a number of isolated processes have intersecting segments that offer savings of cost sufficient to counterbalance the additional cost of diversion to the new place. The complications arising from this question are discussed in detail but cannot be reproduced in this brief survey.

Weber does not, however, analyze the technical factors behind agglomeration in the way that he analyzes weight, distance, and the other technical factors behind transportation and labor cost; he regards the savings of agglomeration as made up of too many heterogeneous factors. He merely summarizes the cost that can be reduced by agglomeration as constituting what he calls the "form value" of the industry. This cost plays the same rôle in agglomeration that the labor cost plays in attracting the industry to the favorable labor place, and the discussion is built up in complete analogy to the discussion of the labor factor. He finds, on the one side, that the attraction of the places of agglomeration depends on the ratio of the form value cost to the weight of the product; this he calls its "form value index." He finds, on the other side, that the divertibility of the manufacturing industry depends on the weight to be transported during the whole process of production, i.e., its "locational weight," mentioned earlier. And he finds that whether the industry actually will be diverted depends upon the two in combination—upon the ratio of the form value to the locational weight; this he calls its "form coefficient."

For the rest, there will be found in Weber's work supplements, general conclusions, and, last but not least, attempts to incorporate the analytical results in a more complete picture. Weber concludes his discussion by applying his results to the general trend of economic evolution, putting his more or less mathematical theory into a historical and sociological setting. This aspect of his work is repeated and completed in a sketch of what he calls a capitalistic theory of location, in which, mainly, he explains the distribution of labor—a matter that could not appropriately be explained in the exposition of pure theory.

AUGUST LOESCH

(1906–1945)

Until recently, location theory has been based on assumptions of static conditions and general equilibrium analysis. The German economist August Loesch in 1940 presented a theory of space economy (*Die Räumliche Ordnung der Wirtschaft*) which could operate under conditions of *imperfect* competition, and, in fact, he attempted to tie his theory in with that of Professor Edward Chamberlin, discussed in Part XIV of this book. In 1938 he wrote a summary of his theory, and since this is the only work of Loesch available in English, it is presented as our selection.

THE NATURE OF ECONOMIC REGIONS *

Impressed by the accidental way in which states are created and smashed, we are looking out for a more natural and lasting spatial order of things. Geographical and cultural regions, however, are from an economic point of view just as artificial units of reference as states are. True enough, they all are of some economic relevance, but this does not alter their essentially non-economic nature. Important as their balance of payments, their price levels, their barter terms of trade may be for them, to *us* these averages and aggregates are entirely arbitrary and accidental. It is independent economic regions that we here discuss, regions not derived from but equivalent to those political, cultural, geographical units.

Even if we already knew the characteristics of economic regions—which we do not—their counterparts in the world of reality would be likely to differ more from each other than from an ideal picture. Hence studying the ideal region is both the only way to learn about the *essential,* and the first step towards investigating the *actual* structure of any real economic region. So we shall deal first with the theoretical nature of such regions, and second with their actual existence.

I

Let us start from very radical assumptions in order to prevent any spatial differences of an uneconomic origin from hiding in our starting points. We assume a vast plain with an equal distribution of raw materials, and a complete absence of any other inequalities, either political or geographical. We further assume that nothing but self-sufficient farmyards are regularly dispersed over that plain. How can any spatial differences possibly result from this initial situation?

Supposing one of those farmers tries to produce a certain commodity beyond his needs, will he be able to sell the surplus? He will be helped by the economies of large scale production, and handicapped by costs of

* From "The Nature of Economic Regions," *Southern Economic Journal,* July, 1938, pp. 71–78.

transportation. Will the balance be in his favor? If his neighbors all have a similar way of living, the demand curve of one of them will be typical for the others as well. Let us assume *d* in Figure 1 to be such an individual demand curve for beer. *OP* being the price at the center of production *P*, the demand of the people living there will be *PQ*. *PR* being the freight from *P* to *R*, the demand of each of the people living in *R* is *RS*. Farther out, at *F*, where the freight is *PF*, no more beer will be sold. Hence *PF* is the maximum shipping radius for beer, and the total demand within that radius is equal to the volume of the cone which we get by rotating the triangle *PQF* around *PQ* as axis. Figure 2 shows that cone. To repeat: its volume, corrected for the density of population, is equal to the

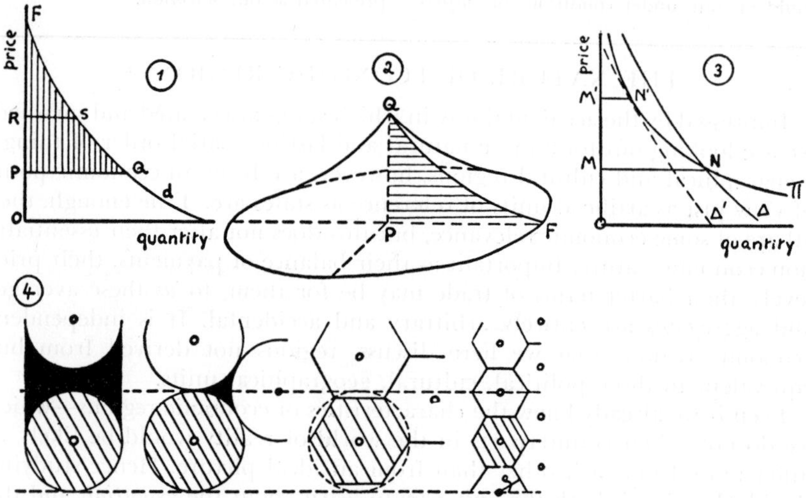

total possible demand if the price at the factory is *OP*. For other prices at the mill we get other cones of demand, and as a final result the curve Δ of Figure 3, that represents the total demand as a function of the price at the mill. π of Figure 3 is a so-called "planning curve," showing the minimum costs at which a given output could be produced if a new factory had to be built for that purpose. Only if the planning curve π intersects or is to the left of the total demand curve Δ, is it possible for our farmer to run a brewery. Otherwise he would produce at a loss.

The shape of a trading area, however, is not a circle, as we have so far assumed. For even if the whole country were filled up with such circular areas that are close enough to just touch each other, a number of people could still successfully try to enter the brewing business. For all the black corners in Figure 4 are left unused, and moreover, as has been shown by Chamberlin,[1] the size of the individual firm will be reduced from *MN* to

[1] For those not acquainted with Chamberlin's theory it may be worth while to point out that his argument is based mainly on two facts: (1) Due to product differentiation, of which differentiation of the seller's location is just a special case, the demand curve facing

M'N' (in Figure 3) without rendering it unprofitable. The way to make use of the corners is to change the shape of the area into a regular hexagon. This will shift the curve $\triangle$ slightly to the left, as the hexagon is somewhat smaller than the circle that circumscribes it. Moreover, by Chamberlin's operation the size of the hexagon will be reduced until it is so small that the corresponding demand curve $\triangle'$ just touches the offer curve in *N'*. Now apparently no more people can enter the brewing business.[2] As the largest possible shipping radius results in a total demand *MN,* so the necessary minimum radius must yield the demand *M'N'*. Figure 4 shows the development from the largest to the smallest possible shipping range.

Two other possibilities of avoiding black corners are conceivable, namely the square and the triangle. But it can be shown [3] that the hexagon has an economic advantage over both: it affords the larger demand per square mile, provided the total area is the same in all cases. *The hexagon is, therefore, the most economical shape for trading areas.* For every commodity, a trading area in the form of a hexagon with a characteristic inner radius ρ is necessary and sufficient to render the production of this commodity profitable.

The trading areas of the various products look like nets of such hexagons, from very small ones to very large ones, depending upon the product. We can throw these nets over our plain at random. In spite of the resulting disorder, every place on the plain would have access to every product. Several considerations, however, which can only be mentioned here, suggest a more orderly and at the same time more economical arrangement. In the first place, we lay our nets in such a way that all of them have one center of production in common. This point will enjoy all the advantages of a large local demand. Secondly, we turn the nets around this center so that we get six sectors where centers of production are frequent, and six others where they are scarce, as is shown on Figures 12 and 13. This arrangement does not deprive any place of its access to every product, and at the same time provides for the best lines of transportation. It can be

the individual seller is not horizontal (as in pure competition where the product is perfectly uniform) but has a negative slope. If e.g. the seller raises his price, not all his customers will buy from his competitors as in a perfect market. To a number of them the special advantages (e.g. of convenient location) offered by him will be worth the higher price. (2) As long as the demand curve is to the right of the cost curve the extra profits thus possible will attract new competitors. They will sell products slightly different from those already in the market, or, as in our case, locate their businesses at places more convenient for part of the buyers. This will shift the demand curves of the old establishments to the left until they just touch the cost curves and all extra profits are wiped out. (See E. Chamberlin, *The Theory of Monopolistic Competition.*)

2 We disregard here the possibility of reducing the area even more through spatial price discrimination.

3 Whilst a more accurate and detailed proof is too lengthy for this short paper, the plausibility of our assertion can readily be seen from the fact that the regular hexagon has the advantage over the circle of using up all the territory, without departing as far from the ideal circular shape as either square or triangle.

shown that the aggregate of freights is a minimum,[4] and the final result is a complicated but orderly system of market areas. How many of these self-sufficient systems will come into existence on our plain depends merely upon the commodity which has the largest necessary shipping radius, as long as there are no economic limits to the size of the central city.

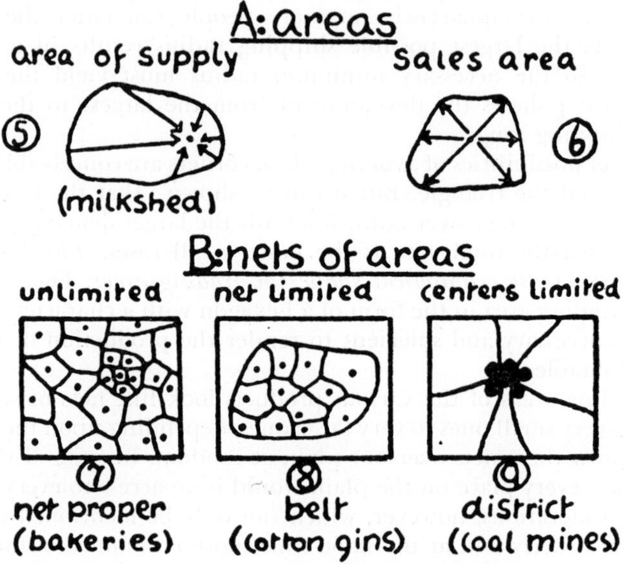

More striking about our result than any particulars is the fact that we suddenly have crowds of economic areas on a plain which we deprived of all spatial inequalities at the outset. We first have the hexagonal market area surrounding every center of production or consumption. Second, we have a net of such areas for every commodity. And third, we have a systematic arrangement of the nets of market areas of the various commodities. It is the latter, the self-sufficient system of market areas as shown in Figure 12, that I should like to call the ideal economic region. How much of it we find in reality will be discussed in the second part of the paper.

II

As soon as we drop the assumption of a uniform plain, the size and shape of our market areas evidently become irregular. Moreover, if we no longer stick to the supposition of a uniform product, the individual areas for the same line of production overlap, and may consequently be full of holes particularly near the periphery. Yet there are numerous instances left where our assumptions are roughly fulfilled and where our results, there-

4 As more centers of production coincide more consumers are able to buy from local mills than under any other arrangement of the nets. Not only the mileage of transports but the mileage of lines of transportation as well is reduced.

fore, must hold true without much modification, as factual investigations indeed seem to indicate.

Actually it is not quite accurate to compare the numerous market areas of a commodity to a net. Due to the overlapping just mentioned they often rather resemble fish scales or an irregular layer of slabs of slate. In spite of this modification the essential characteristics of a net are mostly

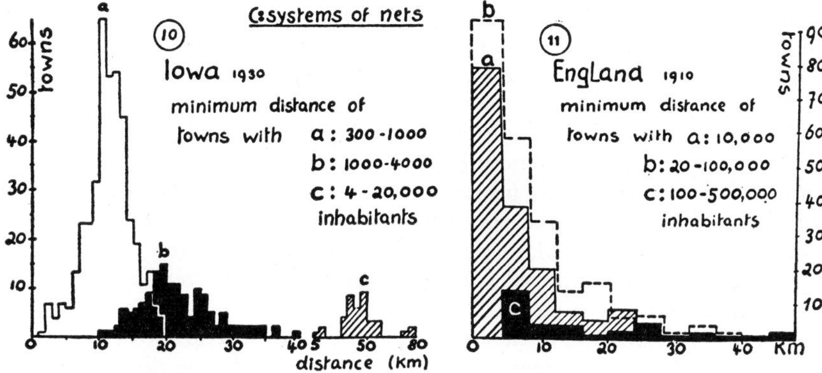

retained, and as a matter of fact most of the maps showing trading areas that were prepared either by scholars or by business men do not give any consideration to the overlapping at all. Far more important than this modification of the structure of our nets are the changes in their extension. In some instances, for which bakeries may serve as an example (Figure 7), the nets still cover the whole territory under consideration. In fact, a survey made by the author of about half the American industry

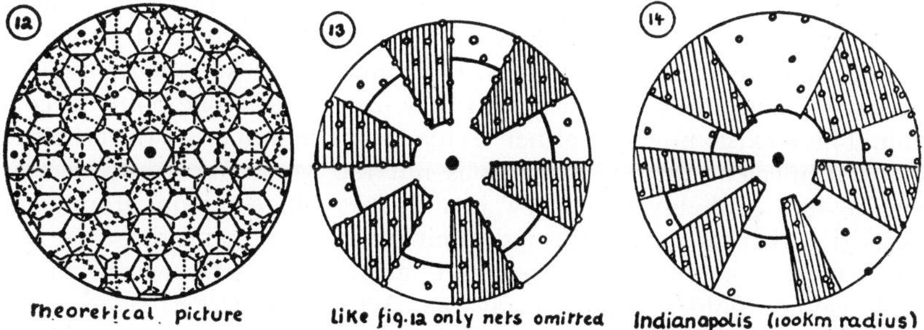

would seem to indicate that the importance of this type of production is rather underrated. Nevertheless, the very nets or at least their centers are often compressed on a relatively small space, and we may speak then of belts and districts respectively. The former case may be exemplified by the net of the areas of supply of the cotton gins that is naturally limited by the cotton belt. And an illustration of the concentration of the centers of production only are the mines in a coal district (see Figures 8 and 9 respectively). Instead of tracing out the areas, which is a very difficult task, we can show their character just as clearly by measuring the minimum distance of their centers from each other. This is done in Figures 10 and 11, not for centers of a single production but for towns of a supposedly similar economic function. In Iowa, with its rather equal distribution of production, the distances between towns increase with their size, just as in our theoretical picture based on assumptions approximately fulfilled in Iowa. In England, on the other hand, the cities cluster in the coal districts and show the same distance from each other irrespective of size. Such concentrations of the nets or their centers may have purely economic reasons such as the advantages due to the proximity of many establishments of the same branch. But it may also be a reflection of the limited geographical extension of factors of economic consequence although not of economic nature. It is worth noting, however, that these non-economic factors and their economic reflections are not co-extensive. For instance, the area where cotton *could* be grown is larger than the actual cotton belt.

In addition to the limited size of the nets, and the overlapping of the individual market areas, a third deviation from the ideal pattern is worth mentioning. In our theoretical deduction we had to cope with the problem of how the various nets should be located, while the distribution of the centers of production within a net was conspicuous for its regularity. Actually this too is a problem, and a very difficult one at that. Neither of the two traditional instruments of determining the geographical distribution of production can solve it: the theory of location proper cannot because it is applicable only to a single establishment, not to a whole industry; and the theory of comparative costs fails because it is applicable only to trade between men, not between countries. The only adequate solution of the location of all the interdependent centers of production is a system of locational equations which the author hopes to present later.

The systems of nets come off worse in the real world than either the nets or the individual market areas. It is simply impossible to arrange all the irregular nets in such a way that they have at least one point in common. There exists nowhere either a city with a complete set of industries or a self-sufficient region. But this is not the worst. We could at least imagine and probably find a few actual cases where regions trade their specialties with each other through their central cities, and through them alone. In such an instance a systematic arrangement of towns as in our ideal region would still be conceivable. Actually, however, small places which in every other respect entirely depend upon neighboring cities are the centers of large market areas. As far as their particular products are concerned, even metropolitan cities or the whole nation may be tributary to those little places, the industries of which neither need nor attract a large local market. Furthermore, while the regional system of nets of market areas centers in a large city, not every big city dominates such a system. Many mining towns, for instance, have not much of an economic function towards their hinterland. In contrast with such specialized cities, a regional center is characterized by a variety of production and trade that links it to the surrounding country. If, now, we disregard all the market areas of the type just described, a substructure of economic regions is left. They *differ* from the ideal pattern in the important respect that they are not self-sufficient; they *correspond* to the ideal inasmuch as they too are based (1) on the advantages of a large local concentration of production, consumption or trade; (2) on the most economical layout of lines of communication.

This regional substructure can be discovered almost everywhere but it is not everywhere of equal importance. Its importance can be measured by comparison with those market areas that have to be eliminated from a regional analysis as was just pointed out. To give some examples: regionalism prevails in southern Germany.[5] The distribution of the undisputed regional centers: Frankfurt, Nürnberg, München, Zürich, Strassburg, with Stuttgart in the middle is very regular. There should be one more center to the south of München but the Alps make this obviously impossible. The rise of München over Augsburg that had the advantage of an earlier start is worth noting. München has the better location from the point of view of our theory. It is right in the middle of the region, and at the proper distance from the neighboring centers. The German Ruhr district, on the other hand, hardly displays any regional pattern whatever. According as the systematic or the chaotic distribution of the nets of market areas prevails in a given case, we may stress or disregard the regional substructure. From this it follows that while the regional concept will be most realistic with respect to some parts of a country, it would be difficult and not very useful to divide a state up into its regions.

Finally, as to the relation between economic and other regions, it is essential for the regional system of market areas to have a center. In rare and particularly fortunate cases these economic centers are the same time cultural and political ones, thus becoming the true heart of their region, as Paris is for France.

III

To summarize, we found three main types of economic areas: simple market areas, nets of such areas, and systems of nets. Or, if we want to give a popular name to each, we may speak of markets, belts, and regions. In this sequence they become more complex, more self-sufficient, and unfortunately less real. On the one end there are the individual market areas, most simple, most real, and most dependent upon trade. The systems of market areas, or regions, on the other hand, are very complex; in an ideal case quite self-sufficient, but harder to find in reality. Many commodities are produced and traded outside of any system. And whatever systems we do find, overlap even more than the market areas of a single commodity. A clear economic region is a fortunate accident rather than a natural

[5] This has very ably been shown by Walter Christaller, *Die zentralen Orte in Süddeutschland.*

subdivision of states. Still, beneath a sphere of irregular market areas, we find a regional substructure of varying importance almost everywhere. Between the simple area of sale or supply and the full regional system is the net. The geographical extension of these nets or of their centers is often small. In this case these belts or districts of production or consumption are very conspicuous, but should still be distinguished from regions. A region is a system of *various* areas, an organism rather than just an organ.

PART TEN
Marginalism

Marginal-utility theory was founded in the last quarter of the nineteenth century by the trinity of Jevons, Menger, and Walras, all of whom came to substantially the same theoretical position although not acquainted with each others' work. Gossen (*Entwickelung der Gesetze des Menschlichen Verkehrs,* 1854) and Senior (*An Outline of the Science of Political Economy,* 1836) had anticipated much of the work of these founders, but Gossen's work was forgotten soon after publication, while Senior, after anticipating several important aspects of utility theory, rested his main value theory on the Ricardian subjective cost principle.

Utility theory first rose to dominance in Austria, where Menger was followed by his great pupils, von Wieser and Böhm-Bawerk. It made slow progress in Germany, and because the historical school was so well entrenched there, Menger had to defend his method in a series of polemic articles. The mathematical variant of the theory, introduced by Walras, did not meet with a warm reception in France but was taken over, expanded, and implemented by several important Italian economists—Pareto, Pantaleoni, and Barone. In England Jevons met with considerable opposition, perhaps because of his attacks on the firmly established followers of Mill, but by 1895 Smart's translation of von Wieser and Böhm-Bawerk into English, and Marshall's attempted synthesis of marginal and classical economics, gave impetus to popularization of the new doctrine. In the United States John Bates Clark, Frank Fetter, Irving Fisher, and Donald Davenport were among the economists who made original contributions in the field of marginal-utility economics.

The classical school had rejected desirability or utility as a measure of value because there seemed to be too great a discrepancy between the values of goods and their prices. Adam Smith had cited the classic example of water and diamonds, and Ricardo fell back on a comparison of gold and iron. It seemed to them that the less useful article commanded the higher price, and they apparently failed to realize that scarcity played a great role in value. Useful water, which commanded no price in England, lacked exchange value because of its abundance.

The new marginal theory seemed revolutionary when it first appeared. It explains prices on grounds of utility and regards cost of production as a derivative rather than a determinant of price. In other words, where goods come into being through production the factors of production are cost goods, to be valued in the same manner as the goods they produce.

Subjective utility is thus the determinant in both exchange value and distribution, since distribution involves only a pricing of the factors of production. The concept of the use value or utility of a single unit of a commodity being determined by the value of the last increment of a unit, or by the value of a unit in its least important use, is called *marginal utility.* This term was never used by any of the three founders of the theory, but it happened to be the term Smart used as a translation of the German *Grenznutzen* when he translated von Wieser's *Natural Value* in 1893, and it has become standard usage in English-speaking countries.

Another change in emphasis made by the marginalists was the focusing on subjective exchange value as the central problem of economics. In order to formulate a determinate theory, the marginalists claimed the philosophic right of abstract speculation and set up hedonistic psychology and a static capitalistic system as being universal. Thus, there has been a rebirth of the *homo economicus* of the classical school, but he is now shown as a force represented by supply and demand curves, to be regarded like the forces in treatises on mechanics. Because of the emphasis on hedonism, the marginal-utility school has also been called the psychological school. Man is depicted as a completely rational, predictable being, whose chief motivation is to obtain pleasure and avoid pain or sacrifice.

Like the classical school before it, marginalism came to the conclusion that the greatest well-being and the optimum utilization of resources would result from absolutely free competition. There was the same abhorrence of state intervention by most of the writers.

The marginalist school has been criticized on many grounds; these criticisms will be taken up in detail in our discussion of the historical and institutional schools later in this volume.

The important differences between the several writers of the marginalist school—between Jevons and Menger for example—are analyzed in the selections on the individual economists. Marshall has been included here because although his theory contains numerous different strains and facets, including many elements of classical economics, he seems basically a marginalist.

For reasons of convenience rather than logic, the marginalist and the mathematical schools have been separated. Those economists who, like Walras, use the mathematical method have been placed in a separate section even when their theory is essentially marginalist.

CARL MENGER

(1840–1921)

Carl Menger was the founder of the Austrian school, so-called because all of the writers in this aspect of economics were associated with the University of Vienna.

After graduation from the University of Vienna, Menger became a government economist; not until several years after the publication of his famous Grundsätze der Volkswirtschaftslehre (*Principles of Economics*) in 1871 was he offered his first university post. He led an uneventful academic life until his retirement in 1903, and his teaching lived on in the works of his pupils, especially Friedrich von Wieser and Eugen von Böhm-Bawerk. His actual influence was negligible outside of Austria because he allowed his book to go out of print and did not arrange for a second edition. There was no English translation until 1951.

Menger's theory of value differs in some important respects from the theory of Walras and Jevons, the other two founders of marginal-utility economics. First, he makes no use of mathematics and his examples are down-to-earth, so the average reader is not repelled by the presentation. Secondly, his subjective theory of value is not geared to utilitarianism or any other particular psychological school. Consequently, the growing attacks on hedonism, which led to the rejection of Jevons' work, had little effect on the influence of Menger's views. Lastly, Menger's approach is more explicitly atomistic than either Jevons' or Walras'. To Menger, the behavior of the individual holds the key to economic behavior, and the behavior of the economic order as a whole is then merely the sum of the behavior of the participating individuals.

Like later Austrian economists, Menger introduces a gradation of goods and services to explain the relationship of value to complementarity. That is, economic goods are divided into goods of "higher" and "lower" economic orders, depending on whether they are producers' or consumers' goods. Exchange is the result of differences in the relative subjective valuations of different individuals and is carried on until the ratio of utilities at the margin is the same for all individuals concerned. Menger does not use the term *marginal utility* (which was introduced by von Wieser), but he clearly had a marginal concept in mind.

Menger's theory of distribution, in which he developed a theory of "negative imputation," is a primitive form of the marginal-productivity theory. This traces the value of each productive factor by postulating a combination of the various factors minus the unknown factor and, through addition, arrives at the value of the factor and its product.

Menger was defender of the deductive abstract method of economic analysis in the famous *Methodenstreit* with Schmoller in the latter half of the nineteenth century. He insisted that both the inductive and deductive methods had their place in economic analysis, and as a matter of fact, Menger himself wrote several minor studies of a historical nature on the origins of money.

The following selections, drawn from his *Principles of Economics,* present Menger's approach to value, exchange, distribution, and economic method in general.

ECONOMY AND ECONOMIC GOODS *

Needs arise from our drives and the drives are imbedded in our nature. An imperfect satisfaction of needs leads to the stunting of our nature. Failure to satisfy them brings about our destruction. . . . Thus the attempt to provide for the satisfaction of our needs is synonymous with the attempt to provide for our lives and well-being. It is the most important of all human endeavors, since it is the prerequisite and foundation of all others.

In practice, the concern of men for the satisfaction of their needs is expressed as an attempt to attain command of all the things on which the saatisfaction of their needs depends. If a person has command of all the consumption goods necessary to satisfy his needs, their actual satisfaction depends only on his will. We may thus consider his objective as having been attained when he is in possession of these goods, since his life and well-being are then in his own hands. The quantities of consumption goods a person must have to satisfy his needs may be termed his *requirements.* The concern of men for the maintenance of their lives and well-being becomes, therefore, an attempt to provide themselves with their requirements.

But if men were concerned about providing themselves with their requirements for goods only when they experienced an immediate need of them, the satisfaction of their needs, and hence their lives and well-being, would be very inadequately assured.

If we suppose the inhabitants of a country to be entirely without stocks of foodstuffs and clothing at the beginning of winter, there can be no doubt that the majority of them would be unable to save themselves from destruction, even by the most desperate efforts directed to the satisfaction of their needs. But the further civilization advances, and the more men come to depend upon procuring the goods necessary for the satisfaction of their needs by a long process of production, the more compelling becomes the necessity of arranging in advance for the satisfaction of their needs—that is, of providing their requirements for future time periods. . . . Civilized men strive to ensure the satisfaction of their needs for many years to come. Indeed, they not only plan for their entire lives, but as a rule, extend their plans still further in their concern that even their descendants shall not lack means for the satisfaction of their needs. . . .

The concern of men for the satisfaction of their needs thus becomes an attempt to *provide in advance* for meeting their requirements in the future, and we shall therefore call a person's requirements those quantities of goods that are necessary to satisfy his needs within the time period covered by his plans.

There are two kinds of knowledge that men must possess as a prerequisite for any successful attempt to provide in advance for the satis-

* From *Principles of Economics,* translated by James Dingwall and Bert F. Hoselitz (Glencoe, Illinois, The Free Press, 1950).

faction of their needs. They must become clear: (a) about their requirements—that is, about the quantities of goods they will need to satisfy their needs during the time period over which their plans extend, and (b) about the quantities of goods at their disposal for the purpose of meeting these requirements.

All provident activity directed to the satisfaction of human needs is based on knowledge of these two classes of quantities. Lacking knowledge of the first, the activity of men would be conducted blindly, for they would be ignorant of their objective. Lacking knowledge of the second, their activity would be planless, for they would have no conception of the available means.

In what follows, it will first be shown how men arrive at a knowledge of their requirements for future time periods; it will then be shown how they estimate the quantities of goods that will be at their disposal during these time periods; and finally a description will be given of the activity by which men endeavor to direct the quantities of goods (consumption goods and means of production) at their disposal to the most effective satisfaction of their needs.

Human Requirements

REQUIREMENTS FOR GOODS OF FIRST ORDER (CONSUMPTION GOODS)

Human beings experience directly and immediately only needs for goods of first order—that is, for goods that can be used directly for the satisfaction of their needs. If no requirements for these goods existed, none for goods of higher order could arise. Requirements for goods of higher order are thus dependent upon requirements for goods of first order, and an investigation of the latter constitutes the necessary foundation for the investigation of human requirements in general. We shall first, accordingly, be occupied with human requirements for goods of first order, and then with an exposition of the principles according to which human requirements for goods of higher order are regulated.

The quantity of a good of first order necessary to satisfy a concrete human need [1] (and hence also the quantity necessary to satisfy all the needs for a good of first order arising in a certain period of time) is determined directly by the need itself (by the needs themselves) and bears a direct quantitative relationship to it (them). If, therefore, men were always correctly and completely informed, as a result of previous experience, about the concrete needs they will have, and about the intensity with which these needs will be experienced during the time period for which they plan, they could never be in doubt about the quantities of goods

[1] The term "concrete human need" recurs from time to time in the text. Menger uses the term to refer to a need (or rather a portion of a need) that is satisfied by consumption of a single unit of a good. When an individual consumes successive units of a good, Menger pictures him as satisfying successive "concrete needs" of diminishing psychological importance. At some points he adopts a different terminology, and speaks of the consumption of successive units of a commodity as successive "acts of satisfaction."

necessary for the satisfaction of their needs—that is, about the magnitude of their requirements for goods of first order.

But experience tells us that we are often more or less in doubt whether certain needs will be felt in the future at all. . . .

Even with needs that we know in advance will be experienced in the time period for which we plan, we may be uncertain about the quantities involved. We are well aware that these needs will make themselves felt, but we do not know beforehand in exactly what degree—that is, we do not know the exact quantities of goods that will be necessary for their satisfaction. But these are the very quantities here in question.

In the case of needs about which there is uncertainty as to whether they will arise at all in the time periods for which men make their plans, experience teaches us that, in spite of their deficient foresight, men by no means fail to provide for their eventual satisfaction. Even healthy persons living in the country are, to the extent permitted by their means, in possession of a medicine chest, or at least of a few drugs for unforeseen emergencies. Careful householders have fire extinguishers to preserve their property in case of fire, weapons to protect it if necessary, probably also fire- and burglar-proof safes, and many similar goods. Indeed, even among the goods of the poorest people I believe that some goods will be found that are expected to be utilized only in unforeseen contingencies.

The circumstance that it is uncertain whether a need for a good will be felt during the period of our plans does not, therefore, exclude the possibility that we will provide for its eventual satisfaction, and hence does not cause the reality of our requirements for goods necessary to satisfy such needs to be in question. On the contrary, men provide in advance, and as far as their means permit, for the eventual satisfaction of these needs also, and include the goods necessary for their satisfaction in their calculations whenever they determine their requirements as a whole.

But what has been said here of needs whose appearance is altogether uncertain is fully as true where there is no doubt that a need for a good will arise but only uncertainty as to the intensity with which it will be felt, since in this case also men correctly consider their requirements to be fully met when they are able to have at their disposal quantities of goods sufficient for all anticipated eventualities.

A further point that must be taken into consideration here is the *capacity* of human needs *to grow*. If human needs are capable of growth and, as is sometimes maintained, capable of infinite growth, it could appear as if this growth would extend the limits of the quantities of goods necessary for the satisfaction of human needs continually, indeed even to complete infinity, and that therefore any advance provision by men with respect to their requirements would be made utterly impossible.

On this subject of the capacity of human needs for infinite growth, it appears to me, first of all, that the concept of infinity is applicable only to unlimited progress in the development of human needs, but not to the quantities of goods necessary for the satisfaction of these needs during a given period of time. Although it is granted that the series is infinite, each individual element of the series is nevertheless finite. Even if human needs can be considered unlimited in their development into the most distant periods of the future, they are nevertheless capable of quantitative determination for all given, and especially for all economically significant, time periods. Thus, even under the assumption of uninterrupted progress in the development of human needs, we have to deal with finite and never with infinite, and thus completely indeterminate, magnitudes if we concern ourselves only with definite time periods.

If we observe people in provident activity directed to the satisfaction of their future needs, we can easily see that they are far from letting the capacity of their needs to grow escape their attention. On the contrary, they are most diligently concerned to take account of it. A person expecting an increase in his family or a higher social position will pay due attention to his increased future needs in the construction and furnishing of dwellings and in the purchase of carriages and similar durable goods. As a rule, and as far as his means will permit, he will attempt to take account of the higher claims of the future, not in a single connection only, but with respect to his holdings of goods as a whole. We can observe an analogous phenomenon in the activities of municipal governments. We see municipalities constructing waterworks, public buildings (schools, hospitals, etc.), parks, streets, and so on, with attention not only to the needs of the present, but with due consideration to the increased needs of the future. Naturally this tendency to give attention to future needs is even more distinctly evident in the activities of national governments.

To summarize what has been said, it appears that human requirements for consumption goods are magnitudes whose quantitative determination with respect to future time periods poses no fundamental difficulties. They are magnitudes about which, in activities directed to the satisfaction of their needs, men actually endeavor to attain clarity within feasible limits and insofar as a practical necessity compels them—that is, their attempts to determine these magnitudes are limited, on the one hand, to those time periods for which, at any time, they plan to make provision and, on the other hand, to a degree of exactness that is sufficient for the practical success of their activity.

REQUIREMENTS FOR GOODS OF HIGHER ORDER (MEANS OF PRODUCTION)

If our requirements for goods of first order for a coming time period are already directly met by existing quantities of these goods, there can be no question of a further provision for these same requirements by means of higher order. But if these requirements are not met, or are not completely met, by existing goods of first order (that is, if they are not met directly), requirements for goods of higher order for the time period in question do arise. These requirements are the quantities of goods of higher order that are necessary, in the existing state of technology of the relevant branches of production, for supplying our full requirements for goods of first order.

The simple relationship just presented with respect to our requirements for the means of production is to be observed, however, as we shall see in what follows, only in rare cases. An important modification of this principle arises from the casual interrelationships between goods.

It was demonstrated earlier that it is impossible for men to employ any one good of higher order for the production of corresponding goods of lower order unless they are able, at the same time, to have the complementary goods at their disposal. Now what was said earlier of goods in general becomes more sharply precise here when we take into account the available quantities of goods. It was shown earlier that we can change goods of higher order into goods of lower order, and thus use them for the satisfaction of human needs, only if we have the complementary goods simultaneously at our disposal. This principle can now be restated in the following terms: *We can bring quantities of goods of higher order to the production of given quantities of goods of lower order, and thus finally to the meeting of our requirements, only if we are in the position of having the complementary quantities of the other goods of higher order simultaneously at our disposal.* Thus, for instance, even the largest quantity of land cannot be employed for the production of a quantity of grain, however small, unless we have at our disposal the (complementary) quantities of seed, labor services, etc., that are necessary for the production of this small quantity of grain.

Hence requirements for a single good of higher order are never encountered. On the contrary, we often observe that, whenever the requirements for a good of lower order are not at all or are only incompletely met, requirements for each of the corresponding goods of higher order are experienced only jointly with quantitatively corresponding requirements for the other complementary goods of higher order. . . .

From what has been said, we derive the principle that, *with respect to given future time periods, our effective requirements for particular goods of higher order are dependent upon the availability of complementary quantities of the corresponding goods of higher order. . . .*

The further civilization progresses with a highly developed division of labor, the more accustomed do people in various lines become to producing quantities of goods of higher order under the implicit and as a rule correct assumption that other persons will produce the corresponding quantities of the complementary goods. Manufacturers of opera glasses very seldom produce the glass lenses, the ivory or tortoise-shell cases, and the bronze parts, used in assembling the opera glasses. On the contrary, it is known that the producers of these glasses generally obtain the separate parts from specialized manufacturers or artisans and only assemble these parts, adding perhaps a few finishing touches. The glass-cutter who makes the lenses, the fancy-goods worker who makes the ivory or tortoise-shell cases, and the bronze-worker who makes the bronze castings, all operate under the implicit assumption that requirements for their products do exist. And yet nothing is more certain than that the effective requirements for the products of each one of them are dependent upon the production of the complementary quantities in such a fashion that, if the production of glass lenses were to suffer an interruption, the effective requirements for the other goods of higher order necessary for the production of telescopes, opera-glasses, and similar goods, would become latent. At this point, economic disturbances would appear that laymen usually consider completely abnormal, but which are, in reality, entirely in accordance with economic laws.

THE TIME LIMITS WITHIN WHICH HUMAN NEEDS ARE FELT

In our present investigation, the only topic still remaining to be taken into consideration is the problem of time, and we must demonstrate for what time periods men actually plan their requirements.

On this question, it is clear, in the first place, that our requirements for goods of first order appear to be met, with reference to a given future time period, if, within this time period, we will be in the position of having *directly* at our disposal the quantities of goods of first order that we require. It is different if we must meet our requirements for goods of first or, in general, of lower order indirectly (that is, by means of quantities of the corresponding goods of higher order), because of the lapse of time that is inevitable in any production process. Let us designate as Period I the time period that begins now and extends to the point in time when a good of first order can be produced from the corresponding goods of second order now at our disposal. Let us call Period II the time period following Period I and extending to the point in time when a good of first order can be produced from the goods of third order now available to us. And similarly, let us designate the following time periods III, IV, and so on. A sequence of time periods is thus defined for each particular kind of good. For each of these time periods we have immediate and direct requirements for the good of first order, and these requirements are actually met since, during these time periods, we come to have direct command of the necessary quantities of the good of first order.

Suppose, however, that we should try to meet our requirements for a good of first order during Period II by means of goods of fourth order. It is clear that this would be physically impossible, and that an actual provision of our requirements for the good of first order within the posited time period could result only from the use of goods of first or second order.

The same observation can be made not only with respect to our requirements for goods of first order, but with respect to our requirements for all goods of lower order in relation to the available goods of higher order. We cannot, for example, provide our requirements for goods of third order during Period V by obtaining command, during that time period, of the corresponding quantities of goods of sixth order. On the contrary, it is clear that for this purpose we would already have had to obtain command of the latter goods during Period II.[2]

If the requirements of a people for grain for the current year were not directly covered in late autumn by the then existing stocks of grain, it would be much too late to attempt to employ the available land, agricultural implements, labor services, etc., for that purpose. But autumn would be the proper time to provide for the grain requirements of the following year by utilizing the above-mentioned goods of higher order. Similarly, to meet our requirements for the labor services of competent teachers a decade from now, we must already, at the present time, educate capable persons for this purpose.

Human requirements for goods of higher order, like those for goods of lower order, are not only magnitudes that are quantitatively determined in strict accordance with definite laws, and that can be estimated beforehand by men where a practical necessity exists, but they are magnitudes also which, within certain time limits, men do calculate with an exactness sufficient for their practical affairs. Moreover, the record of the past demonstrates that, on the basis of previous experience as to their needs and as to the processes of production, men continually improve their ability to estimate more exactly the quantities of the various goods that will be needed to satisfy their needs, as well as the particular time periods within which these requirements for the various goods will arise. . . .

THE THEORY OF VALUE *

The Original Measure of Value

THE DEPENDENCE OF SEPARATE SATISFACTIONS ON PARTICULAR GOODS (OBJECTIVE FACTOR)

. . . If we summarize what has been said, we obtain the following principles as the result of our investigation thus far:

(1) The importance that goods have for us and which we call value is merely imputed. Basically, only satisfactions have importance for us, because the maintenance of our lives and well-being depend on them. But we logically impute this importance to the goods on whose availability we are conscious of being dependent for these satisfactions.

(2) The magnitudes of importance that different satisfactions of concrete needs (the separate acts of satisfaction that can be realized by means of individual goods) have for us are unequal, and their measure lies in the degree of their importance for the maintenance of our lives and welfare.

[2] In this paragraph Menger implicitly assumes his time periods to be of equal duration. Reference to the definitions of the second paragraph preceding will confirm that this need not be the case.—TR.

* From *Principles of Economics,* translated by James Dingwall and Bert F. Hoselitz (Glencoe, Illinois. The Free Press, 1950).

(3) The magnitudes of the importance of our satisfactions that are imputed to goods—that is, the magnitudes of their values—are therefore also unequal, and their measure lies in the degree of importance that the satisfactions dependent on the goods in question have for us.
(4) In each particular case, of all the satisfactions assured by the whole available quantity of a good, only those that have the least importance to an economizing individual are dependent on command of a given portion of the whole quantity.
(5) The value of a particular good or of a given portion of the whole quantity of a good at the disposal of an economizing individual is thus for him equal to the importance of the least important of the satisfactions assured by the whole available quantity and achieved with any equal portion. For it is with respect to these least important satisfactions that the economizing individual concerned is dependent on the availability of the particular good, or given quantity of a good.

Thus, in our investigation to this point, we have traced the differences in the value of goods back to their ultimate causes, and have also, at the same time, found the ultimate, and original, measure by which the values of all goods are judged by men.

If what has been said is correctly understood, there can be no difficulty in solving any problem involving the explanation of the causes determining the differences between the values of two or more concrete goods or quantities of goods.

If we ask, for example, why a pound of drinking water has no value whatsoever to us under ordinary circumstances, while a minute fraction of a pound of gold or diamonds generally exhibits a very high value, the answer is as follows: Diamonds and gold are so rare that all the diamonds available to mankind could be kept in a chest and all the gold in a single large room, as a simple calculation will show. Drinking water, on the other hand, is found in such large quantities on the earth that a reservoir can hardly be imagined large enough to hold it all. Accordingly, men are able to satisfy only the most important needs that gold and diamonds serve to satisfy, while they are usually in a position not only to satisfy their needs for drinking water fully but, in addition, also to let large quantities of it escape unused, since they are unable to use up the whole available quantity. Under ordinary circumstances, therefore, no human need would have to remain unsatisfied if men were unable to command some particular quantity of drinking water. With gold and diamonds, on the other hand, even the least significant satisfactions assured by the total quantity available still have a relatively high importance to economizing men. Thus concrete quantities of drinking water usually have *no* value to economizing men but concrete quantities of gold and diamonds a *high* value.

All this holds only for the ordinary circumstances of life, when drinking water is available to us in copious quantities and gold and diamonds in very small quantities. In the desert, however, where the life of a traveller is often dependent on a drink of water, it can by all means be imagined that more important satisfactions depend, for an individual, on a pound of water than on even a pound of gold. In such a case, the value of a pound of water would consequently be greater, for the individual concerned, than the value of a pound of gold. And experience teaches us that such a relationship, or one that is similar, actually develops where the economic situation is as I have just described.

THE INFLUENCE OF DIFFERENCES IN THE QUALITY OF GOODS ON THEIR VALUE

Human needs can often be satisfied by goods of different types and still more frequently by goods that differ, not as to type, but as to kind. Where we deal with given complexes of human needs, on the one side, and with the quantities of goods available for their satisfaction, on the other side, the needs do not, therefore, always stand opposite quantities of homogeneous goods, but often opposite goods of different types, and still more frequently opposite goods of different kinds.

For greater simplicity of exposition I have, until now, omitted consideration of the differences between goods, and have, in the preceding sections, considered only cases in which quantities of completely homogeneous goods stand opposite needs of a specific type (stressing particularly the way in which their importance decreases in accordance with the degree of completeness of the satisfaction already attained). In this way, I was able to give greater emphasis to the influence that differences in the available quantities exercise on the value of goods.

The cases that now remain to be taken into consideration are those in which given human needs may be satisfied by goods of different types or kinds and in which, therefore, given human requirements stand opposite available quantities of goods of which separate portions are qualitatively different.

In this connection, it should first be noted that differences between goods, whether they be differences of type or of kind, cannot affect the value of the different units of a given supply if the satisfaction of human needs is in no way affected by these differences. Goods that satisfy human needs in an identical fashion are for this very reason regarded as completely homogeneous from an economic point of view, even though they may belong to different types or kinds on the basis of external appearance.

If the differences, as to type or kind, between two goods are to be responsible for differences in their value, it is necessary that they also have different capacities to satisfy human needs. In other words, it is necessary that they have what we call, from an economic point of view, differences in *quality*. An examination of the influence that differences in quality exercise on the value of particular goods is therefore the subject of the following investigation.

From an economic standpoint, the qualitative differences between goods may be of two kinds. Human needs may be satisfied either in a *quantitatively* or in a *qualitatively* different manner by means of equal quantities of qualitatively different goods. With a given quantity of beech-wood, for instance, the human need for warmth may be satisfied in a *quantitatively* more intensive manner than with the same quantity of fir. But two equal quantities of foodstuffs of equal food value may satisfy the need for food in *qualitatively* different fashions, since the consumption of one dish may, for example, provide enjoyment while the other may provide either no enjoyment or only an inferior one. With goods of the first category, the inferior quality can be fully compensated for by a larger quantity, but with goods of the second category this is not possible. Fir, alder, or pine can replace beech-wood for heating purposes, and if coal of inferior carbon content, oak bark of inferior tannin content, and the ordinary labor services of tardy or less efficient day-laborers are only available to economizing men in sufficiently large quantities, they can generally replace the more highly qualified goods perfectly. But even if unpalatable foods or beverages, dark and wet rooms, the services of mediocre physicians, etc., are available in the largest quantities, they can never satisfy our needs as well, *qualitatively,* as the corresponding more highly qualified goods.

When economizing individuals appraise the value of a good, it is purely a question, as we have seen, of estimating the importance of satisfaction of those needs with respect to which they are dependent on command of the good. The quantity of a good that will bring about a given satisfaction is, however, only a secondary factor in valuation. For if smaller quantities of a more highly qualified good will satisfy a human need in the same (that is, in a quantitatively and qualitatively identical) manner as larger quantities of a less qualified good, it is evident that the smaller quantities of the more highly qualified good will have the same value to economizing men as the larger quantities of the less qualified good. Thus equal quantities of goods having different qualities of the first kind will display values that are unequal in the proportion indicated. If, for example, in determining the value of oak bark we take account exclusively of its tannin content, and seven hundred-weight of one grade has the same effectiveness as eight hundred-weight of another grade, it will also have the same value as the latter quantity to the artisans using the bark. Merely reducing these goods to quantities of equal economic effectiveness (a procedure actually employed in the economic activities of men in all such cases) thus completely removes the difficulty in determining the value of given quantities of different qualities (so far as their effectiveness is merely quantitatively different). . . .

The question of the influence of different qualities on the values of particular goods is more complicated when the qualitative differences between the goods cause needs to be satisfied in qualitatively different ways. There can be no doubt, after what has been said about the general principle of value determination, that it is the importance of the needs that would remain unsatisfied if we did not have command of a particular good of not only the general type but also the specific quality corresponding to these needs that is, in this case too, the factor determining its value. The difficulty I am discussing here does not, therefore, lie in the general principle of value determination being inapplicable to these goods, but rather in the determination of the particular satisfaction that depends on a particular concrete good when a whole group of needs stands opposite goods whose various units are capable of satisfying these needs in qualitatively different ways. In other words, it lies in the practical application of the general principle of value determination to human economic activity. The solution to this problem arises from the following considerations.

Economizing individuals do not use the quantities of goods available to them without regard to differences in quality when these exist. A farmer who has grain of different grades at his disposal does not, for example, use the worst grade for seeding, grain of medium quality as cattle feed, and the best for food and the production of beverages. Nor does he use the grains of different grades indiscriminately for one purpose or another. Rather, with a view to his requirements, he employs the best grade for seeding, the best that remains for food and beverages, and the grain of poorest quality for fattening cattle.

With goods whose units are homogeneous, the total available quantity of a good stands opposite the whole set of concrete needs that can be satisfied by means of it. But in cases where the different units of a good satisfy human needs in qualitatively different ways, the total available quantity of a good no longer stands opposite the whole set of needs; each available quantity of specific quality instead stands opposite corresponding specific needs of the economizing individuals.

If, with respect to a given consumption purpose, a good of a certain quality cannot be replaced at all by goods of any other quality, the principle of value determination previously demonstrated applies fully and directly to particular quantities of that good. Thus the value of any particular unit of such a good is equal to the importance of the least important satisfaction that is provided for by the total available quantity of this precise quality of good, since it is with respect to this satisfaction that we are actually dependent on command of the particular unit of this quality.

But human needs can be satisfied by means of goods of different qualifications, although in qualitatively different ways. If goods of one quality can be replaced by goods of another quality, though not with the same effectiveness, the value of a unit of the goods of superior quality is equal to the importance of the least important satisfaction that is provided for by the goods of superior quality minus a value quota [3] that is greater:

[3] "*Werthquote.*" Menger presents the argument underlying this proposition at length on pages 370–372. But an explanatory note may perhaps be helpful due to the brevity and peculiar form of the present passage.

Assume that the least important satisfaction rendered by a unit of the superior good

(1) the smaller the value of the goods of inferior quality by which the particular need in question can also be satisfied, and (2) the smaller the difference to men between the importance of satisfying the particular need with the superior good and the importance of satisfying it with the inferior one.

Thus we arrive at the result that, even in cases in which a complex of needs stands opposite a quantity of goods of different qualities, satisfactions of given intensities always depend on each partial quantity or on each concrete unit of these goods. Hence, in all the cases discussed, the principle of value determination that I formulated above maintains its full applicability.

THE SUBJECTIVE CHARACTER OF THE MEASURE OF VALUE. LABOR AND VALUE. ERROR.

When I discussed the nature of value, I observed that value is nothing inherent in goods and that it is not a property of goods. But neither is value an independent thing. There is no reason why a good may not have value to one economizing individual but no value to another individual under different circumstances. The *measure* of value is entirely subjective in nature, and for this reason a good can have great value to one economizing individual, little value to another, and no value at all to a third, depending upon the differences in their requirements and available amounts. What one person disdains or values lightly is appreciated by another, and what one person abandons is often picked up by another. While one economizing individual esteems equally a given amount of one good and a greater amount of another good, we frequently observe just the opposite evaluations with another economizing individual.

Hence not only the *nature* but also the *measure* of value is subjective. Goods always have value to certain economizing individuals and this value is also *determined* only by these individuals.

The value an economizing individual attributes to a good is equal to

has an importance of 5 in Use A, that the least important satisfaction rendered by a unit of the inferior good in Use B has an importance of 2, and that a unit of the inferior good would render a satisfaction with an importance of 3 if it were to replace a unit of the superior good in Use A. Menger contends that the use-value of a unit of a superior good that can be replaced by an inferior good is equal, not to the importance of the least important satisfaction actually rendered by a unit of the superior good, but to the importance of the satisfactions dependent on continued command of that unit. In the present instance, if command of a unit of the superior good is lost and a unit of the inferior good is moved from Use B to Use A to take its place, the satisfactions lost to the consumer are: (1) a satisfaction in Use B with an importance of 2, which is lost because one less unit of the inferior good is employed in Use B, and (2) a satisfaction in Use A with an importance of 2 (the difference between the 5 units lost because one unit less of the superior good is employed in Use A and the 3 units gained because of the employment of a unit of the inferior good in its place). The use-value of a unit of the superior good is therefore 4, the sum of these two items. The "value quota" mentioned by Menger in the text is the difference between the least important satisfaction that the superior good would render in Use A and its use-value calculated in this way. The "value-quota" in this example is thus 5 minus 4, or 1.—TR.

the importance of the particular satisfaction that depends on his command of the good. There is no necessary and direct connection between the value of a good and whether, or in what quantities, labor and other goods of higher order were applied to its production. A non-economic good (a quantity of timber in a virgin forest, for example) does not attain value for men if large quantities of labor or other economic goods were applied to its production. Whether a diamond was found accidentally or was obtained from a diamond pit with the employment of a thousand days of labor is completely irrelevant for its value. In general, no one in practical life asks for the history of the origin of a good in estimating its value, but considers solely the services that the good will render him and which he would have to forgo if he did not have it at his command. Goods on which much labor has been expended often have no value, while others, on which little or no labor was expended, have a very high value. Goods on which much labor was expended and others on which little or no labor was expended are often of equal value to economizing men. The quantities of labor or of other means of production applied to its production cannot, therefore, be the determining factor in the value of a good. Comparison of the value of a good with the value of the means of production employed in its production does, of course, show whether and to what extent its production, an act of *past* human activity, was appropriate or economic. But the quantities of goods employed in the production of a good have neither a necessary nor a directly determining influence on its value.

Equally untenable is the opinion that the determining factor in the value of goods is the quantity of labor or other means of production that are necessary for their *reproduction*. A large number of goods cannot be reproduced (antiques, and paintings by old masters, for instance) and thus, in a number of cases, we can observe value but no possibility of reproduction. For this reason, any factor connected with reproduction cannot be the determining principle of value in general. Experience, moreover, shows that the value of the means of production necessary for the reproduction of many goods (old-fashioned clothes and obsolete machines, for instance) is sometimes considerably higher and sometimes lower than the value of the products themselves.

The determining factor in the value of a good, then, is neither the quantity of labor or other goods necessary for its production nor the quantity necessary for its reproduction, but rather the magnitude of importance of those satisfactions with respect to which we are conscious of being dependent on command of the good. This principle of value determination is universally valid, and no exception to it can be found in human economy.

The importance of a satisfaction to us is not the result of an arbitrary decision, but rather is measured by the importance, which is not arbitrary, that the satisfaction has for our lives or for our well-being. The relative degrees of importance of different satisfactions and of successive acts of satisfaction are nevertheless matters of judgment on the part of economizing men, and for this reason, their knowledge of these degrees of importance is, in some instances, subject to error. . . .

But what has been said by no means excludes the possibility that stupid men may, as a result of their defective knowledge, sometimes estimate the importance of various satisfactions in a manner contrary to their real importance. Even individuals whose economic activity is conducted rationally, and who therefore certainly endeavor to recognize the true importance of satisfactions in order to gain an accurate foundation for their economic activity, are subject to error. Error is inseparable from all human knowledge.

Men are especially prone to let themselves be misled into overestimating the importance of satisfactions that give intense momentary pleasure but contribute only fleetingly to their well-being, and so into underestimating the importance of satisfactions on which a less intensive but longer enduring well-being depends. In other words, men often esteem passing, intense enjoyments more highly than their permanent welfare, and sometimes even more than their lives.

If men are thus already often in error with respect to their knowledge of the subjective factor of value determination, when it is merely a question of appraising their own states of mind, they are even more likely to err when it is a question of their perception of the objective factor of value determination, especially when it is a question of their knowledge of the magnitudes of the quantities available to them and of the different qualities of goods.

For these reasons alone it is clear why the determination of the value of particular goods is beset with manifold errors in economic life. But in addition to value fluctuations that arise from changes in human needs, from changes in the quantities of goods available to men, and from changes in the physical properties of goods, we can also observe fluctuations in the values of goods that are caused simply by *changes in the knowledge* men have of the importance of goods for their lives and welfare.

The Laws Governing the Value of Goods of Higher Order

THE PRINCIPLE DETERMINING THE VALUE OF GOODS OF HIGHER ORDER

Among the most egregious of the fundamental errors that have had the most far-reaching consequences in the previous development of our science is the argument that goods attain value for us because goods were employed in their production that had value to us. Later, when I come to the discussion of the prices of goods of higher order, I shall show the specific causes that were responsible for this error and for its becoming the foundation of the accepted theory of prices (in a form hedged about with all sorts of special provisions, of course). Here I want to state, above all, that this argument is so strictly opposed to all experience that it would have to be rejected even if it provided a *formally* correct solution to the problem of establishing a principle explaining the value of goods.

But even this last purpose cannot be achieved by the argument in question, since it offers an explanation only for the value of goods we may designate as "products" but not for the value of all other goods, which appear as original factors of production. It does not explain the value of goods directly provided by nature, especially the services of land. It does not explain the value of labor services. Nor does it even, as we shall see later, explain the value of the services of capital. For the value of all these goods cannot be explained by the argument that goods derive their value from the value of the goods expended in their production. Indeed, it makes their value completely incomprehensible.

This argument, therefore, provides neither a formally correct solution nor one that conforms with the facts of reality, to the problem of discovering a universally valid explanation of the value of goods. On the one hand, it is in contradiction with experience; and on the other hand, it is patently inapplicable wherever we have to deal with goods that are not the product of the combination of goods of higher order. The value of goods of lower order cannot, therefore, be determined by the value of the goods of higher order that were employed in their production. On the contrary, it is evident that the value of goods of higher order is always and without exception determined by the prospective value of the goods of lower order in whose production they serve. The existence of our *requirements* for goods of higher order is dependent upon the goods they serve to produce having expected economic character and hence expected *value*. In securing our requirements for the satisfaction of our needs, we do not need command of goods that are suitable for the production of goods of lower order that have no expected value (since we have no requirements for them). We therefore have the principle that the value of goods of higher order is dependent upon the expected value of the goods of lower order they serve to produce. Hence goods of higher order can attain value, or retain it once they have it, only if, or as long as, they serve to produce goods that we expect to have value for us. If this fact is established, it is clear also that the value of goods of higher order cannot be the *determining* factor in the prospective value of the corresponding goods of lower order. Nor can the value of the goods of higher order already expended in producing a good of lower order be the determining factor in its present value. On the contrary, the value of goods of higher order is, in all cases, regulated by the prospective value of the goods of lower order to whose production they have been or will be assigned by economizing men.

The prospective value of goods of lower order is often—and this must be carefully observed—very different from the value that similar goods have in the present. For this reason, the value of the goods of higher order by means of which we shall have command of goods of lower order at some future time is by no means measured by the current value of similar goods of lower order, but rather by the prospective value of the goods of lower order in whose production they serve.

Suppose, for example, that we have the saltpetre, sulphur, charcoal, specialized labor services, appliances, etc., necessary for the production of a certain quantity of gunpowder, and that thus, by means of these goods, we shall have this quantity of gunpowder at our command in three months time. It is clear that the value this gunpowder is expected to have for us in three months time need not necessarily be equal to, but may be greater or less than, the value of an identical quantity of gunpowder at the present time. Hence also, the magnitude of the value of the above goods of higher order is measured, not by the value of gunpowder at present, but by the prospective value of their product at the end of the production period. Cases can even be imagined in which a good of lower or first order is completely valueless at present (ice in winter, for example), while simultaneously available corresponding goods of higher order that assure quantities of the good of lower order for a future time period (all the materials and implements necessary for the production of artificial ice, for example) have value with respect to this future time period—and vice versa.

Hence there is no necessary connection between the value of goods of lower or first order in the present and the value of currently available goods of higher order serving for the production of such goods. On the contrary, it is evident that the former derive their value from the relationship between requirements and available quantities in the present, while the latter derive their value from the prospective relationship between the requirements and the quantities that will be available at the future points in time when the products created by means of the goods of higher order will become available. If the prospective future value of a good of lower order rises, other things remaining equal, the value of the goods of higher order whose possession assures us future command of the good of lower order rises also. But the rise or fall of the value of a good of lower order available in the present has no necessary causal connection with the rise or fall of the value of currently available corresponding goods of higher order.

Hence the principle that the value of goods of higher order is governed, not by the value of corresponding goods of lower order of the present, but rather by the prospective value of the product, is the universally valid principle of the determination of the value of goods of higher order.

Only the satisfaction of our needs has direct and immediate significance to us. In each concrete instance, this significance is measured by the importance of the various satisfactions for our lives and well-being. We next attribute the exact quantitative magnitude of this importance to the specific goods on which we are conscious of being directly dependent for the satisfactions in question—that is, we attribute it to economic goods of first order, as explained in the principles of the previous section. In cases in which our requirements are not met or are only incompletely met by goods of first order, and in which goods of first order therefore attain value for us, we turn to the corresponding goods of the next higher order in our efforts to satisfy our needs as completely as possible, and attribute the value that we attributed to goods of first order in turn to goods of second, third, and still higher orders whenever these goods of higher order have economic character. The value of goods of *higher order* is therefore, in the final analysis, nothing but a special form of the importance we attribute to our lives and well-being. Thus, as with goods of first order, the factor that is ultimately responsible for the value of goods of higher order is merely the importance that we attribute to those satisfactions with respect to which we are aware of being dependent on the availability of the goods of higher order whose value is under consideration. But due to the casual connections between goods, the value of goods of higher order is not measured directly by the expected importance of the final satisfaction, but rather by the expected value of the corresponding goods of lower order.

THE PRODUCTIVITY OF CAPITAL

The transformation of goods of higher order into goods of lower order takes place, as does every other process of change, in time. The times at which men will obtain command of goods of first order from the goods of higher order in their present possession will be more distant the higher the order of these goods. While it is true, as we saw earlier, that the more extensive employment of goods of higher order for the satisfaction of human needs brings about a continuous expansion in the quantities of available consumption goods, this extension is only possible if the provident activities of men are extended to ever more distant time periods. . . .

Thus by relinquishing their collecting economy, and by making progress in the employment of goods of higher orders for the satisfaction of their needs, economizing men can most assuredly increase the consumption goods available to them accordingly—but only on condition that they lengthen the periods of time over which their provident activity is to extend in the same degree that they progress to goods of higher order.

There is, in this circumstance, an important restraint upon economic progress. The most anxious care of men is always directed to assuring themselves the consumption goods necessary for the maintenance of their lives and well-being in the present or in the immediate future, but their anxiety diminishes as the time period over which it is extended becomes longer. This phenomenon is not accidental but deeply imbedded in human nature. To the extent that the maintenance of our lives depends on the satisfaction of our needs, guaranteeing the satisfaction of earlier needs must necessarily precede attention to later ones. And even where not our lives but merely our continuing well-being (above all our health) is dependent on command of a quantity of goods, the attainment of well-being in a nearer period is, as a rule, a prerequisite of well-being in a later period. Command of the means for the maintenance of our well-being at some distant time avails us little if poverty and distress have already undermined our health or stunted our development in an earlier period. Similar considerations are involved even with satisfactions having merely the importance of enjoyments. All experience teaches that a present enjoyment or one in the near future usually appears more important to men than one of equal intensity at a more remote time in the future. . . .

The circumstance that places a restraint upon the efforts of economizing men to progress in the employment of goods of higher orders is thus the necessity of first making provision, with the goods at present available to them, for the satisfaction of their needs in the immediate future; for only when this has been done can they make provision for more distant time periods. In other words, the economic gain men can obtain from more extensive employment of goods of higher orders for the satisfaction of their needs is dependent on the condition that they *still have further quantities of goods available for more distant time periods* after they have met their requirements for the immediate future.

In the early stages and at the beginning of every new phase of cultural development, when a few individuals (the first discoverers, inventors, and enterprisers) are first making the transition to the use of goods of the next higher order, the portion of these goods that had existed previously but which until then had had no application of any sort in human economy, and for which there were therefore no requirements, naturally have non-economic character. When a hunting people is passing over to sedentary agriculture, land and materials that were not previously used and are now employed for the first time for the satisfaction of human needs (lime, sand, timber, and stones for building, for example) usually maintain their non-economic character for some time after the transition has begun. It is therefore not the limited quantities of these goods that prevents economizing men in the first stages of civilization from making progress in the employment of goods of higher orders for the satisfaction of their needs.

But there is, as a rule, another portion of the complementary goods of higher order, which has already been serving for the satisfaction of human needs in some branch or other of production before the transition to the employment of a new order of goods, and which therefore previously exhibited economic character. The seed grain and labor services needed by an individual passing from the stage of collecting economy to agriculture are examples of this kind.

These goods, which the individual making the transition previously used as goods of lower order, and which he might continue to use as goods of lower order, must now be employed as goods of higher order if he wishes to take advantage of the economic gain mentioned earlier. In other words, he can procure this gain only by employing goods, which are available to him, if he so chooses, for the *present* or for the *near future,* for the satisfaction of the needs of a *more distant time period.*

Meanwhile, with the continuous development of civilization and with progress in the employment of further quantities of goods of higher order by economizing men, a large part of the other, previously non-economic, goods of higher order (land, limestone, sand, timber, etc., for example) attains economic character. When this occurs, each individual can participate in the economic gains connected with employment of goods of higher order in contrast to purely collecting activity (and, at higher levels of civilization, with the employment of goods of higher order in contrast to the limitations of means of production of lower order) only if he already has command of quantities of economic goods of higher order (or quantities of economic goods of any kind, when a brisk commerce has already developed and goods of all kinds may be exchanged for one another) in the present for future periods of time—in other words, only if he possesses *capital.*

With this proposition, however, we have reached one of the most important truths of our science, the "productivity of capital." The proposition must not be understood to mean that command of quantities of economic goods in an earlier period for a later time can contribute anything by itself *during* this period to the increase of the consumption goods available to men. It merely means that command of quantities of economic goods for a certain period of time is *for economizing individuals* a means to the better and more complete satisfaction of their needs, and therefore a *good*—or rather, an *economic good,* whenever the available quantities of capital services are smaller than the requirements for them.

The more or less complete satisfaction of our needs is therefore no less dependent on command of quantities of economic goods for certain periods of time (on capital services) than it is on command of other economic goods. For this reason, capital services are objects to which men attribute value, and as we shall see later, they are also objects of commerce.

Some economists represent the payment of interest as a reimbursement for the abstinence of the owner of capital. Against this doctrine, I must point out that the abstinence of a person cannot, by itself, attain goods-character and thus value. Moreover, capital by no means always originates from abstinence, but in many cases as a result of mere seizure (whenever formerly non-economic goods of higher order attain economic character because of society's increasing requirements, for example). Thus the payment of interest must not be regarded as a compensation of the owner of capital for his abstinence, but as the exchange of one economic good (the use of capital) for another (money, for instance). . . .

THE VALUE OF COMPLEMENTARY QUANTITIES OF GOODS OF HIGHER ORDER

In order to transform goods of higher order [4] into goods of lower order, the passage of a certain period of time is necessary. Hence, whenever eco-

[4] It is not just the technical means of production that must be regarded as goods of higher order, but in general, all goods that can be used for the satisfaction of human needs only by being combined with other goods of higher order. The commodities that

nomic goods are to be produced, *command of the services of capital is necessary for a certain period of time.* The length of this period varies according to the nature of the production process. In any given branch of production, it is longer the higher the order of the goods to be directed to the satisfaction of human needs. But some passage of time is inseparable from any process of production.

During these time periods, the quantity of economic goods of which I am speaking (capital) is *fixed,* and not available for other productive purposes. In order to have a good or a quantity of goods of lower order at our command at a future time, it is not sufficient to have fleeting possession of the corresponding goods of higher order at some single point in time, but instead necessary that we retain command of these goods of higher order for a period of time that varies in length according to the nature of the particular process of production, and that we *fix* them in this production process for the duration of that period.

In the preceding section, we saw that command of quantities of economic goods for given periods of time has value to economizing men, just as other economic goods have value to them. From this it follows that the aggregate present value of all the goods of higher order necessary for the production of a good of lower order can be set equal to the prospective value of the product to economizing men only if the value of the services of capital during the production period is included.

Suppose, for example, we wish to determine the value of the goods of higher order that assure us command of a given quantity of grain a year hence. The value of the seed grain, the services of land, the specialized agricultural labor services, and all the other goods of higher order necessary for the production of the given quantity of grain will indeed be equal to the *prospective* value of the grain at the end of the year, but only on condition that the value of a year's command of these economic goods to the economizing individuals concerned is included in the sum. The *present* value of these goods of higher order by themselves is therefore equal to the value of the prospective product minus the value of the services of the capital employed. . . .

The value of goods to the economizing individuals concerned is, as I have already stated several times, the most important foundation of price formation. Now if, in ordinary life, we see that buyers of goods of higher order never pay the full prospective price of a good of lower order for the complementary means of production technically necessary for its production, that they are always only in a position to grant, and actually do grant, prices for them that are somewhat lower than the price of the product, and that the sale of goods of higher order thus has a certain

a wholesale merchant can pass on to the retailer only by employing capital, incurring costs of shipping, and using various specific labor services, must be regarded as goods of higher order. The same is true of the commodities in the hands of a grocer. Even the speculator adds to the objects of his speculation at least his entrepreneurial activities and his capital services, and often storage services, warehousing, etc., as well.

similarity to discounting, the prospective price of the product forming the basis of the computation,[5] these facts are explained by the preceding argument. . . .

The process of transforming goods of higher order into goods of lower or first order, provided it is economic in other respects, must also always be planned and conducted, with some economic purpose in view, by an economizing individual. This individual must carry through the economic computations of which I have just been speaking, and he must actually bring the goods of higher order, including technical labor services, together (or cause them to be brought together) for the purpose of production. The question as to which functions are included in this so-called *entrepreneurial activity* has already been posed several times. Above all we must bear in mind that an entrepreneur's own *technical* labor services are often among the goods of higher order that he has at his command for purposes of production. When this is the case, he assigns them, just like the services of other persons, their roles in the production process. The owner of a magazine is often a contributor to his own magazine. The industrial entrepreneur often works in his own factory. Each of them is an entrepreneur, however, not because of his technical participation in the production process, but because he makes not only the underlying economic calculations but also the actual decisions to assign goods of higher order to particular productive purposes. Entrepreneurial activity includes: (a) obtaining *information* about the economic situation; (b) economic *calculation*—all the various computations that must be made if a production process is to be efficient (provided that it is economic in other respects); (c) the *act of will* by which goods of higher order (or goods in general—under conditions of developed commerce, where any economic good can be exchanged for any other) are assigned to a particular production process; and finally (d) *supervision* of the execution of the production plan so that it may be carried through as economically as possible. In small firms, these entrepreneurial activities usually occupy but an inconsiderable part of the time of the entrepreneur. In large firms, however, not only the entrepreneur himself, but often several helpers, are fully occupied with these activities. But however extensive the activities of these helpers may be, the four functions listed above can always be observed in the actions of the entrepreneur, even if they are ultimately confined (as in corporations) to determining the allocation of portions of wealth to particular productive purposes only by general categories, and to the selection and control of persons. After what has been said, it will be evident

[5] Since, other things being equal, the productiveness of a production process and the value of the capital services used are both greater the longer the time period required for the production process, the values of goods of higher order, which can be employed in productive processes of very different duration, and which therefore assure us, at our choice, consumption goods of different values at different points in time, are brought into equilibrium with respect to the present.

that I cannot agree with Mangoldt, who designates "risk bearing" as the *essential* function of entrepreneurship in a production process, since this "risk" is only incidental and the chance of loss is counterbalanced by the chance of profit.

In the early stages of civilization and even later in the case of small manufactures, entrepreneurial activity is usually performed by the same economizing individual whose technical labor services also constitute one of the factors in the production process. With progressive division of labor and an increase in the size of enterprises, entrepreneurial activity often occupies his full time. For this reason, entrepreneurial activity is just as necessary a factor in the production of goods as technical labor services. It therefore has the character of a good of higher order, and value too, since like other goods of higher order it is also generally an economic good. Hence whenever we wish to determine the present value of complementary quantities of goods of higher order, the prospective value of the product determines the total value of all of them together only if the value of entrepreneurial activity is included in the total.

Let me summarize the results of this section. The aggregate present value of all the complementary quantities of goods of higher order (that is, all the raw materials, labor services, services of land, machines, tools, etc.) necessary for the production of a good of lower or first order is equal to the prospective value of the product. But it is necessary to include in the sum not only the goods of higher order technically required for its production but also the services of capital and the activity of the entrepreneur. For these are as unavoidably necessary in every economic production of goods as the technical requisites already mentioned. Hence the *present* value of the technical factors of production by themselves is not equal to the full prospective value of the product, but always behaves in such a way that a margin for the value of the services of capital and entrepreneurial activity remains.

THE VALUE OF INDIVIDUAL GOODS OF HIGHER ORDER

We have seen that the value of a particular good (or of a given quantity of goods) to the economizing individual who has it at his command is equal to the importance he attaches to the satisfactions he would have to forgo if he did not have command of it. From this we could infer, without difficulty, that the value of each unit of goods of higher order is likewise equal to the importance of the satisfactions assured by command of a unit if we were not impeded by the fact that a good of higher order cannot be employed for the satisfaction of human needs by itself but only in combination with other (the complementary) goods of higher order. Because of this, however, the opinion could arise that we are dependent, for the satisfaction of concrete needs, not on command of an individual concrete good (or concrete quantity of some one kind of good) of higher order, but rather on command of complementary quantities of goods of higher order, and that therefore only aggregates of complementary goods of higher order can independently attain value for an economizing individual.

It is, of course, true that we can obtain quantities of goods of lower order only by means of *complementary* quantities of goods of higher order. But it is equally certain that the various goods of higher order need not always be combined in the production process in fixed proportions (in the manner, perhaps, that is to be observed in the case of chemical reactions, where only a certain weight of one substance combines with an equally fixed weight of another substance to yield a given chemical compound). The most ordinary experience teaches us rather that a given quantity of some one good of lower order can be produced from goods of higher order that stand in very different quantitative relationships with one another. In fact, one or several goods of higher order that are complementary to a group of certain other goods of higher order may often be omitted altogether without destroying the capacity of the remaining complementary goods to produce the good of lower order. The services of land, seed, labor services, fertilizer, the services of agricultural implements, etc., are used to produce grain. But no one will be able to deny that a *given* quantity of grain can also be produced without the use of fertilizer and without employing a large part of the usual agricultural implements, provided only that the other goods of higher order used for the production of grain are available in correspondingly larger quantities.

If experience thus teaches us that some complementary goods of higher order can often be omitted entirely in the production of goods of lower order, we can much more frequently observe, not only that given products can be produced by varying quantities of goods of higher order, but also that there is generally a very wide range within which the proportions of goods applied to their production can be, and actually are, varied. Everyone knows that, even on land of homogeneous quality, a given quantity of grain can be produced on fields of very different sizes if more or less intensively tilled—that is, if larger or smaller quantities of the other complementary goods of higher order are applied to them. . . .

But even where particular goods of higher order cannot be replaced by quantities of other complementary goods, and a diminution of the available quantity of some particular good of higher order causes a corresponding diminution of the product (in the production of some chemical, for instance), the corresponding quantities of the other means of production do not necessarily become valueless when this one production good is lacking. The other means of production can, as a rule, still be applied to the production of other consumption goods, and so in the last analysis to the satisfaction of human needs, even if these needs are usually less important than the needs that could have been satisfied if the missing quantity of the complementary good under consideration had been available.

As a rule, therefore, what depends on a given quantity of a good of higher order is not command of an exactly corresponding quantity of product, but only a portion of the product and often only its higher quality. Accordingly, the value of a given quantity of a particular good of higher order is not equal to the importance of the satisfactions that depend on the whole product it helps to produce, but is equal merely to the importance of the satisfactions provided for by the portion of the product that would remain unproduced if we were not in a position to command the given quantity of the good of higher order. Where the result of a diminution of the available quantity of a good of higher order is not a decrease in the quantity of product but a worsening of its quality, the value of a given quantity of a good of higher order is equal to the difference in importance between the satisfactions that can be achieved with the more highly qualified product and those that can be achieved with the less qualified product. In both cases, therefore, it is not satisfactions provided by the whole product that a given quantity of a particular good of higher order helps to produce that are dependent on command of it, but only satisfactions of the importance here explained.

Even where a diminution of the available quantity of a particular good of higher order causes the product (some chemical compound, for example) to diminish proportionately, the other complementary quantities of goods of higher order do not become valueless. Although their complementary factor of production is now missing, they can still be applied to the production of other goods of lower order, and thus directed to the satisfaction of human needs, even if these needs are, perhaps, somewhat less important than would otherwise have been the case. Thus in this case too, the full value of the product that would be lost to us for lack of a particular good of higher order is not the determining factor in its value. Its value is equal only to the difference in importance between the satisfactions that are assured if we have command of the good of higher order whose value we wish to determine and the satisfactions that would be achieved if we did not have it at our command.

If we summarize these three cases, we obtain a general law of the determination of the value of a concrete quantity of a good of higher order. Assuming in each instance that all available goods of higher order are employed in the most economic fashion, the value of a concrete quantity of a good of higher order is equal to the difference in importance between the satisfactions that can be attained when we have command of the given quantity of the good of higher order whose value we wish to determine and the satisfactions that would be attained if we did not have this quantity at our command.

This law corresponds exactly to the general law of value determination since the difference referred to in the law of the preceding paragraph represents the importance of the satisfactions that depend on our command of a given good of higher order.

If we examine this law with respect to what was said earlier about the value of the complementary quantities of goods of higher order required for the production of a consumption good, we obtain a corollary principle: the value of a good of higher order will be greater (1) the greater the prospective value of the product if the value of the other complementary goods necessary for its production remains equal, and (2) the lower, other things being equal, the value of the complementary goods.

THE VALUE OF THE SERVICES OF LAND, CAPITAL, AND LABOR, IN PARTICULAR

Land occupies no exceptional place among goods. If it is used for consumption purposes (ornamental gardens, hunting grounds, etc.), it is a good of first order. If it is used for the production of other goods, it is, like many others, a good of higher order. Whenever there is a question, therefore, of determining the value of land or the value of the services of land, they are subject to the general laws of the determination of value. If certain pieces of land have the character of goods of higher order, their value is subject also to the laws of value determination of goods of higher order that I have explained in the preceding section.

A widespread school of economists has recognized correctly that the value of land cannot validly be traced back to labor or to the services of capital. From this, however, they have deduced the legitimacy of assigning land an exceptional position among goods. But the methodological blunder involved in this procedure is easily recognized. That a large and important group of phenomena cannot be fitted into the general laws of a science dealing with these phenomena is telling evidence of the need for reforming the science. It does not, however, constitute an argument that would justify the most questionable methodological procedure of separating a group of phenomena from all other objects of observation exactly similar in general nature, and elaborating special highest principles for each of the two groups.

Recognition of this mistake has led, therefore, in more recent times to numerous attempts to fit land and the services of land into the framework of a system of economic theory with all other goods, and to trace their values and the prices they fetch back to human labor or to the services of capital, in conformity with the accepted principles.

But the violence done to goods in general, and to land in particular, by such an attempt is obvious. A piece of land may have been wrested from the sea with the greatest expenditure of human labor; or it may be the alluvial deposit of some river and thus have been acquired without any labor at all. It may have been originally overgrown with jungle, covered with stones, and reclaimed later with great effort and economic sacrifice; or it may have been free of trees and fertile from the beginning. Such items of its past history are of interest in judging its *natural* fertility, and certainly also for the question of *whether the application of economic goods to this piece of land* (improvements) *were appropriate and economic.* But its history is of no relevance when its general economic relationships, and especially its *value,* are at issue. For these have to do with the importance goods attain for us solely because they assure us future satisfactions. . . .

Thus the newer attempts to explain the value of land or the services of land by reducing them to labor services or to the services of capital must be regarded only as an outcome of the effort to make the accepted theory of ground-rent (a part of our science that stands, relatively, in the least contradiction with the phenomena of real life) consistent with prevalent misconceptions of the highest principles of our science. It must further be protested against the accepted theory of rent, especially in the form in which it was expressed by Ricardo, that it brought to light merely an isolated factor having to do with differences in the value of land but not a principle explaining the value of the services of land to economizing men, and that the isolated factor was mistakenly advanced as the principle.

Differences in the fertility and situation of pieces of land are doubtless among the most important causes of differences in the value of the services of land and of land itself. But beyond these there exist still other causes of differences in the value of these goods. Differences in fertility and situation are not even responsible for these other causes, much less a general principle explaining the value of land and services of land. If all pieces of land had the same fertility and equally favorable locations, they would yield no rent at all, according to Ricardo. But although a single factor accounting for differences between the rents they yield may then indeed be absent, it is quite certain that neither all the differences between the rents nor rent itself would, of necessity, disappear. It is evident rather that even the most unfavorably situated and least fertile pieces of land in a country where land is scarce would yield a rent, a rent that could find no explanation in the Ricardian theory.

Land and the services of land, in the concrete forms in which we observe them, are objects of our value appraisement like all other goods. Like other goods, they attain value only to the extent that we depend on command of them for the satisfaction of our needs. And the factors determining their value are the same as those we encountered earlier in our investigation of the value of goods in general. A deeper understanding of the differences in their value can, therefore, also only be attained by approaching land and the services of land from the general points of view of our science and, insofar as they are goods of higher order, relating them to the corresponding goods of lower order and especially to their complementary goods.

In the preceding section we obtained the result that the aggregate value of the goods of higher order necessary for the production of a consumption good (including the services of capital and entrepreneurial activity) is equal to the prospective value of the product. Where services of land are applied to the production of goods of lower order, the value of these services, together with the value of the other complementary goods, will be equal to the prospective value of the good of lower or first order to whose production they have been applied. As this prospective value is higher or lower, other things remaining equal, the aggregate value of the complementary goods will be higher or lower. As for the separate value of actual pieces of land or services of land, it is regulated, like the value of other goods of higher order, in accordance with the principle that the value of a good of higher order will, other things being equal, be greater (1) the greater the value of the prospective product, and (2) the smaller the value of the complementary goods of higher order.[6]

The value of services of land is therefore not subject to different laws than the value of the services of machines, tools, houses, factories, or any other kind of economic good.

The existence of the special characteristics that land, and the services of land, as well as many other kinds of goods, exhibit is by no means denied. In any country, land is usually available only in quantities that cannot be easily increased; it is fixed as to situation; and it has an extraordinary variety of grades. All the peculiarities of value phenomena we are able to observe in the case of land and the services of land can be traced back to these three factors. Since these factors have bearing only upon the quantities and qualities of land available to economizing men in general and to the inhabitants of certain territories in particular, the peculiarities in question are factors in the determination of value that influence not just the value of land and the services of land but, as we saw, the value of all goods. The value of land thus has no exceptional character.

The fact that the prices of *labor services,* like the prices of the services of land, cannot without the greatest violence be traced back to the prices of their costs of production has led to the establishment of special principles for this class of prices as well. It is said that the most common labor must support the laborer and his family, since his labor services could not otherwise be contributed permanently to society; and that his labor cannot provide him with much more than the minimum of subsistence, since otherwise an increase of laborers would take place which would reduce the price of labor services to the former low level. The minimum of subsistence is therefore, in this theory, the principle that governs the price of the most common labor, while the higher prices of other labor services are explained by reducing them to capital investment or to rents for special talents.

But experience teaches us that there are labor services that are completely useless, and even injurious, to economizing men. They are there-

6 The value of a piece of land is determined by the expected value of its services, and not the other way around. The value of a piece of land is nothing but the expected value of all its future services discounted to the present. Hence the higher the expected value of the services of land and the lower the value of the services of capital (rate of interest), the higher will be the value of land. We shall see later that the value of goods is the foundation for their prices. That the price of land can regularly be observed to rise rapidly in periods of a people's economic growth is due to an increase in land rent on the one hand, and to a decrease in the rate of interest on the other.

fore not goods. There are other labor services that have goods-character but not economic character, and hence no value. (In this second category belong all labor services that are available to society, for some reason or other, in such large quantities that they attain non-economic character—the labor services connected with some unpaid office, for example). Hence too (as we shall see later) labor services of these categories cannot have prices. Labor services are therefore not always goods or economic goods simply because they are labor services; they do not have value as a matter of necessity. It is thus not always true that every labor service fetches a price, and still less always a *particular* price.

Experience also informs us that many labor services cannot be exchanged by the laborer even for the most necessary means of subsistence, while a quantity of goods ten, twenty, or even a hundred, times that required for the subsistence of a single person can easily be had for other labor services. Wherever the labor services of a man actually exchange for his bare means of subsistence, it can only be the result of some fortuitous circumstance that his labor services are exchanged, in conformity with the general principles of price formation, for that particular price and no other. Neither the means of subsistence nor the minimum of subsistence of a laborer, therefore, can be the direct cause or determining principle of the price of labor services.[7]

In reality, as we shall see, the *prices* of actual labor services are governed, like the prices of all other goods, by their *values*. But their values are governed, as was shown, by the magnitude of importance of the satisfactions that would have to remain unsatisfied if we were unable to command the labor services. Where labor services are goods of higher order, their values are governed (proximately and directly) in accordance with the principle that the value of a good of higher order to economizing men is greater (1) the greater the prospective value of the product, provided the value of the complementary goods of higher order is constant, and (2) the lower, other things being equal, the value of the complementary goods. . . .

The inadequacy of the theory that explained the prices of goods by the prices of the goods of higher order that served to produce them naturally also made itself felt wherever the price of the *services of capital* came in question. I explained the ultimate causes of the economic character and value of goods of this kind earlier in the present chapter, and pointed out the error in the theory that represents the price of the services of capital as a compensation for the abstinence of the owners of capital. In truth, the price that can be obtained for the services of capital is, as we have seen, no less a consequence of their economic character and of their *value*, than is the case with the prices of other goods. The determining

[7] A laborer's standard of living is determined by his income, and not his income by his standard of living. In a strange confusion of cause and effect, however, the latter relationship has nevertheless often been maintained.

principle of the value of the services of capital is the same as the principle determining the value of goods in general.[8]

The fact that the *prices* of the services of land, capital, and labor, or, in other words, rent, interest, and wages, cannot be reduced without the greatest violence . . . to quantities of labor or costs of production, has made it necessary for the proponents of these theories to develop principles of price formation for these three kinds of goods that are entirely different from the principles that are valid for all other goods. In the preceding sections, I have shown with respect to goods of all kinds that all phenomena of *value* are the same in nature and origin, and that the magnitude of value is *always* governed according to the same principles. Moreover, as we shall see in the next two chapters, the *price* of a good is a consequence of its *value* to economizing men, and the magnitude of its price is always determined by the magnitude of its value. It is also evident, therefore, that rent, interest, and wages are all regulated according to the same general principles. In the present section, however, I have dealt merely with the *value* of the services of land, capital, and labor. On the basis of the results obtained here I shall state the principles according to which the prices of these goods are governed after I have explained the general theory of price.

One of the strangest questions ever made the subject of scientific debate is whether rent and interest are justified from an ethical point of view or whether they are "immoral." Among other things, our science has the task of exploring why and under what conditions the services of land and of capital display economic character, attain value, and can be exchanged for quantities of other economic goods (prices). But it seems to me that the question of the legal or moral character of these facts is beyond the sphere of our science. Wherever the services of land and of capital bear a price, it is always as a consequence of their value, and their value to men is not the result of arbitrary judgments, but a necessary consequence of their economic character. The prices of these goods (the services of land and of capital) are therefore the necessary products of the economic situation under which they arise, and will be more certainly obtained the more developed the legal system of a people and the more upright its public morals.

It may well appear deplorable to a lover of mankind that possession of capital or a piece of land often provides the owner a higher income for a given period of time than the income received by a laborer for the most strenuous activity during the same period. Yet the cause of this is not immoral, but simply that the satisfaction of more important human needs depends upon the services of the given amount of capital or piece of land than upon the services of the laborer. The agitation of those who

[8] A special characteristic of *price formation* in the case of the services of capital is due . . . to the fact that these services cannot ordinarily be sold without transferring the capital itself into the hands of the buyer of the services of capital. There is a resulting risk for the owner of the capital for which he must be compensated by a premium.

would like to see society allot a larger share of the available consumption goods to laborers than at present really constitutes, therefore, a demand for nothing else than paying labor above its value. For if the demand for higher wages is not coupled with a program for the more thorough training of workers, or if it is not confined to advocacy of freer competition, it requires that workers be paid not in accordance with the value of their services to society, but rather with a view to providing them with a more comfortable standard of living, and achieving a more equal distribution of consumption goods and of the burdens of life. A solution of the problem on this basis, however, would undoubtedly require a complete transformation of our social order.

FRIEDRICH VON WIESER

(1851–1926)

Friedrich von Wieser, perhaps the greatest disciple of Carl Menger, was born in Vienna and trained in law and economics. His first teaching post was at the University of Prague; in 1903 he became a professor at the University of Vienna. He also held high posts in the Austrian government, serving at one time as minister of commerce.

In 1889, while still at the University of Prague, he published *Der Natürliche Werth* (*Natural Value*), which several critics have regarded as the most competent summary of Austrian doctrine available.

In 1914 he published his *Theorie der Gesellschaftlichen Wirtschaft* (*Social Economics*) as the theoretical part of a great German-Austrian coöperative treatise on social economics, under the direction of Max Weber. Here he took upon himself the task of analyzing the entire range of economic doctrine from the standpoint of Austrian theory. He passed from the economy of the individual (*i.e.*, simple economy) to the economy of the group (*i.e.*, social economy), to the state economy, and finally, to the world economy.

Von Wieser's original contributions to Austrian theory lie mainly in the fields of cost and distribution. His theory of alternative opportunity costs or transfer costs is notably different from Marshall's cost-of-production theory. Costs, he showed, are not prices necessary to evoke supplies of the factors of production, but payments that are needed to attract the productive factors from alternative uses. Value is a maximization of alternative opportunities, and the multitude of alternative uses will determine the final position and value of the various cost items. As defined in monetary terms, von Wieser's theory states that the opportunity cost of any commodity is the amount of money necessary to induce employment of the factors of production in this particular task, rather than elsewhere.

This theory of cost marked a radical departure from the classical traditions. The Austrians assumed a fixed stock of cost factors and explained the value of the individual cost factor in terms of the value of the products. Classical theorists, on the other hand, occupied themselves with an explanation of the cost factors as such and estimated the value of a product by the extent that such factors became incorporated in the product. Cost problems became for the Austrians essentially a question of *imputation,* that is, of allocating the value of the product among the factors in the productive process.

Von Wieser's theory of opportunity costs completed the structure of Austrian economics and was soon adopted by other writers, such as Wicksteed and Davenport. It is now an accepted part of the modern theory of distribution.

In the first selection we have a restatement of the theory of the Austrian school written especially for English readers by von Wieser in 1891.

THE AUSTRIAN SCHOOL AND THE THEORY OF VALUE *

The agents of production, land, capital, and labour, derive their value from the value of their products, ultimately, therefore, from the utility of those products. As stock is valued by the expected dividend, so is the field by the expected crop. A simple idea; yet thereby hangs one of the weightiest problems. Land, capital, and labour yield a return only

* From "The Austrian School and the Theory of Value," *Economic Journal,* 1891, pp. 110–121.

by their combined agency. Now what is the clue to the distribution amongst the separate effective factors of this joint return? The comparison with stocks and dividends is of no further use to us here, for one share in an investment is like another, while land, capital and labour are diverse. Even if labour alone be considered, the difficulty still confronts us. How are we to divide a machine, constructed by a number of labourers according to the instructions and under the direction of the inventor, so as to refer every part to its true originator?

Theorists have hitherto set down this problem as insoluble, and insoluble it is as commonly stated. It is impossible, to put it briefly, to give a reply to the question as to which part of the child is derived from the father and which from the mother. The question in itself is an absurdity. But it is just in this sense that the problem does not admit of statement, if it is to be correctly stated in the light of practical economy. What is required in economy is, not physical division of the product amongst all its creative factors, but the practical *imputation* of it, imputation in the sense used by a magistrate in speaking of a legal 'charge.' A sophist might maintain the impossibility of determining, amongst the thousand conditions, without the conjunction of which a murder could not have been effected, what share in the deed fell on the murderer; the judge, unperplexed by such scruples, sifts those thousand causes solely to get at the responsible author, and charges him with the whole of the deed. Who would accuse him of offending nature and logic thereby? And as he is concerned with the responsible author, so in economy, it is always amongst the thousand implicated causes with the practically determining factor that we have to do.

A field cultivated with the same expenditure of capital and labour as another field of greater fertility yields a larger return. This surplus crop is by no means produced by the field alone, capital and labour as well are wrought into it; nevertheless every agriculturist will rightly charge not the capital nor the labour with the crop, but, simply and solely, the better field, the value of which is raised by just the amount of the surplus. Such a judgment, so far from being illogical, embodies a great practical truth. In imputing the return by this method, I am enabled to find the correct adjustment of the economic measurement, which has to be carried out in the case of the commodities of production. It would, for example, be impossible for me to decide whether to purchase a machine and what price to consent to give for it, if I did not know how to calculate the work it would do for me, *i.e.*, what share in the total return to my undertaking should be imputed to it in particular. Without the art of imputation there would be no business calculations, no economic method, no economy, just as without the system of criminal charge, there could be no society. Fortunately the practice of it is universal, everyone, be he never so stupid and inexperienced, applying it though with varying degrees of acuteness.

These rules of economic imputation as used in practical life the Austrian school has endeavoured to connect by way of theory. The principle under which it formulates them points back to its general principle for estimating value. If I say 'free commodities have no value for me,' this means that I do not 'charge' them with the utility which they afford. The reason for this is, that I do not feel myself to be dependent upon them; if that supply which happens to be next to hand were for some reason or other to be withdrawn from my possession, I could take any other quantity from the abundance everywhere about me and use it. I impute utility only to those commodities which are not to be had in profusion, and on which I feel myself dependent in consequence, I meanwhile reflecting, that with every portion lost from my possession I lose a definite utility not to be had without it. Now the agriculturist, in losing a cow from his yard, does not forfeit with her the whole return on his farming, but suffers only a certain diminution in it, just as in the opposite event of his introducing some improved machinery he gains a certain increase. In these diminishing and increasing returns, varying with the variations in productive combinations, the principle of imputed returns finds its simplest elucidation, notwithstanding the many difficulties arising by the way. Space fails me to explain my meaning more precisely. I will only specify further, that in the particular instance account must be taken of supply, demand, circumstances of allied products, technical progress, &c., in short of all the well-known conditions, from which experts are able with so much success to infer what importance to attach now to this, now to that, element in production.

The most momentous consequence of the theory of imputation is, I take it, that it is false, with the Socialists, to impute to labour alone the entire productive return. Land and Capital as well must find recognition as collaborating factors in production, from the point of view of practical economy; excepting the case of their being available in superabundant quantities, which, however, can only be true of Land. The fact of fertility alone does not constitute an adequate condition for imputing rent to land, any more than utility as such makes a commodity valuable. Productive imputation requires the conjunction of utility and scarcity. But in the case of land, if scarcity be assumed, the charge of rent arises, whatever the form of land-tenure, and whether the produce is sold in the market or not. Even in a socialistic state a surplus reaped from better soil must be taken into account as soon as inferior soils are cultivated; the occupier farming the better land will be made responsible for a larger yield in view of the nature of the soil.

A further complication of value is afforded by the cost of production. Experience shows, that in very many cases the value of products is less than equivalent to the utility they bestow, because it is adjusted to the measure of the expense required for their production. Hence a great many theorists have concluded that value is not derived from utility, but is governed by another principle, viz., cost of production. But what is the cost, and how is it measured? The readiest way of expressing in figures the expenditure of materials and labour required to produce any article is to give the supplies to be consumed, the number of working days, the number of tons of coal, the time during which machinery is at work, the figure of each of the infinite number of items used in the production, and so on. This runs up a long list, but the items are incapable of being added up; these magnitudes are as mere bulk incomparable, incommensurable, and cannot be concentrated in one term. To sum them, every item must be put down in terms of value—but how is this to be determined? We can tell at once. The value of the productive elements is determined on the ground of utility as afforded by the products, and this holds good of the labour no less than of the coals, the machinery, and all the other means of production. To insist then on cost of production is ultimately to insist on some utility. There is no new principle to be discovered, none save utility.

Estimation of cost shows us in each particular case what utility the productive elements would confer if they were consumed otherwise than in turning out the produce desired. It shows us, for example, that the utility of the materials and labour, by the aid of which an important telegraphic communication is set up, would have amounted to very much less in those other uses, from which they have been withdrawn in order to do this. From this however it follows, that it is impossible to estimate the value of the communication as highly as its own high utility would absolutely warrant, since it can only be,—and precisely if it can be,—set up at the much smaller sacrifice of that utility which is involved in the cost of production. This extraneous utility is in this case the 'marginal utility' which affords a measure for the value. To value a product by its cost means then to impute as much utility to it as is to be *imputed to all its productive elements taken together*. Taken thus, products present themselves not merely according to their sources, but according to their value as well, as *the syntheses of their productive elements*. That product which requires them in greater quantity has the greater value. Consequently cost of production determines the *relative* value of produce, while the *absolute* value of the commodities consumed in the cost is determined by the value of the forthcoming produce.

Labour, like land and capital, owes the reward imputed to it not only to its productiveness, but also to its scarcity, *i.e.*, to the fact that it is not to be had in free abundance. Labour, however, has yet another motive force in itself, by which it can influence the estimation of value. Everyone is personally concerned to evade the toils and perils of labour. Value may accrue to products from this consideration, inasmuch as the man who possesses them is spared the toils and dangers of acquiring them. This is Ricardo's fundamental idea, and on its development he lavished all the keenness of his intellect. The Austrian school has not passed carelessly over this motive force and its theoretic expositions, but has devoted a very thorough-going attention to them. On this occasion I shall limit myself to a single comment. If Ricardo's idea were correct, and commodities were, in the strict sense of the word, of no importance to us, except that the possession of them saved us labour, which we should otherwise have to apply elsewhere, then the difference between rich and poor would perforce be quite other than what it unfortunately is. The rich man's privileges would consist only in possessing those things which the poor man will also possess, but which he must first give himself the trouble of acquiring; his prerogative would lie, not in greater enjoyment or a more secure existence, but in greater ease. What nation would not eagerly exchange the facts of life for this Utopia!

Finally there are further complications involved in the nature of land and capital. The first problem confronting us here is that of the rent of the soil, and it is not the most difficult. Ricardo's theory of rent is nothing else than an application of the theory of imputation, and that to the simplest conceivable case. Ricardo discloses the reasons why certain differences occurring in the returns from the cultivation of land must be imputed to just those portions of the soil in relation to which they arise, as constituting *their* share of reward, as rent. The value of the soil presents a much harder problem; the same is true of interest and the value of capital. Concerning these I shall say nothing, for special reasons, till the next section.

By our investing a certain amount of capital during a certain time in a certain product, we deprive ourselves of the interest which some other investment of our capital would fetch. The sacrifice of utility which we make in production consists therefore not only in the consumption of capital, but also in the sacrifice of interest, which is larger in proportion as the capital is larger and the period of investment longer. Accordingly, the current interest for the given interval of time is to be reckoned in the cost of production, and determines, together with the other elements of cost, the value of the products. I will not touch now on the knotty question, whether rent, too, is to be reckoned in the cost of production.

It has been objected that interest is a surplus of profit over expenditure, that it is conditioned by the value of the products and cannot, therefore, itself determine the value of the products. But is not the value of the productive commodities also conditioned by the value of the produce? And yet we say that it, as cost value, itself jointly determines the same. Equally are we entitled to say the same of interest. The value of iron depends on the value of iron products, but the relative value of the iron products is determined by the mass of iron required. The rate of interest depends upon the value of the goods, but the relative value of the goods is determined by the quantity of capital required and by the length of time during which it is invested.

We have asserted that the value of capital is based on the value of the produce into which capital is transposed. Experience does not wholly verify this theory. The sum of 105 gulden, which I am entitled to demand after a year's interval, constitutes the base on which its capital value is reckoned, but that value is not an equivalent amount. It is reckoned as somewhat less, deduction being made for interest. How is this deduction justified? In this way does the Austrian school state the problem of interest, the solution of which is essential to the complete solution of the problem of the value of capital.

The problem of the value of land moreover stands in connection with it. A piece of land contains for its owner the promise of rent for an indefinite number of years, and therefore its value ought to be equal to the sum of this whole series of years, which might even be taken as infinite. Actually, however, the value of land is rated much lower, viz., as the product of the annual rent multiplied by twenty, thirty, or some such shorter term of years.

The Austrian school does not maintain its unanimity over the theory of interest. As it is impossible for me to set forth here all our attempts to explain it, the reader will forgive me if I merely set forth my own. . . .

I start from the notion of imputation. A portion of the product must be assigned to capital. But of this share we must first replace as much of the capital as was consumed. Now experience shows that this being done, the reward of capital as a rule is not exhausted, a surplus of clear profit remaining over. That capital is in this sense productive is just as truly a fact of experience as that the soil always brings forth fresh produce.

I ask the reader to note that hitherto I have spoken only of produce in kind, and not yet of its value. The aggregate gross income of capital, considered in kind, contains in itself the replacement of capital in kind, besides a surplus produce, viz. net profit. If the total capital $= x$, and the net profit $= 5$, then, assuming that all the capital is consumed, the total gross produce is $x + 5$. But if this is so, if the total produce is greater than was the total capital, then its *value* must also be greater, and that by just the amount of net profit. The value of 100 items must be less than that of 105, just as that of the field cleared of its harvest must be less than the value of field *plus* crop. The difference between the value of capital and the value of gross profits can only disappear if capital ceases to be productive and yield profit.

From these considerations the following conclusions emerge:—

1.—The value of circulating capital is found by *discounting, i.e.,* by deduction of interest from gross income.

2.—If a capital of 100 can after a year be converted into 105, then is a sum of 100, which can only be claimed after a year, of less value than 100. Future goods have, therefore, less value than present goods.

3.—The capital value of a perpetual rental may be found by summing the several instalments, but only after their future value has been reduced to present value by continuous discounting. An abbreviated method for arriving at the same result is that of *capitalization, i.e.,* the multiplication of the yearly rental by a figure, the key to which is derived from the current rate of interest, *e.g.,* if this be 5 per cent., multiply by 20. This abbreviated procedure yields mathematically the same result as the longer method of discounting interest and compound interest.

This gives us, besides, the rule for reckoning the value of land.

4.—The value of fixed capital is reckoned by corresponding combinations, either through discounting or capitalizing, attention being given to the principle of amortization or sinking fund.

Value is, in the first instance, estimated by every one from a personal standpoint as 'value in use.' In the exchange of commodities, however, these individual estimates join issue, and thence arises price or 'value in exchange.' Prof. Sax explains price as the average of individual estimates of value; in the opinion of the other Austrian economists it obeys another law.

The maximum price which the consumer can ever afford to give does not exceed what he, according to his own estimate of money, looks upon as the full equivalent of the value in use which the commodities he is buying will have for him. And if he wishes to buy several items of the same commodity he measures the value of an item by marginal utility. A wealthier purchaser therefore, whose need is equally insistent, will be able to afford a higher price, since he in his pecuniary estimates will equate with the same value in use a larger sum of money. In practice, however, even the wealthiest of purchasers will consent to this higher price only if he must do so in order to keep off less wealthy bidders, who else could take the goods out of the market. Yet if so much of the commodity is offered, that even for lower bidders something is left over, the price must be adjusted to their estimates, in order that everything may find a sale; and then, since the price in the same market is the same for all buyers, the bidders of greater purchasing power pay less than what they by their estimates of money and goods were ready to give. The more goods there are, the deeper must be the strata of population having lower money-estimates of goods, who are thereby admitted to purchase. That money-equivalent, which obtains with the last group of buyers thus admitted for the last item bought (viz., of a commodity of which a number is always bought), and which determines the price, we may call the marginal equivalent.

Thus we see exchange value and price following the law of margins like value in use, with this qualification, that they are determined directly, not by marginal utility but by marginal equivalence, in which, not only supply and demand, but also the wealth of the purchasers is taken into account. Rare articles of luxury, *e.g.*, precious stones, fetch very high prices, because the rich contend for them with the poor and the richest with the rich. Stock goods supplied for imperative needs command very low prices, corresponding to the purchasing power of the lowest strata of the population. According to the economic stratification of any given nation, we may reproduce in terms of money the marginal utility of stock commodities by a very low equivalent, and that of articles of luxury by a very high equivalent. Hence from prices as such we can draw no inference whatever as to the national economic significance implied by commodities, in virtue of the relation of their supply to need as such; the picture they reveal is distorted, because it is unequally projected. Prices cannot be taken without qualification as the social expression of the valuation of commodities; they are the results of a conflict waged over those commodities, in which power besides need, and more than need, has decided the issue.

Production follows prices. That which can be sold dear is produced more eagerly at greater cost in larger quantities. To this extent is our production diverted from its purely economic aim, to minister to wants as such and allay them as far as possible. Those misshapen prices which are engendered by monopolies may be abolished by the suppression of monopolies, and those which, especially in the matter of wages, arise from the distress in the position of the labourer, may be removed by a general coalition of labourers; but those which result from inequality in the means of purchasers are, I take it, inextricably bound up with our economic *régime*.

Value in use and value in exchange, understood in the sense we have employed hitherto, are to be distinguished not only in extension but also in intension. Value in use is not only particular but also subjective; value in exchange is not only general but also objective. There is no doubt a subjective exchange-value as well, which plays an extremely important part in economy, but for brevity's sake there shall be no mention of that here.

If value is understood as subjective, then the question, why commodities are valuable, becomes equivalent to, why do men prize commodities? The phenomenon requiring explanation is, the love of men for material goods, *auri sacra fames,* side by side with the love of men for men, and their love for moral goods. The Austrian school, while indicating utility as the root and measure of that love, seeks to establish this principle in the sphere of material objects, as the utilitarians do in estimating moral values. And yet how complicated even in the material world is the calculus of self-interest! We value commodities for the sake of their utility, yet we do not value utility when it is coupled with abundance; in other commodities we value as a rule not the total, but only the marginal, utility; in the cost of production we value, instead of the utility of the product itself, the utility of other extraneous products; and finally through it all runs the difficulty of imputing the reward of production.

What on the other hand is the nature of value in exchange as objective? It informs us respecting the ratio of the prices of commodities, telling us that such a commodity has such a price, while it brings it into comparison with the prices other commodities are commanding at the same time. It is concerned only with the relations between commodities, nowhere with those between men. There is no definition under which we may combine both conceptions of value, the subjective and the objective. We must be content with showing their mutual relation.

In economy, both find application. Every decision arrived at by any one respecting a commodity is based upon his subjective judgment of value. Price and exchange-value on the other hand furnish the general principles of exchange and of the calculus of production.

Theory has to examine both phenomena. I will restrict myself to showing why it may not neglect subjective values. The reason is, that it would thereby leave unexplained all individual decisions in economic matters, *e.g.* it would not even explain why any one buys. For by objective standards wares and prices have the same value; by objective standards we give equals for equals, for which we should have no motive. But further, exchange-value itself, considered objectively, can only find its explanation in the laws of subjective value, obeyed by buyer and seller in concluding a bargain. If commodities which are to be had in abundance fetch no price, this can only be owing to the fact that they have subjectively no value for anyone. The law, that in the same market equal portions of the same commodity are equal in price, could not hold, did not every owner always assign equal value to equal portions. Price follows marginal equivalent because subjective value follows marginal utility; it only adjusts itself to cost of production, because every producer subjectively for himself assigns a value to products as syntheses of their productive elements. Rent is paid for land, interest for capital, wages for labour, because in subjective valuation a share of the aggregate return is imputed to land, a share to capital, a share to labour; nor could any more precisely quantitative expression be found for price, were it not that subjective value, by its bearing on supply, number, and cost of production, already admitted of computation. Motives it is true are ever coming into play through the conflict of price, which are wanting in the personal calculus; on the other hand monopoly suppresses the effect of the influence of cost, and other such differences: nevertheless without the subjective influences of the estimation of values, no dealings in price would ultimately be conceivable, nor could the law of price be maintained.

I must abstain from any complete demonstration of this governing idea, and will pursue it a little further in one direction only. In reply to a passage in my book on *Natural Value,* Prof. Edgeworth has said that the difference between the valuations under an Economic and those under a Socialistic *régime* is most briefly and appropriately expressed by the statement that in the former case the tendency to maximum utility is, while in the latter case it is not, subject to the condition 'that there should be only one rate of exchange in a market.' With the same request as he then made, that my forced brevity may not be taken for want of courtesy, I remark that in my judgment, of course, not 'one rate of exchange,' but nevertheless 'one rate of value' would still obtain under socialism. If a million tons of grain are lying ready for distribution among the citizens, each ton, assuming it is of equal quality, will have to be held equal in value to any other. In consumption the several tons will not afford equal degrees of utility, but equal utility will be imputed to them as their value. I admit that, when goods are not sold to citizens, but distributed among them, equal prices will not come to be paid for equal items, nevertheless equality in judgments on value would manifest itself in many other directions, chiefly in the calculus of production. Thus, to take as example a simple though comparatively unimportant case, the effective capacity of two machines would be judged by the quantity of products they yielded, in which it would not occur to any one to assume the value of those products, equal quality being assumed, as other than equal. If it were not essentially required in economic procedure, that we should regard a number of commodities, similar in quality but affording different degrees of utility, as economically equal, the fact of their being held as equal in price would be an offence against economic procedure, detrimental to either buyer, or seller, or both. If there were no better explanation of this fact than competition, if its foundation did not lie deep in the nature of each individual economic subject, economy would go astray wherever and whenever it proceeded on the principle of prices reckoned in this manner.

I touch at this point on the difference, alluded to at the outset, which exists between Jevons and the Austrian school respecting the conception of value and the principle of the law of value. For us, Jevons holds too closely to the narrower view, which sees in price the only manifestation of value. We conform to an idea always firmly maintained in Germany, when we say that in economy value decides everything, not only the price of the bargain, but also what amount of consumption, productive employment, and outlay entering into it is permissible. But while the older German school suffers this general function of value to depend ultimately on bare usefulness, to which it gives the empty name of value-in-use (*Gebrauchswerth*), we explain the determining cause as value in its true, complete meaning, value with all the principal laws revealing themselves in price; value as following the law of margins and the cost of production; value as demanding productive imputation, rent and interest. But precisely on this ground do we hold the view that the current mode of reckoning in economy by exchange-value is not a dictum of the market, but, in spite of many peculiarities conditioned by the market, a dictum of economy itself.

THE ECONOMIC PRINCIPLE IN STATE ECONOMY *

To the extent to which the state computes by exchange value in its private and administrative enterprises, it is obviously guided strictly by the economic principle like any other entrepreneur. The highest net yield is sought. This may be ascertained by a numerical comparison of the costs incurred and the utility secured. However, it is perfectly evident that there is no violation of economic principle if the state in these enterprises,

* From *Social Economics* by Friedrich von Wieser. Translated by A. Ford Hinrichs. Copyright 1927 by Greenberg: Publisher.

rather than reckon by exchange value, in exceptional cases considers the simple social use-value. In every such instance the state would arrive at its decision with a view to that result which under the given conditions it regards as the highest possible.

From this reasoning it follows that the state in its national economic administration obeys the economic principle even when it does not calculate directly by exchange value but by public economic use-value. The latter also leads to the maximum utility. However, the indirect productivity of administrative institutions does not lend itself so readily or exactly to verification as does the direct productivity of a private enterprise after the regular working routine of the latter has once been entered upon. A manufactured article is the fully controlled resultant of productive means. It is quite feasible to calculate the precise gains to be expected from products for which certain costs have been incurred. The indirect advancement of industry which is anticipated from an administrative institution can never be foreseen with equal certainty; the private initiative of free entrepreneurs is an imponderable, though it may be the decisive factor in the problem. When the opportunities offered by the administration are taken advantage of on a long and broad scale the results may be great. But it is quite within the range of possibilities that though the administration has done its best, the results lag behind and are meagre because private initiative fails to take advantage of the opportunities offered.

If one follows this train of thought from the national economic administration into the broader fields of the state's activity that is animated by its estimation of the general social interest, it is evident that here also the economic principle as such maintains its validity. But its obedience to mathematical rule and expression is wholly lost. The state determines the numerical expression only for the partial values which it acquires at market prices: costs for the services of employees and purchases of supplies. These may be entered item by item in official budgets and final accountings; but against these costs, no figure can ever be set for the total value of the effects of the state's administration, no figure which shall serve as a spur to its efforts and set the ultimate limit for the amount of its disbursements. Who would seek to give arithmetical expression to the "benefits" of a victorious war and to equate these numerically against its costs and other sacrifices! And yet when the existence of the state is endangered, national consciousness will sound a call to war. The intensity-values of the interests to be protected are carefully appraised. Definite decisions are arrived at as soon as public opinion had agreed upon its verdict in the appraisal or sentiments. But throughout this process, numerical expressions for those things which are intensely felt cannot be found, are not sought and are considered of minor importance. Under other conditions to be sure the conflict of opinion regarding political decisions arises largely from an uncertainty as to their consequences when numerical data are lacking.

In any event the state's economic plan should be in harmony with the economic principle; less important interests should be kept in the background while the most vital ones allowed by the available means are assured. The more abundant these means are, the larger will be the amounts brought forward from the common force and the greater the effects anticipated. The richer state can offer its citizens greater military protection; the poorer one must be content with a more modest military display. To this extent the plan of state economy even where it is determined by aggregate valuations is controlled precisely like the economy which computes according to partial value and desires to extend the margin of use as far as possible.

When scheduling the plan for the state's expenditures, it is of particular importance that the state is bound to act as a protective association. The amount of its expenditures to meet this duty must therefore always depend upon the nature, degree and imminence of the danger against which it is to protect the people. A rushing torrent requires more extensive precautionary measures than a quiet pool. During a period in which the great nations are pushing their armaments to the extreme and national passions and jealousies are inflamed it is not safe for any state unduly to curtail its military outlays. The poorer state will not set a standard of its military preparation only to accord with its economic power. It must also consider the general state of preparedness. Even a state whose wealth is declining may feel compelled in times of danger to increase its military budget.

Such conditions give rise to the much invoked rule that whereas in private economies expenditures have to be adjusted to the available income, in the case of the state income must be adjusted to expenses. As it is formulated, however, the rule has too broad a meaning. In its expenditures as well the state must be guided by the revenues which a dutiful observance of economic margins permits it to secure from the incomes of its citizens. These problems we shall presently discuss more fully. However, it is true that the state more frequently than the private citizens is under the necessity of suddenly and substantially increasing its necessary expenditures. The reason for doing so is to be found in the uniqueness of the economic task that faces the state. The principal problem of the private economy is the economic approval or disapproval of the needs to be satisfied and the acquisition of the required means. By its partial satisfactions and labors it is possible for this economy to adjust itself with a certain fluidity to the point indicated by Gossen's Law of Satiety through the marginal utility. But, as has just been shown, in so far as the public economy is serving the ends of a protective association, it is bound to accept the measure of its expenditures for the greater part from facts which are beyond its control. The increasing imminence of war may suddenly endanger national life and all its values for which, under the quiet conditions of peace, no consideration or foresight was necessary.

WILLIAM STANLEY JEVONS

(1835–1882)

W. S. Jevons was born in Liverpool, England, educated at the University of London, and at nineteen made assayer of the mint in Australia. Returning to England, he became a professor at Owens College in Manchester and later at the University of London.

Jevons was one of the three economists (the other two were Menger and Walras) who almost simultaneously seized upon the notion of subjective utility at the margin as the basis for constructing a new type of economic theory. Jevons' *Theory of Political Economy* (1871) was the outstanding English book on economics between the publication of Mill's *Principles* in 1848 and the appearance of Marshall's work in 1890.

In Jevons' system, established in embryo as early as 1862, a mathematical treatment of economics is fused with an avowed hedonistic philosophy. The cardinal feature of the structure is the strict dependence of value on utility which, in turn, rests upon pleasure and pain. Jevons then introduces an additional utility function—the utility of a commodity depending upon the stock of that commodity. Thus, the total utility of a commodity is equal to the sum of the amounts of utility contributed by each additional quantity of it. The degree of utility at any point is a declining function of incremental additions to the stock of goods. The "final degree of utility," is then defined as the amount of satisfaction associated with the consumption of the final increment of a stock of goods, divided by the increase in the physical stock. It is at this point that Jevons' concept differs somewhat from the more familiar concept of marginal utility derived from Menger and von Wieser: the former is a ratio, whereas the latter is a quantity of satisfaction.

The conclusion follows that when a commodity is capable of serving several different uses, it will be distributed among them so that the final degree of utility of that commodity in each of its alternative uses will be equal. Exchange between two individuals will cease when "the ratio of exchange of any two commodities [is] . . . the reciprocal of the ratio of the final degrees of utility of the quantities of commodity available for consumption," which is merely a clumsy way of saying that in equilibrium marginal utilities will be proportionate to prices.

Jevons' theory of exchange between two individuals is converted into a theory of competitive exchange on the market through the concept of the trading body—a group of buyers and sellers of undefined number. The trading bodies act like two individuals, and the theory of competitive exchange in reality turns out to be an analysis of barter-exchange between two individuals—a case of bilateral monopoly. The ratio of exchange under bilateral monopoly is indeterminate, as Edgeworth was soon to show, and hence it may be seen that Jevons failed to supply a theory of the formation of market price on the basis of utility.

Jevons' theory of distribution is simple. Profits are resolved into wages, superintendence, insurance against risk, and interest. The interest theory contains noteworthy hints of a marginal-productivity theory of capital as well as an Austrian view of interest as the result of the greater productivity of "roundabout" production. In these terms, labor is a residual claimant and wages depend upon the particular deduction of rent, taxes, and interest.

Jevons' system was mathematical but lacked the symmetry of the Austrian variant of marginal theory; it also adhered to Benthamite psychology, which was becoming increasingly discredited in Jevons' own time. These factors militated against popular acceptance of his ideas. He did prove a major influence, however, on Philip Wicksteed, a British clergyman and lecturer, whose *Common Sense of Political Economy* remains one of the most scintillating works in the neo-classical tradition. Through Wicksteed, Jevons influenced some of the theoreticians of the Fabian socialist movement.

The genius of Jevons was many-sided. Besides writing his text in economics and a famous textbook on deductive logic, he pioneered in inductive and statistical studies of specific problems, such as the coal question and the state in relation to labor.

The following selection from the *Theory of Political Economy* gives the gist of Jevons' exposition of value, exchange, and distribution.

THEORY OF POLITICAL ECONOMY *

Introduction

The science of Political Economy rests upon a few notions of an apparently simple character. Utility, wealth, value, commodity, labour, land, capital, are the elements of the subject; and whoever has a thorough comprehension of their nature must possess or be soon able to acquire a knowledge of the whole science. . . . Accordingly, I have devoted the following pages to an investigation of the conditions and relations of the above-named notions.

Repeated reflection and inquiry have led me to the somewhat novel opinion, that *value depends entirely upon utility.* Prevailing opinions make labour rather than utility the origin of value; and there are even those who distinctly assert that labour is the *cause* of value. I show, on the contrary, that we have only to trace out carefully the natural laws of the variation of utility, as depending upon the quantity of commodity in our possession, in order to arrive at a satisfactory theory of exchange, of which the ordinary laws of supply and demand are a necessary consequence. This theory is in harmony with facts; and, whenever there is any apparent reason for the belief that labour is the cause of value, we obtain an explanation of the reason. Labour is found often to determine value, but only in an indirect manner, by varying the degree of utility of the commodity through an increase or limitation of the supply. . . .

It is clear that Economics, if it is to be a science at all, must be a mathematical science. There exists much prejudice against attempts to introduce the methods and language of mathematics into any branch of the moral sciences. Many persons seem to think that the physical sciences form the proper sphere of mathematical method, and that the moral sciences demand some other method—I know not what. My theory of Economics, however, is purely mathematical in character. Nay, believing that the quantities with which we deal must be subject to continuous variation, I do not hesitate to use the appropriate branch of mathematical science, involving though it does the fearless consideration of infinitely small quantities. The theory consists in applying the differential calculus to the familiar notions of wealth, utility, value, demand, supply, capital, interest, labour, and all the other quantitative notions belonging to the

* From *Theory of Political Economy* (London, Macmillan and Co., Ltd., 1888).

daily operations of industry. As the complete theory of almost every other science involves the use of that calculus, so we cannot have a true theory of Economics without its aid.

To me it seems that *our science must be mathematical, simply because it deals with quantities.* Wherever the things treated are capable of being *greater or less,* there the laws and relations must be mathematical in nature. The ordinary laws of supply and demand treat entirely of quantities of commodity demanded or supplied, and express the manner in which the quantities vary in connection with the price. In consequence of this fact the laws *are* mathematical. Economists cannot alter their nature by denying them the name; they might as well try to alter red light by calling it blue. Whether the mathematical laws of Economics are stated in words, or in the usual symbols, x, y, z, p, q, etc., is an accident, or a matter of mere convenience. If we had no regard to trouble and prolixity, the most complicated mathematical problems might be stated in ordinary language, and their solution might be traced out by words. In fact, some distinguished mathematicians have shown a liking for getting rid of their symbols, and expressing their arguments and results in language as nearly as possible approximating to that in common use. . . .

These attempts, however distinguished and ingenious their authors, soon disclose the inherent defects of the grammar and dictionary for expressing complicated relations. The symbols of mathematical books are not different in nature from language; they form a perfected system of language, adapted to the notions and relations which we need to express. They do not constitute the mode of reasoning they embody; they merely facilitate its exhibition and comprehension. If, then, in Economics, we have to deal with quantities and complicated relations of quantities, we must reason mathematically; we do not render the science less mathematical by avoiding the symbols of algebra—we merely refuse to employ, in a very imperfect science, much needing every kind of assistance, that apparatus of appropriate signs which is found indispensable in other sciences.

Many persons entertain a prejudice against mathematical language, arising out of a confusion between the ideas of a mathematical science and an exact science. They think that we must not pretend to calculate unless we have the precise data which will enable us to obtain a precise answer to our calculations; but, in reality, there is no such thing as an exact science, except in a comparative sense. Astronomy is more exact than other sciences, because the position of a planet or star admits of close measurement; but, if we examine the methods of physical astronomy, we find that they are all approximate. Every solution involves hypotheses which are not really true: as, for instance, that the earth is a smooth, homogeneous spheroid. Even the apparently simpler problems in statics or dynamics are only hypothetical approximations to the truth.

We can calculate the effect of a crowbar, provided it be perfectly inflexible and have a perfectly hard fulcrum—which is never the case. The data are almost wholly deficient for the complete solution of any one problem in natural science. Had physicists waited until their data were perfectly precise before they brought in the aid of mathematics, we should have still been in the age of science which terminated at the time of Galileo. . . .

The greater or less accuracy attainable in a mathematical science is a matter of accident, and does not affect the fundamental character of the science. There can be but two classes of sciences—those which are *simply logical,* and *those which, besides being logical, are also mathematical.* If there be any science which determines merely whether a thing be or be not —whether an event will happen, or will not happen—it must be a purely logical science; but if the thing may be greater or less, or the event may happen sooner or later, nearer or farther, then quantitative notions enter, and the science must be mathematical in nature, by whatever name we call it. . . .

Many readers may, even after reading the preceding remarks, consider it quite impossible to create such a calculus as is here contemplated, because we have no means of defining and measuring quantities of feeling, like we can measure a mile, or a right angle; or any other physical quantity. I have granted that we can hardly form the conception of a unit of pleasure or pain, so that the numerical expression of quantities of feeling seems to be out of the question. But we only employ units of measurement in other things to facilitate the comparison of quantities; and if we can compare the quantities directly, we do not need the units. . . .

To return, however, to the topic of the present work, the theory here given may be described as *the mechanics of utility and self-interest.* Oversights may have been committed in tracing out its details, but in its main features this theory must be the true one. Its method is as sure and demonstrative as that of kinematics or statics, nay, almost as self-evident as are the elements of Euclid, when the real meaning of the formulae is fully seized.

I do not hesitate to say, too, that Economics might be gradually erected into an exact science, if only commercial statistics were far more complete and accurate than they are at present, so that the formulae could be endowed with exact meaning by the aid of numerical data. These data would consist chiefly in accurate accounts of the quantities of goods possessed and consumed by the community, and the prices at which they are exchanged. There is no reason whatever why we should not have those statistics, except the cost and trouble of collecting them, and the unwillingness of persons to afford information. The quantities themselves to be measured and registered are most concrete and precise. . . .

The deductive science of Economics must be verified and rendered useful by the purely empirical science of Statistics. Theory must be invested with the reality and life of fact. But the difficulties of this union are immensely great . . . I make hardly any attempt to employ statistics in this work, and thus I do not pretend to any numerical precision. But, before we attempt any investigation of facts, we must have correct theoretical notions; and of what are here presented, I would say, in the words of Hume, in his *Essay on Commerce,* "If false, let them be rejected: but no one has a right to entertain a prejudice against them merely because they are out of the common road."

I wish to say a few words, in this place, upon the relation of Economics to Moral Science. The theory which follows is entirely based on a calculus of pleasure and pain; and the object of Economics is to maximise happiness by purchasing pleasure, as it were, at the lowest cost of pain. The language employed may be open to misapprehension, and it may seem as if pleasures and pains of a gross kind were treated as the all-sufficient motives to guide the mind of man. I have no hesitation in accepting the Utilitarian theory of morals which does uphold the effect upon the happiness of mankind as the criterion of what is right and wrong. But I have never felt that there is anything in that theory to prevent our putting the widest and highest interpretation upon the terms used.

Jeremy Bentham put forward the Utilitarian theory in the most uncompromising manner. According to him, whatever is of interest or importance to us must be the cause of pleasure or of pain; and when the terms are used with a sufficiently wide meaning, pleasure and pain include all the forces which drive us to action. They are explicitly or implicitly the matter of all our calculations, and form the ultimate quantities to be treated in all the moral sciences. The words of Bentham on this subject may require some explanation and qualification, but they are too grand and too full of truth to be omitted. "Nature," he says, "has placed mankind under the governance of two sovereign masters—*pain* and *pleasure*. It is for them alone to point out what we ought to do, as well as to determine what we shall do. On the one hand the standard of right and wrong, on the other the chain of causes and effects, are fastened to their throne. They govern us in all we do, in all we say, in all we think: every effort we can make to throw off our subjection will serve but to demonstrate and confirm it. In words a man may pretend to abjure their empire; but, in reality, he will remain subject to it all the while. The *principle of utility* recognises this subjection, and assumes it for the foundation of that system, the object of which is to rear the fabric of felicity by the hands of reason and of law. Systems which attempt to question it deal in sounds instead of sense, in caprice instead of reason, in darkness instead of light." . . .

The Theory of Utility

My principal work now lies in tracing out the exact nature and conditions of utility. It seems strange indeed that economists have not bestowed more minute attention on a subject which doubtless furnishes the true key to the problem of Economics.

In the first place, utility, though a quality of things, is *no inherent quality*. It is better described as *a circumstance of things* arising out of their relation to man's requirements. As Senior most accurately says, "Utility denotes no intrinsic quality in the things which we call useful; it merely expresses their relations to the pains and pleasures of mankind." We can never, therefore, say absolutely that some objects have utility and others have not. The ore lying in the mine, the diamond escaping the eye of the searcher, the wheat lying unreaped, the fruit ungathered for want of consumers, have no utility at all. The most wholesome and necessary kinds of food are useless unless there are hands to collect and mouths to eat them sooner or later. Nor, when we consider the matter closely, can we say that all portions of the same commodity possess equal utility. Water, for instance, may be roughly described as the most useful of all substances. A quart of water per day has the high utility of saving a person from dying in a most distressing manner. Several gallons a day may possess much utility for such purposes as cooking and washing; but after an adequate supply is secured for these uses, any additional quantity is a matter of comparative indifference. All that we can say, then, is that water, up to a certain quantity, is indispensable; that further quantities will have various degrees of utility; but that beyond a certain quantity the utility sinks gradually to zero; it may even become negative, that is to say, further supplies of the same substance may become inconvenient and hurtful.

Exactly the same considerations apply more or less clearly to every other article. A pound of bread per day supplied to a person saves him from starvation, and has the highest conceivable utility. A second pound per day has also no slight utility; it keeps him in a state of comparative plenty, though it be not altogether indispensable. A third pound would begin to be superfluous. It is clear, then, that *utility is not proportional to commodity:* the very same articles vary in utility according as we already possess more or less of the same article. The like may be said of other things. One suit of clothes per annum is necessary, a second convenient, a third desirable, a fourth not unacceptable, but we sooner or later reach a point at which further supplies are not desired with any perceptible force unless it be for subsequent use.

Let us now investigate this subject a little more closely. Utility must be considered as measured by, or even as actually identical with, the addition made to a person's happiness. It is a convenient name for the aggregate of the favorable balance of feeling produced,—the sum of the pleasure created and the pain prevented. We must now carefully discriminate between the *total utility* arising from any commodity and the utility attaching to any particular portion of it. Thus the total utility of the food we eat consists in maintaining life, and may be considered as infinitely great; but if we were to subtract a tenth part from what we eat daily, our loss would be but slight. We should certainly not lose a tenth part of the whole utility of food to us. It might be doubtful whether we should suffer any harm at all.

Let us imagine the whole quantity of food which a person consumes on an average during twenty-four hours to be divided into ten equal parts. If his food be reduced by the last part, he will suffer but little; if a second tenth part be deficient, he will feel the want distinctly; the subtraction of the third tenth part will be decidedly injurious; with every subsequent subtraction of a tenth part his sufferings will be more and more serious, until at length he will be upon the verge of starvation. Now, if we call each of the tenth parts *an increment,* the meaning of these facts is, that each increment of food is less necessary, or possesses less utility, than the previous one. To explain this variation of utility we may make use of space representations, which I have found convenient in illustrating the laws of economics in my college lectures during fifteen years past.

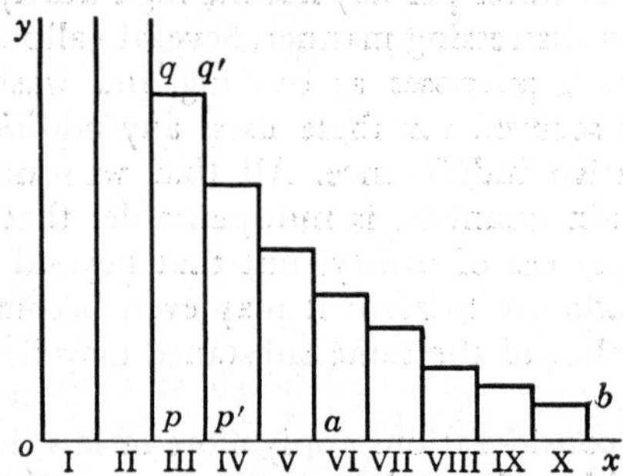

Let the line *ox* be used as a measure of the quantity of food, and let it be divided into ten equal parts to correspond to the ten portions of food mentioned above. Upon these equal lines are constructed rectangles and the area of each rectangle may be assumed to represent the utility of the increment of food corresponding to its base. Thus the utility of the last increment is small, being proportional to the small rectangle on X. As we approach towards *o,* each increment bears a larger rectangle, that standing upon III being the largest complete rectangle. The utility of the next increment, II, is undefined, as also that of I, since these portions of food would be indispensable to life, and their utility, therefore, infinitely great.

We can now form a clear notion of the utility of the whole food, or of any part of it, for we have only to add together the proper rectangles. The utility of the first half of the food will be the sum of the rectangles standing on the line *oa;* that of the second half will be represented by the sum of the smaller rectangles between *a* and *b.* The total utility of the food will be the whole sum of the rectangles, and will be infinitely great.

The comparative utility of the several portions is, however, the most important. Utility may be treated as *a quantity of two dimensions,* one dimension consisting in the quantity of the commodity, and another in the intensity of the effect produced upon the consumer. Now the quantity of the commodity is measured on the horizontal line *ox,* and the intensity of utility will be measured by the length of the upright lines, or *ordinates.*

The intensity of utility of the third increment is measured either by *pq*, or *p′q′*, and its utility is the product of the units in *pp′* multiplied by those in *pq*.

But the division of the food into ten equal parts is an arbitrary supposition. If we had taken twenty or a hundred or more equal parts, the same general principle would hold true, namely, that each small portion would be less useful and necessary than the last. The law may be considered to hold true theoretically, however small the increments are made; and in this way we shall at last reach a figure which is undistinguishable from a continuous curve. The notion of infinitely small quantities of food may seem absurd as regards the consumption of one individual; but when we consider the consumption of a nation as a whole, the consumption may well be conceived to increase or diminish by quantities which are, practically speaking, infinitely small compared with the whole consumption. The laws which we are about to trace out are to be conceived as theoretically true of the individual; they can only be practically verified as regards the aggregate transactions, productions, and consumptions of a large body of people. But the laws of the aggregate depend of course upon the laws applying to individual cases.

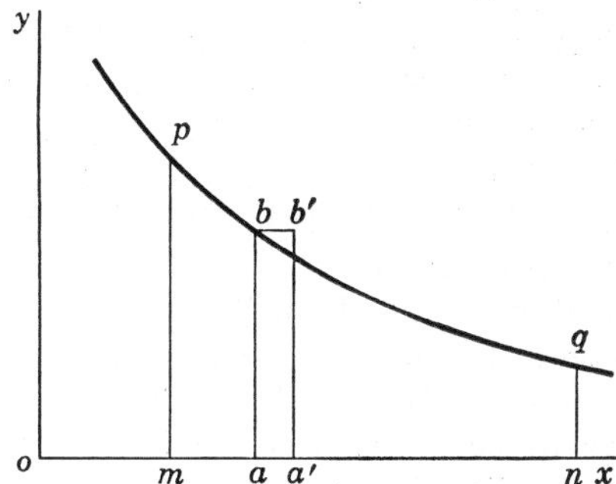

The law of the variation of the degree of utility of food may thus be represented by a continuous curve *pbq*, and the perpendicular height of each point at the curve above the line *ox* represents the degree of utility of the commodity when a certain amount has been consumed.

Thus, when the quantity *oa* has been consumed, the degree of utility corresponds to the length of the line *ab;* for if we take a very little more food, *aa′*, its utility will be the product of *aa′* and *ab* very nearly, and more nearly the less is the magnitude of *aa′*. The degree of utility is thus properly measured by the height of a very narrow rectangle corresponding to a very small quantity of food, which theoretically ought to be infinitely small.

We are now in a position to appreciate perfectly the difference between the *total utility* of any commodity and the *degree of utility* of the commodity at any point. These are, in fact, quantities of altogether different kinds, the first being represented by an area, and the second by a line.

We must consider how we may express these notions in appropriate mathematical language.

Let x signify, as is usual in mathematical books, the quantity which varies independently—in this case the quantity of commodity. Let u denote the *whole utility* proceeding from the consumption of x. Then u will be, as mathematicians say, *a function of x;* that is, it will vary in some continuous and regular, but probably unknown, manner, when x is made to vary. Our great object at present, however, is to express the *degree of utility*.

Mathematicians employ the sign Δ prefixed to a sign of quantity, such as x, to signify that a quantity of the same nature as x, but small in proportion to x, is taken into consideration. Thus Δx means a small portion of x, and $x + \Delta x$ is therefore a quantity a little greater than x. Now when x is a quantity of commodity, the utility of $x + \Delta x$ will be more than that of x as a general rule. Let the whole utility of $x + \Delta x$ be denoted by $u + \Delta u$; then it is obvious that the increment of utility Δu belongs to the increment of commodity Δx; and if, for the sake of argument, we suppose the degree of utility uniform over the whole of Δx, which is nearly true, owing to its smallness, we shall find the corresponding degree of utility by dividing Δu by Δx.

We find these considerations fully illustrated by the last figure, in which oa represents x, and ab is the degree of utility at the point a. Now, if we increase x by the small quantity aa', or Δx, the utility is increased by the small rectangle $abb'a'$, or Δu; and since a rectangle is the product of its sides, we find that the length of the line ab, the degree of utility, is represented by the fraction $\Delta u/\Delta x$.

As already explained, however, the utility of a commodity may be considered to vary with perfect continuity, so that we commit a small error in assuming it to be uniform over the whole increment Δx. To avoid this, we must imagine Δx to be reduced to an infinitely small size, Δu decreasing with it. The smaller the quantities are the more nearly we shall have a correct expression for ab, the degree of utility at the point a. Thus the *limit* of this fraction $\Delta u/\Delta x$, or, as it is commonly expressed, du/dx, is the degree of utility corresponding to the quantity of commodity x. *The degree of utility is,* in mathematical language, *the differential coefficient of u considered as a function of x,* and will itself be another function of x.

We shall seldom need to consider the degree of utility except as regards the last increment which has been consumed, or, which comes to the same thing, the next increment which is about to be consumed. I shall therefore commonly use the expression *final degree of utility,* as meaning the degree of utility of the last addition, or the next possible addition of a very small, or infinitely small, quantity to the existing stock. In ordinary circumstances, too, the final degree of utility will not be great compared with what it might be. Only in famine or other extreme circumstances do we approach the higher degrees of utility. Accordingly we can often treat the lower portions of the curves of variation (pbq) which concern ordinary commercial transactions, while we leave out of sight the portions beyond p or q. It is also evident that we may know the degree of utility at any point while ignorant of the total utility, that is, the area of the whole curve. To be able to estimate the total enjoyment of a person would be an interesting thing, but it would not be really so important as to be able to estimate the additions and subtractions to his enjoyment which circumstances occasion. In the same way a very wealthy person may be quite unable to form any accurate statement of his aggregate wealth, but he may nevertheless have exact accounts of income and expenditure, that is, of additions and subtractions.

The final degree of utility is that function upon which the theory of economics will be found to turn. Economists, generally speaking, have failed to discriminate between this function and the total utility, and from this confusion has arisen much perplexity. Many commodities which are most useful to us are esteemed and desired but little. We cannot live without water, and yet in ordinary circumstances we set no value on it. Why is this? Simply because we usually have so much of it that its final degree of utility is reduced nearly to zero. We enjoy every day the almost infinite utility of water, but then we do not need to consume more than we have. Let the supply run short by drought, and we begin to feel the higher degrees of utility, of which we think but little at other times.

The variation of the function expressing the final degree of utility is the all-important point in economic problems. We may state, as a general law, that *the degree of utility varies with the quantity of commodity, and ultimately decreases as that quantity increases.* No commodity can be named which we continue to desire with the same force, whatever be the quantity already in use or possession. All our appetites are capable of *satisfaction* or *satiety* sooner or later, in fact, both these words mean, etymologically, that we have had *enough,* so that more is of no use to us. It does not follow, indeed, that the degree of utility will always sink to zero. This may be the case with some things, especially the simple animal requirements, such as food, water, air, etc. But the more refined and intellectual our needs become, the less are they capable of satiety. To the desire for articles of taste, science, or curiosity, when once excited, there is hardly a limit. . . .

A few words will suffice to suggest that as utility corresponds to the production of pleasure, or, at least, a favorable alteration in the balance of pleasure and pain, so negative utility will consist in the production of pain, or the unfavorable alteration of the balance. In reality we must be almost as often concerned with the one as with the other; nevertheless, economists have not employed any distinct technical terms to express that production of pain which accompanies so many actions of life. They have fixed their attention on the more agreeable aspect of the matter. It will be allowable, however, to appropriate the good English word *discommodity,* to signify any substance or action which is the opposite of *commodity,* that is to say, *anything which we desire to get rid of,* like ashes or sewage. Discommodity is, indeed, properly an abstract form signifying inconvenience, or disadvantage; but as the noun *commodities* has been used in the English language for four hundred years at least as a concrete term, so we may now convert discommodity into a concrete term, and speak of *discommodities* as substances or things which possess the quality of causing inconvenience or harm. For the abstract notion, the opposite or negative of utility, we may invent the term *disutility,* which will mean something different from inutility, or the absence of utility. It is obvious that utility passes through inutility before changing into disutility, these notions being related as +, o, and —.

The principles of utility may be illustrated by considering the mode in which we distribute a commodity when it is capable of several uses. There are articles which may be employed for many distinct purposes: thus, barley may be used either to make beer, spirits, bread, or to feed cattle; sugar may be used to eat, or for producing alcohol; timber may be used in construction, or as fuel; iron and other metals may be applied to many different purposes. Imagine, then, a community in the possession of a certain stock of barley; what principles will regulate their mode of consuming it? Or, as we have not yet reached the subject of exchange, imagine an isolated family, or even an individual, possessing an adequate stock, and using some in one way and some in another. The theory of utility gives, theoretically speaking, a complete solution of the question.

Let s be the whole stock of some commodity, and let it be capable of two distinct uses. Then we may represent the two quantities appropriated to these uses by x_1 and y_1, it being a condition that $x_1 + y_1 = s$. The person may be conceived as successively expending small quantities of the commodity. Now it is the inevitable tendency of human nature to choose that course which appears to offer the greatest advantage at the moment. Hence, when the person remains satisfied with the distribution he has made, it follows that no alteration would yield him more pleasure, which amounts to saying that an increment of commodity would yield exactly as much utility in one use as in another. Let Δu_1, Δu_2 be the increments of utility which might arise respectively from consuming an increment of commodity in the two different ways. When the distribution is completed, we ought to have $\Delta u_1 = \Delta u_2$; or at the limit we have the equation

$$\frac{du_1}{dx} = \frac{du_2}{dy},$$

which is true when x, y are respectively equal to x_1, y_1. We must, in other words, have the *final degrees of utility* in the two uses equal.

The same reasoning which applies to uses of the same commodity will evidently apply to any two uses, and hence to all uses simultaneously, so that we obtain a series of equations less numerous by a unit than the number of ways of using the commodity. The general result is that commodity, if consumed by a perfectly wise being, must be consumed with a maximum production of utility.

We should often find these equations to fail. Even when x is equal to $^{99}/_{100}$ of the stock, its degree of utility might still exceed the utility attaching to the remaining $^{1}/_{100}$ part in either of the other uses. This would mean that it was preferable to give the whole commodity to the first use. Such a case might perhaps be said to be not the exception but the rule; for whenever a commodity is capable of only one use, the circumstance is theoretically represented by saying that the final degree of utility in this employment always exceeds that in any other employment.

Under peculiar circumstances great changes may take place in the consumption of a commodity. In a time of scarcity the utility of barley as food might rise so high as to exceed altogether its utility, even as regards the smallest quantity, in producing alcoholic liquors; its consumption in the latter way would then cease. In a besieged town the employment of articles becomes revolutionized. Things of great utility in other respects are ruthlessly applied to strange purposes. In Paris a vast stock of horses was eaten, not so much because they were useless in other ways, as because they were needed more strongly as food. A certain stock of horses had, indeed, to be retained as a necessary aid to locomotion, so that the equation of the degrees of utility never wholly failed. . . .

Theory of Exchange

In the popular use of the word value no less than three distinct though connected meanings seem to be confused together. These may be described as

(1) Value in use;
(2) Esteem, or urgency of desire;
(3) Ratio of exchange.

Adam Smith . . . distinguished between the first and the third meanings. He said, "The word value, it is to be observed, has two different meanings, and sometimes expresses the power of purchasing other goods which the possession of that object conveys. The one may be called 'value in use'; the other 'value in exchange.' The things which have the greatest value in use have frequently little or no value in exchange; and, on the contrary those which have the greatest value in exchange have frequently little or no value in use. Nothing is more useful than water: but it will purchase scarce anything; scarce anything can be had in exchange for it. A diamond, on the contrary, has scarce any value in use; but a very great quantity of other goods may frequently be had in exchange for it."

It is sufficiently plain that, when Smith speaks of water as being highly useful and yet devoid of purchasing power, he means *water in abundance,* that is to say, water so abundantly supplied that it has exerted its full useful effect, or its *total utility.* Water, when it becomes very scarce, as in a dry desert, acquires exceedingly great purchasing power. Thus Smith evidently means by value in use, *the total utility of a substance of which the degree of utility has sunk very low, because the want of such substance has been well nigh satisfied.* By purchasing power he clearly means the ratio of exchange for other commodities. But here he fails to point out that the quantity of goods received in exchange depends just as much upon the nature of the goods received, as on the nature of those given for them. In exchange for a diamond we can get a great quantity of iron, or corn, or paving-stones, or other commodity of which there is abundance; but we can get very few rubies, sapphires, or other precious stones. Silver is of high purchasing power compared with zinc, or lead, or iron, but of small purchasing power compared with gold, platinum, or iridium. Yet we might well say in any case that diamond and silver are things of high value. Thus I am led to think that the word value is often used in reality to mean *intensity of desire or esteem for a thing.* A silver ornament is a beautiful object apart from all ideas of traffic; it may thus be valued or esteemed simply because it suits the taste and fancy of its owner, and is the only one possessed. Even Robinson Crusoe must have looked upon each of his possessions with varying esteem and desire for more, although he was incapable of exchanging with any other person. Now, in this sense value seems to be identical with the final degree of utility of a commodity, as defined in a previous page; it is measured by the intensity of the pleasure or benefit which would be obtained from a new increment of the same commodity. No doubt there is a close connection between value in this meaning, and value as ratio of exchange. Nothing can have a high purchasing power unless it be highly esteemed in itself; but it may be highly esteemed apart from all comparison with other things; and, though highly esteemed, it may have a low purchasing power, because those things against which it is measured are still more esteemed.

Thus I come to the conclusion that, in the use of the word value, three distinct meanings are habitually confused together, and require to be thus distinguished—

(1) Value in use = total utility;
(2) Esteem = final degree of utility;
(3) Purchasing power = ratio of exchange.

It is not to be expected that we could profitably discuss such matters as economic doctrines, while the fundamental ideas of the subject are thus jumbled up together in one ambiguous word. The only thorough remedy consists in substituting for the dangerous name *value* that one of the three stated meanings which is intended in each case. In this work, therefore, I shall discontinue the use of the word value altogether, and when, as will be most often the case in the remainder of the book, I need to refer to the third meaning, often called by economists *exchange* or *exchangeable value,* I shall substitute the wholly unequivocal expression *Ratio of Exchange,* specifying at the same time what are the *two articles* exchanged. When we speak of the ratio of exchange of pig-iron and gold, there can be no possible doubt that we intend to refer to the ratio of the number of units of the one commodity to the number of units of the other commodity for which it exchanges, the units being arbitrary concrete magnitudes, but the ratio an abstract number. . . .

There is no difficulty in seeing that, when we use the word Value in the sense of ratio of exchange, its dimension will be simply zero. Value will be expressed, like angular magnitude and other ratios in general, by abstract number. Angular magnitude is measured by the ratio of a line to a line, the ratio of the arc subtended by the angle to the radius of the circle. So value in this sense is a ratio of the quantity of one commodity to the quantity of some other commodity exchanged for it. If we compare the commodities simply as physical quantities, we have the dimensions M divided by M, or MM^{-1}, or M^0. Exactly the same result would be obtained if, instead of taking the mere physical quantities, we were to compare their utilities, for we should then have MU divided by MU or M^0U^0, which, as it really means *unity*, is identical in meaning with M^0.

When we use the word value in the sense of esteem, or urgency of desire, the feeling with which Oliver Twist must have regarded a few more mouthfuls when he "asked for more," the meaning of the word, as already explained, is identical with *degree of utility*, of which the dimension is U. Lastly, the *value in use* of Adam Smith, or the *total utility*, is the integral of .U.*d*M, and has the dimensions MU. We may thus tabulate our results concerning the ambiguous uses of the word *value*—

Popular Expression of Meaning	Scientific Expression	Dimensions
(1) Value in use	Total Utility	MU
(2) Esteem, or Urgency of Desire for more	Final Degree of Utility	U
(3) Purchasing Power	Ratio of Exchange ..	M^0

When a commodity is perfectly uniform or homogeneous in quality, any portion may be indifferently used in place of an equal portion: hence, in the same market, and at the same moment, all portions must be exchanged at the same ratio. There can be no reason why a person should treat exactly similar things differently, and the slightest excess in what is demanded for one over the other will cause him to take the latter instead of the former. In nicely balanced exchanges it is a very minute scruple which turns the scale and governs the choice. A minute difference of quality in a commodity may thus give rise to preference, and cause the ratio of exchange to differ. But where no difference exists at all, or where no difference is known to exist, there can be no ground for preference whatever. If, in selling a quantity of perfectly equal and uniform barrels of flour, a merchant arbitrarily fixed different prices on them, a purchaser would of course select the cheaper ones; and where there was absolutely no difference in the thing purchased, even an excess of a penny in the price of a thing worth a thousand pounds would be a valid ground of choice. Hence follows what is undoubtedly true, with proper explanations, that *in the same open market, at any one moment, there cannot be two prices for the same kind of article*. Such differences as may practically occur arise from extraneous circumstances, such as the defec tive credit of the purchasers, their imperfect knowledge of the market, and so on.

The principle above expressed is a general law of the utmost importance in Economics, and I propose to call it *The Law of Indifference,* meaning that, when two objects or commodities are subject to no important difference as regards the purpose in view, they will either of them be taken instead of the other with perfect indifference by a purchaser. Every such act of indifferent choice gives rise to an equation of degrees of utility, so that in this principle of indifference we have one of the central pivots of the theory.

Though the price of the same commodity must be uniform at any one moment, it may vary from moment to moment, and must be conceived as in a state of continual change. Theoretically speaking, it would not usually be possible to buy two portions of the same commodity *successively* at the same ratio of exchange, because, no sooner would the first portion have been bought than the conditions of utility would be altered. When exchanges are made on a large scale, this result will be verified in practice. If a wealthy person invested £100,000 in the funds [1] in the morning, it is hardly likely that the operation could be repeated in the afternoon at the same price. In any market, if a person goes on buying largely, he will ultimately raise the price against himself. Thus it is apparent that extensive purchases would best be made gradually, so as to secure the advantage of a lower price upon the earlier portions. In theory this effect of exchange upon the ratio of exchange must be conceived to exist in some degree, however small may be the purchases made. Strictly speaking, the ratio of exchange at any moment is that of dy to dx, of an infinitely small quantity of one commodity to the infinitely small quantity of another which is given for it. The ratio of exchange is really a differential coefficient. The quantity of any article purchased is a function of the price at which it is purchased, and the ratio of exchange expresses the rate at which the quantity of the article increases compared with what is given for it.

We must carefully distinguish, at the same time, between the Statics and Dynamics of this subject. The real condition of industry is one of perpetual motion and change. Commodities are being continually manufactured and exchanged and consumed. If we wished to have a complete solution of the problem in all its natural complexity, we should have to treat it as a problem of motion—a problem of dynamics. But it would surely be absurd to attempt the more difficult question when the more easy one is yet so imperfectly within our power. It is only as a purely statical problem that I can venture to treat the action of exchange. Holders of commodities will be regarded not as continuously passing on these commodities in streams of trade, but as possessing certain fixed amounts which they exchange until they come to equilibrium.

It is much more easy to determine the point at which a pendulum will

[1] [Government obligations, in English usage.—*Editor*].

come to rest than to calculate the velocity at which it will move when displaced from that point of rest. Just so, it is a far more easy task to lay down the conditions under which trade is completed and interchange ceases, than to attempt to ascertain at what rate trade will go on when equilibrium is not attained.

The difference will present itself in this form: dynamically we could not treat the ratio of exchange otherwise than as the ratio of dy and dx, infinitesimal quantities of commodity. Our equations would then be regarded as differential equations, which would have to be integrated. But in the statical view of the question we can substitute the ratio of the finite quantities y and x. Thus, from the self-evident principle, stated earlier, that there cannot, in the same market, at the same moment, be two different prices for the same uniform commodity, it follows that *the last increments in an act of exchange must be exchanged in the same ratio as the whole quantities exchanged.* Suppose that two commodities are bartered in the ratio of x for y; then every mth part of x is given for the mth part of y, and it does not matter for which of the mth parts. No part of the commodity can be treated differently from any other part. We may carry this division to an indefinite extent by imagining m to be constantly increased, so that, at the limit, even an infinitely small part of x must be exchanged for an infinitely small part of y, in the same ratio as the whole quantities. This result we may express by stating that the increments concerned in the process of exchange must obey the equation

$$\frac{dy}{dx} = \frac{y}{x}.$$

The use which we shall make of this equation will be seen in the next section [page 407].

The keystone of the whole Theory of Exchange, and of the principal problems of Economics, lies in this proposition—*The ratio of exchange of any two commodities will be the reciprocal of the ratio of the final degrees of utility of the quantities of commodity available for consumption after the exchange is completed.* When the reader has reflected a little upon the meaning of this proposition, he will see, I think, that it is necessarily true, if the principles of human nature have been correctly represented in previous pages.

Imagine that there is one trading body possessing only corn, and another possessing only beef. It is certain that, under these circumstances, a portion of the corn may be given in exchange for a portion of the beef with a considerable increase of utility. How are we to determine at what point the exchange will cease to be beneficial? This question must involve both the ratio of exchange and the degrees of utility. Suppose, for a moment, that the ratio of exchange is approximately that of ten pounds of corn for one pound of beef: then if, to the trading body which possesses corn, ten pounds of corn are less useful than one of beef, that body will desire to carry the exchange further. Should the other body possessing beef find one pound less useful than ten pounds of corn, this body will also be desirous to continue the exchange. Exchange will thus go on until each party has obtained all the benefit that is possible, and loss of utility would result if more were exchanged. Both parties, then, rest in satisfaction and equilibrium, and the degrees of utility have come to their level, as it were.

This point of equilibrium will be known by the criterion, that an infinitely small amount of commodity exchanged in addition, at the same rate, will bring neither gain nor loss of utility. In other words, if increments of commodities be exchanged at the established ratio, their utilities will be equal for both parties. Thus, if ten pounds of corn were of exactly the same utility as one pound of beef, there would be neither harm nor good in further exchange at this ratio.

It is hardly possible to represent this theory completely by means of a diagram, but the accompanying figure may, perhaps, render it clearer. Suppose the line *pqr* to be a small portion of the curve of utility of one commodity, while the broken line *p′qr′* is the like curve of another commodity which has been reversed and superposed on the other. Owing to this reversal, the quantities of the first commodity are measured along the base line from *a* towards *b*, whereas those of the second must be measured in the opposite direction. Let units of both commodities be

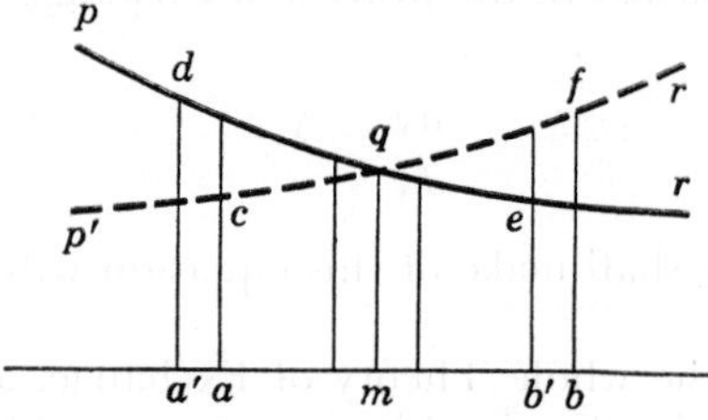

represented by equal lengths: then the little line of *a′a* indicates an increase of the first commodity, and a decrease of the second. Assume the ratio of exchange to be that of unit for unit, or 1 to 1: then, by receiving the commodity *a′a* the person will gain the utility *ad,* and lose the utility *a′c;* or he will make a net gain of the utility corresponding to the mixtilinear figure *cd.* He will, therefore, wish to extend the exchange. If he were to go up to the point *b′*, and were still proceeding, he would, by the next small exchange, receive the utility *be,* and part with *b′f;* or he would have a net loss of *ef.* He would, therefore, have gone too far; and it is pretty obvious that the point of intersection, *q,* defines the place where he would stop with the greatest advantage. It is there that a net gain is converted into a net loss, or rather where, for an infinitely small quantity, there is neither gain nor loss. To represent an infinitely small quantity, or even an exceedingly small quantity, on a diagram is, of course, impossible; but on either side of the line *mq* I have represented the utilities of a small quantity of commodity more or less, and it is apparent that the net gain or loss upon the exchange of these quantities would be trifling.

To represent this process of reasoning in symbols, let Δx denote a small increment of corn, and Δy a small increment of beef exchanged for it. Now our Law of Indifference comes into play. As both the corn and the beef are homogeneous commodities, no parts can be exchanged at a different ratio from other parts in the same market: hence, if x be the whole quantity of corn given for y the whole quantity of beef received, Δy must have the same ratio to Δx as y to x; we have then,

$$\frac{\Delta y}{\Delta x} = \frac{y}{x}, \quad \text{or} \quad \Delta y = \frac{y}{x} \Delta x.$$

In a state of equilibrium, the utilities of these increments must be equal in the case of each party, in order that neither more nor less exchange would be desirable. Now the increment of beef, Δy, is y/x times as great as the increment of corn, Δx, so that, in order that their utilities shall be equal, the degree of utility of beef must be x/y times as great as the degree of utility of corn. Thus we arrive at the principle that *the degrees of utility of commodities exchanged will be in the inverse proportion of the magnitudes of the increments exchanged.*

Let us now suppose that the first body, A, originally possessed the quantity a of corn, and that the second body, B, possessed the quantity b of beef. As the exchange consists in giving x of corn for y of beef, the state of things after exchange will be as follows:—

A holds $a - x$ of corn, and y of beef,
B holds x of corn, and $b - y$ of beef.

Let $\phi_1(a - x)$ denote the final degree of utility of corn to A, and $\phi_2 x$ the corresponding function for B. Also let $\psi_1 y$ denote A's final degree of utility for beef, and $\psi_2(b - y)$ B's similar function. Then, as explained previously A will not be satisfied unless the following equation holds true:—

$$\phi_1(a - x) \cdot dx = \psi_1 y \cdot dy; \text{ or } \frac{\phi_1(a - x)}{\psi_1 y} = \frac{dy}{dx}.$$

Hence, substituting for the second member by the equation given previously, we have

$$\frac{\phi_1(a - x)}{\psi_1 y} = \frac{y}{x}.$$

What holds true of A will also hold true of B, *mutatis mutandis.* He must also derive exactly equal utility from the final increments, otherwise it will be for his interest to exchange either more or less, and he will disturb the conditions of exchange. Accordingly the following equation must hold true:

$$\psi_2(b - y) \cdot dy = \phi_2 x \cdot dx;$$

or, substituting as before,

$$\frac{\phi_2 x}{\psi_2(b - y)} = \frac{y}{x}.$$

We arrive, then, at the conclusion, that whenever two commodities are exchanged for each other, and *more or less can be given or received in infinitely small quantities,* the quantities exchanged satisfy two equations, which may be thus stated in a concise form—

$$\frac{\phi_1(a - x)}{\psi_1 y} = \frac{y}{x} = \frac{\phi_2 x}{\psi_2(b - y)}.$$

The two equations are sufficient to determine the results of exchange; for there are only two unknown quantities concerned, namely, x and y, the quantities given and received. . . .

The preceding pages contain, if I am not mistaken, an explanation of the nature of value which will, for the most part, harmonise with previous views upon the subject. Ricardo has stated, like most other economists, that utility is absolutely essential to value; but that "possessing utility, commodities derive their exchangeable value from two sources: from their scarcity, and from the quantity of labour required to obtain them." Senior, again, has admirably defined wealth, or objects possessing value, as "those things, and those things only, which are transferable, are limited in supply, and are directly or indirectly productive of pleasure or preventive of pain." Speaking only of things which are transferable, or capable of being passed from hand to hand, we find that two of the clearest definitions of value recognise *utility* and *scarcity* as the essential qualities. But the moment that we distinguish between the total utility of a mass of commodity and the degree of utility of different portions, we may say that it is scarcity which prevents the fall in the final degree of utility. Bread has the almost infinite utility of maintaining life, and when it becomes a question of life or death, a small quantity of food exceeds in value all other things. But when we enjoy our ordinary supplies of food, a loaf of bread has little value, because the utility of an additional loaf is small, our appetites being satiated by our customary meals.

I have pointed out the excessive ambiguity of the word Value, and the apparent impossibility of using it safely. When intended to express the mere fact of certain articles exchanging in a particular ratio, I have proposed to substitute the unequivocal expression—*ratio of exchange.* But I am inclined to believe that a ratio is not the meaning which most persons attach to the word Value. There is a certain sense of esteem or desirableness, which we may have with regard to a thing apart from any distinct consciousness of the ratio in which it would exchange for other things. I may suggest that this distinct feeling of value is probably identical with the final degree of utility. While Adam Smith's often-quoted *value in use* is the total utility of a commodity to us, the *value in exchange* is defined by the *terminal utility,* the remaining desire which we or others have for possessing more.

There remains the question of labour as an element of value. Economists have not been wanting who put forward labour as the *cause of value,* asserting that all objects derive their value from the fact that labour has been expended on them; and it is thus implied, if not stated, that value will be proportional to labour. This is a doctrine which cannot stand for a moment, being directly opposed to facts. . . .

The mere fact that there are many things, such as rare ancient books, coins, antiquities, etc., which have high values, and which are absolutely incapable of production now, disperses the notion that value depends on labour. Even those things which are producible in any quantity by labour seldom exchange exactly at the corresponding values. The market price of corn, cotton, iron, and most other things is, in the prevalent theories of value, allowed to fluctuate above or below its natural or cost value. There may, again, be any discrepancy between the quantity of labour spent upon an object and the value ultimately attaching to it. A great undertaking like the Great Western Railway, or the Thames Tunnel, may embody a vast amount of labour, but its value depends entirely upon the number of persons who find it useful. If no use could be found for the *Great Eastern* steamship, its value would be *nil,* except for the utility of some of its materials. On the other hand, a successful undertaking, which happens to possess great utility, may have a value, for a time at least, far exceeding what has been spent upon it, as in the case of the [first] Atlantic Cable. The fact is, that *labour once spent has no influence on the future value of any article:* it is gone and lost for ever. In commerce bygones are for ever bygones; and we are always starting clear at each moment, judging the values of things with a view to future utility. Industry is essentially prospective, not retrospective; and seldom does the result of any undertaking exactly coincide with the first intentions of its promoters.

But though labour is never the cause of value, it is in a large proportion of cases the determining circumstance, and in the following way:— *Value depends solely on the final degree of utility. How can we vary this degree of utility?—By having more or less of the commodity to consume. And how shall we get more or less of it?—By spending more or less labour in obtaining a supply.* According to this view, then, there are two steps between labour and value. Labour affects supply, and supply affects the degree of utility, which governs value, or the ratio of exchange. In order that there may be no possible mistake about this all-important series of relations, I will re-state it in a tabular form, as follows:—

Cost of production determines supply;
Supply determines final degree of utility;
Final degree of utility determines value.

But it is easy to go too far in considering labour as the regulator of value; it is equally to be remembered that labour is itself of unequal value. Ricardo, by a violent assumption, founded his theory of value on quantities of labour considered as one uniform thing. He was aware that labour differs infinitely in quality and efficiency, so that each kind is more or less scarce, and is consequently paid at a higher or lower rate of wages. He regarded these differences as disturbing circumstances which would have to be allowed for; but his theory rests on the assumed equality of labour. This theory rests on a wholly different ground. I hold labour to be *essentially variable,* so that *its value must be determined by the value of the produce, not the value of the produce by that of the labour.* I hold it to be impossible to compare *à priori* the productive powers of a navvy, a carpenter, an iron-puddler, a schoolmaster, and a barrister. Accordingly, it will be found that not one of my equations represents a comparison between one man's labour and another's. The equation, if there is one at all, is between the same person in two or more different occupations. The subject is one in which complicated action and reaction takes place.

JOHN BATES CLARK

(1847–1938)

John Bates Clark was largely responsible for the indigenous growth of marginal-utility economics in the United States. He appears to have evolved the marginal-utility principle independently and to have applied it in an ingenious manner to problems of distribution and production.

Clark's interest in theoretical, deductive economics is a bit unusual; he was one of the first American graduate students to study in Germany (1873–1875) and was, in fact, the pupil of Roscher and Knies, the founders of the German historical school. In all probability the influence of the German historical school was responsible for Clark's deep interest in ethics and social issues and for his opposition to the teachings of the classical school.

His most important theoretical contribution is *The Distribution of Wealth* (1899), from which the selections herein are taken. This was at once the first systematic theoretical book on marginal-utility economics and, because of the manner in which it extended the marginal principle to cover the problems of production and distribution, an original contribution to economic theory. Clark's interest in distribution stemmed in the first place from his ethical preconceptions; in a just society men should get all that they create, or their fair share of it. He then tried to devise an analytical tool which would relate the results of the pricing process to the standards of social justice. Actually, what he did analyze was the pricing of the factors of production under perfect competition and static conditions. He arrived at the conclusion that the wages of the marginal laborer would just equal the marginal product and that the wage of every unit of labor employed would then equal his marginal product.

It then followed that wages could not rise above this level without causing the marginal laborers to be unemployed, since their cost would now exceed their return. The increased output resulting from the employment of additional labor in a given plant was subject to diminishing returns. Thus, given the supply of capital, the state of technique, and the productivity of labor, the level of wages which would ensure full employment was strictly determined. Labor's demand for wages above this "natural" level could only cause unemployment.

The modern version of the marginal-productivity theory of wages is essentially due to Clark's treatment. Of late, however, more attention has been given to the factors that determine the supply of labor. Clark's theory is a demand theory of wages which assumes a given quantity of labor in its analysis of the marginal product of labor. To be sure, some economists even today continue to argue the validity of the theory. In 1945 and 1946 a heated discussion took place in the pages of the *American Economic Review* regarding the applicability of the marginal-productivity theory of wages. The argument remains unresolved.

Clark did make an important methodological contribution, however, in his stress on the distinction between static and dynamic analysis. According to Clark, five possible types of changes may occur in a dynamic economy: changes in population, tastes, capital, techniques, and forms of industrial organization. Clark held that profits would be nonexistent in a stationary state. Wages and interest would then be the only normal returns, rent being a differential return found in the income of all factors of production. In a dynamic economy, however, change makes profit possible.

Clark's writings influenced an entire generation of economists and established, in fact, an American branch of orthodox economics. In the following selections from *The Distribution of Wealth* Clark's ideas on the subject of distribution in general and on wages, rent, and interest are presented in some detail.

THE DISTRIBUTION OF WEALTH *

Final Productivity the Regulator of Both Wages and Interest

Each unit of labor . . . is worth to its employer what the last unit produces. When the force is complete, no one body of a thousand men can withdraw without lessening the product of the whole society by the same amount that we have attributed to the one that we last set working. The effective value of any unit of labor is always what the whole society with all its capital produces, minus what it would produce if that unit were to be taken away. This sets the universal standard of pay. A unit of labor consists, in the supposed case, of a thousand men, and the product of it is the natural pay of a thousand men. If the men are equal, a thousandth part of this amount is the natural pay of any one of them.

We are seeking, of course, a static standard of wages; but the process that gradually builds up a force of laborers from a thousand to a hundred thousand, and causes capital to modify its forms as the increase of the force goes on, is not a static process. It is a dynamic operation which brings the working force up to its static complement. From the time that the force is complete, however, we leave it unchanged: we let the static condition thus attained continue forever. The importance of going through the illustrative dynamic process, and making up the permanent force unit by unit, lies in the clear view that this gives of the product that can be attributed to the "final" unit.

Actually, no unit is last in time. The hundred thousand men, with the hundred million dollars' worth of capital, work on year after year, and no one division of a thousand can be singled out as constituting the particular division whose product fixes wages. Any one such body of men is always worth to its employers what the final division would produce, if we were to set them working in such an order of succession as, for illustration, we have described. That the men will get this amount, is insured by employers' competition. The final division of a thousand men has in its hands a certain potential product, when it offers its service to employers. If one set of *entrepreneurs* will not give them the value of it; another will, provided that competition is perfect. With an ideally complete and free competitive system, each unit of labor can get exactly what a final unit produces. With an imperfect competition, it still *tends* to get that amount. The final product of labor sets a standard for the pay of labor; and actual wages tend toward it, with variations.

. . . We may now summarize the conclusions that we have thus far reached, concerning the natural standard of wages, in the following series of propositions:—

(1) Labor, like commodities, is subject to a law of marginal appraisal. The rate that the market puts on the final unit of the supply of each

* From *The Distribution of Wealth* (London, Macmillan and Co., Ltd., New York, The Macmillan Co., 1899).

of them, it puts on the entire supply. As the last unit of consumers' goods is a price-making one, so the last unit of labor is the one that fixes wages.

(2) The term *final* does not designate a particular unit that can be identified and separated from others. There is not, for example, in the elevators of the United States a special lot of wheat that is in a strategic position and has a price-making power that other wheat does not possess. Any unit whatever of this commodity is final in the economic sense; inasmuch as, by its presence, it brings the supply to its present actual magnitude. Similarly, the *final, marginal* or *last* unit of labor does not consist of particular men. It is especially necessary to guard against the idea that the final men, whose products fix the general rate of wages, are those who would naturally be employed last, because they are the poorest. We have been careful to say that it is units of labor, as such, that are the basis of the law of wages; and a body of men must be of the average quality of ordinary laborers, if it is to constitute such a unit.

(3) In presenting the law of final utility, it is customary to arrange the units of a commodity in an imaginary series, to present them one at a time and to ascertain how important each one is to the consumer. Yet commodities never come to the market in such an order. The whole present supply of a commodity is offering in the market; but the price that it is bringing is fixed by the importance that would attach to the final unit, *if the supply were offered in such a series of units.*

In like manner, we may find it useful, in presenting the law by which wages are fixed, to go through an imaginary operation of setting men at work, one man at a time or one company of men at a time, and thus to find what importance the market places on the last one. This reveals the operation of a law of diminishing productivity; and whether we take a single man or a body of men as the unit of labor, *any unit can get, as pay, what the last one would produce, if the force were set working in this way.*

(4) The standard of wages thus attained is a static one. So long as the labor and the capital continue unchanged in amount, and produce the same things, by the same processes and under an unchanging form of organization, wages will continue at the rate that this test establishes. Setting men at work in succession is a bit of imaginary dynamics, but what it reveals is a *static law.*

. . . Everywhere do the forms of the capital show differences in earning power; and the owners choose first the most productive forms, and later the less productive. To this fact is due the present low rate of interest. We are utilizing the opportunities for investment that stand late in the series and are low in the scale of productivity.

We have said that no increment of capital can get for its owner more than the last increment produces. We may state this in another way by saying that no form of capital can claim and get for its owners in a year a larger fraction of its cost than the least productive form produces. Under modern conditions, if the man who lends "money" for the procuring of a highly necessary tool demands the whole amount that is secured through the use of it, the *entrepreneur,* who is the borrower, will refuse the money and will use, for the procuring of the tool which is so much needed, the money that formerly went into the tool that was last and least important on the list. In terms of more primitive life, if the man who performs the labor of making a very necessary tool demands the whole product that it creates, the *entrepreneur* will decline to utilize this tool-making labor and will divert to the making of the needed instrument that labor which has been used for the making of the least important part of his working equipment. Capital is, it thus appears, completely transmutable in form. Society can quit making one kind of instrument and make another. Capital-goods are, then, interchangeable; and while this is so, no increment of capital can ever secure for its owner more than the final increment produces.

It is, of course, true that labor also has to change its forms, as capital accumulates. The man who watches a complicated machine is going through a set of movements very different from those executed by a man working with a hand tool. Every time that we change the form of the capital, we change, by that very fact, the character of the labor. Mutual adaptation in form is the general rule for these two producing agents. Change the merely quantitative ratio of one of them to the other, and you make it necessary to transform both of them in character. As with ten units of capital for ten units of labor there will be one grade of instruments and certain kinds of work performed in connection with them, so with eleven units of capital for ten units of labor there will be somewhat different kinds of instruments and different modes of working. This double transformation must, moreover, theoretically extend through the whole mass of capital and the whole process of labor. Everywhere there are to be seen new and improved kinds of capital-goods and new modes of using them.

With this qualification, we may represent the law of interest by the process of building up, increment by increment, the fund of social capital and measuring the product produced by each unit of it. In this imaginary process we have revealed a true law of varying productivity. As we have said, the addition to the product caused by the last unit of capital fixes the rate of interest. Every unit of capital can secure for its owner what the last unit produces, and it can secure no more. The principle of final productivity, in short, acts in two ways, affording a theory of wages and of interest.

The Products of Labor and Capital, as Measured by the Formula for Rent

. . . Labor, as . . . applied to land, is subject to a law of diminishing returns. Put one man on a quarter section of land, containing prairie and forest, and he will get a rich return. Two laborers on the same ground will get less per man; three will get still less; and, if you enlarge the force to ten, it may be that the last man will get wages only. We must, however, be very careful to make sure of the reason why the tenth man gets only his wages. If the men are hired by the owner of the land at the prevalent rate of wages, what has happened is that the force has been enlarged till the last man produces only what is paid to him. In this case . . . wages fix the intensive margin of cultivation of this land. The rate that we must pay to the men decides for us how many of them we can employ on our farm. If, however, our farm is isolated and the workers are a society by themselves, and if there are ten of them to be employed, we shall set them all working and pay to each of them as much as the last one produces. Here it is the product of the marginal labor that fixes the rate of wages, . . . and here, also, the situation illustrates the true law of rent.[1]

All the earlier men in the series create surplus products, over and above the amount created by the last man. They get only what the last one produces, and the farmer-landlord gets the remainder. What goes to the owner of the land is the sum of a series of remainders that are made by taking, in each case, the product that is attributable to one of the earlier men as a minuend and the product that is imputable to the last man as a subtrahend.

Call the product that the single worker creates, when he has the whole field to himself, P^{1st}. Call the additional product that the second man is able to bring into existence P^{2d}, etc.; call the enlargement in the output made by the last man P^{10th}.

$$P^{1st} - P^{10th} = \text{surplus created by the first worker.}$$
$$P^{2d} - P^{10th} = \text{surplus created by the second worker.}$$
$$P^{9th} - P^{10th} = \text{surplus created by the ninth worker.}$$

If we complete the series of such subtractions and add the nine remainders, the sum of them all will be the rent of the piece of land. This is the amount that the owner can keep, from the total created by the different workers aided by the land.

The sum of $P^{1st} + P^{2d} + P^{3d}$, etc., to and including P^{10th}, is the whole product of the field and the labor that is spent on it. It is the sum of all the minuends in the foregoing series, with the product of the final man

[1] The law of rent, as commonly stated, has the defect that is illustrated by the former of these cases, where it is applied to the reward for labor. The farmer who figures in the current statement of the law hires his men at the wages that prevail in the various industries that are carried on about him; and, when he finds that more men will not produce their wages, he quits enlarging his force. Each of the earlier men creates a surplus above his wages. When we are considering the rent of a limited piece of land devoted to one use, the scientific way to calculate the rent is to use as the subtrahend wages, rather than the final product of labor; since it is wages that fix final product. If what we want is a genuine differential product, we must isolate our working society, count the laborers, set them all at work and let the last produce what he can. There will then be a difference between what each of the earlier men produces and this final or standard product. This is, in each case, a true differential product. It is measured by comparing, not products created for the farmer and wages paid by him, but one product with another product.

added to it. $10 \times P^{10th}$ equals the total subtrahend; and the total rent of the field is the difference between these amounts. It is, in other words, the whole product minus ten times the product of the tenth and last unit of labor.

Let us . . . measure the number of laborers by the line AD, and the product of successive increments of labor by AB, A′B′, etc. If we give to these lines an appreciable width, so that a series of them will fill the entire figure, ABCD, that area will measure the product of all the labor and all the capital in our illustrative agricultural community. The capital is virtually all in the form of land; and we are now able to attribute to the land that part of the product which, in effect, it creates.

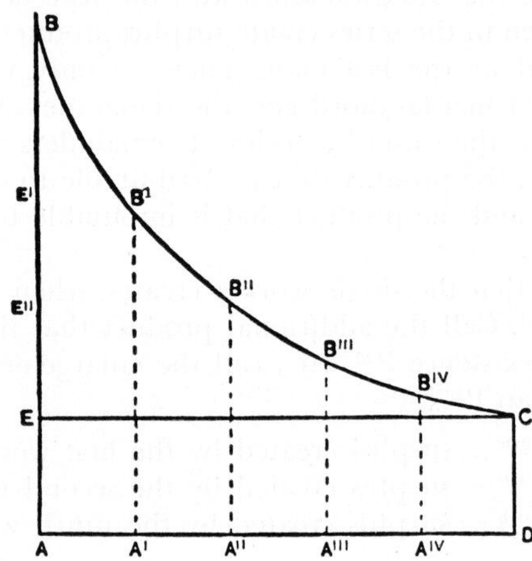

The last unit of labor creates the amount of product that is expressed by DC; and, accordingly, each unit of labor is effectively worth just that amount to the employing farmer, and each unit gets that amount as its wages. AECD measures total wages, and EBC measures the entire rent of the land. This amount we have spoken of as composed of a series of surpluses, or differential products, and we have measured them in each case by subtracting from what we have called the product of one of the earlier increments of labor the product of the last increment. AB minus DC gives such a surplus, and it is a part of the rent. It looks, at a careless view, as though land had the capacity to cut off and claim for itself a part of the product of labor—that is, the surplus part of the product of all the earlier increments of *labor* appears to be the *rent* of the *land.*

In reality, this surplus is the fruit of the aid that the land affords, and is attributable to the land only. A correct conception of the nature of any rent makes it a concrete addition which one producing agent is able to make to the product that is attributable to another producing agent. Land makes its own addition to the product of each unit of labor except the last one. When there was available only a piece of land, with no labor to till it, the product was *nil.* When one unit of labor combined itself with the land, the product was AB; and in this form of statement we impute the whole product to the labor. A second unit of labor now comes, unaided by capital, into the field and adds itself, empty-handed, to the working force. Whatever it produces, it brings into existence by adding to what the field yielded to one man's cultivation. The product thus created by an addition to labor, with no addition to capital, is A′B′. The difference between AB and A′B′, which is the line E′B, measures the surplus that a man can produce when he has the whole field to aid him above what he can create when he is unaided. The last man adds labor and no land to the productive combination; while the first man had land, and the addition that the land itself made to the bare product of labor constitutes the differential quantity which is the rent of the land. The science of rent is a science of economic causation, which traces products to their sources. The rent getter is a product creator.

The third man, also empty-handed, creates the amount A″B″; and E′B + E″E′ measures the contribution that the land has thus far made to the joint product of land and labor. Extending the vertical lines and giving to them width enough to make them fill the area of the entire figure, we have AECD as the product of all the labor, when it is taken unit by unit and made to work virtually unaided. ABCD is what it creates as it is aided by the land, and EBC is the amount that the land contributes to the product of the combination. This measures the difference between the product of ten units of aided labor and ten units of unaided labor.

We can now make the really important application of the principle of diminishing returns, which fixes both marginal productivity and rent. This is the application that is actually making everywhere in the business world. The isolated farm, with its whole capital in land, is an illustration only; while the real field for labor, to which the farm corresponds, is the world, with its whole circle of industries and its complex equipment of capital.

For a fixed area of land read, now, a fixed fund of permanent social capital. It is at this moment an exact sum; and it will, as it were, prolong the conditions of this moment, remaining at exactly its present size. The artificial instruments are, of course, perishing and renewing; but, if there is no need of changing the form of the capital, a worn-out instrument will be replaced by another that is exactly like it. A hoe will replace a hoe, and a ship will succeed a ship; and the new instruments of production will be exact duplicates of the old. This would be clear in a completely static condition. We are, however, to introduce labor, increment by increment, into this general field of industry; and this, of course, compels such a change in the forms of the capital as we have already described. The amount of the capital remaining fixed, the instruments become more numerous and cheaper, as the force of labor enlarges.

Labor, applied to the whole fund of capital, in land and all other instruments, is now subject to the law of diminishing returns. The first unit produces the amount AB, the second produces the amount A′B′, the third creates the quantity A″B″ and the last the quantity DC. This last amount sets the rate of wages, and the area AECD measures the amount of wages. It leaves the amount expressed by the area EBC as the rent of the fund of social capital. All interest is thus a surplus, entirely akin to the rent of land, as that is expressed by the Ricardian formula: it is a concrete product, attributable to the agent that claims it as an income.

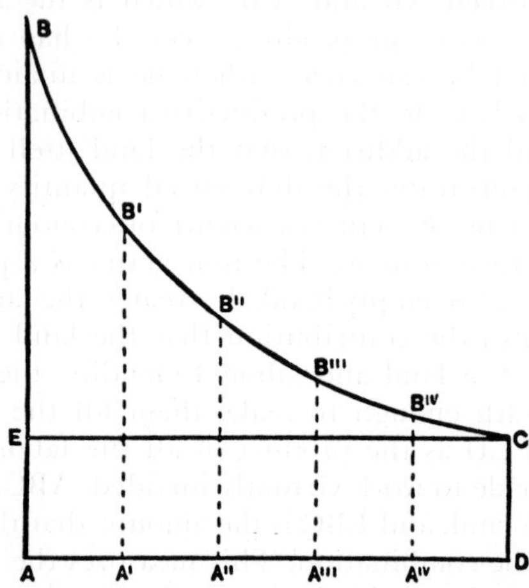

This rent is, moreover, made up of a series of genuine differential gains. It is not like the rent of the farm, in our former illustration, which, as we found, really depends on the rate of wages that prevails elsewhere. The rent of the whole fund of social capital is the sum of a series of differences between certain products and a final, or standard, product. True differentials lie between different products, and not between products and wages. The line DC, which sets the rate of wages, expresses primarily the product of the last unit of labor. We have set all the men in the society working, we have measured the amount created by the last addition to the force, and we have measured the surplus that each earlier unit of labor creates above this amount. The surplus is, in each case, a true differential product; since it is not merely a remainder that is left after paying wages, but is a difference between one product and another. It is the difference between the product of aided labor and that of the labor that is virtually unaided, and the sum of all these differences is the rent of the social fund of capital.

Reverse now the situation. Let labor be the fixed element and let social capital enlarge, changing its forms of course, in the enlarging.

ABCD is the total product. AB is the product of the first unit of capital, A′B′ the product of the second, A″B″ that of the third and DC that of the last. A unit of capital, adding itself with no new labor to the productive combination, enlarges the product by the amount DC. So much can be attributed to any unit of capital, separately considered. The effective importance of every one of the units of capital is the same. While capital-goods are not interchangeable, true capital is completely so; and all parts of it are, therefore, on a plane in their earning capacity. A merchant, a manufacturer or a farmer, if he can offer good security, can hire all the "money" that he needs at the rate that the least necessary sum which he invests in his business will earn for him. Does this imply an exploitation of the earlier units of capital? Does the borrower of these sums rob the lender?

If the final unit of capital produces the amount DC, it will get that amount as interest; and certainly no other unit can get any more. AECD will be the total amount of interest, and EBC will be a surplus; but it will be a surplus that is causally attributable to labor, and to labor only. The difference between the product that is solely due to capital and that which is due to capital and another agent in combination is the effect of the presence and the work of that other agent.

If we were to apply the term *rent* to all such surpluses, we should say that EBC is the rent of the force of laborers that is at work in connection with capital. This amount is made up of a series of differential products. Apparently AB — DC is the difference between the product of the first unit of capital and that of the last, A′B′ — DC is the difference between the product of the second unit of capital and that of the last, etc. *The rent of the labor,* if we use that expression, is the sum of the surplus products connected with the earlier units of capital but not attributable to them as a cause. The laborers seem to get a part of what the earlier units of capital produce; whereas, in reality, this is the difference between what capital and labor jointly produce and what capital alone contributes to the product of the combination. EBC is, therefore, the amount that is imputable to labor only.

One law governs wages and interest—the law of final productivity. By one mode of statement of the law (Fig. 1), we get wages as an amount directly determined by this principle: it is the area AECD of our diagram. Arithmetically stated, the earnings of all labor equal the product of the final unit of labor multiplied by the number of the units. In Fig. 1, in which wages are thus determined, interest is a surplus that is of the nature of rent. By another mode of stating the law (Fig. 2), we get interest as the amount that is positively fixed by the final productivity law, and wages are now the surplus that is akin to rent. These amounts together make up the whole static income of society.

Profit has no place in such static conditions. The two incomes that are permanent and independent of dynamic changes are the products, respectively, of labor and of capital. Each of them is directly determined by the final productivity law, and each is also a remainder—a surplus or a differential quantity. In one use of terms, it is a rent made by subtracting the other income from the whole product of social industry.

Does such a remainder ever go to the persons who naturally get it, merely because it is a remainder and is not claimed by others? In Fig. 1, where EBC, representing interest, is a surplus governed by the law of rent, does the capitalist get this amount merely because labor cannot get it? The whole product is ABCD, and labor can have only AECD. If there is no profit, capital must get the remainder. Do the capitalists, then, come into the possession of this income merely because it is thus left for them by the laborers?

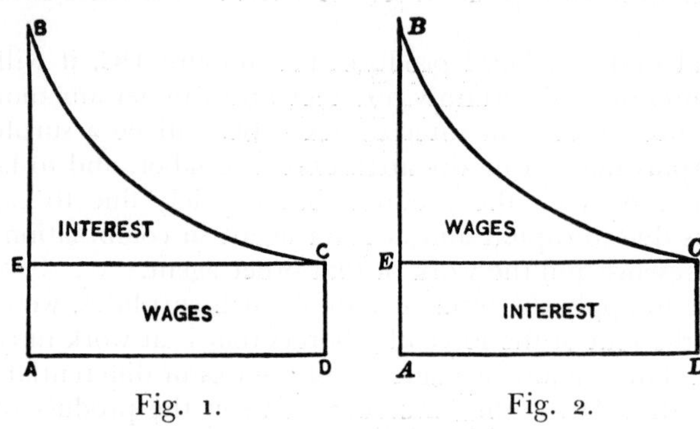

Fig. 1. Fig. 2.

This point is of much consequence. The question at issue is nothing less than whether any static income is determined residually. Clearly it is never so determined. No static income is what it is merely because the deducting of another income from the social product leaves a certain remainder. Any income that is nothing but a remainder must go to the *entrepreneur*. Because EBC, in Fig. 1, is not claimed by labor, it is left in the hands of the *entrepreneur*. Thus far it is a residuum. It is, moreover, important that this amount should thus be left in the employer's hands, for by this means he is made able to pay the interest that the capitalist will claim; but there is in the mere fact that he has this sum nothing that makes it necessary for him to pay it to the capitalist. What the owners of capital can force *entrepreneurs* to pay them, is determined by the final productivity of capital. Employers of capital must pay for the final increment of it just what that increment produces, and they must pay for all other increments at the same rate. If this necessity takes from them the whole amount, EBC, which labor leaves in their hands, then EBC goes to the capitalist. It does so, however, only because the capitalist can claim and get it, by the direct action of the final productivity law. What the capitalist can get under this principle is expressed by Fig. 2. AECD is here the amount of interest, as directly and positively fixed. This amount must pass, in any case, from the *entrepreneurs* to the capitalists.

The *entrepreneur,* then, after paying wages, as indicated by AECD in Fig. 1, has left in his hands EBC, out of which he can pay interest. What he must pay as interest, is *AECD* in Fig. 2. If the area EBC in Fig. 1 were larger than *AECD* in Fig. 2, there would be a remainder left for the *entrepreneur.* This would be a pure profit, the only kind of income that is ever residually determined.

It is clear, on the face of the facts, that the two static incomes—those, namely, of the laborer and of the capitalist—are paid to them by the *entrepreneur,* who receives and sells the product of their joint industry. In the cotton mill, it is the hirer of capital and of labor who puts the goods on the market and from the proceeds pays the workmen and the owners of capital. If he pays first to the capitalist what the final productivity law, as applied to capital, calls for, he has a remainder out of which he must pay wages; and now it is the final productivity law that decides what he must pay as wages. If there is anything left on his hands after the two payments are made, it is a profit; and the terms *profit* and *residual income* are thus synonymous.

This truth we may demonstrate by using our diagrams in a reversed order. In Fig. 2 *AECD* is interest, as directly determined, and *EBC* is the remainder, which is left in the *entrepreneur's* hands for the payment of wages. What the *entrepreneur* must pay to the workmen is AECD of Fig. 1. If that is less than *ECD* of Fig. 2, there is a residuum, or profit, for the *entrepreneur.* Static conditions, however, exclude such a profit by making these two areas equal.

We have, then, established the following propositions:—

(1) Wages and interest are both determined by the law of final productivity.

(2) When, in an illustrative case, one of these incomes is so determined, the other appears to be a residuum.

(3) As a residuum, such an income would be left in the *entrepreneurs'* hands; but it is actually taken from them by a further action of the final productivity law.

(4) *Entrepreneurs'* profit and residual income are synonymous terms.[2]

[2] The above theses appear sharply to contradict the theory of wages advanced by the late President Francis A. Walker, in which wages are called the residual share in distribution. It is an aid in removing causes of confusion from the discussion, and in giving to the theory of this eminent economist what is due to it, to notice the fact that his study was essentially a study of a subject in economic dynamics. If the total product of industry becomes larger than it has been, and if interest, rent and profit do not become any greater than they were, wages must absorb the whole increase. In this view, the residuum may be regarded as a remainder that is left when the former product of the whole industry is subtracted from the present product. Such a view of the power of labor to get all the increase that dynamic changes create would be consistent with the view that, in the merely static adjustment that takes place at all times, wages are determined directly by the law of final productivity, as are other shares of the total product. We might claim that the progress which makes industry, as a whole, more productive makes labor, separately considered, more so, but leaves the productivity of other agents unchanged. Laborers would then, in each static adjustment that takes place, force *entrepreneurs* to give them their product, just as capitalists would do. Statically, wages would be determined directly; while dynamically they would consist partly in a residuum, made by deducting the former product of industry, as a whole, from the present product.

In our view, progress in methods of production makes both labor and capital more productive; and the fruits of progress are thus shared by the two agents, according to the de-

The static conditions assumed in the present study preclude the existence of such *entrepreneurs'* gains.

---

grees of specific productivity that the progress gives to them. Labor, then, does not get the whole difference between the former product of industry and the present product. What we are trying to make clear is that, in a merely static adjustment of shares in distribution, both wages and interest must be determined directly, and not residually. After paying interest, the *entrepreneur* has wages left in his hands; but he is forced to pay it to labor *because it is the product of labor.* In making his bargain, the worker has the benefit of free competition. He is virtually selling his forthcoming product, and can resort to another employer, if the present one refuses to give him the full value of it. The capitalist, in making this contract for the payment of interest, is in the same way selling a product, and can exact the value of it. Without this power, neither laborers nor capitalists could get their shares from the *entrepreneur's* hands. For an early statement of the principles presented in this chapter, the reader is referred to an article by the present writer, in the *Quarterly Journal of Economics,* for April, 1891, on "Distribution as Determined by a Law of Rent."

ALFRED MARSHALL

(1842–1924)

Marshall was born in London and educated at Cambridge University, where he prepared himself for a career in philosophy and ethics. His parallel interest in mathematics led him to translate the doctrines of Ricardo and John Stuart Mill into mathematical language while he was still a young tutor. By 1871, the year in which Jevons' *Theory* and Menger's *Principles* were published, Marshall had already developed a similar approach to the theory of value. His two papers, "The Pure Theory of Domestic Values" and "The Pure Theory of Foreign Trade," which were published in 1879, contain the gist of his approach. His chief work, the *Principles of Economics,* appeared in 1890 and went through eight editions before his death.

Although he was acquainted with the general equilibrium theory of Continental economists and was an adept mathematician, Marshall chose the less vigorous method of partial equilibrium analysis because it served to make economic science a better "engine for discovery" in the investigation of specific problems. His approach to his predecessors was unusually conciliatory, and throughout his career, he tended to phrase his own doctrines so as to minimize the change from the Ricardian tradition. In contrast to the earlier utility theorists, he did not take supply for granted but considered it as "the other blade of a pair of scissors." Underlying demand was marginal utility as reflected in the price offers of buyers. Underlying supply was marginal effort, reflected in the supply prices of sellers. The dual character of the "pair of scissors" was carried over in the theory of distribution. The marginal-productivity theory of wages and interest, later to be refined by J. B. Clark, was accepted as an important explanation of the nature of demand. On the supply side, however, the earnings of factors would tend to approach the marginal sacrifice and disutility of effort involved.

Among Marshall's major contributions was the introduction of time factors into economics, which allowed him to qualify his static analysis by dynamic considerations. It was his distinction between the short run and the long run that signalized the shift from the classical treatment of cost factors. In the long run, when all expenses are variable because all factors are withdrawable, the influence of cost on price is more important than in the short run, because it takes time to adjust supply to changing conditions and it is through this adjustment that cost affects price. Thus, Marshall's emphasis on demand and the short run was seen by him as an extension, not a contradiction, of Ricardian theory.

His partial equilibrium method is illustrated by his discussion of demand. Since the demand schedule relates solely to the relationship between price and quantity demanded, other things must be held constant, or, as Marshall has it, "impounded in *ceteris paribus.*" Thus, the taste of consumers, their money incomes, the number of buyers, and the prices of other commodities are held constant in the discussion of the equilibrium determination of supply and demand. This procedure is still the accepted method of analyzing changes in demand.

Marshall's "box of tools" is familiar to every student of economics: the elasticity coefficient, the distinction between prime and supplementary cost and between money and real cost, the principle of substitution at the margin, external and internal economies, long-run and short-run analysis, and quasi-rent.

The *Principles of Economics* represented work of more than two decades. When it finally appeared in 1890, its success was immediate and complete. No book since *The Wealth of Nations* has had as pervasive an influence on economic thought.

Several generations of eminent British economists passed through Marshall's hands at Cambridge, and his disciples soon held the more important academic chairs in the United Kingdom. Among his important pupils were Edgeworth, who refined the theory of monopoly, and Pigou, who elaborated Marshall's concept of consumers' surplus into a comprehensive theory of social welfare. As late as the 1930's major innovations in economic thought resulted from attempts to remedy the inadequacies in Marshall's system. For example, the incompatibility of decreasing costs and competition led Chamberlin and Robinson to develop the theory of monopolistic competition. Keynes, who was a pupil of Marshall, was moved to demonstrate the possibility of underemployment equilibrium because of the failure of Marshall and his followers to deal with the problem of unemployment and trade cycles.

The following selections set forth in brief the Marshallian system of value and distribution and give Marshall's own estimate of his position in relation to his predecessors, especially Ricardo.

The selection from *Industry and Trade* is especially noteworthy because it is on a different level of discourse from the *Principles;* instead of generalization and abstraction, Marshall used historical analogies and statistics to explain the special role of cartels in the German economy. The article from the *Economic Journal* shows Marshall's optimism, his faith in the benevolence of business men, whom he likened to knights of old, and his fear of the deadening hand of collectivism. These selections are included as an antidote to the narrower impression of Marshall's scope which is conveyed by the *Principles* alone.

PRINCIPLES OF ECONOMICS *

General Theory of Equilibrium of Demand and Supply

§ 1. . . . we have studied the theory of the mutual relations of demand and supply in their most general form; taking as little account as possible of the special incidents of particular applications of the theory, and leaving over for the following Book the study of the bearings of the general theory on the special features of the several agents of production, Labour, Capital, and Land.

The difficulties of the problem depend chiefly on variations in the area of space, and the period of time over which the market in question extends; the influence of time being more fundamental than that of space.

Even in a market of very short period, such as that of a provincial corn-exchange on market-day, the "higgling and bargaining" might probably oscillate about a mean position, which would have some sort of a right to be called the equilibrium price: but the action of dealers in offering one price or refusing another would depend little, if at all, on calculations with regard to cost of production. They would look chiefly at present demand on the one hand, and on the other at the stocks of the commodity already available. It is true that they would pay some attention to such movements of production in the near future as might throw their shadow before; but in the case of perishable goods they would look only a very little way beyond the immediate present. Cost of production has for instance no perceptible influence on the day's bargaining in a fish-market.

In a rigidly stationary state in which supply could be perfectly adjusted to demand in every particular, the normal expenses of production, the

* The selection from Alfred Marshall, *Principles of Economics,* copyright by The Macmillan Co., New York, and used with the publisher's permission.

marginal expenses, and the average expenses (rent being counted in) would be one and the same thing, for long periods and for short. But, as it is, the language both of professed writers on economics and of men of business shows much elasticity in the use of the term Normal when applied to the causes that determine value. And one fairly well marked division needs study.

On the one side of this division are long periods, in which the normal action of economic forces has time to work itself out more fully; in which therefore a temporary scarcity of skilled labour, or of any other of the agents of production, can be remedied; and in which those economies that normally result from an increase in the scale of production—normally, that is without the aid of any substantive new invention—have time to develop themselves. The expenses of a representative firm, managed with normal ability and having normal access to the internal and external economies of production on a large scale, may be taken as a standard for estimating normal expense of production: and when the period under survey is long enough to enable the investment of capital in building up a new business to complete itself and to bear full fruits; then the marginal supply price is that, the expectation of which in the long run just suffices to induce capitalists to invest their material capital, and workers of all grades to invest their personal capital in the trade.

On the other side of the line of division are periods of time long enough to enable producers to adapt their production to changes in demand, in so far as that can be done with the existing provision of specialized skill, specialized capital, and industrial organization; but not long enough to enable them to make any important changes in the supplies of these factors of production. For such periods the stock of material and personal appliances of production has to be taken in a great measure for granted; and the marginal increment of supply is determined by estimates of producers as to the amount of production it is worth their while to get out of those appliances. If trade is brisk all energies are strained to their utmost, overtime is worked, and then the limit to production is given by want of power rather than by want of will to go further or faster. But if trade is slack every producer has to make up his mind how near to prime cost it is worth his while to take fresh orders. And here there is no definite law, the chief operative force is the fear of spoiling the market; and that acts in different ways and with different strengths on different individuals and different industrial groups. For the chief motive of all open combinations and of all informal silent and "customary" understandings whether among employers or employed is the need for preventing individuals from spoiling the common market by action that may bring them immediate gains, but at the cost of a greater aggregate loss to the trade.

§ 2. We next turned aside to consider the relations of demand and supply with reference to things that need to be combined together for the purposes of satisfying a joint demand; of which the most important instance is that of the specialized material capital, and the specialized personal skill that must work together in any trade. For there is no direct demand on the part of consumers for either alone, but only for the two conjointly; the demand for either separately is a derived demand, which rises, other things being equal, with every increase in the demand for the common products, and with every diminution in the supply price of the joint factors of production. In like manner commodities of which there is a joint supply, such as gas and coke, or beef and hides, can each of them have only a derived supply price, governed by the expenses of the whole process of production on the one hand, and on the other by the demand for the remaining joint products.

The composite demand for a thing, resulting from its being used for several different purposes, and the composite supply of a thing, that has several sources of production, present no great difficulty; for the several amounts demanded for the different purposes, or supplied from different sources, can be added together, . . . for combining the demands of the rich, the middle classes and the poor for the same commodity.

Next we made some study of the division of the supplementary costs of a business,—and especially those connected with building up a trade connection, with marketing, and with insurance—among the various products of that business.

§ 3. Returning to those central difficulties of the equilibrium of normal demand and supply which are connected with the element of time, we investigated more fully the relation between the value of an appliance for production and that of the things produced by it.

When different producers have different advantages for producing a thing, its price must be sufficient to cover the expenses of production of those producers who have no special and exceptional facilities; for if not they will withhold or diminish their production, and the scarcity of the amount supplied, relatively to the demand, will raise the price. When the market is in equilibrium, and the thing is being sold at a price which covers these expenses, there remains a surplus beyond their expenses for those who have the assistance of any exceptional advantages. If these advantages arise from the command over free gifts of nature, the surplus is called a producer's surplus or producer's rent: there is a surplus in any case, and if the owner of a free gift of nature lends it out to another, he can generally get for its use a money income equivalent to this surplus.

The price of the produce is equal to the cost of production of that part of it, which is raised on the margin, that is under such unfavourable conditions as to yield no rent. The cost of this part can be reckoned up without reasoning in a circle; and the cost of other parts cannot.

If land which has been used for growing hops, is found capable of yielding a higher rent as market-garden land, the area under hops will undoubtedly be diminished; and this will raise their marginal cost of production and therefore their price. The rent which land will yield for one kind of produce, calls attention to the fact that a demand for the land for that kind of produce increases the difficulties of supply of other kinds; though it does not directly enter into those expenses. And similar arguments apply to the relation between the site values of urban land and the costs of things made on it.

Thus when we are taking a broad view of normal value, when we are investigating the causes which determine normal value "in the long run," when we are tracing the "ultimate" effects of economic causes; then the income that is derived from capital in these forms enters into the payments by which the expenses of production of the commodity in question have to be covered; and estimates as to the probable amount of that income directly control the action of the producers, who are on the margin of doubt as to whether to increase the means of production or not. But, on the other hand, when we are considering the causes which determine normal prices for a period which is short relatively to that required for largely increasing the supply of those appliances for production; then their influence on value is chiefly indirect and more or less similar to that exerted by the free gifts of nature. The shorter the period which we are considering, and the slower the process of production of those appliances, the less part will variations in the income derived from them play in checking or increasing the supply of the commodity produced by them, and in raising or lowering its supply price.

§ 4. This leads to the consideration of some difficulties of a technical character connected with the marginal expenses of production of a commodity that obeys the law of increasing return. The difficulties arise from the temptation to represent supply price as dependent on the amount produced, without allowing for the length of time that is necessarily occupied by each individual business in extending its internal, and still more its external organization; and in consequence they have been most conspicuous in mathematical and semi-mathematical discussions of the theory of value. For when changes of supply price and amount produced are regarded as dependent exclusively on one another without any reference to gradual growth, it appears reasonable to argue that the marginal supply price for each individual producer is the addition to his aggregate expenses of production made by producing his last element; that this marginal price is likely in many cases to be diminished by an increase in his output much more than the demand price in the general market would be by the same cause.

The statical theory of equilibrium is therefore not wholly applicable to commodities which obey the law of increasing return. It should however be noted that in many industries each producer has a special market in which he is well known, and which he cannot extend quickly; and that therefore, though it might be physically possible for him to increase his output rapidly, he would run the risk of forcing down very much the demand price in his special market, or else of being driven to sell his surplus production outside on less favourable terms. And though there are industries in which each producer has access to the whole of a large market, yet in these there remain but few internal economies to be got by an increase of output, when the existing plant is already well occupied. No doubt there are industries as to which neither of these statements is true: they are in a transitional state, and it must be conceded that the statical theory of equilibrium of normal demand and supply cannot be profitably applied to them. But such cases are not numerous; and with regard to the great bulk of manufacturing industries, the connection between supply price and amount shows a fundamentally different character for short periods and for long.

For short periods, the difficulties of adjusting the internal and external organization of a business to rapid changes in output are so great that the supply price must generally be taken to rise with an increase, and to fall with a diminution in the amount produced.

But in long periods both the internal and the external economies of production on a large scale have time to develop themselves. The marginal supply price is not the expenses of production of any particular bale of goods: but it is the whole expenses (including insurance, and gross earnings of management) of a marginal increment in the aggregate process of production and marketing.

§ 5. Some study of the effects of a tax, regarded as a special case of a change in the general conditions of demand and supply suggests that, when proper allowance is made for the interests of consumers, there is on abstract grounds rather less *primâ facie* cause than the earlier economists supposed, for the general doctrine of so-called "Maximum Satisfaction"; *i.e.* for the doctrine that the free pursuit by each individual of his own immediate interest, will lead producers to turn their capital and labour, and consumers to turn their expenditure into such courses as are most conducive to the general interests. We have nothing to do at this stage of our inquiry, limited as it is to analysis of the most general character, with the important question how far, human nature being constituted as it is at present, collective action is likely to be inferior to individualistic action in energy and elasticity, in inventiveness and directness of purpose; and whether it is not therefore likely to waste through practical inefficiency more than it could save by taking account of all the interests affected by any course of action. But even without taking account of the evils arising from the unequal distribution of wealth, there is *primâ facie* reason for believing that the aggregate satisfaction, so far from being already a maximum, could be much increased by collective action in promoting the production and consumption of things in regard to which the law of increasing return acts with especial force.

This position is confirmed by the study of the theory of monopolies. It is the immediate interest of the monopolist so to adjust the production and sale of his wares as to obtain for himself the maximum net revenue, and the course which he thus adopts is unlikely to be that which affords the aggregate maximum satisfaction. The divergence between individual and collective interests is *primâ facie* less important with regard to those things which obey the law of diminishing return, than with regard to those which obey the law of increasing return: but, in the case of the latter, there is strong *primâ facie* reason for believing that it might often be to the interest of the community directly or indirectly to intervene, because a largely increased production would add much more to consumers' surplus than to the aggregate expenses of production of the goods. More exact notions on the relations of demand and supply, particularly when expressed in the form of diagrams, may help us to see what statistics should be collected, and how they should be applied in the attempt to estimate the relative magnitudes of various conflicting economic interests, public and private.

Ricardo's theory of cost of production in relation to value occupies so important a place in the history of economics that any misunderstanding as to its real character must necessarily be very mischievous; and unfortunately it is so expressed as almost to invite misunderstanding. In consequence there is a widely spread belief that it has needed to be reconstructed by the present generation of economists. Cause is shown [elsewhere] for not accepting this opinion; and for holding on the contrary that the foundations of the theory as they were left by Ricardo remain intact; that much has been added to them, and that very much has been built upon them, but that little has been taken from them. It is there argued that he knew that demand played an essential part in governing value, but that he regarded its action as less obscure than that of cost of production, and therefore passed it lightly over in the notes which he made for the use of his friends, and himself; for he never essayed to write a formal treatise: also that he regarded cost of production as dependent—not as Marx asserted him to have done on the mere quantity of labour used up in production, but—on the quality as well as quantity of that labour; together with the amount of stored up capital needed to aid labour, and the length of time during which such aid was invoked.

General View of Distribution

§ 1. The argument of the preceding ten chapters may now be summarized. . . . In the [section preceding this] we traced a continuous thread running through and connecting the applications of the general theory of equilibrium of demand and supply to different periods of time; from those so short that cost of production could exercise no direct influence on value, to those so long that the supply of the appliances of production could be fairly well adjusted to the indirect demand for them, which is derived from the direct demand for the commodities which they produce. In the present Book we have been concerned with another thread of continuity, which lies transversely to the thread connecting different periods of time. It connects the various agents and appliances for production, material and human; and establishes a fundamental unity between them, in spite of their important differences of outward feature.

Firstly, wages and other earnings of effort have much in common with interest on capital. For there is a general correspondence between the causes that govern the supply prices of material and of personal capital: the motives which induce a man to accumulate personal capital *in* his son's education, are similar to those which control his accumulation of material capital *for* his son. There is a continuous transition from the father who works and waits in order that he may bequeath to his son a rich and firmly-established manufacturing or trading business, to one who works and waits in order to support his son while he is slowly acquiring a thorough medical education, and ultimately to buy for him a lucrative practice. Again, there is the same continuous transition from him to one who works and waits in order that his son may stay long at school; and may afterwards work for some time almost without pay while learning a skilled trade, instead of being forced to support himself early in an occupation, such as that of an errand-boy, which offers comparatively high wages to young lads, because it does not lead the way to a future advance.

It is indeed true that the only persons, who, as society is now constituted, are very likely to invest much in developing the personal capital of a youth's abilities are his parents: and that many first-rate abilities go for ever uncultivated because no one, who can develop them, has had any special interest in doing so. This fact is very important practically, for its effects are cumulative. But it does not give rise to a fundamental difference between material and human agents of production: for it is analogous to the fact that much good land is poorly cultivated because those who would cultivate it well have not access to it.

Again, since human beings grow up slowly and are slowly worn out, and parents in choosing an occupation for their children must as a rule look forward a whole generation, changes in demand take a longer time to work out their full effects on supply in the case of human agents than of most kinds of material appliances for production; and a specially long period is required in the case of labour to give full play to the economic forces which tend to bring about a normal adjustment between demand and supply. Thus on the whole the *money* cost of any kind of labour to the employer corresponds in the long run fairly well to the *real* cost of producing that labour.

§ 2. The efficiency of human agents of production on the one hand, and that of material agents on the other, are weighed against one another and compared with their *money* costs; and each tends to be applied as far as it is more efficient than the other in proportion to its money cost. A chief function of business enterprise is to facilitate the free action of this great principle of substitution. Generally to the public benefit, but sometimes in opposition to it, business men are constantly comparing the services of machinery, and of labour, and again of unskilled and skilled labour, and of extra foremen and managers; they are constantly devising and experimenting with new arrangements which involve the use of different factors of production, and selecting those most profitable for themselves.

The efficiency as compared with the cost of almost every class of labour, is thus continually being weighed in the balance in one or more branches of production against some other classes of labour: and each of these in its turn against others. This competition is primarily "vertical": it is a struggle for the field of employment between groups of labour belonging to different grades, but engaged in the same branch of production, and inclosed, as it were, between the same vertical walls. But meanwhile "horizontal" competition is always at work, and by simpler methods: for, firstly, there is great freedom of movement of adults from one business to another within each trade; and secondly, parents can generally introduce their children into almost any other trade of the same grade with their own in their neighbourhood. By means of this combined vertical and horizontal competition there is an effective and closely adjusted balance of payments to services as between labour in different grades; in spite of the fact that the labour in any one grade is mostly recruited even now from the children of those in the same grade.

The working of the principle of substitution is thus chiefly indirect. When two tanks containing fluid are joined by a pipe, the fluid, which is near the pipe in the tank with the higher level, will flow into the other, even though it be rather viscous; and thus the general levels of the tanks will tend to be brought together, though no fluid may flow from the further end of the one to the further end of the other; and if several tanks are connected by pipes, the fluid in all will tend to the same level, though some tanks have no direct connection with others. And similarly the principle of substitution is constantly tending by indirect routes to apportion earnings to efficiency between trades, and even between grades, which are not directly in contact with one another, and which appear at first sight to have no way of competing with one another.

§ 3. There is no breach of continuity as we ascend from the unskilled labourer to the skilled, thence to the foreman, to the head of a department, to the general manager of a large business paid partly by a share of the profits, to the junior partner, and lastly to the head partner of a large private business: and in a joint-stock company there is even somewhat of an anti-climax when we pass from the directors to the ordinary shareholders, who undertake the chief ultimate risks of the business. Nevertheless business undertakers are to a certain extent a class apart.

For while it is through their conscious agency that the principle of substitution chiefly works in balancing one factor of production against another; with regard to them it has no other agency than the indirect influence of their own competition. So it works blindly, or rather wastefully; it forces many to succumb who might have done excellent work if they had been favoured at first: and, in conjunction with the tendency to increasing return, it strengthens those who are strong, and hands over the businesses of the weak to those who have already obtained a partial monopoly.

But on the other hand there is also a constant increase in the forces which tend to break up old monopolies, and to offer to men, who have but little capital of their own, openings both for starting new businesses and for rising into posts of command in large public and private concerns; and these forces tend to put business ability in command of the capital required to give it scope.

On the whole the work of business management is done cheaply—not indeed as cheaply as it may be in the future when men's collective instincts, their sense of duty and their public spirit are more fully developed; when society exerts itself more to develop the latent faculties of those who are born in a humble station of life, and to diminish the secrecy of business; and when the more wasteful forms of speculation and of competition are held in check. But yet it is done so cheaply as to contribute to production more than the equivalent of its pay. For the business undertaker, like the skilled artisan, renders services which society needs, and which it would probably have to get done at a higher cost if he were not there to do them.

The similarity between the causes that determine the normal rewards of ordinary ability on the one hand, and of business power in command of capital on the other, does not extend to the fluctuations of their current earnings. For the employer stands as a buffer between the buyer of goods and all the various classes of labour by which they are made. He receives the whole price of the one and pays the whole price of the others. The fluctuations of his profits go with fluctuations of the prices of the things he sells, and are more extensive: while those of the wages of his employees come later and are less extensive. The earnings at any particular time of his capital and ability are sometimes large, but sometimes also a negative quantity: whereas those of the ability of his employees are never very large, and are never a negative quantity. The wage-receiver is likely to suffer much when out of work; but that is because he has no reserve, not because he is a wage-receiver.

That part of a man's income which he owes to the possession of extraordinary natural abilities is a free boon to him: and from an abstract point of view bears some resemblance to the rent of other free gifts of nature, such as the inherent properties of land. But in reference to normal prices, it is to be classed rather with the profits derived by free settlers from the cultivation of new land, or again with the find of the pearl-fisher. The plot of one settler turns out better and that of another worse than was expected; the good find of one dive of the pearl-fisher compensates for many others that are fruitless: and the high income which one barrister, or engineer, or trader earns by his natural genius has to be counted with the comparative failures of many others; who perhaps appeared of no less promise when young and received as costly an education and start in life, but whose services to production were less than his in proportion to their cost. The ablest business men are generally those who get the highest profits, and at the same time do their work most cheaply; and it would be as wasteful if society were to give their work to inferior people who would undertake to do it more cheaply, as it would be to give a valuable diamond to be cut by a low waged but unskilled cutter.

§ 4. . . . we may call to mind the double relation in which the various agents of production stand to one another. On the one hand they are often rivals for employment; any one that is more efficient than another in proportion to its cost tending to be substituted for it, and thus limiting the demand price for the other. And on the other hand they all constitute the field of employment for each other: there is no field of employment for any one, except in so far as it is provided by the others: the national dividend which is the joint product of all, and which increases with the supply of each of them, is also the sole source of demand for each of them.

Thus an increase of material capital causes it to push its way into new uses; and though in so doing it may occasionally diminish the field of employment for manual labour in a few trades, yet on the whole it will very much increase the demand for manual labour and all other agents of production. For it will much increase the national dividend, which is the common source of the demand for all; and since by its increased competition for employment it will have forced down the rate of interest, therefore the joint product of a dose of capital and labour will now be divided more in favour of labour than before.

This new demand for labour will partly take the form of the opening-out of new undertakings which hitherto could not have paid their way; while a new demand will come from the makers of new and more expensive machinery. For when it is said that machinery is substituted for labour, this means that one class of labour combined with much waiting is substituted for another combined with less waiting: and for this reason alone, it would be impossible to substitute capital for labour in general, except indeed locally by the importation of capital from other places.

It remains true, however, that the chief benefit which an increase of capital confers upon labour is not by opening out to it new employments, but by increasing the joint product of land, labour and capital (or of land, labour and waiting), and by reducing the share of that product which any given amount of capital (or of waiting) can claim as its reward.

§ 5. In discussing the influence which a change in the supply of work of any one industrial group exerts on the field of employment for other kinds of labour, there was no need to raise the question whether the increase of work came from an increase in the numbers or in the efficiency of those in the group: for that question is of no direct concern to the others. In either case there is the same addition to the national dividend: in either case competition will compel them to force themselves to the same extent into uses in which their marginal utility is lower; and will thus lessen to the same extent the share of the joint product which they are able to claim in return for a given amount of work of a given kind.

But the question is of vital importance to the members of that group. For, if the change is an increase of one-tenth in their average efficiency, then each ten of them will have as high an aggregate income as each eleven of them would have if their numbers had increased by one-tenth, their efficiency remaining unchanged.

This dependence of the wages of each group of workers on the numbers and efficiency of others is a special case of the general rule that the environment (or *Conjuncture*) plays a part at least coordinate with a man's energy and ability in governing that net product to which his wages ever approximate under the influence of competition.

The net product to which the normal wages of any group of workers approximate, must be estimated on the assumption that production has been pushed to that limit at which the output can be just marketed with normal profits, but not more: and it must be estimated with reference to a worker of normal efficiency; whose additional output repays an employer of normal ability and normal good fortune and normal resources with normal profits, but not more. (Something must be added to or subtracted from this net product to find the normal wages of a worker whose efficiency is more or less than normal.) The time chosen must be one of normal prosperity; and when the supplies of different kinds of labour are relatively appropriate. For instance if the building trade is exceptionally depressed, or exceptionally prosperous: or if its development is checked by an inadequate supply of bricklayers or carpenters, while the supply of other classes of building operatives is superabundant, then the occasion is one which does not afford a convenient opportunity for estimating the relations of net product to normal wages of either bricklayers or carpenters.

ELEMENTS OF ECONOMICS OF INDUSTRY *

Consumers' Surplus

§ 1. The benefit, which a person gets from purchasing at a low price things which he would rather pay a high price for than go without, has already been called his consumers' surplus. Our aim now is to apply the notion of consumers' surplus as an aid in estimating roughly some of the benefits which a person derives from his environment or his conjuncture.

In order to give definiteness to our notions, let us consider the case of tea purchased for domestic consumption. Let us take the case of a man who, if the price of tea were 20*s*. a pound, would just be induced to buy one pound annually; who would just be induced to buy two pounds if the price were 14*s*., three pounds if the price were 10*s*., four pounds if the price were 6*s*., five pounds if the price were 4*s*., six pounds if the price were 3*s*., and who, the price being actually 2*s*., does purchase seven pounds. We have to investigate the consumers' surplus which he derives from his power of purchasing tea at 2*s*. a pound.

The fact that he would just be induced to purchase one pound if the price were 20*s*., proves that the total enjoyment or satisfaction which he

* From *Elements of Economics of Industry*, fourth edition (London, Macmillan and Co., Ltd., 1907).

derives from that pound is as great as that which he could obtain by spending 20*s.* on other things. When the price falls to 14*s.*, he could, if he chose, continue to buy only one pound. He would then get for 14*s.* what was worth to him at least 20*s.*; and he will obtain a surplus satisfaction worth to him at least 6*s.*, or in other words a consumers' surplus of at least 6*s.* But in fact he buys a second pound of his own free choice, thus showing that he regards it as worth to him at least 14*s.* He obtains for 28*s.* what is worth to him at least 20*s.* + 14*s.*; i.e. 34*s.* His surplus satisfaction is at all events not diminished by buying it, but remains worth at least 6*s.* to him. The total utility of the two pounds is worth at least 34*s.*, his consumers' surplus is at least 6*s.* The fact that each additional purchase reacts on the utility of the purchases which he had previously decided to make, *has already been allowed for, and must not be counted a second time.*

When the price falls to 10*s.*, he might, if he chose, continue to buy only two pounds; and obtain for 20*s.* what was worth to him at least 34*s.*, and derive a surplus satisfaction worth at least 14*s.* But in fact he prefers to buy a third pound: and as he does this freely, we know that he does not diminish his surplus satisfaction by doing it. He now gets for 30*s.* three pounds; of which the first is worth to him at least 20*s.*, the second at least 14*s.*, and the third at least 10*s.* The total utility of the three is worth at least 44*s.*, his consumers' surplus is at least 14*s.*, and so on.

When at last the price has fallen to 2*s.* he buys seven pounds, which are severally worth to him not less than 20, 14, 10, 6, 4, 3, and 2*s.* or 59*s.* in all. This sum measures their total utility to him, and his consumers' surplus is (at least) the excess of this sum over the 14*s.* he actually does pay for them, i.e. 45*s.* This is the excess value of the satisfaction he gets from buying the tea over that which he could have got by spending the 14*s.* in extending a little his purchase of other commodities, of which he had just not thought it worth while to buy more at their current prices; and any further purchases of which at those prices would not yield him any consumers' surplus. In other words, he derives this 45*s.* worth of surplus enjoyment from his conjuncture, from the adaptation of the environment to his wants in the particular matter of tea. If that adaptation ceased, and tea could not be had at any price, he would have incurred a loss of satisfaction at least equal to that which he could have got by spending 45*s.* more on extra supplies of things that were worth to him only just what he paid for them.

The first pound was probably worth to him more than 20*s.* All that we know is that it was not worth less to him. He probably got some small surplus even on that. Again, the second pound was probably worth more than 14*s.* to him. All that we know is that it was worth at least 14*s.* and not worth 20*s.* to him. He would get therefore at this stage a surplus satisfaction of at least 6*s.*, probably a little more.

The significance of the condition that he buys the second pound of his own free choice is shown by the consideration that if the price of 14*s.* had been offered to him on the condition that he took two pounds, he would then have to elect between taking one pound for 20*s.* or two pounds for 28*s.*: and then his taking two pounds would not have proved that he thought the second pound worth more than 8*s.* to him. But as it is, he takes a second pound paying 14*s.* unconditionally for it; and that proves that it is worth at least 14*s.* to him.

It is sometimes objected that as he increases his purchases, the urgency of his need for his earlier purchases is diminished, and their utility falls; therefore we ought to continually redraw the earlier parts of our list of demand prices at a lower level, as we pass along it towards lower prices (i.e. to redraw at a lower level our demand curve as we pass along it to the right). But this misconceives the plan on which the list of prices is made out. The objection would have been valid, if the demand price set against each number of pounds of tea represented the *average* utility of that number. For it is true that, if he would pay just 20*s.* for one pound, and just 14*s.* for a second, then he would pay just 34*s.* for the two; i.e. 17*s.* each on the average. And if our list had had reference to the *average* prices he would pay, and had set 17*s.* against the second pound; then no doubt we should have had to redraw the list as we passed on. For when he has brought a third pound the average utility to him of each of the three will be less than that of 17*s.*; being in fact 14*s.* 8*d.* if, as we go on to assume, he would pay just 10*s.* for a third pound. But this difficulty is entirely avoided on the plan of making out demand prices which is here adopted; according to which his second pound is credited, not with the 17*s.* which represents the average value per pound of the two pounds; but with the 14*s.*, which represents the *additional* utility which a second pound has for him. For that remains unchanged when he has bought a third pound, of which the additional utility is measured by 10*s.*[1]

§ 2. We may now pass from the demand of an individual to that of a market. If we neglect for the moment the fact that the same sum of money represents different amounts of pleasure to different people, we may measure the surplus satisfaction which the sale of tea affords, say, in the London market, by the aggregate of the sums by which the prices shown in a complete list of demand prices for tea exceeds its selling price.

[1] Again it has been objected:—"Of what avail is it to say that the utility of an income of (say) £100 a year is worth (say) £1000 a year?" There would be no avail in saying that. But there might be use, when comparing life in Central Africa with life in England, in saying that, though the things which money will buy in Central Africa may on the average be as cheap there as here, yet there are so many things which cannot be bought there at all, that a person with a thousand a year there is not so well off as a person with three or four hundred a year here. If a man pays 1*d.* toll on a bridge, which saves him an additional drive that would cost a shilling, we do not say that the penny is worth a shilling, but that the penny together with the advantage offered him by the bridge (the part it plays in his conjuncture) is worth a shilling for that day. Were the bridge swept away on a day on which he needed it, he would be in at least as bad a position as if he had been deprived of eleven pence.

Let us then consider the demand curve *DD′* for tea in any large market. Let *OH* be the amount which is sold there at the price *HA* annually, a year being taken as our unit of time. Taking any point *M* in *OH* let us draw *MP* vertically upwards to meet the curve in *P* and cut a horizontal line through *A* in *R*. We will suppose the several lbs. numbered in the order of the eagerness of the several purchasers: the eagerness of the purchaser of any lb. being measured by the price he is just willing to pay for that lb. The figure informs us that *OM* can be sold at the price *PM;* but that at any higher price not quite so many lbs. can be sold. There must be then

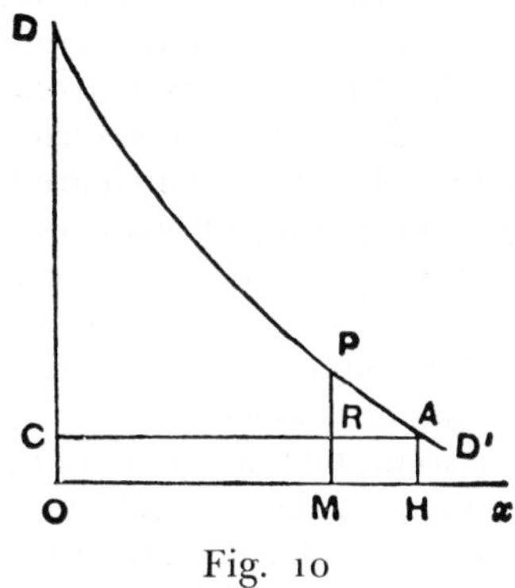

Fig. 10

some individual who will buy more at the price *PM,* than he will at any higher price; and we are to regard the *OM*th lb. as sold to this individual. Suppose for instance that *PM* represents 4*s*., and that *OM* represents a million lbs. The purchaser described above is just willing to buy his fifth lb. of tea at the price 4*s*., and the *OM*th or millionth lb. may be said to be sold to him. If *AH* and therefore *RM* represent 2*s*., the consumers' surplus derived from the *OM*th lb. is the excess of *PM* or 4*s*. which the purchaser of that lb. would have been willing to pay for it over *RM* the 2*s*. which he actually does pay for it. Let us suppose that a very thin vertical parallelogram is drawn of which the height is *PM* and of which the base is the distance along *Ox* that measures the single unit or lb. of tea. It will be convenient henceforward to regard price as measured not by a mathematical straight line without thickness, as *PM;* but by a very thin parallelogram, or as it may be called a thick straight line, of which the breadth is in every case equal to the distance along *Ox* which measures a unit or lb. of tea. Thus we should say that the total satisfaction derived from the *OM*th lb. of tea is represented (or, on the assumption made in the last paragraph above is measured) by the thick straight line *MP;* that the price paid for this lb. is represented by the thick straight line *MR* and the consumers' surplus derived from this lb. by the thick straight line *RP*. Now let us suppose that such thin parallelograms, or thick straight lines, are drawn for all positions of *M* between *O* and *H,* one for each lb. of tea. The thick straight lines thus drawn, as *MP* is, from *Ox* up to the demand curve will each represent the aggregate of the satisfaction derived from a lb. of tea; and taken together thus occupy and exactly fill up the whole area *DOHA*. Therefore we may say that the area *DOHA* represents the aggregate of the satisfaction derived from the consumption of tea. Again, each of the straight lines drawn, as *MR* is, from *Ox* upwards as far as *AC* represents the price that actually is paid for a lb. of tea. These straight lines together make up the area *COHA;* and therefore this area represents the total price paid for tea. Finally each of the straight lines drawn as *RP* is from *AC* upwards as far as the demand curve, represents the consumers' surplus derived from the corresponding lb. of tea. These straight lines together make up the area *DCA;* and therefore this area represents the total consumers' surplus that is derived from tea when the price is *AH*. But it must be repeated that this geometrical measurement is only an aggregate of the measures of benefits which are not all measured on the same scale except on the assumption just made above. Unless that assumption is made the area only represents an aggregate of satisfactions, the several amounts of which are not exactly measured. On that assumption only, its area measures the volume of the total *net* satisfaction derived from the tea by its various purchasers.

We cannot guess at all accurately how much of anything people would buy at prices very different from those which they are accustomed to pay for it: or in other words, what the demand prices for it would be for amounts very different from those which are commonly sold. Our list of demand prices is therefore highly conjectural except in the neighbourhood of the customary price; and the best estimates we can form of the whole amount of the utility of anything are liable to large error. But this difficulty is not important practically. For the chief applications of the doctrine of consumers' surplus are concerned with such changes in it as would accompany changes in the price of the commodity in question in the neighbourhood of the customary price: that is, they require us to use only that information with which we are fairly well supplied. These remarks apply with special force to necessaries.

Again, for some purposes such things as tea and coffee must be grouped together as one commodity: and it is obvious that, if tea were inaccessible, people would increase their consumption of coffee, and vice versa. The loss that people would suffer from being deprived both of tea and coffee would be greater than the sum of their losses from being deprived of either alone: and therefore the total utility of tea and coffee is greater than the sum of the total utility of tea calculated on the supposition that people can have recourse to coffee, and that of coffee calculated on a like supposition as to tea. This difficulty can be theoretically evaded by grouping the two "rival" commodities together under a common demand schedule. On the other hand, if we have calculated the total utility of fuel with reference to the fact that without it we could not obtain hot water to obtain the beverage tea from tea leaves, we should count something twice over if we added to that utility the total utility of tea leaves, reckoned on a similar plan: and again the total utility of agricultural produce includes that of ploughs, and the two may not be added together; though the total utility of ploughs may be discussed in connection with one problem, and that of wheat in connection with another.

Quasi-rents, or Incomes from an Appliance for Production Already Made by Man

§ 1. The farmer pays "rent" to his landlord without troubling himself to distinguish how much of the annual net value of his land is due to the free gift of nature, and how much to the investment of capital by his landlord in the improvement of the land, and in erecting buildings on it. Now the income derived from farm buildings, or houses, is clearly of the same character as the income derived from durable machines; and that income is popularly classed with profits more often than with rent. But yet the farmer's habit of speaking has much justification. For the incomes derived from appliances for production made by man have really something analogous to true rents.

The net incomes derived from appliances for production already made, may be called their *quasi-rents:* partly because we shall find that, when we are considering periods of time too short to enable the supply of such appliances to respond to a change in the demand for them, the stock of them has to be regarded as *temporarily* fixed. For the time they hold nearly the same relation to the price of the things which they take part in producing, as is held by land, or any other free gift of nature, of which the stock is *permanently* fixed; and whose net income is a true rent. Let us take an illustration from manufacture.

§ 2. Let us suppose that an exceptional demand for a certain kind of textile fabrics is caused by, say, a sudden movement of the fashions. The special machinery required for making that fabric will yield for the time a high income, governed by the price that can be got for the produce, and consisting of the excess of the aggregate price of that produce over the direct outlay (including wear-and-tear) incurred in its production; and the quasi-rent, or net income, from the machinery will be for the time greater than normal profits on the original investment.

If later on the tide turns, and the demand is less than had been expected; the factories with the most imperfect appliances, and the worst machinery in other factories will be thrown out of work; while those machines, which it is just worth while to keep in work, will just pay the actual expenses of working them, but will yield no surplus. But the excess of the price got for the goods made by the better appliances over their wear-and-tear, together with the actual expenses of working them, will be the income which these appliances yield during the short period of depression. This quasi-rent or net income derived from the machinery will in this second period be less than normal profits on the original investment.

These remarks may be extended. Appliances for production are of many different kinds: they include not only land, factories and machines, but also business ability and manual skill. The owner of any one of those will not generally apply it to produce anything, unless he expects to gain in return at least enough to compensate him for the immediate and special trouble, sacrifice and outlay involved in this particular operation, and which he could escape by declining to undertake it.

In short periods the supply of these various appliances for production —whether machinery and other material plant, or specialized skill and ability—has not time to be fully adapted to demand; and the producers have to adjust their supply to the demand as best they can with the appliances already at their disposal. On the one hand there is not time materially to increase those appliances if the supply of them is deficient; and on the other, if the supply is excessive, some of them must remain imperfectly employed, since there is not time for the supply to be much reduced by gradual decay, and by conversion to other uses. The particular income derived from them during those times, does not *for the time* affect perceptibly the supply, nor therefore the price, of the commodities produced by them: it is a surplus of total receipts over Prime (money) cost, governed by the more or less accidental relations of demand and supply for that time. And this excess has enough resemblance to that excess value of the produce of land over the direct cost of raising it, which is the basis of rent as ordinarily understood, to justify us in calling it a Quasi-rent.

A Quasi-rent differs however from a true Rent in this way. If true Rent ceased, those gifts of nature which are free and imperishable would remain undiminished, and be ready to contribute their part to production as before. But if the Quasi-rent from any class of appliances for production not made by man fell so low that it did not amount in the long run to normal profits on the investment of capital and effort required to sustain the supply of those appliances; then those appliances would dwindle, and would *not* contribute their part to production as before. In long periods, on the other hand, there is time to adjust the resources of supply to demand.

§ 3. The general principle under discussion may then be put thus. The price of anything and the amount of it that is produced are together governed by the general relations of demand and supply: the price just covers the expenses of production of that part of this amount which is raised at the greatest disadvantage; every other part yields a surplus above its direct cost; and this surplus is a result and not a cause of the selling price. For the price is governed by the relations of supply and demand; and while, of course, the surplus does not affect the demand, so neither does it affect the supply, since it is yielded only by a part of the produce which would be produced even at a lower price.

When we are taking a broad view of normal value extending over a very long period of time, when we are investigating the causes which determine normal value "in the long run," when we are tracing the "ultimate" effects of economic causes, then the income that is derived from capital in these forms enters into the payments by which the expenses of production of the commodity in question have to be covered, and it directly controls the action of the producers who are on the margin of doubt as to whether to increase the means of production or not. But, on the other hand, when we are considering the causes which determine normal prices for a period which is short relatively to that required for largely increasing the supply of those appliances for production, then the stock of these appliances has to be taken as fixed, almost as though they were free gifts of nature. The shorter the period which we are considering, and the slower the process of production of those appliances, the less part will variations in the income derived from them play in checking or increasing the supply of the commodity produced by them, and in raising or lowering its supply price; and the more nearly true will it be that, for the period under discussion, the net income to be derived from them is to be regarded as a producer's surplus or quasi-rent.

This doctrine is however difficult, and easily misunderstood. Further study is required before it can be safely applied to complex issues.

THE SOCIAL POSSIBILITIES OF ECONOMIC CHIVALRY *

The reasonable dissatisfaction, with which every thoughtful person must regard the existing distribution of wealth, is in danger of being perverted towards ill-considered measures of reform by Utopian schemers; who imply, if they do not explicitly state, that, if wealth were equally divided, everyone would have access to means of comfort, refinement, and even luxury which are far out of the reach of any of the working classes at present. But the fact is that very many prosperous artisans' families, certainly many more than a hundred thousand, already enjoy a larger income than they would if the total of £1,700,000,000, at which the income of the United Kingdom is estimated, were divided out equally among its population of forty-three million—that is to say, they would lose by an equal distribution of income.[1]

These facts are consistent with the belief that a vast increase of happiness and elevation of life might be attained if those forms of expenditures which serve no high purpose could be curtailed, and the resources thus set free could be applied for the welfare of the less prosperous members of the working classes; the whole change being so made as not considerably to slacken the springs of productive energy. But they are not

* From "The Social Possibilities of Economic Chivalry," *Economic Journal,* March, 1907, pp. 12–18, 25–26.

1 The statistical position may be looked at in another way. The average annual earnings of the men, women, and children employed in the chief manufacturing industries was estimated by the Board of Trade, as the result of a partial wage census in 1888, to be £48. The returns took insufficient account of the high wages earned by many pieceworkers; and, though they have been criticised as possibly rather too high in some other respects, we may be sure that the average is now over £50. Therefore a family of average ability and average size, all the members of which were employed in manufacture, has now a considerably higher income than it would have under an equal division of income to all persons, including the very young and the very old.

consistent with the common suggestion that by retrenching the lavish expenditure of the rich, and dividing income equally, the whole people would be raised to affluence previously unknown to working men. More's *Utopia* and Morris's *News from Nowhere* stimulate aspiration, and are so beautiful in themselves that they will remain a joy for ever. And they work unmixed good, because they do not profess to be practical. But in recent years we have suffered much from schemes that claim to be practical, and yet are based on no thorough study of economic realities; that lack the subtle beauty of a delicate imagination; and that even propose to tear up by the roots family life, the tree whose fruits and flowers contribute much more than half to the sum total of all that is known of beauty and happiness by the people in general, and especially by the working classes.

CHIVALRY IN WAR AND CHIVALRY IN BUSINESS

Our age is, then, not quite as wasteful and harsh as it is sometimes represented. Much more than a half, possibly even three-quarters, of the total income of the nation is devoted to uses which make for happiness and the elevation of life, nearly as efficiently as is possible with our present limited understanding of the arts of life. Even so, there is a large margin for improvement; and yet in one respect we seem to be going on wrong lines. For it is easier to make believe, even to oneself, that one looks down on wealth, than to work with energy in order to make wealth a thing of which the world may be proud. But in fact material resources enter of necessity so much into the thoughts and cares of nearly everybody that, if the world is not proud of its wealth, it cannot respect itself. Surely, then, it is worth while to make a great effort to enlist wealth in the service of the true glory of the world. And history seems to suggest a route to this end.

War is more cruel even than competition to oust rivals from their work and living; but there grew up around it a chivalry which brought out the noble, emulative side of war, and even something of the finer sympathies. If in the Elysian fields a mediæval warrior be now discussing with late inhabitants of worlds many billions of miles away from our own the experiences of his old world, he may hold up his head as he speaks of the chivalry of war, the thing that occupied people's imagination most in that age.

In the present age our thoughts are occupied with industrial progress, with the marvellous services which we compel nature to render to us in manufacture and transport. But if the talk should turn in the Elysian fields on the elevation of life which we have won by the new methods of business, we should not hold up our heads as bravely as would the mediæval knight. I want to suggest that there is much latent chivalry in business life, and that there would be a great deal more of it if we sought it out and honoured it as men honoured the mediæval chivalry of war. If we do this for a generation or two, then people bringing the latest news from this world may talk boldly of the chivalry of wealth: they may be proud of the elevation of life which has been achieved by training the finer elements of human nature to full account in the production of wealth and in its use.

Chivalry in business includes public spirit, as chivalry in war includes unselfish loyalty to the cause of prince, or of country, or of crusade. But it includes also a delight in doing noble and difficult things because they are noble and difficult: as knightly chivalry called on a man to begin by making his own armour, and to use his armour for choice in those contests in which his skill and resource, his courage and endurance, would be put to the severest tests. It includes a scorn for cheap victories, and a delight in succouring those who need a helping hand. It does not disdain the gains to be won on the way, but it has the fine pride of the warrior who esteems the spoils of a well-fought battle, or the prizes of a tournament, mainly for the sake of the achievements to which they testify, and only in the second degree for the value at which they are appraised in the money of the market.

THE CHIEF MOTIVE TO THE HIGHEST CONSTRUCTIVE WORK IN INDUSTRY IS A CHIVALROUS DESIRE TO MASTER DIFFICULTIES AND OBTAIN RECOGNISED LEADERSHIP

The commonplace and even the sordid sides of business work obtrude themselves on our notice. Some men are known to have become rich by foul means. Many more have prospered by a steady adherence to affairs, largely of a routine character; with but little use of the higher imagination, and perhaps with scarcely any romance in their lives except in their family relations. These two classes of business men come into close contact with the ordinary observer; and, if he rejoices in the æsthetic expenditure of wealth which he has inherited probably from a business ancestor, he is likely to declaim in vigorous but undiscriminating language against those who greedily pursue wealth.

But there can be no doubt that at least one-half of the best ability in the Western world is engaged in business. Unless, therefore, we are convinced that human nature is irredeemably sordid, we must expect that there is much nobility to be found in business; and, if we look for it in the right place, we shall find it. . . .

THE NEED FOR ENLARGING THE HONOUR GIVEN TO THE HIGHEST CONSTRUCTIVE BUSINESS FACULTY IS INCREASED BY THE GROWTH OF BUREAUCRATIC RULE, WHICH IS HOSTILE TO IT

There are many kinds of laboratory experiments which a man can be hired to make at a few hundred pounds a year, but the epoch-making discoveries generally come from men who love their work with a chivalrous love. The true significance of such a man's life is often not recognised till he has passed away, but he is fairly sure that he will be honoured at last. Money is wanted to educate scientific men, to supply them with apparatus, and a moderate income earned without oppressive routine of teaching or other fatigue. But that is all that money can do. That being done, creative science can be evoked only by the force which evokes creative art and creative literature—the force of chivalrous emulation.

A chemist requires only a little space in a laboratory. But many of the most important experiments of a business man require the whole space, the whole material appliances, and the whole staff of a large business to be at his disposal, and often for many years consecutively. If he is working at his own risk, he can put forth his energies with perfect freedom. But if he is a servant of a bureaucracy, he cannot be certain of freedom; he may be given a little freedom for a while, and then a change in administration, or impatience at his failure to strike the true path of progress at his first trial, may cause him to be pulled up sharp; and his chains clank, even when they do not press tightly.

Difficulties of this kind are met not only in the industrial undertakings of Governments, but also in very large joint stock companies, and especially the so-called trusts. The chief owners of the trusts have given, and are giving, an extraordinary amount of thought to devising means whereby the heads of departments and others may be allowed a free hand; and emulation may be brought to bear as a stimulus to their energy and enterprise. Their devices are marvellously ingenious, and among the most instructive episodes in recent economic history, but they have attained only a modicum of success. Experience shows ever more and more that the technical economy to be attained by piling Pelion on Ossa in the agglomeration of vast businesses is nearly always less than was expected, and that the difficulty of the human element ever increases with increasing size. Much can be done by various schemes of reward and promotion as regards junior officials, and even the superior officials are stimulated by congresses and other opportunities for submitting their new ideas to the judgment of brother experts. But no fairly good substitute has been found, or seems likely to be found, for the bracing fresh air which a strong man with a chivalrous yearning for leadership draws into his lungs when he sets out on a business experiment at his own risk.

ECONOMISTS GENERALLY DESIRE INCREASED INTENSITY OF STATE ACTIVITIES FOR SOCIAL AMELIORATION, THAT ARE NOT FULLY WITHIN THE RANGE OF PRIVATE EFFORT: BUT THEY ARE OPPOSED TO THAT VAST EXTENSION OF STATE ACTIVITIES WHICH IS DESIRED BY COLLECTIVISTS

These considerations point towards the watershed which divides the large majority of economists from "Collectivists"—*i.e.,* those who would transfer to the State the ownership and management of land, machinery, and all other agents of production. We are told sometimes that everyone who strenuously endeavours to promote the social amelioration of the people is a Socialist—at all events, if he believes that much of this work can be better performed by the State than by individual effort. In this sense nearly every economist of the present generation is a Socialist. In this sense I was a Socialist before I knew anything of economics; and, indeed, it was my desire to know what was practicable in social reform by State and other agencies which led me to read Adam Smith and Mill, Marx and Lassalle, forty years ago. I have since then been steadily growing a more convinced Socialist in this sense of the word; and I have watched with admiration the strenuous and unselfish devotion to social well-being that is shown by many of the able men who are leading the collectivist movement. I do not doubt that the paths, on which they would lead us, might probably be strewn with roses for some distance. But I am convinced that so soon as collectivist control had spread so far as to considerably narrow the field left for free enterprise, the pressure of bureaucratic methods would impair not only the springs of material wealth, but also many of those higher qualities of human nature, the strengthening of which should be the chief aim of social endeavour. . . .

If collectivism is to work even fairly well, there must be ample provision for enabling anyone who thinks his lot unduly hard to find relief in some way that has not as yet been discovered. . . .

Let us, however, suppose, for the sake of argument, that some workable scheme to this end could be devised. We are then brought face to face with the difficulty already suggested that those improvements in method and in appliances, by which man's power over nature has been acquired in the past, are not likely to continue with even moderate vigour if free enterprise be stopped, before the human race has been brought up to a much higher general level of economic chivalry than has ever yet been attained. The world under free enterprise will fall far short of the finest ideals until economic chivalry is developed. But until it is developed, every great step in the direction of collectivism is a grave menace to the maintenance even of our present moderate rate of progress.

THE SOCIAL POSSIBILITIES OF ECONOMIC CHIVALRY ON THE PART OF INDIVIDUALS AND THE COMMUNITY AS A WHOLE UNDER EXISTING INSTITUTIONS

To conclude:—There is much more economic chivalry in the world than appears at first sight. The most important and progressive business work is scarcely ever without a large chivalrous element, and is often mainly dominated by chivalrous motives. But there is also much getting of wealth that is not chivalrous, and much expenditure that has no touch of nobility. To distinguish that which is chivalrous and noble from that which is not, is a task that needs care and thought and labour; and to perform that task is a first duty for economists sitting at the feet of business men and learning from them. An endeavour should be made so to guide public opinion that it becomes an informal Court of Honour:

that wealth, however large, should be no passport to social success if got by chicanery, by manufactured news, by fraudulent dealing, or by malignant destruction of rivals; and that business enterprise which is noble in its aims and in its methods, even if it does not bring with it a large fortune, may receive its due of public admiration and gratitude, as does that of the progressive student of science, or literature, or art.

The discriminating favour of the multitude at Athens and Florence gave the strongest stimulus to imaginative art. And if coming generations can search out and honour that which is truly creative and chivalric in modern business work, the world will grow rapidly in material wealth and in wealth of character. Noble efforts could be evoked; and even dull men would gradually cease to pay homage to wealth *per se* without inquiring how it had been acquired. Wealth-getting by sordid means would not win its way in society, nor in popular favour; and no political committee, however devoid of high sentiment, would be short-sighted enough to follow a recent example in choosing a candidate who had been proved judicially to owe much of his wealth to base means. Sordid practices would then prevent wealth from yielding that social *éclat* for which sordid men chiefly prize it, would go out of favour with men of ability and common sense, however devoid of high principle.

EMPLOYMENT IN BRITISH AND GERMAN STEEL INDUSTRIES *

A COMPARISON OF THE STEEL INDUSTRIES OF BRITAIN AND GERMANY, WITH SPECIAL REFERENCE TO THE PLEAS THAT GERMANY'S CARTEL AND FISCAL POLICIES IN ASSOCIATION HAVE BENEFITED THE PEOPLE

The tasks involved in cartellization are appropriate to the temper of the German people. The long hours of more or less intensive work, to which they are accustomed, enable them to attend numerous discussions without difficulty: the discipline, to which they have been seasoned in military service, inclines them to submit easily to cartel regulation; and, what is perhaps equally important, the semi-military organization of cartels is well adapted to the purposes of an autocratic rule, which regards peace as the time of preparation for war. Moreover an autocratic Government can exert certain kinds of discipline, which are not congenial to the temper of a self-governing people; and would, partly for that reason, involve lengthy discussions, and obstruct the proceedings of Parliament, if attempted in Britain. For instance, a cartel, which offends the German Government, may find that the charges for the railway traffic, in which it is specially interested, are quietly raised: or those on important rival products may be lowered, or the Protective tarif may be modified to its disadvantage: no such discipline would be tolerable in Britain.

There is another reason for the bias in favour of cartels that is shown

* From *Industry and Trade* (London, Macmillan and Co., Ltd., 1919).

by a Government that is largely under the control of a wealthy minority. It is, that cartel policy is greatly dependent on the aid of a Protective tarif, which tends to enrich many of those who are already rich; though it lowers the purchasing power of incomes generally, and especially those of the poorer classes. This again is an advantage from the point of view of German military autocracy: for the wealth of the rich is more accessible to the tax collector, than are the wages of the working classes, when once the taxes on ordinary necessaries have been pressed as far as they can well go: and the relatively low standard of comfort enjoyed by the German working classes in time of peace has lessened the expenditure needed for maintaining a large army in peace and in war. These injurious influences are apt to be obscured by invalid arguments, one of which calls for attention here. It is to the effect that Germany's system must be advantageous to her working classes, since it enlarges the funds which cartellized industries have at their disposal for the employment of labour: and it is suggested that Britain might therefore advantageously follow her example.

This suggestion seems based on exclusive attention to the interests of some industry that is being overridden in its own market by the foreigner; and to ignore the interests of other British industries, whose alertness enables them to get the better of rivals abroad. No doubt increased employment in the former industry can be given by shutting out its rivals: but, for every million pounds worth of increased employment so given by it, about a million pounds less employment is likely to be given by those industries whose exports have provided Britain with her power of purchasing imports. Capital will gradually shift from those industries, which are doing most to make the country strong; and will pass to those, to which she has so far owed less. Of course they may be "nascent" industries: or they may be such as can properly receive financial aid (direct or indirect) from the State for military, or other exceptional reasons. The easiest, though not the best, way of doing this may be to enable them to sell their products at higher prices and give increased employment, in consequence of the partial exclusion of rival imports: but such action will, as a general rule, only alter the distribution of good employment, and will not increase its total amount. Therefore, unless this shifting of employment is required for some exceptional reason of high policy, its net effect is likely to be an injury to employees as a body.

Protective tarifs and cartel-organization enable the German steel industries to obtain higher gains from their outputs of hardware, textile machinery etc., *when destined for use by Germans,* than they otherwise could; and the German people may perhaps derive a minute indirect gain from this. But that gain is generally only a small part of what has been artificially taken from them. The Steelworks Union is indeed able to boast that it divides out the benefits of the Protective tarif equitably among all steel "users": but, as has just been argued, that is true only with regard to those capitalist users, who apply steel material in business.

Those who use the steel products as utensils in their houses, or buy products made by steel plant, have no place in this arithmetic.

The German people have indeed some relief in regard to the transport industries. For the Government has a special interest in the supply of steel for railways and ships. It buys steel for railways on advantageous terms. And, it allows steel for making ships to be imported freely; by which excellent provision it has conferred great benefits on the people. If that provision were extended generally, Germany would obtain the necessaries of life on the same advantageous terms as Britain does; and the purchasing power of wages would be at least as high relatively to their money value as in Britain. Not long ago it was higher: but now it is much lower in consequence of that Protective system, of which German cartel policy is a part.[1]

[1] An American onlooker says:—"The English workingman gets higher wages than the German workingman. All the salaried men in English factories get higher wages, and work shorter hours, than the salaried men in German factories. The English agents in foreign parts not only get higher salaries, but insist on week-end holidays and on having several afternoons off during the week in order to play golf and tennis; whereas the German agent works every day and Sunday." Professor Carver, *Principles of Political Economy,* 1918, p. 347. The President of the North German Steamship Company, referring in Hong Kong to the question how it was that Germans had already (in 1910) obtained nearly half the trade of the port, though the port belonged to Britain, called attention to the early desertion of the English offices; and added, "But in some of the German offices those lights will be burning up to nine o'clock. That is the answer. We Germans are winning the trade of the world because of our capacity for, our willingness to *work, work, work*" (*The Times,* 21 March, 1919).

The Report of the Board of Trade on *The cost of living in German towns,* 1908, p. lii, sums up its results as to the comparative purchasing power of wages in Germany and England in the building, engineering and printing trades, by saying that "the German rate of money wages per hour is about three-quarters of the English rate: and the cost of rent, food, and fuel nearly one-fifth greater than in England": that is, English real wages are more than half as much again as German. The second half of this statement "is based on the English standard of consumption": the difference would have been rather less, if based on the German standard.

This result is confirmed by the evidence published in several Reports of the Tariff Commission. For instance, in that on *The engineering industries,* 1909, many witnesses referred to the rates of money wages in England and Germany: every one of them said that the rates per week were higher in England, and the hours of work shorter; and twelve gave numerical estimates of the difference. Three of these put it low: an equal number put the money wages per hour in England twice as high as in Germany. The average of all the estimates seems to coincide with the Board of Trade estimate, quoted above, that before the World-war the English money rate per hour was one-third greater than the German. *The Report on the shipping and shipbuilding industries* [Cd. 9092] 1918, p. 27 lays stress on the fact that in the steel industry "competition with Germany was, in the view of the steel makers, rendered difficult by the low wages prevailing there." Of course uniformly high wages throughout all industries in a country do not materially affect the *relative* values of her imports and exports of manufactured products: and therefore they have less influence on the course of trade than is suggested by the consideration of one industry alone. But this does not affect the authority of the Committee on the matter of fact.

PART ELEVEN

Mathematical Economics

In general, mathematical economics is a method rather than a set of principles. Most mathematical economists belong to the general equilibrium school, associated with the University of Lausanne, which has followers in many Continental countries. Mathematics is a logical method. Its propositions are equations, which are, of necessity, abstractions and do not describe human life realistically. Furthermore, there are only a few places in economic analysis where mathematics is indispensable; an excellent mathematician like Alfred Marshall found it advisable to relegate his mathematical apparatus to an appendix, and the main body of his work suffered no decline in quality.

Two French pioneers in mathematical economics were Augustin Cournot (*Recherches sur les Principes Mathématiques de la Théorie des Richesses,* 1838) and E. J. Dupuit ("De la Mesure de l'Utilité des Travaux Publics" in *Annales des Ponts et Chaussées,* 1844); although neither had a really systematic theory, between them they covered most of the problems later taken up by Walras and Pareto and for the first time utilized infinitesimal calculus in treating economic phenomena. The founders of the general equilibrium mathematical method in economics were Walras, a Frenchman, and Pareto, an Italian. Since they both taught at the Swiss University of Lausanne, the label *Lausanne school* is often applied to these men and their followers.

The great contribution of Walras (*Éléments d'Économie Politique Pure,* 1874–1877) was the development of a complete theory of general equilibrium based on a system of differential equations. His assumption was that the quantity of goods sold within a certain market during a given time will be equal to the quantity offered for sale within that time; that is, demand equals supply. Furthermore, under static conditions it is possible to solve the problem of simultaneous prices on the market, since a number of equations can be set up which will just equal the number of unknown prices to be determined. The price of every product is dependent in some way on the price of every other product.

Thus, in general equilibrium analysis as used by the Lausanne school the whole of economics is organized into an interdependent set of propositions stated mathematically. Like the marginalists, these economists concentrate upon problems of exchange and assume equalization of the utilities of individual purchases at the margin, with utility decreasing as consumption increases. In this sense, Gossen, Jevons, and Walras were all members of both the mathematical and the marginalist schools, and the difference between the two bodies of thought lies more in whether expression is literary or mathematical than in basic content. In the same way, in the section on imperfect competition we group Morgenstern with other noted writers on oligopoly although his treatment is rigorously mathematical. The term *mathematical* denotes a distinction of method, not content. In fact, the Swedish economist Wicksell, in his *Lectures on Political Economy,* successfully integrated the Austrian psycho-literary approach and mathematical formulation. The specific differences in the treatment of economic theory by different mathematical economists will be shown in the following sections on Cournot, Walras, and Pareto.

The general equilibrium theory now commonly accepted on the continent of Europe and taken over by Professor Hicks in a recent reformulation of the theory of value (*Value and Capital,* 1939) follows, on the whole, the Paretian model as exemplified by the *Manuale di Economia Politica.* Here Pareto first introduced the technique of indifference curves, adapted from Edgeworth and Fisher, to indicate the indifference of individuals to various combinations of a number of commodities. Thus Pareto hoped to rid economics of the taint of hedonism by eliminating the necessity of measuring values and underlying utilities. He felt that his method made it necessary to presuppose only a scale of preferences and a *comparability* of values.

There were also some attempts to study dynamic conditions by the mathematical method.

ANTOINE AUGUSTIN COURNOT

(1801–1877)

Cournot, a French mathematician, philosopher, and economist, founded the mathematical school of economics. In his major work, *Recherches sur les Principes Mathématiques de la Théorie des Richesses* (*Researches into the Mathematical Principles of the Theory of Wealth,* 1838), he pioneered in the use of calculus, especially differential equations, to represent the functional relationship between prices and quantities sold in a competitive market. Cournot's theory of the firm already contains the modern treatment of firm equilibrium. Here Cournot assumed that total cost and total revenue vary continuously with output and that the equilibrium position is that of the maximization of net revenue—total revenue minus total cost. The modern theory of the firm, for which the condition of maximum profit is the equality of marginal cost and marginal revenue, is merely a polished version of Cournot's maximization of net revenue.

Instead of starting his analysis from the pole of competition, Cournot adopted the case of pure monopoly (one seller) as a general starting point, building up from monopoly to limited, and then to unlimited, competition. In postulating the possible combinations of prices and quantities for an equilibrium solution of the duopoly case (two sellers), Cournot assumed that the duopolist sets the quantity sold and passively observes the price reaction; that is, he supposes that his rival's output is, for all practical purposes, independent of his own. Each duopolist assumes that the rival follows a policy of fixed output, while in reality each gears his own output to his requirements of profit maximization. On the basis of these incorrect assumptions Cournot concluded that eventually each duopolist adjusts his output to the simultaneous output of the other and a determinate equilibrium results; in other words, a stable outcome is predictable on theoretical grounds. On Cournot's assumptions, the solution is determinate not merely for duopoly but also for oligopoly (few sellers).

For many years Cournot's startlingly original ideas remained forgotten. It was only in the seventies that he was rediscovered. Jevons first drew attention to Cournot's work in the theory of demand; a full decade later, Bertrand in France, and later still, Edgeworth in England, revived the discussion of duopoly. Cournot was then criticized for making quantity instead of price the independent variable. If (as in Cournot's case) price is a dependent variable, there is nothing to prevent either duopolist from capturing the entire market by some slight price reduction. Consequently, Cournot's case results in constant price wars and is inherently unstable. In contrast to Cournot, Edgeworth concluded on the basis of the uncertainty of mutual reactions in the duopoly case that an unstable and indeterminate solution would result.

Recent thinking tends to accept Edgeworth's conclusions rather than Cournot's, but there is general agreement that the Cournot model remains the parent of all modern oligopoly theory.

Cournot's major work was not translated into English until 1897. But he had had great influence on French economists and was the spiritual father of the famous mathematical school of Lausanne. Alfred Marshall acknowledged his indebtedness to Cournot and regarded him as the greatest single influence on his thinking.

The following selection, from Chapter VII of his *Researches,* presents Cournot's analysis of duopoly. We shall have occasion to consider this problem again in our section on imperfect-competition theory.

OF THE COMPETITION OF PRODUCERS *

Every one has a vague idea of the effects of competition. Theory should have attempted to render this idea more precise; and yet, for lack of regarding the question from the proper point of view, and for want of recourse to symbols (of which the use in this connection becomes indispensable), economic writers have not in the least improved on popular notions in this respect. These notions have remained as ill-defined and ill-applied in their works, as in popular language.

To make the abstract idea of monopoly comprehensible, we imagined one spring and one proprietor. Let us now imagine two proprietors and two springs of which the qualities are identical, and which, on account of their similar positions, supply the same market in competition. In this case the price is necessarily the same for each proprietor. If p is this price, $D = F(p)$ the total sales, D_1 the sales from the spring (1) and D_2 the sales from the spring (2), then $D_1 + D_2 = D$. If, to begin with, we neglect the cost of production, the respective incomes of the proprietors will be pD_1 and pD_2; and *each of them independently* will seek to make this income as large as possible.

We say *each independently*, and this restriction is very essential, as will soon appear; for if they should come to an agreement so as to obtain for each the greatest possible income, the results would be entirely different, and would not differ, so far as consumers are concerned, from those obtained in treating of a monopoly.

Instead of adopting $D = F(p)$ as before, in this case it will be convenient to adopt the inverse notation $p = f(D)$; and then the profits of proprietors (1) and (2) will be respectively expressed by

$$D_1 \times f(D_1 + D_2), \qquad \text{and} \qquad D_2 \times f(D_1 + D_2),$$

i.e. by functions into each of which enter two variables, D_1 and D_2.

Proprietor (1) can have no direct influence on the determination of D_2: all that he can do, when D_2 has been determined by proprietor (2), is to choose for D_1 the value which is best for him. This he will be able to accomplish by properly adjusting his price, except as proprietor (2), who, seeing himself forced to accept this price and this value of D_1, may adopt a new value for D_2, more favourable to his interests than the preceding one.

Analytically this is equivalent to saying that D_1 will be determined in terms of D_2 by the condition

$$\frac{d[D_1 f(D_1 + D_2)]}{dD_1} = 0,$$

and that D_2 will be determined in terms of D_1 by the analogous condition

$$\frac{d[D_2 f(D_1 + D_2)]}{dD_2} = 0,$$

* From *Researches into the Mathematical Principles of the Theory of Wealth*, translated by Nathaniel T. Bacon (New York, The Macmillan Co., 1897).

whence it follows that the final values of D_1 and D_2, and consequently of D and of p, will be determined by the system of equations

$$(1)\qquad f(D_1 + D_2) + D_1 f'(D_1 + D_2) = 0,$$
$$(2)\qquad f(D_1 + D_2) + D_2 f'(D_1 + D_2) = 0.$$

Let us suppose the curve m_1n_1 (Fig. 1) to be the plot of equation (1), and the curve m_2n_2 that of equation (2), the variables D_1 and D_2 being represented by rectangular coördinates. If proprietor (1) should adopt for D_1 a value represented by $ox_{,}$, proprietor (2) would adopt for D_2 the value $oy_{,}$, which, for the supposed value of D_1, would give him the greatest profit. But then, for the same reason, producer (1) ought to adopt for D_1 the value $ox_{,,}$, which gives the maximum profit when D_2 has the value $oy_{,}$. This would bring producer (2) to the value $oy_{,,}$ for D_2, and so

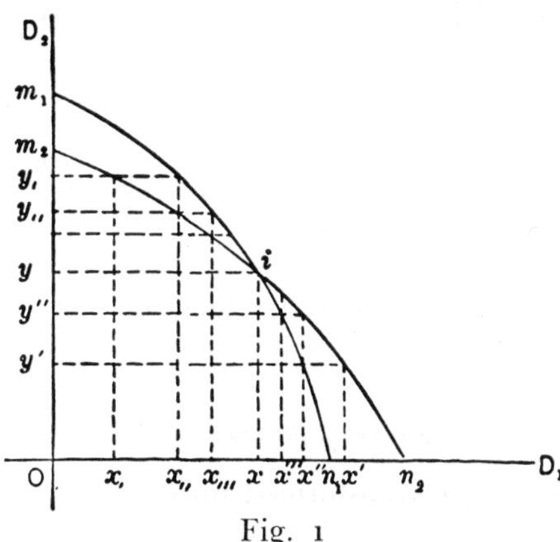

Fig. 1

forth; from which it is evident that an equilibrium can only be established where the coördinates ox and oy of the point of intersection i represent the values of D_1 and D_2. The same construction repeated on a point of the figure on the other side of the point i leads to symmetrical results.

The state of equilibrium corresponding to the system of values ox and oy is therefore *stable; i.e.* if either of the producers, misled as to his true interest, leaves it temporarily, he will be brought back to it by a series of reactions, constantly declining in amplitude, and of which the dotted lines of the figure give a representation by their arrangement in steps.

The preceding construction assumes that $om_1 > om_2$ and $on_1 < on_2$: the results would be diametrically opposite if these inequalities should change sign, and if the curves m_1n_1 and m_2n_2 should assume the disposition represented by Fig. 2. The coördinates of the point i, where the two curves intersect, would then cease to correspond to a state of stable equilibrium. But it is easy to prove that such a disposition of the curves is inadmissible. In fact, if $D_1 = 0$, equations (1) and (2) reduce, the first to

$$f(D_2) = 0,$$

and the second to

$$f(D_2) + D_2 f'(D_2) = 0.$$

The value of D_2 derived from the first would correspond to $p = 0$; the value of D_2 derived from the second corresponds to a value of p which would make the product pD_2 a maximum. Therefore the first root is necessarily greater than the second, or $om_1 > om_2$, and for the same reason $on_2 > on_1$.

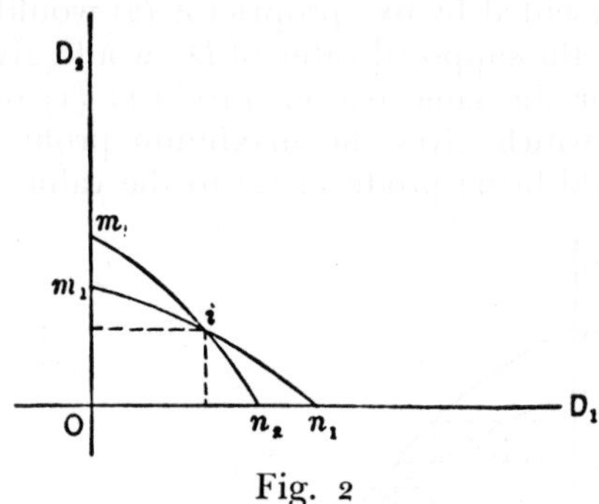

Fig. 2

From equations (1) and (2) we derive first $D_1 = D_2$ (which ought to be the case, as the springs are supposed to be similar and similarly situated), and then by addition:

$$2f(D) + Df'(D) = 0,$$

an equation which can be transformed into

$$D + 2p\frac{dD}{dp} = 0, \tag{3}$$

whereas, if the two springs had belonged to the same property, or if the two proprietors *had come to an understanding*, the value of p would have been determined by the equation

$$D + p\frac{dD}{dp} = 0, \tag{4}$$

and would have rendered the total income Dp a *maximum*, and consequently would have assigned to each of the producers a greater income than what they can obtain with the value of p derived from equation (3).

Why is it then that, for want of an understanding, the producers do not stop, as in the case of a monopoly or of an association, at the value of p derived from equation (4), which would really give them the greatest income?

The reason is that, producer (1) having fixed his production at what it should be according to equation (4) and the condition $D_1 = D_2$, the other will be able to fix his own production at a higher or lower rate with a *temporary benefit.* To be sure, he will soon be punished for his mistake, because he will force the first producer to adopt a new scale of production which will react unfavourably on producer (2) himself. But these successive reactions, far from bringing both producers nearer to the original condition [of monopoly], will separate them further and further from it. In other words, this condition is not one of stable equilibrium; and, although the most favourable for both producers, it can only be maintained by means of a formal engagement; for in the moral sphere men cannot be supposed to be free from error and lack of forethought any more than in the physical world bodies can be considered perfectly rigid, or supports perfectly solid, etc.

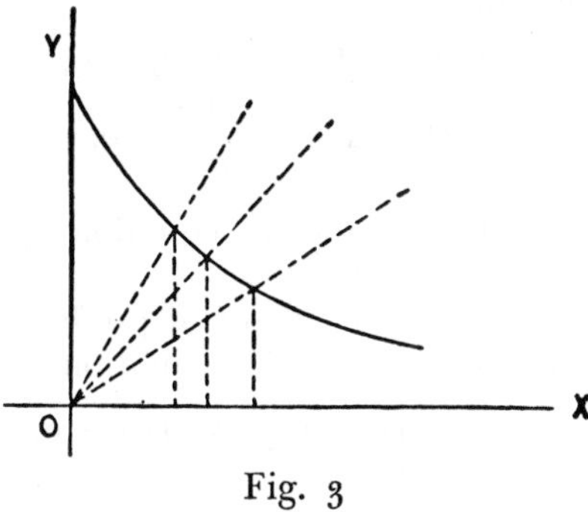

Fig. 3

The root of equation (3) is graphically determined by the intersection of the line $y = 2x$ with the curve $y = -F(x)/F'(x)$; while that of equation (4) is graphically shown by the intersection of the same curve with the line $y = x$. But, if it is possible to assign a real and positive value to the function $y = -F(x)/F'(x)$ for every real and positive value of x, then the abscissa x of the first point of intersection will be smaller than that of the second, as is sufficiently proved simply by the plot of Fig. 3. It is easily proved also that the condition for this result is always realized by the very nature of the law of demand. In consequence the root of equation (3) is always smaller than that of equation (4); or (as every one believes without any analysis) the result of competition is to reduce prices.

If there were 3, 4, . . ., n producers in competition, all their conditions being the same, equation (3) would be successively replaced by the following:

$$D + 3p\frac{dD}{dp} = 0, \qquad D + 4p\frac{dD}{dp} = 0, \qquad \ldots \qquad D + np\frac{dD}{dp} = 0;$$

and the value of p which results would diminish indefinitely with the indefinite increase of the number n.

In all the preceding, the supposition has been that natural limitation of their productive powers has not prevented producers from choosing each the most advantageous rate of production. Let us now admit, besides the n producers, who are in this condition, that there are others who reach the limit of their productive capacity, and that the total production of this class is Δ; we shall continue to have the n equations

$$(5)\begin{cases} f(D) + D_1 f'(D) = 0, \\ f(D) + D_2 f'(D) = 0, \\ \cdots\cdots\cdots \\ f(D) + D_n f'(D) = 0, \end{cases}$$

which will give $D_1 = D_2 = \cdots = D_n$, and by addition,

$$nf(D) + nD_1 f'(D) = 0.$$

But $D = nD_1 + \Delta$, whence

$$nf(D) + (D - \Delta)f'(D) = 0,$$

or

$$D - \Delta + np\frac{dD}{dp} = 0.$$

This last equation will now replace equation (3) and determine the value of p and consequently of D.

Each producer being subject to a cost of production expressed by the functions $\phi_1(D_1)$, $\phi_2(D_2)$, $\cdots$, $\phi_n(D_n)$, the equations of (5) will become

$$(6)\begin{cases} f(D) + D_1 f'(D) - \phi_1'(D_1) = 0, \\ f(D) + D_2 f'(D) - \phi_2'(D_2) = 0, \\ \cdots\cdots\cdots\cdots \\ f(D) + D_n f'(D) - \phi_n'(D_n) = 0, \end{cases}$$

If any two of these equations are combined by subtraction, for instance if the second is subtracted from the first, we shall obtain

$$\begin{aligned} D_1 - D_2 &= \frac{1}{f'(D)}[\phi_1'(D_1) - \phi_2'(D_2)] \\ &= \frac{dD}{dp}[\phi_1'(D_1) - \phi_2'(D_2)]. \end{aligned}$$

As $\frac{dD}{dp}$ is essentially negative, we shall therefore have at the same time

$$D_1 \gtrless D_2, \quad \text{and} \quad \phi_1'(D_1) \lessgtr \phi_2'(D_2).$$

Thus the production of plant *A* will be greater than that of plant *B*, whenever it will require greater expense to increase the production of *B* than to increase the production of *A* by the same amount.

For a concrete example, let us imagine the case of a number of coal mines supplying the same market in competition one with another, and that, in a state of stable equilibrium, mine *A* markets annually 20,000 hectoliters and mine *B*, 15,000. We can be sure that a greater addition to the cost would be necessary to produce and bring to market from mine *B* an additional 1000 hectoliters than to produce the same increase of 1000 hectoliters in the yield of mine *A*.

This does not make it impossible that the costs at mine *A* should exceed those at mine *B* at a lower limit of production. For instance, if the production of each were reduced to 10,000 hectoliters, the costs of production at *B* might be smaller than at *A*.

By addition of equations (6), we obtain

$$nf(D) + Df'(D) - \Sigma\, \phi_n'(D_n) = 0,$$

or

$$D + \frac{dD}{dp}\,[np - \Sigma\, \phi_n'(D_n)] = 0. \tag{7}$$

If we compare this equation with the one which would determine the value of p in case all the plants were dependent on a monopolist, viz.

$$D + \frac{dD}{dp}\,[p - \phi'(D)] = 0, \tag{8}$$

we shall recognize that on the one hand substitution of the term np for the term p tends to diminish the value of p; but on the other hand substitution of the term $\Sigma\phi_n'(D_n)$ for the term $\phi'(D)$ tends to increase it, for the reason that we shall always have

$$\Sigma\, \phi_n'(D_n) > \phi'(D);$$

and, in fact, not only is the sum of the terms $\phi_n'(D_n)$ greater than $\phi'(D)$, but even the average of these terms is greater than $\phi'(D)$, *i.e.* we shall have the inequality

$$\frac{\Sigma\, \phi_n'(D_n)}{n} > \phi'(D).$$

To satisfy one's self of this, it is only necessary to consider that any capitalist, holding a monopoly of productive property, would operate by preference the plants of which the operation is the least costly, leaving the others idle if necessary; while the least favoured competitor will not make up his mind to close his works so long as he can obtain any profit from them, however modest. Consequently, for a given value of p, or for the same total production, the costs will always be greater for competing producers than they would be under a monopoly.

It now remains to be proved that the value of p derived from equation (8) is always greater than the value of p derived from equation (7).

For this we can see at once that if in the expression $\phi'(D)$ we substitute the value $D = F(p)$, we can change $\phi'(D)$ into a function $\psi(p)$; and each of the terms which enter into the summational expression $\Sigma\, \phi_n'(D_n)$, can also be regarded as an implicit function of p, in virtue of the relation

$D = F(p)$ and of the system of equations (6). In consequence the root of equation (7) will be the abscissa of the point of intersection of the curve

$$(a) \qquad y = -\frac{F(x)}{F'(x)},$$

with the curve

$$(b) \qquad y = nx - [\psi_1(x) + \psi_2(x) + \cdots + \psi_n(x)];$$

while the root of equation (8) will be the abscissa of the point of intersection of the curve (a) with one which has for its equation

$$(b') \qquad y = x - \psi(x).$$

As has been already noted, equation (a) is represented by the curve MN (Fig. 4), of which the ordinates are always real and positive; we can represent equation (b) by the curve PQ, and equation (b') by the curve $P'Q'$. In consequence of the relation just proved, viz.,

$$\Sigma\, \psi_n(x) > \psi(x),$$

we find for the value $x = 0$, $OP > OP'$. It remains to be proved that the curve $P'Q'$ cuts the curve PQ at a point I situated below MN, so that the abscissa of the point Q' will be greater than that of the point Q.

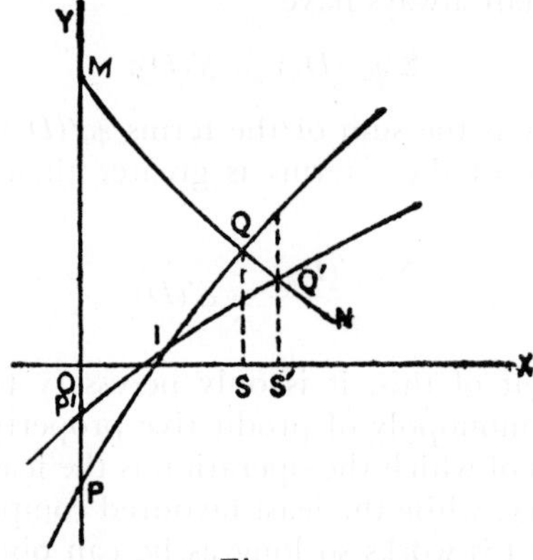

Fig. 4

This amounts to proving that at the points Q and Q', the ordinate of the curve (b) is greater than the ordinate of the curve (b') corresponding to the same abscissa.

Suppose that it were not so, and that we should have

$$x - \psi(x) > nx - [\psi_1(x) + \psi_2(x) + \cdots + \psi_n(x)],$$

or

$$(n-1)x < \psi_1(x) + \psi_2(x) + \cdots + \psi_n(x) - \psi(x).$$

$\psi(x)$ is an intermediate quantity between the greatest and smallest of the terms $\psi_1(x), \psi_2(x), \cdots, \psi_{n-1}(x), \psi_n(x)$; if we suppose that $\psi_n(x)$ denotes the smallest term of this series, the preceding inequality will involve the following inequality:

$$(n - 1)x < \psi_1(x) + \psi_2(x) + \cdots + \psi_{n-1}(x).$$

Therefore x will be smaller than the average of the $n - 1$ terms of which the sum forms the second member of the inequality; and among these terms there will be some which are greater than x. But this is impossible, because producer (k), for instance, will stop producing as soon as p becomes less than $\phi_k'(D_k)$ or $\psi_k(p)$.

Therefore if it should happen that the value of p derived from equations (6), combined with the relations

$$(9) \qquad D_1 + D_2 + \cdots + D_n = D, \qquad \text{and} \qquad D = F(p),$$

should involve the inequality

$$p - \phi_k'(D_k) < 0,$$

it would be necessary to remove the equation

$$f(D) + D_k f'(D) - \phi_k'(D_k) = 0$$

from the list of equations (6), and to substitute for it

$$p - \phi_k'(D_k) = 0,$$

which would determine D_k as a function of p. The remaining equations of (6), combined with equations (9), will determine all the other unknown quantities of the problem.

MARIE ESPRIT LÉON WALRAS

(1834–1910)

Walras was one of the greatest figures in the history of economic thought, both as a founder of marginal-utility economics and as author of the first great work in mathematical economics.

There is no real precedent for his major task, the exposition of the theory of general equilibrium. For although Cournot did pave the way for the theory in his demonstration of the functional interdependence of prices and demand, it remained for Walras to demonstrate it rigorously and comprehensively in his presentation.

Walras studied to be a mining engineer but left engineering school before his training was completed and became a free-lance journalist and an advocate of economic, especially agrarian, reform. In 1870 he was appointed to the chair of political economy at the University of Lausanne, where he remained until 1892; he was succeeded by Vilfredo Pareto.

The classic exposition of his theory may be found in his *Éléments D'Économie Politique Pure* (1874–1877). As in Jevons and Menger, value is based on utility as a function of the quantity demanded. Walras makes use of the term *rareté,* defined as the intensity of the last want satisfied (or the mathematical derivative of effective utility in relation to the quantity possessed). Exchange follows from the desire to equalize *raretés,* and prices, under competitive conditions, will be determined by the intersection of the demand and supply curves. Walras also employs the notion of *prix crié,* the price called by an auctioneer, to depict the process of competitive price formation. By approximations, the equilibrium price will be achieved. In equilibrium, the market exchange of two commodities is such that the ratio of the *raretés* is equal to the ratio of the prices. Walras' exchange equations are not confined to two commodities, but deal with any number of commodities.

Given the equations of supply and demand at equilibrium, and the *numéraire* (the accounting unit) derived from them, the solution of the problem of general equilibrium is determinate, according to Walras; that is, the number of simultaneous equations is equal to the number of unknowns, the number of prices to be ascertained. The problem is determinate, however, in a formal sense only. The necessary data cannot be obtained, and the number of simultaneous equations which would have to be solved is virtually infinite. Indeed, the application of general equilibrium theory is practically impossible here, precisely because its scope is so inclusive. Nevertheless, its conceptual emphasis constitutes an important contribution to economic thought.

The emphasis on the mutual interdependence of economic phenomena, and the demonstration of the logically autonomous character of the competitive order, provide a necessary foundation for more specific economic problems.

Walras believed that a general equilibrium of exchange constitutes a condition of maximum satisfaction for society as a whole. Consequently, he advocated nationalization of land, since the private ownership of land hinders achievement of equilibrium by restricting the mobility of labor, between places and between occupations.

Walras' influence on the various areas of economic thought is somewhat difficult to assess. The theory of general equilibrium was quickly accepted, but economists differed as to the importance that was to be assigned to Walras' theoretical feat. The *Éléments* has not been translated into English, and Walras' elaborate mathematical treatment has repelled many readers. His reputation in England and America is based on the simpler restatements of his doctrine by his followers, such as Wicksell, Edgeworth, Davenport, and especially Pareto. His specific doctrines, apart from his utility analysis, have had little influence on subsequent thought.

In the following article, "Geometrical Theory of the Determination of Prices," Walras gives what is probably the best brief summary of general equilibrium theory available in English. The piece stands by itself, and because geometry is used instead of calculus, it should offer few mathematical difficulties to the reader.

GEOMETRICAL THEORY OF THE DETERMINATION OF PRICES *

I. *The Exchange of Several Commodities among Themselves*

In my *Eléments d'économie politique pure,* passing from the theory of exchange of two commodities to the theory of the exchange of several commodities among themselves, and seeing that in that case the demand or the supply of each of the commodities by each of the traders is a function, not only of the price of that commodity, but also of the price of all the others, I believed it was necessary to adopt exclusively the analytic method of expression and do without the help of diagrams. But since then I have found a means, which I will indicate briefly, of elaborating the theory in question by the method of geometrical representation.

Suppose a party to the exchange with the quantities q_a, q_b, q_c, q_d . . . of the commodities (A), (B), (C), (D), represented by the lines Oq_a, Oq_b, Oq_c, Oq_d . . . (Fig. 1) and having for him the utility expressed by the curves $\alpha_q\alpha_r$, $\beta_q\beta_r$, $\gamma_q\gamma_r$, $\delta_q\delta_r$ . . . I proceed to describe these curves which are the essential and fundamental basis of all the mathematical theory of social wealth.

We may say in ordinary language: "The desire that we have of things or the utility that things have for us, diminishes in proportion to the consumption. The more a man eats, the less hungry he is; the more he drinks, the less thirsty; at least in general and saving certain regrettable exceptions. The more hats and shoes a man has, the less need has he of a new hat or a new pair of shoes; the more horses he has in his stables, the less effort will he make to procure one horse more, always neglecting the action of impulses which the theory has the right to neglect, excepting when accounting for certain special cases." But in mathematical terms we say: "The intensity of the last desire satisfied, is a decreasing function of the quantity of commodity consumed," and we represent these functions by curves, the *quantities consumed* by the ordinates and the *intensity of the last desire satisfied* by the abscissas. For example, take the commodity (A), the intensity of the desire of our consumer which would be $O\alpha_r$ at the beginning of the consumption, would be nil after the consumption of a quantity $O\alpha_q$, the consumer having then arrived at satiety. That intensity of the last desire satisfied, for the sake of brevity, I call *rareté*. The English call it the *final degree of utility,* the Germans *Grenznutzen.* It is not an appreciable quantity, but it is only necessary to

* From "Geometrical Theory of the Determination of Prices," *Annals of the American Academy of Political and Social Science*, July, 1892, pp. 47–64.

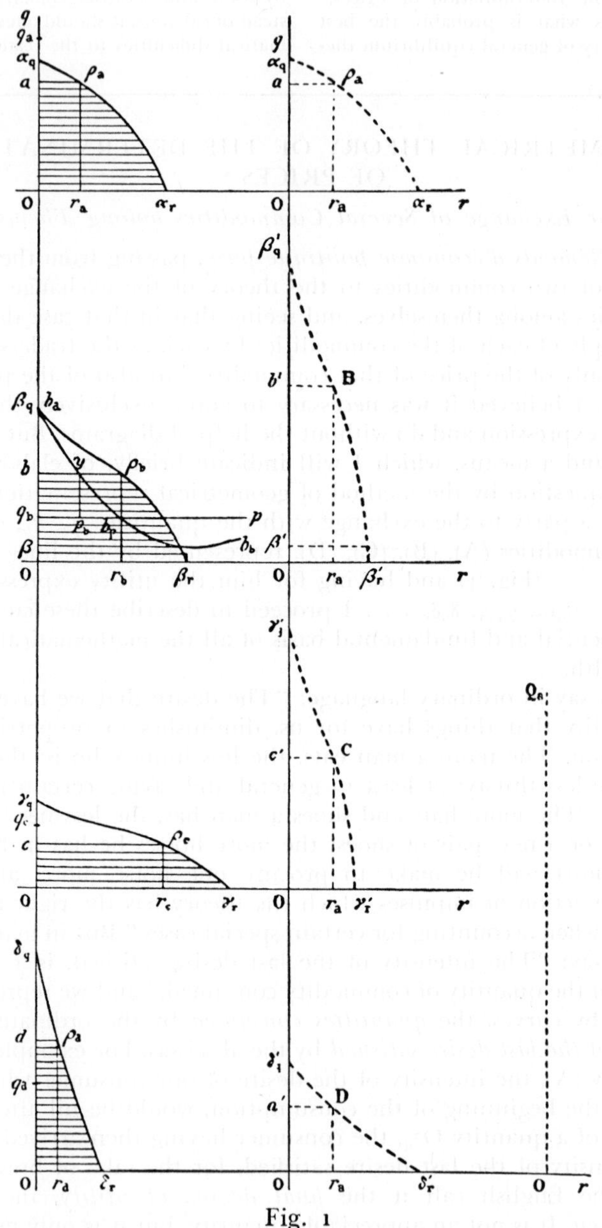

Fig. 1

conceive it in order to found upon the fact of its diminution the demonstration of the great laws of pure political economy.

For the present let p_b, p_c, p_d . . . be the prices of (B), (C), (D), in terms of (A) determined at random on the market. The first problem that we have to solve consists in determining the quantities of (A), (B), (C), (D) . . ., x, y, z, w . . . the first positive and representing the quantities demanded, the second negative and representing the quantities offered, which our trader will add to the quantities q_a, q_b, q_c, q_d, of which he is already possessed or which he will subtract from them, so as to consume the quantities $q_a + x$, $q_b + y$, $q_c + z$, $q_d + w$ . . . represented by the lines Oa, Ob, Oc, Od . . . Just as we employed the general hypothesis above, of a party to the exchange for whom the *rareté* decreased with the quantity consumed, so here we employ the general hypothesis of a party to the exchange who seeks in the exchange the greatest possible satisfaction of his desires. Now the sum of the desires satisfied by a quantity Oa of commodity (A), for example, is the *surface* $Oa\rho_a\alpha_r$. The *effective utility* is the integral described by the *rareté* in relation to the quantity consumed. Consequently the problem, whose solution we are seeking, consists precisely in determining Oa, Ob, Oc, Od . . . under the condition that the sum of the shaded areas $Oa\rho_a\alpha_r$, $Ob\rho_b\beta_r$, $Oc\rho_c\gamma_r$, $Od\rho_d\delta_r$ . . . be a maximum.

In order to furnish that solution very simply in the geometric form, I subject the curves of utility or desire $\beta_q\beta_r$, $\gamma_q\gamma_r$, $\delta_q\delta_r$ . . . to the following transformation. I lay off from the origin O, upon the horizontal axes, the new abscissas equal to $1/p$ of the old abscissas. Also, upon the parallels to the vertical axes drawn through the extremities of the new abscissas, I lay off from the horizontal axes the new ordinates equal to p times the old ordinates. In the figure, $p_b = 2$, $p_c = 3$, $p_d = \frac{1}{2}$ . . . As is easily seen, the new curves $\beta'_q\,\beta'_r$, $\gamma'_q\,\gamma'_r$, $\delta'_q\,\delta'_r$ . . . represent the utility of (A), as spent for (B), for (C), for (D) . . ., or, in other words, the desire the exchanging party has of (A), in order to procure some of (B), of (C), of (D) . . . In short, if we consider the areas $O\beta_q\beta_r$, $O\gamma_q\gamma_r$, $O\delta_q\delta_r$ . . . as the limits of sums of rectangles infinitely small, we may consider the surfaces, $O\beta'_q\beta'_r$, $O\gamma'_q\gamma'_r$, $O\delta'_q\delta'_r$, as the limits of *equal* sums of rectangles infinitely small, each base being p times less, and each height p times greater. Now, each of the rectangles of the former sum represents the effective utility of an increment of commodity; each of the rectangles of the latter sum represents, in the same way, the equal effective utility of the p increments of (A), with which that increment of commodity may be bought.

The curves $\alpha_q\alpha_r$, $\beta'_q\beta'_r$, $\gamma'_q\gamma'_r$, $\delta'_q\delta'_r$ being placed beside each other, I take a vertical length OQ_a, representing the equivalent in (A) of the quantities q_a, q_b, q_c, q_d, of (A), (B), (C), (D) . . . at the prices 1, p_b, p_c, p_d . . . viz: $q_a + q_bp_b + q_cp_c + q_dp_d +$ . . . and I advance it from right to left, in order to satisfy the varying desires in the order of their intensity, until it is sub-divided among the curves into the ordinates $r_a\rho_a = Oa$, $r_aB = Ob'$, $r_aC = Oc'$, $r_aD = Od'$, . . . corresponding to a like abscissa. Now, that abscissa Or_a will represent, in terms of (A), the *rareté* of (A), of (B), of (C), of (D) . . . say, r_a, corresponding to the maximum of effective utility. The ordinates *Oa, Ob′, Oc′, Od′* . . . , will represent, in terms of (A), the quantities to be consumed, of (A), of (B), of (C), and of (D), the only commodities to be consumed being those for which the intensity of the first desire to be satisfied is greater than r_a.

If we carry back the abscissas $Or_a = r_a$, $Or_b = p_b r_a$, $Or_c = p_c r_a$, $Or_d = p_d r_a$ . . . to the curves $a_q\, a_r$, $\beta_q\, \beta_r$, $\gamma_q\, \gamma_r$, $\delta_q\, \delta_r$ . . . we obtain the ordinates *Oa, Ob, Oc, Od* . . . representing the quantities of (A), of (B), of (C), of (D), . . . to be consumed. And so, *in a state of maximum satisfaction, the raretés are proportional to the prices, according to the equations:*

$$\frac{r_a}{1} = \frac{r_b}{p_b} = \frac{r_c}{p_c} = \frac{r_d}{p_d} = \ldots$$

Thus it is, that, given the quantities possessed and the utilities of the commodities, we determine for a party in the exchange the demand or supply of each of the commodities at prices taken at random, which will afford the maximum satisfaction of his wants.

Having given the demand and supply of commodities by all the parties in the exchange at prices taken at random, it remains to determine the current prices at equilibrium, under the condition of the equality of the total effective demand and supply. The solution of the second problem may also be furnished geometrically.

Let us, for an instant, neglect p_c, p_d . . . and seek at first to determine, provisionally, p_b. And, for that purpose, let us inquire how (p_c, p_d . . . being supposed constant) the variations of p_b influence the demand and supply of (B).

If y is positive, that is to say, if the trader is in need of (B), an augmentation of p_b can only diminish y. In short, if he takes at a higher price an equal quantity, he still owes a difference which he cannot pay, without diminishing the quantities of (A), (C), (D) . . . But, then, he will augment the *raretés* of these commodities; and, in consequence, the condition of maximum satisfaction will be less perfectly fulfilled. Hence, the quantity y is too great for a price higher than p_b.

If y is negative, that is to say, if the party is a supplier of (B), there are three possible results. The party, being supposed to supply an equal quantity at a higher price, a surplus is due him, and, by means of that surplus, he can augment his quantities, and consequently diminish his *raretés* of (A), (C), (D) . . . Then, one of three things occurs: Either the surplus is insufficient to reestablish the condition of maximum satisfaction, or it is just sufficient, or it is more than sufficient; and, in consequence, at a price higher than p_b, the party must supply a quantity of (B), either greater than, equal to, or less than y. It is certain, that he will find himself in one of these three cases, according to the amount of the enhancement of p_b. For, if, on the one hand, that enhancement of p_b constantly diminishes the ratio r_b/p_b by increasing the denominator, that same increase of

p_b admits, on the other hand, of a continual lowering in $r_a/1$, r_c/p_c, r_d/p_d . . . by a diminution of the numerators r_a, r_c, r_d, . . . which may finally cause a decrease of the numerator r_b itself.

The variation of p_b, from zero to infinity, therefore, causes the party to the exchange to pass from the side of demand to that of supply; then, from an increasing supply to a decreasing supply. At the price zero, the demand is equal to the excess of the quantity necessary perfectly to satisfy the wants over the quantity possessed; at the price infinity, the amount offered is nil. In the case of the exchange of several commodities, as in the case of the exchange of two commodities with each other, the tendencies may be represented geometrically, for a party to the exchange, by a curve [1] $b_d\, b_p\, b_o$. (Fig. 1). [p. 466]

All the parties to the exchange being not identical, but similar in their tendencies, as far as concerns the commodity (B), it is clear that all the partial curves of demand must be united [2] in a total curve that continually decreases, B_dB_p (Fig. 2), and all the partial curves of supply in a total curve NP, successively increasing and decreasing, from zero to zero, if we take it positively, by making NP′ turn around the horizontal axis, so as to bring it to the position NP. The abscissa Op'_b, of the point of intersection B of the two curves B_dB_p and NP, will be provisionally the current price at equilibrium for which the total effective supply and demand of (B) will be equal. Furthermore, the intersection of the two curves, B_dB_p and NP, may take place either when the second curve rises, or when it falls.

It follows from the nature of the curves, that we shall obtain the provisional current price of (B) by raising it in case of a surplus of effective demand over effective supply, and lowering it, on the contrary, in case of a surplus of effective supply over effective demand. Passing then to the determination of the current price of (C), then to the current price of (D) . . . , we obtain them by the same means. It is quite true that, in determining the price of (C), we may destroy the equilibrium in respect to (B); that, in determining the price of (D), we may destroy the equilibrium in respect to (B), and in respect to (C), and so on. But, as the determinations of the prices of (C), (D) . . . in respect to the demand

1 [The ordinates of this curve have the same meaning as the ordinates of the utility curve for (B) on which it is superposed, but its abscissas represent the price of (B) in terms of (A). Thus in order that the individual may consume Ob, that is buy $q_b\, b$ in addition to his original stock Oq_b the price must be $b\, y$ (in this case 2). If the price rises above $q_b\, b_p$ he ceases to buy and begins to sell. But the curve reaches a minimum point and then approaches $q_b\, p$ as an asymptote. That is as the price rises beyond a certain point, he ceases to stint himself in the enjoyment of (B) and parts with less and less of it.—TRANSLATOR.]

2 [The total *demand* curve for (B) ($B_d\, B_p$ Fig. 2) may evidently be found from the partial curves such as $b_d\, b_p\, b_o$ by selecting on these individual curves the points which correspond to a given abscissa (price) and constructing a corresponding point in the total curve which shall have the same abscissa, but whose ordinate shall be the sum of the ordinates of the individual curves *measured above* $q_b\, p$ as $y\, p_b$. In like manner the ordinates of NP′ are the sum of the individual ordinates *measured below* $q_b\, p$ and corresponding to like abscissas.—TRANSLATOR.]

and supply of (B), will result in a contrary way, we shall always be nearer the equilibrium at the second trial than at the first. We enter here on the theory of trial and error, such as I have developed in my work, and by virtue of which *we arrive at the equilibrium of a market by raising the price of commodities, the demand for which is greater than the supply, and by lowering the price of those, the supply of which is greater than the demand.*

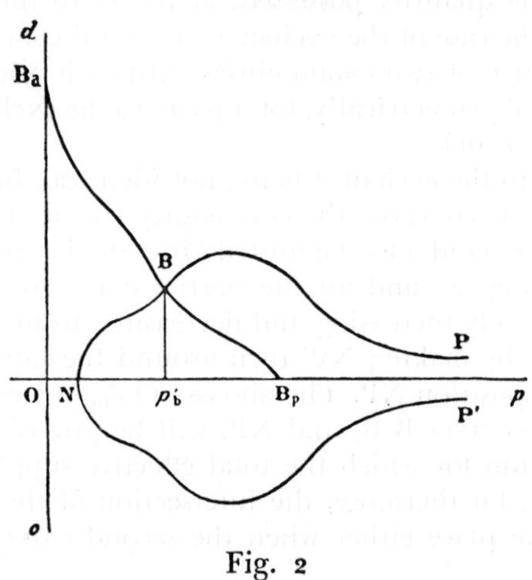

Fig. 2

It is due to the concurrent employment of analytic expression and geometric representation that we have here, in the case of the exchange of several commodities among themselves, not only the idea but the picture of the phenomenon of the determination of prices upon the market. And with this, it seems to me, we possess at last the theory. Some critics, however, laugh at the number of pages I use in demonstrating that we may arrive at a current price by raising in case of an excess of the demand over the supply, and lowering in case of an excess of the supply over the demand. "And you," I said once to one of them, "how do you demonstrate it?" "Well," he answered me, a little surprised and embarrassed, "is there any need of demonstrating it? It seems to me self-evident." "There is nothing evident except axioms, and this is not an axiom. But one naturally follows the mode of reasoning which Jevons has formulated so clearly in his little treatise on *Political Economy,* that a rise, making necessarily a diminution of the demand and an augmentation of the supply, causes equality in case of a surplus of the one over the other." "Precisely." "But there is an error there. A rise necessarily diminishes the demand; but it does not necessarily augment the supply. If you are a supplier of wine, it may well be that you supply less at a million, than at a thousand francs, less at a billion than at a million, simply because you prefer to drink your wine yourself, rather than use the surplus which you could procure by selling it beyond a certain limit. The same is true of labor. We easily conceive that a man, who supplies ten hours a day of his time at the price of one franc an hour, would not supply more than four at the price of 10 francs, or than one at 100 francs. We see, every day, in the large towns, that the laborers, when they earn 20 or 25 francs a day, do not work more than three or four days a week." "But if that is so, how is raising it a means of reaching the current price?" "It is this that the theory explains. Two individuals, who have separated, may meet again, either by moving each, in an opposite direction to the other, or by one going faster than the other. Supply and demand equalize themselves, sometimes in one way, sometimes in another." Is it not worth while to demonstrate rigorously the fundamental laws of a science? We count to-day I do not know how many schools of political economy. The *deductive* school and the *historical* school; the school of *laisser-faire* and the school of *state-intervention,* or *socialisme de la chaire,* the *socialistic* school properly so-called, the *catholic* school, the *protestant* school. For me, I recognize but two: the school of those who do not demonstrate, and the school, which I hope to see founded, of those who do demonstrate their conclusions. It is in demonstrating rigorously the elementary theorems of geometry and algebra, then the theorems of the calculus and mechanics which result from them, in order to apply them to experimental ideas, that we realize the marvels of modern industry. Let us proceed in the same way in political economy, and we shall, without doubt, succeed in dealing with the nature of things in the economic and social order, as they are dealt with in the physical and industrial order.

II. The Exchange of Products and Services with Each Other

It is my present purpose to apply to the theory of production and the theory of capitalization the exclusively geometric method of demonstration according to which I have sketched the theory of exchange in the preceding paragraph.

Now, in formulating the theory of exchange, we suppose the quantities of the commodities to be a given, not an unknown element of the problem. To begin with, in order to arrive at a theory of production, it is necessary to consider commodities as the products resulting from combined productive services, and, in consequence, it is necessary to introduce the quantities of manufactured products into the problem, as so many unknown quantities, adding as is proper, an equal number of determining mathematical conditions. That is what I wish to do here, referring to my *Elements of pure political economy* for definitions and notations.[3]

Suppose, then, the services of land, labor and capital [in the narrow

[3] [These definitions of conceptions peculiar to the author and constituting essential elements of his system of Economics are to be found in the preface to his work (pp. XII–XVI). I have translated by *capitals* the word *capitaux* (which includes all things material or immaterial that are used more than once) and by *services* the word *services* (the successive uses of the capitals).—TRANSLATOR.]

sense] (T), (P), (K) . . . susceptible of being utilized, either directly as consumable services, or indirectly as productive services, that is to say, in the form of the products of the sorts (A), (B), (C), (D) . . . The first problem that we have to solve consists in determining, for each consumer, the supply of services and the demand for services, either in the form of consumable services, or as products. Now the solution of the problem is furnished us by the theory of exchange.

Given, then, a consumer possessed of the quantities q_t, q_p, q_k, of the services (T), (P), (K) . . . and having a desire for these services and a desire for the products, (A), (B), (C), (D) . . . expressed by the curves of utility or desire. Given, also, p_t, p_p, p_k . . . π_b, π_c, π_d, . . . the prices (taken at random) of (T), (P), (K) . . . and of (B), (C), (D) . . . in terms of (A). We will transform the curves of utility or desire of services and products into curves of utility (measured in (A)) of (T), (P), (K) . . . (B), (C), (D) . . . or, in other words, into curves of the desire for (A) to be used in procuring some of (T), (P), (K), . . . (B), (C), (D) . . . This is done by dividing the abscissas and multiplying the ordinates by market prices. The curve of the utility or desire of (A) and the transformed curves of utility, or desire of (T), (P), (K) . . . (B), (C), (D) . . . being placed one under the other, we may advance a vertical line of the length $Q_a = q_t p_t + q_p p_p + q_k p_k + \dots$ from right to left, until it distributes itself among all the curves into ordinates corresponding to a like abscissa r_a. By carrying back the abscissas $p_t r_a$, $p_p r_a$, $p_k r_a$ . . . r_a, $\pi_b r_a$ $\pi_c r_a$, $\pi_d r_a$ . . . to the primitive curves, we obtain the ordinates representing the quantities of labor (T), (P), (K) . . . and of products (A), (B), (C), (D) . . . to be consumed. It is evident that *in the state of maximum satisfaction, the raretés will be proportional to the prices according to the equations:*

$$\frac{r_t}{p_t} = \frac{r_p}{p_p} = \frac{r_k}{p_k} = \dots = \frac{r_a}{1} = \frac{r_b}{\pi_b} = \frac{r_c}{\pi_c} = \frac{r_d}{\pi_d} = \dots$$

Our prices p_t, p_p, p_k, . . . π_b, π_c, π_d . . . for services and products are supposed to be taken at random. We will now suppose, that there have been manufactured, say, the quantities Ω_a, Ω_b, Ω_c, Ω_d . . . of (A), (B), (C), (D) . . . , at random, and, leaving p_t, p_p, p_k . . . as they are, let us determine the prices of (B), (C), (D) . . . by the condition that the demand for the products shall be equal to their supply, that is to the quantity manufactured. The solution of the second problem is likewise furnished us by the theory of exchange. Suppose, then, Δ_b, represented by the ordinate $\pi_b \Delta_b$ (Fig. 3), to be the total demand for (B) at the prices just supposed for services and products. We know, by the theory of exchange, that if, disregarding at first the prices of (C), (D) . . . and seeking to determine provisionally the price of (B), we cause the price to vary from zero to infinity, the demand for (B) will diminish always according to the curve $B_d B_p$. Hence, there exists a price, π'_b, corresponding to the equality of the demand for (B), with the supply Ω_b, which is $> \pi_b$, if, at the price π_b, the demand for (B) is greater than the supply, and which is $< \pi_b$, if, at the price π_b', the supply of (B) is greater than the demand. We shall likewise find a price π_c', corresponding to the equality of the demand for (C), with the supply Ω_c, a price π_d', corresponding to the equality of the demand for (D), with the supply Ω_d, and so on. After the first experiment we proceed to a second, to a third still, and so on, until we have obtained a series of prices, π_b'', π_c'', π_d'' . . . at which the demands for (B), (C), (D) . . . . will be equal to the supplies Ω_b, Ω_c, Ω_d . . . We conclude then that in the matter of production, as in the matter of exchange, *we reach the*

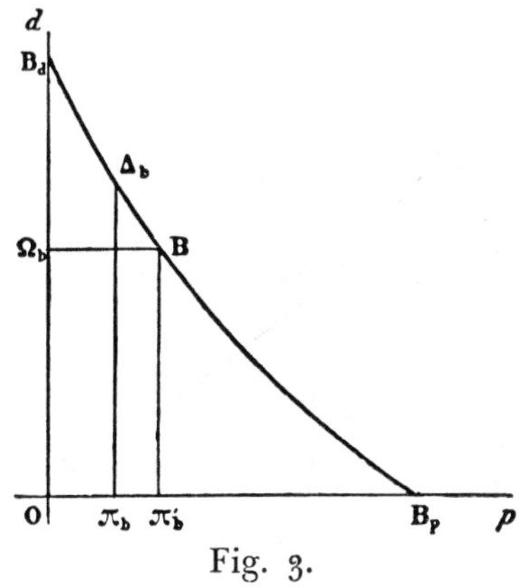

Fig. 3.

equilibrium of market of products in raising the price of those, the demand for which is greater than the supply and lowering the price of those, the supply of which is greater than the demand.

π''_b, π''_c, π''_d . . . are thus the *selling prices* of the quantities, Ω_b, Ω_c, Ω_d . . . of (B), (C), (D) . . . But from the prices, p_t, p_p, p_k . . . of the services, (T), (P), (K) . . . result certain cost prices, p_b, p_c, p_d . . . of the products, (B), (C), (D) . . .[4] And the difference, positive or negative, between the

[4] It is true that, in order to suppose a cost price, common to all the undertakers, it is necessary to suppose that the *fixed expenses* distribute themselves among an equal quantity of products, in order to allow us to make them correspond to the *proportional expenses;* that is, it is necessary to suppose all the parties manufacturing equal quantities of products. The hypothesis is no more real than that of the absence of gain or loss, but it is as rational. If, in short, at a given point, a certain quantity of manufactured products corresponds to the absence of gain and loss, the parties in the transaction, who manufactured less, take the losses, restrain their production and finish by liquidating, those who manufactured more take the gains, develop their production and attract to themselves the business of the others; thus, owing to the distinct nature of proportional expense and fixed expense, production in free competition, after being engaged in a great number of small enterprises, tends to distribute itself among a number less great of medium enterprises, then among a small number of great enterprises, to end finally, first in a *monopoly at cost price,* then in a *monopoly at the price of maximum gain.* This statement is corroborated by the facts. But during the whole period of competition and even during the period of monopoly at cost price, it is always permissible, in order to simplify the theory, to suppose the undertakers manufacturing equal quantities of products and to make the fixed expense correspond to the proportional expense.

selling price and the *cost price,* in the production of (B), (C), (D) . . . results in the gain or loss, $\Omega_b\,(\pi_b'' - p_b)$, $\Omega_c(\pi_c'' - p_c)$, $\Omega_d(\pi_d'' - p_d)$ . . . It is now necessary to determine the manufactured quantities of (B), (C), (D) . . . by the condition that the *selling price* and *cost price* be equal, so that there may be neither gain nor loss to the undertakers. This third problem is the especial problem of the theory of production, and may also be solved geometrically as follows:

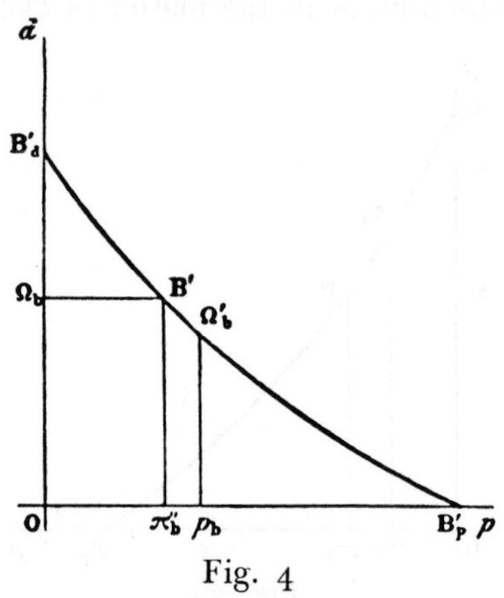

Fig. 4

Let Op_b (Fig. 4) be an abscissa representing the *cost price,* p_b. Let $O\pi''_b$ be an abscissa representing the *selling price,* π_b'', and π''_bB' an ordinate representing the quantity Ω_b of (B), manufactured at random, and demanded at the price π_b''. If we suppose p_t, p_p, p_k, . . . π_c'', π_d'' . . . determined and constant, and that we may vary the price of (B), from zero to infinity, it is certain that the demand for (B) will diminish, always following a curve $B_d'\,B_p'$. Consequently, there exists a demand Ω_b', corresponding to a *selling price,* equal to the *cost price* p_b, which is $\gtrless \Omega_b$, according as π_b'' is $\gtrless p_b$. We might also find a demand Ω_c', corresponding to a *selling price* equal to a *cost price* p_c; a demand Ω_d', corresponding to a *selling price* equal to a *cost price* p_d, and so on. If, then, we substitute the manufactured quantities, Ω_b', Ω_c', Ω_d' . . . for the manufactured quantities, Ω_b, Ω_c, Ω_d . . . and sell them, according to the mechanism of rise and fall of prices described in the preceding paragraphs, we obtain new selling prices which will still be slightly different from p_b, p_c, p_d . . . Proceeding thence to a second, to a third trial, of the two experiments, and so on, we shall obtain at last certain quantities, D_b, D_c, D_d . . . of (B), (C), (D) . . . disposed of at *selling prices* equal to the *cost prices,* p_b, p_c, p_d . . . We may, then, enunciate this important proposition for the theory of production, viz: *we arrive at the equality of the selling price of products and their cost price in productive services by augmenting the quantity of products, of which the selling price exceeds the cost price, and by diminishing the quantity of those whose cost price exceeds their selling price;* by which we see that, strictly speaking, the consideration of the expense of production determines not the *price* but the *quantity* of the products.[5]

Our prices of services p_t, p_p, p_k . . . have always been determined at random. There remains to us a fourth and last problem to solve, which is to determine the way in which the quantities demanded and the quantities supplied are equal. Now, at the point where we are, there are quantities supplied of (T), (P), (K) . . . U_t, U_p, U_k . . . which are determined by the condition of maximum satisfaction, conformably to the solution of our first problem. And, in view of the quantities supplied, there are quantities demanded which are composed of two elements: first, the quantities demanded by the consumers in the way of consumable services u_t, u_p, u_k . . . which are also determined by the condition of maximum satisfaction; then, the quantities demanded by the undertakers in the way of productive services, D_t, D_p, D_k, . . . which are determined by the quantities manufactured of the products (A), (B), (C), (D) . . . the demand for which is equal to the supply, and the selling price equal to the cost price, conformably with the solution of our second and third problems. We may demonstrate exactly as in the theory of exchange, that if, everything else remaining equal, we cause p_t to vary from zero to infinity, (1), the demand for (T), $D_t + u_t$ will diminish, always following a curve T_d T_p (Fig. 5); (2), the supply of (T) will, starting from zero, increase, then diminish and return to zero, following a curve QR; and that, consequently, there exists a price p'_t, at which the supply and demand of (T) are equal, which is $>p_t$, if at the price p_t, the demand for (T) is greater than the supply, and $<p_t$ if at the price p_t, the supply of (T) is greater than the demand. There exists, likewise, a price p'_p, at which the supply and demand of (P) are equal, a price p'_k, at which the supply and demand of (K) are equal, and so on. After a first series of experiments with the prices, p_t, p_p, p_k . . . including, of course, the experiments in the second and third problems, we would proceed to repeat them on the prices, p_t', p_p', p_k' . . . and so on. Hence, *we arrive at the equilibrium of the market for services as in that for products, by raising the price of*

[5] Imagine that instead of saving only himself, Robinson Crusoe had been accompanied by a hundred sailors and passengers who brought with them rice, rum, etc. If all these individuals held a market on the shore in order to exchange their commodities with each other, these would have current prices perfectly determined and entirely independent of the cost of production. This is the problem of exchange and shows how the prices depend only on the *rareté,* that is, the utility and quantity possessed of the commodities. But if, afterwards, these individuals, having found on the island the necessary productive services, proceed to manufacture the same commodities and carry their products to the market, the commodities whose selling price exceeds their cost price would multiply; those whose cost price exceeds their selling price would become rare, until the equality of selling price and cost price was established. This is the problem of production and shows how the consideration of the cost of production determines the quantity and not the price of the products.

that for which the demand is greater than the supply, and lowering the price of that whose supply is greater than the demand.[6]

We must represent to ourselves all the operations as taking place simultaneously which by the requirements of the demonstration we have had to suppose occurring successively; that is to say, in the market of products and in that of services, those who demand raise the price when the demand exceeds the supply, and those who supply lower the price when there is an excess of supply over the demand. The undertakers increase their production in case the selling price exceeds the cost price and reduce it,

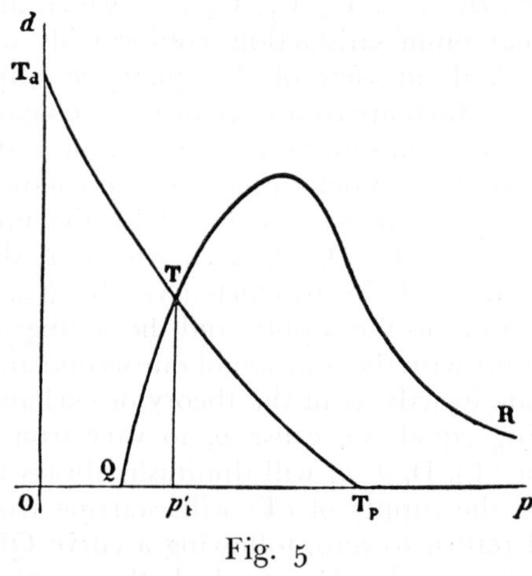

Fig. 5

on the contrary, when the cost price exceeds the selling price. And here, again, thanks to the geometric representation, we shall have an exact and complete picture of the general phenomenon of the establishment of economic equilibrium under the rule of free competition. But, nevertheless, an analytical form of expression will be necessary to a strictly scientific understanding of the matter. From this point of view, then, having defined the elements of the system or the quantities that come into play, it is necessary to distinguish those which are given and those which are unknown, to express by equations the conditions of economic equilibrium, to prove that these equations are in number just equal to the unknown quantities, to show that, by the experiments, we approximate more and more nearly the solution, and to explain the particular conditions of equilibrium so far as concerns the product (A). For all these matters, of which nothing has been said here, I take the liberty of referring the reader to section III of my *Eléments.*

III. The Exchange of Savings for New Capitals

In order to simplify, let us suppose for the present, the equilibrium established as regards the quantities of commodities manufactured as well

[6] The price of the raw materials would be determined as that of productive services.

as the prices of commodities and of services, and let us neglect the changes which may be caused in this equilibrium by our investigation of the special equilibrium of capitalization. Let us, in the same way, neglect the cost of the redemption and insurance of the capitals.

The elements in the equilibrium of capitalization are the quantities produced of new capitals and the rate of interest whence results the prices of the capitals following the general formula $\pi = p/i$.

Suppose, there are produced at random, the quantities D_k, D_{k1}, D_{k11} . . . of capitals of the sorts (K), (K′), (K″) . . . and that there is a rate of interest at random, i. At that rate each man engaged in exchange determines the excess of his income over his consumption, and the total of these individual excesses forms a total excess E, which is the quantity of cash at hand to buy new capitals or the demand of the new capitals in cash at the rate of interest, i. On the other hand, at the current prices for their use, p_k, p_{k1}, p_{k11}, supposed to be determined, and constant, the quantities D_k, D_{k1}, D_{k11} . . . of the capitals (K), (K′), (K″) . . . give a total income $D_k p_k + D_{k1} p_{k1} + D_{k11} p_{k11} + \ldots$, and possess a total value

$$\frac{D_k p_k + D_{k1} p_{k1} + D_{k11} p_{k11} + \ldots}{i}$$

which is the quantity of cash demanded in exchange for the new capitals or the supply of new capitals at the rate of interest i. If, by chance, the two quantities of cash are equal, the rate i will be the rate of the equilibrium of the interest, but generally they will be unequal and it remains to render them equal.

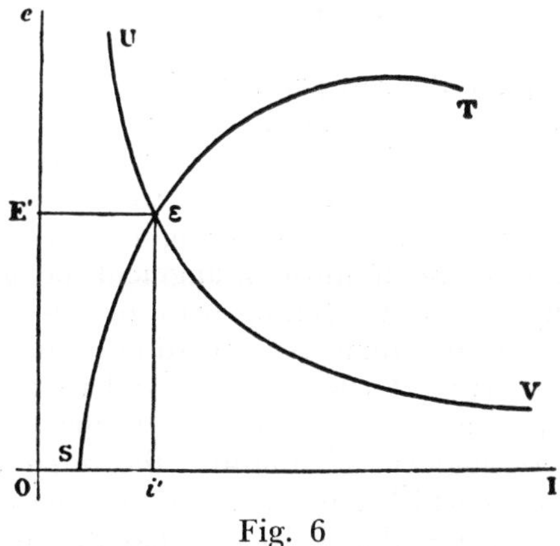

Fig. 6

Now, we may assume that the excess of the income over the consumption is at first nil, at a nil rate, then it multiplies and augments at a positive and increasing rate, then diminishes and returns to zero, if the rate tends to become infinitely great; that is to say, if, with a minimum saving, one may gain a very great increase in his income. In other words, the rate of interest, being an abscissa on the axis OI (Fig. 6), the excess of income over consumption will be the ordinate of a curve, successively increasing and decreasing, S T. As to the value of the new capitals it evidently increases or decreases, according as the rate of interest decreases or increases. In other words, the rate of interest being an abscissa on the axis O I, the value of the new capital may be an ordinate of a curve continually decreasing, U V. Hence, we see immediately that *it is necessary to raise the price of the new capitals by lowering the rate of interest if the demand for new capitals in cash is greater than the supply, and to lower the price of the new capitals by raising the rate of interest, if the supply of the new capitals in cash is greater than the demand.*

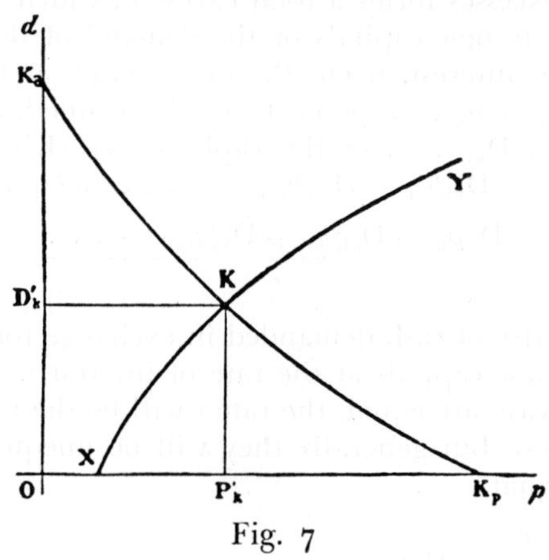

Fig. 7

At this time, there are the cost prices P_k, P_{kl}, P_{kll} . . . of the new capital (K), (K′), (K″) . . . besides the selling prices π_k, π_{kl}, π_{kll} . . . The question is to reduce the selling and cost prices to the equality which generally does not exist between them. Now we may regard as established by the previous demonstrations that in augmenting or diminishing the quantity of a capital (K), we diminish or augment the *rareté* and the price of its use, and consequently the selling price of this capital, and that is to say, that the curve of the quantity in relation to the selling price is the constantly decreasing curve K_d K_p (Fig. 7). And we are equally justified in concluding that in augmenting or diminishing the quantity of the same capital (K), we augment or diminish the *rareté* and the prices of the productive services which enter into the making of the capital and consequently its cost price; that is to say, that the curve of quantity in relation to the cost price is the constantly increasing curve, X Y. Hence, we see immediately and without the necessity of reproducing here the exposition of the successive approximations in regard to the quantities of capital (K), (K′), (K″) . . . that *it is necessary to augment the quantity of a new capital, whose selling price exceeds its cost price and diminish the quantity of that whose cost price exceeds its selling price.*

The equilibrium of capitalization once established, as has just been explained, we have:

$$P_k = \pi_k = \frac{p_k}{i}, \qquad P_{kl} = \pi_{kl} = \frac{p_{kl}}{i}, \qquad P_{kll} = \pi_{kll} = \frac{p_{kll}}{i}$$

or

$$\frac{p_k}{P_k} = \frac{p_{kl}}{P_{kl}} = \frac{p_{kll}}{P_{kll}} = \ldots ;$$

that is to say, the rate of interest is the same for all capital saved.

We may demonstrate geometrically in a very simple manner, at least as far as concerns capitals in consumable services, that *this identity of rate of interest is the condition of the maximum utility of new capitals.*

There are two problems of maximum utility relating to the services or use of new capitals; that connected with the distribution by an individual of his income among his different kinds of desires, and that connected with the distribution by a society of the excess of its income over its consumption among many varieties of capital. The first is solved by means of the construction which was made in the theory of exchange, and referred to at the beginning of the theory of production, involving the proportionality of the *rareté* of a species of capital to the price paid for its use, according to the equations:

$$\frac{r_k}{p_k} = \frac{r_{kl}}{p_{kl}} = \frac{r_{kll}}{p_{kll}} = \ldots$$

It will be understood, without difficulty, that the second problem would be solved by a construction exactly similar to the former. Instead of transforming the curves of the desires for the various services of capitals by dividing the abscissas, and multiplying the ordinates by the prices for their use, p_k, p_{kl}, p_{kll} . . . we should divide the one and multiply the other by the cost prices P_k, P_{kl}, P_{kll} . . . , involving the proportionality of the *raretés* to these prices, viz:

$$\frac{r_k}{P_k} = \frac{r_{kl}}{P_{kl}} = \frac{r_{kll}}{P_{kll}} = \ldots$$

or, dividing the latter system by the former:

$$\frac{p_k}{P_k} = \frac{p_{kl}}{P_{kl}} = \frac{p_{kll}}{P_{kll}} = \ldots$$

which expresses the identity of the rates of interest of all capital.

VILFREDO PARETO

(1848–1923)

Vilfredo Pareto was born in Paris, the son of an Italian marquis who had voluntarily exiled himself from Italy because he opposed the government of his native city, Genoa. Pareto's mother was French. Vilfredo returned to Italy in 1858 and started studies which led to a doctor's degree in engineering. He was a successful engineer and rose to be general manager of the largest steel works in Italy.

It was not until 1893 that his writings attracted the attention of Walras and led to a professorship at the University of Lausanne. The genius of the man may be appreciated by the fact that he was engaged in economic research only between 1892 and 1912; before that time he was an engineer, and afterwards he devoted himself primarily to sociological studies. In spite of the relative brevity of his preoccupation with economics, his exposition of mathematical economics is today considered one of the most erudite and elegant available.

Pareto was an unusual man in many ways. A successful businessman and engineer, he had both a knowledge of industrial processes rare in academic economists and a solid mathematical training. Equally contemptuous of the bourgeoisie and of socialists, he isolated himself in a world of classical study. This attitude was due, perhaps, to his patrician background and to a financial independence which enabled him to select his associates. His disgust with the excesses of parliamentary democracy in Italy led him to leave the country for Switzerland even before he was invited to the University of Lausanne. The extent of Pareto's connection with Italian Fascism has never been firmly established. It is certain that he approved of Mussolini's seizure of power in 1921 and that Mussolini conferred senatorial rank on him, but there is no proof that he ever joined the Fascist Party or even endorsed its teachings.

Pareto's influence on economic theory has been phenomenal. Although he never taught in Italy and spent the years after 1906 in retirement in a country villa in Switzerland, he built up a following which dominated economic teaching in Italy almost completely and in France to a lesser degree. Yet Pareto was never really original; his work was more or less an improvement on that of his predecessor, Walras. Walras, unfortunately, had had a philosophy of agrarian socialism which was gall and wormwood to the academic fraternity in Italy. Pareto regarded both this philosophy and Walras' monetary heresy (for that era) as unnecessary and unscientific; he kept his theory "pure." This trait may have contributed to the extraordinary popularity of his unoriginal though excellent work.

The most mature statement of Pareto's economics is in the *Manuale di Economia Politica* (1906). The theory is aridly pure, static, and general in the sense that it can be applied to *any* economic system. Like that of Walras, it is basically one of general equilibrium under static conditions. He disliked the hedonistic base implicit in marginal-utility economics and therefore attempted to find some way of abandoning the entire concept of measurable utility. Instead, he used the technique of indifference curves that had been formally introduced by Edgeworth. However, Pareto deviated from Edgeworth in one important respect: Edgeworth began with a measurable total utility from which he deduced the definition of indifference curves. Pareto, on the other hand, took his indifference curves as given and divested them of any utility connotation, thus basing economic theory on observable preference scales. He never succeeded, however, in freeing himself completely from utility concepts.

Pareto also made a substantial contribution to welfare economics. The problem in this branch of economics, he believed, was to determine how to achieve the greatest total satisfactions in an economy. Any change imposed on any economic pattern which would result in greater gains than losses may be said to increase the collective welfare. He granted that under some circumstances the collective state could promote welfare better than perfect competition.

Although they are out of our immediate sphere of interest, Pareto's contributions to sociology are so important that they must be mentioned. His great *Trattato di Soziologia Generale* (1916) is as important to sociology as the *Manuale di Economia Politica* is to economics. His sociology is basically an analysis of the political process and is marked by a contempt for political democracy and, to put it mildly, a lack of antipathy for dictatorship. To Pareto, history was a succession of aristocracies or of *élites*. In sociology he did not succeed in repressing his personal predilections and prejudices as well as he had in his economic theory.

MANUAL OF POLITICAL ECONOMY *

General Conception of Economic Equilibrium

The main object of our study is economic equilibrium. We will soon see that this balance results from the antagonism that exists between men's tastes and the obstacles in the way of satisfying them. Our study is therefore divided into three rather distinct parts: first, the study of tastes; second, the study of obstacles; third, the study of the way in which these two factors are combined so as to achieve equilibrium.

The best way of proceeding would be first to study tastes and completely exhaust this subject; then to go on to the study of obstacles and exhaust that also; finally to study equilibrium itself, going back neither over the study of tastes, nor over that of obstacles. But it would be as difficult for the author to do this as it would be for the reader. It is impossible to treat any one of these subjects exhaustively without making frequent references to ideas pertaining to the two others. If the basic nature of these ideas is not made clear, the reader cannot follow the argument; if they are explained, the result is to intermingle the very subjects that we set out to distinguish. Besides, the reader tires quickly of a long discourse whose object he does not see. The author takes this into account and discusses desires and obstacles, not at random, but only to the extent that this would be useful to determine equilibrium. Thus the reader satisfies his legitimate desire to know the destination of the long road he has to travel. . . .

Let us suppose that people find themselves in the presence of certain things capable of satisfying their desires and that we give these things the name "economic goods." If the question is raised, How would one distribute any one of these goods among these individuals? we encounter a question which belongs in the second group of theories.[1] In reality, each man is aware only of one sensation, that which corresponds to the amount of an economic good which is assigned to him; we are not dealing with the problem of the different sensations of one and the same

* From *Manuale di Economia Politica* (Milan, Società Editrice Libraria, 1906).

1 [The second group of theories compares the feelings of one man with those of another and determines how the men should be related to one another in order to achieve certain ends.—*Editor*]

individual, which we would be able to compare among themselves; we can only compare the feelings of one individual with those of another.

If there are two or more things, each individual is aware of two or more different feelings, according to the quantity of things which he has at his disposal; we can then compare these feelings, and among the different possible combinations, decide which one would be chosen by a particular individual. This is a question which belongs in the first group of theories.[2]

If all the allotments of economic goods at the disposal of an individual increase (or diminish), we will soon see that, with the exception of one case which we will discuss later, the new position will be so much more advantageous (or less so) than the former one for the individual in question that in this case there is no problem to resolve. But if, on the other hand, certain quantities increase while others diminish, then the question arises whether or not the new combination is or is not advantageous to the individual. It is in this category that economic problems belong. We see them arise in real life in the process of making a trading agreement, where one gives one thing in order to receive another, and in the processes of production, in which certain goods are transformed into others. We will consider these problems first.

The elements which we are obliged to combine are, on the one hand, a man's tastes and on the other, the obstacles in the way of satisfying them. If, instead of having to consider mankind, we had to study ethereal beings with neither needs nor desires, not having any physical need to eat or drink, there would not be a single economic problem to solve. Going to the other extreme, it would be the same if we supposed that there was not a single barrier to prevent men from satisfying every taste and desire. There are no economic problems for the man who can arrange everything to suit himself.

The problem arises because our tastes meet with certain obstacles, and it is all the more difficult to solve when there are several methods of satisfying our tastes and of surmounting the obstacles. The question therefore arises as to how and why an individual prefers this or that method. Let us examine this problem more closely.

If one only had to choose between two things, or among a small number, the problem would be qualitative and easily solved. Which would you rather have—a barrel of wine or a watch? The answer is easy. But in actual life there are a very large number of things open to choice, and even in regard to two things there are innumerable quantitative combinations among which one could choose. In the course of a year a man could drink 100, 101, 102, . . . litres of wine; and if his watch is not going perfectly, he could get another immediately or perhaps wait one month, two months, . . . one year, two years, . . . before making this purchase, taking good care of his watch in the meantime. To put it in

2 [The first group compares the several feelings of a man placed in different conditions and seeks to decide which of these conditions he will choose.—*Editor*]

another way, there is an infinite number of quantitative variations of things among which we have to choose, and these variations may be very slight, almost imperceptible. We therefore need to construct a theory which will enable us to solve this type of problem.

Let us consider a series of combinations of different quantities of goods. A man can go from one to another of these combinations, finally stopping at one of them. It is very important to know which one is his final choice, and we can arrive at the answer by means of the theory of economic equilibrium.

ECONOMIC EQUILIBRIUM

This can be defined in various ways, all of which in reality go back to the same thing. It can be said that economic equilibrium is that state which maintains itself indefinitely if there is no change in the conditions which are being studied. If for the moment we direct our attention only to the stable equilibrium, we can say that it is determined in such a fashion that if it is only slightly modified, it immediately tends to right itself—to return to its previous state. These two definitions are equivalent.

For example: an individual, under certain given circumstances or conditions, buys a kilogramme of bread every day; if one day he is made to buy 900 grammes of it, and if he becomes free again the next day, he will continue to buy one kilogramme of bread indefinitely. This is what is called a state of equilibrium.

It will be necessary to explain mathematically that once this equilibrium has been attained, these variations, or, if you like, these movements, will not occur; which brings us back to the statement that the system maintains itself indefinitely in the state under consideration.

We can describe as *real* those changes which are necessary to achieve equilibrium. We can describe as *potential* those changes which, while they theoretically could take us out of the state of equilibrium, do not occur in reality because equilibrium sustains itself.

Political economy studies real changes in order to know how these events take place, and it studies potential changes in order to understand the characteristics of certain economic conditions.

If, by some change or other, we could move away from a given economic state, and if we could move indefinitely in the direction of increasing the amounts of all the goods desired by man, we would achieve a state in which every man would have all he wanted. Obviously, this would be an equilibrium position; but also, obviously, things do not proceed thus in the real world. We will have to decide on other equilibrium positions at which we should stop, because not all types of change are open to us, but only those changes which are in the realm of possibility. In other words, there are obstacles which stand in the way of some changes which do not permit man to follow certain roads, and which prevent certain modifications from taking place. Equilibrium results from this very opposition between our tastes and the obstacles in the way of satisfying them.

If these obstacles or hindrances were such that they determined each movement exactly, we would not have to consider tastes at all and consideration of the obstacles would be enough to determine equilibrium. As a matter of fact, this is not the case, at least not in general. Obstacles do not absolutely determine all change; they simply establish certain limits. They impose certain restrictions, but they permit an individual to move in a more or less restricted area according to his own tastes—and among the range of possible movements we will have to seek out those which occur in reality.

These tastes and obstacles are related to every individual that one considers. For an individual, the tastes of other men with whom he is related are a part of the obstacles confronting him.

To have all the given facts of the problem of equilibrium, it is necessary to add another factor to tastes and obstacles; that is, the actual conditions which determine the position of individuals and the way in which goods are transformed. For example: the quantities of salable goods possessed by individuals, the means of manufacture, etc. We will understand this question better as we proceed with our study.

To determine equilibrium, we will assume as a condition that at the moment it takes place, the changes permitted by the obstacles are restrained by our tastes; or, inversely, as a way of saying the same thing, that at this moment the changes permitted by our tastes are restrained by the obstacles in the way. In reality, it is evident, in these two ways, that we are describing that state of affairs in which no movement will take place, and this is, by definition, the characteristic of the state of equilibrium.

It is therefore necessary for us to determine what changes our tastes allow in a state of equilibrium, and what changes they prevent, and in the same way, what changes existing obstacles allow and which ones they prevent.

THE TASTES OF MEN

It is necessary to find a way to deal with tastes in a mathematical fashion. It has been held that they can be inferred from the pleasure that men derive from certain goods. If a thing satisfies men's needs or desires it is said to have *use-value, utility*.

This idea is imperfect and ambiguous in several respects. First, not enough emphasis is given to the point that this *use-value,* this *utility,* is exclusively a relationship between one man and one thing. Also, it has been discussed a great deal, perhaps unwittingly, as if it were an objective characteristic of things. Others, who came closer to the truth, but not close enough, spoke of it as if it were a relation between men in general and one thing in particular. Second, it has not been realized that this *use-value* depends on (was a function of, as the mathematicians say) the quantities consumed. For example, it is meaningless to speak in the abstract of the *use-value* of water, and it is not enough to add, as we have just seen, that this *use-value* is relative to a certain man; it is very different depending on whether this man is dying of thirst or whether he has already drunk as much as he wishes. To be exact, we should speak of the use-value of a certain quantity of water when it is added to a known quantity which has been already consumed.

Pure economics arose principally from the correction of this error of the former school of economic thought. With Jevons it appeared as the correction of theories on value current at that time; with Walras it became, and this marked considerable progress, the theory of a particular case of economic equilibrium, that of free competition. In the meanwhile another case, that of monopoly, had already been studied, but in an entirely different manner, by Cournot. Marshall, Edgeworth, and Irving Fisher have studied economic phenomena in a manner increasingly extensive and general; in our *Lectures* it becomes the general theory of economic equilibrium, and we are proceeding even further along this road in the present work.

Third, the word *utility* has been taken to mean something entirely different in political economy from what it signifies in everyday speech. In the ordinary sense of the word, morphine does not have utility because it is hurtful to the one addicted to it; on the other hand, economically speaking, it has utility for him because it satisfies one of his needs, even though it is injurious to him. Although earlier economists have drawn attention to this ambiguity, it is often forgotten even now; thus it is very important not to use the same word to describe two such different things. We have suggested in our *Lectures* that *economic utility* be designated by the words *ophelimity*. Other authors have subsequently followed this suggestion. . . .

For an individual *ophelimity* is the pleasure he derives from a certain quantity of an article when that quantity is added to a given amount (which could equal zero, let us say) of the same thing already in his possession.

If this certain quantity is very small (infinitely small) and if one divides the pleasure that it brings by the quantity itself, we have what we shall call ELEMENTAL OPHELIMITY.

Finally, if one divides elemental ophelimity by the price, we have WEIGHTED ELEMENTAL OPHELIMITY.

A new refinement has been given to the theory of ophelimity. There is one weak spot in the basic reasoning behind this theory, and this point has been considerably clarified by Professor Irving Fisher. We have been saying that this thing called *pleasure, use-value, economic utility, ophelimity,* is a quantity, but the demonstration of this fact has not been given. Let us suppose that this demonstration has been made; how would we go about measuring this quantity? It would be a mistake to believe that the value of ophelimity could be deduced in a general way through the laws of supply and demand. This can only be done in a particular case, where only the unit of measure for ophelimity remains arbitrary, when it is a question of articles of such nature that the ophelimity of each one of them depends only on the quantity of this article and is independent of how much of other articles may be consumed. . . . But generally speaking, for example when the ophelimity of article A, consumed at the same time with articles B, C, . . . , depends not only on the consumption of A but also on the consumption of B, C, . . . , ophelimity remains undetermined, even after the unit for measuring it has been fixed.

In what follows, it should always be understood that when we speak of ophelimity, we wish simply to indicate one of a series of indices of ophelimity. . . .

INDIFFERENCE LINES OF TASTES

Let us consider a man who is governed by his tastes alone and who has 1 kilogramme of bread and 1 kilogramme of wine. His tastes being given, he is inclined to have a little less bread and a little more wine, or vice versa. He agrees, for example, to have only .9 kilogramme of bread provided that he has 1.2 kilogrammes of wine. In other words, this means that these two combinations, 1 kilogramme of bread and 1 kilogramme of wine, or .9 kilogramme of bread and 1.2 kilogrammes of wine are the same to him; he does not prefer the second more than the first, or the first more than the second. He would not know which one to choose; it is a matter of *indifference* to him whether he is to be satisfied by one or the other of these combinations.

Going on from the combination of 1 kilogramme of bread and 1 kilogramme of wine, we can set up a large number of others among which the choice is a matter of indifference. We have, for example

Bread	1.6	1.4	1.2	1.0	.8	.6
Wine	.7	.8	.9	1.0	1.4	1.8

Such a series, which could be extended infinitely, is called an *indifference series.*

The use of graphs will be of great assistance in understanding this question. Let us construct two axes perpendicular to each other, *o*A and *o*B, and let *o*A be the axis for bread and *o*B for wine. For instance, *oa* represents a quantity of bread, *ob* a quantity of wine; the point *m,* where these two intersect, indicates the combination of one kilogramme of bread and one kilogramme of wine.

We can present in this way the whole preceding series, and by joining all the points in this series in a continuous line, we will obtain the line *nms,* which is called an INDIFFERENCE LINE or an INDIFFERENCE CURVE.[3]

Let us give some sort of index to each one of these combinations. These indices, which will be considered fixed from this point on, ought to satisfy the two following conditions: First, any two combinations between which

[3] This is the expression of Professor F. Y. Edgeworth. He assumes the existence of *utility* (ophelimity) and from this deduces indifference curves; on the other hand, I consider indifference curves as given, and from them I deduce what I find necessary for equilibrium theory, without depending on ophelimity.

the choice is indifferent should have the same index number; second, when of two combinations one is preferred over the other, the preferred combination should have the larger index number.

We thus have INDICES OF OPHELIMITY, or of the pleasure that an individual feels when he enjoys the combination that corresponds to a given index.

It follows from what has been said that all the combinations of one indifference series have the same index, which is the same as saying that all the points along an indifference line have the same index.

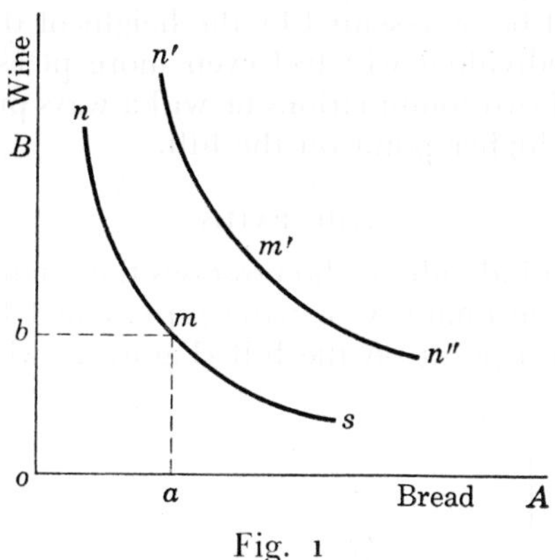

Fig. 1

In Figure 1 let 1 be the index of the line *nms;* let *m'* (for example 1.1 of bread and 1.1 of wine) be a different combination that the individual prefers over combination *m,* and let us give this the index 1.1. Going on further from the combination *m'* we find another indifference series; that is to say, we describe another curve, namely *n'm'n''*. We can go on in this way, it being well understood that we can consider not only combinations that, for one individual, are better than combination *m* but also those that are worse. We will thus have several indifference series, each one having its index; in other words, we will cover that part of the plane *o*AB which we wish to consider with an infinite number of indifference curves, each having its own index.

This gives us a complete picture of an individual's tastes as far as bread and wine are concerned, and this is sufficient for us to determine economic equilibrium. The individual can vanish now, provided that he leaves us this photograph of his tastes.

It is understood, of course, that all types of articles can be dealt with as we have dealt with bread and wine.

The reader who has used topographical maps knows that it is customary there to draw certain curves which designate all the points which, for the same curve, are the same level—are the same distance above sea-level or above any other sort of level.

The curves in Figure 1 are contour curves provided that we regard the indices of ophelimity as representing a height above the plane *o*AB, supposed horizontal, of points on a hill. This is what may be called the hill of the indices of pleasure. There exists an infinite number of others similar to it, according to the arbitrary system of indices selected.

If pleasure can be measured, if ophelimity exists, one of these systems of indices will be precisely that of the values of ophelimity . . . , and the corresponding hill will be the hill of pleasure or of ophelimity.

An individual who is satisfied with a certain combination of bread and wine can be represented by one point on this hill. The pleasure that this individual feels will be represented by the height of this point above the plane *o*AB. The individual will feel even more pleasure when he is at a greater height—of two combinations he will always prefer the one which is represented by a higher point on the hill.

THE PATHS

Let us imagine an individual who possesses the quantity of bread represented by *oa* and the quantity of wine represented by *ab;* we say that the individual is at a point on the hill (Figure 2) which is projected at

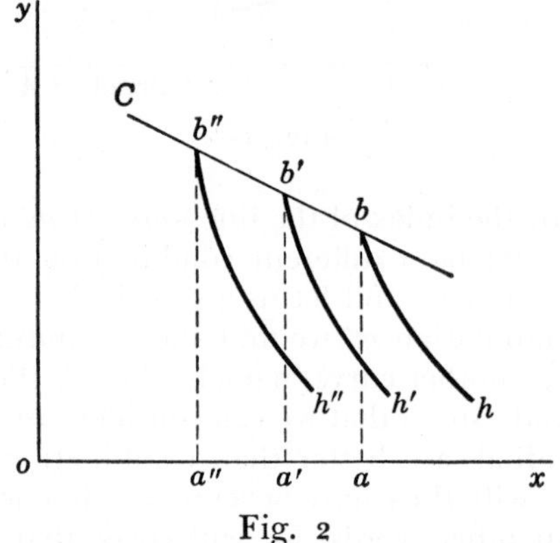

Fig. 2

b on the horizontal plane *xy*, or more briefly that he is at *b*. Let us suppose that at another time the individual had *oa′* of bread and *a′b′* of wine; leaving *b* he will be at *b′*. If later on he has *oa″* of bread and *a″b″* of wine he will have gone from *b′* to *b″*, and so on in this way until he comes to *c*. Let us suppose that the points *b, b′*, and *b″* are very close, and let us join them by a line: we will say that the individual who has successively had the quantity *oa* of bread and *ab* of wine, *oa′* of bread and *a′b′* of wine, etc. has traversed on the hill a *path,* a route, a road, which is projected on the horizontal plane *oxy* along the line *bb′b″ . . . c,* or more briefly, that he has travelled the path *bc*. . . .

EQUILIBRIUM

As we have seen earlier, equilibrium exists when the changes that our tastes would have occasioned are restrained by the obstacles in the way, or vice versa. The general problem of equilibrium is therefore divided into three others, which are: first, to determine what equilibrium is as far as tastes are concerned: second, to determine what equilibrium is in regard to the obstacles, or in regard to the producers; third, to find a point common to both states of equilibrium, which will constitute a point of general equilibrium.

As to the paths, we ought to consider: first, the equilibrium in regard to a given path; second, to consider equilibrium in regard to a number of paths and see how that one which will be followed is chosen.

In dealing with the types of phenomena, we should first consider Type I in regard to the one who trades and the one who engages in production. Later we will study Type II, which is not generally in evidence except for individuals who enter into contracts with others who behave according to Type I.[4]

EQUILIBRIUM IN RELATION TO TASTES

Let us begin by considering an individual who follows a set path and who does his utmost to arrive at the point on this path where his tastes will be most completely satisfied.

If obstacles of the first category [physical in nature] produce on this path a point beyond which he cannot go, and if the positions preceding it are less advantageous to him, obviously he will proceed to this spot, and there he will come to a halt. At this point equilibrium exists as far as tastes are concerned. This point could be a point of tangency to the path and to an indifference curve; it is the highest point on the path which the individual can attain.

The point of tangency could also be the lowest point on the path, and at this point equilibrium would be unstable. For the time being, we will not discuss this case.

Henceforth, we will give consideration to straight paths only, because, in reality, these are the most frequent; but our arguments are of a general nature, and one could, by means of slight modifications or restrictions, apply them to other types of paths.

Let us consider an individual (Figure 3) for whom $t, t', t'', \ldots$ represent the indifference curves of his tastes, the indices of ophelimity increasing from t to t'''. Every week this individual has the quantity *om* of A. Let us suppose that in changing from A to B he follows the straight

[4] [Type I refers to the type of transaction in which a party accepts the going price as given and is interested only in his own personal advantage. In Type II one is concerned with changing the given price and is interested in the different positions he would achieve under different price situations.—*Editor*]

path *mn*. At the point *a*, where the path meets the indifference curve *t*, there is no equilibrium because the individual would rather go from *a* to *b*, on the curve *t′*, where he will have a larger index of ophelimity.

One could say as much for all points where the path crosses indifference curves, but not of the point *c″*, where the path is tangent to an indifference curve. In reality, the individual is only able to go from *c″* towards *b* or towards *b′*, and in these two cases the index of ophelimity declines. His tastes therefore oppose any movement on the part of an individual who has arrived at c″ while moving along the path *mn;* therefore *c″* is the point of equilibrium. It is the same for the analogous points

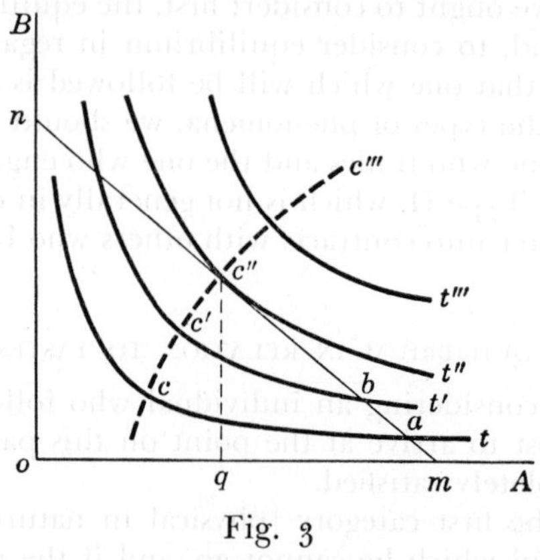

Fig. 3

c, c′, c″, and *c‴*, located on other paths which the individual might theoretically travel. If all these points are joined by a line, one will obtain the line of equilibrium in regard to tastes; and it is thus called THE LINE OF EXCHANGES.

The terminal points which, coming from *m*, precede the points of the exchange line could also be points of equilibrium.

It would be possible to have a path that would reach the quantity zero of A without having been tangent to a single indifferent line. In this case, we would have a terminal point where the path cuts the axis *o*B, and this would mean that on this path not only would the individual choose to give the whole quantity of A which he possesses in order to have some of B, but if he had an even greater quantity of A, he would give it to have some of B.

In arriving at the total of the articles transformed by each individual, one obtains the exchange line for the aggregate of these individuals, and if one wishes, the indifference curves for this aggregate can be represented in the same way. They will result from the indifference curves of the individuals who make up the group. . . .

Economic Equilibrium

EQUILIBRIUM OF TASTES AND PRODUCTION

Let us consider an isolated collective group, and let us suppose that all an individual's expenditures are made for articles that he buys and that all his receipts result from the sale of his labor, of other functions of capital, or of other commodities.

Under these conditions economic equilibrium is determined by the conditions which we have already laid down in regard to tastes and obstacles. We have seen that tastes, and the consideration of the existing quantities of certain goods, determine the relationships between prices and the quantities bought or sold. Furthermore, the theory of production has taught us that, these relationships being given, the prices and the quantities are determined. The problem of equilibrium is thus completely solved.

EQUILIBRIUM IN GENERAL

The preceding theoretical case differs greatly from reality in one respect. In actual life an individual's receipts are far from coming only from the goods that he sells for production. The public debt of civilized nations is enormous; a very small part of this debt has been used for productive purposes, and, at that, often very badly. The individuals who receive payments of the interest on this debt cannot in any way be regarded as people who have placed economic goods in the processes of production. One would have in mind similar considerations when discussing the ever-increasing bureaucracy of modern states, military and naval expenditures, and many of the outlays for public works. We are not in any way seeking to discover here whether or not, and to what extent, these expenditures are more or less useful to society; we are simply establishing the fact that their utility, when it does exist, is of another species than that which results directly from production of an economic nature.

On the other hand, an individual's expenditures are far from being restricted to the economic goods that he buys. Taxes constitute an important part of these outlays. It has been estimated, by calculation which although rough is perhaps not too far wrong, that in certain European countries about 25% of an individual's income is taken away in taxes. The theory which we have explained would therefore be only three-fourths true for most of the amounts which make up a nation's revenue.

It is easy to modify this theory in a way that takes account of the phenomena we have just pointed out. In regard to the income of individuals, it will be enough to distinguish the part that results from economic phenomena from the part that is outside it, and to proceed in the same way as regards expenditures.

The portion of income which is retained by individuals is spent by them according to their tastes; and in the matter of its division among different things, this goes back to the theory, already explained, of equilibrium tastes. The part which is taken out in advance by the public authorities is disbursed according to rules which economic science does not have to study. In the latter case one should suppose that these rules are a part of the given situation concerning the problem to be solved. The laws of supply and demand will follow from the consideration of these two categories of expenses. If only one of them were considered, there could be a marked divergence from real facts. In the case of iron and steel, for example, government orders account for an important part of total production.

As far as equilibrium in regard to obstacles is concerned, it is necessary to take account of the fact that the expenditures of enterprises are not equal, as in the preceding case, to the total incomes of the individuals, but that these outlays constitute only a part of the total, since the remainder has another origin (the public debt, salaries, etc.). The distribution of the portion set aside to buy goods resulting from the productive process is determined by the theory of equilibrium in regard to obstacles. The distribution of the other part of the revenues is determined by the sort of considerations which, like those of the similar case preceding, are beyond the purview of economic science, and which one should therefore borrow from the other sciences; this distribution should be counted here as one of the given factors of the problem.

PROPERTIES OF EQUILIBRIUM

Equilibrium, according to the conditions under which it is obtained, partakes of certain properties which it is important to distinguish.

We will begin by defining a term which it is well to use in order to avoid unduly long expressions. We will say that the members of a group, in a certain position, enjoy *maximum ophelimity,* when it is impossible to find a way of moving out from this position a little in such a way that the ophelimity enjoyed by each individual in the group is either increased or diminished. This is to say that each little change from this position necessarily has the effect of increasing the ophelimity enjoyed by some and diminishing that enjoyed by others; of being agreeable to some, disagreeable to others.

PART TWELVE

Reactions against Orthodoxy: The German Historical School

While Adam Smith's economic concepts found a ready reception in France, where there was a liberal spirit similar to England's, they ran into difficulty in Germany. The German states were ready to expand both commercially and industrially, and they felt that any adoption of free-trade doctrine would completely block progress. In Germany, too, state control and intervention had long been traditional, and few Germans could reconcile themselves to an individualistic, atomistic view of society. In this intellectual environment there grew up a school of economists who were united in their opposition to English classical economics and to the marginal-utility economics which later followed.

In the past there has been a distinction between the older historical school, consisting of Roscher, Hildebrand, and Knies, and the so-called younger school, consisting of Schmoller, Sombart, and Weber. The older writers were satisfied to supplement classical theory, or at most, to criticize it, whereas the members of the younger school often dispensed with it altogether.

Actually, the fundamental unity of the German historical school far supersedes any minor differences. Friedrich List has not in the past been regarded as a member of the German historical school, probably because he was not an academician. Today, however, many competent authorities not only include him but regard him as the founder of the historical school, since his *National System of Political Economy* was the first of a long series of attacks against British classical theory, advocating tariff protection for Germany until such time as England's initial advantage in industry was overcome. The arguments which he used to back up his thesis were based primarily on historical studies.

After 1871 the German historical school became very active in the field of economic policy. Their sponsorship of social reform earned them the sobriquet of "socialists of the chair," although none of them were really members of the Socialist Party.

The historical school believed that economics could be founded on a firm basis only if economists concentrated on concrete historical studies and eschewed armchair theorizing. In the last quarter of the nineteenth century this attitude led to a famous quarrel over method (the *Methodenstreit*), in which the respective champions were Schmoller and Menger;

Menger, on the one hand, defended the Austrian school and abstract theory, while Schmoller claimed that economics could be built only on an evolutionary basis and that the institutional framework which the classical and neo-classical schools took for granted was really nothing more than a stage in the total historical process.

Later, the historical school dropped its intense opposition to abstract theory, but it continued to regard the construction of a historical framework as a necessary basis for further theoretical development. Within this framework various members of the school developed theories of their own. For example, Max Weber introduced an analytical tool, which he called "the ideal type," involving a simplified historical model derived from experience and reality; he brought this to bear upon the particular subject under investigation. Sombart was still another kind of historicist. He attempted to analyze the entire economic history of Europe as a continual process—the rise and development of capitalism.

At its best, the historical school represents a welcome synthesis of history and theory. Theory alone gives an incomplete picture of the economic process, while history must be fused with theory in order to achieve an integrated approach.

The effects of the historical school were manifold. Because of its rejection of marginal-utility economics, it isolated German economists from their fraternity in other countries. As a result, there was a long stagnation of theory in Germany, and not until after World War I did that country produce outstanding theorists like Schneider and Stackelberg. At the same time, the historical school exercised great influence in other countries, especially Scandinavia and the United States. In the latter country the so-called institutional school is very close in method and approach to the German historical school, especially in its later phases.

WERNER SOMBART

(1863–1941)

The writings of Werner Sombart are among the most advanced examples of the work of the German historical school. Some of his later works achieved that rare fusion of history and theory which his predecessors strove for but never attained.

Sombart's father was a prosperous farmer who was elected to the German Reichstag and settled in Berlin. Sombart went to the University of Berlin, where he obtained his doctorate; then he worked for the Bremen chamber of commerce. When he tried to enter academic life, however, his admiration for the works of Karl Marx militated against his chances for appointment in Berlin. As a result, he had to teach at a provincial university. In spite of the fact that he was a very able teacher and wrote a tremendous number of books and articles, it was not until Sombart was fifty-four that the University of Berlin offered him a professorship.

At the turn of the century Sombart began his masterpiece, *Der Moderne Kapitalismus* (*Modern Capitalism,* 1902), in which he attempted to sketch the development of capitalism from Charlemagne to J. P. Morgan. He believed that capitalism was only one episode in the history of mankind—the episode in which money-making was of primary importance. Capitalism molded the entire world in its own image, said Sombart. It caused great movements in population from city to city and from country to country. Business administration became an end in itself. Mass production gave rise to mass markets, the ratio of monopoly and concentration in business increased, and there was an increase in cyclical depression. People had to be disciplined into the passive regularity demanded of a machine tender, and all of civilization had to fit into the tempo of capitalism.

Unfortunately, there is no complete English translation of Sombart's great storehouse of scholarship, and even if there were, its Olympian scope would make the selection of relatively short excerpts summarizing his position difficult. He combined theory and history in excellent fashion, but his theory is different from the value and distribution analysis within the framework of present-day institutions which we customarily call theory. Sombart felt that instead of one *general* economic theory there were *many* theories, covering an infinite plurality of economic systems. This evolutionary institutional approach characterized the work of the younger German historical school, and as we shall see later on, was taken over by the American institutional school. In both cases the main problem under investigation was the operation of the capitalistic system and its predecessors.

Both Sombart and Max Weber were concerned not only with the operational framework but with the "spirit," or *Geist,* of capitalism and analyzed especially the effect of religion and social mores on capitalism. Sombart felt that Protestantism and, above all, Judaism were especially congenial to the capitalistic spirit and structure.

Sombart was deeply indebted to Karl Marx for much spadework in his field of investigation. Unlike Marx, however, he felt that capitalism would not pass away in the foreseeable future, but would endure in altered form, with government control and a rise in the number of coöperatives, for example. Thus, its more objectionable features might be ameliorated, and its product might be more equally shared.

The following article, written by Sombart himself for the *Encyclopaedia of the Social Sciences,* summarizes his masterpiece, *Modern Capitalism.* A part of *Der Bourgeois* (1913) was translated by M. Epstein in 1915, under the title *The Quintessence of Capitalism.* Several important excerpts from this translation are included herein.

CAPITALISM *

Capitalism as a specific economic system cannot be understood without an analysis of the concept of economic system with a view to pointing out the function of this concept in economic science. Economic life is distinguished as a particular sphere of cultural life by the principle of "economy." This principle as a logical concept is removed from the realm of space and time, but "economy" in the sense of economic life is an existential complex with definite spatial and temporal aspects. All culture, and consequently all economy, is historical. As there is in the abstract no religion, no art, no language, no state, but merely a certain religion, a certain art, a certain language, a certain state, so there is no economy in the abstract, but a particularly constituted, historically distinguishable economic life. . . .

Economic science . . . requires a constitutive conception in order to arrange its material in systems. The function of such a conception is to enable us to classify the fundamental characteristics of economic life of a particular time, to distinguish it from the economic organization of other periods and thus to delimit the major economic epochs in history. . . .

These requirements are satisfied by the general conception of the economic system. By an economic system is understood a mode of satisfying and making provisions for material wants which can be comprehended as a unit and wherein each constituent element of the economic process displays some given characteristic. These constituent elements are the economic spirit or outlook—the sum total of the purposes, motives and principles which determine men's behavior in economic life—the form of economic life or the objective system of regulations of economic relations, and the technology employed in economic processes. Defined more precisely, an economic system is a unitary mode of providing for material wants, animated by a definite spirit, regulated and organized according to a definite plan and applying a definite technical knowledge. . . .

The Spirit of the Capitalist System. The special character of capitalism will be brought out most clearly if we consider separately the characteristic forms which the three constituent elements—spirit, form and technology—assume in the capitalist system.

The spirit or the economic outlook of capitalism is dominated by three ideas: acquisition, competition and rationality.

The purpose of economic activity under capitalism is acquisition, and more specifically acquisition in terms of money. The idea of increasing the sum of money on hand is the exact opposite of the idea of earning a livelihood which dominated all precapitalistic systems, particularly the feudal-handicraft economy. In pre-capitalistic systems economic as well as all other thought and action was centered about the human being. Man's

* The selection from Werner Sombart, "Capitalism," *The Encyclopaedia of the Social Sciences,* Volume III. Copyright 1930 by the Macmillan Co., New York, and used with the publisher's permission.

interests as producer or as consumer determined the conduct of individuals and of the community, the organization of the economic life of society as a whole and the ordinary routine of business life in its concrete manifestations. Goods were produced and traded in order adequately to meet the consumers' needs and to provide an ample livelihood for producers and merchants; the standards for the expectations of both consumers and producers were fixed by long established usage. The category of qualitative use value was the determining principle of valuation. All social and individual norms affecting economic processes were grounded in human, personal values. On the other hand, in systems dominated by the idea of acquisition the aim of all economic activity is not referred back to the living person. An abstraction, the stock of material things, occupies the center of the economic stage; an increase of possessions is basic to all economic activity. The idea of such an economic system is expressed most perfectly in the endeavor to utilize that fund of exchange value which supplies the necessary substratum for production activities (capital).

While acquisition constitutes the purpose of economic activity, the attitudes displayed in the process of acquisition form the content of the idea of competition. These attitudes, which are logically inherent in acquisition, may be described as freedom of acquisition from regulation by norms imposed upon the individual from the outside, the lack of quantitative limits to acquisition, its superiority over all other aims and its ruthlessness.

By reason of its freedom from regulation, capitalism rests essentially on the individual's assertion of his natural power. Every economic agent may and should extend his sphere of action as far as the complete exercise of his powers will allow; in case of failure, however, he completely foregoes assistance. Economic activity is closely associated with personal risk, but the economic agent is free to strive for economic success in any way he chooses provided he does not violate the penal code.

There are no absolute limits to acquisition, and the system exercises a psychological compulsion to boundless extension. The fact that capitalistic enterprise has as its purpose a certain mode of utilizing a stock of goods signifies a complete divorce of the aims of capitalistic economy from the personality of the economic agent. The abstract, impersonal character of the aim indicates its limitlessness. Activity in the capitalistic system is no longer determined by the needs, quantitatively and qualitatively limited, of one person or of a group of persons. Profits, no matter how large, can never reach a level sufficiently high to satisfy the economic agent. The positive drive toward boundless acquisition is grounded in the conditions of management. It is empirically true, though not logically inevitable, that any enlargement of business reacts to its own advantage, at least quantitatively through an extension of its sphere of exploitation and sometimes also qualitatively through a reduction of costs. This provides the stimulus to the continuous expansion of a business, often contrary to the expressed wishes of its owners and managers. In this peculiar orientation of human activity upon an infinitely removed goal lies the reason for the dynamic potency of the capitalistic system, a potency which renders intelligible all its remarkable achievements.

Acquisition therefore becomes unconditional, absolute. Not only does it seize upon all phenomena within the economic realm, but it reaches over into other cultural fields and develops a tendency to proclaim the supremacy of business interests over all other values. Wherever acquisition is absolute the importance of everything else is predicated upon its serviceability to economic interests: a human being is regarded merely as labor power, nature as an instrument of production, life as one grand commercial transaction, heaven and earth as a large business concern in which everything that lives and moves is registered in a gigantic ledger in terms of its money value. Ideals oriented upon the value of the human personality loosen their hold upon man's mind; efforts for the increase of human welfare cease to have value. Perfection of the business mechanism appears as the only goal worth striving for; the means become an end. The vague notion of progress comes to include only such developments as advances in technology, reductions in costs, increase in the briskness of trade, growth of wealth. *Fiat quaestus et pereat mundus.*

Acquisition which is quantitatively and qualitatively absolute degenerates eventually into unscrupulousness and ruthlessness. Business draws practical conclusions from the revolutionary supremacy of its ideals and seeks, without consideration for any conflicting interests, to clear all obstacles to the limitless and unqualified exercise of acquisition. The intensity of the acquisitive drive attains a point at which all moral and temperamental inhibitions disappear and all conflicting drives become inhibited. The business man is "unscrupulous" in his choice of ways and means, because the selection is based exclusively on their serviceability in the achievement of the final goal, on their usefulness as instruments of acquisition.

When the direction of economic affairs is oriented solely upon acquisition it is inevitable that those modes of economic behavior should be adopted which seem most rational, most systematic, best adapted to the purpose in hand. In the old, precapitalistic economic organization, which is essentially traditionalistic and static, there sets in a process of rationalization representing a manifestation of the dynamic principle. Economic rationality is thus the third dominating idea of the capitalist system.

Economic rationality is manifested in several aspects of the capitalistic business management—its predilection for long range planning, for the strict adaptation of means to ends, for exact calculation. The genuinely capitalistic enterprise is managed on the basis of a plan which extends as far as possible into the future, thus leading to the introduction, among other things, of roundabout methods of production. The execution of the plan is accomplished by means which are painstakingly examined with reference to maximum serviceability for the purposes in hand—a vivid contrast to the ill considered employment of means in more traditionalistic economies. Underlying the planning and its execution are the evaluation and registration of all business facts in precise quantitative terms and the coordination of these records as a significant whole. This adherence to exact accounting is only natural in a situation where all economic acts are regulated in accordance with their pecuniary value and where management looks to maximized profits as its ultimate aim.

Rationalization permeates, of course, the entire scope of business and affects its technical as well as its commercial aspects. It introduces into the sphere of production the most "rational" methods and stimulates thereby the development of scientific technology. It creates rational factory management and leads to proper departmentalization and departmental coordination. The rationalization of the procedures of manual labor results in the employment of the individual worker most serviceably with respect to the ultimate capitalistic aim. On the commercial side rationalization affects the purchase of production equipment and materials, the sale of the ready product at the most suitable time or in the best market, the creation of new outlets whether through clever salesmanship or through the development of new forms of retailing.

Economic rationality penetrates gradually into other cultural spheres, reaching even those which are only remotely connected with economic life. Under its influence all untamed natural growth disappears and, where it proves disturbing, even the aesthetically individual is mercilessly weeded out. The idea of strict adaptation of means to ends, one of the essential ideological props of capitalism, permeates the totality of culture and leads in the course of time to a purely utilitarian valuation of human beings, objects and events.

While individual action under capitalism is informed by the ideal of highest rationality, the capitalistic system as a whole remains irrational, because the other dominant capitalistic idea, that of acquisition, of the unrestricted assertion by the individual of his power, leaves the regulation of the total economic process to the uncoordinated discretion of individual economic agents. From this coexistence of well nigh perfect rationality and of the greatest irrationality originate the numerous strains and stresses which are peculiarly characteristic of the economic system of capitalism.

The Form of the Capitalist System. The objective, institutional order of capitalism is characteristically free. The dominance of economic individualism has its counterpart in the far reaching independence of the individual economic agents. The restrictions which law and usage impose upon them affect only the most marginal of their activities; essentially restrictions are intended to forestall merely criminal dealings, leaving a wide area of discretion to the individual. "Economic freedom," an aspect of the philosophy of natural rights, assumes, when regarded as an element of the economic order, the form of a system of positive rights conferred upon the individual by law and morals; these positive rights constitute the substance of economic liberalism.

Capitalistic business is typically private, so that economic initiative is lodged with enterprises which are actuated by the quest for private gain. . . .

The structure of capitalist economy is aristocratic. The number of economic agents is small as compared with the total number of persons participating in economic life, with the result that a large majority is subject to the power of a few economic agents. In a regime of economic freedom the relation between the economic agent and the persons controlled by him takes appropriately the legal form of a free contract. The dominance of a minority is explained by the fact that because of the high standard of technical knowledge and organizational skill required under capitalism people of average abilities and fortunes are incapable of assuming the direction of production and can therefore no longer act as economic agents as they could under the handicraft system.

The capitalist system, based as it is upon highly developed occupational specialization and functional separation, is marked by a high degree of decentralization. The principles underlying the division of labor in capitalist industry differ from those which governed handicraft economy to the extent that the segregation of a certain range of activities into a distinct branch of industry is determined not by the outlook and limitations of a living personality but by purely material factors, the causal sequences of the technological processes. Organic articulation enforced by an active, creative person is superseded under capitalism by purposefully directed mechanistic separation and coordination. The degree of specialization depends ultimately upon the advantages which it may bring to the private economic agents in their pursuit of profits.

Capitalist economy rests upon an exchange basis, the links between its constituent elements being the connections and relations established in the market. All production is intended for the market, is characteristically limited to the production of saleable goods; all products enter into commercial traffic. Similarly all means of production emerge from exchange transactions, are purchased in the market. No less important is the fact that the connection between economic agents and the persons controlled by them is established by contract entered into in the market; labor is thus treated as a species of saleable goods. The relationship between wants and their satisfaction through production is established indirectly through the medium of price, which regulates the quantity and character of output. Since the guiding principle of capitalism is gain, there is production only if prices yield profit, if they offer to the individual enterprise the prospect of economic success. This system of satisfying wants is therefore flexible, unlike the systems found in economic organizations oriented directly upon the satisfaction of needs. Distribution of the results of production, involving as it does a conflict between various groups, particularly between the two great classes of recipients of surplus value and of wages, is likewise regulated through the mechanism of pricing.

Finally, the organization of production under capitalism is not limited to any single form. Although large scale production predominates, production on a small scale (e.g. domestic system) also has its place in the system.

The Technology of the Capitalist System must satisfy certain conditions. To begin with, capitalist technology must insure a high degree of productivity. It cannot fall below a certain minimum, because capitalist organization of production, involving necessarily the differentiation between the work of organization and management on the one hand and that of technical execution on the other, would then be impossible. For example, as long as every hunter can manage to subsist on the yield of his daily hunt, there is no room for a capitalist organization of hunting under the leadership of an organizer who does no actual hunting himself. Moreover, this productivity must be as high as possible, because, other things being equal, an increase in productivity means a correspondingly greater profit to the capitalist enterprise. The compensation of the wage earners, which is limited to the amount needed for subsistence, can with increased productivity be produced in a shorter time, and a larger proportion of the total working time remains therefore for the production of profits. Again, an advance in technology, particularly in the technique of transportation, involves capitalist expansion whether through an extension of the markets or an intensive accumulation of stock. Capitalist expansion under these conditions is accompanied by an increase in total profits and, in view of the decline in the costs of production, by a rise in the profit rate.

The technology characteristic of the capitalist system must also lend itself most readily to improvement and perfection. For constant technical improvements are an important weapon in the hands of the capitalist entrepreneur, who seeks to eliminate his competitor and to extend his market by offering goods superior in quality or lower in price. Moreover, such improvements yield a considerable differential profit, since the entrepreneur can realize a profit larger than the average so long as his improvements do not become widely accessible, and thus tend to reduce the socially necessary production costs. It will be observed that the quest for differential profit is an important dynamic factor in capitalist society. . . .

The Capitalistic Enterprise. . . . The capitalistic enterprise has its own aims or, more properly, it has a single, very definite goal, profit; for only this particular goal corresponds to its spiritual essence. While it is in a sense sheer tautology to say that profit is its only goal, for conceptually the capitalistic enterprise is nothing but an instrumentality for the purpose of profit making, it is nevertheless of great significance that in this economic construct the spirit of the capitalist system and the aims of the individual economic agents become merged. Since the aims of these individuals are essentially arbitrary because they are freely determined, it is merely a happy coincidence if the immanent spirit of capitalism, acquisition, appears also as the subjectively experienced motive for individual action in the form of a striving for profit. The motives of capitalistic entrepreneurs are by no means restricted to acquisitive drives; among them we find a motley array—the desire for power, the craving for acclaim, the impulsion to serve the common good, the urge to action. But as all these motives work out in the capitalistic enterprise, they become, by virtue of an inner necessity, subordinate to profit making. For on closer examination it appears that none of the strivings which actuate the entrepreneur has any chance of success unless the capitalistic enterprise itself is successful, unless it yields a surplus above cost. Whatever other desires the entrepreneur may entertain, whatever subjectively conceived purpose his work may serve, he must always, simply because he is a capitalistic entrepreneur, want his enterprise to flourish, and so concentrate his energies upon the making of profit. . . .

In addition to an aim distinct from the purposes of its owners the capitalistic enterprise has a separate intelligence: it is the *locus* of economic rationality which is quite independent of the personality of the owner or of the staff. . . . Rational business methods are steadily and systematically developed and improved by persons who devote all or part of their time to this pursuit, which may itself be directed toward profit making. Thousands upon thousands of people, ranging in occupation from professors of business disciplines to humble bookkeepers, from downtrodden computers to manufacturers of all sorts of office equipment, are engaged in a perpetual quest for ways and means of perfecting economic rationality. As a result of these manifold efforts there exists at present a highly developed and constantly improving system of procedures (supplemented by specifications regarding the physical equipment to be employed therein) designed to insure business efficiency. This system is important primarily because it exists independently of any specific concern and is applicable to any line of business. Such a ready made economic rationality can be bought by the entrepreneur and installed in his concern to regulate it for the future.

Finally, the capitalistic enterprise possesses also the bourgeois virtues of industry, thrift and stability, which the entrepreneur in the early days of capitalism had to cultivate in his own person in order to achieve success. These have now been transferred to the business concern and it is possible for the entrepreneur himself to dispense with them.

The infusion of the capitalist spirit in material objects affects in a number of obvious ways the course of economic activity. In the first place, management becomes more intensive, business planning more definitive. The incorporation of human beings into a material system fixes a definite minimum of energy which must be put forth: just as the speed of the worker is determined by that of the machine, so the tempo of work of the office force, from president to errand boy, is set by an external factor, the routine of the enterprise. The knowledge at the disposal of the executive is also increased thereby; now it far surpasses his personal erudition. Yet he is no longer burdened with the problem of the perfect organization of his business, which formerly consumed a large proportion of his energy; he is relieved of much useless activity and is thereby freed for specifically entrepreneurial work. Secondly, objectification of the capitalist spirit helps also to extend its domain. Thus the spread of the capitalist ideology over the entire world and to all strata of the entrepreneurial class is easily explained by the fact that economic rationality can be readily transmitted. Finally, the same process contributes to the spreading uniformity of economic life. Since economic procedures are objectively selected for their maximum serviceability in the achievement of certain ends, the fact that the ultimate aim is the same wherever capitalism prevails explains the increase in similarity of these economic procedures along with the development of economic rationality.

THE MODERN BUSINESS MAN *

What characterizes the capitalist spirit of our own day—the zenith of capitalism; and how does that spirit differ from the one which filled the old-fashioned bourgeois?

Before attempting to answer these questions, let us realize that there is no one single type of undertaker today, any more than in earlier epochs; that, as in the early capitalist period, a different spirit moves different capitalist undertakers. Let us, then, place the various types in groups. Surprising as it may seem, they are the types we already know as having existed in the past. To-day, too, we find the freebooter, the ground landlord, the bureaucrat, the speculator, the trader and the manufacturer.

Recall the career of a Cecil Rhodes. Does it not remind you of the Genoese merchants on their towers, or possibly even more of Sir Walter Raleigh and Sir Francis Drake? Cecil Rhodes was of the stuff that robber-knights were made of. He was a discoverer and a conqueror whom no stumbling-blocks could retard; beside the sword and the rifle he wielded another mighty weapon—modern stock-exchange gambling. He was partly politician, partly capitalist undertaker; rather more of a diplomat than a trader; he recognized no other power than brute force. It is strange to find in him even one iota of the Puritan spirit. And if we are to compare him with earlier generations, he must be placed alongside the men of the Renaissance.

How different from Cecil Rhodes's world is that of (say) Stumm, or some Silesian mine-owner! Here we are in the atmosphere of the old feudal landed nobility; the ancient relationship between master and man is still met with; the staff of the establishments are arranged in a kind of hierarchy, and business is deliberate and cumbersome. Such are a few of the characteristics of these concerns, the directors of which have much in common with the capitalist landed proprietor of days gone by.

Then there is a third kind of undertaker nowadays who reminds us

* From *The Quintessence of Capitalism*, translated by M. Epstein (New York, E. P. Dutton & Co., Inc., 1915).

of the bureaucrat of old—exact in his work, methodical to a degree, nicely balanced in his judgments, highly gifted as an organizer, very careful before committing himself, an excellent executive official, who to-day may be town clerk of a large town and to-morrow manager of a bank, who frequently enough gives up the control of a Government department for that of a trust. You will find him at the head of state and municipal enterprises. . . .

How different is the persevering tradesman who makes a fortune because of his sure eye for the right conjuncture, or by clever calculations and advantageous agreements with his wholesale house, his customers, and his employees. What has such a man, say a Berlin draper, in common with Cecil Rhodes? What the director of a multiple shop with a gold-mine speculator? And what all these with the manufacturer who runs his factory as was done 100 or 200 years ago, in Bradford or Sedan?

These old friends are still among us, and seemingly their form is unchanged. Nor are they the only types of the modern undertaker. Others have joined the group, which thus becomes quite picturesque. A very common one, usually found in America, may be termed the master-undertaker (since super-undertaker is an ugly word). His great characteristic is that he unites within himself several independent types. He may be freebooter, unscrupulous calculator, landlord, and speculator all in one. Any trust-magnate will serve as an illustration. . . .

In olden times . . . the undertakers were children of the early capitalist spirit; in modern times, they are the children of the perfected capitalist spirit.

What manner of thing is this perfected capitalist spirit? And what have all the types of the modern capitalist undertaker in common?

1. The ideal of both must be our first consideration. What is it? What are the life-values that govern the latter-day business man? What strikes us here is that there has been a peculiar change of perspective in the evaluation of man, a change of perspective which seems to have affected the whole of the rest of life. Man, the flesh-and-blood man, with his joys and sorrows, with his needs and demands, has been forced from his place as the centre round which all economic activities rotate; his throne is now occupied by a few abstractions, such as Acquisitiveness and Business. Man has ceased to be what he was until the end of the early capitalist period—the measure of all things. The economic subjective agent now aims at as high a profit as he can, and strives to make his business flourish exceedingly. The two aims are closely intertwined, as we shall presently observe. Their relationship may be expressed thus: The undertakers wish to see business thriving; as for acquisitiveness, it is forced upon them, even though they may never have set out with that as their goal.

The real interest of undertaking does not always lie in mere gain, certainly not for the dominating personalities who determine the type. Walter Rathenau was, as I think, perfectly right when he once said: "I have never yet met with a business man whose chief aim was to acquire wealth. I will even go so far as to assert that he who is out to make money cannot possibly be a great business man." Something very different occupies the thoughts of the undertaker. His heart is set on seeing his business thrive. Once more Walter Rathenau has expressed it well. "The object of the business man's work, of his worries, his pride and his aspirations is just his undertaking, be it a commercial company, factory, bank, shipping concern, theatre or railway. The undertaking seems to take on form and substance, and to be ever with him, having, as it were, by virtue of his bookkeeping, his organization, and his branches, an independent economic existence. The business man is wholly devoted to making his business a flourishing, healthy, living organism." This view is shared by all the capitalist undertakers of the day in so far as they have expressed themselves on the inner meaning of their activity.

Now, what is really meant by making a business, that is, a capitalist undertaking, flourish? Observe that a business begins with a sum of money and ends with the same, and that therefore its existence is bound up with the realization of a surplus. Success in business can only mean success in realizing this surplus. No profits, no business success. A factory may make very dear or very cheap goods, and their quality may establish their maker's name as a household word throughout the globe, but if the business continues to show a deficit from year to year, it is a failure from the capitalist point of view. To flourish, a concern must be profitable; to prosper, it must pay.

You see now what I meant when I made the statement that the undertakers wish to see business thriving, and as for acquisitiveness, it is forced upon them.

Such being the goal of the capitalist undertaker, the end of his activities is necessarily projected into infinity. In earlier times, when the needs of the community determined economic activities, these had natural boundaries or limits. There can be no such limits when economic activities are determined by acquisitiveness and by flourishing businesses. There is never a point in the future when the total profits are sufficiently great for the undertaker to say: It is enough. Should the development of a business be such that its prosperity ceases to increase, the many-sidedness of modern enterprise will see to it that before long a second, and possibly a third, business is added to the original one. Thus it is that in modern days two equally strong tendencies show themselves—expansion of one and the same business, and the branching out into subsidiary or additional businesses. This very often leads to a kind of inner pressure in the mind of the undertaker. It frequently happens that he really does not want to expand further, but he must. Many a captain of industry has confessed as much. . . .

So much for the nature of the activity itself. What is new is its boundlessness. So long as the needs of the living human being governed economic activities, so long did these have a limit. But with the disappearance of the governing factor, the natural limit fell away. Accordingly the activities of the capitalist undertaker have no bounds. *Non sunt certi denique fines.* Which means that the expenditure of human energy in modern economic activities, extensively and intensively, is strained to the uttermost. Every minute of the day, of the year, nay, of life itself, is devoted to work; and during this working period every power is occupied at highest pressure. Everybody is acquainted with the hard-worked man of to-day. Whether employer or employed, he is constantly on the verge of a breakdown owing to overwork. That he tends to be excited, that he is always on the move, is generally known too. Speed and yet more speed—such is the cry of the age. It rushes onward in one mad race.

The influence of such a life on body and soul is not difficult to gauge. It corrodes the former and dries up the latter. Everything is sacrificed to the Moloch of work; all the higher instincts of heart and mind are crushed out by devotion to business. How much the inner life of modern man has been shattered is best seen if we cast a glance at the kernel of all natural life—the relationship to women. These men have no time for the enjoyment of delicate passions, nor even for gallant flirtations. They seem to be quite incapable of deep erotic emotions. Either they are wholly apathetic so far as love is concerned, or they are content with a brief sensual intoxication. They either do not bother about women at all, or they buy what they require in this respect.

3. Business principles likewise have undergone a change. That was only to be expected when the goal of enterprise has become different. To-day, it may be said, five main rules regulate economic activities.

(*a*) Absolute rationalism is the first. Economic activities are ruled by cold reason, by thought. As we have already seen, that has always been the case; it showed itself in the making of plans, in considering whether any policy was likely to be successful or no, and in calculation generally. The modern capitalist spirit differs from its predecessors only in the degree in which this rule is obeyed. To-day the rule is strictly, one might almost say sternly, enforced. The last trace of traditionalism has vanished. The man of to-day (and the American undertaker may stand as the most perfect type) is filled with the will to apply cold reason to economic activities; moreover, he possesses the determination to make the will effective. Accordingly, he is ever ready to adopt a newer method if it is more rational, whether in the sphere of organization, of production, or of calculation. This naturally implies that, no matter what the cost may be, he is able to leave the old methods the moment the newer ones are available.

(*b*) Production for exchange (as opposed to production for use) is the motto of economic activities. As much profit as possible is their ideal; consequently what matters is not the goodness or the kind of commodities produced but their saleability. How they are sold is secondary, so long as they are sold. Consequently the undertaker is wholly indifferent to the quality of his wares; he will make shoddy goods or cheap substitutes, if only it pays. If cheap and nasty boots yield more profit than good ones, it would be a deadly sin against the holy spirit of capitalism to manufacture good ones. It is no argument against the truth of this to point to a movement in certain industries (the chemical industry is one), the object of which is to improve quality. As well say that the bonuses which the general store offers to its employees on the sale of more expensive articles proves the same thing. What both instances do prove is that they are cases where there is more profit from high-class goods than from inferior articles. The greatest gain is the only criterion in these matters, and an undertaker will make now cheap goods, now dearer, according as the one or the other yields more profit. From the capitalist's standpoint that is only natural.

What follows from this is plain. Since it is inherent in acquisitiveness to enlarge incomings to the uttermost; and since, again, the greater the sale the larger the profits, it is only to be expected that the undertaker will try all he can to increase his sales. Apart from the greater gain, more extended sales will give him certain advantages over competitors. Hence it is by no means remarkable that the desire for greater sales, for new markets, for more customers, is one of the mightiest motive powers in modern capitalism. It is directly responsible for a number of business principles, all of which have one end in view—to make the public buy. The more important of these principles deserve to be mentioned.

(*c*) The first (and the third in the general scheme) may be enunciated as follows: Search out the customer and attack him. That is to-day as self-evident a maxim in all branches of business as it was strange and wrong in the age of early capitalism. In practice it means that you set out to attract the customer's attention and to stir up within him the desire to purchase. You attract his attention by shouting in his ears, or catching his eye by loud, coloured indicators; you strive to make him purchase by suggestion; you seek to convince him that the articles for sale are extraordinarily good or valuable. Advertisement serves both ends—as every one knows; and advertisements, as every one knows also, shatter all sense of propriety, of taste, of good manners, and of dignity. Is it not true to say that modern advertising in its extreme forms is both unæsthetic and immoral?

(*d*) Secondly, sell as cheaply as you can; reduce price to the lowest possible figure so as to attract the public. In the early capitalist age low prices were an abomination. The motto then was (as we have already noted) little business but great profits. To-day we are at the opposite extreme: as much business as possible but small profits. Small profits, quick returns—is not this nowadays the universal motto?

(*e*) Elbow-room is demanded in order to arrive at the wished-for goal. Which means, first, that you require freedom of action, liberty to enter upon or to abstain from any course, as seems best to you. It means emancipation from the trammels of law or morality; it means that you should be allowed to poach on your neighbour's preserves just as he may be allowed to poach on yours; it means that you should be allowed to oust him if you can; it means that you object to interference either from the state or from working men's organizations in making your contracts. You want none of the restraints of an earlier age. The free exercise of your powers shall alone determine economic success or failure.

THE GROWTH OF A CAPITALISTIC POINT OF VIEW IN ECONOMIC LIFE *

During the whole of the period which I have described as the "early capitalistic age," and in which the Jews began to make their influence felt, the same fundamental notions generally prevailed in regard to economic life as characterized the Middle Ages—feudal relationships, manual labour, three estates of the realm, and so forth.

The centre of this whole was the individual man. Whether as producer or as consumer, his interests determined the attitude of the community as of its units, determined the law regulating economic activities and the practices of commercial life. Every such law was personal in its intent; and all who contributed to the life of the nation had a personal outlook. Not that each person could do as he liked. On the contrary, a code of restrictions hedged about his activities in every direction. But the point is that the restrictions were born of the individualistic spirit. Commodities were produced and bought and sold in order that consumers might have their wants sufficiently satisfied. On the other hand, producers and traders were to receive fair wages and fair profits. What was fair, and what sufficient for your need, tradition and custom determined.

And so, producer and trader should receive as much as was demanded by the standard of comfort in their station in life. That was the mediæval view; it was also the view current in the early capitalistic age, even where business was carried on along more or less modern lines. We find its expression in the industrial codes of the day, and its justification in the commercial literature.

Hence, to make profit was looked upon by most people throughout the period as improper, as "unchristian"; the old economic teaching of Thomas Aquinas was observed, at least officially. The religious or ethical rule was still supreme; there was as yet no sign of the liberation of economic life from its religious and ethical bonds. Every action, no matter in what sphere, was done with a view to the Highest Tribunal—the will of God. Need it be pointed out that the attitude of Mammon was as opposed to this as pole is to pole?

Producer and trader should receive sufficient for their need. One outstanding result of this principle was strictly to circumscribe each man's activity in his locality. Competition was therefore quite out of the question. In his own sphere a man might work as he willed—when, how, where —in accordance with tradition and custom. But to cast a look at his neighbour's sphere—that he was forbidden to do. Just as the peasant received his holding—so much field, with pasture and woodland, as would

* From *The Jews and Modern Capitalism,* translated by M. Epstein (Glencoe, Illinois, The Free Press, 1951).

keep him and his family, just as he never even dreamt of adding to his possessions, so, too, the craftsman and the merchant were to rest content with their portions and never covet their neighbour's. The peasant had his land, the town-dweller his customers: in either case they were the source whence sprang his livelihood; in either case they were of a size sufficient for the purpose. Hence, the trader had to be assured of his custom, and many were the ordinances which guarded him against competition. Besides, it was commercial etiquette. You did not run after your customers. You waited until they came, "and then" (in the words of De Foe's sermon), "with God's blessing and his own care, he may expect his share of trade with his neighbours." The merchant who attended fairs did not do otherwise; "day and night he waits at his stall."

To take away your neighbour's customers was contemptible, unchristian, and immoral. A rule for "Merchants who trade in commodities" was: "Turn no man's customers away from him, either by word of mouth or by letter, and do not to another what you would not have another do to you." It was, however, more than a rule; it became an ordinance, and is met with over and over again. In Mayence its wording was as follows: "No one shall prevent another from buying, or by offering a higher price make a commodity dearer, on pain of losing his purchase; no one shall interfere in another's business undertaking, or carry on his own on so large a scale as to ruin other traders." In Saxony it was much the same. "No shopkeeper shall call away the customers from another's shop, nor shall he by signs or motions keep them from buying."

But to attract customers even without interfering with your neighbour's business was regarded as unworthy. As late as the early 18th century in London itself it was not considered proper for a shopkeeper to dress his windows tastefully, and so lure purchasers. De Foe, no less than his later editors, did not mince words in expressing his contempt for such a course, of which, as he mentions apparently with some satisfaction, only a few bakers and toymen were guilty.

To the things that were not permitted belonged also advertising your business and praising your wares. The gentle art of advertising first appeared in Holland sometime about the middle of the 17th century, in England towards its end, in France much later. . . .

To praise your goods or to point out wherein your business was superior to others was equally nefarious. But the last word in commercial impropriety was to announce that your prices were lower than those of the man opposite. "To undersell" was most ungentlemanly: "No blessing will come from harming your neighbour by underselling and cutting prices."

Bad as underselling itself was in the eyes of the people of those days, it was beneath contempt to advertise it. "Since the death of our author," say the editors of the fifth edition (1745) of De Foe's *Complete English Tradesman,* "this underselling practice is grown to such a shameful height that particular persons publickly advertise that they undersell the rest of the trade." It may be asked, Why were the editors so concerned about the matter? The reason is manifest in a subsequent passage. "We have had grocers advertising their underselling one another at a rate a fair trader cannot sell for and live." It is the old cry: fixed profits, a fixed livelihood, a fixed production and fixed prices. . . .

Like the producers, the consumers also received attention. In a certain sense the consumer received even more, for the naïve conception that all production was in the interests of consumption had not yet disappeared. Hence the stress laid on *good* wares, on the principle that commodities should really be what they pretended; and innumerable were the ordinances that were everywhere promulgated to this intent, more especially in the 17th and 18th centuries.

It was long before the purely capitalistic notion gained acceptance that the value in exchange of any commodity was what influenced the undertaker most. We may see how slow its progress was from the conflicting opinions on the subject in England in the 18th century. Sir Josiah Child appears to have been in the minority on this, as on most other questions, when he formulated the demand that every manufacturer should be allowed to judge for himself as to the kind of commodity, and the quality, that he brought into the market. It is curious enough nowadays to read Child's plea for the right of the manufacturer to make shoddy goods. "If we intend to have the trade of the world," he cries, "we must imitate the Dutch, who make the worst as well as the best of all manufactures, that we may be in a capacity of serving all markets and all humours."

In a world of economic ideas such as these, the theory of "just price" was an organic element. Price was not something in the formation of which the individual had a say. Price was determined for him; it was as subject to religious and ethical principles as everything else in economic life. It was to be such as would make for the common good, as well of the consumer as of the producer. Different ages had their own standard for determining it; in Luther's day, for example, the cost of production was the deciding factor. But as commercial intercourse widened, the doctrine of the just price was found to be more and more impossible, and the view that price must be determined by the factors in the market found general acceptance. But be that as it may, the point to accentuate is that price was based on ethical and not (as was held to be the case later) on natural principles. Then people said that the individual *must* not determine price at his own will; whereas later the view was that he *could* not so determine it.

What manner of world was that in which opinions such as these predominated? If we had to describe it in a word, we should say that it was "slow." Stability was its bulwark and tradition its guide. The individual never lost himself in the noise and whirl of business activity. He still had complete control of himself; he was not yet devoid of that native dignity, which does not make itself cheap for the sake of profit. Trade and commerce were everywhere carried on with a dash of personal pride. And all this to a greater extent in the country than in the large towns, where advancing capitalism made itself soonest felt. "The proud and haughty demeanour of the country merchant" is noted by a keen observer of his time. We can almost see the type, in his knee-breeches and long coat, his head bewigged and his manner somewhat stiff. Business with him was an even process; he got through it without much thought or worry, serving his circle of customers in the traditional way, knowing nothing of excitement, and never complaining that the day was too short.

MAX WEBER

(1864–1920)

Max Weber—one of Germany's greatest writers and thinkers, as able a philosopher and sociologist as he was an economist—represents, like Sombart, the later aspects of historicism. The main outlines of the evolutionary development and of the analysis of capitalism had already been sketched by Karl Marx, Schmoller, and others. Weber concerned himself with the relationship between capitalism and specific economic institutions.

The son of a wealthy politician of conservative outlook, Weber was born in Berlin and studied jurisprudence. Upon graduation he established himself as a judge in Berlin. After the appearance in 1892 of his now-famous study on labor in eastern Germany, *Die Lage der Landarbeiter im Ostelbischen Deutschland* (Volume III of *Die Verhältnisse de Landarbeiter in Deutschland,* a series published in Leipzig), he was called to the chair of economics at the University of Freiburg. In 1897 he moved to the University of Heidelberg, and later on he was granted a professorship at the University of Munich.

Weber's immense contribution to sociology cannot be more than mentioned here. His definition of sociology is so broad —he conceives of it as encompassing all the social activities of human beings—that economics becomes but one narrow part of the larger subject. However, his contribution to economics and to economic history is also considerable. Among the more important of his economic studies available in English are: *General Economic History* (*Wirtschaftsgeschichte,* 1923, translated by Frank Knight), *The Protestant Ethic and the Spirit of Capitalism* (*Die Protestantische Ethik und der Geist des Kapitalismus,* 1904–1905, translated by Talcott Parsons), and *The Theory of Social and Economic Organization* (*Wirtschaft und Gesellschaft,* 1921, translated by Talcott Parsons), originally published as Volume III of the collaborative *Grundriss der Sozialökonomik* (1914–1926).

Weber describes capitalism in general as any system of rationally conducted exchange for profit. Modern capitalism is a sub-type, marked by the dominating influence of the bourgeois spirit of calculation and rational accounting. Its outstanding features are "bureaucratic organization" dedicated to pecuniary ends and the disciplined organization of the labor force. Bureaucracy is not a special feature of capitalism. It is present whenever society is so organized that its goals constitute impersonal ends to the participating individuals. Weber's "bureaucracy" and "rational action" illustrate his use of the concept of "the ideal type"—an analytical abstraction in which universal features of social organization are fused into a distinct logical model.

Weber's historical method went unnoticed in the English-speaking world until Talcott Parsons' translation and critical efforts drew attention to this neglected aspect of Weber's system. Weber's methodological outlook, and particularly his stress on the necessity of freeing social science from value judgments, have been noted in England and America. His writings on the relationship between religion and the development of capitalism have also attracted much attention and have been the source of much controversy. In his *Protestant Ethic and the Spirit of Capitalism,* the source of our selection, Weber argued that the development of western capitalism was primarily the result of the favorable ethics of Protestantism. In other studies Weber tested his thesis by analyzing the relationships between religious ethics and social and economic organization in Buddhism, Confucianism, Taoism, and Judaism.

THE PROTESTANT ETHIC AND THE SPIRIT OF CAPITALISM *

Introduction

The impulse to acquisition, pursuit of gain, of money, of the greatest possible amount of money, has in itself nothing to do with capitalism. This impulse exists and has existed among waiters, physicians, coachmen, artists, prostitutes, dishonest officials, soldiers, nobles, crusaders, gamblers, and beggars. One may say that it has been common to all sorts and conditions of men at all times and in all countries of the earth, wherever the objective possibility of it is or has been given. It should be taught in the kindergarten of cultural history that this naïve idea of capitalism must be given up once and for all. Unlimited greed for gain is not in the least identical with capitalism, and is still less its spirit. Capitalism *may* even be identical with restraint, or at least a rational tempering, of this irrational impulse. But capitalism is identical with the pursuit of profit, and forever *renewed* profit, by means of continuous, rational, capitalistic enterprise. . . .

Let us now define our terms somewhat more carefully than is generally done. We will define a capitalistic economic action as one which rests on the expectation of profit by the utilization of opportunities for exchange, that is on (formally) peaceful chances of profit. Acquisition by force (formally and actually) follows its own particular laws, and it is not expedient, however little one can forbid this, to place it in the same category with action which is, in the last analysis, oriented to profits from exchange. . . . The important fact is always that a calculation of capital in terms of money is made, whether by modern book-keeping methods or in any other way, however primitive and crude. Everything is done in terms of balances: at the beginning of the enterprise an initial balance, before every individual decision a calculation to ascertain its probable profitableness, and at the end a final balance to ascertain how much profit has been made. . . .

Whenever money finances of public bodies have existed, money-lenders have appeared, as in Babylon, Hellas, India, China, Rome. They have financed wars and piracy, contracts and building operations of all sorts. In overseas policy they have functioned as colonial entrepreneurs, as planters with slaves, or directly or indirectly forced labour, and have farmed domains, offices, and, above all, taxes. They have financed party leaders in elections and *condottieri* in civil wars. And, finally, they have been speculators in chances for pecuniary gain of all kinds. This kind of entrepreneur, the capitalistic adventurer, has existed everywhere. With the exception of trade and credit and banking transactions, their activities were predominantly of an irrational and speculative character, or directed

* From *The Protestant Ethic and the Spirit of Capitalism,* translated by Talcott Parsons (New York, Charles Scribner's Sons, London, George Allen & Unwin, Ltd., 1930).

to acquisition by force, above all the acquisition of booty, whether directly in war or in the form of continuous fiscal booty by exploitation of subjects. . . .

But in modern times the Occident has developed, in addition to this, a very different form of capitalism which has appeared nowhere else: the rational capitalistic organization of (formally) free labour. . . .

Rational industrial organization, attuned to a regular market, and neither to political nor irrationally speculative opportunities for profit, is not, however, the only peculiarity of Western capitalism. The modern rational organization of the capitalistic enterprise would not have been possible without two other important factors in its development: the separation of business from the household, which completely dominates modern economic life, and closely connected with it, rational bookkeeping. A spatial separation of places of work from those of residence exists elsewhere, as in the Oriental bazaar and in the *ergasteria* of other cultures. The development of capitalistic associations with their own accounts is also found in the Far East, the Near East, and in antiquity. But compared to the modern independence of business enterprises, those are only small beginnings. The reason for this was particularly that the indispensable requisites for this independence, our rational business bookkeeping and our legal separation of corporate from personal property, were entirely lacking, or had only begun to develop. The tendency everywhere else was for acquisitive enterprises to arise as parts of a royal or manorial *household* (of the *oikos*), which is, as Rodbertus has perceived, with all its superficial similarity, a fundamentally different, even opposite, development.

However, all these peculiarities of Western capitalism have derived their significance in the last analysis only from their association with the capitalistic organization of labour. Even what is generally called commercialization, the development of negotiable securities and the rationalization of speculation, the exchanges, etc., is connected with it. For without the rational capitalistic organization of labour, all this, so far as it was possible at all, would have nothing like the same significance, above all for the social structure and all the specific problems of the modern Occident connected with it. Exact calculation—the basis of everything else—is only possible on a basis of free labour.

And just as, or rather because, the world has known no rational organization of labour outside the modern Occident, it has known no rational socialism. Of course, there has been civic economy, a civic food-supply policy, mercantilism and welfare policies of princes, rationing, regulation of economic life, protectionism, and *laissez-faire* theories (as in China). The world has also known socialistic and communistic experiments of various sorts: family, religious, or military communism, State socialism (in Egypt), monopolistic cartels, and consumers' organizations. But although there have everywhere been civic market privileges, companies, guilds, and all sorts of legal differences between town and country, the concept of the citizen has not existed outside the Occident, and that of the bourgeoisie outside the modern Occident. Similarly, the proletariat as a class could not exist, because there was no rational organization of free labour under regular discipline. Class struggles between creditor and debtor classes; landowners and the landless, serfs, or tenants; trading interests and consumers or landlords, have existed everywhere in various combinations. But even the Western mediæval struggles between putters-out and their workers exist elsewhere only in beginnings. The modern conflict of the large-scale industrial entrepreneur and free-wage labourers was entirely lacking. And thus there could be no such problems as those of socialism.

Hence in a universal history of culture the central problem for us is not, in the last analysis, even from a purely economic view-point, the development of capitalistic activity as such, differing in different cultures only in form: the adventurer type, or capitalism in trade, war, politics, or administration as sources of gain. It is rather the origin of this sober bourgeois capitalism with its rational organization of free labour. Or in terms of cultural history, the problem is that of the origin of the Western bourgeois class and of its peculiarities, a problem which is certainly closely connected with that of the origin of the capitalistic organization of labour, but is not quite the same thing. For the bourgeois as a class existed prior to the development of the peculiar modern form of capitalism, though, it is true, only in the Western hemisphere.

. . . Of undoubted importance are the rational structures of law and of administration. For modern rational capitalism has need, not only of the technical means of production, but of a calculable legal system and of administration in terms of formal rules. Without it adventurous and speculative trading capitalism and all sorts of politically determined capitalisms are possible, but no rational enterprise under individual initiative, with fixed capital and certainty of calculations. . . .

Religious Affiliation and Social Stratification

. . . Business leaders and owners of capital, as well as the higher grades of skilled labour, and even more the higher technically and commercially trained personnel of modern enterprises, are overwhelmingly Protestant. This is true not only in cases where the difference in religion coincides with one of nationality, and thus of cultural development, as in Eastern Germany between Germans and Poles. The same thing is shown in the figures of religious affiliation almost wherever capitalism, at the time of its great expansion, has had a free hand to alter the social distribution of the population in accordance with its needs, and to determine its occupational structure. The more freedom it has had, the more clearly is the effect shown. It is true that the greater relative participation of Protestants in the ownership of capital, in management, and the upper ranks of labour in great modern industrial and commercial enterprises, may in part be explained in terms of historical circumstances which extend far back into the past, and in which religious affiliation is not a cause of the economic conditions, but to a certain extent appears to be a result of them. . . . A number of those sections of the old Empire which were most highly developed economically and most favoured by natural resources and situation, in particular a majority of the wealthy towns, went over to Protestantism in the sixteenth century. The results of that circumstance favour the Protestants even to-day in their struggle for economic existence. There arises thus the historical question: why were the districts of highest economic development at the same time particularly favourable to a revolution in the Church? . . .

The emancipation from economic traditionalism appears, no doubt, to be a factor which would greatly strengthen the tendency to doubt the sanctity of the religious tradition, as of all traditional authorities. But it is necessary to note . . . that the Reformation meant not the elimination of the Church's control over everyday life, but rather the substitution of a new form of control for the previous one. It meant the repudiation of a control which was very lax, at that time scarcely perceptible in practice, and hardly more than formal, in favour of a regulation of the whole of conduct which, penetrating to all departments of private and public life, was infinitely burdensome and earnestly enforced. . . . The rule of Calvinism . . . as it was enforced in the sixteenth century in Geneva and in Scotland, at the turn of the sixteenth and seventeenth centuries in large parts of the Netherlands, in the seventeenth in New England, and for a time in England itself, would be for us the most absolutely unbearable form of ecclesiastical control of the individual which could possibly exist. . . . Now how does it happen that at that time those countries which were most advanced economically, and within them the rising bourgeois middle classes, not only failed to resist this unexampled tyranny of Puritanism, but even developed a heroism in its defence? . . .

But further, and especially important: it may be, as has been claimed, that the greater participation of Protestants in the positions of ownership and management in modern economic life may to-day be understood, in part at least, simply as a result of the greater material wealth they have inherited. But there are certain other phenomena which cannot be explained in the same way. . . . That the percentage of Catholics among the students and graduates of higher educational institutions in general lags behind their proportion of the total population, may, to be sure, be largely explicable in terms of inherited differences of wealth. But among the Catholic graduates themselves the percentage of those graduating from the institutions preparing, in particular, for technical studies and industrial and commercial occupations, but in general from those preparing for middle-class business life, lags still farther behind the percentage of Protestants. On the other hand, Catholics prefer the sort of training which the humanistic Gymnasium affords. That is a circumstance to which the above explanation does not apply. . . .

Even more striking is a fact which partly explains the smaller proportion of Catholics among the skilled labourers of modern industry. Among journeymen . . . the Catholics show a stronger propensity to remain in their crafts, that is they more often become master craftsmen, whereas the Protestants are attracted to a larger extent into the factories in order to fill the upper ranks of skilled labour and administrative positions. The explanation of these cases is undoubtedly that the mental and spiritual peculiarities acquired from the environment, here the type of education favoured by the religious atmosphere of the home community and the parental home, have determined the choice of occupation, and through it the professional career.

The smaller participation of Catholics in the modern business life of Germany is all the more striking because it runs counter to a tendency which has been observed at all times including the present. National or religious minorities which are in a position of subordination to a group of rulers are likely, through their voluntary or involuntary exclusion from positions of political influence, to be driven with peculiar force into economic activity. Their ablest members seek to satisfy the desire for recognition of their abilities in this field, since there is no opportunity in the service of the State. This has undoubtedly been true of the Poles in Russia and Eastern Prussia, . . . of the Huguenots in France under Louis XIV, the Nonconformists and Quakers in England, and, last but not least, the Jew for two thousand years. But the Catholics in Germany have shown no striking evidence of such a result of their position . . . in the times when they were persecuted or only tolerated, either in Holland or in England. On the other hand, it is a fact that the Protestants . . . both as ruling classes and as ruled, both as majority and as minority, have shown a special tendency to develop economic rationalism which cannot be observed to the same extent among Catholics either in the one situation or in the other. Thus the principal explanation of this difference must be sought in the permanent intrinsic character of their religious beliefs, and not only in their temporary external historico-political situations. . . .

The Spirit of Capitalism

. . . Sombart, in his discussions of the genesis of capitalism, has distinguished between the satisfaction of needs and acquisition as the two great leading principles in economic history. . . . Enterprises, namely, which are carried on by private entrepreneurs by utilizing capital (money or goods with a money value) to make a profit, . . . may at the same time have a traditionalistic character. This has, in the course even of modern economic history, not been merely an occasional case, but rather the rule, with continual interruptions from repeated and increasingly powerful conquests of the capitalistic spirit. To be sure the capitalistic form of an enterprise and the spirit in which it is run generally stand in some sort of adequate relationship to each other, but not in one of necessary interdependence. Nevertheless, we provisionally use the expression spirit of (modern) capitalism to describe that attitude which seeks profit rationally and systematically in the manner . . . of Benjamin Franklin. This, however, is justified by the historical fact that that attitude of mind has on the one hand found its most suitable expression in capitalistic enterprise, while on the other the enterprise has derived its most suitable motive force from the spirit of capitalism.

But the two may very well occur separately. Benjamin Franklin was filled with the spirit of capitalism at a time when his printing business did not differ in form from any handicraft enterprise. And we shall see that at the beginning of modern times it was by no means the capitalistic entrepreneurs of the commercial aristocracy, who were either the sole or the predominant bearers of the attitude we have here called the spirit of capitalism. It was much more the rising strata of the lower industrial middle classes. Even in the nineteenth century its classical representatives were not the elegant gentlemen of Liverpool and Hamburg, with their commercial fortunes handed down for generations, but the self-made parvenus of Manchester and Westphalia, who often rose from very modest circumstances. As early as the sixteenth century the situation was similar; the industries which arose at that time were mostly created by parvenus. . . .

The form of organization was in every respect capitalistic; the entrepreneur's activity was of a purely business character; the use of capital, turned over in the business, was indispensable; and finally, the objective aspect of the economic process, the book-keeping, was rational. But it was traditionalistic business, if one considers the spirit which animated the entrepreneur: the traditional manner of life, the traditional rate of profit, the traditional amount of work, the traditional manner of regulating the relationships with labour, and the essentially traditional circle of customers and the manner of attracting new ones. . . .

This leisureliness was suddenly destroyed, and often entirely without any essential change in the form of organization, such as the transition to a unified factory, to mechanical weaving, etc. What happened was, on the contrary, often no more than this: some young man from one of the putting-out families went out into the country, carefully chose weavers for his employ, greatly increased the rigour of his supervision of their work, and thus turned them from peasants into labourers. On the other hand, he would begin to change his marketing methods, . . . would take the details into his own hands, would personally solicit customers, visiting them every year, and above all would adapt the quality of the product directly to their needs and wishes. At the same time he began to introduce the principle of low prices and large turnover. There was repeated what everywhere and always is the result of such a process of rationalization: those who would not follow suit had to go out of business. The idyllic state collapsed under the pressure of a bitter competitive struggle, respectable fortunes were made, and not lent out at interest, but always reinvested in the business. The old leisurely and comfortable attitude toward life gave way to a hard frugality in which some participated and came to the top, because they did not wish to consume but to earn, while others who wished to keep on with the old ways were forced to curtail their consumption.

. . . the new spirit, the spirit of modern capitalism, had set to work. The question of the motive forces in the expansion of modern capitalism is not in the first instance a question of the origin of the capital sums which were available for capitalistic uses, but, above all, of the development of the spirit of capitalism. Where it appears and is able to work itself out, it produces its own capital and monetary supplies as the means to its ends, but the reverse is not true.[1] Its entry on the scene was not generally peaceful. . . . Along with clarity of vision and ability to act, it is only by virtue of very definite and highly developed ethical qualities that it has been possible for him [the entrepreneur] to command the absolutely indispensable confidence of his customers and workmen. Nothing else could have given him the strength to overcome the innumerable obstacles, above all the infinitely more intensive work which is demanded of the modern entrepreneur. But these are ethical qualities of quite a different sort from those adapted to the traditionalism of the past. . . .

Now, how could activity, which was at best ethically tolerated, turn into a calling in the sense of Benjamin Franklin? The fact to be explained historically is that in the most highly capitalistic centre of that time, in Florence of the fourteenth and fifteenth centuries, the money and capital market of all the great political Powers, this attitude was considered ethically unjustifiable, or at best to be tolerated. But in the backwoods small bourgeois circumstances of Pennsylvania in the eighteenth century, where business threatened for simple lack of money to fall back into barter, where there was hardly a sign of large enterprise, where only the earliest beginnings of banking were to be found, the same thing was considered the essence of moral conduct, even commanded in the name of duty. To speak here of a reflection of material conditions in the ideal superstructure would be patent nonsense. What was the background of ideas which could account for the sort of activity apparently directed toward profit alone as a calling toward which the individual feels himself to have an ethical obligation? For it was this idea which gave the way of life of the new entrepreneur its ethical foundation and justification.

The attempt has been made, particularly by Sombart, . . . to depict economic rationalism as the salient feature of modern economic life as a whole. Undoubtedly with justification, if by that is meant the extension of the productivity of labour which has, through the subordination of the process of production to scientific points of view, relieved it from its dependence upon the natural organic limitations of the human individual. Now this process of rationalization in the field of technique and economic

[1] This is not to be understood as a claim that changes in the supply of the precious metals are of no economic importance.

organization undoubtedly determines an important part of the ideals of life of modern bourgeois society. . . . It is one of the fundamental characteristics of an individualistic capitalistic economy that it is rationalized on the basis of rigorous calculation, directed with foresight and caution toward the economic success which is sought in sharp contrast to the hand-to-mouth existence of the peasant, and to the privileged traditionalism of the guild craftsman and of the adventurers' capitalism, oriented to the exploitation of political opportunities and irrational speculation.

It might thus seem that the development of the spirit of capitalism is best understood as part of the development of rationalism as a whole, and could be deduced from the fundamental position of rationalism on the basic problems of life. In the process Protestantism would only have to be considered in so far as it had formed a stage prior to the development of a purely rationalistic philosophy. But any serious attempt to carry this thesis through makes it evident that such a simple way of putting the question will not work, simply because of the fact that the history of rationalism shows a development which by no means follows parallel lines in the various departments of life. The rationalization of private law, for instance, if it is thought of as a logical simplification and rearrangement of the content of the law, was achieved in the highest hitherto known degree in the Roman law of late antiquity. But it remained most backward in some of the countries with the highest degree of economic rationalization, notably in England, where the Renaissance of Roman Law was overcome by the power of the great legal corporations, while it has always retained its supremacy in the Catholic countries of Southern Europe. The worldly rational philosophy of the eighteenth century did not find favour alone or even principally in the countries of highest capitalistic development. The doctrines of Voltaire are even to-day the common property of broad upper, and what is practically more important, middle-class groups in the Roman Catholic countries. Finally, if under practical rationalism is understood the type of attitude which sees and judges the world consciously in terms of the worldly interests of the individual ego, then this view of life was and is the special peculiarity of the peoples of the *liberum arbitrium,* such as the Italians and the French are in very flesh and blood. But we have already convinced ourselves that this is by no means the soil in which that relationship of a man to his calling as a task, which is necessary to capitalism, has pre-eminently grown. In fact, one may . . . rationalize life from fundamentally different basic points of view and in very different directions. Rationalism is an historical concept which covers a whole world of different things. . . . We are here particularly interested in the origin of precisely the irrational element which lies in this, as in every conception of a calling.

Asceticism and the Spirit of Capitalism

. . . The emphasis on the ascetic importance of a fixed calling provided an ethical justification of the modern specialized division of labour. In a similar way the providential interpretation of profit-making justified the activities of the business man. The superior indulgence of the *seigneur* and the parvenu ostentation of the *nouveau riche* are equally detestable to asceticism. But, on the other hand, it has the highest ethical appreciation of the sober, middle-class, self-made man. "God blesseth His trade" is a stock remark about those good men who had successfully followed the divine hints. The whole power of the God of the Old Testament, who rewards His people for their obedience in this life, necessarily exercised a similar influence on the Puritan who, following Baxter's advice, compared his own state of grace with that of the heroes of the Bible, and in the process interpreted the statements of the Scriptures as the articles of a book of statutes. . . .

But all the more emphasis was placed on those parts of the Old Testament which praise formal legality as a sign of conduct pleasing to God. They held the theory that the Mosaic Law had only lost its validity through Christ in so far as it contained ceremonial or purely historical precepts applying only to the Jewish people, but that otherwise it had always been valid as an expression of the natural law, and must hence be retained. This made it possible, on the one hand, to eliminate elements which could not be reconciled with modern life. But still, through its numerous related features, Old Testament morality was able to give a powerful impetus to that spirit of self-righteous and sober legality which was so characteristic of the worldly asceticism of this form of Protestantism.

Thus when authors, as was the case with several contemporaries as well as later writers, characterize the basic ethical tendency of Puritanism, especially in England, as English Hebraism they are, correctly understood, not wrong. It is necessary, however, not to think of Palestinian Judaism at the time of the writing of the Scriptures, but of Judaism as it became under the influence of many centuries of formalistic, legalistic, and Talmudic education. Even then one must be very careful in drawing parallels. The general tendency of the older Judaism toward a naïve acceptance of life as such was far removed from the special characteristics of Puritanism. It was, however, just as far—and this ought not to be overlooked—from the economic ethics of mediæval and modern Judaism, in the traits which determined the positions of both in the development of the capitalistic ethos. The Jews stood on the side of the politically and speculatively oriented adventurous capitalism; their ethos was, in a word, that of pariah-capitalism. But Puritanism carried the ethos of the rational organization of capital and labour. It took over from the Jewish ethic only what was adapted to this purpose. . . .

This worldly Protestant asceticism, as we may recapitulate up to this point, acted powerfully against the spontaneous enjoyment of possessions; it restricted consumption, especially of luxuries. On the other hand, it had the psychological effect of freeing the acquisition of goods from the inhibitions of traditionalistic ethics. It broke the bonds of the impulse of acquisition in that it not only legalized it, but (in the sense discussed) looked upon it as directly willed by God. The campaign against the temptations of the flesh, and the dependence on external things, was, as besides the Puritans the great Quaker apologist Barclay expressly says, not a struggle against the rational acquisition, but against the irrational use of wealth.

But this irrational use was exemplified in the outward forms of luxury which their code condemned as idolatry of the flesh, however natural they had appeared to the feudal mind. On the other hand, they approved the rational and utilitarian uses of wealth which were willed by God for the needs of the individual and the community. They did not wish to impose mortification on the man of wealth, but the use of his means for necessary and practical things. The idea of comfort characteristically limits the extent of ethically permissible expenditures. . . .

On the side of the production of private wealth, asceticism condemned both dishonesty and impulsive avarice. What was condemned as covetousness, Mammonism, etc., was the pursuit of riches for their own sake. For wealth in itself was a temptation. But here asceticism was the power "which ever seeks the good but ever creates evil"; what was evil in its sense was possession and its temptations. For, in conformity with the Old Testament and in analogy to the ethical valuation of good works, asceticism looked upon the pursuit of wealth as an end in itself as highly reprehensible; but the attainment of it as a fruit of labour in a calling was a sign of God's blessing. And even more important: the religious valuation of restless, continuous, systematic work in a worldly calling, as the highest means to asceticism, and at the same time the surest and most evident proof of rebirth and genuine faith, must have been the most powerful conceivable lever for the expansion of that attitude toward life which we have here called the spirit of capitalism.

When the limitation of consumption is combined with this release of acquisitive activity, the inevitable practical result is obvious: accumulation of capital through ascetic compulsion to save. The restraints which were imposed upon the consumption of wealth naturally served to increase it by making possible the productive investment of capital. . . . As far as the influence of the Puritan outlook extended, under all circumstances—and this is, of course, much more important than the mere encouragement of capital accumulation—it favoured the development of a rational bourgeois economic life; it was the most important, and above all the only consistent influence in the development of that life. It stood at the cradle of the modern economic man.

To be sure, these Puritanical ideals tended to give way under excessive pressure from the temptations of wealth, as the Puritans themselves knew very well. . . .

In fact the whole history of monasticism is in a certain sense the history of a continual struggle with the problem of the secularizing influence of wealth. The same is true on a grand scale of the worldly asceticism of Puritanism. The great revival of Methodism, which preceded the expansion of English industry toward the end of the eighteenth century, may well be compared with such a monastic reform. We may hence quote here a passage from John Wesley himself which might well serve as a motto for everything which has been said above. For it shows that the leaders of these ascetic movements understood the seemingly paradoxical relationships which we have here analysed perfectly well, and in the same sense that we have given them. He wrote:

"I fear, wherever riches have increased, the essence of religion has decreased in the same proportion. Therefore I do not see how it is possible, in the nature of things, for any revival of true religion to continue long. For religion must necessarily produce both industry and frugality, and these cannot but produce riches. But as riches increase, so will pride, anger, and love of the world in all its branches. How then is it possible that Methodism, that is, a religion of the heart, though it flourishes now as a green bay tree, should continue in this state? For the Methodists in every place grow diligent and frugal; consequently they increase in goods. Hence they proportionately increase in pride, in anger, in the desire of the flesh, the desire of the eyes, and the pride of life. So, although the form of religion remains, the spirit is swiftly vanishing away. Is there no way to prevent this—this continual decay of pure religion? We ought not to prevent people from being diligent and frugal; *we must exhort all Christians to gain all they can, and to save all they can; that is, in effect, to grow rich.*" . . .

As Wesley here says, the full economic effect of those great religious movements, whose significance for economic development lay above all in their ascetic educative influence, generally came only after the peak of the purely religious enthusiasm was past. Then the intensity of the search for the Kingdom of God commenced gradually to pass over into sober economic virtue; the religious roots died out slowly, giving way to utilitarian worldliness. Then, as Dowden puts it, as in *Robinson Crusoe,* the isolated economic man who carries on missionary activities on the side takes the place of the lonely spiritual search for the Kingdom of Heaven of Bunyan's pilgrim, hurrying through the market-place of Vanity. . . .

Finally, it gave him the comforting assurance that the unequal distribution of the goods of this world was a special dispensation of Divine Providence, which in these differences, as in particular grace, pursued secret ends unknown to men. Calvin himself had made the much-quoted statement that only when the people, i.e. the mass of labourers and craftsmen, were poor did they remain obedient to God. In the Netherlands (Pieter de la Court and others), that had been secularized to the effect that the mass of men only labour when necessity forces them to do so. This formulation of a leading idea of capitalistic economy later entered into the current theories of the productivity of low wages. Here also, with the dying out of the religious root, the utilitarian interpretation crept in unnoticed, in the line of development which we have again and again observed. . . .

Now naturally the whole ascetic literature of almost all denominations is saturated with the idea that faithful labour, even at low wages, on the part of those whom life offers no other opportunities, is highly pleasing to God. In this respect Protestant Asceticism added in itself nothing new. But it not only deepened this idea most powerfully, it also created the force which was alone decisive for its effectiveness: the psychological sanction of it through the conception of this labour as a calling, as the best, often in the last analysis the only means of attaining certainty of grace. And on the other hand it legalized the exploitation of this specific willingness to work, in that it also interpreted the employer's business activity as a calling. It is obvious how powerfully the exclusive search for the Kingdom of God only through the fulfilment of duty in the calling, and the strict asceticism which Church discipline naturally imposed, especially on the propertyless classes, was bound to affect the productivity of labour in the capitalistic sense of the word. The treatment of labour as a calling became as characteristic of the modern worker as the corresponding attitude toward acquisition of the business man. . . .

Since asceticism undertook to remodel the world and to work out its ideals in the world, material goods have gained an increasing and finally an inexorable power over the lives of men as at no previous period in history. To-day the spirit of religious asceticism—whether finally, who knows?—has escaped from the cage. But victorious capitalism, since it rests on mechanical foundations, needs its support no longer. The rosy blush of its laughing heir, the Enlightenment, seems also to be irretrievably fading, and the idea of duty in one's calling prowls about in our lives like the ghost of dead religious beliefs. Where the fulfilment of the calling cannot directly be related to the highest spiritual and cultural values, or when, on the other hand, it need not be felt simply as economic compulsion, the individual generally abandons the attempt to justify it at all. In the field of its highest development, in the United States, the pursuit of wealth, stripped of its religious and ethical meaning, tends to become associated with purely mundane passions, which often actually give it the character of sport. . . .

Here we have only attempted to trace the fact and the direction of its influence to their motives in one, though a very important point. But it would also further be necessary to investigate how Protestant Asceticism was in turn influenced in its development and its character by the totality of social conditions, especially economic. The modern man is in general, even with the best will, unable to give religious ideas a significance for culture and national character which they deserve. But it is, of course, not my aim to substitute for a one-sided materialistic an equally one-sided spiritualistic causal interpretation of culture and of history. Each is equally possible, but each, if it does not serve as the preparation, but as the conclusion of an investigation, accomplishes equally little in the interest of historical truth.

PART THIRTEEN
Reactions against Orthodoxy: Institutionalism

A reaction against neo-classical economics similar to that of the historical school in Germany occurred in the United States in the twentieth century. Its proponents came to be known as institutionalists, because of their emphasis on the analysis of social and economic institutions. Yet the movement was not unified and was not really confined to America, so the term *institutionalist school* is used in the loosest sense possible. The predecessors of institutionalism were Sismondi, Marx, and the younger German historical school, especially Sombart and Max Weber.

In almost all the countries in which it has taken root, institutionalism has crystallized a deep interest in social reform. It has stressed an intensive and critical study of the evolution of economic institutions with a view to change and improvement. It has also stressed the interrelationships between the social sciences, especially the bond between economics and sociology. Its principal quarrel with neo-classicism has arisen from the belief of the latter in the stability and rightness of existing economic institutions, especially capitalism.

Thorstein Veblen was the messiah of institutionalism in the United States, and his ideology, at least, came primarily from Marx and the German historical school. His theory, however, was unique in its emphasis on the Darwinian concept of continuous and cumulative change. Society, to Veblen, is a complex of institutions—habitual forms of structure, organization, and behavior which regulate the conduct of individuals. These institutions are subject to constant change, said Veblen, although the process may be imperceptible in the short run. Examples of economic institutions are private property, the wage system, the corporation, and competition. According to Veblen, since these institutions are subject to change, they must be studied from an evolutionary point of view.

The chief contribution of the institutional school is of a critical nature. It has eschewed and even ridiculed formal economic logic and the theoretical systems implicitly based on the permanence of existing economic institutions. Veblen, for instance, was critical of the marginal economics of John Bates Clark, the historical economics of Gustav Schmoller, and the socialist economics of Karl Marx. And yet no institutional methodology at all comparable to that of orthodox economics ever evolved. Like the historical school, the institutional economists believed that a long period of quantitative research on specific problems must precede the construction of any meaningful theory. They did not want to produce just another collection of logical inferences from untested preconceptions and postulates.

The principal institutional writers will be treated in the following section, and it will be noted that each has a distinct approach and area of investigation, though all belong in the same general category. Veblen's non-critical contribution is chiefly in the field of business organization, Commons specialized in the legal aspects of capitalism and the history of labor, while Mitchell stressed quantitative research on the business cycle. Our British representative, Hobson, has written in a great number of fields but is best known for his critical analysis of the human costs of industry and for his underconsumption theory of the business cycle.

The influence of the institutional school is difficult to assess. It has been responsible for many important monographic studies and has numbered in its ranks some of the ablest economists in the United States—Wesley Mitchell, Thorstein Veblen, Paul Homan, Walton Hamilton, John Maurice Clark, Willard Thorp, John R. Commons, and Clarence Ayres, to name but a few. It never did succeed, however, in achieving more than a goal, an ideology, and a point of view. The death of Veblen, Commons, and Mitchell and the advent of Keynesian economics, which possesses a method and theory as well as an ideology, led many respectable heretics to jump on the new bandwagon.

THORSTEIN BUNDE VEBLEN

(1857–1929)

Thorstein Veblen was probably the most original thinker in economics to emerge in America. His learning extended into other fields as well—philosophy, anthropology, and sociology—and it may be said that he was more than an economist: he was a complete social scientist. In addition, he was the spiritual progenitor of respectable economic heterodoxy in the United States. His theories were highly original and influenced an entire generation of brilliant economists who followed him—Wesley Mitchell, Paul Homan, John Ise, Walton Hamilton, and Clarence Ayres, to name a few.

His life was unusual. In material terms, there is no doubt that he was a failure. He had difficulty getting on with people and stumbled from one precarious teaching job to another. He never held a rank higher than assistant professor and by normal standards was probably a poor teacher of undergraduates. Yet he was the finest critical economist of his generation, and in addition, a skillful satirist.

Veblen was very much a product of his own time. He was born on a backwoods farm in Wisconsin on July 30, 1857. Both of his parents were Norwegian immigrants who lived in one of the Scandinavian settlements in the middle west. When Veblen was twenty years old, he entered Carleton College, where John Bates Clark was one of his teachers. His academic career after graduation was extremely checkered. He studied philosophy, first at Johns Hopkins and then at Yale, but after receiving his Ph.D. he was unable to secure a teaching post and spent seven years on the family farm, formally unproductive. In 1891 he started life over again at Cornell as a graduate student in economics, and later he went to the University of Chicago as a graduate fellow. Here he made his reputation, rising to an assistant professorship and managing the newly founded *Journal of Political Economy*. In 1899 he published his famous *Theory of the Leisure Class,* which brought him to country-wide notice.

After comparatively short stays at other universities, he worked as a government employee during World War I and joined the staff of the newly formed New School for Social Research, where he remained until his retirement from teaching in 1926. He died in California in 1929.

Veblenian economics revolves about the irreconcilable conflicts between "pecuniary" and "industrial" employments, the "business enterprise" and the "machine process," the "intangibles of ownership" and the "tangible facts of workmanship." The main stress in Veblen's reasoning is always on technology and institutions. He defines institutions as "group habits of thought" or "methods of action arrived at by habituation and convention generally agreed upon" and regards them as being determined by historical development and in their turn shaping economic phenomena. He is primarily concerned with instincts and human motives as they express themselves in religious, aesthetic, and cultural phenomena—habits of thought which embody rationalizations of basic property interests. In Veblen's works, economic theory becomes at once an analysis of the mode of behavior of the leisure class—the separate culture of the élite—and a somewhat vague theory of economic development.

Veblen's contribution to the theory of economic development is best summarized in his *Theory of Business Enterprise,* published in 1904. To Veblen, the directing force of the industrial system and of modern civilization is business enterprise. Its principal characteristics, and the means by which it dominates modern culture, are the machine process and investment for profit. The machine process standardizes and disciplines all facets of life. The quest for profits causes the making of money to take precedence over the making of goods —"industrial employments" become a by-product of "pecuniary employments." The price of business inefficiency and waste, in the form of advertising, promoter's profits, and speculative and monopoly gains, is paid by the community as a whole in the form of depression and unemployment. Veblen's theory of business cycles, with its emphasis on the place held by equipment industries, the peculiar denial of technical progress as the outstanding factor in the revival, and the notion of chronic self-perpetuating depressions, is significant for its revelation of his over-all pessimism regarding the likelihood of economic amelioration under capitalism.

The selection from his essay on "The Limitations of Marginal Utility" illustrates Veblen's criticism of orthodox doctrine. His positive approach to economic theory is exemplified by excerpts from his most important contribution to economics, *The Theory of Business Enterprise.*

THE LIMITATIONS OF MARGINAL UTILITY *

The limitations of the marginal-utility economics are sharp and characteristic. It is from first to last a doctrine of value, and in point of form and method it is a theory of valuation. The whole system, therefore, lies within the theoretical field of distribution, and it has but a secondary bearing on any other economic phenomena than those of distribution—the term being taken in its accepted sense of pecuniary distribution, or distribution in point of ownership. Now and again an attempt is made to extend the use of the principle of marginal utility beyond this range, so as to apply it to questions of production, but hitherto without sensible effect, and necessarily so. The most ingenious and the most promising of such attempts have been those of Mr. Clark, whose work marks the extreme range of endeavour, and the extreme degree of success in so seeking to turn a postulate of distribution to account for a theory of production. But the outcome has been a doctrine of the production of values, and value, in Mr. Clark's as in other utility systems, is a matter of valuation; which throws the whole excursion back into the field of distribution. Similarly, as regards attempts to make use of this principle in an analysis of the phenomena of consumption, the best results arrived at are some formulation of the pecuniary distribution of consumption goods.

Within this limit range marginal-utility theory is of a wholly statical character. It offers no theory of a movement of any kind, being occupied with the adjustment of values to a given situation. Of this, again, no more convincing illustration need be had than is afforded by the work of Mr. Clark, which is not excelled in point of earnestness, perseverance, or insight. For all their use of the term "dynamic," neither Mr. Clark nor any of his associates in this line of research have yet contributed anything at all appreciable to a theory of genesis, growth, sequence, change, process, or the like, in economic life. They have had something to say as to the bearing which given economic changes, accepted as premises, may have on valuation, and so on distribution; but as to the causes of change or the unfolding sequence of the phenomena of economic life they have had

* From "The Limitations of Marginal Utility," originally published in *Journal of Political Economy,* November, 1909. Reprinted from *What Veblen Taught,* edited by Wesley C. Mitchell. Copyright 1936 by The Viking Press, Inc., New York. Reprinted by permission of The Viking Press, Inc., New York.

nothing to say hitherto; nor can they, since their theory is not drawn in causal terms but in terms of teleology.

In all this the marginal-utility school is substantially at one with the classical economics of the nineteenth century, the difference between the two being that the former is confined within narrower limits and sticks more consistently to its teleological premises. Both are teleological, and neither can consistently admit arguments from cause to effect in the formulation of their main articles of theory. Neither can deal theoretically with phenomena of change, but at the most only with rational adjustment to change which may be supposed to have supervened.

To the modern scientist the phenomena of growth and change are the most obtrusive and most consequential facts observable in economic life. For an understanding of modern economic life the technological advance of the past two centuries—e.g., the growth of the industrial arts—is of the first importance; but marginal-utility theory does not bear on this matter, nor does this matter bear on marginal-utility theory. As a means of theoretically accounting for this technological movement in the past or in the present, or even as a means of formally, technically stating it as an element in the current economic situation, that doctrine and all its works are altogether idle. The like is true for the sequence of change that is going forward in the pecuniary relations of modern life; the hedonistic postulate and its propositions of differential utility neither have served nor can serve an inquiry into these phenomena of growth, although the whole body of marginal-utility economics lies within the range of these pecuniary phenomena. It has nothing to say to the growth of business usages and expedients or to the concomitant changes in the principles of conduct which govern the pecuniary relations of men, which condition and are conditioned by these altered relations of business life or which bring them to pass.

It is characteristic of the school that wherever an element of the cultural fabric, an institution or any institutional phenomenon, is involved in the facts with which the theory is occupied, such institutional facts are taken for granted, denied, or explained away. If it is a question of price, there is offered an explanation of how exchanges may take place with such effect as to leave money and price out of the account. If it is a question of credit, the effect of credit extension on business traffic is left on one side and there is an explanation of how the borrower and lender co-operate to smooth out their respective income streams of consumable goods or sensations of consumption. The failure of the school in this respect is consistent and comprehensive. And yet these economists are lacking neither in intelligence nor in information. They are, indeed, to be credited, commonly, with a wide range of information and an exact control of materials, as well as with a very alert interest in what is going on; and apart from their theoretical pronouncements the members of the school habitually profess the sanest and most intelligent views of current practical questions, even when these questions touch matters of institutional growth and decay.

The infirmity of this theoretical scheme lies in its postulates, which confine the inquiry to generalizations of the teleological or "deductive" order. These postulates, together with the point of view and logical method that follow from them, the marginal-utility school shares with other economists of the classical line—for this school is but a branch or derivative of the English classical economists of the nineteenth century. The substantial difference between this school and the generality of classical economists lies mainly in the fact that in the marginal-utility economics the common postulates are more consistently adhered to at the same time that they are more neatly defined and their limitations are more adequately realized. Both the classical school in general and its specialized variant, the marginal-utility school, in particular, take as their common point of departure the traditional psychology of the early nineteenth-century hedonists, which is accepted as a matter of course or of common notoriety and is held quite uncritically. The central and well-defined tenet so held is that of the hedonistic calculus. Under the guidance of this tenet and of the other psychological conceptions associated and consonant with it, human conduct is conceived of and interpreted as a rational response to the exigencies of the situation in which mankind is placed; as regards economic conduct it is such a rational and unprejudiced response to the stimulus of anticipated pleasure and pain—being, typically and in the main, a response to the promptings of anticipated pleasure, for the hedonists of the nineteenth century and of the marginal-utility school are in the main of an optimistic temper. Mankind is, on the whole and normally, (conceived to be) clear-sighted and far-sighted in its appreciation of future sensuous gains and losses, although there may be some (inconsiderable) difference between men in this respect. Men's activities differ, therefore, (inconsiderably) in respect of the alertness of the response and the nicety of adjustment of irksome pain-cost to apprehend future sensuous gain; but, on the whole, no other ground or line or guidance of conduct than this rationalistic calculus falls properly within the cognizance of the economic hedonists. Such a theory can take account of conduct only in so far as it is rational conduct, guided by deliberate and exhaustively intelligent choice—wise adaptation to the demands of the main chance.

The external circumstances which condition conduct are variable, of course, and so they will have a varying effect upon conduct; but their variation is, in effect, construed to be of such a character only as to vary the degree of strain to which the human agent is subject by contact with these external circumstances. The cultural elements involved in the theoretical scheme, elements that are of the nature of institutions, human relations governed by use and wont in whatever kind and connexion, are not subject to inquiry but are taken for granted as pre-existing in a finished, typical form and as making up a normal and definitive economic situation, under which and in terms of which human intercourse is necessarily carried on. This cultural situation comprises a few large and simple articles of institutional furniture, together with their logical implications or corollaries; but it includes nothing of the consequences or effects caused by these institutional elements. The cultural elements so tacitly postulated as immutable conditions precedent to economic life are ownership and free contract, together with such other features of the scheme of natural rights as are implied in the exercise of these. These cultural products are, for the purpose of the theory, conceived to be given *a priori* in unmitigated force. They are part of the nature of things; so that there is no need of accounting for them or inquiring into them, as to how they have come to be such as they are, or how and why they have changed and are changing, or what effect all this may have on the relations of men who live by or under this cultural situation.

Evidently the acceptance of these immutable premises, tacitly, because uncritically and as a matter of course, by hedonistic economics gives the science a distinctive character and places it in contrast with other sciences whose premises are of a different order. As has already been indicated, the premises in question, so far as they are peculiar to the hedonistic economics, are (*a*) a certain institutional situation, the substantial feature of which is the natural right of ownership, and (*b*) the hedonistic calculus. The distinctive character given to this system of theory by these postulates and by the point of view resulting from their acceptance may be summed up broadly and concisely in saying that the theory is confined to the ground of sufficient reason instead of proceeding on the ground of efficient cause. The contrary is true of modern science, generally (except mathematics), particularly of such sciences as have to do with the phenomena of life and growth. The difference may seem trivial. It is serious only in its consequences. The two methods of inference—from sufficient reason and from efficient cause—are out of touch with one another and there is no transition from one to the other, no method of converting the procedure or the results of the one into those of the other. The immediate consequence is that the resulting economic theory is of a teleological character —"deductive" or "*a priori*" as it is often called—instead of being drawn in terms of cause and effect. The relation sought by this theory among the facts with which it is occupied is the control exercised by future (apprehended) events over present conduct. Current phenomena are dealt with as conditioned by their future consequences; and in strict marginal-utility theory they can be dealt with only in respect of their control of the present by consideration of the future. Such a (logical) relation of control or guidance between the future and the present of course involves an exercise of intelligence, a taking thought, and hence an intelligent agent through whose discriminating forethought the apprehended future may affect the current course of events; unless, indeed, one were to admit something in the way of a providential order of nature or some occult line of stress of the nature of sympathetic magic. Barring magical and providential elements, the relation of sufficient reason runs by way of the interested discrimination, the forethought, of an agent who takes thought of the future and guides his present activity by regard for this future. The relation of sufficient reason runs only from the (apprehended) future in the present, and it is solely of an intellectual, subjective, personal, teleological character and force; while the relation of cause and effect runs only in the contrary direction, and it is solely of an objective, impersonal, materialistic character and force. The modern scheme of knowledge, on the whole, rests, for its definitive ground, on the relation of cause and effect; the relation of sufficient reason being admitted only provisionally and as a proximate factor in the analysis, always with the unambiguous reservation that the analysis must ultimately come to rest in terms of cause and effect. The merits of this scientific animus, of course, do not concern the present argument.

Now, it happens that the relation of sufficient reason enters very substantially into human conduct. It is this element of discriminating forethought that distinguishes human conduct from brute behaviour. And since the economist's subject of inquiry is this human conduct, that relation necessarily comes in for a large share of his attention in any theoretical formulation of economic phenomena, whether hedonistic or otherwise. But while modern science at large has made the causal relation the sole ultimate ground of theoretical formulation; and while the other sciences that deal with human life admit the relation of sufficient reason as a proximate, supplementary, or intermediate ground, subsidiary, and subservient to the argument from cause to effect; economics has had the misfortune—as seen from the scientific point of view—to let the former supplant the latter. It is, of course, true that human conduct is distinguished from other natural phenomena by the human faculty for taking thought, and any science that has to do with human conduct must face the patent fact that the details of such conduct consequently fall into the teleological form; but it is the peculiarity of the hedonistic economics that by force of its postulates its attention is confined to this teleological bearing of conduct alone. It deals with this conduct only in so far as it may be construed in rationalistic, teleological terms of calculation and choice. But it is at the same time no less true that human conduct, economic or otherwise, is subject to the sequence of cause and effect, by force of such elements as habituation and conventional requirements. But facts of this order, which are to modern science of graver interest than the teleological details of conduct, necessarily fall outside the attention of the hedonistic economist, because they cannot be construed in terms of sufficient reason, such as his postulates demand, or be fitted into a scheme of teleological doctrines.

There is, therefore, no call to impugn these premises of the marginal-utility economics within their field. They commend themselves to all serious and uncritical persons at the first glance. They are principles of action which underlie the current, business-like scheme of economic life, and as such, as practical grounds of conduct, they are not to be called in question without questioning the existing law and order. As a matter of course, men order their lives by these principles and, practically, entertain no question of their stability and finality. That is what is meant by calling them institutions; they are settled habits of thought common to the generality of men. But it would be mere absent-mindedness in any student of civilization therefore to admit that these or any other human institutions have this stability which is currently imputed to them or that they are in this way intrinsic to the nature of things. The acceptance by the economists of these or other institutional elements as given and immutable limits their inquiry in a particular and decisive way. It shuts off the inquiry at the point where the modern scientific interest sets in. The institutions in question are no doubt good for their purpose as institutions, but they are not good as premises for a scientific inquiry into the nature, origin, growth, and effects of these institutions and of the mutations which they undergo and which they bring to pass in the community's scheme of life.

To any modern scientist interested in economic phenomena, the chain of cause and effect in which any given phase of human culture is involved, as well as the cumulative changes wrought in the fabric of human conduct itself by the habitual activity of mankind, are matters of more engrossing and more abiding interest than the method of inference by which an individual is presumed invariably to balance pleasure and pain under given conditions that are presumed to be normal and invariable. The former are questions of the life-history of the race or the community, questions of cultural growth and of the fortunes of generations; while the latter is a question of individual casuistry in the face of a given situation that may arise in the course of this cultural growth. The former bear on the continuity and mutations of that scheme of conduct whereby mankind deals with its material means of life; the latter, if it is conceived in hedonistic terms, concerns a disconnected episode in the sensuous experience of an individual member of such a community.

In so far as modern science inquires into the phenomena of life, whether inanimate, brute, or human, it is occupied about questions of genesis and cumulative change, and it converges upon a theoretical formulation in the shape of a life-history drawn in causal terms. In so far as it is a science in the current sense of the term, any science, such as economics, which has to do with human conduct, becomes a genetic inquiry into the human scheme of life; and where, as in economics, the subject of inquiry is the conduct of man in his dealings with the material means of life, the science is necessarily an inquiry into the life-history of material civilization, on a more or less extended or restricted plan. Not that the economist's inquiry isolates material civilization from all other phases and bearings of human culture, and so studies the motions of an abstractly conceived "economic man." On the contrary, no theoretical inquiry into this material civilization that shall be at all adequate to any scientific purpose can be carried out without taking this material civilization in its causal, that is to say, its genetic, relations to other phases and bearings of the cultural complex; without studying it as it is wrought upon by other lines of cultural growth and as working its effects in these other lines. But in so far as the inquiry is economic science, specifically, the attention will converge upon the scheme of material life and will take in other phases of civilization only in their correlation with the scheme of material civilization.

Like all human culture, this material civilization is a scheme of institutions—institutional fabric and institutional growth. But institutions are an outgrowth of habit. The growth of culture is a cumulative sequence of habituation, and the ways and means of it are the habitual response of human nature to exigencies that vary incontinently, cumulatively, but with something of a consistent sequence in the cumulative variations that so go forward—incontinently, because each new move creates a new situation which induces a further new variation in the habitual manner of response; cumulatively, because each new situation is a variation of what has gone before it and embodies as causal factors all that has been effected by what went before; consistently, because the underlying traits of human nature (propensities, aptitudes, and what not) by force of which the response takes place, and on the ground of which the habituation takes effect, remain substantially unchanged.

Evidently an economic inquiry which occupies itself exclusively with the movements of this consistent, elemental human nature under given, stable institutional conditions—such as is the case with the current hedonistic economics—can reach statical results alone; since it makes abstraction from those elements that make for anything but a statical result. On the other hand an adequate theory of economic conduct, even for statical purposes, cannot be drawn in terms of the individual simply—as is the case in the marginal-utility economics—because it cannot be drawn in terms of the underlying traits of human nature simply; since the response that goes to make up human conduct takes place under institutional norms and only under stimuli that have an institutional bearing; for the situation that provokes and inhibits action in any given case is itself in great part of institutional, cultural derivation.

THE THEORY OF BUSINESS ENTERPRISE *

The Use of Loan Credit

Credit serves two main uses in the regular course of such business as is occupied with the conduct of industry: (*a*) that of deferred payments in the purchase and sale of goods—book accounts, bills, checks, and the like belong chiefly under this head; and (*b*) loans or debts—notes, stock shares, interest-bearing securities, deposits, call loans, etc., belong chiefly here. These two categories of credit extension are by no means clearly distinct. Forms of credit which commonly serve the one purpose may be turned to

* Reprinted from *The Theory of Business Enterprise* by Thorstein Veblen; copyright 1904 by Charles Scribner's Sons, 1932 by Ann Bevans and Becky Veblen; used by permission of the publishers.

the other use; but the two uses of credit are, after all, broadly distinguishable. For many purposes of economic theory such a distinction might not be serviceable, or even practicable; it is here made merely for present use. It is chiefly with credit of the latter class, or rather with credit in so far as it is turned to use for the latter purpose, that this inquiry is concerned. . . .

Loan credit in excess of what may serve to transfer the management of industrial materials from the owner to a more competent user—that is to say, in so far as it is not, in effect, of the nature of a lease of industrial plant—serves, on the whole, not to increase the quantity of the material means of industry nor, directly, to enhance the effectiveness of their use; but, taken in the aggregate, it serves only to widen the discrepancy between business capital and industrial equipment. So long as times are brisk this discrepancy ordinarily goes on widening through a progressive extension of credit. Funds obtained on credit are applied to extend the business; competing business men bid up the material items of industrial equipment by the use of funds so obtained; the value of the material items employed in industry advances; the aggregate of values employed in a given undertaking increases, with or without a physical increase of the industrial material engaged; but since an advance of credit rests on the collateral as expressed in terms of value, an enhanced value of the property affords a basis for a further extension of credit, and so on.

Now, the base line of business transactions is the money value (market or exchange value, price) of the items involved, not their material efficiency. The value of the money unit is by conventional usage held to be invariable, and the lenders perforce proceed on this assumption, so long as they proceed at all. Consequently, any increase of the aggregate money values involved in the current industrial business enterprises will afford a basis for an extension of loans, indistinguishable from any other block of capitalized values, even if the increase of capitalized values is due to credit advances previously made on the full cash value of the property hypothecated. The extension of loans on collateral, such as stock and similar values involved in industrial business, has therefore in the nature of things a cumulative character. This cumulative extension of credit through the enhancement of prices goes on, if otherwise undisturbed, so long as no adverse price phenomenon obtrudes itself with sufficient force to convict this cumulative enhancement of capitalized values of imbecility. The extension of credit proceeds on the putative stability of the money value of the capitalized industrial material, whose money value is cumulatively augmented by this extension itself. But the money value of the collateral is at the same time the capitalized value of the property, computed on the basis of its presumptive earning-capacity. These two methods of rating the value of collateral must approximately coincide, if the capitalization is to afford a stable basis for credit; and when an obvious discrepancy arises between the outcome given by the two ratings, then a rerating will be had in which the rating on the basis of earning-capacity must be accepted as definitive, since earnings are the ground fact about which all business transactions turn and to which all business enterprise converges. A manifest discrepancy presently arises in this way between the aggregate nominal capital (capital plus loans) engaged in business, on the one hand, and the actual rate of earning-capacity of this business capital, on the other hand; and when this discrepancy has become patent a period of liquidation begins.

To give a readier view of the part played by loan credit in this discrepancy between the business capital and the earning-capacity of industrial concerns, it will be in place to indicate more summarily what are the factors at play.

The earnings of the business community, taken as a whole, are derived from the marketable output of goods and services turned out by the industrial process—disregarding such earnings as accrue to one concern merely at the cost of another. The effective industrial capital, from the use of which this output, and therefore these earnings, arise, is the aggregate of capitalized material items actually engaged in industry. The business capital, on the other hand, is made up of this capitalized industrial material taken as a fund of values, plus good-will, plus whatever funds are obtained on credit by using this capitalized industrial material as collateral, plus funds obtained on other, non-industrial, property used as collateral. Through the competitive use of funds obtained on credit, as spoken of above, the nominal value of the capitalized industrial material is cumulatively augmented so as to make it approximately equal to its original capitalization plus whatever funds are obtained on credit of all kinds. On this basis of an expanded collateral a further extension of credit takes place, and the funds so obtained are incorporated in the business capital and turned to the like competitive use, and so on. Capital and earnings are counted in terms of the money unit. Counted in these terms, the earnings (industrial output) are also increased by the process of inflation through credit, since the competitive use of funds spoken of acts to bid up prices of whatever products are used in industry, and of whatever speculative property is presumed to have some eventual industrial use. But the nominal magnitude (value) of the earnings is not increased in as large a ratio as that of the business capital; since the demand whereby the values of the output are regulated is not altogether a business demand (for productive goods), but is in great part, and indeed in the last resort mainly, reducible to a consumptive demand for finished goods. . . .

The theoretical result of this summary sketch of loan credit so far seems to be: (*a*) an extension of loan credit beyond that involved in the transference of productive goods from their owners to more competent users is unavoidable under the régime of competitive business—credit extension is normally in some degree "abnormal" or "excessive"; (*b*) such a use of credit does not add to the aggregate of industrially productive equipment nor increase its material output of product, and therefore it does not add materially to the aggregate gross earnings obtained by the body of business men engaged in industry, as counted in material terms of wealth or of permanent values; (*c*) it diminishes the aggregate net profits obtained by the business men engaged in industry, as counted in such terms, in that it requires them to pay interest, to creditors outside the industrial process proper, on funds which, taken as an aggregate, represent no productive goods and have no aggregate productive effect; (*d*) there results an overrating of the aggregate capital engaged in industry, compared with the value of the industrial equipment at the starting-point, by approximately the amount of the aggregate deposits and loans on collateral; (*e*) the overrating swells the business capital, thereby raises the valuation of collateral, and gives rise to a further extension of credit, with further results of a like nature; (*f*) commonly beginning at some point where the extension of credit is exceptionally large in proportion to the material substratum of productive goods, or where the discrepancy between nominal capital and earning-capacity is exceptionally wide, the overrating is presently recognized by the creditor and a settlement ensues; (*g*) on the consequent withdrawal of credit a forced rerating of the aggregate capital follows, bringing the nominal aggregate into approximate accord with the facts of earning-capacity; (*h*) the shrinkage which takes place in reducing the aggregate rating of business capital from the basis of capital goods plus loans to the basis of capital goods alone, takes place at the expense of debtors and nominal owners of industrial equipment, in so far as they are solvent; (*i*) in the period of liquidation the gain represented by the credit inflation goes to the creditors and claimants of funds outside the industrial process proper, except that so much as is cancelled in bad debts is written off; (*j*) apart from secondary effects, such as heightened efficiency of industry due to inflated values, changes of the rate of interest, insolvency, etc., the main final outcome is a redistribution of the ownership of property whereby the creditor class, including holders and claimants of funds, is benefited. . . .

The Theory of Modern Welfare

. . . Suppose prices of finished goods to be stable or to vary by inconsequential fluctuations, negligible for purposes of the argument, and suppose the rate of interest to be in a similarly negligible position. In other words, suppose such a condition as the business community would recognize as ordinary, normal, sound, without ground for pronounced hopes or fears. Under modern circumstances, dominated as the modern situation is by the machine industry, such a state of affairs is unstable, even apart from any disturbance of an extraneous kind. It is unstable by virtue of the forces at work in its own process, and these forces, on the whole, make for a progressive change in the direction of depression.

It has appeared above that the depressing effect which a relatively low (declining) rate of interest has upon industrial business is due to its setting up a discrepancy between the accepted capitalization of older establishments and the cost of new establishments of an equivalent earning-capacity. Now, under the circumstances of the more fully developed machine industry, such as it has stood for a couple of decades past, a similar discrepancy results from the gradual but uninterrupted progressive improvements of industrial processes. "The state of the industrial arts," as the older economists are in the habit of calling it, is no longer to be conceived as stationary, even for the time being. No "statical" theory of the industrial arts or of business prosperity is tenable, even for the purposes of a "statical" theory of the industrial situation. Progressively increasing efficiency of the processes in use is a pervading trait of the industrial situation. No two successive years are now on the same, or virtually the same, plane in respect of the efficiency of the industrial arts; indeed, the "period of production" can no longer safely be construed to begin and end on the same level in this respect. At the same time the progressively wider and more close-knit articulation of the several industries in a comprehensive process is also going forward, and this also affects all branches of industrial business in some degree and in the same direction, as will appear presently.

The items of the equipment (plant, materials, and in a measure even good-will) in which any industrial enterprise invests, and by the use of which the business men in industry turn out their output of vendible goods, are themselves products of the machine industry. Machine processes, ever increasing in efficiency, turn out the mechanical appliances and materials with which the processes are carried on, at an ever decreasing cost; so that at each successive step the result is a process having a higher efficiency at a lower cost. This is now no longer a sporadic effect of ingenious contrivances having a local and limited application, to be handled as trade secrets and exploited as an enduring differential advantage.

The cost of production of "capital goods" is steadily and progressively lowered, as counted in terms of the processes involved in their production. In a competitive market this is reflected, with greater or less promptitude, in the prices of such capital goods to all buyers. But the buyers whose purposes this lower scale of prices particularly subserves are chiefly the new investors who go into business in the way of new industrial establishments or extensions of the old. Each new venture or extension goes into the competitive traffic of producing and selling any line of staple goods with a differential advantage, as against those that have gone before it, in the way of a lower scale of costs. A successively smaller aggregate value of new equipment will turn out a given volume of vendible product. In so far as there is no collusive control of the output or the prices, this means that the newcomers will cut under the scale of prices at which their predecessors have been content to supply the goods. The run of competitive prices is lowered; which means that at the new competitive prices, and with their output remaining on its old footing as regards expenses of production, the older establishments and processes will no longer yield returns commensurate with the old accepted capitalization.[1] From the inherent character of the machine industry itself, therefore, it follows that the earning-capacity of any industrial enterprise enters on a decline from the outset, and that its capitalization, based on its initial putative earning-capacity, grows progressively antiquated from the start. The efficiency of the machine process in the "instrumental industries" sets up a discrepancy between cost and capitalization. So that a progressive readjustment of capitalization to correspond with the lowered earning-capacity is required by the nature of the case. It is also, in the nature of the case, impracticable.

In so far as the process of investment and business management involves the use of credit, in the way of interest-bearing securities or loans equivalent to such securities, this element of credit retards the readjustment by force of the fixed charges which it involves. This retardation (aided as it is by the reluctance of business men to lower their capitalization) is of sufficient effect to hinder recapitalization, on the whole, from overtaking the progressive need of it, with the result that a fair or "ordinary" rate of profits on industrial investments is not permanently attainable in the field of open competition. In order that the rate of interest should effectually further business depression in this way, therefore, it is not necessary that the rate should rise or fall, or that it should be relatively high or low, or that it should be uniform over the field, but only that there should be a rate of interest in each case, and that there should be some appreciable volume of credit involved in industrial investments. Credit is, in fact, a ubiquitous factor in modern industrial business, and its effects in the way indicated are therefore to be counted in as a constant force in the situation.

However, even apart from the presence of this ubiquitous credit element, a similar effect would probably result from the progressive enhancement of industrial efficiency when this enhancement proceeds at such a rate as has been the case for some time past. As has been shown in an earlier chapter, business men keep account of their wealth, their outgo and their income, in terms of money value, not in terms of mechanical serviceability or of consumptive effect. Business traffic and business outcome are standardized in terms of the money unit, while the industrial process and its output are standardized in terms of physical measurements (mechanical efficiency). In the current habits and conventions of the business community, the unit of money is accepted and dealt with as a standard measure. The stability of the standard unit cannot be effectually questioned within the scope of business traffic. According to the practical

[1] The established concerns having been capitalized on the basis of past cost, we can say that in the older establishments, capitalization $= f$ (cost), but in the new establishments with an equal earning-capacity, capitalization $= f(\text{cost}_1 = \text{cost} - \Delta \text{ cost})$; hence the rate of earnings $= f(\text{earnings}/\text{cost})$ will be progressively higher as cost decreases:

$$f\left(\frac{\text{earnings}}{\text{cost}}\right) < f\left(\frac{\text{earnings}}{\text{cost} - \Delta\text{ cost}}\right) < f\left(\frac{\text{earnings}}{\text{cost} - 2\,\Delta\text{ cost}}\right), \text{ etc.}$$

metaphysics of the business community, the money unit is an invariable magnitude, whatever may be true of it in fact. A man imbued with these business metaphysics and not given to fine-spun reflection, as business men commonly are not, is richer or poorer in his own apprehension, according as his balance sheet shows a greater or less number of these standard units of value. Investment, expenses, vendible output, earnings, fixed charges, and capitalization run in terms of this value unit. A reduction of earnings or of capitalization, as rated in terms of the value unit, is felt as an impoverishment. The reduction of capitalization in these terms is, therefore, a hardship, which is only reluctantly and tardily submitted to, even if it carries no hardship in the way of a reduced command over the material means of production, of life, or of comfort. A business man's rating in the business community likewise rests on the pecuniary magnitude of his holdings and his transactions, not on the mechanical serviceability of his establishment or his output; and this business rating is a large part of the business man's everyday ambition. An enhancement of it is a source of secure gratification and self-respect, and a reduction of it has a very substantial contrary effect. A reduction of the pecuniary showing is submitted to only reluctantly and tardily, after it has become unavoidable, and only to the least feasible extent. But under conditions, such as now prevail, which involve the requirement of a progressive rerating of this kind, this reluctant concession never overtakes the need of readjustment,—and the discrepancy between capitalization and earning-capacity is therefore chronic so long as no extraneous circumstances come in temporarily to set aside the trend of business affairs in this respect. It may, therefore, be said, on the basis of this view, that chronic depression, more or less pronounced, is normal to business under the fully developed régime of the machine industry.[2]

This deplorable trend given to business by the excessive prevalence and efficiency of the machine industry can, however, be set aside by several factors more or less extraneous to the industrial system proper. Even within the mechanical system of industry there is at least one factor of some consequence that consistently acts to mitigate the trend indicated, and that may even put it in abeyance from time to time. As has been pointed out above, questions of business are fundamentally questions of price. A decline of prices which widely touches business interests brings depression. Conversely, an appreciable advance in prices, from whatever cause, means improvement in business. Such an advance in prices may come of a speculative movement; which in turn may arise from a variety of circumstances, for the most part circumstances extraneous to the industrial process. For the present, however, the question of a speculative movement is best left on one side. Another factor touches the case more intimately. As has more than once been the case, prices

[2] With the above analysis may be contrasted Marx's discussion of the declining rate of profits and the manner in which he conceives overproduction, speculation, and crises to arise out of the tendency of profits to a minimum. (*Kapital,* vol. III. ch. XV.)

may be advanced through a freer supply of the precious metals, or by an inflation of the currency, or a more facile use of credit instruments as a subsidiary currency mechanism. Now, the growing efficiency of industry has an effect in lowering the (material) cost of production of the precious metals and so increasing the ease with which they are supplied, after the same manner as it affects the supply of goods for industrial or consumptive use. But the increased supply of the precious metals has, of course, an effect upon prices contrary to that exerted by the increasing supply of goods. In so far as this effect is had, it acts to correct or mitigate the trend of business toward chronic depression.

But certain circumstances come in to qualify the salutary effect of a lowered cost of the precious metals. Improvements in the industrial processes affect the (industrial) cost of production of the precious metals in a less degree than the cost of other goods; at least, such seems to have been the case recently. But beyond this, and of graver consequence, is a peculiarity affecting the value of the money metals. The annual product of the money metals is not annually consumed, nor nearly. The use of them as money does not consume them except incidentally and very slowly. The mass of these metals in hand at any given time is very considerable and is relatively imperishable, so that the annual accretion is but a small fraction of the aggregate supply. The lowered cost of the annual supply has therefore but a relatively slight effect upon the aggregate value of the available supply.

The case is different as regards the annual output of vendible products, whether for industrial or consumptive use. In this case, and particularly as regards this matter of new investments and extensions of industrial equipment, the annual output counts for by far the greater factor in making the current value of the available supply, if indeed it is not to be regarded as substantially the only factor that comes in question here. Accordingly, it is only under very exceptional circumstances, at times when the precious metals are supplied with extraordinary freedom, that the increased output of these metals can offset the trend of business toward depression. Ordinarily this factor can count for no more than a mitigation of the "tendency of profits to a minimum." And even this mitigating effect, it may be remarked, appears to be of less radical consequence for the general situation of business now than it was during the earlier phases of the machine industry's régime. The most telling effect of an increased supply of the precious metals seems to be the incitement which it gives to speculative inflation.

It will be noted that the explanation here offered of depression makes it a malady of the affections. The discrepancy which discourages business men is a discrepancy between that nominal capitalization which they have set their hearts upon through habituation in the immediate past and that actual capitalizable value of their property which its current earning-capacity will warrant. But where the preconceptions of the business men engaged have, as commonly happens, in great part been fixed and legalized in the form of interest-bearing securities, this malady of the affections becomes extremely difficult to remedy, even though it be true that these legalized affections, preconceptions, or what not, centre upon the metaphysical stability of the money unit.

But while it is true that depression is primarily a business difficulty and rests on emotional grounds, that does not hinder its having grave consequences for industry and for the material welfare of the community outside the range of business interests. Business enterprise, it is true, proceeds on metaphysical grounds and is swayed by considerations of nominal wealth rather than by considerations of material serviceability; but, none the less, business enterprise and business metaphysics control the course of industry.

Dull times in business means dull times in industry, of course. But a caution is necessary on this head. The yearly output does not usually vary extremely between brisk and dull times, except as measured in price. As measured in material terms the discrepancy in the volume of output between brisk and dull times is much less. The gross output as measured by weight and tale is less in dull than in brisk times, other things equal; but the deficiency as measured in these terms is much less than the price returns would indicate. Indeed, the output as measured by weight and tale need not average very appreciably less during a protracted depression than during a preceding period of good times. The volume of business as well as the volume of output (by weight and tale) of industry may increase during a few years of depression at nearly if not quite as high a rate as during a corresponding period of good times. A transition from dull to brisk times, however, commonly if not invariably involves a rapid increase in values, while a converse transition involves a corresponding shrinkage of values, though commonly a slower shrinkage,—except where a crisis intervenes.

The primary hardship of a period of depression is a persistent lesion of the affections of the business men; the greatest secondary hardship is what falls upon the workmen, in the way of partial unemployment and a decline in wages, with consequent precariousness and reduction of their livelihood. For those workmen who continue to find fairly steady employment during the depression, however, even at reduced wages, the loss is more apparent than real; since the cheapening of goods offsets the decline in wages. Indeed, the cheapening of the means of living is apt to offset the fall in wages fully, for such workmen as have steady work. So that in the case of the workmen also, as well as in that of the business men, the distress which dull times brings is in some part a spiritual, emotional matter.

To the rest of the community, those classes that are outside of business enterprise and outside of the industrial occupations proper, that is to say, those (non-industrial) classes who live on a fixed salary or similar fixed income, dull times are a thinly disguised blessing. They suffer in their affections from the reflected emotional detriment of the business community, but they gain in their ease of livelihood and in their savings by all the difference between the price scale of brisk and of dull times. To these classes an era of prosperity brings substantially nothing but detriment.

Depression is primarily a malady of the affections of the business men. That is the seat of the difficulty. The stagnation of industry and the hardships suffered by the workmen and other classes are of the nature of symptoms and secondary effects. Any proposed remedy, therefore, must be of such a nature as to reach this emotional seat of the trouble and restore the balance between the nominal value of the business capital engaged and the earnings of the business; that is to say, a remedy, to be efficacious, must restore profits to a "reasonable" rate; which means, practically, that prices must be brought to the level on which the accepted capitalization has been made. Such a remedy, to offset the disastrous cheapening of products through mechanical improvements, has been found in business coalitions and working arrangements of one kind and another, looking to the "regulation" of prices and output. Latterly this remedy is becoming familiar to the business community as well as to students of the business situation, and its tangible, direct, and unequivocal efficiency in correcting this main infirmity of modern business is well recognized. So much so, indeed, that its urgent advisability has been formulated in the maxim that "Where combination is possible competition is impossible." . . .

The Natural Decay of Business Enterprise

Broadly, the machine discipline acts to disintegrate the institutional heritage, of all degrees of antiquity and authenticity—whether it be the institutions that embody the principles of natural liberty or those that comprise the residue of more archaic principles of conduct still current in civilized life. It thereby cuts away that ground of law and order on which business enterprise is founded. . . . But the future of business enterprise is bound up with the future of civilization, since the cultural scheme is, after all, a single one, comprising many interlocking elements, no one of which can be greatly disturbed without disturbing the working of all the rest.

In its bearing on the question in hand, the "social problem" at large presents this singular situation. The growth of business enterprise rests on the machine technology as its material foundation. The machine industry is indispensable to it; it cannot get along without the machine process. But the discipline of the machine process cuts away the spiritual, institutional foundations of business enterprise; the machine industry is incompatible with its continued growth; it cannot, in the long run, get along with the machine process. In their struggle against the cultural effects of the machine process, therefore, business principles cannot win in the long run; since an effectual mutilation or inhibition of the machine system would gradually push business enterprise to the wall; whereas with a free growth of the machine system business principles would presently fall into abeyance. . . .

When the question is cast up as to what will come of this conflict of institutional forces—called the Social Problem—it is commonly made a question of remedies: What can be done to save civilized mankind from the vulgarization and disintegration wrought by the machine industry?

Now, business enterprise and the machine process are the two prime movers in modern culture; and the only recourse that holds a promise of being effective, therefore, is a recourse to the workings of business traffic. And this is a question, not of what is conceivably, ideally, idyllically possible for the business community to do if they will take thought and act advisedly and concertedly toward a chosen cultural outcome, but of what is the probable cultural outcome to be achieved through business traffic carried on for business ends, not for cultural ends. It is a question not of what ought to be done, but of what is to take place.

Persons who are solicitous for the cultural future commonly turn to speculative advice as to what ought to be done toward holding fast that which is good in the cultural heritage, and what ought further to be done to increase the talent that has been intrusted to this generation. The practical remedy offered is commonly some proposal for palliative measures, some appeal to philanthropic, æsthetic, or religious sentiment, some endeavor to conjure with the name of one or another of the epiphenomena of modern culture. Something must be done, it is conceived, and this something takes the shape of charity organizations, clubs and societies for social "purity," for amusement, education, and manual training of the indigent classes, for colonization of the poor, for popularization of churches, for clean politics, for cultural missionary work by social settlements, and the like. These remedial measures whereby it is proposed to save or to rehabilitate certain praiseworthy but obsolescent habits of life and of thought are, all and several, beside the point so far as touches the question in hand. Not that it is hereby intended to cast a slur on these meritorious endeavors to save mankind by treating symptoms. The symptoms treated are no doubt evil, as they are said to be; or if they are not evil, the merits of that particular question do not concern the present inquiry. The endeavors in question are beside the point in that they do not fall into the shape of a business proposition. They are, on the whole, not so profitable a line of investments as certain other ventures that are open to modern enterprise. Hence, if they traverse the course of business enterprise and of industrial exigencies, they are nugatory, being in the same class with the labor of Sisyphus; whereas if they coincide in effect with the line along which business and industrial exigencies move, they are a work of supererogation, except so far as they may be conceived to accelerate a change that is already under way. Nothing can deflect the sweep of business enterprise, unless it be an outgrowth of this enterprise itself or of the industrial means by which business enterprise works.

Nothing can serve as a corrective of the cultural trend given by the machine discipline except what can be put in the form of a business proposition. The question of neutralizing the untoward effects of the machine discipline resolves itself into a question as to the cultural work and consequences of business enterprise, and of the cultural value of business principles in so far as they guide such human endeavor as lies outside the range of business enterprise proper. It is not a question of what ought to be done, but of what is the course laid out by business principles; the discretion rests with the business men, not with the moralists, and the business men's discretion is bounded by the exigencies of business enterprise. Even the business men cannot allow themselves to play fast and loose with business principles in response to a call from humanitarian motives. The question, therefore, remains, on the whole, a question of what the business men may be expected to do for cultural growth on the motive of profits.

Something they are doing, as others are, from motives of benevolence, with a well-advised endeavor to maintain the cultural gains of the past and to make the way of life smoother for mankind in the future. But the more secure and substantial results to be looked for in this direction are those that follow incidentally, as by-products of business enterprise, because these are not dependent on the vagaries of personal preference, tastes, and prejudices, but rest on a broad institutional basis.

The effects of business enterprise upon the habits and temper of the people, and so upon institutional growth, are chiefly of the nature of sequelæ. . . . The discipline of business employments is of a conservative nature, tending to sustain the conventions that rest on natural-rights dogma, because these employments train the men engaged in them to think in terms of natural rights. . . . In its severer, more unmitigated form, this discipline in pecuniary habits of thought falls on a gradually lessening proportion of the population. The absolute number of business men, counting principals and subordinates, is, of course, not decreasing. The number of men in business pursuits, in proportion to the population, is also apparently not decreasing; but within the business employments a larger proportion are occupied with office routine, and so are withdrawn from the more effectual training given by business management proper. If such a decrease occurs in any country, it is almost certainly not to be found in any other country than America.

This business discipline is somewhat closely limited both in scope and range. (1) It acts to conserve, or to rehabilitate, a certain restricted line of institutional habits of thought, viz. those preconceptions of natural rights which have to do with property. What it conserves, therefore, is the bourgeois virtues of solvency, thrift, and dissimulation. The nobler and more spectacular aristocratic virtues, with their correlative institutional furniture, are not in any sensible degree fortified by the habits of business life. Business life does not further the growth of manners and breeding, pride of caste, punctilios of "honor," or even religious fervor. (2) The salutary discipline of business life touches the bulk of the population, the working classes, in a progressively less intimate and less exacting manner. It can, therefore, not serve to correct or even greatly to mitigate the matter-of-fact bias given these classes by the discipline of the machine process.

As a direct disciplinary factor the machine process holds over the business employments, in that it touches larger classes of the community and inculcates its characteristic habits of thought more unremittingly. And any return to more archaic methods of industry, such as is sometimes advocated on artistic grounds, seems hopeless, since business interests do not countenance a discontinuance of machine methods. The machine methods that are corrupting the hearts and manners of the workmen are profitable to the business men, and that fact seems to be decisive on the point. A direct, advised return to handicraft, or any similar discontinuance of the machine industry, is out of the question; although something in the way of a partial return to more primitive methods of industry need not be impracticable as a remote and indirect consequence of the working of business enterprise.

WESLEY CLAIR MITCHELL

(1874–1948)

After Veblen's death the leadership of the American institutional school passed to Wesley C. Mitchell, for many years a professor at Columbia University and a pioneer in the empirical investigation of business cycles. He was a founder of the National Bureau of Economic Research, which has continued to this day to carry on important work in quantitative research.

Mitchell was born in a small town in Illinois and later studied at the University of Chicago, where he came under the influence of Thorstein Veblen and John Dewey. Although Veblen shook his faith in orthodox doctrine, his skepticism and satire were not, for Mitchell, an adequate point of departure for the reconstruction of economic science. Under the impact of Dewey's pragmatic philosophy, Mitchell laid stress on the necessarily operational character of a "new" economics which would employ verifiable concepts.

After leaving graduate school, Mitchell taught for several years, first at the University of Chicago and then at the University of California, and was chief of the price section of the War Industries Board during World War I. In 1913 he published his seminal study on *Business Cycles,* which proved a landmark in quantitative research.

Here Mitchell abandoned the nineteenth century theory of monistic causation and developed an "analytical description" of the cycle—a pluralistic theory of the cyclical factors which converge on the business order. The analytical description was obtained through the so-called quantitative method: concrete events were arrayed in statistical series, and institutional and statistical analyses were then fused in the analytical description. Essentially, the analysis was a price-cost approach with emphasis on the differences in timing and amplitude of price fluctuations and the effect of these fluctuations on profit expectations. Business cycles were regarded as self-enforcing and self-generating and were portrayed not as disturbances to a basic equilibrium, but as implicit in the functioning of the economic system as a whole.

In the first edition of his book Mitchell assumed a given institutional situation and ignored all but categories of statistically measurable data. In an introductory volume of the revised edition, *Business Cycles, the Problem and Its Setting* (1927), he paid more attention to the changing institutional patterns of a capitalistic economy. The second chapter of this work has been regarded as the outstanding synthesis of the institutionalists' view of the operation of the money economy.

The study of business cycles depended, in his opinion, on an adequate understanding of the role of money in economic organization. His studies of greenback history had convinced him that the money-making economy formed a quasi-independent institution built around the activity of making and spending money incomes. Business fluctuations were inherent in the nature of the money economy, the structure of the price system, and the discoördination of separate business enterprises. Mitchell, like Veblen, never failed to point to the subordination of industrial and commercial processes to the money-making process.

Mitchell's emphasis on the role of money in economic life is well summarized by the following critical essay on "The Role of Money in Economic Theory." Mitchell probably attached great importance to the role of money because it allowed him to develop economics along quantitative lines.

The second of the articles which follow, "Quantitative Analysis in Economic Theory," illustrates Mitchell's philosophy and his critical approach to received doctrine. Some of Mitchell's other stimulating contributions in this field are to be found in a collection of essays entitled *The Backward Art of Spending Money* (1937) and in the *Lectures Notes on Types of Economic Theory* (1949).

In 1946, in conjunction with Dr. A. F. Burns, he published a methodological volume called *Measuring Business Cycles,* which elaborated new statistical techniques for measuring cyclical movements.

Mitchell died in 1948 without having lived to see the completion of the work which he had initiated thirty-five years earlier. In 1951 a posthumous "progress report" on his latest investigations appeared as *What Happens During Business Cycles.*

THE ROLE OF MONEY IN ECONOMIC THEORY *

Economics has advanced far since Mill declared, "there cannot . . . be intrinsically a more insignificant thing, in the economy of society, than money, except in the character of a contrivance for sparing time and labor." In one way or another, tacitly or explicitly, the types of theory current at present all make money in Dr. Marshall's words "the center around which economic science clusters." The psychological school started by representing economic life as guided by psychic bookkeeping, and has developed economics into "the science that treats phenomena from the standpoint of price." Pure theory in its severer forms drops the subject of valuation altogether and confines itself mainly to the interrelations among "ideal prices." Neoclassical theory makes money the "economist's balance," and shows how the use of money simplifies economic problems both practical and theoretical.

In thus singling out the use of money as bringing system into economic behavior, as providing the basis for exact analysis, current theory is returning to the starting point from which Cournot set out on his researches in 1838. What we call price, what Cournot calls the "abstract idea of *wealth* or of *value of exchange,*" he explains in his first chapter, is "suited for the foundation of a scientific theory," because it is "a definite idea, and consequently susceptible of rigorous treatment in combinations." This abstract idea of wealth "could not have been grasped by men of Teutonic stock, either at the epoch of the Conquest, or even at much later periods, when the feudal law existed in full vigor. . . . Such an idea of wealth as we draw from our advanced state of civilization, and such as is necessary to give rise to a theory, can only be slowly developed as a consequence of the progress of commercial relations." A remarkable anticipation of the outcome of two generations of hard thinking! And Cournot applies his insight: as a first problem he chooses not barter, but foreign exchange—the kind of transaction in which nothing but pecuniary factors are involved.

In singling out the influence of an institutional factor as the basis of rationality, current economics is also in line with current psychology. Psychologists hold that man starts with an immense number of inborn reflexes, instincts, and capacities, inherited generation after generation with num-

* From "The Role of Money in Economic Theory," originally published by the American Economic Association in *American Economic Review,* Supplement, March, 1916. Reprinted from *The Backward Art of Spending Money* (New York and London, McGraw-Hill Book Co., Inc., 1937). Used with the permission of the copyright owner, Augustus M. Kelley.

berless differences as between individuals, but with slight changes as regards the species. The behavior these propensities produce is at first quite unreasoning. But among the inborn capacities is the capacity to learn; that is, the capacity to form innumerable *combinations* among the innumerable original propensities. Practically every activity of mature life is the expression not of any single instinct, but of some combination into which several or many propensities have entered. It is these changing combinations among substantially unchanging elements that differentiate the behavior of the civilized man from that of the savage. And these combinations are formed afresh in every child, primarily in his intercourse with other human beings. Thus intelligence is a social product developed in the individual through the exercise of his inherited propensities, and its special character depends upon the society into which the individual is born. The great social institutions, such as speech, writing, the practical arts, and religion, which are passed on with cumulative changes from one generation to another, play the leading role in this nurture of intelligence. They are standard behavior habits—habits of feeling, thinking, and acting in the face of frequently recurring situations—that have approved themselves to the community. These institutions include among their other elements the abstract concepts that are the most precious products of intelligence because they are the indispensable tools of further thought. By learning to use such concepts in dealing with the situations that confront him, the individual standardizes and rationalizes his own behavior. To find the basis of rationality, then, we must not look inside the individual at his capacity to abstract from the totality of experience the feeling elements, to assess their pleasant or unpleasant characters, and to compare their magnitudes. Rather must we look outside the individual to the habits of behavior slowly evolved by society and painfully learned by himself.

Of course, the use of money is one of these great rationalizing habits. It gives society the technical machinery of exchange, the opportunity to combine personal freedom with orderly cooperation on a grand scale, and the basis of that system of accountancy which Sombart appropriately calls "economic rationalism." It is the foundation of that complex system of prices to which the individual must adjust his behavior in getting a living. Since it molds his objective behavior, it becomes part of his subjective life, giving him a method and an instrument for the difficult task of assessing the relative importance of dissimilar goods in varying quantities, and affecting the interests in terms of which he makes his valuations. Because it thus rationalizes economic life itself, the use of money lays the foundation for a rational theory of that life. Money may not be the root of *all* evil, but it is the root of economic science.

That economists are coming to accept this view is no more due to their study of psychology than it is due to their study of Cournot. It is the result of learning by trial and error. They have tried treating money as a superficial phenomenon: they have tried using hedonism as the basis of economic rationality. But in working out, in treatise after treatise, a reasoned account of how men behave, they have come, without foreseeing what they were doing, to the basis on which Cournot built in 1838. That a serious and long-sustained effort to explain their phase of human behavior has brought economists unwittingly to much the same viewpoint as psychologists have attained by other routes may well raise their confidence.

. . . Economic life may be regarded as a continuous process of providing and using commodities and services. This industrial process includes the work of the farm, the mine, the railway, the warehouse, the store, the engineering office, etc., as well as the work of the factory. It has its elaborately differentiated techniques, resting primarily upon the physical sciences and mathematics, in less measure upon certain branches of biology. It has its technical experts, its organized labor force, and its capital in the shape of material equipment.

Economic life may be regarded also as a process of making and spending money. This business process is shared in by everyone who is getting a money income in any way or laying out money for any purpose. Its technique rises from the simple planning of family budgets, through "the exact science of making change," the arts of bargaining and salesmanship, bookkeeping and accountancy, to the large tasks of financial administration. Its technical experts are business enterprisers, chartered accountants, bankers, brokers, business agents of trade-unions, etc. Its special labor force includes bookkeepers, cashiers, advertising clerks, and the like. Its material equipment is meager; but all capital belongs here in the guise of pecuniary funds.

Making goods and making money are both objective processes: at some points quite distinct from or even opposed to each other; at most points running side by side, concerned with the same objects and supervised by the same men. We habitually interpret these two objective processes in terms of personal and social interest. These interpretations give us two other ways of looking at economics. To be specific:

Economic life may be regarded also as a process of making efforts and gaining satisfactions; or better, the activities of getting and using goods, of making and spending money, have a subjective aspect upon which attention may be focused. In this dim inner realm of consciousness it is difficult to make out the technique; there are no technical experts, no labor forces, no material appliances, and no capital in any sense, except by virtue of fanciful analogies.

Economic life may be regarded finally as the process by which a community seeks its material welfare. On this view every person is a contributor to, a burden upon, or a detractor from the commonweal. Such technical experts as there are must be sought among the people in public or private life who seek to promote social welfare by constructive thinking, by agitation, by philanthropic effort, or by doing their daily work with an eye to its serviceability to the community rather than its profit to themselves. Such accounting as is possible runs in terms of heightening or lowering the community's vitality. The concept of capital merges into the broader concept of resources—soil and climate, mines and forests, industrial equipment, public health, intelligence and general education, the sciences that confer control over nature, the sciences that aid in developing body and mind, and the sciences that bear upon social organization.

Now our interest in economics centers in its bearing upon social welfare in the present and the proximate future. As Professor Pigou and Mr. Hobson have shown, it is feasible even now to set up a tentative criterion of economic welfare, and make investigations into the relations between various features of economic activity as now conducted and welfare as thus conceived. Such work may have as keen theoretical interest, as genuine scientific standing, as work that professes to maintain a serene indifference to the fate of humankind. But its successful prosecution on a scientific basis presupposes considerable knowledge of how economic processes actually work at present. While the understanding of these processes has been the chief aim of economic investigation for a century, no one fancies that this fundamental task has yet been adequately performed. In the interests of social welfare itself we need clearer insight into the industrial process of making goods, the business process of making money, and the way in which both sets of activities are related to each other and to the individual's inner life.

Into our conjoint attack upon these problems a clear recognition of the role played by money promises to bring more definite order and more effective cooperation. It helps us to formulate our tasks in ways that suggest definite things to try next. For example, to find the basis of economic rationality in the development of a social institution directs our attention away from that dark subjective realm, where so many economists have groped, to an objective realm, where behavior can be studied in the light of common day. It shows the high promise of that effort to frame an "institutional theory" of value which certain of our colleagues have begun. It helps us to keep in mind the fateful distinction between those elements in human nature that are inherited and hence presumably unchanging, and those other elements that are acquired and hence presumably susceptible of modification—a distinction around which turns so much of our thinking concerning days to come. To realize that our theoretical inquiries cluster about the workings of an institution bridges the gulf that has existed to the detriment of both between economic theory and economic history. It establishes upon a common plane the work of those who seek to know how economic organization has developed in the past, of those who seek to know how it functions in the present, and of those who seek to know what changes it promises to undergo in the future. To differentiate sharply between making money and making goods brings into its proper prominence the problem of the relations between business management and industrial efficiency. It prepares us to face that subtler problem of the dissimilar habits of thought drilled into men by the daily work of the countinghouse and of the factory. By going in for a realistic treatment of business life we may hope to arouse a keener interest and a wider cooperation in economic theory. For we shall be analyzing the actual processes with which men of affairs are concerned; we shall be treating problems that have meaning to legislators, administrators, and judges; we shall be stating our hypotheses in ways that facilitate their practical testing; and we shall be reaching conclusions that have a clearer bearing upon our hopes and fears for the future.

The current tendency to make money "the center around which economic science clusters," then, is a tendency to be fostered. For that course promises (1) to clarify economic theory by giving it a better framework, (2) to render economic theory more useful by directing attention to those actual processes with which all serious proposals for governmental regulation and social reorganization must deal, (3) to make economics more realistic and therefore more interesting intellectually as well as practically, and, finally, (4) to make economic theory more profound by orienting the economist for a fruitful study of his aspect of human behavior.

QUANTITATIVE ANALYSIS IN ECONOMIC THEORY *

The economist of today has at his disposal a wider array of "thorough realistic statistics" than had the economist of yesterday, a more powerful technique, and more opportunities to get assistance. All this is recognized by everyone. But the crucial question remains: What use can we make of these data, this refined technique, and these research assistants in solving the fundamental problems of economic science? Are not these the problems qualitative analysis has posed? When a theorist puts any one of his problems to a statistician, does the answer he gets ever quite meet his questions? And when a statistician attempts to test an economic theory, is his test ever conclusive? In fine, what evidence have we that quantitative analysis is taking over the task upon which qualitative analysis, with all its shortcomings, does make headway?

One view is that, despite all the gains it has made, quantitative analysis shows no more promise of providing a statistical complement of pure theory than it showed when Dr. Marshall pronounced his dicta. I think this view is correct, if the pure theory we have in mind is theory of the type cultivated by Jevons, or by Dr. Marshall himself. Indeed, I incline to go further and say that there is slight prospect that quantitative analysis will ever be able to solve the problems that qualitative analysis has framed, in their present form. What we must expect is a recasting of the old problems into new forms amenable to statistical attack. In the course

* From "Quantitative Analysis in Economic Theory," originally published by the American Economic Association in *American Economic Review,* March, 1925. Reprinted from *The Backward Art of Spending Money* (New York and London, McGraw-Hill Book Co., Inc., 1937). Used with the permission of the copyright owner, Augustus M. Kelley.

of this reformulation of its problems, economic theory will change not merely its complexion but also its content.

Let me illustrate the reaction of methods upon problems by citing an example. In the course of his investigations into economic cycles, Professor Henry L. Moore needed to formulate "the concrete laws of demand for the representative crops." He approached this task by quoting Dr. Marshall's qualitative analysis of demand. But with Marshall's formulation of the problem it was impossible to get quantitative results. For Marshall treated the relation between demand and price on the assumptions (1) that the changes in the two variables are infinitesimal, (2) that the conditions remain constant, and (3) that the shape of the demand curve is known. Professor Moore, on the contrary, had to derive his curves of demand, and to deal with the real world where no factor is known to remain constant and where changes in demand and price are finite. Attacking his problem by mathematical statistics, Moore obtained equations expressing the relations between the demands for and the prices of corn, hay, oats, and potatoes; he determined the precision of these equations as formulas for predicting prices, and he measured the elasticity of demand for each crop. As he pointed out in concluding the discussion, his results do not solve Marshall's problem. But is not Moore's problem more significant theoretically, as well as more relevant to economic practice? If quantitative analysis can give us empirically valid demand curves and coefficients of elasticity for numerous commodities, shall we not have a better theory of demand than qualitative analysis can supply?

From this concrete illustration of the reaction of quantitative method upon economic theory, we may pass to a broader range of considerations. Jevons preached that "The deductive science of Economics must be verified and rendered useful by the purely empirical science of Statistics." But the deductive theory for which Jevons wished a statistical complement was "based on a calculus of pleasure and pain." Today there seems little likelihood that we shall have a quantitative proof—or disproof—of the calculus of pleasure and pain. That problem is passing off the stage.

Belonging to a younger generation than Jevons, Dr. Marshall formally repudiated hedonism; but he conceived of economic behavior as controlled by two opposing sets of motives, the motives that impel us toward consumption and the motives that repel us from labor and waiting. Money was to him "the center around which economic science clusters" because it is the economist's instrument for measuring the force of these motives. One task that he hoped quantitative method would perform was that of rendering these measures more precise. Is there a better chance that we shall attain a statistical measurement of the force of motives than that we shall measure pleasures and pains?

I doubt it. For the quantitative data of the economist are limited to objective phenomena. Of course, the theorist who so wishes may interpret these data in subjective terms, such as pleasure or the strength of desire.

But these interpretations are something that the theorist adds to the data, not something that he draws out of them. In the present state of our knowledge of human nature, such interpretations smack more of metaphysics than of science. Economists who practice quantitative analysis are likely to be chary of deserting the firm ground of measurable phenomena for excursions into the subjective.

That such excursions are not imperative is readily shown. The theoretical purpose of Jevons' calculus of pleasure and pain, of Marshall's opposing sets of motives, and of the simultaneous equations used by the mathematical writers was to lay a foundation in the behavior of individuals on which could be built an explanation of mass phenomena. Of course, the theorists have never supposed that any individual could really tell just how many units of one article he would give for successive units of another; but that mattered little because the theorists have not been interested in the individuals as such. They presented the whole construction scrupulously as a conceptual device for getting insight into what happens in the real markets where the money incomes and costs of living of millions of men are fixed.

Now, the quantitative workers derive their data directly from these real markets. They start with the mass phenomena which the qualitative analysts approached indirectly through their hypothetical individuals. With the fuller reports they are obtaining and the more powerful technique they are developing, properly equipped investigators can study the relations between the actual responses of prices to changes in supply and of supply to changes in prices. They can work out demand schedules that hold empirically within the ranges and periods covered by experience. They can trace the changes in the consumption of commodities by whole communities or by large groups. They can investigate the relations between monetary changes and "real" incomes, between saving and spending, between different forms of economic organization and production. With all these fascinating problems and numberless others before them in shape for attack, it seems unlikely that the quantitative workers will retain a keen interest in imaginary individuals coming to imaginary markets with ready-made scales of bid and offer prices. Their theories will probably be theories about the relationships among the variables that measure objective processes. There is little likelihood that the old explanations will be refuted by these investigators, but much likelihood that they will be disregarded.

If my forecast is valid, our whole apparatus of reasoning on the basis of utilities and disutilities, or motives, or choices, in the individual economy, will drop out of sight in the work of the quantitative analysts, going the way of the static state. The "psychological" element in the work of these men will consist mainly of objective analysis of the economic behavior of groups. Motives will not be disregarded, but they will be treated as problems requiring study, instead of being taken for granted as constituting explanations.

The obsolescence of the older type of reasoning in economics will be promoted by the change which is coming over our thinking about human nature. Psychologists are moving rapidly toward an objective conception and a quantitative treatment of their problems. Their emphasis upon stimulus and response sequences, upon conditioned reflexes; their eager efforts to develop performance tests, their attempts to build up a technique of experiment, favor the spread of the conception that all of the social sciences have a common aim—the understanding of human behavior; a common method—the quantitative analysis of behavior records, and a common aspiration—to devise ways of experimenting upon behavior.

This conception, that economics is one among a number of sciences all dealing with aspects of human behavior, need be no monopoly of the quantitative workers. But it will be especially congenial to their way of thinking. And it will put them in a better position than ever before to cooperate with quantitative analysts in other fields. What Jeremy Bentham's idea that all our actions are determined by pleasure and pain once did to provide a common program for jurists, economists, psychologists, penologists, and educators, may be done again by the idea that all these groups, together with the political scientists, sociologists, anthropologists, and historians, are engaged in the study of human behavior. On that basis the problems of each of these groups are significant for all the others, their technical methods are suggestive, their results pertinent. . . .

I do not mean that we can expect the rapid crystallization of a new system of economic theory built by quantitative analysis. Quite the contrary. The literature that the quantitative workers are due to produce will be characterized not by general treatises, but by numberless papers and monographs. Knowledge will grow by accretion as it grows in the natural sciences, rather than by the excogitation of new systems. Books will pass out of date more rapidly. The history of economic theory will receive less attention. Economists will be valued less on their erudition and more on their creative capacity. The advances will be achieved not only by conceiving new hypotheses, but also by compiling statistics from fresh fields, by inventing new technical methods, by refining upon old measures, and perhaps by devising experiments upon certain types of behavior. It will be harder for anyone to cover the whole field, perhaps quite impossible. From time to time someone will try to give a comprehensive survey of the results of quantitative research, but such books will not have the prestige won by the treatises by Adam Smith, Ricardo, Mill, and Marshall.

Of the content of this quantitative economics we can form but uncertain surmises. One topic, however, is fairly sure to receive much attention—the topic defined twenty-four years ago at the thirteenth annual meeting of the American Economic Association by Dr. Veblen. This is the relation between business and industry, between making money and making goods, between the pecuniary and the technological phases of economic life.

In qualitative analysis this problem has been sadly slurred over. The quantitative workers cannot so blink it. Much of their data will consist of two great groups of time series. One group shows variations in the output, stocks, shipment, or orders for economic goods expressed in physical units—bushels, pounds, yards, ton-miles, names on payrolls, hours of work, accident rates, labor turnover, and so on through a list that will grow with the growth of statistics. The second group of time series shows variations in quantities expressed in monetary units. The relations between these two groups of series will be an obvious problem of just the kind that quantitative workers enjoy attacking. They cannot content themselves by staying always on the money level of analysis, or always on the commodity level; and they cannot pass back and forth between the two levels without realizing what they are doing, as could the classical economists and their followers. Out of this technical characteristic of the statistical data we may expect to come a close scrutiny of the relations between our pecuniary institutions and our efficiency in producing and distributing goods. Such topics as the economic serviceability of advertising, the reactions of an unstable price level upon production, the effect of various systems of public regulation upon the services rendered by public utilities will be treated with incisive vigor as we become able to make the indispensable measurements. And investigations of this type will broaden out into a constructive criticism of that dominant complex of institutions known as the money economy—a constructive criticism which may guide the efforts of our children to make that marvelously flexible form of organization better fitted to their needs.

A bolder generalization may be hazarded. If our present beliefs are confirmed, that the human nature which men inherit remains substantially the same over millenniums, and that the changes in human life are due mainly to the evolution of culture, economists will concentrate their studies to an increasing degree upon economic institutions—the aspect of culture which concerns them. For whatever hopes we may cherish for the future of our race are bound up with the fortunes of the factor that certainly admits of change and perhaps admits of control. The quantitative workers will have a special predilection for institutional problems, because institutions standardize behavior, and thereby facilitate statistical procedure.

With the growing prominence of institutional problems, the fundamental issue of welfare is inextricably involved. What quantitative analysis promises here is to increase the range of objective criteria by which we judge welfare, and to study the variations of these criteria in relation to one another. The statistical worker is in no better position than any other student to specify what mankind should aim at; but in view of the multiplicity of our competing aims and the limitations of our social resources his help in measuring objective costs and objective results is indispensable to convert society's blind fumbling for happiness into an intelligent process of experimentation.

In speaking of experimentation, I do not forget the difficulty of making experiments in the social sciences. That difficulty seems to me almost insuperable, as long as we hold to the old conceptions of human nature. But the behavioristic concept promises to diminish this handicap under which economics and its sister sciences have labored. For we can try experiments upon group behavior. Indeed, we are already trying such experiments. We have experimental schools, in which the physical and social environments of the children are made to vary, with the aim of studying the relations between the stimuli offered by the schools and the learning response. So, too, we experiment with different systems of remunerating labor, different forms of publicity, different organizations for distributing products, different price policies, different methods of supervising public utilities, and the like.

Of course, these experiments upon group behavior lack the rigor of the experimenting done in physical laboratories. The limits within which human beings can be manipulated are narrow; the behavior processes under scrutiny cannot be isolated from complicating processes, except as one applies the method of partial correlation to statistical records. Hence the work of experimenting in the social sciences requires a technique different from that of the natural sciences. The experimenter must rely far more upon statistical considerations and precautions. The ideal of a single crucial experiment cannot be followed. The experiments must be repeated upon numerous individuals or groups; the varieties of reactions to the stimuli must be recorded and analyzed; the representative character of the samples must be known before generalizations can be established. This whole procedure may have more in common with the quantitative study of data drawn from common experience than with the procedure of the man who deals with electric currents passing through a vacuum tube. But whatever approaches are made toward controlling the conditions under which groups act will be eagerly seized upon and developed with results which we cannot yet foresee.

In collecting and analyzing such experimental data as they can obtain, the quantitative workers will find their finest, but most exacting, opportunities for developing statistical technique—opportunities even finer than are offered by the recurrent phenomena of business cycles. It is conceivable that the tentative experimenting of the present may develop into the most absorbing activity of economists in the future. If that does happen, the reflex influence upon economic theory will be more radical than any we can expect from the quantitative analysis of ordinary behavior records. The most dazzling developments of the future may lie in this direction; but they are hardly more than a rosy glow upon the eastern horizon.

So far my argument has run as follows: the increase of statistical data, the improvement of statistical technique, and the endowment of social research are enabling economists to make a larger use of quantitative analysis; in preparing for their work, the quantitative theorists usually find it necessary to formulate problems in a way different from that adopted by qualitative theorists; this technical necessity of restating problems promises to bring about radical changes in economic theory, in particular to make the treatment of behavior more objective, to emphasize the importance of institutions, and to promote the development of an experimental technique.

All this seems plausible as I reel it off; yet it runs counter to prevailing views. According to the classical concept of method, the business of the statistician is merely to verify conclusions established by deduction, and to discover disturbing causes that do not reveal themselves "to a reasoner engaged in the development of the more capital economic doctrines." Thus said Cairnes. And even now some of the most distinguished statistical economists hold that their function is not to recast economic theory, but to provide a statistical complement for it. Professor Henry L. Moore, whose reformulation of Marshall's problem of the relations between demand and price I have cited, has taken this position. What justification is there for a different opinion? Why should a freer use of quantitative analysis produce radical changes in economic theory?

I think there is a deeper-lying reason for my conclusion than is generally recognized. Our qualitative theory has followed the logic of Newtonian mechanics; our quantitative work rests on statistical conceptions. Between the mechanical type of theory and the statistical type of theory there are differences that will force changes in our fundamental conceptions as we shift our emphasis from one type to the other.

Let me expand this statement. In the hedonistic calculus which Jevons followed, man is placed under the governance of two sovereign masters, pain and pleasure, which play the same role in controlling human behavior that Newton's laws of motion play in controlling the behavior of the heavenly bodies. Dr. Marshall's conception of economic behavior as controlled by two opposing sets of motives is scarcely less mechanical in its logic. Indeed, any theorist who works by ascribing motives to men and arguing what they will do under guidance of these forces will produce a mechanical type of explanation.

Intermixed with speculation of this type in economics, there has usually been an element of broad observation upon average behavior. Quantitative work with statistics means the expansion and systematization of this element of observation. It has its counterpart in physics, introduced by Clerk-Maxwell, just as speculation about the force of motives has its counterpart in Newtonian mechanics. . . .

The difference between the mechanical and the statistical conceptions of nature has been clearly worked out in physics. The mechanical view involves the notions of sameness, of certainty. of invariant laws; the statistical view involves the notions of variety, of probability, of approximations. . . .

A close correspondence between the results based on speculation and the results based on statistical observation is not to be expected in economics, for three reasons. First, the cases summed up in our statistics seldom if ever approach in number the millions of millions of molecules, or atoms, or electrons of the physicist. Second, the units in economic aggregates are less similar than the molecules or atoms of a given element. Third, we cannot approach closely the isolation practices of the laboratory. For these reasons the elements of variety, of uncertainty, of imperfect approximation are more prominent in the statistical work of the social sciences than in the statistical work of the natural sciences. And because our statistical results are so marked by these imperfections they do not approach so closely to the results of our reasoning on the basis of assumed premises. Hence the development of statistical method may be expected to make more radical changes in economic than it makes in physical theory.

Of course, this lack of close agreement between the results attainable on the statistical and the mechanical views of nature in economics might be advanced as a reason for holding more strictly to the mechanical type of work. But that would be a wrong conclusion, provided our aim in economics is to understand the world of which we are a part. On this proviso, we seem bound to argue: the mechanical type of speculation works with the notions of sameness, of certainty, of invariant laws. In economics these notions do not fit the phenomena closely. Hence, we must put our ultimate trust in observation. And as fast as we can raise our observations to a scientific level we must drop the cruder, yet not wholly valueless, approximations attained by the mechanical type of work.

JOHN ROGERS COMMONS

(1862–1945)

John R. Commons was born in rural Ohio. He was educated at Oberlin College, where he helped earn his way by working as a typographer. Henry George's *Progress and Poverty* was the major influence in turning his interest from journalism to economics.

At Johns Hopkins he pursued graduate studies, and becoming a protégé of Richard T. Ely, subscribed enthusiastically to the socio-ethical approach to economics that Ely had learned in Germany. Unfortunately, however, he did not impress all of his other professors and failed in some of the courses presenting orthodox theory with which he could not agree.

In the years from 1890 to 1899 he taught successively at Wesleyan, Oberlin, the University of Indiana, and Syracuse University, and did a great deal of writing. His writings, however, offended several wealthy donors to Syracuse, who considered them anti-capitalist, and in 1899 Commons was forced out of academic life, although he was considered an excellent teacher by his students.

During the following five years he acted as investigator for the United States Industrial Commission, worked for the reformist National Civic Federation, and edited a special report of the United States Commissioner of Labor, learning at first hand much which later influenced his economic thinking.

In 1904 Richard Ely, his early sponsor, succeeded in creating a chair for Commons at the University of Wisconsin. This reentry into academic life occurred at the time when the reform movement led by Governor La Follette was at its height, providing a receptive atmosphere for Commons' ideas. In fact, he was actually able to help cast the economic life of Wisconsin into a more liberal, enlightened mold. Concretely, he helped set up the Wisconsin Industrial Commission and codified and improved social and labor legislation.

He was also director of the American Bureau of Industrial Research, which published a monumental eleven-volume *Documentary History of American Industrial Society* (1910–1911). This research supplied the basis for the classic *History of Labor in the United States* (four volumes, 1918–1932), on which Commons collaborated. He next wrote several other books in applied economics, primarily in the field of labor, and from time to time assisted in important government investigations, such as unemployment insurance and the famous Pittsburgh Plus basing-point case in 1923.

In 1924, at the age of sixty-two, Commons wrote his first theoretical book, *The Legal Foundations of Capitalism.* Here he combined Ely's historico-institutional approach with the distillation of thirty-five years of actual observation of economic processes. Here he also combined legal and economic reasoning in a way that had not been used before. The strands of his theory were even more fully developed in a later book, *Institutional Economics* (1934), which presents perhaps the most mature formulation of his concepts. The theme of this book is the influence of collective action on individual action. Conflicting interest groups, maintained Commons, need collective control, and this control should be exercised by the sovereign, the state. The most important state instrumentality controlling individual action is, he believed, the courts. People want security, but because of class conflict and the limiting institution of private property, security can be achieved only through the action of the state.

Commons next pointed out that the property "rights" recognized by society are relative and are evolved by the courts. As submerged groups, such as workers, organize and gain political power, the courts may strengthen their rights (the right of the workers to their jobs, for instance) until they become property rights in every recognized sense.

Commons classified all economic transactions as (1) bargaining, (2) managerial, or

(3) rationing, depending on the number of parties involved and on their relative bargaining positions. Commons defined custom as the repetition of acts and transactions by continuing groups (the persons in the groups may change). He concluded by saying that economic institutions are customs which arise out of the continuing transactions of going concerns. By "going concerns" Commons meant such units as the family, the corporation, the trade union, the church, and the state.

Commons' economics clearly bears little resemblance to traditional value theory. It deviates from, but complements considerably, the institutional economics of Veblen and Mitchell. In Commons' area of investigation, economics, law, politics, sociology, and history all merge into an integral set of concepts. This synthesis will be apparent to the student reading the following selections from *Institutional Economics.*

INSTITUTIONAL ECONOMICS *

Method

I. FROM CORPORATIONS TO GOING CONCERNS

In the year 1893 the people of the State of Indiana made a demand upon the legislature for an equalization of taxes upon the property of the great public utility corporations—such as railways running across the state—with the property of farmers, manufacturers, and business men. Property at that time meant corporeal property and incorporeal property, the physical goods of lands, buildings, railway tracks, stocks of inventories on hand; and the debts and shares of stock owned by individuals or corporations. The incorporeal property escaped the assessors, partly because concealed, partly because the *situs* for taxation purposes followed the domicile of the owner, which, in the case of corporations, was deemed to be the state under whose laws the charter was granted and in which the corporation was required to have its legal office. In response to the demand the legislature of Indiana changed the assessment of these corporations from the valuation of their physical property in Indiana to the total market value of their stocks and bonds, as bought and sold on the New York Stock Exchange, and then prorated that value to the State of Indiana in the proportion that the mileage in Indiana bore to the total mileage in all the states.

What happened was that a corporation which hitherto had only a legal existence in the state of its incorporation, because it was an invisible legal entity existing only in contemplation of law, now became an economic going concern existing in its transactions wherever it carried on business and gained thereby the net income which gave value to its stocks and bonds on the stock exchange.

The State of Ohio copied this legislation and it went from Ohio to the United States Supreme Court where it was sustained in 1897. The Court found that the sum total of all the corporeal property of the Adams Express Company in Ohio was only $23,400; but Ohio's share, according to

* The selection from John R. Commons, *Institutional Economics.* Copyright 1934 by The Macmillan Co., New York, and used with the publisher's permission.

mileage, of the total market value of all the stocks and bonds was $450,000, an intangible property about twelve times as valuable as the corporeal property. The Adams Express Company, instead of a corporation located in New York, becomes a going concern existing wherever it does business. . . .

The significant point, however, is that . . . the Court . . . disregarded the domicile of the corporation in the state of its creation, and passed from a legal corporation existing only in law to an economic going concern existing wherever it does business.

This transition in meaning, while it had been going on in many other cases, involved still another transition from the older economists' meaning of an "exchange," as a physical transfer of commodities, to the institutional meaning of a transaction as a legal transfer of ownership. It was ownership that fixed prices and permitted competition, and it was the transfer of ownership, instead of physical exchange, that determined whether competition was fair or discriminatory.

2. FROM EXCHANGE TO TRANSACTIONS

John Locke's meaning of Labor was his personification of Law, Economics, and Ethics. Labor, with him, meant justification of ownership as well as the existence of material things that were owned. This double meaning of Ownership and Material Wealth continued to be the meaning of the orthodox economists for two hundred years, and they therefore concealed the field of institutional economics. It was this concealed ownership side of the double meaning of Wealth that angered the heterodox economists from Marx and Proudhon in the middle of the Nineteenth Century to Sorel at the opening of the Twentieth Century. We shall distinguish the two meanings and yet discover a correlation of materials and ownership, not in Locke's personification of Labor, but in a *unit of economic activity*, a Transaction, and in that expectation of beneficial transactions which is a larger unit of economic activity, a Going Concern.

This falls in with an analogy to the recent correlation of the separate sciences of physics, chemistry, and astronomy, by the discovery of a unit of activity common to all of them. Roughly speaking, the former units in physics had been molecules, the units in chemistry had been atoms, the units in astronomy had been planets and stars. And the "energies" which made these units go were heat, electricity, chemical affinity, gravity. But nowadays the unit common to all of them is a unit of activity, the interaction of corpuscular wave-lengths, and the concept of "energy" disappears. Four hundred million million vibrations per second are the color red in the human mind, but they are that many wave-lengths in physics, chemistry, and astronomy.

This analogy roughly describes the problem of correlating law, economics, and ethics. It is the problem of discovering a unit of activity common to them.

In the field of economics the units had been, first, Locke's and Ricardo's material *commodities owned* and the *individuals* who owned the commodities, while the "energy" was human *labor*. Next, the units continued to be the same or similar physical commodities and their ownership, but the individuals became those who *consumed* commodities and the "energy" became the stimuli of *wants*, depending upon the quantity and kind of commodity wanted. The first was the objective side, the other the subjective side of the same relation between the individual and the forces of nature, the latter, however, in the form of materials, owned by the individuals. An "exchange," so called, was a labor process of delivering and receiving commodities, or a "subjective exchange-value." In any case, by analogy to the older physical science, these opposing energies of labor and want, magnified into "elasticities" of supply and demand, could be physically correlated by the materialistic metaphor of an automatic tendency towards equilibrium of commodities in exchange against each other, analogous to the atoms of water in the ocean, but personified as "seeking their level" at Ricardo's "margin of cultivation" or Menger's "marginal utility." This equilibrium was accomplished by the "neo-classicists," led by Alfred Marshall (1890).

There was no need of a further correlation with law or ethics—in fact these latter were necessarily excluded, because the relations on which the economic units were constructed were relations between man and nature, not between man and man. One was Ricardo's relation between human labor and the resistance of nature's forces; the other was Menger's relation between the quantity wanted of nature's forces and the quantity available. Neither statute law, nor ethics, nor custom, nor judicial decision had anything to do with either of these relationships; or rather, all these might be eliminated by assuming that ownership was identical with the materials owned, in order to construct a theory of pure economics based solely on the physical exchange of materials and services.

The latter was done. This identity of ownership and materials was accepted as a matter of custom, without investigation. It was assumed that all commodities were owned, but the ownership was assumed to be identical with the physical thing owned, and therefore was overlooked as something to be taken for granted. The theories were worked out as physical materials, omitting anything of property rights, because they were "natural."

The historical and ethical schools of economists, led by Roscher, Schmoller, and others, revolted against these eliminations of ownership. These schools, even in their culminating form of the "ideal typus" as proposed by Rickert and Max Weber, never were able to incorporate into what remained merely descriptions or subjective ideals of historical process, the economic principles derived from Ricardo and Menger. This, however, can be done if we discover a unit of activity common to law, economics, and ethics.

If the subject-matter of political economy is not only individuals and nature's forces, but is human beings getting their living out of each other by mutual transfers of property rights, then it is to law and ethics that we look for the critical turning points of this human activity.

The courts of law deal with human activity in its relation, not of man to nature, but to the *ownership* of nature by man. But they deal with this activity only at a certain point, the point of *conflict of interests* between plaintiff and defendant. But classical economic theory, based on relations of man to nature, had no conflict of interests in its units of investigation, since its units were *commodities* and *individuals* with ownership omitted. These ultimate units produced, in fact, along with the analogy of equilibrium, a *harmony* of interests rather than a *conflict* of interests. Hence the ultimate unit to be sought in the problem of correlating law, economics, and ethics is a unit of conflicting interests of ownership.

But this is not enough. The ultimate unit of activity must also be a unit of *mutually dependent interests.* The relation of man to man is one of interdependence as well as conflict.

Still further, this ultimate unit must be one which not only is continually *repeating* itself, with variations, but also one whose repetitions are expected by the participants to continue, in the future, substantially similar to what they are in the present and have been in the past. The unit must contain security of expectations. This kind of expectation we name *Order.*

This meaning of Order is derived from the fact that the future is wholly uncertain except as based upon reliable inferences drawn from experiences of the past; and also from the fact that it may properly be said that man lives in the future but acts in the present. For these reasons the unit of activity contains a factor that indicates anticipation, or, literally, the act of seizing beforehand the limiting or strategic factors upon whose present control it is expected the outcome of the future may also be more or less controlled, provided there is security of expectations. This is indeed the dominant characteristic of human activity, distinguishing it from all the physical sciences. We shall later separate it out abstractedly and give it the general name of *Futurity.* But the orderly expectations, assumed by all economists under the name of "security," which is a special case of the general principle of Futurity, we name, for our present purposes, simply Order.

Thus, the ultimate unit of activity, which correlates law, economics, and ethics, must contain in itself the three principles of *conflict, dependence,* and *order.* This unit is a Transaction. A transaction, with its participants, is the smallest unit of institutional economics. Transactions intervene between the production of labor, of the classical economists, and the pleasures of consumption, of the hedonic economists, simply because it is society that, by its rules of order, controls ownership of and access to the forces of nature. Transactions, as thus defined, are not the "exchange of commodities," in the physical sense of "delivery," they are the alienation and acquisition, between individuals, of the *rights* of future ownership of physical things, as determined by the collective working rules of society.

The *transfer of these rights* must therefore be negotiated between the parties concerned, according to the working rules of society, before labor can produce, or consumers can consume, or commodities be physically delivered to other persons.

When we analyze transactions, which are the transfers of ownership, we find that they resolve themselves into three types, which may be distinguished as Bargaining, Managerial, and Rationing transactions. These are functionally interdependent and together constitute the whole which we name a Going Concern. A going concern is a joint expectation of beneficial bargaining, managerial, and rationing transactions, kept together by "working rules" and by control of the changeable strategic or "limiting" factors which are expected to control the others. When the expectations cease then the concern quits going and production stops.

This going concern is itself a larger unit, and is analogous to that which in biology is Filmer's "organism," or in physics is Locke's "mechanism." But its components are not living cells, nor electrons, nor atoms—they are Transactions.

We shall here anticipate our subsequent investigational trials and errors and shall set up the conclusions of our historical research by constructing a formula of a bargaining transaction, and then distinguish it from the formulae of managerial and rationing transactions.

(*1*) *Bargaining Transactions.* By a study of the theories of economists, in the light of decisions of courts, the bargaining unit is found to consist of *four* parties, two buyers and two sellers, all of whom are treated legally as *equals* by the ruling authority that decides disputes. The resulting formula may be pictured in terms of the offers made by the participants, as follows, where the buyers offer to pay $100 and $90 respectively, for a commodity, and the sellers offer to accept $110 and $120 respectively.

FORMULA OF BARGAINING TRANSACTION—LEGAL EQUALS

B $100	B^1 $ 90
S $110	S^1 $120

On the other hand, managerial and rationing transactions are, in law and economics, the relation of a superior to an inferior. In the managerial transaction the superior is an individual or a hierarchy of individuals, giving orders which the inferiors must obey, such as the relations of foreman to worker, or sheriff to citizen, or manager to managed. But in the rationing transaction the superior is a collective superior or its official spokesman. These are of various kinds, such as a board of directors of a corporation, or a legislature, or a court of law, or an arbitration tribunal, or a communist or fascist government, or a cartel, or a trade union, or a taxing authority, which prorates among inferiors the burdens and benefits of the concern. The formula of a managerial or rationing transaction is therefore the picture of a relation between *two* parties instead of four, as follows:

Formula of Managerial and Rationing Transactions

Legal Superior
Legal Inferior

It should be kept in mind that the formula of a transaction is not a copy of nature or reality—it is merely a mental configuration of the least unit of economic theory—a unit of investigation by means of which reality may be understood.

Here it is first necessary to distinguish the double and even triple meaning of the word Exchange, already referred to as used by the early economists, which served to conceal the marketing process of bargaining from the labor process of managing, and from the authoritative process of rationing, as well as the legal from the economic process.

The concept of exchange had its historical origin in the precapitalistic period of markets and fairs. The merchant then was a peddler who carried his goods or coins to market and physically exchanged them with other merchants. Yet he really combined in himself two entirely different activities not made use of by the economists: the labor activity of physical delivery and physical acceptance of commodities, and the legal activity of alienation and acquisition of their ownership. The one was physical delivery of physical control over commodities or metallic money, the other was legal transfer of legal control. The one was an Exchange, the other a Transaction.

The difference is fundamental and was not incorporated in economic theory, because materials were not distinguished from their ownership. The *individual* does not transfer ownership. Only the state, or, in medieval times, the "market overt," by operation of law as interpreted by the courts, transfers ownership by reading intentions into the minds of participants in a transaction. The two kinds of transfer have been separated in capitalistic industry. Legal control is transferred at the centers of capitalism, like New York, London, or Paris, but physical control is transferred at the ends of the earth by laborers acting under the commands of those who have legal control. The transfer of legal control is the outcome of a Bargaining Transaction. The transportation of commodities and the delivery of physical control is a labor process of adding "place utility" to a material thing. This labor process, from the legal standpoint, we distinguish as Managerial Transactions.

The individualistic economists necessarily added to their meaning of Exchange the mutual grant of considerations. But this was treated, not objectively as alienation of ownership, but subjectively as a pleasure-pain choice between commodities; whereas, from the legal bargaining standpoint, it is the volitional negotiations of the persuasion or coercion between persons deemed to be legally equal and free, which terminate in reciprocal transfers of *legal control* of commodities and money by operation of existing law in view of the expectations of what the courts will do in case of dispute.

It was the latter meaning of an Exchange which the common-law judges of England, in the Sixteenth Century, recognized in their decisions of disputes between conflicting merchants, by taking over the bargaining customs of merchants on the markets and deciding disputes in conformity with those customs, in so far as they approved the custom. These customs, when taken over by the courts, became an Anglo-American law, technically known as the doctrines of *assumpsit* and *quantum meruit.*

Broadly interpreted these doctrines run as follows: Let it be inferred, in the ordinary course of trade according to the custom of merchants, that, when a person had acquired a commodity or money from another person, he did not intend robbery or theft or deceit, but intended to accept responsibility to pay for it or to deliver a commodity or service in exchange (*implied assumpsit*); and further, he did not intend, by economic coercion or physical duress, to overcome the will of the other person as to the terms of the transfer of ownership, but intended to pay or perform what was fair or reasonable (*quantum meruit*).

This inference of intention to accept responsibility and a moral duty to pay or perform was necessary because the courts were called upon, in case of a dispute, to create a legal duty by enforcing obedience of payment or performance implied in the negotiations. And this applied not only to deferred performance or payment, usually known as debt, but also to immediate performance or payment, usually known as a sale or cash transaction. It is these negotiations and intended alienation and acquisition of legal ownership, in consideration of payment or performance, that we name a Bargaining Transaction, leaving the physical "exchange" to the labor process, which we name physical delivery, enforced by the law of managerial transactions if necessary.

Parallel to these doctrines of *assumpsit* and *quantum meruit* the courts, in developing the law of freedom from duress, constructed an ethical standard of the "willing buyer and willing seller" by making inferences as to what was going on in the minds of participants. This willingness has been, since then, the standard set up for the decision of disputes arising from bargaining transactions, whether commodity bargains on the produce markets, wage bargains on the labor markets, stock and bond bargains on the stock exchange, interest bargains on the money markets, or rent and land bargains on the real estate markets. In all of these bargains the doctrines of *assumpsit, quantum meruit,* and *duress* have had an explicit or implied influence in questions of transfer of ownership.

How, then, shall the economist construct a unit of activity, the bargaining transaction, which shall fit this evolution of the common law, derived, as it is, from thousands of decisions of courts? We have found that economists had already constructed the formula as above, applicable to markets. The bargaining consists of four parties, two buyers and two sellers, each, however, governed by the past and expected decisions of the courts in case of dispute, if a conflict of interests reaches that crisis. Out of a universal formula which may thus be constructed so as to include these four participants offering to transfer ownership, and acting in line with customs approved in legal decisions, may be derived four economic and legal relations between man and man, so intimately bound together that a change in one of them will change the magnitudes of one or more of the other three. They are the issues derived from a fourfold conflict of interests latent in every bargaining transaction, and the decisions of the American courts on economic disputes are readily classified in these four directions. Each decision has for its object the establishment of working rules as precedents which shall bring expectation of mutuality and order out of the conflict of interests. All of these relate to ownership of materials and not to the materials.

(1) The first issue is, Equal or Unequal Opportunity, which is the legal doctrine of Reasonable and Unreasonable Discrimination. Each buyer is choosing between the best two sellers, and each seller is choosing between the best two buyers. If a seller, for example a railroad company, or telegraph company, or steel corporation, charges a higher price to one buyer and therefore a lower price to that buyer's competitor, for exactly similar service, then the first buyer, under modern conditions of narrow margins of profit, is unreasonably discriminated against, and eventually may be bankrupted. But if there is good ground for the discrimination, such as a difference in quantity, cost, or quality, then the discrimination is reasonable and therefore lawful. The same doctrine appears in many cases of labor arbitration and commercial arbitration.

(2) Another issue, inseparable from the first, is that of Fair or Unfair Competition. The two buyers are competitors and the two sellers are competitors, and may use unfair methods in their competition. The decisions on unfair competition have built up, during three hundred years, the modern asset of good-will, the biggest asset of modern business.

(3) The third issue, inseparable from the other two, is that of Reasonable or Unreasonable Price or Value. One of the two buyers will buy from one of the two sellers. The price will depend on the three economic conditions, Opportunity for Choice, Competition of buyer with buyer and seller with seller, and Equality or Inequality of Bargaining Power between the actual buyer and the actual seller, who are nevertheless equals in law. This reasonable price is gradually constructed, in the minds of successive courts, on the three prerequisites of Equal Opportunity, Fair Competition, and Equality of Bargaining Power.

(4) Finally, in the American decisions appears the dominant issue of Due Process of Law. It is this issue which we name a "working rule," which regulates individual transactions. The Supreme Court of the United States has acquired authority to overrule state legislatures, the Federal Congress, and all executives, in all cases where these are deemed by the Court to deprive individuals or corporations of property or liberty "without due process of law." Due process of law is the working rule of the Supreme Court for the time being. It changes with changes in custom

and class dominance, or with changes in judges, or with changes in the opinions of judges, or with changes in the customary meanings of property and liberty. If a state legislature or the Federal Congress, or a lower court, or an executive, deprives any of the four participants in a transaction of his equal choice of opportunities, or his liberty of competition, or his bargaining power in fixing a price, that act of deprivation is a "taking" of both his property and his liberty. If the deprivation cannot be justified to the satisfaction of the Court, then it is a deprivation of property and liberty *without* due process of law, and is therefore unconstitutional and void, and will be enjoined.

Thus, if the formula of a bargaining transaction is properly constructed in the minds of both the economists and the lawyers, with its four participants ruled by the Supreme Court, with its essential attributes of conflict, dependence, and order (due process of law)—just as the formula of the atom or star is being reconstructed in physics, chemistry, and astronomy, with its constituents of protons, electrons, radio-activity, etc.—so also a unit of activity is constructed, common to law, economics, politics, and social ethics.

(2) *Managerial Transactions.* But there are two other, yet inseparable, units of activity: the Managerial and Rationing Transactions, each exhibiting a legal, economic, and ethical correlation.

A managerial transaction grows out of a relation between two persons instead of four. While the habitual assumption back of the decisions in bargaining transactions is that of equality of willing buyers and willing sellers, the assumption back of managerial transactions is that of superior and inferior. One person is a legal superior who has legal right to issue commands. The other is a legal inferior who, while the relation lasts, is bound by the legal duty of obedience. It is the relation of foreman and worker, sheriff and citizen, manager and managed, master and servant, owner and slave. The superior gives orders, the inferior must obey.

From the economic standpoint the managerial transaction is the one whose purpose is the production of wealth, including what we have already named as the physical meaning of Exchange considered as the adding of "place utilities" by transportation and delivery of commodities; whereas the bargaining transaction has for its purpose the distribution of wealth and the inducements to produce and deliver wealth. The universal principle of bargaining transactions is scarcity, while that of managerial transactions is efficiency.

Psychologically and ethically, also, the managerial transaction differs from the bargaining transaction. The ethical psychology, or what we name negotiational psychology of bargaining transactions is that of *persuasion or coercion,* depending on opportunity, competition, and bargaining power; because the parties, although deemed to be legally equal, may be economically unequal (coercion) or economically equal (persuasion). The negotiational psychology of managerial transactions is *command and obedience,* because one of the parties is both legally and economically inferior.

This managerial transaction, in the case of labor, is inseparable from, but distinguishable from, the bargaining transaction. As a bargainer, the modern wage-earner is deemed to be the legal *equal* of his employer, induced to enter the transaction by persuasion or coercion; but once he is permitted to enter the *place of employment* he becomes legally *inferior,* induced by commands which he is required to obey. The distinction is clear if the two sets of terms are distinguished as the bargaining terms of employer and employee, or rather of owner and wage-earner, and the managerial terms of foreman or superintendent, and workman.

Here again is a double meaning of the historic word "exchange," based on failure to make use of the distinction between bargaining and managing. The proprietor, in modern industry, has two representatives, the agent and the foreman, often combined in one person. The agent is one whose acts are deemed legally to bind his principal, the employer, on the doctrine of Agency, which began long before the doctrines of *assumpsit* and *quantum meruit* but had the same underlying principle of implying an intention to transfer the ownership of property. The foreman is an agent for certain important purposes, such as liability of the employer for accidents or accepting an employee's output, where his behavior binds the employer to an assumed debt. He is, as such, an agent, but he is also only another employee placed in charge of the technological process. The distinction has been made clear by the modern differentiation of the "employment department" from the "production department." The employment department is governed by the law of principal and agent; the production department by the law of manager and managed.

Historically the failure of economists to distinguish, in their theories, between agent and employee traces back to the double meaning—legal and technological—of the terms employer and employee, master and servant, owner and slave. But this modern differentiation of two departments gives us the clue for going back and making the historical difference of meaning.

Apparently, therefore, no place was left, in the traditional economic meaning of the word "exchange," for this institutional distinction. Hence the word "exchange" is now found to have had a third meaning—the "exchange" of the laborer's product with a foreman, which is both a physical delivery under order and a transfer of ownership by the laborer of his product to the employer, acting through the employer's agent, in consideration of the transfer of ownership of money by the proprietor, or his agent, to the laborer. The latter transfer of ownership is a detail of the bargaining transaction, with its doctrine of persuasion or coercion, and the laborer is a wage-earner. The former is the managerial transaction of command and obedience, and the laborer is just a bundle of the mechanical labor-power of Ricardo and Marx.

Recent economic theory, since the incoming of "scientific management," has furnished two pairs of terms and two units of measurement which permit the above-mentioned double meaning of "exchange" to be clearly distinguished. The units of measurement are the man-hour and the dollar. The pairs of terms are input-output and outgo-income. Scientific management has restored the labor-theory of Ricardo and Marx, but under the name of Efficiency. The ratio of output per hour (physical use-values) to input per hour (average labor) is the measure of efficiency. This is not an "exchange" at all—between the worker and the foreman—it is the physical process of overcoming the resistance of nature under the supervision of management. The unit of measurement of efficiency is the man-hour.

But the unit of measurement in the bargaining transaction is the dollar. It measures the ratio of outgo to income. The outgo is the alienation of ownership. The income is the acquisition of ownership. The dollar, then, is the measure of relative scarcities in bargaining transactions, while the man-hour is the measure of relative efficiencies in managerial transactions.

There are many cases at common law setting down the rights and duties of these managerial transactions, distinguished from bargaining transactions. They may be brought under the more general rule of the right of an owner to control the behavior of those who enter upon his premises, either as customers, visitors, trespassers, or employees. Hence, in the case of employees, the managerial transaction consists of the superior and the inferior, each governed by the law of command and obedience that has been created by the common-law method of making new law by deciding disputes which arise out of managerial transactions.

The managerial transaction has come to the front in recent years out of the investigations of scientific management. It involves, like the bargaining transaction, a certain amount of negotiation, even though, in law it is based solely upon the will of the superior. This inclusion of negotiation arises mainly from the modern freedom of labor, with its liberty of the laborer to quit without giving reason. Under such an institutional set-up, it is inevitable that something that may look like bargaining comes to the front in managerial transactions. But it is not bargaining—it is managing, though it is an important phase in the negotiations of the bargaining transaction which accompany it. As it is stated figuratively by an eminent manager of a great corporation, "We never give an order; we sell the idea to those who must carry it out." And Mr. Henry S. Dennison, from his own managing experience, has given the most careful analysis of the up-to-date managerial transaction, under the title, "job analysis of managing." His own summary gives an adequate idea of the most recent advance of scientific management in the meaning of managerial transactions.

JOB ANALYSIS OF MANAGING

Understanding	*Observing* (Watching the operation, supervising, includes selecting what to observe and method of recording, mental or physical.) *Evaluating* (Interpreting the observed facts; relating them to other facts and to policies; determining relative significance.)
Devising	*Conceiving* (Imagining possibilities—goals.) *Analyzing* (Analyzing goal and possibilities and relating observed and evaluated facts thereto.) *Contriving* (Determining methods, means, incentives, operatives.)
Persuading	*Directing* (Giving orders—in absolute strictness not managing, but operating.) *Teaching* (Establishing the necessary understanding of goals, means, methods, and incentives.) *Inducing* (Inspiring—"instructing the desires"; the emotional partner to teaching.)

(*3*) *Rationing Transactions.* Finally, Rationing Transactions differ from Bargaining and Managing Transactions in that they are the negotiations of reaching an agreement among several participants who have authority to apportion the benefits and burdens to members of a joint enterprise. A borderline case is a partnership transaction as to sharing the future burdens and benefits of a joint undertaking. A little more explicit is the activity of a board of directors of a corporation in making up its budget for the ensuing year. Quite similar, and more distinctive, is the activity of members of a legislative body in apportioning taxes or agreeing on a protective tariff—known as "log-rolling" in America. The so-called "collective bargaining," or "trade agreement," is a rationing transaction between an association of employers and an association of employees, or between any association of buyers and an association of sellers. Dictatorship and all associations for control of output, like cartels, are a series of rationing transactions. A judicial decision of an economic dispute is a rationing of a certain quantity of the national wealth, or equivalent purchasing power, to one person by taking it forcibly from another person. In these cases there is no bargaining, for that would be bribery, and no managing which is left to subordinate executives. Here is simply that which is sometimes named "policy-shaping," sometimes named "justice," but which, when reduced to economic quantities, is the rationing of wealth or purchasing power, not by parties deemed equal, but by an authority superior to them in law.

We can distinguish two kinds of rationing, output-rationing and price-rationing. Fixing the quantities apportioned to participants without fixing the prices is output-rationing, but fixing the prices and leaving the quantities to the will of the buyer or seller is price-rationing. Soviet Russia and many cartels ration the output, but Soviet Russia also, in many of its "state trusts," like the post-office, fixes prices and leaves to individuals the decision as to quantities. The great field of taxation is a price-rationing, by charging to taxpayers the cost of public services, such as education or highways, without any bargaining by the taxpayer or any regard to the individual benefits he receives from the public services rendered.

These three units of activity exhaust all the activities of the science of economics. Bargaining transactions *transfer ownership* of wealth by voluntary agreement between legal equals. Managerial transactions *create wealth* by commands of legal superiors. Rationing transactions apportion the burdens and benefits of wealth creation by the *dictation* of legal superiors. Since they are units of social activity among equals, or between superiors and inferiors, they are ethical in character as well as legal and economic.

(*4*) *Institutions.* These three types of transactions are brought together in a larger unit of economic investigation, which, in British and American practice, is named a Going Concern. It is these going concerns, with the working rules that keep them agoing, all the way from the family, the corporation, the trade union, the trade association, up to the state itself, that we name Institutions. The passive concept is a "group"; the active is a "going concern."

The difficulty in defining a field for the so-called Institutional Economics is the uncertainty of meaning of the word institution. Sometimes an institution seems to be analogous to a building, a sort of framework of laws and regulations, within which individuals act like inmates. Sometimes it seems to mean the "behavior" of the inmates themselves. Sometimes anything additional to or critical of the classical or hedonic economics is deemed to be institutional. Sometimes anything that is "dynamic" instead of "static," or a "process" instead of commodities, or activity instead of feelings, or management instead of equilibrium, or control instead of laissez-faire, seems to be institutional economics.

All of these notions are doubtless involved in institutional economics, but they may be said to be metaphors or descriptions, whereas a *science* of economic behavior requires analysis into principles—which are similarities of cause, effect, or purpose—and a synthesis in a unified system of principles. And institutional economics, furthermore, cannot separate itself from the marvellous discoveries and insight of the pioneer classical and psychological economists. It should incorporate, however, in addition, the equally important discoveries of the communistic, anarchistic, syndicalistic, fascistic, coöperative, and unionistic economists. Doubtless it is the effort to cover by enumeration all of these uncoördinated activities that gives to the name institutional economics that reputation of a miscellaneous, nondescript, yet merely descriptive character, similar to that which has long since relegated from economics the early crude Historical School.

If we endeavor to find a universal principle, common to all behavior known as institutional, we may define an institution as Collective Action in Control of Individual Action.

Collective action ranges all the way from unorganized Custom to the many organized Going Concerns, such as the family, the corporation, the holding company, the trade association, the trade union, the Federal Reserve System, the "group of affiliated interests," the State. The principle common to all of them is more or less control of individual action by collective action.

This control of the acts of one individual always results in, and is intended to result in, a benefit to other individuals. If it be the enforcement of a contract, then the debt is exactly equal to the credit created for the benefit of the other person. A debt is a duty capable of being enforced collectively, while a credit is an equivalent right created by creating the duty. The resulting social relation is an Economic Status, consisting of the expectations towards which each party is directing his economic behavior. On the debt and duty side it is the status of Conformity to collective action. On the credit and right side it is a status of Security created by the expectation of said Conformity. This is known as "incorporeal" property.

Or, the collective control takes the form of a *tabu* or prohibition of certain acts, such as interference, infringement, trespass, and this prohibition creates an economic status of Liberty for the person thus made immune. But the liberty of one person may be accompanied by prospective benefit or damage to a correlative person, and the economic status thus created is Exposure to the Liberty of the other. An employer is exposed to the liberty of the employee to work or quit, and the employee is exposed to the liberty of the employer to hire or fire. This exposure-liberty relation is coming to be distinguished as "intangible" property, such as the good-will of a business, franchises to do business, patents, trademarks, and so on in great variety.

The working rules which determine for individuals the limits of these correlative and reciprocal economic relationships may be laid down and enforced by a corporation, or a cartel, or a holding company, or a cooperative association, or a trade union, or an employers' association, or a trade association, or a joint trade agreement of two associations, or a stock exchange or board of trade, or a political party, or the state itself through the United States Supreme Court in the American system. Indeed, these economic collective acts of private concerns are at times more powerful than the collective action of the political concern, the State.

Stated in the language of ethics and law, to be developed below, all collective acts establish social relations of right, duty, no right, and no duty. Stated in the language of individual behavior, what they require is performance, avoidance, forbearance by individuals. Stated in the language of the resulting economic status of individuals, what they provide is Security, Conformity, Liberty, and Exposure. Stated in language of cause, effect, or purpose, the common principles running through all economic behavior as a limiting and complementary interdependent relationship are Scarcity, Efficiency, Futurity, the Working Rules of collective action, and Sovereignty. Stated in language of the operation of working rules on individual action they are expressed by the auxiliary verbs of what the individual can, cannot, must, must not, may, or may not *do*. He "can" or "cannot," because collective action will or will not come to his aid. He "must" or "must not," because collective action will compel him. He "may," because collective action will permit him and protect him. He "may not," because collective action will prevent him.

It is because of these behavioristic auxiliary verbs that the familiar term "working rules" is appropriate to indicate the universal principle of cause, effect, or purpose, common to all collective action. Working rules are continually changing in the history of an institution, including the state and all private associations, and they differ for different institutions. They are sometimes known as *maxims* of conduct. Adam Smith names them *canons* of taxation, and the Supreme Court names them the *Rule of Reason,* or *Due Process of Law*. But, whatever their differences and different names, they have this similarity, that they indicate what individuals can, must, or may, do or not do, enforced by Collective Sanctions.

Analysis of these collective sanctions furnishes that correlation of economics, jurisprudence, and ethics, which is prerequisite to a theory of institutional economics. David Hume found the unity of these social sciences in the principle of scarcity and the resulting conflict of interests. Adam Smith isolated economics on the assumptions of divine providence, earthly abundance, and the resulting harmony of interests. Institutional economics goes back to Hume. Taking our cue from Hume and the modern rise of such a term as "business ethics," ethics deals with the rules of conduct arising from conflict of interests and enforced by the *moral* sanctions of collective opinion. Economics deals with the same rules of conduct enforced by the collective sanctions of economic *gain* or *loss*. Jurisprudence deals with the same rules enforced by the organized sanctions of *physical force*. Institutional economics is continually dealing with the relative merits of these three types of sanctions.

From this universal principle of collective action in control of individual action by different kinds of sanctions arise the ethical and legal relations of rights, duties, no-rights, no-duties, and the economic relations not only of Security, Conformity, Liberty, and Exposure, but also of Assets and Liabilities. In fact, it is from the field of corporation finance, with its changeable assets and liabilities, rather than from the field of individual wants and labor, or pains and pleasures, or wealth and happiness, or utility and disutility, that institutional economics derives a large part of its data and methodology. Institutional economics is concerned with the Assets and Liabilities of Concerns contrasted with Adam Smith's Wealth of Nations. Between nations it is the Credits and Debits in the balance of international payments.

Collective action is even more universal in the unorganized form of Custom than it is in the organized form of Concerns. Yet even a going concern is also a Custom. Custom has not given way to free contract and competition, as was asserted by Sir Henry Maine. Customs have merely changed with changes in economic conditions, and they may today be so mandatory that even a dictator cannot overrule them. The business man who refuses or is unable to make use of the modern customs of the credit system, by refusing to accept or issue checks on solvent banks, although the checks are merely private arrangements and not legal tender, simply cannot continue in business by carrying on transactions. These instruments are customary tender, instead of legal tender, backed by the powerful sanctions of profit, loss, and competition, which compel conformity. Other mandatory customs might be mentioned, such as coming to work at seven o'clock and quitting at six, or the customary standards of living.

But these customary standards are always changing; they lack precision, and therefore give rise to disputes over conflicts of interest. If such disputes arise, then the officers of an organized concern, such as a credit association, the manager of a corporation, a stock exchange, a board of trade, a commercial or labor arbitrator, or finally, the courts of law up to the Supreme Court of the United States, reduce the custom to precision and add an organized legal or economic sanction.

This is done through the Common-Law Method of Making Law by the Decision of Disputes. The decisions, by becoming precedents, become the working rules, for the time being, of the particular organized concern. The historic "common law" of Anglo-American jurisprudence is only a special case of the universal principle common to all concerns that survive, of making new law by deciding conflicts of interest, thus giving greater precision and organized compulsion to the unorganized working rules of custom or ethics. The common-law *method* is universal in all collective action, but the technical "common law" of the English and American lawyers is a body of decisions going back to feudal times. In short, the common-law *method,* or way of acting, is itself a custom, with variabilities, like other customs. It is the way in which collective action of all going concerns acts on individual action in time of conflict. It differs from statutory law in that it is judge-made law at the time of decision of disputes.

Collective Action is more than *control* of individual action—it is, by the very act of control, as indicated by the auxiliary verbs, a *liberation* of individual action from coercion, duress, discrimination, or unfair competition, by means of restraints placed on other individuals.

And Collective Action is more than restraint and liberation of individual action—it is *expansion* of the will of the individual far beyond what he can do by his own puny acts. The head of a great corporation gives orders which execute his will at the ends of the earth.

Since liberation and expansion for some persons consist in restraint, for their benefit, of other persons, and while the short definition of an institution is collective action in control of individual action, the derived definition is: collective action in restraint, liberation, and expansion of individual action.

These individual actions are really *trans*-actions—that is, actions between individuals—as well as individual behavior. It is this shift from commodities, individuals, and exchanges to transactions and working rules of collective action that marks the transition from the classical and hedonic schools to the institutional schools of economic thinking. The shift is a change in the ultimate unit of economic investigation, from commodities and individuals to transactions between individuals.

If it be considered that, after all, it is the individual who is important, then the individual with whom we are dealing is the Institutionalized Mind. Individuals begin as babies. They learn the custom of language, of coöperation with other individuals, of working towards common ends, of negotiations to eliminate conflicts of interest, of subordination to the working rules of the many concerns of which they are members. They meet each other, not as physiological bodies moved by glands, nor as "globules of desire" moved by pain and pleasure, similar to the forces of physical and animal nature, but as prepared more or less by habit, induced by the pressure of custom, to engage in those highly artificial transactions created by the collective human will. They are not found in physics, or biology, or subjective psychology, or in the German Gestalt psychology, but are found where conflict, interdependence, and order among human beings are preliminary to getting a living. Instead of individuals the participants are citizens of a going concern. Instead of forces of nature they are forces of human nature. Instead of the mechanical uniformities of desire of the hedonistic economists, they are highly variable personalities. Instead of isolated individuals in a state of nature they are always participants in transactions, members of a concern in which they come and go, citizens of an institution that lived before them and will live after them. . . .

Reasonable Value

. . . The one great advantage of the competitive system is that it shifts bankruptcy to individuals, whereas bankruptcy of a coöperative bankrupts the whole or a part of an entire social class. If an individual business concern fails, then its competitors absorb its customers, and business as a whole goes on. But if a coöperative fails, then all of its members fail, and, worst of all, they lose confidence in each other and even in their government.

Collective bargaining has its difficulties, as well as coöperation. But it does this much. It lets the business man keep the chances of bankruptcy. There is one field of agricultural concerted action where it seems to be successful. The liquid milk farmers do not take over the marketing process by coöperative marketing. They only make trade agreements, as to prices and practices, with the middlemen who continue to do the marketing. They do not displace Capitalism, nor do they arbitrarily set their prices by agricultural dictatorship. They bargain collectively, and resort to arbitration, if necessary. Arbitration is rationing by a judiciary in individual or collective disputes.

Thus arbitration is a subdivision of the fifth kind of Rationing Transaction, which we name Judicial Decision. When an arbitrator or judge decides a dispute between plaintiff and defendant, he transfers from one person to another person an amount of money or goods, present or expected. He does this, not by log-rolling, because he is superior over the litigants; nor by dictatorship, because he is himself bound by custom, precedent, or by statute in the form of a constitution, a by-law or a trade agreement; not by coöperation, because he acts with authority; not by collective bargaining, though he listens to the pleadings and arguments of the representatives of the parties; and not by individual bargaining because this would be bribery. He does it by the judicial procedure of rendering a mere opinion, after weighing all the facts and arguments.

JOHN ATKINSON HOBSON

(1858–1940)

Hobson was born in Derbyshire of respectable middle-class parents and was educated in the classics at Oxford. Here he acquired an interest in economics and social reform. For this last quarter of the nineteenth century was a period of social ferment, a provocative era during which philosophers and historians, like John Ruskin and Arnold Toynbee, were questioning the validity of the classical doctrines. Part and parcel of this increasing concern with the social evils which had followed industrialism was the agitation aroused by the great increase in individual poverty at the same time that there was a great increase in national wealth. There was therefore a widespread growth of the feeling that social justice was not compatible with laissez-faire economics, and at Oxford this feeling was rampant.

After graduation, Hobson was instructor in the classics successively at several famous public schools, but he found increasingly that the work was unsuitable for his temperament and talents. He then tried to obtain a teaching post in economics at a university, but his views were most unacceptable to the academic powers. He was therefore forced to earn his living as a lecturer and writer, and since he had no formal training in economics, his lecturing and writing tended toward the popular, rather than the intellectual, level of exposition. This popular quality remains a major flaw in his works as far as professional economists are concerned. So great, however, were Hobson's intelligence and acumen that many of his books turned out to be genuine contributions to economic thought, in spite of his lack of formal training in analysis and in spite of the fact that, as a popular writer, he had to spread himself over too wide a range of subjects.

His first book, *The Physiology of Industry* (1889), written with A. F. Mummery, is a case in point. Here he contended that depression could be caused by general gluts due to the absence of effective demand. This was the argument that had been advanced against Ricardo's and Say's belief that a *general* glut or oversupply is impossible. Hobson's thesis was considered so heretical by the academic fraternity in 1889 that he was classed as unsound and not fit for a teaching post. Not until he published his *Evolution of Modern Capitalism* in 1894 was he partially restored to good standing.

For his part, Hobson disagreed vehemently with the premises and methods of orthodox political economy, although he conceded the logic of academic economists. Their major fault, he declared, was their failure to grapple with important social and economic problems, and he thereupon set out to evolve his own system. He was, however, no Marxist, and his economics was typical of middle-class, rather than proletarian, reformers: the aim was to change society for the better without revolution. Also, Hobson considered economics to be an organic part of human life and believed that the human, as well as the monetary, costs had to be considered in economic analysis. He argued, for instance, that fatigue and monotony were as important costs to humanity as a whole as rent, raw materials, and labor were to the entrepreneur. In the creation of wealth, "illth" (human cost) is also created, said Hobson. These ideas are best set forth and summarized by Hobson himself in his most important book, *Work and Wealth: A Human Valuation* (1914). Since Hobson wrote on a great variety of subjects, it is impossible to discuss all his books in this brief compass. Three important books, in addition to those noted above, are his *The Economics of Distribution* (1900), *Taxation in the New State* (1920), and *The Economics of Unemployment* (1922). The following selections from *Work and Wealth* and *The Physiology of Industry* give the gist of Hobson's point of view.

WORK AND WEALTH *

Preface

The goods and services that constitute our national income are valued severally and collectively with a fair amount of accuracy in terms of money. For a gold standard, though by no means perfect for the work of monetary measurement, is stable and has a single definite meaning to all men. By means of it we can estimate the rates of growth or decline in our industry, as an aggregate or in its several departments, and the quantities of output and consumption of the various products. We can compare the growth of our national wealth with that of other nations.

But how far can these measurements of concrete wealth furnish reliable information regarding the vital values, the human welfare, which all economic processes are designed to yield? Though it will be generally admitted that every increase of economic wealth is in some measure conducive to welfare, every decrease to illfare, nobody will pretend even approximately to declare what that measure is, or to lay down any explicit rules relating wealth to welfare, either for an individual or a nation. Indeed, even the general assumption that every growth of wealth enhances welfare cannot be admitted without qualification. An injurious excess of income is possible for an individual, perhaps for a nation, and the national welfare which an increased volume of wealth seems capable of yielding might be more than cancelled by a distribution which bestowed upon a few an increased share of the larger wealth, or by an aggravation of the toil of the producers.

Such obvious considerations drive us to seek some intelligible and consistent method of human valuation for economic goods and processes. To find a standard of human welfare as stable and as generally acceptable as the monetary standard is manifestly impossible. Indeed, the difficulties attending any sort of calculus of vital values might appear insuperable, were it not for one reflection. Every statesman, social reformer, philanthropist, every public-spirited citizen, does possess and apply to the conduct of affairs some such standard or criterion as we are seeking. Some notion or idea, more or less clear and explicit, of the general welfare, crossed and blurred no doubt by other interests and passions, is an operative and directive influence in his policy. Moreover, though idiosyncrasies will everywhere affect this operative ideal, there will be found among persons of widely different minds and dispositions a substantial body of agreement in their meaning of human welfare. The common social environment partly evokes, partly imposes, this agreement. In fact, all cooperative work for social progress implies the existence of some such standard as we are seeking. The complex image of human values which it contains is always slowly changing, and varies somewhat among different sorts and conditions of men. But for the interpretation of economic goods

* From *Work and Wealth: A Human Valuation* (New York, The Macmillan Co., 1914).

and processes it has, at any time, a real validity. For it is anchored to certain solid foundations of human nature, the needs and functions to which, alike in the individual and in the society, we give the term 'organic.'

Only by considering the organic nature of man and of human society can we trace an intelligible order in the evolution of industry. The wants of man, and therefore the economic operations serving them must be treated as organic processes. This term, borrowed from biology, must be extended so as to cover the entire physical and spiritual structure of human society, for no other term is so well fitted to describe the nature of the federal unity which society presents. The standard of values thus set up is the current estimate of 'organic welfare.'

The justification of these terms and of this mode of human valuation is to be found in their application to the task before us. These tools will be found to do the work better than any others that are available.

In seeking to translate economic values into human by reference to such a standard of organic welfare, I take as the aptest material for experiment the aggregate of goods and services that constitute the real income of the British nation. In order to reduce that income to terms of human welfare, I first examine separately the economic costs of production and the economic utilities of consumption which meet in this concrete wealth, analysing them into human cost and human utility, the debit and credit sides of the account of welfare. Analysis of the productive processes will, of course, disclose the fact that not all 'economic' costs have human costs attached to them, but that human utilities of varying value inhere in many sorts of productive work. Surveying the different orders of productive energy, from the finest arts to the lowest modes of routine toil, we discover that any two bodies of economic wealth, possessing the same pecuniary value, may differ enormously in the quantity of human cost they carry. For that cost will depend upon the nature of the work, the nature of the workers, and the distribution of the work among the workers. This line of enquiry opens out, in form at any rate, a complete criticism of current English industry, from the humanist standpoint. A similar analysis applied on the consumption side resolves the economic utility of the goods and services into human utility. Here again out of economic utilities much human cost emerges, just as out of economic costs much human utility. Equal quantities of income yield in their consumption widely diverse quantities of human utility or welfare.

Piecing together the two sides of our enquiry into the production and consumption of the income, we perceive, as might be expected, that a sound human economy conforms to the organic law of distribution, 'from each according to his power, to each according to his needs,' and that, precisely so far as the current processes of economic distribution of work and of its product contravene this organic law, waste accrues and illfare displaces welfare. The economic distinction between costs and unearned surplus furnishes in effect a faithful measure of the extent and forms of divergence between the economic and the human 'law' of distribution. For when this surplus income is traced, backward to the human costs involved in its production, forward to the human injuries inflicted by the excessive and bad consumption it sustains, it is seen to be the direct efficient cause of all the human defects in our economic system. Growing in magnitude with the development of the modern arts of industry and commerce, it is the concrete embodiment of the social-economic problem. The absorption and utilisation of the surplus for the betterment of the working-classes and the enrichment of public life are essential conditions for the humanisation of industry.

The first half of the book is occupied with the general exposition and illustration of this method of human valuation. The second part applies the humanist principles thus established, to the discussion of some of the great practical issues of social-economic reconstruction in the fields of business and politics. The medley of overlapping conflicts between capital and labour, producer and consumer, competition and combination, the individual and society, is sifted so as to discover lines of industrial reformation based upon a conception of organic harmony. The reconstruction of the business, so as adequately to represent in its operation the respective interests of capital, ability, labour and the consumer, is seen to be the first desideratum of reform. Here, as in the wider oppositions between business and business, trade and trade, and nation and nation (misconceived as economic units), the more rational standpoint of a humanist valuation suggests modes of reconcilement following an evolution of economic structure in which the corporate or coöperative spirit finds clearer and stronger expression. The most debated question, how far ordinary human nature can yield economic motives to social service strong and reliable enough to enable society to dispense with some of the incentives to competitive greed, hitherto deemed indispensable supports to industry, is discussed in several of the later chapters. The practicable limits of industrial reformation are found to depend upon the reality and importance assigned to 'the social will' as a power operative for industrial purposes, in other words upon the strength of the spiritual unity of society. A final chapter is given to a discussion of the limitations of the scientific and quantitative methods in the interpretation and direction of social-economic life. It is contended that the art of social as of individual conduct must always defy exact scientific guidance, the methods of science being incompetent closely to predict or direct the creative element in organic processes.

The processes of human valuation and judgment, therefore, whether applied to industry or to other activities and achievements, must ultimately belong to the art rather than to the science of society, the statesman and the citizen absorbing and assimilating the history of the past which science presents in its facts and laws, but using his free constructive faculty to make the history of the future. The failures of the individual statesman or citizen in the performance of this artistic work are due to the fact that a larger artist, whose performance the most enlightened individual can but slightly apprehend, viz. society itself, takes an over-ruling part in the process.

This brief presentation of the argument, dwelling unavoidably upon intellectual method, may possibly have failed to convey the intensely practical purpose which I have kept in mind throughout the preparation of the book. That purpose is to present a full and formal exposure of the inhumanity and vital waste of modern industry by the close application of the best-approved formulas of individual and social welfare, and to indicate the most hopeful measures of remedy for a society sufficiently intelligent, courageous and self-governing to apply them.

Such a work evidently presents a large front for hostile criticism. Its scope has often compelled a rigorous compression in the discussion of important controversial topics, and has precluded all entrance upon the more detailed issues in the policy of reconstruction. But I venture to hope that many readers, who may disagree with the particular valuations and interpretations offered in these chapters, will be led to accept the broader outlines of the method of human valuation here proposed, and will recognise the importance of a better application of this method in the solutions of the practical problems of economic reform.

Real Income: Cost and Utility

. . . We are confronted at the outset by the position of an economic science which conceives production entirely in terms of 'cost', consumption entirely in terms of 'utility'. Indeed, the economic doctrine of value hinges almost entirely upon this antithesis. For it is mainly owing to its 'costs' that a limit of scarcity is set on each 'supply', while it is the 'utility' accorded by consumers that gives economic force and meaning to 'demand'. Hence production is conceived as a process which rolls up costs into commodities, consumption as a process that unrolls them into utilities.

Now an organic interpretation of industry cannot accept this mode of conceiving the productive and consumptive functions. Considerations of the organic origins of industry lend no support to the assumption that production is all 'cost' and no 'utility', consumption all 'utility' and no 'cost'. On the contrary, in our human analysis of economic processes we shall rather expect to find costs and utilities, alike in their sense of pains and pleasures and of organic losses and organic gains, commingled in various degrees in all productive and consumptive processes.

Our aim will be to set out, as well as we can, reliable rules for examining the productive and consumptive history of the various sorts of concrete marketable goods so as to discover the human elements of cost and utility contained in each, and by a computation of these positives and negatives to reach some estimate of the aggregate human value contained in the several sorts of commodities which form the concrete income of the nation and in this income as a whole. Only by some such process is it possible to reach a knowledge of the real wealth of nations.

We may state the problem provisionally in three questions:

1. What are the concrete goods and services which constitute the real national income?
2. How are these goods produced?
3. How are they consumed?

But in truth the consideration of the so-called 'concrete' nature of these goods is as irrelevant to our analysis as that of the money ticket placed on them. For from the standpoint of welfare these goods are nothing but the activities of those who produce and consume them, or, if it be preferred, the human processes of production and consumption. The human meaning of any given stock of wheat in our national supply will consist of the efforts of body and mind, the thought and desire and directed skill, put into the several processes of preparing the soil, sowing, tending, reaping and marketing the wheat, undergone by the farmer in Manitoba or in Norfolk, the merchant, shipper, miller, baker who convey it from the farm and convert it into bread, and finally the activities of mastication, digestion and assimilation with the accompanying satisfaction as it passes into the physical system of the consumer. And so with every other sort of concrete marketable goods or services. From the standpoint of human value, they are wholly resolvable into the physical and mental activities and feelings of the human beings who produce and consume them. It is the balance of the desirable over the undesirable in these several activities and feelings that constitutes the human value of any stock of marketable goods. The standard of desirability will be the conception of the organic well-being of the society to which the individuals whose activities and feelings are concerned belong.

Or the several stages of interpretation may be expressed as follows. A given money income must first be resolved into the concrete goods which it expresses: those goods must then be resolved into the various efforts of production and satisfactions of consumption, estimated according to the current ideas and desires of the individuals who experience them: these current individual estimates of the desirable must be adjusted by reference to an ideal standard of the socially desirable. The extent of this latter process of adjustment will, of course, depend upon how far the actual current ideas and feelings of individuals are kept in essential harmony with the true standard of social well-being by the natural evolution of an organic society.

Our task in seeking to devise a method for the human interpretation or valuation of Industry consists then in confronting the goods which form the net consumable income of the community, and in finding answers to the two related questions:

What are the net human costs involved in their production?

What are the net human utilities involved in their consumption?

A simple sum in subtraction should then give us the result we seek—so far as any such quantitative calculus is valid and feasible.

Now though economists, of course, are well aware that many of the processes of production contain elements of pleasure and utility to the producers, while some of the processes of consumption contain elements of pain and cost to the consumers, they have, rightly from their standpoint, ignored these qualifications in their general formulae, and have represented 'goods' from the producer's side as consisting entirely of accumulated costs, while from the consumer's side they constitute pure utility. Though our brief preliminary survey of the origins of industry indicates that no such sharp distinction between production and consumption can ultimately be maintained, and that throughout the whole continuous career of goods from cradle to grave the activities bestowed on them are composites of pleasure and pain, cost and utility, organic gain and organic loss, socially desirable and socially undesirable, it will be expedient to take our start from the commonly-accepted economic position, and to give separate consideration to the human values underlying processes of production on the one hand, processes of consumption on the other.

The general lines along which such an investigation must proceed are unmistakable.

In order to express business 'costs' in terms of human cost, we require to know three things:

1. The quality and kind of the various human efforts involved in the business 'cost'.
2. The capacities of the human beings who give out these efforts.
3. The distribution of the effort among those who give it out.

Corresponding strictly to this analysis of 'costs' of Production will be the analysis of 'utility' of Consumption. There we shall want to know:

1. The quality and kind of the satisfaction or utility yielded by the 'economic utility' that is sold to consumers.
2. The capacities of the consumers who get this 'economic utility'.
3. The distribution of the economic utility among the consuming public.

The humanist criticism of Industry is condensed into this analysis. The humanist requires that the effort expended on any sort of production shall be such as to contain a minimum of painful or injurious or otherwise undesirable activity. His complaint is that Industry, as actually organised and operated under a system which treats all forms of productive human effort as marketable goods, does not secure this human economy. The humanist requires that the persons set to give out undesirable effort, 'human cost', shall be those best capable of sustaining this loss. Weak women or children, for example, shall not be set to do work heavy or dangerous in its incidence, when strong men are available who could do it easily and safely. The humanist requires that undesirable or humanly costly work shall not merely be confined to classes of persons capable of performing it most easily and safely, but that the distribution of such effort shall, as regards length of time and intensity of pace, be such as to reduce the human cost per unit of product to a minimum. The humanist criticism of Industry upon the Costs side consists in pointing out that there is no adequately reliable or normal tendency for the business economy of costs to conform to this three-fold human economy.

Similarly, turning to the consumption side, the humanist points out: 1. That many of the 'goods' sold to consumers are inherently destitute of human utility, or, worse, are repositories of disutility; and that money values is no true key to human utility. 2. That the amount of utility or welfare to be got out of any goods depends upon the character, the natural or acquired capacity, of the particular consumers or classes of consumers into whose hands they fall. 3. That a true economy of consumption, therefore, involves their distribution among consumers in proportion to their capacity to use them for purposes of welfare. It is contended that the current working of our industrial system, on its distributive and consumptive side, makes no reliable provision for securing that the maximum of human utility shall attach to the consumption of the national income. . . .

The Human Costs of Labour

. . . Where the conditions of work are such as to involve a daily repetition of . . . pain, its accumulative effect constitutes one of the heaviest of human costs, a lowering of mentality and of moral resistance closely corresponding to the decline of physical resistance. Drink and other sensational excesses are the normal reactions of this lowered morale. Thus fatigue ranks as a main determinant of the 'character' of the working-classes and has a social significance in its bearing upon order and progress not less important than its influence upon the individual organism.

I have dwelt in some detail upon these phenomena of fatigue, because they exhibit most clearly the defects of the working life which carry heaviest human costs. These defects are excessive duration of labour, excessive specialisation, excessive repetition, excessive strain and excessive speed. Though separate for purposes of analysis, these factors closely interact. Mere duration of labour does not necessarily involve fatigue, provided it carries the elements of interest, variety, and achievement. The degree of specialisation or subdivision of labour counts on the whole more heavily. But even a high degree of specialisation is alleviated, where it contains many little changes of action or position, and affords scope for the satisfaction attending expert skill. It is the constant repetition of an identical action at a prescribed pace that brings the heaviest burden of monotony.

It is upon this combination of conditions that the first count against the dominion of machinery is based. The brief physiological consideration we have brought to bear upon the problem of fatigue gives clearer significance to monotony as a 'cost'. It implies, not merely a dull and distasteful occupation, but one which, taxing continually the same muscles and the same nerve-centres, increases the poison of fatigue. Hand labour of a narrow order, or machine-tending however light, entails this heavy cost, if maintained over a long period of time.

But where monotonous repetition is closely directed by the action of a machine, as regards its manner and its pace, there is a special nervous cost. For a hand-worker, however dull or heavy is the work, retains some slight power of varying the pace and perhaps of changing his position or mode of work. A worker who either feeds a machine or adjusts his movements in obedience to those of a machine, as for instance a cutter in the clothing trade or in shoemaking, has no such liberty. The special cost here entailed is that of trying to make an organism conform in its movements to a mechanism. Now a human being, or any other organism, has certain natural rhythms of movement for work, related to the rhythms of heart and lungs and other organic processes, and there are natural limits also to the pace at which he can efficiently, or even possibly, continue working. A machine also has rhythms and a maximum efficiency pace. But the rhythms of a machine are determined by its mechanical construction and the apparatus which furnishes its power: they are continuously uniform, and are capable of being speeded up beyond the capacity of the human tender.

A human rhythm is really labour-saving, in as much as it eases the strain to work in accordance with a natural swing. To set a man to follow the rhythm of a machine not only loses this economy, but entails an extra effort of conformity. The tendency to speed up a machine, so as to get the most out of it, is liable to take out of the machine-tender even more than he is capable of recognising in the way of nervous strain. Where considerable muscular activity is also required in following a high pace set by a machine, an appalling burden of human costs may be accumulated in a factory day.

When to such direct human costs of labour are added the risks of industrial accident or of industrial diseases, the physical injuries involved in bad atmosphere, heat, noise and other incidental pains and inconveniences which beset many branches of industry, we begin to realise with more distinctness the meaning of 'costs of labour' in the human as distinguished from the economic sense. . . .

The Distribution of Human Costs

. . . Though the physical, moral and social injuries, due to alternating periods of over and under work, are generally admitted, the full costs of such irregularity . . . are far from being adequately realized. While some attempts at 'decasualization' are being made, the larger and more wasteful irregularities of seasonal and cyclical fluctuations are still regarded as irremediable. By the workers themselves and even by social reformers, the injury inflicted upon wages and the standard of living by irregularity of employment is appreciated far more adequately than the related injury inflicted on the physique and morale of the worker by sandwiching periods of over-exertion between intervals of idleness.

This brief survey, however, is no place for a discussion of the causes and remedies of irregular employment. It must suffice to note that over a large number of the fields of industry the excesses and defects of such irregularity prevail to an extent which adds greatly to the total human cost of the products. So far as our nation is concerned, there is no reason to hold that this waste is increasing. Evidence of hours of labour and of unemployment, indeed, appear to indicate that it is somewhat diminishing. But the unequal time-distribution of human costs must continue to rank as a great enhancement of the aggregate of such costs.

But not less injurious than the unequal treatment of equals, is the equal treatment of unequals. The bad human economy of working immature children is a lesson which even the most 'civilised' nations have been exceedingly slow to learn. The bad human economy of working old persons of declining vigour, when able-bodied adult labour is available, is so far from being generally recognised that employers are actually commended on the ground of humanity for keeping at labour their aged employees, when younger and stronger workers are available. Fortunately, the larger provision for retiring pensions attests the growing recognition of this aggravation of the human costs of industry. In both cases alike, the employment of the young and of the old, the error arises from a short-sighted view of the interests of the single person or his single family, instead of a far-sighted view of the welfare of the community. It is often a source of immediate gain to a working-class family to put the children out to wage-earning as early as possible, and to keep old people working as long as they can get work to do. It does not pay the nation, even in the economic sense, that either of these things should be done. The case of child-labour is, of course, the more serious, in that it evidently entails not merely a wasteful strain upon feeble organisms, but an even heavier future cost in stunted growth and impaired efficiency throughout an entire life.

When the play of current economic forces places upon women work which men could perform more easily, or creates women's industries with conditions of labour involving excessive strains upon the organism, the double human costs are even heavier. For if excessive fatigue or nervous strain affects a woman as worker, the injurious costs are likely to be continued and enhanced through her capacity for motherhood. To use up or damage its women by setting them to hard wage labour in mill and workshop is probably the greatest human waste a nation could practise or permit. For some of the prevailing tendencies of modern industrialism appear to be more 'costly' in their bearing upon women than on men. In regard to factory work, and all other industrial work involving a long continuous muscular or nervous strain, or, as in shop labour with its long hours of standing, medical authorities are unanimous in holding that women suffer more than men. 'If a like amount of physical toil and effort be imposed on women, they suffer to a larger degree,' states Sir W. MacCormac. Statistics of employment from various countries agree in showing that the amount of morbidity, as measured by the number of days lost by illness, is greater among working-women than among working-men, and that the mortality of working-women is greater than that of working-men, notwithstanding the fact that the average life of a female is longer than that of a male. Long hours and speeding-up of machinery thus evidently inflict graver organic costs on women than on men. Where piecework is in vogue, it furnishes a stronger stimulus to over-strain in women, because the general lowness of their wage gives a larger importance to each addition. . . .

The Human Law of Distribution

. . . In the ordinary economic account 'costs' appear entirely on the Production side of the account, 'utility' entirely on the Consumption side. Production is regarded not as good or desirable in itself, but only as a means towards an end, Consumption. On the other hand, all parts of Consumption are regarded as in themselves desirable and good, and are assessed as Utilities according to the worth which current desires, expressed in purchasing power, set upon them.

Our human valuation refuses to regard work as a mere means to consumption. It finds life and welfare in the healthy functioning of productive activities, as well as in the processes of repair and growth which form sound consumption.

If all production could be reduced to Art and Exercise, the creative and the re-creative functions, all consumption to the satisfaction of physical and spiritual needs, we should appear to have reached an ideal economy, in which there would be no human costs and a maximum amount of human utility. The conditions of a complete individual life would seem to be attained. But we are not concerned with a society in which completeness of the individual life is the sole end, but with a society in which the desires, purposes and welfare of the individuals are comprised in the achievement of a common life. For this reason I have included under the head of Utility on the Productive side of our account, not only the Art and Exercise which are directly conducive to individual well-being, but a quantum of Labour which represents the economic measure of the inter-dependency, or solidarity, of the so-called individuals. Such labour is the so-called 'sacrifice' required of 'individuals' in the interest of the society to which they belong. To the individualist it appears a distortion of the free full development of his nature, an interference with his perfect life. But it is, of course, neither sacrifice nor distortion. For the so-called individual is nowise, except in physical structure,[1] completely divided from his fellows. He is a social being and this social nature demands recognition and expression in economic processes. It requires

[1] Even there he is not separated in physical functions. The sexual, philoprogenitive, and the gregarious instincts, which are rooted in physical structure, negate physical individualism. So does the structure of his brain, which in solitude decays or becomes diseased.

him to engage in some special work which has for its direct end the welfare of society, in addition to the work of using his own powers for his own personal ends. How far this routine labour for society can be taken into his conception of his human nature, and so become a source of personal satisfaction, is a question we shall discuss later on. At present it will suffice to recognise that each man's fair contribution to the routine labour of the world, though irksome to him, is not injurious but serviceable to his 'human' nature. Thus interpreted, it stands on the utility, not on the cost, side of the account. It must be distinguished from its excess, which we here term 'toil', and from work, which whether from an abuse of the creative faculty or of social control, is bad and degrading in its nature and is here termed mal-production.

A similar distinction between the narrowly personal and the broader social interpretation of welfare is applicable on the consumption side. It is clearly not enough that the income which is to furnish consumption should suffice only to make provision for the satisfaction of the material and spiritual needs of the individual—or even of his family. The expenditure of every man should contain a margin—which I here call 'abundance' —from which he may contribute voluntarily to the good of others. There will be public needs or emergencies, which are not properly covered by State services but remain a call upon the public spirit of persons of discernment and humanity. There are also the calls of hospitality and comradeship, and the wider claim of charity, the willing help to those in need, a charity that is spontaneous, not organised, that degrades neither him who gives nor him who receives, because it is the natural expression of a spirit of human brotherhood. For the sting alike of condescension and of degradation would be removed from charity, when both parties feel that such acts of giving are an agreeable expression of a spirit of fellowship. From the consumption which is thus applied to the satisfaction of sound personal needs, or which overflows in 'abundance' to meet the needs of others, we distinguish sharply that excessive quantity of consumption, which in our Table ranks as 'Satiety', and those base modes of consumption which in their poisonous reactions on personal and social welfare strictly correspond to the base forms of production.

Such are the general lines of demarcation between the strictly business and the human valuation of the productive and consumptive processes. . . .

It is commonly asserted and assumed that . . . *laissez-faire* theory is dead, and that the attainment of a harmony of social welfare, by the free intelligent play of individual self-interest in the direction of economic forces, has been displaced by some theory of conscious coöperative or corporate direction in which the State takes a leading part. But at this very time, when the policy of every civilised nation is engaged more and more in checking monopolies and industrial privileges upon the one hand, and in placing restraints upon the havoc of unfettered competition on the other, a distinct and powerful revival of an economic theory of production and distribution undistinguishable in its essentials from the crude 18th century *laissez-faire* has set in. Largely influenced by the desire to apply mathematics, so as to secure a place for economics as an 'exact' science, many English and American economists have committed themselves to a 'marginalist' doctrine, which for its efficiency rests upon assumptions of infinite divisibility of the factors of production, and frictionless mobility of their flow into all the channels of industry and commerce. These assumptions granted, capital and labour flow into all employments until the last drop in each is equally productive, the products of the 'marginal' or final drops exchanging on a basis of absolute equality and earning for their owners an equal payment. Among English economists Mr. Wicksteed has set out this doctrine in all its economic applications most fully. He shows how by a delicate balance of preferences 'at the margins' i. e. in reference to the last portion of each supply of or demand for anything that is bought or sold, there must be brought about an exact equivalence of utility, of worth, and of remuneration, for the marginal increments in all employment. 'So far as the economic forces work without friction, they secure to everyone the equivalent of his industrial significance at the part of the industrial organism at which he is placed.' Elsewhere he asseverates that, as regards the workers in any employment, this means that 'they are already getting as much as their work is worth,' and that if they are to get more, this 'more' can only be got either out of 'communal funds,' or by making their work worth more. The same application of the marginalist doctrine is made by Professor Chapman. 'The theory, then, merely declares that each person will tend to receive as his wage *his value*—that is, the value of this marginal product—no more and no less. In order to get more than he actually does get, he must become more valuable,—work harder, for instance—that is, he must add more to the product in which he participated.' This is precisely the old '*laissez-faire, laissez-aller*' teaching, fortified by the conception that some special virtue attaches to the equalising process which goes on 'at the margin' of each employment of the factors of production.

The 'law of distribution' which emerges is that every owner of any factor of production 'tends to receive as remuneration' exactly what it is 'worth'. Now this 'law' is doubly defective. Its first defect arises from the fact that economic science assigns no other meaning to the 'worth' or 'value' of anything than what it actually gets in the market. To say, therefore, that anybody 'gets what he is worth', is merely an identical proposition, and conveys no knowledge. The second defect is the reliance upon a 'tendency' which falsely represents the normal facts and forces. It is false in three respects. It assumes in the first place an infinite divisibility of the several factors, necessary to secure the accurate balance of 'preferences' at the margins. It next assumes perfect mobility or freedom of access for all capital and labour into all avenues of employment. Finally, it assumes a statical condition of industry, so that the adjustment of the factors on a basis of equal productivity and equal remuneration at the margins may remain undisturbed. All three assumptions are unwarranted. Very few sorts of real capital or labour approach the ideal of infinite divisibility which marginalism requires. An individual worker, sometimes a group, is usually the minimal 'drop' of labour, and capital is only infinitely divisible when it is expressed in terms of money, instead of plants, machines or other concrete units. Still less is it the case that capital or labour flows or 'tends' to flow with perfect accuracy and liberty of movement into every channel of employment where it is required, so as to afford equality of remuneration at the several margins. Lastly, in most industrial societies the constant changes taking place, in volume and in methods of industry, entail a corresponding diversity in the productivity and the remuneration of the capital and labour employed in the various industries 'at the margin.'

THE PHYSIOLOGY OF INDUSTRY *

The competition among individuals in an ordinary commercial society tends continually to the establishment of actual Over-Supply. . . . Two considerations, which, according to most modern economists, furnish efficient checks to a condition of Over-Supply . . . are—

I. A fall in general prices, which, by causing an increased demand for Commodities, is alleged to provide an economical use for what would otherwise have been Over-Supply.

II. Such a fall in the rate of interest (or profit) as will act as a check upon Saving, and restore the proper relation between production and consumption.[1]

. . . Though the community can have no interest in creating a condition of general Over-supply or Under-consumption, the result may be brought about by the conflicting interests of individuals, because, though there is a strict limit to the amount of saving which a community may do in a given state of general demand, there is no such limit to the saving power of the individual. . . . Two economic checks . . . are alleged to be efficient preventives of any evil results which might arise from an excessive rate of production. . . . An actual condition of Over-production

* From *The Physiology of Industry,* written with A. F. Mummery (London, John Murray, 1889).

[1] So persistent is the assumption among economic writers that the machinery of commerce is a self-adjusting one which cannot get much out of working order, that they seldom take the trouble to distinctly state the nature of the economic checks to Over-Production. But the general tenour of their reasoning is in complete accord with the following statement of Läveleye:—'When there is a lack of equilibrium between production and consumption certain influences come into play, which tend to restore this in the following way:—Too many shoes are made. To sell the surplus shoemakers will lower their prices. This will have two results: First, the fall of price will increase the number of consumers; secondly, shoemakers, finding themselves at a loss, will make fewer shoes, until the equilibrium is here again established.' (Läveleye, 'Elements of Pol. Econ.,' p. 99.) This argument, irrefutable as applied to the interests of any single branch of production, is considered a sufficient answer to those who have asserted the possibility of general Over-Production.

must exist before either of these economic forces can be set in operation. The first force, that of a general fall of prices, . . . can have no power to restore a right relation between production and consumption. The second force, that of falling profit, is seen to operate by acting as a check upon production, and can only act by thus lowering the source of all incomes. The fall of average income thus brought about has been already identified with the phenomena called Depression of Trade. It is, therefore, clear that the self-acting checks on which Political Economy has hitherto relied to prevent any evil results which might arise from an increase of production without a corresponding increase of consumption, are unable to achieve this end. The one check, that of falling prices, is entirely inoperative; the other, that of falling profit, is the immediate cause of the very malady which it is supposed to prevent.

PART FOURTEEN

Neo-Classical Economics: Imperfect-Competition and Oligopoly Theories

The writers to be analyzed in this section belong in the general framework of equilibrium economics but have concentrated on what, for want of a better name, has been called *monopolistic* or *imperfect-competition* theory. In building their theoretical structures, almost all the classical and neo-classical writers implicitly accepted perfect competition, with all its corollaries, as the norm and explained away deviations from the norm as exceptions. Most of them said a few words somewhere about monopoly, but it too was treated as a special case, and no analysis was made of the great variety of market situations between the poles of perfect competition on the one hand and pure monopoly on the other. The contribution of the writers in this section is that they recognized this lacuna in neo-classical theory and attempted to remedy it; that in taking monopoly as their center of attention, they analyzed the market behavior of competing monopolists, thus exploring areas in which competition and monopoly are intermixed. They also attempted to deal with the field of oligopoly—that is, with the theory of markets in which there are only a few sellers.

Problems of duopoly and oligopoly had been analyzed by the French mathematical economist Augustin Cournot as early as 1838. Unfortunately, his book achieved no notice, and it was only in 1883 that it was even reviewed in the *Journal des Savants.* Here he showed that a determinate equilibrium solution can be obtained for the duopoly problem and that the solution can be extended from duopoly to oligopoly. (See the selection from his *Researches,* pp. 452–459.) Technically speaking, the entire theory of monopolistic competition consisted in applying to a wider field, and with greater finesse, methods of analysis which were already to be found in Cournot, and later, in Alfred Marshall's mathematical appendix.

In setting forth his concepts of monopolistic competition, Cournot gave as an example the owner of a unique mineral spring. Having a perfect monopoly, the owner can set the price, within reasonable limits, at almost any point he wishes. Logically, he will select the price where profit per unit multiplied by the number of units sold will be at a maximum.

Next Cournot set up a duopoly situation, with two owners of such springs. Cournot held that each duopolist believes that his rival will continue to produce a definite quantity, irrespective of his own production. He then mentally deducts what he thinks will be the quantity of his competitor's output from the total quantity marketable at each price. Then he obtains his own individual demand function and attempts to equate his marginal revenue to his marginal cost. This process results in a pair of outputs, and the pair is constantly changing, as each competitor finds that he has guessed wrong about his competitor's production, until they reach a point where they are guessing right and their outputs are justified. Actually, it is questionable whether a firm will long continue to base its output decision on the assumption that its rival's output is fixed.

The following selections trace further the development of imperfect-competition and oligopoly theories and indicate the relationship of each to the main body of neo-classical doctrine. It will be noted that Professor Chamberlin follows the Marshallian tradition of specific equilibrium, while Stackelberg, since he is of the Lausanne general equilibrium school, can trace his descent more directly from Cournot.

Finally, the treatment of oligopoly theory necessitates some examination of the new concepts introduced by Professors Morgenstern and von Neumann in 1944 and generally referred to as the theory of games. Actually, this theory is much larger than the imperfect-competition and oligopoly theories, which become special cases within the over-all framework. In this approach, which is discussed more fully later in this section, all economic and business behavior is viewed as some form of strategy.

PIERO SRAFFA

(1898–)

The next major contribution to imperfect-competition theory came from Piero Sraffa, an Italian-born economist who has been teaching at Cambridge University for many years. In his article in the *Economic Journal* on "The Laws of Returns under Competitive Conditions" he made the important point that the increasing returns that result from the internal economies of a firm are incompatible, by its own definition, with the concept of perfect competition. In other words, reductions in cost which come from an increase in a firm's scale of production or from distributing overhead over a large number of product units cannot be fitted into perfect-competition analysis.

Therefore, it was necessary to turn from the theory of perfect competition to the theory of monopoly, which supplies an analytical apparatus for relating variations in cost to changes in the size of the firm. But, as he next pointed out, many market situations fall between competition and monopoly. Another great weakness in perfect-competition theory, according to Sraffa, is the assumption that the consumer is indifferent to where he purchases a product. Sraffa noted that sometimes customers will even pay more to get the same goods from one firm rather than another. Furthermore, *selling* costs, which are extremely important and indeed often larger than production costs, had been thoroughly overlooked in the theory of the neo-classical economists.

Sraffa's article started the now-famous controversy on increasing returns in the *Economic Journal* (1930–1932). This controversy was brought to an end in 1933 by the appearance of two books attempting to reconstruct the whole theory of value on an imperfect-competition basis. These were *The Theory of Monopolistic Competition* by Professor Edward Chamberlin of Harvard and *The Economics of Imperfect Competition* by Professor Joan Robinson of Cambridge. Since the books appeared almost simultaneously, both writers are entitled to laurels as pioneers.

THE LAWS OF RETURNS UNDER COMPETITIVE CONDITIONS *

At present the laws of returns are of special importance owing to the part they play in the study of the problem of value. But they are naturally much older than the particular theory of value in which they are employed, and it is precisely from their secular age and their original applications that they derive both their prestige and their weakness in their modern application. We are disposed to accept the laws of returns as a matter of course, because we have before our eyes the great and indisputable services rendered by them when performing their ancient function, and we often neglect to ask ourselves whether the old barrels are still able to hold the new wine.

The law of diminishing returns has long been associated mainly with the problem of rent, and from this point of view the law as formulated by the classical economists with reference to land was entirely adequate.

* From "The Laws of Returns under Competitive Conditions," *Economic Journal,* December, 1926, pp. 535–550.

It had always been perfectly obvious that its operation affected, not merely rent, but also the cost of the product; but this was not emphasised as a cause of variation in the relative price of the individual commodities produced, because the operation of diminishing returns increased in a like measure the cost of all. This remained true even when the English classical economists applied the law to the production of corn, for, as Marshall has shown, "the term 'corn' was used by them as short for agricultural produce in general" (*Principles,* VI. i. 2, note).

The position occupied in classical economics by the law of increasing returns was much less prominent, as it was regarded merely as an important aspect of the division of labour, and thus rather as a result of general economic progress than of an increase in the scale of production.

The result was that in the original laws of returns the general idea of a functional connection between cost and quantity produced was not given a conspicuous place; it appears, in fact, to have been present in the minds of the classical economists much less prominently than was the connection between demand and demand price.

The development which has emphasised the former aspect of the laws of returns is comparatively recent. At the same time it has removed both laws from the positions which, according to the traditional partition of political economy, they used to occupy, one under the heading of "distribution" and the other under "production," and has transferred them to the chapter of "exchange-value"; there, merging them in the single "law of non-proportional returns," it has derived from them a law of supply in a market such as can be co-ordinated with the corresponding law of demand; and on the symmetry of these two opposite forces it has based the modern theory of value.

In order to reach this result it was found necessary to introduce certain modifications into the form of the two laws. Very little was necessary as regards the law of diminishing returns, which merely required to be generalised from the particular case of land to every case in which there existed a factor of production of which only a constant quantity was available. The law of increasing returns, however, had to be subjected to a much more radical transformation: the part played in it by the division of labour—now limited to the case of independent subsidiary factories coming into existence as the production of an industry increases—was greatly restricted; while consideration of that greater internal division of labour, which is rendered possible by an increase in the dimensions of an individual firm, was entirely abandoned, as it was seen to be incompatible with competitive conditions. On the other hand, the importance of "external economies" was more and more emphasised—that is, of the advantage derived by individual producers from the growth, not of their own individual undertakings, but of the industry in its aggregate.

Even in their present form, however, the two laws have preserved the characteristic of originating from forces of profoundly diverse nature. Such heterogeneousness, while not constituting in itself an insurmountable obstacle when it is attempted to coordinate them and employ them conjointly in problems mainly relating, not to the causes, but to the effects of variations in cost, involves a fresh difficulty when it is sought to classify the various industries according as they belong to one or the other category. It is, in fact, in the very nature of the bases of the two laws that the wider the definition which we assume for "an industry"—that is, the more nearly it includes all the undertakings which employ a given *factor* of production, as, for example, agriculture or the iron industry—the more probable will it be that the forces which make for diminishing returns will play an important part in it; the more restrictive this definition—the more nearly it includes, therefore, only those undertakings which produce a given type of consumable *commodity,* as, for example, fruit or nails—the greater will be the probability that the forces which make for increasing returns will predominate in it. In its effects this difficulty is parallel to that which, as is well known, arises from the consideration of the element of time, whereby the shorter the period of time allowed for the adjustments, the greater is the likelihood of decreasing returns, while the longer that period is, the greater is the probability of increasing returns.

The really serious difficulties make their appearance when it is considered to what extent the supply curves based on the laws of returns satisfy the conditions necessary to enable them to be employed in the study of the equilibrium value of single commodities produced under competitive conditions. This point of view assumes that the conditions of production and the demand for a commodity can be considered, in respect to small variations, as being practically independent, both in regard to each other and in relation to the supply and demand of all other commodities. It is well known that such an assumption would not be illegitimate merely because the independence may not be absolutely perfect, as, in fact, it never can be; and a slight degree of interdependence may be overlooked without disadvantage if it applies to quantities of the second order of smalls, as would be the case if the effect (for example, an increase of cost) of a variation in the industry which we propose to isolate were to react partially on the price of the products of other industries, and this latter effect were to influence the demand for the product of the first industry. But, of course, it is a very different matter, and the assumption becomes illegitimate, when a variation in the quantity produced by the industry under consideration sets up a force which acts directly, not merely upon its own costs, but also upon the costs of other industries; in such a case the conditions of the "particular equilibrium" which it was intended to isolate are upset, and it is no longer possible, without contradiction, to neglect collateral effects.

It unfortunately happens that it is precisely into this latter category that the applications of the laws of returns fall, in the great majority of cases. As regards diminishing returns, in fact, if in the production of a particular commodity a considerable part of a factor is employed, the total amount of which is fixed or can be increased only at a more than proportional cost, a small increase in the production of the commodity will necessitate a more intense utilisation of that factor, and this will affect in the same manner the cost of the commodity in question and the cost of the other commodities into the production of which that factor enters; and since commodities into the production of which a common special factor enters are frequently, to a certain extent, substitutes for one another (for example, various kinds of agricultural produce), the modification in their price will not be without appreciable effects upon demand in the industry concerned. If we next take an industry which employs only a small part of the "constant factor" (which appears more appropriate for the study of the particular equilibrium of a single industry), we find that a (small) increase in its production is generally met much more by drawing "marginal doses" of the constant factor from other industries than by intensifying its own utilisation of it; thus the increase in cost will be practically negligible, and anyhow it will still operate in a like degree upon all the industries of the group. Excluding these cases, and excluding—if we take a point of view embracing long periods—the numerous cases in which the quantity of a means of production may be regarded as being only temporarily fixed in respect to an unexpected demand, very little remains: the imposing structure of diminishing returns is available only for the study of that minute class of commodities in the production of which the whole of a factor of production is employed. Here, of course, by "a commodity" is to be understood an article in regard to which it is possible to construct, or at least to conceive, a demand schedule which is tolerably homogeneous and independent of the conditions of supply, and not, as is frequently implied, a collection of diverse articles, such as agricultural products or ironware.

It is not by mere chance that, notwithstanding the profoundly diverse nature of the two laws of returns, the same difficulties also arise, in almost identical form, in connection with increasing returns. Here again we find that in reality the economies of production on a large scale are not suitable for the requirements of the supply curve: their field of action is either wider or more restricted than would be necessary. On the one hand, reductions in cost which are due to "those *external* economies which result from the general progress of industrial environment" to which Marshall refers (*Principles,* V. xi. 1) must, of course, be ignored, as they are clearly incompatible with the conditions of the particular equilibrium of a commodity. On the other hand, reductions in cost connected with an increase in a firm's scale of production, arising from internal economies or from the possibility of distributing the overhead charges over a larger number of product units, must be put aside as being incompatible with competitive conditions. The only economies which could be taken into consideration would be such as occupy an intermediate position between these two extremes; but it is just in the middle that nothing, or almost nothing, is to be found. Those economies which are external from the point of view of the individual firm, but internal as regards the industry in its aggregate, constitute precisely the class which is most seldom to be met with. As Marshall has said in the work in which he has intended to approach most closely the actual conditions of industry, "the economies of production on a large scale can seldom be allocated exactly to any one industry: they are in great measure attached to groups, often large groups, of correlated industries." [1] In any case, in so far as external economies of the kind in question exist, they are not likely to be called forth by *small* increases in production. Thus it appears that supply curves showing decreasing costs are not to be found more frequently than their opposite.

Reduced within such restricted limits, the supply schedule with variable costs cannot claim to be a general conception applicable to normal industries; it can prove a useful instrument only in regard to such exceptional industries as can reasonably satisfy its conditions. In normal cases the cost of production of commodities produced competitively—as we are not entitled to take into consideration the causes which may make it rise or fall—must be regarded as constant in respect of small variations in the quantity produced.[2] And so, as a simple way of approaching the problem of competitive value, the old and now obsolete theory which makes it dependent on the cost of production alone appears to hold its ground as the best available.

This first approximation, as far as it goes, is as important as it is useful: it emphasises the fundamental factor, namely, the predominant influence of cost of production in the determination of the normal value of commodities, while at the same time it does not lead us astray when we desire to study in greater detail the conditions under which exchange takes place in particular cases, for it does not conceal from us the fact that we cannot find the elements required for this purpose within the limits of its assumptions.

When we proceed to a further approximation, while keeping to the path of free competition, the complications do not arise gradually, as would be convenient; they present themselves simultaneously as a whole.

1 *Industry and Trade,* p. 188.

2 The absence of causes which tend to cause the cost either to increase or diminish appears to be the most obvious and plausible way from which constant costs can arise. But as these constitute the most dangerous enemy of the symmetry between demand and supply, those writers who accept this doctrine, in order to be able to relegate the constant costs to the category of theoretical limiting cases which in reality cannot exist, have persuaded themselves that they are something extremely complicated and improbable, since they "can only result from the accidental balancing of two opposite tendencies; the tendency to diminution of cost . . . and the tendency to increase of cost . . ." (Sidgwick, *Principles of Political Economy,* 1st ed., p. 207; to the same effect see, *e.g.,* Marshall, *Principles,* IV. xiii, 2, and *Palgrave's Dictionary, sub voce* Law of Constant Return). The dictum of Edgeworth, that "to treat *variables* as *constants* is the characteristic vice of the unmathematical economist," might to-day be reversed: the mathematical economists have gone so far in correcting this vice that they can no longer conceive of a constant except as the result of the compensation of two equal and opposite variables.

If diminishing returns arising from a "constant factor" are taken into consideration, it becomes necessary to extend the field of investigation so as to examine the conditions of simultaneous equilibrium in numerous industries: a well-known conception, whose complexity, however, prevents it from bearing fruit, at least in the present state of our knowledge, which does not permit of even much simpler schemata being applied to the study of real conditions. If we pass to external economies, we find ourselves confronted by the same obstacle, and there is also the impossibility of confining within statical conditions the circumstances from which they originate.

It is necessary, therefore, to abandon the path of free competition and turn in the opposite direction, namely, towards monopoly. Here we find a well-defined theory in which variations of cost connected with changes in the dimensions of the individual undertaking play an important part. Of course, when we are supplied with theories in respect to the two extreme cases of monopoly and competition as part of the equipment required in order to undertake the study of the actual conditions in the different industries, we are warned that these generally do not fit exactly one or other of the categories, but will be found scattered along the intermediate zone, and that the nature of an industry will approximate more closely to the monopolist or the competitive system according to its particular circumstances, such as whether the number of autonomous undertakings in it is larger or smaller, or whether or not they are bound together by partial agreements, etc. We are thus led to believe that when production is in the hands of a large number of concerns entirely independent of one another as regards control, the conclusions proper to competition may be applied even if the market in which the goods are exchanged is not absolutely perfect, for its imperfections are in general constituted by frictions which may simply retard or slightly modify the effects of the active forces of competition, but which the latter ultimately succeed in substantially overcoming. This view appears to be fundamentally inadmissible. Many of the obstacles which break up that unity of the market which is the essential condition of competition are not of the nature of "frictions," but are themselves active forces which produce permanent and even cumulative effects. They are frequently, moreover, endowed with sufficient stability to enable them to be made the subject of analysis based on statical assumptions.

Of these effects two, which are closely interconnected, are of special importance because they are to be found with great frequency in industries in which competitive conditions appear to prevail; and they also possess a special interest because, as they relate to certain of the most characteristic features of the theoretical conception of competition, they show how seldom it is for these conditions to be realised in their integrity, and how a slight divergence from them suffices to render the manner in which equilibrium is attained extremely similar to that peculiar to monopoly. These two points in which the theory of competition differs radically from the actual state of things which is most general are: first, the idea that the competing producer cannot deliberately affect the market prices, and that he may therefore regard it as constant whatever the quantity of goods which he individually may throw on the market; second, the idea that each competing producer necessarily produces normally in circumstances of individual increasing costs.

Everyday experience shows that a very large number of undertakings—and the majority of those which produce manufactured consumers' goods—work under conditions of individual diminishing costs. Almost any producer of such goods, if he could rely upon the market in which he sells his products being prepared to take any quantity of them from him at the current price, without any trouble on his part except that of producing them, would extend his business enormously. It is not easy, in times of normal activity, to find an undertaking which systematically restricts its own production to an amount less than that which it could sell at the current price, and which is at the same time prevented by competition from exceeding that price. Business men, who regard themselves as being subject to competitive conditions, would consider absurd the assertion that the limit to their production is to be found in the internal conditions of production in their firm, which do not permit of the production of a greater quantity without an increase in cost. The chief obstacle against which they have to contend when they want gradually to increase their production does not lie in the cost of production—which, indeed, generally favours them in that direction—but in the difficulty of selling the larger quantity of goods without reducing the price, or without having to face increased marketing expenses. This necessity of reducing prices in order to sell a larger quantity of one's own product is only an aspect of the usual descending demand curve, with the difference that instead of concerning the whole of a commodity, whatever its origin, it relates only to the goods produced by a particular firm; and the marketing expenses necessary for the extension of its market are merely costly efforts (in the form of advertising, commercial travellers, facilities to customers, etc.) to increase the willingness of the market to buy from it—that is, to raise that demand curve artificially.

This method of regarding the matter appears the most natural, and that which adheres to the reality of things. No doubt it is possible, from the formal point of view, to reverse these relations and regard every purchaser as being perfectly indifferent in his choice between the different producers, provided the latter, in order to approach him, are prepared to incur marketing expenses varying greatly in different cases, and to reckon these increased marketing expenses in the cost of production of each. In this way increasing individual costs can be obtained to any desired extent and a perfect market in which there is an unlimited demand, at current prices, for the products of each. But the question of allocating the marketing expenses cannot be decided from the point of view of formal correctness, for on that basis the two methods are equivalent; nor can it be decided according to the fact that these charges are actually paid by the purchaser or the seller, as this does not affect their incidence or their effects in any way. What is important is to ascertain how the various forces at work can be grouped in the most homogeneous manner, so that the influence of each of them on the equilibrium resulting from their opposition may be more readily estimated. From this point of view the second of the methods mentioned must be rejected, since it entirely conceals the effects which the circumstances from which the marketing expenses originate exercise in disturbing the unity of the market. It alters in a misleading way, moreover, the customary and well defined significance of the expression "cost of production," with the result of rendering it dependent upon elements quite extraneous to the conditions under which the production of a given undertaking takes place. It consequently misrepresents the manner in which the actual process of determining the price and the quantity produced by each undertaking is affected.

By adhering to the first point of view, therefore, we are led to ascribe the correct measure of importance to the chief obstacle which hinders the free play of competition, even where this appears to predominate, and which at the same time renders a stable equilibrium possible even when the supply curve for the products of each individual firm is descending—that is, the absence of indifference on the part of the buyers of goods as between the different producers. The causes of the preference shown by any group of buyers for a particular firm are of the most diverse nature, and may range from long custom, personal acquaintance, confidence in the quality of the product, proximity, knowledge of particular requirements and the possibility of obtaining credit, to the reputation of a trademark, or sign, or a name with high traditions, or to such special features of modelling or design in the product as—without constituting it a distinct commodity intended for the satisfaction of particular needs—have for their principal purpose that of distinguishing it from the products of other firms. What these and the many other possible reasons for preference have in common is that they are expressed in a willingness (which may frequently be dictated by necessity) on the part of the group of buyers who constitute a firm's clientele to pay, if necessary, something extra in order to obtain the goods from a particular firm rather than from any other.

When each of the firms producing a commodity is in such a position the general market for the commodity is subdivided into a series of distinct markets. Any firm which endeavours to extend beyond its own market by invading those of its competitors must incur heavy marketing expenses in order to surmount the barriers by which they are surrounded; but, on the other hand, within its own market and under the protection of its own barrier each enjoys a privileged position whereby it obtains advantages which—if not in extent, at least in their nature—are equal to those enjoyed by the ordinary monopolist.

Nor is it necessary to stress the customary conception of monopoly to make this case fit into it. In it also, in fact, we find that the majority of the circumstances which affect the strength of a monopolist (such as the possession of unique natural resources, legal privileges, the control of a greater or less proportion of the total production, the existence of rival commodities, etc.) exercise their influence essentially by affecting the elasticity of the demand for the monopolised goods. Whatever the causes may be, this is the only decisive factor in estimating the degree of independence which a monopolist has in fixing prices: the less elastic the demand for his product, the greater is his hold on his market. The extreme case, which may properly be called "absolute monopoly," is that in which the elasticity of the demand for the products of a firm is equal to unity [3]; in that case, however much the monopolist raises his prices, the sums periodically expended in purchasing his goods are not even partially diverted into different channels of expenditure, and his price policy will not be affected at all by the fear of competition from other sources of supply. So soon as this elasticity increases, competition begins to make itself felt, and becomes ever more intense as the elasticity grows, until to infinite elasticity in the demand for the products of an individual undertaking a state of perfect competition corresponds. In the intermediate cases the significance of a moderate elasticity in the demand is that, although the monopolist has a certain freedom in fixing his prices, whenever he increases them he is forsaken by a portion of his purchasers, who prefer to spend their money in some other manner. It matters little to the monopolist if they spend it in purchasing goods very different from his own, or goods identical with them, but supplied by other producers who have not increased their price; in either case he must undergo—if only in a slight degree—actual competition from such goods, since it is precisely the possibility of buying them that leads the purchasers gradually to give up using his product as he increases the price. The direct effects are thus equal whether the sums set free as the result of an increase in price by an undertaking are expended on a large number of different commodities, or whether they are employed preponderatingly in the purchase of one or a few rival commodities which are more or less available for buyers, as occurs in the case of an undertaking which, while controlling only a small part of the total production of a commodity, has the advantage of possessing a particular market of its own. But the indirect effects in the two cases are substantially different.

The method indicated by Marshall in regard to manufactures designed for particular tastes is applicable for the study of this latter case. "When

[3] The elasticity of demand for the products of a monopolist cannot, of course, be less than unity in respect to prices immediately above the equilibrium price—that is, in respect to that part of the demand curve which alone counts in regard to the determination of the power of a monopolist in his own market; a question which is quite distinct from that of the magnitude of the gains obtainable by the monopoly, as the latter is dependent, not so much on the ratio of change, as on the absolute measure of the demand and the demand price.

we are considering an individual producer," he writes, "we must couple his supply curve, not with the general demand curve for his commodity in a wide market, but with the particular demand curve of his own special market" (*Principles,* V. xii. 2). If we extend this method to those industries in which each firm has more or less a particular market, we must not restrict its employment to the occasions when we are considering the individual producer, but we must adhere to it also when we examine the manner in which equilibrium is attained in the trade as a whole; for it is clear that such particular curves can by no means be compounded so as to form a single pair of collective demand and supply curves. The method mentioned above is the very same as that followed in cases of ordinary monopoly, and in both cases, in fact, the individual producer determines his selling price by the well-known method which makes his monopoly revenue or his profits the maximum obtainable.

The peculiarity of the case of the firm which does not possess an actual monopoly but has merely a particular market is that, in the demand schedule for the goods produced by it, the possible buyers are entered in descending order according to the price which each of them is prepared to pay, not rather than go entirely without, but rather than not buy it from that particular producer instead of elsewhere. That is to say, that two elements enter into the composition of such demand prices—the price at which the goods can be purchased from those other producers who, in the order of a purchaser's preference, immediately follow the producer under consideration, and the monetary measure of the value (a quantity which may be positive or negative) which the purchaser puts on his preference for the products of the firm in question.

For convenience in discussion it may be assumed that initially, in an industry in which like conditions prevail, each producer sells at a price which barely covers his costs. The individual interest of each producer will urge him to increase his price quickly so as to obtain the maximum profit. But in proportion as this practice spreads throughout the trade the various demand schedules will be modified as a result; for, as each buyer finds that the prices of the substitutes upon which he was able to reckon are increased, he will be inclined to pay a higher price for the products of the firm whose customer he is. So that, even before the first increase in price has been completely carried into effect, the conditions will be created which may permit every one of the concerns to make a further increase—and so on in succession. Naturally this process speedily reaches its limit. The customers lost by a firm whenever it raises its prices have recourse in part to other suppliers, and these will return to it when the others also have raised their prices; but in part they entirely give up buying the goods and definitely drop out of the market. Thus, every business has two classes of marginal customers—those who are at the margin only from its own individual standpoint and fix a limit for the excess of its prices over the prices generally ruling, and those who are at the margin from the standpoint of the general market and fix a limit for the general increase in price of the product.

It is, of course, possible that a general rise in the prices of a product may affect the conditions of demand and supply of certain firms in such a way as to make it advantageous for them to lower their prices rather than conform with the rise. But in an industry which has attained a certain degree of stability in its general structure, in regard of its methods of production, the number of undertakings composing it, and its commercial customs—in respect to which, therefore, statical assumptions are more nearly justified—this alternative is much less likely to be adopted than its opposite. In the first place, it involves great elasticity in the demand for the products of an individual business and rapidly diminishing costs for it—that is to say, a state of things the almost inevitable and speedy result of which is complete monopolisation, and which, therefore, is not likely to be found in a trade operated normally by a number of independent firms. In the second place, the forces which impel producers to raise prices are much more effective than those which impel them to reduce them; and this not merely owing to the fear which every seller has of spoiling his market, but mainly because an increase of profit secured by means of a cut in price is obtained *at the cost* of the competing firms, and consequently it impels them to take such defensive action as may jeopardise the greater profits secured; whereas an increase of profit obtained by means of a rise in prices not only does not injure competitors but brings them a positive *gain*, and it may therefore be regarded as having been more durably acquired. An undertaking, therefore, when confronted with the dual possibility of increasing its profits by raising its selling prices, or by reducing them, will generally adopt the first alternative unless the additional profits expected from the second are considerably greater.

These same reasons may serve to dispel the doubt, which might at first sight arise, whether in the case considered above the equilibrium may be indeterminate, as it is generally considered to be in the analogous case of multiple monopoly. In the first place, even in this case, as Edgeworth has noticed, "the extent of indeterminateness diminishes with the diminution of the degree of correlation between the articles" produced by the different monopolists [4]; that is to say, in our case, with the diminution of the elasticity of demand for the products of the individual firm—a limitation, it may be added, the effectiveness of which is the greater in proportion as the rapidity of decrease in the individual cost with the increase in the quantity produced becomes less. Both these conditions, as has been said above, are generally present to a large extent in the case we are considering. Moreover, the indeterminateness of the equilibrium in the case of multiple monopoly is necessarily dependent upon the assumption that at any moment each of the monopolists is *equally* inclined either to raise or to reduce his price, according as one or the other may suit

[4] *The Pure Theory of Monopoly,* in Papers Relating to P. E., Vol. I. p. 121.

him best from the point of view of immediate gain—a supposition which, at least in our case, is not, as we have said, justified.[5]

The conclusion that the equilibrium is in general determinate does not mean that generalising statements can be made regarding the price corresponding to that equilibrium; it may be different in the case of each undertaking, and is dependent to a great extent upon the special conditions affecting it.

The only case in which it would be possible to speak of a general price would be that of a trade in which the productive organisation of the different undertakings was uniform, and in which their particular markets were alike as regards the nature and attachment of the customers. In that case, as may readily be seen, the general price of the product, through the independent action of a number of firms, each of which is prompted only by its individual interests, would tend to reach the same level as that which would be fixed by a single monopolistic association in accordance with the ordinary principles of monopoly. This result, far from being conditioned by the existence of an almost complete isolation of the individual markets, requires only a very slight degree of preference for a particular firm in each of the groups of customers. In itself, this case is of no importance, because it is extremely unlikely that such uniformity would actually be found; but it is representative of a tendency, which prevails even in actual cases where the conditions of the various undertakings differ among each other, whereby the cumulative action of slight obstacles to competition produces on prices effects which approximate to those of monopoly.

It should be noted that in the foregoing the disturbing influence exercised by the competition of new firms attracted to an industry the conditions of which permit of high monopolist profits has been neglected. This appeared justified, in the first place because the entrance of new-comers is frequently hindered by the heavy expenses necessary for setting up a connection in a trade in which the existing firms have an established goodwill—expenses which may often exceed the capital value of the profits obtainable; in the second place, this element can acquire importance only when the monopoly profits in a trade are considerably above the normal level of profits in the trade in general, which, however, does not prevent the prices from being determined up to that point in the manner which has been indicated.

It might seem, moreover, that the importance of the marketing difficulties as a limit to the development of the productive unit has been

[5] The determinateness of the equilibrium would be more evident if, instead of regarding the various units of the same goods produced by different undertakings as rival commodities, we had regarded each unit as being composed of two commodities having, within each particular market, a joint demand, one of which (the commodity itself) is sold under competitive conditions, and the other (the special services, or the distinguishing features added to it by each producer) is sold under monopolistic conditions. This point of view, however, is more artificial and less in conformity with the customary method of regarding the matter.

over-estimated as compared with the effect in the same direction exercised by the more than proportionate increase in the expenditure which a firm must sometimes incur in order to furnish itself with the additional means of production which it requires; but it will generally be found that such increases in costs are an effect, and not a determining cause, of the market conditions which render it necessary or desirable for a firm to restrict its production. Thus, the limited credit of many firms, which does not permit any one of them to obtain more than a limited amount of capital at the current rate of interest, is often a direct consequence of its being known that a given firm is unable to increase its sales outside its own particular market without incurring heavy marketing expenses. If it were known that a firm which is in a position to produce an increased quantity of goods at a lower cost is also in a position to sell them without difficulty at a constant price, such a firm could encounter no obstacle in a free capital market. On the other hand, if a banker, or the owner of land on which a firm proposes to extend its own plant, or any other supplier of the firm's means of production, stands in a privileged position in respect to it, he can certainly exact from it a price higher than the current price for his supplies, but this possibility will still be a direct consequence of the fact that such a firm, being in its turn in a privileged position in regard to its particular market, also sells its products at prices above cost. What happens in such cases is that a portion of its monopoly profits are taken away from the firm, not that its cost of production is increased.

But these are mainly aspects of the process of diffusion of profits throughout the various stages of production and of the process of forming a normal level of profits throughout all the industries of a country. Their influence on the formation of the prices of single commodities is relatively unimportant, and their consideration is therefore beyond the scope of this article.

EDWARD HASTINGS CHAMBERLIN

(1899–   )

In his celebrated article on "The Laws of Returns under Competitive Conditions," Sraffa argued that the creation of "private" markets and the practice of non-price competition were no longer exceptional or secondary phenomena, but stable and cumulative factors which pointed to a monopolistic equilibrium solution. On these grounds he advised economists to reconstruct the theory of value on the basis of the individual firm as monopolist of its particular market.

In their attempted reconstruction of value theory, both Professor Edward Chamberlin and Professor Joan Robinson stress the joint influence of monopolistic and competitive elements in the determination of equilibrium. The distinguishing characteristic of monopolistic or imperfect competition is the presence of differentiated products and consumer preferences, rather than the absence of a large number of sellers. There has been some disagreement between Professors Robinson and Chamberlin as to the compatibility of their views regarding the essential features of the new orientation, but it is not necessary for our purposes to judge the controversy. It is perhaps fair to say that Mrs. Robinson devotes more attention to pure monopoly than to monopolistic competition and throws little light on the determination of price under the latter except in her analysis of the former. Her contribution to the new theory consists, for the most part, in an elegant refinement of elementary price theory and an extension of the traditional theory of monopoly along Marshallian lines. On the whole, however, their books cover much the same ground, and since Chamberlin's work is more often referred to by American economists, a selection from it has been chosen for inclusion here.

In general, the theoretical apparatus of both economists is similar. Both introduce the concepts, for instance, of marginal cost and marginal revenue. These are defined as the change in total cost (or total revenue) resulting from a unit change in output. The marginal cost curve lies below the average cost curve when the latter is falling and above it when it is rising. The equilibrium point of profit maximization of the firm occurs where marginal cost just equals marginal revenue. Furthermore, the theory can be applied to product differentiation and to advertising. Perfect-competition theorists regarded products as homogeneous and infinitely divisible, leaving out of account such features as branding and packaging. The utilization of advertising to build up demand was considered an extra-economic phenomenon. On Chamberlin's showing, equilibrium is attained when the marginal increment of the anticipated sales increase for the firm just equals the increment of advertising cost incurred.

In the final part of the selection, Professor Chamberlin applies his methods to distribution problems, a field neglected in the first edition of his book.

THE THEORY OF MONOPOLISTIC COMPETITION *

Introduction

Economic literature affords a curious mixture, confusion and separation of the ideas of competition and monopoly. On the one hand, analysis has revealed the differences between them and has led to the perfection

* Reprinted by permission of the publishers from Edward Chamberlin, *Theory of Monopolistic Competition*. Cambridge, Mass.: Harvard University Press, Copyright, 1948, by The President and Fellows of Harvard College.

and refinement of a separate body of theory for each. Although the two forces are complexly interwoven, with a variety of design, throughout the price system, the fabric has been undone and refashioned into two, each more simple than the original and bearing to it only a partial resemblance. Furthermore, it has, in the main, been assumed that the price system is like this—that all the phenomena to be explained are *either* competitive *or* monopolistic, and therefore that the expedient of two purified and extreme types of theory is adequate.

On the other hand, the facts of intermixture in real life have subtly worked against that complete theoretical distinction between competition and monopoly which is essential to a clear understanding of either. Because *actual* competition (rarely free of monopoly elements) is supposedly explained by the theory of *pure* competition, familiar results really attributable to monopolistic forces are readily associated with a theory which denies them. This association of the theory of competition with facts which it does not fit has not only led to false conclusions about the facts; it has obscured the theory as well. This is the more serious because the mixture of the two forces is a chemical process and not merely a matter of addition. Slight elements of monopoly have a way of playing unexpected logical tricks, with results quite out of proportion to their seeming importance.

. . . The first step in the formulation of a theory of prices must be a clear definition of the two fundamental forces of competition and monopoly, and an examination of each in isolation.

The second step must be a synthesis of the two. This brings us back to the assertion that price theories have followed, in the main, the two extreme channels, without (conscious) recognition of a middle course. Quantitatively, competitive theory has dominated—indeed, the theory of competition has been so generally accepted as the underlying explanation of the price system that the presumption is in its favor; its inadequacy remains to be proved. Hints at the ubiquity of monopoly elements and at the possibility of an intermediate theory are not entirely lacking, however. Thus Professor Knight remarks that "in view of the fact that practically every business is a partial monopoly, it is remarkable that the theoretical treatment of economics has related so exclusively to complete monopoly and perfect competition," and Veblen, ". . . it is very doubtful if there are any successful business ventures within the range of modern industries from which the monopoly element is wholly absent." Such fragmentary recognition of the problem is not hard to find. Yet, with the exception of the theory of duopoly, the middle ground between competition and monopoly remains virtually unexplored and the possibilities of applying such a theory relatively little appreciated.

"Pure competition" is taken as a point of departure, the adjective "pure" being chosen deliberately to describe competition unalloyed with monopoly elements. It is a much simpler and less inclusive concept than "perfect" competition, for the latter may be interpreted to involve perfection in many other respects than in the absence of monopoly. It may imply, for instance, an absence of friction in the sense of an ideal fluidity or mobility of factors such that adjustments to changing conditions which actually involve time are accomplished instantaneously in theory. It may imply perfect knowledge of the future and the consequent absence of uncertainty. It may involve such further "perfection" as the particular theorist finds convenient and useful to his problem. Two illustrations will serve to bring out the contrast between pure and perfect competition. The actual price of wheat approximates very inaccurately its normal price, yet the individual wheat farmer possesses not a jot of monopoly power. The market, though a very imperfect one, is purely competitive. On the other hand, monopoly may exist under conditions which are "perfect," or "ideal," in other respects. The static state and perfect competition are wrongly treated as synonymous by J. B. Clark. There is no reason whatever why monopoly of all sorts and degrees should not be present in a state where the conditions as to population, the supply of capital, technology, organization, and wants remained unchanged. "Pure" and "perfect" competition must not be identified; and to consider the theory of monopolistic competition vaguely as a theory of "imperfect" competition is to confuse the issues.

. . . With differentiation appears monopoly, and as it proceeds further the element of monopoly becomes greater. Where there is any degree of differentiation whatever, each seller has an absolute monopoly of his own product, but is subject to the competition of more or less imperfect substitutes. Since each is a monopolist and yet has competitors, we may speak of them as "competing monopolists," and of the forces at work as those of "monopolistic competition." . . .

It is this latter problem which is of especial interest and importance. In all of the fields where individual products have even the slightest element of uniqueness, competition bears but faint resemblance to the pure competition of a highly organized market for a homogeneous product. Consider, for instance, the competitive analysis as applied to the automobile industry. How is one to conceive of demand and supply curves for "automobiles in general" when, owing to variations in quality, design, and type, the prices of individual units range from several hundred to many thousands of dollars? How define the number of units which would be taken from or put upon the market at any particular price? How fit into the analysis a wide variety of costs based mostly upon a correspondingly wide variety of product? These difficulties are great; perhaps they are not insurmountable. The real one is neither of definition nor of interpretation, and cannot be surmounted. Competitive theory does not fit because competition throughout the group is only partial and is highly uneven. The competition between sport roadsters and ten-ton trucks must be virtually zero; and there is probably more justification for drawing up a joint demand schedule for Fords and house room than for Fords and Locomobiles. These are, perhaps, extreme cases, but the fact that each producer throughout the group has a market at least partially distinct from those of the others introduces forces, absent under pure competition, which materially alter the result. Prices throughout are adjusted in some measure according to the monopoly principle. Furthermore, advertising and selling outlays are invited by the fact that the market of each seller is limited, whereas the very nature of a purely competitive market precludes a selling problem. The theory of pure competition, in explaining the adjustment of economic forces in such an industry, is a complete misfit.

Because most prices involve monopoly elements, it is monopolistic competition that most people think of in connection with the simple word "competition." In fact, it may almost be said that under pure competition the buyers and sellers do not really compete in the sense in which the word is currently used. One never hears of "competition" in connection with the great markets, and the phrases "price cutting," "underselling," "unfair competition," "meeting competition," "securing a market," etc., are unknown. No wonder the principles of such a market seem so unreal when applied to the "business" world where these terms have meaning. They are based on the supposition that each seller accepts the market price and can dispose of his entire supply without materially affecting it. Thus there is no problem of choosing a price policy, no problem of adapting the product more exactly to the buyers' (real or fancied) wants, no problem of advertising in order to change their wants. The theory of pure competition could hardly be expected to fit facts so far different from its assumptions. But there is no reason why a theory of value cannot be formulated which will fit them—a theory concerning itself specifically with goods which are not homogeneous. This is the purpose of the later chapters of this book. . . .

Product Differentiation and the Theory of Value

INTRODUCTION

Under pure competition, the individual seller's market being completely merged with the general one, he can sell as much as he pleases at the going price. Under monopolistic competition, however, his market being separate to a degree from those of his rivals, his sales are limited and defined by three new factors: (1) his price, (2) the nature of his product, and (3) his advertising outlays.

The divergence of the demand curve for his product from the horizontal imposes upon the seller a price problem, absent under pure competition, which is the same as that ordinarily associated with the monopolist. Depending upon the elasticity of the curve and upon its position relative to the cost curve for his product, profits may be increased, perhaps by raising the price and selling less, perhaps by lowering it and selling more. That figure will be sought which will render the total profit a maximum. . . .

GROUP EQUILIBRIUM

Let us turn now to what we may call the group problem, or the adjustment of prices and "products" of a number of producers whose goods are close substitutes for each other. The group contemplated is one which would ordinarily be regarded as composing one imperfectly competitive market: a number of automobile manufacturers, of producers of pots and pans, of magazine publishers, or of retail shoe dealers. From our point of view, each producer within the group is a monopolist, yet his market is interwoven with those of his competitors, and he is no longer to be isolated from them. The question now to be asked is: what characterizes the system of relationships into which the group tends to fall as a result of their influence one upon another? . . .

One difficulty encountered in describing the group equilibrium is that the widest variations may exist in all respects between the different component firms. Each "product" has distinctive features and is adapted to the tastes and needs of those who buy it. Qualitative differences lead to wide divergences in the curves of cost of production, and buyers' preferences account for a corresponding variety of demand curves, both as to shape (elasticity) and as to position (distance from the x and y axes). The result is heterogeneity of prices, and variation over a wide range in outputs (scales of production) and in profits. Many such variations are, of course, temporary, and are constantly in process of being eliminated. We are concerned, however, only with those which persist over a long period of time. To a very considerable extent the scheme of prices is the result of conditions unique to each product and to its market—it defies comprehensive description as a "group" problem, even when monopolistic forces are given their full value in the explanation.

The matter may be put in another way by saying that the "imperfection" of competition is not uniform throughout what is regarded as an imperfectly competitive market. It is not as though a few elements of friction, such as imperfect knowledge, or partial indifference to economic gain, spread an even haze over the whole; nor as though immobility of resources gave a general tendency for "normal" results to be retarded in working themselves out. These factors would apply with equal force in all portions of the field, at least over periods long enough for chance short time irregularities to be ironed out. But the differentiation of the product is not, so to speak, "uniformly spaced"; it is not distributed homogeneously among all of the products which are grouped together. Each has its own individuality, and the size of its market depends on the strength of the preference for it over other varieties. Again, if high average profits lead new competitors to invade the general field, the markets of different established producers cannot be wrested from them with equal facility. Some will be forced to yield ground, but not enough to reduce their profits below the minimum necessary to keep them in business. Others may be cut to the minimum, and still others may be forced to drop out because only a small demand exists or can be created for their particular variety of product. Others, protected by a strong prejudice in favor of theirs, may be virtually unaffected by an invasion of the general field—their monopoly profits are beyond the reach of competition.

These variations will give no real difficulty in the end. Exposition of the group theory is facilitated, however, by ignoring them for the present. We therefore proceed under the heroic assumption that both demand and cost curves for all the "products" are uniform throughout the group. We shall return later to a recognition of their diversity, and to the manner in which allowance for it is to be made. Meanwhile, it may be remarked that diversity of "product" is not entirely eliminated under our assumption. It is required only that consumers' preferences be evenly distributed among the different varieties, and that differences between them be not such as to give rise to differences in cost. This might be approximately true where very similar products were differentiated by trade-marks. It is also approximately realized in the fairly even geographical distribution of small retail establishments in the outlying districts of a city.

Another complication in the group problem arises in connection with the number of competitors included within the group and the manner in which their markets "overlap." . . . This complication may be adequately recognized by considering first the case where numbers are very large, then the case where they are small. Specifically, we assume for the present that any adjustment of price or of "product" by a single producer spreads its influence over so many of his competitors that the impact felt by any one is negligible and does not lead him to any readjustment of his own situation. A price cut, for instance, which increases the sales of him who made it, draws inappreciable amounts from the markets of each of his many competitors, achieving a considerable result for the one who cut, but without making incursions upon the market of any single competitor sufficient to cause him to do anything he would not have done anyway. . . .

As new resources flow into the field, [cost] curves may be raised (by an increase in the price of the productive factors employed); they may be lowered (by improvements in the organization of the group as a whole—"external economies"); or they may remain the same (owing to the absence of both of these tendencies or to their cancellation one against the other). These three possibilities correspond respectively to the familiar increasing, decreasing, and constant cost of competitive theory. . . . No allowance [need be] made for a shift in the curves; in other words, the assumption [may be] made that conditions of constant cost obtained for the group as a whole. This assumption will be continued throughout, and for two reasons: (1) the theory in this form is widely applicable to the facts, and (2) where it is not applicable, its extension to cover cases of increasing and decreasing cost for the group is easily made.

First, as to its applicability. . . . Variations in output by a single producer will, if he is one of many producers, have a negligible effect upon the total output for all and hence upon cost tendencies for the product as a whole. Similarly, whenever the quantity of resources employed in one field of production is small relative to their quantity employed generally, an increase or decrease in output within this one field will have a negligible effect upon the prices of the productive factors employed and hence upon costs. An increase in the manufacture of scissors will not appreciably affect the price of steel. Nor will an increased output of rubber boots raise the price of rubber. What conditions obtain in any particular case is, of course, a question of fact. It is only meant to point out that tendencies towards increasing (or decreasing) cost with respect to particular kinds of resources or factors of production are transmitted to finished products almost always with diminished force and often with a force which is negligible. To this must be added the fact that the resources themselves may be obtained at fairly constant cost. If increased supplies of cement, sand, and gravel are readily available, expansion of the building industry will be possible at constant costs so far as these materials are a factor. In sum, it is likely that many fields of production are subject to conditions of approximately constant cost so far as the prices of the resources involved are concerned.

Do improvements in the organization of resources with larger output—"external economies"—result generally in a tendency to diminishing cost? The answer is yes, where they are appreciable. But it must be realized that such economies include only those made possible by the expansion of this particular field, exclusive of (*a*) those arising from the expansion of smaller fields (the individual establishments) within it—"internal economies"—and (*b*) those arising from the expansion of larger fields of which it is a part—the largest of which would be industry generally. The former are excluded because they may be realized to the full, independently of the output of the group . . . ; the latter, for a similar reason, because, since the group in question is small relative to larger fields of which it is a part, its expansion or contraction has a negligible effect upon economies in this larger field. To illustrate, an expansion of the retail grocery trade does not enable the individual grocer to approximate any more closely the most effective conditions of production within his own shop; neither does it contribute appreciably to such economies as are made possible by a large volume of retailing generally. In the group problem, then, the only economies which may be admitted as lowering the cost curves with increase of output are those which are due to the expansion of the group itself. Whether such economies exist in any particular case is, again, a matter of fact. Wherever they do not or where they are of only negligible importance, the result is a tendency to constant cost for the group.

The theory as developed for the case of constant cost may also be applicable if there are opposing tendencies of increasing and decreasing cost which approximately offset each other. Thus, expansion of the automobile industry may lead to (1) higher costs because of increased demand for materials, and (2) lower costs because of improved organization within the industry, the two roughly balancing each other and giving a net result of constant cost.

Secondly, the theory is not developed to include the cases of increasing and decreasing cost for the group because to do so in detail is not necessary. Where increasing costs obtain, the curves of all producers will rise as the resources employed in the field are increased, and fall as they are diminished, equilibrium being reached at a higher or at a lower point as the case may be. (Rents will be affected as in purely competitive theory, and are here to be included within the cost curves of the individual producers.) Similarly, in the case of decreasing cost the curves of all producers will fall as resources are increased and rise as they are diminished, the equilibrium being correspondingly lower or higher. These observations need not be repeated at every stage of the argument. Regardless of the cost tendency for the group, the equilibrium is always defined in the same manner with respect to the individual curves, and the divergences from the norms of purely competitive theory are always of the same sort. Our interest lies primarily in these matters, and they are most clearly revealed in the simple case of constant cost, to which attention will be confined from this point on. . . .

When both "product" and price are variable, an equilibrium adjustment will be reached for both which is a combination of that for each in isolation. Under given conditions with regard to the "products" and prices of his competitors, each seller will choose that combination of price and "product" for himself which will maximize his profit. For each variety of "product" possible to him there will be a price which will render his profit a maximum *relative* to that "product." From these relative maxima he will choose the largest of all. Readjustments will be necessary as his competitors do the same thing, until finally a point is reached, as for each variable in isolation, where no one can better his position by a further move. At the same time, resources will flow into the field in order to reduce profits which are higher than the competitive minimum, or out of it in order to raise them to this minimum, so that the number of producers finally occupying the field will be such as to leave the costs of each exactly covered and no more.

A graphic summary of this comprehensive equilibrium is attempted in Fig. 1, although, in fact, because of the difficulties of reducing "product" variation to graphic terms, it shows little more than price equilibrium. *PP′* must be regarded as the cost curve for the optimum "product" and *dd′* as the demand curve for it. (Let the dotted line *pp′* be ignored for the moment.) The equilibrium price is *AR,* for, *R* being the point at which *dd′* and *PP′* are tangent to each other, it is evident that either a higher or a lower price would give unit costs in excess of price. Since, by definition, the "product" is the optimum one, either a better or a poorer "product" would likewise leave unit costs, for the amount which could be sold, in excess of the price *OE.* A better "product" would, by raising the cost curve, move its intersection with *EZ* further to the right than it would move the demand (measured along *EZ*). A poorer "product" would similarly, by lowering the cost curve, move its intersection with *EZ* to the left by a shorter distance than it would decrease the demand (measured along *EZ*). The total output in the field under these conditions of equilibrium will be *OA* multiplied by the number of producers.

The conclusion seems to be warranted that just as, for a given "product," price is inevitably higher under monopolistic than under pure competition, so, for a given price, "product" is inevitably somewhat inferior. After all, these two propositions are but two aspects of a single one. If a seller could, by the larger scale of production which is characteristic of pure

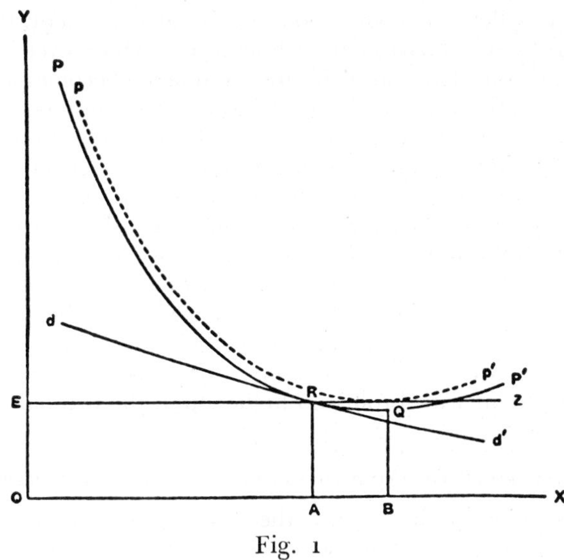

Fig. 1

as compared with monopolistic competition, give the same "product" for less money, he could, similarly, give a better "product" for the same money. This is illustrated in Fig. 1. If competition were pure, *dd'* would be horizontal, and competitive pressure would lower it to the point of tangency with *PP'* at *Q*, where the price would be *BQ*, lower than *AR*. But if the price were now held constant at *AR*, and any seller could dispose of any amount he pleased at that price (as under pure competition), each would expand his output to approximately *OB*, and the extra profits there being realized would be reduced, not by a fall in price, which is impossible by hypothesis, but by general improvement of the "product" with consequent rise in cost curves to the position of the dotted line *pp'*, whose minimum point equals *AR*. It follows that the impossibility of selling all he pleases at the going price creates a tendency not only towards higher prices, but also towards inferior product. Against these forces must, of course, be offset the gain through increased variety and freedom of choice.

THE SMALL GROUP: OLIGOPOLY PLUS MONOPOLISTIC COMPETITION

Having now considered the problems of . . . equilibrium within a group large enough to render each member of it a negligible influence upon the others, we pass to . . . [the case] of a group of relatively few sellers, perhaps only two. . . .

. . . A cut by one seller may lead to a smaller reduction by the one next to him and soon dissipate itself without spreading far. Or, under other circumstances, it might force those nearest him to meet it in full, this in turn forcing others, and so on indefinitely (as blocks in a row will tumble if the first one is started). In this latter case, *through the chain relationships,* a single seller may bring about a general movement, though he be but a negligibly small part of the whole group. Here, even though numbers are large, consideration of indirect influence becomes a factor, with the results already traced in this connection where numbers are small.

The general conclusion must be that the considerations relevant to competition between small numbers are much more generally applicable than might at first be supposed. Certainly, over a wide range of economic activity, the price not only *must,* on account of a differentiated product, be higher than the purely competitive level by at least an amount corresponding to what has been called "a sort of ideal"; it *may* rest at any higher point up to a figure which would maximize the joint profits of those whose markets are related. The extent to which such high prices are prevalent in the economic system is disguised by the fact that they are quite consistent with profits no higher than the ordinary competitive level. . . .

THE DIVERSITY OF CONDITIONS SURROUNDING EACH PRODUCER

The development of the "group" theory has, so far, employed the device of assuming the market of each seller to be of the same size and elasticity, and the cost conditions of each to be identical. Actually, of course, they differ widely. The demand curves for particular products vary both in location with reference to the x and y axes, and in elasticity, depending upon the vagaries of consumers' preferences, the quality of the product, the number and degree of perfection of available substitutes, the class of customers to which appeal is made, and upon many other factors. Similarly, the cost curves vary, both as to location and as to shape, for the simple reason that the products themselves are different. Finally, the two curves vary in their position relative to each other. . . .

Our statement of the group problem must be modified by recognizing that the demand curves are not adjusted uniformly to a position tangent to the cost curves. In so far as profits are higher than the general competitive level in the field as a whole or in any portion of it, new competitors will, *if possible,* invade the field and reduce them. If this were always possible, as hitherto assumed, the curves would always be tangent and monopoly profits would be eliminated. In fact it is only partially possible. As a result, some (or all) of the curves may lie at various distances to the right of the point of tangency, leaving monopoly profits scattered throughout the group—and throughout the price system.

Our theory has now taken into account that which pure competition omits—the special forces at work within the market of each seller. The existence of factors affecting each *variety* of the product can no more be ignored in the theory of value than can the existence of special forces affecting each general *class* of products. To ignore these latter would be to accept as a complete explanation of prices a theory explaining only the general price level. Absurd as this would be, it is only different in degree from stopping short with general classes of products and neglecting all the variety of economic forces at work within these classes. To smooth and perfect competition in this way not only gives a *general* bias to the results; it also levels down and removes at one sweep a whole class of differential elements which forms an essential part of the price structure.

PURE AND MONOPOLISTIC COMPETITION COMPARED

In the development of the theory of pure competition, it was shown that the equilibrium price is that one which equates demand and supply *for the reason that this is the only price consistent with maximum profits for each producer.* Comparison between monopolistic and pure competition is facilitated by restating the central thesis . . . in terms of this earlier argument. Where monopoly elements are present, the equilibrium price is *for this same reason,* inevitably higher than the one indicated by the intersection of the competitive demand and cost curves.

Let *DD′* and *PP′* (Fig. 2*a*) be the demand and cost curves, respectively, for a good sold under conditions of pure competition.[1] There are many buyers and sellers and the good is perfectly standardized. The equilibrium price is *AR*. In Fig. 2*b* the conditions with respect to the individual producer are shown, and . . . the horizontal scale is that of Fig. 2*a* divided by the number of sellers. (If there are fifty sellers, *oa* is 1/50 of *OA*.) The vertical scale is the same in the two figures. The demand and cost curves for the product of the individual producer are, respectively, *ee′* and *pp′*. He adjusts his output to *oa,* his most efficient scale of production, and the price, *ar,* exactly covers his costs. His profits are a maximum, for any other adjustment would reduce them below the necessary minimum included in the cost curve.

Now let the product be differentiated, and let us suppose the differentiation to be of such nature that the curves of cost production are not materially affected. Let us assume, further, that the demand curve for the general market, *DD′*, is unaltered by the fact of differentiation. The demand curve for the goods of any one producer does not remain unaltered, however. The fact of differentiation tips it slightly, so that it may be represented by the solid line *dd′* (Fig. 2*b*), passing through *r*.

1 Conditions of constant cost alone are taken up. The argument would be analogous for increasing and for decreasing costs.

Reactions . . . may now be quickly summarized. Each producer's profits will be increased by raising his price, and this rise will attract new competitors to the field. The curve *dd'* will be moved to the left to the position of the dotted line, and prices for all will settle at *bq,* where this line is tangent to the curve of cost of production, *pp'*.[2] The output of each is *ob,* and to obtain the total for all, this must be multiplied by the number of sellers. Turning now to Fig. 2*a,* it is seen that this total must be *OB,* the amount which will be purchased at the price of *BQ*. This amount, although produced by a larger number of establishments than would be present under purely competitive conditions, is smaller (by *BA*) than the competitive output, the reason being that each is producing on a reduced scale. The total cost of this volume is not *OBHP,* as the competitive cost curve indicates, but *OBQM,* which is greater. Although

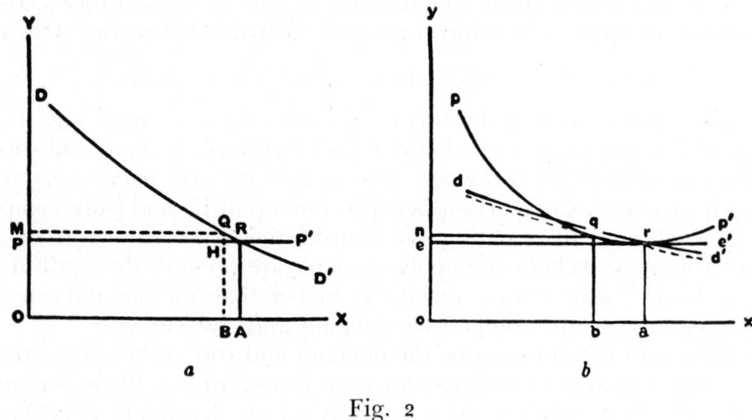

Fig. 2

the equilibrium price is higher under monopolistic competition than under pure competition, the result is not, therefore (as might be expected), a discrepancy between cost and price.

Although higher than the intersection of the demand and supply curves, the price of *BQ* in Fig. 2*a* is perfectly stable. As was the case in the theory of pure competition, the reason must be sought in the conditions pertaining to the individual sellers. It is that *BQ* is the only price consistent with maximum profits for them. The necessity for distinguishing carefully between the equilibrium price and the purely competitive price is again brought to the fore. The two are always divergent when the product is differentiated. Indeed, in this case, the answer to the price problem is not to be had from the purely competitive assumptions or graphic representations. It is impossible to tell from Fig. 2*a* what the price will be, for the point *Q* is derived from Fig. 2*b,* pertaining to the individual seller.

It might seem that this difficulty would be obviated by drawing the

2 Possibilities of the price rising higher than this are omitted for the sake of brevity. Their explanation would be analogous.

curve of costs above the competitive cost curve and parallel to it, representing the costs which must be covered under the conditions of monopolistic competition, instead of under the conditions of pure competition. Such a cost curve would pass through *Q*, and, in the case of constant cost, would be horizontal, being an extension of *MQ* in Fig. 2*a*. But such a curve is not a cost curve, for it does not show the cost at which different amounts of the good can be produced; it can play no part in determining the price *BQ*. It can be drawn only *after BQ* has been defined by the demand and cost curves of the individual products, and, being the locus of these individual equilibria for different total volumes of product, it is as much a curve of demand as of cost. It is defined by the equilibrium price, and can contribute nothing to the explanation of it. This cannot be said of a true cost curve—either *PP′* or *pp′*.

The question is squarely presented of whether competitive theory should be applied at all where monopoly elements are present. We may grant that economic principles work out only in the rough, and that the *actual* price may be neither *AR* nor *BQ;* nevertheless, it tends towards or approximates *BQ*, not *AR*. The price problem for a differentiated product cannot be forced into the mould of competitive demand and cost curves without introducing into the conclusions definite errors—the price is always too low, the cost of production is too low, the scale of production is too large, and the number of producers is too small.

Monopolistic Competition and the Productivity Theory of Distribution

Without raising controversial questions about the productivity theory itself, let it be accepted, for purposes of this argument, as valid under the conditions of pure competition to which it has always (until recently) been implicitly or explicitly related. Its central tenet, that factors of production are paid according to their "marginal productivity," is subject to a variety of interpretations. For our purposes, three possible meanings seem to be important. "Marginal productivity" may refer (*a*) to the physical product, (*b*) to the value of the physical product, or (*c*) to the revenue; which is added, in any case, by the presence of the marginal unit of a factor.

As to the first, it is conceivable that, even in an economic system characterized by a high degree of division of labor, factors of production might be paid literally in their physical product. Farm workers, restaurant employees, and domestic servants are laborers who receive at least a part of their wages in the product which they have helped to produce; and there might be mentioned also the case of a large distilling company which recently paid its stockholders a dividend in whisky. Ordinarily, however, income receivers consume little or none of the product of the enterprise with which they are associated, and it can be marketed so much more effectively by the enterprise itself than by individuals that it would obviously be absurd (and often impossible, as in the case of services) to pay incomes in product and place the burden of exchange upon the income receivers.

For this reason, although "marginal product" has ordinarily meant physical product, the proposition that factors are paid according to their "marginal productivity" has meant that they are paid, not the product itself, but the money obtained from its sale. Thus the second meaning of "marginal productivity," referring to the value of the physical product, merely recognizes the fact of exchange: it is the equivalent of the physical product in money terms, the physical product multiplied by its selling price. It is this meaning which will be adhered to throughout this chapter.

The marginal revenue product (or marginal value product, as it has usually been called), on the other hand, is, in general, quite dissociated from the physical product or its money equivalent. It refers to the added *revenue*—the total revenue (price per unit multiplied by the number of

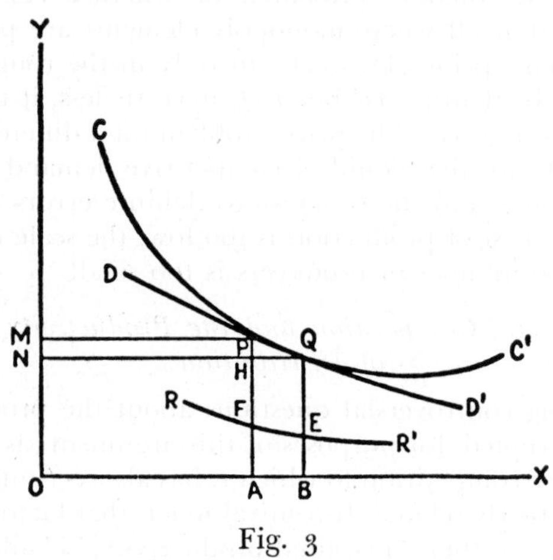

Fig. 3

units) when the last unit of the factor is used less the total revenue when it is not used. In Fig. 3, if the amount of product is increased from *OA* to *OB* by the addition of another laborer, the value of the marginal product is *ABQH;* the marginal revenue product is *OBQN-OAPM* (or *ABQH-NHPM*). The marginal revenue product may be defined most neatly by the use of the marginal revenue curve. It is the marginal physical product multiplied by the marginal revenue.[3] If *RR′* in Fig. 3 is the marginal revenue curve, it is *ABEF*.

Now it is evident that the entrepreneur is always and everywhere, whether under pure or under monopolistic competition, interested only in the marginal revenue products of the factors he employs. But under pure competition, since he can change his output without appreciable effect upon the price, this will always be identical with the value of the

[3] Strictly speaking, each unit of the marginal product must be multiplied by its own marginal revenue and the sum taken.

marginal product. In other words, under pure competition, the demand curve for the product of an individual producer being a horizontal line, his marginal revenue curve coincides with it. Marginal revenue is always equal to selling price. Hence marginal product and marginal revenue product *to the individual competitor* are always identical. Thus it is that, interested only in a factor's marginal revenue product, the entrepreneur arrives nevertheless at paying it its marginal product.

This is shown graphically in Figs. 4*a* and 4*b*. Figure 4*b* is the familiar diagram showing the demand and cost curves (*md* and *cc'*, respectively) for an individual producer under pure competition; Fig. 4*a* shows the demand and cost curves (*DD'* and *MC*, respectively, constant cost being assumed) for the product of *all* the producers. The two figures thus show the *same* facts from two different points of view. It is clear from Fig. 4*b* that, as I have argued, the value of the marginal product (*abqh*) is equal

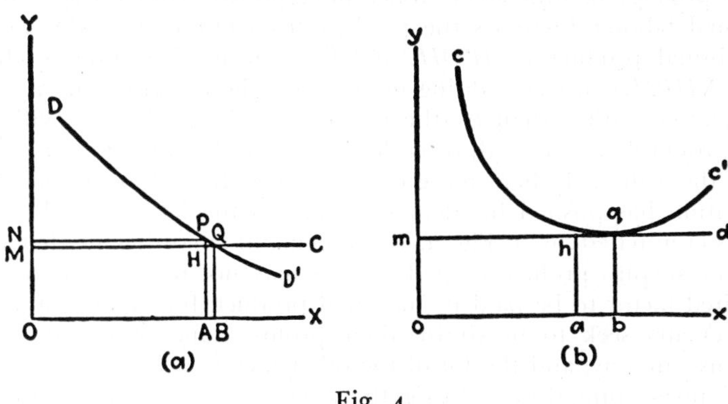

Fig. 4

to the marginal revenue product (*obqm-oahm*) in the eyes of the individual producer. There is an apparent contradiction to this in Fig. 4*a*, where the value of the marginal product is *ABQH* and the marginal revenue product is less than this, *ABQH-MHPN* (equal to *OBQM-OAPN*). But it must not be forgotten that the marginal revenue product in which the individual seller is interested is his own, not that for the market as a whole. If we assume the elasticity of *DD'* between *P* and *Q* in Fig. 4*a* to be unity, then as an individual seller increases his product by the amount *AB*, he adds nothing to the value of the whole supply, and therefore nothing to the revenue derived by all producers together from its sale. But he adds proportionately to the value of his own (Fig. 4*b*), for the sacrifice in price is spread over a large number of producers whereas the greater volume is enjoyed by himself alone. It is for this reason that price will settle at *BQ* (Fig. 4*a*) instead of at *AP* (or at any other point), where the value of the whole supply may be the same. And it is for this reason that each factor will receive the value of its marginal product under pure competition.

Turning to monopolistic competition, let it first be recalled that the number of variables in the problem has increased. Output is now conditioned only in part by price. It is a function also of the "product" in its various phases, and of selling costs. The relation of product variation to the productivity theory will not be taken up here. It is assumed that variations in the proportions of the factors result in different amounts of the *same* product, not in different *kinds* of product. (We may, if we like, suppose that the optimum "product" has been found and that the decisions to be made have been correspondingly narrowed.) . . .

Let us look, then, for the moment, at the price-quantity relationships under monopolistic competition. Because of the sloping demand curve for the product of an individual producer, it appears at once that the marginal revenue product of a factor to him is inevitably smaller than the value of its marginal product. If *DD′* in Fig. 3 is the demand curve for the product of one seller under monopolistic competition, and an additional laborer increases the product from *OA* to *OB*, the value of his marginal product is *ABQH*, and his marginal revenue product is *ABQH-NHPM*. Since, in adding more labor, the entrepreneur is guided by the latter, rather than by the former, it follows that he will never find it profitable and he will often find it impossible to pay to *any* of the factors the value of their marginal products. It will be impossible if competition has pushed his demand curve to the left until all surplus profit is eliminated, as in Fig. 3. If the demand curve lies further to the right, the surplus profit obtained may or may not be enough to permit each hired factor to be paid its marginal product, but if we assume that entrepreneurs seek to maximize their profits, none of it will be put to this use anyway, and the lot of the other factors is in nowise changed. There is no escaping the conclusion that even a slight element of monopoly necessarily reduces the remuneration of all factors employed in a given firm below the value of their marginal products.[4]

It should be emphasized that the deviations of the distributive shares from their marginal products are always in one direction—the share is always smaller. This fortifies conclusions stressed elsewhere in the general theory of monopolistic competition, that pure competition is an extreme, a limit, rather than a norm. Actual prices, distributive shares, and conditions of production generally do not tend toward or oscillate about what they would be under pure competition. Rather, they tend toward norms in the definition of which the monopoly elements must be given full

[4] It should be remarked parenthetically that the cost curve which is relevant to variations in one factor while the others are held constant is not the long-run curve which is usually envisaged in our study, where resources are most effectively organized with reference to each volume of output. Assuming them most effectively organized with reference to the output *OB*, the point *Q* would lie on this latter curve. Since a variation in any one factor from this point without changing the others would, in general, involve conditions of production somewhat less effective than the optimum ones for the resulting outputs, the curve here relevant would lie above the curve defined by the most efficient organization of factors for each output at all points except *Q*, being tangent to it at that point. . . .

recognition. Except where the conditions are actually those of pure competition, competitive theory is a distortion of reality rather than an approximation to it.

Let it be noted that *all* factors (not merely any one, say, labor) receive less than their marginal products; yet it is evident from the figure that this is consistent with a total paid to them which is exactly equal to the total product valued at its selling price. Only minimum profits are included in the cost curve: there is no excess which might be attributed to "exploitation." [5] This requires looking into. Apparently each factor produces more than it gets, yet there is nothing left over after all have been paid.

The answer lies in the fact that the sum of the incomes computed on the basis of marginal products is greater than the total product. The two will be equal only when the productivity function is a homogeneous function of the first degree, i.e., when a small proportionate change in *all* the factors together will yield a proportionate change in product. This will be true only where both average costs and average revenue (price) remain constant with such a change. In other words, it will be true only under pure competition, where, for small deviations from equilibrium (the minimum point on the cost curve) both demand and cost curves are approximately horizontal. At this point the value of the marginal product and the marginal revenue product are equal, and total payments to the factors in terms of either will exactly equal the total income to be distributed. As the demand curve is tipped more and more from the horizontal, under monopolistic competition, so that its point of tangency with the cost curve lies further and further to the left of this minimum point, the discrepancy between marginal products and marginal revenue products increases. The sum of the latter continues to exhaust the total product; the sum of the former grows more and more in excess of it. In the case of firms, the demand curves for whose products lie above the cost curves, there is, of course, a monopoly profit, and this suggests the possibility of increasing the incomes of the *hired* factors to some extent, perhaps even to the value of their marginal products. It is impossible, however, even here, for *all* factors to get their marginal products: hired factors would gain at the expense of the profits share, entrepreneurship receiving now not only less than its marginal product as before, but even less than its marginal revenue product. (Entrepreneurship, or any other factor, may, of course, receive less than its marginal revenue product consistent with getting more than its supply price.) Furthermore, it seems obvious that to pay any particular factor, say labor, more in such firms would be to establish uneven rates of pay for the same work in different enterprises. The remedy is clearly to eliminate the monopoly profits by a price adjustment in favor of the consumer rather than to turn a part of them over to labor.

[5] Cf. Mrs. Robinson, *The Economics of Imperfect Competition*, pp. 283 ff., for a different view.

Evidently the Pigovian definition of exploitation as a wage less than the marginal physical product of labor valued at its selling price is appropriate only to conditions of pure competition, where, if labor receives less than the value of its marginal product, employers are, in fact, pocketing a part of the revenue which the marginal laborer brings in, and where the relation between marginal products and the total product is such that it is possible for labor and all factors to be paid the full value of their marginal products without exceeding the amount to be distributed. It is not appropriate to monopolistic competition, where these conditions do not hold. Here *all* factors are necessarily "exploited" in this sense in order that total payments may be brought within the bounds of the amount available to be paid; it would be impossible for employers to avoid the charge of "exploitation" without going into bankruptcy. Yet Mrs. Robinson adopts such a competitive definition for this field, and even considers how the "exploitation" might be removed, discovering, naturally enough, that, in general, it could not be, except by setting up conditions of "perfect" competition!

HEINRICH VON STACKELBERG

(1905–1946)

In contrast to the Chamberlin-Robinson approach, which centered attention on cases where possible indeterminacy through mutual interdependence is at a minimum, is the theory presented by Heinrich von Stackelberg in *Marktform und Gleichgewicht* (*Market Structure and Equilibrium*, 1934), which consistently emphasized the interdependence of firms and the problems of oligopoly. The conventional theory of monopolistic or imperfect competition is thus of little relevance here.

For Stackelberg, the "pure" duopoly case is the simplified form of the central problem of monopoly theory. Under pure duopoly, equilibrium is achieved only by accident, when one firm adopts the price and production policies of the other. Apart from this occurrence, an infinite number of situations is possible, increasing in complexity as more firms enter the picture and duopoly becomes oligopoly. Unlike the Chamberlin model, Stackelberg's pure oligopoly case does not allow for product differentiation, which is only included later on as an additional variable increasing the difficulty of arriving at a determinate solution. Equilibrium in the oligopoly case results only through a highly fortuitous combination of circumstances. In actuality, oligopoly gives rise to destructive competition and a chaotic market situation.

This view is also in contrast to the neoclassical theory, in which the assumption of many sellers made it possible to ignore the interdependent reactions of competing rivals, since the market situation as a whole could not be altered by any single participant. When the number of firms is small, however, it is impossible for any firm to treat the ruling price as a given datum. Each firm, by changing its policies, can now bring about a change in the policies of its rivals, which, in turn, will affect its own decisions. In short, the distinguishing characteristic of oligopoly is mutual and circular interdependence of decision-making among the participating firms. This situation will be approximated when the number of sellers has become so small that no seller can ignore the effect of his price and output policies upon those of his competitors. Oligopoly situations are likely to be extremely unstable unless there is some type of mutual agreement. Due to the presence of uncertainty and mutual interdependence, any error of estimate by one producer will be compounded immediately, producing chaotic market conditions. Outright collusion, with direct negotiations among rivals, may occur, but "spontaneous co-ordination"—a mutually recognized *modus vivendi* among firms—is the more frequent method of circumventing the dangers of instability. Each firm adjusts its own policies to the expected reactions of rivals. Eventually price and output reach generally acceptable levels, comparable to those determined by collusive agreements but reached without direct negotiation.

Stackelberg also has an admirable discussion of the many forms of market structures, considered from both producer and consumer standpoints, and of the disturbing frequency with which they fail to achieve equilibrium. He is most realistic in showing that where disequilibrium results, equilibrium may be imposed through an instrumentality like a cartel or through state action. He further points out that whereas a liberal, democratic state cannot, an authoritarian state can, eliminate market structures which fail to achieve equilibrium. From that point he develops a defense of authoritarian interventionism. Since the free play of forces will not result in economic equilibrium, the economy is in need of regulation by the state. He is prescient in showing how wages, rent, and profits are determined, not by natural market equilibrium, but by price controls, arbitration, wage negotiations, and compulsory cartels.

MARKET STRUCTURE AND EQUILIBRIUM *

A System of Market Structures

Of the different characteristics by which one could differentiate market structures, only the number of sellers and buyers and the magnitude of the volume realized by any one of them is of interest to us here; only these two factors—as will become even clearer in what is to follow—are relevant for the question of the law of movement and of the functioning of the market mechanism. First of all, we deal with the number of economic units. At first glance this characteristic leads to many possible combinations, as each side of the market may show any number of economic units. In the course of the inquiry it will be shown, however, that the forms of each side of the market can be gathered up in three typical categories which represent all cases: if one side of the market consists of only one economic unit, it represents a monopoly; if it consists of a few economic units, then we have an oligopoly; if it shows very many economic units, then we have "free competition." Both last-named categories are not separated from each other by a fixed border line. Yet they represent in their consequences two basically different cases; how the transition occurs will be shown in the course of the inquiry.

As each side of the market may belong in any one of the three defined categories, there arise altogether nine typical market structures. Each of these market structures must be appropriately named. If nothing is said about one side of the market it should be construed as taking the form of free competition. If there is a monopoly on both sides of the market, this market form will be named *bilateral monopoly*. Analogous to it is the expression *bilateral oligopoly*. If both sides appear in "free competition," we shall simply talk about *free competition*. If a *supply monopoly* faces a *demand oligopoly*, then we have a *restricted supply monopoly*. The term *restricted demand monopoly* is to be understood in a parallel fashion. We get, therefore, the following systematic scheme:

TYPE OF DEMAND	TYPE OF SUPPLY		
	Free Competition	*Oligopoly*	*Monopoly*
Free competition	Free competition	Supply oligopoly	Supply monopoly
Oligopoly	Demand oligopoly	Bilateral oligopoly	Restricted supply monopoly
Monopoly	Demand monopoly	Restricted demand monopoly	Bilateral monopoly

Duopolistic Market Structures—General Analysis

There exists a far-reaching analogy between demand duopoly, supply duopoly, the supply as it affects two demand monopolists, the demand as it affects two supply monopolists, and indirect bilateral monopoly. This

* From *Marktform und Gleichgewicht* (Vienna, Springer, 1934).

permits us to treat at one time the special problems of these market structures and their relationships. In particular, we want to discover when the individual positions are the most favorable ones for any duopolist or monopolist, and when, therefore, duopoly structures arise.

The major characteristic of the above-mentioned five market structures is the appearance of two economic organisms, each of which does some business in the market or fixes a market price and influences thereby the ophelimity index or the profit of the other one. Let us call the two economic organisms *A* and *B,* and let us call the quantity of commodities exchanged by them or the prices fixed by them *x* and *y*. We can say, therefore, that the ophelimity index of each of these two economic organisms depends on these two magnitudes. On this basis we can furnish a general analysis equally valid for price and quantity policy. Inasmuch as *x* and *y* may stand for quantities as well as for prices, we shall refer in what is to follow merely to the values of *x* and *y*.

Since we are dealing with only two organisms, the problem lends itself to graphical presentation. This sort of presentation is necessary, since otherwise the relationships become too complicated. We construct a system of rectangular coordinates, with *x* on the abscissa and *y* on the ordinate. Each point in the first quadrant represents a specific combination of both values. Each point also represents an ophelimity index (gain) of *A* and *B*. All points on the same ophelimity index form an indifference curve *à la* Pareto. The first quadrant, therefore, shows two groups of indifference curves: one for *A* and one for *B*. These indifference curves may, a priori, have any conceivable shape. . . .

For *A,* any value of *y* realized by *B* is an independent magnitude. He will choose that value of *x* which gives him the largest ophelimity index for any given value of *y*. That is, he will choose the optimum point which lies on a line parallel to the *x* axis at the distance *y*. We may immediately exclude the case in which this particular point lies in infinity, since an infinitely large price or quantity is impossible. As long as this point is not on the *y* axis, it must be a point where a line parallel to the *x* axis is tangent to one of *A*'s indifference curves. Since we can always assume the existence of a maximum, we can postulate that each indifference curve of *A* has a point of tangency with a line parallel to the *x* axis. Furthermore, we must assume that the ophelimity index rises in the direction of the point of tangency; otherwise, the point of tangency would be not an ophelimity maximum, but a minimum.

To each value of *y, A* assigns a point of horizontal tangency to one of his indifference curves. The locus of all these points of tangency, *i.e.,* the path of all points where indifference curves have horizontal tangents, forms the reaction curve of *A* to *B*'s values of *y*. This reaction curve assigns an *x* to each value of *y;* that is, it defines *x* as a function of *y*.

Since each *y* has a corresponding point on this curve, *A*'s reaction curve will always slope upward. Depending on the particular shape of the indifference curves, the reaction curve may form an angle with the x axis which will be greater than, equal to, or less than, ninety degrees.

Figure 1 shows the four most typical shapes of indifference curves of A. From these, any other combination can be derived.

Indifference curves for B are shown in Figure 2. They are constructed on the same principle as those shown for A.

Let a and b denote the reaction curves of A and B, respectively. If B considers A's value of x as a given independent magnitude, then B will always obtain that value of y which corresponds to the value of x via B's reaction curve. In that case, A will look for the optimum point, not on a line parallel to the x axis, but on the reaction curve b. This is the point where the reaction curve b is tangent to one of A's indifference curves. This point is on the reaction curve a only if the reaction curve b is horizontal at the point of tangency. We define this point as the independence point of A. In a corresponding fashion, we define the independence point of B.

If both economic organisms attempt to realize their independence points, we obtain a point which represents A's and B's independence values. We

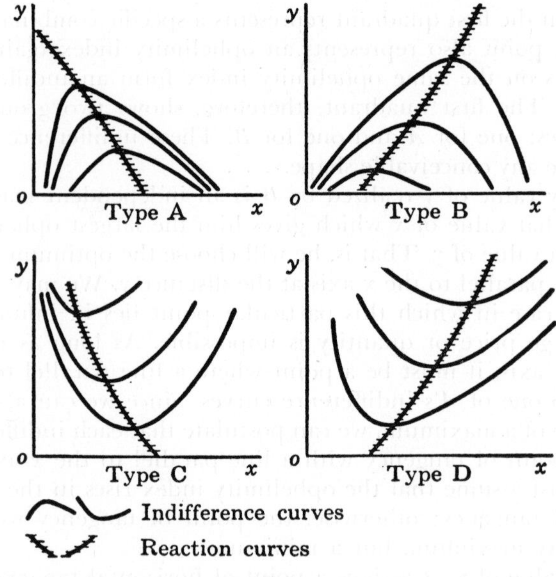

Fig. 1

Type A: Ophelimity indices decrease in an upward direction; reaction curve has negative slope.

Type B: Like A, except that reaction curve has positive slope.

Type C: Like A, except that ophelimity indices increase in an upward direction.

Type D: Like C, except that reaction curve has positive slope.

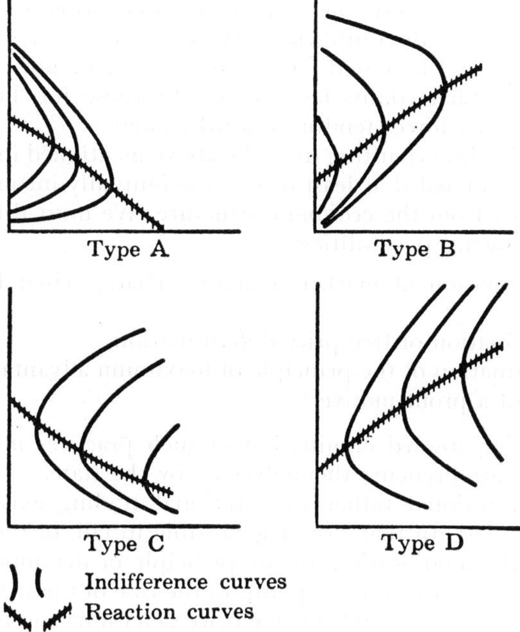

Fig. 2

define this point as the Edgeworth-Bowley duopoly point; at the intersection of both reaction curves, we have the Cournot duopoly point. The combination which is determined at this point will be realized if each of the two economic organisms is influenced by the behavior of the other one, *i.e.,* if it tends toward a dependency position. . . .

The Achievement of Equilibrium as the Objective of Economic Policy

The four forms of the market, demand oligopoly, supply oligopoly, bilateral oligopoly, and bilateral monopoly, are all incompatible with the two basic principles of a free capitalistic economy: *i.e.,* the striving to maximize profits and the freedom of price determination. Furthermore, the coexistence of a number of markets which are characterized by simple or restricted demand or supply monopolies is also incompatible with these basic principles. Since it is a safe assumption that there are such market relations in an economy, the following propositions will generally hold: the more the market forms of an economy deviate from "free competition," the greater the incompatibility of the circulatory mechanism of such an economy with the above-mentioned basic principles. This incompatibility has the practical effect of endangering and disturbing the whole economic mechanism to an unlimited degree; it also becomes a force tending to change the organization of the whole economy. The objective here is to survey those economic changes which bring about the elimination of just such a disequilibrium. Whatever forces there are tending toward a change will be tested only as to whether or not they eliminate disequilibrium. What counts here is not the cause for, but simply the occurrence of, such forces tending toward change.

The disequilibrium resulting from the above-mentioned incompatibility can only be eliminated if at least one of the mutually incompatible practices is excluded from the economic structure. We must differentiate between the following possibilities:

1. The elimination of market structures characterized by disequilibrium.
2. The elimination of free price determination.
3. The elimination of the principle of maximum advantages, especially the principle of a profit motive.

Action looking toward elimination of such practices might be taken either by the entrepreneurs themselves or by the state.

Wherever traditional rather than rational trading exists, disequilibrium does not exist. In that case it is possible to talk of the elimination, or at least of the modification, of the principle of maximum advantage. The same is true, up to a certain point, in the case of the new co-operative movement, where the principle of free price determination is also changed or modified. It is impossible to eliminate the profit motive within the capitalistic sector of the economy, since the former is generally taken as an essential characteristic of the latter. Therefore, we must account here only for two things: the elimination of market structures characterized by disequilibrium, and the elimination of free price determination.

All theoreticians who have dealt with the problem of oligopoly have pointed to the fact that it is in the interest of the oligopolist to combine with other oligopolists and thereby transform oligopoly into monopoly. It is thus that we can interpret the formation of cartels, combines, and trusts as a change-over from the complex case of oligopoly to the relatively simpler case of monopoly. We recognize, however, that this process of concentration from oligopoly into monopoly cannot inevitably assure economic equilibrium, although the creation of monopolies eliminates the disequilibrium which is identified with the known market relations between monopolies. Consequently, it might become necessary to combine the monopolies in competing and complementary goods, a process which could end only in a complete unification of total production. This would be impossible to achieve through private agreement in an economy built upon individual initiative. Moreover, this concentration must result in the creation of bilateral monopolies. The lack of equilibrium in these market structures, *i.e.,* bilateral monopolies, can be eliminated if both monopolists unite in a vertical combination. Yet even in that case there exists the danger of irreconcilable conflict to a much higher degree than in the case of oligopoly. The unification of oligopolists into monopoly not only eliminates the disequilibrium characteristic of oligopoly but presents the possibility of higher gain as well; a vertical combination between monopolists, however, generally means a compromise between both parties. The common gain can only be increased if the monopolist buyer at the same time enjoys a monopoly position in the market for his output.

Conflict between labor unions and employer associations, which occasionally transform the ideology of class warfare into reality, can be considered in our context as an example of irreconcilable antagonism on a bilaterally monopolized labor market, and one which cannot be ameliorated by voluntary co-operation between the participants. . . .

In general, we can say that equilibrium conditions established by the economic participants themselves do not guarantee a smoothly functioning circulatory mechanism. In particular, the profit motive, which is the driving force behind the establishment of these new equilibria, has at the same time monopolistic tendencies toward exploitation; economic productivity decreases, and frictions in the economy are generally increased in an unlimited degree. The truth of this argument becomes obvious in the light of present-day conditions.

Liberal economic policy has always rejected state interference in the economic system. . . . We shall, however, examine briefly the degree to which governmental economic policy may have an equilibrating function.

The formation of state-sponsored cartels may then be considered, without further comment, as the elimination of the market structure beset by disequilibrium. Price regulations, which usually are an inevitable adjunct thereto, represent the simultaneous end to free price formation. Nearly all governmental domestic policies in the economic field may have the same effect. Price control, wage and hour laws, production controls, usury laws, measures against unfair competition and the misuse of economic power, and many other controls may acquire the same significance: the end of free price determination. In liberal states, government intervention in the economy results primarily from parliamentary compromises and is not part of an over-all plan. Consequently, the market structure, being subjected to this unplanned intervention, suffers from more frictions than ever before.

Things are different, however, when a powerful state, in pursuit of a single aim, superimposes upon the economy an over-all plan. Here exists the possibility of consciously supplementing, through economic policy, business cycles whose behavior otherwise would not necessarily conform with the will of the state. Economic policy, then, has two functions: (1) to supplement automatic economic forces when they fail to function properly, (2) to construct an economic system which not merely functions, but functions in a way desired by the state. . . .

The Fascist-Corporate Market

An interesting example of an integral market regulation by the state is Italy. The market organized along corporate lines, as we find it in the Fascist economic constitution, has developed over the years to such a degree that it appears possible to give a short theoretical description of its price determination. This is the reason why we have dedicated the following final paragraphs to the theoretical analysis of the corporate market organization. . . .

The Fascist economic system in Italy has received different interpretations, three of which we shall select here.

The idea which rejects in the most radical way not only the results but the methods of hitherto existing economic theory is the teaching of Ugo Spirito which culminates in the dogma of the "identity of the individual and the state." That means: the individual is only justified in existing insofar as he is a partial function of the state. Accordingly, all his acts basically are acts of the state.

A different idea is the one of Gino Arias which is connected with the concept of the "corporate conscience" (*coscienza corporativa*). According to this, the individual member of the corporate state acts freely because, as a result of the existence of the "corporate conscience" within himself, he can never be at variance with the state and the collective interests of the nation respectively.

Both these normative ideas—because this is what they are in view of their obvious difference from reality—would mean, in our frame of reference, an abolition of the principle of maximum gain in the sense hitherto used. If human beings were to realize through an evolutionary and educational process the dogma of Spirito, a lack of equilibrium in the markets—insofar as they would still exist—could not exist any more, because the state, whose executive organs would be the individuals, cannot conflict with itself. If Arias' conception were to become a reality, the lack of equilibrium would be eliminated by the fact that the "corporate conscience" would stop the individuals, who act on their own responsibility and on their own initiative, from doing anything which could cause disorder in the national economic mechanism.

Both concepts, however, are merely dogmas, utopias, which cannot describe in any way the actual state of affairs. The closest approach to the real conditions was probably made by the two scientists who work together in this field: Alberto De'Stefani and Luigi Amorose.[1] They explained that the free play of forces under present-day circumstances did not guarantee either a "desired" equilibrium or an equilibrium at all and that the economy, therefore, was in need of the regulating, connecting,

[1] A. De'Stefani and L. Amoroso: "Lo Stato e la vita economica," *Rivista Italiana di statistica, economia e finanza,* Anno IV (1932), pp. 201 ff. By the same authors: "La logica del sistema corporativa," *Rivista internationale di scienze sociale e discipline ausiliare,* Anno 41, Ser. 3, vol. 4 (1933), pp. 393 ff.

and equalizing guidance of the state. This is said to be the economic function of the corporate state.

We can agree fully with this concept; we want now to test briefly this equalizing and goal-setting function of the corporate state.

A short schematic description of the market organization, as it has been programmatically announced in the Fascist economic constitution and as it is partly realized and partly still in a state of development, will be given in advance of the theoretical analysis. . . .

The regulation of the labor market occurs in such a way that both syndicates sit down at the bargaining table and attempt to conclude an agreement which is then binding for all those who belong to that particular branch of production. If an agreement is not concluded, an attempt to secure agreement is made on a higher level. If the arbitration is unsuccessful, then the decision is made by a labor court which not only has to adjust the interests of the participants but primarily has to further the over-all productivity of the economy. The state, too, according to this point of view, can cause the labor court to intervene. It is the aim of these institutions to see not only that an agreement is reached between the parties dealing in the market but that it is in accord, as well, with the will of the state as a representative of the nation.

In the same way in which the syndicates regulate the relations in the labor market, it becomes the task of the corporations to regulate the relationships among the different branches of production. The corporate regulation of these material markets (markets of intermediate products in the widest sense) occurs in the same way as the syndicalist regulation of the labor market. What is of significance is the participation of the employees in the regulation of the relations between the branches of production and, furthermore, the fact that the regulation, as a task of the corporations, is a function of the state.

In order to obtain the result of the above-sketched picture of the corporate market, corresponding to our market theory, we merely need to cite the short and succinct formulation by Erwin von Beckerath:

"This regulation schematically shows that both parts of the labor market, employer and employees, were united in recognized syndicates which monopolized the formulations of the conditions of employment. Thus, two monopolistic organizations faced each other between which, following the teachings of economic theory, no natural equilibrium exists. If the Carta del Lavoro leaves it up to the representatives of both syndicate groups at first to find the artificial (conscious) equilibrium, then its aim is to use in the wage determination the insight of the participants in the market conditions; yet the state reserves for itself the decision in case the parties do not correspond to the threefold requirements which the Carta del Lavoro requires from the wage. In short, the state has the power to put the seal of its will on the agreement by permitting its publication or by forcing upon the participants a deviating equilibrium. In this case, the labor courts are used; this has not frequently happened so far.

"In the same fashion, in accordance with the Carta, there exists the possibility that the other economic markets too can be regulated just as the labor market."

In accordance with the organizational idea of the corporate economy, all markets are changed over into the form of a bilateral monopoly. Here, however, free price determination is eliminated and in its stead a price is set which is fixed in the last analysis by the state but which rests on the expert knowledge and interest of the participants. This "conventional" price [2] appears to each market participant as a given magnitude independent of his own individual behavior. If at such a price no adjustment occurs of the amount supplied and the amount demanded, the state can correct the price at any time.

The deciding factor is the restriction on price determination by the state. It is possible that the price deviates from the "normal price" for political or socio-political reasons (for instance in the labor market). If such reasons do not exist, then, in the ideal case, because of the principle of maximum productivity of the economy (which time and again is expressed in the Carta del Lavoro) the normal turnover is reached at the normal price.

If we compare the "natural" equilibrium in a market with "free competition"—practically nonexistent in a pure form—with the "conventional" equilibrium on the bilaterally monopolised corporate market which is diametrically opposed to free competition—an equilibrium created through the lasting intervention of the state—we see that the corporate market leads in principle to the same result as "free competition." The factual deviations of the corporate equilibrium from the ideal case would not be judged differently, in the last analysis, than the factual deviations of the approximately competitive markets of the past free capitalistic economy from their theoretical ideals. It is thus shown that the corporate organization of the market, among other things, neutralises the very structural changes which have led to the abolition of the natural equilibrium in a free capitalistic economy and realizes a new equilibrium.

[2] This price is quite similar to the *prix crié* which Schumpeter has introduced into the problem of bilateral monopoly.

OSKAR MORGENSTERN

(1902–   )

The theoretical vacuum created by the limitations of existing price theory with regard to problems of oligopoly has finally led to an entirely new approach. Because of the dominant element of uncertainty in the oligopoly case, analogy has been made to the general aspects of military strategy. The role of the entrepreneur has been compared to that of a military commander on a battlefield, and economic theorists have been urged to turn from Marshall to Clausewitz for guidance.

The analogy of the oligopoly case to "games" suggests itself immediately. At the turn of the century, Edgeworth likened the monopolist to a chess player who takes account of the opponent's probable moves before moving himself. The same note reappeared in Pigou's *Economics of Welfare* (1920, p. 233). He also suggested, elsewhere, that if the relative probabilities of the various potential relationships between firms could be postulated, it might be possible, with proper limiting assumptions, to demarcate a range within which the price level would come to be situated. The solution of this problem was advanced in 1944 by two members of the faculty of Princeton University, Professors John von Neumann and Oskar Morgenstern, in their *Theory of Games and Economic Behavior.* Here the authors liken economic behavior to games of strategy and tactics, where the outcome is determined by the mutually interdependent personal action of opposing individuals. The theory is not limited by its authors to the oligopoly case, but is supposed to be relevant to all types of markets; that is to say, nothing less than an entire revolution in economic method is here proposed.

The theory of games has received widespread attention and has caused a considerable stirring in the area of utility theory. For one thing, it is a *general* theory and is capable of treating problems of collusion as well as of competition, since both become special cases. What is really needed at the present time is an empirical testing of the theory.

It is difficult to say whether this "games" approach is likely to yield a substitute theory in years to come. We may suspend judgment until such time as the authors bring the theory out of its present rarefied setting so that it may be brought to bear upon the significant practical problems. In its original form, unfortunately, the theory of games does not seem susceptible of comparison with received economic doctrine. We may note, furthermore, that the theory involves serious difficulties in cases of more than three persons, while special assumptions are frequently introduced to arrive at a determinate solution. The theory assumes that the participants remain independent and play a sort of guessing game of strategy to arrive at price and output determination. It assumes a "card game" in which the probability of obtaining one card or the other may be calculated if the players play independently, *i.e.*, if the cards are dealt by random chance. Oligopoly, however, seems to be analogous to a situation in which the players mark their cards or secretly combine into groups, so probability analysis does not always seem appropriate.

The theory of games requires a highly involved and lengthy exposition which unfortunately does not lend itself to compression. However, the following two articles—one an expository review by Professor Leonid Hurwicz of *The Theory of Games and Economic Behavior,* the other a translated article in which Professor Morgenstern gives a non-mathematical discussion of the subject—will together serve as a satisfactory introduction to this new and important field of economics.

THE THEORY OF ECONOMIC BEHAVIOR *

To a considerable extent this review is of an expository nature. This seems justified by the importance of the book, its use of new and unfamiliar concepts and its very length which some may find a serious obstacle.

The existence of the gap which the book attempts to fill has been known to the economic theorists at least since Cournot's work on duopoly, although even now many do not seem to realize its seriousness. There is no adequate solution of the problem of defining "rational economic behavior" on the part of an individual when the very rationality of his actions depends on the probable behavior of other individuals: in the case of oligopoly, other sellers. Cournot and many after him have attempted to sidetrack the difficulty by assuming that every individual has a definite idea as to what others will do under given conditions. Depending on the nature of this expected behavior of other individuals, we have the special, well-known solutions of Bertrand and Cournot, as well as the more general Bowley concept of the "conjectural variation." Thus, the individual's "rational behavior" is determinate *if* the pattern of behavior of "others" can be assumed *a priori* known. But the behavior of "others" cannot be known *a priori* if the "others," too, are to behave rationally! Thus a logical *impasse* is reached.

The way, or at least *a* way, out of this difficulty had been pointed out by one of the authors over a decade ago. It lies in the rejection of a narrowly interpreted maximization principle as synonymous with rational behavior. Not that maximization (of utility [1] or profits) would not be desirable if it were feasible, but there can be no true maximization when only one of the several factors which decide the outcome (of, say, oligopolistic competition) is controlled by the given individual.

Consider, for instance, a duopolistic situation [2] where each one of the duopolists A and B is *trying* to maximize his profits. A's profits will depend not only on his behavior ("strategy") but on B's strategy as well. Thus, *if* A could control (directly or indirectly) the strategy to be adopted by B, he would select a strategy for himself and one for B so as to maximize his

* By Leonid Hurwicz. From "The Theory of Economic Behavior," a review of the *Theory of Games and Economic Behavior*, in *American Economic Review*, December, 1945, pp. 909–923. Reprinted by permission of the American Economic Association.

[1] A side-issue of considerable interest discussed in the *Theory of Games* is that of measurability of the utility function. The authors need measurability in order to be able to set up tables of the type to be presented later in the case where utility rather than profit is being maximized. The proof of measurability is not given; however, an article giving the proof is promised for the near future and it seems advisable to postpone comment until the proof appears. But it should be emphasized that the validity of the core of the *Theory of Games* is by no means dependent on measurability or transferability of the utilities and those who feel strongly on the subject would perhaps do best to substitute "profits" for "utility" in most of the book in order to avoid judging the achievements of the *Theory of Games* from the point of view of an unessential assumption.

[2] It is assumed that the buyers' behavior may be regarded as known.

own profits. But he cannot select B's strategy. Therefore, he can in no way make sure that by proper choice of his own strategy his profits will actually be unconditionally maximized.

It might seem that in such a situation there is no possibility of defining rational behavior on the part of the two duopolists. But it is here that the novel solution proposed by the authors comes in. An example will illustrate this.

Suppose each of the duopolists has three possible strategies at his disposal.[3] Denote the strategies open to duopolist A by A_1, A_2, and A_3, and those open to duopolist B by B_1, B_2, and B_3. The profit made by A, to be denoted by a, obviously is determined by the choices of strategy made by the

A's Profits

B's choice of strategies / A's choice of strategies	B_1	B_2	B_3
A_1	a_{11}	a_{12}	a_{13}
A_2	a_{21}	a_{22}	a_{23}
A_3	a_{31}	a_{32}	a_{33}

Table 1a

B's Profits

B's choice of strategies / A's choice of strategies	B_1	B_2	B_3
A_1	b_{11}	b_{12}	b_{13}
A_2	b_{21}	b_{22}	b_{23}
A_3	b_{31}	b_{32}	b_{33}

Table 1b

two duopolists. This dependence will be indicated by subscripts attached to a, with the first subscript referring to A's strategy and the second subscript to that of B; thus, *e.g.*, a_{13} is the profit which will be made by A if he chooses strategy A_1 while B chooses the strategy B_3. Similarly, b_{13} would denote the profits by B under the same circumstances. The possible outcomes of the "duopolistic competition" may be represented in the following two tables:

Table 1a shows the profits A will make depending on his own and B's choice of strategies. The first row corresponds to the choice of A_1, etc.; columns correspond to B's strategies. Table 1b gives analogous information regarding B's profits.

In order to show how A and B will make decisions concerning strategies we shall avail ourselves of a numerical example given in Tables 2a and 2b.

Now let us watch A's thinking processes as he considers his choice of strategy. First of all, he will notice that by choosing strategy A_3 he will

[3] Actually the number of strategies could be very high, perhaps infinite.

be sure that his profits cannot go down below 5, while either of the remaining alternatives would expose him to the danger of going down to 3 or even to 1. But there is another reason for his choosing A_3. Suppose there is a danger of a "leak": B might learn what A's decision is before he makes his own. Had A chosen, say, A_1, B—if he knew about this—would obviously choose B_3 so as to maximize his own profits; this would leave A with a profit of only 1. Had A choosen A_2, B would respond by selecting B_2, which again would leave A with a profit below 5 which he could be sure of getting if he chose A_3.

One might perhaps argue whether A's choice of A_3 under such circumstances is the only way of defining rational behavior, but it certainly is *a* way of accomplishing this and, as will be seen later, a very fruitful one.

A's Profits

B's choice of strategies / A's choice of strategies	B_1	B_2	B_3
A_1	2	8	1
A_2	4	3	9
A_3	5	6	7

Table 2a

B's Profits

B's choice of strategies / A's choice of strategies	B_1	B_2	B_3
A_1	11	2	20
A_2	9	15	3
A_3	8	7	6

Table 2b

The reader will verify without difficulty that similar reasoning on B's part will make him choose B_1 as the optimal strategy. Thus, the outcome of the duopolistic competition is determinate and can be described as follows: A will choose A_3, B will choose B_1, A's profit will be 5, B's 8.

An interesting property of this solution is that neither duopolist would be inclined to alter his decision, even if he were able to do so, after he found out what the other man's strategy was.

To see this, suppose B has found out that A's decision was in favor of strategy A_3. Looking at the third row of Table 2b, he will immediately see that in no case could he do better than by choosing B_1, which gives him the highest profit consistent with A's choice of A_3. The solution arrived at is of a very stable nature, independent of finding out the other man's strategy.

But the above example is artificial in several important respects. For one thing, it ignores the possibility of a "collusion" or, to use a more neutral term, coalition between A and B. In our solution, yielding the strategy combination (A_3, B_1), the joint profits of the two duopolists amount to 13; they could do better than that by acting together. By agreeing to choose the strategies A_1 and B_3 respectively, they would bring their joint profits up to 21; this sum could then be so divided that both would be better off than under the previous solution.

A major achievement of the *Theory of Games* is the analysis of the conditions and nature of coalition formation. How that is done will be shown below. But, for the moment, let us eliminate the problem of coalitions by considering a case which is somewhat special but nevertheless of great theoretical interest: the case of *constant sum* profits. An example of such a case is given in Tables 3a and 3b.

A's Profits

B's choice of strategies / A's choice of strategies	B_1	B_2	B_3
A_1	2	8	1
A_2	4	3	9
A_3	5	6	7

Table 3a

B's Profits

B's choice of strategies / A's choice of strategies	B_1	B_2	B_3
A_1	8	2	9
A_2	6	7	1
A_3	5	4	3

Table 3b

Table 3a is identical with Table 2a. But figures in Table 3b have been selected in such a manner that the joint profits of the two duopolists always amount to the same (10), no matter what strategies have been chosen. In such a case, A's gain is B's loss and *vice versa*. Hence, it is intuitively obvious (although the authors take great pains to show it rigorously) that no coalition will be formed.

The solution can again be obtained by reasoning used in the previous case and it will again turn out to be (A_3, B_1) with the respective profits 5 and 5 adding up to 10. What was said above about stability of solution and absence of advantage in finding the opponent [4] out still applies.

There is, however, an element of artificiality in the example chosen that is responsible for the determinateness of the solution. To see this it will suffice to interchange 5 and 6 in Table 3a. The changed situation is por-

[4] In this case the interests of the two duopolists are diametrically opposed and the term "opponents" is fully justified; in the previous example it would not have been.

trayed in Table 4 which gives A's profits for different choices of strategies.[5]

There is no solution now which would possess the kind of stability found in the earlier example. For suppose A again chooses A_3; then if B should find that out, he would obviously "play" B_2 which gives him the highest possible profit consistent with A_3. But then A_3 would no longer be A's optimum strategy: he could do much better by choosing A_1; but if he does so, B's optimum strategy is B_3, not B_2, etc. There is no solution which would not give at least one of the opponents an incentive to change his decision if he found the other man out! There is no stability.[6]

A's Profits

B's choice of strategies / A's choice of strategies	B_1	B_2	B_3
A_1	2	8	1
A_2	4	3	9
A_3	6	5	7

Table 4

What is it in the construction of the table that insured determinateness in the case of Table 3 and made it impossible in Table 4? The answer is that Table 3 has a *saddle point* ("minimax") while Table 4 does not.

The saddle point has the following two properties: it is the highest of all the row minima and at the same time it is lowest of the column maxima. Thus, in Table 3a the row minima are respectively 1, 3, and 5, the last one being highest among them (*Maximum Minimorum*); on the other hand, the column maxima are respectively 5, 8, and 9 with 5 as the lowest (*Minimum Maximorum*). Hence the combination (A_3, B_1) yields both the highest row minimum and the lowest column maximum, and, therefore, constitutes a saddle point. It is easy to see that Table 4 does *not* possess a saddle point. Here 5 is still the *Maximum Minimorum*, but the *Minimum Maximorum* is given by 6; the two do not coincide, and it is the

[5] The table for B's profits is omitted because of the constant sum assumption. Clearly, in the constant sum case, B may be regarded as minimizing A's profits since this implies maximization of his own.

[6] There is, however, a certain amount of determinateness, at least in the negative sense, since certain strategy combinations are excluded: *e.g.* (A_2, B_1); A would never choose A_2 if he knew B had chosen B_1, and *vice versa*.

absence of the saddle point that makes for indeterminateness in Table 4.

Why is the existence of a unique saddle point necessary (as well as sufficient) to insure the determinateness of the solution? The answer is inherent in the reasoning used in connection with the earlier examples: if A chooses his strategy so as to be protected in case of any leakage of information concerning his decision, he will choose the strategy whose row in the table has the highest minimum value, *i.e.,* the row corresponding to the *Maximum Minimorum*—A_3 in case of Table 4—for then he is sure he will not get less than 5, even if B should learn of this decision. B, following the same principle, will choose the column (*i.e.,* strategy) corresponding to the *Minimum Maximorum*—B_1 in Table 4—thus making sure he will get at least 4, even if the information does leak out.

In this fashion both duopolists are sure of a certain minimum of profit —5 and 4, respectively. But this adds up to only 9. The residual—1—is still to be allocated and this allocation depends on outguessing the opponent. It is this residual that provides an explanation, as well as a measure, of the extent of indeterminacy. Its presence will not surprise economists familiar with this type of phenomenon from the theory of bilateral monopoly. But there are cases when this residual does equal zero, that is, when the *Minimum Maximorum* equals the *Maximum Minimorum,* which (by definition) implies the existence of the saddle point and complete determinacy.

At this stage the authors of the *Theory of Games* had to make a choice. They could have accepted the fact that saddle points do not always exist so that a certain amount of indeterminacy would, in general, be present. They preferred, however, to get rid of the indeterminacy by a highly ingenious modification of the process which leads to the choice of appropriate strategy.

So far our picture of the duopolist making a decision on strategy was that of a man reasoning out which of the several possible courses of action is most favorable (*"pure strategy"*). We now change this picture and put in his hands a set of dice which he will throw to determine the strategy to be chosen. Thus, an element of chance is introduced into decision making ("mixed strategy").[7] But not everything is left to chance. The duopolist A must in advance formulate a rule as to what results of the throw—assume that just one die is thrown—would make him choose a given strategy. In order to illustrate this we shall use a table that is somewhat simpler, even if less interesting than those used previously. In this new table (Table 5) [8] each duopolist has only two strategies at his disposal.

An example of a rule A might adopt would be:

> If the result of the throw is 1 or 2, choose A_1;
> if the result of the throw is 3, 4, 5, or 6, choose A_2.

[7] The authors' justification for introducing "mixed strategies" is that leaving one's decision to chance is an effective way of preventing "leakage" of information since the individual making the decision does not himself know which strategy he will choose.

[8] In Table 5 there is no saddle point.

A's Profits

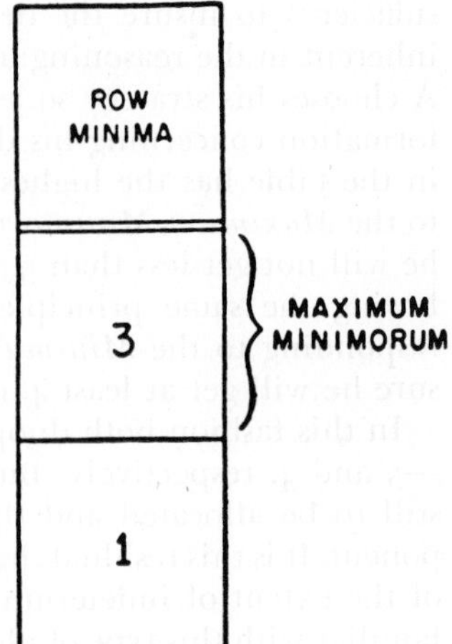

B's choice of strategies / A's choice of strategies	B_1	B_2	ROW MINIMA
A_1	5	3	3 (MAXIMUM MINIMORUM)
A_2	1	5	1

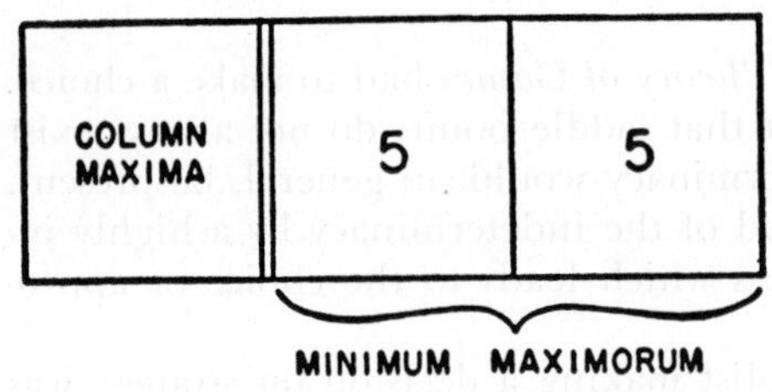

COLUMN MAXIMA	5	5

MINIMUM MAXIMORUM

Table 5

If this rule were followed, the probability that A will choose A_1 is ⅓, that of his choosing A_2 is ⅔. If a different rule had been decided upon (say, one of choosing A_1 wherever the result of the throw is 1, 2, or 3), the probability of choosing A_1 would have been ½. Let us call the fraction giving the probability of choosing A_1 A's *chance coefficient;* in the two examples, A's chance coefficients were ⅓ and ½ respectively.[9]

As a special case the value of the chance coefficient might be zero (meaning, that is, definitely choosing strategy A_2) or one (meaning that A is definitely choosing strategy A_1); thus in a sense "pure strategies" may be regarded as a special case of mixed strategies. However, this last statement is subject to rather important qualifications which are of a complex nature and will not be given here.

[9] Since the probability of choosing A_2 is always equal to one minus that of choosing A_1, specification of the probability of choosing A_1 is sufficient to describe a given rule. However, when the number of available strategies exceeds two, there are several such chance coefficients to be specified.

Now instead of choosing one of the available strategies the duopolist A must choose the optimal (in a sense not yet defined) chance coefficient. How is the choice of the chance coefficient made? The answer lies in constructing a table which differs in two important respects from those used earlier. Table 6 provides an example. Each row in the table now corresponds to a possible value of A's chance coefficient; similarly, columns correspond to possible values of B's chance coefficient. Since the chance coefficient may assume any value between zero and one (including the latter two values), the table is to be regarded merely as a "sample." This is indicated by spaces between rows and between columns. [See p. 642.]

The numbers entered in the table are the average values (mathematical expectations) corresponding to the choice of chance coefficients indicated by the row and column.[10] (One should mention that Table 6 is only an expository device: the actual procedures used in the book are algebraic and much simpler computationally.)

If we now assume with the authors that each duopolist is trying to maximize the mathematical expectation of his profits (Table 6) rather than the profits themselves (Table 5), it might seem that the original source of difficulty remains if a saddle point does not happen to exist. But the

[10] To see this we shall show how, *e.g.*, we have obtained the value in the second row and third column of Table 6 (*viz.*, 3).

We construct an auxiliary table (valid only for this particular combination of chance coefficients (A's 1/3, B's 2/3).

This table differs from Table 5 only by the omission of row minima and column maxima and by the insertion of the probabilities of choosing the available strategies corresponding to the second row and third column of Table 6. The computation of the mathematical expectation is indicated in Table 6.

COMPUTATION OF THE MATHEMATICAL EXPECTATION FOR THE 2ND ROW, 3RD COLUMN IN TABLE 6

A's choice of strategies \ B's choice of strategies		B_1	B_2
	A's chance coefficients \ B's chance coefficients	$\frac{2}{3}$	$\frac{1}{3}$
A_1	$\frac{1}{3}$	5	3
A_2	$\frac{2}{3}$	1	5

$$\tfrac{1}{3} \times \tfrac{2}{3} \times 5 + \tfrac{1}{3} \times \tfrac{1}{3} \times 3 + \tfrac{2}{3} \times \tfrac{2}{3} \times 1 + \tfrac{2}{3} \times \tfrac{1}{3} \times 5 = \tfrac{27}{9} = 3$$

Mathematical Expectations of A's Profits

A's chance coefficients \ B's chance coefficients	0	$\frac{1}{3}$	$\frac{2}{3}$	1	ROW MINIMA
0	5	$3\frac{2}{3}$	$2\frac{1}{3}$	1	1
$\frac{1}{3}$	$4\frac{1}{3}$	$3\frac{2}{3}$	3	$2\frac{1}{3}$	$2\frac{1}{3}$
$\frac{2}{3}$	$3\frac{2}{3}$	$3\frac{2}{3}$	$3\frac{2}{3}$	$3\frac{2}{3}$	$3\frac{2}{3}$ MAXIMUM MINIMORUM
1	3	$3\frac{2}{3}$	$4\frac{1}{3}$	5	3
COLUMN MAXIMA	5	$3\frac{2}{3}$ MINIMUM MAXIMORUM	$4\frac{1}{3}$	5	

Table 6

mixed strategies were not introduced in vain! It is shown (the theorem was originally proved by von Neumann in 1928) that in the table of mathematical expectations (like Table 6) a saddle point *must* exist; the problem is always determinate.[11]

The reader who may have viewed the introduction of dice into the decision-making process with a certain amount of suspicion will probably agree that this is a rather spectacular result. Contrary to the initial impression, it *is* possible to render the problem determinate. But there is a price to be paid: acceptance of mixed strategies, assumption that only the mathematical expectation of profit (not its variance, for instance) matters, seem to be necessary. Many an economist will consider the price too

[11] In Table 6 the saddle point is in the third row second column; it is to be stressed that Table 5 has no saddle point.

high. Moreover, one might question the need for introducing the determinateness into a problem of this nature. Perhaps we should consider as the "solution" the interval of indeterminacy given by the two critical points: the *Minimum Maximorum* and *Maximum Minimorum*.

As indicated earlier in this review, one should not ignore, in general, the possibility of a collusion. This is especially evident when more complex economic situations are considered.

We might, for instance, have a situation where there are two sellers facing two buyers. Here a "coalition" of buyers, as well as one of sellers, may be formed. But it is also conceivable that a buyer would bribe a seller into some sort of coöperation against the other two participants. Several other combinations of this type can easily be found.

When only *two* persons enter the picture, as in the case of duopoly (where the rôle of buyers was ignored), it was seen that coalition would not be formed if the sum of the two persons' profits remained constant. But when the number of participants is *three* or more, subcoalitions can profitably be formed even if the sum of all participants' profits is constant; in the above four-person example it might pay the sellers to combine against the buyers even if (or, perhaps, especially if) the profits of all four always add to the same amount.

Hence, the formation of coalitions may be adequately treated without abandoning the highly convenient constant-sum assumption. In fact, when the sum is known to be non-constant, it is possible to introduce (conceptually) an additional fictitious participant who, by definition, loses what all the real participants gain and *vice versa*. In this fashion a non-constant sum situation involving, say, three persons may be considered as a special case of a constant-sum four-person situation. This is an additional justification for confining most of the discussion (both in the book and in the review) to the constant-sum case despite the fact that economic problems are as a rule of the non-constant sum variety.

We shall now proceed to study the simplest constant-sum case which admits coalition formation, that involving three participants. The technique of analysis presented earlier in the two-person case is no longer adequate. The number of possibilities increases rapidly. Each of the participants may be acting independently; or else, one of the three possible two-person coalitions (A and B *vs.* C, A and C *vs.* B, B and C *vs.* A) may be formed. Were it not for the constant-sum restriction, there would be the additional possibility of the coalition comprising all three participants.

Here again we realize the novel character of the author's approach to the problem. In most [12] of traditional economic theory the formation—or

[12] In his *Grundlagen einer reinen Kostentheorie* (Vienna, 1932) H. von Stackelberg does point out (p. 89) that "the competitors [duopolists] must somehow unite; they must . . . supplement the economic mechanics, which in this case is inadequate, by economic politics." But no rigorous theory is developed for such situations (although an outline of possible developments is given). This is where the *Theory of Games* has made real progress.

absence—of specific coalitions is *postulated.* Thus, for instance, we discuss the economics of a cartel without rigorously investigating the necessary and sufficient conditions for its formation. Moreover, we tend to exclude *a priori* such phenomena as collusion between buyers and sellers even if these phenomena are known to occur in practice. The *Theory of Games,* though seemingly more abstract than economic theory known to us, approaches reality much more closely on points of this nature. A complete solution to the problems of economic theory requires an answer to the question of coalition formation, bribery, collusion, etc. This answer is now provided, even though it is of a somewhat formal nature in the more complex cases; and even though it does not always give sufficient insight into the actual workings of the market.

Let us now return to the case of three participants. Suppose two of them are sellers, one a buyer. Traditional theory would tell us the quantity sold by each seller and the price. But we know that in the process of bargaining one of the sellers might bribe the other one into staying out of the competition. Hence the seller who refrained from market operations would make a profit; on the other hand, the nominal profit made by the man who did make the sale would exceed (by the amount of bribe) the actual gain made.

It is convenient, therefore, to introduce the concept of *gain:* the bribed man's gain is the amount of the bribe, the seller's gain is the profit made on a sale minus the bribe, etc. A given distribution of gains among the participants is called an *imputation.* The imputation is not a number: it is a set of numbers. For instance, if the gains of the participants in a given situation were g_A, g_B, g_C, it is the set of these three g's that is called the imputation. The imputation summarizes the outcome of the economic process. In any given situation there are a great many possible imputations. Therefore, one of the chief objectives of economic theory is that of finding those among all the possible imputations which will actually be observed under rational behavior.

In a situation such as that described (three participants, constant-sum) each man will start by asking himself how much he could get acting independently, even if the worst should happen and the other two formed a coalition against him. He can determine this by treating the situation as a two-person case (the opposing coalition regarded as one person) and finding the relevant *Maximum Minimorum,* or the saddle point, if that point does exist; the saddle point would, of course, exist if "mixed strategies" are used. Next, the participant will consider the possibility of forming a coalition with one of the other two men. Now comes the crucial question: under what conditions might such a coalition be formed?

Before discussing this in detail, let us summarize, in Table 8, all the relevant information.

Table 8

I.	If A acts alone, he can get	5
	If B acts alone, he can get	7
	If C acts alone, he can get	10.
II.	If A and B form a coalition, they can get	15
	If A and C form a coalition, they can get	18
	If B and C form a coalition, they can get	20.
III.	If A, B, and C act together, they can get	25.

Among the many possible imputations, let us now consider the three given in Table 9.

Table 9

	A	B	C
#1	6.5	8.3	10.2
#2	5.0	9.5	10.5
#3	4.0	10.0	11.0

It will be noted that under imputation #1, B and C are each better off than if they had been acting individually: they get respectively 8.3 and 10.2 instead of 7 and 10. Hence, there is an incentive for B and C to form a coalition since without such a coalition imputation #1 would not be possible. But once the coalition is formed, they can do better than under #1; *viz.*, under #2, where each gets more (9.5 and 10.5 instead of 8.3 and 10.2, respectively). In such a case we say that imputation #2 *dominates* imputation #1. It might seem that #3, in turn, dominates #2 since it promises still more to both B and C. But it promises too much: the sum of B's and C's gains under #3 is 21, which is more than their coalition could get (*cf.* Table 8)! Thus #3 is ruled out as unrealistic and cannot be said to dominate any other imputation.

Domination is an exceptionally interesting type of relation. For one thing, it is not transitive: we may have an imputation i_1 dominating the imputation i_2 and i_2 dominating i_3, without thereby implying that i_1 dominates i_3; in fact, i_1 might be dominated by i_3.[13] Moreover, it is easy to construct examples of, say, two imputations, neither of which dominates the other one.[14]

To get a geometric picture of this somewhat unusual situation one may turn to Figure 1, where points on the circle represent different possible

[13] *I.e.*, domination may be a *cyclic* relation. For instance, consider the following three imputations in the above problem: #1 and #2 as in Table 9, and #4, where

	A	B	C
#4	6.0	7.0	12.0.

Here #2 (as shown before) dominates #1 (for the coalition B, C), #4 dominates #2 (for coalition A, C), but at the same time #1 dominates #4 (for the coalition A, B): the cycle is completed.

[14] For instance, #2 and #3 in Table 9.

imputations. (The reader must be cautioned that this is merely a geometrical analogy, though a helpful one.) Let us now say that point #1 dominates point #2 if #2 is less than 90° (clockwise) from #1. It is easy to see in Figure 1 that #1 dominates #2 and #2 dominates #3, but in spite of that, #1 does not dominate #3.

This geometrical picture will help define the very fundamental concept of a *solution.*

Consider the points (imputations) #1, 3, 5, and 7 in Figure 1. None of them dominates any other since any two are either *exactly* or more than 90° apart. But any other point on the circle is dominated by at least (in this case: exactly) one of them: all points between #1 and #3 are dominated by #1, etc. There is no point on the circle which is not dominated by one of the above four points. Now we *define* a solution as a set of points (imputations) with two properties: (1) no element of the set dominates any other element of the set, and (2) any point outside the set must be dominated by at least one element within the set.

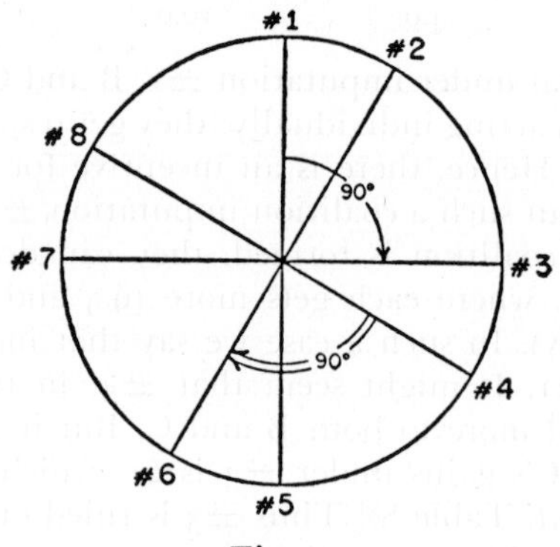

Fig. 1

We have seen that the points #1, 3, 5, 7 do have both of these properties; hence, the four points together form a solution. It is important to see that none of the individual points by itself can be regarded as a solution. In fact, if we tried to leave out any one of the four points of the set, the remaining three would no longer form a solution; for instance, if #1 were left out, the points between #1 and #3 are not dominated by any of the points #3, 5, 7. This violates the second property required of a solution and the three points by themselves are not a solution. On the other hand, if a fifth point were added to #1, 3, 5, 7, the resulting five element set would not form a solution either; suppose #2 is the fifth point chosen; we note that #2 is dominated by #1 and it also dominates #3. Thus, the first property of a solution is absent.

Contrary to what would be one's intuitive guess, an element of the solution may be dominated by points outside the solution: #1 is dominated by #8, etc.

There can easily be more than one solution. The reader should have no trouble verifying the fact that #2, 4, 6, 8 also form a solution, and it is clear that infinitely many other solutions exist.

Does there always exist at least one solution? So far this question remains unanswered. Among the cases examined by the authors none has been found without at least one solution. But it has not yet been proved that there must always be a solution. To see the theoretical possibility of a case without a solution we shall redefine slightly our concept of domination (*cf.* Figure 2): #1 dominates #2 if the angle between them (measured clockwise) does not exceed 180°.

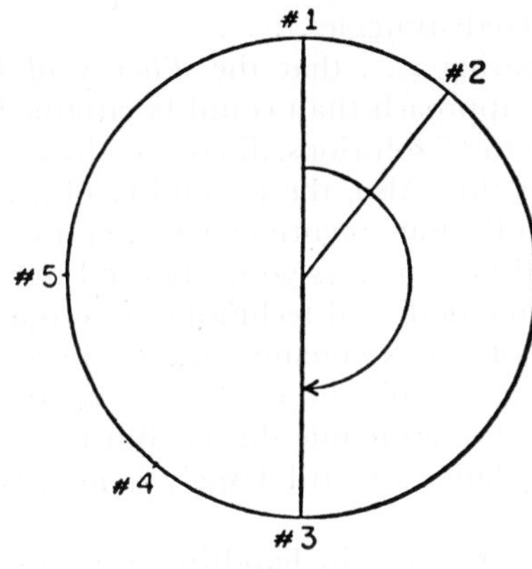

Fig. 2

Hence, in Figure 2 point #1 dominates #3, but not #4, etc. It can now be shown that in this case *no* solution exists. For suppose there is one; then we may, without loss of generality, choose #1 as one of its points. Clearly, #1 by itself does not constitute a solution, for there are points on the circle (*e.g.*, #4) not dominated by #1; thus the solution must have at least two points. But any other point on the circle either is dominated by #1 (*e.g.*, #2), or it dominates #1 (*e.g.*, #4), or both (#3), which contradicts the first requirement for the elements of a solution. Hence there is no solution consisting of two points either. *A fortiori,* there are no solutions containing more than two points. Hence we have been able to construct an example without a solution. But whether this type of situation could arise in economics (or in games, for that matter) is still an open question.

Now for the economic interpretation of the concept of solution. Within the solution there is no reason for switching from one imputation to another since they do not dominate each other. Moreover, there is never a good reason for going outside a given solution: any imputation outside the solution can be "discredited" by an imputation within the solution which dominates the one outside. But, as we have seen, the reverse is also usually true: imputations within the solution may be dominated by those outside. If we are to assume that the latter consideration is ignored, the given solution acquires an institutional, if not accidental, character. According to the authors, a solution may be equivalent to what one would call the "standards of behavior" which are accepted by a given community.

The multiplicity of solutions can then be considered as corresponding to alternative institutional setups; for a given institutional framework only one solution would be relevant. But even then a large number of possibilities remains since, in general, a solution contains more than one imputation. More indeterminancy yet would be present if we had refrained from introducing mixed strategies. . . .

It will stand repeating . . . that the *Theory of Games* does offer a greater generality of approach than could be attained otherwise. The existence of "discriminatory" solutions, discovered by purely analytical methods, is an instance of this. Also, the possibility of accounting for various types of deals and collusions mentioned earlier in connection with the three-person and four-person cases go far beyond results usually obtained by customarily used methods and techniques of economic theory.

The potentialities of von Neumann's and Morgenstern's new approach seem tremendous and may, one hopes, lead to revamping, and enriching in realism, a good deal of economic theory. But to a large extent they are only potentialities: results are still largely a matter of future developments.

The difficulties encountered in handling, even by the more powerful mathematical methods, the situations involving more than three persons are quite formidable. Even the problems of monopoly and monopsony are beyond reach at the present stage of investigation. The same is true of perfect competition, though it may turn out that the latter is not a "legitimate" solution since it excludes the formation of coalitions which may dominate the competitive imputations. A good deal of light has been thrown on the problem of oligopoly, but there again the results are far from the degree of concreteness desired by the economic theorist.

OLIGOPOLY, MONOPOLISTIC COMPETITION, AND THE THEORY OF GAMES *

My assigned task is to show briefly the relation between the problem of imperfect competition, oligopoly, and monopoly on the one hand and the theory of games of strategy [1] on the other. I need not here describe the current views on these problems. I wish, however, to pay my respects to those who have made such valiant efforts to solve them by means of

* "Oligopoly, Monopolistic Competition, and the Theory of Games," *American Economic Review,* Supplement, May, 1948, pp. 10–18. Reprinted by permission of the American Economic Association.

[1] John von Neumann and Oskar Morgenstern, *Theory of Games and Economic Behavior* (Princeton, 1944, 2nd rev. ed., 1947).

theories that have attracted world-wide attention. This remark is called for, lest the following considerations be misunderstood, involving, as they do, the proposal for a radical departure from the present views. Yet this proposal may not be unwelcome since there seems to be a growing conviction that the current theories have run up against such serious obstacles that a fundamental reorientation is necessary. Because of lack of time I may be permitted to state the ideas of the theory of games positively rather than in detailed contrast with the existing theories.

The present piecemeal investigation of individual cases with a wide variety of assumptions and constellations shows the lack of unifying principles of sufficient power. Or, to put it differently, the currently used tools such as the marginal revenue, marginal cost concepts together with product differentiation and the attempt to determine a maximum of profits do not seem strong enough to unlock the exceedingly complex problems. In the background, moreover, is the undeniable and disturbing fact, already well known to Cournot, that when there are but few participants in a market, they reflect about each others' behavior and try to set their course accordingly. Here, indeed, is the crux of the matter and the difficulty should be squarely faced rather than relegated to an inferior role. It is in this domain where the need for a new approach becomes most convincing.

The theory of games of strategy cannot be presented here, because it is incompressible, in spite—or perhaps because—of the fact that it is still in its beginnings. New concepts and new tools of analysis had to be evolved and they would all require careful scrutiny. This it is impossible to do. Neither can I give applications to the American scene.

Another difficulty lies in the mathematical character of the theory. Moreover, the mathematics used are of a rather uncommon kind. They are not merely incidental but concern the very structure of the whole theory. Indeed, a state has been reached where some of the most important results of the theory could be found only by means of mathematics and cannot even any longer be translated adequately into words, precisely as it happens in physical theory. But the concepts which are used can perhaps become accessible for a qualitative description. I want to emphasize that the mathematical nature of the theory is something innate and not just a dressing up of fundamentally simple ideas. Of course, I do believe that a genuinely mathematical and axiomatic theory is superior to any nonmathematical treatment.

I shall now state what the fundamental problem is: We wish to know how the individual, pursuing his maximum interest, should behave on all types of markets. This is a question of rational behavior, of judging quantitatively any situation in which he may be placed so that with his information he can assure himself of the maximum gain or utility. Economic theory must therefore indicate how the firm or the individual should behave under all conceivable conditions. This is a tall order. Current theory asserts that for free competition an ordinary maximum problem results: the firm achieves its maximum when its marginal costs equal marginal revenue and should produce until these two are equated. This is supposed to be exhaustive because the data are allegedly given immutably. Likewise the individual as a consumer can gain his maximum utility. Monopoly theory proceeds similarly, and all maxima are assumed to be obtained simultaneously.

The disconcerting difficulties of oligopoly and monopolistic competition arise because now specific assumptions about the reactions of others are unavoidable. Yet the belief that one is dealing with clear-cut maximum problems is not affected. But if one looks more closely the maximization even under free competition has only been achieved by quietly assuming that the participants in the market do not form coalitions, combinations, etc., which would greatly reduce the effective number of actors. When the number of sellers or buyers or of both is small anyway, the maximum character of the problem becomes exceedingly doubtful even on a purely intuitive basis. Now it is one of the decisive steps in the theory of games to show that one is not confronted with maximum problems (unless dealing with an absolutely isolated Robinson Crusoe, and its formal equivalent) but with a fundamentally different situation.

Where is the difference? It lies in the fact that the theory of competition assumes that the individual or firms are in full control of all the variables that determine the outcome of any transaction undertaken. This is only achieved by the wholly inadmissible trick of holding everything else constant and of forbidding, tacitly no doubt, the previously mentioned agreements among the participants. In a bilateral monopoly, clearly, neither of the two opposing parties controls all the variables determining the outcome. Each has merely one partial set of variables while the result, i.e., the prices and the quantity traded, depends on both partial sets of variables together; i.e., on all variables. In this case no trick whatever will help disguise the fundamental fact that, while each of the participants wishes to maximize his own gain, the problem as a whole is not a maximum problem. It is a situation not taken care of anywhere in current economic theory. It is not even treated in classical mathematics. Furthermore, this kind of problem does not occur in mechanics from which economic theory has taken its images, concepts, and logical methods. I need hardly say more to indicate the extreme seriousness of this problem.

When we have a duopoly or oligopoly against oligopsony, or generally a few sellers against comparatively few or even against many buyers, the situation remains substantially the same: there is no maximum problem. The conjectures of people or firms about each other's behavior are as important as ever. Unless a general theory can be made embodying all these facts, the efforts are bound to fizzle out in a maze of incomplete discussions of partly understood cases. The theory of perfect competition as now generally taught at best remains at the outskirts of the vast field for which a theory must be established. The empirical unreality of its restraining assumptions is matched by the insufficiency of its methodical principles.

If the mechanical, physical model used at present in economics and the methods appropriate to it fail in providing a theory at once realistic and logically satisfactory, is there another model? It will have to fulfill the customary three requirements: it should be similar to the reality it is to model, it must be mathematically manageable, and it must lead to numerical-computational results. Games of strategy appear to fulfill the first requirement and, if a theory can be made, then economic reality can be modeled by suitable games. That is to say, it is more plausible to compare the sparring and jockeying between the large automobile companies to a game of poker with its bluffing, its bids and overbids, or, equivalently, to a military situation, rather than to some mechanical process such as a dance of molecules. Wage negotiations, e.g., between the coal miners and the operators, also have essential traits found nowhere but in games of strategy. Whether a theory can actually be made can only be decided by the success of the attempt.

There can be little doubt that it is intuitively satisfactory to relate games of strategy to economic behavior. Economists and businessmen speak sometimes in passing, but with good instinct, of economic warfare, of a "business strategy," or of the "rules of the game," say of the gold standard. In the same sense, the games we are thinking of are not the ordinary classical games of chance, but those of strategy where the outcome depends primarily on the behavior of the players although frequently chance factors also intervene as they do anywhere in the world.

I wish to emphasize the claim that there is not merely an analogy between the two fields of games of strategy and economics but a strict identity. Thus the theory is not only related to monopolistic situations but deals with all types of markets, with all kinds of economic and rational behavior.

Consider first a two-person game. Each of the two players wishes to win and if he does, it is at the expense of the other. In that case we have a zero-sum game; in economics presumably both parties gain from an exchange; hence the sum of their gains and losses is greater than zero and variable. Each player (or duopolist, if we neglect the buyers for the time being) wishes to gain the maximum. So he has to devise a strategy against the other. The same is true of the other player and there is a clear opposition of interests. Now it may be as disastrous to have one's own strategy found out as it would be profitable to discover the other's scheme. There are games where "being found out" does not matter; they are a minority and are called "strictly determined" and reliable and safe strategies exist. For all other games the chief thing is to protect oneself against the calamity of "being found out." Can it be shown that even in those cases strategies always exist that offer the necessary protection to each of the two players, thus making the game again strictly determined?

The answer is yes. It is based on the empirical observation that the participants playing, say matching pennies, will substitute random statistical behavior (within the rules of the game) for any direct plan of action, or so-called "pure" strategy, that could be discovered by the opponent. To demonstrate this—which makes every zero-sum two-person game strictly determined—a rigorous mathematical proof has been given. It involves a very deep-lying theorem of the so-called "min-max" type which was first proved in 1928 by von Neumann and which, incidentally, reappears in a certain system of simultaneous economic equations. Each particular two-person game must, of course, be solved computationally, but the fundamental theorem assures that the solution always exists and that the best strategy can always be found. This is more than can be said of many economic problems today involving market transactions. Even in the few cases where the existence of a solution has been determined, it is an open question whether it is meaningful, in view of the inappropriateness of the model currently used. Only for the case of the isolated Robinson Crusoe or, equivalently, the strictly organized communistic society can we be sure that a meaningful solution in the form of a maximum can always be found, although the computational difficulties may be immense or in fact insuperable.

The transition from the Robinson Crusoe type of economy to the simplest form of exchange transaction is characterized by the appearance of another "will," controlling part of all the variables which determine the outcome. When the number of participants increases further, entirely new phenomena again appear. When we have three or more players, structural properties of greatest importance in economics emerge. I shall try to give an idea of them by mentioning the principal concepts of the general theory in a qualitative way. The chief point is that the addition of every single new player produces a new situation. The analysis therefore builds up gradually from that of individual behavior, in the tradition of what is best in modern economic theory. Whether there will emerge a convenient asymptotic behavior of the theory when the number of participants becomes really large, remains to be seen. It is our belief, however, that no short cuts are possible.

If we consider three or more participants in a game, or equivalently in a market, we observe immediately the tendency to form coalitions of some of the players against the others. The urge to combine springs from the fact that in combinations it is easier to obtain one's maximum gain than by proceeding independently. These coalitions will necessarily oppose each other as the individual players in a two-person game. Coalitions will therefore have a value for the members, which is expressed by the so-called "characteristic function" upon which the entire theory is based. In order to be admitted to a coalition and to enjoy this advantage over being left alone, payments to others may be necessary. These "compensations," arising out of higgling and bargaining, must also be taken care of by the theory. It suffices to think of the formation of a cartel with production quotas, profit sharing, etc., and of the operation of labor unions, to get a proper empirical background. In all these cases monopolistic elements come to the fore. They are thus viewed as something fundamental in economic and social organization and do not appear as mere appendices of an allegedly basic free competition of the Lausanne type.

If it is at all accepted that fundamental tendencies to form coalitions are at work, then economic theory must account for them by giving these forces their proper role. Clearly, free competition will not continue to prevail when people can gain by combining. On the other hand, a monopoly may be upset by coalitions of its customers, etc. Any investigation of such markets that should neglect these tendencies will fail to describe innate instabilities and the theory must necessarily remain incomplete. The influence the recognition of this situation will have upon legal theory and practice is an interesting prospect.

The outcome of a game or of a market transaction is the making of payments; i.e., the "imputation" or "distribution" of the spoils. The question arises whether there is only one such imputation compatible with stability, where the imputation may also include the compensations paid to members of the coalition. This imputation would represent the solution of the game. Now it is of the utmost importance to realize that solutions with such single imputations are only found for those fundamentally uninteresting games where there is no advantage in combining into monopolistic coalitions. These games are properly called "inessential."

For the "essential" games the advantage in combining expresses the complementarity or non-additivity of value which has given so much trouble in economic theory. Individually the parts of a coalition are worth less than all put together. In the case of essential games there is never a solution made up of one single imputation or distribution. There are only solutions consisting of a set of alternative imputations. Assume that a given (essential) game has only one single solution: it would consist of a number of imputations. But only one of these imputations could materialize at a given time. Is one of these imputations or schemes of payments, e.g., the one that actually materializes, superior to any other, does one "dominate" the others? The answer is no, provided these other imputations, too, belong to the solution. And also that no other imputation will materialize. A solution is thus defined as a set of those imputations which are undominated by each other.

With these remarks we are in the heart of the theory because now we get insight into the structure of stability of a market or a social organization. There are clearly other possibilities for payments and profits than those expressed by the imputations belonging to the solution. Why should they then not be adopted? Surely they must be more advantageous to some members of the market, who must, therefore, strive to see them enforced? This is true. But if one of these imputations which are outside of the solution, and which thus do not belong to the "accepted standard of behavior," should be seriously considered by those who would profit under the scheme, that imputation would in turn be promptly upset or discredited by another one. Other combinations of players would be found who "are convinced or can be convinced" that another safe imputation exists which is to their advantage and that they could thus disturb the other group in their intended acceptance of the desired imputation. The upsetting imputation in turn would inevitably belong to the solution and would thus not be endangered by any other imputation, also part of the solution.

You may find these ideas somewhat unfamiliar and perhaps difficult and you may in particular object to the circular or implicit manner in which I have characterized a solution. You may also ask how one could be sure of the existence of a solution for all conceivable games. Yet you will probably agree that social organizations can be described by a criterion of "soundness" which is inevitably of this circular nature. But aside from the intuitive appeal these ideas may or may not have, they find rigorous mathematical formulation and were subjected to the most painstaking scrutiny of which modern logic is capable. The chief characteristic of a solution is the lack of transitivity of the imputations belonging to the solution. The stability of the imputation that actually materializes thus does not lie in its undisputed superiority over all others. This would only be the case if we had a clear maximum before us according to current economic theory. The stability rests instead with those other "virtual" imputations of the solution, which, though not materialized, could replace the chosen scheme of distribution without themselves being clearly better or superior. They would derive their stability from the same condition. There is thus no conflict between these imputations and that is why any one of them and all together are sound and form an accepted standard of behavior to which they impart an inner stability.

Here you will observe the much greater complexity of forms and concepts to which the theory of games leads. When present economic theory worries about indeterminateness, say of the price range in bilateral monopoly or duopoly, it is concerned but with trivial cases and has really not touched upon the great wealth of interrelationships to be expected in social phenomena. In fact, the theory of games even shows that single solutions of many imputations each must, for numerous games, give place to many solutions each again consisting of multiple imputations. Thus we often find several conflicting standards of behavior but each free from inner contradictions. This is a rigorous expression of the fact that on the same physical background of economic life quite different organizations and income distributions may be established. This indicates a wide divergence of the theory of games from physical theory, the current model of economics, where uniquely defined numbers or aggregates of numbers predominate and consequently much simpler notions of the stability of a price system and a scheme of distribution prevail.

I want to mention further that the theory of games almost automatically produces information about the role of monopolistic privileges and of discrimination. The theory shows that privileges cannot always be maintained by the privileged players even if anchored in the rules of the game. On the other hand, discrimination arises in spite of the general assumption of complete information of all participants. This is rather surprising and shows that discrimination is not, as seems to be widely thought, due to incomplete information. It is of a much deeper nature. An indication of this is also the demonstration that exploitation of the losing players by the winners is not always carried to the limit in the interest of stability of the standard of behavior. All this will be significant in the further study of monopoly and oligopoly.

What about the relation between the solutions for a bilateral monopoly as seen today and that obtained from the theory of games? The results agree fully when only one unit is transacted; but then both agree—fortunately! —with common sense. When the number of units is left for the market to decide, both approaches obtain the same volume of transactions, but the theory of games already shows that price may actually vary more widely than currently assumed, due to the fact that all sorts of premiums and rebates are also permitted. Considering a market of a monopolist selling to two buyers the theory of games again yields partly different results. The reason is that it admits of coalitions and collusions or understandings between the two buyers, or between one of the buyers and the seller, etc., so that the possible prices and the number of units transacted differ from the accepted views. There are indeed different prices for the two buyers, an interesting case for monopoly in general. It is unknown in detail what would happen in very much larger markets save that the complexity of relationships increases fast in conformity with what we observe in the world around us. One cannot in the least be sure that the margins between the possible prices would narrow as current theory desires, so that ultimately unique prices prevail when arbitrarily many buyers and sellers are present. On the other hand, entirely new vistas appear even for very small markets when account is taken of the important possibility that some participants may not have as fine utility scales and as clear a discernment of their advantages as others. But this can only be mentioned here. At any rate I have shown you that one has moved far away even now from marginal costs and marginal revenue as prime factors in the theory of price.

In summarizing I should like to stress these points: (1) The theory of games of strategy is strictly empirical and thus far purely static. Its full development awaits a greatly expanded body of information about the economy as does the current version of economic theory. Yet it can be developed much farther even with the existing descriptive knowledge (e.g., in the field of location of industry). (2) Its logico-mathematical foundations and techniques appear more natural to the subject matter of economics than those used otherwise, which stem from the glamorous but distant and alien field of theoretical physics. (3) The complications it presents are due to the need to take better into account the extraordinary wealth of phenomena of the social and economic world of which we all have now only very inadequate ideas. But the conceptual structure, of which I tried to give a general notion, has, I believe, a considerable intuitive appeal making the access to the exact, quantitative formulation easier than would otherwise be the case.

PART FIFTEEN
Welfare Economics

It is primarily with the theoretical problem of utility that welfare economics is concerned. That is, welfare economics asks the question, How can the total welfare (or utility) of the people in a community be maximized? The generally accepted answer is that the total welfare has been maximized when there exists no further act through which one or more people can be made better off, *i.e.,* their utilities or satisfactions increased, without one or more people being made worse off, *i.e.,* their utilities or satisfactions decreased. In other words, as long as it is possible, through any act or policy, to increase at least one person's utility without simultaneously decreasing someone else's, there is room for increasing the total welfare.

The first and most obvious difficulty which presents itself is that of measuring utility. How can we tell whether a certain act will increase the satisfactions of some people without decreasing the satisfactions of others? It is probably impossible to conceive of a single act that would not have some sort of unfavorable effect on someone. Perhaps even more important is the impossibility of measuring and comparing the utilities enjoyed by different individuals. Utility is a subjective thing and is not susceptible to objective measurement, as is, say, weight, distance, or speed.

The Cambridge economists in England—the so-called neo-classicists, notably Professors Alfred Marshall, A. C. Pigou, and R. F. Kahn—and their American contemporaries, Irving Fisher, Frank Knight, and perhaps Edward Chamberlin, recognized this difficulty a long time ago. Unfortunately, however, they seemed neither prone nor able to offer an adequate and realistic solution to the problem. They argued that since it could not be shown that individuals derived *different* utilities from a given act or policy or, say, from a given money income, it must be assumed instead that they all derived the *same* utilities. That is, since it could not be proven otherwise, *they assumed that individuals possess equal ability to enjoy themselves and to enjoy life.*[1]

Now if welfare economics is to have the objectivity of a science, it cannot depend to any large extent on something as subjective as utility. Accordingly, many economists outside of the Cambridge circle refused to accept welfare economics as a scientific branch of, or approach to, eco-

[1] See Tibor Scitovsky, "The State of Welfare Economics," *American Economic Review,* June, 1951.

nomic inquiry, and during the interwar period welfare economics was forced into the background of economic thinking.

In place of welfare economics a new school of thought developed during the interwar period, with Professors Abba P. Lerner and Oscar Lange as two of its outstanding exponents. Like the welfare economists these theorists concerned themselves with the problem of maximizing utility by providing an optimum allocation and distribution of resources under perfect competition, but unlike the welfare economists they considered themselves to be "theoretical socialists." The Cambridge economists had based their theories on the principal assumption that individuals possess an equal ability to enjoy themselves and to enjoy life. Logically, the only other group that could readily accept this assumption and work with it as a basic tool for further analysis was the socialists.

In 1936 Lord Keynes published his revolutionary work, *The General Theory of Employment, Interest and Money,* in which economists saw, among other things, how public policy might be formulated for the purpose of maintaining a high level of income and employment, with the ultimate effect of increasing economic welfare. As a result of this concern with full employment and welfare, economists began to assume an increasingly important role as policy makers, and they soon realized that they would have to see what welfare economics had to offer if they were to formulate intelligent and rational public policy. Accordingly, in the late 1930's welfare economics was reborn, and it has since become an important part of modern economic theory. Although new developments and ideas have occurred in welfare theory since the late thirties, it is still too early to tell whether they will have lasting significance. Furthermore, there have been relatively few of these original contributions. Much recent work has amounted to nothing more than a re-exposition and refinement of the earlier theories.

ARTHUR CECIL PIGOU

(1877-)

Professor Pigou, now professor emeritus at Cambridge University, was Alfred Marshall's successor in the chair of economics there. He has written on a variety of topics in economics, especially in the fields of public finance and business cycles, but he is perhaps most famous for his classic *Economics of Welfare* (1920). He is at present looked upon as the senior member and dean of the so-called Cambridge school, composed of the followers of, and the elaborators on, the work of Alfred Marshall. Other famous members of this school are R. F. Kahn, Piero Sraffa, and Joan Robinson. Until 1936 John Maynard Keynes also belonged to this group.

Like Marshall, Pigou assumes that the capacities of individuals to enjoy are roughly equal for purposes of economics and that the impossibility of measuring utility subjectively does not really affect the validity of the Cambridge type of analysis. Taking as his guiding principle the desirability of maximizing social and economic welfare, he sets up important categories of welfare. Everything else being equal, a given unit of wealth will yield the most social welfare if it is divided as equally as possible. Likewise, optimum production will result if productive resources are so distributed that the net social yield of the marginal product is equal in all alternative uses. He then considers how laissez-faire, monopoly, and government regulation compare in achieving the maximization of welfare. He comes to the conclusion that free competition and laissez-faire will result in a scale of production and investment less than the optimum in industries of increasing returns.

The following selections, which are concerned with the size and distribution of the national dividend in relation to social welfare, are from the 1920 edition of *The Economics of Welfare*. In addition, a recent article in the *American Economic Review* brings his position on the subject up to date.

THE ECONOMICS OF WELFARE *

The Relation of Economic Welfare to the National Dividend

Let us begin with the relation between economic welfare and the average volume of the national dividend. Here the necessary mediation through consumable income raises no difficulties. In general, anything that increases or diminishes the average volume of the national dividend will affect the average volume of the national consumable income in the same sense. We need not, therefore, trouble to maintain the distinction between them, but may treat national dividend and consumable income as, for this purpose—not, of course, for all purposes—practically equivalent terms. For economy of language I shall, in fact, adopt this plan. With this understanding it is tempting to maintain that any cause which increases the volume of the dividend, provided that it neither injures its distribution nor increases its variability, will increase economic welfare. But this proposition is not valid. The quantity of economic welfare associated with any

* From *The Economics of Welfare* (London, Macmillan and Co., Ltd., 1920).

volume of the dividend depends, not only on the satisfaction yielded by consumption, but also on the dissatisfaction involved in production. There must, therefore, be some point after which an addition to the resources expended in production, while still adding something to the dividend, would involve a direct loss of satisfaction greater than the indirect gain. Suppose, for example, that the whole community was compelled by law to work for eighteen hours a day, and—which is in fact improbable—that this policy made the national dividend larger. It is practically certain that the satisfaction yielded by the extra product would be enormously less than the dissatisfaction caused by the extra labour. And the same thing is true if extra work is done, not under compulsion, but because some workpeople have formed an erroneous estimate of their own interests. No doubt, in the modern world, apart from military conscription, we have to do, not with forced, but with voluntary labour. No doubt too, hours of labour cannot be carried *far* beyond the point to which the workpeople's interests, rightly interpreted, would lead them, without causing a diminution, instead of an increase, in the national dividend. Hence, it is unlikely that we shall often meet in practice with any considerable expansions of the national dividend that are injurious to economic welfare. Still the mere fact that injurious expansions are possible invalidates the proposition suggested above.

Nor is the somewhat obvious disharmony just displayed the only one that may arise. It is fairly plain that, if two regions, between which capital or labour have hitherto been unable to move, with the result that a unit of capital or labour in one of them is producing a considerably larger output than a similar unit in the other, are brought into communication, economic welfare is bound to be increased. For hereafter labour (or capital) will be so distributed between the two regions that nothing could be gained by movement, and the amount of labour exercised (or capital created) will be such that the exercise (or creation) of any additional unit would destroy more satisfaction than the product for which it might be responsible could yield. If, therefore, there is to be harmony, it is necessary that the opening up of communication between the two regions shall also cause the national dividend to increase. It can be shown, however, that this need not happen. Working along the lines of an argument developed by Cournot in his chapter on "The Competition of Markets," we perceive that the abolition of obstacles between the two regions *may* cause the aggregate quantity of labour exercised, or capital created, to be *smaller* than it was before. Suppose, for example, that one group of workpeople is assembled at A and another at B; that the marginal hour's work at A yields a much smaller return than the marginal hour's work of similar quality yields at B; and that at both places the return yielded per hour's work is smaller the greater is the quantity of work that is done there. The removal of an obstacle which has hitherto prevented workmen at A from going to B at once causes a migration. Since, after the change, an hour's work both at B and at A yields more return than an hour's work at A formerly yielded, the men who were originally at A may be led to provide more hours' work than they provided before. But the men originally at B, finding that an hour's work there now yields a less return than it used to yield, may be led to provide fewer hours' work than they provided before. It is evident that conditions of demand and supply at A and B *may* be such that the diminution in the amount of work provided by the natives of B will be greater than the increase in that provided by the natives of A; in such wise that the quantity of labour forthcoming in both regions together is made smaller by the removal of the obstacle between them. Suppose again that in agricultural districts the capital employed is yielding a low return, while in manufacturing districts isolated from them it is yielding a high return; that the demand is elastic in the agricultural districts and very inelastic in the manufacturing districts; and that the supply is about equally elastic in the two sets of districts. On these suppositions, after the removal of the obstacles that separated them, say, by the development of banking, the amount of capital made available in manufacturing districts would remain practically unchanged; but the amount made available in agricultural districts would, on account of the increase in cost, be greatly diminished. On balance, therefore, there would be a smaller aggregate of capital than before in the two sets of districts taken together. These examples show that the abolition of obstacles to movement between two districts *may* diminish the aggregate quantity of resources available for production in the two together. Further, mathematical analysis enables us to conclude that, when an obstacle selected at random is removed, an increase and a decrease in the quantity of productive resources that come into being are about equally *probable,* or, if we prefer to put it so, will occur about equally often. This result does not, of course, imply that an increase and a decrease in the magnitude of the national dividend are about equally probable. For, whether or not the aggregate quantity of resources available for work is diminished, such resources as are available are necessarily employed, on the average, under conditions more favourable to production. Thus, in our example of the two groups of workpeople assembled at A and B, let us suppose that, before the obstacle was removed, x hours' work was forthcoming at A and y hours' work at B, and that, after it is removed, $(x + y - h)$ hours' work are performed at B and no hours' work at A. Then each one of the $(x - h)$ hours now added to the work done at B necessarily yields a larger product than it would have yielded had it continued to be performed at A. The addition that is made in this way to the efficiency of productive resources will bring about an enhanced product, not only on all occasions when the aggregate quantity of resources is increased, but also on some occasions when it is diminished. Hence, more often than not the removal of an obstacle to movement between two regions will increase the national dividend. It is easy to show, however, that sometimes it will diminish it. Suppose, for example, that in the region, where, before the obstacle is removed, production per unit of labour or capital is larger than in the other, there is not room to employ more than a few further units except at a greatly reduced return. In these circumstances, when the obstacle is removed, the output as well as the capital and labour employed there, will be practically the same (if the demand is perfectly inelastic, *exactly* the same) as before; while capital and labour having been withdrawn from the other region in order to take the place of those units that it is no longer worth while to provide in the first, the output in the other region will be smaller than before. This proves that the removal of the obstacle *may* lessen the national dividend. Since, therefore, it *must* increase economic welfare, there may, or in other words, sometimes will, be disharmony. Some causes that injure the national dividend will increase economic welfare, and *vice versa.*

. . . Broadly and generally then we may lay down the following proposition: *Any cause which, without the exercise of compulsion or pressure upon people to make them work more than their wishes and interests dictate, increases productive efficiency, and, therewith, the average volume of the national dividend, provided that it neither injures the distribution nor augments the variability of the country's consumable income, will, in general, increase economic welfare.*

This proposition, it will be observed, is purely qualitative in form, and states nothing about the quantitative relation between an expansion of the national dividend and additions to economic welfare. To remedy this deficiency completely is, of course, impossible. It is not impossible, however, to throw some further light on the matter. To this end we may begin by leaving out of account the reactions that may be produced by the fact of consumption upon capacity for deriving enjoyment from consumption. When this is done, the familiar "law of diminishing utility" instructs us that a given expansion of the national dividend is likely to be accompanied by a *less than proportionate* increase in economic welfare. This conclusion is, moreover, reinforced by a further consideration. The satisfaction which a man obtains from his economic environment is, in great part, derived, not from the *absolute,* but from the *comparative,* magnitude of his income. Mill wrote: "Men do not desire to be *rich,* but to be richer than other men. . . ." An ordinary man's satisfaction does not, of course, depend entirely upon his comparative, but partly at least upon his absolute, income. It cannot be maintained seriously that an increase in the latter will add *nothing whatever* to the satisfactions which constitute his economic welfare. But there is good reason to believe that it will add considerably less to these satisfactions than might have been thought probable at a first careless glance.

It remains to take account of the reactions which the fact of consumption may produce on taste. *Prima facie* it would seem that those reactions may enable a given expansion in the average volume of the dividend to augment economic welfare more largely by indirect means than it is able to do directly. Obviously, the amount of economic satisfaction that a community obtains from a given economic environment depends, not only on the environment, but also, in an at least equal degree, upon the mentality of the people concerned. Jevons observed long ago that a small change in wants and tastes might often by itself lead to a very great increase in economic welfare. And he added a characteristic illustration: "While the great Irish famine was at its worst, abundance of salmon and other fish could have been had for the trouble of catching; scarcely any of the starving peasantry would consent to touch it." . . . It follows that, if a cause, which directly increases the output of any of the goods or services contained in the national dividend, thereby indirectly increases people's capacity for deriving satisfaction from these goods and services, it will, to that extent, make an important indirect contribution to economic welfare. And in fact it can be shown that this frequently happens. For in the economic world "infant," or undeveloped, demands are to be found equally with "infant," or undeveloped, industries. People may be given a taste for a particular thing, or the keenness of their desire for it may be permanently increased, through the temporary use of, or acquaintance with, it. When machines are sent out on trial, or articles presented in sample-packets, or pictures exhibited free to the public, the popular taste for these objects tends to be augmented. When public-houses, or lotteries, or libraries are easily accessible, the taste for drink, or gambling, or literature is not merely gratified, but is also stimulated. When cleanliness, or light, or model dwellings, or model plots of agricultural land are set up, though it is only to be seen, and not owned, by the neighbours, the object lesson may still succeed and make plain superiorities hitherto unrecognised. . . . No doubt sometimes the increase in taste for one thing is associated with a substantially equivalent decline in taste for another thing that fulfils the same purpose,—*e.g.* wool as against cotton,—and does not, therefore, lead to any appreciable increase in aggregate welfare. But, frequently, as a consideration of the examples cited above will show, there is a genuine creation or development of a new taste. The indirect benefits which are thus conferred upon economic welfare by an increase in the dividend have the further characteristic that they may be permanent, even though the increase in any part of the dividend is itself only temporary. For, peoples' tastes being altered in an enduring manner, they will continue to obtain more satisfaction than they did before, if and when the supply of the commodity they have become trained to like falls again to its original amount.

This line of reasoning is, however, subject to an important qualification. It is true that experience of a particular thing will often enable people to get increased satisfaction out of it. But it is at least arguable that, after a point, as growing wealth gives a man command over more and more luxuries, the satisfaction that he gains from each new one is, as it were, taken out of relaxed interest in the others, so that the economic satisfaction which he achieves on the whole is not substantially increased. He may be conceived, in short, as a vessel able, according to his temperament, to "contain" a certain limited amount of economic satisfaction. When satiety point is reached, further new satisfactions can only be admitted at the cost of driving out an equivalent volume of other satisfactions. There can be no doubt that this conception embodies a large element of truth. It need not be denied that a rich man accustomed to a yacht would be much hurt at the time by having to do without his yacht: but, when he had got accustomed to a new and lower standard of living, provided that it still remained fairly high, it might well be that he would be no less happy than before. *Per contra,* a man accustomed to a standard of living represented, say, by £3000 a year, may well get quite as much satisfaction out of life as another man of similar temperament with £300,000 a year and accustomed to the standard which that income implies. These considerations suggest that the reactions which take place between consumption and taste may, on the whole, lessen rather than augment the beneficial effects which a given expansion of the dividend is likely to have upon economic welfare. It must be noted, however, that they are relevant to a change from riches to greater riches, rather than to one from poverty to less poverty; and, looked at as a whole, every modern nation, when its real income is balanced against its population, is still very poor. Hence, as things actually are, I am inclined to think that the reactions which occur between consumption and taste are likely, on the whole, to make the benefit to economic welfare resulting from a given expansion of the dividend a little larger than it would be if there were no reactions. But this conclusion in the present state of economic science, is, of course, little better than a guess.

We now turn to the relation between economic welfare and the proportion of the national dividend accruing to poor persons. Here the distinction between total income and consumed income is more important, because, generally speaking, the richer a man is, the larger proportion of his income he is likely to save, so that, if his total income is, say, twenty times as large, his consumed income may be only, say, five times as large. Nevertheless, it is evident that any transference of income from a relatively rich man to a relatively poor man of similar temperament, since it enables more intense wants to be satisfied at the expense of less intense wants, must increase the aggregate sum of satisfaction. The old "law of diminishing utility" thus leads securely to a second main proposition, which may be stated as follows: *Any cause which increases the proportion of the national dividend received by poor persons, provided that it does not lead to a contraction of the dividend and does not injuriously affect its variability, will, in general, increase economic welfare.* This conclusion is further fortified by the fact that, of the satisfaction yielded by the incomes of rich people, a specially large proportion comes from their *relative* rather than their *absolute* amount, and, therefore, will not be destroyed if the incomes of all rich people are diminished together.

It must be conceded, of course, that, if the rich and the poor were two races with different mental constitutions, such that the rich were inherently capable of securing a greater amount of economic satisfaction from any given income than the poor, the possibility of increasing welfare by this type of change would be seriously doubtful. Furthermore, even without any assumption about inherent racial difference, it may be maintained that a rich man, from the nature of his upbringing and training, is capable of obtaining considerably more satisfaction from a given income—say a thousand pounds—than a poor man would be. For, if anybody accustomed to a given standard of living suddenly finds his income enlarged, he is apt to dissipate the extra income in forms of exciting pleasure, which, when their indirect, as well as their direct, effects are taken into account, may even lead to a positive loss of satisfaction. To this argument, however, there is a sufficient answer. It is true that at any given moment the tastes and temperament of persons who have long been poor are more or less adjusted to their environment, and that a sudden and sharp rise of income is likely to be followed by a good deal of foolish expenditure, which involves little or no addition to economic welfare. If, however, the higher income is maintained for any length of time, this phase will pass; whereas, if the increase is gradual or, still better, if it comes about in such a way as not to be directly perceived—through a fall in prices, for example—the period of foolishness need not occur at all. In any case, to contend that the folly of poor persons is so great that a rise of income among them will not promote economic welfare in any degree, is to press paradox beyond the point up to which discussion can reasonably be called upon to follow. The true view, as I conceive it, is admirably stated by Messrs. Pringle and Jackson in their special report to the Poor Law Commissioners: "It is in the unskilled and least educated part of the population that drink continues to hold its ground; as greater regularity of employment and higher wages are achieved by sections of the working-classes, the men rise in respectability and character. That the drink bill is diminishing, while wages are rising throughout the country, is one of the most hopeful indications of progress we possess." The root of the matter is that, even when, under existing conditions, the mental constitution of poor persons is such that an enlarged income will at the moment yield them little benefit, yet, after a time—more especially if the time is long enough to allow a new generation to grow up—the possession of such an income will make possible the development in them, through education and otherwise, of capacities and faculties adapted for the enjoyment of the enlarged income. Thus, in the long run differences of temperament and taste between rich and poor are overcome by the very fact of a shifting of income between them. Plainly, therefore, they cannot be used as an argument to disprove the benefits of a transference. . . .

It should be noticed that the conclusion set out above is not exactly equivalent to the proposition that economic welfare will be increased by anything that, *ceteris paribus*, renders the national dividend less unequal.

If the community consisted of two members only, it would, indeed, coincide with this. But, in a community consisting of more than two members, the meaning of "rendering the distribution of the dividend less unequal" is ambiguous. . . . With that criterion . . . assuming similarity of temperament among the members of the community, a diminution in the inequality of distribution *probably,* though not necessarily, increases the aggregate sum of satisfaction. . . .

We come next to the relation between economic welfare and the variability of the national dividend as a whole. Here, since it is possible by deliberate action greatly to diminish the variability of the community's consumable income, while leaving that of the national dividend unchanged, the distinction between national dividend and consumable income has much greater importance than it had in any previous portion of this discussion. This fact makes the argument a complicated one.

The first step is as follows. . . . If a given quantity of resources is consumed by two similar men, economic welfare is larger, the more evenly this quantity is shared between them. When the number of our imaginary group . . . [is] increased from two similar men to many similar men, . . . economic welfare *is likely* to be larger, the more evenly consumption is divided among them . . . It is obvious that the result thus achieved is equally applicable when, for many similar men at one moment, we substitute one man at many similar moments. When the aggregate consumption of an individual, whose tastes and needs over a series of years are constant, is given, economic welfare is likely to be larger the more evenly that consumption is spread over these years. From this proposition we proceed to the further proposition, that the economic welfare of a group of individuals is likely to be larger the more evenly the consumption of the representative or average member of that group is distributed through time. By an extension of the reasoning . . . it is readily shown that this latter proposition has equal validity with that just enunciated, when the evenness of the distribution through time of the representative member's consumption is measured by the arithmetical average of the standard, or mean square, deviations of the several members.

The second step of the argument has to do with the relation between the variability of the consumption of the representative member and the variability of the aggregate consumption of the whole community. When the variability of the community's consumption is given, the variability of the representative man's consumption will partly depend on how far mutual insurance arrangements provide, in effect, that those who are temporarily prosperous shall assist the temporarily unfortunate. Let us suppose, however, that the state of these arrangements is given. Then, if people were perfectly mobile between different places and occupations, anything that made the whole community's consumption less variable would necessarily also make the representative man's less variable. When perfect mobility does not exist this need not happen; for the consumption of the community as an aggregate *might* be made steadier by a cause which made less steady the consumption of each several part of it. It is plain, however, that the generality of economic causes affecting the variability of consumption will not act in this way. One reason is that they are blind causes, "random in the technical sense" from the present point of view; and a cause which diminishes variability in one part of a group is most unlikely, unless it is specially selected for that end, so to react on variability in other parts that it increases the variability of the whole. A second reason is that by far the most important of these causes, those, namely, that act through the bounty of Nature or through business confidence, impinge directly upon the whole, without being specialised to any part. When these causes are at work, the variability of the representative man's consumption necessarily rises and falls with that of consumption in the community as a whole.

The third step concerns the relation between the variability of the aggregate *consumption* of the community and the variability of the *income of consumable goods*—or consumable income—accruing to it. These two variabilities will be different if people in good times store up consumable goods in warehouses and shops against the bad times that may follow. But, though they may be different, it is obvious that the two are correlated. Other things being equal, the variability of consumption is certain to be greater the greater is the variability of the consumable income.

The fourth and final step in the argument concerns the relation between the variability of the consumable income of the community and that of the aggregate dividend accruing to it. It is plain that the former variability will, in general, be considerably smaller than the latter, because many people invest in producers' goods, not a constant proportion of their income, but the surplus that is left to them after living up to their normal standard of life. This means that the quantity of resources invested in producers' goods will in bad times be diminished much more than the national dividend, and in good times expanded much more than the national dividend. Hence, the part of the dividend that constitutes consumable income must vary less than the whole dividend varies. This is certain. But it is also certain that, other things being equal, the variability of the consumable income of the community will be greater the greater is the variability of the aggregate dividend accruing to it.

There results from the above analysis my third main proposition: *Any cause which diminishes the variability of the national dividend, provided that it neither diminishes its volume nor injures its distribution, will, in general, increase economic welfare.*

There remains the last of the four attributes of the national dividend . . . namely the variability of that part of it which accrues to the poorer members of the community. Here, as in the preceding section, we must study first the relation between economic welfare and the variability of consumption. Experience shows that the rate, at which the "desiredness" of consumable income to an individual diminishes, itself diminishes as the magnitude of his consumption increases. It follows that the difference between the economic satisfaction yielded by a constant consumption x and a consumption the average volume of which is x, but which oscillates from $(x + h)$ to $(x - h)$, is greater the smaller is x. Hence, other things being equal, a given absolute variability in the consumption of a poor man, or a group of poor men, is more detrimental to economic welfare than an equal absolute variability in the consumption of a rich man or a rich group. This conclusion is emphasised by the reflection that, among poor persons, variability of consumption often involves, not merely loss of satisfaction at the moment, but also physical, and perhaps moral, damage injurious to their productive power in the future; while among rich people there are not likely to be any significant reactions of this kind. It follows that the economic welfare of rich and poor jointly will be increased by any system of transferences which, while leaving the average consumption of each group unaltered, makes the consumption of the poor less variable at the cost of making that of the rich in a corresponding degree more variable. It is, of course, conceivable that, by means of elaborate systems of borrowing, poor persons might establish for themselves a perfectly stable consumption in spite of their income being unstable; so that no advantage could be got by stabilising their income at the cost of rendering unstable the income of better-to-do persons. In practice, however, it is quite certain that they will not succeed in doing this. Consequently, from what has been said it is legitimate to infer a fourth main proposition: *Any cause which diminishes the variability of the part of the national dividend accruing to the poor, even though it increases in corresponding measure the variability of the part accruing to the rich, will, other things being equal, increase economic welfare. . . .*

The National Dividend and Equality of Marginal Social Net Products

Concerned as we are with the *average volume* of the national dividend as a continuing flow, we naturally understand by the resources directed to making it, not a stock of resources, but a similarly continuing flow; and we conceive the distribution of these resources among different occupations on the analogy, not of a stagnant pond divided into a number of sections, but rather of a river divided into a number of streams. This conception involves, no doubt, many minor difficulties in connection both with the varying durability of the equipment employed in different industries and with the dynamic, or changing, tendencies of industry as a whole. In spite of these difficulties, however, the general idea is exact enough for the present purpose. That purpose is to provide a suitable definition for the concept which is fundamental throughout this Part, namely, *the value of marginal social net product*. The essential point is that this too must be conceived as a flow—as the result *per year* of the employment *per year* of the marginal increment of some given quantity of resources. On this basis we may proceed to work out our definition.

The most obvious element in the marginal social net product of any flow of resources employed in any occupation is the direct physical net product. This is equal to the difference between the aggregate flow of physical product for which that flow of resources, *when appropriately organised,* is responsible and the aggregate flow of physical product for which a flow of resources differing from that flow by a small (marginal) increment, *when appropriately organised,* would be responsible. In this statement the phrase *when appropriately organised* is essential. If we were thinking of marginal physical net product in the sense of the difference between the products of two adjacent *quantities* of resources, we should normally imagine the resources to be organised suitably to one of these quantities and, therefore, not to the other. Since, however, our interest is in the difference between the products of two adjacent *flows* of resources, it is natural to conceive each of the two flows as organised in the manner most appropriate to itself. This is the conception we need. It is excellently illustrated by Professor J. B. Clark. The marginal increment of capital invested in a railway corporation is in reality, he writes, "a difference between two kinds of plant for carrying goods and passengers. One of these is the railroad as it stands, with all its equipment brought up to the highest pitch of perfection that is possible with the present resources. The other is the road built and equipped as it would have been if the resources had been by one degree less. A difference in all-round quality between an actual and a possible railroad is in reality the final increment of capital now used by the actual corporation. The product of that last unit of capital is the difference between what the road actually produces and what it would have produced if it had been been made one degree poorer." [1]

So much being understood, it must next be observed that the marginal social net product of any given flow of resources in any occupation may include, over and above the direct physical net product just described, indirect physical effects outside the occupation in which the resources we are contemplating are invested. It might happen, for example, as will be explained more fully in a later chapter, that costs are thrown upon other people not directly concerned, through, say, uncompensated damage done to surrounding woods by sparks from railway engines. All such effects must be included—some of them will be positive, others negative elements—in reckoning up the full physical net product of the marginal increment of any volume of resources turned into any occupation. Further, it may happen that, besides the physical product, there will also be effects that are not physical—modifications, for example, in people's tastes, that cause them to get more or less satisfaction than before from some of their possessions or purchases. When there is any product of this kind we must add it to the physical product already described. The result is the full marginal social net product of the given volume of resources.

[1] *The Distribution of Wealth,* p. 250. I have substituted "produced" for "earned" in the sentence quoted above. . . .

The *value* of this marginal social net product is the money value of the economic satisfaction due to it. When there is no element present other than the direct physical addition made to output in the industry directly concerned, this money value is identical with the marginal increment of product multiplied by the price per unit at which the product is sold when the given volume of resources is being employed in producing it. For example, the value of the marginal net product per year of a million units of resources invested in weaving is equal to the number of bales of cloth by which the output of a million *plus* a small increment, say a million and one, exceeds the output of a million units, multiplied by the money value of a bale of cloth when this output is being produced. This, it should be observed in passing, is different from, and must by no means be confused with, the excess of the money value of the whole product when a million and one units of resources are being employed over the money value of the whole product when a million units are being employed. When there are in the marginal social net product other elements besides the direct physical product, our statement must assume a more general form. The value of the marginal social net product of any volume of resources in any occupation is defined as, and is measured by, the money value of the difference made by the marginal increment of those resources so employed to the sum total of economic welfare.

On the basis of this definition it can be shown that, provided there are no costs of movement between different occupations, and provided conditions are such that only one arrangement of resources will make the values of the marginal net products in all occupations equal, that arrangement must make the national dividend larger than it would be under any other arrangement. If the national dividend consisted of one sort of commodity only, manufactured by means of a number of different occupations, this conclusion would be obvious; for, if the value of the marginal net product of resources in one of the occupations was smaller than in another, the aggregate quantity of this single commodity could be directly increased by a transference. . . . The national dividend . . . is larger or smaller in period A than in period B according as, apart from compulsion to work or certain exceptional obstacles to movement, the amount of economic satisfaction derived from it by a representative member of the group to which it accrues is larger or smaller. Now, the value of the marginal net product of resources in any use is the money measure of the satisfaction which the marginal increment of resources in that use is yielding to the representative man. Plainly, therefore, whenever the value of the marginal net product of resources is less in any one use than it is in any other, the money measure of satisfaction in the aggregate, and, therefore, the national dividend as here defined, can be increased by transferring resources from the use where the value of the marginal net product is smaller to the use where it is larger. It follows from this that, since, *ex hypothesi,* there is only one arrangement of resources that will make the values of the marginal net products equal in all uses, this arrangement is necessarily the one that makes the national dividend, as here defined, a maximum.

So far we have premised that there are no costs involved in moving resources from one occupation (or place) to another. But it is obvious that in fact there are costs—sometimes serious costs—in the way of movement. We have, therefore, to inquire in what, if any, respects this fact makes it necessary to modify the conclusions set out above. The kernel of the matter can be displayed as follows. Suppose that between two points A and B the movement of a unit of resources can be effected at a capital cost which is equivalent to an annual charge of *n* shillings for every year during which a unit that is moved continues in productive work in its new home. In these circumstances the national dividend will be increased by the movement of resources from A to B, so long as the annual value of the marginal net product at B exceeds that at A by more than *n* shillings; and it will be injured by any movement of resources which occurs after the excess of the value of the marginal net product at B has been reduced below *n* shillings. If the initial distribution of resources between A and B is such that the value of the marginal net product at B exceeds (or falls short of) the value of the marginal net product at A by any number of shillings less than *n*, say by $(n - h)$ shillings, the existing arrangement—that under when the values of the marginal net products at the two points differ by $(n - h)$ shillings—is the best arrangement from the standpoint of the national dividend, not indeed absolutely, but *relatively to the fact of the initial distribution and the existing costs of movement.* It is not, be it noted, the best arrangement relatively to the existing costs of movement alone. We cannot say that, when the costs of movement are equivalent to *n* shillings, the national dividend is best served by a distribution under which the values of the marginal net products at A and B differ by such and such a defined number of shillings. The only accurate statement is: when the costs of movement between A and B are equivalent to *n* shillings, the national dividend is best served by the maintenance of the existing distribution, whatever that may be, provided that this distribution does not involve a divergence in the values of marginal net products greater than *n* shillings; and, if the existing distribution does involve a divergence greater than *n* shillings, by a new distribution brought about by the transference of sufficent resources to bring the divergence down to *n* shillings.

We have thus inquired what is the best distribution of resources from the standpoint of the national dividend (*a*) where there are not, and (*b*) where there are, costs of movement. For completeness we must compare with one another the two arrangements that are respectively best in these two sets of conditions. In this connection it is well to recall the possibility . . . that certain special obstacles to movement (and cost is, of course, one form of obstacle) *may,* though injuring economic welfare, at the same time increase the national dividend. This, however, is an exceptional possibility of little relevance to practice. Apart from this, it is obvious that, since the scheme, which is best for the dividend (and economic welfare) when there are costs, is only best because the additional advantage to be got from an arrangement yielding equal values of marginal net products would be less than the costs of getting it, the dividend will be larger if no costs exist and the distribution of resources is adjusted to no costs, than it will be if costs exist and the distribution is adjusted to that fact. Similarly, the dividend will be increased if costs of movement are lessened, though not destroyed, and the distribution of resources is adjusted accordingly.

The foregoing analysis rests upon the assumption that there is only one arrangement of resources which makes the values of marginal social net products everywhere equal—or as nearly equal as, in view of costs of movement, it is to the interest of the national dividend that they should be made. This assumption would be justified if the value of the marginal social net product of resources employed in each several use was always smaller the greater the volume of resources employed there. That condition, it will be noticed, is not equivalent to the condition that what economists call "the law of diminishing returns" prevails in each several use. Diminishing returns in this sense rule when the increment of product due to the increase by a unit in the quantity of resources occupied in producing some commodity is smaller, the greater is the quantity of resources so employed. The law of diminishing returns thus refers to (marginal) physical output, and our condition to (marginal) physical output multiplied by value per unit; and it may easily happen that the expansion of an industry involves a diminution in this complex quantity, even though actual physical production obeys the law of increasing returns. But, when the law of increasing returns is acting strongly, it is evident that even our condition may very well *not* be fulfilled. Hence, the conclusions set out above require to be restated in a modified form. Allowance being made for costs of movement, it is true that the dividend cannot reach the maximum attainable amount *unless* the values of the marginal social net products of resources in all uses are equal. For, if they are not equal, the dividend can always be increased by a transference of resources from the margin of some uses to the margin of others. But, when the values of the marginal social net products in all uses are equal, the dividend *need not* attain an unequivocal maximum. For, if several arrangements are possible, all of which make the values of the marginal social net products equal, each of these arrangements does, indeed, imply what may be called a *relative maximum* for the dividend; but only one of these maxima is the unequivocal, or absolute, maximum. All of the relative maxima are, as it were, the tops of hills higher than the surrounding country, but only one of them is the highest hill-top of all. Furthermore, it is not necessary that all positions of relative maximum should represent larger dividends than all positions which are not maxima. On the contrary, a scheme of distribution approximating to that which yields the absolute maximum, but not itself fulfilling the condition of equal marginal yields, would probably imply a larger dividend than most of the schemes which do fulfil this condition and so constitute relative maxima of a minor character. A point near the summit of the highest hill may be higher than any summit except the highest itself. It is, therefore, very important to inquire in what conditions, in any industry or use, different quantities of investment may yield equal values of marginal social net products.

The answer is as follows. In an industry in which production obeys the law of diminishing returns and demand is not capable of being developed by acquaintance with the commodity supplied, this state of things is impossible. But there are two sets of conditions in which it is not impossible. First, the employment of additional resources in the production of a commodity may, after a time, enable improved methods of organisation to be developed. This means that conditions of increasing return prevail, in such wise that the marginal (physical) net product of a greater quantity of resources exceeds the marginal (physical) net product of a smaller quantity: and, whenever this happens, it is *possible,* though, of course, it is not *necessary,* that the value of the marginal (physical) net product of several different quantities of resources will be the same. Secondly, the employment of additional resources in the production of a commodity may, after a time, lead to an increase in the price per unit offered by consumers of any given quantity of it. For their taste for it may be lastingly enhanced—obvious examples are afforded by the taste for music and tobacco—through experience of it. When this happens the value per unit of a larger product will (after an appropriate interval of time) be greater than the value per unit of a smaller product. It follows that, even for commodities whose production obeys the law of diminishing returns, there *may* be, though, of course, there need not be, several different quantities of invested resources the values of whose marginal social net products are the same.

The practical outcome of this analysis is plain. Even though the values of marginal social net products were equal in all occupations, it would not follow that the national dividend was incapable of increase. On the contrary, in any industry where the conditions are such that there is not only one, but more than one, volume of investment which would yield a marginal social net product equal in value to that obtainable elsewhere, unless it so happens that the volume actually hit upon is that one of these which is the most favourable to the national dividend, an opening for improvement must exist. Benefit could be secured by a *temporary* bounty (or temporary protection) so arranged as to jerk the industrial system out of its present poise at a position of relative maximum, and induce it to settle down again at the position of absolute maximum—the highest hill-top of all. This is the analytical basis of the argument for the protection, or other encouragement, of infant industries; and, if the right infants are selected, the right amount of protection accorded, and this protection removed again at the right time, the argument is perfectly valid. Benefit could also be secured by a *permanent* bounty so arranged as to force the industrial system from the summit of the hill-top on which it is found to any position, that overtops its present site, on the slope of a higher hill. The conditions in which interference may be expected to have this effect, rather than that of shifting the economic system to a different position on the hill that it is on already, are somewhat special. But it can be shown that, in certain states of demand and supply, *some* rates of bounty *must* have this effect. These possibilities have considerable practical importance. It must be clearly understood, however, that the possible advantage of particular disturbances of, and departures from, existing arrangements that involve equality in the values of marginal social net products affords no argument in favour of disturbances or departures in general. It is true that, when the values of the marginal social net products of resources in all uses are equal, *some* disturbances and departures would augment the national dividend. But the *majority* of possible movements would not do this. Any change from a distribution of resources involving equality in the values of marginal net products in all uses, which was not specially arranged with a view to increasing the national dividend, would probably in fact diminish it.

This general conclusion may, moreover, be extended in an important way. Just as the national dividend is likely to be damaged by a change in the distribution of resources that brings about inequality, instead of equality, in the values of marginal social net products, so also, subject to the same conditions as above, it is likely to be damaged by a change that brings about greater inequality instead of less inequality. This conclusion cannot, however, be laid down without explanation. If the uses in which resources are employed were only two in number, its meaning would be perfectly clear and its validity undoubted. In fact, however, these uses are very numerous. This circumstance gives rise to a difficulty . . . The meaning of the concept of greater or less equality among a large number of values is ambiguous. Are we to measure the degree of equality by the mean deviation from the average value, or by the standard deviation, or by the "probable error," or by some other statistical measure? If we use the standard deviation as our criterion, the reasoning . . . shows that an increase in the degree of inequality subsisting among the values of marginal net products in different uses will *probably* lead to a decrease in the national dividend. But the probability is of a lower order than the probability that an increase in the degree of inequality when there are only two uses, and, therefore, no ambiguity about the meaning of this increase, will have that effect. A probability of the same order as that probability arises only where the increase of inequality is brought about by a group of (one or more) changes of individual values, *each one of which taken by itself* tends to increase inequality. Thus, if the distribution of resources is so altered that a number of values of marginal net products which are below the average are all reduced, or if a number which are above the average are all increased, the probability that the dividend will be decreased is of a fairly high order. But, if a cause comes into play, which, while increasing the degree of inequality among the values of marginal net products on the whole, yet diminishes *some* values that are above the average and increases *some* that are below it, the probability may be of a much lower order. This type of difficulty is not, however, of great practical importance, because the obstacles to equality with which we have to deal are, for the most part, general obstacles, and operate in the same sense at nearly all points where they operate at all.

SOME ASPECTS OF WELFARE ECONOMICS *

My book *The Economics of Welfare,* not revised since 1932, stood aside from some significant logical problems which arise out of the fact that real income is made up of a number of different things, the quantities of which vary in different proportions. It is with these problems, together with some semi-philosophical questions about utility, that "the new Welfare Economics," as it likes to be named, principally deals. The technique of indifference curves, preference maps and so on, which it employs, is, of course, machinery. Here I shall confine myself to fundamental issues.

I. THE PURPOSE OF WELFARE ECONOMICS

Welfare Economics is concerned to investigate the dominant influences through which the economic welfare of the world, or of a particular country, is likely to be increased. The hope of those who pursue it is to suggest lines of action—or non-action—on the part of the State or of private persons that might foster such influences. Nobody supposes that economic welfare is coincident with the whole of welfare or that the State ought to pursue it relentlessly without regard for other goods—liberty, for instance, the amenities of the family, spiritual needs and so on. But here we are not concerned with these things; only with economic welfare, that is to say, the part of welfare that is associated with the economic aspects of life. First and foremost we have to satisfy ourselves as to what that is and, more particularly, to decide whether or not it is the sort of thing to which the notions of greater or less and increase or decrease can properly be applied. For, if they cannot, Welfare Economics, every part and aspect of it, vanishes and leaves not a wrack behind.

II. THE MEANING OF ECONOMIC WELFARE

Let us consider first a single individual. What do we mean by the economic welfare of such an individual? It will be generally agreed that this must be somehow resident in his state of mind or consciousness. When we speak loosely of "material welfare," in the sense of a man's income or possessions, that is not welfare as we are thinking of it here. Material welfare may be a *means* to welfare, but it certainly is not identical with

* From "Some Aspects of Welfare Economics," *American Economic Review,* June, 1951, pp. 287–298. Reprinted by permission of the American Economic Association and by courtesy of Macmillan and Co., Ltd., London.

or a part of it. As it seems to me, welfare must be taken to refer either to the goodness of a man's state of mind or to the satisfactions embodied in it. If we were prepared to say that the goodness of satisfactions depended simply on their intensity it might not be necessary to make this distinction. But it is generally felt, in a vague way, that some sorts of satisfaction are in their nature better than others, and that quite irrespective of whether or not they entail dissatisfactions later on. If this is right, a situation containing more satisfaction is not necessarily "better" than one containing less. For the present purpose, I propose to make welfare refer to satisfactions, not goodness, thus leaving it possible that in certain circumstances, a government "ought"—granted that it "ought" to promote goodness—to foster a situation embodying less welfare (but more goodness) in preference to one embodying more welfare.

A man's welfare then consists in his satisfactions. But what does satisfaction mean? Not simply happiness or pleasure; for a man's desires may be directed to other things than these and may be satisfied. It might seem that, when his desire attitude is given, his satisfaction depends straightforwardly on the extent to which his desires are fulfilled. But the satisfaction yielded when a desire is satisfied does not always bear the same proportion to the intensity of the desire. Not only may people make mistakes, desiring certain objects in the hope of satisfactions which they do not in fact yield, but also, as Sidgwick observed, "I do not judge pleasures to be greater or less exactly in proportion as they exercise more or less influence in stimulating the will to actions likely to sustain or produce them." [1] Some economists, neglecting this point, have employed the term "utility" indifferently for satisfactions and for desiredness. I shall employ it here to mean satisfactions, so that we may say that a man's economic welfare is made up of his utilities. For a full treatment we should need to bring into account also such dissatisfactions or disutilities as men may suffer from work, or, what is not quite the same thing, such further satisfactions or utilities as leisure yields to them. It would not be difficult to do this but doing it would complicate and lengthen the discussion. I shall not, therefore, trespass into that field.

III. MEASURABILITY AND COMPARABILITY IN PRINCIPLE OF SATISFACTIONS ENJOYED BY THE SAME INDIVIDUAL

I said in Section I that, if economic welfare were not something to which the notion of greater or less were applicable, Welfare Economics would vanish away. It is sometimes thought that this notion *cannot* be applicable unless satisfactions are measurable.

Now for magnitudes of any kind to be measurable means that a unique and reciprocal correspondence, a one-one relation, can be established between the magnitudes in question and cardinal numbers. Extensive magnitudes, such as lengths, are in general measurable in this sense. Pleasures, satisfactions, utilities, are intensive magnitudes and are not

[1] *Methods of Ethics* (Macmillan & Co., England, 1893), p. 126.

measurable. They are not the sort of thing that we can correlate with a series of cardinal numbers.

It is true, no doubt, that an intensive magnitude may sometimes be correlated with an extensive magnitude and so may be capable of being measured indirectly. This would be true of satisfactions if, by a miracle, they were correlated rigidly with levels of temperature or speed of pulse. Moreover, there is in fact available in our field an "extensive" magnitude of the kind required, namely the amount of money that a man would be willing to pay in order to avoid losing a given satisfaction, or pleasure. Marshall, it will be remembered, laid stress on the advantage which economics has over other social sciences in possessing this measuring rod. Apart, however, from complications about the relation between the intensity of desires and the intensity of the satisfactions that result when a desired object is secured, to which I have already referred, neither Marshall nor anybody else claims that money enables us to measure anything more than small parts of a man's satisfaction. If I have an income of £1,000, it is reasonable to say that the satisfaction I get (or, more strictly expect) when I spend £2 on a small increment of one commodity is likely to be twice as great as what I get when I spend £1 on a small increment of another. But nobody supposes that the satisfaction I get from the whole of my £1,000 income will be only 1,000 times as large as what I get from the expenditure of a single marginal pound. Money does not, therefore, enable us to correlate satisfactions with a series of cardinal numbers, that is, to measure it in the sense understood here. We must concede that they are not measurable in that sense.

This, however, is far from entailing that satisfactions are not in principle *comparable*. The following passage from Bertrand Russell makes this clear. "Those mathematicians who are accustomed to an exclusive emphasis on numbers will think that not much can be said with definiteness concerning magnitudes incapable of measurement. This, however, is by no means the case. The immediate judgments of equality, upon which (as we saw) all measurements depend, are still possible where measurement fails, as are also the immediate judgments of greater and less. Doubt only arises where the difference is small; and all that measurement does in this respect is to make the margin of doubt smaller—an achievement which is purely psychological and of no philosophical importance. Quantities not susceptible of numerical measurement can thus be arranged in a scale of greater and smaller magnitudes, and this is the only strictly quantitative achievement of even numerical measurement. We can know that one magnitude is greater than another and that a third is intermediate between them; also, since the differences of magnitudes are always magnitudes, there is always (theoretically at least) an answer to the question whether the difference of one pair of magnitudes is greater than, less than or the same as, the difference of another pair of the same kind. . . . Without numerical measurement, therefore, the quantitative relations of magnitudes have all the definiteness of which they are capable—nothing is added, from the theoretical standpoint, by the assignment of correlated numbers." [2]

A corollary follows—or seems to follow. Given that we are able in principle to say that the difference between one pair of magnitudes is greater or less than the difference between another pair, we must presumably also be able to say that about differences between differences. This entails that, in spite of the fact that utilities are not measurable, it is still legitimate in principle to imagine a marginal utilities curve and to say, not merely that it slopes down or up, but also that it slopes more or less steeply as we move along it from right to left.

It is indeed impossible even in principle to draw a base line for the curve. Non-measurability entails that. It is thus meaningless to say that the utility derived by one individual in a given period from x units of a commodity is twice, or any other multiple, of the utility derived from y units, or to say, for example, that the curve is a rectangular hyperbola or bears some specifiable relation to a rectangular hyperbola. This entails that we cannot compare the damage done to welfare by a given proportionate change in a man's income when he is enjoying incomes of different sizes. Such questions as whether a tax proportioned to income will inflict equal sacrifice upon him whatever the size of his income or whether a tax progressive in some given form and degree is required to do this, are unanswerable, not merely from lack of data, but in principle. Thus the non-measurability of utility rules out one type of question, which, were utility measurable, it would be legitimate to ask—and which, assuming that it *is* measurable, I did ask in Chapter 7, Part II of my *Study in Public Finance*. This does not, however, reduce the domain of Welfare Economics very seriously, nor does it seriously matter that such questions as whether aggregate welfare would be increased if the population were larger but individual satisfactions smaller are in principle, not merely in practice, unanswerable.

IV. COMPARABILITY IN FACT

So far I have been discussing comparability in principle; are satisfactions or utilities the sort of things which can be held in the relation of greater or less or is it nonsense to maintain this of them in the way that it is nonsense to maintain that one is more red or more liquid than another? I have answered that question. But, granted that these things are comparable in principle, it is a quite different question whether they can be actually compared. If we found that they could not be actually compared, it would not follow that they are incomparable in principle. If all thermometers and kindred gadgets were destroyed, this would not upset at all the comparability in principle of temperatures. *Per contra,* to find, as we have done, that utilities, differences among utilities and differences among these differences are comparable in principle does not

[2] Russell, *Principles of Mathematics* (Cambridge University Press, England, 1903), pp. 182–83.

imply that all or any of them can be compared in fact. Subject, however, to a qualification to be mentioned presently, it is generally agreed that, when an individual chooses satisfaction A in preference to satisfaction B, this *indicates* that satisfaction A is or, more strictly, is expected to be greater than satisfaction B. Choice thus provides an objective test of the comparative magnitudes of different utilities or satisfactions to a given individual. It does the same for marginal utilities or satisfactions, that is the utilities derived from marginal increments of different sorts of goods. But nobody chooses or can choose between the *excess* of marginal utility A over marginal utility B and the *excess* of marginal utility C over marginal utility D. Hence these second differences, though, as I have maintained, comparable in principle, are not comparable in fact—at all events by means of this kind of test. The point, however, is not important for our main argument.

V. INTER-PERSONAL COMPARISONS

So far we have been considering only the comparability of satisfactions as affecting the same person. Once we reject solipsism and admit the existence of other people, what has already been said should suffice to show that the utilities enjoyed by different people are not in their nature incomparable—it is not nonsense to say that A is happier than B. But the question whether they are comparable in fact is a more difficult one. The test of choice is not available here as it is for intra-personal comparisons. No doubt, a parent can choose satisfaction A for one of his sons as against satisfaction B for another; and, if he is impartial between them, this should mean that he judges satisfaction A to be the greater. But I do not think we can appeal to this because the parent's choice is not a direct one and, in framing his decision, he is really faced with the very problem that confronts us here. We cannot, therefore, shift our burden upon him. The issue for Welfare Economics is important. For, if the satisfactions of different individuals cannot be compared, a large part of that subject is undermined. We are not, indeed, precluded from saying that, if one person has more of something and nobody else has less of anything, the welfare of the whole group, so long as their desires are unchanged, is increased. But we are precluded from saying anything about the implication of transfers between richer and poorer persons. To ask whether inter-personal comparisons of satisfactions or utilities are in fact possible is thus not an idle question.

Now, if we take random groups of people of the same race and brought up in the same country, we find that in many features that *are* comparable by objective tests they are on the average pretty much alike; and, indeed, for fundamental characters we need not limit ourselves to people of the same race and country. On this basis we are entitled, I submit, to infer by analogy that they are probably pretty much alike in other respects also. In all practical affairs we act on that supposition. We cannot prove that it is true. But we do not need to do so. Nobody can prove that anybody besides himself exists, but, nevertheless, everybody is quite sure of it. We do not, in short, and there is no reason why we should, start from a *tabula rasa,* binding ourselves to hold every opinion which the natural man entertains to be guilty until it is proved innocent. The burden is the other way. To deny this is to wreck, not merely Welfare Economics, but the whole apparatus of practical thought. On the basis of analogy, observation and intercourse, interpersonal comparisons *can,* as I think, properly be made; and, moreover, unless we have a special reason to believe the contrary, a given amount of stuff may be presumed to yield a similar amount of satisfaction, not indeed as between *any* one man and any other, but as between representative members of groups of individuals, such as the citizens of Birmingham and the citizens of Leeds. This is all that we need to allow this branch of Welfare Economics to function. Of course, in working it out, positive conclusions can only be reached subject to very important qualifications—of which something will have to be said presently.

VI. PROGRAMME

With this background I shall now review the implications and limitations of two propositions in Welfare Economics, on the assumption that satisfactions or utilities, though not measurable, are comparable in principle and can in fact be compared both intra-personally and inter-personally. The two propositions, put at their crudest, are: first, any additions to the real income of an individual makes satisfaction larger; secondly, transfers of money income from better-to-do people to worse-to-do people make satisfaction larger.

VII. THE FIRST PROPOSITION IN A ONE-COMMODITY WORLD

In the conditions supposed the amount of satisfaction that our individual gets depends partly on the state of his desires and partly on how much of the commodity is available to him. If the state of his desires is fixed, it will be generally agreed that in all ordinary circumstances his utility will be greater the more of the commodity that he has. If the state of his desires changes spontaneously, this changing is an additional factor affecting welfare, and nothing can be said about its consequences until the exact nature of the change is known. We rule out, therefore, spontaneous changes in desire attitudes. Our proposition is obviously subject to the condition that such spontaneous changes are excluded. On this basis, if the state of an individual's desires were independent of the amount that he has, nothing further would need to be said. But the amount that he has may react upon and partly determine the state of his desires. What are the implications of this possibility, and in what conditions is it to be expected that these reactions will make our proposition invalid?

It is commonly supposed that, besides more stuff with a given desire attitude entailing more utility, so also does a keener desire attitude with a given quantity of stuff. If this were always so, when an increase of stuff, in the familiar manner of appetite growing with eating, made desire more intense, the increase of stuff would enhance satisfaction in a double way, partly through itself and partly through its effects. In fact, however, enhanced desire with a given quantity of stuff does not necessarily entail more utility or satisfaction. For unsatisfied desire may be painful. If a man with a given income of food per day becomes hungrier, the utility associated with the food he has increases, but the disutility of the food he has not increases too; and the last state of that man may be worse than the first. The ordinary form of diagrammatic analysis fails to bring out this point, though it could easily be modified so as to make it do so. The point, however, is not, I think, of large practical importance, and, for a broad view, may be left out of account. In general, then, an enhancement of desire increases the utility derived from a given provision of our commodity and a contraction of desire has the opposite effect.

It follows that an increase in the quantity of stuff available, not only when it leaves a man's desire attitude unaltered, but also, *a fortiori*, when it expands it, must entail an increase of utility. But having more of a thing may cause a man's desire attitude towards it to become *less* keen, not more. Or, to put the same thing the other way round, when he has become accustomed to having less he may find himself more happy with any given quantity than he used to be. It may even happen that the total satisfaction he gets from the smaller is as large as what he used to get from the larger quantity.

Thus—for this illustration we may waive the assumptions of one individual and a one-commodity world—consider two undergraduates precisely alike in temperament and constitution. One is poor and goes on a cheap Continental holiday, stopping the night at youth hostels; the other does an exactly similar tour at much greater expense and stopping at luxury hotels. Each of them is conditioned by habit and experience to his circumstance. Is there any reason to suppose that the rich undergraduate has a better time—achieves more utility—than the poor one? Yet again in prewar days well-to-do people had elaborate meals and had a number of servants to work for them. Now they have much simpler meals and do their own work. After they have become accustomed to the new conditions, are they less happy than before? It is very doubtful whether a moderately well-to-do man is appreciably happier now than he would be if transplanted back to the pre-railway age and attuned to the conditions of that age. This is in no way incompatible with a man preferring *at any given moment* to have more rather than less. Nor is it incompatible with the fact that the process of *becoming* better-off often yields satisfaction. In the process there is a prize, and, so far, progress, even among the fairly well-to-do, is not merely illusion. But there is a great deal of illusion about it. From a long-run standpoint, *after incomes in excess of a certain moderate level have been attained,* further increases in it may well not be significant for economic welfare.

The italicised words in that sentence are, of course, vital. What the "certain moderate level of income," to which they refer, is can only be guessed at. My own guess is that, even in this country and most certainly, for example, in Asia, a large number of people have incomes well below it. It follows that over a very wide area, in spite of reactions of having on desiring, having more does in fact entail more satisfaction.

VIII. THE FIRST PROPOSITION IN A MANY-COMMODITY WORLD

Let us now abandon the assumption that real income consists of a single sort of commodity—or of bundles of different commodities in each of which the proportions of these commodities are the same. When we do this it is still possible to say, in a straightforward physical sense, that one real income is larger than another, provided that it contains more of some item and not less of any item. There is, therefore, still meaning in the assertion that, other things being equal, a man's economic welfare is increased if his real income becomes larger; and the discussion of the preceding section remains appropriate without fundamental change.

It may perhaps be suggested that for most practical issues this is good enough, for, while technical knowledge and skill are always going forward in some fields, it is unlikely that they are actually going backwards in any. This may be thought to imply that the representative man's real income is unlikely to expand in some of its parts and at the same time to contract in others. That, however, is wrong. This is immediately obvious as regards agricultural products; some crops will often have a better harvest this year than last, others a worse one. But, over and above that, it is easy to see that, when technique improves as regards some commodity, the quantity of another commodity where it has not improved may not remain stationary, but may fall off. Even when technique has improved in respect of both of two commodities, the output of one of them may fall off. What happens, as a moment's reflection shows, depends on the general conditions of demand. The case, therefore, of some commodities available to our representative man increasing while others decrease is far from being a freak case of no practical importance. On the contrary, it is very important indeed. The relation between alterations of this kind in real income and in economic welfare cannot be ignored.

When this kind of alteration has taken place it is plainly impossible to say in any physical sense that actual real income has become larger or has become smaller. As physical entities the first and second actual real incomes are incommensurable.[3] Fortunately, however, we need not stop here. As was said just now, if a man with given desire attitudes comes to have more of something and not less of anything else, his satisfaction

[3] In the *Economics of Warfare,* I *defined* an increase in actual income as an alteration in its content such that, with tastes and distribution constant, more satisfaction would be yielded by it after the alteration than before (p. 54). On that basis our problem was to find an *index* of real income changes that would, or probably would, move up or down as real income so defined moved up or down. The problem here is essentially the same, but approached from a different angle.

will be increased. Moreover, we may presume, in a general way and subject to qualifications, that, alike before and after a change in his real income, he will dispose of his purchasing power among different commodities in a way that gives him more satisfaction than he would get from any other disposition. If then the conditions are such that in the new situation he *could* get more income of the old proportionate pattern, or more of some items and not less of any, we may infer that his economic welfare is greater in the new situation than in the old. That is to say, if in the second situation his *potential* real income of the first situation's pattern is greater than his actual real income in the first, we can infer that his utility or satisfaction will be greater in the second situation. *Per contra,* if in the first situation his potential real income (of the second situation's pattern) is greater than the actual real income in the second, his satisfaction will be greater in the first situation.

There is indeed a difficulty. For may it not happen that, not only is the potential real income of the pattern proper to the first situation larger in the second situation than the actual real income of the first situation, but *also* the potential real income of the pattern proper to the second situation is larger in the first situation than the actual real income of the second situation? If this happens, we are forced to the absurd conclusion that our man's aggregate satisfaction is at once greater in the second situation than in the first, and also greater in the first situation than in the second. The emergence of this contradiction proves that the state of things we are supposing cannot exist. If the potential real income of the pattern of the first situation is larger in the second situation than the actual real income of the first situation, it *must* happen that the potential real income of the pattern proper to the second situation is smaller, not larger, in the first situation than the actual real income of the second situation.

This conclusion seems inevitable in logic, but, none the less, unless we can see *how* it comes about that this must happen, we shall be left with the feeling of intellectual discomfort. Why then must it happen? The explanation is that a man's tastes help to determine what his actual real incomes in the two situations are. The discord we have been contemplating is impossible because, though it would occur *if* his actual real incomes were such and such, in fact his tastes, being, on our assumptions, the same in the two situations, *prevent* his actual real incomes from being such and such.[4]

This analysis, it will be observed, does not in all circumstances enable us in principle to decide whether the economic welfare of an individual with a given desire attitude is greater in one situation than in another. For it may happen that in each situation his potential real income of the other situation's pattern is *less* than the actual real income of that situa-

[4] Professor Samuelson's "Evaluation of Real National Income" in *Oxford Economic Papers,* Vol. 2, No. 1 (Jan., 1950), p. 24, when he corrects a mistake in the *Economics of Welfare.*

tion. When this is so, it is easy to see that no inference about his comparative economic welfare in the two situations can be drawn. If this is not obvious immediately, it can easily be made so with the help of algebraic symbols.

IX. THE FIRST PROPOSITION AS REGARDS GROUPS OF PEOPLE

Our first proposition when applied to a group of people is obviously subject to all the limitations which we have found to be necessary as regards a single individual. Are there any further limitations?

Suppose first that our group consists of a number of exactly similar persons enjoying identical real incomes and that in consequence of technical advance all these real incomes are increased by equal amounts of some items unaccompanied by a decrease in any others. If people *only* wanted things so as not to be inferior to other people, this development would clearly leave economic welfare unaltered. And no doubt to some extent people do want things for this sort of distinction motive. If it were not for this, it would be difficult for an academic person like myself to conceive how anybody could possibly have ever wanted such things as top hats or frock coats or crinolines or bustles. But it would be absurd to suggest that people *only* want things as a means to distinction. Though, therefore, the economic welfare of groups is not in fact increased by an expansion in real income as much as we should expect it to be if we ignored this characteristic, there is no ground for suggesting that it is not increased at all. So far what is true of individuals is also true of groups.

But in real life changes in technique do not affect all members of a group—a national group for instance—similarly. This opens up new possibilities. Even in a one-commodity world it might happen that a development which increased potential real income as a whole injured particular sections of the group—landlords, for example, or capitalists or wage-earners. If all the persons affected were similar and were initially in receipt of identical incomes, a contraction in the incomes of some might outweigh from the standpoint of welfare a more than equivalent expansion in the incomes of others. With people of different tastes and different initial incomes the same thing is true, and the likelihood of a decrease in aggregate welfare is greater. The change in productivity, since we are supposing it to entail an increase in aggregate income, *could,* of course, be accompanied by a set of transfers—compensations—so arranged that in the final result some persons had more real income and none had less. In that event aggregate economic welfare *would be* increased. But to say that in that event it *is* increased is, to my mind, to use words in a misleading way. The correct statement is, I think, that the improvement in productivity necessarily entails a *potential* increase in aggregate economic welfare, but does not necessarily entail an actual increase.

In a many-commodity world we saw in Section VII that it is often impossible in principle to say whether or not actual real income has increased between two years, but usually possible to say whether potential real income has. With a single person, we have found that an increase in potential real income over the actual income of an earlier time necessarily entails an increase in economic welfare, provided that the person's desire attitudes are the same before and after the change. With a group within which distribution is different after the change from what it was before, we can only say that an increase in potential real income necessarily entails a potential increase, not an *actual* increase, in economic welfare. If productivity changes make things predominantly consumed by poor persons (or by persons specially keen on those things) more abundant and things predominantly consumed by rich persons (or by persons indifferent to those things) less abundant, aggregate economic welfare may be increased even though aggregate potential real income is diminished; just as in opposite conditions it may be diminished even though aggregate potential real income is increased.

All this is true and from an academic point of view significant. But the paradox that technical advance may for this sort of reason be adverse to welfare is not I think—apart from advance in the machinery of war—significant practically. For our paradox can only become a fact if technical advances that increase potential real income as a whole at the same time damage the relatively poor. But experience hitherto does not suggest that technical advance in fact acts in that way. On the contrary, mechanical improvements are more readily made in respect of mass-produced goods, which poor people predominantly buy, and in transport, which directly or indirectly cheapen poor men's goods in a larger proportion than rich men's goods. As Leroy-Beaulieu observed long ago: "The man of fashion who is fitted for his clothes by a tailor gains nothing from the great reduction of prices which shops selling clothes ready-made offer to the less comfortable section of the population." [5]

[5] *La Répartition des Richesses*, p. 87.

PART SIXTEEN
Economic Stability and Employment

In this final section some of the more important contributions to the general theory of employment and output under capitalism are presented. Of the more recent writers in this field, Keynes and Schumpeter are perhaps the most famous. Also noteworthy are Wicksell and the other Swedish forerunners of Keynes, and R. F. Kahn, who introduced the concept of the investment multiplier. A long line of great economists—including Malthus, Sismondi, Marx, Veblen, Hobson, and Mitchell, who appear earlier in this volume—had flashes of insight about one or another facet of Keynesian economics. However, none of them succeeded in developing a comprehensive theory of the cycle. It was the genius of Keynes that combined original ideas with the contributions of his predecessors and wove them into a *general* theory exploring the operation of the whole capitalistic system in prosperity and depression. As far as public policy is concerned, Keynes' great contribution was to show that Say's Law does not operate, that there is no automatic tendency toward full employment, and that an economy can be in equilibrium at *any* level of employment. Because it deals with the output and distribution of the product of the economy as a whole, this type of economics has been called *macro-economics.*

Schumpeter's theory differs from both Keynes' and the Swedish economists' in that he utilizes the Walrasian concept of general equilibrium and stresses the role of innovation in causing cyclical movements.

Finally, it may be mentioned that the emphasis on macro-economics in recent years has encouraged the gathering and the theoretical elaboration of national-income and national-product statistics, resulting in tremendous advances in economic measurement.

KNUT WICKSELL

(1851–1926)

Wicksell started his academic career as a student of mathematics and philosophy at the University of Uppsala. Later his interest turned to economics, which he studied abroad, in England, Germany, and France. He then returned to Sweden and from 1900 to 1916 was professor of economics at the University of Lund.

In methodology, Wicksell was in the tradition of the Lausanne school, using mathematical formulations, but he concentrated primarily upon problems of capital and interest. More than anyone up to this time, he succeeded in integrating monetary and so-called general economic theory. At the turn of the century, in *Geldzins und Güterpreise* (*Interest and Prices*, 1898), he attempted to analyze the dynamic phenomena of the economic system as a whole, instead of the static equilibrium which occupied the attention of most of the economists of his time. Here he advanced an explanation for the simultaneous existence of a drop in price and a low interest rate, a situation which seemed paradoxical to his contemporaries because according to the quantity theory of money, prevalent in his day, a low interest rate indicated a plentiful supply of money and such an abundance of money should result in a rise in price. Wicksell's solution of the paradox was to differentiate between the "market" interest rate and the "natural" interest rate, the rate which just equalizes the supply of, and the demand for, money. Because the market interest rate is controlled by commercial bank policy, it determines the supply and demand of loanable funds only and not necessarily the total movements of physical capital. Even when it appears to be low, the bank interest rate may be higher than the natural interest rate as Wicksell defined it.

He also analyzed price equilibrium at given levels of national income, and he was one of the pioneers in time analysis and in the setting up of model sequences. While he did not succeed in thoroughly integrating the theory of price and the theory of money, he was certainly the first to make the attempt. Starting from the premise that the price of any one commodity is determined by supply and demand, he asked why a similar explanation could not be sought for situations where the general price level rises or falls. He felt that the answer to this problem could be found in his analysis of savings and investments.

Wicksell was the spiritual father of the so-called Stockholm school of savings and investment, which numbered among others Ohlin, Myrdal, Lundberg, and Hammarskjöld. While they often disagreed with the master on specific issues, they attacked similar problems and used much the same methodology as he did.

The following article, published in the *Economic Journal* in 1907, presents the gist of Wicksell's thinking on economic problems.

THE INFLUENCE OF THE RATE OF INTEREST ON PRICES *

The thesis which I humbly submit to criticism is this. If, other things remaining the same, the leading banks of the world were to lower their rate of interest, say 1 per cent. below its ordinary level, and keep it so for some years, then the prices of all commodities would rise and rise and rise without any limit whatever; on the contrary, if the leading banks

* From "The Influence of the Rate of Interest on Prices," *Economic Journal*, June, 1907, pp. 213–219.

were to *raise* their rate of interest, say 1 per cent. above its normal level, and keep it so for some years, then all prices would *fall* and fall and fall without any limit except Zero.

Now this proposition cannot be proved directly by experience, because the fact required in its hypothesis never happens.

The supposition was that the banks were to lower or raise their interest, *other things remaining the same,* but that, of course, the banks never do; why, indeed, should they? Other things remaining the same, the bank-rate is sure to remain the same too, or if, by any chance, *e.g.,* by mistake, it were altered, it would very soon come round to its proper level. My thesis is, therefore, only an abstract statement, and somebody, perhaps, will ask: what is the use of it then? But I venture to assert that it may be of very great use all the same. Everybody knows the statement of Newton that, if the attraction of the sun were suddenly to cease, then the planets would leave their orbits in the tangential direction; this, too, of course, is only an abstract proposition, because the solar attraction never ceases, but it is most useful nevertheless; indeed, it is the very corner-stone of celestial mechanics; and in the same way I believe that the thesis here propounded, if proved to be true, will turn out to be the corner-stone of the mechanics of prices, or rather one of its corner-stones, the influence of the supply of precious metals and of the demand for commodities from the gold-producing countries being the other.

Before going further, however, we must answer one more question. Our supposition might be not only unreal as to facts, but even logically impossible; and then, of course, its use would be *nil.* According to the general opinion among economists, the interest on money is regulated in the long run by the profit on capital, which in its turn is determined by the productivity and relative abundance of real capital, or, in the terms of modern political economy, by its *marginal productivity.* This remaining the same, as, indeed, by our supposition it is meant to do, would it be at all possible for the banks to keep the rate of interest either higher or lower than its normal level, prescribed by the simultaneous state of the average profit on capital?

This question deserves very careful consideration, and, in fact, its proper analysis will take us a long way towards solving the whole problem.

Interest on money and profit on capital are not the same thing, nor are they *immediately* connected with each other; if they were, they could not differ at all, or could only differ a certain amount at every time. There is no doubt *some* connecting link between them, but the proper nature and extent of this connection is not so very easy to define.

If we look only at credit transactions between individuals, without any interference of banks, the connection between interest and profit indeed seems obvious. If by investing your capital in some industrial enterprise you can get, after due allowance for risk, a profit of, say, 10 per cent., then, of course, you will not lend it at a much cheaper rate; and if the borrower has no recourse but to individuals in the same situation as you, he will not be able to get the money much cheaper than that.

But it is a very different thing with the modern forms of credit, which almost always imply the mediation of some bank or professional money-lender. The banks in their lending business are not only not limited by their own capital; they are not, at least not immediately, limited by any capital whatever; by concentrating in their hands almost all payments, they themselves create the money required, or, what is the same thing, they accelerate *ad libitum* the rapidity of the circulation of money. The sum borrowed to-day in order to buy commodities is placed by the seller of the goods on his account at the same bank or some other bank, and can be lent the very next day to some other person with the same effect. As the German author, Emil Struck, justly says in his well-known sketch of the English money market: in our days demand and supply of money have become about the same thing, the demand to a large extent creating its own supply.

In a *pure* system of credit, where all payments were made by transference in the bank-books, the banks would be able to grant at any moment any amount of loans at any, however diminutive, rate of interest.

But then, what becomes of the connecting link between interest and profit? In my opinion there is no such link, except precisely *the effect on prices,* which would be caused by their difference.

When interest is low in proportion to the existing rate of profit, and if, as I take it, *the prices thereby rise,* then, of course, trade will require more sovereigns and bank-notes, and therefore the sums lent will *not* all come back to the bank, but part of them will remain in the boxes and purses of the public; in consequence, the bank reserves will melt away while the amount of their liabilities very likely has increased, which will force them to raise their rate of interest.

The reverse of all this, of course, will take place when the rate of interest has accidentally become too high in proportion to the average profit on capital. So far, you will easily remark, my proposition is quite in accordance with well-known facts of the money market. If it be not true, if, on the contrary, as Thomas Tooke asserted, and even Ricardo in his earlier writings seems to have believed, a low rate of interest, by cheapening, as they put it, one of the elements of production, would lower prices, and a high rate of interest raise them—a most specious argument, resting, however, on the unwarrantable assumption that the remuneration of the other factors of production could, under such circumstances, remain the same—then the policy of banks must be the very reverse of what it really is; they would lower their rates when prices were getting high and reserves becoming low, they would raise them in the opposite case.

A more direct proof of my thesis is required, however, and might be given in some such way as this. If as a merchant I have sold my goods to the amount of £100 against a bill or promissory note of three months, and I get it discounted at once by a bank or a bill broker, the rate of discount being 4 per cent. per annum, then in fact I have received a cash price for my goods amounting to £99. If, however, the bill is taken by the bank at 3 per cent., then the cash price of my goods have *ipso facto* risen, if only a quarter of 1 per cent.; very likely not even that, because competition probably will force me to cede part of my extra profit to the buyer of the goods. In other cases, however, when long-term credit comes into play, the immediate rise of prices might be very much greater than that. If the rate of discount remains low, the interest on long loans is sure to go down too; building companies and railway companies will be able to raise money, say at 4 per cent. instead of 5 per cent., and therefore, other things being the same, they can offer, and by competition will be more or less compelled to offer for wages and materials, anything up to 25 per cent. *more* than before, 4 per cent. on £125 being the same as 5 per cent. on £100.

But, further—and this is the essential point to which I would call your special attention—the upward movement of prices, whether great or small in the first instance, *can never cease* so long as the rate of interest is kept lower than its normal rate, *i.e.*, the rate consistent with the then existing marginal productivity of real capital. When all commodities have risen in price, a *new level of prices* has formed itself which in its turn will serve as basis for all calculations for the future, and all contracts. Therefore, if the bank-rate now goes up to its normal height, the level of prices will not go down; it will simply remain where it is, there being no forces in action which could press it down; and, consequently, if the bank-rate *remains lower* than its normal height, a new impetus towards forcing up the prices will follow, and so on. The opposite of all this will take place when the rate of interest has become too high in proportion to average profit, and so in both cases a difference between the two rates remaining, the movement of prices can never cease, just as the electric current never ceases as long as the difference of tension between the poles remains.

The proposition that a low rate of interest will raise prices, a high rate of interest lower prices, is in some respects anything but new; it has been stated more than once, but a formidable objection was always triumphantly brought against it in the shape of statistical facts; indeed, if you consider the figures given, *e.g.*, by Sauerbeck in his well-known tables in the *Journal of the Statistical Society*, you will generally find that high prices do not correspond with a low rate of interest, and *vice versa;* it rather comes the opposite way, interest and prices very often rising and falling together. But this objection quite loses its importance; nay, more, it turns into a positive support of our theory, as soon as we fix our eyes on the relativity of the conception of interest on money, its necessary connection with profit on capital. The rate of interest is never high or low in itself, but only in relation to the profit which people can make with the money in their hands, and this, of course, varies. In good times, when trade is brisk, the rate of profit is high, and, what is of great consequence, is generally expected to remain high; in periods of depression it is low, and expected to remain low. The rate of interest on money follows, no doubt, the same course, but not at once, not of itself; it is, as it were, dragged after the rate of profit by the movement of prices and the consequent changes in the state of bank reserve, caused by the difference between the two rates. In the meantime this difference acts on prices in just the same way as would be the case if, according to our original supposition, profit on capital were to remain constant, and interest on money were to rise or fall spontaneously. In one word, the interest on money is, in reality, very often low when it seems to be high, and high when it seems to be low. This I believe to be the proper answer to the objection stated above, as far as the influence of credit on prices is regarded; occasionally, of course, as in times of wild speculation or panics, the problem is complicated very much by the action of other factors, which need not here be taken into consideration.

Granted, then, our theory to be true in the main or in the abstract, what will be its practical consequences? to what extent would the leading money institutions be able to regulate prices?

A single bank, of course, has no such power whatever; indeed, it cannot put its rates, whether much higher or much lower than prescribed by the state of the market; if it did, it would in the former case lose all profitable business; in the latter case its speedy insolvency would be the inevitable consequence.

Not even all the banks of a single country united could do it in the long run; a too high or too low rate would influence its balance of trade, and thereby cause an influx or reflux of gold in the well-known way, so as to force the banks to apply their rates to the state of the universal money market.

But supposing, as, indeed, we have done, that all the leading banks of the commercial world were to follow the same course, then gold could have no reason to go to one place more than to another, and so the action exercised on prices would have its sway without any hindrance from the international movement of money. Still, even then it would, under the present circumstances, have its obvious limits. As I remarked at the outset, the influence of credit or the rate of interest is only one of the factors acting on prices; the other is the volume of metallic money itself, especially, in our times, the supply of gold, and so long as the gold itself remains the standard of value, this factor evidently will take the lead in the long run. Were the production of gold materially to diminish while the demand for money be unaltered, the banks no doubt, by lowering their rate of interest, might for a while profitably react against the otherwise inevitable pressure on prices, but only for a while, because, even if the rather unnecessary stiffness of present bank legislations could be slackened, the ever-growing demand for gold for industrial purposes would gradually reduce the bank stores, and could only be checked by raising the price of gold—that is, by lowering the average money prices.

The other extreme, which at present seems much more likely to occur: a plethora of gold supply, and the rise of prices thereby caused, could not be effectually met in any way, so long as free coinage of gold exists.

On the other hand, if this most essential step on the way to a rational monetary system should be taken, if the free coining of gold, like that of silver, should cease, and eventually the bank-note itself, or rather the unity in which the accounts of banks are kept, should become the standard of value, then, and not till then, the problem of keeping the value of money steady, the average level of money prices at a constant height, which evidently is to be regarded as the fundamental problem of monetary science, would be solvable theoretically and practically to any extent. And the means of solving it need not be sought in some more or less fantastic scheme like that of a central issuing bank for all the world, as it is sometimes proposed, but simply in a proper manipulation of general bank-rates, lowering them when prices are getting low, and raising them when prices are getting high.

Nor would this system be at all artificial, because the point about which the rate of interest would then oscillate, and to which it would constantly gravitate, would be precisely what I have called above its normal level, that one prescribed by the simultaneous state of the marginal productivity of real capital, the alterations of which we, of course, cannot control, but only have to comply with.

When this paper was read at the British Association meeting it was objected by Mr. Palgrave that the banks could not possibly be charged with the regulation of prices, their liberty of action—if I understood him right—being, in his view, restricted by the necessity of protecting their own reserves as well from getting too low in consequence of an unfavourable balance of trade, as from running to an unprofitable height by an influx of gold. This, no doubt, is true, but it must not be forgotten that the international rate policy of banks has, as it were, *two degrees of freedom,* in so far as the international movement of gold can be checked or modified, not only by raising the rate of discount in the country *from* which the metal flows, but also by lowering it in the country, or countries, *to* which gold is flowing. In other words, the action of the banks against each other, which has for its object the proper distribution of money, or the levelling of the *niveau* of prices between different countries, might logically be concomitant with a *common* action for the purpose of keeping the universal value of money and level of prices at a constant height, which, however, under present circumstances only can be done within the limits prescribed by the general supply of gold.

On the other hand, it was remarked by Professor Edgeworth that if the free coinage of gold be suppressed, the Governments themselves have in their hand the regulating of general prices. This, too, is true, at any rate so long as the present large production of gold persists; and even if it should cease, and gold becomes scarce, the Governments, no doubt, might supplant the lack in currency by a judicious emission of paper-money. . . .

BERTIL OHLIN

(1899–)

The heritage of Knut Wicksell fell on the shoulders of a group of very able younger economists in Sweden, especially Professors Lindahl, Myrdal, and Ohlin, who were soon referred to as the Stockholm school. They shared Wicksell's passion for social reform, and during the great depression, attempted to apply Wicksellian analysis to cyclical problems. In general, their method was to set up models indicating various levels of equilibrium and then try to show the effect of entrepreneurial decisions on the models set up.

Lindahl's analysis sought to determine the conditions which influence the direction of entrepreneurial anticipations. Myrdal went further and queried how, with the *ex-post* data on which analysis was based, one would be able to tell whether businessmen's *ex-ante* anticipations were correct, and if they were not, to discern the direction of drift from the *ex-ante* equilibrium. While they used the Wicksellian apparatus as a foundation, these economists made the theory sharper and more realistic by taking into account such assumptions as waste or under-utilization of resources, imperfect foresight, and monopolistic competition.

Businessmen's anticipations determine investment *ex-ante,* which is the important variable since it, in turn, accounts for changes in both income and savings. Savings adapt themselves to investment by *ex-post* gains or losses. Changes in income, in turn, determine variations in the level of employment. Monetary equilibrium, or the equality between *ex-ante* saving and investment, can result at a level of less than full employment or full resource utilization. Thus, the Swedish economists evolved a theory of unemployment equilibrium as an alternative to the Keynesian underemployment equilibrium.

Manipulation of the interest rate, according to the Swedish school, can help adapt flexible prices to changes in inflexible prices (for example, wage rates) but cannot in itself guarantee full employment. Correction of the interest rate can only remove the monetary causes of instability and adapt the monetary structure to the non-monetary causes (such as technical innovations) of economic change.

Unlike John Maynard Keynes (who is discussed later in this volume), the Stockholm school has never achieved a complete theory of the operation of the economy as a whole. However, since the school is still in a state of growth and has not yet evolved its final product, it is perhaps best to reserve judgment on the ultimate position of its over-all contributions in the history of economic thought. The very essence of the philosophy of Wicksell and his followers is experimentalism, a contempt for orthodoxy and an awareness of the cumulative and continuing nature of economic change. They do not have any strong confidence in the "unseen hand" of Adam Smith or in laissez-faire economics. They believe that man can control his destiny in economics, and they therefore place great reliance on deliberate governmental intervention and planning.

The following selection by Professor Ohlin, himself a leading member of the Stockholm school, describes post-Wicksellian theory in some detail.

SOME NOTES ON THE STOCKHOLM THEORY OF SAVINGS AND INVESTMENT *

A. The Development and Characteristics of the Stockholm Theory

Among the circumstances which explain the present trend of theoretical analysis in Swedish economics one should, I think, first mention the writings of Wicksell, which naturally attracted more attention in Sweden than elsewhere. His *Geldzins und Güterpreise* of 1898 and his later books and papers on money contained the embryo of "a theory of output as a whole," although this fact was not clearly perceived until the late 'twenties, when Professor Lindahl presented his elaboration of Wicksell. Wicksell started from the fact that the price of an individual commodity is determined by supply and demand. If its price rises, one says that it is due to a rise in demand relative to supply. Naturally, if the prices paid for all commodities taken together rise—and thus the general price level is raised—a similar explanation should be possible. Wicksell attempted to give such an explanation through his analysis of saving and investment. Thus, he broke both with the Say doctrine that supply creates its own demand and with the accepted view that the theory of relative prices and the theory of money are two entirely different things, although he never arrived at a real unification of these theories.

Wicksell's analysis was concentrated on the process of price movements, in which credit plays a large rôle. Credit and savings have a time dimension. For this and other reasons he came to study time-using processes. The most famous is his so-called "cumulative" process, which proved to be an important "type model" of economic development, i.e., a "model sequence."

Professor Lindahl—as will be shown below—followed up the Wicksellian analysis. He showed that it was useful in a study of changes in employment and output as well as in prices. Furthermore, he showed that Wicksell's cumulative process depended on special assumptions concerning the entrepreneurs' expectations, thereby utilizing the analysis of "anticipations" which had been presented in Professor Myrdal's work, *Pricing and the Change Factor,* 1927. This work was the second of the circumstances which have vitally affected Swedish research in the field under discussion during the last decade. Myrdal discusses the influence of the uncertain future on price formation. To what extent are economic actions influenced by anticipations of future events, i.e. by expectations? In the static equilibrium price theory of the textbooks, this question had been neglected. Of the pre-depression treatises only Marshall seems to have had it in mind. If he did not make much progress himself in this field, at least he used a terminology which protects him from much of the criticism which can be directed towards other writers. In fact, Keynes' analysis of expectations in Ch. 5—which in many ways is similar to the

* From "Some Notes on the Stockholm Theory of Savings and Investment," *Economic Journal:* Part I, March, 1937, pp. 53–69; Part II, June, 1937, pp. 221–229.

general view in Stockholm—can be regarded as the following up of numerous suggestions in Marshall's "Principles."

Myrdal tries to build these expectations into the static price equilibrium, and thus to give a picture of the forces existing at a certain moment of time. He does not attempt to construct a dynamic price theory which considers the *rate* of change and thus gives an account of a process in time. His theory can be regarded as the last step which a static theory can take in the direction of dynamics. In constructing his equilibrium Myrdal eliminates time from change, but not anticipations of time. In other words, he assumes a timeless adjustment, but with all friction and cost and expectations. While this may appear to be a peculiar construction, it is no doubt more realistic than the earlier static equilibrium. In any case, it enabled Myrdal to concentrate on the influence of expectations. . . .

The third decisive factor in the development of the Stockholm theory was Lindahl's book on *The Means of Monetary Policy* (published in 1930 but circulated in proof a year earlier), which I have already mentioned. He used Myrdal's expectation analysis to follow the Wicksellian line of approach by means of periods of time, perhaps somewhat under the influence of Mr. D. H. Robertson in this latter respect. Some essential parts of Lindahl's theory can be briefly indicated.

Already Wicksell had stressed that consumption purchases are governed by that part of individual incomes which people want to consume, whereas investment purchases are not directly governed by the part of income people want to save. The decisions to save and the decisions to invest are taken largely by different individuals, and there is no mechanism which guarantees that the volume of savings and of investment will always be equal. This is the very essence of the Wicksellian approach. Wicksell goes on to investigate what rôle the rate of interest can play in making them equal, and what happens when they are not made equal. Lindahl does not concentrate his attention to the same extent on the investment activity. He starts from the formula:

$$E(1 - s) = PQ;$$

E is income, s savings ratio, P the price level of consumption goods, and Q the quantity of consumption goods. Regarded as a picture of a brief period, during which equilibrium exists, this equation is implicit in the equilibrium theory of prices. It can be used, however, for an analysis of a process in time, which is divided into different periods. Lindahl studies the conditions under which the components of the equation change, the volume of consumption goods as well as their prices. In so doing he naturally has to pay a great deal of attention, although not in my opinion sufficient, to the volume of real investment. He does not confine his discussion of policy to monetary policy in a narrow sense, but analyses also the effects of changes in the financial policy of the State, e.g. the financing of deficits by borrowing. Thus, he departs a long way from the quantity theory of money approach, by which it was natural in any discussion of price problems, etc., to ask how the quantity of money could be affected. In fact, he follows Wicksell in assuming a perfect credit economy, where the quantity of money has no significance. It would carry me too far to describe his argument concerning Wicksell's cumulative process. Among other things he introduces the hypothesis of unused resources and discusses alternative "models," based on different assumptions as to the disposition to save, etc., demonstrating that they behave rather differently under the impact of the same original change. He also investigates the importance of long- and short-term interest rates, and finds Wicksell's concept of a "normal" rate of interest to be of little or no use. . . .

The high degree of unanimity between the writers mentioned . . . make[s] it justifiable to talk about a Stockholm school of thought. (The only non-resident in Stockholm is Lindahl, who worked in Stockholm for many years.) It must not be supposed, however, that the different members of this school agree on everything. As in my attempt below to illuminate certain aspects of the Stockholm theory I shall follow the version used by myself, I have to add that my terminology has been viewed with great scepticism by some of the younger Stockholm economists, chiefly because of my way of defining income so as to make savings and investment always equal *ex definitione*. Personally, however, I am to-day more than ever convinced that this set of definitions permits a simpler, more realistic and more easily understandable description of economic processes than the rather different definitions used by other members of the Stockholm school.

Let me begin by enumerating the characteristics of what I propose to call the "Stockholm Theory of Processes of Contraction and Expansion," meaning thereby the analysis of changes in employment, output and prices. Firstly, in the discussion of special partial processes attention is concentrated on the reaction of the economic system as a whole, i.e. possible influence on the *total* volume of output and monetary demand. Monetary theory is therefore made a part of the general price theory. The analysis has not as yet been pushed far enough to make it include a theory of business cycles. . . . Secondly, care is taken to state clearly when concepts like income and savings refer to plans or expectations for the future and when they are concerned with a period that is already finished. Thirdly, with the exception of Myrdal (whose position is not quite clear) all use a period method of analysis. In this respect the procedure is similar to D. H. Robertson's. Fourthly, as in Hawtrey's and Keynes' theories, attention is concentrated on the action of the individual entrepreneurs or consumers, and not much is said about what this involves with regard to the movements of the currency units. . . . Fifthly, it has been found that the reasoning to be precise enough must be casuistic. Wide use is, therefore, made of "type models" like Wicksell's cumulative process. For the construction of such models, simplifying assumptions are necessary. Hence each of them throws light on only one aspect of the processes of expansion or contraction.

B. Some Aspects of Process Analysis

1.

To analyse and explain what happens or what will happen in certain circumstances it is necessary to register the relevant events. One needs a system of book-keeping which is relative to time. Not only is the time sequence of events as a rule important, the same is often true of the time-lags. It is therefore practical to use periods of time as a basis for the book-keeping. At the end of each period one can survey the registrations which refer to that period. This answers the question what has happened during a passed period. It is an account *ex-post.*

This, however, explains nothing, for it does not describe the causal or functional relations. As economic events depend on man's actions, one has to investigate what determines these actions. They always refer to a more or less distant future. Hence, one must study those expectations about the future which govern the actions, keeping in mind that expectations are based on the experience of the past, although only partly the *immediate* past. This analysis of the forward-looking type can be called *ex-ante,* using Myrdal's convenient expressions. It goes without saying that actions depend not only on ideas about the future, but also on actual conditions at the moment of action; e.g. the supply of capital instruments and commodity stocks, the character of existing contracts, etc. The *ex-post* description supplies knowledge about these things directly, and at the same time it throws light on those past events, which influence expectations to a greater or smaller extent. Obviously a combination of *ex-post* and *ex-ante* analysis amounts simply to this: after a description of actual events during a certain, finished period, and of the differences between these events and the expectations which existed at the beginning of the period, follows an account of those expectations for the future which more or less govern actions during the next period. The registration of events during this second period reveals again that expectations do not all come true, a fact which influences expectations and actions during the third period, etc.

2.

Let me indicate briefly the concepts required for the *ex-post registration* in the general process analysis. For each individual or firm one has the following equation:

$$R - O - D = E = S + C;$$

R is *revenue,* i.e. the value of sales; O is *current costs,* i.e. payments to factors of production and to other firms for goods used up during this period; D is *depreciation items,* i.e. the computed costs for the period in question which are due to the use of things which are reckoned as products of earlier periods, minus corresponding appreciation items, which I leave out for the sake of simplicity; E is *net income,* of which one part C has been *used for consumption* while the rest is *savings* S. $R - O$ may be called *gross income* G, which is equal to $D + E$. I shall, however, not make use of this concept below.

These definitions are based on the picture of the transactions looked at from the "income side." If we now regard it from the "expenditure side" we get

$$X = I + C;$$

X is *total expenditure,* I is *investment expenditure,* and C is *consumption expenditure.* I includes both O (which is, of course, a kind of investment, but for a space of time shorter than one period) and the investment of a more durable kind. I consists of *reinvestment* I^r and *new investment* I^n.

Returning to the income side, we see that the revenue which is not net income is the return of money which has earlier been invested, either during the same period—this sum is equal to O—or during earlier periods—which sum is equal to D. $O + D$ can be called "old savings made available" or *"free capital."* These sums indicate a flow which is "available" for new investment expenditure. "Free capital" plus the new savings can be called *"waiting,"* W, which is thus equal to: $O + D + S$.

If we sum up all these things for all firms and individuals—that is, for society as a whole—we get the following identities. The distinction between reinvestment and new investment is made in such a way that the sum of investment, which is equal to free capital, is called reinvestment, while the rest is new investment.

Revenue $R =$ Total expenditure X.
Free capital $O + D =$ Reinvestment I^r.
Savings $S =$ New investment I^n.
Waiting $W =$ Investment I.
Net income $E =$ New investment $I^n +$ Consumption C.

The net income is, of course, equal to the sum total of all individual positive net incomes after deduction of all negative net incomes. Similarly, savings for society as a whole are equal to the sum of all positive savings minus all negative ones. An individual has a negative saving when he uses for consumption more than his income. This occurs always when his income is negative. But in other cases also—if his consumption exceeds his net income—he has to use a part of his fortune or take credit. Thus the savings for society are the sum of all positive savings minus negative incomes, consumption of one's own fortune and consumption credit.

This set of definitions, which refers to industrial, not financial transactions, is somewhat similar to Keynes' new terminology, which is based on the same type of identities. My investment I includes, however, more than Keynes' investment. I shall put off the discussion of the depreciation term D until a later part of this paper, where I comment on Keynes, who has made the important distinction between automatic depreciation—which can be called "time depreciation"—and depreciation caused by use of the different assets—"use depreciation." It should be mentioned already here that the computation of the depreciation terms depends upon the expectations, and that therefore book-keeping, including the closing of the accounts—the registration, grouping together, and interpretation of events—is not a pure *ex-post* manœuvre, but a combination of *ex-post* and *ex-ante*.

3.

I come now to the *ex-ante phenomena*—that is, the psychological causation. Purchases of goods and services are either intended for investment or for consumption purposes. Consider first investment purchases. The entrepreneur has certain *expectations* concerning future events beyond his control and a certain knowledge about his productive apparatus, contracts, etc. On this basis he makes certain *plans* concerning his own investments during the coming periods, and these plans are actually carried out as far as *his own* actions during this period are concerned. For the period is chosen so that he does not change his plans until the beginning of the next period. Much ought to be said about the implications of this assumption, and about the necessity for periods of different lengths, but I must pass over it here. Plans are regarded as a special sort of expectations. The difference is that plans concern his own actions, while other expectations do not. Plans are often in terms of alternatives, to be realised under different sets of expected conditions.

The investment plans are of course based on expected revenue from the investment in question and on the expected costs entailed, including the expected rates of interest. In brief, the plans are based on *the profit expectations*. But it would be wrong to assume that entrepreneurs plan to carry out all the investments which they think will yield a return, exceeding the rate of interest which they expect to pay. (Keynes' statement that the investment demand for capital depends on the relations of the marginal efficiency of capital to the interest rates, amounts practically to this.) Of all the possible investments which seem profitable, only some are planned for the next period and actually begun. This may be due to the fact that the present cash and credit resources of the firm are not large enough to permit more, or that the expected cash and credit resources put a check on the investments. Sometimes, however, strong business firms which could easily borrow huge sums for profitable-looking investment prefer not to do so. They are averse to an increase of their indebtedness. It is an open question whether this can be regarded as evidence that they reckon on unfavourable developments, which would make the investment unprofitable, as probable enough to make it not worth while, or whether the explanation must run in other terms. . . . In any case it is clear that the cash and credit resources, which the firm has at its disposal at the beginning of a period and acquires during the period, provide an upper limit for its *ability to buy,* and that the expectations concerning them set a limit to its investment plans; while the profit expectations and the expectations with regard to future cash and credit resources influence the *desire to buy.* As long as the latter does not touch the former limit, it determines the investment plans. (The above refers to investment in producers' goods. A similar, but somewhat different, reasoning explains the investment in durable consumers' goods.)

Like investment purchases, *the demand for non-durable consumption goods and services* is influenced by expectations and by knowledge concerning the actual situation of the consumer. On the basis of these circumstances consumption plans are made for the future, and as far as purchases during the first coming period are concerned, these plans are realised. Of course, the plans are not definite, for the consumer has not one precise expectation, e.g. about what prices will be during the next period or how much cash he will receive. But he usually plans to spend a certain sum for consumption purposes, and has alternative purchase plans concerning the distribution of this sum between different lines of consumption. The important thing for an analysis of changes in employment, output and prices is the sum total he plans to spend and does actually give out. On what does this sum total of planned consumption depend? First of all on the consumer's income expectations. Not his expected income during the first coming period only, but on what he expects to earn over a long period in the future. If a man gets a temporary, well-paid job which gives him a much higher salary than he is used to and more than he can expect to earn later on, his standard of consumption will obviously be much affected by consideration of this latter fact. . . .

Returning to the other circumstances which affect consumption plans, one must list chiefly two types: the expectations concerning future prices, and the expectations concerning future needs in comparison with the consumer's present needs. It is not necessary to dwell on these factors, the importance of which is obvious. The latter has been much discussed in the standard works on the theory of interest. The present and expected future position with regard to cash or credit plays the same rôle for consumption demand as for investment demand. . . .

It goes without saying that a similar analysis of expectations, etc., is required to explain supply as to explain demand. But this is chiefly only another side of the entrepreneurs' investment plans, and need not detain us. I also pass over the analysis of the so-called period of investment. To be of any use this must be an *ex-ante* concept. . . .

4.

Let us turn now to *a comparison of the ex-post and the ex-ante concepts.* Every one of the former has got a corresponding one among the latter. Thus we may simply fix an *a* at the bottom of each letter to indicate that it is *anticipated,* i.e., *expected or planned* income, savings, investment, etc., instead of *realised.* E.g. $E_a = S_a + C_a$.

Consider the relation of planned savings S_a to planned new investment I^n_a. There is no reason for assuming that they should be equal. But when the period is finished, new investment I^n is equal to savings S. How does this equality "come about"? The answer is that the inequality of S_a and I_a sets in motion a process which makes realised income differ from expected income, realised savings from planned savings and realised new investment differ from the corresponding plan. These differences we can call: *unexpected income E_u, unexpected new investment I_u and unintentional savings S_u* ("unintentional" is preferable to unexpected in this connection). The business man who, after the closing of his accounts, finds that he has had a larger net income than he expected and that therefore the surplus over and above his consumption is greater than his planned savings, has provided "unintentional savings" which is equal to this extra surplus. Unexpected new investment which, like unintentional saving, may, of course, be negative, can mean simply that stocks at the end of the period are different from what the entrepreneur expected.

All this is very simple. Many readers may wonder if it is worth bothering about in such detail. The answer is that unless the difference between *ex-ante* and *ex-post* concepts is kept quite clear, confusion is bound to ensue. The profit concept in Keynes' *Treatise on Money*—which in most places was an *ex-post* concept where certain items had been deducted and reckoned as belonging to the next period, but which was used in the causal analysis as if it had been an *ex-ante* concept—is a case in point. Subsequently I shall demonstrate that even in Keynes' "General Theory" a similar though perhaps less important lack of precision is to be found.

To avoid misunderstanding of the above terminology, I wish to stress the fact that income has nothing to do with the actual receipt of cash. The term is used very much in the sense of the ordinary business account. It is not surprising, therefore, that—according to my experience—people with practical experience of business but with no training in economic theory find the system of terms I have sketched and their use in analysis of real problems relatively easy. . . .

5.

Let me now indicate very briefly how an account of various processes can be given with the above terms. Considerations of space force me to make it somewhat "short-hand." Assume that people decide to reduce their savings and increase their consumption during the next period by 10 million, as compared with the realised savings and consumption during the period which has just finished. They expect their income to be unchanged. Assume further that the planned investment is equal to the realised investment during the last period. What will be the result? Retail sales of consumption goods will rise 10 million and the stocks of retailers will at the end of the period be down, e.g. 7 million, the remaining 3 million being the extra income of the retailers. This latter sum is "unintentional" savings. Thus realised saving is down only 7 million, or the same amount as realised investment. For the next period planned investment by retailers will be higher. Furthermore, their income expectations will be more favourable, and therefore their planned consumption greater also. Both investment purchases and consumption purchases will be greater during this second period than during the former, if consumers' disposition to save is the same. Output will rise, or prices go up, or both. While planned savings will be a little greater than during the former period—owing to the retailers' expectations of greater income—planned investment will go up more. For stocks of consumption goods will need refilling. Thus, during this period also, planned new investment will exceed the planned savings, and the process of expansion of the sum of transactions—and thereby quantities, or prices, or both—will go on.

The discrepancy between planned savings and planned investment can be regarded as the cause of the process. A similar development will follow if the original change is an increase of planned investment unaccompanied by any growth in planned savings.

This, however, is only one side of the story. Even if planned savings and planned investment should happen to be equal, a process of expansion is possible. The only thing then required is that expected incomes grow, and that consequently consumers increase their purchases. This fact has often been overlooked by writers who, under the influence of Wicksell or Keynes, start from the saving-investment analysis.

6. THE SPEED OF REACTIONS

Obviously, in each case one has to study the actual transactions in their relation to the plans and expectations. The different reactions depend on that. As these reactions often go in opposite directions, it is necessary to consider the relative strength and speed of these tendencies. What happens first?

Take a simple case. Assume that the wheat crop in important producing countries promises to be unusually large, as in 1928. The price of wheat then falls so heavily that the expected total value of the crop is lower than its average value, and lower than in previous years. Consequently farmers expect lower incomes during the next year. (This is one illustration of the impossibility of making any general assumption that everybody expects his income during the next period to be what it was during the last one.) So far nobody else expects higher incomes. On the contrary, wheat merchants are apt to have more pessimistic income expectations owing to the fall in the value of their stock of wheat. Farmers and perhaps merchants decide to reduce their consumption purchases, and carry this out. But does not a compensatory increase in demand for consumption goods come from consumers who get their bread cheaper, and therefore have more money left for other things? Perhaps, but not at once. Mills do not reduce their prices immediately nor bakers their bread prices. Hence, to begin with, a decline in the total demand for consumption goods ensues. This may set up pessimistic profit expectations in some lines of industry—those selling to the farmers—and lead to a decline in investment, employment, and workers' income expectations, etc. Some such thing may have happened during the period immediately before the great depression, contributing towards its outbreak and severity. . . .

Turn for a moment to the case above of a reduction in planned savings. I tacitly assumed that the banking system did not change its credit conditions. If, however, banks should immediately curtail credit—perhaps because they find that the flow of money into savings accounts is reduced—then investment purchases may be curtailed to the same extent as consumption purchases are increased. Hence, total purchases do not grow during the first period, compared with the last one, and what happens during the second one is uncertain. There is no greater probability that an expansion is caused than a contraction.

Obviously, the effects of a certain primary change varies with the time sequence and the speed of the secondary reactions. The consequences of changes in wage rates, tariffs, etc., will be different under different conditions.

The alternative processes which are caused do, of course, assume different developments with regard to the quantity or the velocity of the means of payments. But it is the time sequences and the time-lags between the various reactions—both the psychological reactions and the actual transactions—which govern the process much more than the construction of the monetary and banking system. Except when the latter reacts by causing a change in credit conditions, it has very little influence. It does not, therefore, seem very practical—although it is quite possible—to study the processes in terms of what happens to the velocity of money, i.e. by following the monetary units round their way in the economic system, in order to find out whether they are hoarded or not, etc. It is better to direct attention to the circumstances which make people change supply and purchases, and to analyse the speed of these reactions, studying the monetary mechanism only as one factor among several. The reactions of purchases depends, e.g., on (1) the speed with which profit and other income expectations are affected (see the crop-variation case above); (2) the speed with which (*a*) the amounts of cash in the hands of different firms or individuals are changed, and (*b*) the willingness of credit institutions and others to give credit is affected; (3) the actual cash and credit position when the primary change occurs. The latter circumstances concern the ability to buy, the first one the willingness to buy within the limits of ability. If the actual resources of many people are ample, then factor No. (2) is of little consequence.

It seems probable that in many cases the changes in the willingness to buy exercise the decisive influence. Hence, it is not then the speed with which the means of payments move, but rather the speed of the psychological reactions which is the governing factor. E.g. during a severe depression many firms have more cash and credit facilities than they need for any purchases under consideration.

7. THE SOURCES OF INCREASED SAVINGS DURING AN EXPANSION

If the interest level is reduced, or the profit expectations raised or public works started, and thereby the total volume of investment expanded, while the planned saving is, to begin with, unchanged, how then is a larger volume of saving—corresponding to the increased investment—called forth? The answer is simple. At the end of each period some individuals and firms find that they have had larger incomes than they expected. In other words, realised savings exceed planned savings. Secondly, the negative incomes which reduce the net savings for society as a whole are reduced. Thirdly, as incomes and expected incomes rise, planned savings grow also.

There is in this explanation no room for such expressions as the common one, that "the expansion of investment has been financed by credit expansion," e.g. the printing of new notes, "injection of new money," and the like. Whether the note circulation is increased or not is immaterial, and has nothing to do with the question how the savings which correspond to the increased investment are called forth. Even when the State finances public works with the printing of new notes, the increased investment is matched by increased "real" savings. At the end of the period some people hold more cash than at its beginning. This is evidence that they have had an income which they have not consumed, i.e. that they have saved. *Ex-post* there is *ex definitione* equality between savings and investment. The usefulness of this construction is that one has to show through what process it is "brought about," even though, as in this case, planned savings differed from planned investment. This process has little or nothing to do with the question whether new notes are printed or not. It is just as possible during a period of constant quantity of money. Naturally, in that case the velocity increases. But to say that either the quantity of money or its velocity, or both, must increase is a truism and no explanation. It amounts to saying that in order that the total money value of transactions shall be able to rise, MV must rise; but MV *is* the total money value of transactions. Hence, it would seem that the quantity theory of money approach and the "injection of new money" idea has led to some confusion.

Are the new savings called forth by the larger investment "forced"? This is, of course, a matter of terminology. To talk about forced savings seems, however, unfortunate, as the people with fixed incomes who reduce their consumption when prices go up, nevertheless probably save less than before. A "forced levy" is therefore a better term. But it is not certain that prices go up. Output may expand at constant prices. In any case, the extra savings come from people who get larger incomes than they expected. Hence, the thing to be stressed is this "unintentional" saving. As already explained the decline in negative incomes and the later rise in planned positive savings and reduction in planned negative savings are also part of the process.

The character of the further process depends on which kind of new savings are created. To the extent that increased investment leads to larger planned savings, without any increase in expected income, it is void of expansionary force. Consumption demand is then reduced as much as investment purchases expanded. If this condition is not fulfilled, total purchases grow, incomes rise, unintentional savings rise, and later planned savings also. But this latter increase in planned savings comes later than it should have done to prevent the process of expansion from continuing.

8. THE RATE OF INTEREST

Obviously the rate of interest cannot—with the terminology used above—be determined by the condition that it equalises the supply of and the demand for savings, or, in other words, equalises savings and investment. For savings and investment are equal *ex definitione,* whatever interest level exists on the market. Nor can one say that the rate of interest equalises planned savings and planned investment, for it obviously does not do this. How, then, is the height of the interest level determined?

The answer is that the rate of interest is simply the price of credit, and that it is therefore governed by the supply of and demand for credit. The banking system—through its ability to give credit—*can* influence, and to some extent does affect, the interest level. As a matter of fact, it is often useful as a first approximation to analyse practical problems on the assumption that the banking system fixes the rates of interest which make the interest "level." Does this mean that its height has no connection with the disposition of individuals and firms to save and with other elements in the price system? Of course not. But it has such a connection only indirectly. One object of interest theory is to explain the nature of this connection.

Given a certain disposition to save and certain income expectations, i.e. certain consumption and savings plans, the level of the rate of interest relatively to profit expectations, etc., determines the volume of investment and the way in which production, trade and prices develop. Thus, incomes are made to differ from expected incomes, savings from planned savings, and investment from planned investment in such a way that savings and investment agree. *Ceteris paribus,* increased investment without a corresponding increase in planned savings raises the sum total of purchases and, thus, production or prices or both. But it should be noted that the "*ceteris paribus*" assumption includes "constant income expectations." If they rise, and consumption with them, an expansion will result even if planned saving should happen to be equal to planned investment. The essence of the matter is simple: how do consumption purchases plus investment purchases vary from one period to another? But to explain this, plans and expectations and their relation to the "realisations" of earlier periods have to be considered.

Other things being equal, a change in the interest level will cause a different kind of economic development. An important conclusion follows. Which rate of interest one wants to call "normal" depends on what kind of economic development one considers "normal." Some people regard a constant price level of some sort as natural, and they are then entitled to call the rate of interest "normal"—if there is one—which leads to this constancy. But there is, of course, no special reason for looking at the price situation alone instead of at the economic situation in general. In brief, the rate of interest, or rather the combination of rates of interest, which is compatible with the economic development one chooses to call "normal," is also normal, and so is the volume of savings and of investment which goes with it. If the interest level should be lower and the volume of investment greater than what corresponds to this development, then a process of relative expansion—of output or price or both—is the outcome. Thereby the total quantity of savings is increased. As this economic development is *ex definitione* not "normal," the extra savings can also be called "not normal." Part of them is of the "unintentional" kind, the rest is planned on the basis of income expectations which are enlarged by the process in question.

According to Wicksell, who used different, somewhat ambiguous terms, a cumulative process of expansion was bound to ensue as long as the actual rate of interest was lower than the normal rate. What is the situation in this respect with the above terminology? Obviously, to say that the process of relative expansion continues so long as the actual rate falls short of the normal rate is a mere tautology, at least if we assume, as Wicksell did, that a lower rate always leads to greater investment than a higher rate. Wicksell's idea was that the normal rate—which he thought of as closely related to a natural rate corresponding to the marginal productivity of capital or of round-about methods of production in some Böhm-Bawerkian sense—changed very slowly if at all through the increase in savings caused by the process of expansion. Hence, he expected prices to continue to rise until the actual rate of interest on the market was raised. This latter opinion is not tenable, except perhaps if certain special assumptions are made as to expectations concerning the future. In a general analysis one has to stress the point that expectations and, thereby, the "normal" rate can change any day. There is, in my opinion, nothing more "physical" about it, as the Austrian theory wanted us to believe. The cumulative process—meaning a continuing rise in total purchases relative to the "normal" development—goes on as long as *expectations are such* that the investment purchases and the consumption purchases involve a relative rise in total purchases. This rather meaningless conclusion is not without importance, as it shows clearly that the "cumulative" character of the process depends on the fact that certain kinds of expectations are set up. A rise in the prices of consumption goods will, under certain conditions—e.g. if entrepreneurs at every moment expect existing prices to continue—raise the subjective value of capital goods and increase the demand for them, leading indirectly to greater income expectations and incomes and to a higher demand for consumption goods, etc., independently—in my opinion—of any shift of productive agents from one line of industry to another.

The important thing to stress is that the distinction between "normal" and "not normal" interest rates and savings depends on arbitrary assumptions that one kind of economic development, e.g. a constant wholesale price level, is "normal." Besides, it is far from certain that there is always one interest level which guarantees the existence of this normal development. On the one hand, it is possible that *no* interest level can do this. On the other hand, a great many and rather different interest levels may satisfy the condition of being compatible with this development. Obviously, in a dynamic analysis one has to give up the idea of an equilibrium rate of interest in the sense of the static equilibrium theory.

. . . On static assumptions it is possible to define a certain interest level and the corresponding volume of savings which is compatible with the maintenance of static equilibrium. Savings and interest rates which are not compatible with this equilibrium get a flavour of being "abnormal" or "artificial." But on dynamic assumptions such ideas have to be given up. It is, of course, conceivable that someone may in the future define a dynamic equilibrium in such a way as to make it useful for the analysis of practical problems, and that thus the distinction between equilibrium and non-equilibrium interest rates and savings may become important. But until this has been done—I doubt if it will ever happen—it seems necessary to emphasise the looseness of all ideas about "normalcy" in connection with interest rates, etc., and to attempt the study of time-using processes with the aid of more relativistic terms.

The reasoning so far is only an indication of the effects produced when the banking system fixes certain interest rates. But does the banking system actually alone determine the height of these rates? Of course not. Only the discount rate is usually fixed by the central bank. As to the other rates, e.g. the bond yield, the banking system is only one of many factors which affect demand, supply, and price. This requires further explanation.

Here again it is important to distinguish between an *ex-post* and *ex-ante* analysis. *Ex-post* one finds equality between the total quantity of new credit during the period, and the sum total of positive individual savings. (Of course, a person who uses his own savings is then said to give credit to himself; this supply and this demand offset one another and exert no influence on the price of credit.) Thus, there is a connection between the rate of interest, which is the price of credit, and the process of economic activity, of which the flow of saving is a part.

To explain how the rates of interest are actually determined, we need, however, a causal analysis which runs chiefly in *ex-ante* terms. What governs the demand and supply of credit? Two ways of reasoning are possible. One is *net* and deals only with *new* credit, and the other is *gross* and includes the outstanding *old* credits. The willingness of certain individuals during a given period to *increase* their holdings of various claims and other kinds of assets *minus* the willingness of others to *reduce* their corresponding holdings gives the supply curves for the different kinds of new credit during the period. Naturally, the quantities each individual is willing to supply depend on the interest rates. In other words, the plans are in the nature of alternative purchase and sales plans. Similarly, the total supply of *new* claims *minus* the reduction in the outstanding volume of *old* ones gives the demand—also a function of the rates of interest—for the different kinds of credit during the period. The prices fixed on the market for these different claims—and thereby the rates of interest—are governed by this supply and demand in the usual way.

The demand for claims of different sorts can be explained partly in terms of the same expectation-analysis as demand for investment goods. In discussing this latter question above nothing was said about the former, i.e. the way people planned to handle their own savings and "free capital." Except when they want to use them for direct investment—purchases of goods for investment purposes—they must decide in favour of acquiring claims, including cash. The psychology behind the choice between the different possibilities in this respect has been much illuminated by Keynes' discussion of "liquidity-preference."

A similar kind of reasoning can, of course, be applied *gross,* i.e. including the old claims which were outstanding when the period began. People's willingness to hold the different claims and other kinds of assets every day governs the supply of credit. The total supply of claims, etc., governs the demand for credit. In each market for the different claims, etc., supply and demand are made equal by price. These prices for interest-bearing claims on certain fixed sums determine the rates of interest. It is quite obvious that this reasoning in gross terms leads to the same result as the net analysis above.

I must pass over the question about the differences between the different kinds of credits, e.g.—(1) the length of the contract and the right to get the sum back on short or long notice and (2) the security given and the credit-worthiness of the borrower. The changing valuation of these things, and the ideas concerning the profit possibilities of other assets than claims, affect demand, supply, and price in the different markets.

Let me add a few words about the market which is given a special position by Keynes, the demand and supply for cash and claims "quickly" convertible into cash. It goes without saying, that the interest rates existing at any given moment fulfil the condition that they make people willing to hold as cash—which term in the following includes the last-mentioned claims—the total amount outstanding. But the same is true of all other claims and assets. The total quantity of cash is not fixed by the banking system at a certain figure, but depends on the economic development and on the actions of a number of individuals just as does the quantity of bonds outstanding. The "market" for cash has no key position in relation to the other markets. It is not even certain that the rate of interest obtained on cash holdings is zero. . . . Of course, one can ask: how intensely does each individual prefer holding a certain part of his fortune in form *A* (cash) rather than in form *B*? It is simpler and clearer to ask directly what sums people want to hold in form *A*, what in form *B*, etc., in a certain price situation and with certain expectations, e.g. with a certain constellation of interest rates, share prices, etc. There is no need of a theory of interest in terms of differentials, similar to the Ricardian theory of rent.

In my opinion, the theory of interest can be regarded as falling into three parts: (1) An analysis of the markets for claims and other assets, where their prices and, thus, the rates of interest are determined. This includes the phenomena of credit policy by banks, e.g. open-market operations. (2) An explanation of what kinds of processes with regard to the quantities of planned and unintentional savings and investment result from the existence of certain interest rates or, rather, from certain movements in interest rates. (3) An account of the connection between these processes and the transactions on the markets first mentioned. One process is apt to increase the willingness to hold long-term bonds, while another process reduces it, and this changed willingness is much dependent on the changes in incomes and in planned savings. Consumers buy consumption goods, business men buy capital goods, i.e. invest in a real sense, but there is a third kind of purchases to be explained—namely, "financial investment," i.e. the purchases of bonds, shares and bank deposits and the failure to use savings either for real or financial investment, which is identical with an increase in cash. It is noteworthy that Keynes, who has presented so interesting an analysis of the desire to vary cash holdings and of the psychology of financial investment, i.e. the willingness to buy bonds, shares, etc., on the one hand, pays so little attention to the connection between changes in production, income and savings on the one hand and the *ability* to make financial investments on the other. Without a consideration of this latter circumstance, the analysis of the markets for claims of different maturity, where the rates of interest are determined, is incomplete. Such a theory as I have here only briefly indicated is of course different from any equilibrium theory of the text-book kind. But it agrees with that theory and differs from Keynes' construction in one essential respect: it brings out the relation of the rates of interest to the other elements of the price system and to their movements, whereas Keynes' construction—unless it is interpreted in a way which he probably does not accept—seems to regard the rates of interest as determined largely "outside" the price system, or at least as having almost no connection with the system of mutually interdependent prices and quantities.

9. SOME ASPECTS OF A THEORY OF EMPLOYMENT

As Mr. Keynes has—rightly, I think—put much emphasis on the consequences of his theoretical approach for the theory of employment and unemployment, I shall add a few words about the attitude towards this problem in the Stockholm theory. . . .

(*a*) Permanent unemployment need not be "due to" a failure to reduce wages. In other words, it is far from certain that a reduction in wage rates would reduce unemployment to what one calls a "frictional" minimum. In the post-war discussion economists have sometimes *assumed* that there is an equilibrium wage which would make demand equal the available quantity of labour and, thus, lead to a state of no unemployment, except of the frictional type. Thereafter, they have proceeded to state that the existence of permanent unemployment is a *proof* that "wages are too high." It is evident that nothing is proved and that the latter statement is simply a repetition of the original assumption. Once the static equilibrium reasoning is given up, it becomes obvious that the relation between wages and unemployment is much more complicated. The level of wage rates is only one element of many, which have to get into certain relationships in order that the available labour force shall be employed. . . .

(*b*) When labour is set free through labour-saving technical changes there is no automatic compensation in increased employment elsewhere. What is set free is not "purchasing power," which will buy more of other goods than those cheapened by the invention, so that the expansion of output of such goods will provide employment for the discarded labourers. On the contrary, it is "productive power" which is made available, and it will not be re-employed unless some new impulse to expansion comes forward.

(*c*) Wage increases can lead to larger output and employment. The effect depends chiefly on how the investment demand of entrepreneurs reacts. Under certain conditions it will grow when wages go up, e.g. because people expect prices to rise later on. Under other conditions the opposite is true. The reaction of consumption demand is easier to determine. The outcome with regard to output and employment depends much on the speed of the various reactions of different kinds of investment demand as well as consumption demand. The possible rise in employment has nothing, as such, to do with a rise in prices or costs of living. The Stockholm theory thus denies the validity of the "orthodox" thesis which Keynes defends—namely, that an increase in employment must be accompanied by a reduction in the real wage. . . .

Obviously, wage changes affect the course of events differently during different cyclical processes. As a first approximation one can say that wage changes are in the short run "neutral" towards employment, as they increase the "cost side" of output as much as the "demand side." It depends on the price policy pursued by the sellers and on the effects of wage changes on investment and consumption demand, whether the quantity of labour employed goes up or down in the short run. (To analyse a great many such processes is the essential part of a "dynamic" theory of wages and employment.) In the "longer run" the tendencies towards a change in the combination of productive factors must of course also be considered.

JOHN MAYNARD KEYNES

(1883–1946)

Measured either by the originality of his ideas or by the influence of his writings, John Maynard Keynes stands out as one of the greatest economists of all time. More than any other writer, he succeeded in swinging the main focus of economics from micro-economics (the study of individual economic men) to macro-economics (the study of groups and measurable aggregates). Furthermore, he shifted the field of economic inquiry to the central problem of discovering what factors govern the level of employment in an economy.

Keynes was born in Cambridge, the son of an economics professor, John Neville Keynes. He was educated at Eton and Cambridge, where he first majored in mathematics but later turned to philosophy and economics. After college he took a civil service post in the India Office. From 1908 to 1914 he was a teaching fellow at Cambridge and helped edit the *Economic Journal.* It was during this period that he began his lifelong specialization in money, credit, and prices.

He joined the British Treasury in 1915 and later served as its representative at the Paris Peace Conference. He believed that the reparations and indemnities the Allies insisted on were unrealistic and would crush Germany, and framed this belief in one of his earliest books, *The Economic Consequences of the Peace* (1919). He felt so strongly on this score that he withdrew as representative from the Conference when he saw that his ideas had no chance for incorporation in the final peace treaty.

After the war he combined teaching at Cambridge with an active business life, including interests in insurance, investments, and publishing. His writings during this period were political in nature, and he was usually to be found on the liberal side.

In 1930 he published his two-volume *Treatise on Money,* in which he crystallized many of the ideas he had been developing in his Cambridge course. Although in this book he did not yet effectively integrate monetary theory with the main body of economic thought, he was moving in that direction, and he used certain Keynesian equations and symbols for the first time.

In 1936 he brought out his famous *General Theory of Employment, Interest and Money,* which he had developed during a seminar on monetary economics at Cambridge. This has turned out to be one of the most influential books ever written in economics. Here he made it plain that he was completely breaking with traditional theory, which held that there is a natural tendency for the economy to reach equilibrium at full employment. By taking output as a variable, Keynes showed that equilibrium can be reached at a level less than—often considerably less than—full employment.

Keynes defined aggregate income of society (Y) as that earned in producing consumer (C) and investment (I) goods. Therefore Y equals C plus I. Since we are considering the economy as a *whole,* these symbols also have consumption functions. That is, I will also equal the amount of money society *spends* on investment goods and the like. If a society decides to save more, without a corresponding rise in investment, effective demand will fall, output will fall with it, and employment will fall thereafter. The level of employment is thus determined by the demand for goods, which in turn depends upon the current rate of consumption of the community. Willingness to invest helps decide the level of output. This willingness depends upon the relationship between the marginal efficiency of capital, *i.e.,* the rate of return over cost, and the rate of interest. Stable economic conditions bring out entrepreneurial confidence and induce investment.

The effect of an increment of investment on the size of the increment of aggregate income of a community is at least partly dependent on that community's propensity to save. Keynes called the ratio between an increment of investment and the resultant increment in aggregate income the *multiplier*. This multiplier is usually measured as the reciprocal of the amount saved by the community. Thus, if a community tends to save one-third of its income, the investment multiplier will be three. Because consumption habits are normally constant, savings tend to go up with an increase in aggregate income. If interest rates are raised, there will be no inducement to invest; hence a drop in output and employment may be expected.

The *General Theory* was published in the midst of the Great Depression, when many governments were seeking something other than the apologetics of traditional economics and welcomed new ideas. Keynes advocated a decrease in the rate of bank interest to make investment more attractive, as well as progressive income taxation, which by making income distribution more equal would induce a higher aggregate capacity to consume. He also advocated government investment, through public works and other means, as a "pump-priming" process when private investment falls off.

In the following selections, important chapters from the *General Theory of Employment, Interest and Money* have been fitted together with several of Keynes' famous articles to give the student an overall view of the Keynesian system.

A younger colleague of Lord Keynes, and one of the ablest members of the Cambridge school of economics, is R. F. Kahn (1905–), who has made outstanding contributions to imperfect-competition theory and welfare economics as well as to business-cycle theory.

In 1931, five years before the *General Theory* of Keynes, Professor Kahn published "The Relation of Home Investment to Unemployment" (reprinted in full in *Readings in Business Cycles and National Income,* edited by Alvin H. Hansen and Richard V. Clemence, New York, W. W. Norton & Company, 1953). In this article he showed how the equations which Keynes had previously developed in his *Treatise on Money* (1930) could be used in the formulation of the concept of the employment multiplier—the relationship between net investment and the eventual level of employment. That is, the first wave of investment and subsequent spending will result in further waves of investment and spending, in each case minus the amount hoarded throughout the economy. The size of the multiplier effect will depend on the propensity of an economy or country to consume. Furthermore, Professor Kahn showed that the effect of an investment in public works by the government will be modified by savings, relief, and unemployment compensation. Because of the way in which the multiplier principle evolved, it is customary to refer to it as the Kahn-Keynes multiplier.

THE GENERAL THEORY *

I have called this book the *General Theory of Employment, Interest and Money,* placing the emphasis on the prefix *general.* The object of such a title is to contrast the character of my arguments and conclusions with those of the *classical* [1] theory of the subject, upon which I was brought up and which dominates the economic thought, both practical and theoretical, of the governing and academic classes of this generation,

* From *The General Theory of Employment, Interest and Money* by John Maynard Keynes. Reprinted by permission of Harcourt, Brace and Company, Inc.

1 "The classical economists" was a name invented by Marx to cover Ricardo and James Mill and their *predecessors,* that is to say for the founders of the theory which culminated in the Ricardian economics. I have become accustomed, perhaps perpetrating a solecism, to include in "the classical school" the *followers* of Ricardo, those, that is to say, who adopted and perfected the theory of the Ricardian economics, including (for example) J. S. Mill, Marshall, Edgeworth and Prof. Pigou.

as it has for a hundred years past. I shall argue that the postulates of the classical theory are applicable to a special case only and not to the general case, the situation which it assumes being a limiting point of the possible positions of equilibrium. Moreover, the characteristics of the special case assumed by the classical theory happen not to be those of the economic society in which we actually live, with the result that its teaching is misleading and disastrous if we attempt to apply it to the facts of experience.

THE GENERAL THEORY OF EMPLOYMENT *

It is generally recognized that the Ricardian analysis was concerned with what we now call long-period equilibrium. Marshall's contribution mainly consisted in grafting on to this the marginal principle and the principle of substitution, together with some discussion of the passage from one position of long-period equilibrium to another. But he assumed, as Ricardo did, that the amounts of the factors of production in use were given and that the problem was to determine the way in which they would be used and their relative rewards. Edgeworth and Professor Pigou and other later and contemporary writers have embroidered and improved this theory by considering how different peculiarities in the shapes of the supply functions of the factors of production would affect matters, what will happen in conditions of monopoly and imperfect competition, how far social and individual advantage coincide, what are the special problems of exchange in an open system and the like. But these more recent writers like their predecessors were still dealing with a system in which the amount of the factors employed was given and the other relevant facts were known more or less for certain. This does not mean that they were dealing with a system in which change was ruled out, or even one in which the disappointment of expectation was ruled out. But at any given time facts and expectations were assumed to be given in a definite and calculable form; and risks, of which, tho admitted, not much notice was taken, were supposed to be capable of an exact actuarial computation. The calculus of probability, tho mention of it was kept in the background, was supposed to be capable of reducing uncertainty to the same calculable status as that of certainty itself; just as in the Benthamite calculus of pains and pleasures or of advantage and disadvantage, by which the Benthamite philosophy assumed men to be influenced in their general ethical behavior.

Actually, however, we have, as a rule, only the vaguest idea of any but the most direct consequences of our acts. Sometimes we are not much concerned with their remoter consequences, even tho time and chance may make much of them. But sometimes we are intensely concerned with

* Reprinted by permission of the publishers from John Maynard Keynes, "The General Theory of Employment," *Quarterly Journal of Economics*. Cambridge, Mass.: Harvard University Press, Copyright, 1937, by The President and Fellows of Harvard College. Pp. 212–223.

them, more so, occasionally, than with the immediate consequences. Now of all human activities which are affected by this remoter preoccupation, it happens that one of the most important is economic in character, namely, Wealth. The whole object of the accumulation of Wealth is to produce results, or potential results, at a comparatively distant, and sometimes at an *indefinitely* distant, date. Thus the fact that our knowledge of the future is fluctuating, vague and uncertain, renders Wealth a peculiarly unsuitable subject for the methods of the classical economic theory. This theory might work very well in a world in which economic goods were necessarily consumed within a short interval of their being produced. But it requires, I suggest, considerable amendment if it is to be applied to a world in which the accumulation of wealth for an indefinitely postponed future is an important factor; and the greater the proportionate part played by such wealth-accumulation the more essential does such amendment become.

By "uncertain" knowledge, let me explain, I do not mean merely to distinguish what is known for certain from what is only probable. The game of roulette is not subject, in this sense, to uncertainty; nor is the prospect of a Victory bond being drawn. Or, again, the expectation of life is only slightly uncertain. Even the weather is only moderately uncertain. The sense in which I am using the term is that in which the prospect of a European war is uncertain, or the price of copper and the rate of interest twenty years hence, or the obsolescence of a new invention, or the position of private wealth-owners in the social system in 1970. About these matters there is no scientific basis on which to form any calculable probability whatever. We simply do not know. Nevertheless, the necessity for action and for decision compels us as practical men to do our best to overlook this awkward fact and to behave exactly as we should if we had behind us a good Benthamite calculation of a series of prospective advantages and disadvantages, each multiplied by its appropriate probability, waiting to be summed.

How do we manage in such circumstances to behave in a manner which saves our faces as rational, economic men? We have devised for the purpose a variety of techniques, of which much the most important are the three following:

(1) We assume that the present is a much more serviceable guide to the future than a candid examination of past experience would show it to have been hitherto. In other words we largely ignore the prospect of future changes about the actual character of which we know nothing.

(2) We assume that the *existing* state of opinion as expressed in prices and the character of existing output is based on a *correct* summing up of future prospects, so that we can accept it as such unless and until something new and relevant comes into the picture.

(3) Knowing that our own individual judgment is worthless, we endeavor to fall back on the judgment of the rest of the world which is perhaps better informed. That is, we endeavor to conform with the be-

havior of the majority or the average. The psychology of a society of individuals each of whom is endeavoring to copy the others leads to what we may strictly term a *conventional* judgment.

Now a practical theory of the future based on these three principles has certain marked characteristics. In particular, being based on so flimsy a foundation, it is subject to sudden and violent changes. The practice of calmness and immobility, of certainty and security, suddenly breaks down. New fears and hopes will, without warning, take charge of human conduct. The forces of disillusion may suddenly impose a new conventional basis of valuation. All these pretty, polite techniques, made for a well-panelled Board Room and a nicely regulated market, are liable to collapse. At all times the vague panic fears and equally vague and unreasoned hopes are not really lulled, and lie but a little way below the surface.

Perhaps the reader feels that this general, philosophical disquisition on the behavior of mankind is somewhat remote from the economic theory under discussion. But I think not. Tho this is how we behave in the market place, the theory we devise in the study of how we behave in the market place should not itself submit to market-place idols. I accuse the classical economic theory of being itself one of these pretty, polite techniques which tries to deal with the present by abstracting from the fact that we know very little about the future.

I daresay that a classical economist would readily admit this. But, even so, I think he has overlooked the precise nature of the difference which his abstraction makes between theory and practice, and the character of the fallacies into which he is likely to be led.

This is particularly the case in his treatment of Money and Interest. And our first step must be to elucidate more clearly the functions of Money.

Money, it is well known, serves two principal purposes. By acting as a money of account it facilitates exchanges without its being necessary that it should ever itself come into the picture as a substantive object. In this respect it is a convenience which is devoid of significance or real influence. In the second place, it is a store of wealth. So we are told, without a smile on the face. But in the world of the classical economy, what an insane use to which to put it! For it is a recognized characteristic of money as a store of wealth that it is barren; whereas practically every other form of storing wealth yields some interest or profit. Why should anyone outside a lunatic asylum wish to use money as a store of wealth?

Because, partly on reasonable and partly on instinctive grounds, our desire to hold Money as a store of wealth is a barometer of the degree of our distrust of our own calculations and conventions concerning the future. Even tho this feeling about Money is itself conventional or instinctive, it operates, so to speak, at a deeper level of our motivation. It takes charge at the moments when the higher, more precarious conventions have weakened. The possession of actual money lulls our disquietude;

and the premium which we require to make us part with money is the measure of the degree of our disquietude.

The significance of this characteristic of money has usually been overlooked; and in so far as it has been noticed, the essential nature of the phenomenon has been misdescribed. For what has attracted attention has been the *quantity* of money which has been hoarded; and importance has been attached to this because it has been supposed to have a direct proportionate effect on the price-level through affecting the velocity of circulation. But the *quantity* of hoards can only be altered either if the total quantity of money is changed or if the quantity of current money-income (I speak broadly) is changed; whereas fluctuations in the degree of confidence are capable of having quite a different effect, namely, in modifying not the amount that is actually hoarded, but the amount of the premium which has to be offered to induce people not to hoard. And changes in the propensity to hoard, or in the state of liquidity-preference as I have called it, primarily affect, not prices, but the rate of interest; any effect on prices being produced by repercussion as an ultimate consequence of a change in the rate of interest.

This, expressed in a very general way, is my theory of the rate of interest. The rate of interest obviously measures—just as the books on arithmetic say it does—the premium which has to be offered to induce people to hold their wealth in some form other than hoarded money. The quantity of money and the amount of it required in the active circulation for the transaction of current business (mainly depending on the level of money-income) determine how much is available for inactive balances, *i.e.* for hoards. The rate of interest is the factor which adjusts at the margin the demand for hoards to the supply of hoards.

Now let us proceed to the next stage of the argument. The owner of wealth, who has been induced not to hold his wealth in the shape of hoarded money, still has two alternatives between which to choose. He can lend his money at the current rate of money-interest or he can purchase some kind of capital-asset. Clearly in equilibrium these two alternatives must offer an equal advantage to the marginal investor in each of them. This is brought about by shifts in the money-prices of capital-assets relative to the prices of money-loans. The prices of capital-assets move until, having regard to their prospective yields and account being taken of all those elements of doubt and uncertainty, interested and disinterested advice, fashion, convention and what else you will which affect the mind of the investor, they offer an equal apparent advantage to the marginal investor who is wavering between one kind of investment and another.

This, then, is the first repercussion of the rate of interest, as fixed by the quantity of money and the propensity to hoard, namely, on the prices of capital-assets. This does not mean, of course, that the rate of interest is the only fluctuating influence on these prices. Opinions as to their prospective yield are themselves subject to sharp fluctuations, precisely for the reason already given, namely, the flimsiness of the basis of knowledge on which they depend. It is these opinions taken in conjunction with the rate of interest which fix their price.

Now for stage three. Capital-assets are capable, in general, of being newly produced. The scale on which they are produced depends, of course, on the relation between their costs of production and the prices which they are expected to realize in the market. Thus if the level of the rate of interest taken in conjunction with opinions about their prospective yield raise the prices of capital-assets, the volume of current investment (meaning by this the value of the output of newly produced capital-assets) will be increased; while if, on the other hand, these influences reduce the prices of capital-assets, the volume of current investment will be diminished.

It is not surprising that the volume of investment, thus determined, should fluctuate widely from time to time. For it depends on two sets of judgments about the future, neither of which rests on an adequate or secure foundation—on the propensity to hoard and on opinions of the future yield of capital-assets. Nor is there any reason to suppose that the fluctuations in one of these factors will tend to offset the fluctuations in the other. When a more pessimistic view is taken about future yields, that is no reason why there should be a diminished propensity to hoard. Indeed, the conditions which aggravate the one factor tend, as a rule, to aggravate the other. For the same circumstances which lead to pessimistic views about future yields are apt to increase the propensity to hoard. The only element of self-righting in the system arises at a much later stage and in an uncertain degree. If a decline in investment leads to a decline in output as a whole, this may result (for more reasons than one) in a reduction of the amount of money required for the active circulation, which will release a larger quantity of money for the inactive circulation, which will satisfy the propensity to hoard at a lower level of the rate of interest, which will raise the prices of capital-assets, which will increase the scale of investment, which will restore in some measure the level of output as a whole.

This completes the first chapter of the argument, namely, the liability of the scale of investment to fluctuate for reasons quite distinct (*a*) from those which determine the propensity of the individual to *save* out of a given income and (*b*) from those physical conditions of technical capacity to aid production which have usually been supposed hitherto to be the chief influence governing the marginal efficiency of capital.

If, on the other hand, our knowledge of the future was calculable and not subject to sudden changes, it might be justifiable to assume that the liquidity-preference curve was both stable and very inelastic. In this case a small decline in money-income would lead to a large fall in the rate of interest, probably sufficient to raise output and employment to the full. In these conditions we might reasonably suppose that the whole of the available resources would normally be employed; and the conditions required by the orthodox theory would be satisfied.

My next difference from the traditional theory concerns its apparent conviction that there is no necessity to work out a theory of the demand and supply of output *as a whole*. Will a fluctuation in investment, arising for the reasons just described, have any effect on the demand for output as a whole, and consequently on the scale of output and employment? What answer can the traditional theory make to this question? I believe that it makes no answer at all, never having given the matter a single thought; the theory of effective demand, that is the demand for output as a whole, having been entirely neglected for more than a hundred years.

My own answer to this question involves fresh considerations. I say that effective demand is made up of two items—investment-expenditure determined in the manner just explained and consumption-expenditure. Now what governs the amount of consumption-expenditure? It depends mainly on the level of income. People's propensity to spend (as I call it) is influenced by many factors such as the distribution of income, their normal attitude to the future and—tho probably in a minor degree—by the rate of interest. But in the main the prevailing psychological law seems to be that when aggregate income increases, consumption-expenditure will also increase but to a somewhat lesser extent. This is a very obvious conclusion. It simply amounts to saying that an increase in income will be divided in some proportion or another between spending and saving, and that when our income is increased it is extremely unlikely that this will have the effect of making us either spend less or save less than before. This psychological law was of the utmost importance in the development of my own thought, and it is, I think, absolutely fundamental to the theory of effective demand as set forth in my book. But few critics or commentators so far have paid particular attention to it.

There follows from this extremely obvious principle an important, yet unfamiliar, conclusion. Incomes are created partly by entrepreneurs producing for investment and partly by their producing for consumption. The amount that is consumed depends on the amount of income thus made up. Hence the amount of consumption-goods which it will pay entrepreneurs to produce depends on the amount of investment-goods which they are producing. If, for example, the public are in the habit of spending nine-tenths of their income on consumption-goods, it follows that if the entrepreneurs were to produce consumption-goods at a cost more than nine times the cost of the investment-goods they are producing, some part of their output could not be sold at a price which would cover its cost of production. For the consumption-goods on the market would have cost more than nine-tenths of the aggregate income of the public and would therefore be in excess of the demand for consumption-goods, which by hypothesis is only the nine-tenths. Thus entrepreneurs will make a loss until they contract their output of consumption-goods down to an amount at which it no longer exceeds nine times their current output of investment goods.

The formula is not, of course, quite so simple as in this illustration. The proportion of their income which the public will choose to consume will not be a constant one, and in the most general case other factors are also relevant. But there is always a formula, more or less of this kind, relating the output of consumption-goods which it pays to produce to the output of investment-goods; and I have given attention to it in my book under the name of the *Multiplier*. The fact that an increase in consumption is apt in itself to stimulate this further investment merely fortifies the argument.

That the level of output of consumption-goods, which is profitable to the entrepreneur, should be related by a formula of this kind to the output of investment-goods depends on assumptions of a simple and obvious character. The conclusion appears to me to be quite beyond dispute. Yet the consequences which follow from it are at the same time unfamiliar and of the greatest possible importance.

The theory can be summed up by saying that, given the psychology of the public, the level of output and employment as a whole depends on the amount of investment. I put it in this way, not because this is the only factor on which aggregate output depends, but because it is usual in a complex system to regard as the *causa causans* that factor which is most prone to sudden and wide fluctuation. More comprehensively, aggregate output depends on the propensity to hoard, on the policy of the monetary authority as it affects the quantity of money, on the state of confidence concerning the prospective yield of capital-assets, on the propensity to spend and on the social factors which influence the level of the money-wage. But of these several factors it is those which determine the rate of investment which are most unreliable, since it is they which are influenced by our views of the future about which we know so little.

This that I offer is, therefore, a theory of why output and employment are so liable to fluctuation. It does not offer a ready-made remedy as to how to avoid these fluctuations and to maintain output at a steady optimum level. But it is, properly speaking, a Theory of Employment because it explains *why*, in any given circumstances, employment is what it is. Naturally I am interested not only in the diagnosis, but also in the cure; and many pages of my book are devoted to the latter. But I consider that my suggestions for a cure, which, avowedly, are not worked out completely, are on a different plane from the diagnosis. They are not meant to be definitive; they are subject to all sorts of special assumptions and are necessarily related to the particular conditions of the time. But my main reasons for departing from the traditional theory go much deeper than this. They are of a highly general character and are meant to be definitive.

I sum up, therefore, the main grounds of my departure as follows:

(1) The orthodox theory assumes that we have a knowledge of the future of a kind quite different from that which we actually possess. This false rationalization follows the lines of the Benthamite calculus. The hypothesis of a calculable future leads to a wrong interpretation of the principles of behavior which the need for action compels us to adopt, and to an underestimation of the concealed factors of utter doubt, precariousness, hope and fear. The result has been a mistaken theory of the rate of interest. It is true that the necessity of equalizing the advantages of the choice between owning loans and assets requires that the rate of interest should be *equal* to the marginal efficiency of capital. But this does not tell us at what *level* the equality will be effective. The orthodox theory regards the marginal efficiency of capital as setting the pace. But the marginal efficiency of capital depends on the price of capital-assets; and since this price determines the rate of new investment, it is consistent in equilibrium with only one given level of money-income. Thus the marginal efficiency of capital is not determined, unless the level of money-income is given. In a system in which the level of money-income is capable of fluctuating, the orthodox theory is one equation short of what is required to give a solution. Undoubtedly the reason why the orthodox system has failed to discover this discrepancy is because it has always tacitly assumed that income *is* given, namely, at the level corresponding to the employment of all the available resources. In other words it is tacitly assuming that the monetary policy is such as to maintain the rate of interest at that level which is compatible with full employment. It is, therefore, incapable of dealing with the general case where employment is liable to fluctuate. Thus, instead of the marginal efficiency of capital determining the rate of interest, it is truer (tho not a full statement of the case) to say that it is the rate of interest which determines the marginal efficiency of capital.

(2) The orthodox theory would by now have discovered the above defect, if it had not ignored the need for a theory of the supply and demand of output as a whole. I doubt if many modern economists really accept Say's Law that supply creates its own demand. But they have not been aware that they were tacitly assuming it. Thus the psychological law underlying the Multiplier has escaped notice. It has not been observed that the amount of consumption-goods which it pays entrepreneurs to produce is a function of the amount of investment-goods which it pays them to produce. The explanation is to be found, I suppose, in the tacit assumption that every individual spends the whole of his income either on consumption or on buying, directly or indirectly, newly produced capital goods. But, here again, whilst the older economists expressly believed this, I doubt if many contemporary economists really do believe it. They have discarded these older ideas without becoming aware of the consequences.

THE THEORY OF THE RATE OF INTEREST *

Perhaps the following is a useful way of indicating the precise points of departure of the theory of the rate of interest expounded in my *General Theory of Employment, Interest and Money* from what I take to be the orthodox theory. Let us begin with four propositions, which, although they may be unfamiliar in form, are not inconsistent with the orthodox theory and which that theory has no reason, so far as I am aware, to reject.

(1) Interest on money *means* precisely what the books on arithmetic say that it means; that is to say, it is simply the premium obtainable on current cash over deferred cash, so that it measures the marginal preference (for the community as a whole) for holding cash in hand over cash for deferred delivery. No one would pay this premium unless the possession of cash served some purpose, i.e., had some efficiency. Thus we can conveniently say that interest on money measures the marginal efficiency of money measured in terms of itself as a unit.[1]

(2) Money is not peculiar in having a marginal efficiency measured in terms of itself. Surplus stocks of commodities in excess of requirements and other capital assets representing surplus capacity may, indeed, have a negative marginal efficiency in terms of themselves, but normally capital assets of all kinds have a positive marginal efficiency measured in terms of themselves. If we know the relation between the present and expected prices of an asset in terms of money we can convert the measure of its marginal efficiency in terms of itself into a measure of its marginal efficiency in terms of money by means of a formula which I have given in my *General Theory*.

(3) The effort to obtain the best advantage from the possession of wealth will set up a tendency for capital assets to exchange, in equilibrium, at values proportionate to their marginal efficiencies in terms of a common unit. That is to say, if r is the money rate of interest (i.e., r is the marginal efficiency of money in terms of itself) and y is the marginal efficiency of a capital asset A in terms of money, then A will exchange in terms of money at a price such as to make $y = r$.

(4) If the demand price of our capital asset A thus determined is not less than its replacement cost, new investment in A will take place, the scale of such investment depending on the capacity available for the

* From "The Theory of the Rate of Interest," in *The Lessons of Monetary Experience; Essays in Honor of Irving Fisher* (New York, Farrar & Rinehart, Inc.; copyright 1937 by Arthur D. Gayer).

[1] This implies a slightly different definition of marginal efficiency from that which I have given in my *General Theory,* namely the substitution of "market value" for "replacement cost." The meaning of "marginal efficiency of capital" of which I make use—and which is, in my opinion, the only definition of the term which makes good sense—was first introduced into economic theory by Irving Fisher in his *Theory of Interest* (1930), under the designation "the rate of return over cost." This conception of his is, I think, the most important and fruitful of his recent original suggestions.

production of *A,* i.e., on its elasticity of supply, and on the rate at which *y,* its marginal efficiency, declines as the amount of investment in *A* increases. At a scale of new investment at which the marginal cost of producing *A* is equal to its demand price as above, we have a position of equilibrium. Thus the price system resulting from the relationships between the marginal efficiencies of different capital assets including money, measured in terms of a common unit, determines the aggregate rate of investment.

These propositions are not, I think, inconsistent with the orthodox theory, or in any way open to doubt. They establish that relative prices (and, under the influence of prices, the scale of output) move until the marginal efficiencies of all kinds of assets are equal when measured in a common unit; and consequently that the marginal efficiency of capital is equal to the rate of interest. But they tell us nothing as to the forces which determine what this common level of marginal efficiency will tend to be. It is when we proceed to this further discussion that my argument diverges from the orthodox argument.

Put shortly, the orthodox theory maintains that the forces which determine the common value of the marginal efficiency of various assets are independent of money, which has, so to speak, no autonomous influence, and that prices move until the marginal efficiency of money, i.e., the rate of interest, falls into line with the common value of the marginal efficiency of other assets as determined by other forces. My theory, on the other hand, maintains that this is a special case and that over a wide range of possible cases almost the opposite is true, namely, that the marginal efficiency of money is determined by forces partly appropriate to itself, and that prices move until the marginal efficiency of other assets fall into line with the rate of interest.

Let me proceed to give the further propositions, which, I suggest, the orthodox theory requires.

(5) The marginal efficiency of money in terms of itself has the peculiarity that it is independent of its quantity. In this respect it differs from other capital assets. This is a consequence of the Quantity Theory of Money strictly stated (a matter to which we shall return later). Thus, unless we import considerations from outside, the money rate of interest is indeterminate, for the demand schedule for money is a function solely of its supply. Nevertheless, a determinate value for r can be derived from the condition that the value of an asset *A,* of which the marginal efficiency in terms of money is y, must be such that $y = r$. For provided that we know the scale of investment, we know y and the value of *A,* and hence we can deduce r. In other words, the rate of interest depends on the marginal efficiency of capital assets other than money. This must, however, be supplemented by another proposition; for it requires that we should already know the scale of investment. This further proposition is as follows.

(6) The scale of investment will not reach its equilibrium level until

the point is reached at which the elasticity of supply of output as a whole has fallen to zero.

Hence follows the final synthesis of this theory. The equilibrium rate of aggregate investment, corresponding to the level of output for a further increase in which the elasticity of supply is zero, depends on the readiness of the public to save. But this in turn depends on the rate of interest. Thus for each level of the rate of interest we have a given quantity of saving. This quantity of saving determines the scale of investment. The scale of investment settles the marginal efficiency of capital, to which the rate of interest must be equal. Our system is therefore determinate. To each possible value of the rate of interest there corresponds a given volume of saving; and to each possible value of the marginal efficiency of capital there corresponds a given volume of investment. Now the rate of interest and the marginal efficiency of capital must be equal. Thus the position of equilibrium is given by that common value of the rate of interest and of the marginal efficiency of capital at which the saving determined by the former is equal to the investment determined by the latter.

Now my departure from the orthodox theory takes place, as I have said, at propositions (5) and (6), for which I substitute:

(5)* The marginal efficiency of money in terms of itself is, in general, a function of its quantity (though not of its quantity alone), just as in the case of other capital assets.

(6)* Aggregate investment may reach its equilibrium rate under proposition (4) above, before the elasticity of supply of output as a whole has fallen to zero.

Before we examine the grounds for substituting (5)* and (6)* for (5) and (6), let us stop for a moment to consider more fully the meaning and the practical implications of the special postulates of the orthodox theory.

Let us begin with proposition (5). So far as the active circulation is concerned, it is sufficiently correct as a first approximation to regard the demand for money as proportionate to the effective demand, i.e., to the level of money income; which amounts to saying that the income velocity of the active circulation is independent of the quantity of money. This is, I say, only a first approximation because the demand for money in the active circulation is also to some extent a function of the rate of interest, since a higher rate of interest may lead to a more economical use of active balances, though this only means that the active balances are partially under the same influence as the inactive balances. But we also require the postulate that the amount of the inactive balances is independent of the rate of interest. I do not see, however, how this can be the case, except in conditions of long-period equilibrium, by which I mean a state of expectation which is both definite and constant and has lasted long enough for there to be no hangover from a previous state of expectation.

In ordinary conditions, on the other hand, this postulate would have awkward consequences quite incompatible with experience. It would mean, for example, that "open-market operations" by a central bank would have no effect, other than momentary, on the rate of interest, the price of bonds remaining the same whatever quantity of them the central bank may buy or sell; the effect of the central bank's action on prices being such as to modify the demand for money to just the same extent as that by which the central bank was altering the supply of money.

Let us now turn to proposition (6). A zero elasticity of supply for output as a whole means that an increase of demand in terms of money will lead to no change in output; that is to say, prices will rise in the same proportion as the money demand rises. Inflation will have no effect on output or employment, but only on prices. This is what I mean by saying that the orthodox theory of the rate of interest involves a strict interpretation of the Quantity Theory of Money, namely that P changes in the same proportion as M. This does not, of course, mean that T and V in the equation $PT = MV$ are irrevocably fixed; but the above, in conjunction with proposition (5), does mean that T and V are neither of them a function of M and that they do not change merely as a result of inflation in the quantity of money. Otherwise interpreted, a zero elasticity of supply for output as a whole involves a zero elasticity of supply for employment, i.e., there is, in my terminology, full employment. Indeed the condition in which the elasticity of supply for output as a whole is zero, is, I now think, the most convenient criterion for defining full employment.

It seems, therefore, that the orthodox theory requires (1) that there should be a state of definite and constant expectation and (2) that there should be a state of full employment. These limitations mean that it is a particular theory applicable only to certain conditions; and this is my justification for calling my own theory a *general theory*, of which the orthodox theory is a limiting case. Perhaps I am wrong in making the orthodox theory employ these postulates. For I am under the disadvantage that no one has ever thought it worth while to write down the postulates which the orthodox theory is supposed to require. But I do not at present see any alternative.

If I am right, the orthodox theory is wholly inapplicable to such problems as those of unemployment and the trade cycle, or, indeed, to any of the day-to-day problems of ordinary life. Nevertheless it is often in fact applied to such problems. The postulates which it requires, not having been stated, have escaped notice, with the result that deep-seated inconsistencies have been introduced into economic thought. The orthodox theory of the rate of interest properly belongs to a different stage of economic assumptions and abstractions from that in which any of us are thinking today. For the rate of interest and the marginal efficiency of capital are particularly concerned with the *indefinite* character of actual expectations; they sum up the effect on men's market decisions of all sorts of vague doubts and fluctuating states of confidence and courage. They belong, that is to say, to a stage of our theory where we are no longer assuming a definite and calculable future. The orthodox theory, on the other hand, is concerned with a simplified world where there is always full employment, and where doubt and fluctuations of confidence are ruled out, so that there is no occasion to hold inactive balances, and prices must be constantly at a level which, merely to satisfy the transactions motive and without leaving any surplus to be absorbed by the precautionary and speculative motives, causes the whole stock of money to be worth a rate of interest equal to the marginal efficiency of capital which corresponds to full employment. The orthodox theory is, for example, particularly applicable to the stationary state.[2] For in such conditions, not only is proposition (5) valid for the same reasons that apply in the case of the long period; but the stock of capital being fixed and new investment being zero, the marginal efficiency of capital must depend on the amount of this given stock and prices must be at a level which equates the amount of money, demanded for active balances at a rate of interest equal to this fixed marginal efficiency of capital, to the fixed supply of money in existence.

There is one other comment worth making. It leads to considerable difficulties to regard the marginal efficiency of money as wholly different in character from the marginal efficiency of other assets. Equilibrium requires, as we have seen above (proposition 3), that the prices of different kinds of assets measured in the same unit must move until their marginal efficiencies measured in that unit are equal. But if the marginal efficiency of money in terms of itself is always equal to the marginal efficiency of other assets, irrespective of the price of the latter, the whole price system in terms of money becomes indeterminate. It is the elements of elasticity (a) in the desire to hold inactive balances and (b) in the supply of output as a whole, which permits a reasonable measure of stability in prices. If these elasticities are zero there is a necessity for the whole body of prices and wages to respond immediately to every change in the quantity of money. This assumes a state of affairs very different from that in which we live. For the two elasticities named above are highly characteristic of the real world; and the assumption that both of them are zero assumes away three-quarters of the problems in which we are interested.

THE THEORY OF PRICES *

I

So long as economists are concerned with what is called the Theory of Value, they have been accustomed to teach that prices are governed by the conditions of supply and demand; and, in particular, changes in marginal cost and the elasticity of short-period supply have played a prominent part. But when they pass in volume II, or more often in a separate treatise, to the Theory of Money and Prices, we hear no more of

[2] Unless we suppose that a constant money wage is compatible with a constant level of employment which is less than full employment.

* From *The General Theory of Employment, Interest and Money* by John Maynard Keynes. Reprinted by permission of Harcourt, Brace and Company, Inc.

these homely but intelligible concepts and move into a world where prices are governed by the quantity of money, by its income-velocity, by the velocity of circulation relatively to the volume of transactions, by hoarding, by forced savings, by inflation and deflation *et hoc genus omne;* and little or no attempt is made to relate these vaguer phrases to our former notions of the elasticities of supply and demand. If we reflect on what we are being taught and try to rationalise it, in the simpler discussions it seems that the elasticity of supply must have become zero and demand proportional to the quantity of money; whilst in the more sophisticated we are lost in a haze where nothing is clear and everything is possible. We have all of us become used to finding ourselves sometimes on the one side of the moon and sometimes on the other, without knowing what route or journey connects them, related, apparently, after the fashion of our waking and our dreaming lives.

. . . The division of Economics between the Theory of Value and Distribution on the one hand and the Theory of Money on the other hand is, I think, a false division. The right dichotomy is, I suggest, between the Theory of the Individual Industry or Firm and of the rewards and the distribution between different uses of a *given* quantity of resources on the one hand, and the Theory of Output and Employment *as a whole* on the other hand. So long as we limit ourselves to the study of the individual industry or firm on the assumption that the aggregate quantity of employed resources is constant, and, provisionally, that the conditions of other industries or firms are unchanged, it is true that we are not concerned with the significant characteristics of money. But as soon as we pass to the problem of what determines output and employment as a whole, we require the complete theory of a Monetary Economy.

Or, perhaps, we might make our line of division between the theory of stationary equilibrium and the theory of shifting equilibrium—meaning by the latter the theory of a system in which changing views about the future are capable of influencing the present situation. *For the importance of money essentially flows from its being a link between the present and the future.* We can consider what distribution of resources between different uses will be consistent with equilibrium under the influence of normal economic motives in a world in which our views concerning the future are fixed and reliable in all respects;—with a further division, perhaps, between an economy which is unchanging and one subject to change, but where all things are foreseen from the beginning. Or we can pass from this simplified propaedeutic to the problems of the real world in which our previous expectations are liable to disappointment and expectations concerning the future affect what we do to-day. It is when we have made this transition that the peculiar properties of money as a link between the present and the future must enter into our calculations. But, although the theory of shifting equilibrium must necessarily be pursued in terms of a monetary economy, it remains a theory of value and distribution and not a separate "theory of money". Money in its significant attributes is, above all, a subtle device for linking the present to the future; and we cannot even begin to discuss the effect of changing expectations on current activities except in monetary terms. We cannot get rid of money even by abolishing gold and silver and legal tender instruments. So long as there exists any durable asset, it is capable of possessing monetary attributes and, therefore, of giving rise to the characteristic problems of a monetary economy.

II

In a single industry its particular price-level depends partly on the rate of remuneration of the factors of production which enter into its marginal cost, and partly on the scale of output. There is no reason to modify this conclusion when we pass to industry as a whole. The general price-level depends partly on the rate of remuneration of the factors of production which enter into marginal cost and partly on the scale of output as a whole, *i.e.* (taking equipment and technique as given) on the volume of employment. It is true that, when we pass to output as a whole, the costs of production in any industry partly depend on the output of other industries. But the more significant change, of which we have to take account, is the effect of changes in *demand* both on costs and on volume. It is on the side of demand that we have to introduce quite new ideas when we are dealing with demand as a whole and no longer with the demand for a single product taken in isolation, with demand as a whole assumed to be unchanged.

III

If we allow ourselves the simplification of assuming that the rates of remuneration of the different factors of production which enter into marginal cost all change in the same proportion, *i.e.* in the same proportion as the wage-unit, it follows that the general price-level (taking equipment and technique as given) depends partly on the wage-unit and partly on the volume of employment. Hence the effect of changes in the quantity of money on the price-level can be considered as being compounded of the effect on the wage-unit and the effect on employment.

To elucidate the ideas involved, let us simplify our assumptions still further, and assume (1) that all unemployed resources are homogeneous and interchangeable in their efficiency to produce what is wanted, and (2) that the factors of production entering into marginal cost are content with the same money-wage so long as there is a surplus of them unemployed. In this case we have constant returns and a rigid wage-unit, so long as there is any unemployment. It follows that an increase in the quantity of money will have no effect whatever on prices, so long as there is any unemployment, and that employment will increase in exact proportion to any increase in effective demand brought about by the increase in the quantity of money; whilst as soon as full employment is reached, it will thenceforward be the wage-unit and prices which will increase in exact proportion to the increase in effective demand. Thus if there is perfectly elastic supply so long as there is unemployment, and perfectly inelastic supply so soon as full employment is reached, and if effective demand changes in the same proportion as the quantity of money, the Quantity Theory of Money can be enunciated as follows: "So long as there is unemployment, *employment* will change in the same proportion as the quantity of money; and when there is full employment, *prices* will change in the same proportion as the quantity of money."

Having, however, satisfied tradition by introducing a sufficient number of simplifying assumptions to enable us to enunciate a Quantity Theory of Money, let us now consider the possible complications which will in fact influence events:

(1) Effective demand will not change in exact proportion to the quantity of money.

(2) Since resources are not homogeneous, there will be diminishing, and not constant, returns as employment gradually increases.

(3) Since resources are not interchangeable, some commodities will reach a condition of inelastic supply whilst there are still unemployed resources available for the production of other commodities.

(4) The wage-unit will tend to rise, before full employment has been reached.

(5) The remunerations of the factors entering into marginal cost will not all change in the same proportion.

Thus we must first consider the effect of changes in the quantity of money on the quantity of effective demand; and the increase in effective demand will, generally speaking, spend itself partly in increasing the quantity of employment and partly in raising the level of prices. Thus instead of constant prices in conditions of unemployment, and of prices rising in proportion to the quantity of money in conditions of full employment, we have in fact a condition of prices rising gradually as employment increases. The Theory of Prices, that is to say, the analysis of the relation between changes in the quantity of money and changes in the price-level with a view to determining the elasticity of prices in response to changes in the quantity of money, must, therefore, direct itself to the five complicating factors set forth above.

We will consider each of them in turn. But this procedure must not be allowed to lead us into supposing that they are, strictly speaking, independent. For example, the proportion, in which an increase in effective demand is divided in its effect between increasing output and raising prices, may affect the way in which the quantity of money is related to the quantity of effective demand. Or, again, the differences in the proportions, in which the remunerations of different factors change, may influence the relation between the quantity of money and the quantity of effective demand. The object of our analysis is, not to provide a machine, or method of blind manipulation, which will furnish an infallible answer, but to provide ourselves with an organised and orderly method of thinking out particular problems; and, after we have reached a provisional conclusion by isolating the complicating factors one by one, we then have to go back on ourselves and allow, as well as we can, for the probable interactions of the factors amongst themselves. This is the nature of economic thinking. Any other way of applying our formal principles of thought (without which, however, we shall be lost in the wood) will lead us into error. It is a great fault of symbolic pseudo-mathematical methods of formalising a system of economic analysis, such as we shall set down in section VI of this chapter, that they expressly assume strict independence between the factors involved and lose all their cogency and authority if this hypothesis is disallowed; whereas, in ordinary discourse, where we are not blindly manipulating but know all the time what we are doing and what the words mean, we can keep "at the back of our heads" the necessary reserves and qualifications and the adjustments which we shall have to make later on, in a way in which we cannot keep complicated partial differentials "at the back" of several pages of algebra which assume that they all vanish. Too large a proportion of recent "mathematical" economics are mere concoctions, as imprecise as the initial assumptions they rest on, which allow the author to lose sight of the complexities and interdependencies of the real world in a maze of pretentious and unhelpful symbols.

IV

(1) The primary effect of a change in the quantity of money on the quantity of effective demand is through its influence on the rate of interest. If this were the only reaction, the quantitative effect could be derived from the three elements—(*a*) the schedule of liquidity-preference which tells us by how much the rate of interest will have to fall in order that the new money may be absorbed by willing holders, (*b*) the schedule of marginal efficiencies which tells us by how much a given fall in the rate of interest will increase investment, and (*c*) the investment multiplier which tells us by how much a given increase in investment will increase effective demand as a whole.

But this analysis, though it is valuable in introducing order and method into our enquiry, presents a deceptive simplicity, if we forget that the three elements (*a*), (*b*) and (*c*) are themselves partly dependent on the complicating factors (2), (3), (4) and (5) which we have not yet considered. For the schedule of liquidity-preference itself depends on how much of the new money is absorbed into the income and industrial circulations, which depends in turn on how much effective demand increases and how the increase is divided between the rise of prices, the rise of wages, and the volume of output and employment. Furthermore, the schedule of marginal efficiencies will partly depend on the effect which the circumstances attendant on the increase in the quantity of money have on expectations of the future monetary prospects. And finally the multiplier will be influenced by the way in which the new income resulting from the increased effective demand is distributed between different classes of consumers. Nor, of course, is this list of possible interactions complete. Nevertheless, if we have all the facts before us, we shall have enough simultaneous equations to give us a determinate result. There will be a determinate amount of increase in the quantity of effective demand which, after taking everything into account, will correspond to, and be in equilibrium with, the increase in the quantity of money. Moreover, it is only in highly exceptional circumstances that an increase in the quantity of money will be associated with a *decrease* in the quantity of effective demand.

The ratio between the quantity of effective demand and the quantity of money closely corresponds to what is often called the "income-velocity of money";—except that effective demand corresponds to the income the expectation of which has set production moving, not to the actually realised income, and to gross, not net, income. But the "income-velocity of money" is, in itself, merely a name which explains nothing. There is no reason to expect that it will be constant. For it depends, as the foregoing discussion has shown, on many complex and variable factors. The use of this term obscures, I think, the real character of the causation, and has led to nothing but confusion.

. . . The distinction between diminishing and constant returns partly depends on whether workers are remunerated in strict proportion to their efficiency. If so, we shall have constant labour-costs (in terms of the wage-unit) when employment increases. But if the wage of a given grade of labourers is uniform irrespective of the efficiency of the individuals, we shall have rising labour-costs, irrespective of the efficiency of the equipment. Moreover, if equipment is non-homogeneous and some part of it involves a greater prime cost per unit of output, we shall have increasing marginal prime costs over and above any increase due to increasing labour-costs.

Hence, in general, supply price will increase as output from a given equipment is increased. Thus increasing output will be associated with rising prices, apart from any change in the wage-unit.

(3) Under (2) we have been contemplating the possibility of supply being imperfectly elastic. If there is a perfect balance in the respective quantities of specialised unemployed resources, the point of full employment will be reached for all of them simultaneously. But, in general, the demand for some services and commodities will reach a level beyond which their supply is, for the time being, perfectly inelastic, whilst in other directions there is still a substantial surplus of resources without employment. Thus as output increases, a series of "bottle-necks" will be successively reached, where the supply of particular commodities ceases to be elastic and their prices have to rise to whatever level is necessary to divert demand into other directions.

It is probable that the general level of prices will not rise very much as output increases, so long as there are available efficient unemployed resources of every type. But as soon as output has increased sufficiently to begin to reach the "bottle-necks", there is likely to be a sharp rise in the price of certain commodities.

Under this heading, however, as also under heading (2), the elasticity of supply partly depends on the elapse of time. If we assume a sufficient interval for the quantity of equipment itself to change, the elasticities of supply will be decidedly greater eventually. Thus a moderate change in effective demand, coming on a situation where there is widespread unemployment, may spend itself very little in raising prices and mainly in increasing employment; whilst a larger change, which, being unforeseen, causes some temporary "bottle-necks" to be reached, will spend itself in raising prices, as distinct from employment, to a greater extent at first than subsequently.

(4) That the wage-unit may tend to rise before full employment has been reached, requires little comment or explanation. Since each group of workers will gain, *cet. par.*, by a rise in its own wages, there is naturally for all groups a pressure in this direction, which entrepreneurs will be more ready to meet when they are doing better business. For this reason a proportion of any increase in effective demand is likely to be absorbed in satisfying the upward tendency of the wage-unit.

Thus, in addition to the final critical point of full employment at which money-wages have to rise, in response to an increasing effective demand in terms of money, fully in proportion to the rise in the prices of wage-goods, we have a succession of earlier semi-critical points at which an increasing effective demand tends to raise money-wages though not fully in proportion to the rise in the price of wage-goods; and similarly in the case of a decreasing effective demand. In actual experience the wage-unit does not change continuously in terms of money in response to every small change in effective demand; but discontinuously. These points of discontinuity are determined by the psychology of the workers and by the policies of employers and trade unions. In an open system, where they mean a change relatively to wage-costs elsewhere, and in a trade cycle, where even in a closed system they may mean a change relatively to expected wage-costs in the future, they can be of considerable practical significance. These points, where a further increase in effective demand in terms of money is liable to cause a discontinuous rise in the wage-unit, might be deemed from a certain point of view, to be positions of semi-inflation, having some analogy (though a very imperfect one) to the absolute inflation . . . which ensues on an increase in effective demand in circumstances of full employment. They have, moreover, a good deal of historical importance. But they do not readily lend themselves to theoretical generalisations.

(5) Our first simplification consisted in assuming that the remunerations of the various factors entering into marginal cost all change in the same proportion. But in fact the rates of remuneration of different factors in terms of money will show varying degrees of rigidity and they may also have different elasticities of supply in response to changes in the

money-rewards offered. If it were not for this, we could say that the price-level is compounded of two factors, the wage-unit and the quantity of employment.

Perhaps the most important element in marginal cost which is likely to change in a different proportion from the wage-unit, and also to fluctuate within much wider limits, is marginal user cost. For marginal user cost may increase sharply when employment begins to improve, if (as will probably be the case) the increasing effective demand brings a rapid change in the prevailing expectations as to the date when the replacement of equipment will be necessary.

Whilst it is for many purposes a very useful first approximation to assume that the rewards of all the factors entering into marginal prime-cost change in the same proportion as the wage-unit, it might be better, perhaps, to take a weighted average of the rewards of the factors entering into marginal prime-cost, and call this the *cost-unit*. The cost-unit, or, subject to the above approximation, the wage-unit, can thus be regarded as the essential standard of value; and the price-level, given the state of technique and equipment, will depend partly on the cost-unit and partly on the scale of output, increasing, where output increases, *more* than in proportion to any increase in the cost-unit, in accordance with the principle of diminishing returns in the short period. We have full employment when output has risen to a level at which the marginal return from a representative unit of the factors of production has fallen to the minimum figure at which a quantity of the factors sufficient to produce this output is available.

V

When a further increase in the quantity of effective demand produces no further increase in output and entirely spends itself on an increase in the cost-unit fully proportionate to the increase in effective demand, we have reached a condition which might be appropriately designated as one of true inflation. Up to this point the effect of monetary expansion is entirely a question of degree, and there is no previous point at which we can draw a definite line and declare that conditions of inflation have set in. Every previous increase in the quantity of money is likely, in so far as it increases effective demand, to spend itself partly in increasing the cost-unit and partly in increasing output.

It appears, therefore, that we have a sort of asymmetry on the two sides of the critical level above which true inflation sets in. For a contraction of effective demand below the critical level will reduce its amount measured in cost-units; whereas an expansion of effective demand beyond this level will not, in general, have the effect of increasing its amount in terms of cost-units. This result follows from the assumption that the factors of production, and in particular the workers, are disposed to resist a reduction in their money-rewards, and that there is no corresponding motive to resist an increase. This assumption is, however, obviously well founded in the facts, due to the circumstance that a change, which is not an all-round change, is beneficial to the special factors affected when it is upward and harmful when it is downward.

If, on the contrary, money-wages were to fall without limit whenever there was a tendency for less than full employment, the asymmetry would, indeed, disappear. But in that case there would be no resting-place below full employment until either the rate of interest was incapable of falling further or wages were zero. In fact we must have *some* factor, the value of which in terms of money is, if not fixed, at least sticky, to give us any stability of values in a monetary system.

The view that *any* increase in the quantity of money is inflationary (unless we mean by *inflationary* merely that prices are rising) is bound up with the underlying assumption of the classical theory that we are *always* in a condition where a reduction in the real rewards of the factors of production will lead to a curtailment in their supply.

VI

. . . We can, if we wish, express the substance of the above in symbolic form.

Let us write MV = D where M is the quantity of money, V its income-velocity [this definition differing in minor respects from the usual definition] and D the effective demand. If, then, V is constant, prices will change in the same proportion as the quantity of money provided that e_p $\left(=\frac{Ddp}{pdD}\right)$ is unity. This condition is satisfied . . . if $e_o = 0$ or if $e_w = 1$. The condition $e_w = 1$ means that the wage-unit in terms of money rises in the same proportion as the effective demand, since $e_w = \frac{DdW}{WdD}$; and the condition $e_o = 0$ means that output no longer shows any response to a further increase in effective demand, since $e_o = \frac{DdO}{OdD}$. Output in either case will be unaltered.

Next, we can deal with the case where income-velocity is not constant. by introducing yet a further elasticity, namely the elasticity of effective demand in response to changes in the quantity of money,

$$e_d = \frac{MdD}{DdM}.$$

This gives us

$$\frac{Mdp}{pdM} = e_p \cdot e_d \text{ where } e_p = 1 - e_e \cdot e_o (1 - e_w);$$

so that

$$\begin{aligned} e &= e_d - (1 - e_w) e_d \cdot e_e \cdot e_o \\ &= e_d (1 - e_e \cdot e_o + e_e \cdot e_o \cdot e_w) \end{aligned}$$

where e without suffix $\left(=\frac{Mdp}{pdM}\right)$ stands for the apex of this pyramid and measures the response of money-prices to changes in the quantity of money.

Since this last expression gives us the proportionate change in prices in response to a change in the quantity of money, it can be regarded as a generalised statement of the Quantity Theory of Money. I do not myself attach much value to manipulations of this kind; and I would repeat the warning . . . that they involve just as much tacit assumption as to what variables are taken as independent (partial differentials being ignored throughout) as does ordinary discourse, whilst I doubt if they carry us any further than ordinary discourse can. Perhaps the best purpose served by writing them down is to exhibit the extreme complexity of the relationship between prices and the quantity of money, when we attempt to express it in a formal manner. It is, however, worth pointing out that, of the four terms e_d, e_w, e_e and e_o upon which the effect on prices or changes in the quantity of money depends, e_d stands for the liquidity factors which determine the demand for money in each situation, e_w for the labour factors (or, more strictly, the factors entering into prime-cost) which determine the extent to which money-wages are raised as employment increases, and e_e and e_o for the physical factors which determine the rate of decreasing returns as more employment is applied to the existing equipment.

If the public hold a constant proportion of their income in money, $e_d = 1$; if money-wages are fixed, $e_w = 0$; if there are constant returns throughout so that marginal return equals average return, $e_e e_o = 1$; and if there is full employment either of labour or of equipment, $e_e e_o = 0$.

Now $e = 1$, if $e_d = 1$ and $e_w = 1$; or if $e_d = 1$, $e_w = 0$ and $e_e \cdot e_o = 1$; or if $e_d = 1$ and $e_o = 0$. And obviously there is a variety of other special cases in which $e = 1$. But in general e is not unity; and it is, perhaps, safe to make the generalisation that on plausible assumptions relating to the real world, and excluding the case of a "flight from the currency" in which e_d and e_w become large, e is, as a rule, less than unity.

VII

So far, we have been primarily concerned with the way in which changes in the quantity of money affect prices in the short period. But in the long run is there not some simpler relationship?

This is a question for historical generalisation rather than for pure theory. If there is some tendency to a measure of long-run uniformity in the state of liquidity-preference, there may well be some sort of rough relationship between the national income and the quantity of money required to satisfy liquidity-preference, taken as a mean over periods of pessimism and optimism together. There may be, for example, some fairly stable proportion of the national income more than which people will not readily keep in the shape of idle balances for long periods together, provided the rate of interest exceeds a certain psychological minimum; so that if the quantity of money beyond what is required in the active circulation is in excess of this proportion of the national income, there will be a tendency sooner or later for the rate of interest to fall to the neighbourhood of this minimum. The falling rate of interest will then, *cet. par.*, increase effective demand, and the increasing effective demand will reach one or more of the semi-critical points at which the wage-unit will tend to show a discontinuous rise, with a corresponding effect on prices. The opposite tendencies will set in if the quantity of surplus money is an abnormally low proportion of the national income. Thus the net effect of fluctuations over a period of time will be to establish a mean figure in conformity with the stable proportion between the national income and the quantity of money to which the psychology of the public tends sooner or later to revert.

These tendencies will probably work with less friction in the upward than in the downward direction. But if the quantity of money remains very deficient for a long time, the escape will be normally found in changing the monetary standard or the monetary system so as to raise the quantity of money, rather than in forcing down the wage-unit and thereby increasing the burden of debt. Thus the very long-run course of prices has almost always been upward. For when money is relatively abundant, the wage-unit rises; and when money is relatively scarce, some means is found to increase the effective quantity of money.

During the nineteenth century, the growth of population and of invention, the opening-up of new lands, the state of confidence and the frequency of war over the average of (say) each decade seem to have been sufficient, taken in conjunction with the propensity to consume, to establish a schedule of the marginal efficiency of capital which allowed a reasonably satisfactory average level of employment to be compatible with a rate of interest high enough to be psychologically acceptable to wealth-owners. There is evidence that for a period of almost one hundred and fifty years the long-run typical rate of interest in the leading financial centres was about 5 per cent., and the gilt-edged rate between 3 and 3½ per cent.; and that these rates of interest were modest enough to encourage a rate of investment consistent with an average of employment which was not intolerably low. Sometimes the wage-unit, but more often the monetary standard or the monetary system (in particular through the development of bank-money), would be adjusted so as to ensure that the quantity of money in terms of wage-units was sufficient to satisfy normal liquidity-preference at rates of interest which were seldom much below the standard rates indicated above. The tendency of the wage-unit was, as usual, steadily upwards on the whole, but the efficiency of labour was also increasing. Thus the balance of forces was such as to allow a fair measure of stability of prices;—the highest quinquennial average for Sauerbeck's index number between 1820 and 1914 was only 50 per cent. above the lowest. This was not accidental. It is rightly described as due to a balance of forces in an age when individual groups of employers were strong enough to prevent the wage-unit from rising much faster than the efficiency of production, and when monetary systems were at the same time sufficiently fluid and sufficiently conservative to provide an average supply of money in terms of wage-units which allowed to prevail the lowest average rate of interest readily acceptable by wealth-owners under the influence of their liquidity-preferences. The average level of employment was, of course, substantially below full employment, but not so intolerably below it as to provoke revolutionary changes.

To-day and presumably for the future the schedule of the marginal efficiency of capital is, for a variety of reasons, much lower than it was in the nineteenth century. The acuteness and the peculiarity of our contemporary problem arises, therefore, out of the possibility that the average rate of interest which will allow a reasonable average level of employment is one so unacceptable to wealth-owners that it cannot be readily established merely by manipulating the quantity of money. So long as a tolerable level of employment could be attained on the average of one or two or three decades merely by assuring an adequate supply of money in terms of wage-units, even the nineteenth century could find a way. If this was our only problem now—if a sufficient degree of devaluation is all we need—we, to-day, would certainly find a way.

But the most stable, and the least easily shifted, element in our contemporary economy has been hitherto, and may prove to be in future, the minimum rate of interest acceptable to the generality of wealth-owners. If a tolerable level of employment requires a rate of interest much below the average rates which ruled in the nineteenth century, it is most doubtful whether it can be achieved merely by manipulating the quantity of money. From the percentage gain, which the schedule of marginal efficiency of capital allows the borrower to expect to earn, there has to be deducted (1) the cost of bringing borrowers and lenders together, (2) the income and sur-taxes and (3) the allowance which the lender requires to cover his risk and uncertainty, before we arrive at the net yield available to tempt the wealth-owner to sacrifice his liquidity. If, in conditions of tolerable average employment, this net yield turns out to be infinitesimal, time-honoured methods may prove unavailing.

To return to our immediate subject, the long-run relationship between the national income and the quantity of money will depend on liquidity-preferences. And the long-run stability or instability of prices will depend on the strength of the upward trend of the wage-unit (or, more precisely, of the cost-unit) compared with the rate of increase in the efficiency of the productive system.

CONCLUDING NOTES ON THE SOCIAL PHILOSOPHY TOWARDS WHICH THE GENERAL THEORY MIGHT LEAD *

I

The outstanding faults of the economic society in which we live are its failure to provide for full employment and its arbitrary and inequitable distribution of wealth and incomes. The bearing of the foregoing theory on the first of these is obvious. But there are also two important respects in which it is relevant to the second.

Since the end of the nineteenth century significant progress towards the removal of very great disparities of wealth and income has been achieved through the instrument of direct taxation—income tax and surtax and death duties—especially in Great Britain. Many people would wish to see this process carried much further, but they are deterred by two considerations; partly by the fear of making skilful evasions too much worth while and also of diminishing unduly the motive towards risk-taking, but mainly, I think, by the belief that the growth of capital depends upon the strength of the motive towards individual saving and that for a large proportion of this growth we are dependent on the savings of the rich out of their superfluity. Our argument does not affect the first of these considerations. But it may considerably modify our attitude towards the second. For we have seen that, up to the point where full employment prevails, the growth of capital depends not at all on a low propensity to consume but is, on the contrary, held back by it; and only in conditions of full employment is a low propensity to consume conducive to the growth of capital. Moreover, experience suggests that in existing conditions saving by institutions and through sinking funds is more than adequate, and that measures for the redistribution of incomes in a way likely to raise the propensity to consume may prove positively favourable to the growth of capital.

The existing confusion of the public mind on the matter is well illustrated by the very common belief that the death duties are responsible for a reduction in the capital wealth of the country. Assuming that the State applies the proceeds of these duties to its ordinary outgoings so that taxes on incomes and consumption are correspondingly reduced or avoided, it is, of course, true that a fiscal policy of heavy death duties has the effect of increasing the community's propensity to consume. But inasmuch as an increase in the habitual propensity to consume will in general (*i.e.* except in conditions of full employment) serve to increase at the same time the inducement to invest, the inference commonly drawn is the exact opposite of the truth.

Thus our argument leads towards the conclusion that in contemporary conditions the growth of wealth, so far from being dependent on the ab-

* From *The General Theory of Employment, Interest and Money* by John Maynard Keynes. Reprinted by permission of Harcourt, Brace and Company, Inc.

stinence of the rich, as is commonly supposed, is more likely to be impeded by it. One of the chief social justifications of great inequality of wealth is, therefore, removed. I am not saying that there are no other reasons, unaffected by our theory, capable of justifying some measure of inequality in some circumstances. But it does dispose of the most important of the reasons why hitherto we have thought it prudent to move carefully. This particularly affects our attitude towards death duties; for there are certain justifications for inequality of incomes which do not apply equally to inequality of inheritances.

For my own part, I believe that there is social and psychological justification for significant inequalities of incomes and wealth, but not for such large disparities as exist to-day. There are valuable human activities which require the motive of money-making and the environment of private wealth-ownership for their full fruition. Moreover, dangerous human proclivities can be canalised into comparatively harmless channels by the existence of opportunities for money-making and private wealth, which, if they cannot be satisfied in this way, may find their outlet in cruelty, the reckless pursuit of personal power and authority, and other forms of self-aggrandisement. It is better that a man should tyrannise over his bank balance than over his fellow-citizens; and whilst the former is sometimes denounced as being but a means to the latter, sometimes at least it is an alternative. But it is not necessary for the stimulation of these activities and the satisfaction of these proclivities that the game should be played for such high stakes as at present. Much lower stakes will serve the purpose equally well, as soon as the players are accustomed to them. The task of transmuting human nature must not be confused with the task of managing it. Though in the ideal commonwealth men may have been taught or inspired or bred to take no interest in the stakes, it may still be wise and prudent statesmanship to allow the game to be played, subject to rules and limitations, so long as the average man, or even a significant section of the community, is in fact strongly addicted to the money-making passion.

II

There is, however, a second, much more fundamental inference from our argument which has a bearing on the future of inequalities of wealth; namely, our theory of the rate of interest. The justification for a moderately high rate of interest has been found hitherto in the necessity of providing a sufficient inducement to save. But we have shown that the extent of effective saving is necessarily determined by the scale of investment and that the scale of investment is promoted by a *low* rate of interest, provided that we do not attempt to stimulate it in this way beyond the point which corresponds to full employment. Thus it is to our best advantage to reduce the rate of interest to that point relatively to the schedule of the marginal efficiency of capital at which there is full employment.

There can be no doubt that this criterion will lead to a much lower rate of interest than has ruled hitherto; and, so far as one can guess at the schedules of the marginal efficiency of capital corresponding to increasing amounts of capital, the rate of interest is likely to fall steadily, if it should be practicable to maintain conditions of more or less continuous full employment—unless, indeed, there is an excessive change in the aggregate propensity to consume (including the State).

I feel sure that the demand for capital is strictly limited in the sense that it would not be difficult to increase the stock of capital up to a point where its marginal efficiency had fallen to a very low figure. This would not mean that the use of capital instruments would cost almost nothing, but only that the return from them would have to cover little more than their exhaustion by wastage and obsolescence together with some margin to cover risk and the exercise of skill and judgment. In short, the aggregate return from durable goods in the course of their life would, as in the case of short-lived goods, just cover their labour-costs of production *plus* an allowance for risk and the costs of skill and supervision.

Now, though this state of affairs would be quite compatible with some measure of individualism, yet it would mean the euthanasia of the rentier, and, consequently, the euthanasia of the cumulative oppressive power of the capitalist to exploit the scarcity-value of capital. Interest to-day rewards no genuine sacrifice, any more than does the rent of land. The owner of capital can obtain interest because capital is scarce, just as the owner of land can obtain rent because land is scarce. But whilst there may be intrinsic reasons for the scarcity of land, there are no intrinsic reasons for the scarcity of capital. An intrinsic reason for such scarcity, in the sense of a genuine sacrifice which could only be called forth by the offer of a reward in the shape of interest, would not exist, in the long run, except in the event of the individual propensity to consume proving to be of such a character that net saving in conditions of full employment comes to an end before capital has become sufficiently abundant. But even so, it will still be possible for communal saving through the agency of the State to be maintained at a level which will allow the growth of capital up to the point where it ceases to be scarce.

I see, therefore, the rentier aspect of capitalism as a transitional phase which will disappear when it has done its work. And with the disappearance of its rentier aspect much else in it besides will suffer a sea-change. It will be, moreover, a great advantage of the order of events which I am advocating, that the euthanasia of the rentier, of the functionless investor, will be nothing sudden, merely a gradual but prolonged continuance of what we have seen recently in Great Britain, and will need no revolution.

Thus we might aim in practice (there being nothing in this which is unattainable) at an increase in the volume of capital until it ceases to be scarce, so that the functionless investor will no longer receive a bonus; and at a scheme of direct taxation which allows the intelligence and determination and executive skill of the financier, the entrepreneur *et hoc genus omne* (who are certainly so fond of their craft that their labour could be obtained much cheaper than at present), to be harnessed to the service of the community on reasonable terms of reward.

At the same time we must recognise that only experience can show how far the common will, embodied in the policy of the State, ought to be directed to increasing and supplementing the inducement to invest; and how far it is safe to stimulate the average propensity to consume, without foregoing our aim of depriving capital of its scarcity-value within one or two generations. It may turn out that the propensity to consume will be so easily strengthened by the effects of a falling rate of interest, that full employment can be reached with a rate of accumulation little greater than at present. In this event a scheme for the higher taxation of large incomes and inheritances might be open to the objection that it would lead to full employment with a rate of accumulation which was reduced considerably below the current level. I must not be supposed to deny the possibility, or even the probability, of this outcome. For in such matters it is rash to predict how the average man will react to a changed environment. If, however, it should prove easy to secure an approximation to full employment with a rate of accumulation not much greater than at present, an outstanding problem will at least have been solved. And it would remain for separate decision on what scale and by what means it is right and reasonable to call on the living generation to restrict their consumption, so as to establish, in course of time, a state of full investment for their successors.

III

In some other respects the foregoing theory is moderately conservative in its implications. For whilst it indicates the vital importance of establishing certain central controls in matters which are now left in the main to individual initiative, there are wide fields of activity which are unaffected. The State will have to exercise a guiding influence on the propensity to consume partly through its scheme of taxation, partly by fixing the rate of interest, and partly, perhaps, in other ways. Furthermore, it seems unlikely that the influence of banking policy on the rate of interest will be sufficient by itself to determine an optimum rate of investment. I conceive, therefore, that a somewhat comprehensive socialisation of investment will prove the only means of securing an approximation to full employment; though this need not exclude all manner of compromises and of devices by which public authority will co-operate with private initiative. But beyond this no obvious case is made out for a system of State Socialism which would embrace most of the economic life of the community. It is not the ownership of the instruments of production which it is important for the State to assume. If the State is able to determine the aggregate amount of resources devoted to augmenting the instruments and the basic rate of reward to those who own them, it will have accomplished all that is necessary. Moreover, the necessary measures of socialisation can be introduced gradually and without a break in the general traditions of society.

Our criticism of the accepted classical theory of economics has consisted not so much in finding logical flaws in its analysis as in pointing out that its tacit assumptions are seldom or never satisfied, with the result that it cannot solve the economic problems of the actual world. But if our central controls succeed in establishing an aggregate volume of output corresponding to full employment as nearly as is practicable, the classical theory comes into its own again from this point onwards. If we suppose the volume of output to be given, *i.e.* to be determined by forces outside the classical scheme of thought, then there is no objection to be raised against the classical analysis of the manner in which private self-interest will determine what in particular is produced, in what proportions the factors of production will be combined to produce it, and how the value of the final product will be distributed between them. Again, if we have dealt otherwise with the problem of thrift, there is no objection to be raised against the modern classical theory as to the degree of consilience between private and public advantage in conditions of perfect and imperfect competition respectively. Thus, apart from the necessity of central controls to bring about an adjustment between the propensity to consume and the inducement to invest, there is no more reason to socialise economic life than there was before.

To put the point concretely, I see no reason to suppose that the existing system seriously misemploys the factors of production which are in use. There are, of course, errors of foresight; but these would not be avoided by centralising decisions. When 9,000,000 men are employed out of 10,000,000 willing and able to work, there is no evidence that the labour of these 9,000,000 men is misdirected. The complaint against the present system is not that these 9,000,000 men ought to be employed on different tasks, but that tasks should be available for the remaining 1,000,000 men. It is in determining the volume, not the direction, of actual employment that the existing system has broken down.

Thus I agree with Gesell that the result of filling in the gaps in the classical theory is not to dispose of the "Manchester System," but to indicate the nature of the environment which the free play of economic forces requires if it is to realise the full potentialities of production. The central controls necessary to ensure full employment will, of course, involve a large extension of the traditional functions of government. Furthermore, the modern classical theory has itself called attention to various conditions in which the free play of economic forces may need to be curbed or guided. But there will still remain a wide field for the exercise of private initiative and responsibility. Within this field the traditional advantages of individualism will still hold good.

Let us stop for a moment to remind ourselves what these advantages are. They are partly advantages of efficiency—the advantages of decentralisation and of the play of self-interest. The advantage to efficiency of the decentralisation of decisions and of individual responsibility is even greater, perhaps, than the nineteenth century supposed; and the reaction against the appeal to self-interest may have gone too far. But, above all, individualism, if it can be purged of its defects and its abuses, is the best safeguard of personal liberty in the sense that, compared with any other system, it greatly widens the field for the exercise of personal choice. It is also the best safeguard of the variety of life, which emerges precisely from this extended field of personal choice, and the loss of which is the greatest of all the losses of the homogeneous or totalitarian state. For this variety preserves the traditions which embody the most secure and successful choices of former generations; it colours the present with the diversification of its fancy; and, being the handmaid of experiment as well as of tradition and of fancy, it is the most powerful instrument to better the future.

Whilst, therefore, the enlargement of the functions of government, involved in the task of adjusting to one another the propensity to consume and the inducement to invest, would seem to a nineteenth-century publicist or to a contemporary American financier to be a terrific encroachment on individualism, I defend it, on the contrary, both as the only practicable means of avoiding the destruction of existing economic forms in their entirety and as the condition of the successful functioning of individual initiative.

For if effective demand is deficient, not only is the public scandal of wasted resources intolerable, but the individual enterpriser who seeks to bring these resources into action is operating with the odds loaded against him. The game of hazard which he plays is furnished with many zeros, so that the players *as a whole* will lose if they have the energy and hope to deal all the cards. Hitherto the increment of the world's wealth has fallen short of the aggregate of positive individual savings; and the difference has been made up by the losses of those whose courage and initiative have not been supplemented by exceptional skill or unusual good fortune. But if effective demand is adequate, average skill and average good fortune will be enough.

The authoritarian state systems of to-day seem to evolve the problem of unemployment at the expense of efficiency and of freedom. It is certain that the world will not much longer tolerate the unemployment which, apart from brief intervals of excitement, is associated—and, in my opinion, inevitably associated—with present-day capitalistic individualism. But it may be possible by a right analysis of the problem to cure the disease whilst preserving efficiency and freedom.

IV

I have mentioned in passing that the new system might be more favourable to peace than the old has been. It is worth while to repeat and emphasise that aspect.

War has several causes. Dictators and others such, to whom war offers, in expectation at least, a pleasurable excitement, find it easy to work on the natural bellicosity of their peoples. But, over and above this, facilitating their task of fanning the popular flame, are the economic causes of war, namely, the pressure of population and the competitive struggle for markets. It is the second factor, which probably played a predominant part in the nineteenth century, and might again, that is germane to this discussion.

I have pointed out in the preceding chapter that, under the system of domestic *laissez-faire* and an international gold standard such as was orthodox in the latter half of the nineteenth century, there was no means open to a government whereby to mitigate economic distress at home except through the competitive struggle for markets. For all measures helpful to a state of chronic or intermittent under-employment were ruled out, except measures to improve the balance of trade on income account.

Thus, whilst economists were accustomed to applaud the prevailing international system as furnishing the fruits of the international division of labour and harmonising at the same time the interests of different nations, there lay concealed a less benign influence; and those statesmen were moved by common sense and a correct apprehension of the true course of events, who believed that if a rich, old country were to neglect the struggle for markets its prosperity would droop and fail. But if nations can learn to provide themselves with full employment by their domestic policy (and, we must add, if they can also attain equilibrium in the trend of their population), there need be no important economic forces calculated to set the interest of one country against that of its neighbours. There would still be room for the international division of labour and for international lending in appropriate conditions. But there would no longer be a pressing motive why one country need force its wares on another or repulse the offerings of its neighbour, not because this was necessary to enable it to pay for what it wished to purchase, but with the express object of upsetting the equilibrium of payments so as to develop a balance of trade in its own favour. International trade would cease to be what it is, namely, a desperate expedient to maintain employment at home by forcing sales on foreign markets and restricting purchases, which, if successful, will merely shift the problem of unemployment to the neighbour which is worsted in the struggle, but a willing and unimpeded exchange of goods and services in conditions of mutual advantage.

V

Is the fulfilment of these ideas a visionary hope? Have they insufficient roots in the motives which govern the evolution of political society? Are the interests which they will thwart stronger and more obvious than those which they will serve?

I do not attempt an answer in this place. It would need a volume of a different character from this one to indicate even in outline the practical measures in which they might be gradually clothed. But if the ideas are correct—an hypothesis on which the author himself must necessarily base what he writes—it would be a mistake, I predict, to dispute their potency over a period of time. At the present moment people are unusually expectant of a more fundamental diagnosis; more particularly ready to receive it; eager to try it out, if it should be even plausible. But apart from this contemporary mood, the ideas of economists and political philosophers, both when they are right and when they are wrong, are more powerful than is commonly understood. Indeed the world is ruled by little else. Practical men, who believe themselves to be quite exempt from any intellectual influences, are usually the slaves of some defunct economist. Madmen in authority, who hear voices in the air, are distilling their frenzy from some academic scribbler of a few years back. I am sure that the power of vested interests is vastly exaggerated compared with the gradual encroachment of ideas. Not, indeed, immediately, but after a certain interval; for in the field of economic and political philosophy there are not many who are influenced by new theories after they are twenty-five or thirty years of age, so that the ideas which civil servants and politicians and even agitators apply to current events are not likely to be the newest. But, soon or late, it is ideas, not vested interests, which are dangerous for good or evil.

JOSEPH ALOIS SCHUMPETER

(1883–1950)

Joseph Schumpeter was born in Moravia and educated in law and economics at the University of Vienna. After a varied career as professor, cabinet minister, banker, and jurist, he settled down to a teaching post at the University of Bonn in 1925. The coming of Hitler caused him to migrate again, this time to Harvard, where he remained as professor of economics until his death.

Schumpeter's output was voluminous, and some of his more important books and articles, his great *Epochen der Dogmen- und Methodengeschichte* (*History of Economic Thought,* 1914) for example, have not yet been made available in English. To attempt to place him in any school of economics is fruitless, since his genius had so many facets that he was a master of almost all the variants of the science. To Schumpeter, there were only two schools of economics—good economics and bad economics. However, his most important works, *Theorie der Wirtschaftlichen Entwicklung* (*The Theory of Economic Development,* 1911) and *Business Cycles* (1939), are in the field of what may be called business-cycle theory. Like Wesley Mitchell, Schumpeter believed that the study of the cycle was the best way of gaining an insight into the entire capitalistic process. Unlike Mitchell, he was willing both to theorize before all the statistics had been gathered and to use models and successive approximations as theoretical tools. He went beyond Keynes in that he was interested not merely in a theory of employment and output as a whole but in the entire picture of the capitalistic process. In his *Capitalism, Socialism, and Democracy* (1942) he regarded pure capitalism as disappearing because of the collapse of its supporting institutions, to be supplanted first by a mixed economy and then by socialism. Yet he was neither a Marxist nor a socialist. Instead he was an objective scientific investigator, with no particular axe to grind. He was no man's pupil, and he founded no school.

Schumpeter's great theoretical concept is that cycles result from innovations and successive adaptations to innovations by the business system under capitalism. To Schumpeter the innovation is not necessarily an invention in the patent-office sense. It may be a new way of doing old things or a new combination of factors. In his model the innovation is introduced from the outside, and the resultant effects on stationary-flow equilibrium are noted. In his abstraction, only one cause of change is allowed to operate, but he nowhere claimed that innovation was the only cause of change or that disturbance must come from outside the model.

The emergence of successful innovations causes a "wave" or "herd" of new businessmen to plunge into the new field with the expectation of profit, and these mass rushes stir up secondary waves of business activity. Furthermore, Schumpeter emphasized the role of capitalistic credit institutions in financing innovations and creating mass purchasing power.

In 1911 Schumpeter was optimistic about the growth capacity of capitalism; in his model each new equilibrium position resulting from new adaptation to innovation was at a higher level than at the last depression phase of the cycle. In his *Capitalism, Socialism, and Democracy,* some thirty years later, he showed the effect that the Great Depression had had on his thinking. In this work, he believed capitalism to be dying because of the crumbling of two of its most important walls—freedom of contract and ownership of property in the corporeal sense.

The following selections from some of Schumpeter's more important writings give us the essence of his method and outlook.

THE EXPLANATION OF THE BUSINESS CYCLE *

I always thought, and still think, that in order to find out whether or not cycles are a phenomenon *sui generis,* clearly standing out as such from the rest of industrial fluctuations and arising from *within* the economic system, we ought, in the first instance, to assume the absence of outside disturbances—non-economic ones, or economic ones which cannot be produced or avoided by economic action, both of which we are going to call "casual"—acting on the system. We shall, then, see either that the economic system *never* (and not only not under "static" conditions) evolves that particular kind of fluctuations of itself, in which case outside disturbances *must* be looked upon as responsible for them; or else that the economic system would of itself display "cyclical" movement, in which case we should have to recognise the presence of a problem of a "normal cycle"; we should, moreover, have to conclude that the whole of purely economic phenomena cannot be exhausted by means of the "static" apparatus; and we should, finally, have to look upon the influence of outside disturbances as a fifth set of problems within the genus of industrial fluctuations, which would, indeed, also form part of any comprehensive survey of all that happens *in* cycles (because outside disturbances of some kind never fail to arise and always must react upon the cyclical movement), but which would have to be kept aloof in a theory of causation, in a sense which I hope is now quite clear. . . .

We only need, however, look at the way in which any disturbing element acts in order to be confronted with a distinction, both natural and important, which points in our direction. If, say, a war breaks out and upsets existing equilibrium, people can try to adapt themselves to altered conditions by infinitesimal steps, reducing, for instance, their consumption or, in their business, accepting the higher takings they get and paying their higher expenses, adjusting the quantity of their product accordingly. They may not be able to so adapt themselves and perish. They will, in so adapting themselves, be of course subject to all sorts of error. Still, we have here a well-defined type of behaviour admirably fitting in with "static" theory; and a type of behaviour, too, which we have before our eyes in real life, *for this is the only way in which the majority of people do act and are capable of acting.* But however high we may put the explanatory value of error and friction, this is emphatically *not* the way in which booms arise, and *not* the kind of events of which booms *fundamentally* consist, as will be seen as we go on.

There evidently is another way of reacting, clearly distinguishable from this, although shading off into this on the border. People can also drop their attitude of passive adaptation, they can react by doing new things or things in a new way, incompatible with the fundamental arrangements that exist. The clerk, instead of reducing consumption, can go into business

* From "The Explanation of the Business Cycle," *Economica,* December, 1927, pp. 290–299, 304–308.

for himself; the manufacturer can change his cotton-mill into an ammunition factory. Some people—never all nor ever more than a minority—do that. This is a different kind of behaviour and not within reach of marginal variations; and it is productive of different consequences.

Now, on the one hand, although, if distinguishable, these two kinds of reaction are both of them invariably set into motion by any "initiating impulse," it is only the first of them which can be said to follow automatically from the outside impulse by virtue of a causal connection exhaustively described—and determined—by theory. The second kind of reactions is not gripped by our analytic machine—although of course their consequences are—unless we "put a new arm" to it, which is precisely what I have been trying to do since 1912; and they cannot, with any certainty, be relied on to happen, or be predicted to happen, in any definite way in practice: they *could* fail to show up, in which case there would be no boom; whilst *if* they show up, it is never the *mere* occurrence of the disturbance which produces them, but *a certain attitude of certain people.*

Again this attitude, on the other hand, exists and shows itself quite independently of the presence of any disturbance. To avoid misunderstanding—of course, the type of behaviour we are glancing at now always has to do with a given environment, and environment always includes some sort of disturbance. But if there were not the one disturbance there would be another. And if there be none, the "impulse" would be *created* by our type. There is always scope for this. Industrial and commercial methods are never perfect in any sense except relatively to the average light and energy of the business community. Knowledge—scientific and other—is always far in advance of actual practice, not only in things which it could not, or not yet, pay to carry out, but also in things which it would. Results of invention—not only, again, impracticable ones—are always offering themselves, but may lie unused indefinitely. Why? Because doing what has not yet stood the test of experience is no mere act of ordinary business practice, such as we primarily think of when applying our theoretic apparatus, and such as the average man of business can be relied on to do promptly, but something else which wants an *attitude* and an *aptitude,* different indeed from what is required for the act of invention, but equally rare—an attitude and aptitude more of character—"power," "leadership"—than of intellect. Hence there are always great prizes to be won by those who have them: the business community does not, and cannot, proceed to new methods, as it were, *in line:* some rush ahead, others lag behind; and the latter are forced onwards or ruined by competition setting in from those who lead. Nor are these things mere frictions such as theory can afford to neglect; fundamental phenomena of modern industrial life depend on them for explanation—the business cycle among them, for the explanation of the nature of which this set of facts—which lies outside the domain of static theory but still within the economic system itself—is both necessary and sufficient, as I hope to show. Meanwhile, we only want to point out that willingness and capacity to do new things will always and necessarily find, or be able to create, the opportunity on which to act, being, in fact, itself the one fundamental "initial impulse" of industrial and commercial change.

In this sense, therefore, I claim "independence" of the cycle and of those booms and depressions *which form the normal cycle* of impulses from without: in the face of the facts, first, that such events do also lead to booms and depressions displaying a very similar mechanism and very similar features; second, that every one of the "normal cycles" is, as a matter of fact, powerfully influenced and coloured by some disturbances from without—*any* given situation being subject to such disturbances, which may help on, or rein in, any given upward or downward movement, and offer, as it were, part of the material of which the fabric of every boom consists, but which, if absent, would be supplemented by other material always at hand.

I also submit that this distinction of phenomena, which in reality always go on together and react upon one another, is no matter of theoretic nicety. For to the distinction in theory corresponds a distinction in reality. If we are furnished with sufficient details of a case, we are always able to tell whether it belongs to the static or non-static sphere—a movement of the rate of interest, for instance. Nor is this all. It is of very considerable practical importance to distinguish between booms of different nature, and it makes a great difference both to diagnosis and to remedial policy, whether we have to do, say, with a crisis of deflation or with the depression of a normal cycle. Neglect of this distinction vitiates, I think, part of what I otherwise consider most valuable results of recent research.

Our fourth proposition is the one due to Juglar: "La cause unique de la dépression c'est la prospérité." That is to say, that the phenomena which we have got in the habit of calling "depression" are no irregular heap of disturbances, but can be understood as the reaction of business life to the situation created by the boom or, more precisely, as the movement of business life towards a new state of equilibrium conforming to the data created by the boom—such being what I may term "normal" depression as distinguished from "abnormal" havoc, incidentally wrought by panic, and productive of consequences of its own. It is important to note that by reaction I do not mean a psychological one, although this, too, must always play an important, though secondary, part, a part, that is, which is secondary not only in importance but also as to its position in the chain of causation. The new data, created by the boom and upsetting all the bases of industrial and commercial calculation, are an "objective" fact. As such they enforce "objective" adjustments. And these and the losses they entail would account for what happens in the period of depression, even if nobody lost his head or turned, by zoological miracle, into a "bear."

It may not be superfluous to ask the reader to bear in mind two more points: we should not, of course, be justified in applying the same sort of reasoning to the boom. There are authorities who barely escape this sort of *perpetuum mobile* reasoning, according to which there would be booms because there are depressions, and depressions because there are booms. This reasoning derives some support from the fact that depressions, by lowering prices of materials, machines, labour and "going concerns," affords the opportunity of buying cheaply. I need not stay to show why this support is insufficient. But I want to emphasise that we are doing nothing of the sort.

As will be readily seen, moreover, *all* theories of the cycle—including those of, say, Marx, Hawtrey, Pigou—are at liberty to accept this proposition. Whatever their explanations may be, they all consider what happens in depression to be the consequence of something which happened in the boom, or, anyhow, before the crisis or depression itself.

We shall, therefore, have explained the cycle when we have explained those booms which are so clearly before our eyes ever since (at least) the Napoleonic wars, which we can so well distinguish from other fluctuations, and in which we can, I think, equally well distinguish what they owe to their own and to extraneous impulses. Those booms consist in the carrying out of innovations in the industrial and commercial organism. By innovations I understand such changes of the combinations of the factors of production as cannot be effected by infinitesimal steps or variations on the margin. They consist primarily in changes in methods of production and transportation, or in changes in industrial organisation, or in the production of a new article, or in the opening up of new markets or of new sources of material. *The recurring periods of prosperity of the cyclical movement are the form progress takes in capitalistic society.*

By saying this we mean to state a fact requiring both proof and explanation. Whilst we hope to be able to contribute, by our two last propositions, something towards the latter, it is impossible here to satisfy the reader as to the former. . . . The reader needs only to make the experiment. If he cares to survey the industrial history from, say, 1760 onwards, he will discover two things; he will find, first, that very many booms are unmistakably characterised by revolutionary changes in some branch of industry which, in consequence, *leads* the boom—railways for instance in the 'forties, or steel in the 'eighties, or electricity in the 'nineties—and that, if he will take a bird's-eye view of our industrial organism, he will be able to follow up every one of its leading features to a source originating in a boom. And he will find, secondly, that *all* the booms which he may find himself unable so to characterise can be shown, by other and independent reasons, to be casual phenomena outside the cyclical movement and distinguishable from it, such as the booms ending in the collapses of 1793, 1799, 1810 and 1922, which, to my mind, lead to the most palpable mistakes both of analysis and policy if mixed up with the cyclical ones. It is equally important—and possible—to distinguish cyclical depressions from mere "breaks" such as the crises of 1866 and 1901—even as a doctor must distinguish between the going down of the temperature of his patient owing to his progress towards health, and the breaks the curve of temperature may occasionally display for all sorts of reasons.

Further corroboration is afforded our proposition by the fact, brought out beyond doubt by statistical investigation and quite universally admitted, of the prominence of the constructional trades, both as to priority in time and as to amplitude of fluctuation, within the events of the cycle. I do not know one modern writer who would deny it. But if the fact be undeniable, it evidently fits in admirably with our thesis: it could not indeed prove it, for there is no such thing as statistical proof. But it is eminently apt to serve as verification; for it derives a very natural explanation by our thesis, which alone, in fact, gives it its proper significance and sheds on it its true light. . . .

Innovations would be powerless to produce booms, if they went on continuously in time. By this we mean, that if it were possible to choose units of time such that to each of them would correspond one new thing done—it need of course be no "invention" carried out—then the disturbances which would still be caused would be small as compared with the whole of the industrial life of a nation, so that they would be capable of being continuously absorbed—just as simple "growth" is—without producing consequences important enough to show. There would be no cycles, though still, of course, irregular disturbances owing to wars, earthquakes, and the like.

Therefore, the problem of causation of the cycles reduces itself to the question (the answer to which contains what we shall call in a sense not now admitting any more of ambiguity, the only "cause" of cycles):

Why is it that industrial and commercial change is not continuously distributed in time, but proceeds by leaps which, it is easy to understand, must fundamentally alter the bases of calculation and upset the existing equilibrium beyond the possibility of all people adapting themselves successfully by marginal variations?

It is simply because as soon as any step in a new direction has been successfully made, it at once and thereby becomes easy to follow. Business life, like any other, consists mainly of routine work based on well-tried experience, partly ancestral; only within the boundaries of routine do people function both promptly and similarly; it is only to routine work that received theory applies; outside routine most people find it difficult—and are often unable to act; those who can are rare and therefore not subject to competitive conditions, whence the phenomenon of profit; but whenever in a given situation (which theory has the right and the duty to assume to be in the first instance "static") new things have been successfully done by some, others can, on the one hand, copy their behaviour in the same line—whence prominence of one industry at the time—and on the other hand, get the courage to do similar things in other lines, the spell being broken and many details of the behaviour of the first leaders being applicable outside their own field of action. And therefore the first success draws other people in its wake and finally crowds of them, which is what the boom consists in.

I beg leave to ask the reader not to be deterred by what must necessarily look like a highly abstract if not one-sided view of the thing. Of course this is *no* theory of the cycle, if we understand by this a complete explanation of all that happens. This can only be found in a reasoned history of industrial life. It is only the backbone of it. . . .

There is . . . the fact of booms as well as depressions becoming milder —the last real "crash" in Europe having taken place in 1873. Now there are many ways of accounting for this, all of them compatible with our theory. But there is one which we can, I think, directly derive from it, viz., the steadying influence of great units, especially of trusts. As the industrial units tend to grow, the management tends more and more to be divorced from ownership. Therefore, whereas the rising men had, in the times of our fathers, typically to found new businesses and to get their things done by under-selling the old ones, the rising men of a later period are not confined to this method, but can and do conquer leading positions in the new big units now existing, and impose on them their plans. It is evident that, as far as this is being done and as far as, consequently, the new things tend more and more to grow out of the units already existing, the simple change of the managers does what formerly had to be done by a struggle in the markets, conducive to bankruptcies and other well-known features of depressions; and this of course tends to mitigate them and to prevent many losses. . . .

The features of depression explain themselves not wholly by equilibrium being upset by new enterprise pouring forth new products at prices with which all firms cannot compete, and driving up prices of means of production beyond what they can afford to pay, nor even by the secondary waves, which it would be easy to insert in our picture. . . .

It is only the fact that society is not "static," that the industrial and commercial process is always being reorganised and revolutionised, that accounts for the phenomenon of a sort of money which is indeed still a "ticket"—in J. Stuart Mill's sense—admitting holders to the "national heap" of goods, but not or not yet also a "certificate" representing productive service rendered. Although the device once evolved will then serve many purposes, it would never have been evolved without the innovators', the entrepreneurs' demand for mobile resources, which always remains its *raison d'être*.

. . . Just as in strict theory there is no other demand for the creation *ad hoc* of purchasing power but that of the entrepreneur, there would in strict theory be no other sources from which to satisfy it but such creation. It is not so in practice because that constant revolution of industrial and commercial methods is constantly yielding profits, the first, most natural and most important source of "mobile resources" or of "savings," which however would not exist in a static state, from which we have to start in order to avoid explaining things by what are their consequences; nor would there be in a static state nearly as much motive to save out of other resources besides profits as there actually is. The analytic value of this proposition does not depend on what important or unimportant rôle "creation of credit" may play in a given country at a given time. Situations are possible of great wealth and little activity in which this rôle would be nil. To point to such, or nearly such, situations would be easy but irrelevant.

But as the innovators' or entrepreneurs' demand for credit could not, in the highly abstract case we are considering, be met by *other* resources, so it always *could* be met by this. That is to say, saving, though still of primary importance, turns out to be a shade less important than one would think. "Mobile resources" are not necessarily the result of previous saving, just as economic progress is not *primarily* the result of an increase in factors of production, but the result of applying the quantities of them already existing to ever new ends and by ever changing methods. As we have seen, this is done by withdrawing them from the uses they are serving and the persons who manage them, in order to hand them over to those who will use them better, by means of purchasing power created in favour of the latter and of a consequent rise in prices which cuts down the demand of the former. It remains true, as Ricardo knew, and as we do not deny, that no wealth can be created by "banking operations." It even remains true, although in a sense not quite natural, that productive forces must be saved before there can be new production. But those "banking operations" are an important device for bringing about a better arrangement of productive forces; and if saving there be it is not the usual sort of saving, but what we may term "forced saving."

It is not possible here to unfold all the applications by which this analysis lights up many points of the theory of money, credit, interest and other matters, which cannot, I submit, be dealt with satisfactorily without it. I only wish to show or rather hint at how it links up with the theory of the cycle.

The periods of prosperity or booms being the periods in which "innovations" in, or reorganisations of, the productive process are mainly taken in hand, they consequently are the periods of creation of new purchasing power as, in fact, is shown by statistics. This, and not simply fluctuation of the "K" in the Marshall-Pigou-Keynes formula, accounts for the rise of prices in every boom, which could hardly be explained otherwise. There may be a lag because of the presence of accumulated stock, and a rise in articles of consumption before a rise in the *rate* of wages, because of the presence, at the beginning, of unemployment. This is why the Spiethoff index is so much better than some others, but this does not alter any fundamentals.

The periods of depression, being typically the periods in which the changes in the productive organisms, especially those embodied in new industrial plants which now have got into working order—the theoretical turning-point—begin to make themselves felt and to exert their pressure on the rest of the community, are consequently periods of deflation. This explains the downward movement of prices we observe. It is, first, deflation of the sort we have been describing as self-deflation. But it is, naturally, aggravated by what I may term autonomous deflation by frightened banks, who not only see and expect difficulties arising with their debtors but also anticipate difficulties with depositors and sources of rediscount. Here, too, there may be lags through producers trying to keep prices up and through frozen credits defying the endeavours to contract them, but here, too, this does not affect the basic argument, although it very much does affect the situation.

No more need be said about the function which this movement of general prices—the upward one as well as the downward one—actually fulfils. It is clear enough. Nor need we stay to explain how far and why we are unable to accept Mr. Hawtrey's dictum by which he so gallantly exposed himself to attack, viz., that the cycle is a "purely monetary phenomenon," which most undoubtedly it is not. We rather think it our duty to explain how far we do agree with him.

We agree with him, first, in recognising that the fundamental cause, whilst in its nature independent of the machinery of money and credit, could not without it produce the particular kind of effects it does. Booms and consequently depressions are not the work of banks: their "cause" is a non-monetary one and entrepreneurs' demand is the initiating cause even of so much of the cycle as can be said to be added by the act of banks. But booms and depressions would not without banks be what they are, and it remains utterly misleading to say, as has been said ever since Fullarton, that banks are only following the lead of demand and unable "to force their money on people"; for it lies with them to satisfy *this* and to create *additional* demand in a sense quite different from the sense in which it would be true of sellers of a commodity: the latter acting under the pressure of cost which is absent, within limits, in the case of the former. So there is for banks a range of freedom of action to which nothing corresponds in other branches of business: this range would exist even without national or international understandings which, however, powerfully extend it.

It follows—which is indeed a second point of agreement—that banks can and do, even without knowing it, exert influence on the pace of prosperity and depression, although . . . more on the former than on the latter; and they do more than this. They not only finance innovators' or entrepreneurs' demand, but also the demand of other people, who simply want more credit because they see prices rise. They are even specially willing to give in to those people, for they are their old customers. Hence, they help the coming up of a secondary wave of the boom to which, although it also increases forced savings, it is impossible to attribute the function of the "primary wave." Other waves may and often do follow, and among them the great wave of mere speculative punting, all of which makes prices rise still more. It is these things which make up the physiognomy of both boom and depression, and which we have looked to when warning the reader not to judge our theory merely from what we said in the first part of this paper. They are, in fact, the bridge which leads from what we consider the keystone to the complexities of the "real" phenomenon. . . .

We also agree as to the practical possibility of stopping any normal boom by a proper management of credit. It may be difficult, and discount policy may be insufficient to effect it except in quiet times. Into this we cannot enter; but it is surely possible. This does not imply indeed that it is in any sense desirable. But inasmuch as I am strongly under the impression that these discussions and the theoretic views of the parties to them are influenced by views held as to policy, and that such views are suspected to be at the bottom of every theory propounded, I am most anxious to say that I do not wish to advocate or fight any policy whatever. And although I feel debarred from entering upon questions of desirability of measures by the purely scientific character of my argument—the mixing up of which with practical policy I should indeed look upon as a misdemeanour—I still wish, in order to appease suspicions, to say that if I think that the cycle cannot be successfully held to be merely an "evil," serving no social interests whatever, I do not mean thereby to imply that it is to be complimented on the way it fulfils what we have seen to be its "function." It may well be argued that it does its work at very great costs, that these costs might be saved or reduced by proper arrangements and that a policy of keeping the level of prices stable might do but little harm to improvement, while greatly reining-in secondary phenomena which are universally (or nearly so) felt to be evils and are the main source of error, losses, unemployment, and so on. Some slackening down of improvement might even be held to be no more than a reasonable price to pay for benefits such as these.

THE INSTABILITY OF CAPITALISM *

STABILITY AND PROGRESS

We see that there is, indeed, one element in the capitalist process, embodied in the type and function of the entrepreneur, which will, *by its mere working and from within*—in the absence of all outside impulses or disturbances and even of "growth"—destroy any equilibrium that may have established itself or been in process of being established; that the action of that element is not amenable to description by means of infinitesimal steps; and that it produces the cyclical "waves" which are essentially the form "progress" takes in competitive capitalism and could be discovered by the theory of it, if we did not know of them by experience. But by a mechanism at work in, and explaining the features of, periods

* From "The Instability of Capitalism," *Economic Journal,* September, 1928, pp. 383–386.

of depression, a new equilibrium always emerges, or tends to emerge, which absorbs the results of innovation carried out in the preceding periods of prosperity. The new elements find their equilibrium proportions; the old ones adapt themselves or drop out; incomes are rearranged; prosperity inflation is corrected by automatic self-deflation through the repayment of credits out of profits, through the new consumers' goods entering the markets and through saving stepping into the place of "created" credits. So the instabilities, which arise from the process of innovation, tend to right themselves, and do not go on accumulating. And we may phrase the result we reach in our terminology by saying that there is, through instability of the *System,* no economic instability of the *Order.*

The instability due to what we conceive to be the basic factor of purely economic change is, however, of very different importance in the two historic types of capitalism. . . .

Innovation in competitive capitalism is typically embodied in the foundation of new firms—the main lever, in fact, of the rise of industrial families; improvement is forced on the whole branch by the processes of underselling and of withdrawing from them their means of production, workmen and so on shifting to the new firms; all of which not only means a large amount of disturbance as an incident, but is also effective in bringing about the result, and to change "internal" economies into "external" ones, only *as far as* it means disturbance. The new processes do not, and generally cannot, evolve out of the old firms, but place themselves side by side with them and attack them. Furthermore, for a firm of comparatively small size, which is no power on the money market and cannot afford scientific departments or experimental production and so on, innovation in commercial or technical practice is an extremely risky and difficult thing, requiring supernormal energy and courage to embark upon. But as soon as the success is before everyone's eyes, everything is made very much easier by this very fact. It can now, with much-diminished difficulty, be copied, even improved upon, and a whole crowd invariably does copy it—which accounts for the leaps and bounds of progress as well as for setbacks, carrying in their wake not only the primary disturbance, inherent to the process, but a whole string of secondary ones and *possibilities,* although no more than possibilities, of recurrent catastrophes or crises.

All this is different in "trustified" capitalism. Innovation is, in this case, not any more embodied *typically* in new firms, but goes on, within the big units now existing, largely independently of individual persons. It meets with much less friction, as failure in any particular case loses its dangers, and tends to be carried out as a matter of course on the advice of specialists. Conscious policy towards demand and taking a long-time view towards investment becomes possible. Although credit creation still plays a rôle, both the power to accumulate reserves and the direct access to the money market tend to reduce the importance of this element in the life of a trust—which, incidentally, accounts for the phenomenon of prosperity coexisting with stable, or nearly stable, prices which we have had the opportunity of witnessing in the United States 1923–1926. It is easy to see that the three causes alluded to, whilst they accentuated the waves in competitive, must tend to soften them down in trustified, capitalism. Progress becomes "automatised," increasingly impersonal and decreasingly a matter of leadership and individual initiative. This amounts to a fundamental change in many respects, some of which reach far out of the sphere of things economic. It means the passing out of existence of a system of selection of leaders which had the unique characteristic that success in *rising* to a position and success in *filling* it were essentially the same thing—as were success of the firm and success of the man in charge—and its being replaced by another more akin to the principles of appointment or election, which characteristically divorce success of the concern from success of the man, and call, just as political elections do, for aptitudes in a candidate for, say, the presidency of a combine, which have little to do with the aptitudes of a good president. There is an Italian saying, "Who enters the conclave as prospective pope, will leave it as a cardinal," which well expresses what we mean. The types which rise, and the types which are kept under, in a trustified society are different from what they are in a competitive society, and the change is spreading rapidly to motives, stimuli and styles of life. For our purpose, however, it is sufficient to recognise that the only fundamental cause of instability inherent to the capitalist system is losing in importance as time goes on, and may even be expected to disappear.

Instead of summing up a very fragmentary argument, I wish to emphasise once more, in concluding, that no account whatsoever has been taken of any but purely economic facts and problems. Our diagnosis is, therefore, no more sufficient as a basis for prediction than a doctor's diagnosis to the effect that a man has no cancer is a sufficient basis for the prediction that he will go on living indefinitely. Capitalism is, on the contrary, in so obvious a process of transformation into something else, that it is not the fact, but only the interpretation of this fact, about which it is possible to disagree. Towards this interpretation I have wished to contribute a negative result. But it may be well, in order to avoid misunderstanding, to state expressly what I believe would be the positive result of a more ambitious diagnostic venture, if I may presume to do so in one short and imperfect sentence: Capitalism, whilst economically stable, and even gaining in stability, creates, by rationalising the human mind, a mentality and a style of life incompatible with its own fundamental conditions, motives and social institutions, and will be changed, although not by economic necessity and probably even at some sacrifice of economic welfare, into an order of things which it will be merely matter of taste and terminology to call Socialism or not.

CRUMBLING WALLS *

THE OBSOLESCENCE OF THE ENTREPRENEURIAL FUNCTION

In our discussion of the theory of vanishing investment opportunity, a reservation was made in favor of the possibility that the economic wants of humanity might some day be so completely satisfied that little motive would be left to push productive effort still further ahead. Such a state of satiety is no doubt very far off even if we keep within the present scheme of wants; and if we take account of the fact that, as higher standards of life are attained, these wants automatically expand and new wants emerge or are created, satiety becomes a flying goal, particularly if we include leisure among consumers' goods. However, let us glance at that possibility, assuming, still more unrealistically, that methods of production have reached a state of perfection which does not admit of further improvement.

A more or less stationary state would ensue. Capitalism, being essentially an evolutionary process, would become atrophic. There would be nothing left for entrepreneurs to do. They would find themselves in much the same situation as generals would in a society perfectly sure of permanent peace. Profits and along with profits the rate of interest would converge toward zero. The bourgeois strata that live on profits and interest would tend to disappear. The management of industry and trade would become a matter of current administration, and the personnel would unavoidably acquire the characteristics of a bureaucracy. Socialism of a very sober type would almost automatically come into being. Human energy would turn away from business. Other than economic pursuits would attract the brains and provide the adventure.

For the calculable future this vision is of no importance. But all the greater importance attaches to the fact that many of the effects on the structure of society and on the organization of the productive process that we might expect from an approximately complete satisfaction of wants or from absolute technological perfection can also be expected from a development that is clearly observable already. Progress itself may be mechanized as well as the management of a stationary economy, and this mechanization of progress may affect entrepreneurship and capitalist society nearly as much as the cessation of economic progress would. In order to see this it is only necessary to restate, first, what the entrepreneurial function consists in and, secondly, what it means for bourgeois society and the survival of the capitalist order.

We have seen that the function of entrepreneurs is to reform or revolutionize the pattern of production by exploiting an invention or, more generally, an untried technological possibility for producing a new commodity or producing an old one in a new way, by opening up a new source of supply of materials or a new outlet for products, by reorganizing

* From *Capitalism, Socialism, and Democracy* (New York and London, Harper & Brothers. Copyright, 1942, by Joseph A. Schumpeter).

an industry and so on. Railroad construction in its earlier stages, electrical power production before the First World War, steam and steel, the motorcar, colonial ventures afford spectacular instances of a large genus which comprises innumerable humbler ones—down to such things as making a success of a particular kind of sausage or toothbrush. This kind of activity is primarily responsible for the recurrent "prosperities" that revolutionize the economic organism and the recurrent "recessions" that are due to the disequilibrating impact of the new products or methods. To undertake such new things is difficult and constitutes a distinct economic function, first, because they lie outside the routine tasks which everybody understands and, secondly, because the environment resists in many ways that vary, according to social conditions, from simple refusal either to finance or to buy a new thing, to physical attack on the man who tries to produce it. To act with confidence beyond the range of familiar beacons and to overcome that resistance requires aptitudes that are present in only a small fraction of the population and that define the entrepreneurial type as well as the entrepreneurial function. This function does not essentially consist in either inventing anything or otherwise creating the conditions which the enterprise exploits. It consists in getting things done.

This social function is already losing importance and is bound to lose it at an accelerating rate in the future even if the economic process itself of which entrepreneurship was the prime mover went on unabated. For, on the one hand, it is much easier now than it has been in the past to do things that lie outside familiar routine—innovation itself is being reduced to routine. Technological progress is increasingly becoming the business of teams of trained specialists who turn out what is required and make it work in predictable ways. The romance of earlier commercial adventure is rapidly wearing away, because so many more things can be strictly calculated that had of old to be visualized in a flash of genius.

On the other hand, personality and will power must count for less in environments which have become accustomed to economic change—best instanced by an incessant stream of new consumers' and producers' goods —and which, instead of resisting, accept it as a matter of course. . . .

THE DESTRUCTION OF THE INSTITUTIONAL FRAMEWORK OF CAPITALIST SOCIETY

. . . The capitalist process in much the same way in which it destroyed the institutional framework of feudal society also undermines its own.

. . . The very success of capitalist enterprise paradoxically tends to impair the prestige or social weight of the class primarily associated with it and . . . the giant unit of control tends to oust the bourgeoisie from the function to which it owed that social weight. The corresponding change in the meaning, and the incidental loss in vitality, of the institutions of the bourgeois world and of its typical attitudes are easy to trace.

On the one hand, the capitalist process unavoidably attacks the economic standing ground of the small producer and trader. What it did to the pre-capitalist strata it also does—and by the same competitive mechanism—to the lower strata of capitalist industry. Here of course Marx scores. It is true that the facts of industrial concentration do not quite live up to the ideas the public is being taught to entertain about it. The process has gone less far and is less free from setbacks and compensatory tendencies than one would gather from many a popular exposition. In particular, large-scale enterprise not only annihilates but also, to some extent, creates space for the small producing, and especially trading, firm. Also, in the case of the peasants and farmers, the capitalist world has at last proved both willing and able to pursue an expensive but on the whole effective policy of conservation. In the long run, however, there can be little doubt about the fact we are envisaging, or about its consequences. Outside of the agrarian field, moreover, the bourgeoisie has shown but little awareness of the problem [1] or its importance for the survival of the capitalist order. The profits to be made by rationalizing the organization of production and especially by cheapening the tortuous way of commodities from the factory to the ultimate consumer are more than the mind of the typical businessman can resist.

Now it is important to realize precisely what these consequences consist in. A very common type of social criticism which we have already met laments the "decline of competition" and equates it to the decline of capitalism because of the virtues it attributes to competition and the vices it attributes to modern industrial "monopolies." In this schema of interpretation, monopolization plays the role of arteriosclerosis and reacts upon the fortunes of the capitalist order through increasingly unsatisfactory economic performance. We have seen the reasons for rejecting this view. Economically neither the case for competition nor the case against concentration of economic control is anything like as strong as this argument implies. And, whether weak or strong, it misses the salient point. Even if the giant concerns were all managed so perfectly as to call forth applause from the angels in heaven, the political consequences of concentration would still be what they are. The political structure of a nation is profoundly affected by the elimination of a host of small and medium-sized firms the owner-managers of which, together with their dependents, henchmen and connections, count quantitatively at the polls and have a hold on what we may term the foreman class that no management of a large unit can ever have; the very foundation of private property and free contracting wears away in a nation in which its most vital, most concrete, most meaningful types disappear from the moral horizon of the people.

On the other hand, the capitalist process also attacks its own institutional framework—let us continue to visualize "property" and "free contracting" as *partes pro toto*—within the precincts of the big units. Ex-

[1] Although some governments did; the government of imperial Germany did much to fight this particular kind of rationalization, and there is now a strong tendency to do the same in this country.

cepting the cases that are still of considerable importance in which a corporation is practically owned by a single individual or family, the figure of the proprietor and with it the specifically proprietary interest have vanished from the picture. There are the salaried executives and all the salaried managers and submanagers. There are the big stockholders. And then there are the small stockholders. The first group tends to acquire the employee attitude and rarely if ever identifies itself with the stockholding interest even in the most favorable cases, i.e., in the cases in which it identifies itself with the interest of the concern as such. The second group, even if it considers its connection with the concern as permanent and even if it actually behaves as financial theory would have stockholders behave, is at one remove from both the functions and the attitudes of an owner. As to the third group, small stockholders often do not care much about what for most of them is but a minor source of income and, whether they care or not, they hardly ever bother, unless they or some representatives of theirs are out to exploit their nuisance value; being often very ill used and still more often thinking themselves ill used, they almost regularly drift into an attitude hostile to "their" corporations, to big business in general and, particularly when things look bad, to the capitalist order as such. No element of any of those three groups into which I schematized the typical situation unconditionally takes the attitude characteristic of that curious phenomenon, so full of meaning and so rapidly passing, that is covered by the term Property.

Freedom of contracting is in the same boat. In its full vitality it meant individual contracting regulated by individual choice between an indefinite number of possibilities. The stereotyped, unindividual, impersonal and bureaucratized contract of today—this applies much more generally, but *a potiori* we may fasten upon the labor contract—which presents but restricted freedom of choice and mostly turns on a *c'est à prendre ou à laisser,* has none of the old features the most important of which become impossible with giant concerns dealing with other giant concerns or impersonal masses of workmen or consumers. The void is being filled by a tropical growth of new legal structures—and a little reflection shows that this could hardly be otherwise.

Thus the capitalist process pushes into the background all those institutions, the institutions of property and free contracting in particular, that expressed the needs and ways of the truly "private" economic activity. Where it does not abolish them, as it already has abolished free contracting in the labor market, it attains the same end by shifting the relative importance of existing legal forms—the legal forms pertaining to corporate business for instance as against those pertaining to the partnership or individual firm—or by changing their contents or meanings. The capitalist process, by substituting a mere parcel of shares for the walls of and the machines in a factory, takes the life out of the idea of property. It loosens the grip that once was so strong—the grip in the sense of the legal right and the actual ability to do as one pleases with one's own; the grip also in the sense that the holder of the title loses the will to fight, economically, physically, politically, for "his" factory and his control over it, to die if necessary on its steps. And this evaporation of what we may term the material substance of property—its visible and touchable reality—affects not only the attitude of holders but also that of the workmen and of the public in general. Dematerialized, defunctionalized and absentee ownership does not impress and call forth moral allegiance as the vital form of property did. Eventually there will be *nobody* left who really cares to stand for it—nobody within and nobody without the precincts of the big concerns.